CONTENTS

THE NATIONWIDE
FOOTBALL ANNUAL
2017–2018

Published by SportsBooks Limited, 9 St Aubyns Place, York, YO24 1EQ
First published in 1887

A CIP catalogue record for this book is available from the British Library.

Editorial compilation by Stuart Barnes

ISBN-13 9781907524547

Front cover shows Michy Batshuayi scoring the goal against West Bromwich Albion which clinched the Premier League title for Chelsea.
Back cover: Manchester United celebrate winning the Europa League.

Printed and bound in the UK by CPI Group (UK) Ltd, Croydon CRO 4YY

COMMENT

By Stuart Barnes

Goal-line technology has proved a success in the Premier League. It's now being introduced to the Championship. Video evidence to assist referees will start from the third round of the FA Cup in the new season. Football, it seems, is catching up with the modern world. Would now not be a good time to address another anachronism – the overlong, overblown summer transfer window? Through June and July, the market for players is buoyant. Then it becomes a tiresome distraction as the new season approaches, continuing to the end of August and culminating in the mad scramble that has become deadline day. This year, it stretches nearly four weeks beyond the start of the English Football League season, to almost three weeks after the Premier League kicks-off. Surely, it's time for all deals to be done and dusted before both get under way, so we can all concentrate on the game itself. Arsenal's Arsene Wenger has argued that the present system is archaic. Former England manager Glenn Hoddle believes the window for the top division should close 24 hours before the first matches. England defender Phil Jagielka has described it as a 'circus' – unsettling players and causing uncertainty among clubs. Other leading figures have voiced similar views. Should influential voices like these not be heard?

~

On the subject of transfers, there is a growing reluctance by clubs to divulge how much they have paid for a particular player. The price is described as 'undisclosed,' even if it is acknowledged that the fee represents a record for that particular club. Two early examples this summer were Liam Boyce's move to Burton Albion from Ross County (around £500,000) and Bournemouth's signing of Nathan Ake from Chelsea (around £20m). It may not suit the club, nor the player, nor his agent for the fee to be revealed. But, in the end, is it not their supporters who matter most and should be kept fully in the picture?

~

Every two years, England's failure at a major championship is dissected by a critical public and media. The latest embarrassment, against Iceland in Euro 2016, remains a vivid memory. What followed, Sam Allardyce's 67 days as manager, was beyond satire. 'Not too many England managers left with a 100 percent win record,' said Michael Owen, with tongue firmly in cheek. So the performance of England's under-20 team in winning the World Youth Cup this summer proved a breath of fresh air. It showed what meticulous planning, shrewd management and astute execution can do on the national stage. The hope is for some of those players to make a successful transition to the under-21 squad, then go on to develop at full international level. To do that, they will need plenty of experience in the Premier League. And there comes the stumbling block, with chances often few and far between because of the preponderance of overseas players. This was highlighted by some of the under-21 side beaten by Germany on penalties in the European Championship semi-finals in Poland. Leicester's Demarai Gray and Ben Chilwell, along with Chelsea's Nathaniel Chalobah, now with Watford, were key players at the tournament. Yet the trio made just 17 starts between them last season. It's a worrying statistic.

~

The arrival of a new club in league football is always welcome, even though it has often meant the demise of others with long-standing membership. The fact that Forest Green Rovers will be the smallest in the EFL adds to the interest. And when they insist on a vegan diet for the players and ban red meat being served to supporters on match days, this is clearly a club breaking with convention. The progress of the 'little club on the hill' – as Rovers are known – will be watched with some fascination by supporters way beyond their Gloucestershire home in Nailsworth (pop 5,800).

ENGLAND WORLD CHAMPIONS AGAIN –
51 YEARS ON

England became world champions during the summer for the first time in more than half a century – led by a coach born four days before Bobby Moore famously lifted the Jules Rimet Trophy at Wembley in 1966. Paul Simpson's under-20 side won the World Youth Cup in South Korea, beating Venezuela 1-0 in the final with a goal by Everton's Dominic Calvert-Lewin. It was the culmination of detailed preparation, which included a mini-tournament in South Korea in November 2016, an intensive build-up and total confidence shown by the squad under Simpson, who joined the FA as a national specialist coach before stepping up when Aidy Boothroyd succeeded Gareth Southgate in charge of the national under-21 squad. Previously, he played more than 800 games for ten clubs, including Manchester City, Derby and Wolves, and managed five Football League teams. 'The players told me they could win it,' said Simpson. 'They have been absolutely committed and this is the reward.' After topping their group, England defeated Costa Rica, Mexico and Italy, then held on to Calvert-Lewin's 34th minute goal with the help of a penalty save by Newcastle's Freddie Woodman and resolute defending late on. Dominic Solanke, ahead of his move from Chelsea to Liverpool, was named the tournament's best player – an award once given to Diego Maradona, Lionel Messi and Sergio Aguero. Woodman was chosen as the best goalkeeper.

GROUP A

	P	W	D	L	F	A	Pts
England Q	3	2	1	0	5	1	7
South Korea Q	3	2	0	1	5	2	6
Argentina	3	1	0	2	6	5	3
Guinea	3	0	1	2	1	9	1

Match-day 1: England 3 (Calvert-Lewin 37, Armstrong 52, Solanke 90) Argentina 0. Att: 15,510 (Jeonju). **Match-day 2**: England 1 (Cook 53) Guinea 1 (Tomori 59 og). Att: 5,992 (Jeonju). **Match-day 3**: England 1 (Dowell 56) South Korea 0. Att: 35,279 (Suwon)

GROUP B

	P	W	D	L	F	A	Pts
Venezuela Q	3	3	0	0	10	0	9
Mexico Q	3	1	1	1	3	3	4
Germany Q	3	1	1	1	3	4	4
Vanuatu	3	0	0	3	4	13	0

GROUP C

	P	W	D	L	F	A	Pts
Zambia Q	3	2	0	1	6	4	6
Portugal Q	3	1	1	1	4	4	4
Costa Rica Q	3	1	1	1	2	2	4
Iran	3	1	0	2	4	6	3

GROUP D

	P	W	D	L	F	A	Pts
Uruguay Q	3	2	1	0	3	0	7
Italy Q	3	1	1	1	4	3	4
Japan Q	3	1	1	1	4	5	4
South Africa	3	0	1	2	1	4	1

GROUP E

	P	W	D	L	F	A	Pts
France Q	3	3	0	0	9	0	9
New Zealand Q	3	1	1	1	3	3	4
Honduras	3	1	0	2	3	6	3
Vietnam	3	0	1	2	0	6	1

GROUP F

	P	W	D	L	F	A	Pts
USA Q	3	1	2	0	5	4	5
Senegal Q	3	1	1	1	2	1	4
Saudi Arabia Q	3	1	1	1	3	4	4
Ecuador	3	0	2	1	4	5	2

KNOCK-OUT STAGE

Last 16: England 2 (Lookman 35, 63) Costa Rica 1 (Leal 89). Att: 4,428 (Jeonju). Italy 2 France 1, Mexico 1 Senegal 0, Portugal 3 South Korea 1, Uruguay 1 Saudi Arabia 0, USA 6 New Zealand 0, Venezuela 1 Japan 0 (aet), Zambia 4 Germany 3 (aet)

Quarter-finals: England 1 (Solanke 47) Mexico 0. Att: 5,953 (Cheonan). Italy 3 Zambia 2 (aet), Uruguay 2 Portugal 2 (aet, Uruguay won 5-4 on pens), Venezuela 2 USA 1 (aet)

Semi-finals: England 3 (Solanke 66, 88, Lookman 77) Italy 1 (Orsolini 2). Att: 5,329 (Jeonju). Venezuela 1 Uruguay 1 (aet, Venezuela won 4-3 on pens)

FINAL

ENGLAND 1 VENEZUELA 0
Suwon (30,346), Sunday, June 11 2017

England (4-2-3-1): Woodman, Kenny, Tomori, Clarke-Salter, Walker-Peters, Cook (capt), Onomah, Dowell (Ojo 62), Solanke, Lookman (Maitland-Niles 76), Calvert-Lewin, **Booked:** Tomori, Dowell. **Coach**: Paul Simpson

Scorer – England: Calvert-Lewin (34). **Half-time**: 1-0

England squad: Henderson (Manchester Utd), Woodman (Newcastle), Southwood (Reading); Clarke-Salter (Chelsea), Connolly (Everton), Kenny (Everton), Fry (Middlesbrough), Konsa (Charlton), Tomori (Chelsea); Walker-Peters (Tottenham); Cook (Bournemouth), Dowell (Everton), Ejaria (Liverpool), Maitland-Niles (Arsenal), Ojo (Liverpool), Onomah (Tottenham); Armstrong (Newcastle), Calvert-Lewin (Everton), Chapman (Middlesbrough), Lookman (Everton), Solanke (Chelsea)

ENGLAND RETAIN TOULON TROPHY

The day before victory in South Korea, another young England line-up retained the Toulon Trophy – a tournament for international development players held annually in France. Gareth Southgate's under-21s won it in 2016. This time, a team comprising under 18, 19 and 20 players topped their group, defeated Scotland 3-0 in the semi-finals and beat Ivory Coast in the final. England led though Sheffield United's David Brooks, voted Player of the Tournament, conceded an 87th minute equaliser, then won 5-3 on penalties, converting all their spot-kicks through Ike Ugbo, Elliott Embleton, Harvey Barnes, Callum Slattery and Ronaldo Vieira.

GROUP A

	P	W	D	L	F	A	Pts
England Q	3	3	0	0	10	2	9
Angola	3	1	1	1	6	3	4
Japan	3	0	2	1	3	4	2
Cuba	3	0	1	2	3	13	1

Match-day 1: England 1 (Ugbo 51) Angola 0. **Match-day 2**: England 7 (Barnes 19, 50, Hirst 34, 59, 70 pen, Brooks 66, Taylor-Crossdale 82 pen) Cuba 1 (Saucedo 38). **Match-day 3**: England 2 (Hirst 26 pen, Taylor-Crossdale 78 pen) Japan 1 (Ando 59)

GROUP B

	P	W	D	L	F	A	Pts
Ivory Coast Q	3	2	1	0	5	3	7
Wales	3	1	2	0	3	2	5
France	3	1	1	1	7	3	4
Bahrain	3	0	0	3	1	8	0

Match-day 1: Wales 0 France 0. **Match-day 2**: Wales 1 (James 83 pen) Bahrain 0. **Match-day 3**: Wales 2 (Thomas 8, 88) Ivory Coast 2 (Tiehi 56, Krasso 68)

GROUP C

	P	W	D	L	F	A	Pts
Czech Rep Q	3	2	1	0	5	2	7
Scotland Q	3	2	0	1	5	4	6
Brazil	3	1	1	1	1	1	4
Indonesia	3	0	0	3	1	5	0

Match-day 1: Scotland 2 (Burke 2, 61) Czech Rep 3 (Chveja 36, Sasinka 46, Graiciar 65). **Match-day 2**: Scotland 1 (Taylor 36) Brazil 0. **Match-day 3**: Scotland 2 (Hardie 33, 69) Indonesia 1 (Putra 24)

Semi-finals: England 3 (Barnes 7, 74, Embleton 56) Scotland 0, Ivory Coast 2 Czech Rep 1.
Third place match: Scotland 3 (Hardie 49, Wighton 63, Granecny 88 og) Czech Rep 0

FINAL

ENGLAND 1 IVORY COAST 1 (England won 5-3 on pens)
Aubange: Saturday, June 10 2017

England (3-4-3): Schofield, Grant, Worrall (capt), Tymon (Tanganga 52), James, Embleton, Vieira, Mitchell (Slattery 77), Brooks (Uwakwe 65), Hirst (Ugbo 58), Barnes. **Booked**: Grant, Vieira, Schofield. **Coach**: Neil Dewsnip
Scorers – England: Brooks (14). **Ivory Coast**: Loba (87 pen). **Half-time**: 1-0

England squad: Balcombe (Brentford), Schofield (Huddersfield); Grant (Chelsea), James (Chelsea), Tanganga (Tottenham), Tymon (Hull), Worrall (Nottm Forest); Barnes (Leicester), Brooks (Sheffield Utd), Mitchell (Manchester Utd), Moore (Leicester), Slattery (Southampton), Uwakwe (Chelsea), Vieira (Leeds); Bolton (Manchester City), Embleton (Sunderland), Hirst (Sheffield Wed), Kemp (West Ham), Taylor-Crossdale (Chelsea), Ugbo (Chelsea)

ENGLAND ON THE SPOT AGAIN

A tournament that started on the wrong foot, then picked up sufficient pace to raise genuine hopes of success, came to an end in familiar fashion for an England team. For the eighth time in ten major championships, there was defeat in a penalty shoot-out, this time in a European under-21 semi-final against Germany which had gone to spot-kicks after a 2-2 scoreline at the end of 120 minutes. Jordan Pickford, Everton's new £30m signing from Sunderland who had saved a penalty in the opening group match against Sweden, gave his side the initial advantage by denying Yannick Gerhardt. But Tammy Abraham also had his effort kept out – and after Ben Chilwell and James Ward-Prowse held their nerve, Nathan Redmond's failure gave the Germans and their coach Stefan Kuntz victory by 4-3. Kuntz had been among the scorers in the shoot-out to end England's chances in Euro 96 at Wembley. This time, his team were technically superior and dominated possession, without quelling their opponents' competitive spirit. It was rewarded with an equaliser from Demarai Gray, followed by Abraham's goal early in the second-half to establish a 2-1 lead, held until 20 minutes from the end of normal time. Previously, England improved after a stuttering goalless draw against the Swedes. They came from behind to defeat Slovakia 2-1 with goals by Alfie Mawson and Redmond, then swept aside Poland 3-0, with Gray, Jacob Murphy and Lewis Baker (pen) on the mark. England now move on to qualifying for the 2019 tournament in Italy and San Marino in the new season when there will be a much-changed line up, with 18 of the 23-strong squad in Poland no longer eligible for under-21 football. They are paired with Scotland, Holland and Ukraine in a group completed by Latvia and Andorra.

GROUP A

Match-day 1
England 0 **Sweden** 0. Att: 11,672 (Kielce)
England (4-2-3-1): Pickford, Holgate, Chambers, Mawson, Chilwell, Ward-Prowse, Chalobah, Murphy (Gray 70), Baker, Abraham, Redmond
Poland 1 (Lipski 1) **Slovakia** 2 (Valijent 20, Sanfranko 78). Att: 14,911 (Lublin)

Match-day 2
England 2 (Mawson 50, Redmond 61) **Slovakia** 1 (Chrien 23). Att: 12,087 (Kielce)
England (4-1-2-1-2): Pickford, Holgate (Murphy 46), Chambers, Mawson, Chilwell, Chalobah, Baker, Ward-Prowse, Swift (Gray 80), Abraham (Woodrow 88), Redmond. Booked: Ward-Prowse, Murphy, Baker
Poland 2 (Moneta 6, Kownacki 90) **Sweden** 2 (Strandberg 36, Une-Larsson 41). Att: 14,651 (Lublin)

Match-day 3
England 3 (Gray 6, Murphy 69, Baker 82 pen) **Poland** 0. Att: 13,176 (Kielce)
England (4-1-2-1-2): Pickford, Holgate, Chambers, Mawson, Chilwell, Chalobah (Hughes 39), Baker, Ward-Prowse (Abraham 73), Swift, Redmond (Murphy 46), Gray. Booked: Mawson
Slovakia 3 (Chrien 5, Mihalik 23, Satka 73) **Sweden** 0. Att: 11,203 (Lublin)

	P	W	D	L	F	A	Pts
England Q	3	2	1	0	5	1	7
Slovakia	3	2	0	1	6	3	6
Sweden	3	0	2	1	2	5	2
Poland	3	0	1	2	3	7	1

GROUP B

Match-day 1
Portugal 2 (Guedes 37, Bruno Fernandes 88) **Serbia** 0. Att: 10,724 (Bydgoszcz). **Spain** 5 (Saul 10, Marco Asensio 16, 54, 72, Deulofeu 35 pen) **Macedonia** 0. Att: 8,269 (Gdynia)

Match-day 2
Portugal 1 (Bruma 77) **Spain** 3 (Niguez 21, Sandro 65, Wiliams 90). Att: 13,862 (Gdynia).

Serbia 2 (Gacinovic 24, Djurdjevic 90) **Macedonia** 2 (Bardhi 64 pern, Gjorgiev 83). Att: 5,121 (Bydgoszcz)

Match-day 3
 Macedonia 2 (Bardhi 40, Markoski 80) **Portugal** 4 (Edgar le 2, Bruma 22, 90, Daniel Podence 57). Att: 7,533 (Gdynia). **Serbia** 0 **Spain** 1 (Suarez 38). Att: 12,058 (Bydgoszcz)

	P	W	D	L	F	A	Pts
Spain Q	3	3	0	0	9	1	9
Portugal	3	2	0	1	7	5	6
Serbia	3	0	1	2	2	5	1
Macedonia	3	0	1	2	4	11	1

GROUP C

Match-day 1
Denmark 0 **Italy** 2 (Pellegrini 54, Petagna 86). Att: 8,754 (Krakow). **Germany** 2 (Meyer 44, Gnabry 50) **Czech Republic** 0. Att: 14,051 (Tychy)

Match-day 2
Czech Republic 3 (Travnik 24, Havlik 79, Luftner 85) **Italy** 1 (Berardi 70). Att: 13,251 (Tychy)
Germany 3 (Selke 53, Kempf 73, Amiri 79) **Denmark** 0. Att: 9,298 (Krakow)

Match-day 3
Czech Republic 2 (Schick 27, Chory 54) **Denmark** 4 (Andersen 23, Zohore 35, 73, Ingvartsen 90). Att: 9,047 (Krakow). **Italy** 1 (Bernardeschi 30) **Germany** 0. Att: 14,039 (Tychy)

	P	W	D	L	F	A	Pts
Italy Q	3	2	0	1	4	3	6
Germany Q	3	2	0	1	5	1	6
Czech Rep	3	1	0	2	5	7	3
Denmark	3	1	0	2	4	7	3

SEMI-FINALS

England 2 (Gray 41, Abraham 50) **Germany** 2 (Selke 35, Platte 70). Att: 13,214 (Tychy) – aet, Germany won 4-3 on pens
England (4-2-3-1): Pickford, Holgate (Iorfa 106), Chambers, Mawson, Chilwell, Chalobah (Murphy 66), Hughes (Swift 85), Ward-Prowse, Baker, Gray (Redmond 73), Abraham. **Booked**: Hughes, Chilwell, Holgate
Germany (4-1-4-1): Pollersbeck, Toljan, Jung (Kehrer 80), Kempf, Gerhardt, Haberer (Kohr 102), Philipp, Meyer, Arnold, Gnabry (Amiri 87), Selke (Platte 63). **Booked**: Selke, Gnabry, Kempf, Arnold
Referee: G Mazeika (Lithuania). **Half-time**: 1-1
Penalties: Arnold 0-1, Baker 1-1, Gerhardt 1-1, Abraham 1-1, Philipp 1-2, Chilwell 2-2, Meyer 2-3, Ward-Prowse 3-3, Amiri 3-4, Redmond 3-4
Spain 3 (Saul 53, 65, 74) **Italy** 1 (Bernardeschi 62). Att: 13,105 (Krakow)

FINAL

Germany 1 (Weiser 40) **Spain** 0. Att: 14,059 (Krakow, June 30, 2017)

England squad: Gunn (Manchester City), Mitchell (Derby), Pickford (Everton); Chambers (Arsenal), Chilwell (Leicester), Hause (Wolves), Holding (Arsenal), Holgate (Everton), Iorfa (Wolves), Mawson (Swansea), Stephens (Southampton), Targett (Southampton); Baker (Chelsea), Chalobah (Chelsea), Grealish (Aston Villa), Hughes (Derby), Swift (Reading), Ward-Prowse (Southampton); Abraham (Chelsea), Gray (Leicester), Jacob Murphy (Norwich), Redmond (Southampton), Woodrow (Fulham)

DAY BY DAY DIARY 2016–17

JULY 2016

19 Leicester captain Wes Morgan signs a new contract through to 2019, but the club lose recruitment chief Steve Walsh to Everton.

20 The FA, Premier League and English Football League declare a crackdown on verbal and physical dissent and aggressive conduct towards match officials. Liverpool sign Newcastle's Georginio Wijnaldum for £25m.

21 Wolves owner Steve Morgan sells the club to a Chinese corporation, Fosun International, for £45m.

22 Sam Allardyce is appointed England's new manager and says his aim is to give the country 'the national team the fans deserve.' Steve Bruce, who wanted the job, resigns as Hull manager, unhappy at the club's preparations for a return to the Premier League. His assistant, Mike Phelan, is appointed caretaker.

23 David Moyes, former Manchester United and Everton manager, replaces Sam Allardyce at Sunderland.

24 The new England boss appoints Sammy Lee, his former assistant at Bolton, as his No 2. UEFA fine Liverpool £13,400 and Sevilla £14,200 for crowd trouble at the Europa League Final in Basle.

25 The scheduled first match between Jose Mourinho's Manchester United and Pep Guardiola's Manchester City, a friendly in China, is postponed because of an unplayable pitch in Beijing.

26 Steven Pressley resigns after nine months as Fleetwood manager.

27 The FA announce that a fourth substitution will be allowed during extra-time of FA Cup ties from the quarter-finals onwards.

28 Shay Given announces his retirement from international football after winning 134 caps in a 20-year career with the Republic of Ireland.

29 Wolves manager Kenny Jackett is sacked by the club's new owners. Uwe Rosler, formerly in charge of Leeds, Wigan and Brentford, is appointed Fleetwood's new manager.

30 Walter Zenga, former Sampdoria and Palermo coach, succeeds Kenny Jackett at Molineux. After impressing with the Republic of Ireland at Euro 2016, goalkeeper Darren Randolph signs a new four-year contract with West Ham.

AUGUST 2016

1 Manchester City pay Schalke £37m for 20-year-old Germany winger Leroy Sane. Walsall break their 37-year-old transfer record by signing Cyprus striker Andreas Makris from Anorthosis Famagusta for an undisclosed fee surpassing the previous highest of £175,000.

2 Hibernian manager Neil Lennon, sent off during the Europa League qualifying defeat by Brondby, is given a five-match European ban by UEFA for 'acts of violence against the referee'. Gylfi Sigurdsson signs a new four year contract with Swansea.

3 Former Everton manager Roberto Martinez is appointed Belgium's new head coach. Manchester City sign 19-year-old Brazilian winger Gabriel Jesus from Palmeiras for £27m. A crowd of more than 58,000 watch Wayne Rooney's testimonial match at Old Trafford between Manchester United and his former club Everton, with proceeds of £1.2m going to children's charities.

4 Ross McCormack becomes Scotland's most expensive player when joining Aston Villa from Fulham for £12m. In their first match at the London Stadium, West Ham defeat Domzale 3-0 to reach the Europa League play-offs 4-2 on aggregate, watched by a crowd of nearly 54,000. Aberdeen, Scotland's remaining team in the tournament after defeats for Hearts and Hibernian in previous qualifying ties, lose 2-1 on aggregate to another Slovenian side, Maribor.

5 Jeremy Peace sells West Bromwich Albion to billionaire Guochuan Lai for around £150m,

the fourth Midlands club to be taken over by Chinese investors after Wolves, Aston Villa and Birmingham. James Milner, winner of 61 caps, retires from international football after a meeting with England manager Sam Allardyce.

6 Kasper Schmeichel signs a new five-year contract with Leicester. On the opening day of the Football League season, newly-promoted Grimsby defeat Morecambe 2-0 and Cheltenham draw 1-1 with Leyton Orient.

7 Manchester United beat Leicester 2-1 in the Community Shield. Celtic open their defence of the Scottish Premiership title with a 2-1 victory over Hearts.

8 Paul Pogba flies in to Manchester in a private jet for a medical ahead of a world record £89.3m move from Juventus to Manchester United. West Ham sign Andre Ayew from Swansea for a club record £20.5m. Kyle Lafferty, Norwich and Northern Ireland striker, is fined £23,000 for breaching FA betting rules.

9 Four years after leaving Old Trafford for Juventus on a free transfer, Paul Pogba completes his return on a salary reported to be £290,000 a week. The fee overtakes Gareth Bale's £85.3m move from Tottenham to Real Madrid in August, 2013. Another huge transfer takes Everton's John Stones to Manchester City for £47.5m – the second highest fee for a defender after the £50m move of David Luiz from Chelsea to Paris Saint-Germain in the summer of 2014. Eight Championship sides lose to lower league opposition in the first round of the League Cup, including Rotherham, who are beaten 5-4 on their own ground by Morecambe.

10 Claudio Ranieri is rewarded for leading Leicester to the Premier League title with a new four-year contract.

11 Swansea break their transfer record with the £15.5m purchase of Atletico Madrid striker Borja Baston.

12 Former Sheffield United midfielder Jose Baxter is banned for 12 months by the FA after failing a drugs test for a second time.

13 Leicester begin their defence of the Premier League title with a 2-1 defeat at Hull.

15 Everton sign Yannick Bolasie from Crystal Palace for £28m, a record fee for the London club. Accrington are fined £5,000 for fielding an ineligible player, Janoi Donacien, in their opening two matches of the season, both of them won. The fine is suspended and the league and cup results stand.

16 Burnley pay a club record £7.3m for Andelecht's Belgium midfielder Steven Defour.

17 Riyad Mahrez ends speculation about his future by signing a new contract with Leicester through to 2020.

18 Derby's Chris Baird retires from international football after winning 79 caps with Northern Ireland. Hull's Sam Clucas signs a new three-year contract.

19 Watford break their transfer record for the second time in two months, paying Juventus £13m for Argentina midfielder Roberto Pereyra. Celtic's Scott Brown calls time on his international career after winning 50 caps with Scotland. Manchester City's Kelechi Iheanacho signs a two-year contract extension through to 2021.

20 Crystal Palace pay a club record £27m for Liverpool's Christian Benteke.

21 Barcelona's Neymar scores the winning penalty as Brazil beat Germany 5-4 in a shoot-out after the Olympic Final ends 1-1 in Rio de Janeiro.

22 Reece Burke, West Ham's 19-year-old centre-back, signs a new four-year contract with the the club.

23 Celtic reach the Champions League group stage by beating Hapoel Beer Sheva 5-4 on aggregate in the play-offs. League of Ireland champions Dundalk, who came through two qualifying rounds, lose 3-1 to Legia Warsaw over the two legs.

24 Manchester City go through with a 6-0 aggregate victory over Steaua Bucharest. Robbie Keane announces that his record-breaking, 18-year Republic of Ireland international career will end in the upcoming friendly with Oman. Greg Clarke, former Football League chairman, succeeds Greg Dyke as chairman of the FA. Danny Drinkwater signs a new five-year contract with Leicester.

25 Manchester City sign Barcelona goalkeeper Claudio Bravo for £15.4, signalling the end of Joe Hart's ten years at the club. For the second successive season, West Ham are knocked out of the Europa League by the Romanian side Astra Giurgiu, this time 2-1 on aggregate in the play-off round.

26 Thierry Henry joins the coaching team of Belgium coach Roberto Martinez. Cedric Soares signs new four-year contract with Southampton.

27 Arsenal sign Germany defender Shkodran Mustafi from Valencia for £35m and Deportivo Coruna striker Lucas Perez for £17m. Derby buy Matej Vydra from Watford for £12.5m, a record fee for both clubs.

28 The day after scoring for Nottingham Forest in a 3-1 win over Leeds, 19-year-old winger Oliver Burke overtakes Ross McCormack as the most expensive Scottish player when joining Red Bull Leipzig for £13m – a record fee for the Championship club.

29 Two more record signings, this time for Southampton, who pay Lille £16m for Morocco midfielder Sofiane Boufal, and for Bristol City, who receive an initial £11m from Aston Villa for Jonathan Kodjia – a fee that could rise to a Championship record £15m.

30 Two clubs make record £13m signings from Tottenham. West Bromwich Albion bring in Nacer Chadli and Hull acquire Ryan Mason.

31 Premier League clubs spend £155m on transfer deadline day, taking the total outlay for the summer window to a record £1.16bn. Chelsea pay the day's biggest fee, £34m, to bring David Luiz back to Stamford Bridge, two years after selling him to Paris Saint Germain for £50m. Three clubs pay record fees, two of them for the second time in a matter of weeks. Leicester sign Algeria striker Islam Slimani from Sporting Lisbon for £29.7m, while Burnley pay Derby £10.5m for Jeff Hendrick. Sunderland also set a new mark of £13.6m for Gabon international midfielder Didier N'Dong from Lorient. Two major loan moves take Joe Hart to Torino and Arsenal's Jack Wilshere to Bournemouth. Robbie Keane marks his 146th appearance for the Republic of Ireland with his 68th goal in a 4-0 win over Oman. Manchester United's Bastian Schweinsteiger also bows out of international football after his 121st cap for Germany in a 2-0 victory over Finland.

SEPTEMBER 2016

1 Danny Simpson signs a new three-year contract with Leicester. Brazil businessman Diego Lemos completes a takeover of Morecambe from club chairman Peter McGuigan.

2 Sergio Aguero is banned for three matches by the FA for elbowing Winston Reid in Manchester City's win over West Ham.

4 Sam Allardyce makes a winning start as England manager in their opening World Cup qualifier against Slovakia. Adam Lallana's first international goal in stoppage-time brings a 1-0 victory as Wayne Rooney overtakes David Beckham to become his country's record outfield player with 116 caps. Robert Snodgrass scores a hat-trick in Scotland's 5-1 win over Malta, while Northern Ireland also make a good start away from home, holding the Czech Republic to a goalless draw.

5 Wales open their campaign by beating Moldova 4-0, with Joe Allen on the mark for his country for the first time and Gareth Bale scoring two goals, one a penalty. Jeff Hendrick and Daryl Murphy net their first goals for the Republic of Ireland who draw 2-2 away to Serbia.

6 Sam Allardyce sees Marcus Rashford score a hat-trick on his debut for England's under-21 side, who beat Norway 6-1 in a European Championship qualifier.

7 Christian Eriksen signs a new four-year contract with Tottenham. The Scottish FA introduce a fourth substitute for Scottish Cup ties going into extra-time.

8 Roberto Martinez is reported to have received a £10m pay-off after being sacked by Everton in May 2016.

9 Eric Dier signs a new five-year contract with Tottenham.

10 Moussa Dembele scores a hat-trick as Celtic beat Rangers 5-1 in the first 'Old Firm' match since Rangers were liquidated and demoted in 2012.

11 Crystal Palace defender Pape Souare is ruled out for the rest of the season after sustaining thigh and jaw injuries in a car crash on the M4 motorway.

12 A bronze statue of Alan Shearer, the Premier League's record scorer with 260 goals, is unveiled at St James' Park, Newcastle, one of his former clubs.

13 Celtic are beaten 7-0 by Barcelona in their opening Champions League group game, the club's worst defeat in European competition. Manchester City's first match, against Borussia Monchengladbach, is called off shortly before kick-off because of safety concerns around the Etihad Stadium following a thunderstorm. After reviewing video evidence, the FA ban Burton's Kyle McFadzean for three matches for elbowing Paul Gladon during the match against Wolves.

14 City's game is played 24 hours later, with Sergio Aguero scoring a hat-trick in a 4-0 victory. Tottenham, playing their home games at Wembley because of the crowd reduction at White Hart Lane, lose 2-1 to Monaco in front of a club record attendance of 85,011. Leicester win 3-0 in Bruges on their debut in the tournament.

15 Aleksander Ceferin, a Slovenian lawyer, is chosen to succeed Michel Platini as president of UEFA. Dundalk become the first Irish club to gain a point in European competition, drawing 1-1 away from home with Alkmaar in their opening Europa League fixture.

17 A drone circling over the stadium causes Bradford's home game with Bristol Rovers to be halted for three minutes by referee Andy Haines.

18 Dele Alli signs a new six-year contract with Tottenham.

19 Stoke manager Mark Hughes is fined £8,000 by the FA for improper conduct during an incident with fourth official Jon Moss during the game against Tottenham. Rangers suspend Joey Barton following an altercation with manager Mark Warburton.

20 England women beat Belgium 2-0 to top their qualifying group for the 2017 European Championship.

21 Danny Rose signs a new contract through to 2021 with Tottenham.

22 The English Football League rule out Premier League B teams and non English clubs from their plans for a new League Three in 2019.

23 Martin O'Neill, the Republic of Ireland manager, and assistant Roy Keane sign new contracts through to the 2018 World Cup. Burnley's Andre Gray is banned for four matches and fined £25,000 by the FA for homophobic abuse on social media dating back to 2012 when he was playing non-league football.

24 Aston Villa, with a starting line-up worth £60m and Newcastle, whose players cost £63m, draw 1-1 in the most 'expensive' ever Football League match. Fourteen players are sent off in the day's programme.

25 Manchester City win their first Women's Super League title by defeating defending champions Chelsea 2-0.

26 The FA launch an immediate investigation after England manager Sam Allardyce is filmed by the *Daily Telegraph* attempting to negotiate a £400,000 business deal with undercover reporters, offering advice on how to get round third-party ownership rules on players, mocking his predecessor Roy Hodgson and criticising Hodgson's No 2 Gary Neville. Andy Hessenthaler becomes the first league managerial casualty of the season, sacked by Leyton Orient after five months in the job with his side 14th in the table.

27 Sam Allardyce is forced out of his £3m-a-year 'dream' job, reportedly with a seven-figure pay-off, after 67 days and a single match. A meeting with FA chairman Greg Clarke and chief executive Martin Glenn is followed by the announcement of his departure by 'mutual agreement.' The governing body condemn him for 'inappropriate conduct' and a 'serious error of judgement.' Allardyce apologises and regrets 'embarrassing comments.' Derby manager Nigel Pearson is suspended by the club after an altercation with owner Mel Morris. Leyton Orient captain Robbie Weir is sent off after 20 seconds for a lunging tackle on Plymouth's Ben Purrington.

28 The FA turn to Gareth Southgate, manager of the England under-21 side, to take charge of the senior team's next four games.

29 Tommy Wright, Barnsley's assistant manager, is dismissed by the club after *Daily Telegraph* footage of him accepting a £5,000 payment. Tony Mowbray resigns as Coventry manager with his side bottom of League One. Newport's Warren Feeney is sacked with his team at the foot of League Two. Celtic are fined 10,000 euros (£8,616) after fans waved Palestine flags during a Champions League play-off with the Israeli club Hapoel Be'er Sheva. Rangers manager Mark Warburton is banned for one match by the Scottish FA for abusing match officials during the defeat by Aberdeen. Dundalk pass another European milestone – defeating Maccabi Tel Aviv 1-0 in their second Europa League group match.

30 Slovakia defender Jan Durica is fined £4,000 by FIFA for suggesting England's World Cup qualifying win over his side was fixed by the referee.

OCTOBER 2016

1 Arsene Wenger reaches 20 years as manager of Arsenal amid speculation that he could take over the England job at the end of his current contract with the club.

2 Roberto di Matteo, manager of Aston Villa for four months, is sacked after a single win in the opening 11 Championship matches. Alberto Cavasin, former Fiorentina and Sampdoria coach, becomes Leyton Orient's sixth manager in two years. Manchester City women complete the double by beating Birmingham 1-0 after extra-time in the Continental Cup Final.

3 Swansea, without a Premier League win since the opening day of the season, sack Francesco Guidolin, after eight months in charge, on his 61st birthday. He is replaced by Le Havre's former United States coach Bob Bradley, who becomes the first American to manage in the Premier League.

4 Paul Trollope, manager of Cardiff for four-and-a-half months, is dismissed with his side second from bottom.

5 Neil Warnock takes over at Cardiff, his 13th managerial appointment at a league club.

6 Captain Seamus Coleman scores his first Republic of Ireland goal for a 1-0 World Cup qualifying victory over Georgia. Wales draw 2-2 in Austria. England under 21s, with Aidy Boothroyd taking over from Gareth Southgate, defeat Kazakhstan 1-0 to ensure qualification for the 2017 European Championship Finals. Queens Park Rangers are fined £7,500 by the FA for misconduct by players against Fulham.

7 Micky Mellon leaves Shrewsbury to become manager of Tranmere, where he had two spells as a player. Graham Westley, former Peterborough, Preston and Stevenage manager, takes over at Newport. Hartlepool manager Craig Hignett is given a three match touchline ban by the FA for abusive language during the game against Plymouth.

8 England defeat Malta 2-0 in Gareth Southgate's first match in charge in front of a Wembley crowd of nearly 82,000. James McArthur's 89th minute goal gives Scotland a 1-1 draw with Lithuania. Kyle Lafferty comes off the bench to score twice in Northern Ireland's 4-0 victory over San Marino. Nigel Pearson's contract with Derby is terminated by mutual consent.

9 Two goals by James McClean point the Republic of Ireland to a 3-1 win in Moldova. Wales falter in their third qualifier, held 1-1 at home by Georgia.

10 Wayne Rooney insists he will fight for his England future after being dropped by Gareth Southgate for the World Cup qualifier in Slovenia. Nottingham Forest manager Philippe Montanier is given a two match touchline ban and fined £3,000 by the FA for abusing a match official after the game against Sheffield Wednesday. Leeds manager Garry Monk receives a one-match ban and £2,000 fine for misconduct during the game against Bristol City. Huddersfield's David Wagner is fined £2,000 for his behaviour in the match with Reading.

11 An outstanding performance by Joe Hart rescues a point for England in a goalless draw against Slovenia. Scotland suffer a damaging 3-0 defeat in Slovakia. Northern Ireland are beaten 2-0 in their away game against Germany.

12 Steve McClaren returns as manager of Derby, 17 months after being sacked by the club. Steve Bruce takes over at Aston Villa, his ninth managerial appointment. Craig Gardner signs a new two-year contract with West Bromwich Albion.

13 Chelsea sign a kit deal with Nike worth a reported £90m over 15 seasons. Mike Phelan is appointed Hull manager, after nearly three months as caretaker.

14 Ched Evans, Chesterfield and former Wales striker, is cleared of rape following a retrial at Cardiff Crown Court.

15 Charlton's home game against Coventry is halted for five minutes after hundreds of plastic toy pigs are thrown onto the pitch by supporters of both clubs protesting about their respective owners.

17 Manchester City post record revenues for 2015–16 of £391.8m and profits of £20.5m.

18 Aston Villa's Jack Grealish is banned for three games by the FA after being caught on camera stamping on Conor Coady, of Wolves.

19 Mesut Ozil scores a hat-trick in Arsenal's 6-0 Champions League win over Ludogorets. Lionel Messi scores three for Barcelona in their 4-0 victory over Manchester City.

20 Alan Stubbs, manager of Rotherham for 14 matches, is sacked with his team bottom of the Championship and replaced by Kenny Jackett, formerly in charge of Wolves. Bury are fined £12,500 by the FA for failing to control their players during the match against Rochdale.

21 The FA ban Brentford's Alan McCormack for five matches and fine him £6,000 for abusing a female assistant referee during the game against Cardiff – an offence 'aggravated' by a reference to gender.

22 Paul Hurst leaves Grimsby to become Shrewsbury's new manager after the two clubs agree a compensation package.

23 Karl Robinson, the third longest serving manager behind Arsenal's Arsene Wenger and Exeter's Paul Tisdale, is sacked after six-and-a-half-years at MK Dons, with his side a point away from the bottom four.

24 The FA announce a new overseas broadcast rights deal for the FA Cup, reported to be worth £820m over six seasons, commencing in 2018–19. Moussa Sissoko is banned for three matches after being caught on camera elbowing Harry Arter in Tottenham's match against Bournemouth.

25 There are two more managerial casualties in the Championship, taking the total to six in October. Walter Zenga, in charge at Wolves for 87 days, is sacked after a run of one point from five matches. Gary Caldwell, Wigan's promotion-winning manager, is dismissed with his side second from bottom.

26 Agent Mino Raiolo is reported to be receiving £24m for brokering Paul Pogba's world record £89.3m move from Juventus to Manchester United. Swindon are fined £10,000 by the FA for failing to control their players during the game against AFC Wimbledon.

27 The FA begin an investigation into violent clashes between rival fans at West Ham's League Cup tie against Chelsea. Hull's Adama Diomande is banned for three matches on video evidence for striking Bristol City's Marlon Pack.

28 Celtic captain Scott Brown comes out of international retirement after two months to help Scotland's faltering World Cup qualifying campaign. Tony Pulis, the West Bromwich Albion manager, signs a one-year extension to his contract. Newport's Paul Bignot is banned for six matches by the FA for violent conduct against Cheltenham.

30 Gareth Bale agrees a new six-year contract with Real Madrid said to be worth £108m after tax.

31 Sunderland manager David Moyes is banned for one match and fined £8,000 by the FA for swearing at the fourth official in a League Cup tie against Southampton.

NOVEMBER 2016

1 Arsenal reach the last 16 of the Champions League for the 17th successive season, with two group matches to spare. London Mayor Sadiq Khan orders an investigation into the finances of the London Stadium, West Ham's new home, after a rise in conversion costs from £272m to £323m.

2 Leicester set a Champions League record, becoming the first newcomers to the competition to keep a clean sheet in their first four group games. Manchester United manager Jose Mourinho is given a one-match touchline ban and fined a total of £58,000 by the FA for two misconduct charges involving referees Mark Clattenburg and Anthony Taylor. Warren Joyce, manager of United's reserve team, is appointed Wigan's new manager. Liverpool's Danny Ings is ruled out for the rest of the season with another knee injury, the first of which kept him out for most of the previous campaign.

3 The chairman of the London Stadium operators, David Edmonds, resigns amid the controversy over finances. A new three-year sponsor for the EFL (League) Cup is announced – Thai energy drinks company Carabao.

4   Rochdale's Calvin Andrew receives one of the longest bans in English football history – 12 matches for smashing an elbow into the face of Oldham's Peter Clarke in an off-the-ball incident caught on camera. The FA consider the normal three-game ban for violent conduct 'clearly insufficient.'

5   Another Championship manager is sacked – Jimmy Floyd Hasselbaink following Queens Park Rangers' match against Nottingham Forest with his side 17th in the table. Paul Lambert, formerly in charge of Blackburn, Aston Villa and Norwich, is appointed the new Wolves manager.

6   Aston Villa's Alan Hutton retires from international football after winning 50 caps for Scotland.

7   Marcus Bignot, manager of National League club Solihull and a former Queens Park Rangers defender, takes charge at Grimsby.

8   Gareth Bale is voted Wales' Player of the Year for the fourth successive year and sixth time in all.

9   Burton's Kyle McFadzean is banned for four games by the FA after being caught on camera stamping on Barnsley's Sam Winnall – his second such suspension of the season for violent conduct.

10 Joey Barton's two-year contract with Rangers is terminated after six troubled months and eight appearances for the club.

11 England consolidate their position at the top of their World Cup qualifying group with a 3-0 win over Scotland, who are left second from bottom. Conor McLaughlin scores his first goal for Northern Ireland, who defeat Azerbaijan 4-0. Ian Holloway is appointed manager of Queens Park Rangers for the second time – ten years after his first spell in charge ended. Accrington manager John Coleman receives a two-match touchline ban for misbehaviour during the match against Crawley.

12 James McClean's third goal in two games gives the Republic of Ireland a 1-0 away win over Austria. Wales falter again, conceding an 85th minute equaliser to Serbia and having to settle for a second successive 1-1 home draw.

13 Barnet manager Martin Allen undergoes minor heart surgery.

14 Two more managerial departures. Russell Slade is sacked after six months at Charlton with his side 15th. Mansfield's Adam Murray resigns with his team 18th. Frank Lampard announces he is leaving New York City at the end of his contract.

15 England, on the brink of a notable victory over Spain in the last of Gareth Southgate's four matches as interim manager, concede goals in the 89th minute and the sixth minute of stoppage-time to draw 2-2. Northern Ireland lose 3-0 at home to Croatia in another friendly international. The English Football League call off plans for an extra division after talks with the FA break down. Steven Gerrard calls time on his spell with LA Galaxy.

16 England captain Wayne Rooney apologises to Gareth Southgate for a late night drinking session after the win over Scotland. Bury's David Flitcroft is the latest managerial casualty, after seven successive League One defeats. Former Leeds and Rotherham manager Steve Evans taks over at Mansfield. Twelve EFL clubs are fined for fielding weakened teams in the Checkatrade Trophy – Luton and Portsmouth £15,000, Fleetwood £5,000 and Blackpool, Bradford, Bristol Rovers, Charlton, MK Dons, Millwall, Peterborough, Sheffield United and Southend all £3,000.

17 Gordon Strachan, Scotland's under-pressure manager, is given a vote of confidence by the Scottish FA. The governing body ban former Rangers midfielder Joey Barton for one match for breaking betting rules. Rochdale's Calvin Andrew has his 12-match ban reduced to nine games on appeal.

18 Robbie Keane announces his departure from LA Galaxy after five seasons at the club. Derby terminate their naming rights agreement with sports drink manufacturer iPro and revert to Pride Park as their stadium name from January, 2017.

19 As the FA investigate the incident involving Wayne Rooney – and claims about other players – the captain attacks what describes as 'disgraceful' coverage.

20 Three Wales players, Joe Allen, Gareth Bale and Aaron Ramsey, are shortlisted by UEFA for their team of the year.

21 Steven Gerrard turns down the offer of the vacant manager's job at MK Dons. Port Vale's Anthony Grant, sent off against Fleetwood and banned for one game, is given an additional five-match suspension and £2,000 fine by the FA for returning to the pitch at the end of the game to remonstrate with referee John Brooks. Oldham have a transfer embargo imposed for non-payment of bills.

22 Leicester reach the Champions League knock-out stage as group winners by beating Club Bruges 2-1. Tottenham go out after a 2-1 defeat in their return match with Monaco. Borussia Dortmund's 8-4 win over Legia Warsaw is a record aggregate score for the competition.

23 Manchester City and Arsenal ensure runners-up places in their groups. Celtic are knocked out and also miss out on a place in the Europa League. Alberto Cavasin, manager of Leyton Orient for 52 days, is sacked after losing eight of his ten matches in all competitions. His assistant, Andy Edwards, is given the job until the end of the season.

24 Steven Gerrard ends his illustrious playing career to pursue a new one in coaching. Wayne Rooney overtakes Ruud van Nistelrooy to become Manchester United's all-time record scorer in Europe with his 39th goal in a 4-0 Europa League win over Feyenoord. Leicester's Danny Drinkwater is banned by the FA for three matches after being caught on camera elbowing Watford's Valon Behrami.

25 Karl Robinson returns to management a month after his dismissal by MK Dons, filling the vacant job at Charlton.

26 Crystal Palace winger Wilfried Zaha, winner of two England caps in friendlies, switches international allegiance to the Ivory Coast, country of his birth.

27 Celtic win their 100th major trophy – the first under Brendan Rodgers – by beating Aberdeen 3-0 in the Scottish League Cup Final.

28 West Bromwich Albion manager Tony Pulis is ordered to pay Crystal Palace £3.7m in damages and compensation, and accused of 'deceit' by a judge, after losing a High Court action against his former club over a £2m bonus. Kenny Jackett resigns as Rotherham manager after 39 days and five games in charge. Newcastle's Jack Colback is fined £25,000 by the FA for breaking betting rules. Norwich are fined £15,000 for the behaviour of their players against Queens Park Rangers.

29 Wembley's arch is lit up in green as a mark of respect for the 19 players and coaching staff of the Brazilian club Chapecoense who died in a plane crash on the way to a match in Colombia. Ben Woodburn, aged 17 years and 45 days, replaces Michael Owen as Liverpool's youngest-ever scorer with their second goal in a 2-0 win over Leeds in the quarter-finals of the EFL Cup.

30 Gareth Southgate is appointed permanent England manager on a four-year contract. Manchester United manager Jose Mourinho receives his second one-match ban in a month for improper conduct – this one for kicking a water bottle in frustration during the match with West Ham. It is accompanied by a £16,000 fine. Harry Kane signs a new contract through to 2022 with Tottenham.

DECEMBER 2016

1 In his first press conference, Gareth Southgate tells the England players that drinking heavily in the public eye is 'not intelligent' and they have to ask themselves 'how good they want to be.' He says Wayne Rooney will remain captain.

2 Robbie Neilson leaves Hearts to become the new MK Dons manager. Martin Allen ends his fourth spell as Barnet manager to take over at National League club Eastleigh. Tottenham's Jan Vertonghen signs a new contract through to 2019.

3 Clubs hold a minute's silence for victims of the plane crash in Colombia. Two Preston players, Jermaine Beckford and Eoin Doyle, are sent off for fighting each other during their team's defeat by Sheffield Wednesday and are fined by the club.

4 Ian Cathro, Newcastle's assistant coach, succeeds Robbie Neilson at Tynecastle.

5 Everton's Yannick Bolasie and Sunderland's Duncan Watmore are ruled out for the rest of the season with knee injuries.

6 Lucas Perez scores a hat-trick as Arsenal beat Basle 4-1 to finish top of their Champions League group.

7 Leicester, showing ten changes for their final group match, suffer the biggest-ever defeat by an English team in the tournament – 5-0 against Porto.

8 Manchester United reach the knockout stage of the Europa League. Southampton and the Irish club Dundalk fail to qualify from their groups.

9 Leeds owner Massimo Cellino is suspended from all football activities for 18 months and fined £250,000 by the FA for breaking agent regulations in the transfer of Ross McCormack to Fulham in 2014. The club are also fined £250,000. Agent Derek Day is banned for 18 months – 11 of which are suspended – and fined £75,000.

10 Hull's Robert Snodgrass publicly apologises after diving to win a penalty against Crystal Palace.

11 Cristiano Ronaldo is voted the world's best player for the fourth time after winning Euro 2016 with Portugal and the Champions League with Real Madrid. Barcelona's Lionel Messi is named runner-up, with Antoine Griezmann of Atletico Madrid third.

12 The FA sign a 12-year extension of their England kit deal with Nike worth a reported £400m. Chelsea's Cesar Azpilicueta signs a new three-and-a-half-year contract with the club.

13 Chelsea are fined £100,000 by the FA for a players' brawl in the game against Manchester City – the club's fifth penalty in 19 months for failing to control their players. City are fined £35,000.

14 Birmingham sack Gary Rowett with his side on the fringe of a play-off place. The club say it is a 'strategic, long term' decision. Rowett is replaced by former Watford and West Ham manager Gianfranco Zola.

15 West Bromwich Albion and Watford are each fined £45,000 by the FA for a players' melee. Brighton's Kazenga LuaLua is given a four-match ban and £8,000 fine for threatening behaviour towards a match official after being sent off in the Football League Trophy match against AFC Wimbledon. Bury caretaker-manager Chris Brass is given the job until the end of the season.

16 Ilkay Gundogan is ruled out for the rest of Manchester City's season with knee ligament damage. Everton's Gareth Barry, Leighton Baines and Mason Holgate sign contract extensions. Reece Oxford, West Ham's highly-rated defender, signs a new four-and-a-half-year deal on his 18th birthday.

17 Thirteen players are booked in Crawley's 3-1 League Two win over Newport, nine of them from the Welsh side.

18 Premier League champions Leicester are named the top team and Claudio Ranieri wins the coach's prize at the BBC Sports Personality of the Year awards.

19 FIFA fine all four home nations for players wearing poppies on their shirts in World Cup qualifiers around Armistice Day – England £35,000 for 'several incidents,' Scotland and Wales £15,700 and Northern Ireland £11,700.

20 Newcastle's Jonjo Shelvey is banned for five matches and fined £100,000 by the FA for racially abusing Romain Saiss, Wolves' Moroccan midfield player. Notts County manager John Sheridan receives a five-match touchline ban and £2,500 fine from the governing body for abusive language towards referee Eddie Ilderton and fourth official Matthew Donohue during the match against Wycombe. The Football League fine Shrewsbury £8,000 – with three-quarters of the sum suspended – for fielding two ineligible players in a 3-0 defeat at Charlton.

21 Russell Slade, former Charlton and Cardiff manager, takes charge at Coventry. Chelsea coach Steve Holland is appointed England's assistant manager. Reading and Sheffield Wednesday are both fined £15,000 by the FA for a players' confrontation.

22 Crystal Palace manager Alan Pardew is sacked after a single win in 11 Premier League matches. Hugo Lloris signs a three-year contract extension with Tottenham. West Ham's Diafra Sakho is ruled out of Senegal's squad for the Africa Cup of Nations with a back injury.

23 Three months after being forced out of the England job, Sam Allardyce returns to club football as Alan Pardew's replacement.

24 Chelsea agree to sell Oscar to Chinese Super League club Shanghai SIPG for £52m, a record fee for the Premier League club. Ben Foster signs a new two-and-a-half-year contract with West Bromwich Albion.

26 Port Vale manager Bruno Ribeiro resigns after six matches without a win leaves his side 17th in the table. In one of the season's most bizarre incidents, Watford mascot Harry the Hornet throws himself in front of Wilfried Zaha after the Palace forward's yellow card for diving during the match at Vicarage Road.

27 Bob Bradley, manager of Swansea for 85 days, is sacked after two wins in 11 matches, 29 goals conceded and with his team second from bottom. Harry the Hornet escapes FA disciplinary action, but is spoken to by the club 'about his responsibilities.'

28 Premier League official Mark Clattenburg is named the world's best referee at the Globe Soccer awards, having taken charge of the FA Cup, Champions League and Euro 2016 finals in 2016.

29 Wales manager Chris Coleman is ruled out of the running for the vacant Swansea job by his wife Charlotte on social media. Carlos Tevez, former Manchester City, Manchester United and West Ham striker, becomes the world's highest-paid player when signing for the Chinese Super League club Shanghai Shenhua for £615,000 a week.

30 James McClean signs a new two-and-a-half-year contract with West Bromwich Albion.

31 Chris Coleman receives an OBE in the New Year Honours for leading Wales to the last four of Euro 2016. Michael O'Neill, who took Northern Ireland to the finals, is awarded an MBE. So are Alex Scott, the Arsenal women's captain and winner of 136 England caps, and Sian Massey-Ellis, a Premier League and Football League assistant referee.

JANUARY 2017

2 John Sheridan, manager of Notts County for seven months, is sacked after nine successive defeats leaves his side a point off the relegation zone.

3 Hull, bottom-of-the-table, sack Mike Phelan two-and-a-half months after being appointed manager on a permanent basis. Gillingham dismiss Justin Edinburgh with his side 17th. Paul Clement, assistant to Carlo Ancelotti at Bayern Munich and a former Derby manager, fills the vacant Swansea job. Bristol City manager Lee Johnson and his assistant John Pemberton are both fined £2,000 by the FA for improper conduct at the end of the game against Wolves.

4 Ady Pennock, a former defender with the club, takes over at Gillingham until the end of the season.

5 Leeds owner Massimo Cellino sells half of his stake in the club to Italian businessman Andrea Radrizzani. Morecambe manager Jim Bentley receives a two-match touchline ban from the FA after being sent off during the home defeat by Cheltenham.

6 Marco Silva, former Sporting Lisbon and Olympiacos coach, takes charge at Hull. Everton sign Charlton forward Ademola Lookman for a League One record fee of £11m.

7 Stoke, West Bromwich Albion and Bournemouth lose FA Cup third round ties to teams from lower divisions.

8 Crewe's Steve Davis, appointed in November 2011 and the second longest-serving manager in League Two behind Morecambe's Jim Bentley, is sacked and replaced by academy manager David Artell, a former club captain. Chesterfield's Danny Wilson also loses his job after a run of poor results.

9 Robert Page, manager of Northampton for eight months, is sacked after eight defeats in ten matches. Peter Crouch, 35, signs a new one-year contract with Stoke.

10 FIFA decide to increase the number of teams at the World Cup from 32 to 48, starting in 2026. There will be 16 groups of three followed by the knockout stage.

11 Chelsea are given the go-ahead by local council planners for a new £500m, 60,000-seater stadium at Stamford Bridge. Notts County owner Ray Trew sells the club to Nottingham businessman Alan Hardy for a reported £3.5m. Kelly Smith, 38, record scorer for the England women's team, announces her retirement after 117 appearances and 46 goals.

12 Former England manager Graham Taylor dies, aged 72, following a heart attack. West Ham manager Slaven Bilic announces that midfielder Dimitri Payet no longer wants to play for the club. Ten days after losing his job at Notts County, John Sheridan is appointed manager of bottom-of-the-table Oldham for the third time. He replaces Stephen Robinson, sacked after six months in charge. Kevin Nolan, former Leyton Orient manager, takes over at Notts County. Three Arsenal players sign new contracts – Laurent Koscielny and Olivier Giroud until 2020 and Francis Coquelin until 2021.

13 The managerial merry-go-round continues. Ten days after his dismissal by Gillingham, Justin Edinburgh is appointed by Northampton. Caretaker Paul Warne is named Rotherham manager until the end of the season. Sheffield Wednesday are fined £15,000 by the FA for a breach of regulations over the loan of Sergiu Bus to Italian club Salernitana.

14 Philippe Montanier, manager of Nottingham Forest for seven months, is sacked with his side three points away from the relegation zone.

15 Hartlepool dismiss Craig Hignett, their manager for 11 months, after a run of one win in nine matches.

16 Oldham have their transfer embargo lifted.

17 Manchester City's Bacary Sagna is fined £40,000 by the FA for questioning the integrity of referee Lee Mason over the sending-off of Fernandinho against Burnley. Former Wigan manager Gary Caldell takes over at Chesterfield.

18 Dave Jones returns to management with Hartlepool, his first appointment since being sacked by Sheffield Wednesday in December, 2013.

19 Arsenal captain Per Mertesacker, out for the first half of the season with a knee injury, signs a one-year extension to his contract.

20 Steven Gerrard returns to Liverpool as a coach at the club's academy. West Bromwich Albion receive a club record £11.8m from Stoke for Saido Berahino. Manchester City pay a record fee of £175,000 for a 13-year-old – defender Finley Burns from Southend.

22 Ryan Mason has emergency surgery on a fractured skull after a clash of heads with Gary Cahill in Hull's match at Chelsea.

23 A winding-up petition against Southend is dismissed by a judge after the club pay off a debt to Revenue and Customs.

24 Middlesbrough owner Steve Gibson rejects a bid of around £50m by a Chinese consortium for a 50 per cent stake in the club.

25 Southampton reach the League Cup Final, defeating Liverpool 2-0 on aggregate. Philippe Coutinho signs a new five-year contract with Liverpool.

26 Manchester United win the second semi-final, beating Hull 3-2 over the two legs. Luton manager Nathan Jones is given a one-match touchline ban and £500 fine by the FA for abusive language towards match officials at the end of the game against Wycombe.

27 Arsenal manager Arsene Wenger is given a four-match touchline ban and £25,000 fine by the FA for his behaviour towards referee Jon Moss and fourth official Anthony Taylor during the game against Burnley. Sunderland's Papy Djilobodji is also banned for four games after being caught on camera striking West Bromwich Albion's Darren Fletcher.

28 Two non-league clubs – Lincoln and Sutton – reach the last 16 of the FA Cup for the first time. Kilmarnock's Kris Boyd scores the Scottish Premier League's fastest-ever goal after 10 seconds against Ross County.

29 Dimitri Payet is accused by West Ham joint chairman David Sullivan of showing a lack of 'commitment and respect' to the club after rejoining Marseille for £25m. Danny Webb, son of former Chelsea defender David Webb, is appointed Leyton Orient manager until the end of the season.

30 Nigel Clough turns down the chance to follow in the footsteps of his father Brian as Nottingham Forest manager to stay with Burton. Ryan Mason returns home after a week in hospital in London. Wolves pay a club record £13m for Benfica winger Helder Costa.

31 Watford's Odion Ighalo becomes the latest player to move to China, joining Changchun Yatai for £20m – a record fee for the Premier League club. Burnley sign Robbie Brady from Norwich for £13m – a record for both clubs. Brentford receive a record £12m from Aston

Villa for Scott Hogan. Premier League clubs record a transfer window profit for the first time, despite spending a six-year January high of £215m. They bring in £40m more, according to finance analysts Deloitte.

FEBRUARY 2017

1   The Scottish League decide to retain a three-week mid-season break for the Premiership next season. Fleetwood are fined £4,000 by the FA for failing to keep accurate records of players' whereabouts for doping tests.

2   Saido Berahino, Stoke's new signing from West Bromwich Albion, is revealed to have served a two-month ban for failing an out-of-competition drugs test in September, 2016. The FA fine Queens Park Rangers £40,000 and Fulham £36,000 for clashes between players. Rangers coach Marc Bircham and Fulham's Marco Cesarini are both fined £2,000 for their involvement.

3   An 18-month ban imposed on Leeds chairman Massimo Cellino for breaking agent regulations is reduced by the FA on appeal to a year. The governing body also cut a £250,000 fine to £100,000 and reduce that of his club from £250,000 to £200,000.

4   Aidy Boothroyd, interim manager of England's under-21 team, is appointed by the FA to take charge for the summer's European Championship.

5   Cameroon win the Africa Cup of Nations Final 2-1 after Arsenal's Mohamed Elneny puts Egypt ahead.

6   Leicester manager Claudio Ranieri receives 'unwavering support' from the club's owners after his side drop to within a point of the relegation zone.

7   Greg Clarke threatens to resign as FA chairman if his proposals for reforming the governing body are not approved by the Government.

8   Chris Brunt signs a new contract to stay at West Bromwich Albion until at least the summer of 2018.

9   Joint caretaker-managers Gary Brazil and Jack Lester are told to stay in charge at Nottingham Forest until the end of the season after three wins in four matches.

10 Thirteen players are reported to have tested positive for social drugs since 2012, with their names not disclosed by the FA.

11 Mystery surrounds the departure of manager Mark Warburton from Rangers. The club say he resigned. Warburton denies doing so.

12 Harry Winks, Tottenham's England under-21 midfielder, signs a new contract through to 2022.

14 West Ham manager Slaven Bilic is fined £8,000 by the FA for throwing a TV microphone to the ground during the game against West Bromwich Albion. His assistant, Nikola Jurcevic, is fined the same amount after admitting a separate misconduct charge.

15 Mark Clattenburg, the Premier League's top referee, quits to become Saudi Arabia's new head of referees. Lee Clark leaves Kilmarnock to become Bury's new manager. Kevin Nugent, Charlton's assistant manager, takes over at Barnet.

16 Manchester City are fined £35,000 by the FA for failing to provide accurate information of their players' whereabouts for doping tests. Hull are fined £20,000 for failing to control their players against Arsenal. Championship clubs agree to introduce goal-line technology for the 2017–18 season. The FA post a record turnover of £370m for 2015–16. Zlatan Ibrahimovic scores a hat-trick in Manchester United's 3-0 win over St Etienne in the Europa League round of 16 first leg.

17 Leyton Orient captain Liam Kelly is banned for six games by the FA after being caught on camera pushing over a ball-boy during the win at Plymouth. The governing body deem the standard three-match suspension for violent conduct 'clearly insufficient.'

18 Lincoln become the first non-league side to reach the last eight of the FA Cup since Queens Park Rangers in 1914. They beat Burnley 1-0 at Turf Moor with an 89th minute goal from Sean Raggett.

20 Sutton go out with flying colours, beaten 2-0 by Arsenal after victories over three league sides – Leeds, AFC Wimbledon and Cheltenham.

21 Manchester City's 5-3 win over Monaco goes into the Champions League record books – the first time eight goals have been scored in the first leg of a knockout tie. Blackburn manager Owen Coyle is sacked with his side second from bottom. Wycombe manager Gareth Ainsworth is given a one-match touchline ban and £500 fine by the FA for misconduct during the match against Crewe.

22 Manchester United reach the last 16 of the Europa League with a 4-0 aggregate win over St Etienne. Adam Lallana signs a new three-year contract with Liverpool. Tony Mowbray, formerly in charge at Coventry, succeeds Owen Coyle at Blackburn. Three months after leaving Barnet to become manager of Eastleigh, Martin Allen is dismissed by the National League club, having won only two of 14 games.

23 Claudio Ranieri, who led Leicester to their historic Premier League title win, is sacked – less than three weeks after receiving 'unwavering support' from the club's Thai owners. They claim a change of manager is essential because of fears of relegation. Tottenham go out of the Europa League at the first knockout stage, beaten 3-2 on aggregate by Gent after Dele Alli is sent off and Harry Kane scores an own goal in the second leg. Barnsley manager Paul Heckingbottom is given a one-match touchline ban and £2,000 fine by the FA for misconduct during the match against Wolves.

24 Blackburn's Hope Akpan has a three-match ban for violent conduct extended to four games for pushing referee Scott Duncan after being sent off against Sheffield Wednesday. His club are fined £5,000 for their players' response to the incident. Celtic are fined £10,000 by UEFA for crowd disturbances at the Champions League match against Manchester City.

25 Manager Neil Warnock signs a one-year extension to his contract after leading Cardiff away from relegation trouble.

26 Manchester United beat Southampton 3-2 in the EFL Cup Final with an 87th minute goal from Zlatan Ibrahimovic.

27 Huddersfield manager David Wagner receives a two-match touchline ban and £6,000 fine from the FA for an altercation with Leeds' manager Garry Monk, who is banned for one game and fined £3,000. Both clubs are fined £10,000.

28 Motherwell sack manager Mark McGhee after a run of poor results, culminating a 5-1 home defeat by Dundee.

MARCH 2017

1 Middlesbrough's Adam Clayton signs a contract extension through to 2021.

2 Leandro Bacuna is banned for six matches for barging an assistant referee during Aston Villa's win over Derby. The FA rule that the standard three game ban for violent conduct is insufficient.

3 The law-making International FA Board, meeting at Wembley, give the go-ahead for video technology to assists referees from the third round of the FA Cup next season.

4 BT agree a £1.2bn deal with UEFA to show Champions League and Europa League matches for another four years.

5 Russell Slade is sacked after ten weeks as manager of Coventry with his side 13 points adrift at the bottom of League One.

6 Coventry appoint Mark Robins manager for the second time, four years after he left the club to take over at Huddersfield.

7 Arsenal suffer a second 5-1 loss to Bayern Munich and go out of the Champions League at the round of 16 stage for the seventh successive season. The 10-2 aggregate is the heaviest defeat for an English team in the tournament's knockout stage. Zlatan Ibrahimovic is banned for three matches after being caught on camera elbowing Tyrone Mings in Manchester United's game against Bournemouth.

8 Barcelona make Champions League history by retrieving a 4-0 deficit from the first leg of their Champions League last 16 match against Paris Saint-Germain. They win the return game 6-1 with three goals in the final seven minutes in front of a 96,000 crowd at the Nou Camp. The FA rule that a three-match ban for Tyrone Mings for stamping on the head of Zlatan Ibrahimovic is 'clearly insufficient' and impose five games.

9 Bournemouth are fined £35,000 by the FA for failing to provide accurate information of their players' whereabouts for doping tests. Tottenham's Ben Davies signs a new four-year contract. Graham Westley, manager of Newport for five months, is sacked with his side 11 points adrift at the bottom of League Two.

10 Norwich manager Alex Neil is sacked after a single win in seven games leaves his side nine points away from a play-off place.

11 Lincoln's FA Cup adventure comes to an end with a 5-0 defeat by Arsenal in a sixth round tie. Pedro Caixinha, Portuguese coach with Qatari club Al-Gharafa, is appointed the new Rangers manager.

12 Steve McClaren is dismissed by Derby for the second time, with his team ten points adrift of the play-offs after his six months in charge. Craig Shakespeare is appointed Leicester manager until the end of the season after winning both games as caretaker.

13 Wigan's Warren Joyce becomes the 15th managerial departure of the season in the Championship. Joyce, in charge for four months, is dismissed a fortnight after eye surgery with Wigan second from bottom.

14 Leicester reach the Champions League quarter-finals with a 3-2 aggregate win over Sevilla. A month after leaving Rangers, Mark Warburton is named Nottingham Forest's new manager. Three months after his departure from Birmingham, Gary Rowett takes over at Derby.

15 Leicester are left as England's only survivors, with Manchester City beaten on away goals by Monaco after a 6-6 aggregate scoreline. Former Oldham manager Stephen Robinson takes charge at Motherwell.

16 Middlesbrough manager Aitor Karanka is sacked with his team second from bottom after ten matches without a win. Manchester United reach the Europa League quarter-finals by beating Rostov 2-1 on aggregate. Sheffield Wednesday manager Carlos Carvalhal is fined £2,000 by the FA for improper conduct during the match against Aston Villa.

17 Manchester United are fined £20,000 by the FA for their players' behaviour following the sending-off of Ander Herrera during the FA Cup defeat by Chelsea. Scunthorpe manager Graham Alexander is given a one-match touchline ban and £1,000 fine for abusive language after his side conceded three penalties in nine minutes against Gillingham.

18 FA Cup heroes Lincoln are beaten 3-2 on aggregate by York in the semi-finals of the FA Trophy.

20 Leyton Orient survive an immediate winding-up order in the High Court after paying a tax bill. Owner Francesco Becchetti is ordered to pay off debts or sell the club.

22 Gareth Southgate suffers his first defeat as England manager – 1-0 away to Germany. In another friendly, Scotland are held 1-1 by Canada.

23 Everton agree a deal to buy land on the banks of the River Mersey for a new 50,000-seater stadium.

24 Seamus Coleman sustains a broken leg in the Republic of Ireland's goalless World Cup qualifier against Wales. Neil Taylor is shown a straight red card for his challenge on the Everton defender.

26 Jermain Defoe returns to the England side after an absence of more than three years and scores in a 2-0 World Cup qualifying win over Lithuania. A goal by Jamie Ward after 90 seconds puts Northern Ireland on the way to victory over Norway by the same scoreline. Chris Martin comes off the bench to revive Scotland's chances of qualifying with an 88th minute winner against Slovenia.

27 Manchester City are fined £35,000 by the FA for their players' behaviour after conceding a penalty against Liverpool.

28 An experimental Republic of Ireland side, with four new caps, lose 1-0 at home to Iceland in a friendly international.

29 Vauxhall decide to end their multi-million pound sponsorship of the four home nations' international teams after the 2018 World Cup.

30 Danny Webb resigns after two months as manager of relegation-bound Leyton Orient, having won two of his 12 games in charge. His assistant, Omer Riza, takes over until the end of the season – the club's fifth manager of the season. Manchester City women reach the

Champions League semi-finals with a 2-0 aggregate win over Danish side Fortuna Hjørring.

31 Burton defender Ben Turner is banned for five games and fined £8,000 by the FA for racially abusing Brentford's Nico Yennaris.

APRIL 2017

1 Rotherham are the first team to be relegated – with seven Championship matches still to play.

2 Celtic clinch their sixth successive title with eight games to spare, Scott Sinclair scoring a hat-trick in a 5-0 victory against Hearts. Coventry beat Oxford 2-1 in the Football League Trophy Final, watched by a crowd of more than 74,000 at Wembley.

3 Tom Davies, Everton's 18-year-old midfielder, signs a new contract through to 2022.

4 Leeds defender Liam Cooper, caught on camera stamping on Reading's Reece Oxford, is banned for six matches by the FA because of the severity of the offence.

5 Liverpool are fined £100,000 by the Premier League and banned for two years from signing academy players from other clubs for a breach of rules involving an approach to a 12-year-old at Stoke. A year of the ban is suspended. Paul Warne, Rotherham's caretaker-manager for four months, is given the job on a permanent basis.

6 Celtic manager Brendan Rodgers signs a new four-year contract. Manchester United's Jesse Lingard agrees a new deal through to 2021. Football League clubs agree to increase the number of home-grown players on team sheets from six to seven from the 2007-18 season. They also decide for at least one club-developed player to be included from 2018-19

7 Figures show Premier League clubs paying £174m to agents over the last two transfer windows, with Manchester City (£26m), Chelsea (£25m) and Manchester Utd (£19m) spending the most. Newcastle (£10m), Charlton (£608,000) and Portsmouth (£175,000) are the highest spenders in the other divisions. Two St Johnstone players, Danny Swanson and Richard Foster, are fined by the club for fighting each other at half-time of the match against Hamilton

8 Sheffield United and Doncaster are the first Football League clubs to win promotion.

9 Marcus Bignot, Grimsby manager for five months, is sacked, with players reportedly refusing to sign new contracts while he remained in the job. Brighton's Anthony Knockaert is named Championship Player of the Year. Billy Sharp (Sheffield United) and John Marquis (Doncaster) win the League One and League Two awards.

10 Former Arsenal and England captain Tony Adams is appointed head coach of Spanish club Granada.

11 The Champions League quarter-final between Borussia Dortmund and Monaco is postponed following three explosions near the Dortmund team bus. Defender Marc Bartra has surgery on his wrist to remove fragments of glass from a shattered window.

12 The first leg game goes on 24 hours later, against Dortmund's wishes, and they are beaten 3-2.

13 Russell Slade is appointed Grimsby manager for the second time, having been in charge from 2004–06. It's his third job of the season after spells with Coventry and Charlton.

15 Kevin Nugent, with a single win in 11 games, is sacked after two months as Barnet manager.

16 John Terry announces he is leaving Chelsea at the end of the season after a 22-year association with the club.

17 Gianfranco Zola resigns as Birmingham manager after two wins in 22 league games. Brighton are promoted to the Premier League.

18 Harry Redknapp returns to league management at St Andrew's on a temporary basis, nearly two years after leaving Queens Park Rangers. Leicester's Champions League run comes to an end with a 2-1 aggregate defeat by Atletico Madrid. Glen Johnson signs a one-year contract extension with Stoke.

19 Ross County's Alex Schalk is banned for two matches by the Scottish FA for a dive which won his side a penalty against Celtic.

20 Manchester United reach the Europa League semi-finals with an extra-time goal from Marcus Rashford for a 3-2 aggregate win over Anderlecht. The victory is clouded by a knee injury sustained by leading scorer Zlatan Ibrahimovic, who is ruled out for the remainder of the season and into the 2017-18 campaign and is later released by the club. The FA fine Huddersfield £12,500 and Burton £5,000 for a players' melee – Huddersfield's second punishment of the season.

21 Ugo Ehiogu, former Aston Villa, Middlesbrough and England defender, dies aged 44 after suffering a cardiac arrest at Tottenham's training centre, where he was under-23 coach.

22 Chelsea reach the FA Cup Final with a 4-2 win over Tottenham. Aberdeen defeat Hibernian 3-2 in the first Scottish Cup semi-final. Leyton Orient are relegated after 112 years in the Football League. Lincoln return, after an absence of six years, as National League champions.

23 Arsenal set up an all-London final at Wembley by beating Manchester City 2-1 after extra-time. Celtic go through to meet Aberdeen with a 2-0 victory over Rangers. Chelsea's N'Golo Kante is named the Professional Footballers' Association Player of the Year.

24 Newcastle clinch promotion back to the Premier League at the first attempt. Dave Jones, Hartlepool manager for three months, is sacked after his side drop into the bottom two with two matches to play.

25 Neil Taylor has a standard one-match sending-off ban doubled by FIFA for the tackle which left Seamus Coleman with a broken leg in the Wales-Republic of Ireland World Cup qualifier.

26 Joey Barton admits his career may be over after an 18-month FA ban for breaching betting rules. The Burnley player is also fined £30,000 after admitting to 1,260 bets on matches. Chelsea win the FA Youth Cup for the sixth time in eight seasons. Two clubs, West Ham and Newcastle, are visited by Revenue and Customs officers investing suspected tax fraud.

27 Birmingham captain Paul Robinson is banned for three games by the FA after being caught on camera hitting out at Aston Villa's James Chester.

28 Liverpool's Dejan Lovren signs a new contract through to 2021.

29 Sunderland are relegated after ten seasons in the Premier League.

MAY 2017

2 The FA face widespread calls to follow the lead of Scotland's governing body and crack down on players diving.

3 Michael Brown, caretaker-manager of relegated Port Vale for five months, is appointed on a permanent basis.

4 Crawley, fourth from bottom in League Two, sack manager Dermot Drummy. Swindon's Luke Williams leaves the club after relegation.

5 Manchester City are fined £300,000 and banned from signing academy players for two years by the Premier League for a breach of rules involving approaches to an 11-year-old at Everton and a 15-year-old at Wolves. The FA ban Accrington's Paddy Lacey for 14 months for a drugs offence.

6 Hartlepool are relegated after 96 years in the Football League, going down after Newport score an 89th minute winner against Notts County to stay up. Portsmouth win the League Two title.

7 Newcastle are Championship winners after Brighton concede an 89th minute equaliser against Aston Villa. Celtic's Brendan Rodgers in named Scotland's Manager of the Year. Scott Sinclair, his leading scorer, is voted Player of the Year by the Scottish PFA.

8 Middlesbrough are relegated from the Premier League after losing 3-0 to Chelsea, who move to the brink of becoming champions. Chelsea's N'Golo Kante adds the football writers' Footballer of the Year award to his PFA title. Ched Evans rejoins Sheffield United, from Chesterfield, five years after being released by the club when sent to prison.

9 Mike Flynn is appointed permanent manager after leading Newport away for relegation. Football League figures show that more than 18 million fans watched matches during the season, the highest since 1959.

10 Harry Redknapp signs a one-year contract after keeping Birmingham in the Championship.

11 Manchester United reach the Europa League Final with a 2-1 aggregate victory over Celta Vigo. Michail Antonio, West Ham's Player of the Year, signs a new four-year contract.

12 Chelsea become Premier League champions in Antonio Conte's first season in English football. They make sure by beating West Bromwich Albion 1-0 with a goal by substitute Michy Batshuayi. Kevin Mirallas signs a contract extension through to 2020 with Everton.

14 Hull are relegated from the Premier League. Forest Green become the smallest club in the

Football League. The team from Nailsworth (pop 5,800) in Gloucestershire beat Tranmere 3-1 in the National League Play-off Final. Tottenham legends past and present – among them Pat Jennings, Ossie Ardiles, Martin Chivers, David Ginola and Glenn Hoddle – are paraded before the final game at White Hart Lane before the stadium is demolished, after 118 years, in readiness for a new one next door.

15 Telecoms company Vodafone pull out of a £20m deal to sponsor West Ham's London Stadium.

16 Walter Mazzarri, manager of Watford for a year, is sacked after five successive defeats.

17 Nottingham Forest are taken over by a Chinese consortium. The club's previous Thai owners retain a minority stake. Cristiano Ronaldo overtakes Jimmy Greaves as the all-time leading scorer in Europe's five major leagues, scoring twice for Real Madrid against Celta Vigo to take his tally to 368.

18 The FA address the problem of players diving by introducing a retrospective two-match ban for offenders. Greek shipping magnate Evangelos Marinakis buys Reading from Fawaz Al Hasawi.

20 Millwall's 1-0 victory over Bradford in the League One Play-off Final is marred by an invasion of the Wembley pitch by supporters at the final whistle. Inverness are relegated from the Scottish Premiership.

21 Scottish champions Celtic become the first team since Rangers in 1899 to complete a league season without losing. Leading scorer Scott Sinclair adds the football writers' Footballer of the Year award to his PFA prize. Arsenal miss out on a Champions League place for the first time in 20 years.

22 Chelsea's Antonio Conte is named the League Managers' Association and Premier League Manager of the Year. David Moyes resigns as manager of relegated Sunderland.

23 Sam Allardyce resigns after leading Crystal Palace away from the threat of relegation. Former Leeds and Liverpool winger Harry Kewell takes over at Crawley. Arsenal captain Laurent Koscielny is ruled out of the FA Cup Final against Chelsea after losing an appeal against his sending off in the final Premier League game against Everton. Italian businessman Andrea Radrizzani completes a takeover of Leeds, ending Massimo Cellino's controversial three years as owner of the club.

24 Two nights after a bomb attack in their city killed 22 people and injured many more, Manchester United defeat Ajax 2-0 in the Europa League Final to win a Champions League place. Chelsea cancel their victory parade because of the bombing.

25 Two managers resign – Marco Silva after Hull's relegation and Garry Monk after failing to agree a new deal with Leeds. Norwich appoint Borussia Dortmund's Daniel Farke as their new manager. Wilfried Zaha signs a five-year extension to his contract with Crystal Palace. Dundee United's Simon Murray is booked twice for diving and sent off in the first leg of the Scottish Premiership Play-off Final against Hamilton. The red card is later rescinded after a successful appeal against the first yellow.

26 Manchester City make the first big signing of the summer, paying £43m for Monaco midfielder Bernardo Silva. Antonio Valencia signs a new contract with Manchester United through to 2019.

27 Arsenal win the FA Cup for a record 13th time and manager Arsene Wenger achieves a record seventh success. His side are 2-1 winners over favourites Chelsea, who have Victor Moses sent off for a second yellow card, this one for diving. Celtic complete a season's Treble by beating Aberdeen 2-1 in the Scottish Cup Final with a stoppage-time goal by substitute Tom Rogic.

28 Blackpool defeat Exeter 2-1 in the League Two Play-off Final. Michael Carrick extends his contract with Manchester United by a year.

29 Huddersfield reach the Premier League for the first time, beating Reading 4-3 on penalties after a goalless 120 minutes. Inverness sack manager Richie Foran after relegation from the Scottish Premiership.

30 Arsenal manager Arsene Wenger ends months of speculation about his future by signing a new two-year contract.

31 Former Porto and Valencia coach Nuno Espirito Santo becomes the fourth Wolves manager in ten months, following the departure of Paul Lambert. Paul Cook leaves promoted Portsmouth to take charge at Wigan.

JUNE 2017

1 Manchester City's Yaya Toure agrees a one-year contract extension. Henry McClelland, chairman of Scottish League Two club Annan, is fined £3,000 – with £2,000 suspended – by the Scottish FA for placing more than 4,000 football bets, including 430 involving his own club.

2 Liam Boyce scores his first international goal to give Northern Ireland a 1-0 win over New Zealand. In another friendly, the Republic of Ireland lose 3-1 to Mexico in New Jersey, with Stephen Gleeson on the mark for the first time for the Republic. Kenny Jackett, former Rotherham and Wolves manager, takes charge of Portsmouth. Keith Wyness, Aston Villa's chief executive, is banned from all football-related activity for three weeks and fined £10,000 by the FA for posting an offensive message on social media. Neil McCann, who led Dundee away from the threat of relegation from the Scottish Premiership as caretaker following the dismissal of Paul Hartley, is appointed permanent manager.

3 Real Madrid win the Champions League for the third time in four years, beating Juventus 4-1 at the Principality Stadium, Cardiff.

4 Former Scotland international Lee McCulloch is confirmed as Kilmarnock manager after three months as caretaker The Republic Ireland defeat Uruguay 3-0 in a friendly international.

5 Former Bury manager David Flitcroft takes charge of Swindon.

6 David Wagner, manager of promoted Huddersfield, agrees a new contract with the club.

7 Liverpool apologise to Southampton over allegations of an illegal approach to Virgil van Dijk and end their interest in the player.

8 Manchester City pay a world record fee of £34.9m for a goalkeeper – Benfica's Ederson. England reach the World Youth Cup Final by beating Italy 3-1.

9 Former Leeds manager Garry Monk takes charge at Middlesbrough. Hull appoint former Russia and CSKA Moscow coach Leonid Slutsky. Former Sunderland manager David Moyes is fined £30,000 by the FA for telling a BBC reporter 'she might get a slap'. Tony Mowbray signs a new two-year contract with relegated Blackburn.

10 A stoppage-time goal by new captain Harry Kane gives England a 2-2 World Cup qualifying draw against Scotland at Hampden Park after they trail to two free-kicks by Leigh Griffiths – the Celtic player's first goals for his country. Stuart Dallas also scores in added time to keep Northern Ireland on track for the play-offs with a 1-0 victory in Azerbaijan.

11 Wales draw for the fifth time in six qualifiers – 1-1 away to Serbia. The Republic of Ireland share the same scoreline with Austria. England under-20s become the country's first world champions since Bobby Moore's team in 1966. They beat Venezuela 1-0 in the final in Suwon, South Korea, with a goal by Everton's Dominic Calvert-Lewin.

12 A winding-up petition against relegated Leyton Orient is dismissed in the High Court after creditors are paid.

13 Two goals by Harry Kane are not enough to save England from a 3-2 defeat by ten-man France in a friendly international. Kane's second is a penalty, awarded by the video assistant referee for a trip on Dele Alli by Raphael Varane, who is sent off two minutes into the second-half.

14 Southampton, eighth in the Premier League and League Cup finalists, sack Claude Puel after one season as manager. Manchester United sign Benfica central defender Victor Lindelof for £30.7m. Hull receive a club record £17m from Leicester for Harry Maguire.

15 Jordan Pickford becomes the most expensive English goalkeeper in a £30m move from Sunderland to Everton – a record fee for both clubs. Everton also sign Ajax midfielder Davy Klaassen for £23.6m. Aberdeen's Derek McInness turns down the vacant Sunderland's manager's job.

16 Jordan Pickford saves a penalty as England draw 0-0 with Sweden in their opening match of the European under-21 Championship in Poland.

18 Thomas Christiansen, former coach to the Cypriot club Apoel Nicosia, is, appointed the new Leeds manager.

19 England come from behind to beat Slovakia 2-1 to revive their chances of qualifying for the semi-finals.

20 Burton pay an undisclosed club record fee, reported to be around £500,000 for Ross County's Liam Boyce, the Scottish Premiership season's leading scorer.

21 The Premier League write to all 20 clubs asking if they would be interested in piloting safe standing at their grounds.

22 England under-21s defeat Poland 3-0 to top their group and qualifying for the semi-finals. Liverpool sign former Chelsea winger Mohamed Salah from Roma for £34.3m. The FA end all sponsorship with betting companies, including mutually terminating a deal with Ladbrokes.

23 Mauricio Pellegrino, former Liverpool and Argentina defender, is named Southampton's new manager. Leyton Orient, relegated and run-down under the three-year ownership of Francesco Becchetti, are taken over by a consortium headed by businessman Nigel Travis, a life-long supporter of the club. Huddersfield break their transfer record with the £3.5m signing of Porto striker Laurent Depoitre.

24 Arsenal, Chelsea and the FA agree to give the proceeds from the 2017 Community Shield match to the Grenfell Tower fire disaster fund.

25 Frank de Boer, former Inter Milan and Ajax coach, is appointed Crystal Palace's new manager.

26 League One Shrewsbury become the first English club to seek permission for a safe standing area at their ground, pioneered by Celtic in 2016. Michael Appleton leaves Oxford to become Leicester's assistant manager.

27 England under-21s are knocked out by Germany, who win a penalty shoot-out 4-3 after a 2-2 scoreline. The FA are accused in a FIFA report of flouting bidding rules in their unsuccessful attempt to stage the 2018 World Cup.

28 The Crown Prosecution Service announce that six people face criminal trials over the 1989 Hillsborough disaster. There are no charges brought against Sheffield Wednesday or the FA. Bristol City pay a club record £5.3m for Senegal international striker Famara Diedhiou from the French club Angers.

29 Simon Grayson leaves Preston to become Sunderland's new manager. Kieran Trippier signs a new five-year contract with Tottenham.

30 Two clubs break their transfer records. Bournemouth pay £20m for Chelsea's Nathan Ake. Huddersfield sign Manchester City's Aaron Mooy for £8m. Clubs are advised to make a stadium check for the cladding thought to have contributed to the Grenfell Tower fire disaster.

JULY 2017

1 Spaniard Pep Clotet, former assistant at Leeds and Swansea, is appointed Oxford manager.

2 Angelo Ogbonna signs a new five-year contract with West Ham.

3 Burnley's Michael Keane joins Everton for an initial £25m fee. Former Chelsea stalwart John Terry signs a one-year contract with Aston Villa.

4 Rangers suffer a humiliating 2-1 aggregate defeat by Progres Niederkorn, a team of part-time players from Luxembourg, in the first qualifying round of the Europa League.

5 Arsenal sign Lyon striker Alexandre Lacazette for a club record £46.5m. Huddersfield break their transfer record for the third time in a fortnight, spending £11.4m on Montpellier striker Steve Mounie. Former Norwich manager Alex Neil takes over at Preston.

6 Arsenal captain Per Mertesacker announces he will retire at the end of the 2017-18 season and become the club's academy manager.

7 West Ham's Pedro Obiang signs a new contract through to 2022.

8 Wolves break their transfer record with the £15m signing of Porto midfielder Ruben Neves.

9 Wayne Rooney returns to Everton on a free transfer after 13 years at Manchester United. Chelsea sign Germany defender Antonio Rudiger from Roma for an initial £29m.

10 Manchester United sign Everton's Romelu Lukaku for £75m – the most expensive transfer between Premier League clubs.

14 Manchester City sign Tottenham's Kyle Walker for an initial £45.

15 Chelsea sign Monaco midfielder Tiemoue Bakayoko for £39.7m. England become European under-19 champions, beating Portugal 2-1 in the final in Georgia.

ENGLISH TABLES 2016–2017

PREMIER LEAGUE

		P	Home W	D	L	F	A	Away W	D	L	F	A	GD	Pts
1	Chelsea	38	17	0	2	55	17	13	3	3	30	16	52	93
2	Tottenham	38	17	2	0	47	9	9	6	4	39	17	60	86
3	Manchester City	38	11	7	1	37	17	12	5	5	43	22	41	78
4	Liverpool	38	12	5	2	45	18	10	5	4	33	24	36	76
5	Arsenal	38	14	3	2	39	16	9	3	7	38	28	33	75
6	Manchester Utd	38	8	10	1	26	12	10	5	4	28	17	25	69
7	Everton	38	13	4	2	42	16	4	6	9	20	28	18	61
8	Southampton	38	6	6	7	17	21	6	4	9	24	27	-7	46
9	Bournemouth	38	9	4	6	35	29	3	6	10	20	38	-12	46
10	WBA	38	9	2	8	27	22	3	7	9	16	29	-8	45
11	West Ham	38	7	4	8	19	31	5	5	9	28	33	-17	45
12	Leicester	38	10	4	5	31	25	2	4	13	17	38	-15	44
13	Stoke	38	7	6	6	24	24	4	5	10	17	32	-15	44
14	Crystal Palace	38	6	2	11	24	25	6	3	10	26	38	-13	41
15	Swansea	38	8	3	8	27	34	4	2	13	18	36	-25	41
16	Burnley	38	10	3	6	26	20	1	4	14	13	35	-16	40
17	Watford	38	8	4	7	25	29	3	3	13	15	39	-28	40
18	Hull	38	8	4	7	28	35	1	3	15	9	45	-43	34
19	Middlesbrough	38	4	6	9	17	23	1	7	11	10	30	-26	28
20	Sunderland	38	3	5	11	16	34	3	1	15	13	35	-40	24

Chelsea, Tottenham, Manchester City, Manchester Utd into Champions League group stage, Liverpool into play-off round; Arsenal into Europea League group stage, Everton into third qualifying round
Prize money (league position = amount received): 1 £153.2m, 2 £148.5m, 3 £149.4m, 4 £148.4m, 5 £142.7m, 6 £143.6m, 7 £132.4m, 8 £127.6m, 9 £123.9m, 10 £120m, 11 £121.8m, 12 £120.9m, 13 £113.4m, 14 £115.1m, 15 £109.5m, 16 £107.6m, 17 £108.5m, 8 £103.8m, 19 £104.6m, 20 £99.9m

Biggest win: Hull 1 Tottenham 7
Highest aggregate score: Everton 6 Bournemouth 3; Swansea 5 Crystal Palace 4
Highest attendance: 75,397 (Manchester Utd v WBA)
Lowest attendance: 10,890 (Bournemouth v Middlesbrough)
Player of Year: N'Golo Kante (Chelsea)
Manager of Year: Antonio Conte (Chelsea)
Golden Boot: 29 Harry Kane (Tottenham)
Golden Glove: 16 clean sheets Thibaut Courtois (Chelsea)
PFA Team of Year: De Gea (Manchester Utd), Walker (Tottenham), Luiz (Chelsea), Cahill (Chelsea), Rose (Tottenham), Alli (Tottenham), Hazard (Chelsea), Kante (Chelsea), Mane (Liverpool), Kane (Tottenham), Lukaku (Everton)
Leading league scorers: 29 Kane (Tottenham); 25 Lukaku (Everton); 24 Sanchez (Arsenal); 20 Aguero (Manchester City), Diego Costa (Chelses); 18 Alli (Tottenham); 17 Ibrahimovic (Manchester Utd); 16 Hazard (Chelsea), King (Bournemouth); 15 Benteke (Crystal Palace), Defoe (Sunderland), Llorente (Swansea); 14 Son Heung-min (Tottenham); 13 Coutinho (Liverpool), Mane (Liverpool), Vardy (Leicester); 12 Giroud (Arsenal); 11 Firmino (Liverpool); 10 Deeney (Watford), Vokes (Burnley), Walcott (Arsenal)

SKY BET CHAMPIONSHIP

		P	Home W	D	L	F	A	Away W	D	L	F	A	GD	Pts
1	Newcastle	46	15	3	5	49	23	14	4	5	36	17	45	94
2	Brighton	46	17	3	3	46	14	11	6	6	28	26	34	93
3	Reading	46	16	5	2	35	16	10	2	11	33	48	4	85
4	Sheffield Wed	46	15	2	6	36	22	9	7	7	24	23	15	81
5	Huddersfield*	46	15	2	6	34	26	10	4	9	22	32	-2	81
6	Fulham	46	10	8	5	45	32	12	6	5	40	25	28	80
7	Leeds	46	14	4	5	32	16	8	5	10	29	31	14	75
8	Norwich	46	15	4	4	55	22	6	6	12	30	47	16	70
9	Derby	46	11	8	4	33	20	7	5	11	21	30	4	67
10	Brentford	46	11	5	7	42	25	7	5	11	33	40	10	64
11	Preston	46	11	6	6	40	26	5	8	10	24	37	1	62
12	Cardiff	46	11	4	8	31	26	6	7	10	29	35	-1	62
13	Aston Villa	46	12	8	3	33	20	4	6	13	14	28	-1	62
14	Barnsley	46	6	11	6	32	33	9	2	12	32	34	-3	58
15	Wolves	46	8	4	11	25	30	8	6	9	29	28	-4	58
16	Ipswich	46	8	10	5	30	24	5	6	12	18	34	-10	55
17	Bristol City	46	11	4	8	33	26	4	5	14	27	40	-6	54
18	QPR	46	9	4	10	30	32	6	4	13	22	34	-14	53
19	Birmingham	46	8	5	10	25	31	5	9	9	20	33	-19	53
20	Burton	46	9	4	10	28	30	4	9	10	21	33	-14	52
21	Nottm Forest	46	12	4	7	42	30	2	5	16	20	42	-10	51
22	Blackburn	46	8	8	7	29	30	4	7	12	24	35	-12	51
23	Wigan	46	5	8	10	19	26	5	4	14	21	31	-17	42
24	Rotherham	46	5	6	12	23	34	0	2	21	17	64	-58	23

*Also promoted

Biggest win: Norwich 7 Reading 1; QPR 0 Newcastle 6
Highest aggregate score: Burton 3 Brentford 5; Norwich 7 Reading 1; Wolves 4 Fulham 4
Highest attendance: 52,301 (Newcastle v Leeds)
Lowest attendance: 3,725 (Burton v QPR, Burton v Fulham)
Player of Year: Anthony Knockaert (Brighton)
Manager of Year: Chris Hughton (Brighton)
Top league scorer: 27 Chris Wood (Leeds)
PFA Team of Year: Stockdale (Brighton), Bruno (Brighton), Dunk (Brighton), Lascelles (Newcastle), Sessegnon (Fulham), Cairney (Fulham), Knockaert (Brighton), Mooy (Huddersfield), Shelvey (Newcastle), Gayle (Newcastle), Wood (Leeds)
Leading league scorers: 27 Wood (Leeds); 23 Abraham (Bristol City), Gayle (Newcastle), Murray (Brighton); 19 Kodjia (Aston Villa); 18 Kermorgant (Reading); 16 Jerome (Norwich); 15 Hogan (Aston Villa – 14 for Brentford), Knockaert (Brighton), Vibe (Brentford); 14 Assombalonga (Nottm Forest), Ince (Derby), Winnall (Sheffield Wed – 11 for Barnsley); 12 Cairney (Fulham), Forestieri (Sheffield Wed), Graham (Blackburn), Hugill (Preston), Jota (Brentford), Kachunga (Huddersfield), Ritchie (Newcastle), Zohore (Cardiff)

SKY BET LEAGUE ONE

		P	W	D	L	F	A	W	D	L	F	A	GD	Pts
				Home						Away				
1	Sheffield Utd	46	17	3	3	42	16	13	7	3	50	31	45	100
2	Bolton	46	13	7	3	35	16	12	4	7	33	20	32	86
3	Scunthorpe	46	14	6	3	46	22	10	4	9	34	32	26	82
4	Fleetwood	46	12	8	3	34	20	11	5	7	30	23	21	82
5	Bradford	46	11	12	0	36	17	9	7	7	26	26	19	79
6	Millwall*	46	13	6	4	34	17	7	7	9	32	40	9	73
7	Southend	46	11	7	5	39	27	9	5	9	31	26	17	72
8	Oxford	46	11	4	8	33	27	9	5	9	32	25	13	69
9	Rochdale	46	13	7	3	48	25	6	5	12	23	37	9	69
10	Bristol Rov	46	13	6	4	42	26	5	6	12	26	44	-2	66
11	Peterborough	46	9	6	8	39	33	8	5	10	23	29	0	62
12	MK Dons	46	7	6	10	29	37	9	7	7	31	21	2	61
13	Charlton	46	9	8	6	31	19	5	10	8	29	34	7	60
14	Walsall	46	11	5	7	34	29	3	11	9	17	29	-7	58
15	AFC Wimbledon	46	8	8	7	34	25	5	10	8	18	30	-3	57
16	Northampton	46	9	5	9	35	29	5	6	12	25	44	-13	53
17	Oldham	46	8	9	6	19	18	4	8	11	12	26	-13	53
18	Shrewsbury	46	10	5	8	26	26	3	7	13	20	37	-17	51
19	Bury	46	9	3	11	36	33	4	8	11	25	40	-12	50
20	Gillingham	46	8	9	6	32	30	4	5	14	27	49	-20	50
21	Port Vale	46	10	6	7	32	31	2	7	14	13	39	-25	49
22	Swindon	46	7	6	10	23	24	4	5	14	21	42	-22	44
23	Coventry	46	8	7	8	22	24	1	5	17	15	44	-31	39
24	Chesterfield	46	7	5	11	26	39	2	5	16	17	39	-35	37

*Also promoted

Biggest win: Bristol Rov 5 Northampton 0; Scunthorpe 5 Gillingham 0
Highest aggregate score: MK Dons 5 Northampton 3
Highest attendance: 31,003 (Sheffield Utd v Chesterfield)
Lowest attendance: 1,907 (Rochdale v Walsall)
Player of Year: Billy Sharp (Sheffield Utd)
Manager of Year: Chris Wilder (Sheffield Utd)
Top league scorer: 30 Billy Sharp
PFA Team of Year: Moore (Sheffield Utd, Freeman (Sheffield Utd), Beevers (Bolton), Wheater (Bolton), Meredith (Bradford), Duffy (Sheffield Utd), Fleck (Sheffield Utd), Morris (Scunthorpe), Otzumer (Walsall), Sharp (Sheffield Utd), Vaughan (Bury)
Leading league scorers: 30 Sharp (Sheffield Utd); 24 Vaughan (Bury); 19 Morris (Scunthorpe); 17 Gregory (Millwall); 16 Cox (Southend), Taylor (Bristol Rov); 15 Henderson (Rochdale), Ozturen (Walsall); 14 Ball (Fleetwood), Jones (Bradford – 9 for Port Vale); 13 Bodin (Bristol Rov), Holmes (Charlton), Maguire (Oxford), O'Brien (Millwall), Wright (Gillingham); 12 Agard (MK Dons), Toney (Scunthorpe – 6 for Shrewsbury); 11 Ajose (Swindon – 6 for Charlton), Madden (Scunthorpe), Morison (Millwall), Wordsworth (Southend)

SKY BET LEAGUE TWO

			Home					Away					
		P	W	D	L	F	A	W	D	L	F	A	GD	Pts
1	Portsmouth	46	14	4	5	48	19	12	5	6	31	21	39	87
2	Plymouth	46	13	3	7	41	29	13	6	4	30	17	25	87
3	Doncaster	46	14	6	3	40	22	11	4	8	45	33	30	85
4	Luton	46	11	7	5	38	26	9	10	4	32	17	27	77
5	Exeter	46	8	5	10	36	29	13	3	7	39	27	19	71
6	Carlisle	46	10	7	6	34	34	8	10	5	35	34	1	71
7	Blackpool*	46	10	9	4	40	24	8	7	8	29	22	23	70
8	Colchester	46	14	4	5	43	27	5	8	10	24	30	10	69
9	Wycombe	46	11	6	6	29	21	8	6	9	29	32	5	69
10	Stevenage	46	11	1	11	42	33	9	6	8	25	30	4	67
11	Cambridge	46	9	5	9	30	26	10	4	9	28	24	8	66
12	Mansfield	46	9	7	7	31	21	8	8	7	23	29	4	66
13	Accrington	46	10	7	6	36	29	7	7	9	23	27	3	65
14	Grimsby	46	9	6	8	32	31	8	5	10	27	32	-4	62
15	Barnet	46	6	9	8	27	31	8	6	9	30	33	7	57
16	Notts Co	46	7	7	9	25	30	9	1	13	29	46	-22	56
17	Crewe	46	8	7	8	35	26	6	11	6	23	41	-9	55
18	Morecambe	46	6	4	13	24	38	8	6	9	23	35	-20	52
19	Crawley	46	8	7	8	29	30	5	5	13	24	41	-18	51
20	Yeovil	46	8	8	7	25	24	3	9	11	24	40	-15	50
21	Cheltenham	46	8	7	8	27	25	4	7	12	22	44	-20	50
22	Newport	46	6	8	9	26	35	6	4	13	25	38	-22	48
23	Hartlepool	46	7	8	8	28	30	4	6	14	26	45	-21	46
24	Leyton Orient	46	4	1	18	19	40	6	5	12	28	47	-40	36

* Also promoted

Biggest win: Accrington 5 Leyton Orient 0; Crewe 5 Grimsby 0; Hartlepool 0 Cambridge 5; Plymouth 6 Newport 1; Portsmouth 6 Cheltenham 1; Stevenage 6 Hartlepool 1; Yeovil 5 Crawley 0

Highest aggregate score: Mansfield 4 Accrington 4

Highest attendance: 18,625 (Portsmouth v Plymouth)

Lowest attendance: 1,045 (Accrington v Wycombe)

Player of Year: John Marquis (Doncaster)

Manager of Year: Paul Cook (Portsmouth)

Top league scorer: 26 John Akinde (Barnet), John Marquis

PFA Team of Year: McCormick (Plymouth), Mellor (Blackpool), Bradley (Plymouth), Burgess (Portsmouth), Stevens (Portsmouth), Adams (Carlisle), Berry (Cambridge), Coppinger (Doncaster), Carey (Plymouth), Hylton (Luton), Marquis (Doncaster)

Leading league scorers: 26 Akinde (Barnet), Marquis (Doncaster); 21 Hylton (Luton); 20 Collins (Crawley), Godden (Stevenage); 19 Bogle (Grimsby); 17 Berry (Cambridge), Wheeler (Exeter); 16 Porter (Colchester), Hylton (Luton); 14 Amond (Hartlepool), Carey (Plymouth), Dagnall (Crewe), Stead (Notts Co), Wyke (Carlisle); 13 Kee (Accrington), Naismith (Portsmouth), Reid (Exeter), Rowe (Doncaster), Watkins (Exeter)

PREMIER LEAGUE RESULTS 2016–2017

	Arsenal	Bournemouth	Burnley	Chelsea	Crystal Palace	Everton	Hull	Leicester	Liverpool	Manchester City	Manchester Utd	Middlesbrough	Southampton	Stoke	Sunderland	Swansea	Tottenham	Watford	WBA	West Ham
Arsenal	–	3-1	2-1	3-0	2-0	3-1	2-0	1-0	3-4	2-2	2-0	0-0	2-1	3-1	2-0	3-2	1-1	1-2	1-0	3-0
Bournemouth	3-3	–	2-1	1-3	0-2	1-0	6-1	1-0	4-3	0-2	1-3	4-0	1-3	2-2	1-2	2-0	0-0	2-2	1-0	3-2
Burnley	0-1	3-2	–	1-1	3-2	2-1	1-1	1-0	2-0	1-2	0-2	1-0	1-0	1-0	4-1	0-1	0-2	2-0	2-2	1-2
Chelsea	3-1	3-0	3-0	–	1-2	5-0	2-0	3-0	1-2	2-1	4-0	3-0	4-2	4-2	5-1	3-1	2-1	4-3	1-0	2-1
Crystal Palace	3-0	1-1	0-2	0-1	–	0-1	4-0	2-2	2-4	1-2	1-2	1-0	3-0	4-1	0-4	1-2	0-1	1-0	0-1	0-1
Everton	2-1	6-3	3-1	0-3	1-1	–	4-0	4-2	0-1	4-0	1-1	3-1	3-0	1-0	2-0	2-1	1-1	1-0	3-0	2-0
Hull	1-4	3-1	1-1	0-2	3-1	2-2	–	2-1	2-0	0-3	0-1	4-2	0-2	0-2	0-2	2-1	1-7	2-0	1-1	2-1
Leicester	0-0	1-1	3-0	0-3	3-1	0-2	3-1	–	3-1	4-2	0-3	2-2	0-0	4-1	2-0	2-1	1-6	3-0	1-2	1-0
Liverpool	3-1	2-2	2-1	1-1	5-0	3-1	5-1	4-1	–	1-0	0-0	3-0	0-0	0-0	2-0	2-3	2-0	6-1	2-1	2-2
Manchester City	2-1	4-0	1-1	1-3	2-0	1-1	3-1	4-1	1-1	–	0-0	1-1	1-1	1-1	2-1	2-1	2-2	2-0	3-1	3-1
Manchester Utd	1-1	1-1	0-0	2-0	1-2	0-0	0-0	0-0	1-1	1-2	–	1-0	2-0	1-1	3-1	1-1	1-0	2-0	0-0	1-1
Middlesbrough	1-2	2-0	0-0	0-1	3-1	1-0	1-0	3-0	0-3	2-2	1-3	–	1-2	0-1	1-0	3-0	1-2	0-1	1-1	1-3
Southampton	0-2	0-0	3-1	0-2	1-0	1-1	0-0	2-2	0-0	0-3	1-0	1-0	–	1-2	1-1	1-0	1-4	1-1	1-2	1-3
Stoke	1-4	0-1	2-0	1-2	2-3	0-3	3-1	2-1	1-2	1-4	1-1	2-0	0-0	–	2-0	3-1	0-4	2-0	1-1	0-0
Sunderland	1-4	0-1	0-0	1-2	5-4	1-0	3-0	2-0	2-2	0-2	0-3	1-2	0-4	1-3	–	0-2	0-0	1-0	2-1	2-2
Swansea	0-4	0-3	3-2	0-1	1-0	3-2	0-2	1-1	1-2	1-3	1-3	0-0	2-1	2-0	3-0	–	1-3	0-0	2-1	1-4
Tottenham	2-0	4-0	2-1	1-2	1-1	3-2	3-1	2-1	1-1	0-5	2-1	2-1	2-1	4-0	1-0	5-0	–	4-0	4-0	3-2
Watford	1-3	2-2	2-1	3-0	1-1	1-2	1-0	0-1	1-0	0-4	3-1	0-0	3-4	0-1	1-0	3-1	1-4	–	2-0	1-1
WBA	3-1	2-1	4-0	0-1	0-2	0-0	3-1	0-1	2-3	0-4	0-2	0-0	0-1	1-0	2-0	3-1	1-1	3-1	–	4-2
West Ham	1-5	1-0	1-0	1-2	3-0	0-0	1-0	2-3	0-4	0-4	0-2	1-1	0-3	1-1	1-0	1-0	1-0	2-4	2-2	–

SKY BET CHAMPIONSHIP RESULTS 2016–2017

	Aston Villa	Barnsley	Birmingham	Blackburn	Brentford	Brighton	Bristol City	Burton	Cardiff	Derby	Fulham	Huddersfield	Ipswich	Leeds	Newcastle	Norwich	Nottm Forest	Preston	QPR	Reading	Rotherham	Sheffield Wed	Wigan	Wolves
Aston Villa	–	1-3	1-0	2-2	1-0	1-1	2-0	2-1	3-1	1-0	1-0	1-1	0-1	1-1	1-1	2-0	2-2	2-2	1-0	1-3	3-0	2-0	1-0	1-1
Barnsley	1-1	–	2-2	2-0	0-3	1-1	2-2	2-1	3-1	2-0	2-4	1-1	1-1	3-2	0-2	2-1	2-5	0-0	3-2	1-2	4-0	1-1	0-0	1-3
Birmingham	0-3	–	–	1-0	1-2	1-2	1-1	1-0	0-0	2-0	2-0	2-0	1-1	1-2	0-2	3-0	2-2	0-0	1-4	1-2	4-2	2-1	0-1	1-3
Blackburn	1-0	2-0	1-0	–	3-2	1-2	0-2	0-2	0-0	1-0	0-1	1-1	3-2	2-1	1-2	0-1	1-0	3-2	3-1	2-3	4-2	1-1	1-0	1-1
Brentford	3-0	0-2	1-3	3-2	–	3-3	2-0	2-1	1-1	4-0	0-2	0-1	0-0	2-0	1-2	5-0	1-0	5-0	3-1	4-1	4-2	1-1	0-0	0-1
Brighton	1-1	2-0	1-2	1-0	0-2	–	0-1	4-1	0-0	3-0	2-1	1-0	1-0	2-0	0-1	5-0	3-0	2-2	3-0	3-0	3-0	2-2	1-2	1-2
Bristol City	3-1	3-2	1-1	0-2	3-3	1-0	–	0-0	2-3	1-1	0-2	4-0	1-1	2-0	1-2	1-2	3-0	2-2	2-1	2-4	1-0	2-2	2-1	3-1
Burton	1-1	0-0	2-0	1-1	4-1	0-1	0-0	–	2-0	1-1	0-2	0-1	2-0	2-3	0-1	1-2	1-0	1-2	2-1	0-1	2-1	1-1	1-0	2-1
Cardiff	1-0	3-4	2-0	2-1	1-0	0-1	1-0	2-0	–	0-2	2-2	3-2	3-1	0-2	1-2	0-1	1-0	0-1	0-2	0-1	5-0	1-1	0-1	3-1
Derby	0-0	2-1	1-0	1-2	3-4	0-0	1-0	0-0	1-0	–	2-2	3-2	0-1	1-0	0-2	1-0	3-0	2-0	1-0	3-2	2-1	2-0	0-1	1-3
Fulham	3-1	2-0	1-1	2-2	1-1	1-2	2-2	3-1	2-1	0-2	–	5-0	3-1	1-1	1-3	2-2	3-2	3-1	1-2	5-0	2-1	1-1	3-2	1-0
Huddersfield	1-0	4-2	1-1	1-1	0-1	1-4	0-3	1-1	2-2	2-2	1-4	–	1-0	2-1	1-3	3-0	3-2	3-2	1-2	2-3	2-1	1-1	3-0	1-0
Ipswich	0-0	2-1	1-1	3-2	1-1	0-0	2-0	2-0	1-1	0-3	0-2	5-0	–	1-1	3-1	1-1	0-2	1-0	3-0	2-3	2-1	0-1	3-0	0-0
Leeds	2-0	3-0	1-2	2-1	1-0	2-0	2-1	2-0	3-0	0-1	1-1	0-1	1-0	–	0-2	4-3	3-1	4-1	2-2	4-1	2-2	1-0	3-0	0-2
Newcastle	2-0	3-0	4-0	0-1	3-1	2-0	2-2	1-0	3-2	1-0	1-3	1-2	0-2	1-1	–	1-1	3-1	0-1	4-0	7-1	4-0	0-1	2-1	3-1
Norwich	1-0	0-1	3-1	0-1	5-0	2-0	3-0	4-3	1-2	2-2	3-1	2-0	1-1	2-3	2-2	–	5-1	1-1	2-2	1-1	3-1	0-1	4-3	3-1
Nottm Forest	2-1	0-1	3-1	3-2	2-1	3-0	0-1	1-1	3-0	0-1	1-1	2-0	1-2	2-1	2-1	1-2	–	1-1	2-1	3-0	5-1	1-2	1-0	0-2
Preston	2-0	1-2	2-1	4-2	1-1	2-0	1-0	1-1	0-0	1-2	1-2	3-1	1-1	1-4	1-2	1-3	1-1	–	2-1	3-0	1-1	1-2	1-0	1-2
QPR	0-1	2-1	1-1	0-2	3-0	1-2	2-2	1-1	2-1	0-1	2-1	1-0	2-1	3-0	0-6	2-1	2-0	0-2	–	1-1	2-1	1-2	2-1	1-2
Reading	1-2	0-0	1-1	3-1	3-2	1-2	2-2	3-0	2-1	1-0	0-1	1-0	1-0	1-0	0-1	3-1	1-0	1-3	0-1	–	2-1	1-2	2-1	0-1
Rotherham	0-2	0-1	1-1	1-1	1-2	0-2	2-2	3-1	1-2	1-3	0-1	2-3	2-0	0-2	0-1	5-1	2-2	2-1	1-0	0-2	–	0-2	3-2	2-2
Sheffield Wed	1-0	2-0	3-0	2-1	1-2	1-2	3-2	1-1	1-1	0-1	1-2	2-0	1-1	0-2	2-1	5-1	2-1	2-1	1-0	1-0	1-0	–	2-1	0-0
Wigan	1-0	3-2	1-1	3-0	0-1	0-1	0-1	C-0	0-0	0-1	0-3	0-1	1-1	1-1	0-1	2-2	2-0	0-0	1-0	0-3	1-0	0-1	–	2-1
Wolves	1-0	0-4	1-2	0-0	3-1	0-2	3-1	3-1	3-1	4-4	0-1	0-1	0-0	0-1	0-1	1-2	1-0	1-2	1-2	2-0	1-0	0-2	0-1	–

SKY BET LEAGUE ONE RESULTS 2016-2017

	Bolton	Bradford	Bristol Rov	Bury	Charlton	Chesterfield	Coventry	Fleetwood	Gillingham	Millwall	MK Dons	Northampton	Oldham	Oxford	Peterborough	Port Vale	Rochdale	Scunthorpe	Sheffield Utd	Shrewsbury	Southend	Swindon	Walsall	Wimbledon
Bolton	–	0-0	1-1	0-0	1-2	0-0	1-0	1-0	4-0	2-0	2-1	1-0	2-0	0-2	3-0	3-1	2-1	2-1	1-0	2-1	1-1	1-2	4-1	1-1
Bradford	2-2	–	1-1	1-1	0-0	2-0	3-1	2-1	2-2	1-1	2-2	1-0	1-0	2-1	1-0	2-1	4-0	0-0	3-3	2-0	1-1	2-1	1-0	3-0
Bristol Rov	1-2	1-1	–	4-2	1-5	2-1	4-1	2-1	2-1	3-4	0-0	5-0	0-1	2-3	1-2	4-1	2-2	1-1	0-0	2-0	2-0	1-0	1-1	2-0
Bury	0-2	0-2	3-0	–	2-0	1-0	2-1	0-0	2-1	2-3	0-2	3-0	0-1	2-3	5-1	4-1	0-1	2-1	1-3	3-0	1-4	1-0	1-0	1-2
Charlton	1-1	0-1	4-1	0-1	–	3-0	3-0	0-1	3-0	0-0	0-2	3-0	1-1	2-0	1-1	2-0	1-3	2-1	1-1	3-0	2-1	3-0	3-1	1-2
Chesterfield	1-0	0-1	1-0	1-2	1-2	–	1-0	0-1	3-3	1-3	0-2	3-1	0-1	0-4	3-3	2-0	1-3	0-3	1-4	1-1	0-4	3-1	2-0	0-2
Coventry	2-2	0-2	1-0	1-2	1-2	2-0	–	0-1	2-1	0-0	1-2	3-1	0-0	2-1	1-0	2-0	2-0	0-1	1-2	1-1	0-2	1-3	2-0	0-0
Fleetwood	2-4	2-1	0-1	1-0	0-0	0-0	1-0	–	2-1	1-4	1-4	0-0	1-0	2-0	3-3	1-1	2-0	0-1	1-2	1-0	0-2	2-1	2-0	2-2
Gillingham	0-4	3-1	3-1	2-1	2-2	1-1	0-1	0-1	–	1-1	2-1	3-1	1-2	2-1	2-1	1-1	3-0	2-2	1-2	3-0	1-1	4-1	0-0	2-2
Millwall	0-2	1-1	2-1	2-1	2-2	2-3	0-1	0-1	2-3	–	2-1	0-1	1-0	1-2	0-2	2-0	3-0	3-1	2-1	0-1	2-1	4-0	0-0	0-0
MK Dons	1-1	1-2	0-0	3-1	1-1	2-3	1-1	0-1	3-2	2-1	–	5-3	3-0	0-3	1-0	2-0	2-3	3-1	2-3	2-1	1-0	2-0	2-0	1-0
Northampton	0-1	1-2	2-3	0-0	2-1	3-1	3-0	1-1	0-0	2-1	1-0	–	0-0	0-1	1-1	2-0	1-0	1-1	1-1	2-1	1-0	1-1	2-0	1-0
Oldham	1-0	1-0	0-2	0-0	1-1	2-1	0-0	1-1	1-1	1-0	1-0	0-0	–	2-1	2-0	0-0	1-1	1-0	2-1	2-3	2-2	0-2	0-0	0-0
Oxford	2-4	1-0	0-2	5-1	1-1	3-1	4-1	1-3	1-1	1-0	1-2	0-1	1-1	–	2-1	2-0	1-0	2-0	1-2	2-1	0-2	2-1	0-0	1-3
Peterborough	1-0	1-2	4-2	2-1	0-2	5-2	0-2	2-1	1-1	5-1	1-1	2-3	2-2	1-2	–	2-2	2-3	0-3	0-1	2-1	1-4	2-2	4-0	0-1
Port Vale	0-2	1-1	0-2	3-1	1-0	1-0	0-2	0-2	0-1	0-0	1-0	1-0	1-0	2-1	0-0	–	3-0	2-2	2-1	1-1	3-0	4-0	4-0	2-0
Rochdale	1-0	1-1	3-1	2-0	0-0	3-0	2-0	0-2	3-0	1-3	1-0	1-1	1-0	2-1	2-0	3-0	–	1-0	1-2	1-0	3-0	4-1	4-0	0-0
Scunthorpe	1-0	3-2	3-1	3-2	2-1	0-0	2-1	0-2	5-0	3-0	1-0	1-1	1-0	0-0	3-2	3-2	1-1	–	2-2	0-1	3-0	4-1	0-0	1-2
Sheffield Utd	2-0	3-0	1-0	0-0	2-1	3-2	0-1	0-2	2-2	2-1	1-1	1-0	2-4	2-1	1-1	4-0	1-1	1-1	–	2-1	0-3	4-0	0-1	4-0
Shrewsbury	0-2	1-0	2-0	4-3	0-0	1-1	2-3	0-2	1-3	1-2	2-4	2-4	3-0	2-0	1-1	0-3	1-0	3-1	0-3	–	1-0	1-1	1-1	2-1
Southend	0-1	3-0	1-1	1-1	3-1	1-0	0-0	0-2	1-3	1-0	2-1	1-3	3-1	3-1	1-0	1-0	3-0	3-1	2-4	1-1	–	1-1	3-2	3-0
Swindon	0-1	1-1	1-2	3-0	1-1	1-0	1-0	1-0	1-0	1-0	0-0	1-3	0-0	1-2	0-1	1-0	3-0	1-2	2-4	1-1	0-0	–	1-0	0-0
Walsall	1-0	1-1	3-1	3-3	1-2	1-0	1-0	0-1	1-2	1-4	0-1	2-1	2-1	1-1	1-4	0-2	0-2	1-4	4-1	3-2	0-0	1-0	–	3-1
Wimbledon	1-2	2-3	0-1	5-1	2-1	2-1	1-1	2-2	2-0	2-2	0-0	0-1	0-0	2-1	0-0	4-0	3-1	1-2	2-3	1-1	0-2	0-0	1-0	–

SKY BET LEAGUE TWO RESULTS 2016–2017

	Accrington	Barnet	Blackpool	Cambridge	Carlisle	Cheltenham	Colchester	Crawley	Crewe	Doncaster	Exeter	Grimsby	Hartlepool	Leyton Orient	Luton	Mansfield	Morecambe	Newport	Notts Co	Plymouth	Portsmouth	Stevenage	Wycombe	Yeovil
Accrington	–	1-0	2-1	2-0	2-1	1-1	3-0	0-0	0-1	2-2	0-2	2-0	2-0	1-0	1-0	4-4	1-2	1-0	0-1	0-1	2-0	0-3	1-1	1-1
Barnet	2-0	–	1-1	0-1	1-1	3-1	2-1	1-1	4-1	3-2	0-2	2-2	1-3	0-0	1-4	0-2	0-1	2-2	1-0	1-0	2-0	1-0	0-2	1-1
Blackpool	0-0	2-2	–	1-1	2-2	3-0	4-1	0-0	2-1	1-2	1-2	2-0	3-2	2-0	0-2	0-1	1-2	0-0	4-0	1-0	3-1	1-0	0-2	2-2
Cambridge	2-1	1-1	0-0	–	2-2	3-1	1-1	2-0	2-1	1-2	3-0	3-0	2-0	4-0	0-3	1-3	3-2	4-1	4-0	0-1	3-1	1-0	1-2	1-0
Carlisle	1-1	1-1	1-4	0-3	–	1-1	0-1	3-1	0-2	2-1	0-1	1-3	3-0	3-0	0-3	5-2	1-1	2-1	1-2	1-0	0-3	0-0	1-0	2-1
Cheltenham	3-0	2-2	2-2	0-1	1-1	–	0-3	1-1	0-2	0-1	0-2	0-1	3-2	2-2	1-0	0-0	1-1	2-1	1-2	1-3	2-3	0-2	1-0	2-0
Colchester	1-2	2-1	2-2	2-0	4-1	2-0	–	2-3	4-0	0-1	2-3	3-2	2-1	3-0	2-1	2-0	3-1	0-0	2-1	0-0	2-3	1-1	1-0	2-0
Crawley	0-0	1-1	1-0	0-1	3-3	0-0	2-0	–	0-3	1-1	1-2	3-2	1-0	3-0	2-1	2-0	1-3	3-1	2-1	0-0	1-2	1-2	1-0	2-0
Crewe	0-1	1-1	1-0	1-3	1-1	0-0	1-1	0-2	–	3-1	0-2	0-1	3-3	3-1	1-2	2-2	2-1	2-1	2-1	1-2	1-2	2-1	2-1	0-1
Doncaster	2-2	3-2	0-1	1-0	2-2	3-0	2-1	0-2	3-1	–	2-1	0-0	4-0	3-1	1-2	2-2	2-3	0-3	2-3	1-2	3-1	2-2	2-2	4-1
Exeter	0-2	0-2	2-0	1-2	2-3	3-0	1-1	0-2	4-0	1-3	–	1-1	4-0	3-1	0-2	1-0	2-3	1-2	0-1	0-1	1-1	1-1	4-2	0-1
Grimsby	2-0	2-2	2-0	1-2	2-2	0-1	2-0	0-1	0-2	1-5	0-3	–	2-1	1-2	2-0	3-0	2-0	1-1	1-2	3-0	4-3	5-2	1-2	4-2
Hartlepool	2-0	0-2	0-1	0-5	1-1	1-2	1-3	4-0	0-1	2-1	1-3	0-3	–	1-3	1-2	1-2	3-2	0-1	2-3	0-2	3-0	0-1	0-2	1-1
Leyton Orient	1-0	3-1	1-2	1-1	1-2	2-3	0-1	1-1	3-2	0-0	3-1	1-1	2-1	–	1-2	2-0	0-4	3-1	2-1	1-2	4-1	0-2	0-2	0-1
Luton	1-0	3-1	1-0	2-0	0-0	1-1	2-3	3-0	0-0	3-1	1-1	2-1	3-0	2-0	–	1-1	2-0	0-4	3-1	3-2	2-0	2-0	1-1	1-0
Mansfield	4-4	0-1	1-0	0-0	2-0	1-1	1-2	3-0	0-0	1-1	0-1	2-1	0-0	1-0	1-1	–	0-1	1-1	3-2	2-0	1-3	2-1	1-1	1-0
Morecambe	1-2	0-1	2-1	2-3	0-1	2-2	1-0	1-1	2-1	3-1	1-0	1-2	0-1	1-2	0-2	1-1	–	1-1	4-1	1-0	1-2	2-2	1-2	2-3
Newport	1-0	2-2	1-3	2-0	2-3	0-1	0-2	0-1	1-1	1-0	0-1	0-0	2-2	0-4	0-4	2-3	1-1	–	4-1	1-3	2-3	0-2	1-1	2-0
Notts Co	1-0	1-0	0-1	2-1	3-1	1-0	2-1	3-1	2-0	2-0	1-2	1-0	0-0	3-1	0-0	2-0	1-2	0-1	–	2-1	2-3	1-1	0-1	2-0
Plymouth	0-1	0-2	0-3	2-1	1-2	1-1	3-0	2-0	2-1	1-0	2-1	4-1	2-0	2-3	0-3	4-0	1-0	2-0	1-2	–	1-2	1-1	1-2	2-1
Portsmouth	2-0	5-1	2-0	1-1	2-0	3-0	2-0	3-0	2-1	0-1	3-1	0-1	1-0	2-1	2-1	4-0	2-0	6-1	1-2	1-1	–	3-0	4-2	3-1
Stevenage	0-3	1-0	0-0	1-2	0-2	0-2	3-0	2-4	4-2	3-4	0-2	2-2	0-1	4-1	1-1	0-1	0-1	0-3	3-0	1-1	3-0	–	3-0	2-2
Wycombe	1-1	0-1	0-0	1-0	0-1	3-3	0-2	1-2	3-3	2-1	1-0	2-1	2-0	1-0	2-0	0-1	0-1	4-2	3-3	4-2	1-0	1-0	–	1-0
Yeovil	1-1	0-1	0-3	1-1	2-1	0-3	0-0	2-1	0-3	0-3	0-0	0-0	1-2	1-1	0-4	0-0	0-1	0-1	2-0	2-1	2-1	1-1	1-0	–

HIGHLIGHTS OF THE PREMIER LEAGUE SEASON 2016–17

AUGUST 2016

13 Hull, down to 13 fit senior players and without a manager after the resignation of Steve Bruce, overcome title holders Leicester 2-1 with goals by Adama Diomande and Robert Snodgrass. It's the first opening day defeat for English champions since Arsenal in 1989. An 87th minute own goal by Paddy McNair on his Sunderland debut gives Manchester City victory by the same scoreline in Pep Guardiola's first game in charge. Three other new managers share the spoils. Watford, under Walter Mazzarri, lead through Etienne Capoue's first goal for the club. But they lose Ben Watson to a straight red card for bringing down Shane Long and Claude Puel's Southampton level through a debut strike from Nathan Redmond. Former Southampton manager Ronald Koeman's first game with Everton also ends 1-1, against Tottenham. So does Middlesbrough's return to the Premier League against Stoke, with Alvaro Negredo on the mark on his debut. Another player opening his account is Leroy Fer, whose goal gives Swansea a 1-0 win at Burnley.

14 Sadio Mane makes a scoring debut and Philippe Coutinho scores twice as Liverpool win a rousing opener at the Emirates. They come from behind to lead 4-1 before Arsenal, fielding a makeshift defence through injuries, pull back to 4-3. Jose Mourinho makes a winning start with Manchester United as new-signing Zlatan Ibrahimovic continues his record of scoring on his debut for clubs in Italy, Spain and France by rounding off a 3-1 scoreline at Bournemouth.

15 Chelsea, under their new manager Antonio Conte, open with a 2-1 victory over West Ham, secured by an 89th minute goal from Diego Costa.

19 Zlatan Ibrahimovic scores both goals, one from the penalty spot, in Manchester United's 2-0 defeat of Southampton as Friday night football makes its bow.

20 Two of the promoted teams take pride of place with 2-0 victories. Burnley account for Liverpool, despite having just 19 percent possession; Hull, still down to the bare bones, are winners at Swansea. Sergio Aguero and substitute Nolito share the goals in Manchester City's 4-1 victory at Stoke, one of Aguero's a penalty after his midweek double spot-kick miss against Steaua Bucharest in the Champions League. Victor Wanyama opens his account for Tottenham with the only one against Crystal Palace. So does Michy Batshuayi with an 80th minute equaliser for Chelsea at Watford, followed seven minutes later by another late winner from Diego Costa. Everton also come from behind away to West Bromwich Albion to prevail 2-1, with Gareth Barry netting the decider on his 100th appearance for the club.

21 Middlesbrough, the third promoted side, win 2-1 at Sunderland, courtesy of a brace from Cristhian Stuani at Sunderland in the resumption of the Tees-Wear derby. West Ham mark their Premier League debut at the Olympic Stadium with a 1-0 win over Bournemouth, who lose Harry Arter to a second yellow card.

27 Hull are denied another notable result in stoppage-time when Manchester United substitute Marcus Rashford scores the only goal of the game. Leicester open their account by beating Swansea 2-1, despite Riyad Mahrez having a penalty saved by Lukasz Fabianski – one of six spot-kicks awarded in the day's programme. Bournemouth's Artur Boruc denies Yohan Cabaye in a 1-1 draw at Crystal Palace, while Everton's Leighton Baines fires his penalty against the post and is fortunate to see the ball rebound into the net off goalkeeper Shay Given for the only goal against Stoke. Santi Cazorla sets Arsenal on the way to a 3-1 success at Watford, for whom record-signing Roberto Pereyra scores on his debut. His new team have six players booked, resulting in a £25,000 FA fine. James Milner, in Liverpool's 1-1 draw at Tottenham, and Jermain Defoe for Sunderland, who share the same scoreline with Southampton, are also on the spot

28 Two goals by Raheem Sterling point Manchester City towards a 3-1 victory over West Ham, but the result loses some of its shine by an FA charge against Sergio Aguero for elbowing Winston Reid. City head the table on goal difference after three matches, with Chelsea and Manchester United also having maximum points from their opening three matches.

SEPTEMBER 2016

10 Pep Guardiola wins his first competitive clash with Jose Mourinho as City overcome United 2-1 in the Manchester derby at Old Trafford, despite the absence of the suspended Sergio Aguero. Kevin De Bruyne takes the individual honours, scoring their first goal and paving the way for the second from Kelechi Iheanacho. Liverpool mark the opening of their £115m Main Stand by beating Leicester 4-1, with Roberto Firmino on the mark twice in front of a crowd of more than 53,000, the club's biggest since 1977. Tottenham's Son Heung-min also nets twice, in a 4-0 win at Stoke, while three players score for the first time for their clubs. Record signing Christian Benteke puts Crystal Palace on the way to a 2-1 victory at Middlesbrough; Jose Holebas completes Watford's 4-2 success at West Ham, achieved after a brace by Michail Antonio puts the home side 2-0 ahead; Steven Defour earns Burnley a 1-1 draw with Hull.

11 Diego Costa rescues a point for Chelsea, his second goal of the game after 81 minutes delivering a 2-2 scoreline at Swansea.

12 Romelu Lukaku's hat-trick gives Everton a 3-0 win at Sunderland, his goals coming in an 11-minute spell in the second-half.

16 Jordan Henderson fires a spectacular goal from 30 yards as Liverpool defeat Chelsea 2-1 at Stamford Bridge.

17 Gareth Barry marks his 600th Premier League appearance with a goal in Everton's 3-1 win over Middlesbrough, their fourth in five matches for the club's best start since 1978. Ilkay Gundogan scores on his Manchester City debut, but the shine is taken off a 4-0 victory over Bournemouth by the dismissal of Nolito for putting his head into Adam Smith's face. Hull's Jake Livermore also receives a straight red card, this one for deliberate handball. The resulting penalty by Alexis Sanchez is saved by Eldin Jakupovic, but Sanchez is on the mark twice, while Granit Xhaka scores his first for the club from 30 yards in Arsenal's 4-1 away success. Islam Slimani opens his account with two headed goals on his league debut for Leicester, who defeat Burnley 3-0. Another record buy, Nacer Chadli, nets his first two for West Bromwich Albion, one from the penalty spot, as West Ham are beaten 4-2.

18 Watford condemn Manchester United to a third defeat in eight days – one of them in the Europa League – with a 3-1 success, earned by Etienne Capoue's fourth goal in five games, a first for the club by Camilo Zuniga and Troy Deeney's penalty, won by on loan Zuniga. Watford end a run of 11 successive defeats by United, dating back to 1986, while Jose Mourinho loses three in a row in the same season for the first time since 2002 as Porto coach. James Tomkins and Andros Townsend score their first goals for Crystal Palace, 4-1 winners over Stoke, who concede four for the third time in four matches. Sunderland have Adnan Januzaj sent off for a second yellow card in a 1-0 defeat at Tottenham.

24 Jose Mourinho relegates Wayne Rooney to the Manchester United substitutes' bench and the move pays off with four first-half goals for a 4-1 victory over Leicester, one of them from record signing Paul Pogba, his first for the club. Demarai Gray's consolation is his first for Leicester. Two teams score three times in the first-half, James Milner converts the first of his two penalties in that period as Liverpool overcome Hull 5-1, Ahmed Elmohamady having been sent off for deliberate handball. Alexis Sanchez, with his 47th goal in 100 appearances in all competitions, puts Arsenal on the way to a 3-0 success against Chelsea to end their rivals' superiority in recent meetings. Manchester City return to the Liberty Stadium three days after a League Cup victory to defeat Swansea 3-1. Sergio Aguero is back from suspension with two goals, one a penalty, while Fernando Llorente gets his first for the home side. Jermain Defoe looks to have put Sunderland on the way to their first three points of the season with his second goal of the game, but Crystal Palace hit back to level, then win 3-2 with Christian Benteke's 94th minute header. There is also a brace for Son Heung-min in Tottenham's 2-1 win at Middlesbrough. Another stoppage-time goal, from West Bromwich Albion's Salomon Rondon, rescues a point for Tony Pulis in his 1,000th game in management. It cancels out Joe Allen's first for Stoke.

25 Charlie Austin's fifth goal in four Premier League and Europa League games sets Southampton on the way to a 3-0 away win over West Ham.

26 Jeff Hendrick opens his account for Burnley in their 2-0 defeat of Watford. At the end of the month, Manchester City lead Tottenham by four points, with Arsenal, Liverpool and Everton by a point further back.

OCTOBER 2016

1 Dimitri Payet delivers a candidate for goal of the season with a solo run past five players to earn West Ham a point against Middlesbrough. Isaac Success lives up to his name by coming off the bench to score his first goal for Watford in a 2-2 draw with Bournemouth. Swansea's 2-1 home defeat by Liverpool is followed by the dismissal of manager Francesco Guidolin.

2 Manchester City's flying start, six wins out of six, is checked at Tottenham, who beat them 2-0 with Aleksandar Kolarov's own goal and Dele Alli's strike. Spurs can even afford to miss a penalty, Claudio Bravo saving from Erik Lamela. Arsene Wenger, celebrating 20 years as Arsenal manager, admits his side are lucky to come away from Burnley with three points after Laurent Koscielny's only goal of the game in stoppage-time goes in off his hand.

15 Maarten Stekelenburg takes pride of place by saving penalties from Kevin De Bruyne and Sergio Aguero – both conceded by Phil Jagielka – to earn Everton a 1-1 draw against Manchester City at the Etihad. Another outstanding goalkeeping performance, by Ben Foster, looks to have given West Bromwich Albion victory over Tottenham, until Dele Alli finally beats him with an 89th minute equaliser. Mike Phelan's first match as Hull's permanent manager is one to forget – a 6-1 drubbing at Bournemouth, for whom Junior Stanislas scores two goals, one a penalty. Bob Bradley, the first American to manage in the Premier League, begins his bid to improve Swansea's fortunes with a 3-2 defeat by Arsenal. Theo Walcott nets twice for the home side, but they lose Granit Xhaka to a straight red card for lunging at Modou Barrow and Swansea have chances to draw level after record-signing Borja Baston's first goal for the club. Also dismissed, for two yellows in the space of 60 seconds in the second-half, is West Ham's Aaron Cresswell on his first appearance of the season following a knee ligament injury. His side hold on to 1-0 advantage at Crystal Palace, who pay for Christian Benteke's penalty miss. Joe Allen takes his tally for club and country to five goals in four games with a brace in Stoke's first win of the season – 2-0 against Sunderland.

16 Southampton's Charlie Austin has seven in six games in all competitions after two in the 3-1 win over Burnley, one a penalty.

17 Stalemate at Anfield as Manchester United's defensive discipline and organisation earn a goalless draw against Liverpool.

22 Ahmed Musa and Christian Fuchs score their first goals for Leicester in a 3-1 win over Crystal Palace. Yannick Bolasie opens his account for Everton with an equaliser at Burnley, but the home side take the points with Scott Arfield's 90th minute strike. West Ham are also late winners, Winston Reid breaking the deadlock in stoppage-time against Sunderland. Two long-distance finishes from Xherdan Shaqiri deliver a 2-0 success for Stoke at Hull.

23 On his return to Stamford Bridge, Jose Mourinho's plan to frustrate Chelsea as Manchester United did against Liverpool lasts just 30 seconds. Pedro puts his former side ahead and they go on to win 4-0, with N'Golo Kante's first goal for the club rounding off the scoring.

29 Olivier Giroud, a peripheral figure in Arsenal's successful start to the season, finally makes his mark as they overwhelm Sunderland with three goals in six second-half minutes to win 4-1 at the Stadium of Light. Giroud comes off the bench to score with his first two touches, supplementing a brace from Alexis Sanchez to leave Sunderland with the worst record after ten matches in Premier League history – two points and a goal difference of minus 13. Two each by Sergio Aguero and Ilkay Gundogan provide a 4-0 success for Manchester City against West Bromwich Albion to end a run of six matches without a win in all competitions – Pep Guardiola's worst as a manager. Gaston Ramirez stakes a claim for goal of the season, running 70 yards to put Middlesbrough on the way to a 2-0 success against Bournemouth. Joel Matip scores his first for Liverpool in a 4-2 victory at Crystal Palace, whose goals come from James McArthur. Manchester United have Ander Herrera dismissed for a second yellow card and manager Jose Mourinho sent to the stands for touchline protests in a goalless draw with Burnley.

31 On-loan Wilfried Bony registers his first goals for Stoke, a brace accounting for former club Swansea 3-1.

NOVEMBER 2016

5 A stunning performance by Chelsea, a first victory for Sunderland against the odds and two dramatic stoppage-time goals deliver an enthralling day's football. Eden Hazard is on the mark twice and Marcos Alonso scores his first goal for Chelsea, who overwhelm Everton 5-0 for a fifth successive win since switching to a 3-4-3 formation. Sunderland have manager David Moyes serving a touchline ban, fall behind at Bournemouth and lose Steven Pienaar to a second yellow card. But Victor Anichebe, playing with a cracked rib, marks his first Premier League start for the club with his first goal, then wins the penalty which Jermain Defoe converts for the team's first success at the 11th attempt. Manchester City are brought down to earth after beating Barcelona in midweek when Marten de Roon's first for Middlesbrough earns 1-1 a draw at the Etihad in the second minute of time added on. Ashley Barnes, out for most of Burnley's promotion campaign with a knee injury, celebrates even later, his match winner for 3-2 against Crystal Palace coming in the 94th minute.

6 Liverpool, like Chelsea, maintain impressive momentum to overcome Watford 6-1, with Georginio Wijnaldum opening his account for the club, Sadio Mané netting twice and the team making it 30 goals in 11 games, Watford's consolation is a first for Daryl Janmaat. There is also a first for West Bromwich Albion's Matt Phillips, who scores the winner for a 2-1 scoreline at Leicester. Harry Kane returns from a seven-week lay-off with an ankle injury to convert the penalty which gives Tottenham a 1-1 draw against Arsenal at the Emirates and enables manager Mauricio Pochettino to remain unbeaten in his first five top-flight north London derbies – a club record. Hull come from behind to end a run of six successive defeats by defeating Southampton 2-1, captain Michael Dawson heading the winner. The win is clouded by injuries to Abel Hernandez (groin) and Will Keane (knee), while Manchester United's 3-1 success at Swansea – Zlatan Ibrahimović netting twice – is also overshadowed as Jose Mourinho publicly criticises Chris Smalling and Luke Shaw for crying off through injury.

19 Yaya Toure makes a major impact on his first appearance of the season for Manchester City. The midfielder, frozen out after comments by his agent angered manager Pep Guardiola, scores both goals in a 2-1 victory away to Crystal Palace. But there is more concern for Guardiola when injury dogged Vincent Kompany collides with his goalkeeper Claudio Bravo and has to go off with knee ligament damage. Three other teams in the leading group are involved in dramatic finishes. Tottenham, trailing West Ham 2-1 at home, equalise in the 89th minute through Harry Kane, who then converts a stoppage-time penalty. There is still time for West Ham's Winston Reid to be shown a second yellow card. Tottenham's first goal, from Harry Winks, is his first for the club on his first Premier League start. Substitute Olivier Giroud heads an equaliser for Arsenal at Old Trafford while Seamus Coleman is also on the mark in the 89th minute to give Everton the same 1-1 scoreline, against Swansea. Victor Anichebe is again Sunderland's match-winner, his two goals setting up a 3-0 win over Hull. Neither a ten-minute second half stoppage for a floodlights' failure, nor the dismissal of Papy Djilobodji for a second yellow, can disturb the home side's authority. On-loan Nathan Ake marks his first Bournemouth start with his first goal for a 1-0 success at Stoke, who pay for Bojan Krkic's penalty miss.

21 West Bromwich Albion produce their best performance under Tony Pulis for a 4-0 victory over Burnley.

26 Bob Bradley describes his first victory as Swansea manager as 'crazy.' They lead Crystal Palace 3-1, trail 3-4, then win 5-4 with two stoppage-time goals from substitute Fernando Llorente. Leroy Fer also scores twice as Palace concede from four set-plays for a sixth successive defeat. Sergio Aguero's brace for a 2-1 success by Manchester City at Burnley takes his tally to 33 goals in 34 Premier League games. Alvaro Negredo also nets twice for Middlesbrough at Leicester, but his side are denied victory by the last kick of the game – Islam Slimani's penalty which gives the home side a 2-2 draw. Tottenham surrender the division's only unbeaten record when going down 2-1 to Chelsea at Stamford Bridge, where the club have not won now for 26 years.

29 Jose Mourinho is sent to the stands for the second time in a month for another touchline rant, this time during a 1-1 draw with West Ham which leaves Manchester United 11 points behind leaders Chelsea and seemingly out of the title race with just a third of the season gone. Josh Sims, 19, makes an immediate impact on his Southampton debut, providing the assist for Charlie Austin's goal after 44 seconds which proves enough for victory over Everton on Ronald Koeman's first return to St Mary's. Alex Sanchez scores twice in Arsenal's 3-1 victory over Bournemouth. Watford's Miguel Britos is sent off for a second yellow card in the 1-0 home defeat by Stoke. Chelsea end the month a point ahead of Liverpool and Manchester City and three clear of Arsenal.

DECEMBER 2016

3 Chelsea come from behind to win a highly-charged, top-of-the-table match at the Etihad. Goals by Diego Costa, Willian and Eden Hazard deliver a 3-1 success against Manchester City, who have two players shown straight red cards in stoppage-time. Sergio Aguero is sent off for a two-footed lunge at David Luiz and banned for four matches, having already served a three-game suspension earlier in the season. In the mass brawl that follows, Fernandinho grabs Cesc Fabregas by the throat and consequently misses three fixtures. Alexis Sanchez fires a hat-trick in 14 second-half minutes, and sets up a goal for Mesut Ozil, as Arsenal overwhelm West Ham 5-1 at the London Stadium. Tottenham also hit five, without reply, against Swansea, with two goals each from Harry Kane and Christian Eriksen - Kane's first a disputed penalty. Two by Christian Benteke point Crystal Palace to a 3-0 victory over Southampton. His first leaves Fraser Forster red-faced after the goalkeeper miskicks an intended clearance. West Bromwich Albion climb to sixth with a 3-1 win over Watford, who have Christian Kabalese on the scoresheet for the first time, but lose Roberto Pereyra to a straight red for manhandling James McClean.

4 Bournemouth end Liverpool's 15-match unbeaten run in all competitions on a remarkable afternoon at Dean Court. They twice trail by two goals, then score three times in the final 17 minutes to prevail 4-3. Nathan Ake gets the winner in stoppage-time, with substitute Ryan Fraser having played a key role in the comeback.

10 Struggling Leicester revive memories of their historic title success with a 4-2 win over Manchester City. Jamie Vardy and Andy King score in the opening five minutes and Vardy goes on to record a hat-trick to end a 16-match goal drought in all competitions. It's also a red-letter day for Theo Walcott, who scores his 100th career goal as Arsenal come from behind to defeat Stoke 3-1. Stefano Okaka nets his first two goals for Watford, who beat Everton 3-2 with a starting line-up of 11 different nationalities - Troy Deeney the only English player. Romelu Lukaku gets both Everton goals and there is also a brace for Swansea's Fernando Llorente in their 3-0 victory over Sunderland. The day's most embarrassed player is Hull's Robert Snodgrass, who dives to win a penalty in the 3-3 draw with Crystal Palace and later publicly apologises.

11 Henrikh Mkhitaryan, out of favour at Manchester United for much of the season, follows up his first goal for the club in their midweek Europa League win by becoming the first Armenian player to score in the Premier League with the only goal against Tottenham. Diego Costa's fifth in six games gives Chelsea victory over West Bromwich Albion by the same scoreline.

13 Arsenal suffer their first defeat since the opening day of the Premier League season, going down 2-1 at Everton to an 86th minute goal by Ashley Williams, his first for the club. The home side's success is marred by a second yellow card for Phil Jagielkla, ruling him out of the upcoming Merseyside derby. On his first league start of the campaign, Bournemouth's Marc Pugh scores the only goal of the game with Leicester.

14 A hat-trick by Salomon Rondon - all headers - in the space of 13 second-half minutes gives West Bromwich Albion a 3-1 victory over Swansea. Adam Lallana strikes twice as Liverpool win 3-0 at Middlesbrough. So does Christian Eriksen for Tottenham, who defeat Hull by the same scoreline. Chelsea continue to set the pace, Cesc Fabregas netting the only goal at

Sunderland. Stoke have Marko Arnautovic shown a straight red card for a studs-up challenge on Sofiane Boufal in a goalless draw with Southampton.

17 A year to the day since Jose Mourinho left Stamford Bridge for the second time with Chelsea in disarray, Antonio Conte's team record their 11th straight victory. Diego Costa scores the only goal against Crystal Palace, whose manager Alan Pardew is sacked five days later after a single win in 11. Daniel Amartey heads his first for Leicester, who retrieve a 2-0 deficit for a point at Stoke. But they have Jamie Vardy shown a straight red card for a two-footed challenge on Mame Biram Diouf and six bookings costs them a £25,000 FA fine. Zlatan Ibrahimovic takes his tally to ten in nine games in all competitions for Manchester United, a brace accounting for West Bromwich Albion 2-0 at The Hawthorns. Alvaro Negredo also gets two, one a penalty, as Middlesbrough defeat Swansea 3-0. Hull's luck is out at West Ham, where they hit the woodwork three times, have another effort cleared off the line and lose 1-0 to Mark Noble's disputed penalty.

18 Leroy Sane opens his account for Manchester City in a 2-1 victory over Arsenal, whose manager Arsene Wenger admits to a 'horrible week' for his team. Jay Rodriguez is on the mark twice as Southampton come from behind to win 3-1 at Bournemouth.

19 The Merseyside derby is heading for a goalless draw until Sadio Mane gives Liverpool three points with a 95th minute goal at Goodison Park.

26 Chelsea make light of the absence of Diego Costa and N'Golo Kante to beat Bournemouth 3-0 for a club-record 12th successive win. At the bottom, Swansea's 4-1 home defeat by West Ham is followed by the sacking of manager Bob Bradley. Record-signing Andre Ayew scores for the first time as his side move away from trouble with a third successive victory. Troy Deeney's 100th goal for Watford, from the penalty spot, puts a damper on Sam Allardyce's first game in charge of Crystal Palace. His new team have the chance to go 2-0 up with a penalty of their own, but Christian Benteke's kick is saved by Heurelho Gomes and they have to settle for a 1-1 draw. Goal of the day comes from Henrikh Mkhitaryan in Manchester United's 3-1 success against Sunderland – a backheel volley 'scorpion' kick which is allowed to stand despite TV replays showing the player in an offside position. Busiest referee is Craig Pawson, who books 11 players in Burnley's 1-0 win over Middlesbrough, six of them from the home side who face a £25,000 FA fine.

28 Dele Alli scores twice as Tottenham come from behind to win 4-1 at Southampton, who have Nathan Redmond shown a straight red card for fouling Alli and conceding a penalty which Harry Kane fires over.

31 In the first meeting of Jurgen Klopp and Pep Guardiola in English football, Klopp's Liverpool defeat Manchester City with an eighth minute header from Georginio Wijnaldum at Anfield. Willian is on the mark twice as Chelsea equal the top-flight record of 13 successive victories in a single season with a 4-2 success against Stoke, who have Bruno Martins Indi on the mark for the first time. A hat-trick by Andre Gray powers Burnley to a 4-1 win over Sunderland. Manchester United also end the year strongly, thanks to Anthony Martial and Paul Pogba goals in the 85th and 86th minutes against Middlesbrough. They deliver a 2-1 scoreline watched, on his 75th birthday, by Sir Alex Ferguson, renowned for late comebacks during his time as manager. A day to remember, too, for Hal Robson Kanu, who marks his first start for West Bromwich Albion at Southampton with his first goal for the club – and the first since his memorable strike against Belgium in the quarter-finals of Euro 2016. Southampton have Virgil van Dijk sent off for a second yellow card in their 2-1 defeat.

JANUARY 2017

1 Another spectacular 'scorpion' kick goal, this time from Olivier Giroud, puts Arsenal on the way to a 2-0 win over Crystal Palace. Harry Kane also makes headlines, scoring twice and providing two assists for Dele Alli's brace in Tottenham's 4-1 victory at Watford.

2 Manchester City have Fernandinho sent off for the third time in six Premier League and Champion League matches – this one for a two-footed lunge on Burnley's Johann Berg Gudmundsson. City make light of the loss to come out on top 2-1, gaining ground on Liverpool, who are held 2-2 at Sunderland, for whom Jermain Defoe converts two penalties.

Also shown a straight red card is West Ham's Sofiane Feghouli, for a challenge on Manchester United's Phil Jones after 15 minutes. This is rescinded by the FA, the fourth time the club have been successful in five appeals against dismissals. United win 2-0 to extend their unbeaten run in all competitions to 13 matches. On-loan Enner Valencia comes off the bench to score his first goal for Everton, who defeat Southampton 3-0. Hull's 3-1 loss to West Bromwich Albion is followed by the dismissal of manager Mike Phelan.

3 Three goals down to Bournemouth with 20 minutes remaining, Arsenal launch a dramatic comeback, completed by Olivier Giroud's equaliser in stoppage-time after the home side have Simon Francis shown a straight red card for his challenge on Aaron Ramsey. Another late goal, from substitute Angel Rangel two minutes from the end of normal time, gives Swansea a 2-1 victory at Crystal Palace. It follows Alfie Mawson's first for the club and provides an immediate boost for new manager Paul Clement.

4 Chelsea's winning run comes to an end at White Hart Lane. They go down 2-0 to Tottenham, for whom Dele Alli takes his tally to seven goals in four games with two near-identical headers. After the Christmas and New Year programmes, Chelsea (49) lead Liverpool by five points, with Tottenham and Manchester City on 42 and Arsenal with 41.

14 West Ham and Chelsea overcome the absence of key players to record 3-0 victories. Andy Carroll hails the best goal of his career, a spectacular scissor-kick for West Ham against Crystal Palace as London Stadium supporters turn against Dimitri Payet following his refusal to play for the club again. Chelsea are missing Diego Costa at Leicester, but a brace by wing-back Marcos Alonso have them coasting. Harry Kane celebrates the birth of his daughter with a hat-trick against West Bromwich Albion, while Arsenal are also 4-0 winners, away to Swansea, Alex Iwobi forcing two own goals from Jack Cork and Kyle Naughton. Hull's new manager, Marco Silva, makes a successful start, with Abel Hernandez scoring twice in a 3-1 win over Bournemouth on his first start for two months after a groin injury. Also on the mark twice is Marko Arnautovic in Stoke's 3-1 success at Sunderland. A good day, too, for Joey Barton, who comes off the bench to score the only goal against Southampton on his return to Burnley after the cancellation of his contract with Rangers. Vicarage Road pays its respects to the late Graham Taylor on an emotional afternoon when the match with Middlesbrough fails to match the occasion, ending goalless.

15 Pep Guardiola admits Manchester City's title chances are over after the worst defeat of his managerial career. City lose 4-0 at Everton, who score with all four of their shots on target – two of them delivering first goals for the club for 18-year-old Tom Davies and 19-year-old new signing Ademola Lookman. At Old Trafford, James Milner puts Liverpool ahead from the penalty spot and Zlatan Ibrahimovic levels for Manchester United six minutes from the end of normal time.

21 Wayne Rooney shares the day's honours with Swansea. Rooney overtakes Sir Bobby Charlton as Manchester United's all-time leading scorer with his 250th goal for the club – a stoppage-time free kick which earns a 1-1 draw at Stoke. Swansea deliver a shock result at Anfield. They lead 2-0 with goals by Fernando Llorente, are pegged back by two from Roberto Firmino, then win with one from Gylfi Sigurdsson to move out of the relegation zone – and end Liverpool's 12-month unbeaten home record. Tottenham also come from behind at the Etihad for a 2-2 draw after two errors by goalkeeper Hugo Lloris put Manchester City in the driving seat. Dimitri Payet's demand for a move looks to have fostered a new-found team spirit for West Ham, who win 3-1 at Middlesbrough with a brace by Andy Carroll and on-loan Jonathan Calleri's first for the club.

22 Chelsea take advantage of their title rivals dropping points by beating Hull 2-0. The result is overshadowed by a sickening collision between Gary Cahill and Ryan Mason which leaves the Hull midfield player with a fractured skull. There is late drama at the Emirates after Arsenal lead through Shkodran Mustafi's first goal for the club, then have Granit Xhaka shown a straight red card for lunging at Steven Defour. Andre Gray levels for Burnley from the penalty spot in the 93rd minute and Arsene Wenger is sent to the stands for protesting. But his side prevail with a 98th minute spot-kick from Alexis Sanchez – their second controversial injury-time winner of the season against Sean Dyche's side.

31 Arsenal, with Arsene Wenger starting a four-match touchline ban, suffer a shock 2-1 home defeat by Watford. Goals by Younes Kaboul and Troy Deeney in the space of three first-half minutes provide the club's first league victory over Arsenal since 1988 – achieved on the eve of Graham Taylor's funeral. With Tottenham held to a goalless draw at Sunderland, Chelsea's grip at the top strengthens after a 1-1 draw at Liverpool. Simon Mignolet's penalty save from Diego Costa, denies Antonio Conte's side an even more commanding position. With 56 points, they lead Tottenham (47), Arsenal (47) and Liverpool (46). At the other end of the table, Sam Allardyce has his first league win with Crystal Palace, 2-0 at Bournemouth.

FEBRUARY 2017

1 Peter Crouch scores his 100th Premier League goal in Stoke's 1-1 draw with Everton. Manchester City return to the London Stadium three weeks after a 5-0 FA Cup victory and hand out another drubbing to West Ham – this time 4-0, with new-signing Gabriel Jesus scoring his first goal for the club.

4 Romelu Lukaku takes pride of place on an eventful day at both ends of the table. The Everton striker scores after 30 seconds against Bournemouth, finishes with four goals and sets up another for James McCarthy in a 6-3 victory described as manager Ronald Koeman as a 'crazy game.' Josh King nets twice for Bournemouth, who concede three or more goals for the tenth league match. Eden Hazard caps a man-of-the-match performance with a brilliant solo goal as Chelsea force Arsenal out of the title reckoning with a 3-1 win. A brace for Jermain Defoe and a first goal for the club for Didier Ndong boost Sunderland, who score three times in the final five minutes of the first-half in a crushing 4-0 away win over relegation rivals Crystal Palace. No-one is more delighted than Jack Rodwell, who has his first league victory in 38 starts for Sunderland. Despite losing captain Michael Dawson to a calf injury in the warm-up, Hull also achieve a notable success, beating Liverpool 2-0 away and effectively ending their interest in the title. On-loan Alfred N'Diaye is on the mark on his debut. Southampton's new signing, Manolo Gabbiadini, puts them ahead in his first match, but it's not enough to prevent a sixth defeat in seven games as West Ham come from behind to prevail 3-1 at St Mary's. Pedro Obiang featuring among their scorers for the first time. Another first-time marksman is on loan M'Baye Niang in Watford's 2-1 win over Burnley, who have Jeff Hendrick shown a straight red card after six minutes for lunging at Jose Holebas.

5 Leicester drop to within a point of the relegation zone after a 3-0 home defeat by Manchester United, failing to score for the fifth successive match. Gabriel Jesus hits both Manchester City goals for a 2-1 win against Swansea, his winner coming in stoppage-time.

11 Tottenham's title challenge looks to be over after a 2-0 defeat at Liverpool, who end a run of five league games without a victory thanks to two goals in the space of three second-half minutes from Sadio Mane. Arsenal return to winning ways by the same scoreline against Hull with two from Alexis Sanchez, the first allowed to stand after the ball goes in off his hand, the second a penalty when Sam Clucas handles a goal-bound header from Lucas Perez and receives a straight red card. There is also a brace for Manolo Gabbiadini as Southampton bring Sunderland down to earth by winning 4-0 at the Stadium of Light. West Ham manager Slaven Bilic is sent to the stands for throwing a TV microphone to the ground after Gareth McAuley's 94th minute goal gives West Bromwich Albion a 2-2 draw at the London Stadium.

12 Martin Olsson scores for the first time for Swansea, who continue their revival under Paul Clement and leave Claudio Ranieri threatening major changes to his struggling Leicester side after a 2-0 defeat. Robbie Brady, Burnley's record signing, also opens his account. A 25-yard free-kick earns a 1-1 draw with Chelsea and takes his new side's tally at Turf Moor to 29 points out of an overall total of 30.

13 Manchester City's 2-0 victory at Bournemouth is overshadowed when Gabriel Jesus sustains a broken bone in his right foot and is ruled out for two months.

25 Former Chelsea midfielder Frank Lampard, a guest of honour at Stamford Bridge, sees them stretch their lead by beating Swansea 3-1. Patrick van Aanholt scores his Crystal Palace goal for a 1-0 win over relegation rivals Middlesbrough, while Idrissa Gueye's first for Everton sets up a 2-0 victory over Sunderland. Gareth McAuley is on the mark on his 500th club appearance in England to give West Bromwich Albion a 2-1 success against Bournemouth. Two players are sent off for second yellow cards – Burnley's Ashley Barnes at Hull and West Ham's Michail Antonio at Watford. Both matches are drawn 1-1.

26 Harry Kane's third hat-trick in nine Premier League and FA Cup matches takes him past 100 career goals as Tottenham overcome Stoke 4-0. They move on to 53 points, ten behind Chelsea, with Manchester City on 52 and Arsenal with 50.

27 Four days after Claudio Ranieri's shock dismissal, Leicester end a run of six matches without a win. Jamie Vardy scores twice – his first league goals since December – as they defeat Liverpool 3-1.

MARCH 2017

4 Manchester United and Arsenal suffer setbacks in their bid for Champions League places. Leading scorer Zlatan Ibrahimovic has a penalty saved by Artur Boruc as United are held 1-1 by Bournemouth, who play with ten men for the second-half following Andrew Surman's second yellow card. Arsenal lose 3-1 at Liverpool and drop out of the top four after a third defeat in four games. Fernando Llorente's stoppage-time header, his second of the game, earns Swansea a 3-2 victory over Burnley, achieved despite a controversial penalty awarded against them for a clear handling offence by Burnley's Sam Vokes. Andre Gray converts it, his second of the afternoon, and two other players are on the mark twice. Nathan Redmond helps Southampton to a 4-3 win at Watford, who have Abdoulaye Doukoure on the scoresheet for the first time, while Marko Arnautovic's brace for Stoke accounts for Middlesbrough 2-0. Goal of the day is scored by Andros Townsend, who runs 85 yards to complete a 2-0 success for Crystal Palace away to West Bromwich Albion.

5 Two by Harry Kane set up Tottenham for a club record ninth successive Premier League home win – 3-2 against Everton.

6 Chelsea respond to Tottenham's victory by defeating West Ham 2-1 away and restoring a ten-point lead at the top.

11 Josh King completes a hat-trick in stoppage-time to give Bournemouth a 3-2 success against West Ham which ends their run of eight games without a win. King also misses a penalty and so does team-mate Benik Afobe. On-loan Oumar Niasse comes off the bench to score twice for Hull, who overcome relegation rivals Swansea 2-1. Morgan Schneiderlin nets his first for Everton in a 3-0 victory over West Bromwich Albion.

18 Gary Cahill gives away a penalty, then scores the decider after 87 minutes as Chelsea win 2-1 away to Stoke, who have Phil Bardsley sent off in extra-time for a second yellow card. Days after declining to sign a lucrative new contract, Romelu Lukaku becomes the first player to 20 Premier League goals for the season – and the first in an Everton shirt to reach that mark in the top division since Gary Lineker in 1986. Lukaku nets twice in stoppage-time, while Dominic Calvert-Lewin claims his first for the club in a 4-0 victory over Hull, who have Tom Huddlestone shown a straight red for his challenge on Idrissa Gueye. West Bromwich Albion defender Craig Dawson heads in two corners against Arsenal, who suffer a fourth league defeat (3-1) in five games – Arsene Wenger's worst run as manager. Leicester, revitalised under Craig Shakespeare, put relegation worries behind them with a third successive win, 3-2 at West Ham. Crystal Palace take another step to safety with their third on the trot, 1-0 against Watford, courtesy of Troy Deeney's own goal.

19 Middlesbrough, with Steve Agnew as caretaker following the dismissal of manager Aitor Karanka on the back of ten league games without a win, remain deep in trouble, losing 3-1 at home to Manchester United. Tottenham make it ten successive league victories at White Hart for the first time for 30 years by defeating Southampton 2-1. The top of the table shows Chelsea (69), Tottenham (59), Manchester City (57), Liverpool (56). The bottom four are Sunderland (20), Middlesbrough (22), Hull (24), Swansea (27).

APRIL 2017

1 Chelsea's lead is cut when Crystal Palace score twice in the first 11 minutes through Wilfried

Zaha and Christian Benteke for a shock 2-1 success at Stamford Bridge. The result offers some hope for Tottenham, who win 2-0 at Burnley, with Eric Dier on the mark for the first time this season. Hull's chances of staying up are boosted when an 85th minute goal by on-loan Andrea Ranocchia, his first for the club, delivers a 2-1 victory over faltering West Ham. But Sunderland look doomed after conceding the only one of the game to Miguel Britos, his first for Watford. Another first-timer is Matthew Pennington, who levels for Everton in the Merseyside derby. But Liverpool quickly regain the advantage through Philippe Coutinho and go on to prevail 3-1. Leicester caretaker-manager Craig Shakespeare joins the likes of Jose Mourinho and Pep Guardiola by winning his first four Premier League games – this latest one 2-0 against Stoke.

4 Everton's Ashley Williams receives a straight red card for handling Luke Shaw's shot in the last minute of stoppage-time, enabling Zlatan Ibrahimovic to give Manchester United a 1-1 draw from the resulting penalty. Also dismissed, for a second yellow card, is Watford's Miguel Britos in a 2-0 win over West Bromwich Albion.

5 Two goals by Eden Hazard launch Chelsea back to winning ways, 2-1 against Manchester City, and they are on the verge of restoring a ten-point advantage as Tottenham trail 1-0 at Swansea with the clock showing 88 minutes. But Dele Alli equalises and his side score twice more in injury-time to keep their hopes alive. Hull also come from behind to boost their chances of staying up, Lazar Markovic recording his first goal for the club in the 4-2 defeat of Middlesbrough, who look to be joining Sunderland in the Championship.

8 Tottenham put the pressure back on Chelsea by beating Watford 4-0 in a lunchtime match, Son Heung-min scoring twice and Dele Alli netting his 13th goal in 15 league games. But the leaders respond by winning 3-1 at Bournemouth, with Eden Hazard again on the mark. West Ham, without a victory in seven matches, ease the pressure as Cheikhou Kouyate scores the only goal against Swansea, whose own relegation worries intensify.

9 Sunderland's woes continue with Sebastian Larsson's straight red card for his challenge on Ander Hererra in a 3-0 home defeat by Manchester United. A week after signing a new five-year contract, Tom Davies puts Everton ahead after 30 seconds against Leicester, matching Chelsea's Pedro and Everton's Romelu Lukaku for the season's fastest goal. Lukaku nets twice to end Leicester's winning run under Craig Shakespeare 4-2.

10 Arsenal fall seven points adrift of a Champions League place when losing 3-0 to Crystal Palace, who move further away from trouble with a fifth win in six games, rounded off by Luka Milivojevic's first goal for the club from the penalty spot.

15 Tottenham win a seventh successive match in the top flight for the first time since 1967, Vincent Janssen's first goal from open play completing a 4-0 scoreline against Bournemouth. Manchester City's Vincent Kompany, back after another debilitating injury, celebrates wildly after putting them on the way to a 3-0 victory at Southampton with a header. Fellow central defender Phil Jagielka also makes headlines with his third goal in three games for Everton, this one paving the way for a 3-1 win over Burnley. Sunderland end a seven-game goal drought in a 2-2 draw with West Ham, but are still nine points from safety. West Ham have Sam Byram sent off for a second yellow card.

16 Chelsea's lead is cut to four points after a 2-0 defeat at Old Trafford, Marcus Rashford and Ander Herrera scoring Manchester United's goals.

22 Hull are forced to play for 65 minutes with ten men following Oumar Niasse's straight red card – later rescinded – for a challenge on Watford's M'Baye Niang. But they stay firm for a 2-0 victory, completed by a 30-yard drive from Sam Clucas. Hull stay two points ahead of Swansea, who beat Stoke by the same scoreline. Tom Carroll scores his first goal for the club after Stoke's Marko Arnautovic misses a penalty. Josh King takes his tally to 11 in 13 matches as Bournemouth are 4-0 winners against Middlesbrough, who have Gaston Ramirez sent off for a second yellow card.

23 Two goals by Christian Benteke give Crystal Palace a third straight success at Anfield, their 2-1 win putting Liverpool's Champions League aspirations in jeopardy.

25 Three days after beating Tottenham 4-2 to reach the FA Cup Final, Chelsea restore a seven-point lead over their title rivals by beating Southampton by the same scoreline, Diego Costa scoring twice.

26 Tottenham respond by winning at Crystal Palace, Christian Eriksen scoring the only goal of the game. Middlesbrough collect their first three points in 17 games, Marten de Roon netting the only one of their match with Sunderland.

27 United's Marouane Fellaini is shown a straight red card for butting Sergio Aguero – 19 seconds after being booked for fouling the City striker – in a goalless Manchester derby.

29 Sunderland are relegated, with four fixtures still to play, by a 1-0 home defeat against Bournemouth, failing to score for the 11th time in 13 games. Eldin Jakupovic saves a last-minute penalty from Dusan Tadic to earn Hull a goalless draw at Southampton. Burnley win their first away match of the season, 2-0 against Crystal Palace.

30 Chelsea turn on the style at Goodison Park, Pedro's 25-yard drive paving the way for a 3-0 win over Everton. But Totenham hang in there to defeat Arsenal 2-0 and ensure finishing above their north London rivals for the first time in 22 years. Swansea manager Paul Clement accuses Marcus Rashford of 'deceiving' referee Neil Swarbrick to win a penalty in a 1-1 draw at Old Trafford. Middlesbrough are also unhappy about Kevin Friend's decision to award a spot-kick for Leroy Sane's fall during the 2-2 draw with Manchester City in which on-loan Calum Chambers scores his first goal for the home side. At the end of the month, Chelsea have 81 points, four more than Tottenham, followed by Liverpool and City on 66, United 65 and Arsenal 60. Hull remain two points clear of Swansea.

MAY 2017

5 Tottenham falter, losing to Manuel Lanzini's goal, the only one of the match, at West Ham.

6 Hull miss the chance to consolidate their position when going down 2-0 to Sunderland – their first home defeat under Marco Silva. Swansea take advantage to move above their rivals, Fernando Llorente heading the only goal against Everton. Sam Vokes is on the mark twice in Burnley's 2-2 draw with West Bronmwich Albion, who end a run of five games without a goal.

7 Arsenal end Manchester United's 25-match unbeaten league run – 12 of them draws – with a 2-0 victory. It's Arsene Wenger's first success in 15 competitive fixtures against a Jose Mourinho side. James Milner fails from the penalty spot for the first time in more than seven years, Fraser Forster's save earning Southampton a goalless draw at Liverpool.

8 Middlesbrough are relegated after going down 3-0 to Chelsea, who move to within one win of the title.

12 Chelsea are crowned champions with a 1-0 victory over West Bromwich Albion, delivered by substitute Michy Batshuayi's 82nd minute goal at The Hawthorns.

13 Swansea move close to safety, beating Sunderland 2-0 with goals by leading scorer Fernando Llorente and Kyle Naughton, the defender's first for six years. Two by Olivier Giroud help keep Arsenal's hopes of a Champions League place alive, their 4-1 success against Stoke following up the 2-0 midweek defeat of Southampton, also away from home. Josh King takes his tally to 13 goals in 16 games with Bournemouth's winner against Burnley (2-1). Leicester's Riyad Mahrez has a penalty disallowed in the 2-1 defeat by Manchester City for kicking the ball twice after he slips when taking it.

14 Hull lose 4-0 at Crystal Palace and are relegated, with Swansea staying up. Liverpool win by the same scoreline at West Ham to keep Champions League qualification in their own hands. Philippe Coutinho netting twice. On an emotional afternoon at White Hart Lane, Tottenham defeat Manchester United 2-1 in the final game at the old stadium before it is demolished after 118 years and replaced by a new one next door.

15 John Terry leads Chelsea's title party by scoring their 100th goal of the season in all competitions. The champions are 4-3 winners over Watford, who have Sebastian Prodl sent off for a second yellow card.

16 Two goals by Alexis Sanchez give Arsenal a 2-0 victory over Sunderland, but they remain outsiders for a Champions League place behind Manchester City, 3-1 winners over West Bromwich Albion, and Liverpool.

18 Harry Kane scores four goals in Tottenham's 6-1 win at Leicester to overtake Everton's Romelu Lukaku as the league's leading marksman. Son Heung-min nets the other two.

21 On the final day of the season, Arsenal miss out on a Champions League place for the first time in 20 years, Harry Kane scores his fourth Premier League hat-trick in four months and John Terry bows out after 22 years at Chelsea. Arsene Wenger's side overcome the loss of captain Laurent Koscielny – shown a straight red card after 13 minutes for lunging at Enner Valencia – to beat Everton 3-1, But it's not enough to prevent Manchester City, 5-0 winners at Watford, and Liverpool, who defeat relegated Middlesbrough 3-0, from holding on to third and fourth places respectively. Sergio Aguero nets twice for City at Vicarage Road in Walter Mazzarri's last game in charge of the home side following his midweek sacking. Kane retains the Golden Boot with 29 goals in 30 appearances as Tottenham swamp relegated Hull 7-1 on their own ground. Terry, 36, takes his leave of Stamford Bridge on his 717th appearance, wearing the number 26 shirt and playing a stage-managed 26 minutes before being substituted. Chelsea win – for a record 30th time – 5-1, Michy Batshuayi scoring twice in two minutes at the end after relegated Sunderland lead through Javi Manquillo's first for the club. Elsewhere, young and old make their mark. Josh Harrop, 21, marks his Manchester United debut with a goal in the 2-0 win over Crystal Palace, while 16-year-old Angel Gomes comes on as a late substitute. Peter Crouch, 36, becomes the first player in Premier League history to score 50 headed goals as Stoke win 1-0 at Southampton

HOW CHELSEA BECAME CHAMPIONS

AUGUST 2016

15	Chelsea 2 (Hazard 47 pen, Diego Costa 89) West Ham 1 (Collins 77). Att: 41,542
20	Watford 1 (Capoue 55) Chelsea 2 (Batshuayi 80, Diego Costa 87). Att: 20,772
27	Chelsea 3 (Hazard 9, Willian 41, Moses 89) Burnley 0. Att: 41,607

SEPTEMBER 2016

11	Swansea 2 (Sigurdsson 59 pen, Fer 62) Chelsea 2 (Diego Costa 18, 81). Att: 20,865
16	Chelsea 1 (Diego Costa 61) Liverpool 2 (Lovren 17, Henderson 36). Att: 41,514
24	Arsenal 3 (Sanchez 11, Walcott 14, Ozil 40) Chelsea 0. Att: 60,028

OCTOBER 2016

1	Hull 0 Chelsea 2 (Willian 61, Diego Costa 67). Att: 21,257
15	Chelsea 3 (Diego Costa 7, Hazard 33, Moses 80) Leicester 0. Att: 41,547
23	Chelsea 4 (Pedro 1, Cahill 21, Hazard 62, Kante 70) Manchester Utd 0. Att: 41,424
30	Southampton 0 Chelsea 2 (Hazard 6, Diego Costa 55). Att: 31,827

NOVEMBER 2016

5	Chelsea 5 (Hazard 19, 56, Alonso 20, Diego Costa 42, Pedro 65) Everton 0. Att: 41,429
20	Middlesbrough 0 Chelsea 1 (Diego Costa 41). Att: 32,704
26	Chelsea 2 (Pedro 45, Moses 51) Tottenham 1 (Eriksen 11) Att: 41,513

DECEMBER 2016

3	Manchester City 1 (Cahill 45 og) Chelsea 3 (Diego Costa 60, Willian 70, Hazard 90). Att: 54,457
11	Chelsea 1 (Diego Costa 76) WBA 0. Att: 41,622
14	Sunderland 0 Chelsea 1 (Fabregas 40). Att: 41,008
17	Crystal Palace 0 Chelsea 1 (Diego Costa 43. Att: 25,259
26	Chelsea 3 (Pedro 24, Hazard 49 pen, S Cook 90 og) Bournemouth 0. Att: 41,384

31   Chelsea 4 (Cahill 34, Willian 57, 65, Diego Costa 85) Stoke 2 (Martins Indi 46, Crouch 64). Att: 41,601

JANUARY 2017

4   Tottenham 2 (Alli 45, 54) Chelsea 0. Att: 31,491
14   Leicester 0 Chelsea 3 (Alonso 6, 51, Pedro 71). Att: 32,066
22   Chelsea 2 (Diego Costa 45, Cahill 81) Hull 0. Att: 41,605
31   Liverpool 1 (Wijnaldum 57) Chelsea 1 (Luiz 24). Att: 53,157

FEBRUARY 2017

4   Chelsea 3 (Alonso 13, Hazard 53, Fabregas 85) Arsenal 1 (Giroud 90). Att: 41,490
12   Burnley 1 (Brady 24) Chelsea 1 (Pedro 7). Att: 21,744
25   Chelsea 3 (Fabregas 19, Pedro 72, Diego Costa 84) Swansea 1 (Llorente 45). At: 41,612

MARCH 2017

6   West Ham 1 (Lanzini 90) Chelsea 2 (Hazard 25, Diego Costa 50). Att: 56,984
18   Stoke 1 (Walters 38 pen) Chelsea 2 (Willian 13, Cahill 87). Att: 27,724

APRIL 2017

1   Chelsea 1 (Fabregas 5) Crystal Palace 2 (Zaha 9, Benteke 11). Att: 41,489
5   Chelsea 2 (Hazard 10, 35) Manchester City 1 (Aguero 26). Att: 41,528
8   Bournemouth 1 (King 42) Chelsea 3 (A Smith 17 og, Hazard 20, Alonso 68). Att: 11,283
16   Manchester Utd 2 (Rashford 7, Herrera 49) Chelsea 0. Att: 75,272
25   Chelsea 4 (Hazard 5, Cahill 45, Diego Costa 54, 89) Southampton 2 (Romeu 24, Bertrand 90). Att: 41,168
30   Everton 0 Chelsea 3 (Pedro 66, Cahill 79, Willian 86). Att: 39,595

MAY 2017

8   Chelsea 3 (Diego Costa 23, Alonso 34, Matic 65) Middlesbrough 0. Att: 41,500
12   WBA 0 Chelsea 1 (Batashuayi 82). Att: 25,367 (Chelsea clinched title)
15   Chelsea 4 (Terry 22, Azpilicueta 36, Batshuayi 49, Fabregas 88) Watford 3 (Capoue 24, Janmaat 51, Okaka 74). Att: 41,473
21   Chelsea 5 (Willian 8, Hazard 61, Pedro 77, Batshuayi 90, 90) Sunderland 1 (Manquillo 3). Att: 41,618

ENGLISH FOOTBALL LEAGUE PLAY-OFFS 2016–17

Huddersfield Town sought a new approach and new ideas when appointing a Continental coach to take charge of the team for the first time. Eighteen months later, that vision paid rich dividends when David Wagner's players held their nerve in a penalty shoot-out to win the Championship Play-off Final – a match with an estimated £200m price tag – in his first full season. Victory for the former Borussia Dortmund coach, brought the club promotion to the Premier League for the first time – and top flight football for the first time since 1972, in the days of the old First Division. A tense match against Jaap Stam's Reading was still goalless after extra-time – and the teams remained locked after four penalties each. Then, on-loan Liverpool goalkeeper Danny Ward, hero of their semi-final shoot-out win over Sheffield Wednesday, saved from substitute Jordan Obita, offering record-buy Christopher Schindler the chance to drive the winner into the bottom corner. The £1.8m signing from 1860 Munich, one of five German players in the team, also had a key role during the season, missing just two matches as Huddersfield finished fifth.

Steve Morison followed up his two goals in **Millwall**'s semi-final win over Scunthorpe with an 85th minute winner against Bradford in the League One Final. But he admitted afterwards that an unpleasant pitch invasion by the club's own supporters had ruined the big day for him and his side. There was also a shadow over **Blackpool**'s success. Supporters boycotted the 2-1 win over Exeter City – the continuation of long-standing protests against the club's owners – with fewer than 6,000 present at the national stadium to see goals by Brad Potts and Mark Cullen secure an immediate return to League One. **Forest Green Rovers** become the smallest in the Football League, the team from Nailsworth (pop 5,800) in Gloucestershire beating Tranmere 3-1 in the National League Final. Kaiyne Woolery, on loan from Wigan, scored twice.

SEMI-FINALS, FIRST LEG

CHAMPIONSHIP
Fulham 1 (Cairney 65) **Reading** 1 (Obita 53). Att: 23,717. **Huddersfield** 0 **Sheffield Wednesday** 0. Att: 20,357

LEAGUE ONE
Bradford 1 (McArdle 77) **Fleetwood** 0. Att: 15,696. **Millwall** 0 **Scunthorpe** 0. Att: 12,568

LEAGUE TWO
Blackpool 3 (Cullen 19, 47, 67 pen) **Luton** 2 (Potts 26, Vassell 28). Att: 3,882. **Carlisle** 3 (Moore-Taylor 32 og, O'Sullivan 71, S Miller 73) **Exeter** 3 (Grant 15, Harley 45, Wheeler 56). Att: 9,708

NATIONAL LEAGUE
Aldershot 0 **Tranmere** 3 (Stockton 3, 75, Norwood 48). Att: 5,614. **Dagenham** 1 (Maguire-Drew 45) **Forest Green** 1 (Noble 29 pen). Att: 2,208

SEMI-FINALS, SECOND LEG

CHAMPIONSHIP
Reading 1 (Kermorgant 49 pen) **Fulham** 0. Att: 22,044 (Reading won 2-1 on agg). **Sheffield Wed** 1 (Fletcher 51) **Huddersfield** 1 (Lees 73 og). Att: 32,625 (aet, agg 1-1, Huddersfield won 4-3 on pens)

LEAGUE ONE
Fleetwood 0 **Bradford** 0. Att: 5,076 (Bradford won 1-0 on agg) **Scunthorpe** 2 (Toney 19, Dawson 81) **Millwall** 3 (Morison 45, 58, Gregory 52). Att: 7,190 (Millwall won 3-2 on agg)

LEAGUE TWO
Exeter 3 (Watkins 10, 79, Stacey 90) **Carlisle** 2 (Kennedy 81, O'Sullivan 90). Att: 7,450 (Exeter won 6-5 on agg). **Luton** 3 (Mellor 37 og, Cuthbert 45, Hylton 57 pen) **Blackpool** 3 (Delfouneso 22, Gnanduillet 76, Moore 90 og). Att: 10,032 (Blackpool won 6-5 on agg)

NATIONAL LEAGUE
Forest Green 2 (Doidge 34, Marsh-Brown 45) **Dagenham** 0. Att: 3,237 (Forest Green won 3-1 on agg) **Tranmere** 2 (Stockton 31, Norwood 90) **Aldershot** 2 (Mensah 43, Hughes 50 og). Att: 10,261 (Tranmere won 5-2 on agg)

FINALS

CHAMPIONSHIP – MONDAY, MAY 29 2017
Huddersfield Town 0 **Reading** 0 – aet, Huddersfield Town won 4-3 on pens. Att: 76,682 (Wembley)
Huddersfield Town (4-2-3-1): Ward, Smith (capt) (Cranie 88), Hefele, Schindler, Lowe, Mooy, Hogg, Kachunga (Quaner 66), Brown (Palmer 99), Van la Parra, Wells. **Subs not used:** Coleman, Holmes-Dennis, Whitehead, Hudson. **Booked:** Hogg, Kachunga, Smith. **Manager:** David Wagner
Reading (3-4-1-2): Al Habsi, Tiago Ilori, Moore, Van den Berg (Obita 64), Gunter (capt), Evans, Williams, Blackett, Swift (Kelly 100), Kermorgant, Grabban (McCleary 74). **Subs not used:**

Jaakkola, Beerens, Mendes, Popa. **Booked**: Van den Berg, Kermorgant, Obita. **Manager**: Jaap Stam
Referee: N Swarbrick (Lancs)

LEAGUE ONE – SATURDAY, MAY 20 2017
Bradford City 0 **Millwall** 1 (Morison 85). Att: 53,320 (Wembley)
Bradford City (4-4-2): Doyle, McMahon, McArdle, Knight-Percival, Meredith, Law (Dieng 74),
Cullen, Vincelot (capt), Marshall, Wyke, Clarke (Jones 74). **Subs not used**: Sattelmaier, Darby,
Hiwula, Gilliead, Kilgallon. **Booked**: Meredith. **Manager**: Stuart McCall
Millwall (4-4-2): Archer, Romeo, Webster, Hutchinson, Craig (capt), Wallace (Onyedinma 89),
Abdou, Williams, O'Brien (Ferguson 70), Gregory (Butcher 90), Morison. **Subs not used**: King,
Worrall, Thompson, Cooper. **Booked**: O'Brien. **Manager**: Neil Harris
Referee: S Hooper (Wilts). **Half-time**: 0-0

LEAGUE TWO – SUNDAY, MAY 28 2017
Blackpool 2 (Potts 3, Cullen 64) **Exeter City** 1 (Wheeler 40). Att: 23,380 (Wembley)
Blackpool (3-5-2): Slocombe, Aimson, Robertson, Aldred (capt) (Osayi-Samuel 30), Mellor,
Payne (Black 62), Daniel, Danns, Potts, Cullen (Flores 75), Vassell. **Subs not used**: Lyness,
Nolan, Delfouneso, Gnanduillet. **Booked**: Cullen, Osayi-Samuel, Slocombe, Flores, Daniel.
Manager: Gary Bowyer
Exeter City (4-3-3): Pym, Stacey, Brown (Sweeney 58), Moore-Taylor (capt), Woodman (Holmes
72), James, Harley, Wheeler, Watkins, Grant (Reid 58). **Subs not used**: Olejnik, Tillson,
McAlinden, Croll. **Manager**: Paul Tisdale
Referee: D England (South Yorks). **Half-time**: 1-1

NATIONAL LEAGUE – SUNDAY, MAY 14 2017
Tranmere Rovers 1 (Jennings 22) **Forest Green Rovers** 3 (Woolery 12, 44, Doidge 41). Att:
18,801 (Wembley)
Tranmere Rovers (4-4-2): Davies, Ridehalgh (capt), McNulty, Ihiekwe, Buxton, Norwood,
Hughes, Maynard, Jennings (Cook 61), Stockton, Mangan (Dunn 53). **Subs not used**: Turner,
Gumbs, Collins. **Booked**: Buxton. **Manager**: Micky Mellon
Forest Green Rovers (4-2-3-1): Russell, Pinnock, Monthe, Ellis, Bennett, Cooper, Traore
(Wedgbury 81), Marsh-Brown (Wishart 61), Noble (capt), Woolery, Doidge (Mullings 76). **Subs
not used**: Tilt, Bugiel. **Booked**: Cooper, Bennett, Noble. **Manager**: Mark Cooper
Referee: A Backhouse (Cumbria). **Half-time**: 1-3

PLAY-OFF FINALS – HOME & AWAY
1987: Divs 1/2: Charlton beat Leeds 2-1 in replay (Birmingham) after 1-1 agg (1-0h, 0-1a).
Charlton remained in Div 1 Losing semi-finalists: Ipswich and Oldham. **Divs 2/3: Swindon** beat
Gillingham 2-0 in replay (Crystal Palace) after 2-2 agg (0-1a, 2-1h). Swindon promoted to
Div 2. Losing semi-finalists: Sunderland and Wigan; Sunderland relegated to Div 3. **Divs 3/4:**
Aldershot beat Wolves 3-0 on agg (2-0h, 1-0a) and promoted to Div 3. Losing semi-finalists:
Bolton and Colchester; Bolton relegated to Div 4
1988: Divs 1/2: Middlesbrough beat Chelsea 2-1 on agg (2-0h, 0-1a) and promoted to Div 1;
Chelsea relegated to Div 2. Losing semi-finalists: Blackburn and Bradford City. **Divs 2/3: Wal-**
sall beat Bristol City 4-0 in replay (h) after 3-3 agg (3-1a, 0-2h) and promoted to Div 2. Losing
semi-finalists: Sheffield Utd and Notts County; Sheffield Utd relegated to Div 3. **Divs 3/4:**
Swansea beat Torquay 5-4 on agg (2-1h, 3-3a) and promoted to Div 3. Losing semi-finalists:
Rotherham and Scunthorpe.; Rotherham relegated to Div 4
1989: Div 2: Crystal Palace beat Blackburn 4-3 on agg (1-3a, 3-0h). Losing semi-finalists:
Watford and Swindon. **Div 3: Port Vale** beat Bristol Rovers 2-1 on agg (1-1a, 1-0h). Losing
semi-finalists: Fulham and Preston **Div.4: Leyton Orient** beat Wrexham 2-1 on agg (0-0a, 2-1h).
Losing semi-finalists: Scarborough and Scunthorpe

PLAY-OFF FINALS AT WEMBLEY

1990: Div 2: Swindon 1 Sunderland 0 (att: 72,873). Swindon promoted, then demoted for financial irregularities; Sunderland promoted. Losing semi-finalists: Blackburn and Newcastle Utd **Div 3: Notts County** 2 Tranmere 0 (att: 29,252). Losing semi-finalists: Bolton and Bury. **Div 4: Cambridge Utd** 1 Chesterfield 0 (att: 26,404). Losing semi-finalists: Maidstone and Stockport County

1991: Div 2: Notts County 3 Brighton 1 (att: 59,940). Losing semi-finalists: Middlesbrough and Millwall. **Div 3: Tranmere** 1 Bolton 0 (att: 30,217). Losing semi-finalists: Brentford and Bury. **Div 4: Torquay** 2 Blackpool 2 – Torquay won 5-4 on pens (att: 21,615). Losing semi-finalists: Burnley and Scunthorpe

1992: Div 2: Blackburn 1 Leicester 0 (att: 68,147). Losing semi-finalists: Derby and Cambridge Utd. **Div 3: Peterborough** 2 Stockport 1 (att: 35,087). Losing semi-finalists: Huddersfield and Stoke. **Div 4: Blackpool** 1 Scunthorpe 1 aet, Blackpool won 4-3 on pens (att: 22,741). Losing semi-finalists: Barnet and Crewe

1993: Div 1: Swindon 4 Leicester 3 (att: 73,802). Losing semi-finalists: Portsmouth and Tranmere. **Div 2: WBA** 3 Port Vale 0 (att: 53,471). Losing semi-finalists: Stockport and Swansea. **Div 3: York** 1 Crewe 1 aet, York won 5-3 on pens (att: 22,416). Losing semi-finalists: Bury and Walsall

1994: Div 1: Leicester 2 Derby 1 (att: 73,671). Losing semi-finalists: Millwall and Tranmere. **Div 2: Burnley** 2 Stockport 1 (att: 44,806). Losing semi-finalists: Plymouth Argyle and York. **Div 3: Wycombe** 4 Preston 2 (att: 40,109). Losing semi-finalists: Carlisle and Torquay

1995: Div 1: Bolton 4 Reading 3 (att: 64,107). Losing semi-finalists: Tranmere and Wolves. **Div 2: Huddersfield** 2 Bristol Rov 1 (att: 59,175). Losing semi-finalists: Brentford and Crewe. **Div 3: Chesterfield** 2 Bury 0 (att: 22,814). Losing semi-finalists: Mansfield and Preston

1996: Div 1: Leicester 2 Crystal Palace 1 aet (att: 73,573). Losing semi-finalists: Charlton and Stoke. **Div 2: Bradford City** 2 Notts Co 0 (att: 39,972). Losing semi-finalists: Blackpool and Crewe. **Div 3: Plymouth Argyle** 1 Darlington 0 (att: 43,431). Losing semi-finalists: Colchester and Hereford

1997: Div 1: Crystal Palace 1 Sheffield Utd 0 (att: 64,383). Losing semi-finalists: Ipswich and Wolves. **Div 2: Crewe** 1 Brentford 0 (att: 34,149). Losing semi-finalists: Bristol City and Luton. **Div 3: Northampton** 1 Swansea 0 (att: 46,804). Losing semi-finalists: Cardiff and Chester

1998: Div 1: Charlton 4 Sunderland 4 aet, Charlton won 7-6 on pens (att: 77, 739). Losing semi-finalists: Ipswich and Sheffield Utd. **Div 2: Grimsby** 1 Northampton 0 (att: 62,988). Losing semi-finalists: Bristol Rov and Fulham. **Div 3: Colchester** 1 Torquay 0 (att: 19,486). Losing semi-finalists: Barnet and Scarborough

1999: Div 1: Watford 2 Bolton 0 (att: 70,343). Losing semi-finalists: Ipswich and Birmingham. **Div 2: Manchester City** 2 Gillingham 2 aet, Manchester City won 3-1 on pens (att: 76,935). Losing semi-finalists: Preston and Wigan. **Div 3: Scunthorpe** 1 Leyton Orient 0 (att: 36,985). Losing semi-finalists: Rotherham and Swansea

2000: Div 1: Ipswich 4 Barnsley 2 (att: 73,427). Losing semi-finalists: Birmingham and Bolton. **Div 2: Gillingham** 3 Wigan 2 aet (att: 53,764). Losing semi-finalists: Millwall and Stoke. **Div 3: Peterborough** 1 Darlington 0 (att: 33,383). Losing semi-finalists: Barnet and Hartlepool

PLAY-OFF FINALS AT MILLENNIUM STADIUM

2001: Div 1: Bolton 3 Preston 0 (att: 54,328). Losing semi-finalists: Birmingham and WBA. **Div 2: Walsall** 3 Reading 2 aet (att: 50,496). Losing semi-finalists: Stoke and Wigan. **Div 3: Blackpool** 4 Leyton Orient 2 (att: 23,600). Losing semi-finalists: Hartlepool and Hull.

2002: Div 1: Birmingham 1 Norwich 1 aet, Birmingham won 4-2 on pens, (att: 71,597).

Losing semi-finalists: Millwall and Wolves. **Div 2: Stoke** 2 Brentford 0 (att: 42,523). Losing semi-finalists: Cardiff and Huddersfield. **Div 3: Cheltenham** 3 Rushden & Diamonds 1 (att: 24,368). Losing semi-finalists: Hartlepool and Rochdale

2003: Div 1: Wolves 3 Sheffield Utd 0 (att: 69,473). Losing semi-finalists: Nott'm Forest and Reading. **Div 2: Cardiff** 1 QPR. 0 aet (att: 66,096). Losing semi-finalists: Bristol City and Oldham. **Div 3: Bournemouth** 5 Lincoln 2 (att: 32,148). Losing semi-finalists: Bury and Scunthorpe

2004: Div 1: Crystal Palace 1 West Ham 0 (att: 72,523). Losing semi-finalists: Ipswich and Sunderland. **Div 2: Brighton** 1 Bristol City 0 (att: 65,167). Losing semi-finalists: Hartlepool and Swindon. **Div 3: Huddersfield** 0 Mansfield 0 aet, Huddersfield won 4-1 on pens (att: 37,298). Losing semi-finalists: Lincoln and Northampton

2005: Championship: West Ham 1 Preston 0 (att: 70,275). Losing semifinalists: Derby Co and Ipswich. **League 1: Sheffield Wed** 4 Hartlepool 2 aet (att: 59,808). Losing semi-finalists: Brentford and Tranmere **League 2: Southend** 2 Lincoln 0 aet (att: 19532). Losing semi-finalists: Macclesfield and Northampton

2006: Championship: Watford 3 Leeds 0 (att: 64,736). Losing semi-finalists: Crystal Palace and Preston. **League 1: Barnsley** 2 Swansea 2 aet (att: 55,419), Barnsley won 4-3 on pens. Losing semi-finalists: Huddersfield and Brentford. **League 2: Cheltenham** 1 Grimsby 0 (att: 29,196). Losing semi-finalists: Wycombe and Lincoln

PLAY-OFF FINALS AT WEMBLEY

2007: Championship: Derby 1 WBA 0 (att: 74,993). Losing semi-finalists: Southampton and Wolves. **League 1: Blackpool** 2 Yeovil 0 (att: 59,313). Losing semi-finalists: Nottm Forest and Oldham. **League 2: Bristol Rov** 3 Shrewsbury 1 (att: 61,589). Losing semi-finalists: Lincoln and MK Dons

2008: Championship: Hull 1 Bristol City 0 (att: 86,703). Losing semi-finalists: Crystal Palace and Watford. **League 1: Doncaster** 1 Leeds 0 (att: 75,132). Losing semi-finalists: Carlisle and Southend. **League 2: Stockport** 3 Rochdale 2 (att: 35,715). Losing semi-finalists: Darlington and Wycombe

2009: Championship: Burnley 1 Sheffield Utd 0 (att: 80,518). Losing semi-finalists: Preston and Reading. **League 1: Scunthorpe** 3 Millwall 2 (att: 59,661). Losing semi-finalists: Leeds and MK Dons. **League 2: Gillingham** 1 Shrewsbury 0 (att: 53,706). Losing semi-finalists: Bury and Rochdale

2010: Championship: Blackpool 3 Cardiff 2 (att: 82,244). Losing semi-finalists: Leicester and Nottm Forest. **League 1: Millwall** 1 Swindon 0 (att:73,108). Losing semi-finalists: Charlton and Huddersfield. **League 2: Dagenham & Redbridge** 3 Rotherham 2 (att: 32,054). Losing semi-finalists: Aldershot and Morecambe

2011: Championship: Swansea 4 Reading 2 (att: 86,581). Losing semi-finalists: Cardiff and Nottm Forest. **League 1: Peterborough** 3 Huddersfield 0 (Old Trafford, att:48,410). Losing semi-finalists: Bournemouth and MK Dons. **League 2: Stevenage** 1 Torquay 0 (Old Trafford, att: 11,484. Losing semi-finalists: Accrington and Shrewsbury

2012: Championship: West Ham 2 Blackpool 1 (att: 78,523). Losing semi-finalists: Birmingham and Cardiff. **League 1: Huddersfield** 0 Sheffield Utd 0 aet, Huddersfield won 8-7 on pens (att: 52,100). Losing semi-finalists: MK Dons and Stevenage. **League 2: Crewe** 2 Cheltenham 0 (att: 24,029). Losing semi-finalists: Southend and Torquay

2013: Championship: Crystal Palace 1 Watford 0 (att: 82,025). Losing semi-finalists: Brighton and Leicester. **League 1: Yeovil** 2 Brentford 1 (att: 41,955). Losing semi-finalists: Sheffield Utd and Swindon. **League 2: Bradford** 3 Northampton 0 (att: 47,127). Losing semi-finalists: Burton and Cheltenham

2014: Championship: QPR 1 Derby 0 (att: 87,348). Losing semi-finalists: Brighton and Wigan. **League 1: Rotherham** 2 Leyton Orient 2 aet, Rotherham won 4-3 on pens (att: 43,401). Losing semi-finalists: Peterborough and Preston. **League 2: Fleetwood** 1 Burton 0 (att: 14,007). Losing semi-finalists: Southend and York)

2015: Championship: Norwich 2 Middlesbrough 0 (att: 85,656). Losing semi-finalists: Brentford and Ipswich. **League 1: Preston** 4 Swindon 0 (att: 48,236). Losing semi-finalists: Chesterfield and Sheffield Utd. **League 2: Southend** 1 Wycombe 1 aet, Southend won 7-6 on pens (att: 38,252). Losing semi-finalists: Stevenage and Plymouth

2016: Championship: Hull 1 Sheffield Wed 0 (att 70,189). Losing semi-finalists: Brighton and Derby. **League 1: Barnsley** 3 Millwall 1 (att 51,277). Losing semi-finalists: Bradford and Walsall. **League 2: AFC Wimbledon** 2 Plymouth 0 (att 57,956). Losing semi-finalists: Accrington and Portsmouth)

HISTORY OF THE PLAY-OFFS

Play-off matches were introduced by the Football League to decide final promotion and relegation issues at the end of season 1986-87. A similar series styled 'Test Matches' had operated between Divisions One and Two for six seasons from 1893-98, and was abolished when both divisions were increased from 16 to 18 clubs.

Eighty-eight years later, the play-offs were back in vogue. In the first three seasons (1987-88-89), the Finals were played home-and-away, and since they were made one-off matches in 1990, they have featured regularly in Wembley's spring calendar, until the old stadium closed its doors and the action switched to the Millennium Stadium in Cardiff in 2001.

Through the years, these have been the ups and downs of the play-offs:

1987: Initially, the 12 clubs involved comprised the one that finished directly above those relegated in Divisions One, Two and Three and the three who followed the sides automatically promoted in each section. Two of the home-and-away Finals went to neutral-ground replays, in which **Charlton** clung to First Division status by denying Leeds promotion while **Swindon** beat Gillingham to complete their climb from Fourth Division to Second in successive seasons, via the play-offs. Sunderland fell into the Third and Bolton into Division Four, both for the first time. **Aldershot** went up after finishing only sixth in Division Four; in their Final, they beat Wolves, who had finished nine points higher and missed automatic promotion by one point.

1988: Chelsea were relegated from the First Division after losing on aggregate to **Middlesbrough**, who had finished third in Division Two. So Middlesbrough, managed by Bruce Rioch, completed the rise from Third Division to First in successive seasons, only two years after their very existence had been threatened by the bailiffs. Also promoted via the play-offs: **Walsall** from Division Three and **Swansea** from the Fourth. Relegated, besides Chelsea: Sheffield Utd (to Division Three) and Rotherham (to Division Four).

1989: After two seasons of promotion-relegation play-offs, the system was changed to involve the four clubs who had just missed automatic promotion. That format has remained. Steve Coppell's **Crystal Palace**, third in Division Two, returned to the top flight after eight years, beating Blackburn 4-3 on aggregate after extra time. Similarly, **Port Vale** confirmed third place in Division Three with promotion via the play-offs. For **Leyton Orient**, promotion seemed out of the question in Division Four when they stood 15th on March 1. But eight wins and a draw in the last nine home games swept them to sixth in the final table, and two more home victories in the play-offs completed their season in triumph.

1990: The play-off Finals now moved to Wembley over three days of the Spring Holiday weekend. On successive afternoons, **Cambridge Utd** won promotion from Division Four and **Notts Co** from the Third. Then, on Bank Holiday Monday, the biggest crowd for years at a Football League fixture (72,873) saw Ossie Ardiles' **Swindon** beat Sunderland 1-0 to reach the First Division for the first time. A few weeks later, however, Wembley losers **Sunderland** were promoted instead, by default; Swindon were found guilty of "financial irregularities" and stayed in Division Two.

1991: Again, the season's biggest League crowd (59,940) gathered at Wembley for the First Division Final in which **Notts Co** (having missed promotion by one point) still fulfilled their ambition, beating Brighton 3-1. In successive years, County had climbed from Third Division to First via the play-offs – the first club to achieve double promotion by this route. Bolton were denied automatic promotion in Division Three on goal difference, and lost at Wembley to an extra-time goal by **Tranmere**. The Fourth Division Final made history, with Blackpool beaten 5-4 on penalties by **Torquay** – first instance of promotion being decided by a shoot-out. In the table, Blackpool had finished seven points ahead of Torquay.

1992: Wembley that Spring Bank Holiday was the turning point in the history of **Blackburn**. Bolstered by Kenny Dalglish's return to management and owner Jack Walker's millions, they beat Leicester 1-0 by Mike Newell's 45th-minute penalty to achieve their objective – a place in the new Premier League. Newell, who also missed a second-half penalty, had recovered from a broken leg just in time for the play-offs. In the Fourth Division Final **Blackpool** (denied by penalties the previous year) this time won a shoot-out 4-3 against Scunthorpe., who were unlucky in the play-offs for the fourth time in five years. **Peterborough** climbed out of the Third Division for the first time, beating Stockport County 2-1 at Wembley.

1993: The crowd of 73,802 at Wembley to see **Swindon** beat Leicester 4-3 in the First Division Final was 11,000 bigger than that for the FA Cup Final replay between Arsenal and Sheffield Wed Leicester rallied from three down to 3-3 before Paul Bodin's late penalty wiped away **Swindon**'s bitter memories of three years earlier, when they were denied promotion after winning at Wembley. In the Third Division Final, **York** beat Crewe 5-3 in a shoot-out after a 1-1 draw, and in the Second Division decider, **WBA** beat Port Vale 3-0. That was tough on Vale, who had finished third in the table with 89 points – the highest total never to earn promotion in any division. They had beaten Albion twice in the League, too.

1994: Wembley's record turn-out of 158,586 spectators at the three Finals started with a crowd of 40,109 to see Martin O'Neill's **Wycombe** beat Preston 4-2. They thus climbed from Conference to Second Division with successive promotions. **Burnley**'s 2-1 victory in the Second Division Final was marred by the sending-off of two Stockport players, and in the First Division decider **Leicester** came from behind to beat Derby Co and end the worst Wembley record of any club. They had lost on all six previous appearances there – four times in the FA Cup Final and in the play-offs of 1992 and 1993.

1995: Two months after losing the Coca-Cola Cup Final to Liverpool, Bruce Rioch's **Bolton** were back at Wembley for the First Division play-off Final. From two goals down to Reading in front of a crowd of 64,107, they returned to the top company after 15 years, winning 4-3 with two extra-time goals. **Huddersfield** ended the first season at their new £15m. ground with promotion to the First Division via a 2-1 victory against Bristol Rov – manager Neil Warnock's third play-off success (after two with Notts Co). Of the three clubs who missed automatic promotion by one place, only **Chesterfield** achieved it in the play-offs, comfortably beating Bury 2-0.

1996: Under new manager Martin O'Neill (a Wembley play-off winner with Wycombe in 1994), **Leicester** returned to the Premiership a year after leaving it. They had finished fifth in the table, but in the Final came from behind to beat third-placed Crystal Palace by Steve Claridge's shot in the last seconds of extra time. In the Second Division **Bradford City** came sixth, nine points behind Blackpool (3rd), but beat them (from two down in the semi-final first leg) and then clinched promotion by 2-0 v Notts County at Wembley. It was City's greatest day since they won the Cup in 1911. **Plymouth Argyle** beat Darlington in the Third Division Final to earn promotion a year after being relegated. It was manager Neil Warnock's fourth play-off triumph in seven seasons after two with Notts County (1990 and 1991) and a third with Huddersfield in 1995.

1997: High drama at Wembley as **Crystal Palace** left it late against Sheffield Utd in the First Division play-off final. The match was scoreless until the last 10 seconds when David Hopkin lobbed Blades' keeper Simon Tracey from 25 yards to send the Eagles back to the Premiership after two seasons of Nationwide action. In the Second Division play-off final, **Crewe** beat Brentford 1-0 courtesy of a Shaun Smith goal. **Northampton** celebrated their first Wembley appearance with a 1-0 victory over Swansea thanks to John Frain's injury-time free-kick in the Third Division play-off final.

1998: In one of the finest games ever seen at Wembley, **Charlton** eventually triumphed 7-6 on penalties over Sunderland. For Charlton, Wearside-born Clive Mendonca scored a hat-trick and

Richard Rufus his first career goal in a match that lurched between joy and despair for both sides as it ended 4-4. Sunderland defender Michael Gray's superb performance ill deserved to end with his weakly struck spot kick being saved by Sasa Ilic. In the Third Division, the penalty spot also had a role to play, as **Colchester**'s David Gregory scored the only goal to defeat Torquay, while in the Second Division a Kevin Donovan goal gave **Grimsby** victory over Northampton.

1999: Elton John, watching via a personal satellite link in Seattle, saw his **Watford** side overcome Bolton 2-0 to reach the Premiership. Against technically superior opponents, Watford prevailed with application and teamwork. They also gave Bolton a lesson in finishing through match-winners by Nick Wright and Allan Smart. **Manchester City** staged a remarkable comeback to win the Second Division Final after trailing to goals by Carl Asaba and Robert Taylor for Gillingham, Kevin Horlock and Paul Dickov scored in stoppage time and City went on to win on penalties. A goal by Spaniard Alex Calvo-Garcia earned **Scunthorpe** a 1-0 success against Leyton Orient in the Third Division Final.

2000: After three successive play-off failures, **Ipswich** finally secured a place in the Premiership. They overcame the injury loss of leading scorer David Johnson to beat Barnsley 4-2 with goals by 36-year-old Tony Mowbray, Marcus Stewart and substitutes Richard Naylor and Martijn Reuser. With six minutes left of extra-time in the Second Division Final, **Gillingham** trailed Wigan 2-1. But headers by 38-year-old player-coach Steve Butler and fellow substitute Andy Thomson gave them a 3-2 victory. Andy Clarke, approaching his 33rd birthday, scored the only goal of the Third Division decider for **Peterborough** against Darlington.

2001: **Bolton**, unsuccessful play-off contenders in the two previous seasons, made no mistake at the third attempt. They flourished in the new surroundings of the Millennium Stadium to beat Preston 3-0 with goals by Gareth Farrelly, Michael Ricketts – his 24th of the season – and Ricardo Gardner to reach the Premiership. **Walsall**, relegated 12 months earlier, scored twice in a three-minute spell of extra time to win 3-2 against Reading in the Second Division Final, while **Blackpool** capped a marked improvement in the second half of the season by overcoming Leyton Orient 4-2 in the Third Division Final.

2002: Holding their nerve to win a penalty shoot-out 4-2, **Birmingham** wiped away the memory of three successive defeats in the semi-finals of the play-offs to return to the top division after an absence of 16 years. Substitute Darren Carter completed a fairy-tale first season as a professional by scoring the fourth spot-kick against Norwich. **Stoke** became the first successful team to come from the south dressing room in 12 finals since football was adopted by the home of Welsh rugby, beating Brentford 2-0 in the Second Division Final with Deon Burton's strike and a Ben Burgess own goal. Julian Alsop's 26th goal of the season helped **Cheltenham** defeat League newcomers Rushden & Diamonds 3-1 in the Third Division decider.

2003: **Wolves** benefactor Sir Jack Hayward finally saw his £60m investment pay dividends when the club he first supported as a boy returned to the top flight after an absence of 19 years by beating Sheffield Utd 3-0. It was also a moment to savour for manager Dave Jones, who was forced to leave his previous club Southampton because of child abuse allegations, which were later found to be groundless. **Cardiff**, away from the game's second tier for 18 years, returned with an extra-time winner from substitute Andy Campbell against QPR after a goalless 90 minutes in the Division Two Final. **Bournemouth**, relegated 12 months earlier, became the first team to score five in the end-of-season deciders, beating Lincoln 5-2 in the Division Three Final.

2004: Three tight, tense Finals produced only two goals, the lowest number since the Play-offs were introduced. One of them, scored by Neil Shipperley, gave **Crystal Palace** victory over West Ham, the much-travelled striker tapping in a rebound after Stephen Bywater parried Andy Johnson's shot. It completed a remarkable transformation for Crystal Palace, who were 19th in the table when Iain Dowie left Oldham to become their manager. **Brighton** made an immediate return to Division One in a poor game against Bristol City which looked set for extra-time until Leon Knight netted his 27th goal of the campaign from the penalty spot after 84 minutes. **Huddersfield** also went back up at the first attempt, winning the Division Three Final in a penalty shoot-out after a goalless 120 minutes against Mansfield.

2005: Goals were few and far between for Bobby Zamora during **West Ham**'s Championship season – but what a difference in the Play-offs. The former Brighton and Tottenham striker scored three times in the 4-2 aggregate win over Ipswich in the semi-finals and was on the mark again with the only goal against Preston at the Millennium Stadium. **Sheffield Wed** were eight minute away from defeat against Hartlepool in the League One decider when Steven MacLean made it 2-2 from the penalty spot and they went on to win 4-2 in extra-time. **Southend**, edged out of an automatic promotion place, won the League Two Final 2-0 against Lincoln, Freddy Eastwood scoring their first in extra-time and making the second for Duncan Jupp. **Carlisle** beat Stevenage 1-0 with a goal by Peter Murphy in the Conference Final to regain their League place 12 months after being relegated.

2006: From the moment Marlon King scored his 22nd goal of the season to set up a 3-0 win over Crystal Palace in the semi-final first leg, **Watford** had the conviction of a team going places. Sure enough, they went on to beat Leeds just as comfortably in the final. Jay DeMerit, who was playing non-league football 18 months earlier, headed his side in front. James Chambers fired in a shot that hit a post and went in off goalkeeper Neil Sullivan. Then Darius Henderson put away a penalty after King was brought down by Shaun Derry, the man whose tackle had ended Boothroyd's playing career at the age of 26. **Barnsley** beat Swansea on penalties in the League One Final, Nick Colgan making the vital save from Alan Tate, while Steve Guinan's goal earned **Cheltenham** a 1-0 win over Grimsby in the League Two Final. **Hereford** returned to the Football League after a nine-year absence with Ryan Green's extra-time winner against Halifax in the Conference Final.

2007: Record crowds, plenty of goals and a return to Wembley for the finals made for some eventful and entertaining matches. Stephen Pearson, signed from Celtic for £650,000 in the January transfer window, took **Derby** back to the Premier League after an absence of five seasons with a 61st minute winner, his first goal for the club, against accounted for West Bromwich Albion. It was third time lucky for manager Billy Davies, who had led Preston into the play-offs, without success, in the two previous seasons. **Blackpool** claimed a place in the game's second tier for the first time for 30 years by beating Yeovil 2-0 – their tenth successive victory in a remarkable end-of-season run. Richard Walker took his tally for the season to 23 with two goals for **Bristol Rov**, who beat Shrewsbury 3-1 in the League Two Final. Sammy McIlroy, who led Macclesfield into the league in 1997, saw his Morecambe side fall behind in the Conference Final against Exeter, but they recovered to win 2-1.

2008: Wembley has produced some unlikely heroes down the years, but rarely one to match 39-year-old Dean Windass. The **Hull** striker took his home-town club into the top-flight for the first time with the only goal of the Championship Final against Bristol City – and it was a goal fit to grace any game. In front of a record crowd for the final of 86,703, Fraizer Campbell, his 20-year-old partner up front, picked out Windass on the edge of the penalty box and a sweetly-struck volley flew into the net. **Doncaster**, who like Hull faced an uncertain future a few years earlier, beat Leeds 1-0 in the League One Final with a header by James Hayer from Brian Stock's corner. Jim Gannon had lost four Wembley finals with **Stockport** as a player, but his first as manager brought a 3-2 win against Rochdale in the League Two Final with goals by Anthony Pilkington and Liam Dickinson and a Nathan Stanton own goal. Exeter's 1-0 win over Cambridge United in the Conference Final took them back into the Football League after an absence of five seasons.

2009: Delight for Burnley, back in the big time after 33 years thanks to a fine goal from 20 yards by Wade Elliott, and for their town which became the smallest to host Premier League football. Despair for Sheffield Utd, whose bid to regain a top-flight place ended with two players, Jamie Ward and Lee Hendrie, sent off by referee Mike Dean. Martyn Woolford capped a man-of-the-match performance with an 85th minute winner for Scunthorpe, who beat Millwall 3-2 to make an immediate return to the Championship, Matt Sparrow having scored their first two goals. Gillingham also went back up at the first attempt, beating Shrewsbury with Simeon Jackson's header seconds from the end of normal time in the League Two Final. Torquay returned to the Football League after a two-year absence by beating Cambridge United 2-0 in the Conference Final.

2010: Blackpool, under the eccentric yet shrewd Ian Holloway, claimed the big prize two years almost to the day after the manager was sacked from his previous job at Leicester. On a scorching afternoon, with temperatures reaching 106 degrees, they twice came back from a goal down to draw level against Cardiff through Charlie Adam and Gary Taylor-Fletcher, then scored what proved to be the winner through Brett Ormerod at the end of a pulsating first half. **Millwall**, beaten in five previous play-offs, reached the Championship with the only goal of the game against Swindon from captain Paul Robinson. **Dagenham & Redbridge** defeated Rotherham 3-2 in the League Two Final, Jon Nurse scoring the winner 20 minutes from the end. **Oxford** returned to the Football League after an absence of four years with a 3-1 over York in the Conference Final.

2011: Scott Sinclair scored a hat-trick as **Swansea** reached the top flight, just eight years after almost going out of the Football League. Two of his goals came from the penalty spot as Reading were beaten 4-2 in the Championship Final, with Stephen Dobbie netting their other goal. The day after his father's side lost to Barcelona in the Champions League Final, Darren Ferguson led **Peterborough** back to the Championship at the first attempt with goals by Tommy Rowe, Craig Mackail-Smith and Grant McCann in the final 12 minutes against Huddersfield. John Mousinho scored the only one of the League Two Final for **Stevenage**, who won a second successive promotion by beating Torquay. **AFC Wimbledon**, formed by supporters in 2002 after the former FA Cup-winning club relocated to Milton Keynes, completed their rise from the Combined Counties to the Football League by winning a penalty shoot-out against Luton after a goalless draw in the Conference Final.

2012: **West Ham** were third in the Championship and second best to Blackpool in the final. But they passed the post first at Wembley, thanks to an 87th minute goal from Ricardo Vaz Te which gave Sam Allardyce's side a 2-1 victory. Allardyce brought the Portuguese striker to Upton Park from Barnsley for £500,000 – a fee dwarfed by the millions his goal was worth to the club. Goalkeepers took centre stage in the League One Final, with **Huddersfield** and Sheffield United still locked in a marathon shoot-out after a goalless 120 minutes. Alex Smithies put the 21st penalty past his opposite number Steve Simonsen, who then drove over the crossbar to give Huddersfield victory by 8-7. Nick Powell, 18, lit up the League Two Final with a spectacular volley as **Crewe** beat Cheltenham 2-0. **York** regained a Football League place after an absence of eight years by beating Luton 2-1 in the Conference decider.

2013: Veteran Kevin Phillips, a loser in three previous finals, came off the bench to fire **Crystal Palace** into the Premier League with an extra-time penalty. Wilfried Zaha was brought down by Marco Cassetti and 39-year-old Phillips showed nerves of steel to convert the spot-kick. A goalline clearance by Joel Ward then denied Fernando Forestieri as Watford sought an equaliser. **Yeovil** upset the odds by reaching the Championship for the first time. They defeated Brentford 2-1, Paddy Madden scoring his 23rd goal of the season and on-loan Dan Burn adding the second. **Bradford**, back at Wembley three months after their Capital One Cup adventure, swept aside Northampton 3-0 in the League Two Final with goals from James Hanson, Rory McArdle and Nahki Wells. **Newport** returned to the Football League after a 25-year absence by defeating Wrexham 2-0 in the Conference Final.

2014: An immediate return to the Premier League for **Queens Park Rangers** seemed unlikely when Gary O'Neil was sent off for bringing down Derby's Johnny Russell. There was still more than half-an-hour to go of a match Derby had dominated. But Rangers held on and with 90 minutes nearly up Bobby Zamora punished a mistake by captain Richard Keogh to score the only goal. **Rotherham** retrieved a 2-0 deficit against Leyton Orient with two goals by Alex Revell in the League One Final and won the eventual penalty shoot-out 4-3 for a second successive promotion. **Fleetwood** achieved their sixth promotion in ten seasons with a 1-0 victory over Burton, courtesy of a free-kick from Antoni Sarcevic in the League Two Final. Liam Hughes and Ryan Donaldson were on the mark as **Cambridge United** returned to the Football League after a nine-year absence by beating Gateshead 2-1 in the Conference Final, two months after winning the FA Trophy at Wembley

2015: **Norwich** were rewarded for a flying start with a return to the Premier League at the first attempt. Cameron Jerome put them ahead against Middlesbrough after 12 minutes of the Championship Final and Nathan Redmond made it 2-0 three minutes later, a scoreline they maintained without too many problems. Jermaine Beckford's hat-trick put **Preston** on the way to a record 4-0 victory over Swindon in the League One Final. **Southend**, who like Preston were denied automatic promotion on the final day of the regular season, beat Wycombe 7-6 on penalties after the League Two Final ended 1-1. **Bristol Rovers** were also penalty winners, by 5-3 against Grimsby in the Conference decider, so making an immediate return to the Football League.

2016: A goal worthy of winning any game took Hull back to the Premier League at the first attempt. Mohamed Diame, their French-born Senegal international midfielder, curled a 25-yard shot into the top corner after 72 minues for a 1-0 win over Sheffield Wednesday. Another spectacular goal, by Adam Hammill, helped Barnsley beat Millwall 3-1 on their return to Wembley for the League One Final after winning the Johnstone's Paint Trophy. AFC Wimbledon achieved their sixth promotion since being formed by supporters in 2002, defeating favourites Plymouth 2-0 in the League Two Final. Grimsby ended a six-year absence from the Football League with a 3-1 victory over Forest Green in the National League decider

Play-off attendances

1987	20	310,000	2003	15	374,461
1988	19	305,817	2004	15	388,675
1989	18	234,393	2005	15	353,330
1990	15	291,428	2006	15	340,804
1991	15	266,442	2007	15	405,278 (record)
1992	15	277,684	2008	15	382,032
1993	15	319,907	2009	15	380,329
1994	15	314,817	2010	15	370,055
1995	15	295,317	2011	15	310,998
1996	15	308,515	2012	15	332,930
1997	15	309,085	2013	15	346,062
1998	15	320,795	2014	15	307,011
1999	15	372,969	2015	15	367,374
2000	15	333,999	2016	15	393,145
2001	15	317,745	2017	15	323,727
2002	15	327,894			

THE THINGS THEY SAY ...

'We played for England, we played for Manchester and we played for the people who died' – **Paul Pogba**, Manchester United midfielder, dedicating United's Europa League victory to the victims of the city's concert bombing.

'We are a great team only on paper, not on the pitch' – **Antonio Conte**, Chelsea manager, after his team's indifferent start to the season.

'To arrive in my first season and to repeat what Claudio (Ranieri) did, I am very proud. I found fantastic players and great men' – **Antonio Conte** after their Premier League title triumph.

'The adventure was amazing and will live with me for ever. All I dreamt of was staying with the club I love. But my dream died' – **Claudio Ranieri**, title-winning **Leicester** manager after his sacking.

'We are duty-bond to put the club's long-term interests above all sense of personal sentiment' – **Aiyawatt Srivaddhanaprabha**, Leiceter's vice-chairman.

'I shed a tear for Claudio, for football and for my club. They should be building statues to him, not sacking him' – **Gary Lineker**, former Leicester striker.

ENGLISH HONOURS LIST

PREMIER LEAGUE

	First	Pts	Second	Pts	Third	Pts
1992–3a	Manchester Utd	84	Aston Villa	74	Norwich	72
1993–4a	Manchester Utd	92	Blackburn	84	Newcastle	77
1994–5a	Blackburn	89	Manchester Utd	88	Nottm Forest	77
1995–6b	Manchester Utd	82	Newcastle	78	Liverpool	71
1996–7b	Manchester Utd	75	Newcastle	68	Arsenal	68
1997–8b	Arsenal	78	Manchester Utd	77	Liverpool	65
1998–9b	Manchester Utd	79	Arsenal	78	Chelsea	75
1999 00b	Manchester Utd	91	Arsenal	73	Leeds	69
2000–01b	Manchester Utd	80	Arsenal	70	Liverpool	69
2001 02b	Arsenal	87	Liverpool	80	Manchester Utd	77
2002–03b	Manchester Utd	83	Arsenal	78	Newcastle	69
2003–04b	Arsenal	90	Chelsea	79	Manchester Utd	75
2004–05b	Chelsea	95	Arsenal	83	Manchester Utd	77
2005 06b	Chelsea	91	Manchester Utd	83	Liverpool	82
2006–07b	Manchester Utd	89	Chelsea	83	Liverpool	68
2007–08b	Manchester Utd	87	Chelsea	85	Arsenal	83
2008–09b	Manchester Utd	90	Liverpool	86	Chelsea	83
2009–10b	Chelsea	86	Manchester Utd	85	Arsenal	75
2010–11b	Manchester Utd	80	Chelsea	71	Manchester City	71
2011–12b	*Manchester City	89	Manchester Ud	89	Arsenal	70
2012–13b	Manchester Utd	89	Manchester City	78	Chelsea	75
2013–14b	Manchester City	86	Liverpool	84	Chelsea	82
2014–15b	Chelsea	87	Manchester City	79	Arsenal	75
2015–16b	Leicester	81	Arsenal	71	Tottenham	70
2016–17b	Chelsea	93	Tottenham	86	Manchester City	78

* won on goal difference. Maximum points: a, 126; b, 114

FOOTBALL LEAGUE

FIRST DIVISION

1992–3	Newcastle	96	West Ham	88	††Portsmouth	88
1993–4	Crystal Palace	90	Nottm Forest	83	††Millwall	74
1994–5	Middlesbrough	82	††Reading	79	Bolton	77
1995–6	Sunderland	83	Derby	79	††Crystal Palace	75
1996–7	Bolton	98	Barnsley	80	††Wolves	76
1997–8	Nottm Forest	94	Middlesbrough	91	††Sunderland	90
1998–9	Sunderland	105	Bradford City	87	††Ipswich	86
1999–00	Charlton	91	Manchester City	89	Ipswich	87
2000–01	Fulham	101	Blackburn	91	Bolton	87
2001–02	Manchester City	99	WBA	89	††Wolves	86
2002–03	Portsmouth	98	Leicester	92	††Sheffield Utd	80
2003–04	Norwich	94	WBA	86	††Sunderland	79

CHAMPIONSHIP

2004–05	Sunderland	94	Wigan	87	††Ipswich	85
2005–06	Reading	106	Sheffield Utd	90	Watford	81
2006–07	Sunderland	88	Birmingham	86	Derby	84
2007–08	WBA	81	Stoke	79	Hull	75
2008–09	Wolves	90	Birmingham	83	††Sheffield Utd	80
2009–10	Newcastle	102	WBA	91	††Nottm Forest	79
2010–11	QPR	88	Norwich	84	Swansea	80
2011–12	Reading	89	Southampton	88	West Ham	86

2012–13	Cardiff	87	Hull	79	††Watford	77
2013-14	Leicester	102	Burnley	93	††Derby	85
2014-15	Bournemouth	90	Watford	89	Norwich	86
2015-16	Burnley	93	Middlesbrough	89	††Brighton	89
2016-17	Newcastle	94	Brighton	93	††Reading	85

Maximum points: 138 ††Not promoted after play–offs

SECOND DIVISION

1992–3	Stoke	93	Bolton	90	††Port Vale	89
1993–4	Reading	89	Port Vale	88	††Plymouth Argyle	85
1994–5	Birmingham	89	††Brentford	85	††Crewe	83
1995–6	Swindon	92	Oxford Utd	83	††Blackpool	82
1996–7	Bury	84	Stockport	82	††Luton	78
1997–8	Watford	88	Bristol City	85	Grimsby	72
1998–9	Fulham	101	Walsall	87	Manchester City	82
1999–00	Preston	95	Burnley	88	Gillingham	85
2000–01	Millwall	93	Rotherham	91	††Reading	86
2001–02	Brighton	90	Reading	84	††Brentford	83
2002–03	Wigan	100	Crewe	86	††Bristol City	83
2003–04	Plymouth Argyle	90	QPR	83	††Bristol City	82

LEAGUE ONE

2004–05	Luton	98	Hull	86	††Tranmere	79
2005–06	Southend	82	Colchester	79	††Brentford	76
2006–07	Scunthorpe	91	Bristol City	85	Blackpool	83
2007-08	Swansea	92	Nottm Forest	82	Doncaster	80
2008-09	Leicester	96	Peterborough	89	††MK Dons	87
2009–10	Norwich	95	Leeds	86	Millwall	85
2010–11	Brighton	95	Southampton	92	††Huddersfield	87
2011–12	Charlton	101	Sheffield Wed	93	††Sheffield Utd	90
2012–13	Doncaster	84	Bournemouth	83	††Brentford	79
2013-14	Wolves	103	Brentford	94	††Leyton Orient	86
2014-15	Bristol City	99	MK Dons	91	Preston	89
2015-16	Wigan	87	Burton	85	††Walsall	84
2016-17	Sheffield Utd	100	Bolton	86	††Scunthorpe	82

Maximum points: 138 †† Not promoted after play–offs

THIRD DIVISION

1992–3a	Cardiff	83	Wrexham	80	Barnet	79
1993–4a	Shrewsbury	79	Chester	74	Crewe	73
1994–5a	Carlisle	91	Walsall	83	Chesterfield	81
1995–6b	Preston	86	Gillingham	83	Bury	79
1996–7b	Wigan	87	Fulham	87	Carlisle	84
1997–8b	Notts Co	99	Macclesfield	82	Lincoln	75
1998–9b	Brentford	85	Cambridge Utd	81	Cardiff	80
1999–00b	Swansea	85	Rotherham	84	Northampton	82
2000–01b	Brighton	92	Cardiff	82	*Chesterfield	80
2001–02b	Plymouth Argyle	102	Luton	97	Mansfield	79
2002–03b	Rushden & D	87	Hartlepool Utd	85	Wrexham	84
2003–04b	Doncaster	92	Hull	88	Torquay	81

* Deducted 9 points for financial irregularities

LEAGUE TWO

2004–05b	Yeovil	83	Scunthorpe	80	Swansea	80
2005–06b	Carlisle	86	Northampton	83	Leyton Orient	81
2006–07b	Walsall	89	Hartlepool	88	Swindon	85
2007–08b	MK Dons	97	Peterborough	92	Hereford	88

2008-09*b*	Brentford	85	Exeter	79	Wycombe	78
2009-10*b*	Notts Co	93	Bournemouth	83	Rochdale	82
2010-11*b*	Chesterfield	86	Bury	81	Wycombe	80
2011-12*b*	Swindon	93	Shrewsbury	88	Crawley	84
2012-13*b*	Gillingham	83	Rotherham	79	Port Vale	78
2013-14*b*	Chesterfield	84	Scunthorpe	81	Rochdale	81
2014-15*b*	Burton	94	Shrewsbury	89	Bury	85
2015-16*b*	Northampton	99	Oxford	86	Bristol Rov	85
2016-17*b*	Portsmouth	87	Plymouth	87	Doncaster	85

Maximum points: *a*, 126; *b*, 138;

FOOTBALL LEAGUE 1888–1992

1888-89*a*	Preston	40	Aston Villa	29	Wolves	28
1889-90*a*	Preston	33	Everton	31	Blackburn	27
1890-1*a*	Everton	29	Preston	27	Notts Co	26
1891-2*b*	Sunderland	42	Preston	37	Bolton	36

OLD FIRST DIVISION

1892-3*c*	Sunderland	48	Preston	37	Everton	36
1893-4*c*	Aston Villa	44	Sunderland	38	Derby	36
1894-5*c*	Sunderland	47	Everton	42	Aston Villa	39
1895-6*c*	Aston Villa	45	Derby	41	Everton	39
1896-7*c*	Aston Villa	47	Sheffield Utd	36	Derby	36
1897-8*c*	Sheffield Utd	42	Sunderland	39	Wolves	35
1898-9*d*	Aston Villa	45	Liverpool	43	Burnley	39
1899-1900*d*	Aston Villa	50	Sheffield Utd	48	Sunderland	41
1900-1*d*	Liverpool	45	Sunderland	43	Notts Co	40
1901-2*d*	Sunderland	44	Everton	41	Newcastle	37
1902-3*d*	The Wednesday	42	Aston Villa	41	Sunderland	41
1903-4*d*	The Wednesday	47	Manchester City	44	Everton	43
1904-5*d*	Newcastle	48	Everton	47	Manchester City	46
1905-6*e*	Liverpool	51	Preston	47	The Wednesday	44
1906-7*e*	Newcastle	51	Bristol City	48	Everton	45
1907-8*e*	Manchester Utd	52	Aston Villa	43	Manchester City	43
1908-9*e*	Newcastle	53	Everton	46	Sunderland	44
1909-10*e*	Aston Villa	53	Liverpool	48	Blackburn	45
1910-11*e*	Manchester Utd	52	Aston Villa	51	Sunderland	45
1911-12*e*	Blackburn	49	Everton	46	Newcastle	44
1912-13*e*	Sunderland	54	Aston Villa	50	Sheffield Wed	49
1913-14*e*	Blackburn	51	Aston Villa	44	Middlesbrough	43
1914-15*c*	Everton	46	Oldham	45	Blackburn	43
1919-20*f*	WBA	60	Burnley	51	Chelsea	49
1920-1*f*	Burnley	59	Manchester City	54	Bolton	52
1921-2*f*	Liverpool	57	Tottenham	51	Burnley	49
1922-3*f*	Liverpool	60	Sunderland	54	Huddersfield	53
1923-4*f*	*Huddersfield	57	Cardiff	57	Sunderland	53
1924-5*f*	Huddersfield	58	WBA	56	Bolton	55
1925-6*f*	Huddersfield	57	Arsenal	52	Sunderland	48
1926-7*f*	Newcastle	56	Huddersfield	51	Sunderland	49
1927-8*f*	Everton	53	Huddersfield	51	Leicester	48
1928-9*f*	Sheffield Wed	52	Leicester	51	Aston Villa	50
1929-30*f*	Sheffield Wed	60	Derby	50	Manchester City	47
1930-1*f*	Arsenal	66	Aston Villa	59	Sheffield Wed	52
1931-2*f*	Everton	56	Arsenal	54	Sheffield Wed	50
1932-3*f*	Arsenal	58	Aston Villa	54	Sheffield Wed	51

Season	First	Pts	Second	Pts	Third	Pts
1933–4 f	Arsenal	59	Huddersfield	56	Tottenham	49
1934–5 f	Arsenal	58	Sunderland	54	Sheffield Wed	49
1935–6 f	Sunderland	56	Derby	48	Huddersfield	48
1936–7 f	Manchester City	57	Charlton	54	Arsenal	52
1937–8 f	Arsenal	52	Wolves	51	Preston	49
1938–9 f	Everton	59	Wolves	55	Charlton	50
1946–7 f	Liverpool	57	Manchester Utd	56	Wolves	56
1947–8 f	Arsenal	59	Manchester Utd	52	Burnley	52
1948–9 f	Portsmouth	58	Manchester Utd	53	Derby	53
1949–50 f	*Portsmouth	53	Wolves	53	Sunderland	52
1950–1 f	Tottenham	60	Manchester Utd	56	Blackpool	50
1951–2 f	Manchester Utd	57	Tottenham	53	Arsenal	53
1952–3 f	*Arsenal	54	Preston	54	Wolves	51
1953–4 f	Wolves	57	WBA	53	Huddersfield	51
1954–5 f	Chelsea	52	Wolves	48	Portsmouth	48
1955–6 f	Manchester Utd	60	Blackpool	49	Wolves	49
1956–7 f	Manchester Utd	64	Tottenham	56	Preston	56
1957–8 f	Wolves	64	Preston	59	Tottenham	51
1958–9 f	Wolves	61	Manchester Utd	55	Arsenal	50
1959–60 f	Burnley	55	Wolves	54	Tottenham	53
1960–1 f	Tottenham	66	Sheffield Wed	58	Wolves	57
1961–2 f	Ipswich	56	Burnley	53	Tottenham	52
1962–3 f	Everton	61	Tottenham	55	Burnley	54
1963–4 f	Liverpool	57	Manchester Utd	53	Everton	52
1964–5 f	*Manchester Utd	61	Leeds	61	Chelsea	56
1965–6 f	Liverpool	61	Leeds	55	Burnley	55
1966–7 f	Manchester Utd	60	Nottm Forest	56	Tottenham	56
1967–8 f	Manchester City	58	Manchester Utd	56	Liverpool	55
1968–9 f	Leeds	67	Liverpool	61	Everton	57
1969–70 f	Everton	66	Leeds	57	Chelsea	55
1970–1 f	Arsenal	65	Leeds	64	Tottenham	52
1971–2 f	Derby	58	Leeds	57	Liverpool	57
1972–3 f	Liverpool	60	Arsenal	57	Leeds	53
1973–4 f	Leeds	62	Liverpool	57	Derby	48
1974–5 f	Derby	53	Liverpool	51	Ipswich	51
1975–6 f	Liverpool	60	QPR	59	Manchester Utd	56
1976–7 f	Liverpool	57	Manchester City	56	Ipswich	52
1977–8 f	Nottm Forest	64	Liverpool	57	Everton	55
1978–9 f	Liverpool	68	Nottm Forest	60	WBA	59
1979–80 f	Liverpool	60	Manchester Utd	58	Ipswich	53
1980–1 f	Aston Villa	60	Ipswich	56	Arsenal	53
1981–2 g	Liverpool	87	Ipswich	83	Manchester Utd	78
1982–3 g	Liverpool	82	Watford	71	Manchester Utd	70
1983–4 g	Liverpool	80	Southampton	77	Nottm Forest	74
1984–5 g	Everton	90	Liverpool	77	Tottenham	77
1985–6 g	Liverpool	88	Everton	86	West Ham	84
1986–7 g	Everton	86	Liverpool	77	Tottenham	71
1987–8 h	Liverpool	90	Manchester Utd	81	Nottm Forest	73
1988–9 j	††Arsenal	76	Liverpool	76	Nottm Forest	64
1989–90 j	Liverpool	79	Aston Villa	70	Tottenham	63
1990–1 j	Arsenal	83	Liverpool	76	Crystal Palace	69
1991–2 g	Leeds	82	Manchester Utd	78	Sheffield Wed	75

Maximum points: a, 44; b, 52; c, 60; d, 68; e, 76; f, 84; g, 126; h, 120; j, 114
*Won on goal average †Won on goal diff ††Won on goals scored No comp 1915–19 –1939–46

OLD SECOND DIVISION 1892–1992

Year						
1892–3a	Small Heath	36	Sheffield Utd	35	Darwen	30
1893–4b	Liverpool	50	Small Heath	42	Notts Co	39
1894–5c	Bury	48	Notts Co	39	Newton Heath	38
1895–6c	*Liverpool	46	Manchester City	46	Grimsby	42
1896–7c	Notts Co	42	Newton Heath	39	Grimsby	38
1897–8c	Burnley	48	Newcastle	45	Manchester City	39
1898–9d	Manchester City	52	Glossop	46	Leicester Fosse	45
1899–1900d	The Wednesday	54	Bolton	52	Small Heath	46
1900–1d	Grimsby	49	Small Heath	48	Burnley	44
1901–2d	WBA	55	Middlesbrough	51	Preston	42
1902–3d	Manchester City	54	Small Heath	51	Woolwich Arsenal	48
1903–4d	Preston	50	Woolwich Arsenal	49	Manchester Utd	48
1904–5d	Liverpool	58	Bolton	56	Manchester Utd	53
1905–6e	Bristol City	66	Manchester Utd	62	Chelsea	53
1906–7e	Nottm Forest	60	Chelsea	57	Leicester Fosse	48
1907–8e	Bradford City	54	Leicester Fosse	52	Oldham	50
1908–9e	Bolton	52	Tottenham	51	WBA	51
1909–10e	Manchester City	54	Oldham	53	Hull	53
1910–11e	WBA	53	Bolton	51	Chelsea	49
1911–12e	*Derby	54	Chelsea	54	Burnley	52
1912–13e	Preston	53	Burnley	50	Birmingham	46
1913–14e	Notts Co	53	Bradford PA	49	Woolwich Arsenal	49
1914–15e	Derby	53	Preston	50	Barnsley	47
1919–20f	Tottenham	70	Huddersfield	64	Birmingham	56
1920–1f	*Birmingham	58	Cardiff	58	Bristol City	51
1921–2f	Nottm Forest	56	Stoke	52	Barnsley	52
1922–3f	Notts Co	53	West Ham	51	Leicester	51
1923–4f	Leeds	54	Bury	51	Derby	51
1924–5f	Leicester	59	Manchester Utd	57	Derby	55
1925–6f	Sheffield Wed	60	Derby	57	Chelsea	52
1926–7f	Middlesbrough	62	Portsmouth	54	Manchester City	54
1927–8f	Manchester City	59	Leeds	57	Chelsea	54
1928–9f	Middlesbrough	55	Grimsby	53	Bradford City	48
1929–30f	Blackpool	58	Chelsea	55	Oldham	53
1930–1f	Everton	61	WBA	54	Tottenham	51
1931–2f	Wolves	56	Leeds	54	Stoke	52
1932–3f	Stoke	56	Tottenham	55	Fulham	50
1933–4f	Grimsby	59	Preston	52	Bolton	51
1934–5f	Brentford	61	Bolton	56	West Ham	56
1935–6f	Manchester Utd	56	Charlton	55	Sheffield Utd	52
1936–7f	Leicester	56	Blackpool	55	Bury	52
1937–8f	Aston Villa	57	Manchester Utd	53	Sheffield Utd	53
1938–9f	Blackburn	55	Sheffield Utd	54	Sheffield Wed	53
1946–7f	Manchester City	62	Burnley	58	Birmingham	55
1947–8f	Birmingham	59	Newcastle	56	Southampton	52
1948–9f	Fulham	57	WBA	56	Southampton	55
1949–50f	Tottenham	61	Sheffield Wed	52	Sheffield Utd	52
1950–1f	Preston	57	Manchester City	52	Cardiff	50
1951–2f	Sheffield Wed	53	Cardiff	51	Birmingham	51
1952–3f	Sheffield Utd	60	Huddersfield	58	Luton	52
1953–4f	*Leicester	56	Everton	56	Blackburn	55
1954–5f	*Birmingham	54	Luton	54	Rotherham	54

Year	Team	Pts	Team	Pts	Team	Pts
1955–6f	Sheffield Wed	55	Leeds	52	Liverpool	48
1956–7f	Leicester	61	Nottm Forest	54	Liverpool	53
1957–8f	West Ham	57	Blackburn	56	Charlton	55
1958–9f	Sheffield Wed	62	Fulham	60	Sheffield Utd	53
1959–60f	Aston Villa	59	Cardiff	58	Liverpool	50
1960–1f	Ipswich	59	Sheffield Utd	58	Liverpool	52
1961–2f	Liverpool	62	Leyton Orient	54	Sunderland	53
1962–3f	Stoke	53	Chelsea	52	Sunderland	52
1963–4f	Leeds	63	Sunderland	61	Preston	56
1964–5f	Newcastle	57	Northampton	56	Bolton	50
1965–6f	Manchester City	59	Southampton	54	Coventry	53
1966–7f	Coventry	59	Wolves	58	Carlisle	52
1967–8f	Ipswich	59	QPR	58	Blackpool	58
1968–9f	Derby	63	Crystal Palace	56	Charlton	50
1969–70f	Huddersfield	60	Blackpool	53	Leicester	51
1970–1f	Leicester	59	Sheffield Utd	56	Cardiff	53
1971–2f	Norwich	57	Birmingham	56	Millwall	55
1972–3f	Burnley	62	QPR	61	Aston Villa	50
1973–4f	Middlesbrough	65	Luton	50	Carlisle	49
1974–5f	Manchester Utd	61	Aston Villa	58	Norwich	53
1975–6f	Sunderland	56	Bristol City	53	WBA	53
1976–7f	Wolves	57	Chelsea	55	Nottm Forest	52
1977–8f	Bolton	58	Southampton	57	Tottenham	56
1978–9f	Crystal Palace	57	Brighton	56	Stoke	56
1979–80f	Leicester	55	Sunderland	54	Birmingham	53
1980–1f	West Ham	66	Notts Co	53	Swansea	50
1981–2g	Luton	88	Watford	80	Norwich	71
1982–3g	QPR	85	Wolves	75	Leicester	70
1983–4g	†Chelsea	88	Sheffield Wed	88	Newcastle	80
1984–5g	Oxford Utd	84	Birmingham	82	Manchester City	74
1985–6g	Norwich	84	Charlton	77	Wimbledon	76
1986–7g	Derby	84	Portsmouth	78	††Oldham	75
1987–8h	Millwall	82	Aston Villa	78	Middlesbrough	78
1988–9j	Chelsea	99	Manchester City	82	Crystal Palace	81
1989–90j	†Leeds	85	Sheffield Utd	85	†† Newcastle	80
1990–1j	Oldham	88	West Ham	87	Sheffield Wed	82
1991–2j	Ipswich	84	Middlesbrough	80	†† Derby	78

Maximum points: *a*, 44; *b*, 56; *c*, 60; *d*, 68; *e*, 76; *f*, 84; *g*, 126; *h*, 132; *j*, 138 * Won on goal average † Won on goal difference †† Not promoted after play-offs

THIRD DIVISION 1958–92

Year	Team	Pts	Team	Pts	Team	Pts
1958–9	Plymouth Argyle	62	Hull	61	Brentford	57
1959–60	Southampton	61	Norwich	59	Shrewsbury	52
1960–1	Bury	68	Walsall	62	QPR	60
1961–2	Portsmouth	65	Grimsby	62	Bournemouth	59
1962–3	Northampton	62	Swindon	58	Port Vale	54
1963–4	*Coventry	60	Crystal Palace	60	Watford	58
1964–5	Carlisle	60	Bristol City	59	Mansfield	59
1965–6	Hull	69	Millwall	65	QPR	57
1966–7	QPR	67	Middlesbrough	55	Watford	54
1967–8	Oxford Utd	57	Bury	56	Shrewsbury	55
1968–9	*Watford	64	Swindon	64	Luton	61
1969–70	Orient	62	Luton	60	Bristol Rov	56
1970–1	Preston	61	Fulham	60	Halifax	56
1971–2	Aston Villa	70	Brighton	65	Bournemouth	62
1972–3	Bolton	61	Notts Co	57	Blackburn	55

1973–4	Oldham	62	Bristol Rov	61	York	61
1974–5	Blackburn	60	Plymouth Argyle	59	Charlton	55
1975–6	Hereford	63	Cardiff	57	Millwall	56
1976–7	Mansfield	64	Brighton	61	Crystal Palace	59
1977–8	Wrexham	61	Cambridge Utd	58	Preston	56
1978–9	Shrewsbury	61	Watford	60	Swansea	60
1979–80	Grimsby	62	Blackburn	59	Sheffield Wed	58
1980–1	Rotherham	61	Barnsley	59	Charlton	59
†1981–2	**Burnley	80	Carlisle	80	Fulham	78
†1982–3	Portsmouth	91	Cardiff	86	Huddersfield	82
†1983–4	Oxford Utd	95	Wimbledon	87	Sheffield Utd	83
†1984–5	Bradford City	94	Millwall	90	Hull	87
†1985–6	Reading	94	Plymouth Argyle	87	Derby	84
†1986–7	Bournemouth	97	Middlesbrough	94	Swindon	87
†1987–8	Sunderland	93	Brighton	84	Walsall	82
†1988–9	Wolves	92	Sheffield Utd	84	Port Vale	84
†1989–90	Bristol Rov	93	Bristol City	91	Notts Co	87
†1990–1	Cambridge Utd	86	Southend	85	Grimsby	83
†1991–2	Brentford	82	Birmingham	81	††Huddersfield	78

* Won on goal average ** Won on goal difference † Maximum points 138 (previously 92) †† Not promoted after play–offs

FOURTH DIVISION 1958–92

1958–9	Port Vale	64	Coventry	60	York	60	Shrewsbury	58
1959–60	Walsall	65	Notts Co	60	Torquay	60	Watford	57
1960–1	Peterborough	66	Crystal Palace	64	Northampton	60	Bradford PA	60
1961–2	Millwall	56	Colchester	55	Wrexham	53	Carlisle	52
1962–3	Brentford	62	Oldham	59	Crewe	59	Mansfield	57
1963–4	*Gillingham	60	Carlisle	60	Workington	59	Exeter	58
1964–5	Brighton	63	Millwall	62	York	62	Oxford Utd	61
1965–6	*Doncaster	59	Darlington	59	Torquay	58	Colchester	56
1966–7	Stockport	64	Southport	59	Barrow	59	Tranmere	58
1967–8	Luton	66	Barnsley	61	Hartlepool Utd	60	Crewe	58
1968–9	Doncaster	59	Halifax	57	Rochdale	56	Bradford City	56
1969–70	Chesterfield	64	Wrexham	61	Swansea	60	Port Vale	59
1970–1	Notts Co	69	Bournemouth	60	Oldham	59	York	56
1971–2	Grimsby	63	Southend	60	Brentford	59	Scunthorpe	57
1972–3	Southport	62	Hereford	58	Cambridge Utd	57	Aldershot	56
1973–4	Peterborough	65	Gillingham	62	Colchester	60	Bury	59
1974–5	Mansfield	68	Shrewsbury	62	Rotherham	58	Chester	57
1975–6	Lincoln	74	Northampton	68	Reading	60	Tranmere	58
1976–7	Cambridge Utd	65	Exeter	62	Colchester	59	Bradford City	59
1977–8	Watford	71	Southend	60	Swansea	56	Brentford	59
1978–9	Reading	65	Grimsby	61	Wimbledon	61	Barnsley	61
1979–80	Huddersfield	66	Walsall	64	Newport	61	Portsmouth	60
1980–1	Southend	67	Lincoln	65	Doncaster	56	Wimbledon	55
†1981–2	Sheffield Utd	96	Bradford City	91	Wigan	91	Bournemouth	88
†1982–3	Wimbledon	98	Hull	90	Port Vale	88	Scunthorpe	83
†1983–4	York	101	Doncaster	85	Reading	82	Bristol City	82
†1984–5	Chesterfield	91	Blackpool	86	Darlington	85	Bury	84
†1985–6	Swindon	102	Chester	84	Mansfield	81	Port Vale	79
†1986–7	Northampton	99	Preston	90	Southend	80	††Wolves	79
†1987–8	Wolves	90	Cardiff	85	Bolton	78	††Scunthorpe	77
†1988–9	Rotherham	82	Tranmere	80	Crewe	78	††Scunthorpe 77
†1989–90	Exeter	89	Grimsby	79	Southend	75	††Stockport	74
†1990–1	Darlington	83	Stockport	82	Hartlepool Utd	82	Peterborough	80
1991–2a	Burnley	83	Rotherham	77	Mansfield	77	Blackpool	76

* Won on goal average Maximum points: †, 138; a, 126; previously 92 †† Not promoted after play–offs

THIRD DIVISION – SOUTH 1920–58

Year	Champion		Runner-up		Third	
1920–1a	Crystal Palace	59	Southampton	54	QPR	53
1921–2a	*Southampton	61	Plymouth Argyle	61	Portsmouth	53
1922–3a	Bristol City	59	Plymouth Argyle	53	Swansea	53
1923–4a	Portsmouth	59	Plymouth Argyle	55	Millwall	54
1924–5a	Swansea	57	Plymouth Argyle	56	Bristol City	53
1925–6a	Reading	57	Plymouth Argyle	56	Millwall	53
1926–7a	Bristol City	62	Plymouth Argyle	60	Millwall	56
1927–8a	Millwall	65	Northampton	55	Plymouth Argyle	53
1928–9a	*Charlton	54	Crystal Palace	54	Northampton	52
1929–30a	Plymouth Argyle	68	Brentford	61	QPR	51
1930–31a	Notts Co	59	Crystal Palace	51	Brentford	50
1931–2a	Fulham	57	Reading	55	Southend	53
1932–3a	Brentford	62	Exeter	58	Norwich	57
1933–4a	Norwich	61	Coventry	54	Reading	54
1934–5a	Charlton	61	Reading	53	Coventry	51
1935–6a	Coventry	57	Luton	56	Reading	54
1936–7a	Luton	58	Notts Co	56	Brighton	53
1937–8a	Millwall	56	Bristol City	55	QPR	53
1938–9a	Newport	55	Crystal Palace	52	Brighton	49
1946–7a	Cardiff	66	QPR	57	Bristol City	51
1947–8a	QPR	61	Bournemouth	57	Walsall	51
1948–9a	Swansea	62	Reading	55	Bournemouth	52
1949–50a	Notts Co	58	Northampton	51	Southend	51
1950–1d	Nottm Forest	70	Norwich	64	Reading	57
1951–2d	Plymouth Argyle	66	Reading	61	Norwich	61
1952–3d	Bristol Rov	64	Millwall	62	Northampton	62
1953–4d	Ipswich	64	Brighton	61	Bristol City	56
1954–5d	Bristol City	70	Leyton Orient	61	Southampton	59
1955–6d	Leyton Orient	66	Brighton	65	Ipswich	64
1956–7d	*Ipswich	59	Torquay	59	Colchester	58
1957–8d	Brighton	60	Brentford	58	Plymouth Argyle	58

THIRD DIVISION – NORTH 1921–58

Year	Champion		Runner-up		Third	
1921–2b	Stockport	56	Darlington	50	Grimsby	50
1922–3b	Nelson	51	Bradford PA	47	Walsall	46
1923–4a	Wolves	63	Rochdale	62	Chesterfield	54
1924–5a	Darlington	58	Nelson	53	New Brighton	53
1925–6a	Grimsby	61	Bradford PA	60	Rochdale	59
1926–7a	Stoke	63	Rochdale	58	Bradford PA	57
1927–8a	Bradford PA	63	Lincoln	55	Stockport	54
1928–9a	Bradford City	63	Stockport	62	Wrexham	52
1929–30a	Port Vale	67	Stockport	63	Darlington	50
1930–1a	Chesterfield	58	Lincoln	57	Wrexham	54
1931–2c	*Lincoln	57	Gateshead	57	Chester	50
1932–3a	Hull	59	Wrexham	57	Stockport	59
1933–4a	Barnsley	62	Chesterfield	61	Stockport	59
1934–5a	Doncaster	57	Halifax	55	Chester	54
1935–6a	Chesterfield	60	Chester	55	Tranmere	54
1936–7a	Stockport	60	Lincoln	57	Chester	53
1937–8a	Tranmere	56	Doncaster	54	Hull	53
1938–9a	Barnsley	67	Doncaster	56	Bradford City	52
1946–7a	Doncaster	72	Rotherham	64	Chester	56
1947–8a	Lincoln	60	Rotherham	59	Wrexham	50
1948–9a	Hull	65	Rotherham	62	Doncaster	50
1949–50a	Doncaster	55	Gateshead	53	Rochdale	51
1950–1d	Rotherham	71	Mansfield	64	Carlisle	62
1951–2d	Lincoln	69	Grimsby	66	Stockport	59

1952–3d	Oldham	59	Port Vale	58	Wrexham	56
1953–4d	Port Vale	69	Barnsley	58	Scunthorpe	57
1954–5d	Barnsley	65	Accrington	61	Scunthorpe	58
1955–6d	Grimsby	68	Derby	63	Accrington	59
1956–7d	Derby	63	Hartlepool Utd	59	Accrington	58
1957–8d	Scunthorpe	66	Accrington	59	Bradford City	57

Maximum points: a, 84; b, 76; c, 80; d, 92 * Won on goal average

TITLE WINNERS

PREMIER LEAGUE
Manchester Utd 13
Chelsea 5
Arsenal 3
Manchester City 2
Blackburn 1
Leicester 1

FOOTBALL LEAGUE CHAMPIONSHIP
Newcastle 2
Reading 2
Sunderland 2
Bournemouth 1
Burnley 1
Cardiff 1
Leicester 1
QPR 1
WBA 1
Wolves 1

DIV 1 (NEW)
Sunderland 2
Bolton 1
Charlton 1
Crystal Palace 1
Fulham 1
Manchester City 1
Middlesbrough 1
Newcastle 1
Norwich 1
Nottm Forest 1
Portsmouth 1

DIV 1 (ORIGINAL)
Liverpool 18
Arsenal 10
Everton 9
Aston Villa 7
Manchester Utd 7
Sunderland 6
Newcastle 4
Sheffield Wed 4
Huddersfield 3
Leeds 3
Wolves 3
Blackburn 2
Burnley 2
Derby 2

Manchester City 2
Portsmouth 2
Preston 2
Tottenham 2
Chelsea 1
Ipswich 1
Nottm Forest 1
Sheffield Utd 1
WBA 1

LEAGUE ONE
Brighton 1
Bristol City 1
Charlton 1
Doncaster 1
Leicester 1
Luton 1
Norwich 1
Scunthorpe 1
Sheffield Utd 1
Southend 1
Swansea 1
Wigan 1
Wolves 1

DIV 2 (NEW)
Birmingham 1
Brighton 1
Bury 1
Chesterfield 1
Fulham 1
Millwall 1
Plymouth 1
Preston 1
Reading 1
Stoke 1
Swindon 1
Watford 1
Wigan 1
Notts Co 1

DIV 2 (ORIGINAL)
Leicester 6
Manchester City 6
Sheffield Wed 5
Birmingham 4
Derby 4
Liverpool 4
Ipswich 3
Leeds 3

Middlesbrough 3
Notts County 3
Preston 3
Aston Villa 2
Bolton 2
Burnley 2
Chelsea 2
Grimsby 2
Manchester Utd 2
Norwich 2
Nottm Forest 2
Stoke 2
Tottenham 2
WBA 2
West Ham 2
Wolves 2
Blackburn 1
Blackpool 1
Bradford City 1
Brentford 1
Bristol City 1
Bury 1
Coventry 1
Crystal Palace 1
Everton 1
Fulham 1
Huddersfield 1
Luton 1
Millwall 1
Newcastle 1
Oldham 1
Oxford Utd 1
QPR 1
Sheffield Utd 1
Sunderland 1

LEAGUE TWO
Chesterfield 2
Brentford 1
Burton 1
Carlisle 1
Gillingham 1
MK Dons 1
Northampton 1
Notts County 1
Portsmouth 1
Swindon 1
Walsall 1
Yeovil 1

APPLICATIONS FOR RE-ELECTION (System discontinued 1987)

14	Hartlepool	4	Norwich	2	Oldham
12	Halifax	3	Aldershot	2	QPR
11	Barrow	3	Bradford City	2	Rotherham
11	Southport	3	Crystal Palace	2	Scunthorpe
10	Crewe	3	Doncaster	2	Southend
10	Newport	3	Hereford	2	Watford
10	Rochdale	3	Merthyr	1	Blackpool
8	Darlington	3	Swindon	1	Brighton
8	Exeter	3	Torquay	1	Bristol Rov
7	Chester	3	Tranmere	1	Cambridge Utd
7	Walsall	2	Aberdare	1	Cardiff
7	Workington	2	Ashington	1	Carlisle
7	York	2	Bournemouth	1	Charlton
6	Stockport	2	Brentford	1	Mansfield
5	Accrington	2	Colchester	1	Port Vale
5	Gillingham	2	Durham	1	Preston
5	Lincoln	2	Gateshead	1	Shrewsbury
5	New Brighton	2	Grimsby	1	Swansea
4	Bradford PA	2	Millwall	1	Thames
4	Northampton	2	Nelson	1	Wrexham

RELEGATED CLUBS (TO 1992)

1892–3   In Test matches, Darwen and Sheffield Utd won promotion in place of Accrington and Notts Co
1893–4   Tests, Liverpool and Small Heath won promotion Darwen and Newton Heath relegated
1894–5   After Tests, Bury promoted, Liverpool relegated
1895–6   After Tests, Liverpool promoted, Small Heath relegated
1896–7   After Tests, Notts Co promoted, Burnley relegated
1897–8   Test system abolished after success of Burnley and Stoke, League extended Blackburn and Newcastle elected to First Division
Automatic promotion and relegation introduced

FIRST DIVISION TO SECOND DIVISION

1898–9   Bolton, Sheffield Wed
1899–00   Burnley, Glossop
1900–1   Preston, WBA
1901–2   Small Heath, Manchester City
1902–3   Grimsby, Bolton
1903–4   Liverpool, WBA
1904–5   League extended Bury and Notts Co, two bottom clubs in First Division, re–elected
1905–6   Nottm Forest, Wolves
1906–7   Derby, Stoke
1907–8   Bolton, Birmingham
1908–9   Manchester City, Leicester Fosse
1909–10   Bolton, Chelsea
1910–11   Bristol City, Nottm Forest
1911–12   Preston, Bury
1912–13   Notts Co, Woolwich Arsenal
1913–14   Preston, Derby
1914–15   Tottenham, *Chelsea
1919–20   Notts Co, Sheffield Wed
1920–1   Derby, Bradford PA
1921–2   Bradford City, Manchester Utd
1922–3   Stoke, Oldham
1923–4   Chelsea, Middlesbrough
1924–5   Preston, Nottm Forest
1925–6   Manchester City, Notts Co

1926 7	Leeds, WBA
1927–8	Tottenham, Middlesbrough
1928–9	Bury, Cardiff
1929–30	Burnley, Everton
1930–1	Leeds, Manchester Utd
1931–2	Grimsby, West Ham
1932–3	Bolton, Blackpool
1933–4	Newcastle, Sheffield Utd
1934–5	Leicester, Tottenham
1935–6	Aston Villa, Blackburn
1936–7	Manchester Utd, Sheffield Wed
1937–8	Manchester City, WBA
1938–9	Birmingham, Leicester
1946–7	Brentford, Leeds
1947–8	Blackburn, Grimsby
1948–9	Preston, Sheffield Utd
1949 50	Manchester City, Birmingham
1950–1	Sheffield Wed, Everton
1951–2	Huddersfield, Fulham
1952–3	Stoke, Derby
1953–4	Middlesbrough, Liverpool
1954–5	Leicester, Sheffield Wed
1955–6	Huddersfield, Sheffield Utd
1956–7	Charlton, Cardiff
1957–8	Sheffield Wed, Sunderland
1958–9	Portsmouth, Aston Villa
1959–60	Luton, Leeds
1960–61	Preston, Newcastle
1961–2	Chelsea, Cardiff
1962 3	Manchester City, Leyton Orient
1963–4	Bolton, Ipswich
1964 5	Wolves, Birmingham
1965–6	Northampton, Blackburn
1966–7	Aston Villa, Blackpool
1967–8	Fulham, Sheffield Utd
1968–9	Leicester, QPR
1969 70	Sheffield Wed, Sunderland
1970 1	Burnley, Blackpool
1971–2	Nottm Forest, Huddersfield
1972–3	WBA, Crystal Palace
1973–4	Norwich, Manchester Utd, Southampton
1974–5	Chelsea, Luton, Carlisle
1975–6	Sheffield Utd, Burnley, Wolves
1976 7	Tottenham, Stoke, Sunderland
1977–8	Leicester, West Ham, Newcastle
1978–9	QPR, Birmingham, Chelsea
1979–80	Bristol City, Derby, Bolton
1980–1	Norwich, Leicester, Crystal Palace
1981–2	Leeds, Wolves, Middlesbrough
1982–3	Manchester City, Swansea, Brighton
1983–4	Birmingham, Notts Co, Wolves
1984–5	Norwich, Sunderland, Stoke
1985–6	Ipswich, Birmingham, WBA
1986–7	Leicester, Manchester City, Aston Villa
1987–8	Chelsea**, Portsmouth, Watford, Oxford Utd
1988–9	Middlesbrough, West Ham, Newcastle
1989–90	Sheffield Wed, Charlton, Millwall
1990–1	Sunderland, Derby
1991–2	Luton, Notts Co, West Ham

* Subsequently re–elected to First Division when League extended after the war
** Relegated after play–offs

SECOND DIVISION TO THIRD DIVISION

1920–1	Stockport
1921–2	Bradford City, Bristol City
1922–3	Rotherham, Wolves
1923–4	Nelson, Bristol City
1924–5	Crystal Palace, Coventry
1925–6	Stoke, Stockport
1926–7	Darlington, Bradford City
1927–8	Fulham, South Shields
1928–9	Port Vale, Clapton Orient
1929–30	Hull, Notts County
1930–1	Reading, Cardiff
1931–2	Barnsley, Bristol City
1932–3	Chesterfield, Charlton
1933–4	Millwall, Lincoln
1934–5	Oldham, Notts Co
1935–6	Port Vale, Hull
1936–7	Doncaster, Bradford City
1937–8	Barnsley, Stockport
1938–9	Norwich, Tranmere
1946–7	Swansea, Newport
1947–8	Doncaster, Millwall
1948–9	Nottm Forest, Lincoln
1949–50	Plymouth Argyle, Bradford PA
1950–1	Grimsby, Chesterfield
1951–2	Coventry, QPR
1952–3	Southampton, Barnsley
1953–4	Brentford, Oldham
1954–5	Ipswich, Derby
1955–6	Plymouth Argyle, Hull
1956–7	Port Vale, Bury
1957–8	Doncaster, Notts Co
1958–9	Barnsley, Grimsby
1959–60	Bristol City, Hull
1960–1	Lincoln, Portsmouth
1961–2	Brighton, Bristol Rov
1962–3	Walsall, Luton
1963–4	Grimsby, Scunthorpe
1964–5	Swindon, Swansea
1965–6	Middlesbrough, Leyton Orient
1966–7	Northampton, Bury
1967–8	Plymouth Argyle, Rotherham
1968–9	Fulham, Bury
1969–70	Preston, Aston Villa
1970–1	Blackburn, Bolton
1971–2	Charlton, Watford
1972–3	Huddersfield, Brighton
1973–4	Crystal Palace, Preston, Swindon
1974–5	Millwall, Cardiff, Sheffield Wed
1975–6	Portsmouth, Oxford Utd, York
1976–7	Carlisle, Plymouth Argyle, Hereford
1977–8	Hull, Mansfield, Blackpool
1978–9	Sheffield Utd, Millwall, Blackburn
1979–80	Fulham, Burnley, Charlton
1980–1	Preston, Bristol City, Bristol Rov
1981–2	Cardiff, Wrexham, Orient
1982–3	Rotherham, Burnley, Bolton
1983–4	Derby, Swansea, Cambridge Utd
1984–5	Notts Co, Cardiff, Wolves
1985–6	Carlisle, Middlesbrough, Fulham

1986-7	Sunderland**, Grimsby, Brighton
1987-8	Sheffield Utd**, Reading, Huddersfield
1988-9	Shrewsbury, Birmingham, Walsall
1989-90	Bournemouth, Bradford City, Stoke
1990-1	WBA, Hull
1991-2	Plymouth Argyle, Brighton, Port Vale

** Relegated after play-offs

THIRD DIVISION TO FOURTH DIVISION

1958-9	Rochdale, Notts Co, Doncaster, Stockport
1959-60	Accrington, Wrexham, Mansfield, York
1960-1	Chesterfield, Colchester, Bradford City, Tranmere
1961-2	Newport, Brentford, Lincoln, Torquay
1962-3	Bradford PA, Brighton, Carlisle, Halifax
1963-4	Millwall, Crewe, Wrexham, Notts Co
1964-5	Luton, Port Vale, Colchester, Barnsley
1965-6	Southend, Exeter, Brentford, York
1966-7	Doncaster, Workington, Darlington, Swansea
1967-8	Scunthorpe, Colchester, Grimsby, Peterborough (demoted)
1968-9	Oldham, Crewe, Hartlepool Utd, Northampton
1969-70	Bournemouth, Southport, Barrow, Stockport
1970-1	Gillingham, Doncaster, Bury, Reading
1971-2	Mansfield, Barnsley, Torquay, Bradford City
1972-3	Scunthorpe, Swansea, Brentford, Rotherham
1973-4	Cambridge Utd, Shrewsbury, Rochdale, Southport
1974-5	Bournemouth, Watford, Tranmere, Huddersfield
1975-6	Aldershot, Colchester, Southend, Halifax
1976-7	Reading, Northampton, Grimsby, York
1977-8	Port Vale, Bradford City, Hereford, Portsmouth
1978-9	Peterborough, Walsall, Tranmere, Lincoln
1979-80	Bury, Southend, Mansfield, Wimbledon
1980-1	Sheffield Utd, Colchester, Blackpool, Hull
1981-2	Wimbledon, Swindon, Bristol City, Chester
1982-3	Reading, Wrexham, Doncaster, Chesterfield
1983-4	Scunthorpe, Southend, Port Vale, Exeter
1984-5	Burnley, Orient, Preston, Cambridge Utd
1985-6	Lincoln, Cardiff, Wolves, Swansea
1986-7	Bolton**, Carlisle, Darlington, Newport
1987-8	Doncaster, York, Grimsby, Rotherham**
1988-9	Southend, Chesterfield, Gillingham, Aldershot
1989-90	Cardiff, Northampton, Blackpool, Walsall
1990-1	Crewe, Rotherham, Mansfield
1991-2	Bury, Shrewsbury, Torquay, Darlington

** Relegated after plays-offs

DEMOTED FROM FOURTH DIVISION TO CONFERENCE

1987	Lincoln
1988	Newport
1989	Darlington
1990	Colchester
1991	No demotion
1992	No demotion

DEMOTED FROM THIRD DIVISION TO CONFERENCE

1993	Halifax
1994-6	No demotion
1997	Hereford
1998	Doncaster

1999	Scarborough
2000	Chester
2001	Barnet
2002	Halifax
2003	Exeter, Shrewsbury
2004	Carlisle, York

DEMOTED FROM LEAGUE TWO TO CONFERENCE/NATIONAL LEAGUE

2005	Kidderminster, Cambridge Utd
2006	Oxford Utd, Rushden & Diamonds
2007	Boston, Torquay
2008	Mansfield, Wrexham
2009	Chester Luton
2010	Grimsby, Darlington
2011	Lincoln, Stockport
2012	Hereford, Macclesfield
2013	Barnet, Aldershot
2014	Bristol Rov, Torquay
2015	Cheltenham, Tranmere
2016	Dagenham, York
2017	Hartlepool, Leyton Orient

RELEGATED CLUBS (SINCE 1993)

1993
Premier League to Div 1: Crystal Palace, Middlesbrough, Nottm Forest
Div 1 to Div 2: Brentford, Cambridge Utd, Bristol Rov
Div 2 to Div 3: Preston, Mansfield, Wigan, Chester

1994
Premier League to Div 1: Sheffield Utd, Oldham, Swindon
Div 1 to Div 2: Birmingham, Oxford Utd, Peterborough
Div 2 to Div 3: Fulham, Exeter, Hartlepool Utd, Barnet

1995
Premier League to Div 1: Crystal Palace, Norwich, Leicester, Ipswich
Div 1 to Div 2: Swindon, Burnley, Bristol City, Notts Co
Div 2 to Div 3: Cambridge Utd, Plymouth Argyle, Cardiff, Chester, Leyton Orient

1996
Premier League to Div 1: Manchester City, QPR, Bolton
Div 1 to Div 2: Millwall, Watford, Luton
Div 2 to Div 3: Carlisle, Swansea, Brighton, Hull

1997
Premier League to Div 1: Sunderland, Middlesbrough, Nottm Forest
Div 1 to Div 2: Grimsby, Oldham, Southend
Div 2 to Div 3: Peterborough, Shrewsbury, Rotherham, Notts Co

1998
Premier League to Div 1: Bolton, Barnsley, Crystal Palace
Div 1 to Div 2: Manchester City, Stoke, Reading
Div 2 to Div 3: Brentford, Plymouth Argyle, Carlisle, Southend

1999
Premier League to Div 1: Charlton, Blackburn, Nottm Forest
Div 1 to Div 2: Bury, Oxford Utd, Bristol City
Div 2 to Div 3: York, Northampton, Lincoln, Macclesfield

2000
Premier League to Div 1: Wimbledon, Sheffield Wed, Watford
Div 1 to Div 2: Walsall, Port Vale, Swindon
Div 2 to Div 3: Cardiff, Blackpool, Scunthorpe, Chesterfield

2001
Premier League to Div 1: Manchester City, Coventry, Bradford City
Div 1 to Div 2: Huddersfield, QPR, Tranmere
Div 2 to Div 3: Bristol Rov, Luton, Swansea, Oxford Utd

2002
Premier League to Div 1: Ipswich, Derby, Leicester
Div 1 to Div 2: Crewe, Barnsley, Stockport
Div 2 to Div 3: Bournemouth, Bury, Wrexham, Cambridge Utd

2003
Premier League to Div 1: West Ham, WBA, Sunderland
Div 1 to Div 2: Sheffield Wed, Brighton, Grimsby
Div 2 to Div 3: Cheltenham, Huddersfield, Mansfield, Northampton

2004
Premier League to Div 1: Leicester, Leeds, Wolves
Div 1 to Div 2: Walsall, Bradford City, Wimbledon
Div 2 to Div 3: Grimsby, Rushden & Diamonds, Notts Co, Wycombe

2005
Premier League to Championship: Crystal Palace, Norwich, Southampton
Championship to League 1: Gillingham, Nottm Forest, Rotherham
League 1 to League 2: Torquay, Wrexham, Peterborough, Stockport

2006
Premier League to Championship: Birmingham, WBA, Sunderland
Championship to League 1: Crewe, Millwall, Brighton
League 1 to League 2: Hartlepool Utd, MK Dons, Swindon, Walsall

2007
Premier League to Championship: Sheffield Utd, Charlton, Watford
Championship to League 1: Southend, Luton, Leeds
League 1 to League 2: Chesterfield, Bradford City, Rotherham, Brentford

2008
Premier League to Championship: Reading, Birmingham, Derby
Championship to League 1: Leicester, Scunthorpe, Colchester
League 1 to League 2: Bournemouth, Gillingham, Port Vale, Luton

2009
Premier League to Championship: Newcastle, Middlesbrough, WBA
Championship to League 1: Norwich, Southampton, Charlton
League 1 to League 2: Northampton, Crewe, Cheltenham, Hereford

2010
Premier League to Championship: Burnley, Hull, Portsmouth
Championship to League 1: Sheffield Wed, Plymouth, Peterborough
League 1 to League 2: Gillingham, Wycombe, Southend, Stockport

2011
Premier League to Championship: Birmingham, Blackpool, West Ham
Championship to League 1: Preston, Sheffield Utd, Scunthorpe
League 1 to League 2: Dagenham & Redbridge, Bristol Rov, Plymouth, Swindon

2012
Premier League to Championship: Bolton, Blackburn, Wolves
Championship to League 1: Portsmouth, Coventry, Doncaster
League 1 to League 2: Wycombe, Chesterfield, Exeter, Rochdale

2013
Premier League to Championship: Wigan, Reading, QPR
Championship to League 1: Peterborough, Wolves, Bristol City
League 1 to League 2: Scunthorpe, Bury, Hartlepool, Portsmouth

2014
Premier League to Championship: Norwich, Fulham, Cardiff
Championship to League 1: Doncaster, Barnsley, Yeovil
League 1 to League 2: Tranmere, Carlisle, Shrewsbury, Stevenage

2015
Premier League to Championship: Hull, Burnley QPR
Championship to League 1: Millwall, Wigan, Blackpool
League 1 to League 2: Notts Co, Crawley, Leyton Orient, Yeovil

2016
Premier League to Championship: Newcastle, Norwich, Aston Villa
Championship to League 1: Charlton, MK Dons, Bolton
League 1 to League 2: Doncaster, Blackpool, Colchester, Crewe

2017
Premier League to Championship: Hull, Middlesbrough, Sunderland
Championship to League 1: Blackburn, Wigan, Rotherham
League 1 to League 2: Port Vale, Swindon, Coventry, Chesterfield

THE THINGS THEY SAY ... ABOUT THE ENGLAND JOB

'This is the role I have always wanted. It is the best job in English football. I will do everything I can to help England give the nation the success our fans deserve. Above all, we have to make the people and the whole country proud' – **Sam Allardyce** after being appointed England manager.

'I am deeply disappointed at this outcome. I recognise I made some comments which have caused embarrassment. I also regret my comments with regard to other individuals' – **Sam Allardyce** on his removal from the job 67 days later after being filmed by the *Daily Telegraph* attempting to negotiate a £400,000 business deal with undercover reporters, offering advice on how to get round third-party ownership rules on players, mocking his predecessor Roy Hodgson and criticising Hodgson's No 2 Gary Neville.

'Allardyce's conduct was inappropriate of an England manager. He accepts he made a significant error of judgement. The manager of the England team is a position which must demonstrate strong leadership and show respect for the integrity of the game' – **FA** statement on his departure.

'It's a catastrophic misjudgement by Sam and his advisors. I didn't think England could stoop any lower from what happened at the Euros. Now here we are a laughing stock of world football. We've got a problem with money. It's greed' – **Alan Shearer**, former England captain.

'Not too many England managers left their post with a 100 percent win record' – **Michael Owen**, former England striker, on Allardyce's victory in his one match in charge.

'With the overall objective of qualifying (for the World Cup), we have kept the team on track. But we have taken over a mess really and had to steady the ship' – **Gareth Southgate** after becoming interim England manager

'We need an environment and culture to enable us to perform at our very best. If we think we are good enough to play the best teams in the world and give ourselves a slight handicap along the way, then good luck with that. So where I will be clear is that there is a level of expectation when you are with England' – **Gareth Southgate** tells his players that drinking heavily in the public eye is 'not intelligent' after being appointed manager on a permanent basis.

ANNUAL AWARDS

FOOTBALL WRITERS' ASSOCIATION

Footballer of the Year: 1948 Stanley Matthews (Blackpool); **1949** Johnny Carey (Manchester Utd); **1950** Joe Mercer (Arsenal); **1951** Harry Johnston (Blackpool); **1952** Billy Wright (Wolves); **1953** Nat Lofthouse (Bolton); **1954** Tom Finney (Preston); **1955** Don Revie (Manchester City); **1956** Bert Trautmann (Manchester City); **1957** Tom Finney (Preston); **1958** Danny Blanchflower (Tottenham); **1959** Syd Owen (Luton); **1960** Bill Slater (Wolves); **1961** Danny Blanchflower (Tottenham); **1962** Jimmy Adamson (Burnley); **1963** Stanley Matthews (Stoke); **1964** Bobby Moore (West Ham); **1965** Bobby Collins (Leeds); **1966** Bobby Charlton (Manchester Utd); **1967** Jack Charlton (Leeds); **1968** George Best (Manchester Utd); **1969** Tony Book (Manchester City) & Dave Mackay (Derby) – shared; **1970** Billy Bremner (Leeds); **1971** Frank McLintock (Arsenal); **1972** Gordon Banks (Stoke); **1973** Pat Jennings (Tottenham); **1974** Ian Callaghan (Liverpool); **1975** Alan Mullery (Fulham); **1976** Kevin Keegan (Liverpool); **1977** Emlyn Hughes (Liverpool); **1978** Kenny Burns (Nott'm Forest); **1979** Kenny Dalglish (Liverpool); **1980** Terry McDermott (Liverpool); **1981** Frans Thijssen (Ipswich); **1982** Steve Perryman (Tottenham); **1983** Kenny Dalglish (Liverpool); **1984** Ian Rush (Liverpool); **1985** Neville Southall (Everton); **1986** Gary Lineker (Everton); **1987** Clive Allen (Tottenham); **1988** John Barnes (Liverpool); **1989** Steve Nicol (Liverpool); Special award to the Liverpool players for the compassion shown to bereaved families after the Hillsborough Disaster; **1990** John Barnes (Liverpool); **1991** Gordon Strachan (Leeds); **1992** Gary Lineker (Tottenham); **1993** Chris Waddle (Sheffield Wed); **1994** Alan Shearer (Blackburn); **1995** Jürgen Klinsmann (Tottenham); **1996** Eric Cantona (Manchester Utd); **1997** Gianfranco Zola (Chelsea); **1998** Dennis Bergkamp (Arsenal); **1999** David Ginola (Tottenham); **2000** Roy Keane (Manchester Utd); **2001** Teddy Sheringham (Manchester Utd); **2002** Robert Pires (Arsenal); **2003** Thierry Henry (Arsenal); **2004** Thierry Henry (Arsenal); **2005** Frank Lampard (Chelsea); **2006** Thierry Henry (Arsenal); **2007** Cristiano Ronaldo (Manchester Utd); **2008** Cristiano Ronaldo (Manchester Utd); **2009** Steven Gerrard (Liverpool); **2010** Wayne Rooney (Manchester Utd); **2011** Scott Parker (West Ham); **2012** Robin van Persie (Arsenal); **2013** Gareth Bale (Tottenham); **2014** Luis Suarez (Liverpool); **2015** Eden Hazard (Chelsea); **2016** Jamie Vardy (Leicester); **2017** N'Golo Kante (Chelsea)

PROFESSIONAL FOOTBALLERS' ASSOCIATION

Player of the Year: 1974 Norman Hunter (Leeds); **1975** Colin Todd (Derby); **1976** Pat Jennings (Tottenham); **1977** Andy Gray (Aston Villa); **1978** Peter Shilton (Nott'm Forest); **1979** Liam Brady (Arsenal); **1980** Terry McDermott (Liverpool); **1981** John Wark (Ipswich); **1982** Kevin Keegan (Southampton); **1983** Kenny Dalglish (Liverpool); **1984** Ian Rush (Liverpool); **1985** Peter Reid (Everton); **1986** Gary Lineker (Everton); **1987** Clive Allen (Tottenham); **1988** John Barnes (Liverpool); **1989** Mark Hughes (Manchester Utd); **1990** David Platt (Aston Villa); **1991** Mark Hughes (Manchester Utd); **1992** Gary Pallister (Manchester Utd); **1993** Paul McGrath (Aston Villa); **1994** Eric Cantona (Manchester Utd); **1995** Alan Shearer (Blackburn); **1996** Les Ferdinand (Newcastle); **1997** Alan Shearer (Newcastle); **1998** Dennis Bergkamp (Arsenal); **1999** David Ginola (Tottenham); **2000** Roy Keane (Manchester Utd); **2001** Teddy Sheringham (Manchester Utd); **2002** Ruud van Nistelrooy (Manchester Utd); **2003** Thierry Henry (Arsenal); **2004** Thierry Henry (Arsenal); **2005** John Terry (Chelsea); **2006** Steven Gerrard (Liverpool); **2007** Cristiano Ronaldo (Manchester Utd); **2008** Cristiano Ronaldo (Manchester Utd); **2009** Ryan Giggs (Manchester Utd); **2010** Wayne Rooney (Manchester Utd); **2011** Gareth Bale (Tottenham); **2012** Robin van Persie (Arsenal); **2013** Gareth Bale (Tottenham); **2014** Luis Suarez (Liverpool); **2015** Eden Hazard (Chelsea); **2016** Riyad Mahrez (Leicester); **2017** N'Golo Kante (Chelsea)

Young Player of the Year: 1974 Kevin Beattie (Ipswich); **1975** Mervyn Day (West Ham); **1976** Peter Barnes (Manchester City); **1977** Andy Gray (Aston Villa); **1978** Tony Woodcock (Nott'm Forest); **1979** Cyrille Regis (WBA); **1980** Glenn Hoddle (Tottenham); **1981** Gary Shaw (Aston Villa); **1982** Steve Moran (Southampton); **1983** Ian Rush (Liverpool); **1984** Paul Walsh (Luton); **1985** Mark Hughes (Manchester Utd); **1986** Tony Cottee (West Ham); **1987** Tony Adams (Arsenal); **1988** Paul Gascoigne (Newcastle); **1989** Paul Merson (Arsenal); **1990** Matthew Le Tissier (Southampton); **1991** Lee Sharpe (Manchester Utd); **1992** Ryan Giggs (Manchester Utd); **1993** Ryan Giggs (Manchester Utd); **1994** Andy Cole (Newcastle); **1995** Robbie Fowler

(Liverpool); **1996** Robbie Fowler (Liverpool); **1997** David Beckham (Manchester Utd); **1998** Michael Owen (Liverpool); **1999** Nicolas Anelka (Arsenal); **2000** Harry Kewell (Leeds); **2001** Steven Gerrard (Liverpool); **2002** Craig Bellamy (Newcastle); **2003** Jermaine Jenas (Newcastle); **2004** Scott Parker (Chelsea); **2005** Wayne Rooney (Manchester Utd); **2006** Wayne Rooney (Manchester Utd); **2007** Cristiano Ronaldo (Manchester Utd); **2008** Cesc Fabregas (Arsenal), **2009** Ashley Young (Aston Villa), **2010** James Milner (Aston Villa), **2011** Jack Wilshere (Arsenal), **2012** Kyle Walker (Tottenham), **2013** Gareth Bale (Tottenham), **2014** Eden Hazard (Chelsea), **2015** Harry Kane (Tottenham), **2016** Dele Alli (Tottenham), **2017** Dele Alli (Tottenham)

Merit Awards: 1974 Bobby Charlton & Cliff Lloyd; **1975** Denis Law; **1976** George Eastham; **1977** Jack Taylor; **1978** Bill Shankly; **1979** Tom Finney; **1980** Sir Matt Busby; **1981** John Trollope; **1982** Joe Mercer; **1983** Bob Paisley; **1984** Bill Nicholson; **1985** Ron Greenwood; **1986** England 1966 World Cup-winning team; **1987** Sir Stanley Matthews; **1988** Billy Bonds; **1989** Nat Lofthouse; **1990** Peter Shilton; **1991** Tommy Hutchison; **1992** Brian Clough; **1993** Manchester Utd, 1968 European Champions; Eusebio; **1994** Billy Bingham; **1995** Gordon Strachan; **1996** Pele; **1997** Peter Beardsley; **1998** Steve Ogrizovic; **1999** Tony Ford; **2000** Gary Mabbutt; **2001** Jimmy Hill; **2002** Niall Quinn; **2003** Sir Bobby Robson; **2004** Dario Gradi; **2005** Shaka Hislop; **2006** George Best; **2007** Sir Alex Ferguson; **2008** Jimmy Armfield; **2009** John McDermott, **2010** Lucas Radebe, **2011** Howard Webb, **2012** Graham Alexander, **2013** Eric Harrison/Manchester Utd Class of '92, **2014** Donald Bell (posthumously; only footballer to win Victoria Cross, World War 1), **2015** Steven Gerrard & Frank Lampard, **2016** Ryan Giggs, **2017** David Beckham

MANAGER OF THE YEAR 1 (chosen by media and sponsors)

1966 Jock Stein (Celtic); **1967** Jock Stein (Celtic); **1968** Matt Busby (Manchester Utd); **1969** Don Revie (Leeds); **1970** Don Revie (Leeds); **1971** Bertie Mee (Arsenal); **1972** Don Revie (Leeds); **1973** Bill Shankly (Liverpool); **1974** Jack Charlton (Middlesbrough); **1975** Ron Saunders (Aston Villa); **1976** Bob Paisley (Liverpool); **1977** Bob Paisley (Liverpool); **1978** Brian Clough (Nott'm Forest); **1979** Bob Paisley (Liverpool); **1980** Bob Paisley (Liverpool); **1981** Ron Saunders (Aston Villa); **1982** Bob Paisley (Liverpool); **1983** Bob Paisley (Liverpool); **1984** Joe Fagan (Liverpool); **1985** Howard Kendall (Everton); **1986** Kenny Dalglish (Liverpool); **1987** Howard Kendall (Everton); **1988** Kenny Dalglish (Liverpool); **1989** George Graham (Arsenal); **1990** Kenny Dalglish (Liverpool); **1991** George Graham (Arsenal); **1992** Howard Wilkinson (Leeds); **1993** Alex Ferguson (Manchester Utd); **1994** Alex Ferguson (Manchester Utd); **1995** Kenny Dalglish (Blackburn); **1996** Alex Ferguson (Manchester Utd); **1997** Alex Ferguson (Manchester Utd); **1998** Arsene Wenger (Arsenal); **1999** Alex Ferguson (Manchester Utd); **2000** Sir Alex Ferguson (Manchester Utd); **2001** George Burley (Ipswich); **2002** Arsene Wenger (Arsenal); **2003** Sir Alex Ferguson (Manchester Utd); **2004** Arsene Wenger (Arsenal); **2005** Jose Mourinho (Chelsea); **2006** Jose Mourinho (Chelsea); **2007** Sir Alex Ferguson (Manchester Utd); **2008** Sir Alex Ferguson (Manchester Utd); **2009** Sir Alex Ferguson (Manchester Utd); **2010** Harry Redknapp (Tottenham), **2011** Sir Alex Ferguson (Manchester Utd), **2012:** Alan Pardew (Newcastle), **2013** Sir Alex Ferguson (Manchester Utd), **2014** Tony Pulis (Crystal Palace), **2015** Jose Mourinho (Chelsea), **2016** Claudio Ranieri (Leicester), **2017** Antonio Conte (Chelsea)

MANAGER OF THE YEAR 2 (Chosen by the League Managers' Association)

1993 Dave Bassett (Sheffield Utd); **1994** Joe Kinnear (Wimbledon); **1995** Frank Clark (Nott'm Forest); **1996** Peter Reid (Sunderland); **1997** Danny Wilson (Barnsley); **1998** David Jones (Southampton); **1999** Alex Ferguson (Manchester Utd); **2000** Alan Curbishley (Charlton Athletic); **2001** George Burley (Ipswich); **2002** Arsene Wenger (Arsenal); **2003** David Moyes (Everton); **2004** Arsene Wenger (Arsenal); **2005** David Moyes (Everton); **2006** Steve Coppell (Reading); **2007** Steve Coppell (Reading); **2008** Sir Alex Ferguson (Manchester Utd); **2009** David Moyes (Everton), **2010** Roy Hodgson (Fulham), **2011** Sir Alex Ferguson (Manchester Utd), **2012:** Alan Pardew (Newcastle), **2013** Sir Alex Ferguson (Manchester Utd), **2014** Brendan Rodgers (Liverpool), **2015** Eddie Howe (Bournemouth), **2016** Claudio Ranieri (Leicester), **2017** Antonio Conte (Chelsea)

SCOTTISH FOOTBALL WRITERS' ASSOCIATION

Footballer of the Year: 1965 Billy McNeill (Celtic); 1966 John Greig (Rangers); 1967 Ronnie Simpson (Celtic); 1968 Gordon Wallace (Raith); 1969 Bobby Murdoch (Celtic); 1970 Pat Stanton (Hibernian); 1971 Martin Buchan (Aberdeen); 1972 David Smith (Rangers); 1973 George Connelly (Celtic); 1974 World Cup Squad; 1975 Sandy Jardine (Rangers); 1976 John Greig (Rangers); 1977 Danny McGrain (Celtic); 1978 Derek Johnstone (Rangers); 1979 Andy Ritchie (Morton); 1980 Gordon Strachan (Aberdeen); 1981 Alan Rough (Partick Thistle); 1982 Paul Sturrock (Dundee Utd); 1983 Charlie Nicholas (Celtic); 1984 Willie Miller (Aberdeen); 1985 Hamish McAlpine (Dundee Utd); 1986 Sandy Jardine (Hearts); 1987 Brian McClair (Celtic); 1988 Paul McStay (Celtic); 1989 Richard Gough (Rangers); 1990 Alex McLeish (Aberdeen); 1991 Maurice Malpas (Dundee Utd); 1992 Ally McCoist (Rangers); 1993 Andy Goram (Rangers); 1994 Mark Hateley (Rangers); 1995 Brian Laudrup (Rangers); 1996 Paul Gascoigne (Rangers); 1997 Brian Laudrup (Rangers); 1998 Craig Burley (Celtic); 1999 Henrik Larsson (Celtic); 2000 Barry Ferguson (Rangers); 2001 Henrik Larsson (Celtic); 2002 Paul Lambert (Celtic); 2003 Barry Ferguson (Rangers); 2004 Jackie McNamara (Celtic); 2005 John Hartson (Celtic); 2006 Craig Gordon (Hearts); 2007 Shunsuke Nakamura (Celtic); 2008 Carlos Cuellar (Rangers); 2009 Gary Caldwell (Celtic); 2010 David Weir (Rangers); 2011 Emilio Izaguirre (Celtic); 2012 Charlie Mulgrew (Celtic); 2013 Leigh Griffiths (Hibernian); 2014 Kris Commons (Celtic); 2015 Craig Gordon (Celtic); 2016 Leigh Griffiths (Celtic); 2017 Scott Sinclair (Celtic)

PROFESSIONAL FOOTBALLERS' ASSOCIATION SCOTLAND

Player of the Year: 1978 Derek Johnstone (Rangers); 1979 Paul Hegarty (Dundee Utd); 1980 Davie Provan (Celtic); 1981 Mark McGhee (Aberdeen); 1982 Sandy Clarke (Airdrieonians); 1983 Charlie Nicholas (Celtic); 1984 Willie Miller (Aberdeen); 1985 Jim Duffy (Morton); 1986 Richard Gough (Dundee Utd); 1987 Brian McClair (Celtic); 1988 Paul McStay (Celtic); 1989 Theo Snelders (Aberdeen); 1990 Jim Bett (Aberdeen); 1991 Paul Elliott (Celtic); 1992 Ally McCoist (Rangers); 1993 Andy Goram (Rangers); 1994 Mark Hateley (Rangers); 1995 Brian Laudrup (Rangers); 1996 Paul Gascoigne (Rangers); 1997 Paolo Di Canio (Celtic); 1998 Jackie McNamara (Celtic); 1999 Henrik Larsson (Celtic); 2000 Mark Viduka (Celtic); 2001 Henrik Larsson (Celtic); 2002 Lorenzo Amoruso (Rangers); 2003 Barry Ferguson (Rangers); 2004 Chris Sutton (Celtic); 2005 John Hartson (Celtic) and Fernando Ricksen (Rangers); 2006 Shaun Maloney (Celtic); 2007 Shunsuke Nakamura (Celtic); 2008 Aiden McGeady (Celtic); 2009 Scott Brown (Celtic); 2010 Steven Davis (Rangers); 2011 Emilio Izaguirre (Celtic); 2012 Charlie Mulgrew (Celtic); 2013 Michael Higdon (Motherwell); 2014 Kris Commons (Celtic); 2015 Stefan Johansen (Celtic); 2016 Leigh Griffiths (Celtic); 2017 Scott Sinclair (Celtic)

Young Player of the Year: 1978 Graeme Payne (Dundee Utd); 1979 Ray Stewart (Dundee Utd); 1980 John McDonald (Rangers); 1981 Charlie Nicholas (Celtic); 1982 Frank McAvennie (St Mirren); 1983 Paul McStay (Celtic); 1984 John Robertson (Hearts); 1985 Craig Levein (Hearts); 1986 Craig Levein (Hearts); 1987 Robert Fleck (Rangers); 1988 John Collins (Hibernian); 1989 Billy McKinlay (Dundee Utd); 1990 Scott Crabbe (Hearts); 1991 Eoin Jess (Aberdeen); 1992 Phil O'Donnell (Motherwell); 1993 Eoin Jess (Aberdeen); 1994 Phil O'Donnell (Motherwell); 1995 Charlie Miller (Rangers); 1996 Jackie McNamara (Celtic); 1997 Robbie Winters (Dundee Utd); 1998 Gary Naysmith (Hearts); 1999 Barry Ferguson (Rangers); 2000 Kenny Miller (Hibernian); 2001 Stilian Petrov (Celtic); 2002 Kevin McNaughton (Aberdeen); 2003 James McFadden (Motherwell); 2004 Stephen Pearson (Celtic); 2005 Derek Riordan (Hibernian); 2006 Shaun Maloney (Celtic); 2007 Steven Naismith (Kilmarnock); 2008 Aiden McGeady (Celtic); 2009 James McCarthy (Hamilton); 2010 Danny Wilson (Rangers); 2011: David Goodwillie (Dundee Utd); 2012 James Forrest (Celtic); 2013 Leigh Griffiths (Hibernian); 2014 Andy Robertson (Dundee Utd); 2015 Jason Denayer (Celtic); 2016 Kieran Tierney (Celtic); 2017 Kieran Tierney (Celtic)

SCOTTISH MANAGER OF THE YEAR

1987 Jim McLean (Dundee Utd); 1988 Billy McNeill (Celtic); 1989 Graeme Souness (Rangers); 1990 Andy Roxburgh (Scotland); 1991 Alex Totten (St Johnstone); 1992 Walter Smith

(Rangers); **1993** Walter Smith (Rangers); **1994** Walter Smith (Rangers); **1995** Jimmy Nicholl (Raith); **1996** Walter Smith (Rangers); **1997** Walter Smith (Rangers); **1998** Wim Jansen (Celtic); **1999** Dick Advocaat (Rangers); **2000** Dick Advocaat (Rangers); **2001** Martin O'Neill (Celtic); **2002** John Lambie (Partick Thistle); **2003** Alex McLeish (Rangers); **2004** Martin O'Neill (Celtic); **2005** Alex McLeish (Rangers); **2006** Gordon Strachan (Celtic); **2007** Gordon Strachan (Celtic); **2008** Billy Reid (Hamilton); **2009** Csaba Laszlo (Hearts), **2010** Walter Smith (Rangers), **2011:** Mixu Paatelainen (Kilmarnock), **2012** Neil Lennon (Celtic), **2013** Neil Lennon (Celtic), **2014** Derek McInnes (Aberdeen), **2015** John Hughes (Inverness), **2016** Mark Warburton (Rangers), **2017** Brendan Rodgers (Celtic)

EUROPEAN FOOTBALLER OF THE YEAR

1956 Stanley Matthews (Blackpool); **1957** Alfredo di Stefano (Real Madrid); **1958** Raymond Kopa (Real Madrid); **1959** Alfredo di Stefano (Real Madrid); **1960** Luis Suarez (Barcelona); **1961** Omar Sivori (Juventus); **1962** Josef Masopust (Dukla Prague); **1963** Lev Yashin (Moscow Dynamo); **1964** Denis Law (Manchester Utd); **1965** Eusebio (Benfica); **1966** Bobby Charlton (Manchester Utd); **1967** Florian Albert (Ferencvaros); **1968** George Best (Manchester Utd); **1969** Gianni Rivera (AC Milan); **1970** Gerd Muller (Bayern Munich); **1971** Johan Cruyff (Ajax); **1972** Franz Beckenbauer (Bayern Munich); **1973** Johan Cruyff (Barcelona); **1974** Johan Cruyff (Barcelona); **1975** Oleg Blokhin (Dynamo Kiev); **1976** Franz Beckenbauer (Bayern Munich); **1977** Allan Simonsen (Borussia Moenchengladbach); **1978** Kevin Keegan (SV Hamburg); **1979** Kevin Keegan (SV Hamburg); **1980** Karl-Heinz Rummenigge (Bayern Munich); **1981** Karl-Heinz Rummenigge (Bayern Munich); **1982** Paolo Rossi (Juventus); **1983** Michel Platini (Juventus); **1984** Michel Platini (Juventus); **1985** Michel Platini (Juventus); **1986** Igor Belanov (Dynamo Kiev); **1987** Ruud Gullit (AC Milan); **1988** Marco van Basten (AC Milan); **1989** Marco van Basten (AC Milan); **1990** Lothar Matthaus (Inter Milan); **1991** Jean-Pierre Papin (Marseille); **1992** Marco van Basten (AC Milan); **1993** Roberto Baggio (Juventus); **1994** Hristo Stoichkov (Barcelona); **1995** George Weah (AC Milan); **1996** Matthias Sammer (Borussia Dortmund); **1997** Ronaldo (Inter Milan); **1998** Zinedine Zidane (Juventus); **1999** Rivaldo (Barcelona); **2000** Luis Figo (Real Madrid); **2001** Michael Owen (Liverpool); **2002** Ronaldo (Real Madrid); **2003** Pavel Nedved (Juventus); **2004** Andriy Shevchenko (AC Milan); **2005** Ronaldinho (Barcelona); **2006** Fabio Cannavaro (Real Madrid); **2007** Kaka (AC Milan); **2008** Cristiano Ronaldo (Manchester United), **2009** Lionel Messi (Barcelona)

WORLD FOOTBALLER OF YEAR

1991 Lothar Matthaus (Inter Milan and Germany); **1992** Marco van Basten (AC Milan and Holland); **1993** Roberto Baggio (Juventus and Italy); **1994** Romario (Barcelona and Brazil); **1995** George Weah (AC Milan and Liberia); **1996** Ronaldo (Barcelona and Brazil); **1997** Ronaldo (Inter Milan and Brazil); **1998** Zinedine Zidane (Juventus and France); **1999** Rivaldo (Barcelona and Brazil); **2000** Zinedine Zidane (Juventus and France); **2001** Luis Figo (Real Madrid and Portugal); **2002** Ronaldo (Real Madrid and Brazil); **2003** Zinedine Zidane (Real Madrid and France); **2004** Ronaldinho (Barcelona and Brazil); **2005** Ronaldinho (Barcelona and Brazil); **2006** Fabio Cannavaro (Real Madrid and Italy); **2007** Kaka (AC Milan and Brazil); **2008** Cristiano Ronaldo (Manchester United and Portugal), **2009** Lionel Messi (Barcelona and Argentina)

FIFA BALLON D'OR (replaces European and World Footballer of the Year)

2010: Lionel Messi (Barcelona). **2011** Lionel Messi (Barcelona), **2012** Lionel Messi (Barcelona), **2013** Cristiano Ronaldo (Real Madrid), **2014:** Cristiano Ronaldo (Real Madrid), **2015** Lionel Messi (Barcelona), **2016** Cristiano Ronaldo (Real Madrid)

FIFA WORLD COACH OF THE YEAR

2010: Jose Mourinho (Inter Milan). **2011** Pep Guardiola (Barcelona), **2012** Vicente del Bosque (Spain), **2013** Jupp Heynckes (Bayern Munich), **2014** Joachim Low (Germany), **2015** Luis Enrique (Barcelona), **2016** Claudio Ranieri (Leicester)

PREMIER LEAGUE

ARSENAL

A season that threatened to deliver nothing more than a campaign to drive Arsene Wenger out of the club was turned on its head by a superb FA Cup victory. With the manager's future in the balance, Arsenal defied the odds to deny champions Chelsea the 'Double' and lift the trophy for the third time in four years. Three days later, Wenger ended months of speculation about his future by agreeing a new two-year contract and began preparing for his 22nd campaign in charge. The challenge is to make them a Premier League force again, regain the Champions League place lost after finishing fifth and try to win round those supporters whose behaviour he branded a disgrace in an interview broadcast hours before their Wembley triumph. When Arsenal defeated Antonio Conte's side 3-0 at the Emirates in late September, few would have predicted how the fortunes of the two teams would swing so significantly. Arsenal finished 18 points adrift of the champions and 11 short of Tottenham – the first time since 1995 that they had lagged behind their north London rivals. They hung on to a top-four place for nearly six months until back to-back 3-1 defeats by Liverpool and West Bromwich Albion, then a 3-0 loss to Crystal Palace, left them seven points adrift. Wins in the last five matches were not enough to overtake Liverpool, who finished a point ahead in fourth place. Along the way, Arsenal had suffered an embarrassing 10-2 aggregate defeat by Bayern Munich in the Champions League's first knockout round.

Bellerin H 27 (6)	Holding R 9	Ospina D.................... 1 (1)
Cazorla S 7 (1)	Iwobi A.................... 18 (8)	Oxlade-Chamberlain A 16 (13)
Cech P 35	Jenkinson C 1	Ozil M 32 (1)
Chambers C 1	Koscielny L 33	Ramsey A 13 (10)
Coquelin F 22 (7)	Lucas Perez 2 (9)	Sanchez A 36 (2)
Debuchy M 1	Maitland-Niles A.......... - (1)	Walcott T 23 (5)
Elneny M 8 (6)	Martinez D 2	Welbeck D 8 (8)
Gabriel 15 (4)	Mertesacker P .... - (1)	Wilshere J 0 (2)
Gibbs K 8 (3)	Monreal N................ 35 (1)	Xhaka G.................... 28 (4)
Giroud O 11 (18)	Mustafi S 26	

League goals (77): Sanchez 24, Giroud 12, Walcott 10, Ozil 8, Iwobi 3, Cazorla 2, Koscielny 2, Mustafi 2, Oxlade-Chamberlain 2, Welbeck 2, Xhaka 2, Bellerin 1, Chambers 1, Lucas Perez 1, Ramsey 1, Opponents 4
FA Cup goals (18): Walcott 5, Ramsey 3, Sanchez 3, Sanchez 2, Welbeck 2, Lucas Perez 1, Monreal 1, Opponents 1
League Cup goals (6): Oxlade-Chamberlain 3, Lucas Perez 2, Xhaka 1
Champions League goals (20): Ozil 4, Walcott 4, Lucas Perez 3, Sanchez 3, Giroud 2, Iwobi 1, Oxlade-Chamberlain 1, Xhaka 1, Opponents 1
Average home league attendance: 59,957. **Player of Year**: Alexis Sanchez

BOURNEMOUTH

Josh King lifted Bournemouth from an awkward position on the fringe of the relegation zone into the upper half of the table with an exceptional scoring streak in the second half of the season. The Norway striker and former Manchester United youth player netted 13 goals in 16 games and finished with 16 for the campaign, four more than in his previous league career. His tally included a hat-trick against West Ham, completed in stoppage-time and delivering a 3-2 victory. King also missed a penalty in that match, which ended a run of eight without a win, including a 6-3 defeat at Everton. His 88th minute goal, which relegated Sunderland, took Bournemouth past 40 points with three fixtures remaining. Then, another winner, this time five minutes from the end of the final home game against Burnley, left them in the top ten. A 1-1 draw in the final match at Leicester took them above West Bromwich Albion and completed a five-match unbeaten finish, rewarded with ninth place. It was an improvement of seven on their first season in the Premier League, an impressive achievement by Eddie Howe and his players.

Afobe B 14 (17)	Federici A 2	Mings T 5 (2)
Ake N 8 (2)	Francis S 34	Mousset L 3 (8)
Allsop R..............................1	Fraser R 19 (9)	Pugh M.................... 16 (5)
Arter H 33 (2)	Gosling D 14 (13)	Smith A 34 (2)
Boruc A 35	Grabban L................... - (3)	Smith B 3 (2)
Cargill B .... - (1)	Gradel M.................. - (11)	Stanislas J 18 (3)
Cook L 4 (2)	Ibe J..................... 13 (12)	Surman A 21 (1)
Cook S............................38	King J................... 31 (5)	Wilshere A 22 (5)
Daniels C 34	Worthington M............. - (1)	Wilson C 16 (4)

League goals (55): King 16, Stanislas 7, Afobe 6, Wilson C 6, Daniels 4, Ake 3, Fraser 3, Cook S 2, Gosling 2, Pugh 2, Arter 1, Smith A 1, Opponents 2
FA Cup goals: None. **League Cup goals (4):** Gosling 1, Grabban 1, Gradel 1, Wilson M 1
Average home league attendance: 11,182. **Player of Year:** Steve Cook

BURNLEY

Sean Dyche's side turned Turf Moor into something of a fortress, upsetting the pre-season odds which pointed to an instant return to the Championship. Ten home victories meant that a good part of the campaign was spent looking up, not down, once a 1-0 defeat by Swansea on the opening day had been absorbed. Until a disappointing finish, the other losses were against teams in the top six – Arsenal, Manchester City, Tottenham and Manchester United. One of those was bitterly disputed, with Laurent Koscielny's stoppage-time winner for Arsenal going in off his hand. The return at the Emirates also produced late drama, Andre Gray equalising in the 93rd minute and Alexis Sanchez winning it for Arsenal with a another penalty in the 98th. Burnley broke briefly into the top ten on three occasions. Each time they were unable to hold on. Only late on were they forced to look over their shoulder – five points above the relegation zone – and any jitters were dispelled, ironically, by the first and only away win, earned by goals from Ashley Barnes and Gray against Crystal Palace. After that, Burnley gained a single point from the final three games against West Bromwich Albion, Bournemouth and West Ham and slipped to 16th.

Agyei D...................... - (3)	Gray A 26 (6)	Lowton M........................36
Arfield S 23 (8)	Gudmundsson J...... 10 (10)	Marney D 21
Bamford P .... - (6)	Heaton T.........................35	Mee B 34
Barnes A.................. 20 (8)	Hendrick J 31 (1)	O'Neill A .... - (3)
Barton J.................. 12 (2)	Janes D 1	Robinson P 3
Boyd G 33 (3)	Jutkiewicz L .... - (2)	Tarkowski J 4 (15)
Brady R 7 (7)	Keane M 35	Vokes S 21 (16)
Defour S 16 (5)	Kightly M 1 (4)	Ward S 37
Flanagan J 3 (3)	Long K 3	Westwood A 6 (3)

League goals (39): Vokes 10, Gray 9, Barnes 6, Boyd 2, Hendrick 2, Keane 2, Arfield 1, Barton 1, Brady 1, Defour 1, Gudmundsson 1, Marney 1, Mee 1, Ward 1
FA Cup goals (4): Vokes 2, Gray 1, Defour 1. **League Cup goals:** None
Average home league attendance: 20,558. **Player of Year:** Tom Heaton

CHELSEA

All the talk was about the arrival of Guardiola and Mourinho in Manchester, Klopp's first full season at Liverpool and Tottenham's resurgence under Pochettino. Antonio Conte's appointment by Chelsea didn't exactly slip under the radar. But when his new side lost to Liverpool and were beaten 3-0 by Arsenal, they were well down in the title reckoning. Conte's response was to switch to a back three and the outcome was remarkable – 13 successive wins to equal the top flight record in a single season and a six-point lead at the top before a 2-0 defeat at Tottenham. Eden Hazard, a pale shadow under Mourinho the previous season, was back to his best, Diego Costa scored 14 goals by the half-way point and, most surprisingly, Victor Moses developed as an effective wing-back. Most significantly, N'Golo Kante repeated the midfield drive and industry which fired Leicester to the 2016 title – and was rewarded with both major Player of the Year awards. Manager of the Year Conte's total confidence in his squad meant no winter transfer business, apart from the £52m departure of Oscar to the Chinese Super League. In the New Year, only Tottenham developed anything approaching a threat. They drew encouragement from Crystal Palace's win at Stamford Bridge and Chelsea's defeat at Old Trafford. But after defeating their rivals in the FA Cup, the leaders scored ten goals against Southampton, Everton and Middlesbrough , then clinched the title with two games to spare, when Michy Batshuayi – a peripheral figure for most of the season – came off the bench to score an 85th minute winner against West Bromwich Albion. The FA Cup Final against Arsenal proved a match too far and something of an embarrassment, with Moses sent off for diving after a league season without a single red card.

Ake N	1 (1)	Courtois T	36	Matic N	30 (5)
Alonso M	30 (1)	Fabregas C	13 (16)	Moses V	29 (5)
Azpilicueta C	38	Hazard E	36	Aina O	- (3)
Batshuayi M	1 (19)	Ivanovic B	6 (7)	Oscar	5 (4)
Begovic A	2	Kante N'Golo	35	Pedro	26 (9)
Cahill G	36 (1)	Kenedy	1	Terry J	6 (3)
Chalobah N	1 (9)	Loftus-Cheek R	- (6)	Willian	15 (19)
Diego Costa	35	Luiz D	33	Zouma K	3 (6)

League goals (85): Diego Costa 20, Hazard 16, Pedro 9, Willian 8, Alonso 6, Cahill 6, Batshuayi 5, Fabregas 5, Moses 3, Azpilicueta 1, Kante 1, Luiz 1, Matic 1, Terry 1, Opponents 2
FA Cup goals (16): Pedro 4, Willian 4, Batshuayi 2, Diego Costa 2, Hazard 1, Ivanovic 1, Kante 1, Matic 1. **League Cup goals** (8): Batshuayi 2, Cahill 2, Fabregas 2, Azpilicueta 1, Moses 1
Average home league attendance: 41,508. **Player of Year**: Eden Hazard

CRYSTAL PALACE

The England job turned into a one-match nightmare, but when it comes to keeping clubs in the Premier League Sam Allardyce has few equals. Three months after being forced out as national team manager, he returned to club football at Selhurst Park when Alan Pardew was sacked after a single win in 11 games. Allardyce, who led Sunderland out of trouble in 2016, took over a side fourth from bottom, one point off the bottom three. After his first eight games in charge, all he had to show was a 2-0 victory at Bournemouth. Then came the recovery – four wins out of five including a 2-1 success against Chelsea at Stamford Bridge. Further wins over Arsenal and Liverpool took them seven points clear and within striking distance of a mid-table finish. But successive home defeats by Tottenham and Burnley, followed by a 5-0 drubbing by Manchester City, had Palace sweating with two fixtures remaining. A second minute goal by Wilfried Zaha calmed nerves and Palace went to make sure of staying up – and sending Hull down- with a 4-0 success. Afterwards, Allardyce admitted it had been the hardest of his rescue acts because of the demanding run-in his team faced and his subsequent resignation suggested this might have been the end of his managerial career. He was replaced by Frank de Boer, former Inter Milan and Ajax coach.

Benteke C	36	Kaikai S	.... - (1)	Sakho M	8
Benteke J	.... - (1)	Kelly M	.... 25 (4)	Sako B	.... - (7)
Bolasie Y	.... - (1)	Ledley J	.... 13 (5)	Schlupp J	.... 11 (4)
Cabaye Y	.... 25 (7)	Lee Chung-Yong	.... 4 (11)	Tomkins J	.... 23 (1)
Campbell F	.... - (12)	Mandanda S	9	Townsend A	.... 30 (6)
Dann S	.... 19 (4)	McArthur J	.... 24 (5)	Van Aanholt P	.... 8 (3)
Delaney D	.... 21 (9)	Milivojevic L	14	Ward J	38
Flamini M	.... 3 (7)	Mutch J	.... - (4)	Wickham C	.... 4 (4)
Fryers E	.... - (8)	Souare P	3	Zaha W	.... 34 (1)
Hennessey W	29	Puncheon J	.... 35 (1)		
Jedinak M	1	Remy L	.... 1 (4)		

League goals (50): Benteke C 15, Zaha 7, McArthur 5, Cabaye 4, Dann 3, Tomkins 3, Townsend 3, Milivojevic 2, Wickham 2, Van Aanholt 2, Campbell 1, Ledley 1, Opponents 2
FA Cup goals (2): Benteke C 2. **League Cup goals (2):** Dann 1, Wickham 1
Average home league attendance: 25,161. **Player of Year:** Wilfried Zaha

EVERTON

Ronald Koeman supervised a season of progress – thanks largely to the prolific Romelu Lukaku – with an improvement of four places on 2016. Outside the top-six teams, they stood alone and unchallenged, building on the club's best start for 38 years and accumulating the most points at Goodison Park, 43, since 1989-90. Lukaku scored a hat-trick in 11 minutes against Sunderland and Gareth Barry marked his 600th Premier League appearance with a goal in the win over Middlesbrough as Everton opened with 13 points from five matches. Lukaku went on to become their first player since Gary Lineker in 1986 to reach 20 goals in the top division and the first since Dixie Dean in 1934 to score in nine successive home games in all competitions. That sequence included four in a 6-3 win over Bournemouth which Koeman called 'a crazy game.' He finished with 25, having been overtaken for the Golden Boot award by Harry Kane's successive hat-tricks for Tottenham. Amid the flood of goals, Lukaku turned down the offer of a new five-year contract, questioning the club's willingness to make major signings. Eight goals conceded in two games against Chelsea and a last-day defeat by Arsenal were also food for thought for his manager.

Baines L	32	Funes Mori R	.... 16 (7)	McCarthy J	.... 7 (5)
Barkley R	.... 32 (4)	Gueye I	.... 32 (1)	Mirallas K	.... 23 (12)
Barry G	.... 23 (10)	Holgate M	.... 16 (2)	Oviedo B	6
Bolasie Y	.... 12 (1)	Jagielka P	.... 25 (2)	Pennington M	.... 2 (1)
Calvert-Lewin D	.... 5 (6)	Kenny J	.... - (1)	Robles J	.... 19 (1)
Cleverley T	.... 4 (6)	Kone A	.... - (6)	Schneiderlin M	.... 12 (2)
Coleman S	26	Lennon A	.... 6 (5)	Stekelenburg M	19
Davies T	.... 18 (6)	Lookman A	.... 3 (5)	Valencia E	.... 5 (16)
Deulofeu G	.... 4 (7)	Lukaku R	.... 36 (1)	Williams A	.... 35 (1)

League goals (62): Lukaku 25, Barkley 5, Coleman 4, Mirallas 4, Jagielka 3, Valencia 3, Baines 2, Barry 2, Davies 2, Bolasie 1, Calvert-Lewin 1, Gueye 1, Lookman 1, McCarthy 1, Pennington 1, Schneiderlinn 1, Williams 1, Opponents 4
FA Cup goals (1): Lukaku 1. **League Cup goals (4):** Kone 2, Barkley 1, Lennon 1
Average home league attendance: 39,310. **Player of Year:** Romelu Lukaku

HULL CITY

A transformation in Hull's fortunes under Marco Silva was not enough to prevent a return to the Championship. The former Sporting Lisbon and Olympiacos coach reshaped his squad with seven signings, five of them on loan, in the January transfer window. The reward was an impressive run at the KCom Stadium which netted 19 points from seven matches. Eldin Jakupovic then saved a last-minute penalty from Dusan Tadic to earn a goalless draw at Southampton and a home game against relegated Sunderland provided a great chance to take another step towards safety. Instead, a 2-0 defeat offered Swansea the same opportunity, which they accepted, and a 4-0 defeat at Crystal Palace in the penultimate fixture left Hull four points adrift. Silva declined to stay on and took the Watford job. He had replaced Mike Phelan, who in a chaotic pre-season at the club took over when Steve Bruce resigned, unhappy at preparations for the new campaign. An injury crisis left Phelan with just 13 fit senior players, but they started with improbable wins over defending champions Leicester and Swansea. Six new players came in during the last few days of the transfer window, including Tottenham's Ryan Mason for record fee of £13m. After nearly three months as caretaker, Phelan was confirmed as manager in mid-October, his first match a 6-1 drubbing at Bournemouth. He was sacked two-and-a-half-months later with Hull bottom. The club's latest appointment, Leonid Slutsky, formerly coached the Russia national team and CKSA Moscow.

Bowen J 1 (6)	Hernandez A 16 (8)	Mbokani D 8 (4)
Clucas S 36 (1)	Huddlestone T 23 (8)	Meyler D 9 (11)
Davies C 25 (1)	Jakupovic E 22	N'Diaye A 15
Dawson M 19 (3)	Keane W 4 (1)	Niasse O 12 (5)
Diomande A 13 (9)	Livermore J 20 (1)	Ranocchia A 15 (1)
Elabdellaoui A 7 (1)	Maguire H 25 (4)	Robertson A 31 (2)
Elmohamady A 28 (5)	Maloney S 2 (7)	Snodgrass R 19 (1)
Evandro 7 (4)	Markovic L 12	Tymon J 4 (1)
Grosicki K 12 (3)	Marshall D 16	
Henriksen M 6 (9)	Mason R 11 (5)	

League goals (37): Snodgrass 7, Hernandez 4, Niasse 4, Clucas 3, Dawson 3, Diomande 2, Maguire 2, Markovic 2, Ranocchia 2, Huddlestone 1, Livermore 1, Maloney 1, Mason 1, Meyler 1, N'Diaye 1, Robertson 1, Opponents 1
FA Cup goals (3): Evandro 1, Hernandez 1, Tymon 1. **League Cup goals** (10): Diomande 2, Snodgrass 2, Dawson 1, Henriksen 1, Huddlestone 1, Maguire 1, Mason 1, Niasse 1
Average home league attendance: 20,761. **Player of Year**: Sam Clucas

LEICESTER CITY

Claudio Ranieri declared there was more chance of ET coming to Piccadilly Circus than of the club retaining the title. Ranieri was proved right – but not in the way he expected. Leicester made the worst start of any Premier League champions, 13 points from first 14 matches, struggling to overcome the loss of midfielder 'roadrunner' N'Golo Kante and showing little sign of benefitting from the £75m investment in new players. The manager admitted to a relegation fight and the slump continued well beyond the midway point of the season. He was given a vote of confidence, but three weeks later when his side dropped to within a point of the bottom three the Thai owners sacked him. Some argued the players betrayed him, others that a change was essential. Most significantly, four days after his dismissal Leicester ended a run of six matches without a goal, beating Liverpool 3-1 with Jamie Vardy scoring for the first time in the league for more than two months. With Craig Shakespeare as caretaker, the improvement was maintained by four more straight wins, along with a victory over Sevilla which brought a place in the last eight of the Champions League. That impressive run came to an end against Atletico Madrid, but Leicester continued to reach out for a place in the top half of the table until a 6-1 home defeat by Tottenham put paid to that. Shakespeare was confirmed as manager in the summer.

Albrighton M 29 (4)	Drinkwater D 27 (2)	Huth R 33
Amartey D 17 (7)	Fuchs C 35 (1)	James M - (1)
Benalouane Y 11	Gray D 9 (21)	King A 15 (8)
Chilwell B 7 (5)	Hernandez L 3 (1)	Mahrez R 33 (3)

Mendy N.........................4	Schlupp J 1 (3)	Vardy J 33 (2)
Morgan W 27	Schmeichel K................30	Wasilewski J.....................1
Musa A..................... 7 (14)	Simpson D............... 34 (1)	Zieler R-R 8 (1)
Ndidi O.........................17	Slimani I................ 13 (10)	
Okazaki S 21 (9)	Ulloa L 3 (13)	

League goals (48): Vardy 13, Slimani 7, Mahrez 6, Okazaki 3, Albrighton 2, Fuchs 2, Huth 2, Musa 2, Ndidi 2, Amartey 1, Chilwell 1, Drinkwater 1, Gray 1, King 1, Morgan 1, Ulloa 1, Opponents 2
FA Cup goals (7): Musa 2, Gray 1, King 1, Morgan 1, Ndidi 1, Opponents 1. **League Cup goals** (2): Okazaki 2. **Community Shield goals** (1): Vardy 1
Champions League goals (11): Mahrez 4, Albrighton 2, Vardy 2, Morgan 1, Okazaki 1, Slimani 1
Average home league attendance: 31,893. **Player of Year**: Kasper Schmeichel

LIVERPOOL

Jurgen Klopp overcame injuries to key players and defensive frailties to bring Champions League football back to Anfield in his first full season as manager. Along with Manchester City, his team came under late pressure to maintain a top-four place behind Chelsea and Tottenham. But an impressive 4-0 victory at West Ham in the penultimate match, with Philippe Coutinho twice on the mark, kept their noses in front of Arsenal. And a goal on the stroke of half-time by Georginio Wijnaldum eased the tension building against relegated Middlesborough on the final afternoon. Coutinho and Adam Lallana added to it for a 3-0 victory to leave them a point clear of Arsenal in fourth place. Lallana, Jordan Henderson and Sadio Mane all had spells out. On their day, Liverpool were unstoppable, scoring four or more goals on seven occasions, while remaining unbeaten, and accumulating 20 points, from games against their top-six rivals. Countering that, they conceded goals too often from set-pieces and dropped too many points against teams from the lower reaches of the table, including defeats by Hull, Swansea, Burnley, Bournemouth and Crystal Palace. A League Cup semi-final defeat by Southampton was another disappointment.

Alexander-Arnold T 2 (5)	Karius L.........................10	Milner J 36
Clyne N 37	Klavan R................. 15 (5)	Moreno A................. 2 (10)
Coutinho P............... 28 (3)	Lallana A 27 (4)	Origi D................ 14 (20)
Ejaria O .... - (2)	Lovren D.........................29	Stewart K................... - (4)
Emre Can................. 26 (6)	Lucas Leiva........... 12 (12)	Sturridge D 7 (13)
Firmino R 34 (1)	Mane S.................... 26 (1)	Wijnaldum G 33 (3)
Grujic M .... - (5)	Matip P 27 (2)	Woodburn B 1 (4)
Henderson J...................24	Mignolet S 28	

League goals (78): Coutinho 13, Mane 13, Firmino 11, Lallana 8, Milner 7, Origi 7, Wijnaldum 6, Emre Can 5, Sturridge 3, Lovren 2, Henderson 1, Matip 1, Opponents 1
FA Cup goals (2): Lucas Leiva 1, Origi 1. **League Cup goals** (12): Sturridge 4, Origi 3, Coutinho 1, Firmino 1, Klavan 1, Woodburn 1, Opponents 1
Average home league attendance: 53,016. **Player of Year**: Sadio Mane

MANCHESTER CITY

A flying start, a sobering finish and an admission that he would have been sacked if his former clubs Bayern Munich and Barcelona had performed in similar fashion. That was Pep Guardiola's introduction to the Premier League, which yielded none of the big prizes he had been hired to deliver. The saving grace was another season of Champions League football, secured after his team were holding on to a top-four place, by a single point, with four matches remaining. They did so with 5-0 scorelines over Crystal Palace and Watford, along with victories over Leicester and West Bromwich Albion. That sequence mirrored what they had achieved in the opening weeks of the season – six straight wins and eight points clear of Chelsea. By the time Antonio Conte's team came away from the Etihad 3-1 winners in early December, there had been a 12-point swing. On their day, City were still a joy to watch. But inconsistency had taken over, defensive shortcomings were being highlighted and Guardiola's decision to dispense with the services of Joe Hart had become a mystery to many. Neither Claudio Bravo nor Willy Caballero matched up to the England goalkeeper, either domestically or in Europe, where they were ousted on away goals by Monaco after a 6-6 aggregate scoreline in the first knockout round. City finished 15 points adrift of champions Chelsea and the last chance of honours went with an FA Cup semi final defeat by Arsenal.

Aguero S................. 25 (6)	Garcia A 1 (3)	Sagna B................. 14 (3)
Bravo C..........................22	Gundogan I 9 (1)	Sane L.................. 20 (6)
Caballero W........... 16 (1)	Iheanacho K........ 15 (5)	Silva D 31 (3)
Clichy G.................. 24 (1)	Jesus Navas 12 (12)	Sterling R 29 (4)
De Bruyne K............. 33 (3)	Kolarov A 27 (2)	Stones J 23 (4)
Delph F 2 (5)	Kompany V 10 (1)	Toure Y 22 (3)
Fernandinho............. 31 (1)	Nasri S .... - (1)	Zabaleta P 11 (9)
Fernando 5 (10)	Nolito 9 (10)	
Gabriel Jesus............. 8 (2)	Otamendi N ,....... 29 (1)	

League goals (80): Aguero 20, Gabriel Jesus 7, Sterling 7, De Bruyne 6, Sane 5, Toure 5, Iheanacho 4, Nolito 4, Silva 4, Gundogan 3, Kompany 3, Fernandinho 2, Clichy 1, Delph 1, Kolarov 1, Otamendi 1, Zabaleta 1, Opponents 5
FA Cup goals (16): Aguero 5, Sane 2, Silva 2, Toure 2, Iheanacho 1, Sterling 1, Stones 1, Zabaleta 1, Opponents 1. **League Cup goals** (2): Clichy 1, Garcia 1
Champions League goals (24): Aguero 8, Gundogan 2, Iheanacho 2, Nolito 2, Sane 2, Silva 2, Sterling 2, De Bruyne 1, Delph 1, Fernandinho 1, Stones 1
Average home league attendance: 54,019. **Player of Year:** David Silva

MANCHESTER UNITED

Just like their neighbours, Jose Mourinho and United were subject to searching questions about their season. The big difference was that they compensated in a big way for Premier League failings by adding the Europa League trophy to the League Cup and – at the manager's insistence – completing a treble after collecting the Community Shield. Most importantly, a 2-0 victory over Ajax in Europe's second-tier tournament not only meant a return to the Champions League but served as a tribute to their city, coming as it did two nights after the Manchester bombing. With a third of the season gone, and Mourinho having been sent off twice for touchline rants, United trailed Chelsea by 11 points and were already out of the title reckoning. They conceded too many late goals and dropped too many points to teams in the lower reaches of the table. Even a club record 25 unbeaten league games had its limitations, with 12 of them drawn. In total, they shared the spoils on 15 occasions, while 18 wins represented the club's lowest number in the Premier League era. To be fair, resources were stretched in final few weeks with injuries to Zlatan Ibrahimovic, Marcos Rojo, Phil Jones, Chris Smalling and Juan Mata. Ibrahimovic, who delivered the League Cup by scoring twice in a fortuitous 3-2 win over Southampton, enjoyed a successful first season in English football, before it was cut short by a serious knee injury which ended his time at Old Trafford.

Bailly E................... 24 (1)	Gomes A..................... - (1)	Mata J 19 (6)
Blind D.................. 20 (3)	Harrop J 1	McTominay S 1 (1)
Carrick M............... 18 (5)	Herrera A 27 (4)	Mitchell D.........................1
Darmian M............. 15 (3)	Ibrahimovic I............ 27 (1)	Mkhitaryan H 15 (9)
De Gea D 35	Pereira J 1	Pogba P 29 (1)
Depay M .... - (4)	Jones P..........................18	Rashford M 16 (16)
Fellaini M 18 (10)	Lingard J 18 (7)	Rojo M 18 (3)
Fosu-Mensah T........... 1 (3)	Martial A................. 18 (7)	Romero S..........................2

Rooney W 15 (10)	Smalling C 13 (5)	Young A 8 (4)
Schneiderlin M .... - (3)	Tuanzebe A 4	
Shaw L 9 (2)	Valencia A 27 (1)	

League goals (54): Ibrahimovic 17, Mata 6, Pogba 5, Rashford 5, Rooney 5, Martial 4, Mkhitaryan 4, Blind 1, Fellaini 1, Harrop 1, Herrera 1, Lingard 1, Rojo 1, Smalling 1, Valencia 1
FA Cup goals (10): Rashford 3, Fellaini 1, Ibrahimovic 1, Martial 1, Mkhitaryan 1, Rooney 1, Schweinsteiger B 1, Smalling 1. **League Cup goals** (14): Ibrahimovic 4, Martial 2, Mata 2, Carrick 1, Fellaini 1, Herrera 1, Lingard 1, Pogba 1, Rashford 1. **Community Shield goals** (2): Ibrahimovic 1, Lingard 1
Europa League goals (22): Ibrahimovic 5, Mkhitaryan 5, Lingard 2, Mata 2, Pogba 2, Rashford 2, Rooney 2, Fellaini 1, Martial 1
Average home league attendance: 75,290. **Player of Year**: Ander Herrera

MIDDLESBROUGH

A shortage of goals was punished by an immediate return to the Championship. Aitor Karanka's side just about coped with 17 in the first half of the season. But the problem became more acute during a run of 16 matches without a win, They dropped into the bottom three with a 2-0 defeat at Stoke and the manager was sacked 12 days later after three-and-a-half-years in charge. He had been critical of club's dealings in the January transfer market, accused fans of creating an 'awful atmosphere' and clashed Middlesbrough stalwart Stewart Downing. Coach Steve Agnew, given the job on a caretaker basis, was unable to arrest the demise, until Marten de Roon's goal accounted for fellow-strugglers Sunderland and offered a glimmer of hope. That was followed by one of their best performances, a 2-2 draw with Manchester City. But it still left them six points from safety and a 3-0 defeat at Stamford Bridge sent them down with two matches remaining. By then, they had added just nine goals to their tally. Further defeats by Southampton and Liverpool left them second from bottom, 12 points adrift. A fortnight after resigning as Leeds manager, Garry Monk took over on Teesside during the summer.

Adomah A 1 (1)	Fabio 21 (3)	Leadbitter G 7 (6)
Ayala D 11 (3)	Fischer V 6 (7)	Negredo A 33 (3)
Bamford P 2 (6)	Forshaw A 30 (4)	Nsue E 4
Barragan A 26	Friend G 20 (4)	Nugent D .... - (4)
Bernardo 10 (1)	Gestede R 4 (12)	Ramirez G 20 (4)
Chambers C 24	Gibson B 38	Rhodes J 2 (4)
Clayton A 32 (2)	Guedioura A .... - (5)	Stuani C 16 (7)
De Roon M 32 (1)	Guzan B 10	Traore A 16 (11)
Downing S 24 (6)	Husband J 1	Valdes V 28

League goals (27): Negredo 9, De Roon 4, Stuani 4, Ramirez 2, Ayala 1, Bamford 1, Chambers 1, Downing 1, Gestede 1, Gibson 1, Leadbitter 1, Opponents 1
FA Cup goals (7): Leadbitter 2, De Roon 1, Downing 1, Gestede 1, Negredo 1, Stuani 1. **League Cup goals** (1): Nugent 1
Average home league attendance: 30,449. **Player of Year**: Ben Gibson

SOUTHAMPTON

A third successive summer of upheaval at St Mary's meant the loss of manager Ronald Koeman, leading scorers Sadio Mane and Graziano Pelle and midfielder Victor Wanyama. In the winter transfer window, Joe Fonte joined the exodus, while injuries cost them the services of Charlie Austin and Virgil van Dijk for large parts of the season. Again, Southampton reorganised and rebuilt, this time under former Nice coach Claude Puel, finishing eighth and reaching the League Cup Final in which they were unlucky to lose to Manchester United. A poor start, two points from four matches, was followed by victories over Swansea, West Ham and Burnley, paving the way for Southampton to climb the table. Four successive defeats around the turn of the year set them back, but eight goals in successive matches against Sunderland and Watford restored momentum, with the £14m winter signing of Napoli's Manolo Gabbiadini paying instant dividends with six goals in his first four matches. Two of them came at Wembley, where fortune favoured United with an 87th minute winner for 3-2. The other major disappointment was failing to qualify for the Europa League knockout stage after being held by the Israeli side Hapoel Beer Sheva at home in the final group game. Overall, Puel's summer dismissal seemed harsh. He was replaced by former Liverpool and Argentine defender Mauricio Pellegrino.

Austin C 11 (4)	Hojbjerg P. 14 (8)	Sims J 1 (6)
Bertrand R 28	Long S 10 (22)	Soares C 30
Boufal S 12 (12)	Martina C.................. 6 (3)	Stephens J................ 15 (2)
Caceres M.......................1	McQueen S 5 (8)	Tadic D 30 (3)
Clasie J................. 12 (4)	Pied J 1 (3)	Targett M 5
Davis S 29 (3)	Redmond N.............. 32 (5)	Ward-Prowse J 22 (8)
Fonte J 17	Reed H 1 (2)	Yoshida M.....................23
Forster F 38	Rodriguez J............... 9 (15)	Van Dijk V.....................21
Gabbiadini M 10 (1)	Romeu O 35	

League goals (41): Redmond 7, Austin 6, Rodriguez 5, Gabbiadini 4, Ward-Prowse 4, Long 3, Tadic 3, Bertrand 2, Boutal 1, Clasie 1, Romeu 1, Yoshida 1, Van Dijk 1, Opponents 2
FA Cup goals (3): Long 1, Van Dijk 1, Yoshida 1. **League Cup goals** (9): Gabbiadini 2, Austin 1, Bertrand 1, Boufal 1, Clasie 1, Hesketh 1, Long 1, Redmond 1
Europa League goals (6): Austin 2, Van Dijk 2, Rodriguez 1, Opponents 1
Average home league attendance: 30,936. **Player of Year**: Oriel Romeu

STOKE CITY

A poor start and a faltering finish put the damper on the bid for a fourth successive top-ten finish. Stoke failed to win any of their opening seven matches, conceding four goals to Manchester City, Tottenham and Crystal Palace. They were up and running with successive victories over Sunderland, Hull and Swansea to move away from the bottom three – and the season continued in up-and-down fashion. Four goals were conceded in four more matches, all to leading teams, but Mark Hughes's side picked up sufficient points to work their way up to ninth – their finishing position in the three previous campaigns. This despite winter-signing Saido Berahino failing to score after a £12m move from West Bromwich Albion where, the striker admitted, he had lost his way. Holding Manchester City to a goalless draw at with a resolute performance at the Etihad maintained that position, before five defeats in the next six dropped them to 13th. At least there was a successful finish, along with a Premier League record achieved by veteran Peter Crouch, who became the first player to score 50 headed goals with the winner at Southampton. It left Stoke 13th, albeit within a point of their target.

Adam C 17 (7)	Cameron G............. 18 (1)	Ngoy J .... (5)
Afellay I 3 (9)	Crouch P................ 13 (14)	Pieters E................. 35 (1)
Allen J 34 (2)	Given S 5	Shaqiri X.......................21
Arnautovic M.................32	Grant L 28	Shawcross R 35
Bardsley P 14 (1)	Imbula G 9 (3)	Sobhi R 8 (9)
Berahino S................ 8 (5)	Johnson G................ 21 (2)	Walters J 13 (10)
Biram Diouf M........ 15 (12)	Krkic B 5 (4)	Whelan G 26 (4)
Bony W.................... 9 (1)	Martins Indi B 35	Wollscheid P 2
Butland J 5	Muniesa M 7 (3)	

League goals (41): Crouch 7, Allen 6, Arnautovic 6, Shaqiri 4, Walters 4, Krkic 3, Bony 2, Adam 1, Biram Diouf 1, Martins Indi 1, Muniesa 1, Shawcross 1, Opponents 4
FA Cup goals: None. **League Cup goals** (5): Crouch 3, Arnautovic 1, Bardsley 1
Average home league attendance: 27,433. **Player of Year**: Lee Grant

SUNDERLAND

They escaped the drop in the previous four seasons under four different managers. This time, under a fifth, there was no reprieve. David Moyes admitted early in the season that the odds were stacked against them – and took no pleasure in being proved correct. There was always a slim chance while Jermain Defoe kept the scoreline ticking over. But when his goals dried up, Sunderland had no-one else to turn to. Moyes, the former Manchester United and Everton manager, came in when Sam Allardyce, who beat the drop in 2016, was appointed England manager three weeks before the start of the campaign. With ten matches gone, his side had just two points on the board. They were finally off the mark with three victories in four games, against Bournemouth, Hull and Leicester, to move off the bottom and retain contact with teams immediately above the relegation zone. A 4-0 win over Crystal Palace, with Defoe netting twice, offered further hope. Then, a run of ten matches with just two goals killed them. The last of those, defeat by Bournemouth, confirmed the inevitable – with four fixtures remaining. When Defoe ended his drought, against Hull, it was no coincidence that Sunderland ended the sequence with a 2-0 win. It was his 15th and last for the club. He left for Bournemouth, while Moyes resigned. In came Preston's Simon Grayson.

Anichebe V 14 (4)	Jones B 25 (2)	McNair P 5 (4)
Asoro J .... - (1)	Kaboul Y............................1	Ndong D 27 (4)
Borini F 19 (5)	Khazri W................. 7 (14)	O'Shea J................. 26 (2)
Cattermole L 8	Kirchoff J 5 (2)	Oviedo B 10
Defoe J 37	Kone L 29 (1)	Pickford J 29
Denayer J................. 22 (2)	Larsson S................. 17 (4)	Pienaar S 10 (5)
Djilobodji P 17 (1)	Lens J .... - (2)	Rodwell J................ 17 (3)
Gibson D................... 7 (5)	Lescott J................... 1 (1)	Van Aanholt P 20 (1)
Gooch L................... 4 (7)	Love D 6 (6)	Watmore D.............. 11 (3)
Honeyman G 2 (3)	Mannone V...................9	
Januzaj A.............. 18 (7)	Manquillo J 15 (5)	

League goals (29): Defoe 15, Anichebe 3, Van Aanholt 3, Borini 2, Jones 1, Khazri 1, Kone 1, Manquillo 1, Ndong 1, Opponents 1
FA Cup goals: None. **League Cup goals (3):** McNair 2, Januzaj 1
Average home league attendance: 41,287. **Player of Year:** Jermain Defoe

SWANSEA CITY

When Paul Clement was appointed early in the New Year, Swansea were rubbing shoulders with Sunderland in the bottom three. Four months later, after victory at the Stadium of Light, they were 14 points ahead and on the brink of survival. The following day, this was confirmed when Hull went down after losing to Crystal Palace – a successful outcome for the club's third manager of the season. The first, Francesco Guidolìn, was sacked on his 61st birthday after a single league win since the opening day. He was replaced by Le Havre's former USA coach Bob Bradley, the first American to manage in the Premier League, who lasted just 85 days before he was fired after two wins in 11 matches and 29 goals conceded. Swansea lacked leadership and a dominant centre-half after losing Ashley Williams to Everton. But Clement, assistant to Carlo Ancelotti at Bayern Munich and before that in charge of Derby, made an immediate impact with four wins out of six to move his new side out of the relegation zone. They were back in trouble with a month of the campaign remaining after losing five out of six, before Fernando Llorente scored vital goals against Stoke and Everton. The former Juventus and Sevilla striker then set them on the way at Sunderland, followed by Kyle Naughton's first goal for six years to complete a 2-0 success.

Amat J	15 (2)	Fer L	27 (7)	Narsingh L	3 (10)
Ayew J	9 (5)	Fernandez F	27	Naughton K	31
Barrow M	12 (6)	Fulton J	9 (2)	Nordfeldt K	1
Baston B	4 (14)	Ki Sung-Yueng	13 (10)	Olsson M	14 (1)
Britton L	16	Kingsley S	12 (1)	Rangel A	8 (10)
Carroll T	16 (1)	Llorente F	28 (5)	Routledge W	24 (3)
Cork J	25 (5)	Mawson A	27	Sigurdsson G	37 (1)
Dyer N	3 (5)	McBurnie O	- (5)	Taylor N	11
Fabianski L	37	Montero J	2 (11)	Van der Hoorn M	7 (1)

League goals (45): Llorente 15, Sigurdsson 9, Fer 6, Mawson 4, Routledge 3, Olsson 2, Ayew 1, Baston 1, Carroll 1, Naughton 1, Rangel 1, Van der Hoorn 1
FA Cup goals: None. **League Cup goals** (4): McBurnie 2, Fulton 1, Sigurdsson 1
Average home league attendance: 20,619. **Player of Year:** Gylfi Sigurdsson

TOTTENHAM HOTSPUR

Tottenham's impressive achievements in their final year at the old White Hart Lane were't enough to make them champions. But the season proved beyond doubt that Mauricio Pochettino's team are now part of the elite of English football and look title-winners in waiting. They finished runners-up for the first time since 1963, were the only side to sustain a challenge to Chelsea, achieved a record tally of Premier League points and scored 14 successive wins at home for the first time in any single top-flight season. Finishing above Arsenal for the first time in 22 years was another cause for celebration. Individually, Harry Kane joined Alan Shearer, Ruud van Nistelrooy and Thierry Henry in scoring 20 Premier League goals in three successive seasons, this one including three hat-tricks in the space of nine league and FA Cup matches, with two more to round things off. Dele Alli enhanced his reputation as one of Europe's most outstanding young players, while the introduction of Victor Wanyama gave the midfield a powerful new presence. Tottenham built on the club's start in the top division since becoming champions in 1960-61, accumulating 17 points from seven games. The ability to come from behind and win matches underlined their character and it was not until a 1-0 defeat at West Ham, with three fixtures remaining, that Chelsea were able to breathe more easily. Kane and his side ran riot in the final two games, the England striker overtaking Everton's Romelu Lukaku for the Golden Boot award with seven goals in away wins over Leicester (6-1) and Hull (7-1). The major disappointment was failing to qualify from their Champions League group, the result of two defeats at Wembley, where they will return in the new season in readiness for a 61,000-seater stadium at White Hart Lane.

Alderweireld T	30	Kane H	29 (1)	Son Heung-min	23 (11)
Alli D	35 (2)	Lamela E	6 (3)	Trippier K	6 (6)
Carroll T	- (1)	Lesniak E	- (1)	Vertonghen J	33
Davies B	18 (5)	Lloris H	34	Vorm M	4 (1)
Dembele M	24 (6)	Nkoudou G-K	- (8)	Walker K	31 (2)
Dier E	34 (2)	Onomah J	- (5)	Wanyama V	35 (1)
Eriksen C	36	Rose D	18	Wimmer K	4 (1)
Janssen V	7 (20)	Sissoko M	8 (17)	Winks H	3 (18)

League goals (86): Kane 29, Alli 18, Son Heung-min 14, Eriksen 8, Wanyama 4, Dier 2, Janssen 2, Rose 2, Alderweireld 1, Davies 1, Dembele 1, Lamela 1, Winks 1, Opponents 2
FA Cup goals (17): Son Heung-min 6, Kane 4, Alli 3, Janssen 2, Davies 1, Eriksen 1. **League Cup goals** (6): Eriksen 2, Janssen 2, Lamela 1, Onomah 1
Champions League goals (6): Kane 2, Alderweireld 1, Alli 1, Son Heung-min 1, Opponents 1.
Europa League (2): Eriksen 1, Wanyama 1
Average home league attendance: 31,639. **Player of Year:** Christian Eriksen

WATFORD

In a season which delivered three record in-and-out transfers for the club, Watford lost the chance of a first top-ten place in the Premier League with a disappointing finish. They were handily placed after successive victories over Sunderland, West Bromwich Albion and Swansea. But after reaching the 40-point mark with six games remaining, they were beaten by relegation-threatened Hull, then found a demanding run-in too much, losing to Liverpool, Leicester, Everton, Chelsea and Manchester City. It left them fourth from bottom, with speculation rife about the position of manager Walter Mazzarri. Neither of his two major signings, costing the best part of £26m, lasted the course. Argentine Roberto Pereyra scored on his debut and had settled in nicely into midfield when he sustained a knee injury and was ruled out for the remainder of the campaign after a dozen starts for the club. Nigerian striker Isaac Success made just two starts, along with many off the bench in between muscle problems. Odion Ighalo, the previous season's leading marksman, also had just one league goal to show for his efforts before Watford accepted a £20m bid from the Chinese Super League club Changchun Yatai during the transfer window. Mazzarri, in charge for a year, was sacked with one game remaining and replaced by Marco Silva, fresh from trying to save Hull from going down.

Amrabat N 25 (4)	Gomes H........................38	Okaka S.................... 10 (9)
Anya I.......................... - (1)	Guedioura A............... 9 (3)	Pantilimon C............... - (2)
Behrami V................ 26 (1)	Holebas J....................33	Pereira D .... - (2)
Britos M 27	Ighalo O................ 14 (4)	Pereyra R................ 12 (1)
Capoue E 37	Janmaat D 18 (9)	Prodl S 32 (1)
Cathcart C 13 (2)	Kabasele C................ 7 (9)	Sinclair J 1 (4)
Cleverley T 16 (1)	Kaboul Y....................22	Success I 2 (17)
Deeney T 31 (6)	Kenedy .... - (1)	Vydra M........................ - (1)
Doucoure A 14 (6)	Mariappa A 6 (1)	Watson B .... - (4)
Eleftheriou A............. - (1)	Mason B 1 (1)	Zarate M........................3
Folivi M .... - (1)	Niang M 15 (1)	Zuniga J 6 (15)

League goals (40): Deeney 10, Capoue 7, Okaka 4, Holebas 2, Janmaat 2, Kabasele 2, Kaboul 2, Niang 2, Pereyra 2, Britos 1, Doucoure 1, Ighalo 1, Success 1, Prodl 1, Zuniga 1, Opponents 1
FA Cup goals (2): Kabasele 1, Sinclair 1. **League Cup goals (1):** Ighalo 1
Average home league attendance: 20,571. **Player of Year:** Sebastian Prodl

WEST BROMWICH ALBION

Tony Pulis achieved his first top-half finish as a Premier League manager – and Albion were looking at matching their highest placing when Jonny Evans scored their 16th goal of the season from a corner in the final match at Swansea. Instead, leading scorer Salomon Rondon missed two gilt-edged chances to seal a victory and his side lost 2-1 to an 85th minute goal from Fernando Llorente, slipping from eighth to tenth in the table. It was their seventh defeat in the final eight games off the back of a 3-1 win over Arsenal, their best of the season, followed by a goalless draw against Manchester United at Old Trafford. The run included a club record five in succession without scoring and mirrored a poor finish in 2016 when Albion failed to win any of their last nine fixtures. Previously, Pulis had completed 1,000 matches as a manager in a 1-1 draw against former club Stoke. His side reached the 'safety' mark of 40 points in the 26th fixture when goals from Craig Dawson and Gareth McAuley accounted for Bournemouth. Dawson then scored with two headers from corners against Arsenal.

Berahino S................ 3 (1)	Field S 4 (4)	Lambert R.................... - (1)
Brunt C................ 27 (4)	Fletcher D................ 37 (1)	Leko J .... - (9)
Chadli N 27 (4)	Foster B........................38	Livermore J.............. 15 (1)
Dawson C........................37	Galloway B.......................3	McAuley G 36
Evans J.................... 30 (1)	Gardner C 2 (7)	McClean J.............. 13 (21)

Morrison J.............. 17 (14)	Phillips M................ 26 (1)	Wilson M 3 (1)
Nyom A 29 (3)	Robson-Kanu H 5 (24)	Yacob C 27 (6)
Olsson J...........................7	Rondon S................ 32 (6)	

League goals (43): Rondon 8, McAuley 6, Chadli 5, Morrison 5, Dawson 4, Phillips 4, Brunt 3, Robson-Kanu 3, Evans 2, Fletcher 2, McClean 1
FA Cup goals (1): Phillips 1. **League Cup goals** (2): McAuley 1, McClean 1
Average home league attendance: 23,876. **Player of Year**: Ben Foster

WEST HAM UNITED

Swopping tight-knit Upton Park for the wide open spaces of the London Stadium was always going to be challenge for Slaven Bilic and his players. Four goals conceded there to Watford and three to Southampton underlined the problem of adapting, with four points from seven games representing the club's worst start to a top flight season. Five more were scored by Arsenal. Then, as West Ham began stitching together wins for the first time, their best player, Dimitri Payet, declared he no longer wanted to play for the club. That resulted in a £25m move back to Marseille, followed closely by a 4-0 defeat against Manchester City. Add to that Andy Carroll's continuing fitness problems and it was no wonder there were those who longed for a return to their former home. Through it all, the team managed to avoid being sucked into a relegation struggle, despite a tendency to drop points from leading positions. Finally, the fans had a cause for celebration – Manuel Lanzini's winner against Tottenham which effectively put their neighbours out of the title reckoning. Another 4-0 defeat, this time against Liverpool, was a sharp reminder of how difficult the season had been, but at least West Ham finished on a high by winning at Burnley to finish 11th, four places down on 2016.

Adrian 16	Fernandes E............. 8 (20)	Payet D 17 (1)
Antonio M 29	Fletcher A................. 2 (14)	Randolph D....................22
Arbeloa A................. 1 (2)	Fonte J...........................16	Reid W 30
Ayew A 16 (9)	Kouyate C....................31	Rice D .... - (1)
Byram S 13 (5)	Lanzimi M................ 31 (4)	Sakho D.................. 2 (2)
Calleri J 4 (12)	Masuaku A............... 11 (2)	Snodgrass R............. 8 (7)
Carroll A 16 (3)	Noble M 29 (1)	Tore G 3 (2)
Collins J 19 (3)	Nordtveit H 11 (5)	Valencia E......................3
Cresswell A 24 (2)	Obiang P................. 21 (1)	Zaza S................... 5 (3)
Feghouli S 11 (10)	Ogbonna A 20	

League goals (47): Antonio 9, Lanzini 8, Carroll 7, Ayew 6, Feghouli 3, Noble 3, Collins 2, Payet 2, Reid 2, Calleri 1, Kouyate 1, Obiang 1, Sakho 1, Opponents 1
FA Cup goals: None. **League Cup goals** (4): Fernandes 1, Fletcher 1, Kouyate 1, Payet 1
Europa League goals (5): Kouyate 2, Noble 2, Feghouli 1
Average home league attendance: 56,972. **Player of Year**: Michail Antonio

CHAMPIONSHIP

ASTON VILLA

Villa had a poor return on the £80m spent on new players in the two transfer windows. They were unable to come to terms with the unforgiving nature of the Championship, falling well short of an immediate return to the Premier League. A single win in the opening 11 games cost Roberto di Matteo his job, with his team already ten points adrift of even the play-offs. Steve Bruce became the club's fifth manager in 20 months, on the back of his record of taking teams into the top flight, and was unbeaten in his first seven games. Villa climbed to within four points of a place in the top-six, then dropped back into the bottom half of the table after nine games without a win left them 16 points adrift and out of contention. Their best spell came late, seven wins out of eight with just one goal conceded. Jonathan Kodjia, an £11m signing from Bristol City, scored seven goals in that sequence, taking his tally for the campaign to 19. That lifted his side into mid-table, but defeats by promotion contenders Reading and Fulham and relegation threatened Blackburn dragged them back.

Adomah A................. 30 (8)	De Laet R 3	Johnstone S 21
Agbonlahor G 4 (9)	Elphick T................ 20 (6)	Kodjia L 36
Amavi J 26 (8)	Gardner G 18 (8)	Kozak L .... - (2)
Ayew J...................... 17 (4)	Gestede R 8 (10)	Lansbury H 17 (1)
Bacuna L 22 (8)	Gollini P 20	McCormack R............. 13 (7)
Baker N 31 (1)	Grealish J 20 (11)	Richards M 1 (1)
Bjarnason B 5 (3)	Green A 4 (11)	Taylor C .... - (1)
Bree J........................ 6 (1)	Hepburn-Murphy R ...... - (3)	Taylor N 14
Bunn M 5 (1)	Hogan S 9 (4)	Traore A .... - (1)
Chester J 45	Hourihane C............. 13 (4)	Tshibola A 5 (3)
Cissokho A 11 (1)	Hutton A.................. 31 (3)	Westwood A 18 (5)
Davis K .... - (6)	Jedinak M 33	

League goals (47): Kodjia 19, Grealish 5, Gestede 4, Adomah 3, Chester 3, McCormack 3, Ayew 2, Agbonlahor 1, Bacuna 1, Baker 1, Gardner 1, Hogan 1, Hourihane 1, Tshibola 1, Opponents 1
FA Cup goals: None. **League Cup goals** (1): Ayew 1
Average home league attendance: 32,107. **Player of Year**: Jonathan Kodjia

BARNSLEY

The loss of key players during the January transfer window had a marked effect on Barnsley's season. Sam Winnall moved Sheffield Wednesday, followed by captain Conor Hourihane and James Bree to Aston Villa. At the time, Barnsley were closing in on a play-off place and actually came within a point of sixth-place Wednesday. They had netted four goals each when beating Rotherham, Wolves and Cardiff and came from behind to score three times in nine minutes for a 3-2 victory over Leeds. After that, results suffered. There was a notable 3-1 victory at Villa Park, with Tom Bradshaw scoring twice, but the final 14 matches yielded just one more success – 2-0 against Blackburn. Fortunately, Barnsley had sufficient points in the bank to hold on to a position just below half-way and they may well have settled for that when setting on the season after winning promotion via the play-offs.

Armstrong A........... 21 (13)	Elder C 5	James M 17 (1)
Bradshaw T............. 28 (14)	Evans C 1 (2)	Janko S 7 (7)
Bree J..................... 18 (1)	Hammill A 22 (15)	Jones G 16 (1)
Brown J .... - (2)	Hedges R................... 2 (6)	Kay J................................1
D'Almeida S .... - (3)	Hourihane C...................25	Kent R.................... 38 (6)
Davies A 46	Jackson A 9 (1)	Kpekawa C................. 4 (3)

Lee E	- (6)	Mowatt A	6 (5)	White A	10
MacDonald A	39	Payne S	- (7)	Williams R	4 (12)
Mawson A	4	Roberts M	40	Winnall S	20 (2)
Moncur G	8 (4)	Scowen J	38 (3)	Yiadom A	31 (1)
Morsy S	12 (2)	Watkins M	34 (8)		

League goals (64): Winnall 11, Watkins 10, Bradshaw 8, Armstrong 6, Hourihane 6, Roberts 4, Hammill 3, Kent 3, Mawson 2, Moncur 2, Scowen 2, James 1, Janko 1, MacDonald 1, Mowatt 1, Williams 1, Opponents 2

FA Cup goals (1): MacDonald 1. **League Cup goals** (1): Scowen 1

Average home league attendance: 13,831. **Player of Year**: Marc Roberts

BIRMINGHAM CITY

Harry Redknapp rolled back the years with a successful relegation rescue act at St Andrew's. The 70-year-old said he felt more like 17 after leading Birmingham to safety on a nerve-shredding final day of the season. He returned to management nearly two years after leaving Queens Park Rangers in a last throw of the dice by the club, whose gamble of replacing Gary Rowett with Gianfranco Zola midway through the campaign had backfired spectacularly. Redknapp's first game, a 1-0 defeat by Aston Villa, left the club two points off the drop zone. His second, in front of the biggest home league crowd since their Premier League exit – nearly 27,000 – brought a 2-0 victory over Huddersfield, despite the dismissal of Che Adams after 23 minutes and Lukas Jutkiewicz having a penalty saved. Adams won his appeal against the red card, freeing him for the final game away to Bristol City, and he scored the goal which kept his side above Nottingham Forest and Blackburn, who also won their final fixtures. Redknapp was rewarded with a one year contract. Rowett's dismissal, with Birmingham on the fringe of a play-off place, was described as a 'strategic, long-term' decision. In the event, Zola failed to win any of his first eight games, the worst start by a manager of the club since 1889. He resigned, with just two in 22 matches, after a home defeat by Burton.

Adams C	28 (12)	Gleeson S	25 (4)	O'Keefe C	- (1)
Bielik K	8 (2)	Grounds J	42	Robinson P	13 (9)
Brown R	1 (7)	Jutkiewicz L	31 (7)	Shotton R	43
Cogley J	9 (5)	Keita C	9 (1)	Sinclair J	3 (2)
Cotterill D	19 (6)	Kieftenbeld M	41 (5)	Solomon-Otabor V	- (3)
Davis D	40 (1)	Kuszczak T	38	Spector J	22
Donaldson C	16 (7)	Legzdins A	8 (2)	Stewart G	6 (15)
Fabbrini D	2 (5)	Maghoma J	20 (7)	Storer J	- (4)
Frei K	3 (10)	Morrison M	30 (1)	Tesche R	19 (5)
Gardner C	19 (1)	Nsue E	18	Wiggins R	1 (1)

League goals (45): Jutkiewicz 11, Adams 7, Donaldson 6, Davis 4, Maghoma 3, Morrison 3, Gardner 2, Grounds 2, Shotton 2, Cotterill 1, Frei 1, Gleeson 1, Kieftenbeld 1, Nsue 1

FA Cup goals (2): Cotterill 1, Jutkiewicz 1. **League Cup goals**: None

Average home league attendance: 18,717. **Player of Year**: David Davis

BLACKBURN ROVERS

Blackburn's demise under the controversial ownership of Venky's continued on the final day of the season when they came off worst in a three-way struggle to avoid the Championship's third relegation place. A 3-1 victory at Brentford was not enough to lift them above Birmingham or Nottingham Forest, who both won their respective matches. The drop intensified protests against the Indian company, who took over the then Premier League club in November 2010 and have since seen attendances dwindle at Ewood Park. Tony Mowbray became the eighth manager of their tenure when Owen Coyle was sacked two days after Rovers made Manchester United work for a 2-1 FA Cup fifth round victory. Mowbray, formerly in charge of Coventry – another relegated club beleaguered by angry fans – took over a side second from bottom after 31 games. He enjoyed some early success, with 1-0 victories over Derby and Wigan, accompanied by a move out of the drop zone. It was a brief respite. Rovers were back there after a run of seven matches without a win and they eventually went down as a result of Forest having a superior goal difference of two.

Akpan H	16 (9)	Greer G	19 (2)	Nyambe R	22 (3)
Bennett E	18 (7)	Guthrie D	22 (2)	Raya D	5
Brown W	3 (2)	Hendrie S	2 (2)	Samuelsen M	1 (2)
Byrne J	3 (1)	Henley A	2	Steele J	41
Conway C	34 (8)	Hoban T	15 (1)	Stokes A	2 (6)
Duffy S	3	Lenihan D	32 (8)	Tomlinson W	- (1)
Emnes M	22 (13)	Lowe J	43	Ward E	6
Evans C	16 (3)	Lucas Joao	3 (10)	Wharton S	1 (1)
Feeney L	21 (14)	Mahoney C	4 (10)	Williams D	39
Gallagher S	35 (8)	Marshall B	22		
Graham D	28 (7)	Mulgrew C	26 (2)		

League goals (53): Graham 12, Gallagher 11, Conway 6, Emnes 4, Bennett 3, Lucas Joao 3, Mulgrew 3, Akpan 1, Brown 1, Guthrie 1, Hoban 1, Marshall 1, Stokes 1, Williams 1, Opponents 4
FA Cup goals (5): Bennett 1, Feeney 1, Gallagher 1, Graham 1, Opponents 1. **League Cup goals** (7): Duffy 2, Stokes 2, Akpan 1, Conway 1, Wharton 1
Average home league attendance: 12,688. **Player of Year**: Derrick Williams

BRENTFORD

Any doubts that Brentford would suffer from the loss of leading marksman Scott Hogan to Aston Villa in the January transfer window were quickly dispelled. Hogan's 14 goals, including a hat-trick against Preston, represented almost half the team's total in the first half of the season. But Spanish winger Jota, returning from a loan spell at Eibar, and Dane Lasse Vibe both netted 11 in the second half to keep their side in the upper reaches of the table. Jota hit a hat-trick against Rotherham; two from Vibe came as a 3-1 deficit at Burton was transformed into a 5-3 victory; in tandem, they scored two each in a 4-0 success against Derby. Two more for Jota helped them complete the double over Queens Park Rangers, followed by a point against their other west London rivals, promotion-chasing Fulham, in front of a near-25,000 crowd at Craven Cottage. That lifted Brentford to tenth – one below their 2016 finish – a position they maintained despite losing the last game to relegation-threatened Blackburn.

Barbet Y	15 (8)	Elder C	6	MacLeod L	10 (3)
Bentley D	45	Field T	13 (2)	McCormack A	2 (9)
Bjelland A	25 (3)	Henry R	12	McEachran J	14 (13)
Bonham J	1	Hofmann P	- (10)	Saunders S	2 (6)
Canos S	13 (5)	Hogan S	25	Sawyers R	39 (4)
Clarke J	19 (11)	Jota	19 (2)	Shaibu J	- (4)
Cole R	- (1)	Jozefzoon F	6 (13)	Vibe L	30 (4)
Colin M	38	Kaikai S	6 (12)	Westbrooke Z	- (1)
Dean H	42	Kerschbaumer K	9 (11)	Woods R	42
Egan J	34	Ledesma E	- (1)	Yennaris N	39 (7)

League goals (75): Vibe 15, Hogan 14, Jota 12, Yennaris 6, Canos 4, Colin 4, Egan 4, Dean 3, Kaikai 3, Clarke 2, Sawyers 2, Barbet 1, Field 1, Jozefzoon 1, Kerschbaumer 1, Opponents 2
FA Cup goals (5): Field 2, Barbet 1, Sawyers 1, Vibe 1. **League Cup goals**: None
Average home league attendance: 10,467. **Player of Year**: Harlee Dean

BRIGHTON & HOVE ALBION

Brighton reached the promised land for the first time – and manager Chris Hughton urged his players to celebrate that achievement and not dwell on the disappointment of surrendering the title to Newcastle. After three play-off failures in the previous four years, they made it to the Premier League, a tribute to Hughton's shrewd guidance of a team whose persistence eventually gained its reward. It was, in every sense, a special season for a club, who in 1997 were 30 minutes away from non-league football and spent the best part of 16 years without a ground of their own. An unbeaten run of 18 matches was the foundation. They went top for the first time at the midway point of the season, overtaking Newcastle, and the two teams were then neck-and-neck until Brighton opened up a seven-point advantage with a win over Wigan, which clinched promotion with three games remaining. Nothing, it seemed, could dislodge them. Instead, they lost at Norwich when David Stockdale conceded identical own goals – two shots hitting the woodwork and the ball bouncing off the goalkeeper into the net each time. A home defeat by Bristol City followed. Then, they conceded an 89th equaliser to Aston Villa, enabling Newcastle to finish a point ahead after beating Barnsley in their final fixture. Hughton was named the Championship's Manager of the Year and Anthony Knockaert won the players' award.

Adekugbe S	1	Hunt R	- (1)	Pocognoli S	17 (3)
Akpom C	1 (9)	Kayal B	1 / (3)	Rosenior L	9 (1)
Baldock S	27 (4)	Knockaert A	44 (1)	Sidwell S	26 (8)
Bong G	24	LuaLua K	(3)	Skalak J	24 (7)
Bruno	42	Maenpaa N	1	Stephens D	33 (6)
Duffy S	31	Manu E	- (2)	Stockdale D	45
Dunk L	43	March S	9 (16)	Tomori F	2 (7)
Goldson C	4 (1)	Murphy J	20 (15)	Towell R	- (1)
Hemed T	20 (17)	Murray G	39 (6)		
Hunemeier U	11	Norwood O	16 (17)		

League goals (74): Murray 23, Knockaert 15, Baldock 11, Hemed 11, March 3, Duffy 2, Dunk 2, Murphy 2, Stephens 2, Hunemeier 1, Pocognoli 1, Sidwell 1
FA Cup goals (3): Hemed 1, Kayal 1, Towell 1. **League Cup goals (9):** Hemed 2, Manu 2, Murphy 2, Adekugbe 1, Baldock 1, LuaLua 1
Average home league attendance: 7,996. **Player of Year:** Anthony Knockaert

BRISTOL CITY

The club kept faith with Lee Johnson throughout a difficult season and were rewarded when the manager led his side to safety with a rousing finish. City were a single point off the relegation zone with six matches remaining after a 5-0 defeat at Preston. Victories over Wolves and Queens Park Rangers pointed the way to safety, they twice came from behind to beat Barnsley and Josh Brownhill's winner at Brighton, his first goal for the club, made them mathematically sure of staying up. Chelsea loanee Tammy Abraham, who broke into England's under-21 team, was on the mark four times in that sequence to finish with 23 for the campaign. City had climbed to sixth after 15 matches, then plummeted when losing 11 of the next 12. There were eight successive defeats, equalling a club record, before the sequence was halted by a 2-2 draw against Sheffield Wednesday. They defeated Rotherham by the only goal, then let slip a 3-0 half-time lead at Derby to finish 3-3. In the January transfer window, Johnson paid £300,000 for Bristol Rovers' leading scorer Matty Taylor, the first player to make that move across the city in 30 years.

Abraham T	40 (1)	Cotterill D	12 (1)	Fielding F	27
Ayling L	1	Djuric M	3 (8)	Flint A	46
Brownhill J	19 (8)	Ekstrand J	1 (1)	Freeman L	14 (4)
Bryan J	39 (5)	Engvall G	- (2)	Giefer F	10

Golbourne S	17 (2)	Moore T	1 (4)	Smith K	21 (2)
Hegeler J	8 (4)	O'Donnell R	8	Taylor M	9 (6)
Kodjia J	4	O'Dowda C	15 (19)	Tomlin L	30 (8)
Little M	26 (2)	O'Neil G	22 (7)	Vyner Z	3
Lucic I	1 (1)	Pack M	29 (4)	Wilbraham A	8 (24)
Magnusson H	26 (2)	Paterson J	16 (6)	Wright B	21
Matthews A	11 (1)	Reid B	18 (12)		

League goals (60): Abraham 23, Tomlin 6, Flint 5, Paterson 4, Wilbraham 4, Reid 3, Cotterill 2, Freeman 2, Pack 2, Taylor 2, Brownhill 1, Bryan 1, Djuric 1, Magnusson 1, O'Neil 1, Wright 1, Opponents 1
FA Cup goals (1): Paterson 1. **League Cup goals** (6): Abraham 3, Reid 1, Tomlin 1, Wilbraham 1
Average home league attendance: 19,256. **Player of Year**: Tammy Abraham

BURTON ALBION

They may have been, by some distance, the smallest club in the Championship, but the performance of Nigel Clough's team was arguably the biggest of the season. Clough turned down the chance to follow in the footsteps of his father Brian by managing Nottingham Forest – and his players repaid that loyalty by staying up against all the odds. A run of seven defeats in eight matches around the midway point of the season threatened to sink them. But Clough made shrewd winter signings – Michael Kightly, Cauley Woodrow, Marvin Sordell and Luke Varney – and was rewarded with goals from all of them. Wins over Queens Park Rangers, Wolves and Norwich came in the space of five matches and they would have had another if Lasse Vigen Christensen's shot had gone in instead of hitting both posts and being gathered by grateful Blackburn goalkeeper Jason Steele. Clough feared that a 5-3 home defeat by Brentford, after leading 3-1, might proved costly. Instead, Burton won at Huddersfield, with a stoppage-time goal from Jackson Irvine, and held their nerve in a testing run-in. Birmingham and Leeds were both beaten, while Varney's equaliser in the penultimate fixture at Barnsley took them to 52 points.

Akins L	30 (8)	Fox B	- (1)	Naylor T	23 (10)
Barker S	- (5)	Harness M	- (10)	O'Gray C	22 (4)
Beavon S	5 (5)	Irvine J	41 (1)	Palmer M	31 (5)
Brayford J	33	Kightly M	10 (2)	Sbarra J	- (1)
Butcher C	- (1)	McCrory D	11 (5)	Sordell M	19 (2)
Bywater S	3 (2)	McFadzean K	29 (2)	Turner B	38 (1)
Choudhury H	6 (7)	McLaughlan J	43	Varney L	4 (11)
Christensen L V	15 (1)	Miller W	4 (11)	Ward J	15 (3)
Dyer L	37 (5)	Mousinho J	28 (4)	Williamson L	8 (6)
Flanagan T	22 (8)	Murphy L	18 (1)	Woodrow C	11 (3)

League goals (49): Irvine 10, Dyer 7, Akins 5, Woodrow 5, Kightly 4, Sordell 4, Ward 4, Naylor 3, McFadzean 1, Miller 1, Murphy 1, O'Grady 1, Palmer 1, Turner 1, Varney 1
FA Cup goals: None. **League Cup goals** (3): Beavon 1, Butcher 1, Reilly 1
Average home league attendance: 5,228. **Player of Year**: Jackson Irvine

CARDIFF CITY

Neil Warnock delivered another rescue act in his 13th managerial appointment at a league club. Cardiff called on his services after sacking Paul Trollope, two months into the season, with the team second from bottom on eight points from 11 matches. Warnock immediately signed three unattached players – Junior Hoilett, Sol Bamba and Marouane Chamakh – and in his first match in charge Bamba scored in 2-1 win over Bristol City. By the midway point, Cardiff had moved away from bottom three. Then, a productive February, which brought ten points and 13 goals from matches against Leeds, Derby, Rotherham and Fulham, lifted them into mid-table. Danish striker Kenneth Zohore, little used under Trollope, netted five times in those games and finished as the leading scorer. Warnock signed a one-year extension to his contract and although Cardiff tailed off somewhat at the tail-end of the season, they still finished just below half-way after signing off with a 3-0 away victory over Huddersfield.

Amos B.........................16	Hoilett J 29 (4)	Murphy B.................. 4 (1)
Bamba S......................26	Huws E.................... 1 (2)	Noone C 17 (17)
Bennett J 23 (1)	Immers L................ 10 (3)	O'Keefe S 3 (5)
Chamakh M.............. - (2)	John D.................... 9 (6)	Peltier I......................28
Connolly M............. 26 (2)	Kennedy M .... - (2)	Pilkington A 21 (13)
Gounongbe F.......... 3 (8)	Lambert R............. 13 (5)	Ralls J 39 (3)
Gunnarsson A...............40	Manga C.............. 16 (5)	Richards A 25 (1)
Halford G................ 9 (7)	Marshall D....................4	Richardson K 2 (4)
Harris K................ 22 (15)	McGregor A....................19	Whittingham P 28 (9)
Harris M................ 1 (1)	Meite I .... - (1)	Wilson B......................3
Healey R 2 (5)	Morrison S 43 (1)	Zohore K................. 24 (5)

League goals (60). Zohore 12, Pilkington 7, Whittingham 7, Ralls 6, Harris K 4, Lambert 4, Morrison 4, Bennett 3, Gunnarsson 3, Bamba 2, Hoilett 2, Noone 2, Connolly 1, Healey 1, Opponents 2
FA Cup goals (1): Pilkington 1. **League Cup goals:** None
Average home league attendance: 16,564. **Player of Year:** Aron Gunnarsson

DERBY COUNTY

Another season of high expectancy at Pride Park – another season of modest achievement, blighted by a poor start and accompanied by managerial upheaval. Nigel Pearson was suspended by the club after an altercation with owner Mel Morris and his contract later terminated by mutual consent. His side had a single win in nine games and scored just three goals. Steve McClaren returned as manager, 17 months after being sacked, and by the end of the year Derby climbed to the fringe of the play-offs. In the process, there was a club record of eight successive home games without conceding a goal. But form dipped again in the New Year, they fell ten points away from a top-six place and McClaren was dismissed again following a 3-0 defeat by Brighton after six months in charge. In came Gary Rowett, surprisingly sacked by Birmingham, and there was a huge satisfaction win for the new man when returning to St Andrew's not long after and coming away with a 2-1 victory. It still left them seven points adrift and their slim hopes were ended by 4-0 defeat at Brentford, with Rowett admitting his sights had been on building a team capable of success in 2017-18.

Anya I.................... 14 (12)	De Sart J 8 (1)	Nugent D................. 11 (6)
Baird C 28 (5)	Forsyth C 3	Olsson M 30
Bennett M.............. - (2)	Hanson J 2 (3)	Pearce A 39 (1)
Bent D................ 22 (15)	Hendrick J 2	Russell J 29 (7)
Blackman N............. 2 (7)	Hughes W 28 (10)	Shackell J 7 (1)
Bryson C............. 23 (11)	Ince T.................... 41 (4)	Vydra M 20 (13)
Butterfield J............ 34 (6)	Johnson B......................33	Weimann A 1 (10)
Camara A................ 3 (12)	Keogh R......................42	Wilson J.................. 3 (1)
Carson S......................46	Lowe M.................... 8 (1)	
Christie C................ 24 (3)	Martin C 3 (2)	

League goals (54). Ince 14, Bent 10, Nugent 6, Vydra 5, Johnson 3, Bryson 2, Hughes 2, Pearce 2, Russell 2, Anya 1, Blackman 1, Butterfield 1, Christie 1 De Sart 1, Forsyth 1, Opponents 2
FA Cup goals (5): Bent 2, Bryson 1, Camara 1, Ince 1. **League Cup goals** (2): Bent 1, Keogh 1
Average home league attendance: 29,042. **Player of Year:** Scott Carson

FULHAM

Fulham swept into the play-offs with considerable momentum after a strong finish to the regular season. It bode well for their chances of a return to the Premier League. Instead, they failed to make home – and numerical – advantage count in the first leg of the semi-final, drawing 1-1 with Reading, who had Paul McShane sent off after 80 minutes. Between them, the two sides had missed 15 out of 25 penalties during the regular campaign, so it was ironic that the outcome was settled from the spot. Yann Kermorgant converted four minutes into the second-half after Tomas Kalas handled to send Jaap Stam's team to Wembley. Fulham's only consolation was to finish as the division's highest scorers on 85, alongside champions Newcastle and Norwich. They had beaten Reading 5-0 at Craven Cottage and won 3-1 at St James' Park with two goals from 16-year-old starlet Ryan Sessegnon. That victory took his side to within two points of a place in the play-offs, which they confirmed with 16 goals in the final six matches

Adeniran D.................. - (1)	Humphrys S .... - (2)	McDonald K 43
Aluko S.................... 44 (1)	Johansen S 35 (1)	Odoi D..................... 21 (9)
Ayite F...................... 22 (9)	Jozabed 1 (6)	Parker S 12 (17)
Bettinelli M........................6	Kalas T........................36	Ream T..................... 28 (6)
Button D........................40	Kebano N 12 (16)	Sessegnon R 17 (8)
Cairney T 44 (1)	Piazon L 19 (10)	Sigurdsson R............ 15 (2)
Christensen L .... - (4)	Madl M................... 14 (2)	Smith M 7 (9)
Cyriac G...................... - (9)	Malone S 34 (2)	Tunnicliffe R 3 (4)
Fredericks R............. 25 (5)	Martin C 27 (4)	Woodrow C................ 1 (4)

Play-offs – appearances: Aluko 2, Ayite 2, Bettinelli 2, Cairney 2, Fredericks 2, Johansen 2, Kalas 2, Malone 2, McDonald 2, Ream 2, Kebano 1 (1), Martin 1 (1), Cyriac – (1), Piazon – (1), Sessegnon – (1)
League goals (85): Cairney 12, Johansen 11, Martin 10, Ayite 9, Aluko 8, Kebano 6, Malone 6, Piazon 5, Sessegnon 5, McDonald 3, Odoi 2, Smith 2, Cyriac 1, Kalas 1, Ream 1, Sigurdsson 1, Opponents 2. **Play-offs goals** (1): Cairney 1
FA Cup goals (6): Johansen 2, Sessegnon 2, Aluko 1, Martin 1. **League Cup goals** (6): Woodrow 2, Adeniran 1, Christensen 1, Piazon 1, Opponents 1.
Average home league attendance: 19,199. **Player of Year**: Tom Cairney

HUDDERSFIELD TOWN

David Wagner transformed Huddersfield from relegation candidates to Wembley winners – with the help of German expertise from the penalty spot. His side finished the league season with more goals conceded than scored. And none of their players managed to find the net in three play-off matches. But they overcame these statistical quirks to reach the Premier League for the first time – 13 years after playing in the game's fourth tier. After a goalless 120 minutes in the final, Reading were defeated in a shoot-out, clinched by Christopher Schindler's spot-kick. The 4-3 scoreline matched their victory over Sheffield Wednesday in the semi-finals, after an own goal 17 minutes from the end of normal time had kept them alive. On that day, Michael Hefele and fellow German Chris Lowe were on the spot in the shoot-out. Wagner, a former Borussia Dortmund coach, became the club's first Continental manager in November 2015 when they were a point off the bottom three. This time, 13 points from five matches represented the club's best start for 66 years. Huddersfield stayed top for two months, faltered with a single win in eight games, then regained a top-six spot and held it for the remainder of the campaign. Wagner, who turned down an offer from Wolfsburg of the Bundesliga shortly before Christmas, eventually gave up on automatic promotion, began rotating his players and lost three of the final four fixtures, while having to defend his decision to field weakened teams.

Billing P	13 (11)	Hudson M	17 (5)	Scannell S	8 (7)
Brown I	12 (3)	Kachunga E	41 (1)	Schindler C	43 (1)
Bunn H	6 (10)	Lolley J	8 (11)	Smith T	40 (2)
Coleman J	3 (2)	Lowe C	39 (2)	Ward D	43
Cranie M	7 (7)	Mooy A	42 (3)	Wells N	31 (12)
Gorenc-Stankovic J	4 (3)	Palmer K	16 (8)	Whitehead D	10 (6)
Hefele M	28 (9)	Paurevic I	- (1)	Van La Parra R	36 (4)
Hogg J	33 (4)	Payne J	10 (13)		
Holmes-Dennis T	7 (2)	Quaner C	9 (7)		

Play-offs – appearances: Brown 3, Hefele 3, Hogg 3, Kachunga 3, Lowe 3, Mooy 3, Smith 3, Schindler 3, Van la Parra 3, Wells 3, Ward 2, Coleman 1, Quaner – (3), Cranie – (2), Holmes-Dennis – (2), Palmer – (1), Payne – (1)
League goals (56): Kachunga 12, Wells 10, Brown 4, Mooy 4, Palmer 4, Smith 4, Hefele 3, Billing 2, Lowe 2, Payne 2, Quaner 2, Schindler 2, Van La Parra 2, Hogg 1, Lolley 1, Opponents 1. **Play-offs – goals (1):** Opponents 1
FA Cup goals (9): Bunn 2, Hefele 2, Payne 2, Brown 1, Palmer 1, Quaner 1. **League Cup goals (1):** Kachunga 1
Average home league attendance: 20,343. **Player of Year:** Aaron Mooy

IPSWICH TOWN

A flying start quickly gave way to a season of major disappointment. It ended with the club's lowest finish, 16th in the second tier, since 1959, prompting speculation about the future of the Championship's longest-serving manager, Mick McCarthy. His side couldn't have wished for a better opening, nor £600,000 signing Grant Ward from Tottenham, who came off the bench for the second-half, scored with his first touch after 39 seconds and went on to register a hat-trick in a 4-2 win over Barnsley. That was as many as Ipswich scored in the next 11 games and as many as Ward netted in the remainder of the campaign. That they avoided being sucked into a relegation struggle was largely down to the goals scored by Tom Lawrence, during a loan spell from Leicester, and a late season flourish which brought three wins out of four at a time when Ipswich were six points away from trouble. They defeated Wigan 3-0, then put together their only back-to-back victories – against Burton and Newcastle. A 3-1 win over champions-to-be Newcastle in a match designated Sir Bobby Robson Day – in memory of the man who managed both clubs – was followed by three goalless defeats to end to finish with.

Berra C	44	Gerken D	2	Samuel D	2 (4)
Best L	5 (6)	Grant C	3 (3)	Sears F	29 (11)
Bialkowski B	44	Huws E	13	Skuse C	40
Bishop E	7 (12)	Kenlock M	16 (2)	Smith T	6 (4)
Bru K	14 (12)	Knudsen J	35 (1)	Spence J	16 (2)
Chambers L	46	Lawrence T	32 (2)	Taylor S	3
Diagouragn T	10 (2)	McGoldrick D	25 (5)	Varney L	4 (11)
Digby P	2 (2)	Moore K	- (11)	Ward G	35 (8)
Douglas J	17 (4)	Murphy D	4	Webster A	21 (2)
Dozzell A	5 (1)	Pitman B	13 (9)	Williams J	1 (7)
Emmanuel J	11 (4)	Rowe D	2 (2)		

League goals (48): Lawrence 9, Sears 7, Ward 6, McGoldrick 5, Chambers 4, Pitman 4, Huws 3, Varney 3, Berra 2, Knudsen 2, Bru 1, Webster 1, Opponents 1
FA Cup goals (2): Lawrence (2). **League Cup goals:** None
Average home league attendance: 16,981. **Player of Year:** Bartosz Bialkowski

LEEDS UNITED

Garry Monk brought a measure of stability and a touch of success to Elland Road, where previous years had been dominated by protesting fans, managerial upheaval and under-achievement. It wasn't enough to offer the chance of a return to the top flight via the play-offs, but at least there were close to five months spent in the top-six before a youthful team showed, according to their manager, that they were not quite ready to handle end-of-season pressures. Leeds, overcame a patchy start to the campaign to climb the table on the back of eight wins out of ten. They went on to challenge the best in the Championship, beating Brighton with two goals from Chris Wood and taking a point at Newcastle with Wood's 95th minute strike. Leeds were then fifth, with a five-point cushion. But a home loss to Wolves, followed by defeat at Burton, allowed fast-finishing Fulham and Sheffield Wednesday to overtake them. Then, they trailed 3-0 to Norwich in front of a home crowd of 34,000 before Wood launched a comeback which brought a 3-3 scoreline by the end. With 27 league goals, and three more in cup ties, he finished the Championship's leading marksman. Monk's subsequent resignation because of a contract dispute came as a shock to supporters. He was replaced by Thomas Christiansen, former coach at Cypriot club Apoel Nicosia.

Alfonso 8 (6)	Coyle 3 (1)	O'Kane E 20 (4)
Antonsson M 6 (10)	Dallas S 20 (11)	Phillips K 23 (10)
Ayling L 42	Diagouraga T 1	Roofe K 28 (14)
Bamba S 2	Doukara S 17 (17)	Sacko H 28 (10)
Barrow M 1 (4)	Green R 46	Taylor C 26 (3)
Bartley K 45	Grimes M 1 (6)	Vieira R 24 (10)
Berardi A 24 (2)	Hernandez P 32 (3)	Wood C 41 (8)
Bridcutt L 22 (3)	Jansson P 34	
Cooper L 8 (3)	Mowatt A 4 (11)	

League goals (61): Wood 27, Bartley 6, Doukara 6, Hernandez 6, Jansson 3, Roofe 3, Dallas 2, Sako 2, Alfonso 1, Antonsson 1, Phillips 1, Vieira 1, Opponents 2
FA Cup goals (2): Dallas 1, Mowatt 1. **League Cup goals (6):** Wood 3, Antonsson 2, Denton T 1
Average home league attendance: 27,698. **Player of Year:** Chris Wood

NEWCASTLE UNITED

Nothing less than an immediate return to the Premier League would have satisfied the St James' Park faithful – and they had double cause to celebrate when their side came from behind to win the title. Newcastle looked like having to settle for the runners-up spot when trailing Brighton by seven points with three games left. But while their rivals faltered, a promotion-clinching victory over Preston was followed by a win at Cardiff. That left them a point behind going into the final round of fixtures, a position that looked like remaining with Brighton on the brink of winning at Villa Park. Then it all changed as Villa equalised in the 89th minute, putting Newcastle back on top with a 3-0 defeat of Barnsley. Three days later, manager Rafael Benitez met owner Mike Ashley, received an assurance that money would be available for team strengthening and committed his future to the club. His team had not been entirely convincing at home, losing five times. A club record 14 victories on their travels compensated. It included the 6-0 defeat of Queens Park Rangers, the club's biggest in the league away since 1962. Dwight Gayle's 23 goals, including hat-tricks against Norwich and Birmingham, made him the first Newcastle player since Alan Shearer to score 20 or more in a season.

Aarons R 1 (3)	Clark C 34	Gayle D.................... 26 (6)
Ameobi S .... - (4)	Colback J 24 (5)	Gouffran Y 33 (6)
Anita V 24 (3)	Darlow K........................34	Haidara M.................. - (1)
Armstrong A .... - (2)	Diame M 27 (10)	Hanley G 5 (5)
Atsu C 15 (17)	Dummett P 44 (1)	Hayden I................. 28 (5)
Ayoze Perez 25 (11)	Elliot R 3	Janmaat D 2

Jesus Gamez	2 (3)	Mitrovic A	11 (14)	Shelvey J	38 (4)
Lascelles J	41 (2)	Murphy D	7 (8)	Sterry J	- (2)
Lazaar A	- (4)	Ritchie M	40 (2)	Tiote C	- (1)
Mbemba C	12	Sels M	9	Yedlin D	21 (6)

League goals (85): Gayle 23, Ritchie 12, Ayoze Perez 9, Atsu 5, Gouffran 5, Murphy 5, Shelvey 5, Mitrovic 4, Clark 3, Diame 3, Lascelles 3, Hayden 2, Hanley 1, Mbemba 1, Yedlin 1, Opponents 3
FA Cup goals (4): Ritchie 2, Gouffran 1, Murphy 1. **League Cup goals** (11): Ayoze Perez 3, Diame 3, Mitrovic 2, Ritchie 2, Gouffran 1
Average home league attendance: 51,106. **Player of Year**: Ciaran Clark

NORWICH CITY

There were times during a topsy-turvy season when Norwich looked every inch a side capable of making an immediate return to the Premier League. There were others when they were ordinary and uninspired. The inconsistency left them hopelessly adrift of automatic promotion and a distance away from the play-offs. Alex Neil's side topped the table three times in the opening few weeks before a run of two wins in 12 games pushed them down into mid-table midway through the campaign. Nelson Oliveira's 'perfect' hat-trick of left foot, right foot and header against Derby ended that sequence. It was followed soon after by 15 goals scored in six matches, which delivered a place four points away from the top-six, but another lean run, this time spanning five games, led to Neil's dismissal. With coach Alan Irvine appointed until the end of the season, Norwich again showed what might have been by thrashing fourth-place Reading 7-1, six of their goals coming in the first-half. They also overcame leaders Brighton, albeit fortuitously with two own goals by goalkeeper David Stockdale, on the way to 20 goals in the final six fixtures. Norwich, joint top scorers on 85 with Newcastle and Fulham, then appointed Borussia Dortmund's Daniel Farke as the new manager.

Bassong S	8 (1)	Jerome C	31 (9)	Oliveira N	16 (12)
Bennett R	24 (9)	Klose T	31 (1)	Olsson M	16 (3)
Brady R	22 (1)	Lafferty K	- (12)	Pritchard A	19 (11)
Canos S	1 (2)	Maddison J	- (3)	Ruddy J	27
Dijks M	15	Martin R	36 (1)	Tettey A	33 (2)
Dorrans G	22 (1)	McGovern M	19 (1)	Thompson L	1 (2)
Godfrey B	- (2)	Mulumbu Y	7 (6)	Whittaker S	7 (5)
Hoolahan W	30 (3)	Murphy Jacob	32 (6)	Wildschut Y	6 (3)
Howson J	37 (1)	Murphy Josh	9 (18)		
Pinto I	37	Naismith S	20 (9)		

League goals (85): Jerome 16, Oliveira 11, Murphy Jacob 9, Hoolahan 7, Dorrans 6, Howson 6, Pritchard 6, Naismith 5, Brady 4, Murphy Josh 4, Dijks 1, Pinto 1, Klose 1, Lafferty 1, Maddison 1, Martin 1, Olsson 1, Wildschut 1, Opponents 3
FA Cup goals (2): Naismith 1, Whittaker 1. **League Cup goals** (10): Canos 2, Godfrey 1, Lafferty 1, Martin 1, Murphy Jacob 1, Murphy Josh 1, Naismith 1, Oliveira 1, Pritchard 1
Average home league attendance: 26,354. **Player of Year**: Wes Hoolahan

NOTTINGHAM FOREST

Forest beat the drop by the skin of their teeth, thanks to Britt Assombalonga's goals at a crucial time. Mark Warburton's side were clinging to a place just above the relegation zone when the Congolese striker, who missed most of the previous season with a knee injury, scored twice in the penultimate home game against Reading for a 3-2 win. Then, in the last one in front of a 28,000 crowd at the City Ground, he netted two more, one from the penalty spot, against Ipswich. Chris

Cohen got his first at home for six years on his 300th appearance for the club in a 3-0 victory which enabled Forest to stay ahead of Blackburn with a superior goal difference of two. Forest had spent much of the season on the fringe of the bottom three, having lost too many matches after scoring first. Philippe Montanier, in charge for seven months, was sacked the day after the collapse of a takeover bid for the club by an American consortium – the sixth manager dismissed since Kuwati Fawaz Al-Hasawi assumed control in 2012. Gary Brazil took over as caretaker for the second time and after a successful start was given the job, supposedly for the remainder of the campaign. Instead, a run of five defeats in seven matches led to Warburton's appointment, a month after his acrimonious departure from Rangers.

Ahmedhodzic A .... - (1)	Henderson S 11 (1)	Pereira H 16 (6)
Assombalonga B 20 (12)	Hobbs J 9	Perquis D...................17
Bendtner N 7 (8)	Iacovitti A 2	Pinillos D................ 14 (2)
Brereton B 13 (5)	Kasami P 19 (6)	Smith J................... 14 (1)
Burke O 4 (1)	Lam T 11 (8)	Stojkovic V...................20
Carayol M 13 (6)	Lansbury H 16 (1)	Traore A 2 (2)
Cash M.................. 18 (10)	Lica 2 (3)	Vaughan D 25 (6)
Clough Z 9 (5)	Lichaj E 39 (2)	Veldwijk L...........................1
Cohen C........................20	Mancienne M 24 (4)	Vellios A 12 (16)
De Vries D.......................1	McCormack R............ 3 (4)	Ward J 13 (5)
Dumitru N................. 6 (4)	Mills M 24 (3)	Worrall J...................21
Fox D 22 (1)	Osborn B 45 (1)	
Grant J 4 (2)	Paterson J.................. - (1)	

League goals (62): Assombalonga 14, Lansbury 6, Vellios 6, Burke 4, Clough 4, Osborn 4, Brereton 3, Bendtner 2, Kasami 2, Lam 2, Lichaj 2, Pereira 2, Perquis 2, Carayol 1, Cohen 1, Dumitru 1, McCormack 1, Mills 1, Pinillos 1, Ward 1, Opponents 2
FA Cup goals: None. League Cup goals (4): Paterson 1, Vaughan 1, Veldwijk 1, Ward 1
Average home league attendance: 20,333. **Player of Year**: Eric Lichaj

PRESTON NORTH END

Simon Grayson's team overcame a miserable start to the season to climb to the fringes of a play-off place, before a disappointing finish resulted in a mid-table finish. They lost five of the first six matches – all by a single-goal margin and were second from bottom after the first month. The boost of a 3-0 victory over Cardiff was immediately overshadowed by a 5-0 defeat by Brentford. Then, Preston settled into a degree of consistency which dispelled any prospect of a relegation struggle. They reached as high as eighth and a 5-0 victory over Bristol City moved them to within five points of Sheffield Wednesday with six fixtures left. That was as good as it got. A tough run-in leaked 13 goals against Leeds, Huddersfield, Norwich and Newcastle, they were held by relegated Rotherham and lost the last game 1-0 to Wolves. It meant a repeat of the previous season's 11th place, with Grayson admitting that if he had been offered, at the start of the season, a finish above Aston Villa he would have taken it. He was later named Sunderland's manager. In came former Norwich manager Alex Neil.

Baptisie A................ 23 (1)	Garner J..........................2	May S........................ 2 (3)
Barkhuizen T.......... 12 (5)	Grimshaw L............ 3 (2)	McGeady A 32 (2)
Beckford J 4 (14)	Horgan D 10 (9)	Pearson B 29 (2)
Boyle A...........................7	Hugill J 35 (9)	Pringle B 7 (3)
Browne A 21 (10)	Humphrey C............ 4 (6)	Robinson C 34 (8)
Browning T 8	Huntington P......... 26 (7)	Spurr T 11 (7)
Clarke T........................42	Johnson D............. 30 (10)	Vermijl M 13 (5)
Cunningham G 40	Lindegaard A...................8	Welsh J..............................6
Doyle E 6 (5)	Makienok S 7 (18)	Wright B...................18
Gallagher P 28 (3)	Maxwell C......................38	

League goals (64): Hugill 12, Robinson 10, McGeady 8, Barkhuizen 6, Clarke 4, Johnson 4, Baptiste 3, Makienok 3, Horgan 2, Vermijl 2, Beckford 1, Cunningham 1, Doyle 1, Gallagher 1, Huntington 1, May 1, Pearson 1, Spurr 1, Opponents 2
FA Cup goals (1): Robinson 1. **League Cup goals** (6): Makienok 3, Doyle 2, Hugill 1
Average home league attendance: 12,607. **Player of Year:** Aiden McGeady

QUEENS PARK RANGERS

Rangers survived a late-season scare to preserve their Championship status. A 5-1 victory over Rotherham took Ian Holloway's side ten points clear of the relegation zone and within reach of a mid-table finish. Instead, six successive defeats, all by a single-goal margin, sent them sliding into a nervy penultimate match against fellow strugglers Nottingham Forest at Loftus Road. They came through 2-0 with goals from Conor Washington and Joel Lynch to go clear and transfer all the pressure on Forest for the final day of the regular campaign. It had been an eventful few months for Holloway in his second spell as manager of the club – ten years after the first ended – following the dismissal of Jimmy Floyd Hasselbaink. His first match brought a 2-1 victory over Norwich after remarkable start, with Norwich's Martin Olsson sent off for handling on the goal line and Tjaronn Chery missing the resulting penalty inside the first two minutes. That, too, was followed by a run of six straight losses, which eventually gave way to a much more settled spell in the New Year.

Bidwell J. 36	Grego-Cox R .... - (1)	Perch J. 29 (3)
Borysiuk A 8 (3)	Hall G. 34	Petrasso M. 1 (1)
Bowler J .... - (1)	Hamalainen N 1 (2)	Polter S 12 (8)
Caulker S. 12 (1)	Henry K 13 (1)	Robinson J. 7
Chery T. 22	Kakay O. .... - (1)	Sandro 3 (3)
Comley B .... - (1)	LuaLua K. .... ? (9)	Shodipo O. 5 (6)
Cousins J. 17 (1)	Luongo M 35	Smith M 13 (3)
Doughty M 2 (2)	Lynch J. 28 (2)	Smithies A. 46
El Khayati A. 1 (5)	Mackie J. 11 (7)	Sylla I. 14 (18)
Freeman L 12 (4)	Manning R 17 (1)	Washington C 26 (14)
Furlong D. 13 (1)	Morrison R 1 (4)	Wszolek P 23 (6)
Gladwin B. 3 (4)	Ngbakoto Y 13 (13)	
Goss S. 3 (3)	Onuoha N 43 (1)	

League goals (52): Sylla 10, Washington 7, Chery 4, Polter 4, Smith 4, Ngbakoto 3, Lynch 3, Onuoha 3, Wszolek 3, Caulker 2, Freeman 2, LuaLua 1, Luongo 1, Mackie 1, Manning 1, Opponents 3
FA Cup goals (1): Bidwell 1. **League Cup goals** (5) Sandro 3, Ngbakoto 1, Washington 1
Average home league attendance: 14,616. **Player of Year:** Alex Smithies

READING

Jaap Stam pledged to stay on and launch another promotion bid after losing a penalty shoot-out at Wembley. The former Manchester United defender led his side to third place in his first season as manager, then on to the Play-off Final with a 2-1 aggregate victory over Fulham, delivered by Yann Kermorgant's spot-kick in normal time. After a goalless 120 minutes, they gained an early advantage when Ali Al Habsi saved Huddersfield's second penalty. Kermorgant, Danny Williams and Liam Kelly put them 3-2 ahead, then Liam Moore drove over the bar, Jordan Obita had his kick saved and they lost 4-3. Reading had moved into the top-six in late October and stayed there for the rest of the season. They were always adrift of the top two, Newcastle and Brighton, but rarely came under pressure to surrender their own position. A 7-1 defeat at Norwich, where six goals were conceded in the first-half, had little effect, Stam describing it as a painful 'one-off.' Reading quickly regrouped to win four of their five final matches, scoring ten goals, to carry plenty of momentum in the knockout phase.

Al Habsi A	46	Kermorgant Y	.... 34 (8)	Quinn S	.... 1 (6)
Beerens R	.... 37 (3)	McCleary G	.... 39 (2)	Rakels D	.... 1 (1)
Blackett T	.... 33 (1)	McShane P	.... 29 (2)	Samuel D	.... 6 (3)
Cooper J	.... - (3)	Meite Y	.... 1 (13)	Swift J	.... 31 (5)
Evans G	.... 24 (11)	Mendes J	.... 2 (10)	Tiago Ilori	.... 2 (3)
Grabban L	.... 7 (9)	Moore L	40	Van den Berg J	.... 25 (2)
Gravenberch D	.... - (2)	Mutch J	.... 8 (1)	Watson T	.... - (3)
Gunter C	46	Obita J	.... 28 (9)	Williams D	.... 36 (5)
Harriott C	.... 3 (9)	Oxford R	.... 2 (3)		
Kelly L	.... 21 (7)	Popa A	.... 4 (4)		

Play-offs – appearances: Al Habsi 3, Blackett 3, Evans 3, Grabban 3, Gunter 3, Kermorgant 3, Moore 3, Swift 3, Williams 3, Tiago Ilori 2 (1), Van den Berg 2 (1), Obita 1 (1), McShane 1, Kelly – (2), McCleary – (2), Mendes – (1)
League goals (68): Kermorgant Y 18, McCleary 9, Swift 8, Beerens 6, Williams 4, Grabban 3, McShane 3, Mendes 3, Evans 2, Obita 2, Samuel 2, Gunter 1, Harriott 1, Kelly 1, Meite 1, Moore 1, Mutch 1, Popa 1, Opponents 1. **Play-offs – goals (2)**: Kermorgant 1, Obita 1
FA Cup goals: None. **League Cup goals** (6): Harriott 2, Beerens 1, Quinn 1, Swift 1, Van den Berg 1
Average home league attendance: 17,505. **Player of Year**: Ali Al Habsi

ROTHERHAM UNITED

Rotherham flirted with relegation in the two previous years, but this time there was no escape. They were the first team in the four divisions to go down – with seven matches still to play – amid another season of managerial upheaval. Alan Stubbs, in charge for 14 matches, was sacked in late October with his team bottom – a position occupied for the remainder of the campaign. Kenny Jackett, formerly in charge of Wolves, resigned after 39 days, five games and a single point. Coach Paul Warne, who had a long playing career at the club, became their sixth manager in 15 months, initially as caretaker, then appointed until the end of the season and finally given the job on a permanent basis, four days after the drop was confirmed by a home defeat by promotion-chasing Fulham which left his side 24 points adrift. He had then suffered 18 losses in 22 league games and admitted he was resigned to looking for another job. Warne never really stood much chance of turning things round, prompting chairman Tony Stewart to insist he had impressed the board 'in a number of areas in what has been a very difficult situation' and deserved the stay in the job. Some light relief came with a first win for three months, 1-0 against Ipswich courtesy of a goal from Tom Adeyemi in the penultimate home game.

Adeyemi T	.... 28 (1)	Ekstrand J	1	Odemwingie P	.... 3 (4)
Ajayi S	17	Fisher D	.... 33 (1)	Price L	.... 16 (1)
Allan S	.... 4 (6)	Forde A	.... 20 (12)	Purrington B	.... 7 (3)
Bailey-King D	.... - (1)	Forster-Caskey J	.... 5 (1)	Smallwood R	.... 20 (5)
Ball D	.... 12 (1)	Frecklington L	.... 18 (4)	Taylor J	.... 35 (7)
Belaid A	.... 14 (3)	Fry D	10	Thorpe T	.... - (2)
Blackstock D	.... 4 (12)	Halford G	.... 10 (4)	Vaulks W	.... 31 (9)
Bray A	.... - (5)	Kelly S	.... 16 (4)	Ward D	.... 40 (1)
Broadfoot K	3	Mattock J	.... 33 (3)	Wilson K	8
Brown I	.... 17 (3)	Morris C	.... 6 (2)	Wood R	.... 28 (1)
Camp L	18	Newell J	.... 28 (6)	Yates J	.... 7 (14)
Clarke-Harris J	.... 2 (5)	McDonnell R	12		

League goals (40): Ward 11, Adeyemi 6, Taylor 4, Brown 3, Belaid 2, Forde 2, Newell 2, Wood 2, Ajayi 1, Blackstock 1, Frecklington 1, Smallwood 1, Vaulks 1, Yates 1, Opponents 2
FA Cup goals (2): Adeyemi 1, Ward 1. **League Cup goals** (4): Yates 2, Forde 1, Halford 1
Average home league attendance: 9,783. **Player of Year**: Tom Adeyemi

SHEFFIELD WEDNESDAY

Wednesday experienced play-off disappointment for the second successive season. They lost at Wembley in 2016 to a spectacular goal by Hull's Mohamed Diame. This time, the chances of a long-cherished return to the Premier League were ended on penalties in the semi-finals against Huddersfield, a side they had beaten twice in the regular season. After a goalless draw in the first leg, Wednesday were favourites to go through at a packed Hillsborough. Steven Fletcher headed in a cross from Barry Bannan, but an own goal by Tom Lees pegged them back. Then, Sam Hutchinson and Fernando Forestieri had spot-kicks saved and the shoot-out was lost 4-3. Wednesday had carried considerable momentum into the knock-out stage with a strong finish to the regular season. A spell of one win in six games had put their place in jeopardy. But after dropping out of the top-six, there were six successive wins – including a second of the campaign against champions-to-be Newcastle – and qualification was confirmed when Kieran Lee scored the only goal at Ipswich in the penultimate match.

Abdi A	11 (5)	Hunt J	31 (1)	Palmer L	15 (6)
Bannan B	42 (1)	Hutchinson S	33	Pudil D	26
Buckley W	2 (9)	Jones D	18 (11)	Reach A	36 (3)
Dawson C	2 (2)	Lee K	26	Rhodes J	14 (4)
Emanuelson U	- (1)	Lees T	35	Sasso V	12 (2)
Fletcher S	22 (16)	Loovens G	29 (3)	Semedo J	2 (8)
Forestieri F	25 (10)	Lucas Joao	7 (3)	Wallace R	32 (9)
Fox M	10	Matias M	1 (1)	Westwood K	43
Hirst G	- (1)	McManaman C	2 (9)	Wildsmith J	1
Hooper G	17 (6)	Nuhiu A	2 (18)	Winnall S	10 (4)

Play-offs – appearances: Bannan 2, Fletcher 2, Forestieri 2, Hunt 2, Lee 2, Lees 2, Loovens 2, Pudil 2, Westwood 2, Wallace 2, Reach 1 (1), Hutchinson 1, Rhodes – (2), Jones – (1), Nuhiu – (1), Winnall – (1)
League goals (60): Forestieri 12, Fletcher 10, Hooper 6, Lee 5, Wallace 5, Reach 3, Rhodes 3, Winnall 3, Hutchinson 2, Pudil 2, Sasso 2, Abdi 1, Bannan 1, Fox 1, Lees 1, Loovens 1, Opponents 2. **Play-offs – goals (1):** Fletcher 1
FA Cup goals: None. **League Cup goals (1):** Lucas Joao 1
Average home league attendance: 27,129 **Player of Year:** Keiren Westwood

WIGAN ATHLETIC

Two managerial changes failed to save Wigan from an immediate return to the game's third tier. Gary Caldwell, who led them to the League One title in 2016, was sacked two-and-a-half months into the season with his side second from bottom. His replacement, Manchester United's reserve team manager Warren Joyce, led a mini-revival with back-to-back wins over Burton and Brentford. It was not maintained and Joyce was dismissed, a fortnight after undergoing eye surgery, having been in charge for four months. Graham Barrow, who had five years as a player with the club, took over as caretaker until the end of the campaign, with Wigan four points from safety. That increased to seven before former Manchester United midfielder Nick Powell returned from a three-month injury lay-off to score a stoppage-time winner against Rotherham. A week later, Powell came off the bench to score a hat-trick in 11 minutes and transform a two-goal deficit against Barnsley into another 3-2 victory. He was also on the mark against Brighton, but too late to prevent a 2-1 defeat which took their opponents into the Premier League. After that, Wigan shared a goalless draw with Cardiff and were relegated when losing to the only goal of the game against Reading in the penultimate game. Fresh from leading Portsmouth to the League Two title, Paul Cook was appointed the new manager.

Dogdan A	17	Burke L	4 (1)	Buxton J	39
Bogle O	12 (2)	Burke R	10	Byrne J	- (2)
Bruce A	- (2)	Burn D	39 (3)	Byrne N	6 (8)

Chow T .... - (1)
Colclough R 2 (8)
Connolly C 14 (3)
Daniels D .... - (1)
Davies C 1 (13)
Flores J .... - (2)
Garbutt L 7 (1)
Gilbey A 11 (4)
Gilks M 13 (1)
Gomez J 12 (3)
Grigg W 24 (9)

Hanson J 14 (3)
Haugaard J 8
Jaaskeklainen J 8 (1)
Jacobs M 39 (4)
Kellett A 4 (1)
Knoyle K .... - (1)
Laurent J .... - (1)
Le Fondre A 3 (9)
MacDonald S 36 (3)
Mandron M 1 (2)
Morgan C 15 (5)

Morsy S 13 (2)
Obertan G 7 (5)
Perkins D 24 (3)
Powell N 10 (11)
Power M 40 (2)
Tunnicliffe R 8 (1)
Warnock S 45
Weir J 1 (3)
Wildschut Y 19 (6)
Woolery K .... - (1)

League goals (40): Powell 6, Grigg 5, Wildschut 4, Bogle 3, Gomez 3, Jacobs 3, Connolly 2, Gilbey 2, Burke R 1, Burn 1, Buxton 1, Davies 1, Le Fondre 1, MacDonald 1, Morsy 1, Obertan 1, Tunnicliffe 1, Opponents 3
FA Cup goals (2): Grigg 1, Wildschut 1. **League Cup goals** (1): Grigg 1
Average home league attendance: 11,722. **Player of Year**: Dan Burn

WOLVERHAMPTON WANDERERS

Eleven home defeats, the worst in the Championship apart from rock bottom Rotherham, exposed Wolves to another disappointing season. It came amid managerial upheaval, first when Kenny Jackett was sacked by the club's new Chinese owners a week the campaign kicked-off. He was replaced by Walter Zenga, former Sampdoria and Palermo coach, who made nine signings by August 27, but lasted just 87 days before he was dismissed after a run of one point from five games. That brought in Paul Lambert, formerly in charge of Blackburn, Aston Villa and Norwich, who had some modest success before five successive defeats left his side a single point off the bottom three. The rollercoaster continued as Wolves reeled off five straight victories, including a 3-1 success against promotion-minded Fulham at Craven Cottage, to banish fears of a relegation struggle. They climbed to 15th and that's where they finished, one place lower than in 2016. Lambert then left and former Porto and Valencia coach Nuno Espirito Santo became the club's fourth manager in ten months.

Batth D...........................39
Bodvarsson J D........ 22 (20)
Borthwick-Jackson C.........6
Burgoyne H.......................6
Cavaleiro I 17 (14)
Coady C 35 (5)
Dicko N 19 (11)
Doherty M 41 (1)
Edwards D 42 (2)
Enobakhare B............. 8 (5)
Evans L 12 (3)
Gibbs-White M 2 (5)

Gladon P................... 1 (1)
Graham J 1 (1)
Helder Costa 30 (5)
Hause K 23 (1)
Henry J 1 (1)
Ikeme C.........................31
Iorfa D 21 (1)
John O .... - (2)
Lonergan A 9 (2)
Marshall B 13 (3)
Mason J 9 (10)
Oniangue P 8 (2)

Price J 17 (2)
Ronan C 3 (1)
Saiss R 19 (5)
Saville G 15 (9)
Silvio 4
Stearman R..................18
Teixeira J 9 (8)
Wallace J 5 (4)
Weimann A 15 (4)
Williamson M 5
Wilson D .... - (1)
Weir J 1 (3)

League goals (54): Edwards 10, Helder Costa 10, Cavaleiro 5, Batth 4, Doherty 4, Bodvarsson 3, Dicko 3, Mason 3, Hause 2, Marshall 2, Oniangue 2, Teixeira 2, Weimann 2, Saville 1, Opponents 1
FA Cup goals (4): Doherty 1, Helder Costa 1, Stearman 1, Weimann 1. **League Cup goals** (4): Coady 1, Helder Costa 1, Mason 1, Wallace 1
Average home league attendance: 21,570. **Player of Year**: Helder Costa

LEAGUE ONE

AFC WIMBLEDON

Throughout their rise to Football League status via the pyramid system, Wimbledon longed for the chance to meet – and beat – arch-rivals MK Dons, the reincarnation of the old Plough Lane club, on equal terms. Their victory in the 2016 League Two play-offs, accompanied by Dons' relegation from the Championship, finally brought them together, initially at stadiummk a fortnight before Christmas when the home side were 1-0 winners. Three months later, Wimbledon turned the tables with goals from Jake Reeves and Lyle Taylor for a 2-0 victory. At that point, they were sitting comfortably in mid-table with no relegation worries and every chance to strike out for a top-half finish. Instead, the goals dried up and they failed to score in eight of the remaining nine matches, the exception being a 3-1 victory over Rochdale. That left them in 15th place, three below Dons but still able to look back on a satisfactory season. One downside was defeat by Sutton in the third round of the FA Cup.

Antwi J .... - (1)	Francomb G.............. 31 (3)	Poleon D ,.............. 19 (22)
Barcham A............... 32 (5)	Fuller R.......................28	Reeves J.....................46
Barnett T 11 (25)	Kaja E...................... - (1)	Robertson C.................13
Beere T................... 3 (5)	Kelly S................. 22 (4)	Robinson P.................43
Bulman D 31 (7)	McDonnell J 3	Shea J.......................36
Charles D 32 (4)	Meades J............... 22 (2)	Sibbick T 1 (1)
Clarke R 7	Nightingale W 10 (2)	Soares T.......................15
Egan A 3 (6)	Oakley G .... - (2)	Taylor L................. 36 (7)
Elliott T 30 (9)	Owens S................... 2 (1)	Whelpdale C ,,..............8 (9)
Fitzpatrick D 2 (4)	Parrett D 20 (12)	

League goals (52): Taylor 10, Elliott 9, Poleon 8, Barcham 5, Parrett 5, Barnett 2, Charles 2, Francomb 2, Kelly 2, Meades 2, Robinson 2, Reeves 1, Robertson 1, Whelpdale 1
FA Cup goals (12): Elliott 4, Poleon 3, Taylor 2, Barnett 1, Parrett 1, Robinson 1. **League Cup goals (2):** Taylor 1, Whelpdale 1. **League Trophy goals (6):** Barnett 2, Poleon 2, Barcham 1, Taylor 1
Average home league attendance: 4,477 **Player of Year:** Tom Elliott

BOLTON WANDERERS

A year on from relegation to League One continuing the club's fall from grace, Bolton bounced back under new manager Phil Parkinson after a flying start to the season and a crucial win at the end of it. They finished runners-up to Sheffield United and there were 22,000 fans to see it. Maximum points from four matches represented the club's best opening for 82 years. It was followed by seven without a win – then five successive victories without conceding a goal. Leading scorer Zach Clough moved to Nottingham Forest in the winter transfer window, but the return of Adam Le Fondre for a second loan spell brought him five goals in five games as Bolton put together another purple patch to open up a six-point cushion in second place. There was another wobble that opened the door to a challenge from Fleetwood – a single goal in five games. But central defender David Wheater's eighth goal of the campaign helped steady the ship by victory over Port Vale. Then, a 3-0 success against Peterborough clinched it – Jem Karacan netting his first for club, followed by Wheater's ninth and another for Le Fondre.

Alnwick B 20 (1)	Clough Z................. 17 (6)	Karacan J 2 (3)
Ameobi S............... 15 (5)	Davies M................. 4 (1)	Le Fondre A 17 (2)
Anderson K 3 (5)	Derik 19 (6)	Long C........................ 3 (7)
Beevers M.....................45	Dervite D 13 (1)	Madine G.......................36
Buxton L........................9	Henry J............... 12 (18)	Morais F.......................19
Clayton M .... - (10)	Howard M 26 (1)	Moxey D 16 (3)

Pratley D	11 (1)	Taylor C	3 (13)	Wheater D	43
Proctor J	7 (14)	Thorpe T	16 (5)	Wilkinson C	2 (7)
Solomon-Otabor V	- (4)	Trotter L	17 (3)	Wilson L	18
Spearing J	36 (1)	Vela J	45 (1)	Woolery K	- (1)
Taylor A	31 (3)	Warbara R	1		

League goals (68): Clough 9, Madine 9, Vela 9, Wheater 9, Beevers 7, Le Fondre 6, Spearing 3, Ameobi 2, Morais 2, Trotter 2, Anderson 1, Clayton 1, Henry 1, Karacan 1, Long 1, Thorpe 1, Wilson 1, Opponents 3
FA Cup goals (5): Ameobi 1, Henry 1, Madine 1, Trotter 1, Vela 1. **League Cup goals** (2): Proctor 1, Woolery 1. **League Trophy goals** (1): Ameobi 1
Average home league attendance: 15,194. **Player of Year**: David Wheater

BRADFORD CITY

Bradford were left to reflect on what might have been after losing the Play-off Final. They enjoyed enough possession and created sufficient chances to have been in front before Steve Morison's 85th minute goal gave Millwall the verdict. Stuart McCall, in his second spell as manager, and his players then had to endure an unpleasant pitch invasion by Millwall fans, which even match-winner Morison admitted had spoiled the occasion for his side. Bradford also had to look back on a home record which, on one hand, showed them unbeaten throughout the campaign – Tottenham were the only other team to do that – but on the other displayed 12 drawn matches. Not until the final few weeks of the season did they produce consistent form at Valley Parade, beating Peterborough, Swindon, Walsall, Oxford and Wimbledon to confirm a top-six place. In the semi-finals, they defeated Fleetwood 1-0 with a 77th minute Rory McArdle goal and maintained the advantage in a goalless draw in the return leg.

Jones A	9 (6)	Hiwula J	26 (15)	Morais F	4 (13)
Anderson P	- (3)	Hudson E	- (1)	Penney M	- (1)
Clarke B	25 (8)	Kilgallom M	6 (1)	Pybus D	- (1)
Cullen J	40	Knight-Percival N	42	Rabiega V	- (1)
Darby S	19 (3)	Law N	37 (3)	Sattelmaier R	2
Devine D	8 (3)	Marshall M	38 (4)	Toner K	2
Dieng T	28 (11)	McArdle R	22 (2)	Vincelot R	45
Doyle C	44	McMahon T	25	Vuckic H	4 (6)
Gilliead A	5 (4)	McNulty M	5 (10)	Webb-Foster R	- (1)
Hanson J	13 (4)	Meredith J	41	Wyke C	16

Play-offs – appearances: Clarke 3, Cullen 3, Doyle 3, Knight-Percival 3, Law 3, Marshall 3, McArdle 3, McMahon 3, Meredith 3, Vincelot 3, Wyke 3, Dieng – (3), Darby – (1), Hiwula – (1), Jones – (1), Gilliead – (1)
League goals (62): Hiwula 9, Clarke 7, Wyke 7, Marshall 6, McMahon 6, Jones 5, Hanson 4, Law 4, Dieng 3, Meredith 2, Vincelot 2, Cullen 1, McArdle 1, McNulty 1, Morais 1, Toner 1, Vyuckic 1. **Play-offs – goals** (1): McArdle 1
FA Cup goals (1): Opponents 1. **League Cup goals**: None. **League Trophy goals** (8): Hiwula 3, Vuckic 3, Dieng 1, Law 1
Average home league attendance: 18,167. **Player of Year**: Mark Marshall

BRISTOL ROVERS

Rovers returned to the game's third tier with a place in the top half of the table at the end of a season which provided plenty of talking points. Not least was the £300,000 sale of leading marksman Matty Taylor to Bristol City, the first from Rovers to City in 30 years, in the winter transfer window. Billy Bodin ensured the goals kept flowing and there were notable contributions from two other players. Ellis Harrison scored four times in the 5-0 defeat of Northampton, including a seven-minute first-half hat trick, while Byron Moore netted the club's fastest-ever league goal, in 11 seconds for victory at Wimbledon. That kept alive slim hopes of a play-off place. But a 3-1 defeat at Gillingham in the next match virtually ruled them out of contention and Rovers' defensive frailties were evident again in the two final fixtures as four goals were conceded to Peterborough, and Millwall. They had also shipped four in their first meeting with Millwall and conceded nine in two games with Charlton.

Boateng H.....................9	Harris R 4 (1)	McChrystal M 3 (1)
Bodin B 27 (9)	Harrison E 25 (12)	Mildenhall S....................4
Broom R ....- (5)	Hartley P 17 (1)	Montano C..............12 (13)
Brown L.....................40	James L 10 (14)	Moore B 12 (15)
Burn J 1 (1)	Lawrence L.................1 (3)	Partington J...............4 (3)
Clarke J 19 (3)	Leadbitter D 28 (2)	Puddy W 7
Clarke O 30	Lines C 40 (4)	Roberts C 2
Clarke-Salter J...........9 (3)	Lockyer T.....................46	Roos K 16 (1)
Colkett C 8 (7)	Lucas J ....- (1)	Sinclair S................37 (1)
Easter J 9 (12)	Lumley J 19	Sweeney R 16
Gaffney R 22 (12)	Mansell L 4 (5)	Taylor M 23 (4)

League goals (68): Taylor 16, Bodin 13, Harrison 8, Gaffney 6, Hartley 5, Clarke O 4, Easter 4, Colkett 3, Lines 3, Moore 2, Clarke-Salter 1, Montano 1, Sinclair 1, Opponents 1
FA Cup goals (6): Gaffney 3, Taylor 2, Brown 1. **League Cup goals** (3): Harrison 1, Hartley 1, Lines 1. **League Trophy goals** (2): Easter 1, Taylor 1
Average home league attendance: 9,302. **Player of Year**: Ollie Clarke

BURY

James Vaughan's goals enabled his side to retain their League One status. He scored 24, second only to Sheffield United's Billy Sharp, including a brace in a 3-0 victory over Northampton in the penultimate match which took Bury to the brink of safety. They lost the final fixture at Southend, but finished with one point to spare over the fourth bottom club, Port Vale. Vaughan's tally included four in a 5-1 victory over Peterborough. He was also on the mark as his side transformed a 3-0 deficit at Walsall into a 3-3 draw. Five successive wins took Bury to second place after ten matches. Losing to leaders Scunthorpe was the start of a dramatic slide which resulted in club record 12 successive defeats, leaving them third from bottom at Christmas. David Flitcroft, the division's manager of the month for September, paid the price after another defeat, 5-0 against Wimbledon in the FA Cup. Caretaker Chris Brass was given the job until the end of the season, but there was another change when Lee Clark left Kilmarnock to become the club's permanent manager.

Barnett L 24	Hope H 17 (16)	Moore T 18 (1)
Beadling T 2	Ismail Z 12 (4)	Murphy J.....................16
Bedeau J 6 (1)	Jones C 12 (1)	Pennant J.................2 (5)
Brown R 7	Kay A..........................42	Pope T 33 (4)
Bryan K 6 (6)	Lainton R 7	Rachubka P...................1
Burgess C 18	Leigh G 45	Soares T 26
Burgess S 14 (2)	Lowe R...................7 (5)	Styles C 12 (1)
Caddis P....................13	Mackreth J 1 (2)	Tutte A..................10 (7)
Cameron N 3 (1)	Maher N 14 (3)	Vaughan J 36 (1)
Clark N 2 (1)	Mayor D 17 (4)	Walker T.................1 (10)
Danns N 13 (5)	Mellis J 31 (4)	Williams B 22
Dudley A..................- (3)	Miller G..................5 (23)	
Etuhu K...................11 (9)	Miller I......................- (3)	

League goals (61): Vaughan 24, Miller G 7, Pope 4, Hope 3, Ismail 3, Mayor 3, Mellis 3, Burgess S 2, Danns 2, Etuhu 2, Soares 2, Barnett 1, Brown 1, Leigh 1, Lowe 1, Tutte 1, Opponents 1
FA Cup goals (2): Hope 2. **League Cup goals** (2): Maher 1, Pope 1. **League Trophy goals** (6): Pope 2, Ismail 1, Kay 1, Miller G 1, Walker 1
Average home league attendance: 3,845. **Player of Year**: James Vaughan

CHARLTON ATHLETIC

Another season of under-achievement and supporters' protests at The Valley. The fans continued to call for a change of ownership as their team struggled to mount any sort of challenge for an immediate return to the Championship. They did see another change of manager, with Russell Slade sacked after six months in charge, having apologised for a 3-0 defeat by Swindon which left his side 15th. Slade, who had made eight summer signings, was replaced by Karl Robinson, a month after his own dismissal by MK Dons. Roland Duchatelet's seventh appointment since the Belgian businessman bought the club in January 2014 had the satisfaction of a 1-0 win over his former club, delivered by a goal from 19-year-old Ademola Lookman, who joined Everton for £11m shortly afterwards. Charlton also had a 4-1 win over Bristol Rovers, with Josh Magennis scoring a hat-trick. But they dropped back into the bottom half of the table after a run of 14 games brought a single victory. And a strong finish to the campaign, four wins in five, was not enough to lift them into the top sector.

Ahearne-Grant K......... 1 (7)	Fox M 24	Mavididi S 3 (2)
Ajose N.................... 17 (4)	Hanlan B .... - (9)	Novak L................ 13 (16)
Aribo J 13 (6)	Holmes R 31 (4)	Page L..........................8
Barnes A .... - (1)	Holmes-Dennis T .... - (1)	Pearce J 23
Bauer P 34 (2)	Jackson J................ 22 (8)	Phillips D.......................8
Botaka J 8 (18)	Da Silva J 6 (4)	Rudd D.........................38
Byrne N 16 (1)	Johnson R 1 (1)	Solly C...........................27
Chicksen A.............. 15 (6)	Konsa E.................. 30 (2)	Teixeira J 15 (5)
Crofts A 41 (4)	Lennon H....................2	Ulvestad F 26 (1)
Foley K 12 (3)	Lookman A.............. 15 (6)	Umerah J.................... - (1)
Forster-Caskey J 12 (3)	Magennis J 36 (3)	Watt T 9 (7)

League goals (60): Holmes 13, Magennis 10, Ajose 6, Lookman 5, Bauer 4, Jackson 4, Teixeira 4, Botaka 2, Forster-Caskey 2, Novak 2, Watt 2, Byrne 1, Chicksen 1, Crofts 1, Pearce 1, Ulvestad 1, Opponents 1
FA Cup goals (4): Lookman 2, Chicksen 1, Jackson 1. **League Cup goals**: None. **League Trophy goals** (1): Ajose 1
Average home league attendance: 11,162. **Player of Year**: Ricky Holmes

CHESTERFIELD

Gary Caldwell learned quickly that success in management can be a fleeting affair. In his first season, the former Scotland defender led Wigan to the League One title and was named the division's manager of the year. In the second, he was sacked by the club after two months, returned in charge of Chesterfield and finished the campaign with his new team relegated. Caldwell took over at the Proact Stadium from Danny Wilson, fired after a patchy campaign took another turn for the worse over the Christmas and New Year period. He inherited a side third from bottom and struggling for goals, a predicament which showed no sign of improving. A first victory, 1-0 against Swindon, did not arrive until his eighth game in charge; the second, 1-0 against Port Vale, came seven matches after that. By then, Chesterfield were nine points from from safety. A 4-0 defeat at home to Southend, in which Dion Donohue was sent off, left them on the brink and the drop was confirmed three days later with a 3-1 reversal at Scunthorpe. They finished bottom 13 points adrift, with a club record 27 defeats.

Allinson L 5	Evans C 20 (5)	Maguire L 10 (1)
Anderson T 34 (1)	Evatt I 29 (1)	McGinn P 17 (1)
Angel.......................... 5 (4)	Faupala D 7 (7)	Mitchell R............. 16 (12)
Ariyibi G 24 (4)	Fulton R 26	Morrison C .... - (1)
Beesley J 4 (3)	Gardner D 22 (12)	Nolan J.................... 28 (2)
Brown R .... - (2)	German R 1 (6)	O'Neil L.........................17
Brownell J.................. - (1)	Graham L........................4	O'Shea J................... 23 (4)
Daley D...................... - (1)	Grimshaw L 10 (3)	Raglan C.........................1
Dennis K................... 26 (9)	Hird S 35	Rowley J..........................7
Dimaio C................... 17 (6)	Humphreys R .... - (2)	Simons R 6 (13)
Donohue D............... 36 (1)	Jones D 11 (3)	Stuckmann T...............15
Ebanks-Blake S 9 (4)	Kakay O 7 (1)	Wakefield C................. - (1)
El-Fitouri S 2	Liddle G 26	Wilkinson C 6 (6)

League goals (43): Dennis 8, O'Shea 6, Evans 5, Wilkinson 4, Anderson 2, Ebanks-Blake 2, Evatt 2, Gardner 2, Mitchell 2, O'Neil 2, Donohue 1, Faupala 1, Hird 1, Liddle 1, McGinn 1, Nolan 1, Rowley 1, Opponents 1
FA Cup goals (2): Evans 1, O'Shea 1. **League Cup goals** (1): McGinn 1. **League Trophy goals** (7): Dennis 2, Dimaio 1, Ebanks-Blake 1, Evans 1, Maguire 1, O'Shea 1
Average home league attendance: 5,929. **Player of Year:** Ian Evatt

COVENTRY CITY

Relegated to the game's fourth tier for the first time in 58 years; victory at Wembley 30 years after their FA Cup triumph. That was the bitter-sweet 'double' Coventry experienced during the season. Throw in three managers, supporters' protests and doubts expressed about continuing to play at the Ricoh Arena and it was a truly bizarre campaign. Tony Mowbray was the first to go, resigning after the opening ten matches without a win. Mark Venus, his No 2, spent three months as caretaker before Russell Slade, formerly in charge of Charlton and Cardiff, was appointed, supposedly until the end of the season, with the team still in the bottom two. He was sacked after ten weeks with Coventry 13 points adrift at the bottom, having won just one of his 13 matches. In came Mark Robins, appointed for the second time, four years after leaving the club to take over at Huddersfield. He had no chance of turning things round and the drop was confirmed – with three games remaining – by a 1-1 draw against Charlton when fans from both sides threw plastic pigs on the pitch in protest at their clubs' respective owners. Robins, at least, had the satisfaction of taking his new side to the League Trophy Final in which goals by Gael Bigirimana and George Thomas delivered a 2-1 win over Oxford in front of a crowd of more than 74,000.

Agyei D...................... 12 (4)	Jones J................... 11 (23)	Sordell M.................. 18 (2)
Beavon S 13 (1)	Kelly-Evans, D........ 13 (11)	Spence K..................... - (1)
Rigirimana G............ 28 (2)	Lameiras R 14 (13)	Sterry J............................16
Burge L..........................33	Maycock C .... - (3)	Stevenson B 22 (6)
Camwell C......................1	McBean J .... - (2)	Stokes C 5 (2)
Charles-Cook R 13 (2)	McCann C....................13	Thomas G 23 (5)
Clarke N.........................18	Page L...........................22	Thomas K 8 (6)
Kelly-Evans D............. - (1)	Rawson F 12 (2)	Tudgay M 21 (7)
Foley L 11 (1)	Reid K 19 (10)	Turnbull J......................36
Folivi M .... - (1)	Reilly C 17 (1)	Vernam C 3 (1)
Gadzhev V 13 (1)	Ricketts S 6 (1)	Willis J............................36
Harries C 6 (2)	Rose A 19 (2)	Wright A 7 (4)
Haynes R 17 (2)	Shipley J.................... - (1)	Yakubu .... - (3)

League goals (37): Thomas G 5, Agyei 4, Sordell 4, Tudgay 4, Thomas K 3, Willis 3, Beavon 2, Reid 2, Rose 2, Stevenson 2, Wright 2, Gadzhev 1, Jones 1, Lameiras 1, McCann 1
FA Cup goals (3): Sordell 2, Sterry 1. League Cup goals (4): Gadzhev 1, Haynes 1, Lameiras 1, Rose 1. League Trophy goals (20): Thomas G 4, Haynes 3, Lameiras 3, Bigirimana 2, Turnbull 2, Willis 2, Agyei 1, Beavon 1, Jones 1, Sordell 1
Average home league attendance: 9,119. Player of Year: Lee Burge

FLEETWOOD TOWN

Fleetwood set new standards in their rise from the ninth tier of English football, overcoming managerial upheaval ten days before the start of the season to reach the play-offs. This time, it came with Uwe Rosler at the helm, following Steven Pressley's resignation. Pressley, who had signed ten players during the summer, blamed 'a number of factors' for his decision to go after nine months as manager. Rosler, formerly in charge of Leeds, Wigan and Brentford, led his side into the leading group early in the New Year on the back of eight unbeaten matches. During that spell, they also overcame Shrewsbury and Southport in replays to reach round three of the FA Cup. The undefeated league sequence stretched to a club record 18 games with a 2-0 away win over Scunthorpe, rewarded with second place at the expense of their rivals. The run ended in a 4-2 home defeat by Bolton, who went on to claim the second automatic promotion place behind Sheffield United. Fleetwood, finishing fourth, lost to the only goal in their semi-final first leg against Bradford and shared a goalless draw in the return.

Ball D 39 (7)	Duckworth M 2 (2)	Kip R .... - (1)
Bell A 44	Eastham A 34 (1)	Long C 15 (3)
Bolger C 29 (3)	Glendon G 19 (7)	McLaughlin C 42
Brannagan C 5 (8)	Godswill Ekpolo 4 (2)	Neal C 17
Burns W 3 (7)	Grant R 44 (2)	Nirennold V 6 (20)
Cairns A 29 (1)	Holloway A 1 (5)	Pond N 30 (2)
Cole D 18 (17)	Hunter A 24 (20)	Ryan J 16
Davies B 22	Jakubiak A .... - (3)	Schwabl M 8 (5)
Davis J 3 (1)	Maguire J 1 (2)	Sowerby J 5 (3)
Dempsey K 35 (3)	Jonsson E 8 (4)	Woolford M 3 (6)

Play-offs – appearances: Ball 2, Bell 2, Cairns 2, Davies 2, Dempsey 2, Eastham 2, Grant 2, McLaughlin 2, Cole 1 (1), Glendon 1 (1), Hunter 1 (1), Bolger 1, Pond 1, Schwabl 1, Burns – (2), Brannagan – (1),
League goals (64): Ball 14, Grant 9, Hunter 8, Bolger 5, Cole 5, Long 4, McLaughlin 4, Bell 2, Dempsey 2, Eastham 2, Nirennold 2, Davies 1, Jonsson 1, Sowerby 1, Woolford 1, Opponents 3. Play-offs goals: None
FA Cup goals (7): Hunter 2, Cole 2, Bell 1, Bolger 1, Holloway 1. League Cup goals (2): Holloway 1, Hunter 1. League Trophy goals (3): Cole 1, Jakubiak 1, Sowerby 1
Average home league attendance: 3,272. Player of Year: Cian Bolger

GILLINGHAM

Gillingham seemed to have shed relegation worries with a run of three wins in four matches, rounded off by a remarkable result against promotion-chasing Scunthorpe. They transformed a 2-0 deficit with three penalties in the space of 11 minutes, all converted by Josh Wright against his former club. That left Ady Pennock's side seven points clear of the bottom four. But eight goals conceded to Bolton and Rochdale, followed by two more defeats against Peterborough and MK Dons, had the danger signals flashing again. Cody McDonald eased the pressure with goals after 90 and 96 minutes for a 3-1 win over Bristol Rovers, only for two further reversals to leave them needing to match Port Vale's result away to Fleetwood to stay up. Although Wright had a penalty saved at Northampton, they survived as both games ended goalless. Gillingham had made a decent cent start to the season, with ten points from five matches. But they failed to maintain it and Pennock, a former defender with the club and former manager of Forest Green, was appointed until the end of the season when Justin Edinburgh was sacked early in the New Year with his side 17th. He was then confirmed in the job.

Bond J. 7	Herd C. 12	Nouble F. 7 (5)
Byrne M. 22 (9)	Hessenthaler J. 24 (4)	O'Hara J. .... - (2)
Cargill B 9	Holy T 6	Oldaker D 2 (3)
Cornick H 4 (2)	Jackson R 30 (4)	Osadebe F 12 (12)
Cundle G .... - (2)	Knott R 15 (2)	Oshilaja A 31 (2)
Dack B 32 (2)	Konchesky P 25	Parker J 5 (11)
Dickenson M 1 (1)	List E 3 (12)	Pask J 7 (3)
Donnelly R. 11 (17)	Martin I. 14 (3)	Quigley J. 8 (2)
Ehmer M. 45	McDonald C 40 (4)	Rehman Z. 10
Emmanuel-Thomas J. 23 (5)	Muldoon O 3 (1)	Wagstaff S 23 (3)
Garmston B. 1 (4)	Nelson S. 33 (1)	Wright J. 41

League goals (59): Wright 13, McDonald 10, Ehmer 7, Emmanuel-Thomas 7, Dack 5, Donnelly 2, Oshilaja 2, Parker 2, Byrne 1, Cargill 1, Hessenthaler 1, Jackson 1, Knott 1, Nouble 1, Osadebe 1, Quigley 1, Wagstaff 1, Opponents 2
FA Cup goals (5): Nouble 2, Hessenthaler 1, McDonald 1, Wagstaff 1. **League Cup goals** (5): Emmanuel Thomas 2, Byrne 1, Dack 1, McDonald 1. **League Trophy goals** (4): Oldaker 2, Emmanuel-Thomas 1, Wright 1
Average home league attendance: 6,129. **Player of Year**: Josh Wright

MILLWALL

Two 86th minute goals paved the way for Millwall's return to the Championship. The first, headed in by Shaun Hutchinson, delivered a 4-3 victory away to Bristol Rovers on the final day of the regular season, enabling them to finish a point ahead of Southend in sixth place. It earned a play-off semi-final against Scunthorpe in which two by Steve Morison in the second leg at Glanford Park set up a 3-2 aggregate victory and a return to Wembley, where they lost to Barnsley in the 2016 final. This time, Morison was on the mark five minutes from the end of normal time to deliver a 1-0 victory. It was followed by an unpleasant pitch invasion by their own supporters, leaving the club's Player of the Year admitting that those responsible had marred the achievement for the team and the club. A run of 17 unbeaten matches had previously taken Millwall into a play-off position and through to the sixth round of the FA Cup. They knocked out Bournemouth, Watford and Leicester. But a 6-0 beating by Tottenham was followed immediately by a single point gained from next four games. After that, it was touch and go whether they would regain a place in the leading group.

Abdou N 6 (6)	King I 10 (1)	Smith H. 7 (2)
Archer J. 36	Martin J. 19 (4)	Thompson B. 36 (2)
Butcher C 9 (21)	Morison J. 35 (3)	Wallace J 14 (2)
Cooper J 13 (2)	Nelson S. 2 (1)	Webster B 44
Craig T. 43	O'Brien A. 35 (8)	Williams S 43 (1)
Cummings S 15 (1)	Onyedinma F. 23 (19)	Worrall D 14 (19)
Ferguson S. 22 (18)	Pavey A .... - (1)	Wylde G. 1 (4)
Gregory L. 35 (2)	Philpot J. .... - (2)	
Hutchinson S 13 (3)	Romeo M 31 (1)	

Play-offs – appearances: Abdou 3, Archer 3, Craig 3, Gregory 3, Hutchinson 3, Morison 3, Wallace 3, Webster 3, Williams 3, O'Brien 2 (1), Romeo 2 (1), Ferguson 1 (2), Cummings 1, Butcher – (2), Onyedinma – (1)

League goals (66): Gregory 17, O'Brien 13, Morison 11, Williams 4, Onyedinma 3, Wallace 3,

Butcher 2, Cooper 2, Ferguson 2, Hutchinson 2, Webster 2, Craig 1, Martin 1, Smith 1, Worrall 1, Opponents 1. **Play-offs goals** (4): Morison 3, Gregory 1
FA Cup goals (11): Smith 3, Cummings 2, Ferguson 2, Morison 2, O'Brien 1, Romeo 1. **League Cup goals** (5): Morison 1, O'Brien 1, Onyedinma 1, Williams 1, Opponents 1. **League Trophy goals** (8): Morison 2, Onyedinma 2, Smith 2, Abdo 1, Worrall 1
Average home league attendance: 9,340. **Player of Year**: Steve Morison

MILTON KEYNES DONS

Karl Robinson's six-and-a-half-years as manager – third longest behind Arsenal's Arsene Wenger and Exeter's Paul Tisdale – came to an end with the sack after a 3-0 home defeat by Southend left his side a point off the drop zone after 15 matches. Steven Gerrard turned down the job, maintaining it came too soon after his retirement as a player. Ritchie Barker took over as caretaker before the permanent appointment of Hearts boss Robbie Neilson. His first league game was a highly-charged affair against arch-rivals Wimbledon, won with a penalty by Dean Bowditch. Dons were then still in the bottom half of the table, but began moving up with 12 goals scored against Swindon, Northampton and Peterborough. Results were patchy after that, ruling out any prospect of closing the gap on the leading teams and challenging for an immediate return to the Championship. Dons, however, managed to reach the mid-point of the table which brought wins over Gillingham, Charlton, Southend and Walsall.

Agard K 33 (9)	Lewington D.................... 36	Reeves B 26 (8)
Aneke C 9 (6)	Martin D 39 (1)	Thomas-Asante B......... - (6)
Baldock G................. 36 (1)	Maynard N 20 (11)	Tilney B 5 (1)
Barnes H 18 (3)	Muirhead R 12 (7)	Tshimanga K .... - (6)
Bowditch D 20 (8)	Ngohbo M 1 (8)	Upson E 40 (2)
Brittain C.................... 2 (4)	Nicholls L 7 (1)	Walsh J............................ 39
Carruthers S............. 18 (5)	O'Keefe S 17 (1)	Williams G B 29 (4)
Colclough R 12 (6)	Potter D 32 (5)	Williams G C 5 (6)
Downing P 34 (3)	Powell D 8 (12)	Wootton S 1
Hendry J.................... 6 (1)	Rasulo G.................... 1 (2)	

League goals (60): Agard 12, Reeves 7, Barnes 6, Bowditch 5, Colclough 5, Aneke 4, O'Keefe 4, Upson 3, Maynard 2, Muirhead 2, Powell 2, Williams G B 2, Carruthers 1, Lewington 1, Potter 1, Walsh 1, Wootton 1, Opponents 1
FA Cup goals (6): Reeves 2, Agard 1, Bowditch 1, Powell 1, Thomas-Asante 1. **League Cup goals** (5): Bowditch 3, Tilney 1, Tshimanga 1. **League Trophy goals** (5): Agard 1, Reeves 1, Tapp F 1, Walsh 1, Opponents 1
Average home league attendance: 10,307. **Player of Year**: George Williams

NORTHAMPTON TOWN

Northampton's record unbeaten league run of 24 matches to the end of the previous League Two title-winning season was extended to 31 before a 3-1 defeat at Chesterfield. They were back to winning ways, and up to fifth, with seven goals scored in successive games against Shrewsbury and Bury. A 6-0 victory over Harrow followed in the FA Cup, but a sudden loss of form sent them sliding, with eight defeats in ten, culminating in a 5-0 reversal against Bristol Rovers. There was also a defeat by Stourbridge, lowest ranked side left in the FA Cup, contributing to the sacking of manager Robert Page. Ten days after his own dismissal by Gillingham, Justin Edinburgh came in to oversee sufficient victories – including 3-0 against Coventry delivered by Keshi Anderson's hat-trick – to establish what looked to be a comfortable mid-table position. Instead, Northampton were grateful for those points in the bank, failing to win any of their final eight fixtures and finishing four off the relegation zone.

114

Anderson K 9 (5)	Hanley R .... - (1)	Potter A 3 (8)
Anderson P 28 (8)	Hooper JJ 5 (5)	Revell A 29 (3)
Beautyman H 11 (10)	Hoskins S 18 (7)	Richards M 28 (14)
Boateng H 11 (5)	Iaciofano J .... - (1)	Smith A 40
Buchanan D 45	McCourt J 17 (9)	Smith M 13 (1)
Byrom J 1 (1)	McDonald R 2 (5)	Sonupe E .... - (1)
Cornell D 6	McWilliams S 2 (3)	Taylor M 43
D'Ath L .... - (1)	Moloney B 19 (4)	Williams L 8
Diamond Z 37 (2)	Nyatanga L 34 (3)	Wylde G 6 (6)
Eardley N 10	O'Toole J-J 34 (6)	Zakuani G 20 (1)
Gorre K 9 (4)	Phillips J 18 (2)	

League goals (60): O'Toole 10, Richards 10, Revell 8, Taylor 7, Anderson P 6, Anderson K 3, Beautyman 3, Hoskins 3, Smith M 2, Zakuani 2, Gorre 1, McCourt 1, Phillips 1, Wylde 1, Opponents 2
FA Cup goals (6): Richards 2, Anderson P 1, Hooper 1, O'Toole 1, Taylor 1. **League Cup goals** (5): Revell 2, Diamond 1, O'Toole 1, Opponents 1. **League Trophy goals** (2): Beautyman 1, Richards 1
Average home league attendance: 6,208. **Player of Year:** Zander Diamond

OLDHAM ATHLETIC

John Sheridan renewed a long-standing connection with the club to lead them away from the threat of relegation for the second successive season. He left in the summer after his first rescue act to take over at Notts County, returning ten days after losing that job to replace Stephen Robinson. Oldham were then bottom, having scored just 12 goals in 24 matches. Sheridan, who spent the last six years of his playing career at Boundary Park, followed by the first spell of three spells as manager in 2006, won his opening match this time against Gillingham, the team's first three points for three months. They went on to win five of his first nine and move away from the bottom four. In the tenth, Connor Ripley saved two stoppage time penalties for a goalless draw at Millwall. There was still plenty of work to do, but Lee Erwin came up with some important goals and Peter Clarke's header for a 1-1 draw against Rochdale in the final home game ensured safety. Oldham finished four points clear, but were still saddled with the fewest goals in the four divisions – 31.

Banks O 24 (10)	Glackin B .... - (1)	O'Neill A 12 (3)
Burgess C 23	Green P 36 (5)	Obadeyi I 10 (5)
Clarke P 46	Holloway A 14 (1)	Osei D 4 (15)
Croft L 5 (15)	Hunt R 9 (1)	Reckord J 12 (1)
Dummigan C 11 (1)	Jahraldo Martin C ...... - (4)	Ripley C 46
Dunne C 13 (1)	Klok M 6 (4)	Stott J 4
Edmundson S 2 (1)	Ladapo F 12 (5)	Taylor C 14 (2)
Erwin L 25 (9)	Law J 19 (3)	Wilson B 25 (1)
Fane O 31 (8)	McKay B 20 (6)	Winchester C 4 (5)
Flynn R 31 (6)	McLaughlin R 31 (5)	Woodland L .... - (1)
Gerrard A 14	Ngoo M 3 (10)	

League goals (31): Erwin 8, Clarke 5, Banks 2, Ladapo 2, Law 2, McLaughlin 2, Obadeyi 2, Burgess 1, Flynn 1, Green 1, Wilson 1, Winchester 1, Opponents 3
FA Cup goals (4): McKay 2, Clarke 1, Flynn 1. **League Cup goals** (2): Flynn 1, Law 1. **League Trophy goals** (11): Erwin 2, McKay 2, Osei 2, Banks 1, Burgess 1, Croft 1, Ladapo 1, Wilson 1
Average home league attendance: 4,514. **Player of Year:** Peter Clarke

OXFORD UNITED

Another eventful season for Oxford, despite losing key players Kemar Roofe and Callum O'Dowda from the side that won promotion and reached Wembley in 2016. They returned to the national stadium for a second successive Football League Trophy Final, losing this time 2-1 to Coventry. In the FA Cup, they knocked out Newcastle 3-0 in the fourth round, then retrieved a two-goal deficit at Middlesbrough before conceding an 86th minute decider. In the league, Oxford were on the fringes of a top-six place through to the final round of matches and would have gone closer had their home form been better. They lost eight matches in front of their own fans, while away there was a spell of six victories out of seven. One of those was a 4-0 success at Chesterfield in which Conor McAleny scored a hat-trick. A month later, he got three more in the 5-1 home win over Bury. His side completed the campaign with successive victories over Port Vale, Millwall and Shrewsbury to finish eighth, four points short of progressing to the play-offs. Manager Michael Appleton left during the summer to become Craig Shakespeare's assistant at Leicester. He was succeeded by Spaniard Pep Clotet, former assistant at Leeds and Swansea.

Carroll C 3 (1)	Long S 2 (1)	Ribeiro C 3
Crowley D 2 (4)	Lundstram J............. 44 (1)	Roberts T................. - (14)
Dunkley C 40	MacDonald A............ 17 (5)	Rothwell J.............. 19 (14)
Eastwood S 46	Maguire C 40 (2)	Ruffels L 14 (6)
Edwards P............... 37 (1)	Martin A 2 (2)	Sercombe L.............. 24 (6)
Hall R..................... 21 (5)	Martinez A 8 (7)	Skarz J 28 (2)
Hemmings K 22 (18)	McAleny C 14 (4)	Taylor R 9 (12)
Johnson M 33 (6)	Nelson C.......................33	Thomas W................. 8 (5)
Ledson R 20 (2)	Raglan C.......................16	Welch-Hayes M.................1

League goals (65): Maguire 13, McAleny 10, Hall 6, Hemmings 6, Dunkley 3, Edwards 3, Johnson 3, Sercombe 3, Thomas 3, Crowley 2, Nelson 2, Ruffels 2, Martinez 1, Ledson 1, Lundstram 1, MacDonald 1, Rothwell 1, Taylor 1, Opponents 3
FA Cup goals (16): Hemmings 5, Martinez 2, Taylor 2, Edwards 1, MacDonald 1, Maguire 1, Nelson 1, Roberts 1, Rothwell 1, Ruffels 1. **League Cup goals** (3): Crowley 1, Sercombe 1, Thomas 1. **League Trophy goals** (16): Henmings 4, Johnson 3, Maguire 3, Edwards 1, MacDonald 1, Roberts 1, Sercombe 1, Taylor 1, Opponents 1
Average home league attendance: 8,297. **Player of Year**: Simon Eastwood

PETERBOROUGH UNITED

For the second successive season, Peterborough fell away in the second half of the season after losing to Premier League opposition in the FA Cup. It cost them in 2016 in the wake of a fourth round tie against West Bromwich Albion. This time, a 4-1 third round defeat by Chelsea at Stamford Bridge put the brake on a promotion challenge. Two points off a play-off place, they lost 5-1 at Bury immediately afterwards and conceded four goals at home to both MK Dons and Southend. Nine defeats in 13 games dropped them to 11th, with little chance of being able to recover lost ground. Overall, eight defeats in front of their own supporters proved too big a handicap. So was the inability to match the leading group, with just seven points gained out of a possible 36 against the teams in the top-six. Peterborough finished 11th, an improvement of two places on the previous campaign.

Alnwick B 4	Bostwick M 38	Grant A...........................11
Anderson H................. - (1)	Chettle C 5 (6)	Hughes A............... 37 (2)
Anderson J................ 5 (2)	Coulthirst S............ 11 (5)	Inman B 5 (6)
Angol L 5 (8)	Da Silva Lopes L....... 32 (6)	Mackail-Smith C....... 14 (4)
Baldwin J........................27	Edwards G 23 (10)	Madison M............... 37 (4)
Ball D.............................6	Forrester C.............. 39 (6)	McGee L........................39
Binnom-Williams J..... 9 (1)	Freestone L....................4	Moncur G................. 5 (8)
Borg A 1 (2)	Gormley J .... - (1)	Moore D..................... - (4)

Morias J 7 (13)	Samuelsen M 4 (7)	Tafazoli R 30 (1)
Nabi A .... - (2)	Santos R .... - (1)	Taylor P 25 (14)
Nichols T 37 (6)	Smith M 39	Tyler M 3
Oduwa N .... - (6)	Stevens M .... - (1)	White H 4 (2)

League goals (62): Nichols 10, Maddison 9, Edwards 7, Mackail-Smith 5, Forrester 4, Morias 3, Bostwick 3, Tafazoli 3, Taylor 3, Coulthirst 2, Da Silva Lopes 2, Moncur 2, Angol 1, Baldwin 1, Ball 1, Hughes 1, Samuelsen 1, Smith 1, Opponents 2
FA Cup goals (7): Coulthirst 2, Edwards 2, Da Silva Lopes 1, Nichols 1, Taylor 1. **League Cup goals** (4): Nichols 2, Da Silva Lopes 1, Taylor 1. **League Trophy goals** (3): Anderson J 1, Moncur 1, Taylor 1
Average home league attendance: 5,581. **Player of Year**: Michael Bostwick

PORT VALE

New Portuguese manager Bruno Ribeiro overhauled the Vale Park squad during the summer, bringing in a large number of foreign players as part of the shake-up. Five successive home wins suggested a successful integration with his home-grown contingent. They were fourth two months into the season, with Alex Jones, on loan from Birmingham, scoring freely. But a slump left them 17th at Christmas, prompting Ribeiro to resign. Vale also lost nine-goal Jones to Bradford after an unsuccessful attempt at a permanent signing. Under caretaker Michael Brown, they dropped into the bottom four after a single win in 14 games. Relief came with victories over Swindon, Shrewsbury and Wimbledon, before the goals dried up at the most crucial part of the campaign. Just one was scored in the final seven fixtures, including a goalless draw at Fleetwood in the final round of matches. They needed to better Gillingham's result on that afternoon, but their rivals also drew, at Northampton, to survive by a point and send Vale down. Brown was later given the job on a permanent basis.

Alnwick J 26	Hart S 9 (2)	Purkiss B 32
Amoros S 7 (3)	Hooper JJ 21 (2)	Reeves W 4 (8)
Bikey A 5 (2)	Jones A 17 (2)	Shalaj G .... - (7)
Boot R 1	Kelly S 9 (12)	Shodipo O 4 (2)
Brown M 1 (2)	Kiko 11 (10)	Smith N........................46
Cicilia R 16 (13)	Knops K 28 (1)	Streete R 36 (1)
De Freitas A 16 (8)	Mac-Intosch C 3	Tanser S 8 (3)
Eagles C 16 (4)	Mbamba C .... - (6)	Taylor R 22
Fasan L 10	Mehmet D 9	Thomas J 23
Foley S 32	Paterson M 10 (6)	Turner D 3 (13)
Forrester A 12 (9)	Tavares P 19 (3)	Walker T 5 (1)
Grant A.....................20	Pereira Q 2 (12)	
Guy C 10 (1)	Pugh D 13 (1)	

League goals (45): Jones 9, Hooper 5, Streete 5, Cicilia 4, Eagles 4, Smith 4, Taylor 4, Forrester 2, Paterson 2, Walker 2, Foley 1, Hart 1, Thomas 1, Opponents 1
FA Cup goals (5): Cicilia 1, Jones 1, Streete 1, Taylor 1, Opponents 1. **League Cup goals** (1): Grant 1. **League Trophy goals** (1): Smith 1
Average home league attendance: 4,813. **Player of Year**: Nathan Smith

ROCHDALE

Rochdale overcame a poor start, worked their way into a play-off place, but could not hold on and finished four points adrift of the top-six. They had to play catch-up after opening with three draws and four defeats which left them bottom. Victory over Fleetwood proved to be the first of ten in succession at home, stretching to the end of the year, with 25 goals scored and just four conceded. Along with Matty Lund's hat-trick at Northampton, where they twice came from behind to win 3-2, this purple patch took them up to fourth. The sequence came to an end, rather unceremoniously, with a 4-0 beating by Oxford which precipitated another lean spell – this time nine games without success. It left them eight points adrift, albeit with fixtures in hand over the teams immediately above them. Rochdale halved the deficit by the end of the season when a ninth-place finish was one short of the club's best-ever in 2015.

Allen J 26 (5)	Lillis J 14	Owusu D .... - (1)
Andrew C 31 (8)	Logan C 24	Rafferty J 36 (4)
Bunney J 28 (1)	Lund M 27 (2)	Rathbone O 18 (9)
Camps C 37 (7)	McDermott D 9 (8)	Redshaw J .... - (1)
Canavan N 23 (2)	McGahey H 30 (6)	Tanser S 5
Cannon A 14 (10)	McNulty J 33 (2)	Taylor J 1
Davies S 16 (13)	Mendez-Laing N 30 (9)	Thompson J 17 (4)
Henderson I 39 (3)	Morley A 2	Vincenti P 3 (11)
Keane K 27 (2)	Noble-Lazarus R 3 (7)	Wilson B 8
Kitching M 4 (1)	Odelusi S 1 (14)	

League goals (71): Henderson 15, Davies 9, Lund 9, Camps 8, Mendez-Laing 8, Andrew 7, Thompson 3, Allen 2, Canavan 2, Cannon 2, Rathbone 2, Bunney 1, McDermott 1, Noble-Lazarus 1, Vincenti 1
FA Cup goals (7): Davies 3, Henderson 2, Camps 1, Mendez-Laing 1. **League Cup goals** (4): Cannon 1, Henderson 1, Lund 1, Mendez-Laing 1. **League Trophy goals** (5): Davies 1, Gillam M 1, Henderson 1, Noble-Lazarus 1, Odelusi 1
Average home league attendance: 3,556. **Player of Year**: Joe Rafferty

SCUNTHORPE UNITED

For the best part of six months of the season, Scunthorpe looked a solid bet for automatic promotion. A formidable record at Glanford Park, alongside a flood of goals from Josh Morris, took them top. Even when Sheffield United's relentless pursuit finally paid off, they held an eight-point cushion in second place. But it all changed when defeat at Southend was followed by Shrewsbury ending a club-best unbeaten run of 26 home league games. There were seven further games without a win, resulting in Bolton and Fleetwood overtaking them and pressure building to hold on to a play-off place. Five successive victories to end the regular campaign saw off that threat, as well as building some momentum for the knockout phase. And when a resolute performance was rewarded with a goalless draw in the first leg at Millwall, Scunthorpe again looked to be in the driving seat. Instead, an early goal by on-loan Ivan Toney was undermined by poor defending. They were pegged back on the stroke of half-time, conceded two more goals in an eight-minute after the break, and although Stephen Dawson made it 3-2 on the night with nine minutes of normal time remaining, it was not enough.

Adelakun H 7 (10)	Hopper T 22 (9)	Toffolo H 21 (1)
Anyon J 7 (1)	Laird S .... - (1)	Toney I 9 (6)
Bishop N 36 (6)	Madden P 28 (6)	Townsend C 24
Goode C 13 (7)	Mantom S 10 (16)	Van Veen K 25 (8)
Clarke J 23	Margetts J .... - (2)	Wallace M 46
Crooks M 8 (4)	Mirfin D 33 (1)	Williams L 1 (6)
Daniels L 39	Morris J 44	Wiseman S 17 (7)
Davies C 3 (16)	Ness J 9 (3)	Wootton K .... - (2)
Dawson S 41 (2)	Smallwood R 6 (10)	
Holmes D 28 (4)	Sutton L 6 (2)	

Play-offs – appearances: Anyon 2, Bishop 2, Clarke 2, Dawson 2, Madden 2, Mirfin 2, Morris 2, Ness 2, Toney 2, Townsend 2, Wallace 2, Davies – (1), Holmes – (1), Mantom – (1), Van Veen – (1)

League goals (80): Morris 19, Madden 11, Van Veen 10, Toney 6, Bishop 5, Hopper 5, Crooks 3, Holmes 3, Adelakun 2, Mantom 2, Mirfin 2, Toffolo 2, Wallace 2, Wiseman 2, Clarke 1, Dawson 1, Smallwood 1, Wootton 1, Opponents 2. **Play-offs – goals** (2): Dawson 1, Toney 1
FA Cup goals (1): Hopper 1. **League Cup goals** (3): Van Veen 2, Morris 1. **League Trophy goals** (8): Adelakun 2, Williams 2, Mantom 1, Margetts 1, Wallace 1, Opponents 1
Average home league attendance: 4,536. **Player of Year:** Murray Wallace

SHEFFIELD UNITED

Chris Wilder led his home-town club back to the Championship with a record-breaking title win. After six years of failing to live up to Bramall Lane's profile and support, United recorded 30 victories and reached 100 points to outpace the rest of the division in Wilder's first season as manager. A poor start, one point from the first four games, prompted a change to a back three – and an immediate improvement. With Billy Sharp a prolific scorer, United worked their way up the table, going top for the first time at the midway point of the campaign. The manager strengthened his squad in the winter transfer window and they clinched promotion, with four games to spare, by coming from behind to win 2-1 at Northampton – where his previous team clinched promotion from League Two almost a year to the day – with an 88th minute goal by John Fleck. A week later, the title was theirs when nearest rivals Bolton were beaten by Oldham. Then, in front of a 31,000 crowd in the final match, they reached a century of points by defeating Chesterfield. Wilder became the first manager to win promotion in successive seasons for two clubs since Neil Warnock in the mid 1990s. He was named the division's Manager of the Year and Sharp won the Player of the Year award for his 30 goals.

Adams C	- (1)	Ebanks-Landell E	29 (5)	O'Connell J	40 (4)
Basham C	42 (1)	Fleck J	41 (3)	O'Shea J	5 (5)
Brayford J	3	Freeman K	39 (2)	Riley J	1 (1)
Brown R	- (2)	Hanson J	10 (3)	Scougall S	6 (19)
Carruthers S	2 (12)	Hussey C	5 (2)	Sharp B	44 (2)
Chapman H	- (12)	Lafferty D	37	Whiteman B	- (2)
Clarke L	12 (11)	Lavery C	6 (21)	Wilson J	7
Coutts P	40 (3)	Long G	3	Wright J	28 (2)
Done M	24 (7)	McNulty M	1 (3)		
Duffy M	38 (1)	Moore S	43		

League goals (92): Sharp 30, Freeman 10, Clarke 7, Duffy 6, Ebanks-Landell 5, Fleck 4, Lafferty 4, Lavery 4, O'Connell 4, Scougall 4, Done 3, O'Shea 3, Basham 2, Coutts 2, Chapman 1, Hanson 1, Wilson 1, Opponents 1
FA Cup goals (8): Chapman 3, Basham 1, Coutts 1, Freeman 1, O'Connell 1, Scougall 1.
League Cup goals (1): Clarke 1. **League Trophy goals** (5): Clarke 1, Coutts 1, O'Connell 1, Slater R 1, Opponents 1
Average home league attendance: 21,892. **Player of Year:** John Fleck/Billy Sharp (joint)

SHREWSBURY TOWN

Another season spent flirting with the drop ended with League One status retained in the final home game. Junior Brown's winner against Southend left his side three points clear of fourth-from-bottom Port Vale, who had a game in hand but an inferior goal difference. Shrewsbury spent the best part of four months in the relegation zone, first under Micky Mellon, then when Mellon left to become manager of Tranmere – where he had two spells as a player – and Grimsby's Paul Hurst took charge. They were still there going into the New Year, before Freddie Ladapo, signed on loan from Crystal Palace in the winter transfer window, instigated a significant change of fortunes. Ladapo scored winning goals against Bradford, Oldham, Bury and Scunthorpe in the space of a month to send his side five points clear by the time they had ended Scunthorpe's

26-match unbeaten home league record. But after beating Charlton 4-3, with Louis Dodds scoring twice, Shrewsbury took just two points from the next six games and were back in trouble. Victory over Rochdale ended that sequence and Brown's header in the penultimate fixture made them safe.

Black I 15 (4)	Lancashire O 13 (3)	Payne S 9 (3)
Brown J 43	Leitch-Smith AJ 8 (8)	Riley J 28 (4)
Deegan G 36 (4)	Leutwiler J 43	Roberts T 10 (2)
Dodds L 29 (9)	Mangan A 2 (8)	Rodman A 18 (2)
Ebanks-Blake S 5 (2)	McGivern R 14 (1)	Sadler M 33 (1)
El-Abd A 24 (4)	McAtee J .... - (1)	Sarcevic A 7 (5)
Grimmer J 22 (2)	Moha 1 (3)	Smith D 5 (5)
Halstead M 3	Morris B 8 (5)	Toney I 19
Humphrys S 3 (11)	Nsiala A 21	Waring G 5 (9)
Jones E 1 (3)	O'Brien J 14 (4)	Whalley S 23 (9)
Ladapo F 10 (5)	Ogogo A 25 (1)	Yates R 9 (3)

League goals (46): Dodds 8, Toney 6, Brown 5, Ladapo 4, Roberts 4, Black 3, Whalley 3, El-Abd 2, Humphrys 2, Payne 2, Sadler 2, Lancashire 1, Leitch-Smith 1, Nsiala 1, Riley 1, Rodman 1
FA Cup goals (5): Dodds 1, Grimmer 1, Leitch-Smith 1, O'Brien 1, Sadler 1. **League Cup goals** (2): Dodds 1, Leitch-Smith 1. **League Trophy goals** (3: Leitch-Smith 2, Toney 1
Average home league attendance: 5,507. **Player of Year**: Mat Sadler

SOUTHEND UNITED

Phil Brown's side looked a good bet for the play-offs when making the most of a favourable run of fixtures with a month or so of the season remaining. They regained sixth place from Millwall when coming from 2-0 down to beat Walsall 3-2 with goals from Nile Ranger, Anton Ferdinand and Simon Cox. Further wins over Wimbledon and Oldham established a three-point lead over their rivals. But defeat by the odd goal in four of the next five games – broken by a 4-0 victory over Chesterfield – left them a point adrift going into the final round of matches. Southend defeated Bury 1-0, only for Millwall to deny them with an 85th minute goal for a 4-3 victory against Bristol Rovers. Millwall also knocked them out of the FA Cup in the first round. The season had started poorly. They were third from bottom after two months. But a single defeat in the next 17 matches, rounded off with 3-1 win over leaders Scunthorpe, put them into the running for promotion.

Amos L 2 (1)	Inniss R 8 (2)	Ranger N 19 (8)
Atkinson W 35 (2)	King A 5 (2)	Robinson T 3 (15)
Barrett A 12	Kyprianou H 2 (1)	Smith T 19
Bridge J 1 (3)	Leonard R 43	Sokolik J 2 (3)
Coker B 29 (2)	McGlashan J 13 (22)	Thompson A 40
Cox S 39 (5)	McLaughlin S 32 (2)	Timlin M 25 (2)
Demetriou J 40 (1)	Mooney D 10 (3)	Walton C 7
Ferdinand A 34	Nouble L .... - (5)	White J 11 (2)
Fortune M-A 16 (16)	O'Neill L 6 (11)	Williams J .... - (7)
Hines Z .... - (5)	Oxley M 20	Wordsworth A 33 (1)

League goals (70): Cox 16, Wordsworth 11, Ranger 8, McLaughlin 7, Fortune 5, Atkinson 4, Leonard 3, McGlashan 3, Ferdinand 2, Robinson 2, Demetriou 1, Kyprianou 1, Mooney 1, O'Neill 1, Thompson 1, Timlin 1, White 1, Opponents 2
FA Cup goals: None. **League Cup goals** (1): McLaughlin 1. **League Trophy goals** (4): Fortune 1, Kyprianou 1, Mooney 1, Wordsworth 1
Average home league attendance: 7,406. **Player of Year**: Ryan Leonard

SWINDON TOWN

Tim Sherwood's appointment as director of football three months into the season was described by chairman Lee Power as 'one of the biggest the club has ever made.' The former Tottenham and Aston Villa manager, who played alongside Power at Norwich in the early 1990s, was tasked with working alongside coach Luke Williams. There was a winning start to the partnership, 3-0 against Charlton, but far from proving a success, it failed to lift Swindon from the fringes of the relegation zone. Worse followed, with their team dropping into the bottom four after losing at Bury in mid-February – and staying there for the remainder of the campaign. Late winners by Conor Thomas, against Millwall, and Nicky Ajose, in the next match at Fleetwood, offered some hope. But Swindon failed to score in their final four matches, with a 2-0 home defeat by Scunthorpe in the penultimate fixture, sealing their fate. They finished six points adrift and Williams left the club shortly afterwards. He was replaced by former Bury manager David Flitcroft. Sherwood departed soon after.

Ajose N.....15	Gladwin B.....15 (3)	Rodgers A.....19 (3)
Barry B.....17 (6)	Goddard J.....28 (14)	Sendles-White J.....5
Branco R.....34	Henry W.....3	Smith T.....4 (4)
Brophy J.....22 (8)	Hylton J.....4 (8)	Starkey J.....1
Colkill C.....19	Iandolo E.....5 (5)	Stewart J.....- (7)
Conroy D.....11 (3)	Ince R.....14	Thomas C.....29 (4)
Delfouneso N.....13 (5)	Jones L.....23 (1)	Thompson N.....34
Doughty M.....13 (1)	Kashii Y.....18 (2)	Twine S.....- (1)
Evans J.....- (1)	Murray S.....13 (5)	Vigouroux L.....43
Fankaty Dabo.....15	Norris L.....18 (21)	Young J.....1 (1)
Feruz I.....4	Obika J.....27 (3)	
Furlong D.....21 (3)	Ormonde-Ottewill B..18 (3)	

League goals (44): Obika 6, Ajose 5, Norris 4, Goddard 3, Doughty 2, Furlong 2, Gladwin 2, Ince 2, Jones 2, Kasim 2, Branco 2, Thompson 2, Barry 1, Colkett 1, Delfouneso 1, Fankaty Dabo 1, Murray 1, Ormonde-Ottewill 1, Rodgers 1, Thomas 1, Opponents 2
FA Cup goals (2): Delfouneso 1, Doughty 1. **League Cup goals** (2): Brophy 1, Stewart 1. **League Trophy goals** (5): Norris 2, Delfouneso 1, Iandolo 1, Branco 1
Average home league attendance: 7,026. **Player of Year**: Lawrence Vigouroux

WALSALL

Walsall reached the play-offs and the League Trophy Final in the two previous seasons. This one was a more mundane affair – a place in the bottom half of the table and little to shout about in any of the knockout competitions. They lost key players in the summer, including leading scorer Tom Bradshaw, and did not have the consistency to make an impression on the table. Their highest position was eighth, achieved by successive home wins against Peterborough, Oldham and Chesterfield. That left them six points short of a top-six place and needing to maintain the momentum to go closer. Instead, they won only one of the last ten matches and finished 14th after losing 4-1 at home to MK Dons in the final round of fixtures. High spot of the campaign was the double recorded over champions Sheffield United – 1-0 at Bramall Lane with a goal by Amadou Bakayoko and 4-1 in the return, in which Erhun Oztumer netted one of his 15 for the campaign. They also defeated United in the League Trophy's group stage.

Bakayoko A.....18 (21)	Etheridge N.....41	Kouhyar O.....2 (4)
Candlin M.....1 (4)	Ginnelly J.....4 (5)	Laird S.....26 (2)
Chambers A.....43	Hayles-Doherty T.....- (1)	MacGillivray C.....5
Cuvelier F.....15 (7)	Henry R.....2	Makris A.....17 (15)
Dobson G.....9 (12)	Jackson S.....24 (14)	McCarthy J.....46
Edwards J.....43	Kinsella L.....5 (3)	Morris K.....28 (7)

Moussa F 14 (8)	Osbourne I 27 (3)	Randall-Hurren W .... - (2)
O'Connell E 17	Oztumer E 34 (7)	Roberts K 4
O'Connor J 40	Preston M 25 (5)	Toner K 16

League goals (51): Oztumer 15, Jackson 7, McCarthy 5, Morris 5, Bakayoko 4, Moussa 4, Edwards 3, Laird 3, Dobson 1, Makris 1, O'Connell 1, Osbourne 1, Preston 1
FA Cup goals: None. **League Cup goals**: None. **League Trophy goals** (9): Bakayoko 6, Kouhyar 1, Laird 1, Morris 1
Average home league attendance: 5,071. **Player of Year**: Jason McCarthy

LEAGUE TWO

ACCRINGTON STANLEY

Accrington faltered at a crucial time for the second successive season. They missed out on automatic promotion in the final round of matches in 2016 – and lost out to Wimbledon in the play-offs. This time, their chances of reaching the knockout phase look slim when dropping into the relegation zone during a spell of seven defeats in eight matches. That sequence ended with victory over Crewe, but they remained in trouble for another month before a strong recovery followed an eventful 4-4 draw at Mansfield, where they led 2-0, 3-1 and 4-3 before conceding an 89th minute equaliser. Stanley went 15 games unbeaten to close to within two points of the leading group. Then, defeat by a Newport side battling to avoid non-league football was followed by a 4-1 home loss to Luton in the penultimate fixture. It not only ended their chances – while ensuring Luton went forward – but meant that in a tightly-packed division they finished in the bottom half of the table, despite winning 3-0 at Stevenage in the last game.

Beckles O 40 (1)	Eagles C 2 (4)	McConville S 41
Boco R 12 (18)	Edwards J 2 (8)	O'Sullivan J 18 (1)
Brown S 27 (1)	Gornell T 10 (19)	Ogle R .... - (1)
Jones C .... - (2)	Hery B .... - (1)	Parish E 11
Chapman A 15	Hewitt S 4 (5)	Pearson M 43
Clare S 6 (2)	Hughes M 36	Rodak M 20
Clark J 35 (7)	Husin N 7 (4)	Rodgers H 19
Conneely S 38	Kee B 37 (2)	Shaw B .... - (2)
Davies A 4	Lacey P 7 (4)	Taylor-Fletcher G .... - (4)
Donacien J 30 (5)	McCartan S 26 (8)	Vyner Z 16

League goals (59): Kee 13, McCartan 11, Pearson 8, Boco 6, McConville 5, Beckles 2, Gornell 2, Hughes 2, Clare 1, Clark 1, Conneely 1, Davies 1, Donacien 1, Edwards 1, Husin 1, Lacey 1, O'Sullivan 1, Rodgers 1
FA Cup goals (7): Kee 2, Beckles 1, Boco 1, Clark 1, McConville 1, O'Sullivan 1. **League Cup goals** (1): Pearson 1. **League Trophy goals** (4): Gornell 2, Clark 1, Taylor-Fletcher 1
Average home league attendance: 1,699. **Player of Year**: Matty Pearson

BARNET

Against a background of managerial upheaval, John Akinde continued to score a sackful of goals. The big man netted 31 to lead Barnet's return to the Football League in 2015 and 23 in their first season back. This time, Akinde contributed 26 to finish the division's top marksman, alongside Doncaster's John Marquis, as they repeated the 15th place of the previous campaign. Barnet lost Martin Allen, who ended his fourth spell as manager to take over at National League Eastleigh with his team a point away from a play-off place. Three players went with him, Bonz N'Gala, Gavin Hoyte and Sam Togwell. Allen's successor, Charlton assistant manager Kevin Nugent, managed a single win in 11 games and was gone after two months in the job. His assistant, Rossi

Eames, took over for the remaining matches and was then given the job permanently, becoming the league's youngest boss at 32.

Akinde J 46	Dembele B...........23	Shomotun F 3 (1)
Akinde S...........- (1)	Fonguck W...........2 (1)	Stephens J...........18
Akinola S 14 (5)	Gambin L...........13 (6)	Sweeney D...........- (4)
Akpa Akpro J-L...........7 (16)	Gash M...........2	Taylor H...........22 (3)
Amaluzor J...........- (11)	Hoyte G...........2	Taylor J...........13 (1)
Batt S...........3 (8)	Johnson E...........33 (3)	Togwell S 11 (1)
Izquierdo R...........10 (4)	Kyei N...........6 (6)	Tomlinson B...........1 (2)
Buchel B...........4	Mason-Clark E...........2 (4)	Tutonda D...........6 (1)
Burgoyne H...........2	Muggleton S...........5 (8)	Vickers J...........22 (1)
Campbell-Ryce J...........23 (9)	N'Gala B...........9 (1)	Vilhete M...........36 (4)
Champion T 22 (4)	Nelson M...........43	Watson R 15 (4)
Clough C...........18	Nicholls A...........11 (6)	Weston C 36 (4)
Cojocarel S 1 (2)	Santos R...........15	
Coulson L 4 (7)	Sesay A 2 (3)	

League goals (57): Akinde J 26, Weston 6, Dembele 4, Gambin 4, Vilhete 3, Akinola 2, Nicholls 2, Santos 2, Akpa Akpro 1, Batt 1, Campbell-Ryce 1, Champion 1, Clough 1, Nelson 1, Tutonda 1, Watson1
FA Cup goals: None. **League Cup goals**: None. **League Trophy goals** (3): Amaluzor 1, Nicholls 1, Weston 1
Average home league attendance: 2,260. **Player of Year**: John Akinde

BLACKPOOL

Boycotting fans took the gloss off Blackpool's immediate return to League One, but none could dispute the size of their team's achievement under Gary Bowyer. One of seven disputing two remaining play-off places on the final day of the regular campaign, they went through by defeating Leyton Orient 3-1. The semi-final against Luton, who had twice beaten them, was finely balanced after Mark Cullen's hat-trick against his former club delivered a 3-2 victory in the first leg. Nathan Delfouneso's goal extended that advantage in the return, but Luton replied with three to lead 5-4. Armand Gnanduillet levelled with a header and an own goal by goalkeeper Stuart Moore in the fifth minute of stoppage-time sent Blackpool to Wembley. Seven years previously, 37,000 supporters had seen their side reach the Premier League with victory over Cardiff. This time, there were fewer than 6,000 at the national stadium – a continuation of long-standing protests against the club's owners, the Oyston family. Blackpool had overcome Exeter on the opening day of the season – and they closed it with a 2-1 victory. Brad Potts scored within three minutes and set up the winner for Cullen in the second-half to give Bowyer – son of Nottinghanm Forest's double European Cup winner Ian – success in his first season in charge.

Almson W 15 (3)	Flores J...........14 (5)	Payne J...........32 (3)
Aldred T 44	Gnanduillet A...........9 (10)	Philliskirk D 10 (8)
Black I 1 (9)	Lyness D...........12 (1)	Potts B 42
Boney M ....- (1)	Matt J...........14 (18)	Pugh D...........18
Cain M 2 (4)	McAlister J...........18 (4)	Robertson C...........44
Cullen M 17 (10)	Mellor K 44	Slocombe S...........34
Daniel C 27 (7)	Nolan E 1 (2)	Taylor A...........38
Danns N 11 (2)	Odelusi S...........1 (6)	Vassell K 27 (2)
Delfouneso N 16 (2)	Osayi-Samuel B...........13 (18)	Yeates M...........2 (3)

Play-offs – appearances: Almson 3, Aldred 3, Cullen 3, Danns 3, Mellor 3, Payne 3, Potts 3, Robertson 3, Slocombe 3, Taylor 2, Vassell 2, Daniel 1, Delfouneso 1 (1), Black – (3), Flores – (2), Samuel – (2), Gnanduillet – (1)

League goals (69): Vassell 11, Potts 10, Cullen 9, Delfouneso 5, Daniel 4, Mellor 4, Osayi-Samuel 4, Flores 3, Gnanduillet 3, Matt 3, Aldred 2, Danns 2, Taylor 2, Cain 1, Odelusi 1, Payne 1, Opponents 4. **Play-offs – goals (8):** Cullen 4, Delfouneso 1, Gnanduillet 1, Potts 1, Opponents 1
FA Cup goals (5): Matt 2, Mellor 1, Osayi-Samuel 1, Potts 1. **League Cup goals (4):** Herron J 1, McAlister 1, Mellor 1, Potts 1. **League Trophy goals (5):** Gnanduillet 2, Vassell 2, Mellor 1
Average home league attendance: 3,456. **Player of Year:** Tom Aldred

CAMBRIDGE UNITED

Cambridge overcame their worst start to a Football League season to build a challenge for the play-offs and sustain it until the final match. Just three draws from the opening eight fixtures left them bottom. They got off the mark by coming from behind to defeat Newport with an 83rd minute goal from Luke Berry, gradually built up a head of steam and five successive wins, leading up to Boxing Day, had them up to seventh. Another dip brought a drop into the bottom half after six without a victory, but again they regrouped, helped by Medy Elito's second-half hat-trick for a 3-0 success at Carlisle. There was a final push in April when four wins of six were rewarded with a place one point off Blackpool in seventh position. On the last day, they faced another side with a chance of going up and it was Wycombe who scored the only goal, leaving Cambridge four points adrift. Berry's 17 goals were supplemented with the four he scored in an FA Cup second round win over Coventry.

Adams B	4 (2)	Gosling J	3 (1)	Mingoia P	40
Berry L	45	Gregory D	1	Newton C	17 (10)
Carroll J	19 (1)	Halliday B	30	Norris W	45
Clark M	17 (10)	Ikpeazu U	20 (9)	O'Neill L	13
Corr B	1 (6)	Keane K	1	Pigott J	5 (5)
Coulsen J	6 (1)	Legge L	43 (1)	Roberts M	26 (1)
Dallison T	5	Lewis P	5 (8)	Taylor G	34 (2)
Davies L	3 (2)	Long S	5 (2)	Wharton S	9
Dunk H	23 (15)	Maris G	17 (6)	Williamson B	17 (16)
Dunne J	28 (5)	McDonagh G	5 (8)		
Elito M	12 (11)	McGurk A	7 (8)		

League goals (58): Berry 17, Ikpeazu 6, Legge 6, Elito 5, Mingoia 5, Maris 4, Corr 2, Dunk 2, Roberts 2, Taylor 2, Clark 1, Dunne 1, Halliday 1, McDonagh 1, Newton 1, O'Neill 1, Wharton 1
FA Cup goals (10): Berry 4, Elito 1, Ikpeazu 1, Legge 1, Mingoia 1, Roberts 1, Williamson 1.
League Cup goals (3): Berry 1, Elito 1, Mingoia 1. **League Trophy goals (3):** Ikpeazu 2, Pigott 1, Opponents 1
Average home league attendance: 4,737. **Player of Year:** Luke Berry

CARLISLE UNITED

A quirk of fate ended Carlisle's promotion bid. Danny Grainger twice brought them level from the penalty spot at Exeter on the final day of the regular season and Jamie Proctor headed in for a 3-2 victory to seal sixth-place. That brought the teams back together in the play-offs. They shared six goals in the first leg at Brunton Park and were locked again on 2-2 going into stoppage-time in the return match. Then, with almost the last kick, Jack Stacey netted the winner for Exeter against the club he played for on loan the previous season. It was a cruel end to the campaign for Keith Curle's side, who started off with a club record 15 games without defeat – eight wins and seven draws. They held an automatic place for three months, but lost leading marksman Charlie Wyke to Bradford and lost their play-off place after seven games without scoring, another club record. Curle, himself, turned down an offer from another club, before fortunes improved with victories over Yeovil and Newport putting them back in contention.

Adams N	41 (1)	Hooper J	- (1)	Miller T	38 (3)
Asamoah D	- (8)	Ibehre J	20 (18)	Nabi S	– (1)
Atkinson D	- (1)	Joachim J-M	- (2)	O'Sullivan J	10 (7)
Bailey J	8 (4)	Jones M	26 (2)	Penn R	- (1)
Brisley S	22 (6)	Joyce L	42 (3)	Proctor J	16 (1)
Brough P	- (1)	Kennedy J	23 (4)	Raynes M	40 (1)
Devitt J	17 (18)	Lambe R	27 (11)	Tomlinson B	- (2)
Ellis M	5 (2)	Liddle G	21	Waring G	2 (7)
Gillesphey M	31 (1)	McKee J	1 (3)	Wright K	- (2)
Gillespie M	46	McQueen A	1 (3)	Wyke C	19 (7)
Grainger D	3	Miller S	19 (11)		

Play-offs – appearances: Adams 2, Bailey 2, Devitt 2, Gillespie 2, Grainger 2, Joyce 2, Lambe 2, Liddle 2, Miller T 2, Proctor 2, Raynes 2, Miller S – (2), O'Sullivan – (2), Kennedy – (1), Waring – (1)

League goals (69): Wyke 14, Ibehre 12, Kennedy 9, Grainger 6, Lambe 6, Miller S 4, Proctor 4, Adams 3, Brisley 3, Raynes 2, Joyce 1, Liddle 1, O'Sullivan 1, Opponents 4. **Play-offs goals (5)**: O'Sullivan 2, Kennedy 1, Miller S 1, Opponents 1

FA Cup goals (5): Ibehre 2, Grainger 1, Kennedy 1, Lambe 1. **League Cup goals (3)**: Jones 1, Miller S 1, Wyke 1. **League Trophy goals (13)**: Wyke 3, Grainger 2, Miller S 2, Lambe 1, McKee 1, Miller T 1, Raynes 1, Salkeld C 1, Opponents 1

Average home league attendance. 5,114. **Player of Year**: Nicky Adams

CHELTENHAM TOWN

Gary Johnson reshaped his struggling side during the winter transfer window, with players in and out of the club throughout January amid worries of a continuing relegation struggle. Cheltenham, back in the Football League after a season's absence, won just one of their first 12 games and went into the New Year second from bottom. The shake-up brought a gradual improvement, which accelerated with successive wins over Yeovil, Leyton Orient and Carlisle. But a single goal in five games in March – during which Johnson underwent a triple heart by-pass operation and his assistant Russell Milton took charge – proved another warning sign. So too did the resurgence of Newport, a side previously thought to have been resigned to a return to non-league football. In the event, Cheltenham overcame Morecambe and Grimsby, then held their nerve to beat Hartlepool with a goal by Danny Wright which took them to 50 points and sent their opponents into a last-day bid for survival.

Arthur K	1 (4)	Hall A	8 (2)	Plavotic T	10 (1)
Barthram J	22 (7)	Holman D	16 (8)	Dickie R	20
Boyle W	21	Jennings J	2 (1)	Rowe J	26 (6)
Brown S	21	Lainton R	1	Smith J	2 (3)
Cooper A	1	Morgan-Smith A	4 (13)	Storer K	18 (5)
Cranston J	30 (8)	Munns J	8 (10)	Suliman E	5 (4)
Davis L	13 (3)	O'Shaughnessy D	26 (1)	Waters B	41 (5)
Dayton J	10 (18)	Onariase E	22	Whitehead D	5 (1)
De Girolamo D	4 (1)	Parslow D	19 (2)	Winchester C	20
Downes A	15 (5)	Pell H	42	Wootton M	10 (6)
Griffiths R	24	Pike A	5	Wright D	34 (7)

League goals (49): Waters 12, Wright 9, Pell 7, Dayton 3, O'Shaughnessy 3, Boyle 2, Dickie 2, Wootton 2, Barthram 1, De Girolamo 1, Downes 1, Hall 1, Holman 1, Munns 1, Onariase 1, Plavotic 1, Winchester 1

FA Cup goals (6): Waters 2, Barthram 1, Holman 1, Pell 1, Wright 1. **League Cup goals (1)**: Pell 1. **League Trophy goals (10)**: De Girolamo 3, Morgan-Smith 2, Jennings 1, O'Shaughnessy 1, Pell 1, Waters 1, Wright 1

Average home league attendance: 3,323. **Player of Year**: Billy Waters

COLCHESTER UNITED

Colchester came up just short after climbing out of the relegation zone to mount a challenge for an immediate return to League One. They went into the final day of the season as one of seven clubs with a chance of filling one of the two play-off places still up for grabs. Tarique Fosu, on loan from Reading, scored both goals in a 2-0 win over Yeovil, but with Carlisle and Blackpool consolidating sixth and seventh places respectively, it was not enough. They finished eighth, a point behind Blackpool, having overcome a ten-match run without a victory which left them second from bottom after 17 games. A week later, they were on the rise after successive wins over Cheltenham and Crewe and by the New Year were up to sixth on the back of a purple patch of 19 points out of 21, with 20 goals scored. It included a 4-1 success against Carlisle in which Kurtis Guthrie scored a hat-trick. A fortnight later they were back among the pack and spent the rest of the season on the fringes.

Akinwande F .... - (1)	Guthrie K 32 (1)	Prosser L 14
Bonne M 1 (17)	James C.................... 13 (1)	Pyke R...................... 4 (8)
Briggs M 11 (4)	Johnstone D 15 (13)	Sembie-Ferris D........... - (7)
Brindley R............... 40 (1)	Kamara G 1 (3)	Slater C 23 (5)
Dickenson B............. 35 (1)	Kent F 13	Szmodics S 16 (3)
Doyley L 2 (1)	Kinsella L 11 (2)	Vincent-Young K 6 (12)
Eastman T 35	Lapslie T....................37	Walker S....................46
Edge C .... - (1)	Loft D 2 (6)	Wright D 31 (11)
Elokobi G.....................29	Murray S................. 15 (1)	Wynter A.................. 10 (5)
Fosu T.................. 14 (19)	O'Sullivan T.............. - (3)	
Garvan O.........................18	Porter C 32 (6)	

League goals (67): Porter 16, Dickenson 12, Guthrie 12, Fosu-Henry 5, Szmodics 5, Eastman 3, Slater 3, Johnstone 2, Wright 2, Bonne 1, Brindley 1, Elokobi 1, Garvan 1, Opponents 3
FA Cup goals (1): Fosu 1. **League Cup goals**: None. **League Trophy goals** (2): Bonne 1, Sembie-Ferris 1
Average home league attendance: 3,973. **Player of Year**: Brennan Dickenson

CRAWLEY TOWN

James Collins played a key role in Crawley avoiding being sucked into a relegation struggle. He scored 20 goals, nine of them in a 12-match sequence, which looked to have pointed the way towards mid-table respectability. Jimmy Smith also made his mark with a hat-trick for a 3-2 victory away to in-form Colchester. Their side then defeated Wycombe to move ten points clear of trouble. After that, they struggled, winning just one of the final 14 games, 3-0 against Leyton Orient. Fortunately, there was enough in the bank to compensate for the slump and Crawley finished five points clear in 19th, an improvement of one place on 2016. Striker Matt Harrold, injured or much of the season, took charge for the final match against Mansfield following the sacking of manager Dermot Drummy. Former Leeds and Liverpool winger Harry Kewell then took over.

Arthur C.................... 3 (3)	Davey A 8 (6)	Payne J................. 23 (9)
Banton J.................. 11 (3)	Djalo A 24 (4)	Roberts J 14 (9)
Bawling B 2 (27)	Garnett A 1 (1)	Smith J.............................46
Beeney M 1	Harrold M 1 (10)	Tajbakhsh A 2 (2)
Blackman A 31 (1)	Henderson C 8 (4)	Watt S ....- (2)
Boldewijn E............. 43 (3)	Lelan J 10 (3)	Yorwerth J................ 14 (7)
Clifford B 26 (10)	McNerney J............... 33 (1)	Young L 42 (1)
Collins J 45	Mersin Y 6 (2)	Yussuf A 6 (10)
Connolly M............. 40 (1)	Morris G 39	
Cox D 20 (2)	Murphy R.................. 7 (8)	

League goals (53): Collins 20, Smith 7, Boldewijn 5, Connolly 3, McNerney 3, Roberts 3, Yorwerth 3, Cox 2, Yussuf 2, Djalo 1, Murphy 1, Payne 1, Opponents 2
FA Cup goals (3): Clifford 1, Harrold 1, Roberts 1. **League Cup goals** (1): Boldewijn 1. **League Trophy goals** (3): Collins 2, Yussuf 1
Average home league attendance: 2,492. **Player of Year**: James Collins

CREWE ALEXANDRA

Chris Dagnall fired Crewe to safety away with an impressive scoring burst at a time when the threat of a second successive relegation was beginning to bite. With a third of the season remaining, they were fourth from bottom, four points off the drop zone, following a 4-0 defeat at Exeter. Steve Davis, the second longest-serving manager in League Two behind Morecambe's Jim Bentley, was sacked a month earlier after five years in charge, with his replacement David Artell initially unable to effect a change in fortunes. Academy manager Artell, a former club captain, had a morale-boosting first win, 5-0 against Grimsby, with Dagnall on the mark twice. He went on to deliver 12 goals in 14 matches, rounded off by a hat-trick on the final day. It came in a 4-1 victory over Barnet which left Crewe, nine points clear of the drop zone. It had been a difficult season on and off the field for the club, who were at the centre of an investigation into allegations of historical child sexual abuse.

Ainley C	6 (21)	Finney O	- (1)	Nugent B	15 (5)
Kiwomya A	22 (12)	Garratt B	46	Pickering H	- (1)
Bakayogo Z	36 (4)	Guthrie J	33	Ray G	18 (5)
Bingham B	25 (5)	Hollands D	23 (1)	Saunders C	1 (4)
Bowery J	18 (1)	Jones J	42 (3)	Turton O	45
Cooke C	18	Kirk C	11 (11)	Udoh D	1 (8)
Cooper G	43 (3)	Lowe R	21 (1)	Wintle R	7 (10)
Dagnall C	39 (2)	Lowery T	2 (5)		
Davis H	25	Ng P	9 (7)		

League goals (58): Dagnall 14, Jones 10, Cooper 9, Kiwomya 7, Lowe 5, Cooke 4, Bowery 2, Ainley 1, Davis 1, Hollands 1, Ray 1, Turton 1, Wintle 1, Opponents 1
FA Cup goals (2): Jones 1, Lowe 1. **League Cup goals** (5): Dagnall 2, Lowe 2, Bingham 1. **League Trophy goals** (5): Ainley 1, Cooper 1, Dagnall 1, Lowe 1, Udoh 1
Average home league attendance: 3,882. **Player of Year**: Chris Dagnall

DONCASTER ROVERS

Darren Ferguson led his side back to League One at the first attempt with a solid season's work which would have been crowned with the title had it not been for late season lapses. The division's highest scorers, with John Marquis leading the charge, looked a solid bet to finish on top when a promotion-clinching victory over Mansfield, achieved by Tommy Rowe's header, left them leading the field six points clear with five games remaining. Instead, they claimed only one point from those matches, the last of which was a 2-1 defeat away to relegated Hartlepool. It meant Doncaster finished third, two points behind Portsmouth and Plymouth. Marquis also drew a blank in those games after a hat-trick against Grimsby took him to 26 goals – two away from Laurie Sheffield's 28 for the club in the 1965-66 campaign. But there was still a major prize for his tally – League Two's Player of the Year award. His team's total of 85 featured 45 away from home, including five at Morecambe and Grimsby and four against Stevenage and Leyton Orient.

Alcock C	24 (3)	Butler A	44	Garrett T	1 (1)
May A	9 (7)	Calder R	5 (10)	Grant C	20 (1)
Baudry M	26 (5)	Coppinger J	38 (1)	Houghton J	32
Beestin A	(3)	Etheridge R	3 (3)	Keegan P	- (6)
Blair M	45	Evina C	13 (3)	Lawlor I	19

Longbottom W............. - (3)	Mason N................... 37 (1)	Rowe T............................46
Lund M...................... 4 (2)	McCullough L............ 6 (1)	Sinclair A................... 1 (3)
Mandeville L 9 (12)	McSheffrey G 3 (9)	Williams A 25 (12)
Marosi M 24 (1)	Middleston H 6 (19)	Wright J................... 18 (4)
Marquis J.......................45	Richardson F............. 3 (1)	

League goals (85): Marquis 26, Rowe 13, Williams 11, Coppinger 10, Mandeville 7, Baudry 5, May 3, Blair 3, Butler 3, Grant 1 Houghton 1, Opponents 2
FA Cup goals (1): Mandeville 1. **League Cup goals** (1) Mandeville 1. **League Trophy goals** (5): Beeston 1, Calder 1, Longbottom 1, Mandeville 1, Williams 1
Average home league attendance: 6,021. **Player of Year**: John Marquis

EXETER CITY

Paul Tisdale's side were unable to complete a major sporting double for their city at the end of an eventful season for the club. The day after Exeter Chiefs won rugby's Premiership Final, they went down 2-1 to Blackpool at Wembley, having climbed off the foot of the table to reach the play-offs. They came through a nail-biting semi-final against Carlisle with a 95th minute winner from Jack Stacey against the team he played for on loan the previous season. Exeter were then behind within three minutes in the final, levelled through leading scorer David Wheeler, but lost to a goal midway through the second-half. Five successive home defeats to start with, a club record, had stretched to nine without a win in front of their own supporters before Mansfield were defeated 2-0 with two goals from Ollie Watkins, later named the Football League's Young Player of the Year. It preceded a run of seven straight wins, equalling the club record, and delivered a rise to fourth in the table. Wheeler scored in each one for an outright club best and was on the mark again as Exeter recovered a 3-0 deficit against Yeovil at St James Park, his 88th minute effort followed by stoppage-time goals from Troy Brown and Reuben Reid. Exeter went on to confirm a play-off spot with their 13th away victory, 3-1 at Doncaster, in the penultimate match.

Ampadu E.................. 6 (2)	James L................... 42 (1)	Simpson R 14 (12)
Archibald-Henville T ... 1 (2)	Jay M .... - (2)	Stacey J.................... 27 (7)
Brown T.................... 28 (2)	McAlinden L 9 (23)	Sweeney P 27 (2)
Byrne A .... - (1)	McCready T............... 1 (1)	Taylor J............................43
Croll L 16 (3)	Moore-Taylor J...................42	Tillson J 9 (11)
Egan K .... - (1)	Oakley M 5 (14)	Watkins O 40 (5)
Grant J 9 (11)	Olejnik B 17 (1)	Wheeler D 33 (5)
Hamon J...........................1	Pym C 28	Woodman C....................33
Harley R 28 (3)	Reid R 31 (5)	
Holmes L 12 (4)	Riley-Lowe C 4 (1)	

Play-offs – appearances: Brown 3, Harley 3, Moore-Taylor 3, Taylor 3, Watkins 3, Wheeler 3, Woodman 3, Grant 2 (1), Stacey 2 (1), James 2, Olejnik 2, Holmes 1 (2), Sweeney 1 (1), Pym 1, Tillson 1, Reid – (2)
League goals (75): Wheeler 17, Reid 13, Watkins 13, Harley 5, Holmes 5, McAlinden 5, Moore-Taylor 5, Grant 4, Taylor 4, Brown 2, James 1, Simpson 1. **Play-offs – goals** (7): Watkins 2, Wheeler 2, Grant 1, Harley 1, Stacey 1
FA Cup goals (1): Reid 1. **League Cup goals** (2): Harley 1, Taylor 1. **League Trophy goals** (6): McAlinden 2, Wheeler 2, Jay 1, Watkins 1
Average home league attendance: 4,166. **Player of Year**: David Wheeler

GRIMSBY TOWN

Grimsby lost two leading scorers, as well as the manager who brought the good times back to Blundell Park, but still had a satisfactory return to the Football League after a six-year absence. Padraig Amond, who netted 30 goals in their successful National League campaign, opted for a summer move to Hartlepool. Paul Hurst left two-and-a-half-months into the new season to become Shrewsbury's new manager. Then, in the winter transfer window, Omar Bogle moved to Wigan after his 19 goals had taken Grimsby to the fringe of a play-off place. More upheaval followed, with Hurst's replacement, Solihull's Marcus Bignot, a former Queens Park Rangers defender, sacked a month from the end of the campaign, with players reportedly refusing to sign new contracts while he remained in the job. In came Russell Slade for his second spell with the club and his third job of the season after managing Coventry and Charlton. Two wins, two defeats and a draw left his new side just below half-way.

Andrew D.................,46	Davies B.............. 22 (3)	McKeown J..................39
Asante A.................. 2 (7)	Disley C................ 15 (13)	Mills Z...........................30
Berrett J 15 (4)	Dyson C............... 14 (2)	Osborne J............. 17 (2)
Bogle O 25 (2)	Gowling L............. 17 (1)	Pearson S............. 30 (4)
Bolarinwa T........... 16 (18)	Gunning G 12 (2)	Summerfield L......... 22 (1)
Boyce A................ 12 (5)	Henderson D...............7	Tuton S..................... 5 (5)
Browne R............... - (5)	Jackson K.............. 15 (5)	Vernon S............... 12 (16)
Chambers A 14 (2)	Jones D .... ,2 (1)	Vose D................... 15 (8)
Clements C..............16	Jones S.................. 16 (2)	Yussuf A 4 (7)
Collins D.................36	Maxwell L.............. 1 (3)	
Comley B.............. 26 (7)	McAllister S.................3	

League goals (59): Bogle 19, Jones 7, Clements 4, Dyson 4, Vernon 3, Berrett 2, Bolarinwa 2, Collins 2, Disley 2, Pearson 2, Vose 2, Yusuf 2, Asante 1, Boyce 1, Chambers 1, Davies 1, Jackson 1, Osborne 1, Summerfield 1, Opponents 1
FA Cup goals: None. **League Cup goals:** None. **League Trophy goals (4):** Boyce 1, Disley 1, Jackson 1, Summerfield 1
Average home league attendance: 5,259. **Player of Year:** Danny Andrew

HARTLEPOOL UNITED

Hartlepool were cast out into non-league football on a dramatic final day of the season at Victoria Park. They came from behind to beat promoted Doncaster 2-1 with goals by 18-year-old substitute Devante Rodney in the 74th and 83rd minutes which gave his side a chance of surviving. But an 89th minute winner for Newport against Notts County meant it was the Welsh team staying up. Hartlepool looked to be safe when three wins in four games, against Crewe, Exeter and Cambridge, left them nine points clear of trouble. But the failure to win any of the next eight, coupled with Newport's revival, cost them dearly. Club president and Sky Sports presenter Jeff Stelling called on air for manager Dave Jones to resign as his team dropped into the bottom two after a home defeat by Barnet. Two days later, the manager was sacked after 13 points in 17 games, leaving defender Matthew Bates in charge for the final two fixtures. The first was a 1-0 defeat at Cheltenham; the second brought an end to the club's 96 years of Football League membership. They had started the season with Craig Hignett in charge. Hignett was dismissed after a run of one win in nine league and FA Cup matches and replaced by Jones, his first appointment since being fired by Sheffield Wednesday in December, 2013.

Alessandra L 39 (7)	Featherstone N..............43	Kavanagh S......................9
Amond P................. 37 (9)	Fewster B .... - (4)	Laurent J............. 18 (7)
Bartlett A 9 (1)	Fryer J.....................14	Magnay C............. 11 (2)
Bates M 19 (1)	Green K .... - (1)	Martin J...........................3
Blackford J .... - (1)	Harrison S............. 35 (3)	Nelson A................. 3 (1)
Carroll J 19 (2)	Hawkes J .... - (2)	Nsiala A................ 20 (1)
Carson T.....................23	Hawkins L.............. 27 (7)	Oates R 17 (8)
Deverdics N 15 (13)	Heardman T.............. - (2)	Paynter B............. 12 (9)
Donnelly L 31 (1)	Jones R 3 (1)	Richards J............. 12 (3)

Richardson K 9 (2)	Simpson C .... - (2)	Walker B................. 19 (1)
Rodney D................... - (4)	Smith C..................... - (1)	Woods M................ 25 (11)
Rooney L 3 (4)	Thomas N 31 (2)	

League goals (54): Amond 14, Alessandra 9, Thomas 9, Featherstone 3, Oates 3, Paynter 3, Magnay 2, Rodney 2, Woods 2, Bates 1, Deverdics 1, Harrison 1, Laurent 1, Nsiala 1, Walker 1, Opponents 1
FA Cup goals (3): Deverdics 1, Paynter 1, Opponents 1. **League Cup goals**: None. **League Trophy goals** (2): Oates 2
Average home league attendance: 3,788

LEYTON ORIENT

Relegation from the Football League is distressing for any club and their fans. For Orient, the end of 112 years of membership was particularly traumatic. They finished 12 points adrift after a shambolic season under owner Francesco Becchetti involving five different managers, a winding up order from Revenue and Customs and league officials admitting to being 'exceptionally concerned' about what had gone on. Once the drop was confirmed, honorary president and previous owner Barry Hearn resigned in protest at Becchetti's tenure. Andy Hessenthaler became the league's first managerial casualty of the campaign, sacked after back-to-back defeats by Yeovil and Notts County. As their predicament deteriorated, he was followed in the hot seat by Alberto Cavasin, Andy Edwards, Danny Webb and Omer Riza. Orient suffered a club record eight successive home defeats on the way to the foot of the table. A 3-2 away win over second-place Plymouth turned the table upside down as Gavin Massey equalised with his second goal of the game after 88 minutes, then set up's Sandro Semedo's 94th minute winner. A 4-0 victory at fellow-strugglers Newport offered further hope, but 15 goals conceded in the next four matches left them needing to miracle to survive. Riza, with seven teenagers in his team had no chance of turning things round and relegation was confirmed by a 3-0 defeat at Crewe with two fixtures remaining. There was more distress when the last home game against Colchester was suspended after a sit-down protest by fans, then completed behind closed doors nearly two hours later.

Abrahams T............... 4 (5)	Dunne A .... - (5)	McCallum P 20 (9)
Adeboyejo V 4 (9)	Erichot Y................. 18 (1)	Mezague T 11 (6)
Alzate S 9 (3)	Gnanduillet A .... - (1)	Moncur F 5 (4)
Atangana N 25 (4)	Grainger C....................3	Moore S..................... 3 (1)
Benedicic Z................ - (1)	Happe D 1 (1)	N'Nomo U.................. 1 (5)
Bowery J................. 9 (8)	Hunt N 34	Ochieng H................. 4 (2)
Cisak A......................28	Janse J..........................8	Palmer O 10 (10)
Clark M...................... 8 (1)	Judd M......................20	Parkes T 41
Clohessy S 2	Kelly L.................. 19 (2)	Pollock A 8 (1)
Collins M 28 (2)	Kennedy C 31 (1)	Sargeant S....................15
Cornick H 9 (2)	Koroma J 12 (10)	Semedo S 35 (7)
Cox D 4	Liburd R 4 (4)	Simpson J................ 12 (2)
Dalby S................... 10 (6)	Massey G 36	Weir R 15 (2)

League goals (47): Massey 8, McCallum 8, Palmer 5, Kelly 4, Koroma 3, Semedo 3, Simpson 3, Abrahams 2, Adeboyejo 1, Alzate 1, Bowery 1, Cornick 1, Cox 1, Dalby 1, Hunt 1, Janse 1, Kennedy 1, Mezague 1, Parkes 1
FA Cup goals: None. **League Cup goals** (2): McCallum 2. **League Trophy goals** (3): McCallum 2, Semedo 1
Average home league attendance: 4,663

LUTON TOWN

A 95th minute own goal by goalkeeper Stuart Moore delivered a cruel end to Luton's promotion chances. Trailing 4-2 on aggregate in the second leg of their play-off against Blackpool at Kenilworth Road, they roared back to transform the semi-final with an own goal by Blackpool's Kelvin Mellor, Scott Cuthbert's header and a penalty won and converted by Danny Hylton. But they were pegged back to 5-5 with 14 minutes of normal time remaining and lost out when Jordan Cook's attempted clearance went in off the luckless Moore. Luton beat their opponents twice in the regular campaign and had moved to within a point of an automatic promotion place in early March after a 4-0 win over Yeovil. But the failure to win any of the five matches remaining in that month left them trailing. They climbed back to fourth and carried plenty of momentum into the play-offs with nine goals in the final three matches against Notts County, Accrington and Morecambe. Hylton's 22 goals were supplemented by five more in other competitions.

Cook J	31 (4)	Lee O	24 (9)	Palmer O	4 (13)
Cuthbert S	37 (1)	Macey M	11	Potts D	22 (1)
D'Ath L	8 (3)	Mackail-Smith C	- (2)	Rea G	36 (3)
Famewo A	1 (1)	Marriott J	25 (14)	Ruddock P	34 (8)
Gambin J	8 (8)	McGeehan C	24	Senior J	9 (1)
Gilliead A	10 (8)	McQuoid J	1 (2)	Sheehan A	31 (3)
Gray J	11 (8)	Moore S	8	Smith J	12 (13)
Hylton D	38 (1)	Mullins J	21 (2)	Vassell I	22 (18)
Justin J	24 (5)	O'Donnell S	27 (3)	Walton C	27

Play-offs – appearances: Cuthbert 2, D'Ath 2, Hylton 2, Justin 2, Lee 2, Moore 2, Potts 2, Rea 2, Ruddock 2, Sheehan 2, Vassell 2, Cook – (1), Marriott – (1), Palmer – (1)
League goals (70): Hylton 21, McGeehan 10, Marriott 8, Vassell 8, Cook 3, Palmer 3, Rea 2, Ruddock 2, Sheehan 2, Cuthbert 1, Gambin 1, Gilliead 1, Gray 1, Justin 1, Lee 1, O'Donnell 1, Smith 1, Opponents 3. **Play-offs – goals** (5): Cuthbert 1, Hylton 1, Potts 1, Vassell 1, Opponents 1
FA Cup goals (10): Hylton 3, Marriott 2, O'Donnell 2, Gray 1, Mullins 1, Rea 1. **League Cup goals** (3): Gray 1, McGeehan 1, Opponents 1. **League Trophy goals** (19): Vassell 5, Hylton 2, Marriott 2, McQuoid 2, Cook 1, Gilliead 1, Gray 1, Mackail-Smith 1, Musonda F 1, Sheehan 1, Smith 1, Opponents 1
Average home league attendance: 8,046. **Player of Year**: Danny Hylton

MANSFIELD TOWN

Mansfield went into the final day of the regular season with a slim chance of reaching the play-offs. They were two points adrift, needing to beat Steve Evans's former club Crawley and hope other results went their way. But after establishing a 2-0 lead with goals by Danny Rose and Ben Whiteman, they were pegged back – and would not have gone through anyway because of wins by teams above them. It meant a mid-table finish in a tightly-packed division. Former Leeds and Rotherham manager Evans took charge after Adam Murray resigned after a 4-0 defeat by Portsmouth which left Mansfield 18th in mid-November. His appointment was described as 'arguably the most significant and most exciting in the club's modern history' by chief executive officer Carolyn Radford. Evans, who began with wins over Crawley at home and Blackpool, led his side to the fringes of the leading group. They closed to within a point of their target before a home defeat by Portsmouth left them with too much to do.

Arquin Y	3 (9)	Clements C	18 (2)	Hemmings A	10 (6)
Baxendale J	3 (9)	Collins L	35 (2)	Henderson D	3 (10)
Bennett R	46	Coulthirst S	15 (5)	Hoban P	13 (8)
Benning M	45	Gobern O	6 (3)	Howkins K	13 (3)
Byrom J	21 (1)	Green M	31 (11)	Hurst K	12 (2)
Chapman A	5	Hamilton C	13 (16)	Iacovitti A	4 (4)

Jensen B.........................3	Potter A 5 (7)	Thomas J .... - (6)
Kean J...........................19	Rose D 25 (12)	White H 18
MacDonald A............ 13 (5)	Rose M 17 (1)	Whiteman B 23
McGuire J 13 (4)	Shearer S................. 24 (1)	
Pearce K........................41	Taft G 9 (4)	

League goals (54): Green 10, Rose D 9, Whiteman 7, Coulthirst 5, Hoban 4, Clements 3, Pearce 3, Arquin 2, Bennett 2, Rose M 2, Benning 1, Henderson 1, Hurst 1, MacDonald 1, Potter 1, White 1, Opponents 1
FA Cup goals (1) Hemmings 1. **League Cup goals** (1): Rose M 1. **League Trophy goals** (10): Green 3, Hoban 2, Clements 1, Hemmings 1, Henderson 1, Pearce 1, Rose D 1
Average home league attendance: 3,774. **Player of Year:** Rhys Bennett

MORECAMBE

A flying start gave way to a difficult season on and off the pitch. Four successive victories put Jim Bentley's side on top of the table, earning League Two's longest-serving boss the season's first Manager of the Month award. The points accumulated proved to be important insurance against a slump at the end of the campaign. In a tightly packed division, Morecambe seemed to have progressed to a comfortable mid-table position on the back of just one defeat in 11 matches, starting early in the New Year. Instead, seven successive defeats sent them tumbling. Victory at Stevenage proved a welcome relief, but it was the only one in the final 13 fixtures, leaving the team in 18th position, an improvement of three on 2016. This came against a background of board concern for the club's future, new owner Diego Lemos being accused of failing to deliver promised investment, the PFA having to pay wages and the imposition of a transfer embargo ahead of the January window.

Barkhuizen T..................14	Jennings J................. 12 (1)	Rose M 43
Conlan L..................... 16 (5)	Jordan L .... - (6)	Stockton C 17 (2)
Duckworth M............. 11 (3)	Kenyon A 14 (5)	Turner R 13 (16)
Dunn J 9 (4)	Massanka N .... - (11)	Wakefield L 22 (3)
Edwards R 43	McGowan A.............. 22 (8)	Whitmore A....................35
Ellison K 39 (6)	Molyneux L 22 (18)	Wildig A.................. 23 (5)
Evans A 7 (7)	Mullin P 28 (12)	Winnard D.....................23
Fleming A 25 (5)	Murphy P 22 (10)	Yawson S .... - (1)
Hawley K .... - (1)	Nizic D 5	
Hedley B..................... - (1)	Roche B 41	

League goals (53): Ellison 8, Mullin 8, Rose 7, Barkhuizen 5, Molyneux 5, Stockton 5, Murphy 3, Dunn 2, Evans 2, Fleming 2, Turner 2, Wildig 2, Edwards 1, Opponents 1
FA Cup goals (2) Winnard 2. **League Cup goals** (6): Dunn 3, Stockton 2, Ellison 1. **League Trophy goals** (8): Stockton 3, Mullin 2, Dunn 1, Edwards 1, Murphy 1
Average home league attendance: 1,703. **Player of Year:** Ryan Edwards

NEWPORT COUNTY

Newport rose like the phoenix to deliver one of the game's greatest escapes. With two months of the season remaining, they looked dead and buried, 11 points adrift at the bottom of the table with 12 games remaining and facing a return to non-league football. The club sacked Graham Westley, manager for five months after a 4-0 home defeat by Leyton Orient, replaced him with coach Mike Flynn as caretaker and saw a remarkable transformation. Flynn won his first two games, against Crewe and Morecambe to close the gap to seven and picked up three more against Crawley, Exeter and Yeovil. A 6-1 thrashing by Plymouth set them back, but they finally broke free from seven months in the relegation zone by beating Accrington and overhauling Hartlepool. That left everything depending on the final round of games. Hartlepool defeated promoted Doncaster and were heading for safety until Irish central defender Mark O'Brien volleyed his first goal in three years in the 89th minute to give Newport a 2-1 victory over Notts County and keep them up. Newport, who confirmed Flynn as manager of his home town club, had started the season with Warren Feeney in charge. He was sacked after 11 games and replaced by Westley, who signed a dozen players in the winter transfer window.

Barnum-Bobb J 15 (11)	Gordon J 2 (8)	O'Hanlon J 5 (2)
Bennett S 38 (1)	Green J 4 (6)	Owen-Evans T 12 (12)
Bignot P 9 (1)	Grego-Cox R 7	Parkin J 8 (2)
Bird R 19	Healey R 13 (4)	Pipe D 21
Bittner J 1 (1)	Jackson M 9 (13)	Randall M 22 (3)
Blanchard M 1	Jebb J 4 (1)	Reid C 9 (1)
Bojai F .... - (1)	John-Lewis L 1 (1)	Rigg S 29 (5)
Butler D................. 38 (2)	Jones D 29 (2)	Rose M 12
Cameron K 6	Labadie J 17 (2)	Samuel A 15 (3)
Compton J 2 (6)	Mcite A 3 (1)	Sheehan J 17 (3)
Day J...........................45	Myrie-Williams J 14 (9)	Tozer B 17 (6)
Demetriou M 12 (5)	Nelson S 12 (2)	Turley J 6
Flynn M..................... 4 (1)	O'Brien M 20	Williams A 8 (8)

League goals (51): Bird 6, Healey 6, Rigg 6, Sheehan 5, Demetriou 4, Parkin 4, Butler 3, Labadie 3, Williams 3, Samuel 2, Barnum-Bobb 1, Compton 1, Gordon 1, Myrie-Williams 1, O'Brien 1, Owen-Evans 1, Randall 1, Tozer 1, Turley 1
FA Cup goals (5): Sheehan 2, Barnum-Bobb 1, Green 1, Healey 1. **League Cup goals** (2): Jackson 1, Randall 1. **League Trophy goals** (4): Barnum-Bobb 1, Bennett 1, Green 1, Myrie-Williams 1
Average home league attendance: 2,861. **Player of Year:** Joe Day

NOTTS COUNTY

Kevin Nolan led County away from the threat of non-league football. They were in trouble, a point off the relegation zone, when John Sheridan was sacked after a ninth successive defeat, 4-0 at Cambridge. That stretched to a club record ten under the single game player-coach Alan Smith had as caretaker. Owner Ray Trew sold the club to Nottingham businessman Alan Hardy, who immediately installed Nolan, formerly in charge of Leyton Orient, as manager. In his first match, County ended the losing sequence with a goalless draw against local rivals Mansfield in front of a crowd of more than 11,000. And they won for the first time for three months, against Crawley, with a 90th minute goal from Jonathan Forte, despite the earlier dismissal of Curtis Thompson for a second yellow card. That was the start of nine victories in 14 matches which lifted them into the relative comfort of the middle reaches of the table. Three defeats in the last four meant they climbed no higher, but the job had been done.

Aborah S.................... 6 (2)	Duffy R......................42	O'Connor M.............. 30 (2)
Ameobi S 13 (4)	Edwards M.....................2	Oliver V.................. 2 (17)
Audel T.................. 12 (4)	Forte J.................. 28 (7)	Osborne S................. 1 (2)
Bola M 10 (3)	Gibson M .... - (1)	Richards J................. 7 (5)
Burke G 2 (3)	Grant J 15 (2)	Rodman A.............. 15 (1)
Campbell A 21 (8)	Hewitt E 23 (6)	Smith A 7 (12)
Campbell T 1 (10)	Hollis H 30 (1)	Snijders G................. 3 (2)
Clackstone J.............. 7 (1)	Howes A 1 (1)	Stead J................. 37 (1)
Collin J.........................43	Laing L 19 (2)	Thompson C 11 (2)
Collins A 3 (15)	Loach S 3	Tootle M 32 (1)
Dickinson C............. 33 (1)	Milsom R................ 36 (2)	Yeates M............... 11 (3)

League goals (54): Stead 14, Forte 8, Grant 6, Ameobi 4, Campbell 4, Duffy 4, Collins 2, Hewitt 2, O'Connor 2, Tootle 2, Audel 1, Hollis 1, Laing 1, Oliver 1, Rodman 1, Opponents 1

FA Cup goals (6): Campbell 3, Collins 1, Forte 1, Laing 1. **League Cup goals**: None. **League Trophy goals** (4): Burke 1, Campbell 1, Forte 1, Snijders 1
Average home league attendance: 5,970. **Player of Year**: Rob Milsom

PLYMOUTH ARGYLE

Plymouth flirted with promotion in the two previous seasons, losing to Wimbledon in the 2016 Play-off Final and reaching the semi-finals before that. This time, they went all the way, finally fulfilling the club's status and support with the runners-up spot and a return to the game's third tier. Derek Adams's team compensated for seven home defeats with club-record performances on their travels – one spell of seven successive league victories and overall 13 wins away from Home Park. They led the division for a total of three months, but the last of those home reversals, against Accrington at a time when Doncaster were ruling the roost, convinced Adams that the title would not be theirs. In the event, Doncaster blew a six-point lead, opening the way for Plymouth to regain the leadership with a promotion-clinching 6-1 win over Newport followed by the 2-1 defeat of Crewe in their final home fixture. It took them a point clear, but a 1-1 draw at Grimsby on the last day of the regular season was not enough to withstand Portsmouth's 6-1 victory over Cheltenham which made them champions with a superior goal difference, both sides having finished on 87 points.

Blissett N 1 (8)	Jervis J 28 (14)	Slew J 19 (13)
Bradley S 43 (1)	Kennedy M 17	Smith C 12 (13)
Bulvitis N 16 (2)	McCormick L..................46	Sokolik J.................. 15 (3)
Carey G............................46	Miller G 27 (4)	Songo'o Y 41 (5)
Donaldson R 14 (12)	Osborne K................. - (1)	Spencer J 17 (8)
Fox D 37 (3)	Purrington B 16 (3)	Tanner C 11 (15)
Garita A 8 (6)	Rooney L .... - (1)	Taylor R 15 (3)
Goodwillie D............. 5 (11)	Sarcevic A 16 (1)	Threlkeld O 33 (3)
Ijaha D 2 (1)	Sawyer G 21	

League goals (71): Carey 14, Jervis 12, Bradley 7, Kennedy 5, Tanner 5, Slew 4, Taylor 4, Spencer 3, Blissett 2, Bulvitis 2, Donaldson 2, Garita 2, Sarcevic 2, Songo'o 2, Threlkeld 2, Goodwillie 1, Smith 1, Sokolik 1
FA Cup goals (3): Carey 1, Fox 1, Slew 1. **League Cup goals**: None. **League Trophy goals** (5): Bulvitis 1, Jervis 1, Slew 1, Smith 1, Tanner 1
Average home league attendance: 9,652. **Player of Year**: Sonny Bradley

PORTSMOUTH

Portsmouth finally began to reverse their fall from the heady days of Premier League football to the game's fourth tier. And they completed the job in some style by becoming champions on the last day of the season. Paul Cook's side went into the final round of fixtures in third place, a point behind Doncaster and two adrift of Plymouth. Both their rivals dropped points, against Hartlepool and Grimsby respectively, opening the way for a 6-1 victory over Cheltenham to make the title theirs with a superior goal difference. Portsmouth had been knocking on the door for an automatic promotion place for much of the season, finally making it with three victories in eight days at beginning of March – Crawley (2-0), Colchester (4-0) and Grimsby (4-0). Defeat at Stevenage in the next game left them 13 points adrift of the top spot. But while Doncaster folded and Plymouth failed to take advantage, Portsmouth came storming through by accumulating an unmatchable 22 points, with 20 goals scored, from their final eight matches. Cook then left the club to take over at Wigan and in came Kenny Jackett, former Rotherham and Wolves manager.

Aborah S.................... 1 (3)	Bennett K 33 (6)	Clarke M..........................33
Baker C 40 (5)	Burgess C 44	Davies T 10 (3)
Barton A 2 (1)	Chaplin C............... 13 (26)	Doyle E............................12

Doyle M 46	Linganzi A................ 12 (7)	Smith M 14 (4)
Evans G 41	Lowe J...................... 5 (9)	Stevens E 45
Forrde D 46	Main C 4 (8)	Talbot D..........................5
Hunt N 4 (16)	Naismith K 22 (15)	Whatmough J 4 (6)
Kabamba N................ 1 (3)	Roberts G 31 (10)	
Lalkovic M 5 (8)	Rose D 33 (5)	

League goals (79): Naismith 13, Roberts 10, Baker 9, Chaplin 8, Bennett 6, Evans 5, Rose 5, Burgess 4, Lowe 4, Smith 3, Doyle E 2, Main 2, Clarke 1, Doyle M 1, Hunt 1, Lalkovic 1, Linganzi 1, Stevens 1, Whatmough 1, Opponents 1
FA Cup goals (1): Evans 1. **League Cup goals** (2): Main 1, Naismith 1. **League Trophy goals** (6): Smith 3, Main 2, Naismith 1
Average home league attendance: 16,823. **Player of Year**: Christian Burgess

STEVENAGE

The loss of leading marksman Matt Godden, coupled to successive home defeats at a crucial time of the season, cost Stevenage a place in the play-offs. Godden scored 13 goals in 14 games to point his side towards fourth place, with a five-point cushion and just five matches remaining. He missed three of them with a broken toe, Morecambe and Mansfield came away from the Lamex Stadium with 1-0 victories and by the time the striker returned for the final game against Accrington, Stevenage had slipped to eighth. They lost that one, too, making it 11 defeats in all in front of their own supporters, although three points would not have been enough because the teams above them all won. In contrast, there were six successive away wins, a record for the club, leading up to the midway point of the campaign. Godden, a summer signing from National League Ebbsfleet, finished with 20 goals, including a hat-trick against Newport.

Conlon T 3 (1)	Hyde J 2 (4)	McQuoid J 10 (6)
Cowans H 12 (6)	Jones J 36	Nthle K 20 (2)
Day C 10 (1)	Kennedy B 26 (10)	Ogilvie C 18
Fox A 7 (2)	Kerr N .... - (1)	Pett T 35 (5)
Franks F 40 (1)	King J...........................36	Schumacher S.......... 27 (1)
Godden M 37 (1)	Lee C 35 (9)	Tonge M................. 13 (14)
Gorman D 15 (10)	Liburd R 2 (11)	Walker T 7 (1)
Gray J....................... - (3)	Loft R...................... - (9)	Wells D 10 (4)
Henry R 32 (1)	McAnuff I 22 (9)	Wilkinson L............. 38 (2)
Hinds K 4 (9)	McKee M 1 (1)	
Hunte C 2 (1)	McKirdy H 6 (5)	

League goals (67): Godden 20, Kennedy 8, Pett 6, Schumacher 5, McAnuff 4, Wilkinson 4, Franks 3, King 3, Walker 3, Lee 2, Gorman 1, Hunte 1, Liburd 1, McKirdy 1, McQuoid 1, Tonge 1, Wells 1, Opponents 2
FA Cup goals: None. **League Cup goals** (1): Kennedy 1. **League Trophy goals** (7): Liburd 2, Franks 1, Godden 1, McKirdy 1, Schumacher 1, Walker 1
Average home league attendance: 2,899. **Player of Year**: Matt Godden

WYCOMBE WANDERERS

Wycombe recovered from an FA Cup hangover to finish just short of the play-offs. They produced an exhilarating performance in a fourth round tie at White Hart Lane, leading 2-0 at half-time with two goals by Paul Hayes, then 3-2 through Garry Thompson, before Tottenham equalised in the 89th minute and scored the winner seven minutes into added-time. Gareth Ainsworth's side were sixth at the time, one of a cluster of teams jostling for positions, but won just once in the next eight matches, dropped into mid-table and were still there with four remaining. Such was the competitive nature of the division, however, that victories over Barnet and leaders Doncaster, followed by a draw at Morecambe, offered them a slim chance. They were a single point adrift going into the final fixture, needing to beat Cambridge and hope all the teams directly the teams above them slipped up. Scott Kashket's goal delivered a 1-0 victory, lifting them above two of them, Cambridge and Stevenage. But it was not quite enough and they finished behind Colchester on goal difference and a point adrift of seventh-place Blackpool.

Akinfenwa A........... 32 (10)	Gape D 29 (3)	O'Nien L 28 (3)
Bean M.................... 15 (4)	Harriman M................38	Pierre A 38 (1)
Blackman J....................42	Hayes P 18 (5)	Rowe D.................... 10 (2)
Bloomfield M............ 24 (9)	Jacobson J....................39	Saunders S 11 (6)
Brown S........................3	Jakubiak A 4 (6)	Southwell D 11 (2)
Cowan-Hall P 20 (8)	Jombati S 23 (2)	Stewart A................ 30 (1)
Dawson C....................1	Kashket S 13 (8)	Thompson G........... 21 (21)
De Havilland W......... 12 (4)	McGinn S 3 (2)	Weston M................. 9 (10)
Freeman N.............. 4 (10)	Muller M................... 7 (2)	Wood S 22 (11)

League goals (58): Akinfenwa 12, Kashket 10, Bloomfield 5, Cowan-Hall 4, Hayes 3, Jacobson 3, O'Nien 3, Thompson 3, Weston 3, Jombati 2, Pierre 2, Wood 2, Gape 1, Jakubiak 1, Saunders 1, Southwell 1, Stewart 1, Opponents 1
FA Cup goals (12): Hayes 3, Kashket 3, Akinfenwa 2, Cowan-Hall 1, Stewart 1, Thompson 1 Wood 1. **League Cup goals**: None. **League Trophy goals (15)**: Akinfenwa 4, Kashket 3, Thompson 3, Freeman 1, Hayes 1, McGinn 1, Rowe 1, Stewart 1
Average home league attendance: 3,917. **Player of Year**: Adebayo Akinfenwa

YEOVIL TOWN

Yeovil showed signs of a promotion challenge after a poor start, but fell away. A single win in the opening seven matches left them second from bottom and fearing another relegation struggle. They then beat Leyton Orient and Cheltenham and climbed out of trouble with successive 1-0 victories over Wycombe, Newport and Crewe. Then, the 5-0 defeat of Crawley had them up to sixth approaching the half-way point of the campaign. But another slump – four points from eight matches – resulted in a drop into the bottom half of the table and they rarely looked like recovering lost ground. Yeovil managed just three wins in 2017, against Plymouth, Morecambe and Crewe. Fortunately, there was enough in the bank to avoid a late scramble for safety. They finished 20th, four points away from trouble and one place worse off than the previous campaign.

Akpa Akpro J-L........... 9 (4)	Harrison S................ 4 (10)	McLeod I 2 (2)
Butcher M................ 27 (7)	Hedges R................. 20 (1)	Mugabi B............... 20 (11)
Campbell T 6 (13)	James T 1 (1)	Shepherd L....................38
Dawson K 39	Jones O .... - (2)	Smith N.................... 33 (1)
Dickson R 34	Khan O 27 (2)	Sowunmi O 4 (8)
Dolan M....................38	Krysiak A 41	Storer J............................1
Eaves T.................. 30 (10)	Lacey A 38 (2)	Ward D 14 (2)
Dolan M....................38	Lawless A 30 (3)	Whitfield B............. 22 (12)
Goodship B 1 (7)	Maddison J 5	

League goals (49): Zoko 8, Khan 6, Dolan 4, Eaves 4, Hedges 4, Lacey 3, Ward 3, Akpa Akpro 2, Butcher 2, Dawson 2, Smith 2, Whitfield 2, Campbell 1, Harrison 1, Lawless 1, Mugabi 1, Shephard 1, Opponents 2
FA Cup goals (3): Hedges 1, Khan 1, Zoko 1. **League Cup goals (2)**: Dolan 1, Opponents 1.
League Trophy goals (16): Zoko 4, Eaves 3, Sowunmi 2, Dawson 1, Khan 1, Lacey 1, McLeod 1, Mugabi 1, Whitfield 1, Opponents 1
Average home league attendance: 3,535. **Player of Year**: Alex Lacey

LEAGUE CLUB MANAGERS 2017–18

Figure in brackets = number of managerial changes at club since the War. †Second spell at club

PREMIER LEAGUE

Arsenal (11)	Arsene Wenger	October 1996
Bournemouth (24)	Eddie Howe	October 2012
Brighton (33)	Chris Hughton	December 2014†
Burnley (24)	Sean Dyche	October 2012
Chelsea (29)	Antonio Conte	July 2016
Crystal Palace (42)	Frank de Boer	June 2017
Everton (18)	Ronald Koeman	June 2016
Huddersfield (28)	David Wagner	November 2015
Leicester (29)	Craig Shakespeare	June 2017
Liverpool (14)	Jurgen Klopp	October 2015
Manchester City (30)	Pep Guardiola	May 2016
Manchester Utd (11)	Jose Mourinho	May 2016
Newcastle (27)	Rafael Benitez	March 2016
Southampton (27)	Maurlcio Pellegrino	June 2017
Stoke (23)	Mark Hughes	May 2013
Swansea (35)	Paul Clement	January 2017
Tottenham (23)	Mauricio Pochettino	May 2014
Watford (35)	Marco Silva	May 2017
WBA (32)	Tony Pulis	January 2015
West Ham (14)	Slaven Bilic	June 2015

† Second spell at club

CHAMPIONSHIP

Aston Villa (26)	Steve Bruce	October 2016
Barnsley (25)	Paul Heckingbottom	June 2016
Birmingham (27)	Harry Redknapp	May 2017
Bolton (23)	Phil Parkinson	June 2016
Brentford (33)	Dean Smith	November 2015
Bristol City (26)	Lee Johnson	February 2016
Burton (3)	Nigel Clough	December 2015
Cardiff (31)	Neil Warnock	October 2016
Derby (26)	Gary Rowell	March 2017
Fulham (32)	Slavisa Jokanovic	December 2015
Hull (29)	Leonid Slutsky	June 2017
Middlesbrough (21)	Garry Monk	June 2017
Millwall (31)	Neil Harris	April 2015
Ipswich (13)	Mick McCarthy	November 2012
Leeds (31)	Thomas Christiansen	June 2017
Norwich (29)	Daniel Farke	May 2017
Nottm Forest (24)	Mark Warburton	March 2017
Preston (29)	Alex Neil	July 2017
QPR (34)	Ian Holloway	November 2016
Reading (22)	Jaap Stam	June 2016
Sheffield Utd (38)	Chris Wilder	May 2016
Sheffield Wed (29)	Carlos Carvalhal	June 2015
Sunderland (30)	Simon Grayson	June 2017
Wolves (26)	Nuno Espirito Santo	May 2017

Number of changes since elected to Football League: Burton 2009

LEAGUE ONE

AFC Wimbledon (1)	Neal Ardley	October 2012
Blackburn (31)	Tony Mowbray	February 2017

Blackpool (31)	Gary Bowyer	June 2016
Bradford (34)	Stuart McCall	June 2016
Bristol Rov (-)	Darrell Clarke	March 2014
Bury (26)	Lee Clark	February 2017
Charlton (24)	Karl Robinson	November 2016
Doncaster (5)	Darren Ferguson	October 2015
Fleetwood (3)	Uwe Rosler	July 2016
Gillingham (25)	Ady Pennock	May 2017
MK Dons (16)	Robbie Neilson	December 2016
Northampton (33)	Justin Edinburgh	January 2017
Oldham (31)	John Sheridan	January 2017
Oxford (3)	Pep Clotet	July 2017
Peterborough (30)	Grant McCann	May 2016
Plymouth (34)	Derek Adams	June 2015
Portsmouth (34)	Kenny Jackett	June 2017
Rochdale (32)	Keith Hill†	January 2013
Rotherham (28)	Paul Warne	April 2017
Scunthorpe (28)	Graham Alexander	March 2016
Shrewsbury (5)	Paul Hurst	October 2016
Southend (28)	Phil Brown	March 2013
Walsall (35)	Jon Whitney	June 2016
Wigan (24)	Paul Cook	June 2017

† Second spell at club. Number of changes since elected to Football League: Peterborough 1960, Wigan 1978, AFC Wimbledon 2011, Fleetwood 2012. Since returning: Doncaster 2003, Shrewsbury 2004, Oxford 2010, Bristol Rov 2015

LEAGUE TWO

Accrington (4)	John Coleman†	September 2014
Barnet (2)	Rossi Eames	May 2017
Cambridge (1)	Shaun Derrty	November 2015
Carlisle (5)	Keith Curle	September 2014
Cheltenham (-)	Gary Johnson	March 2015
Chesterfield (22)	Gary Caldwell	January 2017
Colchester (28)	John McGreal	May 2016
Coventry (35)	Mark Robins	March 2017
Crawley (7)	Harry Kewell	May 2017
Crewe (22)	David Artell	January 2017
Exeter (-)	Paul Tisdale	June 2006
Forest Green (-)	Mark Cooper	May 2016
Grimsby (2)	Russell Slade	April 2017
Lincoln (-)	Danny Cowley	May 2016
Luton (1)	Nathan Jones	January 2016
Mansfield (2)	Steve Evans	November 2016
Morecambe (1)	Jim Bentley	May 2011
Newport (5)	Mike Flynn	May 2017
Notts Co (43)	Kevin Nolan	January 2017
Port Vale (26)	Michael Brown	May 2017
Stevenage (4)	Darren Sarll	May 2016
Swindon (31)	David Flitcroft	June 2017
Wycombe (10)	Gareth Ainsworth	November 2012
Yeovil (6)	Darren Way	December 2015

† Second spell at club. Number of changes since elected to Football League: Wycombe 1993, Yeovil 2003, Morecambe 2007, Stevenage 2010, Crawley 2011, Forest Green 2017. Since returning: Colchester 1992, Carlisle 2005, Accrington 2006, Exeter 2008, Mansfield 2013, Newport 2013, Cambridge 2014, Luton 2014, Barnet 2015, Cheltenham 2016, Grimsby 2016, Lincoln 2017

MANAGERIAL CHANGES 2016–17

PREMIER LEAGUE

Crystal Palace: Out – Alan Pardew (Dec 2016); In – Sam Allardyce; Out (May 2017);
In – Frank de Boer
Hull: Out – Steve Bruce (Jul 2016); In – Mike Phelan; Out (Jan 2017);
In – Marco Silva; Out (May 2017); ; In – Leonid Slutsky
Leicester: Out – Claudio Ranieri (Feb 2017); In – Craig Shakespeare
Middlesbrough: Out – Aitor Karanka (Mar 2017); In – Garry Monk
Southampton: Out – Claude Puel (June 2017); In – Mauricio Pellegrino
Sunderland: Out – Sam Allardyce (Jul 2016); In – David Moyes; Out (May 2017);
In – Simon Grayson
Swansea: Out – Francesco Guidolin (Oct 2016); In – Bob Bradley; Out (Dec 2016);
In – Paul Clement
Watford: Out – Walter Mazzarri (May 2017); In – Marco Silva

CHAMPIONSHIP

Aston Villa: Out – Roberto di Matteo (Oct 2016); In – Steve Bruce
Birmingham: Out – Gary Rowett (Dec 2016); In – Gianfranco Zola; Out (Apr 2017);
In – Harry Redknapp
Blackburn: Out – Owen Coyle (Feb 2017); In – Tony Mowbray
Cardiff: Out – Paul Trollope (Oct 2016); In – Neil Warnock
Derby: Out – Nigel Pearson (Oct 2016); In – Steve McClaren; Out (Mar 2017);
In – Gary Rowett
Leeds: Out – Garry Monk (May 2017); In – Thomas Christiansen
Norwich: Out – Alex Neil (Mar 2017); In – Daniel Farke
Nottm Forest: Out – Philippe Montanier (Jan 2017); In – Mark Warburton
Preston: Out – Simon Grayson (Jun 2017); In – Alex Neil
QPR : Out – Jimmy Floyd Hasselbaink (Nov 2016); In – Ian Holloway
Rotherham: Out – Alan Stubbs (Oct 2016); In – Kenny Jackett; Out (Nov 2016);
In – Paul Warne
Wigan: Out – Gary Caldwell (Oct 2016); In – Warren Joyce; Out (Mar 2017),
In – Paul Cook
Wolves: Out – Kenny Jackett (Jul 2016); In – Walter Zenga; Out – (Oct 2016);
In – Paul Lambert; Out (May 2017); In – Nuno Espirito Santo

LEAGUE ONE

Bury: Out – David Flitcroft (Nov 2016); In – Lee Clark
Charlton: Out – Russell Slade (Nov 2016); In – Karl Robinson
Chesterfield: Out – Danny Wilson (Jan 2017); In – Gary Caldwell
Coventry: Out – Tony Mowbray (Sep 2016); In – Russell Slade; Out (Mar 2017);
In – Mark Robins
Fleetwood: Out – Steven Pressley; In – Uwe Rosler
Gillingham: Out – Justin Edinburgh (Jan 2017); In – Ady Pennock
MK Dons: Out – Karl Robinson (Oct 2016); In – Robbie Neilson
Northampton: Out – Robert Page (Jan 2017); In – Justin Edinburgh
Oldham: Out – Stephen Robinson (Jan 2017); In – John Sheridan
Oxford: Out – Michael Appleton (Jun 2017); In – Pep Clotet
Port Vale: Out – Bruno Ribeiro (Dec 2016); In – Michael Brown
Shrewsbury: Out – Micky Mellon (Oct 2016); In – Paul Hurst
Swindon: Out – Luke Williams (May 2017); In – David Flitcroft

LEAGUE TWO

Barnet:	Out – Martin Allen (Dec 2016); In – Kevin Nugent; Out (Apr 2017); In – Rossi Eames
Crawley:	Out – Dermot Drummy (May 2017); In – Harry Kewell
Crewe:	Out – Steve Davis (Jan 2017); In – David Artell
Grimsby:	Out – Paul Hurst (Oct 2016); In – Marcus Bignot; Out (Apr 2017); In – Russell Slade
Hartlepool:	Out – Craig Hignett (Jan 2017); In – Dave Jones; Out (Apr 2017); In – Craig Harrison
Leyton Orient:	Out – Andy Hessenthaler (Sep 2016); In – Alberto Cavasin; Out (Nov 2016); In – Danny Webb; Out (Mar 2017); In – Omer Riza
Mansfield:	Out – Adam Murray (Nov 2016); In – Steve Evans
Newport:	Out – Warren Feeney (Sep 2016); In – Graham Westley; Out (Mar 2017); In – Mike Flynn
Notts Co:	Out – John Sheridan (Jan 2017); In – Kevin Nolan
Portsmouth:	Out Paul Cook (May 2017); In – Kenny Jackett

THE THINGS THEY SAY ...

'In my situation at a big club, I'm sacked. I'm out. Sure. Definitely' – **Pep Guardiola**, Manchester City manager, admitting he would have been dismissed at former clubs Barcelona and Bayern Munich had he under-achieved as he did in his first season at the Etihad.

'I don't mind criticism because we are in a public job. I believe there is a difference between being criticised and being treated in a way that human beings don't deserve. The lack of respect from some has been a disgrace and I will never forget it' – **Arsene Wenger**, Arsenal manager, on being hounded by some supporters wanting him out.

'A moment of madness' – **Alan Shearer**, Match of the Day pundit, after Arsenal's Laurent Koscielny was sent off after 13 minutes for lunging at Everton's Enner Valencia and missed the FA Cup Final against Chelsea.

'Are you mad?' – **Sandra Redknapp** after husband Harry told her he had agreed to return to management to save Birmingham from relegation.

'After a result like that, I feel 17, not 70' – **Harry Redknapp** after doing exactly that.

'I've never been so high and so low in such a short period. Those people who have ruined it for everyone should hang their heads in shame' – **Steve Morison**, Millwall's League One Play-off Final match-winner, after his own fans invaded the Wembley pitch afterwards.

'I joked before the match about the Germans being able to take penalties' – **David Wagner**, Huddersfield manager, after German-born Chris Lowe and Michael Hefele converted spot-kicks in their play-off semi-final win over Sheffield Wednesday.

'We can't seriously sit here and say it's normal to play a game of football and earn that type of money. But it's the going rate and what would we do if we were offered that amount?' – **Chris Coleman**, Wales manager, on Gareth Bale's new deal with Real Madrid worth a reported £108m over six years.

EMIRATES FA CUP 2016–17

FIRST ROUND

National League North side Brackley beat Gillingham for the second time in four seasons. They are denied when the League One team recover from 2-0 down to force a replay – and it's the same story in the replay. But when the tie goes to extra-time, Brackley win 4-3 as Jimmy Armson completes a hat-trick and Shane Byrne's corner is deflected in off goalkeeper Stuart Nelson. Three other underdogs go through. Solihull retrieve a two-goal deficit to earn a replay against Yeovil and reach the second round for the first time by 4-2 in a penalty shoot-out, Omari Sterling-James netting the decisive spot-kick. Eastleigh are 3-1 winners at Swindon with goals from Jai Reason, Andy Drury and Mikael Mandron (pen), while John McCombe's header gives Macclesfield a 1-0 success at Walsall. Maidstone look like joining them with Bobby-Joe Taylor's penalty. Instead, they concede an equaliser to Rochdale in the final seconds and lose the replay 2-0. Sheffield United's Harry Chapman scores a hat-trick in the round's biggest victory – 6-0 against Leyton Orient.

Alfreton 1 Newport 1	Portsmouth 1 Wycombe 2
Blackpool 2 Kidderminster 0	Sheffield Utd 6 Leyton Orient 0
Bolton 1 Grimsby 0	Shrewsbury 3 Barnet 0
Boreham Wood 2 Notts Co 2	Southport 0 Fleetwood 0
Bradford 1 Accrington 2	St Albans 3 Carlisle 5
Braintree 7 Eastbourne 0	Stockport 0 Woking 4
Bury 2 AFC Wimbledon 2	Taunton 2 Barrow 2
Cambridge 1 Dover 1	Walsall 0 Macclesfield 1
Charlton 3 Scunthorpe 1	Westfields 1 Curzon Ashton 1
Cheltenham 1 Crewe 1	Whitehawk 1 Stourbridge 1
Colchester 1 Chesterfield 2	Yeovil 2 Solihull 2
Crawley 1 Bristol Rov 1	**Replays**
Dagenham 0 Halifax 0	AFC Wimbledon 5 Bury 0
Dartford 3 Sutton 6	Barrow 2 Taunton 1
Eastleigh 1 Swindon 1	Brackley 4 Gillingham 3 (aet)
Exeter 1 Luton 3	Bristol Rovers 4 Crawley 2 (aet)
Gillingham 2 Brackley 2	Coventry 2 Morecambe 1
Hartlepool 3 Stamford 0	Crewe 1 Cheltenham 4
Lincoln 2 Altrincham 1	Curzon Ashton 3 Westfields 1
Maidstone 1 Rochdale 1	Dover 2 Cambridge 4 (aet)
Mansfield 1 Plymouth 2	Fleetwood 4 Southport 1 (aet)
Merstham 0 Oxford 5	Halifax 2 Dagenham 1
Millwall 1 Southend 0	Newport 4 Alfreton 1 (aet)
MK Dons 3 Spennymoor 2	Notts Co 2 Boreham Wood 0
Morecambe 0 Coventry 1	Rochdale 2 Maidstone 0
Northampton 6 Harrow 0	Solihull 1 Yeovil 1
Oldham 2 Doncaster 1	(aet, Solihull won 4-2 on pens)
Peterborough 2 Chesham 1	Stourbridge 3 Whitehawk 0
Port Vale 1 Stevenage 0	Swindon 1 Eastleigh 3

SECOND ROUND

A remarkable recovery saves AFC Wimbledon and leaves little Curzon Ashton heartbroken. Trailing 3-0 after 80 minutes to Adam Morgan's hat-trick, the League One side score three times in three minutes through Tom Elliott, Dominic Poleon and Tyrone Barnett and edge the tie with Elliott's second goal in stoppage-time. Luton also come from behind against Solihull, transforming a two-goal half-time deficit into a 6-2 victory. Brackley's run is ended at Blackpool, but there is plenty of success elsewhere for non-league teams. Sutton, who famously knocked out Coventry in 1989, equalise against Cheltenham (Tony Tubbs) and go through with Roarie Deacon's injury-time strike. Byron Harrison nets both goals as Barrow also come from behind to win 2-1 away to Bristol Rovers. So does Theo Robinson in Lincoln's 3-2 victory against Oldham in which Terry Hawridge is also on the mark. And seventh-tier Stourbridge oust Northampton 1-0, courtesy of Jack Duggan's 86th minute goal. Luke Berry nets all four, one a penalty, for Cambridge, who overwhelm Coventry 4-0, while Scott Kashket and Harry Smith fire hat-tricks for Wycombe and Millwall respectively.

Blackpool 1 Brackley 0	Plymouth 0 Newport 0
Bolton 3 Sheffield Utd 2	Port Vale 4 Hartlepool 0
Bristol Rov 1 Barrow 2	Shrewsbury 0 Fleetwood 0
Cambridge 4 Coventry 0	Stourbridge 1 Northampton 0
Carlisle 1 Rochdale 2	Sutton 2 Cheltenham 1
Charlton 0 MK Dons 0	Woking 0 Accrington 3
Chesterfield 0 Wycombe 5	**Replays**
Curzon Ashton 3 AFC Wimbledon 4	Halifax 0 Eastleigh 2
Eastleigh 3 Halifax 3	Fleetwood 3 Shrewsbury 2
Lincoln 3 Oldham 2	MK Dons 3 Charlton 1
Luton 6 Solihull 2	Newport 0 Plymouth 1
Macclesfield 0 Oxford 0	Oxford 3 Macclesfield 0
Millwall 5 Braintree 2	Peterborough 2 Notts Co 0
Notts Co 2 Peterborough 2	

THIRD ROUND

Five days after the death of Graham Taylor, Lincoln go through to the fourth round for the first time since Taylor's team of 1976. A goal by Nathan Arnold in the first minute of stoppage-time gives them victory over Ipswich on an emotional night at Sincil Bank. Another National League team celebrate late success in a replay. Sutton trail early on, equalise through Roarie Deacon after AFC Wimbledon have Paul Robinson sent off, then go through with goals from Max Biamou in the 90th minute and Dan Fitchett in the sixth minute of added-time. Bournemouth manager Eddie Howe is left to reflect on the decision to change his entire team for the tie against League One Millwall, who take advantage to win 3-0 with Steve Morison, Shaun Cummings and Shane Ferguson on the mark. Two Premier League sides are beaten at home by Championship opposition. Darren Bent and Tom Ince strike in the space of three second-half minutes as Derby come from behind to overcome West Bromwich Albion; Helder Costa and Matt Doherty give Wolves a 2-0 success at Stoke. Wayne Rooney equals Sir Bobby Charlton's club-record 249 goals as Manchester United ease through against Reading, managed by former Old Trafford stalwart Jaap Stam. The meeting of new managers goes the way of Hull's Marco Silva as 17-year-old Josh Tymon's first goal for the club rounds off victory over Swansea's Paul Clement. Stourbridge's run is ended by an 83rd minute goal at Wycombe.

Accrington 2 Luton 1	Hull 2 Swansea 0
Barrow 0 Rochdale 2	Ipswich 2 Lincoln 2
Birmingham 1 Newcastle 1	Liverpool 0 Plymouth 0
Blackpool 0 Barnsley 0	Manchester Utd 4 Reading 0
Bolton 0 Crystal Palace 0	Middlesbrough 3 Sheffield Wed 0
Brentford 5 Eastleigh 1	Millwall 3 Bournemouth 0
Brighton 2 MK Dons 0	Norwich 2 Southampton 2
Bristol City 0 Fleetwood 0	Preston 1 **Arsenal** 2
Cambridge 1 Leeds 2	QPR 1 Blackburn 2
Cardiff 1 Fulham 2	Rotherham 2 Oxford 3
Chelsea 4 Peterborough 1	Stoke 0 Wolves 2
Everton 1 Leicester 2	Sunderland 0 Burnley 0
Huddersfield 4 Port Vale 0	Sutton 0 AFC Wimbledon 0

Tottenham 2 Aston Villa 0
Watford 2 Burton 0
WBA 1 Derby 2
West Ham 0 Manchester City 5
Wigan 2 Nottm Forest 0
Wycombe 2 Stourbridge 1
Replays
AFC Wimbledon 1 Sutton 3

Barnsley 1 Blackpool 2 (aet)
Burnley 2 Sunderland 0
Crystal Palace 2 Bolton 1
Fleetwood 0 Bristol City 1
Lincoln 1 Ipswich 0
Newcastle 3 Birmingham 1
Plymouth 0 Liverpool 0
Southampton 1 Norwich 0

FOURTH ROUND

Two non-league clubs make it to the last 16 for the first time. Sutton overcome Leeds with a penalty from Jamie Collins and are rewarded with a home tie against Arsenal. Leeds count the cost of making ten changes for the tie. So do Brighton, making nine for the visit to Lincoln, who come from behind to win 3-1 with a penalty by Alan Power, Fikayo Tomori's own goal and a Theo Robinson strike. They are not the only teams ousted with below strength line-ups as the competition takes second place to league ambitions. Liverpool are beaten 2-1 at Anfield by Wolves, who never look back after Richard Stearman's opener with just 53 seconds on the clock. Oxford sink Newcastle 3-0 thanks to goals from Kane Hemmings, Curtis Nelson and Toni Martinez – alongside Simon Eastwood's penalty save from Aleksandar Mitrovic with the scoreline 1-0. Millwall's Steve Morison nets the only one of the tie after 85 minutes against Watford, while Wycombe also look set for victory in the tie of the round at White Hart Lane. They lead Tottenham 2-0, then 3-2 before Dele Alli levels in the 89th minute and Son Heung-min nets the winner seven minutes into added-time. Southampton and Arsenal both make ten changes at St Mary's, where Arsene Wenger's side dominate proceedings, particularly Theo Walcott, who scores a hat-trick in a 5-0 success.

Blackburn 2 Blackpool 0
Burnley 2 Bristol City 0
Chelsea 4 Brentford 0
Crystal Palace 0 Manchester City 3
Derby 2 Leicester 2
Fulham 4 Hull 1
Lincoln 3 Brighton 1
Liverpool 1 Wolves 2
Manchester Utd 4 Wigan 0

Middlesbrough 1 Accrington 0
Millwall 1 Watford 0
Oxford 3 Newcastle 0
Rochdale 0 Huddersfield 4
Southampton 0 **Arsenal** 5
Sutton 1 Leeds 0
Tottenham 4 Wycombe 3
Replay
Leicester 3 Derby 1 (aet)

FIFTH ROUND

Lincoln become the first non-league side to reach the last eight since Queens Park Rangers in 1914 with a battling performance at Turf Moor. Luke Waterfall heads Sam Habergham's 89th minute corner back across goal and Sean Raggett's header is ruled to have crossed the line by goal-line technology. It's a good day all round for Lincoln, whose bid to regain Football League membership is boosted by defeats for National League title rivals Forest Green and Dagenham. Sutton's run comes to an end, but they make Arsenal work for a 2-0 victory and go close to reducing the deficit with Roarie Deacon's 30-yard shot against the bar. Millwall account for a third Premier League club – despite losing Jake Cooper to a second yellow card after 52 minutes – with a goal by Shaun Cummings in the last minute of normal time against Leicester. Oxford retrieve a 2-0 deficit at Middlesbrough through Chris Maguire and West Ham loanee Toni Martinez, but go out to substitute Cristhian Stuani's 86th minute goal. Harry Kane's hat-trick for Tottenham ends Fulham's hopes of an upset.

Blackburn 1 Manchester Utd 2
Burnley 0 Lincoln 1
Fulham 0 Tottenham 3
Huddersfield 0 Manchester City 0
Middlesbrough 3 Oxford 2

Millwall 1 Leicester 0
Sutton 0 **Arsenal** 2
Wolves 0 **Chelsea** 2
Replay
Manchester City 5 Huddersfield 1

SIXTH ROUND

Lincoln's 9,000 supporters at the Emirates see their side hold Arsenal until Theo Walcott's goal on the stroke of half-time. After that, Arsenal assume control, enabling manager Arsene Wenger to overtake Sir Alex Ferguson by reaching his 11th semi-final in the tournament. Chelsea's N'Golo Kante delivers the only goal of a heated heavyweight tie against Manchester United in which United have Ander Herrera sent off for a second yellow card and fourth official Mike Jones has to intervene in a touchline clash between managers Antonio Conte and Jose Mourinho. In the last FA Cup tie at White Hart before the famous old stadium is knocked down, Son Heung-min hits a hat-trick as Tottenham end Millwall's run. Their 6-0 win is clouded by an ankle injury sustained by Harry Kane. Completing a big-four line-up for the semi-finals are Manchester City, 2-0 winners at Middlesbrough.

Arsenal 5 Lincoln 0
Chelsea 1 Manchester Utd 0

Middlesbrough 0 Manchester City 2
Tottenham 6 Millwall 0

SEMI-FINALS (both at Wembley)

Chelsea and Tottenham break off from disputing the Premier League title to serve up a compelling match. Willian scores two goals for Chelsea, one a penalty, and Nemanja Matic seals their 4-2 victory with a stunning 30-yard drive. Tottenham suffer the club's seventh successive semi-final defeat in the competition. The following day, there is joy for Arsene Wenger as Alexis Sanchez scores an extra-time winner for Arsenal; disappointment for Manchester City's Pep Guardiola, who will end the season without a trophy for the first time in his managerial career.

Arsenal 2 Manchester City 1 (aet)

Chelsea 4 Tottenham 2

FINAL

No wonder Arsene Wenger was beaming from ear-to-ear. The normally straight-faced Arsenal manager had just become the most successful in the history of the FA Cup, seen his side take the lead role in one of the finest finals of recent years and achieve a record 13th success in the competition by beating the champions. In that moment, Wenger also knew he would be staying at the Emirates after months of speculation about his future, fuelled by Premier League failings and criticism from some supporters. Three days later, he duly signed a new two-year contract, with the manner of his side's third Wembley triumph in four years still being admired. They really had no right to have achieved it, having been stripped of the services of Laurent Koscielny, Shkodran Mustafi and Gabriel Paulista through injury and suspension. It meant an untried and untested back three in which Per Mertesacker had just 37 minutes of football under his belt all season. With the Colombian David Ospina surprisingly preferred in goal to Petr Cech, Arsenal looked vulnerable in the extreme. Instead, Mertesacker's mighty performance spread confidence throughout the team and he surely deserved to have shaded man-of-the-match honours ahead of the irrepressible Alexis Sanchez. Admittedly, Chelsea were a pale shadow of the side that romped to the title. It seemed like a match too far. Yet Antonio Conte's team were second best to such an extent that they were fortunate not to have been on the end of a hiding.

ARSENAL 2 CHELSEA 1
Wembley (89,472); Saturday, May 27 2017

Arsenal (3-4-2-1): Ospina, Holding, Mertesacker (capt), Monreal, Bellerin, Ramsey, Xhaka, Oxlade-Chamberlain (Coquelin 83), Sanchez (Elneny 90), Ozil, Welbeck (Giroud 78). **Subs not used**: Cech, Walcott, Iwobi, Lucas Perez. **Scorers**: Sanchez (4), Ramsey (79). **Booked**: Ramsey, Holding, Xhaka, Coquelin. **Manager**: Arsene Wenger

Chelsea (3-4-3): Courtois, Azpilicueta, Luiz, Cahill (capt), Moses, Kante, Matic (Fabregas 62), Alonso, Pedro (Willian 72), Diego Costa (Batshuayi 88), Hazard. **Subs not used**: Begovic, Terry, Zouma, Ake. **Scorer**: Diego Costa (76). **Booked**: Moses, Kante. **Sent off**: Moses (68). **Manager**: Antonio Conte

Referee: A Taylor (Cheshire). **Half-time**: 1-0

HOW THEY REACHED THE FINAL

Arsenal
Round 3: 2-1 away to Preston (Ramsey, Giroud)
Round 4: 5-0 away to Southampton (Walcott 3, Welbeck 2)
Round 5: 2-0 away to Sutton (Lucas Perez, Walcott)
Round 6: 5-0 home to Lincoln (Walcott, Giroud, Waterfall og, Sanchez, Ramsey)
Semi-finals: 2-1 v Manchester City (Monreal, Sanchez) – aet

Chelsea
Round 3: 4-1 home to Peterborough (Pedro 2, Batshuayi, Willian)
Round 4: 4-0 home to Brentford (Willian, Pedro, Ivanovic, Batshuayi pen)
Round 5: 2-0 away to Wolves (Pedro, Diego Costa)
Round 6: 1-0 home to Manchester Utd (Kante)
Semi-finals: 4-2 v Tottenham (Willian 2, 1 pen, Hazard, Matic)

Leading scorers: 6 Morgan (Curzon Ashton), Son Heung-min (Tottenham); 5 Aguero (Manchester City), Hemmings (Oxford), Mandron (Eastleigh), Robinson (Lincoln), Walcott (Arsenal); 4 Berry (Cambridge), Deacon (Sutton), Elliott (AFC Wimbledon), Kane (Tottenham), Pedro (Chelsea), Willian (Chelsea)

FINAL FACTS AND FIGURES

- Arsenal moved ahead of Manchester United with a record 13th victory in the competition. It was their third Wembley triumph in four years after wins over Aston Villa and Hull.

- Arsene Wenger lifted the trophy for a record seventh time, overtaking George Ramsay's successes between 1887-1920 in his role as Aston Villa's manager-secretary before the role of a manager was defined.

- Aaron Ramsey also scored the winner, in extra-time, in his side's 3-2 success over Hull in 2014.

- Alex Sanchez has now scored seven goals in five matches at Wembley – five of them for Arsenal in FA Cup Finals and semi-finals and two for Chile against England in a friendly international.

- Per Mertesacker had played only 37 minutes of first-team football during the season because of a knee injury.

- Victor Moses became the fifth player sent off in an FA Cup Final after Chris Smalling (Manchester United), Pablo Zabaleta (Manchester City), Jose Reyes (Arsenal) and Kevin Moran (Manchester United).

- Chelsea completed their Premier League title-winning season without having had a player shown a red card.

FA CUP FINAL SCORES & TEAMS

1872 **Wanderers 1** (Betts) Bowen, Alcock, Bonsor, Welch; Betts, Crake, Hooman, Lubbock, Thompson, Vidal, Wollaston. Note: Betts played under the pseudonym 'AH Chequer' on the day of the match **Royal Engineers 0** Capt Merriman; Capt Marindin; Lieut Addison, Lieut Cresswell, Lieut Mitchell, Lieut Renny-Tailyour, Lieut Rich, Lieut George Goodwyn, Lieut Muirhead, Lieut Cotter, Lieut Bogle

1873 **Wanderers 2** (Wollaston, Kinnaird) Bowen; Thompson, Welch, Kinnaird, Howell, Wollaston, Sturgis, Rev Stewart, Kenyon-Slaney, Kingsford, Bonsor **Oxford University 0** Kirke-Smith; Leach, Mackarness, Birley, Longman, Chappell-Maddison, Dixon, Paton, Vidal, Sumner, Ottaway. March 29; 3,000; A Stair

1874 **Oxford University 2** (Mackarness, Patton) Neapean; Mackarness, Birley, Green, Vidal, Ottaway, Benson, Patton, Rawson, Chappell-Maddison, Rev Johnson **Royal Engineers 0** Capt Merriman; Major Marindin, Lieut W Addison, Gerald Onslow, Lieut Oliver, Lieut Digby, Lieut Renny-Tailyour, Lieut Rawson, Lieut Blackman Lieut Wood, Lieut von Donop. March 14; 2,000; A Stair

1875 **Royal Engineers 1** (Renny-Tailyour) Capt Merriman; Lieut Sim, Lieut Onslow, Lieut (later Sir) Ruck, Lieut Von Donop, Lieut Wood, Lieut Rawson, Lieut Stafford, Capt Renny-Tailyour, Lieut Mein, Lieut Wingfield-Stratford **Old Etonians 1** (Bonsor) Thompson; Benson, Lubbock, Wilson, Kinnaird, (Sir) Stronge, Patton, Farmer, Bonsor, Ottaway, Kenyon-Slaney. March 13; 2,000; CW Alcock. aet **Replay – Royal Engineers 2** (Renny-Tailyour, Stafford) Capt Merriman; Lieut Sim, Lieut Onslow, Lieut (later Sir) Ruck, Lieut Von Donop, Lieut Wood, Lieut Rawson, Lieut Stafford, Capt Renny-Tailyour, Lieut Mein, Lieut Wingfield-Stratford **Old Etonians 0** Capt Drummond-Moray; Kinnaird, (Sir) Stronge, Hammond, Lubbock, Patton, Farmer, Bonsor, Lubbock, Wilson, Farmer. March 16; 3,000; CW Alcock

1876 **Wanderers 1** (Edwards) Greig; Stratford, Lindsay, Chappell-Maddison, Birley, Wollaston, C Heron, G Heron, Edwards, Kenrick, Hughes **Old Etonians 1** (Bonsor) Hogg; Rev Welldon, Lyttleton, Thompson, Kinnaird, Meysey, Kenyon-Slaney, Lyttleton, Sturgis, Bonsor, Allene. March 11; 3,500; WS Rawson aet **Replay – Wanderers 3** (Wollaston, Hughes 2) Greig; Stratford, Lindsay, Chappel-Maddison, Birley, Wollaston, C Heron, G Heron, Edwards, Kenrick, Hughes **Old Etonians 0** Hogg, Lubbock, Lyttleton, Farrer, Kinnaird, (Sir) Stronge, Kenyon-Slaney, Lyttleton, Sturgis, Bonsor, Allene. March 18; 1,500; WS Rawson

1877 **Wanderers 2** (Kenrick, Lindsay) Kinnaird; Birley, Denton, Green, Heron, Hughes, Kenrick, Lindsay, Stratford, Wace, Wollaston **Oxford University 1** (Kinnaird og) Allington; Bain, Dunnell, Rev Savory, Todd, Waddington, Rev Fernandez, Otter, Parry, Rawson. March 24; 3,000; SH Wright, aet

1878 **Wanderers 3** (Kinnaird, Kenrick 2) (Sir) Kirkpatrick; Stratford, Lindsay, Kinnaird, Green, Wollaston, Heron, Wylie, Wace, Denton, Kenrick **Royal Engineers 1** (Morris) Friend; Cowan, (Sir) Morris, Mayne, Heath, Haynes, Lindsay, Hedley, (Sir) Bond, Barnet, Ruck. March 23; 4,500; SR Bastard

1879 **Old Etonians 1** (Clerke) Hawtrey; Edward, Bury, Kinnaird, Lubbock, Clerke, Pares, Goodhart, Whitfield, Chevalier, Beaufoy **Clapham Rovers 0** Birkett; Ogilvie, Field, Bailey, Prinsep, Rawson, Stanley, Scott, Bevington, Growse, Keith-Falconer. March 29; 5,000; CW Alcock

1880 **Clapham Rovers 1** (Lloyd-Jones) Birkett; Ogilvie, Field, Weston, Bailey, Stanley, Brougham, Sparkes, Barry, Ram, Lloyd-Jones **Oxford University 0** Parr; Wilson, King, Phillips, Rogers, Heygate, Rev Childs, Eyre, (Dr) Crowdy, Hill, Lubbock. April 10; 6,000; Major Marindin

1881 **Old Carthusians 3** (Page, Wynyard, Parry) Gillett; Norris, (Sir) Colvin, Prinsep, (Sir) Vintcent, Hansell, Richards, Page, Wynyard, Parry, Todd **Old Etonians 0** Rawlinson; Foley, French, Kinnaird, Farrer, Macauley, Goodhart, Whitfield, Novelli, Anderson, Chevallier. April 9; 4,000; W Pierce-Dix

1882 **Old Etonians 1** (Macauley) Rawlinson; French, de Paravicini, Kinnaird, Foley, Novelli, Dunn, Macauley, Goodhart, Chevallier, Anderson **Blackburn Rov 0** Howarth; McIntyre, Suter, Hargreaves, Sharples, Hargreaves, Avery, Brown, Strachan, Douglas, Duckworth. March 25; 6,500; JC Clegg

1883 **Blackburn Olympic 2** (Matthews, Costley) Hacking; Ward, Warburton, Gibson, Astley, Hunter, Dewhurst, Matthews, Wilson, Costley, Yates **Old Etonians 1** (Goodhart) Rawlinson; French, de Paravicini, Kinnaird, Foley, Dunn, Bainbridge, Chevallier, Anderson, Goodhart, Macauley. March 31; 8,000; Major Marindin, aet

1884 **Blackburn Rov 2** (Sowerbutts, Forrest) Arthur; Suter, Beverley, McIntyre, Forrest, Hargreaves, Brown,

Inglis Sowerbutts, Douglas, Lofthouse **Queen's Park 1** (Christie) Gillespie; MacDonald, Arnott, Gow, Campbell, Allan, Harrower, (Dr) Smith, Anderson, Watt, Christie. March 29; 4,000; Major Marindin

1885   Blackburn Rov 2 (Forrest, Brown) Arthur; Turner, Suter, Haworth, McIntyre, Forrest, Sowerbutts, Lofthouse, Douglas, Brown, Fecitt **Queen's Park 0** Gillespie; Arnott, MacLeod, MacDonald, Campbell, Sellar, Anderson, McWhammel, Hamilton, Allan, Gray. April 4; 12,500; Major Marindin

1886   Blackburn Rov 0 Arthur; Turner, Suter, Heyes, Forrest, McIntyre, Douglas, Strachan, Sowerbutts, Fecitt, Brown **WBA 0** Roberts; Green, Bell, Horton, Perry, Timmins, Woodhall, Green, Bayliss, Loach, Bell. April 3; 15,000; Major Marindin **Replay – Blackburn Rov 2** (Sowerbutts, Brown) Arthur; Turner, Suter, Walton, Forrest, McIntyre, Douglas, Strachan, Sowerbutts, Fecitt, Brown **WBA 0** Roberts; Green, Bell, Horton, Perry, Timmins, Woodhall, Green, Bayliss, Loach, Bell. April 10; 12,000; Major Marindin

1887   Aston Villa 2 (Hodgetts, Hunter) Warner; Coulton, Simmonds, Yates, Dawson, Burton, Davis, Albert Brown, Hunter, Vaughton, Hodgetts **WBA 0** Roberts; Green, Aldridge, Horton, Perry, Timmins, Woodhall, Green, Bayliss, Paddock, Pearson. April 2; 15,500; Major Marindin

1888   WBA 2 (Bayliss, Woodhall) Roberts; Aldridge, Green, Horton, Perry, Timmins, Woodhall, Bassett, Bayliss, Wilson, Pearson **Preston 1** (Dewhurst) Mills-Roberts; Howarth, Holmes, Ross, Russell, Gordon, Ross, Goodall, Dewhurst, Drummond, Graham. March 24; 19,000; Major Marindin

1889   Preston 3 (Dewhurst, Ross, Thomson) Mills-Roberts; Howarth, Holmes, Drummond, Russell, Graham, Gordon, Goodall, Dewhurst, Thompson, Ross **Wolves 0** Baynton; Baugh, Mason, Fletcher, Allen, Lowder, Hunter, Wykes, Brodie, Wood, Knight. March 30; 22,000; Major Marindin

1890   Blackburn Rov 6 (Lofthouse, Jack Southworth, Walton Townley 3) Horne; James Southworth, Forbes, Barton, Dewar, Forrest, Lofthouse, Campbell, Jack Southworth, Walton, Townley **Sheffield Wed 1** (Bennett) Smith; Morley, Brayshaw, Dungworth, Betts, Waller, Ingram, Woolhouse, Bennett, Mumford, Cawley. March 29; 20,000; Major Marindin

1891   Blackburn Rov 3 (Dewar, Jack Southworth, Townley) Pennington; Brandon, Forbes, Barton, Dewar, Forrest, Lofthouse, Walton, Southworth, Hall, Townley **Notts Co 1** (Oswald) Thraves; Ferguson, Hendry, Osborne, Calderhead, Shelton, McGregror, McInnes Oswald, Locker, Daft. March 21; 23,000; CJ Hughes

1892   WBA 3 (Geddes, Nicholls, Reynolds) Reader; Nicholson, McCulloch, Reynolds, Perry, Groves, Bassett, McLeod, Nicholls, Pearson, Geddes **Aston Villa 0** Warner; Evans, Cox, Devey, Cowan, Baird, Athersmith, Devey, Dickson, Hodgetts, Campbell. March 19; 32,810; JC Clegg

1893   Wolves 1 (Allen) Rose; Baugh, Swift, Malpass, Allen, Kinsey, Topham, Wykes, Butcher, Griffin, Wood **Everton 0** Williams; Kelso, Howarth, Boyle, Holt, Stewart, Latta, Gordon, Maxwell, Chadwick, Milward. March 25; 45,000; CJ Hughes

1894   Notts Co 4 (Watson, Logan 3) Toone, Harper, Hendry, Bramley, Calderhead, Shelton, Watson, Donnelly, Logan Bruce, Daft **Bolton 1** (Cassidy) Sutcliffe; Somerville, Jones , Gardiner, Paton, Hughes, Tannahill, Wilson, Cassidy, Bentley, Dickenson. March 31; 37,000; CJ Hughes

1895   Aston Villa 1 (Chatt) Wilkes; Spencer, Welford, Reynolds, Cowan, Russell, Athersmith Chatt, Devey, Hodgetts, Smith **WBA 0** Reader; Williams, Horton, Perry, Higgins, Taggart, Bassett, McLeod, Richards, Hutchinson, Banks. April 20; 42,560; J Lewis

1896   Sheffield Wed 2 (Spiksley 2) Massey; Earp, Langley, Brandon, Crawshaw, Petrie, Brash, Brady, Bell, Davis, Spikesley **Wolves 1** (Black) Tennant; Baugh, Dunn, Owen, Malpass, Griffiths, Tonks, Henderson, Beats, Wood, Black. April 18; 48,030; Lieut Simpson

1897   Aston Villa 3 (Campbell, Wheldon, Crabtree) Whitehouse; Spencer, Reynolds, Evans, Cowan, Crabtree, Athersmith, Devey, Campbell, Wheldon, Cowan **Everton 2** (Bell, Boyle) Menham; Meechan, Storrier, Boyle, Holt, Stewart, Taylor, Bell, Hartley, Chadwick, Milward. April 10; 65,891; J Lewis

1898   Nottm Forest 3 (Capes 2, McPherson) Allsop; Ritchie, Scott, Forman, McPherson, Wragg, McInnes, Richards, Benbow, Capes, Spouncer **Derby 1** (Bloomer) Fryer; Methven, Leiper, Cox, Goodall, Bloomer, Boag, Stevenson, McQueen. April 16; 62,017; J Lewis

1899   Sheffield Utd 4 (Bennett, Beers, Almond, Priest) Foulke; Thickett, Boyle, Johnson, Morren, Needham, Bennett, Beers, Hedley, Almond, Priest **Derby 1** (Boag) Fryer; Methven, Staley, Cox, Paterson, May, Arkesden, Bloomer, Boag, McDonald, Allen. April 15; 73,833; A Scragg

1900 Bury 4 (McLuckie 2, Wood, Plant) Thompson; Darroch, Davidson, Pray, Leeming, Ross, Richards, Wood, McLuckie, Sagar, Plant **Southampton 0** Robinson; Meechan, Durber, Meston, Chadwick, Petrie, Turner, Yates, Farrell, Wood, Milward. April 21; 68,945; A Kingscott

1901 Tottenham 2 (Brown 2) Clawley; Erentz, Tait, Morris, Hughes, Jones, Smith, Cameron, Brown, Copeland, Kirwan **Sheffield Utd 2** (Priest, Bennett) Foulke; Thickett, Boyle, Johnson, Morren, Needham, Bennett, Field, Hedley, Priest, Lipsham. April 20; 110,820; A Kingscott **Replay – Tottenham 3** (Cameron, Smith, Brown) Clawley; Erentz, Tait, Morris, Hughes, Jones, Smith, Cameron, Brown, Copeland, Kirwan. **Sheffield Utd 1** (Priest) Foulke; Thickett, Boyle, Johnson, Morren, Needham, Bennett, Field, Hedley, Priest, Lipsham. April 27; 20,470; A Kingscott

1902 Sheffield Utd 1 (Common) Foulke; Thickett, Boyle, Needham, Wilkinson, Johnson, Bennett, Common, Hedley, Priest, Lipsham **Southampton 1** (Wood) Robinson; Fry, Molyneux, Meston, Bowman, Lee, Turner, Wood Brown, Chadwick, Turner. April 19; 76,914; T Kirkham. **Replay – Sheffield Utd 2** (Hedley, Barnes) Foulke; Thickett, Boyle, Needham, Wilkinson, Johnson, Barnes, Common, Hedley, Priest, Lipsham **Southampton 1** (Brown) Robinson; Fry, Molyneux, Meston, Bowman, Lee, Turner, Wood, Brown, Chadwick, Turner. April 26; 33,068; T Kirkham

1903 Bury 6 (Leeming 2, Ross, Sagar, Wood, Plant) Monteith; Lindsey, McEwen, Johnston, Thorpe, Ross, Richards, Wood, Sagar Leeming, Plant **Derby 0** Fryer; Methven, Morris, Warren, Goodall, May, Warrington, York, Boag, Richards, Davis. April 18; 63,102; J Adams

1904 Manchester City 1 (Meredith) Hillman; McMahon, Burgess, Frost, Hynds, Ashworth, Meredith, Livingstone, Gillespie, Turnbull, Booth **Bolton 0** Davies; Brown, Struthers, Clifford, Greenhalgh, Freebairn, Stokes, Marsh, Yenson, White, Taylor. April 23; 61,374; AJ Barker

1905 Aston Villa 2 (Hampton 2) George; Spencer, Miles, Pearson, Leake, Windmill, Brawn, Garratty, Hampton, Bache, Hall **Newcastle 0** Lawrence; McCombie, Carr, Gardner, Aitken, McWilliam, Rutherford, Howie, Appleyard, Veitch, Gosnell. April 15; 101,117; PR Harrower

1906 Everton 1 (Young) Scott; Crelley, W Balmer, Makepeace, Taylor, Abbott, Sharp, Bolton, Young, Settle, Hardman **Newcastle 0** Lawrence; McCombie, Carr, Gardner, Aitken, McWilliam, Rutherford, Howie, Orr, Veitch, Gosnell. April 21; 75,609; F Kirkham

1907 Sheffield Wed 2 (Stewart, Simpson) Lyall; Layton, Burton, Brittleton, Crawshaw, Bartlett, Chapman, Bradshaw, Wilson, Stewart, Simpson **Everton 1** (Sharp) Scott; W Balmer, B Balmer, Makepeace, Taylor, Abbott, Sharp, Bolton, Young, Settle, Hardman. April 20; 84,594; N Whittaker

1908 Wolves 3 (Hunt, Hedley, Harrison) Lunn; Jones, Collins, Rev Hunt, Wooldridge, Bishop, Harrison, Shelton, Hedley, Radford, Pedley **Newcastle 1** (Howie) Lawrence; McCracken, Pudan, Gardner, Veitch, McWilliam, Rutherford, Howie, Appleyard, Speedie, Wilson. April 25; 74,697; TP Campbell

1909 Manchester Utd 1 (Sandy Turnbull) Moger; Stacey, Hayes, Duckworth, Roberts, Bell, Meredith, Halse, J Turnbull, S Turnbull, Wall **Bristol City 0** Clay; Annan, Cottle, Hanlin, Wedlock, Spear, Staniforth, Hardy, Gilligan, Burton, Hilton. April 24; 71,401; J Mason

1910 Newcastle 1 (Rutherford) Lawrence; McCracken, Whitson, Veitch, Low, McWilliam, Rutherford, Howie, Higgins, Shepherd, Wilson **Barnsley 1** (Tufnell) Mearns; Downs, Ness, Glendinning, Boyle, Utley, Tufnell, Lillycrop, Gadsby, Forman, Bartrop. April 23; 77,747; JT Ibbotson **Replay – Newcastle 2** (Shepherd 2, 1pen) Lawrence; McCracken, Carr, Veitch, Low, McWilliam, Rutherford, Howie, Higgins, Shepherd, Wilson **Barnsley 0** Mearns; Downs, Ness, Glendinning, Boyle, Utley, Tufnell, Lillycrop, Gadsby, Forman, Bartrop. April 28; 69,000; JT Ibbotson.

1911 Bradford City 0 Mellors; Campbell, Taylor, Robinson, Gildea, McDonald, Logan, Speirs, O'Rourke, Devine, Thompson **Newcastle 0** Lawrence; McCracken, Whitson, Veitch, Low, Willis, Rutherford, Jobey, Stewart, Higgins, Wilson. April 22; 69,068; JH Pearson **Replay – Bradford City 1** (Speirs) Mellors; Campbell, Taylor, Robinson, Torrance, McDonald, Logan, Speirs, O'Rourke, Devine, Thompson **Newcastle 0** Lawrence; McCracken, Whitson, Veitch, Low, Willis, Rutherford, Jobey, Stewart, Higgins, Wilson. April 25; 58,000; JH Pearson

1912 Barnsley 0 Cooper; Downs, Taylor, Glendinning, Bratley, Utley, Bartrop, Tufnell, Lillycrop, Travers, Moore **WBA 0** Pearson; Cook, Pennington, Baddeley, Buck, McNeal, Jephcott, Wright, Pailor, Bowser, Shearman. April 20; 54,556; JR Shumacher **Replay – Barnsley 1** (Tufnell) Cooper; Downs, Taylor, Glendinning, Bratley, Utley, Bartrop, Harry, Lillycrop, Travers, Jimmy Moore **WBA 0** Pearson; Cook, Pennington, Baddeley, Buck, McNeal, Jephcott, Wright, Pailor, Bowser, Shearman. April 24; 38,555; JR Schumacher. aet

148

1913 **Aston Villa 1** (Barber) Hardy; Lyons, Weston, Barber, Harrop, Leach, Wallace, Halse, Hampton, Stephenson, Bache **Sunderland 0** Butler; Gladwin, Ness, Cuggy, Thomson, Low, Mordue, Buchan, Richardson, Holley, Martin. April 19; 120,081; A Adams

1914 **Burnley 1** (Freeman) Sewell; Bamford, Taylor, Halley, Boyle, Watson, Nesbit, Lindley, Freeman, Hodgson, Mosscrop **Liverpool 0** Campbell; Longworth, Pursell, Fairfoul, Ferguson, McKinley, Sheldon, Metcalfe, Miller, Lacey, Nicholl. April 25; 72,778; HS Bamlett

1915 **Sheffield Utd 3** (Simmons, Fazackerly, Kitchen) Gough; Cook, English, Sturgess, Brelsford, Utley, Simmons, Fazackerly, Kitchen, Masterman, Evans **Chelsea 0** Molyneux; Bettridge, Harrow, Taylor, Logan, Walker, Ford, Halse, Thomson, Croal, McNeil. April 24; 49,557; HH Taylor

1920 **Aston Villa 1** (Kirton) Hardy; Smart, Weston, Ducat, Barson, Moss, Wallace, Kirton, Walker, Stephenson, Dorrell **Huddersfield 0** Mutch; Wood, Bullock, Slade, Wilson, Watson, Richardson, Mann, Taylor, Swann, Islip. April 24; 50,018; JT Howcroft. aet

1921 **Tottenham 1** (Dimmock) Hunter; Clay, McDonald, Smith, Walters, Grimsdell, Banks, Seed, Cantrell, Bliss, Dimmock **Wolves 0** George; Woodward, Marshall, Gregory, Hodnell, Riley, Lea, Burrill, Edmonds, Potts, Brooks. April 23; 72,805; S Davies

1922 **Huddersfield 1** (Smith pen) Mutch; Wood, Wadsworth, Slade, Wilson, Watson, Richardson, Mann, Islip, Stephenson, Billy Smith **Preston 0** Mitchell; Hamilton, Doolan, Duxbury, McCall, Williamson, Rawlings, Jefferis, Roberts, Woodhouse, Quinn. April 29; 53,000; JWP Fowler

1923 **Bolton 2** (Jack, JR Smith) Pym; Haworth, Finney, Nuttall, Seddon, Jennings, Butler, Jack, JR Smith, Joe Smith, Vizard **West Ham 0** Hufton; Henderson, Young, Bishop, Kay, Tresadern, Richards, Brown, Watson, Moore, Ruffell. April 28; 126,047; DH Asson

1924 **Newcastle 2** (Harris, Seymour) Bradley; Hampson, Hudspeth, Mooney, Spencer, Gibson, Low, Cowan, Harris, McDonald, Seymour **Aston Villa 0** Jackson; Smart, Mort, Moss, Milne, Blackburn, York, Kirton, Capewell, Walker, Dorrell. April 26; 91,695; WE Russell

1925 **Sheffield Utd 1** (Tunstall) Sutcliffe; Cook, Milton, Pantling, King, Green, Mercer, Boyle, Johnson, Gillespie, Tunstall **Cardiff 0** Farquharson; Nelson, Blair, Wake, Keenor, Hardy, Davies, Gill, Nicholson, Beadles, Evans. April 25; 91,763; GN Watson

1926 **Bolton 1** (Jack) Pym; Haworth, Greenhalgh, Nuttall, Seddon, Jennings, Butler, JR Smith, Jack, Joe Smith, Vizard **Manchester City 0** Goodchild; Cookson, McCloy, Pringle, Cowan, McMullan, Austin, Browell, Roberts, Johnson, Hicks. April 24; 91,447; I Baker

1927 **Cardiff 1** (Ferguson) Farquharson; Nelson, Watson, Keenor, Sloan, Hardy, Curtis, Irving, Ferguson, Davies, McLachlan **Arsenal 0** Lewis; Parker, Kennedy, Baker, Butler, John, Hulme, Buchan, Brain, Blythe, Hoar. April 23; 91,206; WF Bunnell

1928 **Blackburn 3** (Roscamp 2, McLean) Crawford; Hutton, Jones, Healless, Rankin, Campbell, Thornewell, Puddefoot, Roscamp, McLean, Rigby **Huddersfield 1** (Jackson) Mercer; Goodall, Barkas, Redfern, Wilson, Steele, Jackson, Kelly, Brown, Stephenson, Smith. April 21; 92,041; TG Bryan

1929 **Bolton 2** (Butler, Blackmore) Pym; Haworth, Finney, Kean, Seddon, Nuttall, Butler, McClelland, Blackmore, Gibson, Cook **Portsmouth 0** Gilfillan; Mackie, Bell, Nichol, McIlwaine, Thackeray, Forward, Smith, Weddle, Watson, Cook. April 27; 92,576; A Josephs

1930 **Arsenal 2** (James, Lambert) Preedy; Parker, Hapgood, Baker, Seddon, John, Hulme, Jack, Lambert, James, Bastin **Huddersfield 0** Turner; Goodall, Spence, Naylor, Wilson, Campbell, Jackson, Kelly, Davies, Raw, Smith. April 26; 92,488; T Crew

1931 **WBA 2** (WG Richardson 2) Pearson; Shaw, Trentham, Magee, Bill Richardson, Edwards, Glidden, Carter, WG Richardson, Sandford, Wood **Birmingham 1** (Bradford) Hibbs; Liddell, Barkas, Cringan, Morrall, Leslie, Briggs, Crosbie, Bradford, Gregg, Curtis. April 25; 92,406; AH Kingscott

1932 **Newcastle 2** (Allen 2) McInroy; Nelson, Fairhurst, McKenzie, Davidson, Weaver, Boyd, Richardson, Allen, McMenemy, Lang **Arsenal 1** (John) Moss; Parker, Hapgood, Jones, Roberts, Male, Hulme, Jack, Lambert, Bastin, John. April 23; 92,298; WP Harper

1933 **Everton 3** (Stein, Dean, Dunn) Sagar; Cook, Cresswell, Britton, White, Thomson, Geldard, Dunn, Dean, Johnson, Stein **Manchester City 0** Langford; Cann, Dale, Busby, Cowan, Bray, Toseland, Marshall, Herd, McMullan, Eric Brook. April 29; 92,950; E Wood

1934 **Manchester City 2** (Tilson 2) Swift; Barnett, Dale, Busby, Cowan, Bray, Toseland, Marshall, Tilson, Herd, Brook **Portsmouth 1** (Rutherford) Gilfillan; Mackie, Smith, Nichol, Allen, Thackeray, Worrall, Smith, Weddle, Easson, Rutherford. April 28; 93,258; Stanley Rous

1935 **Sheffield Wed 4** (Rimmer 2, Palethorpe, Hooper) Brown; Nibloe, Catlin, Sharp, Millership, Burrows, Hooper, Surtees, Palethorpe, Starling, Rimmer **WBA 2** (Boyes, Sandford) Pearson; Shaw, Trentham, Murphy, Bill Richardson, Edwards, Glidden, Carter, WG Richardson, Sandford, Wally. April 27; 93,204; AE Fogg

1936 **Arsenal 1** (Drake) Wilson; Male, Hapgood, Crayston, Roberts, Copping, Hulme, Bowden, Drake, James, Bastin **Sheffield Utd 0** Smith; Hooper, Wilkinson, Jackson, Johnson, McPherson, Barton, Barclay, Dodds, Pickering, Williams. April 25; 93,384; H Nattrass

1937 **Sunderland 3** (Gurney, Carter, Burbanks) Mapson; Gorman, Hall, Thomson, Johnston, McNab, Duns, Carter, Gurney, Gallacher, Burbanks **Preston 1** (Frank O'Donnell) Burns; Gallimore, Beattie, Shankly, Tremelling, Milne, Dougal, Beresford, O'Donnell, Fagan, O'Donnell. May 1; 93,495; RG Rudd

1938 **Preston 1** (Mutch pen) Holdcroft; Gallimore, Beattie, Shankly, Smith, Batey, Watmough, Mutch, Maxwell, Beattie, O'Donnell **Huddersfield 0** Hesford; Craig, Mountford, Willingham, Young, Boot, Hulme, Issac, MacFadyen, Barclay, Beasley. April 30; 93,497; AJ Jewell. aet

1939 **Portsmouth 4** (Parker 2, Barlow, Anderson) Walker; Morgan, Rochford, Guthrie, Rowe, Wharton, Worrall, McAlinden, Anderson, Barlow, Parker **Wolves 1** (Dorsett) Scott; Morris, Taylor, Galley, Cullis, Gardiner, Burton, McIntosh, Westcott, Dorsett, Maguire. April 29; 99,370; T Thompson

1946 **Derby 4** (Stamps 2. Doherty, B Turner og) Woodley; Nicholas, Howe, Bullions, Leuty, Musson, Harrison, Carter, Stamps, Doherty, Duncan **Charlton Athletic 1** (B Turner) Bartram; Phipps, Shreeve, Turner, Oakes, Johnson, Fell, Brown, Turner, Welsh, Duffy. April 27; 98,000; ED Smith. aet

1947 **Charlton Athletic 1** (Duffy) Bartram; Croker, Shreeve, Johnson, Phipps, Whittaker, Hurst, Dawson, Robinson, Welsh, Duffy **Burnley 0** Strong; Woodruff, Mather, Attwell, Brown, Bray, Chew, Morris, Harrison, Potts, Kippax. April 26; 99,000; JM Wiltshire. aet

1948 **Manchester Utd 4** (Rowley 2, Pearson, Anderson) Crompton; Carey, Aston, Anderson, Chilton, Cockburn, Delaney, Morris, Rowley, Pearson, Mitten **Blackpool 2** (Shimwell pen, Mortensen) Robinson; Shimwell, Crosland, Johnston, Hayward, Kelly, Matthews, Munro, Mortensen, Dick, Rickett. April 24; 99,000; CJ Barrick

1949 **Wolves 3** (Pye 2, Smyth) Williams; Pritchard, Springthorpe Crook, Shorthouse, Wright, Hancocks, Smyth, Pye, Dunn, Mullen **Leicester 1** (Griffiths) Bradley; Jelly, Scott, Harrison, Plummer, King, Griffiths, Lee, Harrison, Chisholm, Adam. April 30; 99,500; RA Mortimer

1950 **Arsenal 2** (Lewis 2) Swindin; Scott, Barnes, Forbes, L Compton, Mercer, Cox, Logie, Goring, Lewis, D Compton **Liverpool 0** Sidlow; Lambert, Spicer, Taylor, Hughes, Jones, Payne, Baron, Stubbins, Fagan, Liddell. April 29; 100,000; H Pearce

1951 **Newcastle 2** (Milburn 2) Fairbrother; Cowell, Corbett, Harvey, Brennan, Crowe, Walker, Taylor, Milburn, Jorge Robledo, Mitchell **Blackpool 0** Farm; Shimwell, Garrett, Johnston, Hayward, Kelly, Matthews, Mudie, Mortensen, Slater, Perry. April 28; 100,000; W Ling

1952 **Newcastle 1** (G Robledo) Simpson; Cowell, McMichael, Harvey, Brennan, Eduardo Robledo, Walker, Foulkes, Milburn, Jorge Robledo, Mitchell **Arsenal 0** Swindin; Barnes, Smith, Forbes, Daniel Mercer, Cox, Logie, Holton, Lishman, Roper. May 3; 100,000; A Ellis

1953 **Blackpool 4** (Mortensen 3, Perry) Farm; Shimwell, Garrett, Fenton, Johnston, Robinson, Matthews, Taylor, Mortensen, Mudie, Perry **Bolton 3** (Lofthouse, Moir, Bell) Hanson; Ball, Banks, Wheeler, Barrass, Bell, Holden, Moir, Lofthouse, Hassall, Langton. May 2; 100,000; M Griffiths

1954 **WBA 3** (Allen 2 [1pen], Griffin) Sanders; Kennedy, Millard, Dudley, Dugdale, Barlow, Griffin, Ryan, Allen, Nicholls, Lee **Preston 2** (Morrison, Wayman) Thompson; Cunningham, Walton, Docherty, Marston, Forbes, Finney, Foster, Wayman, Baxter, Morrison. May 1; 100,000; A Luty

1955 Newcastle 3 (Milburn, Mitchell, Hannah) Simpson; Cowell, Batty, Scoular, Stokoe, Casey, White, Milburn, Keeble, Hannah, Mitchell **Manchester City 1** (Johnstone) Trautmann; Meadows, Little, Barnes, Ewing, Paul, Spurdle, Hayes, Revie, Johnstone, Fagan. May 7; 100,000; R Leafe

1956 Manchester City 3 (Hayes, Dyson, Johnstone) Trautmann; Leivers, Little, Barnes, Ewing, Paul, Johnstone, Hayes, Revie, Dyson, Clarke **Birmingham 1** (Kinsey) Merrick; Hall, Green, Newman, Smith, Boyd, Astall, Kinsey, Brown, Murphy, Govan. May 5; 100,000; A Bond

1957 Aston Villa 2 (McParland 2) Sims; Lynn, Aldis, Crowther, Dugdale, Saward, Smith, Sewell, Myerscough, Dixon, McParland **Manchester Utd 1** (Taylor) Wood; Foulkes, Byrne, Colman, Blanchflower, Edwards, Berry, Whelan, Taylor, Charlton, Pegg May 4; 100,000; F Coultas

1958 Bolton 2 (Lofthouse 2) Hopkinson; Hartle, Banks, Hennin, Higgins, Edwards, Birch, Stevens, Lofthouse, Parry, Holden **Manchester Utd 0** Gregg; Foulkes, Greaves, Goodwin, Cope, Crowther, Dawson, Taylor, Charlton, Viollet, Webster. May 3; 100,000; J Sherlock

1959 Nottingham Forest 2 (Dwight, Wilson) Thomson; Whare, McDonald, Whitefoot, McKinlay, Burkitt, Dwight, Quigley, Wilson, Gray, Imlach **Luton Town 1** (Pacey) Baynham; McNally, Hawkes, Groves, Owen, Pacey, Bingham, Brown, Morton, Cummins, Gregory. May 2; 100,000; J Clough

1960 Wolves 3 (McGrath og, Deeley 2) Finlayson; Showell, Harris, Clamp, Slater, Flowers, Deeley, Stobart, Murray, Broadbent, Horne **Blackburn 0** Leyland; Bray, Whelan, Clayton, Woods, McGrath, Bimpson, Dobing, Dougan, Douglas, McLeod. May 7; 100,000; K Howley

1961 Tottenham 2 (Smith, Dyson) Brown; Baker, Henry, Blanchflower, Norman, Mackay, Jones, White, Smith, Allen, Dyson **Leicester 0** Banks; Chalmers, Norman, McLintock, King, Appleton, Riley, Walsh, McIlmoyle, Keyworth, Cheesebrough. May 6; 100,000; J Kelly

1962 Tottenham 3 (Greaves, Smith, Blanchflower pen) Brown; Baker, Henry, Blanchflower, Norman, Mackay, Medwin, White, Smith, Greaves, Jones **Burnley 1** (Robson) Blacklaw; Angus, Elder, Adamson, Cummings, Miller, Connelly, McIlroy, Pointer, Robson, Harris. May 5; 100,000; J Finney

1963 Manchester Utd 3 (Law, Herd 2) Gaskell; Dunne, Cantwell, Crerand, Foulkes, Setters, Giles, Quixall, Herd, Law, Charlton **Leicester 1** (Keyworth) Banks; Sjoberg, Norman, McLintock, King, Appleton, Riley, Cross, Keyworth, Gibson, Stringfellow. May 25; 100,000; K Aston

1964 West Ham 3 (Sissons, Hurst, Boyce) Standen; Bond, Burkett, Bovington, Brown, Moore, Brabrook, Boyce, Byrne, Hurst, Sissons **Preston 2** (Holden, Dawson) Kelly; Ross, Lawton, Smith, Singleton, Kendall, Wilson, Ashworth, Dawson, Spavin, Holden. May 2; 100,000; A Holland

1965 Liverpool 2 (Hunt, St John) Lawrence; Lawler, Byrne, Strong, Yeats, Stevenson, Callaghan, Hunt, St John, Smith, Thompson **Leeds 1** (Bremner) Sprake; Reaney, Bell, Bremner, Charlton, Hunter, Giles, Storrie, Peacock, Collins, Johanneson. May 1; 100,000; W Clements. aet

1966 Everton 3 (Trebilcock 2, Temple) West, Wright, Wilson, Gabriel, Labone, Harris, Scott, Trebilcock, Young, Harvey, Temple **Sheffield Wed 2** (McCalliog, Ford) Springett; Smith, Megson, Eustace, Ellis, Young, Pugh, Fantham, McCalliog, Ford, Quinn. May 14; 100,000; JK Taylor

1967 Tottenham 2 (Robertson, Saul) Jennings; Kinnear, Knowles, Mullery, England, Mackay, Robertson, Greaves, Gilzean, Venables, Saul. Unused sub- Jones **Chelsea 1** (Tambling) Bonetti; Allan Harris, McCreadie, Hollins, Hinton, Ron Harris, Cooke, Baldwin, Hateley, Tambling, Boyle. Unused sub: Kirkup. May 20; 100,000; K Dagnall

1968 WBA 1 (Astle) John Osborne; Fraser, Williams, Brown, Talbot, Kaye, Lovett, Collard, Astle Hope, Clark Sub: Clarke rep Kaye 91 **Everton 0** West; Wright, Wilson, Kendall, Labone, Harvey, Husband, Ball, Royle, Hurst, Morrissey. Unused sub: Kenyon. May 18; 100,000; L Callaghan. aet

1969 Manchester City 1 (Young) Dowd; Book, Pardoe, Doyle, Booth, Oakes, Summerbee, Bell, Lee, Young, Coleman. Unused sub: Connor **Leicester 0** Shilton; Rodrigues, Nish, Roberts, Woollett, Cross, Fern, Gibson, Lochhead, Clarke, Glover. Sub: Manley rep Glover 70. April 26; 100,000; G McCabe

1970 Chelsea 2 (Houseman, Hutchinson) Bonetti; Webb, McCreadie, Hollins, Dempsey, R Harris, Baldwin, Houseman, Osgood, Hutchinson, Cooke. Sub: Hinton rep Harris 91 **Leeds 2** (Charlton, Jones) Sprake; Madeley, Cooper, Bremner, Charlton, Hunter, Lorimer, Clarke, Jones, Giles, Gray Unused sub: Bates. April 11; 100,000; E Jennings. aet **Replay – Chelsea 2** (Osgood, Webb) Bonetti, Webb,

McCreadie, Hollins, Dempsey, R Harris, Baldwin, Houseman, Osgood, Hutchinson, Cooke. Sub: Hinton rep Osgood 105 **Leeds 1** (Jones) Harvey; Madeley, Cooper, Bremner, Charlton, Hunter, Lorimer, Clarke, Jones, Giles, Gray Unused sub: Bates. April 29; 62,078; E Jennings. aet

1971 Arsenal 2 (Kelly, George) Wilson; Rice, McNab, Storey, McLintock Simpson, Armstrong, Graham, Radford, Kennedy, George. Sub: Kelly rep Storey 70 **Liverpool 1** (Heighway) Clemence; Lawler, Lindsay, Smith, Lloyd, Hughes, Callaghan, Evans, Heighway, Toshack, Hall. Sub: Thompson rep Evans 70. May 8; 100,000; N Burtenshaw. aet

1972 Leeds 1 (Clarke) Harvey; Reaney, Madeley, Bremner, Charlton, Hunter, Lorimer, Clarke, Jones, Giles, Gray. Unused sub: Bates **Arsenal 0** Barnett; Rice, McNab, Storey, McLintock, Simpson, Armstrong, Ball, George, Radford, Graham. Sub: Kennedy rep Radford 80. May 6; 100,000; DW Smith

1973 Sunderland 1 (Porterfield) Montgomery; Malone, Guthrie, Horswill, Watson, Pitt, Kerr, Hughes, Halom, Porterfield, Tueart. Unused sub: Young **Leeds 0** Harvey; Reaney, Cherry, Bremner, Madeley, Hunter, Lorimer, Clarke, Jones, Giles, Gray. Sub: Yorath rep Gray 75. May 5; 100,000; K Burns

1974 Liverpool 3 (Keegan 2, Heighway) Clemence; Smith, Lindsay, Thompson, Cormack, Hughes, Keegan, Hall, Heighway, Toshack, Callaghan. Unused sub: Lawler **Newcastle 0** McFaul; Clark, Kennedy, McDermott, Howard, Moncur, Smith, Cassidy, Macdonald, Tudor, Hibbitt. Sub: Gibb rep Smith 70. May 4; 100,000; GC Kew

1975 West Ham 2 (Taylor 2) Day; McDowell, Taylor, Lock, Lampard, Bonds, Paddon, Brooking, Jennings, Taylor, Holland. Unused sub: Gould **Fulham 0** Mellor; Cutbush, Lacy, Moore, Fraser, Mullery, Conway, Slough, Mitchell, Busby, Barrett. Unused sub: Lloyd. May 3; 100,000; P Partridge

1976 Southampton 1 (Stokes) Turner; Rodrigues, Peach, Holmes, Blyth, Steele, Gilchrist, Channon, Osgood, McCalliog, Stokes. Unused sub: Fisher **Manchester Utd 0** Stepney; Forsyth, Houston, Daly, Greenhoff, Buchan, Coppell, McIlroy, Pearson, Macari, Hill. Sub: McCreery rep Hill 66. May 1; 100,000; C Thomas

1977 Manchester Utd 2 (Pearson, J Greenhoff) Stepney; Nicholl, Albiston, McIlroy, B Greenhoff, Buchan, Coppell, J Greenhoff, Pearson, Macari, Hill. Sub: McCreery rep Hill 81 **Liverpool 1** (Case) Clemence; Neal, Jones, Smith, Kennedy, Hughes, Keegan, Case, Heighway, Johnson, McDermott. Sub: Callaghan rep Johnson 64. May 21; 100,000; R Matthewson

1978 Ipswich Town 1 (Osborne) Cooper; Burley, Mills, Talbot, Hunter, Beattie, Osborne, Wark, Mariner, Geddis, Woods. Sub: Lambert rep Osborne 79 **Arsenal 0** Jennings; Rice, Nelson, Price, Young, O'Leary, Brady, Hudson, Macdonald, Stapleton, Sunderland. Sub: Rix rep Brady 65. May 6; 100,000; D Nippard

1979 Arsenal 3 (Talbot, Stapleton, Sunderland) Jennings; Rice, Nelson, Talbot, O'Leary, Young, Brady, Sunderland, Stapleton, Price, Rix. Sub: Walford rep Rix 83 **Manchester Utd 2** (McQueen, McIlroy) Bailey; Nicholl, Albiston, McIlroy, McQueen, Buchan, Coppell, J Greenhoff, Jordan, Macari, Thomas. Unused sub: Greenhoff. May 12; 100,000; R Challis

1980 West Ham 1 (Brooking) Parkes; Stewart, Lampard, Bonds, Martin, Devonshire, Allen, Pearson, Cross, Brooking, Pike. Unused sub: Brush **Arsenal 0** Jennings; Rice, Devine, Talbot, O'Leary, Young, Brady, Sunderland, Stapleton, Price, Rix. Sub: Nelson rep Devine 61. May 10; 100,000; G Courtney

1981 Tottenham 1 (Hutchinson og) Aleksic; Hughton, Miller, Roberts, Perryman, Villa, Ardiles, Archibald, Galvin, Hoddle, Crooks. Sub: Brooke rep Villa 68. **Manchester City 1** (Hutchinson) Corrigan; Ranson, McDonald, Reid, Power, Caton, Bennett, Gow, Mackenzie, Hutchison Reeves. Sub: Henry rep Hutchison 82. May 9; 100,000; K Hackett. aet **Replay – Tottenham 3** (Villa 2, Crooks) Aleksic; Hughton, Miller, Roberts, Perryman, Villa, Ardiles, Archibald, Galvin, Hoddle, Crooks. Unused sub: Brooke **Manchester City 2** (Mackenzie, Reeves pen) Corrigan; Ranson, McDonald, Reid, Power, Caton, Bennett, Gow, Mackenzie, Hutchison Reeves. Sub: Tueart rep McDonald 79. May 14; 92,000; K Hackett

1982 Tottenham 1 (Hoddle) Clemence; Hughton, Miller, Price, Hazard, Perryman, Roberts, Archibald, Galvin, Hoddle, Crooks. Sub: Brooke rep Hazard 104 **Queens Park Rangers 1** (Fenwick) Hucker; Fenwick, Gillard, Waddock, Hazell, Roeder, Currie, Flanagan, Allen, Stainrod, Gregory. Sub: Micklewhite rep Allen 50. May 22; 100,000; C White. aet **Replay – Tottenham 1** (Hoddle pen) Clemence; Hughton, Miller, Price, Hazard, Perryman, Roberts, Archibald, Galvin, Hoddle, Crooks. Sub: Brooke rep Hazard 67 **Queens Park Rangers 0** Hucker; Fenwick, Gillard, Waddock, Hazell, Neill, Currie, Flanagan, Micklewhite, Stainrod, Gregory. Sub: Burke rep Micklewhite 84. May 27; 90,000; C White

1983 Manchester Utd 2 (Stapleton, Wilkins) Bailey; Duxbury, Moran, McQueen, Albiston, Davies, Wilkins, Robson, Muhren, Stapleton, Whiteside. Unused sub: Grimes Brighton 2 (Smith, Stevens) Moseley; Ramsey, Gary A Stevens, Pearce, Gatting, Smillie, Case, Grealish, Howlett, Robinson, Smith. Sub: Ryan rep Ramsey 56. May 21; 100,000; AW Grey. aet Replay – Manchester Utd 4 (Robson 2, Whiteside, Muhren pen) Bailey; Duxbury, Moran, McQueen, Albiston, Davies, Wilkins, Robson, Muhren, Stapleton, Whiteside. Unused sub: Grimes Brighton 0 Moseley; Gary A Stevens, Pearce, Foster, Gatting, Smillie, Case, Grealish, Howlett, Robinson, Smith. Sub: Ryan rep Howlett 74. May 26; 100,000; AW Grey

1984 Everton 2 (Sharp, Gray) Southall; Gary M Stevens, Bailey, Ratcliffe, Mountfield, Reid, Steven, Heath, Sharp, Gray, Richardson. Unused sub: Harper Watford 0 Sherwood; Bardsley, Price, Taylor, Terry, Sinnott, Callaghan, Johnston, Reilly, Jackett, Barnes. Sub: Atkinson rep Price 58. May 19; 100,000; J Hunting

1985 Manchester Utd 1 (Whiteside) Bailey; Gidman, Albiston, Whiteside, McGrath, Moran, Robson, Strachan, Hughes, Stapleton, Olsen. Sub: Duxbury rep Albiston 91. Moran sent off 77. Everton 0 Southall; Gary M Stevens, Van den Hauwe, Ratcliffe, Mountfield, Reid, Steven, Sharp, Gray, Bracewell, Sheedy. Unused sub: Harper. May 18; 100,000; P Willis. aet

1986 Liverpool 3 (Rush 2, Johnston) Grobbelaar; Lawrenson, Beglin, Nicol, Whelan, Hansen, Dalglish, Johnston, Rush, Molby, MacDonald. Unused sub: McMahon Everton 1 (Lineker) Mimms; Gary M Stevens, Van den Hauwe, Ratcliffe, Mountfield, Reid, Steven, Lineker, Sharp, Bracewell, Sheedy. Sub: Heath rep Stevens 65. May 10; 98,000; A Robinson

1987 Coventry City 3 (Bennett, Houchen, Mabbutt og) Ogrizovic; Phillips, Downs, McGrath, Kilcline, Peake, Bennett, Gynn, Regis, Houchen, Pickering. Sub: Rodger rep Kilcline 88. Unused sub: Sedgley Tottenham 2 (Allen, Mabbutt) Clemence; Hughton Thomas, Hodge, Gough, Mabbutt, C Allen, P Allen, Waddle, Hoddle, Ardiles. Subs: Gary A Stevens rep Ardiles 91; Claesen rep Hughton 97. May 16; 98,000; N Midgley. aet

1988 Wimbledon 1 (Sanchez) Beasant; Goodyear, Phelan, Jones, Young, Thorn, Gibson Cork, Fashanu, Sanchez, Wise. Subs: Cunningham rep Cork 56; Scales rep Gibson 63 Liverpool 0 Grobbelaar; Gillespie, Ablett, Nicol, Spackman, Hansen, Beardsley, Aldridge, Houghton, Barnes, McMahon. Subs: Johnston rep Aldridge 63; Molby rep Spackman 72. May 14; 98,203; B Hill

1989 Liverpool 3 (Aldridge, Rush 2) Grobbelaar; Ablett, Staunton, Nichol, Whelan, Hansen, Beardsley, Aldridge Houghton, Barnes, McMahon. Subs: Rush rep Aldridge 72; Venison rep Staunton 91 Everton 2 (McCall 2) Southall; McDonald, Van den Hauwe, Ratcliffe, Watson, Bracewell, Nevin, Trevor Steven, Cottee, Sharp, Sheedy. Subs: McCall rep Bracewell 58; Wilson rep Sheedy 77. May 20; 82,500; J Worrall. aet

1990 Manchester Utd 3 (Robson, Hughes 2) Leighton; Ince, Martin, Bruce, Phelan, Pallister, Robson, Webb, McClair, Hughes, Wallace. Subs: Blackmore rep Martin 88; Robins rep Pallister 93. Crystal Palace 3 (O'Reilly, Wright 2) Martyn; Pemberton, Shaw, Gray, O'Reilly, Thorn, Barber, Thomas, Bright, Salako, Pardew. Subs: Wright rep Barber 69; Madden rep Gray 117. May 12; 80,000; A Gunn. aet Replay – Manchester Utd 1 (Martin) Sealey; Ince, Martin, Bruce, Phelan, Pallister, Robson, Webb, McClair, Hughes, Wallace. Unused subs: Robins, Blackmore Crystal Palace 0 Martyn; Pemberton, Shaw, Gray, O'Reilly, Thorn, Barber, Thomas, Bright, Salako, Pardew. Subs: Wright rep Barber 64; Madden rep Salako 79. May 17; 80,000; A Gunn

1991 Tottenham 2 (Stewart, Walker og) Thorstvedt; Edinburgh, Van den Hauwe, Sedgley, Howells, Mabbutt, Stewart, Gascoigne, Samways, Lineker, Allen. Subs: Nayim rep Gascoigne 18; Walsh rep Samways 82. Nottingham Forest 1 (Pearce) Crossley; Charles, Pearce, Walker, Chettle, Keane, Crosby, Parker, Clough, Glover, Woan. Subs: Hodge rep Woan 62; Laws rep Glover 108. May 18; 80,000; R Milford. aet

1992 Liverpool 2 (Thomas, Rush) Grobbelaar; Jones, Burrows, Nicol, Molby, Wright, Saunders, Houghton, Rush, McManaman, Thomas. Unused subs: Marsh, Walters Sunderland 0 Norman; Owers, Ball, Bennett, Rogan, Rush, Bracewell, Davenport, Armstrong, Byrne, Atkinson. Subs: Hardyman rep Rush 69; Hawke rep Armstrong 77. May 9; 80,000; P Don

1993 Arsenal 1 (Wright) Seaman; Dixon, Winterburn, Linighan, Adams, Jensen, Davis, Parlour, Merson, Campbell, Wright. Subs: Smith rep Parlour 66; O'Leary rep Wright 90. Sheffield Wed 1 (Hirst) Woods; Nilsson Worthington, Palmer, Hirst, Anderson, Waddle, Warhurst, Bright, Sheridan, Harkes. Subs: Hyde rep Anderson 85; Bart-Williams rep Waddle 112. May 15; 79,347; K Barratt. aet Replay – Arsenal

2 (Wright, Linighan) Seaman; Dixon, Winterburn, Linighan, Adams, Jensen, Davis, Smith, Merson, Campbell, Wright. Sub: O'Leary rep Wright 81. Unused sub: Selley **Sheffield Wed 1** (Waddle) Woods; Nilsson, Worthington, Palmer, Hirst, Wilson, Waddle, Warhurst, Bright, Sheridan, Harkes. Subs: Hyde rep Wilson 62; Bart-Williams rep Nilsson 118. May 20; 62,267; K Barratt. aet

1994   Manchester Utd 4 (Cantona 2 [2pens], Hughes, McClair) Schmeichel; Parker, Bruce, Pallister, Irwin, Kanchelskis, Keane, Ince, Giggs, Cantona, Hughes. Subs: Sharpe rep Irwin 84; McClair rep Kanchelskis 84. Unused sub: Walsh (gk) **Chelsea 0** Kharine; Clarke, Sinclair, Kjeldberg, Johnsen, Burley, Spencer, Newton, Stein, Peacock, Wise Substitutions Hoddle rep Burley 65; Cascarino rep Stein 78. Unused sub: Kevin Hitchcock (gk) May 14; 79,634; D Elleray

1995   Everton 1 (Rideout) Southall; Jackson, Hinchcliffe, Ablett, Watson, Parkinson, Unsworth, Horne, Stuart, Rideout, Limpar. Subs: Ferguson rep Rideout 51; Amokachi rep Limpar 69. Unused sub: Kearton (gk) **Manchester Utd 0** Schmeichel; Neville, Irwin, Bruce, Sharpe, Pallister, Keane, Ince, Brian McClair, Hughes, Butt. Subs: Giggs rep Bruce 46; Scholes rep Sharpe 72. Unused sub: Gary Walsh (gk) May 20; 79,592; G Ashby

1996   Manchester Utd 1 (Cantona) Schmeichel; Irwin, P Neville, May, Keane, Pallister, Cantona, Beckham, Cole, Butt, Giggs. Subs: Scholes rep Cole 65; G Neville rep Beckham 89. Unused sub: Sharpe **Liverpool 0** James; McAteer, Scales, Wright, Babb, Jones, McManaman, Barnes, Redknapp, Collymore, Fowler. Subs: Rush rep Collymore 74; Thomas rep Jones 85. Unused sub: Warner (gk) May 11; 79,007; D Gallagher

1997   Chelsea 2 (Di Matteo, Newton) Grodas; Petrescu, Minto, Sinclair, Lebouef, Clarke, Zola, Di Matteo, Newton, Hughes, Wise. Sub: Vialli rep Zola 89. Unused subs: Hitchcock (gk), Myers **Middlesbrough 0** Roberts; Blackmore, Fleming, Stamp, Pearson, Festa, Emerson, Mustoe, Ravanelli, Juninho, Hignett. Subs: Beck rep Ravanelli 24; Vickers rep Mustoe 29; Kinder, rep Hignett 74. May 17; 79,160; S Lodge

1998   Arsenal 2 (Overmars, Anelka) Seaman; Dixon, Winterburn, Vieira, Keown, Adams, Parlour, Anelka, Petit, Wreh, Overmars. Sub: Platt rep Wreh 63. Unused subs: Manninger (gk); Bould, Wright, Grimandi **Newcastle 0** Given; Pearce, Pearce, Batty, Dabizas, Howey, Lee, Barton, Shearer, Ketsbaia, Speed. Subs: Andersson rep Pearce 72; Watson rep Barton 77; Barnes rep Ketsbaia 85. Unused subs: Hislop (gk); Albert. May 16; 79,183; P Durkin

1999   Manchester Utd 2 (Sheringham, Scholes) Schmeichel; G Neville, Johnsen, May, P Neville, Beckham, Scholes, Keane, Giggs, Cole, Solskjaer. Subs: Sheringham rep Keane 9; Yorke rep Cole 61; Stam rep Scholes 77. Unused subs: Blomqvist, Van Der Gouw **Newcastle 0** Harper; Griffin, Charvet, Dabizas, Domi, Lee, Hamann, Speed, Solano, Ketsbaia, Shearer. Subs: Ferguson rep Hamann 46; Maric rep Solano 68; Glass rep Ketsbaia 79. Unused subs: Given (gk); Barton. May 22; 79,101; P Jones

2000   Chelsea 1 (Di Matteo) de Goey; Melchiot Desailly, Lebouef, Babayaro, Di Matteo, Wise, Deschamps, Poyet, Weah, Zola. Subs: Flo rep Weah 87; Morris rep Zola 90. Unused subs: Cudicini (gk), Terry , Harley **Aston Villa 0** James; Ehiogu, Southgate, Barry, Delaney, Taylor, Boateng, Merson, Wright, Dublin, Carbone. Subs: Stone rep Taylor 79; Joachim rep Carbone 79; Hendrie rep Wright 88. Unused subs: Enckelman (gk); Samuel May 20; 78,217; G Poll

2001   Liverpool 2 (Owen 2) Westerveld; Babbel, Henchoz, Hyypia, Carragher, Murphy, Hamann, Gerrard, Smicer, Heskey, Owen. Subs: McAllister rep Hamann 60; Fowler rep Smicer 77; Berger rep Murphy 77. Unused subs: Arphexad (gk); Vignal **Arsenal 1** (Ljungberg) Seaman; Dixon, Keown, Adams, Cole, Ljungberg, Grimandi, Vieira, Pires, Henry, Wiltord Subs: Parlour rep Wiltord 76; Kanu rep Ljungberg 85; Bergkamp rep Dixon 90. Unused subs: Manninger (gk); Lauren. May 12; 72,500; S Dunn

2002   Arsenal 2 (Parlour, Ljungberg) Seaman; Lauren, Campbell, Adams, Cole, Parlour, Wiltord, Vieira, Ljungberg, Bergkamp, Henry Subs: Edu rep Bergkamp 72; Kanu rep Henry 81; Keown rep Wiltord 90. Unused subs: Wright (gk); Dixon **Chelsea 0** Cudicini; Melchiot, Desailly, Gallas, Babayaro, Gronkjaer, Lampard, Petit, Le Saux, Floyd Hasselbaink, Gudjohnsen. Subs: Terry rep Babayaro 46; Zola rep Hasselbaink 68; Zenden rep Melchiot 77. Unused subs: de Goey (gk); Jokanovic. May 4; 73,963; M Riley

2003   Arsenal 1 (Pires) Seaman; Lauren, Luzhny, Keown, Cole, Ljungberg, Parlour, Gilberto, Pires, Bergkamp, Henry. Sub: Wiltord rep Bergkamp 77. Unused subs: Taylor (gk); Kanu, Toure, van Bronckhorst **Southampton 0** Niemi; Baird, Svensson, Lundekvam, Bridge, Telfer, Svensson, Oakley, Marsden, Beattie, Ormerod. Subs: Jones rep Niemi 66; Fernandes rep Baird 87; Tessem rep Svensson 75. Unused subs: Williams, Higginbotham. May 17; 73,726; G Barber

2004   Manchester Utd 3 (Van Nistelrooy [2, 1 pen], Ronaldo) Howard; G Neville, Brown, Silvestre, O'Shea, Fletcher, Keane, Ronaldo, Scholes, Giggs, Van Nistelrooy. Subs: Carroll rep Howard, Butt rep Fletcher, Solskjaer rep Ronaldo 84. Unused subs: P Neville, Djemba-Djemba **Millwall 0** Marshall; Elliott, Lawrence, Ward, Ryan, Wise, Ifill, Cahill, Livermore, Sweeney, Harris. Subs: Cogan rep Ryan, McCammon rep Harris 74 Weston rep Wise 88. Unused subs: Gueret (gk); Dunne. May 22; 71,350; J Winter

2005   Arsenal 0 Lehmann; Lauren, Toure, Senderos, Cole, Fabregas, Gilberto, Vieira, Pires, Reyes, Bergkamp Subs: Ljungberg rep Bergkamp 65, Van Persie rep Fabregas 86, Edu rep Pires 105. Unused subs: Almunia (gk); Campbell. Reyes sent off 90. **Manchester Utd 0** Carroll; Brown, Ferdinand, Silvestre, O'Shea, Fletcher, Keane, Scholes, Rooney, Van Nistelrooy, Ronaldo. Subs: Fortune rep O'Shea 77, Giggs rep Fletcher 91 Unused subs: Howard (gk); G Neville, Smith. **Arsenal** (Lauren, Ljungberg, van Persie, Cole, Vieira) beat Manchester Utd (van Nistelrooy, Scholes [missed], Ronaldo, Rooney, Keane) 5-4 on penalties

2006   Liverpool 3 (Gerrard 2, Cisse) Reina; Finnan, Carragher, Hyypiä, Riise, Gerrard, Xabi, Sissoko, Kewell, Cisse, Crouch. Subs: Morientes rep Kewell 48, Kromkamp rep Alonso 67, Hamman rep Crouch 71. Unused subs: Dudek (gk); Traoré **West Ham 3** (Ashton, Konchesky, Carragher (og)) Hislop; Scaloni, Ferdinand, Gabbidon, Konchesky, Benayoun, Fletcher, Reo-Coker, Etherington, Ashton, Harewood. Subs: Zamora rep Ashton 71, Dailly rep Fletcher, Sheringham rep Etherington 85. Unused subs: Walker (gk); Collins. **Liverpool** (Hamann, Hyypiä [missed], Gerrard, Riise) beat **West Ham** (Zamora [missed], Sheringham, Konchesky [missed], Ferdinand [missed]) 3-1 on penalties. May 13; 71,140; A Wiley

2007   Chelsea 1 (Drogba) Cech, Ferreira, Essien, Terry, Bridge, Mikel, Makelele, Lampard, Wright-Phillips, Drogba, J Cole. Subs: Robben rep J Cole 105, Kalou rep Wright Phillips 93, A Cole rep Robben 108. Unused subs: Cudicini (gk); Diarra. **Manchester Utd 0** Van der Sar, Brown, Ferdinand, Vidic, Heinze, Fletcher, Scholes, Carrick, Ronaldo, Rooney, Giggs Subs: Smith rep Fletcher 92, O'Shea rep Carrick, Solskjaer rep Giggs 112. Unused subs: Kuszczak (gk); Evra. May 19; 89,826; S Bennett

2008   Portsmouth 1 (Kanu) James; Johnson, Campbell, Distin, Hreidarsson, Utaka, Muntari, Mendes, Diarra, Kranjcar, Kanu. Subs: Nugent rep Utaka 69, Diop rep Mendes 78, Baros rep Kanu 87. Unused subs: Ashdown (gk); Pamarot. **Cardiff 0** Enckelman; McNaughton, Johnson, Loovens, Capaldi, Whittingham, Rae, McPhail, Ledley, Hasselbaink, Parry. Subs: Ramsey rep Whittingham 62, Thompson rep Hasselbaink 70, Sinclair rep Rae 87. Unused subs: Oakes (gk); Purse. May 17; 89,874; M Dean

2009   Chelsea 2 (Drogba, Lampard) Cech; Bosingwa, Alex, Terry, A Cole, Essien, Mikel, Lampard, Drogba, Anelka, Malouda. Subs: Ballack rep Essien 61. Unused subs: Hilario (gk), Ivanovic, Di Santo, Kalou, Belletti, Mancienne. **Everton 1** (Saha) Howard; Hibbert, Yobo, Lescott, Baines, Osman, Neville, Cahill, Pienaar, Fellaini, Saha. Subs: Jacobsen rep Hibbert 46, Vaughan rep Saha 77, Gosling rep Osman 83. Unused subs: Nash, Castillo, Rodwell, Baxter. May 30; 89,391; H Webb

2010   Chelsea 1 (Drogba) Cech; Ivanovic, Alex, Terry, A Cole, Lampard, Ballack, Malouda, Kalou, Drogba, Anelka. Subs: Belletti rep Ballack 44, J Cole rep Kalou 71, Sturridge rep Anelka 90. Unused subs: Hilario (gk), Zhirkov, Paulo Ferreira, Matic. **Portsmouth 0** James; Finnan, Mokoena, Rocha, Mullins, Dindane, Brown, Diop, Boateng, O'Hara, Piquionne. Subs: Utaka rep Boateng 73, Belhadj rep Mullins 81, Kanu rep Diop 81. Unused subs: Ashdown (gk), Vanden Borre, Hughes, Ben Haim. May 15; 88,335; C Foy

2011   Manchester City 1 (Y Toure) Hart; Richards, Kompany, Lescott, Kolarov, De Jong, Barry, Silva, Y Toure, Balotelli, Tevez. Subs: Johnson rep Balotelli 73, Zabaleta rep Tevez 87, Vieira rep Silva 90. Unused subs: Given (gk), Boyata, Milner, Dzeko. **Stoke 0** Sorensen; Wilkinson, Shawcross, Huth, Wilson, Pennant, Whelan, Delap, Etherington, Walters, Jones. Subs: Whitehead rep Etherington 62, Carew rep Delap 80, Pugh rep Whelan 84. Unused subs: Nash (gk), Collins, Faye, Diao. May 14; 88,643; M Atkinson

2012   Chelsea 2 (Ramires, Drogba) Cech; Bosingwa, Ivanovic, Terry, Cole, Mikel, Lampard, Ramires, Mata, Kalou, Drogba. Subs: Meireles rep Ramires76, Malouda rep Mata 90. Unused subs: Turnbull (gk), Paulo Ferreira, Essien, Torres, Sturridge. **Liverpool 1** (Carroll) Reina; Johnson, Skrtel, Agger, Luis Enrique, Spearing, Bellamy, Henderson, Gerrard, Downing, Suarez. Subs Carroll rep Spearing 55, Kuyt rep Bellamy 78. Unused subs: Doni (gk), Carragher, Kelly, Shelvey, Rodriguez. May 5; 89,102; P Dowd

2013 Wigan 1 (Watson) Robles; Boyce, Alcaraz, Scharner, McCarthy, McArthur, McManaman, Maloney, Gomez, Espinoza, Kone. Subs: Watson rep Gomez 81. Unused subs: Al Habsi (gk), Caldwell, Golobart, Fyvie, Henriquez, Di Santo. **Manchester City 0** Hart, Zabaleta, Kompany, Nastasic, Clichy, Toure, Barry, Silva, Tevez, Nasri, Aguero. Subs: Milner rep Nasri 54, Rodwell rep Tevez 69, Dzeko rep Barry 90. Unused subs: Pantilimon (gk), Lescott, Kolarov, Garcia. Sent off Zabaleta (84). May 11; 86,254; A Marriner

2014 Arsenal 3 (Cazorla, Koscielny, Ramsey) Fabianski; Sagna, Koscielny, Mertesacker, Gibbs, Arteta, Ramsey, Cazorla, Ozil, Podolski, Giroud. Subs: Sanogo rep Podolski 61, Rosicky rep Cazorla 106, Wilshire rep Ozil 106. Unused subs: Szczesny (gk), Vermaelen, Monreal, Flamini. **Hull 2** (Chester, Davies) McGregor; Davies, Bruce, Chester, Elmohamady, Livermore, Huddlestone, Meyler, Rosenior, Quinn, Fryatt. Subs: McShane rep Bruce 67, Aluko rep Quinn 71, Boyd rep Rosenior 102. Unused subs: Harper (gk), Figueroa, Koren, Sagbo. May 17; 89,345; L Probert. ael

2015 Arsenal 4 (Walcott, Sanchez, Mertesacker, Giroud) Szczesny; Bellerin, Koscielny, Mertesacker, Monreal, Coquelin, Cazorla, Ramsey, Ozil, A Sanchez, Walcott. Subs: Wilshere rep Ozil 77, Giroud rep Walcott 77, Oxlade-Chamberlain rep A Sanchez 90. Unused subs: Ospina (gk), Gibbs, Gabriel, Flamini. **Aston Villa 0** Given; Hutton, Okore, Vlaar, Richardson, Cleverley, Westwood, Delph, N'Zogbia, Benteke, Grealish. Subs: Agbonlahor rep N'Zogbia 53, Bacuna rep Richardson 68, C Sanchez rep Westwood 71. Unused subs: Guzan (gk), Baker, Sinclair, Cole. May 30; 89,283; J Moss

2016 Manchester Utd 2 (Mata, Lingard) De Gea, Valencia, Smalling, Blind, Rojo, Carrick, Rooney, Fellaini, Mata, Martial, Rashford. Subs: Darmian rep Rojo 65, Young rep Rashford 71, Lingard rep Mata 90. Unused subs: Romero, Jones, Herrera, Schneiderlin. **Crystal Palace 1** (Puncheon 78) Hennessey, Ward, Dann, Delaney, Souare, Cabaye, Jedinak, Zaha, McArthur, Bolasie, Wickham. Unused subs: Speroni, Adebayor, Sako, Kelly. May 21; 88,619; M Clattenburg

VENUES

Kennington Oval 1872; **Lillie Bridge** 1873; **Kennington Oval** 1874 – 1892 (1886 replay at the **Racecourse Ground, Derby**); **Fallowfield**, Manchester, 1893; **Goodison Park** 1894; **Crystal Palace** 1895 – 1915 (1901 replay at **Burnden Park**; 1910 replay at Goodison Park; 1912 replay at **Bramall Lane**); **Old Trafford** 1915; **Stamford Bridge** 1920 – 1922; **Wembley** 1923 – 2000 (1970 replay at **Old Trafford**; all replays after 1981 at **Wembley**); **Millennium Stadium** 2001 – 2006; **Wembley** 2007 – 2017

SUMMARY OF FA CUP WINS

Arsenal	13	Sheffield Wed	3	Clapham Rov	1
Manchester Utd	12	West Ham	3	Coventry	1
Tottenham	8	Bury	2	Derby	1
Aston Villa	7	Nottm Forest	2	Huddersfield	1
Liverpool	7	Old Etonians	2	Ipswich	1
Chelsea	7	Portsmouth	2	Leeds	1
Blackburn Rov	6	Preston	2	Notts Co	1
Newcastle	6	Sunderland	2	Old Carthusians	1
Everton	5	Barnsley	1	Oxford University	1
Manchester City	5	Blackburn Olympic	1	Royal Engineers	1
The Wanderers	5	Blackpool	1	Southampton	1
WBA	5	Bradford City	1	Wigan	1
Bolton	4	Burnley	1	Wimbledon	1
Sheffield Utd	4	Cardiff	1		
Wolves	4	Charlton	1		

APPEARANCES IN FINALS

(Figures do not include replays)

Arsenal 20	The Wanderers* 5	Notts Co............................ 2
Manchester Utd............ 19	West Ham 5	Queen's Park (Glasgow) 2
Liverpool..................... 14	Derby............................ 4	Blackburn Olympic* 1
Everton........................ 13	Leeds............................ 4	Bradford City* 1
Newcastle 13	Leicester....................... 4	Brighton 1
Chelsea 12	Oxford University 4	Bristol City 1
Aston Villa 11	Royal Engineers 4	Coventry* 1
Manchester City............ 10	Southampton................... 4	Fulham 1
WBA............................ 10	Sunderland 4	Hull 1
Tottenham 9	Blackpool....................... 3	Ipswich* 1
Blackburn Rov............... 8	Burnley.......................... 3	Luton 1
Wolves........................ 8	Cardiff........................... 3	Middlesbrough 1
Bolton 7	Nottm Forest 3	Millwall 1
Preston........................ 7	Barnsley........................ 2	Old Carthusians*............... 1
Old Etonians 6	Birmingham 2	QPR 1
Sheffield Utd................. 6	Bury*............................. 2	Stoke 1
Sheffield Wed................ 6	Charlton......................... 2	Watford............................ 1
Huddersfield 5	Clapham Rov 2	Wigan 1
Portsmouth 5	Crystal Palace................ 2	Wimbledon* 1

(* Denotes undefeated)

APPEARANCES IN SEMI-FINALS

(Figures do not include replays)

29 Arsenal, Manchester Utd; **26** Everton; **24** Liverpool; **22** Chelsea; **21** Aston Villa; **20** WBA, Tottenham; **18** Blackburn; **17** Newcastle; **16** Sheffield Wed; **14** Bolton, Sheffield Utd, Wolves; **13** Derby, Manchester City; **12** Nottm Forest, Sunderland; **11** Southampton; **10** Preston; **9** Birmingham; **8** Burnley, Leeds; **7** Huddersfield, Leicester, Portsmouth, West Ham; **6** Fulham, Old Etonians, Oxford University, Watford; **5** Millwall, Notts Co, The Wanderers; **4** Cardiff, *Crystal Palace, Luton, Queen's Park (Glasgow), Royal Engineers, Stoke; **3** Barnsley, Blackpool, Clapham Rov, Ipswich, Middlesbrough, Norwich, Old Carthusians, Oldham, The Swifts; **2** Blackburn Olympic, Bristol City, Bury, Charlton, Grimsby, Hull, Reading, Swansea, Swindon, Wigan, Wimbledon; **1** Bradford City, Brighton, Cambridge University, Chesterfield, Coventry, Crewe, Darwen, Derby Junction, Marlow, Old Harrovians, Orient, Plymouth Argyle, Port Vale, QPR, Rangers (Glasgow), Shropshire Wand, Wycombe, York

(*A previous and different Crystal Palace club also reached the semi-final in season 1871–72)

NOW IT'S SIX DEBUT GOALS FOR RASHFORD

Marcus Rashford extended a remarkable run of debut goals last season. The 19-year-old Manchester United striker scored a hat-trick in his first match for England's under-21 side in a European Championship qualifier against Norway. A fortnight later, he was on the mark on his League Cup debut against Northampton. The previous season, Rashford scored on his debut for the England senior team against Australia, for United in the Premier League against Arsenal, in the Manchester derby and in a Europa League game with Midtjylland.

ENGLISH LEAGUE CUP 2016–17

FIRST ROUND

Accrington 0 Bradford 0
(aet, Acrington won 11-10 on pens)
Barnet 0 Millwall 4
Barnsley 1 Northampton 2 (aet)
Birmingham 0 Oxford 1 (aet)
Blackpool 4 Bolton 2 (aet)
Brighton 4 Colchester 0
Bristol Rov 1 Cardiff 0 (aet)
Burton 3 Bury 2 (aet)
Cambridge 2 Sheffield Wed 1 (aet)
Carlisle 2 Port Vale 1
Cheltenham 1 Charlton 0
Coventry 3 Portsmouth 2 (aet)
Derby 1 Grimsby 0
Doncaster 1 Nottm Forest 2
Exeter 1 Brentford 0 (aet)
Fleetwood 2 Leeds 2
(aet, Leeds won 5-4 on pens)
Ipswich 0 Stevenage 1

Leyton Orient 2 Fulham 3
Luton 3 Aston Villa 1
Mansfield 1 Blackburn 3
Newport 2 MK Dons 3
Oldham 2 Wigan 1
Peterborough 3 AFC Wimbledon 2
Preston 1 Hartlepool 0
QPR 2 Swindon 2
(aet, QPR won 4-2 on pens)
Reading 2 Plymouth 0
Rochdale 3 Chesterfield 1
Rotherham 4 Morecambe 5 (aet)
Scunthorpe 2 Notts Co 0 (aet)
Sheffield Utd 1 Crewe 2 (aet)
Shrewsbury 2 Huddersfield 1
Southend 1 Gillingham 3
Walsall 0 Yeovil 2 (aet)
Wolves 2 Crawley 1
Wycombe 0 Bristol City 1

SECOND ROUND

Accrington 1 Burnley 0 (aet)
Blackburn 4 Crewe 3 (aet)
Burton 0 Liverpool 5
Chelsea 3 Bristol Rov 2
Crystal Palace 2 Blackpool 0
Derby 1 Carlisle 1
(aet, Derby won 14-13 on pens)
Everton 4 Yeovil 0
Exeter 1 Hull 3
Fulham 2 Middlesbrough 1 (aet)
Luton 1 Leeds 1
Millwall 1 Nottm Forest 2
Morecambe 1 Bournemouth 2
Newcastle 2 Cheltenham 0

Northampton 2 WBA 2
(aet, Northampton won 4-3 on pens)
Norwich 6 Coventry 1
Oxford 2 Brighton 4
Peterborough 1 Swansea 3
Preston 2 Oldham 0
QPR 2 Rochdale 1
Reading 2 MK Dons 2
(aet, Reading won 4-2 on pens)
Scunthorpe 1 Bristol City 2 (aet)
Stevenage 0 Stoke 4
Sunderland 1 Shrewsbury 0
Watford 1 Gillingham 2 (aet)
Wolves 2 Cambridge 1

THIRD ROUND

Bournemouth 2 Preston 3 (aet)
Brighton 1 Reading 2
Derby 0 Liverpool 3
Everton 0 Norwich 2
Fulham 1 Bristol City 2
Leeds 1 Blackburn 0
Leicester 2 Chelsea 4 (aet)
Newcastle 2 Wolves 0

Northampton 1 **Manchester Utd** 3
Nottm Forest 0 Arsenal 4
QPR 1 Sunderland 2
Southampton 2 Crystal Palace 0
Stoke 1 Hull 0
Swansea 1 Manchester City 2
Tottenham 5 Gillingham 0
West Ham 1 Accrington 0

FOURTH ROUND

Arsenal 2 Reading 0
Bristol City 1 Hull 2
Leeds 2 Norwich 2
(aet, Leeds won 3-2 on pens)
Liverpool 2 Tottenham 1

Manchester Utd 1 Manchester City 0
Newcastle 6 Preston 0
Southampton 1 Sunderland 0
West Ham 2 Chelsea 1

FIFTH ROUND

Arsenal 0 **Southampton** 2
Hull 1 Newcastle 1
(aet, Hull won 3-1 on pens)

Liverpool 2 Leeds 0
Manchester Utd 4 West Ham 1

SEMI-FINALS (two legs)

Manchester Utd 2 Hull 0
Hull 2 **Manchester Utd** 1

Southampton 1 Liverpool 0
Liverpool 0 **Southampton** 1

FINAL

MANCHESTER UNITED 3 SOUTHAMPTON 2
Wembley (85,264); Sunday, February 26 2017

Manchester United (4-2-3-1): De Gea, Valencia, Bailly, Smalling (capt), Rojo, Herrera, Pogba, Lingard (Rashford 76), Mata (Carrick 40), Martial (Fellaini 90), Ibrahimovic. **Subs not used**: Romero, Blind, Rooney, Young. **Scorers**: Ibrahimovic (19, 87), Lingard (38). **Booked**: Herrera, Lingard. **Manager**: Jose Mourinho

Southampton (4-3-3): Forster, Soares, Stephens, Yoshida, Bertrand, Ward-Prowse, Romeu, Davis (capt) (Rodriguez 90), Redmond, Tadic (Boufal 77), Gabbiadini (Long 83). **Subs not used**: Hassen, McQueen, Hojbjerg, Caceres. **Scorer**: Gabbiadini (45, 48). **Booked**: Romeu, Stephens, Redmond. **Manager**: Claude Puel

Referee: A Marriner (West Midlands). **Half-time**: 2-1

At the end of a week in which there was widespread condemnation of the sacking of Leicester's title-winning manager Claudio Ranieri, a cracking League Cup Final went some way to repairing football's bruised image. The honours went to Manchester United, courtesy of an 87th minute goal by Zlatan Ibrahimovic, his second of the game, which underlined the impact the 35-year-old Swede had made in his first season in the Premier League. It also presented Jose Mourinho with his first major trophy at Old Trafford and enabled the manager to match the four successes in the tournament achieved by Sir Alex Ferguson and Brian Clough. Southampton were left, justifiably, cursing their luck, notably when the impressive Manolo Gabbiadini had a goal contentiously ruled out for offside with the scoreline blank. They were the better side for lengthy spells, but fortune deserted them again when Oriel Romeu struck a post at 2-2, before Ibrahimovic stole in on Ander Herrera's cross for his 26th goal in all competitions. Consolation for Southampton, and their manager Claude Puel, came with a performance full of pride and purpose – along with the knowledge that the winter transfer signing of Gabbiadini, scorer of six goals in his first four matches for the club, represented one of the shrewdest of the campaign.

PIGS FLY AT THE VALLEY

Charlton's League One match against Coventry came to a halt last season when The Valley pitch was littered with plastic toy pigs thrown from the stands by rival supporters. They were protesting against the owners of their respective clubs. The hold-up lasted five minutes.

HOW THEY REACHED THE FINAL

Manchester United

Round 3: 3-1 away to Northampton (Carrick, Herrera, Rashford)
Round 4: 1-0 home to Manchester City (Mata)
Round 5: 4-1 home to West Ham (Ibrahimovic 2, Martial 2)
Semi-finals v Hull – first leg, 2-0 home (Mata, Fellaini); second leg, 1-2 away (Pogba)

Southampton

Round 3: 2-0 home to Crystal Palace (Austin pen, Hesketh)
Round 4: 1-0 home to Sunderland (Boufal)
Round 5: 2-0 away to Arsenal (Clasie, Bertrand)
Semi-finals: v Liverpool – first leg, 1-0 home (Redmond); second leg, 1-0 away (Long)

LEAGUE CUP – COMPLETE RESULTS

LEAGUE CUP FINALS

1961*	Aston Villa beat Rotherham 3-2 on agg (0-2a, 3-0h)
1962	Norwich beat Rochdale 4-0 on agg (3-0a, 1-0h)
1963	Birmingham beat Aston Villa 3-1 o agg (3-1h, 0-0a)
1964	Leicester beat Stoke 4-3 on agg (1-1a, 3-2h)
1965	Chelsea beat Leicester 3-2 on agg (3-2h, 0-0a)
1966	WBA beat West Ham 5-3 on agg (1-2a, 4-1h)

AT WEMBLEY

1967	QPR beat WBA (3-2)
1968	Leeds beat Arsenal (1-0)
1969*	Swindon beat Arsenal (3-1)
1970*	Man City beat WBA (2-1)
1971	Tottenham beat Aston Villa (2-0)
1972	Stoke beat Chelsea (2-1)
1973	Tottenham beat Norwich (1-0)
1974	Wolves beat Man City (2-1)
1975	Aston Villa beat Norwich (1-0)
1976	Man City beat Newcastle (2-1)
1977†*	Aston Villa beat Everton (3-2 after 0-0 and 1-1 draws)
1978††	Nottm Forest beat Liverpool (1-0 after 0-0 draw)
1979	Nottm Forest beat Southampton (3-2)
1980	Wolves beat Nottm Forest (1-0)
1981†††	Liverpool beat West Ham (2-1 after 1-1 draw)

MILK CUP

1982*	Liverpool beat Tottenham (3-1)
1983*	Liverpool beat Man Utd (2-1)
1984**	Liverpool beat Everton (1-0 after *0-0 draw)
1985	Norwich beat Sunderland (1-0)
1986	Oxford Utd beat QPR (3-0)

LITTLEWOODS CUP

1987	Arsenal beat Liverpool (2-1)
1988	Luton beat Arsenal (3-2)
1989	Nottm Forest beat Luton (3-1)
1990	Nottm Forest beat Oldham (1-0)

RUMBELOWS CUP

1991	Sheffield Wed beat Man Utd (1-0)
1992	Man Utd beat Nottm Forest (1-0)

COCA-COLA CUP

1993	Arsenal beat Sheffield Wed (2-1)
1994	Aston Villa beat Man Utd (3-1)
1995	Liverpool beat Bolton (2-1)
1996	Aston Villa beat Leeds (3-0)
1997***	Leicester beat Middlesbrough (*1-0 after *1-1 draw)
1998	Chelsea beat Middlesbrough (2-0)

WORTHINGTON CUP (at

Millennium Stadium from 2001)

1999	Tottenham beat Leicester (1-0)
2000	Leicester beat Tranmere (2-1)
2001	Liverpool beat Birmingham (5-4 on pens after *1-1 draw)
2002	Blackburn beat Tottenham (2-1)
2003	Liverpool beat Man Utd (2-0)

CARLING CUP (at Wembley from 2008)

2004	Middlesbrough beat Bolton (2-1)
2005*	Chelsea beat Liverpool (3-2)
2006	Man Utd beat Wigan (4-0)
2007	Chelsea beat Arsenal (2-1)
2008*	Tottenham beat Chelsea (2-1)
2009	Man Utd beat Tottenham
	(4-1 on pens after *0-0 draw)
2010	Man Utd beat Aston Villa (2-1)
2011	Birmingham beat Arsenal (2-1)
2012	Liverpool beat Cardiff
	(3-2 on pens after *2-2 draw)

CAPITAL ONE CUP (at Wembley from 2013)

2013	Swansea beat Bradford (5-0)
2014	Manchester City beat Sunderland (3-1)
2015	Chelsea beat Tottenham (2-0)
2016	Manchester City beat Liverpool
	(3-1 on pens after *1-1 draw)

* After extra time. † First replay at Hillsborough, second replay at Old Trafford. †† Replayed at Old Trafford. ††† Replayed at Villa Park. ** Replayed at Maine Road. *** Replayed at Hillsborough

EFL CUP (at Wembley from 2017)

2017	Manchester Utd beat Southampton (3-2)

SUMMARY OF LEAGUE CUP WINNERS

Liverpool	8	Arsenal	2	Oxford Utd	1
Aston Villa	5	Birmingham	2	QPR	1
Chelsea	5	Norwich	2	Sheffield Wed	1
Manchester Utd	5	Wolves	2	Stoke	1
Nottm Forest	4	Blackburn	1	Swansea	1
Manchester City	4	Leeds	1	Swindon	1
Tottenham	4	Luton	1	WBA	1
Leicester	3	Middlesbrough	1		

LEAGUE CUP FINAL APPEARANCES

12 Liverpool; **9**, Manchester Utd; **8** Aston Villa, Tottenham; **7** Arsenal, Chelsea; **6** Nottm Forest; **5** Leicester, Manchester City, Norwich; **3** Birmingham, Middlesbrough, WBA; **2** Bolton, Everton, Leeds, Luton, QPR, Sheffield Wed, Southampton, Stoke, Sunderland, West Ham, Wolves; **1** Blackburn, Bradford, Cardiff, Newcastle, Oldham, Oxford Utd, Rochdale, Rotherham, Swansea, Swindon, Tranmere, Wigan (Figures do not include replays)

LEAGUE CUP SEMI-FINAL APPEARANCES

17 Liverpool; **16** Tottenham; **14** Arsenal, Aston Villa; Manchester Utd; **12** Chelsea; **9** Manchester City, West Ham; **6** Blackburn, Nottm Forest; **5** Birmingham, Everton, Leeds, Leicester, Middlesbrough, Norwich; **4** Bolton, Burnley, Crystal Palace, Ipswich, Sheffield Wed, Sunderland, WBA; **3** QPR, Southampton, Stoke, Swindon, Wolves; **2** Bristol City, Cardiff, Coventry, Derby, Luton, Oxford Utd, Plymouth, Sheffield Utd, Tranmere, Watford, Wimbledon; **1** Blackpool, Bradford, Bury, Carlisle, Chester, Huddersfield, Hull, Newcastle, Oldham, Peterborough, Rochdale, Rotherham, Shrewsbury, Stockport, Swansea, Walsall, Wigan, Wycombe (Figures do not include replays)

FA COMMUNITY SHIELD

LEICESTER CITY 1 MANCHESTER UNTED 2
Wembley (85,437); Sunday, August 7 2016

Leicester City (4-4-2): Schmeichel, Simpson (Hernandez 63), Morgan (capt), Huth (Ulloa 89), Fuchs (Schlupp 80), Mahrez, Drinkwater, King (Mendy 63), Albrighton (Gray 46), Okazaki (Mus 46), Vardy. **Sub not used:** Zieler. **Scorer:** Vardy (52). **Booked:** Simpson, King, Vardy. **Manager:** Claudio Ranieri

Manchester United (4-2-3-1): De Gea, Valencia, Bailly, Blind, Shaw (Rojo 69), Carrick (Herrera 61), Fellaini, Lingard (Mata 63) (Mkhitaryan 90), Rooney (capt) (Schneiderlin 88), Martial (Rashford 70), Ibrahimovic. **Sub not used:** Romero. **Scorers:** Lingard (32), Ibrahimovic (83). **Booked:** Bailly. **Manager:** Jose Mourinho

Referee: C Pawson (South Yorks). **Half-time:** 0-1

CHECKATRADE TROPHY

(Each team awarded one point for drawn group match after 90 minutes. Then penalties with winning team awarded one additional point. Group winners and runners-up through to knock-out stage)

GROUP STAGE – NORTH

GROUP A

	P	W	D	L	F	A	Pts
Cheltenham	3	2	0	1	4	3	6
Blackpool	3	1	1	1	3	3	5
Everton U21	3	1	1	1	4	3	4
Bolton	3	1	0	2	1	3	3

GROUP B

	P	W	D	L	F	A	Pts
Wolves U21	3	2	0	1	8	4	6
Chesterfield	3	2	0	1	5	5	6
Crewe	3	1	0	2	5	5	3
Accrington	3	1	0	2	4	8	3

GROUP C

	P	W	D	L	F	A	Pts
Bradford	3	2	0	1	5	4	6
Morecambe	3	2	0	1	7	7	6
Bury	3	1	1	1	4	4	4
Stoke U21	3	0	1	2	2	5	2

GROUP D

	P	W	D	L	F	A	Pts
Carlisle	3	3	0	0	11	6	9
Oldham	3	1	1	1	8	7	5
Fleetwood	3	1	0	2	3	6	3
Blackburn U21	3	0	1	2	2	5	1

GROUP E

	P	W	D	L	F	A	Pts
Doncaster	3	1	2	0	4	2	6
Mansfield	3	2	0	1	4	4	6
Port Vale	3	1	1	1	1	1	5
Derby U21	3	0	1	2	4	6	1

GROUP F

Rochdale	3	2	1	0	5	3	8
Sunderland U21	3	2	1	0	4	2	7
Notts Co	3	1	0	2	4	5	3
Hartlepool	3	0	0	3	2	5	0

GROUP G

Scunthorpe	3	3	0	0	6	1	9
Cambridge	3	2	0	1	3	3	6
Shrewsbury	3	1	0	2	3	3	3
Middlesbrough U21	3	0	0	3	2	7	0

GROUP H

Walsall	3	3	0	0	8	3	9
Leicester U21	3	1	1	1	1	1	5
Sheffield Utd	3	1	1	1	5	4	4
Grimsby	3	0	0	3	4	10	0

SOUTH

GROUP A

Yeovil	3	2	1	0	6	3	7
Reading U21	3	1	1	1	5	6	5
Portsmouth	3	1	1	1	6	6	4
Bristol Rov	3	0	1	2	2	4	2

GROUP B

AFC Wimbledon	3	2	0	1	5	3	6
Swansea U21	3	2	0	1	4	4	6
Plymouth	3	1	0	2	5	5	3
Newport	3	1	0	2	4	6	3

GROUP C

Swindon	3	1	2	0	3	2	7
Oxford	3	1	2	0	5	3	5
Exeter	3	1	1	1	6	7	4
Chelsea U21	3	0	1	2	4	6	2

GROUP D

Coventry	3	3	0	0	11	5	9
Wycombe	3	2	0	1	8	4	6
West Ham U21	3	0	1	2	3	8	2
Northampton	3	0	1	2	2	7	1

GROUP E

Southampton U21	3	2	1	0	6	1	7
Crawley	3	2	0	1	3	4	6
Charlton	3	0	2	1	1	3	3
Colchester	3	0	1	2	2	4	2

GROUP F

Norwich U21	3	3	0	0	15	2	9
MK Dons	3	1	1	1	4	6	5
Peterborough	3	1	0	2	3	8	3
Barnet	3	0	1	2	3	9	1

GROUP G

Southend	3	2	0	1	3	4	6
Brighton U21	3	1	1	1	3	4	5
Stevenage	3	1	1	1	7	5	4
Leyton Orient	3	1	0	2	3	3	3

GROUP H

Millwall	3	3	0	0	7	2	9
Luton	3	2	0	1	5	4	6
Gillingham	3	1	0	2	4	4	3
WBA U21	3	0	0	3	0	6	0

SECOND ROUND

North: Bradford 1 Cambridge 0; Doncaster 1 Blackpool 1 (Blackpool won 8-7 on pens); Carlisle 2 Mansfield 3; Cheltenham 6 Leicester U21 1; Rochdale 0 Chesterfield 2; Scunthorpe 1 Morecambe 1 (Scunthorpe won 5-3 on pens); Walsall 1 Oldham 3; Wolves U21 1 Sunderland U21 1 (Wolves won 4-3 on pens)

South: AFC Wimbledon1 Brighton U21 2; Coventry 1 Crawley 0; Millwall 1 Wycombe 3; Norwich U21 0 Swansea U21 1; Southampton U21 1 Reading U21 1 (Reading won 4-3 on pens); Southend 1 Oxford 1 (Oxford won 4-3 on pens); Swindon 2 Luton 3; Yeovil 4 MK Dons 1`

THIRD ROUND

Blackpool 1 Wycombe 1 (Wycombe won 5-4 on pens); Cheltenham 0 Bradford 1; Coventry 3 Brighton U21 0; Luton 4 Chesterfield 0; Mansfield 2 Oldham 0; Oxford 4 Scunthorpe 1; Swansea U21 2 Wolves U21 1; Yeovil 4 Reading U21 1

FOURTH ROUND

Luton 5 Yeovil 2; Mansfield 1 Wycombe 2; Oxford 2 Bradford 1; Swansea U21 1 Coventry 1 (Coventry won 4-2 on pens)

SEMI-FINALS

Coventry 2 Wycombe 1; Luton 2 Oxford 3

FINAL

COVENTRY CITY 2 OXFORD UNITED 1
Wembley (74,434); Sunday, April 2 2017

Coventry City (4-2-3-1): Burge, Willis (capt) (Kelly-Evans 60), Stokes, Turnbull, Haynes, Bigirimana, Stevenson, G Thomas (Jones 81), Lameiras, Reid, Beavon (Tudgay 90). **Subs not used:** Charles-Cook, Gadzhev, Folivi, Harries. **Scorers:** Bigirimana (11), G Thomas (55). **Booked:** Bigirimana. **Manager:** Mark Robins

Oxford United (4-4-2): Eastwood, Edwards, Nelson, Dunkley, Johnson, Hall, Lundstram (capt), Ledson (Sercombe 57), Rothwell (Ruffels 90), Maguire, Hemmings. **Subs not used:** Stevens, Ribeiro, Skarz, Long, Carroll. **Scorer:** Sercombe (76). **Booked:** Dunkley, Sercombe. **Manager:** Michael Appleton

Referee: C Sarginson (Staffs). **Half-time:** 1-0.

BUILDBASE FA TROPHY

FIRST ROUND: Alfreton 1 North Ferriby 0; Altrincham 1 Macclesfield 1; Boreham Wood 0 Maidstone 0; Braintree 2 Torquay 0; Bromley 1 Leiston 1; Chelmsford 1 Hitchin 0; Chorley 0 Guiseley 1; Dagenham 1 Worthing 2; Dartford 1 Dover 1; Dulwich Hamlet 2 Royston 2; East Thurrock 1 Aldershot 1; Ebbsfleet 1 Woking 1; Farsley 0 Southport 4; Forest Green 1 Truro 1; Fylde 1 Brackley 1; Gateshead 2 King's Lynn 0; Harlow 2 Eastleigh 0; Harrogate 3 Barrow 3; Kidderminster 4 Telford 0; Nantwich 1 Lincoln 2; Nuneaton 3 Stocksbridge 1; Solihull 1 Matlock 2; South Park 1 North Leigh 1; Stockport 3 Marine 2; Sudbury 2 Gosport 1; Sutton 1 Bath 0; Wealdstone 2 Wingate 2; Welling 8 Hythe 1; Whitehawk 3 Weymouth 2; Witton 1 Chester 1; Wrexham 0 Tranmere 1; York 3 Worcester 1. **Replays:** Aldershot 3 East Thurrock 4 (aet); Barrow 4 Harrogate 2 (aet); Brackley 4 Fylde 0; Chester 2 Witton 1; Dover 1 Dartford 2; Leiston 3 Bromley 5; Macclesfield 2 Altrincham 1; Maidstone 2 Boreham Wood 3; North Leigh 1 South Park 3; Royston 0 Dulwich Hamlet 1; Truro 0 Forest Green 1 (aet); Weymouth 1 Whitehawk 2; Wingate 1 Wealdstone 2 (aet); Woking 0 Ebbsfleet 1

SECOND ROUND: Barrow 3 Matlock 2; Boreham Wood 2 Alfreton 1; Bromley 1 Welling 2; Chester 0 Forest Green 3; Dartford 0 Chelmsford 1; East Thurrock 2 Braintree 5; Gateshead 1

Lincoln 3; Harlow 1 York 2; Kidderminster 3 Ebbsfleet 0; Nuneaton 6 Guiseley 1; Southport 1 Wealdstone 2; Stockport 1 Brackley 1; Sudbury 1 Macclesfield 3; Tranmere 4 South Park 1; Whitehawk 1 Dulwich Hamlet 4; Worthing 2 Sutton 2. **Replays:** Brackley 2 Stockport 0; Sutton 3 Worthing 2 (aet)

THIRD ROUND: Barrow 1 Kidderminster 0; Braintree 0 Dulwich Hamlet 0; Macclesfield 1 Forest Green 0; Nuneaton 0 York 3; Sutton 0 Boreham Wood 0; Tranmere 1 Chelmsford 1; Wealdstone 1 Brackley 4; Welling 1 Lincoln 3. **Replays:** Boreham Wood 5 Sutton 0; Dulwich Hamlet 5 Braintree 2

FOURTH ROUND: Boreham Wood 0 Lincoln 2; Dulwich Hamlet 2 Macclesfield 2; Tranmere 5 Barrow 1; York 1 Brackley 0. **Replay:** Macclesfield 2 Dulwich Hamlet 0

SEMI-FINALS: First leg: Macclesfield 1 Tranmere 1; York 2 Lincoln 1. **Second leg:** Lincoln 1 York 1 (York won 3-2 on agg). Tranmere 0 Macclesfield 1 (Macclesfield won 2-1 on agg)

FINAL

MACCLESFIELD TOWN 2 YORK CITY 3
Wembley (38,224); Sunday, May 21 2017

Macclesfield Town (4-4-2): Flinders, Halls (capt), Fitzpatrick, Byrne (McCombe 68), Pilkington, Browne, Holroyd, James, Norburn (Dudley 85), Hancox (Summerfield 87), Whitaker. **Subs not used:** Ross, Whitehead. **Scorers:** Browne (13), Norburn (45). **Manager:** John Askey.
York City (4-4-2): Letheren, Heslop (capt), Morgan-Smith, Klukowski (Moke 46), Hall (Connolly 69), Oliver, Parkin, Newton, Holmes (Rooney 75), Parslow, Bencherif. **Subs not used:** Simpson, Fenwick. **Scorers:** Parkin (8), Oliver (22), Connolly (86). **Manager:** Gary Mills
Referee: P Tierney (Lancs). **Half-time:** 2-2

WELSH CUP FINAL

Bala 2 (Evans 77, Smith 85) **New Saints** 1 (Draper 65) – Bangor University Stadium. Att: 1,110

FA VASE FINAL

Cleethorpes 0 South Shields 4 (Finnigan 42 pen, Morse 80, Foley 87, 89) – Wembley. Att: 38,224 (combined with FA Trophy Final)

WOMEN'S FA CUP FINAL

Birmingham 1 (Wellings 73) Manchester City 4 (Bronze 18, Christiansen 25, Lloyd 32, Scott 80) Wembley. Att: 35,271

FA SUNDAY CUP FINAL

Hardwick Social (Stockton) 1 (Coleman 23) New Salamis (London) 1 (MacKenzie 67 pen), aet, Hardwick Social won 3-1 on pens, Bramall Lane, Sheffield

FINALS – RESULTS

Associated Members' Cup
1984   (Hull) Bournemouth 2 Hull 1

Freight Rover Trophy – Wembley
1985   Wigan 3 Brentford 1
1986   Bristol City 3 Bolton 0
1987   Mansfield 1 Bristol City 1
         (aet; Mansfield won 5-4 on pens)

Sherpa Van Trophy – Wembley
1988   Wolves 2 Burnley 0
1989   Bolton 4 Torquay 1

Leyland Daf Cup – Wembley
1990   Tranmere 2 Bristol Rov 1

Autoglass Trophy – Wembley
1991   Birmingham 3 Tranmere 2
1992   Stoke 1 Stockport 0
1993   Port Vale 2 Stockport 1
1994   Huddersfield 1 Swansea 1
         (aet; Swansea won 3-1 on pens)

Auto Windscreens Shield – Wembley
1995   Birmingham 1 Carlisle 0
         (Birmingham won in sudden-death
         overtime)
1996   Rotherham 2 Shrewsbury 1
1997   Carlisle 0 Colchester 0
         (aet; Carlisle won 4-3 on pens)
1998   Grimsby 2 Bournemouth 1

(Grimsby won with golden goal in extra-time)

1999	Wigan 1 Millwall 0
2000	Stoke 2 Bristol City 1

LDV Vans Trophy – Millennium Stadium

2001	Port Vale 2 Brentford 1
2002	Blackpool 4 Cambridge Utd 1
2003	Bristol City 2 Carlisle 0
2004	Blackpool 2 Southend 0
2005	Wrexham 2 Southend 0

Football League Trophy – Millennium Stadium

2006	Swansea 2 Carlisle 1

Johnstone's Paint Trophy – Wembley

2007	Doncaster 3 Bristol Rov 2 (aet) (Millennium Stadium)
2008	MK Dons 2 Grimsby 0
2009	Luton 3 Scunthorpe 2 (aet)
2010	Southampton 4 Carlisle 1
2011	Carlisle 1 Brentford 0
2012	Chesterfield 2 Swindon 0
2013	Crewe 2 Southend 0
2014	Peterborough 3 Chesterfield 1
2015	Bristol City 2 Walsall 0
2016	Barnsley 3 Oxford 2

Checkatrade Trophy – Wembley

2017	Coventry 2 Oxford 1

FINALS – AT WEMBLEY

Full Members' Cup (Discontinued after 1992)

1985–86	Chelsea 5 Man City 4
1986–87	Blackburn 1 Charlton 0

Simod Cup

1987–88	Reading 4 Luton 1
1988–89	Nottm Forest 4 Everton 3

Zenith Data Systems Cup

1989–90	Chelsea 1 Middlesbrough 0
1990–91	Crystal Palace 4 Everton 1
1991–92	Nottm Forest 3 Southampton 2

Anglo-Italian Cup (Discontinued after 1996)
* Home club)

1970	*Napoli 0 Swindon 3
1971	*Bologna 1 Blackpool 2 (aet)
1972	*AS Roma 3 Blackpool 1
1973	*Fiorentina 1 Newcastle 2
1993	Derby 1 Cremonese 3 (at Wembley)
1994	Notts Co 0 Brescia 1 (at Wembley)
1995	Ascoli 1 Notts Co 2 (at Wembley)
1996	Port Vale 2 Genoa 5 (at Wembley)

FA Vase

At Wembley (until 2000 and from 2007)

1975	Hoddesdon 2 Epsom & Ewell 1
1976	Billericay 1 Stamford 0*
1977	Billericay 2 Sheffield 1 (replay Nottingham after a 1-1 at Wembley)
1978	Blue Star 2 Barton Rov 1
1979	Billericay 4 Almondsbury Greenway 1
1980	Stamford 2 Guisborough Town 0
1981	Whickham 3 Willenhall 2*
1982	Forest Green 3 Rainworth MF Welfare 0
1983	VS Rugby 1 Halesowen 0
1984	Stansted 3 Stamford 2
1985	Halesowen 3 Fleetwood 1
1986	Halesowen 3 Southall 0
1987	St Helens 3 Warrington 2
1988	Colne Dynamoes 1 Emley 0*
1989	Tamworth 3 Sudbury 0 (replay Peterborough after a 1-1 at Wembley)
1990	Yeading 1 Bridlington 0 (replay Leeds after 0-0 at Wembley)
1991	Guiseley 3 Gresley Rov 1 (replay Bramall Lane Sheffield after a 4-4 at Wembley)
1992	Wimborne 5 Guiseley 3
1993	Bridlington 1 Tiverton 0
1994	Diss 2 Taunton 1*
1995	Arlesey 2 Oxford City 1
1996	Brigg Town 3 Clitheroe 0
1997	Whitby Town 3 North Ferriby 0
1998	Tiverton 1 Tow Law 0
1999	Tiverton 1 Bedlington 0
2000	Deal 1 Chippenham 0
2001	Taunton 2 Berkhamsted 1 (Villa Park)
2002	Whitley Bay 1 Tiptree 0* (Villa Park)
2003	Brigg 2 AFC Sudbury 1 (Upton Park)
2004	Winchester 2 AFC Sudbury 0 (St Andrews)
2005	Didcot 3 AFC Sudbury 2 (White Hart Lane)
2006	Nantwich 3 Hillingdon 1 (St Andrews)
2007	Truro 3 AFC Totton 1
2008	Kirkham & Wesham (Fylde) 2 Lowestoft 1
2009	Whitley Bay 2 Glossop 0
2010	Whitley Bay 6 Wroxham 1
2011	Whitley Bay 3 Coalville 2
2012	Dunston 2 West Auckland 0
2013	Spennymoor 2 Tunbridge Wells 1
2014	Sholing 1 West Auckland 0
2015	North Shields 2 Glossop North End 1*
2016	Morpeth 4 Hereford 1
2017	South Shields 4 Cleethorpes 0

* After extra-time

FA Trophy Finals

1970	Macclesfield 2 Telford 0
1971	Telford 3 Hillingdon 2
1972	Stafford 3 Barnet 0
1973	Scarborough 2 Wigan 1*
1974	Morecambe 2 Dartford 1
1975	Matlock 4 Scarborough 0
1976	Scarborough 3 Stafford 2*
1977	Scarborough 2 Dag & Red 1
1978	Altrincham 3 Leatherhead 1
1979	Stafford 2 Kettering 0
1980	Dag & Red 2 Mossley 1
1981	Bishop's Stortford 1 Sutton 0
1982	Enfield 1 Altrincham 0*
1983	Telford 2 Northwich 1
1984	Northwich 2 Bangor 1 (replay Stoke after a 1-1 at Wembley)
1985	Wealdstone 2 Boston 1
1986	Altrincham 1 Runcorn 0
1987	Kidderminster 2 Burton 1 (replay WBA after a 0-0 at Wembley)
1988	Enfield 3 Telford 2 (replay WBA after a 0-0 at Wembley)
1989	Telford 1 Macclesfield 0*
1990	Barrow 3 Leek 0
1991	Wycombe 2 Kidderminster 1
1992	Colchester 3 Witton 1
1993	Wycombe 4 Runcorn 1
1994	Woking 2 Runcorn 1
1995	Woking 2 Kidderminster 1
1996	Macclesfield 3 Northwich 1
1997	Woking 1 Dag & Red & Redbridge 0*
1998	Cheltenham 1 Southport 0
1999	Kingstonian 1 Forest Green 0
2000	Kingstonian 3 Kettering 2

2001	Canvey 1 Forest Green 0
2002	Yeovil 2 Stevenage 0
2003	Burscough 2 Tamworth 1
2004	Hednesford 3 Canvey 2
2005	Grays 1 Hucknall 1* (Grays won 6-5 on pens)

2006	Grays 2 Woking 0

2007	Stevenage 3 Kidderminster 2
2008	Ebbsfleet 1 Torquay 0
2009	Stevenage 2 York 0
2010	Barrow 2 Stevenage 1*
2011	Darlington 1 Mansfield 0 *
2012	York 2 Newport 0
2013	Wrexham 1 Grimsby 1 * Wrexham won 4-1 on pens)
2014	Cambridge Utd 4 Gosport 0
2015	North Ferriby 3 Wrexham 3* (North Ferriby won 5-4 on pens)
2016	Halifax 1 Grimsby 0
2017	York 3 Macclesfield 2

(*After extra-time)

FA Youth Cup Winners

Year	Winners	Runners-up	Agg
1953	Man Utd	Wolves	9-3
1954	Man Utd	Wolves	5-4
1955	Man Utd	WBA	7-1
1956	Man Utd	Chesterfield	4-3
1957	Man Utd	West Ham	8-2
1958	Wolves	Chelsea	7-6
1959	Blackburn	West Ham	2-1
1960	Chelsea	Preston	5-2
1961	Chelsea	Everton	5-3
1962	Newcastle	Wolves	2-1
1963	West Ham	Liverpool	6-5
1964	Man Utd	Swindon	5-2
1965	Everton	Arsenal	3-2
1966	Arsenal	Sunderland	5-3
1967	Sunderland	Birmingham	2-0
1968	Burnley	Coventry	3-2
1969	Sunderland	WBA	6-3
1970	Tottenham	Coventry	4-3
1971	Arsenal	Cardiff	2-0
1972	Aston Villa	Liverpool	5-2
1973	Ipswich	Bristol City	4-1
1974	Tottenham	Huddersfield	2-1
1975	Ipswich	West Ham	5-1
1976	WBA	Wolves	5-0
1977	Crystal Palace	Everton	1-0
1978	Crystal Palace	Aston Villa	*1-0
1979	Millwall	Man City	2-0
1980	Aston Villa	Man City	3-2
1981	West Ham	Tottenham	2-1
1982	Watford	Man Utd	7-6
1983	Norwich	Everton	6-5
1984	Everton	Stoke	4-2
1985	Newcastle	Watford	4-1
1986	Man City	Man Utd	3-1
1987	Coventry	Charlton	2-1
1988	Arsenal	Doncaster	6-1
1989	Watford	Man City	2-1
1990	Tottenham	Middlesbrough	3-2
1991	Millwall	Sheffield Wed	3-0
1992	Man Utd	Crystal Palace	6-3
1993	Leeds	Man Utd	4-1
1994	Arsenal	Millwall	5-3
1995	Man Utd	Tottenham	†2-2
1996	Liverpool	West Ham	4-1
1997	Leeds	Crystal Palace	3-1

1998	Everton	Blackburn	5-3
1999	West Ham	Coventry	9-0
2000	Arsenal	Coventry	5-1
2001	Arsenal	Blackburn	6-3
2002	Aston Villa	Everton	4-2
2003	Man Utd	Middlesbrough	3-1
2004	Middlesbrough	Aston Villa	4-0
2005	Ipswich	Southampton	3-2
2006	Liverpool	Man City	3-2
2007	Liverpool	Man Utd	††2-2
2008	Man City	Chelsea	4-2
2009	Arsenal	Liverpool	6-2
2010	Chelsea	Aston Villa	3-2
2011	Man Utd	Sheffield Utd	6-3
2012	Chelsea	Blackburn	4-1
2013	Norwich	Chelsea	4-2
2014	Chelsea	Fulham	7-6
2015	Chelsea	Man City	5-2
2016	Chelsea	Man City	4-2
2017	Chelsea	Man City	6-2

(*One match only; †Manchester Utd won 4-3 on pens, ††Liverpool won 4-3 on pens)

CHARITY/COMMUNITY SHIELD RESULTS (POST WAR)
[CHARITY SHIELD]

Year	Winners	Runners-up	Score
1948	Arsenal	Manchester Utd	4-3
1949	Portsmouth	Wolves	*1-1
1950	England World Cup XI	FA Canadian Tour Team	4-2
1951	Tottenham	Newcastle	2-1
1952	Manchester Utd	Newcastle	4-2
1953	Arsenal	Blackpool	3-1
1954	Wolves	WBA	*4-4
1955	Chelsea	Newcastle	3-0
1956	Manchester Utd	Manchester City	1-0
1957	Manchester Utd	Aston Villa	4-0
1958	Bolton	Wolves	4-1
1959	Wolves	Nottm Forest	3-1
1960	Burnley	Wolves	*2-2
1961	Tottenham	FA XI	3-2
1962	Tottenham	Ipswich Town	5-1
1963	Everton	Manchester Utd	4-0
1964	Liverpool	West Ham	*2-2
1965	Manchester Utd	Liverpool	*2-2
1966	Liverpool	Everton	1-0
1967	Manchester Utd	Tottenham	*3-3
1968	Manchester City	WBA	6-1
1969	Leeds	Manchester City	2-1
1970	Everton	Chelsea	2-1
1971	Leicester	Liverpool	1-0
1972	Manchester City	Aston Villa	1-0
1973	Burnley	Manchester City	1-0
1974	Liverpool	Leeds	1-1
	(Liverpool won 6-5 on penalties)		
1975	Derby Co	West Ham	2-0
1976	Liverpool	Southampton	1-0
1977	Liverpool	Manchester Utd	*0-0
1978	Nottm Forest	Ipswich	5-0
1979	Liverpool	Arsenal	3-1
1980	Liverpool	West Ham	1-0
1981	Aston Villa	Tottenham	*2-2
1982	Liverpool	Tottenham	1-0
1983	Manchester Utd	Liverpool	2-0

1984	Everton	Liverpool	1-0
1985	Everton	Manchester Utd	2-0
1986	Everton	Liverpool	*1-1
1987	Everton	Coventry	1-0
1988	Liverpool	Wimbledon	2-1
1989	Liverpool	Arsenal	1-0
1990	Liverpool	Manchester Utd	*1-1
1991	Arsenal	Tottenham	*0-0
1992	Leeds	Liverpool	4-3
1993	Manchester Utd	Arsenal	1-1
	(Manchester Utd won 5-4 on penalties)		
1994	Manchester Utd	Blackburn	2-0
1995	Everton	Blackburn	1-0
1996	Manchester Utd	Newcastle	4-0
1997	Manchester Utd	Chelsea	1-1
	(Manchester Utd won 4-2 on penalties)		
1998	Arsenal	Manchester Utd	3-0
1999	Arsenal	Manchester Utd	2-1
2000	Chelsea	Manchester Utd	2-0
2001	Liverpool	Manchester Utd	2-1

COMMUNITY SHIELD

Year	Winners	Runners-up	Score
2002	Arsenal	Liverpool	1-0
2003	Manchester Utd	Arsenal	1-1
	(Manchester Utd won 4-3 on penalties)		
2004	Arsenal	Manchester Utd	3-1
2005	Chelsea	Arsenal	2-1
2006	Liverpool	Chelsea	2-1
2007	Manchester Utd	Chelsea	1-1
	(Manchester Utd won 3-0 on penalties)		
2008	Manchester Utd	Portsmouth	0-0
	(Manchester Utd won 3-1 on pens)		
2009	Chelsea	Manchester Utd	2-2
	(Chelsea won 4-1 on pens)		
2010	Manchester Utd	Chelsea	3-1
2011	Manchester Utd	Manchester City	3-2
2012	Manchester City	Chelsea	3-2
2013	Manchester Utd	Wigan	2-0
2014	Arsenal	Manchester City	3-0
2015	Arsenal	Chelsea	1-0
2016	Manchester Utd	Leicester	2-1

(Fixture played at Wembley 1974–2000 and from 2007); Millennium Stadium 2001–06; Villa Park 2012) * Trophy shared

FOOTBALL'S CHANGING HOMES

Everton are planning to move from Goodison Park, their home since 1892, to a new 50,000-seater riverside stadium. The club agreed a deal with owners of the Bramley Moore Dock site on the banks of the Mersey and will seeking planning permission for the £300m project, which is expected to be the catalyst for regenerating the area. An initial target for completion is the 2020-21 season. Liverpool City Council will act as guarantor for Everton to pay for the stadium with a 40-year lease, at the end of which the club assumes sole ownership. It will mean a 10,000 increase in capacity and the opportunity to keep pace with some of the leading Premier League teams. Neighbours **Liverpool** have honoured the 96 victims of the Hillsborough disaster and their most successful manager Bob Paisley at Anfied's new main stand. Two public areas around the development are called 96 Avenue and Paisley Square.

Tottenham legends, past and present, saw the end of an era accompany a 2-1 victory over Manchester United – the final match at the old White Hart Lane ground after 118 years of football there. The club play home matches in the new season at Wembley in readiness for a new £800m stadium – the most expensive in the country – which is earmarked for completion in time for the 2018-19 campaign. Spurs will then have a 61,500 capacity, the biggest in London.

Chelsea received council planning permission for the £500m redevelopment of Stamford Bridge, followed by final approval from the Mayor of London, Sadiq Khan. Work on the 60,000-seater arena is expected to take three years, during which Chelsea are likely to take over Wembley when Tottenham move out. **Bournemouth**, who have made a major impact on the Premier League, announced their intention to leave Dean Court and build a new stadium with a much bigger capacity than the present 11,500. For long-term growth and security, the club want a ground they own and are looking for a suitable site. Initial target date for moving is the 2020-21 season. **Swansea** also aim to increase capacity – at 21,000 the second lowest in the top division – and want the local council to relinquish ownership of the Liberty Stadium.

Queens Park Rangers are considering new sites after giving up on plans for a 40,000-seater stadium at Old Oak. They have held talks with Hammersmith and Fulham Council about the possibility of developing a 30,000-capacity community arena at the Linford Christie Stadium, home of Thames Valley Harriers athletics club. Rangers' capacity at Loftus Road, a mile away, is just over 18,000. **AFC Wimbledon** are on course for return to their roots in Plough Lane at the redeveloped greyhound stadium after a decision not to protect the stadium with listed-building status. It meant the club can go ahead with a new 11,000-capacity ground, with provision for an increase to 20,000, planned for 2019. **Coventry** chairman Tim Fisher said the club must leave the Ricoh Arena in order to survive. He has been unable to close a deal on several sites for a new ground and told a supporters' meeting of the possibility of sharing with Coventry rugby's Butts Park Arena. **Gillingham** unveiled plans to secure their future by moving to a new stadium at Mill Hill in Medway, opposite their training ground. The club have asked for backing from supporters, residents and local businesses. Promoted **Plymouth** are to redevelop the Grandstand side of Home Park with a new 5,000-seater stand at a cost of £5m. There are also plans to fill in the corners at the ground, taking capacity to more than 20,000.

Lincoln, another club on the way up, have announced preliminary plans to move. A new stadium would have an initial capacity of 12,000 – 2,000 more than Sincil Bank. It would be part of a long-term City Council development including more than 3,000 new homes, leisure centre and hotel. The club won promotion back to the Football League and reached the last eight of the FA Cup last season.

Aberdeen have faced opposition from some local councillors and residents over plans for a new £50m, 20,000-capacity stadium and training facilities at Kingsford, close to the city bypass. A new £12m main stand at Tynecastle Stadium will take **Hearts'** capacity to more than 20,000. Completion is scheduled for early in the new season.

SCOTTISH TABLES 2016–2017

LADBROKES PREMIERSHIP

				Home				Away					
		P	W	D	L	F	A	W	D	L	F	A	Gd	Pts
1	Celtic	38	17	2	0	47	8	17	2	0	59	17	81	106
2	Aberdeen	38	12	3	4	34	16	12	1	6	40	19	39	76
3	Rangers	38	11	5	3	31	18	8	5	6	25	26	12	67
4	St Johnstone	38	8	3	8	25	25	9	4	6	25	21	4	58
5	Hearts	38	9	5	5	36	20	3	5	11	19	32	3	46
6	Partick	38	6	5	9	21	32	4	7	17	22	-16	42
7	Ross Co	38	6	5	7	28	31	5	8	7	20	27	-10	46
8	Kilmarnock	38	4	7	8	18	23	5	7	7	18	33	20	41
9	Motherwell	38	5	3	11	27	37	5	5	9	19	32	-23	38
10	Dundee	38	5	5	9	18	30	5	2	12	19	32	-24	37
11	Hamilton	38	6	7	6	22	20	1	7	11	15	36	-19	35
12	Inverness	38	5	8	6	27	33	2	5	12	17	38	-27	34

League split after 33 games, with teams staying in top six and bottom six regardless of points
Celtic into Champions League second qualifying round; Rangers, St Johnstone into Europa League first qualifying round; Aberdeen into second qualifying round

Play-offs (on agg): Quarter-final: Dundee Utd 5 Morton 1. **Semi-final:** Dundee Utd 4 Falkirk 3.
Final: Hamilton 1 Dundee Utd 0
Player of Year: Scott Brown (Celtic). **Manager of Year:** Brendan Rodgers (Celtic)
PFA Team of Year: Lewis (Aberdeen), Logan (Aberdeen), Lustig (Celtic), Lindsay (Partick),
Tierney (Celtic), Armstrong (Celtic), Brown (Celtic), McLean (Aberdeen), Hayes (Aberdeen),
Dembele (Celtic), Sinclair (Celtic)
Leading league scorers: 23 Boyce (Ross Co); 21 Sinclair (Celtic); 17 Dembele (Celtic); 15
Armstrong (Celtic), Moult (Motherwell); 14 Doolan (Partick); 12 Griffiths (Celtic), Rooney
(Aberdeen), Walker (Hearts); 11 Miller (Rangers); 10 McGinn (Aberdeen), Swanson (St
Johnstone)

LADBROKES CHAMPIONSHIP

				Home				Away					
		P	W	D	L	F	A	W	D	L	F	A	Gd	Pts
1	Hibernian	36	9	8	1	36	16	10	6	2	24	10	34	71
2	Falkirk	36	8	6	4	31	22	8	6	4	27	18	18	60
3	Dundee Utd	36	11	6	1	31	17	4	6	8	19	25	8	57
4	Morton	36	8	8	2	23	17	5	5	8	21	24	3	52
5	Dunfermline	36	6	7	5	28	25	6	5	7	18	18	3	48
6	Queen of South	36	6	3	9	25	29	5	7	6	21	23	-6	43
7	St Mirren	36	5	6	7	24	23	4	6	8	28	33	-4	39
8	Dumbarton	36	5	6	7	17	20	4	6	8	29	36	-10	39
9	Raith	36	8	5	5	22	20	2	4	12	13	32	-17	39
10	Ayr	36	4	4	10	13	32	3	8	7	20	30	-29	33

Play-offs (on agg) – Semi-finals: Alloa 1 Airdrieonians 1 (aet, Alloa won 4-3 on pens); Brechin
4 Raith 4 (aet, Brechin won 4-3 on pens). **Final:** Brechin 4 Alloa 4 (aet, Brechin won 5-4 on pens)
Player of Year: John McGinn (Hibernian). **Manager of Year:** Jim Duffy (Morton)
PFA Team of Year: Bell (Dundee Utd), Devlin (Ayr), McGregor (Hibernian), O'Ware (Morton),
Stevenson (Hibernian), Mallan (St Mirren), McGinn (Hibernian), Forbes (Morton), Andreu
(Dundee Utd), Dobbie (Queen of South), Cummings (Hibernian)
Leading league scorers: 19 Cummings (Hibernian), Dobbie (Queen of South); 15 Clark
(Dunfermline); 13 Andreu (Dundee Utd); 11 Thomson (Dumbarton); 10 Lyle (Queen of
South), Murray (Dundee Utd), Sibbald (Falkirk)

LADBROKES LEAGUE ONE

			Home				Away						
		P	W	D	L	F	A	W	D	L	F	A	Gd	Pts
1	Livingston	36	13	1	4	43	16	13	2	3	37	16	48	81
2	Alloa	36	8	6	4	35	21	9	5	4	34	23	25	62
3	Airdrieonians	36	8	2	8	27	32	8	2	8	34	34	-5	52
4	Brechin	36	8	3	7	22	20	7	2	9	21	29	-6	50
5	East Fife	36	7	5	6	22	20	5	5	8	19	24	-3	46
6	Queen's Park	36	7	4	7	18	21	5	6	7	19	30	-14	46
7	Stranraer	36	8	3	7	29	25	4	5	9	17	25	-4	44
8	Albion	36	6	4	8	21	22	5	5	8	20	26	-7	42
9	Peterhead	36	4	6	8	25	29	6	4	8	19	30	-15	40
10	Stenhousemuir	36	5	4	9	23	36	6	2	10	22	28	-19	39

Play-offs (on agg): **Semi-finals:** Forfar 6 Annan 4; Peterhead 4 Montrose 1. **Final:** Forfar 7 Peterhead 2
Player of Year: Liam Buchanan (Livingston). **Manager of Year:** David Hopkin (Livingston)
PFA Team of Year: Parry (Alloa), McGeever (Queen's Park), Graham (Alloa), Page (East Fife), Waters (Alloa), Pittman (Livingston), Byrne (Livingston), Kirkpatrick (Alloa), Ryan (Airdrieonians), Buchanan (Livingston), Mullen (Livingston)
Leading league scorers: 23 Ryan (Airdrieonians); 22 Buchanan (Livingston); 18 Russell (Airdrieonians); 16 McAllister (Peterhead), Spence (Alloa); 14 Kirkpatrick (Alloa), Mullen (Livingston)

LADBROKES LEAGUE TWO

			Home				Away						
		P	W	D	L	F	A	W	D	L	F	A	Gd	Pts
1	Arbroath	36	8	5	5	30	18	10	7	1	33	18	27	66
2	Forfar	36	8	5	5	38	28	10	5	3	31	21	20	64
3	Annan	36	12	1	5	35	23	6	3	9	26	35	3	58
4	Montrose	36	5	6	7	22	30	9	4	5	22	23	-9	52
5	Elgin	36	7	7	4	36	22	7	2	9	31	25	20	51
6	Stirling	36	6	6	6	20	25	6	5	7	30	34	-9	47
7	Edinburgh City	36	5	6	7	21	20	6	4	8	17	25	-7	43
8	Berwick	36	6	3	9	28	32	4	7	7	22	33	-15	40
9	Clyde	36	8	4	6	33	30	2	4	12	16	34	-15	38
10	Cowdenbeath	36	4	3	11	15	25	5	5	8	25	30	-15	35

Play-off Final (on agg): Cowdenbeath 1 East Kilbride 1 (aet, Cowdenbeath won 5-3 on pens)
Player of Year: Shane Sutherland (Elgin). **Manager of Year:** Dick Campbell (Arbroath)
PFA Team of Year: Smith (Stirling), Little (Arbroath), O'Brien (Forfar), Hamilton (Arbroath), MacPhee (Elgin), Cameron (Elgin), Reilly (Elgin), Linn (Arbroath), Doris (Arbroath), Sutherland (Elgin), MacDonald (Clyde)
Leading league scorers: 18 Sutherland (Elgin); 17 MacDonald (Clyde); 13 Cameron (Elgin), McCord (Arbroath), Thomson (Berwick); 12 Denholm (Forfar), Doris (Arbroath)

LADBROKES SCOTTISH LEAGUE RESULTS 2016–2017

PREMIERSHIP

	Aberdeen	Celtic	Dundee	Hamilton	Hearts	Inverness	Kilmarnock	Motherwell	Partick	Rangers	Ross Co	St Johnstone
Aberdeen	–	0-1	3-0	2-1	0-0	1 1	5 1	7-2	2-1	2-1	4-0	0-0
	–	1-3			2-0	1-0		1-0	2-0	0-3	1-0	2-2
Celtic	4-1	–	2-1	1-0	4-0	3-0	6-1	2-0	1-0	5-1	2-0	1-0
	1-0	–	2-0	2-0			3-1	2-0	1-1	1-1		4-1
Dundee	1-3	0-1	–	1 1	3-2	2-1	1-1	2-0	0-2	1-2	0-0	3-0
	0-7	1-2	–		0-2	0-2	1-1		0-1	2-1	1-1	
Hamilton	1-0	0-3	0-1	–	3-3	1-1	1-2	1-1	1-1	1-2	1-0	1-1
	1-0		4-0	–	3-0	1-1	0-1	0-1			1-1	1-0
							0-2					
Hearts	0-1	1-2	2-0	3-1	–	5-1	4-0	3-0	1-1	2-0	0-0	2-2
	1-2	0-5	1-0	4-0	–	1-1			2-2	4-1	0-1	
Inverness	1-3	2-2	3-1	1-1	3-3	–	1-1	1-2	0-0	0-1	2-3	2-1
	0-4	2-2	2-1			–	1-1	3-2		2-1	1-1	0-3
Kilmarnock	0-4	0-1	2-0	0-0	2-0	1-1	–	1-2	2-2	1-1	3-2	0-1
	1-2		0-1	0 0	2 1		–	1-2	1-1	0-0	1-2	
Motherwell	1-3	3-4	0-0	4-2	1-3	0-3	0-0	–	2-0	0-2	4-1	1-2
			1-5	0-0	0-3	4-2	3-1	–			0-1	1-2
			2 3									
Partick	1-2	1-4	2-0	2-2	1-2	2-0	0-0	1-1	–	1-2	1-1	0-2
	0-6	0-5		2-0	2-0	1-1		1-0	–	1-2	2-1	0-1
Rangers	2 1	1 2	1-0	1-1	2-0	1-0	3-0	2-1	2-0	–	0-0	1-1
	1-2	1-5		4-0	2-1			1-1	2-0	–	1-1	3-2
Ross Co	2-1	0-4	1-3	1-1	3-2	2-0	1-1	1-3	1-1	1-1	–	0-2
		2-2	2-1	3-2		4-0	1-2	1-2			–	1-2
St Johnstone	0-0	2-4	2-1	3-0	1-0	3-0	0-1	1-1	1-2	1-1	2-4	–
	1-2	2-5	2-0		1-0		0-2		1-0	1-2		–
					1-0							

173

CHAMPIONSHIP

	Ayr	Dumbarton	Dundee Utd	Dunfermline	Falkirk	Hibernian	Morton	Queen of South	Raith	St Mirren
Ayr	–	4-4	0-1	0-0	0-1	0-3	2-1	1-0	0-2	1-1
		2-1	0-0	0-2	1-4	0-4	1-4	0-2	1-0	0-2
Dumbarton	0-3	–	1-0	2-2	2-1	0-1	0-2	0-0	0-0	1-1
	2-2	–	1-0	0-2	0-1	0-1	1-0	1-2	4-0	2-2
Dundee Utd	3-0	2-1	–	1-0	1-0	1-0	2-1	1-1	2-2	2-1
	2-1	2-2	–	1-0	1-1	0-1	1-1	3-3	3-0	3-2
Dunfermline	1-1	4-3	1-3	–	1-1	1-3	2-1	0-1	0-0	4-3
	0-1	5-1	1-1	–	1-2	1-1	3-1	1-1	1-0	1-1
Falkirk	2-0	1-0	3-1	2-1	–	1-2	1-1	2-2	2-4	3-1
	1-1	2-2	3-0	2-0	–	1-2	0-1	2-2	1-0	2-2
Hibernian	1-2	2-0	1-1	2-1	1-1	–	4-0	4-0	1-1	2-0
	1-1	2-2	3-0	2-2	2-1	–	0-0	3-0	3-2	1-1
Morton	2-1	1-1	0-0	2-1	1-1	1-1	–	1-0	1-0	3-1
	1-1	2-1	1-1	0-1	2-2	1-1	–	1-0	2-0	1-4
Queen of South	4-1	1-2	1-4	2-2	2-0	0-0	0-5	–	3-1	2-3
	0-0	1-2	4-2	0-1	0-2	0-1	3-0	–	2-1	0-2
Raith	1-1	3-2	0-0	2-0	0-2	0-0	0-1	1-0	–	3-1
	4-1	1-3	2-1	0-2	1-4	1-1	2-0	1-1	–	2-0
St Mirren	1-1	0-1	0-2	0-1	1-1	0-2	1-1	1-3	1-0	–
	6-2	1-1	3-2	0-0	1-2	2-0	1-1	0-3	5-0	–

	Airdrieonians	Albion	Alloa	Brechin	East Fife	Livingston	Peterhead	Queen's Park	Stenhousemuir	Stranraer
Airdrieonians	–	0-2	2-1	1-0	1-1	2-4	1-3	4 1	0-5	1-0
	–	1-2	0-1	3-1	2-2	0-4	4-1	3-2	1-0	1-2
Albion	1-2	–	0-4	0-2	1-0	0-1	0-1	2-0	4-0	3-2
	3-4	–	1-1	1-0	0-1	0-2	0-0	1 1	1-1	3-0
Alloa	1-2	0-0	–	1-2	2-1	1-3	4-0	1-1	4-1	2-2
	2-1	1-1	–	6-1	3-0	2-2	0-1	2-2	2-1	1-0
Brechin	3-2	1 2	0-1	–	0-1	0-3	2-1	0-0	2-1	2-0
	3-0	1-0	1-2	–	2-1	0-2	0-1	3-1	2-2	0-0
East Fife	0 1	2-2	2-2	1-2	–	3-1	2-0	1-2	0-1	2-0
	0-4	2-0	0-0	3-2	–	2-1	1-2	0-0	1-0	0-0
Livingston	2-0	1-2	3-1	2-1	3-1	–	1-2	1-2	4-1	5-1
	4-2	3-0	2-1	3-0	0-1	–	4 1	4-0	1-0	0-0
Peterhead	2 4	2-2	1-1	1-3	0-3	1-2	–	2 0	0-2	2-0
	1-1	1-1	3-2	0-1	1-1	2-3	–	4-0	0-1	2-2
Queen's Park	1-3	2-1	1-2	2-0	1 0	1-0	0-0	–	0-3	0-2
	2-1	2-0	0 2	1-1	2 2	1-1	2-0	–	0-2	0-1
Stenhousemuir	2-2	1-0	2-2	1-3	0-1	0-4	2-2	1-2	–	0-5
	4-2	0-3	2-4	1-1	3-1	0-1	3-1	0-2	–	1-0
Stranraer	1-2	3-2	2-5	0-1	1-1	1-2	1-0	0-2	3-1	–
	2-1	3-0	1-2	2-0	2-1	0-1	3-3	1-1	3-0	–

LEAGUE TWO

	Annan	Arbroath	Berwick	Clyde	Cowdenbeath	Edinburgh City	Elgin	Forfar	Montrose	Stirling
Annan	–	1-2	3-1	3-2	2-0	1-1	1-0	1-2	2-3	3-2
	–	2-5	2-1	1-0	1-0	1-0	1-0	1-2	5-1	4-1
Arbroath	1-1	–	1-1	4-0	0-0	0-1	3-2	2-0	0-0	5-3
	1-2	–	4-1	1-0	4-1	0-1	3-2	0-1	0-1	1-1
Berwick	2-0	1-1	–	1-1	1-1	1-3	2-4	1-2	1-2	3-2
	4-1	0-2	–	4-3	1-3	3-2	0-1	3-2	0-1	0-1
Clyde	2-3	3-2	3-2	–	5-3	0-0	2-1	0-1	2-1	1-1
	2-1	1-2	1-1	–	0-2	3-1	3-2	2-2	1-2	2-3
Cowdenbeath	2-2	0-2	0-2	1-0	–	2-0	0-1	3-4	2-0	0-2
	0-1	1-2	0-1	1-0	–	1-2	1-1	1-1	0-2	0-2
Edinburgh City	1-0	3-3	1-2	0-1	1-1	–	1-2	2-3	0-1	2-0
	2-0	0-2	2-2	0-0	1-1	–	3-0	0-1	1-1	1-0
Elgin	0-2	0-1	6-0	0-2	3-1	3-0	–	2-2	4-1	2-3
	3-2	0-0	2-2	4-1	0-0	3-1	–	1-1	1-1	2-2
Forfar	5-1	0-1	2-0	4-3	4-3	1-1	3-2	–	1-3	4-1
	2-4	1-1	2-3	3-0	3-1	1-2	1-1	–	0-0	1-1
Montrose	2-2	1-1	0-0	2-1	1-2	0-1	0-5	1-1	–	2-2
	2-3	1-3	2-1	1-1	2-1	3-0	0-3	1-0	–	1-3
Stirling	3-1	2-2	0-0	1-1	1-2	1-1	0-4	0-3	2-0	–
	1-0	1-1	2-2	3-0	0-3	1-0	1-0	0-3	1-2	–

CELTIC'S RECORD-BREAKING
SIXTH SUCCESSIVE TITLE

Even by their own high standards this was a special season for Celtic. A host of records accompanied their sixth successive title, achieved with 38 unbeaten matches, 34 of them victories and four draws. Not since Rangers in 1898-99 have Scottish champions remained undefeated – and that was when the campaign spanned just 18 games. Only Juventus in Italy's Serie A (2011–12), Arsenal in the Premier League (2003 04) and Barry Town in the League of Wales (1997–98) previously managed it over 38 matches in recent history. Celtic's Kolo Toure also played for Arsenal's 'invincible' team. Brendan Rodgers, in his first season as manager after replacing Ronny Deila in May 2016, said: 'It's a monumental achievement by the players – something for their children and grandchildren to be proud of. What makes it so special is that there are so many variables in football over 38 games. I'm not sure it will happen again in my lifetime.' His club also won the Scottish Cup and League Cup and the club swept the board for individual honours. Rodgers was named Manager of the Year, Scott Sinclair won the PFA and football writers' player awards, while Kieran Tierney was voted best young player for the second successive year.

RECORD FACTS AND FIGURES

● Celtic's 106 points bettered their own record of 103 under Martin O'Neill in season 2001–02

● It was a new European best – one point more than Barry Town in 1996-97

● A 2-0 victory over Hearts, secured with goals by Leigh Griffiths and Stuart Armstrong, in the final match left them 30 points clear of second-place Aberdeen, one more than the winning margin under Neil Lennon in 2013-14

● A total of 106 goals scored was one more than the club achieved under O'Neill in the 2003 04 season. They netted four or more on 14 occasions

● Celtic's 34 victories was one more than they delivered in 2001–02

HOW CELTIC WON THE TITLE
AUGUST 2016

7	Hearts 1 (Walker 36 pen) Celtic 2 (Forrest 8, Sinclair 81). Att: 16,777
20	St Johnstone 2 (Swanson 83 pen, MacLean 89) Celtic 4 (Griffiths 28, Sinclair 40, Forrest 44, Christie 90). Att: 6,823
27	Celtic 4 (Griffiths 13, Forrest 42, Sinclair 87 pen, Rogic 90) Aberdeen 1 (Rooney 32). Att: 57,758

SEPTEMBER 2016

10	Celtic 5 (Dembele 33, 42, 83, Sinclair 61, Armstrong 90) Rangers 1 (Garner 44). Att: 58,348
18	Inverness 2 (King 28, Fisher 89) Celtic 2 (Rogic 17, Sinclair 34). Att: 6,061
24	Celtic 6 (Dembele 35, 38, Forrest 52, Griffiths 66, Sinclair 72 pen, Rogic 85) Kilmarnock 1 (Coulibaly 32). Att: 53,532

OCTOBER 2016

1	Dundee 0 Celtic 1 (Brown 47). Att: 8,827
15	Celtic 2 (Sinclair 18, Dembele pen 87) Motherwell 0. Att: 54,159

| 26 | Ross Co 0 Celtic 4 (Roberts 3, Armstrong 83, Sinclair 90, Dembele 90). Att: 6,290 |
| 29 | Aberdeen 0 Celtic 1 (Rogic 23). Att: 17,105 |

NOVEMBER 2016

| 3 | Celtic 3 (Sinclair 48, Griffiths 63, Rogic 83) Inverness 0. Att: 54,152 |
| 18 | Kilmarnock 0 Celtic 1 (Armstrong 44). Att: 10,962 |

DECEMBER 2016

3	Motherwell 3 (Moult 3, 35, Ainsworth 71) Celtic 4 (McGregor 48, Roberts 70, Armstrong 72, Rogic 90). Att: 8,535
9	Partick 1 (Lindsay 61) Celtic 4 (Armstrong 39, 49, Griffiths 50, McGregor 82). Att: 7,609
13	Celtic 1 (Griffiths 36) Hamilton 0. Att: 55,076
17	Celtic 2 (Griffiths 45, Bitton 57) Dundee 1 (Haber 69). Att: 37,404
20	Celtic 1 (Sinclair 16) Partick 0. Att: 55,733
24	Hamilton 0 Celtic 3 (Griffiths 41, Armstrong 54, Dembele 84). Att: 5,003
28	Celtic 2 (Sviatchenko 38, Armstrong 45) Ross Co 0. Att: 55,355
31	Rangers 1 (Miller 12) Celtic 2 (Dembele 33, Sinclair 70). Att: 50,126

JANUARY 2017

| 25 | Celtic 1 (Boyata 72) St Johnstone 0. Att: 51,057 |
| 29 | Celtic 4 (McGregor 29, Sinclair 77, 90 pen, Roberts 80) Hearts 0. Att: 58,247 |

FEBRUARY 2017

1	Celtic 1 (Boyata 57) Aberdeen 0. Att: 53,958
5	St Johnstone 2 (Watson 31, Boyata 43 og) Celtic 5 (Henderson 6, Dembele 61 pen, 75, 85, Sinclair 81). Att: 6,548
18	Celtic 2 (Dembele 34 pen, Forrest 41) Motherwell 0. Att: 56,366
25	Celtic 2 (Dembele 45, 59 pen) Hamilton 0. Att: 54,685

MARCH 2017

1	Inverness 0 Celtic 4 (Sinclair 43, Dembele 45, 73, Armstrong 66). Att: 5,948
12	Celtic 1 (Armstrong 35) Rangers 1 (Hill 87). Att: 58,545
19	Dundee 1 (El Bakhtaoui 76) Celtic 2 (Simunovic 45, Armstrong 52). Att: 8,968

APRIL 2017

2	Hearts 0 Celtic 5 (Sinclair 24, 27, 84 pen, Armstrong 55, Roberts 61). Att 16,539 (Celtic sealed title)
5	Celtic 1 (Sinclair 50) Partick 1 (Azeez 64). Att: 54,047
8	Celtic 3 (Armstrong 23, Sinclair 71, Forrest 76) Kilmarnock 1 (Jones 65). Att: 57,679
16	Ross Co 2 (Gardyne 50, Boyce 90 pen) Celtic 2 (Tierney 34, Roberts 78). Att: 6,205
29	Rangers 1 (Miller 81) Celtic 5 (Sinclair 7 pen, Griffiths 18, McGregor 52, Boyata 66, Lustig 87)

MAY 2017

6	Celtic 4 (Roberts 47, 62, Boyata 52, McGregor 71) St Johnstone 1 (MacLean 49). Att: 52,796
12	Aberdeen 1 (Hayes 12) Celtic 3 (Boyata 3, Armstrong 8, Griffiths 11). Att: 16,015
18	Partick 0 Celtic 5 (Griffiths 18 pen, Rogic 26, Roberts 41, 84, McGregor 82). Att: 7,847
21	Celtic 2 (Griffiths 50 Armstrong 76) Hearts 0. Att: 58,967

SCOTTISH HONOURS LIST

PREMIER DIVISION

	First	Pts	Second	Pts	Third	Pts
1975–6	Rangers	54	Celtic	48	Hibernian	43
1976–7	Celtic	55	Rangers	46	Aberdeen	43
1977–8	Rangers	55	Aberdeen	53	Dundee Utd	40
1978–9	Celtic	48	Rangers	45	Dundee Utd	44
1979–80	Aberdeen	48	Celtic	47	St Mirren	42
1980–81	Celtic	56	Aberdeen	49	Rangers	44
1981–2	Celtic	55	Aberdeen	53	Rangers	43
1982–3	Dundee Utd	56	Celtic	55	Aberdeen	55
1983–4	Aberdeen	57	Celtic	50	Dundee Utd	47
1984–5	Aberdeen	59	Celtic	52	Dundee Utd	47
1985–6	*Celtic	50	Hearts	50	Dundee Utd	47
1986–7	Rangers	69	Celtic	63	Dundee Utd	60
1987–8	Celtic	72	Hearts	62	Rangers	60
1988–9	Rangers	56	Aberdeen	60	Celtic	46
1989–90	Rangers	51	Aberdeen	44	Hearts	44
1990–1	Rangers	55	Aberdeen	53	Celtic	41
1991–2	Rangers	72	Hearts	63	Celtic	62
1992–3	Rangers	73	Aberdeen	64	Celtic	60
1993–4	Rangers	58	Aberdeen	55	Motherwell	54
1994–5	Rangers	69	Motherwell	54	Hibernian	53
1995–6	Rangers	87	Celtic	83	Aberdeen	55
1996–7	Rangers	80	Celtic	75	Dundee Utd	60
1997–8	Celtic	74	Rangers	72	Hearts	67

PREMIER LEAGUE

	First	Pts	Second	Pts	Third	Pts
1998–99	Rangers	77	Celtic	71	St Johnstone	57
1999–2000	Rangers	90	Celtic	69	Hearts	54
2000–01	Celtic	97	Rangers	82	Hibernian	66
2001–02	Celtic	103	Rangers	85	Livingston	58
2002–03	*Rangers	97	Celtic	97	Hearts	63
2003–04	Celtic	98	Rangers	81	Hearts	68
2004–05	Rangers	93	Celtic	92	Hibernian	61
2005–06	Celtic	91	Hearts	74	Rangers	73
2006–07	Celtic	84	Rangers	72	Aberdeen	65
2007–08	Celtic	89	Rangers	86	Motherwell	60
2008–09	Rangers	86	Celtic	82	Hearts	59
2009–10	Rangers	87	Celtic	81	Dundee Utd	63
2010–11	Rangers	93	Celtic	92	Hearts	63
2011–12	Celtic	93	**Rangers	73	Motherwell	62
2012–13	Celtic	79	Motherwell	63	St Johnstone	56

Maximum points 72 except 1986–8, 1991–4 (88), 1994–2000 (108), 2001–10 (114)
* Won on goal difference. **Deducted 10 pts for administration

PREMIERSHIP

	First	Pts	Second	Pts	Third	Pts
2013–14	Celtic	99	Motherwell	70	Aberdeen	68
2014–15	Celtic	92	Aberdeen	75	Inverness	65
2015–16	Celtic	86	Aberdeen	71	Hearts	65
2016–17	Celtic	106	Aberdeen	76	Rangers	67

FIRST DIVISION (Scottish Championship until 1975–76)

	First	Pts	Second	Pts	Third	Pts
1890–1a	††Dumbarton	29	Rangers	29	Celtic	24
1891–2b	Dumbarton	37	Celtic	35	Hearts	30
1892–3a	Celtic	29	Rangers	28	St Mirren	23
1893–4a	Celtic	29	Hearts	26	St Bernard's	22
1894–5a	Hearts	31	Celtic	26	Rangers	21
1895–6a	Celtic	30	Rangers	26	Hibernian	24
1896–7a	Hearts	28	Hibernian	26	Rangers	25
1897–8a	Celtic	33	Rangers	29	Hibernian	22
1898–9a	Rangers	36	Hearts	26	Celtic	24
1899–1900a	Rangers	32	Celtic	25	Hibernian	24
1900–1c	Rangers	35	Celtic	29	Hibernian	25
1901–2a	Rangers	28	Celtic	26	Hearts	22
1902–3b	Hibernian	37	Dundee	31	Rangers	29
1903–4d	Third Lanark	43	Hearts	39	Rangers	38
1904–5a	†Celtic	41	Rangers	41	Third Lanark	35
1905–6a	Celtic	46	Hearts	39	Rangers	38
1906–7f	Celtic	55	Dundee	48	Rangers	45
1907–8f	Celtic	55	Falkirk	51	Rangers	50
1908–9f	Celtic	51	Dundee	50	Clyde	48
1909–10f	Celtic	54	Falkirk	52	Rangers	49
1910–11f	Rangers	52	Aberdeen	48	Falkirk	44
1911–12f	Rangers	51	Celtic	45	Clyde	42
1912–13f	Rangers	53	Celtic	49	Hearts	41
1913–14g	Celtic	65	Rangers	59	Hearts	54
1914–15g	Celtic	65	Hearts	61	Rangers	50
1915–16g	Celtic	67	Rangers	56	Morton	51
1916–17g	Celtic	64	Morton	54	Rangers	53
1917–18f	Rangers	56	Celtic	55	Kilmarnock	43
1918–19f	Celtic	58	Rangers	57	Morton	47
1919–20h	Rangers	71	Celtic	68	Motherwell	57
1920–1h	Rangers	76	Celtic	66	Hearts	56
1921–2h	Celtic	67	Rangers	66	Raith	56
1922–3g	Rangers	55	Airdrieonians	50	Celtic	40
1923–4g	Rangers	59	Airdrieonians	50	Celtic	41
1924–5g	Rangers	60	Airdrieonians	57	Hibernian	52
1925–6g	Celtic	58	Airdrieonians	50	Hearts	50
1926–7g	Rangers	56	Motherwell	51	Celtic	49
1927–8g	Rangers	60	Celtic	55	Motherwell	55
1928–9g	Rangers	67	Celtic	51	Motherwell	50
1929–30g	Rangers	60	Motherwell	55	Aberdeen	53
1930–1g	Rangers	60	Celtic	58	Motherwell	56
1931–2g	Motherwell	66	Rangers	61	Celtic	48
1932–3g	Rangers	62	Motherwell	59	Hearts	50
1933–4g	Rangers	66	Motherwell	62	Celtic	47
1934–5g	Rangers	55	Celtic	52	Hearts	50
1935–6g	Celtic	68	Rangers	61	Aberdeen	61
1936–7g	Rangers	61	Aberdeen	54	Celtic	52
1937–8g	Celtic	61	Hearts	58	Rangers	49
1938–9f	Rangers	59	Celtic	48	Aberdeen	46
1946–7f	Rangers	46	Hibernian	44	Aberdeen	39
1947–8g	Hibernian	48	Rangers	46	Partick	46
1948–9i	Rangers	46	Dundee	45	Hibernian	39
1949–50i	Rangers	50	Hibernian	49	Hearts	43
1950–1i	Hibernian	48	Rangers	38	Dundee	38
1951–2i	Hibernian	45	Rangers	41	East Fife	37
1952–3i	*Rangers	43	Hibernian	43	East Fife	39
1953–4i	Celtic	43	Hearts	38	Partick	35

	First		Second		Third	
1954–5f	Aberdeen	49	Celtic	46	Rangers	41
1955–6†	Rangers	52	Aberdeen	46	Hearts	45
1956–7f	Rangers	55	Hearts	53	Kilmarnock	42
1957–8f	Hearts	62	Rangers	49	Celtic	46
1958–9f	Rangers	50	Hearts	48	Motherwell	44
1959–60f	Hearts	54	Kilmarnock	50	Rangers	42
1960–1f	Rangers	51	Kilmarnock	50	Third Lanark	42
1961–2f	Dundee	54	Rangers	51	Celtic	46
1962–3f	Rangers	57	Kilmarnock	48	Partick	46
1963–4f	Rangers	55	Kilmarnock	49	Celtic	47
1964–5f	*Kilmarnock	50	Hearts	50	Dunfermline	49
1965–6f	Celtic	57	Rangers	55	Kilmarnock	45
1966–7f	Celtic	58	Rangers	55	Clyde	46
1967–8f	Celtic	63	Rangers	61	Hibernian	45
1968–9f	Celtic	54	Rangers	49	Dunfermline	45
1969–70f	Celtic	57	Rangers	45	Hibernian	44
1970–1f	Celtic	56	Aberdeen	54	St Johnstone	44
1971–2f	Celtic	60	Aberdeen	50	Rangers	44
1972–3f	Celtic	57	Rangers	56	Hibernian	45
1973–4f	Celtic	53	Hibernian	49	Rangers	48
1974–5f	Rangers	56	Hibernian	49	Celtic	45

*Won on goal average †Won on deciding match ††Title shared. Competition suspended 1940–46 (Second World War)

SCOTTISH TITLE WINS

Rangers	*54	Hibernian	4	Kilmarnock	1
Celtic	48	Dumbarton	*2	Motherwell	1
Aberdeen	4	Dundee	1	Third Lanark	1
Hearts	4	Dundee Utd	1	(*Incl 1 shared)	

FIRST DIVISION (Since formation of Premier Division)

	First	Pts	Second	Pts	Third	Pts
1975–6d	Partick	41	Kilmarnock	35	Montrose	30
1976–7j	St Mirren	62	Clydebank	58	Dundee	51
1977–8j	*Morton	58	Hearts	58	Dundee	57
1978–9j	Dundee	55	Kilmarnock	54	Clydebank	54
1979–80j	Hearts	53	Airdrieonians	51	Ayr	44
1980–1j	Hibernian	57	Dundee	52	St Johnstone	51
1981–2j	Motherwell	61	Kilmarnock	51	Hearts	50
1982–3j	St Johnstone	55	Hearts	54	Clydebank	50
1983–4i	Morton	54	Dumbarton	51	Partick	46
1984–5j	Motherwell	50	Clydebank	48	Falkirk	45
1985–6j	Hamilton	56	Falkirk	45	Kilmarnock	44
1986–7k	Morton	57	Dunfermline	56	Dumbarton	53
1987–8k	Hamilton	56	Meadowbank	52	Clydebank	49
1988–9j	Dunfermline	54	Falkirk	52	Clydebank	48
1989–90j	St Johnstone	58	Airdrieonians	54	Clydebank	44
1990–1j	Falkirk	54	Airdrieonians	53	Dundee	52
1991–2k	Dundee	58	Partick	57	Hamilton	57
1992–3k	Raith	65	Kilmarnock	54	Dunfermline	52
1993–4k	Falkirk	66	Dunfermline	65	Airdrieonians	54
1994–5l	Raith	69	Dunfermline	68	Dundee	68
1995–6l	Dunfermline	71	Dundee Utd	67	Morton	67
1996–7l	St Johnstone	80	Airdrieonians	60	Dundee	58
1997–8l	Dundee	70	Falkirk	65	Raith	60
1998–9l	Hibernian	89	Falkirk	66	Ayr	62
1999–2000l	St Mirren	76	Dunfermline	71	Falkirk	68
2000–01l	Livingston	76	Ayr	69	Falkirk	56
2001–02l	Partick	66	Airdrie	56	Ayr	52

	First		Second		Third	
2002–03l	Falkirk	81	Clyde	72	St Johnstone	67
2003–04l	Inverness	70	Clyde	69	St Johnstone	57
2004–05l	Falkirk	75	St Mirren	60	Clyde	60
2005–06l	St Mirren	76	St Johnstone	66	Hamilton	59
2006–07l	Gretna	66	St Johnstone	65	Dundee	53
2007–08l	Hamilton	76	Dundee	69	St Johnstone	58
2008–09l	St Johnstone	65	Partick	55	Dunfermline	51
2009–10l	Inverness	73	Dundee	61	Dunfermline	58
2010–11l	Dunfermline	70	Raith	60	Falkirk	58
2011–12l	Ross	79	Dundee	55	Falkirk	52
2012–13l	Partick	78	Morton	67	Falkirk	53

CHAMPIONSHIP

	First	Pts	Second	Pts	Third	Pts
2013–14l	Dundee	69	Hamilton	67	Falkirk	66
2014–15l	Hearts	91	Hibernian	70	Rangers	67
2015–16l	Rangers	81	Falkirk	70	Hibernian	70
2016–17l	Hibernian	71	Falkirk	60	Dundee Utd	57

Maximum points: a, 36; b, 44; c,.40; d 52; e, 60; f, 68; g, 76; h, 84; i, 60; j, 78; k, 88; l, 108
*Won on goal difference

SECOND DIVISION

	First	Pts	Second	Pts	Third	Pts
1921–2a	Alloa	60	Cowdenbeath	47	Armadale	45
1922–3a	Queen's Park	57	Clydebank	52	St Johnstone	50
1923–4a	St Johnstone	56	Cowdenbeath	55	Bathgate	44
1924–5a	Dundee Utd	50	Clydebank	48	Clyde	47
1925–6a	Dunfermline	59	Clyde	53	Ayr	52
1926–7a	Bo'ness	56	Raith	49	Clydebank	45
1927–8a	Ayr	54	Third Lanark	45	King'sPark	44
1928–9b	Dundee Utd	51	Morton	50	Arbroath	47
1929–30a	*LeithAthletic	57	East Fife	57	Albion	54
1930–1a	Third Lanark	61	Dundee Utd	50	Dunfermline	47
1931–2a	*E Stirling	55	St Johnstone	55	Stenhousemuir	46
1932–3c	Hibernian	55	Queen of South	49	Dunfermline	47
1933–4c	Albion	45	Dunfermline	44	Arbroath	44
1934–5c	Third Lanark	52	Arbroath	50	St Bernard's	47
1935–6c	Falkirk	59	St Mirren	52	Morton	48
1936–7c	Ayr	54	Morton	51	St Bernard's	48
1937–8c	Raith	59	Albion	48	Airdrieonians	47
1938–9c	Cowdenbeath	60	Alloa	48	East Fife	48
1946–7d	Dundee Utd	45	Airdrieonians	42	East Fife	31
1947–8e	East Fife	53	Albion	42	Hamilton	40
1948–9e	*Raith	42	Stirling	42	Airdrieonians	41
1949–50e	Morton	47	Airdrieonians	44	St Johnstone	36
1950–1e	*Queen of South	45	Stirling	45	Ayr	36
1951–2e	Clyde	44	Falkirk	43	Ayr	39
1952–3	E Stirling	44	Hamilton	43	Queen's Park	37
1953–4e	Motherwell	45	Kilmarnock	42	Third Lanark	36
1954–5e	Airdrieonians	46	Dunfermline	42	Hamilton	39
1955–6b	Queen's Park	54	Ayr	51	St Johnstone	49
1956–7b	Clyde	64	Third Lanark	51	Cowdenbeath	45
1957–8b	Stirling	55	Dunfermline	53	Arbroath	47
1958–9b	Ayr	60	Arbroath	51	Stenhousemuir	46
1959–60b	St Johnstone	53	Dundee Utd	50	Queen of South	49
1960–1b	Stirling	55	Falkirk	54	Stenhousemuir	50
1961–2b	Clyde	54	Queen of South	53	Morton	44
1962–3b	St Johnstone	55	E Stirling	49	Morton	48

182

	First	Pts	Second	Pts	Third	Pts
1963–4b	Morton	67	Clyde	53	Arbroath	46
1964–5b	Stirling	59	Hamilton	50	Queen of South	45
1965–6b	Ayr	53	Airdrieonians	50	Queen of South	47
1966–7b	Morton	69	Raith	58	Arbroath	57
1967–8b	St Mirren	62	Arbroath	53	East Fife	49
1968–9b	Motherwell	64	Ayr	53	East Fife	48
1969–70b	Falkirk	56	Cowdenbeath	55	Queen of South	50
1970–1b	Partick	56	East Fife	51	Arbroath	46
1971–2b	*Dumbarton	52	Arbroath	52	Stirling	50
1972–3b	Clyde	56	Dunfermline	52	Raith	47
1973–4h	Airdrieonians	60	Kilmarnock	58	Hamilton	55
1974–5b	Falkirk	54	Queen of South	53	Montrose	53

SECOND DIVISION (MODERN)

	First	Pts	Second	Pts	Third	Pts
1975–6d	*Clydebank	40	Raith	40	Alloa	35
1976–7f	Stirling	55	Alloa	51	Dunfermline	50
1977–8f	*Clyde	53	Raith	53	Dunfermline	48
1978–9f	Berwick	54	Dunfermline	52	Falkirk	50
1979–80f	Falkirk	50	E Stirling	49	Forfar	46
1980–1f	Queen's Park	50	Queen of South	46	Cowdenbeath	45
1981–2t	Clyde	59	Alloa	50	Arbroath	50
1982–3f	Brechin	55	Meadowbank	54	Arbroath	49
1983–4t	Forfar	63	East Fife	47	Berwick	43
1984–5f	Montrose	53	Alloa	50	Dunfermline	49
1985–6f	Dunfermline	57	Queen of South	55	Meadowbank	49
1986–7f	Meadowbank	55	Raith	52	Stirling	52
1987–8f	Ayr	61	St Johnstone	59	Queen's Park	51
1988–9f	Albion	50	Alloa	45	Brechin	43
1989–90f	Brechin	49	Kilmarnock	48	Stirling	47
1990–1f	Stirling	54	Montrose	46	Cowdenbeath	45
1991–2f	Dumbarton	52	Cowdenbeath	51	Alloa	50
1992–3f	Clyde	54	Brechin	53	Stranraer	53
1993–4f	Stranraer	56	Berwick	48	Stenhousemuir	47
1994–5g	Morton	64	Dumbarton	60	Stirling	58
1995–6g	Stirling	81	East Fife	67	Berwick	60
1996–7g	Ayr	77	Hamilton	74	Livingston	64
1997–8g	Stranraer	61	Clydebank	60	Livingston	59
1998–9g	Livingston	77	Inverness	72	Clyde	53
1999–2000g	Clyde	65	Alloa	64	Ross Co	62
2000–01g	Partick	75	Arbroath	58	Berwick	54
2001–02g	Queen of South	67	Alloa	59	Forfar Athletic	53
2002–03g	Raith	59	Brechin	55	Airdrie	54
2003–04g	Airdrie	70	Hamilton	62	Dumbarton	60
2004–05g	Brechin	72	Stranraer	63	Morton	62
2005–06g	Gretna	88	Morton	70	Peterhead	57
2006–07g	Morton	77	Stirling	69	Raith	62
2007–08g	Ross	73	Airdrie	66	Raith	60
2008–09g	Raith	76	Ayr	74	Brechin	62
2009–10g	*Stirling	65	Alloa	65	Cowdenbeath	59
2010–11g	Livingston	82	*Ayr	59	Forfar	59
2011–12g	Cowdenbeath	71	Arbroath	63	Dumbarton	58
2012–13g	Queen of South	92	Alloa	67	Brechin	61

LEAGUE ONE

	First	Pts	Second	Pts	Third	Pts
2013–14g	Rangers	102	Dunfermline	63	Stranraer	51
2014–15g	Morton	69	Stranraer	67	Forfar	66
2015–16g	Dunfermline	79	Ayr	61	Peterhead	59

| 2016–17g | Livingston...............81 | Alloa........................62 | Aidrieonians...............52 |

Maximum points: a, 76; b, 72; c, 68; d, 52e, 60; f, 78; g, 108 *Won on goal average/goal difference

THIRD DIVISION (MODERN)

1994–5	Forfar..................... 80	Montrose...................67	Ross Co 60
1995–6	Livingston................ 72	Brechin......................63	Caledonian Th 57
1996–7	Inverness................ 76	Forfar 67	Ross Co 77
1997–8	Alloa 76	Arbroath.....................68	Ross Co 67
1998–9	Ross Co 77	Stenhousemuir 64	Brechin 59
1999–2000	Queen's Park........... 69	Berwick......................66	Forfar 61
2000–01	*Hamilton................ 76	Cowdenbeath.............76	Brechin 72
2001–02	Brechin 73	Dumbarton.................61	Albion 59
2002–03	Morton 72	East Fife....................71	Albion 70
2003–04	Stranraer 79	Stirling 77	Gretna 68
2004–05	Gretna 98	Peterhead 78	Cowdenbeath.............. 51
2005–06	*Cowdenbeath......... 76	Berwick......................76	Stenhousemuir 73
2006–07	Berwick 75	Arbroath.....................70	Queen's Park.............. 68
2007–08	East Fife................ 88	Stranraer....................65	Montrose..................... 59
2008–09	Dumbarton 67	Cowdenbeath.............63	East Stirling 61
2009–10	Livingston................ 78	Forfar 63	East Stirling 61
2010–11	Arbroath 66	Albion........................61	Queen's Park.............. 59
2011–12	Alloa 77	Queen's Park.............63	Stranraer.................... 58
2012–13	Rangers.................... 83	Peterhead 59	Queen's Park.............. 56

LEAGUE TWO

	First...................... Pts	Second .... Pts	Third .... Pts
2013–14	Peterhead................76	Annan........................63	Stirling 58
2014–15	Albion 71	Queen's Park 61	Arbroath 56
2015–16	East Fife................62	Elgin 59	Clyde 57
2016–17	Arbroath..................66	Forfar 64	Annan........................ 58

Maximum points: 108 * Won on goal difference

RELEGATED FROM PREMIER DIVISION/PREMIER LEAGUE/PREMIERSHIP

1975–6	Dundee,	St Johnstone	1998–9	Dunfermline
1976–7	Kilmarnock,	Hearts	1999–2000	No relegation
1977–8	Ayr,	Clydebank	2000–01	St Mirren
1978–9	Hearts,	Motherwell	2001–02	St Johnstone
1979–80	Dundee,	Hibernian	2002–03	No relegation
1980–1	Kilmarnock,	Hearts	2003–04	Partick
1981–2	Partick,	Airdrieonians	2004–05	Dundee
1982–3	Morton,	Kilmarnock	2005–06	Livingston
1983–4	St Johnstone,	Motherwell	2006–07	Dunfermline
1984–5	Dumbarton,	Morton	2007–08	Gretna
1985–6	No relegation		2008–09	Inverness
1986–7	Clydebank, Hamilton		2009–10	Falkirk
1987–8	Falkirk, Dunfermline, Morton		2010–11	Hamilton
1988–9	Hamilton		2011–12	Dunfermline, *Rangers
1989–90	Dundee		2012–13	Dundee
1990–1	No relegation		2013–14	Hibernian, **Hearts
1991–2	St Mirren, Dunfermline		2014–15	St Mirren
1992–3	Falkirk, Airdrieonians		2015–16	Dundee Utd
1993–4	St J'stone, Raith, Dundee		2016–17	Inverness
1994–5	Dundee Utd			
1995–6	Falkirk, Partick		*Following administration, liquidationand new	
1996–7	Raith		club formed.	
1997–8	Hibernian		**Deducted 15 points for administration	

RELEGATED FROM FIRST DIVISION/CHAMPIONSHIP

1975–6	Dunfermline, Clyde	1996–7	Clydebank, East Fife
1976–7	Raith, Falkirk	1997–8	Partick, Stirling
1977–8	Alloa, East Fife	1998–9	Hamilton, Stranraer
1978–9	Montrose, Queen of South	1999–2000	Clydebank
1979–80	Arbroath, Clyde	2000–01	Morton, Alloa
1980–1	Stirling, Berwick	2001–02	Raith
1981–2	E Stirling, Queen of South	2002–03	Alloa Athletic, Arbroath
1982–3	Dunfermline, Queen's Park	2003–04	Ayr, Brechin
1983–4	Raith, Alloa	2004–05	Partick, Raith
1984–5	Meadowbank, St Johnstone	2005–06	Brechin, Stranraer
1985–6	Ayr, Alloa	2006–07	Airdrie Utd, Ross Co
1986–7	Brechin, Montrose	2007–08	Stirling
1987–8	East Fife, Dumbarton	2008–09	*Livingston, Clyde
1988–9	Kilmarnock, Queen of South	2009–10	Airdrie, Ayr
1989–90	Albion, Alloa	2010–11	Cowdenbeath, Stirling
1990–1	Clyde, Brechin	2011–12	Ayr, Queen of South
1991–2	Montrose, Forfar	2012–13	Dunfermline, Airdrie
1992–3	Meadowbank, Cowdenbeath	2013–14	Morton
1993–4	Dumbarton, Stirling, Clyde,	2014–15	Cowdenbeath
	Morton, Brechin	2015–16	Livingston, Alloa
1994–5	Ayr, Stranraer	2016–17	Raith, Ayr
1995–6	Hamilton, Dumbarton		*relegated to Division Three for breaching
			insolvency rules

RELEGATED FROM SECOND DIVISION/LEAGUE ONE

1993–4	Alloa, Forfar, E Stirling,	2004–05	Arbroath, Berwick
	Montrose, Queen's Park,	2005–06	Dumbarton
	Arbroath, Albion,	2006–07	Stranraer, Forfar
	Cowdenbeath	2007–08	Cowdenbeath, Berwick
1994–5	Meadowbank, Brechin	2008–09	Queen's Park, Stranraer
1995–6	Forfar, Montrose	2009–10	Arbroath, Clyde
1996–7	Dumbarton, Berwick	2010–11	Alloa, Peterhead
1997–8	Stenhousemuir, Brechin	2011–12	Stirling
1998–9	East Fife, Forfar	2012–13	Albion
1999–2000	Hamilton	2013–14	East Fife, Arbroath
2000–01	Queen's Park, Stirling	2014–15	Stirling
2001–02	Morton	2015–16	Cowdenbeath, Forfar
2002–03	Stranraer, Cowdenbeath	2016–17	Peterhead, Stenhousemuir
2003–04	East Fife, Stenhousemuir		

RELEGATED FROM LEAGUE TWO

2015–16	East Stirling

THE THINGS THEY SAY ...

'London Stadium is like a new house. You love it, but not the same' – **Slaven Bilic**, West Ham manager, on his team's problems settling in after the move from Upton Park.

'You know when your kid runs out in the road and you quickly grab them, you don't know whether to give them a smack or a cuddle. That's how I feel' – **Lee Johnson**, Bristol City manager, after his side surrendered a three-goal half-time lead to draw 3-3 at Derby.

'At 2-1 down I'm thinking "What am I doing here at my age?" At 3-2 up I'm thinking "this is why I'm here"' – **Neil Warnock**, Cardiff manager on his side's comeback win against Bristol City.

SCOTTISH PREMIERSHIP 2016–2017

(appearances and scorers)

ABERDEEN

Burns W 7 (6)	Maddison J 10 (4)	Ross F .... - (3)
Christie R 7 (6)	McGinn N 30 (6)	Shinnie G 35 (1)
Considine A....................36	McLean K 36 (2)	Stockley J 8 (19)
Hayes J...........................32	O'Connor A 25 (7)	Storey M 2 (12)
Jack R 25 (1)	Pawlett P 6 (12)	Storie C .... - (2)
Lewis J 38	Reynolds M 22 (4)	Taylor A 28 (3)
Logan S 37 (1)	Rooney A 32 (6)	Wright S 1 (4)

League goals (74): Rooney 12, McGinn 10, Hayes 9, Christie 6, Considine 6, Stockley 5, McLean 4, O'Connor 3, Pawlett 3, Wright 3, Jack 2, Logan 2, Maddison 2, Shinnie 2, Taylor 2, Storey 1, Opponents 2
Scottish Cup goals (10): Rooney 3, McGinn 2, Christie 1, Hayes 1, Logan 1, Shinnie 1, Opponents 1.
League Cup goals (5): Rooney 2, McGinn 1, McLean 1, Opponents 1
Europa League goals (8): Rooney 3, Burns 1, Hayes 1, Logan 1, McGinn 1, Stockley 1
Average home league attendance: 12,640. **Player of Year:** Andrew Considine

CELTIC

Aitchison J .... - (2)	Eboue K 1 (3)	McGregor C 20 (11)
Armstrong S 25 (6)	Forrest J 23 (5)	O'Connell E 2
Bailly L .... - (1)	Gamboa C 13 (4)	Ralston A........................1
Bitton N 16 (10)	Gordon C 34 (1)	Roberts P 20 (12)
Boyata D.........................17	Griffiths L 15 (8)	Rogic T 15 (7)
Brown S...........................33	Henderson L 5 (5)	Simunovic J 24 (1)
Miller C 1	Izaguirre E 10 (2)	Sinclair S 30 (5)
Christie R 3 (2)	Janko S 1 (1)	Sviatchenko E 23 (5)
Ciftci N .... - (1)	Johnston M 1	Tierney K 24
De Vries D.........................4	Lustig M 28 (1)	Toure K 5 (4)
Dembele M 20 (9)	Mackay-Steven G 4 (4)	

League goals (106): Sinclair 21, Dembele 17, Armstrong 15, Griffiths 12, Roberts 9, Rogic 7, Forrest 6, McGregor 6, Boyata 5, Bitton 1, Brown 1, Christie 1, Henderson 1, Lustig 1, Simunovic 1, Sviatchenko 1, Tierney 1
Scottish Cup goals (17): Dembele 5, Sinclair 3, Armstrong 2, Lustig 2, Brown 1, Griffiths 1, McGregor 1, Rogic 1, Tierney 1. **League Cup goals (11):** Dembele 5, Rogic 3, Forrest 2, Sinclair 1
Champions League goals (16): Dembele 5, Griffiths 5, Roberts 2, Brown 1, Rogic 1, Opponents 1
Average home league attendance: 54,624. **Player of Year:** Scott Sinclair

DUNDEE

Bain S 36	Higgins D................... 2 (2)	O'Hara M 26 (2)
Curran J 1	Holt K 37	Ojamaa H 9 (5)
Duffy M 4 (4)	Kerr C 35 (1)	Ross N 11 (8)
El-Bakhtaoui F 15 (15)	Klok M .... - (2)	Teijsse Y 3 (6)
Etxabeguren J 14 (3)	Low N...............................2	Vincent J 27 (1)
Gadzhalov K............. 15 (3)	Loy R 4 (9)	Wighton C 19 (12)
Gomis K 22	McGowan P............... 35 (1)	Williams D 11 (12)
Haber M 27	Mitchell D........................2	
Hateley T 26 (1)	O'Dea D.........................35	

League goals (38): Haber 8, O'Hara 6, O'Dea 4, El-Bakhtaoui 3, Holt 3, Loy 3, McGowan 3, Gadzhalov 2, Wighton 2, Kerr 1, Low 1, Opponents 2
Scottish Cup goals: None. **League Cup goals (15):** Stewart 6, Hemmings 3, Duffy 1, Etxabeguren 1, Loy 1, McGowan 1, O'Dea 1, Teijsse 1
Average home league attendance: 6,431. **Player of Year:** Cammy Kerr

HAMILTON ACADEMICAL

Adams B 2 (3)	Gogic A 3 (4)	Roy R .... - (1)
Bingham R 23 (7)	Hughes R .... - (2)	Sarris G 30
Boyd S .... 1(2)	Imrie D 36 (1)	Seaborne D 10 (1)
Brophy E 7 (21)	Kurakins A 1	Skondras G 11 (2)
Crawford A 31 (2)	Kurtaj G 5 (9)	Sowah L 6 (1)
Cunningham R .... - (2)	Longridge L 9 (7)	Templeton D 1 (2)
D'Acol A 24 (5)	Lyton D 5 (1)	Thomson R .... (1)
Devlin M 28	MacKinnon D 32 (1)	Tierney R .... - (2)
Doherty G 23 (6)	Matthews R 17	Want S .... - (2)
Donati M 26 (5)	McMann S 21 (2)	Watson C 2
Gillespie G 28 (3)	Redmond D 15 (12)	Woods C 21

League goals (37): Crawford 8, D'Acol 7, Bingham 5, Imrie 4, Brophy 2, Devlin 2, Donati 2, Doherty 1, Gillespie 1, Longridge 1, Lyon 1, Redmond 1, Skondras 1, Templeton 1
Scottish Cup goals (3): Bingham 2, Redmond 1. **League Cup goals** (11): Imrie 3, Crawford 2, D'Acol 2, Longridge 2, Donati 1, McGregor J 1
Average home league attendance: 2,530. **Player of Year:** Ali Crawford

HEART OF MIDLOTHIAN

Ozturk A 2 (3)	Henderson E .... - (1)	Rherras F 17 (2)
Djoum A 30 (3)	Hughes A 8	Rossi I 20
Avlonitis A 8 (1)	Johnsen B 22 (12)	Sammon C 9 (10)
Beith A .... - (2)	Kitchen P 26 (3)	Smith L 12 (8)
Bikey D .... - (2)	Martin M 5 (8)	Souttar J 22
Brandon J 1	Moha 3 (8)	Sowah L 11
Buaben P 11 (9)	Muirhead R 6 (12)	Struna A 13
Cowie D 34	Nicholson S 13 (6)	Tziolis A 14 (2)
Currie R 1 (8)	Noring V 3	Walker A 28 (6)
Esmael Goncalves 15	Nowak K 17	Watt T 12 (4)
Hamilton J 35	Paterson C 20	Zanatta D .... - (1)

League goals (55): Walker 12, Paterson 8, Esmael Goncalves 7, Djoum 6, Johnsen 5, Cowie 3, Nicholson 3, Muirhead 2, Buaben 1, Martin 1, Nowak 1, Rherras 1, Sammon 1, Struna 1, Tziolis 1, Watt 1, Opponents 1
Scottish Cup goals (6): Walker 2, Currie 1, Esmael Goncalves 1, Johnsen 1, Martin 1. **League Cup goals** (2): Paterson 1, Walker 1
Europa League goals (7): Rossi 2, Buaben 1, Ozturk 1, Paterson 1, Sammon 1, Opponents 1
Average home league attendance: 16,325. **Player of Year:** Jamie Walker

INVERNESS CALEDONIAN THISTLE

Amer H 8 (5)	Gilchrist C .... - (1)	Mulraney J 10 (16)
Boden S 3 (10)	Horner I 5 (5)	Polworth L 26 (6)
Cole L 13 (8)	King B 17 (9)	Raven D 19 (2)
Doran A 6 (11)	Laing L 14	Sutherland A .... - (1)
Doumbouya L 17 (2)	Mackay C 1	Tansey G 37
Draper R 35 (2)	McKay Billy 14	Tremarco C 29
Ebbe D .... - (3)	McKay Brad 25 (1)	Vigurs I 28 (4)
Esson R 6	McNaughton K 5 (4)	Warren G 33
Fisher A 9 (12)	McCart J 9 (2)	
Fon Williams O 31	Meekings J 18	

League goals (44): Fisher 8, Tansey 7, Doumbouya 5, McKay Billy 4, Tremarco 4, Draper 3, Polworth 3, Warren 2, Boden 1, Cole 1, Doran 1, King 1, McKay Brad 1, Meekings 1, Raven 1, Vigurs 1
Scottish Cup goals (2): Cole 1, Doumbouya 1. **League Cup goals** (15): Boden 4, Vigurs 4, Tremarco 3, King 2, Draper 1, Warren 1
Average home league attendance: 3,945. **Player of Year:** Greg Tansey

KILMARNOCK

Adams C	4 (5)	
Addison M	8 (3)	
Ajer K	16	
Bojaj F	2	
Boyd K	22 (5)	
Boyd S	18 (1)	
Boyle W	11	
Burn J	6 (2)	
Cameron I	- (2)	
Coulibaly S	18 (3)	
Dicker G	36	
Frizzell A	8 (7)	
Graham W	- (3)	
Green G	2 (2)	
Hawkshaw D	7 (8)	
Hendrie L	32	
Jones J	29 (8)	
Kiltie G	7 (4)	
Longstaff L	16	
MacDonald J	24	
McFadzean C	1 (3)	
McKenzie R	25 (3)	
Morrison L	- (1)	
Osborne K	1	
Roberts C	4 (6)	
Sammon C	14 (1)	
Smith M	7 (3)	
Smith S	25 (1)	
Taylor G	34	
Tyson N	11 (6)	
Umerah J	- (4)	
Waddington M	- (1)	
Webb J	- (1)	
Wilson I	16 (4)	
Woodman F	14	

League goals (36): Boyd K 8, Coulibaly 8, Sammon 5, McKenzie 4, Jones 3, Longstaff 3, Boyd S 1, Dicker 1, Frizzell 1, Smith M 1, Smith S 1
Scottish Cup goals: None. **League Cup goals (5):** Coulibaly 3, Boyle 1, McKenzie 1
Average home league attendance: 4,963. **Player of Year:** Kris Boyd

MOTHERWELL

Ainsworth L	10 (20)	
Blyth J	1 (7)	
Bowman R	11 (13)	
Cadden C	36	
Campbell A	6 (1)	
Chalmers J	7 (1)	
Clay C	31 (4)	
Ferguson D	7 (3)	
Frear E	11 (4)	
Gordon S	2 (2)	
Griffiths R	4	
Hammell S	24 (1)	
Hastie J	- (3)	
Heneghan B	37	
Johnson M	4	
Jules Z	6 (4)	
Lasley K	25 (3)	
Livingstone A	- (2)	
Lucas L	6 (4)	
MacLean R	4 (3)	
McDonald S	34 (1)	
McFadden J	- (6)	
McHugh C	19	
McManus S	25	
McMillan J	9 (5)	
Moult L	30 (1)	
Pearson S	10 (1)	
Samson C	34	
Tait R	25	
Thomas D	- (4)	

League goals (46): Moult 15, McDonald 9, Ainsworth 4, Cadden 3, Bowman 2, McFadden 2, McHugh 2, Campbell 1, Clay 1, Frear 1, Johnson 1, Jules 1, Pearson 1, Tait 1, Opponents 2
Scottish Cup goals (1): Moult 1. **League Cup goals (9):** Johnson 3, Cadden 2, McDonald 2, Moult 2
Average home league attendance: 4,485. **Player of Year:** Lewis Moult

PARTICK THISTLE

Amoo D	14 (11)	
Azeez A	19 (19)	
Barton A	30 (1)	
Booth C	31	
Cerny T	27	
Devine D	28 (2)	
Doolan K	29 (8)	
Dumbuya M	8	
Edwards R	33 (5)	
Elliott C	26 (5)	
Erskine C	25 (11)	
Gordon Z	12 (2)	
Keown N	14	
Lamont M	- (1)	
Lawless S	24 (6)	
Lindsay L	36	
McCarthy A	3 (2)	
McDaid D	- (3)	
McLaughlin N	- (1)	
Nesbit K	- (3)	
Osman A	30 (1)	
Pogba M	- (2)	
Ridgers M	1 (1)	
Scully R	6 (1)	
Stuckmann T	4 (1)	
Welsh S	18 (3)	
Wilson D	- (1)	

League goals (38): Doolan 14, Lindsay 6, Erskine 5, Welsh 3, Azeez 2, Lawless 2, Amoo 1, Barton 1, Booth 1, Edwards 1, Osman 1, Opponents 1
Scottish Cup goals (5): Erskine 2, Barton 1, Lawless 1, Osman 1. **League Cup goals (10):** Erskine 2, Welsh 2, Amoo 1, Azeez 1, Doolan 1, Lawless 1, Lindsay 1, Pogba 1
Average home league attendance: 4,282. **Player of Year:** Kris Doolan

RANGERS

Alnwick J 1	Garner J.................21 (10)	O'Halloran M..... 6 (10)
Barjonas J................. 1 (3)	Halliday A................24 (8)	Rossiter J..................... 3 (1)
Barton J.....................5	Hill C 23 (1)	Senderos P 3
Bates D 7	Hodson L 10 (1)	Tavernier J 35 (1)
Beerman M 6 (1)	Holt J 28 (3)	Toral J-M 12
Burt L................. - (1)	Hyndman E..............13	Waghorn M.......... 20 (12)
Crooks M 1 (1)	Kiernan R 24	Wallace L...................27
Dodoo J 5 (15)	Kranjcar N 4 (5)	Wilson A 2
Föderingham W 37	McKay B 28 (7)	Wilson D 19 (2)
Forrester H 7 (14)	Miller K 32 (5)	Windass J 14 (7)

League goals (56): Miller 11, Garner 7, Waghorn 7, McKay 5, Hyndman 4, Dodoo 3, Forrester 3, Halliday 3, Hill 3, Wallace 3, Toral 2, Hodson 1, Kiernan 1, Kranjcar 1, Tavernier 1, Opponents 1
Scottish Cup goals (10): Garner 3, Miller 3, Waghorn 2, Hill 2, Toral 1. **League Cup goals (20):** Waghorn 7, Dodoo 2, Halliday 2, Hill 2, Kranjcar 2, Holt 1, McKay 1, Tavernier 1, Windass 1, Opponents 1
Average home league attendance: 48,893. **Player of Year:** Kenny Miller

ROSS COUNTY

Boyce L 34	Fox S........................35	Morrison G 1 (4)
Burke C 4 (2)	Franks J.................... 9 (9)	Naismith J 14 (2)
Chow T 26 (4)	Fraser M....................33	O'Brien J 8 (8)
Cikos E.....................5	Gardyne M 28 (5)	Quinn P 19
Curran C 26 (8)	Graham B 1	Routis C 23 (7)
Davies A 31	Lalkovic M 2 (4)	Schalk A 15 (17)
Dingwall R .... - (1)	Malcolm B 1	Tumility R 2 (5)
Dingwall T............ 4 (10)	McCarey A 3 (1)	Woods M 27 (2)
Dow R 13 (10)	McEveley J 19 (3)	Van der Weg K 29 (4)
Dykes D .... - (2)	McLaughlin C............. 1- (1)	
Foster R..................... 1	McShane I 9 (3)	

League goals (48): Boyce 23, Curran 5, Schalk 5, McEveley 3, Routis 3, Gardyne 2, Burke 1, Chow 1, Davies 1, Dow 1, Franks 1, Woods 1, Opponents 1
Scottish Cup goals (6): Routis 2, Boyce 1, Chow 1, O'Brien 1, Quinn 1. **League Cup goals (11):** Graham 6, Schalk 3, Curran 2
Average home league attendance: 4,213. **Player of Year:** Liam Boyce

ST JOHNSTONE

Alston B 25 (10)	Foster R.....................33	Scobbie T 14 (2)
Anderson S 26	Gormley J .... - (1)	Shaughnessy J...............38
Clark Z 26	Hurst G..................... - (1)	Smith C 2
Comrie A.................... - (1)	Kane C 14 (11)	Swanson D.............. 28 (2)
Coulson M................ 7 (7)	MacLean S 30 (2)	Thomson C 2 (7)
Craig L 27 (9)	Mannus A 12 (2)	Watson K 3 (1)
Cummins G 17 (13)	McKay B 2	Wotherspoon D 20 (13)
Davidson M 19 (4)	Millar C 14 (3)	
Easton B....................37	Paton P 22 (6)	

League goals (50): Swanson 10, MacLean 9, Craig 5, Cummins 5, Kane 5, Anderson 3, Davidson 3, Alston 2, Foster 1, Paton 1, Shaughnessy 1, Thomson 1, Watson 1, Wotherspoon 1, Opponents 2
Scottish Cup goals (2): Alston 1, MacLean 1. **League Cup goals (14):** Swanson 5, MacLean 2, Anderson 1, Craig 1, Cummins 1, Kane 1, McKay 1, Shaughnessy 1, Wotherspoon 1
Average home league attendance: 4,392. **Player of Year:** Danny Swanson

BETFRED SCOTTISH LEAGUE CUP 2016

(Each group team awarded three points for a win; one point for a drawn match after 90 minutes; then penalties with winners awarded one additional point. Group winners and four best runners-up through to knock-out stage to join four clubs competing in Europe – Aberdeen, Celtic, Hearts, Hibernian)

GROUP A

	P	W	D	L	F	A	Pts
Peterhead	4	2	1	1	8	6	8
East Fife	4	2	1	1	5	4	8
Dundee	4	2	1	1	15	5	7
Forfar	4	1	1	2	4	11	5
Dumbarton	4	0	2	2	7	13	2

GROUP B

St Johnstone	4	3	1	0	11	2	10
Falkirk	4	2	0	2	5	4	6
Stirling Alb	4	2	0	2	6	7	6
Brechin	4	1	1	2	5	8	5
Elgin	4	1	0	3	6	12	3

GROUP C

Inverness	4	3	1	0	15	3	10
Dundee Utd	4	2	2	0	10	3	10
Dunfermline	4	2	0	2	7	7	6
Cowdenbeath	4	1	0	3	4	11	3
Arbroath	4	0	1	3	1	13	1

GROUP D

Alloa	4	4	0	0	10	2	12
Raith	4	2	1	1	5	4	8
Ross Co	4	2	1	1	11	4	7
Cove	4	1	0	3	4	13	3
Montrose	4	0	0	4	1	8	0

GROUP E

Partick	4	4	0	0	9	2	12
Queen of South	4	3	0	1	6	2	9
Airdrieonians	4	1	1	2	5	7	5
Queen's Park	4	1	1	2	5	7	4
Stenhousemuir	4	0	0	4	2	9	0

GROUP F

Rangers	4	4	0	0	10	0	12
Motherwell	4	3	0	1	9	3	9
Stranraer	4	2	0	2	5	8	6
Annan	4	1	0	3	4	7	3
East Stirling	4	0	0	4	1	11	0

GROUP G

Hamilton	4	3	0	1	10	5	9
Ayr	4	3	0	1	5	2	9
St Mirren	4	3	0	1	7	5	9
Livingston	4	1	0	3	6	7	3
Edinburgh City	4	0	0	4	2	11	0

GROUP H

Morton	4	3	1	0	5	0	11
Kilmarnock	4	2	1	1	5	5	7
Clyde	4	1	1	2	4	5	5
Albion Rov	4	0	3	1	1	2	5
Berwick	4	0	2	2	3	6	2

SECOND ROUND

Alloa 1 Inverness 0; Ayr 1 **Aberdeen** 2; **Celtic** 5 Motherwell 0; Dundee Utd 3 Partick 1; Hamilton 1 Morton 2; Hibernian 1 Queen of South 3; Rangers 5 Peterhead 0; St Johnstone 3 Hearts 2

THIRD ROUND

Aberdeen 1 St Johnstone 0; **Celtic** 2 Alloa 0; Morton 2 Dundee Utd 1; Rangers 5 Queen of South 0

SEMI-FINALS

Morton 0 **Aberdeen** 2; (at Hampden Park); Rangers 0 **Celtic** 1; (at Hampden Park)

FINAL

ABERDEEN 0 CELTIC 3
Hampden Park (49,629); Sunday, November 27 2016

Aberdeen (4-2-3-1): Lewis, Logan, Taylor, O'Connor (Stockley 65), Considine, Jack (capt), Shinnie, Hayes (McGinn 71), McLean, Maddison, Rooney (Burns 79). **Subs not used:** Alexander, Reynolds, Pawlett, Storey. **Manager:** Derek McInnes

Celtic (4-2-3-1): Gordon, Lustig, Simunovic, Sviatchenko, Izaguirre, Brown (capt), Armstrong, Roberts (Dillon 65), Rogic (McGregor 77), Forrest (Griffiths 90), Dembele. **Subs not used:** De Vries, Toure, Gamboa, Mackay-Steven. **Scorers:** Rogic (17), Forrest (37), Dembele (64 pen). **Booked:** Brown, Bitton. **Manager:** Brendan Rodgers

Referee: J Beaton. **Half-time:** 0-2

SCOTTISH LEAGUE CUP FINALS

1946 Aberdeen beat Rangers (3-2)
1947 Rangers beat Aberdeen (4-0)
1948 East Fife beat Falkirk (4-1 after 0-0 draw)
1949 Rangers beat Raith Rov (2-0)
1950 East Fife beat Dunfermline Athletic (3-0)
1951 Motherwell beat Hibernian (3-0)
1952 Dundee beat Rangers (3-2)
1953 Dundee beat Kilmarnock (2-0)
1954 East Fife beat Partick (3-2)
1955 Hearts beat Motherwell (4-2)
1956 Aberdeen beat St Mirren (2-1)
1957 Celtic beat Partick (3-0 after 0-0 draw)
1958 Celtic beat Rangers (7-1)
1959 Hearts beat Partick (5-1)
1960 Hearts beat Third Lanark (2-1)
1961 Rangers beat Kilmarnock (2-0)
1962 Rangers beat Hearts (3-1 after 1-1 draw)
1963 Hearts beat Kilmarnock (1-0)
1964 Rangers beat Morton (5-0)
1965 Rangers beat Celtic (2-1)
1966 Celtic beat Rangers (2-1)
1967 Celtic beat Rangers (1-0)
1968 Celtic beat Dundee (5-3)
1969 Celtic beat Hibernian (6-2)
1970 Celtic beat St Johnstone (1-0)
1971 Rangers beat Celtic (1-0)
1972 Partick beat Celtic (4-1)
1973 Hibernian beat Celtic (2-1)
1974 Dundee beat Celtic (1-0)
1975 Celtic beat Hibernian (6-3)
1976 Rangers beat Celtic (1-0)
1977† Aberdeen beat Celtic (2-1)
1978† Rangers beat Celtic (2-1)
1979 Rangers beat Aberdeen (2-1)
1980 Dundee Utd beat Aberdeen (3-0 after 0-0 draw)
1981 Dundee Utd beat Dundee (3-0)
1982 Rangers beat Dundee Utd (2-1)
1983 Celtic beat Rangers (2-1)
1984† Rangers beat Celtic (3-2)
1985 Rangers beat Dundee Utd (1-0)
1986 Aberdeen beat Hibernian (3-0)
1987 Rangers beat Celtic (2-1)
1988† Rangers beat Aberdeen (5-3 on pens after 3-3 draw)
1989 Rangers beat Aberdeen (3-2)
1990† Aberdeen beat Rangers (2-1)
1991† Rangers beat Celtic (2-1)
1992 Hibernian beat Dunfermline Athletic (2-0)
1993† Rangers beat Aberdeen (2-1)
1994 Rangers beat Hibernian (2-1)
1995 Raith Rov beat Celtic (6-5 on pens after 2-2 draw)
1996 Aberdeen beat Dundee (2-0)
1997 Rangers beat Hearts (4-3)

1998 Celtic beat Dundee Utd (3-0)
1999 Rangers beat St Johnstone (2-1)
2000 Celtic beat Aberdeen (2-0)
2001 Celtic beat Kilmarnock (3-0)
2002 Rangers beat Ayr (4-0)
2003 Rangers beat Celtic (2-1)
2004 Livingston beat Hibernian (2-0)
2005 Rangers beat Motherwell (5-1)
2006 Celtic beat Dunfermline Athletic (3-0)
2007 Hibernian beat Kilmarnock (5-1)
2008 Rangers beat Dundee Utd (3-2 on pens after 2-2 draw)
2009† Celtic beat Rangers (2-0)
2010 Rangers beat St Mirren (1-0)
2011† Rangers beat Celtic (2-1)
2012 Kilmarnock beat Celtic (1-0)
2013 St Mirren beat Hearts (3-2)
2014 Aberdeen beat Inverness Caledonian Thistle (4-2 on pens after 0-0 draw)
2015 Celtic beat Dundee Utd (2-0)
2016 Ross Co beat Hibernian (2-1)
2017 Celtic beat Aberdeen (3-0)
(† After extra time; Skol Cup 1985-93, Coca-Cola Cup 1995-97, Co-operative Insurance Cup 1999 onwards)

SUMMARY OF SCOTTISH LEAGUE CUP WINNERS

Rangers	27	East Fife	3	Motherwell	1
Celtic	16	Hibernian	3	Partick	1
Aberdeen	7	Dundee Utd	2	Raith	1
Hearts	4	Kilmarnock	2	Ross Co	1
Dundee	3	Livingston	1	St Mirren	1

HAT-TRICK OF PENALTY SAVES

Cammy Bell saved three penalties from three different players in Dundee United's 3-1 Scottish Championship victory at Dunfermline last season. The former Rangers goalkeeper denied Gavin Reilly, Nicky Clark and Paul McMullan in the first 33 minutes. Cambridge United's Will Norris kept out two stoppage-time spot-kicks as his nine-man side defeated Accrington 2-1 in League Two. Norris saved from Chris Eagles after Leon Legge was sent off for bringing down Terry Gornell. Then, he denied Gornell after Brad Halliday was dismissed for handling on the line.

BARKER BACK AFTER FOUR YEARS

Four-and-a-half-years after a career-threatening knee injury, Shaun Barker made his comeback last season. The 34-year-old defender came off the bench to help Burton see out a 1-0 Championship win over Derby in the first competitive match between the two clubs. Barker sustained the injury in March, 2012 while playing for Derby.

IRN-BRU SCOTTISH CHALLENGE CUP
2016-17

First round: Berwick 0 Spartans 3; Celtic U20 5 Annan 1; Clyde 0 Partick U20 5; Cove 2 Dundee U20 1; Cumbernauld 0 Hamilton U20 3; East Stirling 0 Montrose 3; Formartine 2 Aberdeen U20 5; Inverness U20 0 Arbroath 3; Motherwell U20 2 Edinburgh City 1; Queen's Park 5 Kilmarnock U20 2; Rangers U20 4 Stirling Univ 0; Ross Co U20 2 Brora 3 (aet); St Johnstone U20 1 Turriff 2; Stirling Alb 2 Hearts U20 3

Second round: Aberdeen U20 1 Forfar 3; Albion Rov 2 Hamilton U20 0; Arbroath 2 East Fife 3 (aet); Brechin 4 Cove 1; Cowdenbeath 1 Celtic U20 2; Elgin 2 Hearts U20 0; Motherwell U20 1 Airdrieonians 2; Partick U20 1 Queen's Park 1 (aet, Queen's Park won 6-5 on pens); Peterhead 3 Brora 2; Rangers U20 1 Stenhousemuir 3; Stranraer 7 Spartans 1; Turriff 1 Montrose 0

Third round: Albion Rov 3 St Mirren 4 (aet); Alloa 3 East Fife 0; Ayr 3 Airdrieonians 2 (aet); Brechin 1 Dunfermline 5; Dundee Utd 3 Peterhead 2 (aet); Falkirk 6 Elgin 1; Forfar 3 Raith 2; Livingston 5 Celtic U20 1; Queen of South 7 Stenhousemuir 1; Queen's Park 2 Morton 0; Stranraer 1 Dumbarton 0

Fourth round: Ayr 1 Falkirk 0 (aet); Bala 2 Alloa 4; Crusaders 1 Livingston 2 (Livingston fielded ineligible player – replay ordered); Dunfermline 2 Queen's Park 1; Forfar 1 New Saints 3; Hibernian 1 St Mirren 2; Queen of South 2 Linfield 0 (aet); Stranraer 0 Dundee Utd 1. **Replay:** Crusaders 0 Livingston 3

Fifth round: Dunfermline 0 Dundee Utd 1; Livingston 0 New Saints 3; Queen of South 2 Alloa 0; St Mirren 2 Ayr 1

Semi-finals: Queen of South 2 Dundee Utd 3; St Mirren 4 New Saints 1

FINAL
DUNDEE UNITED 2 ST MIRREN 1
Fir Park, Motherwell (8,089); Saturday, March 25 2017
Dundee United (4-2-3-1): Bell (capt), Murdoch, Edjenguele, Durnan, Robson, Telfer, Flood, Coote (Donaldson 89), Andreu, Van der Velden (Mikkelsen 58), Murray (Nicholls 80). **Subs not used:** Zwick, Dixon, Toshney, Van der Struijk. **Scorers:** Andreu (37), Mikkelsen (75). **Booked:** Flood, Murray. **Manager:** Ray McKinnon
St Mirren (4-4-2): O'Brien, Irvine, MacKenzie, Baird, Eckersley, Magennis (O'Keefe 84), Mallan, McGinn (capt), Morgan, Loy, Sutton. **Subs not used:** Langfield, Demetriou, Webster, Fjelde, Whyte, Watters. **Scorer:** Loy (38). **Booked:** Mallan, Loy. **Manager:** Jack Ross
Referee: N Walsh. **Half-time:** 1-1

WILLIAM HILL SCOTTISH FA CUP 2016–17

FIRST ROUND

Beith 6 Strathspey 0
BSC Glasgow 3 Rothes 1
Civil Service 1 Hawick 1
Clachnacuddin 1 Stirling Univ 2
Dalbeattie 1 Wick 3
Deveronvale 0 Gretna 3
East Kilbride 9 Vale of Leithen 1
Edinburg Univ 0 Whitehill 1
Forres 2 Lossiemouth 2
Fort William 1 Brora 4
Gala 3 Fraserburgh 1
Girvan 1 Huntly 2

Inverurie 0 Buckie 6
Keith 0 Banks O'Dee 1
Nairn 2 Preston 3
Selkirk 0 Linlithgow 3
Turriff 1 Bonnyrigg 1
Leith 0 Cumbernauld 0

Replays
Cumbernauld 1 Leith 0
Bonnyrigg 4 Turriff 1
Hawick 6 Civil Service 2
Lossiemouth 0 Forres 4

SECOND ROUND

Annan 0 East Stirling 0
Arbroath 3 Stirling Univ 1
BSC Glasgow 0 Beith 1
Banks O'Dee 2 Formartine 2
Berwick 2 Hawick 3
Bonnyrigg 2 Cove 1
Brora 0 Clyde 2
Buckie 1 Gretna 1
Cowdenbeath 0 East Kilbride 1
Cumbernauld 2 Forres 2
Edinburgh City 0 Forfar 0

Gala 0 Elgin 4
Huntly 0 Spartans 2
Linlithgow 0 Stirling Alb 3
Preston 0 Montrose 3
Wick 4 Whitehill 1

Replays
Forfar 0 Edinburgh City 1
East Stirling 1 Annan 2
Formartine 7 Banks O'Dee 2
Forres 4 Cumbernauld 0
Gretna 2 Buckie 6

THIRD ROUND

Albion Rov 2 Queen of South 1
Airdrieonians 1 Livingston 2
Beith 0 Morton 6
Bonnyrigg 0 Dumbarton 0
Brechin 0 Ayr 1
Buckie 3 Dunfermline 5
Clyde 5 Arbroath 0
East Fife 1 Edinburgh City 1
Elgin 8 Hawick 1
Formartine 4 Annan 0

Forres 2 Stenhousemuir 2
Peterhead 0 Alloa 1
Queen's Park 2 Montrose 0
Stirling Alb 2 Wick 0
St Mirren 5 Spartans 1
Stranraer 2 East Kilbride 1

Replays
Dumbarton 0 Bonnyrigg 1
Edinburgh City 0 East Fife 1
Stenhousemuir 3 Forres 1

FOURTH ROUND

Aberdeen 4 Stranraer 0
Albion Rov 0 **Celtic** 3
Alloa 2 Dunfermline 3
Ayr 0 Queen's Park 0
Bonnyrigg 1 Hibernian 8
Dundee 0 St Mirren 2
Elgin 1 Inverness 2
Kilmarnock 0 Hamilton 1
Livingston 0 East Fife 1
Morton 2 Falkirk 0
Partick 4 Formartine 0

Raith 1 Hearts 1
Rangers 2 Motherwell 1
Ross Co 6 Dundee Utd 2
St Johnstone 2 Stenhousemuir 0
Stirling Alb 2 Clyde 2

Replays
Clyde 3 Stirling Alb 2
Hearts 4 Raith 2 (aet)
Queen's Park 2 Ayr 2
(aet, Ayr won 5-4 on pens)

FIFTH ROUND

Ayr 1 Clyde 1
Celtic 6 Inverness 0
Dunfermline 1 Hamilton 1
East Fife 2 St Mirren 3
Hearts 0 Hibernian 0
Ross Co 0 **Aberdeen** 1
Rangers 2 Morton 1

St Johnstone 0 Partick 1
Replays
Clyde 1 Ayr 2 (aet)
Hamilton 1 Dunfermline 1
(aet, Hamilton won 3-0 on pens)
Hibernian 3 Hearts 1

SIXTH ROUND

Aberdeen 1 Partick 0
Celtic 4 St Mirren 1

Hibernian 3 Ayr 1
Rangers 6 Hamilton 0

SEMI-FINALS (both at Hampden Park)

Celtic 2 Rangers 0

Hibernian 2 **Aberdeen** 3

FINAL

CELTIC 2 ABERDEEN 1
Hampden Park (48,713); Saturday, May 27 2017

Celtic (4-1-2-3): Gordon, Lustig, Simunovic, Boyata, Tierney (Rogic 26), Brown (capt), McGregor, Armstrong, Roberts (Sviatchenko 90), Griffiths, Sinclair. **Subs not used**: De Vries, Gamboa, Bitton, Forrest, Dembele. **Scorers**: Armstrong (11), Rogic (90). **Booked**: Rogic.
Manager: Brendan Rodgers
Aberdeen (4-3-3): Lewis, Logan, Taylor, Reynolds, Considine, Shinnie (capt), Jack (Wright (90), McLean, McGinn (Connor 75), Stockley (Rooney 62), Hayes. **Subs not used**: Alexander, Storey, Ross, Pawlett. **Scorer**: Hayes (9). **Booked**: Taylor. **Manager**: Derek McInnes
Referee: R Madden. **Half-time**: 1-1

SCOTTISH FA CUP FINALS

1874 Queen's Park beat Clydesdale (2-0)
1875 Queen's Park beat Renton (3-0)
1876 Queen's Park beat Third Lanark (2-0 after 1-1 draw)
1877 Vale of Leven beat Rangers (3-2 after 0-0, 1-1 draws)
1878 Vale of Leven beat Third Lanark (1-0)
1879 Vale of Leven awarded Cup (Rangers withdrew after 1-1 draw)
1880 Queen's Park beat Thornliebank (3-0)
1881 Queen's Park beat Dumbarton (3-1)
1882 Queen's Park beat Dumbarton (4-1 after 2-2 draw)
1883 Dumbarton beat Vale of Leven (2-1 after 2-2 draw)
1884 Queen's Park awarded Cup (Vale of Leven withdrew from Final)
1885 Renton beat Vale of Leven (3-1 after 0-0 draw)
1886 Queen's Park beat Renton (3-1)
1887 Hibernian beat Dumbarton (2-1)
1888 Renton beat Cambuslang (6-1)
1889 Third Lanark beat Celtic (2-1)
1890 Queen's Park beat Vale of Leven (2-1 after 1-1 draw)
1891 Hearts beat Dumbarton (1-0)
1892 Celtic beat Queen's Park (5-1)
1893 Queen's Park beat Celtic (2-1)
1894 Rangers beat Celtic (3-1)
1895 St Bernard's beat Renton (2-1)
1896 Hearts beat Hibernian (3-1)
1897 Rangers beat Dumbarton (5-1)
1898 Rangers beat Kilmarnock (2-0)

1899 Celtic beat Rangers (2-0)
1900 Celtic beat Queen's Park (4-3)
1901 Hearts beat Celtic (4-3)
1902 Hibernian beat Celtic (1-0)
1903 Rangers beat Hearts (2-0 after 0-0, 1-1 draws)
1904 Celtic beat Rangers (3-2)
1905 Third Lanark beat Rangers (3-1 after 0-0 draw)
1906 Hearts beat Third Lanark (1-0)
1907 Celtic beat Hearts (3-0)
1908 Celtic beat St Mirren (5-1)
1909 Cup withheld because of riot after two drawn games in final
between Celtic and Rangers (2-2, 1-1)
1910 Dundee beat Clyde (2-1 after 2-2, 0-0 draws)
1911 Celtic beat Hamilton (2-0 after 0-0 draw)
1912 Celtic beat Clyde (2-0)
1913 Falkirk beat Raith (2-0)
1914 Celtic beat Hibernian (4-1 after 0-0 draw)
1915-19 No competition (World War 1)
1920 Kilmarnock beat Albion (3-2)
1921 Partick beat Rangers (1-0)
1922 Morton beat Rangers (1-0)
1923 Celtic beat Hibernian (1-0)
1924 Airdrieonians beat Hibernian (2-0)
1925 Celtic beat Dundee (2-1)
1926 St Mirren beat Celtic (2-0)
1927 Celtic beat East Fife (3-1)
1928 Rangers beat Celtic (4-0)
1929 Kilmarnock beat Rangers (2-0)
1930 Rangers beat Partick (2-1 after 0-0 draw)
1931 Celtic beat Motherwell (4-2 after 2-2 draw)
1932 Rangers beat Kilmarnock (3-0 after 1-1 draw)
1933 Celtic beat Motherwell (1-0)
1934 Rangers beat St Mirren (5-0)
1935 Rangers beat Hamilton (2-1)
1936 Rangers beat Third Lanark (1-0)
1937 Celtic beat Aberdeen (2-1)
1938 East Fife beat Kilmarnock (4-2 after 1-1 draw)
1939 Clyde beat Motherwell (4-0)
1940-6 No competition (World War 2)
1947 Aberdeen beat Hibernian (2-1)
1948† Rangers beat Morton (1-0 after 1-1 draw)
1949 Rangers beat Clyde (4-1)
1950 Rangers beat East Fife (3-0)
1951 Celtic beat Motherwell (1-0)
1952 Motherwell beat Dundee (4-0)
1953 Rangers beat Aberdeen (1-0 after 1-1 draw)
1954 Celtic beat Aberdeen (2-1)
1955 Clyde beat Celtic (1-0 after 1-1 draw)
1956 Hearts beat Celtic (3-1)
1957† Falkirk beat Kilmarnock (2-1 after 1-1 draw)
1958 Clyde beat Hibernian (1-0)
1959 St Mirren beat Aberdeen (3-1)
1960 Rangers beat Kilmarnock (2-0)
1961 Dunfermline beat Celtic (2-0 after 0-0 draw)
1962 Rangers beat St Mirren (2-0)
1963 Rangers beat Celtic (3-0 after 1-1 draw)
1964 Rangers beat Dundee (3-1)
1965 Celtic beat Dunfermline (3-2)
1966 Rangers beat Celtic (1-0 after 0-0 draw)

1967 Celtic beat Aberdeen (2-0)
1968 Dunfermline beat Hearts (3-1)
1969 Celtic beat Rangers (4-0)
1970 Aberdeen beat Celtic (3-1)
1971 Celtic beat Rangers (2-1 after 1-1 draw)
1972 Celtic beat Hibernian (6-1)
1973 Rangers beat Celtic (3-2)
1974 Celtic beat Dundee Utd (3-0)
1975 Celtic beat Airdrieonians (3-1)
1976 Rangers beat Hearts (3-1)
1977 Celtic beat Rangers (1-0)
1978 Rangers beat Aberdeen (2-1)
1979† Rangers beat Hibernian (3-2 after two 0-0 draws)
1980† Celtic beat Rangers (1-0)
1981 Rangers beat Dundee Utd (4-1 after 0-0 draw)
1982† Aberdeen beat Rangers (4-1)
1983† Aberdeen beat Rangers (1-0)
1984† Aberdeen beat Celtic (2-1)
1985 Celtic beat Dundee Utd (2-1)
1986 Aberdeen beat Hearts (3-0)
1987† St Mirren beat Dundee Utd (1-0)
1988 Celtic beat Dundee Utd (2-1)
1989 Celtic beat Rangers (1-0)
1990† Aberdeen beat Celtic (9-8 on pens after 0-0 draw)
1991† Motherwell beat Dundee Utd (4-3)
1992 Rangers beat Airdrieonians (2-1)
1993 Rangers beat Aberdeen (2-1)
1994 Dundee Utd beat Rangers (1-0)
1995 Celtic beat Airdrieonians (1-0)
1996 Rangers beat Hearts (5-1)
1997 Kilmarnock beat Falkirk (1-0)
1998 Hearts beat Rangers (2-1)
1999 Rangers beat Celtic (1-0)
2000 Rangers beat Aberdeen (4-0)
2001 Celtic beat Hibernian (3-0)
2002 Rangers beat Celtic (3-2)
2003 Rangers beat Dundee (1-0)
2004 Celtic beat Dunfermline (3-1)
2005 Celtic beat Dundee Utd (1-0)
2006† Hearts beat Gretna (4-2 on pens after 1-1 draw)
2007 Celtic beat Dunfermline (1-0)
2008 Rangers beat Queen of the South (3-2)
2009 Rangers beat Falkirk (1-0)
2010 Dundee Utd beat Ross Co (3-0)
2011 Celtic beat Motherwell (3-0)
2012 Hearts beat Hibernian (5-1)
2013 Celtic beat Hibernian (3-0)
2014 St Johnstone beat Dundee Utd (2-0)
2015 Inverness beat Falkirk (2-1)
2016 Hibernian beat Rangers (3-2)
2017 Celtic beat Aberdeen (2-1)
† After extra time

SUMMARY OF SCOTTISH CUP WINNERS

Celtic 37, Rangers 33, Queen's Park 10, Hearts 8, Aberdeen 7, Clyde 3, Hibernian 3, Kilmarnock 3, St Mirren 3, Vale of Leven 3, Dundee Utd 2, Dunfermline 2, Falkirk 2, Motherwell 2, Renton 2, Third Lanark 2, Airdrieonians 1, Dumbarton 1, Dundee 1, East Fife 1, Inverness 1, Morton 1, Partick 1, St Bernard's 1, St Johnstone 1

VANARAMA NATIONAL LEAGUE 2016–2017

| | | P | | Home | | | | | Away | | | | | |
			W	D	L	F	A	W	D	L	F	A	GD	PTS
1	Lincoln	46	17	4	2	48	17	13	5	5	35	23	43	99
2	Tranmere	46	16	3	4	43	19	13	5	5	36	20	40	95
3	Forest Green*	46	12	9	2	46	25	13	2	8	42	31	32	86
4	Dagenham	46	12	5	6	37	28	14	1	8	42	25	26	84
5	Aldershot	46	15	5	3	38	13	8	8	7	28	24	29	82
6	Dover	46	13	5	5	48	28	11	2	10	37	35	22	79
7	Barrow	46	12	8	3	40	20	8	7	8	32	33	19	75
8	Gateshead	46	9	9	5	38	23	10	4	9	34	28	21	70
9	Macclesfield	46	9	3	11	30	29	11	5	7	34	28	7	68
10	Bromley	46	11	3	9	33	37	7	5	11	26	29	-7	62
11	Boreham Wood	46	8	7	8	23	21	7	6	10	26	27	1	58
12	Sutton	46	13	6	4	41	25	2	7	14	20	38	-2	58
13	Wrexham	46	10	5	8	23	24	5	8	10	24	37	-14	58
14	Maidstone	46	8	5	10	29	39	5	8	10	30	36	-16	58
15	Eastleigh	46	8	7	8	28	26	6	8	9	28	37	-7	57
16	Solihull	46	8	3	12	35	38	7	7	9	27	37	-13	55
17	Torquay	46	9	5	9	34	28	5	6	12	20	33	-7	53
18	Woking	46	9	7	7	32	30	5	4	14	34	50	14	53
19	Chester	46	8	3	12	37	35	6	7	10	26	36	-8	52
20	Guiseley	46	9	6	8	32	31	4	6	13	18	36	-17	51
21	York	46	7	8	8	33	31	4	9	10	22	39	-15	50
22	Braintree	46	6	4	13	23	36	7	5	11	28	40	-25	48
23	Southport	46	7	5	11	32	41	3	4	16	20	56	-45	39
24	North Ferriby	46	6	2	15	17	40	6	1	16	15	42	-50	39

*also promoted

Player of Year: Ricky Miller (Dover). **Manager of Year:** Danny Cowley (Lincoln).
Leading league scorers: 40 Miller (Dover); 25 Doidge (Forest Green); 19 Cheek (Braintree), Harrison (Barrow); 18 Hawkins (Dagenham), Johnson (Gateshead); 17 Alabi (Chester), Ugwu (Woking)
Team of Year: Farman (Lincoln), Vaughan (Tranmere), Raggett (Lincoln), McNulty (Tranmere), Habergham (Lincoln), Woodyard (Lincoln), Noble (Forest Green), Harris (Tranmere), Doidge (Forest Green, Miller (Dover), Whitely (Dagenham)

CHAMPIONS

1979–80	Altrincham	1993–94	Kidderminster	2007–08*	Aldershot
1980–81	Altrincham	1994–95	Macclesfield	2008–09*	Burton
1981–82	Runcorn	1995–96	Stevenage	2009–10*	Stevenage
1982–83	Enfield	1996–97*	Macclesfield	2010–11*	Crawley
1983–84	Maidstone	1997–98*	Halifax	2011–2012*	Fleetwood
1984–85	Wealdstone	1998–99*	Cheltenham	2012–13*	Mansfield
1985–86	Enfield	1999–2000*	Kidderminster	2013–14*	Luton
1986–87*	Scarborough	2000–01*	Rushden	2014–15*	Barnet
1987–88*	Lincoln	2001–02*	Boston	2015–16*	Cheltenham
1988–89*	Maidstone	2002–03*	Yeovil	2016–17*	Lincoln
1989–90*	Darlington	2003–04*	Chester	*Promoted to Football League	
1990–91*	Barnet	2004–05*	Barnet	Conference – Record	
1991–92*	Colchester	2005–06*	Accrington	attendance: 11,085 Bristol	
1992–93*	Wycombe	2006–07*	Dagenham	Rov v Alfreton, April 25, 2015	

VANARAMA NATIONAL LEAGUE RESULTS 2016-2017

(home \ away)	Aldershot	Barrow	Boreham Wood	Braintree	Bromley	Chester	Dagenham	Dover	Eastleigh	Forest Green	Gateshead	Guiseley	Lincoln	Macclesfield	Maidstone	N Ferriby	Solihull	Southport	Sutton	Torquay	Tranmere	Woking	Wrexham	York
York	0-0	2-0	1-1	1-1	3-0	1-0	1-0	2-2	1-1	2-1	6-1	6-1	1-1	1-3	1-1	0-1	1-2	2-0	2-2	2-0	1-0	1-0	2-1	–
Wrexham	2-0	2-0	0-1	0-1	1-1	4-3	3-0	1-1	1-1	3-0	2-2	2-3	0-0	1-0	2-1	1-3	2-1	0-1	1-1	3-1	0-1	1-1	–	2-1
Woking	4-0	2-1	2-1	1-3	2-1	3-2	0-1	4-2	2-1	1-0	1-1	0-3	1-3	0-3	2-4	1-2	0-3	4-1	1-0	3-1	3-1	–	1-1	1-0
Tranmere	3-1	2-1	0-2	0-2	1-4	0-1	1-4	2-3	1-1	0-1	0-1	4-2	1-1	2-3	0-1	1-1	2-3	0-0	1-1	3-0	–	3-1	3-2	1-0
Torquay	1-1	1-0	2-0	1-3	2-0	1-0	0-1	2-0	3-0	5-5	2-1	1-2	1-2	1-2	2-0	2-0	1-2	1-2	2-0	–	1-2	2-0	3-0	2-0
Sutton	2-0	0-0	2-2	1-0	1-0	1-0	2-0	4-0	1-0	2-2	3-1	1-1	2-1	0-0	3-0	1-1	3-0	1-1	–	2-3	0-0	3-2	1-1	2-2
Southport	2-1	0-0	3-0	3-1	3-1	3-1	1-0	2-1	4-3	3-0	3-0	5-1	1-1	1-2	3-0	4-0	4-2	–	4-0	1-0	0-3	0-0	1-0	2-0
Solihull	1-2	0-3	0-0	0-0	0-1	1-1	0-3	2-0	3-0	4-4	0-0	0-1	1-1	2-3	0-2	1-4	–	0-1	2-2	0-1	0-3	2-0	1-2	1-2
N Ferriby	2-0	0-2	1-1	1-1	0-2	3-0	0-1	0-6	1-1	2-3	2-0	0-1	0-1	0-1	1-2	–	1-4	2-4	0-2	2-1	0-1	0-3	0-1	0-1
Maidstone	2-0	4-1	1-1	2-0	0-2	3-2	2-0	2-1	2-3	2-0	3-0	2-1	0-3	0-2	–	3-0	1-4	4-2	2-2	1-0	0-1	3-2	1-3	1-0
Macclesfield	0-2	0-1	0-2	0-0	0-0	0-1	1-4	0-1	0-1	0-1	2-3	0-0	2-1	–	3-0	1-0	1-3	3-1	1-2	2-0	4-2	3-1	1-0	1-1
Lincoln	0-0	1-2	3-1	3-0	1-0	0-0	2-0	0-1	3-1	1-1	3-1	3-0	–	2-1	3-0	6-1	1-4	4-0	0-0	2-0	4-2	2-1	1-3	1-1
Guiseley	1-0	1-0	3-1	0-0	1-4	1-1	2-0	0-4	2-2	3-1	1-1	–	2-1	2-1	1-2	6-1	1-4	3-0	4-0	0-1	0-1	1-1	2-3	1-1
Gateshead	1-1	4-1	1-1	1-1	0-2	3-0	0-1	4-2	3-1	3-1	–	3-0	2-3	3-0	1-2	0-1	1-0	5-1	1-1	3-0	0-1	4-3	0-0	2-1
Forest Green	1-1	2-0	1-1	1-1	0-2	3-2	2-1	3-0	1-0	–	1-0	3-0	1-1	3-0	0-4	2-0	2-2	2-0	3-1	1-2	0-0	3-3	3-0	1-0
Eastleigh	1-2	3-1	0-2	2-1	3-1	0-1	2-4	3-0	–	1-1	3-1	1-2	2-0	2-1	2-4	3-0	0-0	0-1	2-3	3-0	0-2	2-1	0-1	1-4
Dover	1-0	3-1	2-1	0-3	3-2	5-0	2-0	–	4-0	4-3	2-4	2-5	1-1	1-1	3-0	0-6	1-4	3-0	1-3	2-1	2-3	1-3	3-0	2-2
Dagenham	3-1	0-2	2-1	0-4	1-3	3-0	–	2-0	3-0	1-2	2-0	1-1	1-1	2-2	3-2	0-1	0-3	3-0	2-5	4-0	1-4	1-0	3-0	1-0
Chester	2-0	1-4	0-2	0-1	0-1	–	3-0	5-0	0-5	1-5	3-2	2-5	2-3	2-3	1-3	3-0	0-3	3-1	0-1	0-1	0-3	2-1	3-1	3-0
Bromley	2-2	4-1	0-5	0-1	–	0-1	1-3	1-2	0-5	1-2	3-2	0-2	1-1	1-3	0-0	3-0	3-1	3-1	1-0	1-3	0-2	2-1	4-3	3-0
Braintree	2-0	4-1	1-2	–	2-2	0-1	3-2	1-2	0-5	0-1	0-0	0-4	0-4	2-4	0-0	0-0	1-4	0-3	2-0	1-3	0-2	2-1	2-0	1-1
Boreham Wood	0-1	1-1	–	0-1	2-2	1-1	1-1	2-0	1-1	2-2	1-1	4-1	2-0	2-4	0-1	3-0	0-3	2-1	0-0	2-0	2-1	2-1	0-1	1-1
Barrow	1-1	–	1-1	2-1	2-2	0-1	0-2	1-2	3-1	1-4	4-1	1-0	3-0	0-1	2-0	2-0	2-4	1-4	0-0	1-1	3-1	2-0	4-1	2-0
Aldershot	–	2-2	2-0	2-0	4-0	2-0	3-1	3-1	0-4	0-4	3-0	1-0	0-0	1-2	2-0	2-0	2-0	2-1	2-0	1-1	3-1	4-0	2-0	0-0

NATIONAL LEAGUE NORTH

	P	W	D	L	F	A	GD	Pts
Fylde	42	26	10	6	109	60	49	88
Kidderminster	42	25	7	10	76	41	35	82
Halifax*	42	24	8	10	81	43	38	80
Salford	42	22	11	9	79	44	35	77
Darlington	42	22	10	10	89	67	22	76
Chorley	42	20	14	8	60	41	19	74
Brackley	42	20	13	9	66	43	23	73
Stockport	42	19	16	7	59	41	18	73
Tamworth	42	21	6	15	73	67	6	69
Gloucester	42	18	10	14	69	61	8	64
Harrogate	42	16	11	15	71	63	8	59
Nuneaton	42	14	13	15	67	69	-2	55
FC United	42	14	12	16	69	68	1	54
Curzon Ashton	42	14	10	18	63	72	-9	52
Boston	42	12	11	19	54	72	-18	47
Bradford PA	42	12	7	23	46	74	-28	43
Telford	42	10	12	20	38	57	-19	42
Alfreton	42	11	9	22	62	95	-33	42
Gainsborough	42	8	12	22	51	84	-33	36
Worcester	42	7	14	21	44	63	-19	35
Stalybridge	42	8	5	29	40	89	-49	29
Altrincham	42	4	9	29	39	91	-52	21

*also promoted. Play-off Final: Halifax 2 Chorley – Darlington
ineligible for play-offs; replaced in semi-finals by Chorley

NATIONAL LEAGUE SOUTH

	P	W	D	L	F	A	GD	Pts
Maidenhead	42	30	8	4	93	29	64	98
Ebbsfleet*	42	29	9	4	96	30	66	96
Dartford	42	25	9	8	83	45	38	84
Chelmsford	42	23	13	6	89	47	42	82
Poole	42	20	11	11	63	49	14	71
Hungerford	42	19	13	10	67	49	18	70
Hampton	42	19	12	11	81	56	25	69
Wealdstone	42	18	12	12	62	58	4	66
Bath	42	18	8	16	71	52	19	62
St Albans	42	16	11	15	72	66	6	59
Eastbourne	42	16	10	16	82	70	12	58
Hemel Hempstead	42	15	12	15	74	83	-9	57
E Thurrock	42	14	14	14	73	65	8	56
Oxford City	42	15	7	20	48	73	-25	52
Weston SM	42	14	6	22	63	69	-6	48
Welling	42	12	7	23	64	69	-5	43
Whitehawk	42	12	7	23	51	72	-21	43
Concord	42	10	12	20	57	75	-18	42
Truro	42	11	7	24	53	99	-46	40
Gosport	42	9	9	24	45	101	-56	36
Bishop's Stortford	42	8	3	31	29	104	-75	27
Margate	42	7	4	31	26	81	-55	25

*also promoted. Play-off Final: Ebbsfleet 2 Chelmsford 1 –
Poole and Hungerford ineligible for play-offs; replaced in semi-finals by Hampton

OTHER LEAGUES 2016–17

DAFABET WELSH PREMIER LEAGUE

	P	W	D	L	F	A	GD	Pts
New Saints	32	28	1	3	101	26	75	85
Connah's Quay	32	16	10	6	45	24	21	58
Bala	32	16	9	7	61	46	15	57
Bangor	31	16	4	12	53	53	0	52
Carmarthen	32	10	9	13	40	46	-6	39
Cardiff MU	32	10	6	16	41	41	0	36
Newtown	32	12	9	11	59	41	18	45
Cefn Druids	32	9	12	11	40	48	-8	39
Llandudno	32	7	14	11	31	45	-14	35
Aberystwyth	32	10	4	18	41	63	-22	34
Rhyl	32	8	6	18	38	76	-38	30
Airbus	32	5	6	21	37	78	-41	21

League split after 22 games, with teams playing ten further games and remaining in top six and bottom six regardless of results. **Cup Final:** New Saints 4 Barry 0

RYMAN PREMIER LEAGUE

	P	W	D	L	F	A	GD	Pts
Havant	46	28	10	8	88	43	45	94
Bognor Regis*	46	27	11	8	87	41	46	92
Dulwich Hamlet	46	22	14	10	89	55	34	80
Enfield	46	21	13	12	86	57	29	76
Wingate & F	46	23	6	17	63	61	2	75
Tonbridge	46	21	11	14	66	55	11	74
Leiston	46	21	10	15	98	66	32	73
Billericay	46	21	9	16	77	56	21	72
Needham Mkt	46	20	12	14	76	80	-4	72
Harlow	46	20	7	19	76	72	4	67
Lowestoft	46	18	10	18	63	73	-10	64
Staines	46	16	13	17	78	68	10	61
Leatherhead **	46	16	12	18	72	72	0	57
Worthing	46	16	8	22	73	85	-12	56
Folkestone	46	15	10	21	75	82	-7	55
Kingstonian	46	16	7	23	65	73	-8	55
Met Police	46	15	9	22	54	72	-18	54
Hendon	46	14	12	20	68	88	-20	54
Burgess Hill	46	14	12	20	59	80	-21	54
Merstham	46	15	11	20	70	72	-2	53
Harrow	46	14	11	21	60	80	-20	53
Canvey Is	46	13	13	20	63	92	-29	52
Sudbury	46	12	10	24	57	85	-28	46
Grays	46	11	5	30	46	101	-55	38

*Also promoted. **3 pts deducted for ineligible player. **Play-off Final:** Bognor Regis 2 Dulwich Hamlet 1

EVOSTICK NORTH PREMIER LEAGUE

	P	W	D	L	F	A	GD	PTS
Blyth	46	31	8	7	114	44	70	101
Spennymoor*	46	25	12	9	96	48	48	87
Stourbridge	46	25	10	11	84	51	33	85
Workington	46	26	5	15	73	56	17	83
Nantwich	46	23	12	11	86	59	27	81
Whitby	46	23	10	13	64	56	8	79
Buxton	46	22	12	12	81	54	27	78
Grantham	46	22	10	14	74	57	17	76
Matlock	46	22	9	15	68	58	10	75
Warrington	46	22	8	16	65	57	8	74
Ashton	46	19	11	16	85	78	7	68
Rushall	46	18	10	18	60	60	0	64
Stafford	46	16	15	15	63	60	3	63
Barwell	46	16	14	16	58	53	5	62
Hednesford	46	18	7	21	68	65	3	61
Mickleover	46	19	3	24	68	71	-3	60
Coalville	46	15	10	21	71	79	-8	55
Marine	46	14	13	19	62	74	-12	55
Halesowen	46	13	12	21	46	70	-24	51
Sutton Coldfield	46	12	11	23	49	79	-30	47
Corby	46	12	10	24	49	72	-23	46
Frickley	46	12	3	31	47	97	-50	39
Ilkeston	46	7	6	33	31	86	-55	27
Skelmersdale	46	5	9	32	40	118	-78	24

*Also Promoted. **Play-off Final:** Spennymoor 1 Stourbridge 0

EVOSTICK SOUTH PREMIER LEAGUE

	P	W	D	L	F	A	GD	PTS
Chippenham	46	31	10	5	94	47	47	103
Leamington*	46	27	11	8	74	32	42	92
Merthyr	46	25	14	7	92	42	50	89
Hitchin	46	24	14	8	79	45	34	86
Slough	46	26	7	13	84	56	28	85
Banbury	46	24	8	14	67	40	27	80
Biggleswade	46	21	11	14	85	59	26	74
Frome	46	20	14	12	80	67	13	74
Kettering	46	21	10	15	84	66	18	73
Weymouth	46	16	18	12	79	58	21	66
Chesham	46	18	10	18	67	62	5	64
Basingstoke	46	18	8	20	65	72	-7	62
King's Lynn	46	14	18	14	60	69	-9	60
Stratford	46	13	17	16	64	66	2	56
St Ives	46	15	11	20	49	70	-21	56
Dunstable	46	16	6	24	46	65	-19	54
Redditch	46	13	11	22	54	75	-21	50
Dorchester	46	12	12	22	52	80	-28	48
St Neots	46	14	6	26	66	101	-35	48
Kings Langley	46	11	14	21	57	72	-15	47
Cambridge	46	12	11	23	46	72	-26	47
Cirencester	46	11	9	26	54	92	-38	42
Hayes	46	10	11	25	48	81	-33	41
Cinderford	46	8	3	35	49	106	-57	27

*Also promoted. **Play-off Final:** Leamington 2 Hitchin 1 (aet)

PRESS AND JOURNAL HIGHLAND LEAGUE

	P	W	D	L	F	A	GD	Pts
Buckie	34	26	4	4	130	36	94	82
Cove	34	25	7	2	109	30	79	82
Brora	34	26	3	5	116	36	80	81
Formartine	34	22	7	5	82	47	35	73
Fraserburgh	34	19	6	9	77	48	29	63
Forres	34	17	7	10	84	63	21	58
Turriff	34	18	4	12	56	42	14	58
Wick	34	15	8	11	75	52	23	53
Inverurie	34	14	8	12	71	53	18	50
Keith	34	15	2	17	74	88	-14	47
Clachnacuddin	34	11	8	15	53	77	-24	41
Lossiemouth	34	11	5	18	52	70	-18	38
Nairn	34	9	7	18	57	74	-17	34
Huntly	34	9	7	18	54	97	-43	34
Deveronvale	34	9	3	22	51	75	-24	30
Rothes	34	7	5	22	37	106	-69	26
Fort William	34	3	2	29	44	136	-92	11
Strathspey	34	2	3	29	28	120	-92	9

Cup Final: Cove 2 Formartine 1

FERRARI PACKAGING LOWLAND LEAGUE

	P	W	D	L	F	A	GD	Pts
East Kilbride	30	24	3	3	89	21	68	75
East Stirling	30	21	5	4	107	43	64	68
Spartans	30	17	5	8	69	30	39	56
Univ of Stirling	30	16	5	9	60	53	7	53
Dalbeattie	30	14	5	11	60	50	10	47
Cumbernauld	30	13	8	9	51	43	8	47
BSC	30	12	6	12	63	56	7	42
Whitehill	30	13	1	16	53	64	-11	37
Gretna	30	12	4	14	44	65	-21	40
Gala	30	11	7	12	55	77	-22	40
Edinburgh Univ	30	10	7	13	40	42	-2	37
Civil Service	30	10	7	13	59	68	-9	37
Vale of Leithen	30	11	4	15	52	66	-14	37
Hawick	30	8	1	21	58	93	-35	25
Selkirk	30	6	5	19	58	86	-28	23
Preston	30	5	1	24	41	102	-61	16

Cup Final: Spartans 3 BSC 0

PREMIER LEAGUE UNDER-23
DIVISION ONE

	P	W	D	L	F	A	GD	Pts
Everton	22	15	3	4	48	21	27	48
Manchester City	22	13	6	3	54	33	21	45
Liverpool	22	13	4	5	47	27	20	43
Arsenal	22	10	3	9	40	32	8	33
Chelsea	22	7	9	6	40	32	8	30
Manchester Utd	22	6	8	8	29	38	-9	26
Sunderland	22	6	7	9	27	37	-10	25
Derby	22	6	6	10	31	42	-11	24
Leicester	22	5	8	9	31	42	-11	23
Tottenham	22	6	4	12	33	44	-11	22
Reading	22	6	4	12	36	56	-20	22
Southampton	22	5	6	11	28	40	-12	21

DIVISION TWO

	P	W	D	L	F	A	GD	Pts
Swansea	22	17	1	4	43	22	21	52
Wolves	22	12	5	5	42	30	12	41
Newcastle	22	11	4	7	34	30	4	37
Fulham	22	10	3	9	39	33	6	33
West Ham*	22	9	6	7	32	26	6	33
Blackburn	22	9	5	8	24	28	-4	32
Aston Villa	22	8	6	8	34	32	2	30
Brighton	22	7	7	8	20	22	-2	28
WBA	22	6	4	12	25	33	-8	22
Middlesbrough	22	5	6	11	25	34	-9	21
Stoke	22	4	8	10	25	36	-11	20
Norwich	22	4	4	13	18	35	-17	17

* Also promoted **Play-off Final**: Newcastle 1 West Ham 2

FA WOMEN'S PREMIER LEAGUE
NORTH DIVISION

	P	W	D	L	F	A	GD	Pts
Blackburn	20	17	3	0	59	20	39	54
Middlesbrough	20	14	1	5	60	31	29	43
Leicester	20	10	4	6	44	37	7	34
Stoke	20	8	6	6	43	37	6	30
Derby	20	9	2	9	39	35	4	29
WBA	20	8	3	9	33	37	-4	27
Fylde*	20	8	5	7	36	30	6	26
Bradford	20	7	1	12	40	40	0	22
Huddersfield	20	5	5	10	37	53	-16	20
Nottm Forest	20	5	3	12	27	49	-22	18
Newcastle	20	2	1	17	16	65	-49	7

*Deducted 3 points for ineligible player

SOUTH DIVISION

	P	W	D	L	F	A	GD	Pts
Tottenham	20	17	1	2	58	13	45	52
Coventry	20	15	3	2	55	15	40	48
Cardiff	20	14	2	4	72	19	53	44
Charlton	20	13	3	4	55	25	30	42
Crystal Palace	20	9	6	5	48	23	25	33
Basildon	20	8	3	9	29	42	-13	27
Lewes	20	7	4	9	31	36	-5	25
Portsmouth	20	5	2	13	31	66	-35	17
West Ham	20	1	6	13	12	59	-47	9
Swindon	20	2	2	16	20	60	-40	8
QPR	20	2	2	16	11	64	-53	8

Play-off Final: Tottenham 3 Blackburn 0. **Cup Final**: Tottenham 0 Charlton 0 (aet, Tottenham won 4-3 on pens)

FA WOMEN'S SUPER LEAGUE 2016

	P	W	D	L	F	A	GD	Pts
Manchester City	16	13	3	0	36	4	32	42
Chelsea	16	12	1	3	42	17	25	37
Arsenal	16	10	2	4	33	14	19	32
Birmingham	16	7	6	3	18	13	5	27
Liverpool	16	7	4	5	27	23	4	25
Notts Co	16	4	4	8	16	26	-10	16
Sunderland	16	2	4	10	17	41	-24	10
Reading	16	1	6	9	15	26	-11	9
Doncaster	16	1	0	15	8	48	-40	3

Continental Cup Final: Manchester City 1 Birmingham 0 (aet)

WORLD RECORD FOR NEW SAINTS

Welsh Premier League champions New Saints broke a 44-year-old world record last season for the longest winning run in top-flight football. A 2-0 victory over Cefn Druids was their 27th in a row in all competitions – one more than Johan Cruyff's Ajax in 1972. Saints won 21 league games, four in two Welsh cups and two in the Scottish Challenge Cup, in which they were invited to play. The sequence ended in their next match when held to a 3-3 draw by Newtown after conceding a stoppage-time equaliser. The Scottish fifth-tier team East Kilbride thought they had broken the record last season, but the official mark can be set only by clubs playing in their country's top division. Saints, previously known as Total Network Solutions before a merger with Oswestry Town, have been champions for six successive years. In last season's Champions League qualifying, they beat Tre Penne from San Marino in the first round, then lost to Apoel Nicosia (Cyprus). In 2005, Saints were beaten 6-0 on aggregate in first qualifying by Liverpool, with Steven Gerrard scoring five of the goals over the two legs.

IRISH FOOTBALL 2016–17

SSE AIRTRICITY LEAGUE OF IRELAND

PREMIER DIVISION

	P	W	D	L	F	A	Pts
Dundalk	33	25	2	6	73	28	77
Cork City	33	21	7	5	65	23	70
Derry City	33	17	11	5	48	29	62
Shamrock Rov	33	16	7	10	46	34	55
Sligo Rov	33	13	10	10	42	35	49
Bray Wdrs	33	13	7	13	39	40	46
St Patrick's Ath	33	13	6	14	45	41	45
Bohemians	33	12	5	16	30	37	41
Galway Utd	33	10	8	15	44	54	38
Finn Harps	33	8	8	17	23	49	32
Wexford Youths	33	6	5	22	31	70	23
Longford Town	33	2	8	23	25	71	14

Leading scorer: 18 Sean Maguire (Cork City). **Player of Year**: Daryl Horgan (Dundalk). **Young Player of Year**: Sean Maguire. **Goalkeeper of Year**: Mark McNulty (Cork City). **Personality of Year**: Stephen Kenny (Dundalk)

FIRST DIVISION

	P	W	D	L	F	A	Pts
Limerick	28	24	3	1	96	26	75
Drogheda Utd	28	15	7	6	42	29	52
Cobh Ramblers	28	15	5	8	40	33	50
UCD	28	14	6	8	57	40	48
Waterford Utd	28	10	3	15	43	65	33
Shelbourne	28	9	3	16	36	42	30
Cabinteely	28	4	4	20	19	54	16
Athlone Town	28	3	5	20	26	62	14

Leading scorer: 13 Gary O'Neill (UCD). **Player of Year**: Shane Duggan (Limerick)

DAILY MAIL CUP FINAL

Cork City 1 (Maguire) **Dundalk** 0. Aviva Stadium, November 6, 2016
Cork City: McNulty, Bennett, Bolger (O'Sullivan), Beattie, Dooley, O'Connor, Morrissey (Healy), Sheppard, Browne, Maguire, Buckley
Dundalk: Rogers, Gannon, Gartland, Boyle, Shields (Mountney), O'Donnell, Horgan, McMillan (Kilduff), Finn, McEleney (Shields), Massey
Referee: R Rogers (Dublin)

EA SPORTS LEAGUE CUP FINAL

Limerick 1 (Lynch) **St Patricks Ath** 4 (Fagan, Byrne, McGrath, Kelly). Markets Field, Limerick, September 17, 2016

NORTHERN IRELAND

DANSKE BANK PREMIERSHIP

	P	W	D	L	F	A	Pts
Linfield	38	27	8	3	87	24	89
Crusaders	38	27	6	5	83	36	87
Coleraine	38	18	11	9	56	42	65
Ballymena Utd	38	18	5	15	75	73	59
Cliftonville	38	17	7	14	55	50	58
Glenavon	38	13	13	12	55	55	52
Dungannon Swifts	38	14	10	14	67	59	52
Ards	38	13	8	17	61	70	47
Glentoran	38	12	10	16	45	53	46
Ballinamallard Utd	38	10	5	23	45	72	35
Carrick Rgrs	38	5	7	26	31	79	22
Portadown*	38	7	4	27	28	75	13

*12 pts deducted for irregular payments

Leading scorer: 25 Andrew Mitchell (Dungannon Swifts). **Manager of Year**: David Healey (Linfield). **Player of Year**: Jamie Mulgrew (Linfield). **Young Player of Year**: Paul Smyth (Linfield). **Goalkeeper of Year**: Roy Carroll (Linfield)

BELFAST TELEGRAPH CHAMPIONSHIP – DIVISION ONE

	P	W	D	L	F	A	Pts
Warrenpoint Town	32	22	6	4	78	35	72
Institute	32	16	9	7	64	39	57
Ballyclare Comrades	32	15	6	11	64	56	51
PSNI	32	13	10	9	49	44	49
Dergview	32	12	6	14	67	55	42
Loughall	32	12	3	17	54	59	39
H&W Welders	32	15	6	11	52	41	51
Knockbreda	32	14	4	14	56	52	46
Larne	32	11	7	14	52	51	40
Lurgan Celtic	32	12	3	17	56	71	39
Armagh City	32	9	7	16	41	55	34
Annagh Utd	32	4	7	21	32	107	19

Leading scorer: 25 Stephen Murray (Warrenpoint Town). **Player of Year**: John McGuigan (Warrenpoint Town)

TENNENT'S IRISH CUP FINAL

Linfield 3 (Waterworth 3) **Coleraine** 0. Windsor Park, May 6 2017

Linfield: Carroll, Haughey, Stafford, Callagher, Clarke, Smyth (Casement), Mulgrew, Lowry, Quinn, Burns (Stewart), Waterworth

Coleraine: Johns, Kane, Ogilby, McConaghie, Mullan, McGonigle (Allan), Lyons, Harkin, McCauley, Bradley, McLaughlin (Parkhill)

Referee: K Kennedy (Lisburn)

LEAGUE CUP FINAL

Ballymena Utd 2 (Jenkins, McCloskey) **Carrick Rgrs** 0. Seaview, Belfast, February 18, 2017

COUNTY ANTRIM SHIELD FINAL

Linfield 3 (Stewart, Stafford, Lowry) **Crusaders** 1 (Owens). Showgrounds, Ballymena, February 7, 2017

UEFA CHAMPIONS LEAGUE 2016–17

FIRST QUALIFYING ROUND, FIRST LEG

New Saints 2 (Quigley 13, Mullan 40) Tre Penne 1 (Fraternali 16). Att: 712

FIRST QUALIFYING ROUND, SECOND LEG

Tre Penne 0 New Saints 3 (Quigley 45, Edwards 47, Draper 90). Att: 743 (New Saints won 5-1 on agg)

FIRST QUALIFYING ROUND, ON AGGREGATE

Alashkert 3 Santa Coloma 0; Lincoln Red Imps 3 Flora Tallinn 2; Valletta 2 Torshavn 2 (Valletta won on away goals)

SECOND QUALIFYING ROUND, FIRST LEG

Crusaders 0 Copenhagen 3 (Santander 6, Cornelius 40, Jensen 53). Att: 2,069. Dundalk 1 (McMillan 66) Hafnarfjardar 1 (Lennon 77). Att: 3,111. Lincoln Red Imps 1 (Casciaro 48) Celtic 0. Att: 1,632. New Saints 0 Apoel Nicosia 0. Att: 1,056

SECOND QUALIFYING ROUND, SECOND LEG

Apoel Nicosia 3 (Alexandrou 54, Sotoriou 73, De Vincenti 90 pen) New Saints 0. Att: 10,548 (Apoel Nicosia won 3-0 on agg). Celtic 3 (Lustig 23, Griffiths 26, Roberts 29) Lincoln Red Imps 0. Att: 55,632 (Celtic won 3-1 on agg). Copenhagen 6 (Pavlovic 16, Mitchell 45 og, Cornelius 49, 77, Jensen 59, Gregus 69) Crusaders 0. Att: 6,924 (Copenhagen won 9-0 on agg). Hafnarfjardar 2 (Hewson 18, Finnhogason 77) Dundalk 2 (McMillan 52, 62). Att: 1,850 (Agg 3-3, Dundalk won on away goals)

SECOND QUALIFYING ROUND, ON AGGREGATE

Astana 2 Zalgiris 0; Bate Borisov 4 SJK 2; Crvena Zvezda 4 Valletta 2; Dinamo Zagreb 5 Vardar 3; Dukla Trencin 6 Olimpija Ljubljana 2 (Dukla Trencin won on away goals); Dynamo Tbilisi 3 Alashkert 1; Hapoel Beer Sheva 3 Sheriff Tiraspol 1; Legia Warsaw 3 Zrinjski Mostar 1; Ludogorets 5 Mladost Podgorica 0; Partizani Tirana 2 Ferencvaros 2 (aet, Partizani Tirana won 3-1 on pens); Qarabag 3 Dudelange 1, Rosenborg 5 Norrkoping 4; Salzburg 3 Liepaja 0

THIRD QUALIFYING ROUND, FIRST LEG

Bate Borisov 1 (Gordeychuk 70) Dundalk 0. Att: 11,321. Astana 1 (Logvinenko 19) Celtic 1 (Griffiths 78). Att: 29,000

THIRD QUALIFYING ROUND, SECOND LEG

Celtic 2 (Griffiths 45 pen, Dembele 90 pen) Astana 1 (Ibraimi 62). Att: 52,952. (Celtic won 3-2 on agg). Dundalk 3 (McMillan 45, 60, Benson 90) Bate Borisov 0. Att: 4,645. (Dundalk won 3-1 on agg)

THIRD QUALIFYING ROUND, ON AGGREGATE

Ajax 3 PAOK Salonika 2; Apoel Nicosia 4 Rosenborg 2; Copenhagen 4 Astra Giurgiu 1; Dinamo Zagreb 3 Dynamo Tbilisi 0; Hapoel Beer Sheva 1 Olympiacos 0; Legia Warsaw 1 Dukla Trencin 0; Ludogorets 6 Crvena Zvezda 4; Monaco 4 Fenerbahce 3; Rostov 4 Anderlecht 2; Salzburg 3 Partizani Tirana 0; Steaua Bucharest 3 Sparta Prague 1; Viktoria Plzen 1 Qarabag 1 (Viktoria Plzen won on away goal); Young Boys 2 Shakhtar Donetsk 2 (aet, Young Boys won 4-2 on pens)

PLAY-OFFS, FIRST LEG

Celtic 5 (Rogic 9, Griffiths 40, 45, Dembele 73, Brown 85) Hapoel Beer Sheva 2 (Maranhao

55, Melikson 57). Att: 52,659. **Dundalk** 0 Legia Warsaw 2 (Nikolic 56 pen, Prijovic 90). Att: 30,417 (Aviva Stadium. Dublin). Steaua Bucharest 0 **Manchester City** 5 (Silva 13, Aguero 41, 78, 89, Nolito 49). Att: 45,327

PLAY-OFF, SECOND LEG

Hapoel Beer Sheva 2 (Sahar 21, Hoban 48) **Celtic** 0. Att: 15,383 (Celtic won 5-4 on agg). Legia Warsaw 1 (Kucharczyk 90) **Dundalk** 1 (Benson 19). Att: 29,066 (Legia Warsaw won 3-1 on agg). **Manchester City** 1 (Delph 56) Steaua Bucharest 0. Att: 40,064 (Manchester City won 6-0 on agg)

PLAY-OFFS, ON AGGREGATE

Borussia Monchengladbach 9 Young Boys 2; Copenhagen 2 Apoel Nicosia 1; Dinamo Zagreb 3 Salzburg 2 (aet); Ludogorets 4 Viktoria Plzen 2; Monaco 3 Villarreal 1; Porto 4 Roma 1; Rostov 5 Ajax 2

GROUP A

September 13, 2016
Basle 1 (Steffen 80) **Ludogorets** 1 (Cafu 45). Att: 30,852
Paris SG 1 (Cavani 1) **Arsenal** 1 (Sanchez 78). Att: 46,440
Arsenal (4-2-3-1): Ospina, Bellerin, Mustafi, Koscielny, Monreal, Coquelin (Xhaka 71), Cazorla, Iwobi, Ozil (Elneny 85), Oxlade-Chamberlain (Giroud 63), Sanchez. **Booked**: Coquelin
Sent off: Giroud (90)

September 28, 2016
Arsenal 2 (Walcott 7, 26) **Basle** 0. Att: 59,993
Arsenal (4-2-3-1): Ospina, Bellerin, Mustafi, Koscielny, Monreal (Gibbs 75), Cazorla, Xhaka, Walcott (Oxlade-Chamberlain 70), Ozil, Iwobi (Elneny 70), Sanchez
Ludogorets 1 (Natanael 16) **Paris SG** 3 (Matuidi 41, Cavani 56, 60). Att: 17,155

October 19, 2016
Arsenal 6 (Sanchez 12, Walcott 42, Oxlade-Chamberlin 46, Ozil 56, 83, 87) **Ludogorets** 0. Att: 59,944
Arsenal (4-2-3-1): Ospina, Bellerin, Mustafi, Koscielny, Gibbs, Cazorla (Elneny 57), Coquelin, Walcott (Perez 62), Ozil, Oxlade-Chamberlain, Sanchez (Iwobi 73)
Paris SG 3 (Di Maria 40, Lucas Moura 62, Cavani 90 pen) **Basle** 0. Att: 46,488

November 1, 2016
Basle 1 (Zuffi 76) **Paris SG** 2 (Matuidi 44, Meunier 90). Att: 34,639
Ludogorets 2 (Cafu 12, Keseru 15) **Arsenal** 3 (Xhaka 20, Giroud 41, Ozil 87). Att: 30,862
Arsenal (4-2-3-1): Ospina, Jenkinson, Mustafi, Koscielny, Gibbs, Coquelin, Xhaka (Elneny 87), Ramsey (Oxlade-Chamberlain 75), Ozil, Sanchez (Iwobi 90), Giroud. **Booked**: Coquelin, Xhaka, Jenkinson

November 23, 2016
Arsenal 2 (Giroud 45 pen, Verratti 60 og) **Paris SG** 2 (Cavani 18, Lucas Moura 77). Att: 59,628
Arsenal (4-2-3-1): Ospina, Jenkinson (Oxlade-Chamberlain 81), Mustafi, Koscielny, Gibbs, Coquelin (Walcott 80), Ramsey, Sanchez, Ozil, Iwobi (Xhaka 78), Giroud. **Booked**: Coquelin, Koscielny
Ludogorets 0 **Basle** 0. Att: 20,821

December 6, 2016
Basle 1 (Doumbia 78) **Arsenal** 4 (Lucas Perez 8, 16, 47, Iwobi 53). Att: 36,000
Arsenal (4-2-3-1): Ospina, Gabriel, Holding, Koscielny, Gibbs, Xhaka, Ramsey (Giroud 70), Lucas Perez, Ozil (Walcot 74), Iwobi, Sanchez (Elneny 70). **Booked**: Gibbs
Paris SG 2 (Cavani 61, Di Maria 90) **Ludogorets** 2 (Misidjan 15, Wanderson 69). Att: 42,650

	P	W	D	L	F	A	Pts
Arsenal Q	6	4	2	0	18	6	14
Paris SG Q	6	3	3	0	13	7	12
Ludogorets	6	0	3	3	6	15	3
Basle	6	0	2	4	3	12	2

GROUP B

September 13, 2016
Benfica 1 (Cervi 12) **Besiktas** 1 (Anderson Talisca 90). Att: 42,126
Dynamo Kiev 1 (Harmash 26) **Napoli** 2 (Milik 36, 45). Att: 35,137

September 28, 2016
Besiktas 1 (Quaresma 29) **Dynamo Kiev** 1 (Tsyhankov 65). Att: 33, 938
Napoli 4 (Hamsik 20, Mertens 51, 58, Milik 54 pen) **Benfica** 2 (Goncalo Guedes 70, Salvio 86). Att: 41, 281

October 19, 2016
Dynamo Kiev 0 **Benfica** 2 (Salvio 9 pen, Cervi 55). Att: 25,991
Napoli 2 (Mertens 30, Gabbiadini 69 pen) **Besiktas** 3 (Adriano 13, Aboubakar 38, 86). Att: 28,502

November 1, 2016
Benfica 1 (Salvio 45 pen) **Dynamo Kiev** 0. Att: 51,641
Besiktas 1 (Quaresma 79 pen) **Napoli** 1 (Hamsik 82). Att: 35,552

November 23, 2016
Besiktas 3 (Tosun 58, Quaresma 83 pen, Aboubakar 89) **Benfica** 3 (Goncalo Guedes 10, Nelson Semedo 25, Fejsa 32). Att: 36,063
Napoli 0 **Dynamo Kiev** 0. Att: 33,736

December 6, 2016
Benfica 1 (Jimenez 87) **Napoli** 2 (Callejon 60, Mertens 79). Att: 55,634
Dynamo Kiev 6 (Besyedin 9, Yarmolenko 31 pen, Buyalsky 33, Gonzalez 45, Sydorchuk 60, Junior Moraes 77) **Besiktas** 0. Att: 14,036

	P	W	D	L	F	A	Pts
Napoli Q	6	3	2	1	11	8	11
Benfica Q	6	2	2	2	10	10	8
Besiktas	6	1	4	1	9	14	7
Dynamo Kiev	6	1	2	3	8	6	5

GROUP C

September 13, 2016
Barcelona 7 (Messi 4, 28, 61, Neymar 50, Iniesta 59, Suarez 76, 89) **Celtic** 0. Att: 73,290
Celtic (5-4-1): De Vries, Gamboa, Lustig, Toure, Sviatchenko (O'Connell 68), Tierney, Roberts (Armstrong 68), Brown, Bitton (McGregor 76), Sinclair, Dembele. **Booked**: Brown

September 14, 2016
Manchester City 4 (Aguero 8, 28 pen, 77, Iheanacho 90) **Borussia Monchengladbach** 0. Att: 30,270
Manchester City (4-2-3-1): Bravo, Zabaleta, Otamendi, Stones, Kolarov, Gundogan (Clichy 81), Fernandinho, Jesus Navas, De Bruyne, Sterling (Sane 79), Aguero (Iheanacho 83). **Booked**: Otamendi

September 28, 2016
Borussia Monchengladbach 1 (Hazard 34) **Barcelona** 2 (Turan 65, Pique 74). Att: 46,283
Celtic 3 (Dembele 3, 47, Sterling 20 og) **Manchester City** 3 (Fernandinho 11, Sterling 28, Nolito 55). Att: 57,814

Celtic (4-2-3-1): Gordon, Lustig, Sviatchenko, Toure, Tierney, Brown, Bitton (Griffiths 84), Forrest (Roberts 81), Rogic (Armstrong 57), Sinclair, Dembele
Manchester City (4-1-4-1): Bravo, Zabaleta, Otamendi, Kolarov, Clichy (Stones 73), Fernandinho, Sterling, Gundogan, Silva, Nolito (Fernando 76), Aguero

October 19, 2016
Barcelona 4 (Messi 17, 61, 69, Neymar 89) **Manchester City** 0. Att: 96,290
Manchester City (4-2-3-1): Bravo, Zabaleta (Clichy 57), Otamendi, Stones, Kolarov, Gundogan (Aguero 79), Fernandinho, Sterling, Silva, Nolito (Caballero 57), De Bruyne. **Booked**: Silva, Fernandinho, Sterling. **Sent off**: Bravo (53)
Celtic 0 **Borussia Monchengladbach** 2 (Stindl 57, Hahn 77). Att: 57,814
Celtic (4-2-3-1): Gordon, Lustig, Sviatchenko, Toure, Tierney, Brown, Bitton (McGregor 63), Forrest (Roberts 73), Rogic (Griffiths 72), Sinclair, Dembele. **Booked**: Tierney

November 1, 2016
Borussia Monchengladbach 1 (Stindl 32) **Celtic** 1 (Dembele 76 pen). Att: 46,283
Celtic (4-2-3-1): Gordon, Gamboa (Henderson 85), Lustig, Sviatchenko, Izaguirre, Brown, Armstrong, Forrest (Roberts 60), Rogic (McGregor 69), Sinclair, Dembele. **Booked**: Izaguirre
Manchester City 3 (Gundogan 39, 74, De Bruyne 51) **Barcelona** 1 (Messi 21). Att: 53,340
Manchester City (4-2-3-1): Caballero, Zabaleta, Otamendi, Stones, Kolarov, Gundogan, Fernandinho (Fernando 60), Sterling (Jesus Navas 71), Silva, De Bruyne (Nolito 89), Aguero.
Booked: Sterling, Kolarov

November 23, 2016
Borussia Monchengladbach 1 (Raffael 23) **Manchester City** 1 (Silva 45). Att: 45, 921
Manchester City (3-2-4-1): Bravo, Stones, Otamendi, Kolarov, Gundogan, Fernandinho, Jesus Navas, De Bruyne, Silva, Sterling (Sagna 68), Aguero. **Booked**: Fernandinho. **Sent off**: Fernandinho ((63)
Celtic 0 **Barcelona** 2 (Messi 24, 56 pen). Att: 57,937
Celtic (4-2-3-1): Gordon, Lustig, Simunovic, Sviatchenko, Izaguirre, Brown, Armstrong, McGregor (Roberts 72), Rogic (Bitton 64), Sinclair (Forrest 46), Dembele. **Booked**: Sviatchenko, Armstrong, Lustig

December 6, 2016
Barcelona 4 (Messi 16, Turabn 50, 53, 67) **Borussia Monchengladbach** 0. Att: 67,157
Manchester City 1 (Iheanacho 8) **Celtic** 1 (Roberts 4). Att: 51,297
Manchester City (3-5-2): Caballero, Sagna, Adarabioyo, Clichy, Maffeo (Jesus Navas 62) Zabaleta, Fernando, Gundogan, Sane, Nolito, Iheanacho. **Booked**: Gundogan
Celtic (4-1-4-1): Gordon, Lustig, Simunovic, Sviatchenko, Izaguirre, Brown, Roberts, Armstrong, Rogic, Forrest (Mackay-Steven 51). Dembele (Griffiths 73). **Booked**: Lustig, Brown

	P	W	D	L	F	A	Pts
Barcelona Q	6	5	0	1	20	4	15
Manchester City Q	6	2	3	1	12	10	9
Borussia M'gladbach	6	1	2	3	5	12	5
Celtic	6	0	3	3	5	16	3

GROUP D

September 13, 2016
Bayern Munich 5 (Lewandowski 28 pen, Muller 45, Kimmich 54, 61, Bernat 90) **Rostov** 0. Att: 70,000
PSV Eindhoven 0 **Atletico Madrid** 1 (Saul 43). Att: 33,989

September 28, 2016
Atletico Madrid 1 (Carrasco 35) **Bayern Munich** 0. Att: 48,242
Rostov 2 (Poloz 8, 37) **PSV Eindhoven** 2 (Propper 14, De Jong 45). Att: 12,646

October 19, 2016
Bayern Munich 4 (Muller 13, Kimmich 21, Lewandowski 60, Robben 84) **PSV Eindhoven** 0.
Att: 70,000
Rostov 0 **Atletico Madrid** 1 (Carrasco 62). Att: 15,400

November 1, 2016
Atletico Madrid 2 (Griezmann 28, 90) **Rostov** 1 (Azmoun 30). Att: 40,392
PSV Eindhoven 1 (Arias 16) **Bayern Munich** 2 (Lewandowski 34 pen, 74). Att: 34,700

November 23, 2016
Atletico Madrid 2 (Gameiro 55, Griezmann 66) **PSV Eindhoven** 0. Att: 37,891
Rostov 3 (Azmoun 44, Poloz 50 pen, Noboa 67) **Bayern Munich** 2 (Douglas Costa 35, Bernat 52). Att: 15,211

December 6, 2016
Bayern Munich 1 (Lewandowski 28) **Atletico Madrid** 0. Att: 70,000
PSV Eindhoven 0 **Rostov** 0. Att: 33,400

		P	W	D	L	F	A	Pts
Atletico Madrid	Q	6	5	0	1	7	2	15
Bayern Munich	Q	6	4	0	2	14	6	12
Rostov		6	1	2	3	6	12	5
PSV Eindhoven		6	0	2	4	4	11	2

GROUP E

September 14, 2016
Bayer Leverkusen 2 (Mehmedi 9, Calhanoglu 15) **CSKA Moscow** 2 (Dzagoev 36, Eremenko 38). Att: 23,459
Tottenham 1 (Alderweireld 45) **Monaco** 2 (Bernardo Silva 15, Lemar 31). Played at Wembley. Att: 85,011 (English record)
Tottenham (4-2-3-1): Lloris, Walker, Alderweireld, Vertonghen, Davies, Dier (Sissoko 81), Alli, Son Heung-min (Dembele 45), Eriksen, Lamela (Janssen 71), Kane. **Booked**: Kane

September 27, 2016
CSKA Moscow 0 **Tottenham** 1 (Son Heung-min 71). Att: 26,153
Tottenham (4-1-4-1): Lloris, Trippier, Alderweireld, Vertonghen, Davies, Wanyama, Lamela, Eriksen, Alli (Winks 82), Son Heung-min, Janssen (N'Koudou 67). **Booked**: Wanyama
Monaco 1 (Glik 90) **Bayer Leverkusen** 1 (Hernandez 73). Att: 8,100

October 18, 2016
Bayer Leverkusen 0 **Tottenham** 0. Att: 28,887
Tottenham (4-2-3-1): Lloris, Trippier, Dier, Vertonghen, Rose, Alli, Wanyama, Lamela (Sissoko 71), Eriksen, Son Heung-min (Onomah 90), Janssen (Dembele 64). **Booked**: Lamela
CSKA Moscow 1 (Traore 34) **Monaco** 1 (Bernardo Silva 87). Att: 24,125

November 2, 2016
Monaco 3 (Germain 12, Falcao 29, 41) **CSKA Moscow** 0. Att: 10,029
Tottenham 0 **Bayer Leverkusen** 1 (Kampl 65). Played at Wembley. Att: 85,512 (English record)
Tottenham (4-2-3-1): Lloris, Walker, Dier, Vertonghen, Davies, Wanyama, Dembele (Janssen 30), Sissoko, Alli, Eriksen (Winks 66), Son-Heung-min (Nkoudou 73)

November 22, 2016
CSKA Moscow 1 (Natcho 76 pen) **Bayer Leverkusen** 1 (Volland 16). Att: 19,164
Monaco 2 (Sidibe 49, Lemar 53) **Tottenham** 1 (Kane 52 pen). Att: 13,100
Tottenham (4-2-3-1): Lloris, Trippier, Dier, Wimmer, Rose, Wanyama, Dembele (Eriksen 65), Alli, Winks (Sissoko 74), Son Heung-min (Janssen 65), Kane. **Booked**: Dier, Dembele, Trippier

December 7, 2016
Bayer Leverkusen 3 (Yurchenko 30, Brandt 48, De Sanctis 82 og) **Monaco** 0. Att: 21,928
Tottenham 3 (Alli 38, Kane 45, Akinfeev 77 og) **CSKA Moscow** 1 (Dzagoev 33). Played at Wembley. Att: 62, 034
Tottenham (4-2-3-1): Lloris, Walker, Dier, Vertonghen, Rose, Wanyama (Alderweireld 68), Winks, Son Heung-min (Nkoudou 62), Alli, Eriksen, Kane (Onomah 82)

	P	W	D	L	F	A	Pts
Monaco Q	6	3	2	1	9	7	11
Bayer Leverkusen Q	6	2	4	0	8	4	10
Tottenham	6	2	1	3	6	6	7
CSKA Moscow	6	0	3	3	5	11	3

GROUP F

September 14, 2016
Legia Warsaw 0 **Borussia Dortmund** 6 (Gotze 7, Papastathopoulos 16, Bartra 51, Guerreiro 51, Castro 76, Aubameyang 87). Att: 27,304
Real Madrid 2 (Ronaldo 89, Alvaro Morata 90) **Sporting Lisbon** 1 (Bruno Cesar 47). Att: 72,179

September 27, 2016
Borussia Dortmund 2 (Aubameyang 43, Schurrle 87) **Real Madrid** 2 (Ronaldo 17, Varane 68). Att: 65,849
Sporting Lisbon 2 (Ruiz 28, Dost 37) **Legia Warsaw** 0. Att: 40,094

October 18, 2016
Real Madrid 5 (Bale 16, Jodlowiec 20 og, Marco 37, Lucas 68, Alvaro Morata 84) **Legia Warsaw** 1 (Radovic 22 pen). Att: 70,251
Sporting Lisbon 1 (Bruno Cesar 67) **Borussia Dortmund** 2 (Aubameyang 9, Weigl 43). Att: 46,609

November 2, 2016
Borussia Dortmund 1 (Ramos 12) **Sporting Lisbon** 0. Att: 65,849
Legia Warsaw 3 (Odjidja-Ofoe 40, Radovic 58, Moulin 83) **Real Madrid** 3 (Bale 1, Benzema 35, Kovacic 85). Player behind closed doors – previous crowd trouble

November 22, 2016
Borussia Dortmund 8 (Kagawa 17, 18, Sahin 20, Dembele 29, Reus 32, 52, 90, Passlack 81) **Legia Warsaw** 4 (Prijovic 10, 24, Kucharczyk 57, Nikolic 83). Att: 55,094 (record Champions League aggregate score)
Sporting Lisbon 1 (Adrien Silva 81 pen) **Real Madrid** 2 (Varane 29, Benzema 87). Att: 50,046

December 7, 2016
Legia Warsaw 1 (Guilherme 30) **Sporting Lisbon** 0. Att: 28,232
Real Madrid 2 (Benzema 28, 53) **Borussia Dortmund** 2 (Aubameyang 60, Reus 88). Att: 76,894

	P	W	D	L	F	A	Pts
Borussia Dortmund Q	6	4	2	0	21	9	14
Real Madrid Q	6	3	3	0	16	10	12
Legia Warsaw	6	1	1	4	9	24	4
Sporting Lisbon	6	1	0	5	5	8	3

GROUP G

September 14, 2016
Club Bruges 0 **Leicester** 3 (Albrighton 5, Mahrez 29, 61 pen). Att: 20,970
Leicester (4-4-2): Schmeichel, Hernandez, Morgan, Huth, Fuchs, Albrighton, Drinkwater, Amartey, Mahrez (Gray 81), Slimani (Ulloa 63), Vardy (Musa 70). **Booked**: Slimani, Ulloa
Porto 1 (Otavio 13) **Copenhagen** 1 (Cornelius 52). Att: 34,325

September 27, 2016
Copenhagen 4 (Denswil 54 og, Delaney 64, Santander 69, Jorgensen 90) **Club Bruges** 0. Att: 25,605
Leicester 1 (Slimani 25) **Porto** 0. Att: 31,805
Leicester (4-4-2): Schmeichel, Hernandez, Morgan, Huth, Fuchs, Mahrez (Gray 88), Drinkwater, Amartey, Albrighton, Slimani (King 82), Vardy (Musa 90). **Booked**: Vardy, Slimani, Huth

October 18, 2016
Club Bruges 1 (Vossen 12) **Porto** 2 (Layun 68, Andre Silva 90 pen). Att: 23,325
Leicester 1 (Mahrez 41) **Copenhagen** 0. Att: 31,037
Leicester (4-4-2): Schmeichel, Simpson, Morgan, Huth, Fuchs, Mahrez (Amartey 90), King, Drinkwater, Albrighton, Slimani (Ulloa 88), Vardy (Okazaki 85). **Booked**: Fuchs

November 2, 2016
Copenhagen 0 **Leicester** 0. Att: 34,146
Leicester (3-4-3): Schmeichel, Morgan, Huth, Fuchs, Hernandez, Amartey, Drinkwater, Schlupp (Okazaki 71), Mahrez, Vardy, Musa. **Booked**: Drinkwater, Huth, Hernandez, Morgan
Porto 1 (Andre Silva 37) **Club Bruges** 0. Att: 32,210

November 22, 2016
Copenhagen 0 **Porto** 0. Att: 32,036
Leicester 2 (Okazaki 5, Mahrez 30 pen) **Club Bruges** 1 (Izquierdo 52). Att: 31,443
Leicester (4-4-2): Zieler, Simpson, Morgan, Huth, Fuchs, Mahrez (Schlupp 68), King, Drinkwater, Albrighton (Amartey 77), Okazaki (Gray 68), Vardy. **Booked**: Zieler

December 7, 2016
Club Bruges 0 **Copenhagen** 2 (Mechele 9 og, Jorgensen 15). Att: 18,981
Porto 5 (Andre Silva 6, 64 pen, Corona 26, Brahimi 44, Diogo Jota 77) **Leicester** 0. Att: 39,310 (record defeat by English club)
Leicester (4-4-2): Hamer, Hernandez, Wasilewski, Morgan, Chilwell, Gray, Mendy, Drinkwater (Barnes 46), Schlupp (Albrighton 46), Musa (Ulloa 46), Okazaki. **Booked**: Chilwell

	P	W	D	L	F	A	Pts
Leicester Q	6	4	1	1	7	6	13
Porto Q	6	3	2	1	9	3	11
Copenhagen	6	2	3	1	7	2	9
Club Bruges	6	0	0	6	2	14	0

GROUP H

September 14, 2016
Juventus 0 **Sevilla** 0. Att: 33,261
Lyon 3 (Tolisso 1, Ferri 49, Cornet 57) **Dinamo Zagreb** 0. Att: 43,754

September 27, 2016
Dinamo Zagreb 0 **Juventus** 4 (Pjanic 24, Higuain 31, Dybala 57, Semper 86 og). Att: 23,875
Sevilla 1 (Ben Yedder 53) **Lyon** 0. Att: 36,741

October 18, 2016
Dinamo Zagreb 0 **Sevilla** 1 (Nasri 37). Att: 6,021
Lyon 0 **Juventus** 1 (Cuadrado 76). Att: 53,907

November 2, 2016
Juventus 1 (Higuain 14 pen) **Lyon** 1 (Tolisso 85). Att: 40,356
Sevilla 4 (Vietto 31, Escudero 66, Nzonzi 80, Ben Yedder 87) **Dinamo Zagreb** 0. Att: 35,215

November 22, 2016
Dinamo Zagreb 0 **Lyon** 1 (Lacazette 72). Att: 7,834

Sevilla 1 (Pareja 10) **Juventus** 3 (Marchisio 45 pen, Bonucci 84, Mandzukic 90). Att: 38,942

December 7, 2016
Juventus 2 (Higuain 52, Rugani 72) **Dinamo Zagreb** 0. Att: 39,380
Lyon 0 **Sevilla** 0. Att: 52,423

	P	W	D	L	F	A	Pts
Juventus Q	6	4	2	0	11	2	14
Sevilla Q	6	3	2	1	7	3	11
Lyon	6	2	2	2	5	3	8
Dinamo Zagreb	6	0	0	6	0	15	0

ROUND OF 16, FIRST LEG

February 14, 2017
Benfica 1 (Mitroglou 49) **Borussia Dortmund** 0. Att: 55,124
Paris SG 4 (Di Maria 18, 55, Draxler 40, Cavani 71) **Barcelona** 0. Att: 46,484

February 15, 2017
Bayern Munich 5 (Robben 11, Lewandowski 53, Thiago Alcantara 56, 64, Muller 88) **Arsenal** 1 (Sanchez 30 pen). Att: 70,000
Arsenal (4-4-1-1): Ospina, Bellerin, Mustafi, Koscielny (Gabriel 49), Gibbs, Oxlade-Chamberlain, Xhaka, Coquelin (Giroud 77), Iwobi (Walcott 66), Ozil, Sanchez. **Booked**: Mustafi, Sanchez, Xhaka
Real Madrid 3 (Benzema 19, Kroos 49, Casemiro 54) **Napoli** 1 (Insigne 8). Att: 78,000

February 21, 2017
Bayer Leverkusen 2 (Bellerabi 48, Savic 68 og) **Atletico Madrid** 4 (Saul 17, Griezmann 25, Gameiro 59 pen, Torres 86). Att: 29,300
Manchester City 5 (Sterling 27, Aguero 58, 71, Stones 77, Sane 82) **Monaco** 3 (Falcao 32, 61, Mbappe-Lottin 41). Att: 53,351
Manchester City (4-3-3): Caballero, Sagna, Stones, Otamendi, Fernandinho (Zabaleta 62), Toure, De Bruyne, Silva, Sterling (Jesus Navas 89) Aguero (Fernando 87), Sane. **Booked**: Aguero, Fernandinho, Otamendi, Zabaleta

February 22, 2017
Porto 0 **Juventus** 2 (Pjaca 72, Dani Alves 74). Att: 49,229
Sevilla 2 (Sarabia 25, Correa 62) **Leicester** 1 (Vardy 73). Att: 38,834
Leicester (4-4-2): Schmeichel, Simpson, Morgan, Huth, Fuchs, Mahrez, Drinkwater, Ndidi, Albrighton (Amartey 87), Musa (Gray 58), Vardy

ROUND OF 16, SECOND LEG

March 7, 2017
Arsenal 1 (Walcott 20) **Bayern Munich** 5 (Lewandowski 55 pen, Robben 68, Douglas Costa 78, Vidal 80, 85). Att: 59,911 (Bayern Munich won 10-2 on agg – record defeat by English team in knockout stage)
Arsenal (4-3-3): Ospina, Bellerin, Mustafa, Koscielny, Monreal, Oxlade-Chamberlain, Xhaka, Ramsey (Coquelin 72), Walcott, Giroud (Ozil 72), Sanchez (Lucas Perez 72). **Booked**: Walcott, Oxlade-Chamberlain, Xhaka. **Sent off**: Koscielny (53)
Napoli 1 (Mertens 24) **Real Madrid** 3 (Sergio Ramos 51, 57, Morata 90). Att: 56,695 (Real Madrid won 6-2 on agg)

March 8, 2017
Barcelona 6 (Suarez 3, Kurzawa 41 og, Messi 50 pen, Neymar 88, 90 pen, Sergi Roberto 90)
Paris SG 1 (Cavani 62). Att: 96,290 (Barcelona won 6-5 on agg)
Borussia Dortmund 4 (Aubameyang 4, 61, 85, Pulisic 59) **Benfica** 0. Att: 65,849 (Borussia Dortmund won 4-1 on agg)

March 14, 2017
Juventus 1 (Dybala 42 pen) **Porto** 0. Att: 41,161 (Juventus won 3-0 on agg)
Leicester 2 (Morgan 27, Albrighton 55) **Sevilla** 0. Att: 31,520 (Leicester won 3-2 on agg)
Leicester (4-4-2): Schmeichel, Simpson, Morgan, Huth, Fuchs, Mahrez (Amartey 90), Drinkwater,
Ndidi, Albrighton, Okazaki (Slimani 64), Vardy. **Booked**: Vardy, Schmeichel, Ndidi, Mahrez

March 15, 2017
Atletico Madrid 0 **Bayer Leverkusen** 0. Att: 49,133 (Atletico Madrid won 4-2 on agg)
Monaco 3 (Mbappe-Lottin 8, Fabinho 29, Bakayoko 77) **Manchester City** 1 (Sane 71). Att:
15,700 (agg 6-6, Monaco won on away goals)
Manchester City (4-1-4-1): Caballero, Sagna, Stones, Kolarov, Clichy (Iheanacho 84),
Fernandinho, Sterling, De Bruyne, Silva, Sane, Aguero. **Booked**: Sagna, De Bruyne, Sterling

QUARTER-FINALS, FIRST LEG

April 11, 2017
Borussia Dortmund v Monaco – postponed, attack on Dortmund team bus
Juventus 3 (Dybala 7, 22, Chiellini 55) **Barcelona** 0. Att: 41,092

April 12, 2017
Atletico Madrid 1 (Griezmann 20 pen) **Leicester** 0. Att: 51,423
Leicester (4-4-1-1): Schmeichel, Simpson, Benalouane, Huth, Fuchs, Mahrez, Ndidi,
Drinkwater, Albrighton, Okazaki (King 46), Vardy (Slimani 78). **Booked**: Albrighton, Benaloune,
Huth
Bayern Munich 1 (Vidal 26) **Real Madrid** 2 (Ronaldo 47, 77). Att: 70,000
Borussia Dortmund 2 (Dembele 57, Kagawa 84) **Monaco** 3 (Mbappe-Lottin 19, 79, Bender 35
og). Att: 65,849

QUARTER-FINALS, SECOND LEG

April 18, 2017
Leicester 1 (Vardy 61) **Atletico Madrid** 1 (Saul 26). Att: 31,548 (Atletico Madrid won 2-1 on agg)
Leicester (4-4-1-1): Schmeichel, Simpson, Morgan (Amartey 84), Benalouane (Chilwell 46),
Fuchs, Mahrez, Ndidi, Drinkwater, Albrighton, Okazaki (Ulloa 46), Vardy
Real Madrid 4 (Ronaldo 76, 105, 109, Marco Asensio 112) **Bayern Munich** 2 (Lewandowski
53 pen, Sergio Ramos 78 og). Att: 78,346 (aet, Real Madrid won 6-3 on agg)

April 19, 2017
Barcelona 0 **Juventus** 0. Att: 96,290 (Juventus won 3-0 on agg)
Monaco 3 (Mbappe-Lottin 3, Falcao 17, Germain 81) **Borussia Dortmund** 1 (Reus 48). Att:
17,135 (Monaco won 6-3 on agg)

SEMI-FINALS, FIRST LEG

May 2, 2017
Real Madrid 3 (Ronaldo 10, 73, 86) **Atletico Madrid** 0. Att: 77,609

May 3, 2017
Monaco 0 **Juventus** 2 (Higuain 29, 59). Att: 16,762

SEMI-FINALS, SECOND LEG

May 9, 2017
Juventus 2 (Mandzukic 33, Dani Alves 44) **Monaco** 1 (Mbappe-Lottin 69). Att: 40,244
(Juventus won 4-1 on agg)

May 10, 2017
Atletico Madrid 2 (Saul 12, Griezmann 16 pen) **Real Madrid** 1 (Isco 42). Att: 53,422 (Real
Madrid won 4-2 on agg)

FINAL

JUVENTUS 1 REAL MADRID 4
Principality Stadium, Cardiff (65,842); Saturday, June 3 2017

Juventus (4-2-3-1): Buffon (capt), Barzagli (Cuadrado 66), Bonucci, Chiellini, Sandro, Pjanic (Marchisio 70), Khedira, Dani Alves, Dybala (Lemina 78), Mandzukic, Higuain. **Subs not used**: Neto, Benatia, Asamoah, Lichtsteiner. **Scorer**: Mandzukic (27). **Booked**: Dybala, Pjanic, Sandro, Cuadrado. **Sent off**: Cuadrado (84). **Coach**: Max Allegri

Real Madrid (4-3-1-2): Navas, Daniel Carvajal, Varane, Sergio Ramos (capt), Marcelo, Kroos (Alvaro Morata 89), Casemiro, Modric, Isco (Marco Asensio 82), Benzema (Bale 77), Ronaldo. **Subs not used**: Kiko Casilla, Nacho, Kovacic, Danilo. **Scorers**: Ronaldo (20, 64), Casemiro (61), Marco Asensio (90). **Booked**: Sergio Ramos, Daniel Carvajal, Kroos, Marco Asensio. **Coach**: Zinedine Zidane

Referee: F Brych (Germany). **Half-time**: 1-1

Leading scorers: 12 Ronaldo (Real Madrid); 11 Messi (Barcelona); 8 Cavani (Paris SG), Lewandowski (Bayern Munich); 7 Aubameyang (Borussia Dortmund); 6 Griezmann (Atletico Madrid); Mbappe-Lottin (Monaco); 5 Aguero (Manchester City), Benzema (Real Madrid), Falcao (Monaco), Higuain (Juventus), Mertens (Napoli)

FINAL FACTS AND FIGURES

● Cristiano Ronaldo became the first player to score in three Champions League Finals, having previously netted for Real in 2014 and for Manchester United against Chelsea in 2008.

● Ronaldo overtook Barcelona's Lionel Messi as leading marksman in this season's tournament.

● The Portugal captain scored his 600th career goal in all competitions for club and country.

● Real were the first club to retain to retain the trophy in the Champions League era.

● They have won their last six finals since losing to Liverpool in 1981.

● Zinedine Zidane became the first coach to win back-to-back trophies since Arrigo Sacchi with AC Milan (1989, 1990).

● Juventus have lost their last five finals since beating Ajax in 1996.

● Juan Cuadrado became the third player to be sent off in a Champions League Final, after Jens Lehmann (Arsenal) in 2006 and Didier Drogba (Chelsea) in 2008.

EUROPEAN CUP/CHAMPIONS LEAGUE FINALS

1956	Real Madrid 4 Reims 3 (Paris)
1957	Real Madrid 2 Fiorentina 0 (Madrid)
1958†	Real Madrid 3 AC Milan 2 (Brussels)
1959	Real Madrid 2 Reims 0 (Stuttgart)
1960	Real Madrid 7 Eintracht Frankfurt 3 (Glasgow)
1961	Benfica 3 Barcelona 2 (Berne)
1962	Benfica 5 Real Madrid 3 (Amsterdam)
1963	AC Milan 2 Benfica 1 (Wembley)
1964	Inter Milan 3 Real Madrid 1 (Vienna)
1965	Inter Milan 1 Benfica 0 (Milan)
1966	Real Madrid 2 Partizan Belgrade 1 (Brussels)
1967	Celtic 2 Inter Milan 1 (Lisbon)
1968†	Manchester Utd 4 Benfica 1 (Wembley)
1969	AC Milan 4 Ajax 1 (Madrid)

1970†	Feyenoord 2 Celtic 1 (Milan)
1971	Ajax 2 Panathinaikos 0 (Wembley)
1972	Ajax 2 Inter Milan 0 (Rotterdam)
1973	Ajax 1 Juventus 0 (Belgrade)
1974	Bayern Munich 4 Atletico Madrid 0 (replay Brussels after a 1-1 draw Brussels)
1975	Bayern Munich 2 Leeds Utd 0 (Paris)
1976	Bayern Munich 1 St. Etienne 0 (Glasgow)
1977	Liverpool 3 Borussia Moenchengladbach 1 (Rome)
1978	Liverpool 1 Brugge 0 (Wembley)
1979	Nottm Forest 1 Malmo 0 (Munich)
1980	Nottm Forest 1 Hamburg 0 (Madrid)
1981	Liverpool 1 Real Madrid 0 (Paris)
1982	Aston Villa 1 Bayern Munich 0 (Rotterdam)
1983	SV Hamburg 1 Juventus 0 (Athens)
1984†	Liverpool 1 AS Roma 1 (Liverpool won 4-2 on penalties) (Rome)
1985	Juventus 1 Liverpool 0 (Brussels)
1986†	Steaua Bucharest 0 Barcelona 0 (Steaua won 2-0 on penalties) (Seville)
1987	Porto 2 Bayern Munich 1 (Vienna)
1988†	PSV Eindhoven 0 Benfica 0 (PSV won 6-5 on penalties) (Stuttgart)
1989	AC Milan 4 Steaua Bucharest 0 (Barcelona)
1990	AC Milan 1 Benfica 0 (Vienna)
1991†	Red Star Belgrade 0 Marseille 0 (Red Star won 5-3 on penalties) (Bari)
1992	Barcelona 1 Sampdoria 0 (Wembley)
1993	Marseille 1 AC Milan 0 (Munich)
1994	AC Milan 4 Barcelona 0 (Athens)
1995	Ajax 1 AC Milan 0 (Vienna)
1996†	Juventus 1 Ajax 1 (Juventus won 4-2 on penalties) (Rome)
1997	Borussia Dortmund 3 Juventus 1 (Munich)
1998	Real Madrid 1 Juventus 0 (Amsterdam)
1999	Manchester Utd 2 Bayern Munich 1 (Barcelona)
2000	Real Madrid 3 Valencia 0 (Paris)
2001	Bayern Munich 1 Valencia 1 (Bayern Munich won 5-4 on penalties) (Milan)
2002	Real Madrid 2 Bayer Leverkusen 1 (Glasgow)
2003†	AC Milan 0 Juventus 0 (AC Milan won 3-2 on penalties) (Manchester)
2004	FC Porto 3 Monaco 0 (Gelsenkirchen)
2005†	Liverpool 3 AC Milan 3 (Liverpool won 3-2 on penalties) (Istanbul)
2006	Barcelona 2 Arsenal 1 (Paris)
2007	AC Milan 2 Liverpool 1 (Athens)
2008†	Manchester Utd 1 Chelsea 1 (Manchester Utd won 6-5 on penalties) (Moscow)
2009	Barcelona 2 Manchester Utd 0 (Rome)
2010	Inter Milan 2 Bayern Munich 0 (Madrid)
2011	Barcelona 3 Manchester Utd 1 (Wembley)
2012†	Chelsea 1 Bayern Munich 1 (Chelsea won 4-3 on pens) (Munich)
2013	Bayern Munich 3 Borussia Dortmund 1 (Wembley)
2014†	Real Madrid 4 Atletico Madrid 1 (Lisbon)
2015	Barcelona 3 Juventus 1 (Berlin)
2016	Real Madrid 1 Atletico Madrid 1 (Real Madrid won 5-3 on pens) (Milan)
2017	Real Madrid 4 Juventus 1 (Cardiff)

† aet
● Champions League since 1993

WOMEN OWNERS IN OPPOSITION

Southampton were involved in a history-making Europa League group match last season. It was a meeting of two women owners, the Premier League club's Katharina Liebherr and Hapoel Beer Sheva's Alona Barkat. Southampton were knocked out by an away goal scored by the Israeli side in the second leg at St Mary's.

UEFA EUROPA LEAGUE 2016–17

FIRST QUALIFYING ROUND (selected results)

FIRST LEG

Aberdeen 3 (Logan 68, McGinn 90 pen, Rooney 90 pen) Fola Esch 1 (Klein 70). Att: 12,570.
AIK 2 (Affane 27, Johansson 51) **Bala** 0. Att: 6,127. **Connah's Quay** 0 Stabaek 0. Att: 573.
Differdange 1 (Er Ralik 39) **Cliftonville** 1 (Lavery 88). Att: 1,355. Gothenburg 5 (Engvall 11,
Rieks 12, Salomonsson 36, Hysen 80, 81) **Llandudno** 0. Att: 6,074
Hearts 2 (Buaben 28 pen, Kalimullin 36 og) Infonet 1 (Harin 21). Att: 14,417. **Linfield** 0 **Cork
City** 1 (Maguire 63 pen). Att: 2,093. Reykjavik 2 (Palmason 40, Fridjonsson 79 pen) **Glenavon**
1 (Kelly 14). Att: 502. **Shamrock Rov** 0 RoPS 2 (Lahdenmaki 26, Saksela 74). Att: 1,908. **St
Patrick's** 1 (Fagan 7) Jeunesse D'Esch 0. Att: 1,200

SECOND LEG

Bala 0 AIK 2 (Avdie 9, Strandberg 25). Att: 890 (AIK won 4-0 on agg). **Cliftonville** 2 (McDaid
3, Donnelly 76) Differdange 0. Att: 1,168 (Cliftonville won 3-1 on agg). **Cork City** 1 (Maguire
50 pen) **Linfield** 0 (Stafford 52). Att: 3,521 (Cork City won 2-1 on agg). Fola Esch 1 (Hadji
45) **Aberdeen** 0. Att: 1,789 (Aberdeen won 3-2 on agg). **Glenavon** 0 Reykjavik 6 (Chopart 6,
30, Fridjonsson 53 pen, Andersen 69, Hauksson 79, Fazlagie 80). Att: 1,250 (Reykjavik won
8-1 on agg)
Infonet 2 (Harin 51, Voskoboinikov 63) **Hearts** 4 (Paterson 2, Rossi 9, 52, Ozturk 45).
Att: 1,354 (Hearts won 6-3 on agg). Jeunesse D'Esch 2 (Stumpf 22, 87) **St Patrick's** 1
(Dennehy 73). Att: 1,378 (agg 2-2, St Patrick's won on away goal). **Llandudno** 1 (Hughes
72) Gothenburg 2 (Smedberg-Dalence 36, Skold 54). Att: 841 (Gothenburg won 7-1 on agg).
RoPS 1 (Muinonen 27) **Shamrock Rov** 1 (McCabe 22 pen). Att: 1,525 (RoPS won 3-1 on agg).
Stabaek 0 **Connah's Quay** 1 (Morris 16). Att: 384 (Connah's Quay won 1-0 on agg)

SECOND QUALIFYING ROUND (selected results)

FIRST LEG

Aberdeen 3 (Stockley 71, Rooney 75, Burns 90) Ventspils 0. Att: 10,672. Birkirkara 0 **Hearts**
0. Att: 1,868. **Cliftonville** 2 (McGuinness 18, Donnelly 49) AEK Larnaca 3 (Trickovski 60,
Charalambous 64, Tomas 76). Att: 1,352. Dinamo Minsk 1 (Korytko 25) **St Patrick's** 1 (Fagan
54). Att: 1,286. Hacken 1 (Owoeri 84) **Cork City** 1 (Maguire 65 pen). Att: 2,022. **Hibernian** 0
Brondby 1 (Wilczek 1). Att: 13,454. Vojvodina 1 (Palocevic 86) **Connah's Quay** 0. Att: 4,276

SECOND LEG

AEK Larnaca 2 (Boljevic 45, Tomas 48) **Cliftonville** 0. Att: 2,122 (AEK Larnaca won 5-2 on
agg). Brondby 0 **Hibernian** 1 (Gray 63). Att: 11,548 (aet, agg 1-1, Brondby won 5-3 on pens).
Connah's Quay 1 (Wilde 66) Vojvodina 2 (Meleg 9, 50 pen). Att: 809 (Vojvodina won 3-1 on
agg). **Cork City** 1 (O'Connor 26) Hacken 0. Att: 5,334 (Cork City won 2-1 on agg). **Hearts** 1
(Sammon 73) Birkirkara 2 (Bubalovic 55, Herrera 67). Att: 14,301 (Birkirkara won 2-1 on
agg). **St Patrick's** 0 Dinamo Minsk 1 (Rassadkin 19). Att: 2,400 (Dinamo Minsk won 2-1 on
agg). Ventspils 0 **Aberdeen** 1 (Rooney 79). Att: 2,100 (Aberdeen won 4-0 on agg)

THIRD QUALIFYING ROUND (selected results)

FIRST LEG

Aberdeen 1 (Hayes 88) Maribor 1 (Novakovic 83). Att: 17,105. Genk 1 (Bailey 31) **Cork City**
0. Att: 7,765. Domzale 2 (Crnic 11 pen, 49) **West Ham** 1 (Noble 18 pen). Att: 8,458

SECOND LEG

Cork City 1 (Bennett 63) Genk 2 (Buffel 13, Dewaest 41). Att: 6,745 (Genk won 3-1 on agg). Maribor 1 (Lewis 90 og) **Aberdeen** 0. Att: 9,796 (Maribor won 2-1 on agg). **West Ham** 3 (Kouyate 8, 25, Feghouli 81) Domzale 0. Att: 53,914 (West Ham won 4-2 on agg)

PLAY-OFFS
FIRST LEG

Astra Giurgiu 1 (Alibec 83) **West Ham** 1 (Noble 45 pen). Att: 3,360

SECOND LEG

West Ham 0 Astra Giurgiu 1 (Teixeira 45). Att: 56,932 (Astra Giurgiu won 2-1 on agg)

ON AGGREGATE

Alkmaar 3 Vojvodina 0; Anderlecht 6 Slavia Prague 0; Astana 4 Bate Borisov 2; Austria Vienna 4 Rosenborg 2; Fenerbahce 5 Grasshoppers 0; Genk 4 Lokomotiv Zagreb 2; Gent 6 Shkendija Tetovo 1; Krasnodar 4 Partizani Tirana 0; Maccabi Tel Aviv 3 Hajduk Split 3 (aet, Maccabi Tel Aviv won 4-3 on pens); Olympicos 3 Arouna 1; Osmanllspor 3 Midtjylland 0; PAOK Salonika 5 Dinamo Tbilisi 0; Panathinaikos 4 Brondby 1; Qabala 3 Maribor 2; Qarabag 3 Gothenburg 1; Rapid Vienna 4 Dukla Trencin 2; Sassuolo 4 Crvena Zvezda 1; Shakhtar Donetsk 4 Basaksehir 1; Slovan Liberec 4 AEK Larnaca 0; Sparta Prague 3 Sonderjyske 2; St Etienne 2 Beitar Jerusalem 1

GROUP A

Match-day 1: Feyenoord 1 (Vilhena 79) **Manchester Utd** 0. Att: 31,000. Zorya Luhansk 1 (Grechyshkin 52) Fenerbahce 1 (Kjaer 90). Att: 16,050
Match-day 2: Fenerbahce 1 (Emenike 18) Feyenoord 0. Att: 16,500. **Manchester Utd** 1 (Ibrahimovic 69) Zorya Luhansk 0. Att: 58,179
Match-day 3: Feyenoord 1 (Jorgensen 55) Zorya Luhansk 0. Att: 35,100. **Manchester Utd** 4 (Pogba 31 pen, 45, Martial 34 pen, Lingard 48) Fenerbahce 1 (Van Persie 83). Att: 73,063
Match-day 4: Fenerbahce 2 (Sow 2, Lens 59) **Manchester Utd** 1 (Rooney 89). Att: 35,378. Zorya Luhansk 1 (Forster 44) Feyenoord 1 (Jorgensen 15). Att: 16,855
Match-day 5: Fenerbahce 2 (Stoch 59, Kjaer 67) Zorya Luhansk 0. Att: 16,145. **Manchester Utd** 4 (Rooney 35, Mata 69, Jones 75 og, Lingard 90) Feyenoord 0. Att: 64,628
Match-day 6: Feyenoord 0 Fenerbahce 1 (Sow 22). Att: 32,000. Zorya Luhansk 0 **Manchester Utd** 2 (Mkhitaryan 48, Ibrahimovic 88). Att: 25,900

	P	W	D	L	F	A	Pts
Fenerbahce Q	6	4	1	1	8	6	13
Manchester Utd Q	6	4	0	2	12	4	12
Feyenoord	6	2	1	3	3	7	7
Zorya Luhansk	6	0	2	4	2	8	2

GROUP B

Match-day 1: Apoel Nicosia 2 (Vinicius 75, De Camargo 87) Astana 1 (Maksimovic 45). Att: 12,008. Young Boys 0 Olympiacos 1 (Cambiasso 42). Att: 11,132
Match-day 2: Astana 0 Young Boys 0. Att: 21,328. Olympiacos 0 Apoel Nicosia 1 (Sotiriou 10). Att: 24,378
Match-day 3: Olympiacos 4 (Figueiras 25, Elyounoussi 33, Seba 34, 65) Astana 1 (Kabanaga 54). Att: 21,480. Young Boys 3 (Hoarau 18, 52, 82 pen) Apoel Nicosia 1 (Efrem 14). Att: 9,553
Match-day 4: Apoel Nicosia 1 (Sotiriou 69) Young Boys 0. Att: 14,200. Astana 1 (Despotovic 8) Olympiacos 1 (Seba 29). Att: 12,158

Match-day 5: Astana 2 (Anicic 59, Despotovic 84) Apoel Nicosia 1 (Efrem 31). Att: 9,143. Olympiacos 1 (Fortounis 48) Young Boys 1 (Hoarau 58). Att: 24,131
Match-day 6: Apoel Nicosia 2 (Da Costa 20 og, De Camargo 83) Olympiacos 0. Att: 14,779. Young Boys 3 (Frey 63, Hoarau 66, Schick 71) Astana 0. Att: 7,616

	P	W	D	L	F	A	Pts
Apoel Nicosia Q	6	4	0	2	8	6	12
Olympiacos Q	6	2	2	2	7	6	8
Young Boys	6	2	2	2	7	4	8
Astana	6	1	2	3	5	11	5

GROUP C

Match-day 1: Anderlecht 3 (Teodorczyk 14, Santos 41 og, Capel 77) Qabala 1 (Dabo 20). Att: 11,638. Mainz 1 (Bungert 57) St Etienne 1 (Beric 88). Att: 20,275
Match-day 2: Qabala 2 (Yeini 57 pen, Zenjov 62) Mainz 3 (Muto 41, Cordoba 68, Oztunali 78). Att: 6,500. St Etienne 1 (Roux 90) Anderlecht 1 (Tielemans 62 pen). Att: 23,258
Match-day 3: Mainz 1 (Malli 10 pen) Anderlecht 1 (Teodorczyk 65). Att: 21,317. St Etienne 1 (Ricardinho 70 og) Qabala 0. Att: 22,855
Match-day 4: Anderlect 6 (Stanciu 9, 41, Tielemans 62, Teodorczyk 89, 90 pen, Bruno 90) Mainz 1 (De Blasis 15). Att: 13,275. Qabala 1 (Yeini 39) St Etienne 2 (Tannane 46, Beric 53). Att: 5,600
Match-day 5: Qabala 1 (Ricardinho 15 pen) Anderlecht 3 (Tielemans 10, Bruno 90, Teodorczyk 90). Att: 4,501. St Etienne 0 Mainz 0. Att: 21,750
Match-day 6: Anderlecht 2 (Chipciu 21, Stanciu 31) St Etienne 3 (Porvaldsson 62, 67, Monnet-Paquet 74). Att: 13,583. Mainz 2 (Hack 29, De Blasis 40) Qabala 0. Att: 12,860

	P	W	D	L	F	A	Pts
St Etienne Q	6	3	3	0	8	5	12
Anderlecht Q	6	3	2	1	16	8	11
Mainz	6	2	3	1	8	10	9
Qabala	6	0	0	6	5	14	0

GROUP D

Match-day 1: Alkmaar 1 (Wuytens 60) Dundalk 1 (Kilduff 89). Att: 10,003. Maccabi Tel Aviv 3 (Medunjanin 26, 70, Kjartansson 50) Zenit St Petersburg 4 (Kokorin 76, Da Silveira 84, Giuliano 86, Djordjevic 90). Att: 10,855
Match-day 2: Dundalk 1 (Kilduff 72) Maccabi Tel Aviv 0. Att: 5,543. Zenit St Petersburg 5 (Kokorin 26, 59, Giuliano 48, Criscito 66 pen, Shatov 80) Alkmaar 0. Att: 15,275
Match-day 3: Alkmaar 1 (Muhren 72) Maccabi Tel Aviv 2 (Scarione 24, Golasa 81). Att: 12,016. Dundalk 1 (Benson 52) Zenit St Petersburg 2 (Mak 71, Giuliano 77). Att: 5,550
Match-day 4: Maccabi Tel Aviv 0 Alkmaar 0. Att:11,356. Zenit St Petersburg 2 (Giuliano 42, 78) Dundalk 1 (Horgan 52). Att: 17,723
Match-day 5: Zenit St Petersburg 2 (Kokorin 44, Kerzhakov 90) Maccabi Tel Aviv 0. Att: 15,843. Dundalk 0 Alkmaar 1 (Weghorst 9). Att: 5,500
Match-day 6: Alkmaar 3 (Rienstra 7, Haps 43, Tankovic 68) Zenit St Petersburg 2 (Giuliano 58, Wuytens 80 og). Att: 13,713. Maccabi Tel Aviv 2 (Ben Haim 21 pen, Micha 38) Dundalk 1 (Dasa 27 og). Att: 9,891

	P	W	D	L	F	A	Pts
Zenit St Petersburg Q	6	5	0	1	17	8	15
Alkmaar Q	6	2	2	2	6	10	8
Maccabi Tel Aviv	6	2	1	3	7	9	7
Dundalk	6	1	1	4	5	8	4

GROUP E

Match-day 1: Astra Giurgiu 2 (Alibec 18, Sapunaru 74) Austria Vienna 3 (Holzhauser 17 pen,Friesenbichler 33, Grunwald 58). Att: 3,300. Viktoria Plzen 1 (Bakos 11) Roma 1 (Perotti 4 pen). Att: 10,326
Match-day 2: Austria Vienna 0 Viktoria Plzen 0. Att: 16,509. Roma 4 (Strootman 15, Fazio 45, Silva Dornellas 47 og, Salah 54) Astra Giurgiu 0. Att: 13,509
Match-day 3: Roma 3 (El Shaarawy 19, 34, Florenzi 69) Austria Vienna 2 (Holzhauser 16, Prokop 82, Kayode 84). Att: 16,478. Viktoria Plzen 1 (Horava 86) Astra Giurgiu 2 (Horava 64 og, Alibec 41). Att: 9,440
Match-day 4: Astra Giurgiu 1 (Stan 19) Viktoria Plzen 1 (Krmencik 25). Att: 1,450. Austria Vienna 2 (Kayode 2, Grunwald 89) Roma 4 (Dzeko 5, 65, De Rossi 18, Nainggolan 78). Att: 32,751
Match-day 5: Austria Vienna 1 (Rotpuller 57) Astra Giurgiu 2 (Florea 79, Budescu 88 pen). Att: 14,127. Roma 4 (Dzeko 11, 61, 88, Mateju 82 og) Viktoria Plzen 1 (Zeman 18). Att: 13,798
Match-day 6: Astra Giurgiu 0 Roma 0. Att: 7,100. Viktoria Plzen 3 (Horava 44, Duris 72, 84) Austria Vienna 2 (Holzhauser 19, Rotpuller 40). Att: 9,117

	P	W	D	L	F	A	Pts
Roma Q	6	3	3	0	16	7	12
Astra Giurgiu Q	6	2	2	2	7	10	8
Viktoria Plzen	6	1	3	2	7	10	6
Austria Vienna	6	1	2	3	11	14	5

GROUP F

Match-day 1: Rapid Vienna 3 (Schwab 51, Joclinton 59, Colley 60 og) Genk 2 (Bailey 29, 90 pen). Att: 21,800. Sassuolo 3 (Koşok 60, Defrel 76, Politano 82) Athletic Bilbao 0. Att: 7,032
Match-day 2: Athletic Bilbao 1 (Benat 59) Rapid Vienna 0. Att: 34,039. Genk 3 (Karelis 8, Bailey 25, Buffel 61) Sassuolo 1 (Politano 65). Att: 9,130
Match-day 3: Genk 2 (Brabec 40, Ndidi 83) Athletic Bilbao 0. Att: 9,530. Rapid Vienna 1 (Schaub 7) Sassuolo 1 (Schrammel 66 og). Att: 22,200
Match-day 4: Athletic Bilbao 5 (Aduriz 8, 24 pen, 44 pen, 74, 90 pen) Genk 3 (Bailey 28, Ndidi 51, Susic 80). Att: 33,417. Sassuolo 2 (Defrel 34, Pellegrini 45) Rapid Vienna 2 (Jelic 85, Kvilitaia 90). Att: 7,838
Match-day 5: Athletic Bilbao 0 (Garcia 10, Aduriz 58, Martinez 79) Sassuolo 2 (Balenziaga og, Ragusa 83). Att: 37,806. Genk 1 (Karelis 11) Rapid Vienna 0. Att: 9,406
Match-day 6: Rapid Vienna 1 (Joclinton 72) Athletic Bilbao 1 (Saborit 84). Att: 21,500. Sassuolo 0 Genk 2 (Heynen 58, Trossard 80). Att: 1,154

	P	W	D	L	F	A	Pts
Genk Q	6	4	0	2	13	9	12
Athletic Bilbao Q	6	3	1	2	10	11	10
Rapid Vienna	6	1	3	2	7	8	6
Sassuolo	6	1	2	3	9	11	5

GROUP G

Match-day 1: Panathinaikos 1 (Berg 5) Ajax 2 (Traore 34, Riedewald 67). Att: 13,019. Standard Liege 1 (Dossevi 3) Celta Vigo 1 (Rossi 13). Att: 10,723
Match-day 2: Ajax 1 (Dolberg 28) Standard Liege 0. Att: 31,352. Celta Vigo 2 (Guidetti 84, Wass 89) Panathinaikos 0. Att: 15,726
Match-day 3: Celta Vigo 2 (Fontas 29, Orellana 82) Ajax 2 (Ziyech 22, Younes 71). Att: 18,397. Standard Liege 2 (Edmilson 45 pen, Belfodil 82) Panathinaikos 2 (Ibarbo 12, 36). Att: 14,463

Match-day 4: Ajax 3 (Dolberg 41, Ziyech 67, Younes 71) Celta Vigo 2 (Guidetti 79, Aspas 86). Att: 44,545. Panathinaikos 0 Standard Liege 3 (Cisse 61, Belfodil 75, 90). Att: 10,837
Match-day 5: Ajax 2 (Schone 39, Tete 50) Panathinaikos 0. Att:41,011. Celta Vigo 1 (Aspas 8) Standard Liege 1 (Laifis 81). Att: 16,470
Match-day 6: Panathinaikos 0 Celta Vigo 2 (Guidetti 4, Orellana 76 pen). Att: 4,005
Standard Liege 1 (Raman 84) Ajax 1 (El Ghazi 27). Att: 20,344

	P	W	D	L	F	A	Pts
Ajax Q	6	4	2	0	11	6	14
Celta Vigo Q	6	2	3	1	10	7	9
Standard Liege	6	1	4	1	8	6	7
Panathinaikos	6	0	1	5	3	13	1

GROUP H

Match-day 1: Braga 1 (Pinto 24) Gent 1 (Milicevic 6). Att: 8,903. Konyaspor 0 Shakhtar Donetsk 1 (Ferreyra 76). Att: 26,860
Match-day 2: Gent 2 (Saief 17, Neto 33) Konyaspor 0. Att: 15,870. Shakhtar Donetsk 2 (Stepanenko 5, Kovalenko 56) Braga 0. Att: 11,938
Match-day 3: Konyaspor 1 (Milosevic 9) Braga 1 (Hassan 55). Att: 24,968. Shakhtar Donetsk 5 (Kovalenko 12, Ferreyra 30, Bernard 45, Taison 75, Malyshev 85) Gent 0. Att: 10,505
Match-day 4: Braga 3 (Velazquez 34, Eduardo 45, Horta 90) Konyaspor 1 (Rangelov 30). Att: 7,729. Gent 3 (Coulibaly 1, Osorio 83, Milicevic 89) Shakhtar Donetsk 5 (Marlos 36 pen, Taison 41, Stepanenko 45, Fred 67, Ferreyra 87). Att: 14,526
Match-day 5: Gent 2 (Coulibaly 32, Milicevic 40) Braga 2 (Stojiljkovic 14, Hassan 36). Att: 19,650. Shakhtar Donetsk 4 (Bardakci 10 og, Dentinho 36, Eduardo 66, Bernard 74) Konyaspor 0. Att: 10,021
Match-day 6: Braga 2 (Stojiljkovic 43, Vukcevic 89) Shakhtar Donetsk 4 (Kryvtsov 22, 62, Taison 39, 66). Att: 15,084. Konyaspor 0 Gent 1 (Coulibaly 90). Att: 10,720

	P	W	D	L	F	A	Pts
Shakhtar Donetsk Q	6	6	0	0	21	5	18
Gent Q	6	2	2	2	9	13	8
Braga	6	1	3	2	9	11	6
Konyaspor	6	0	1	5	2	12	1

GROUP I

Match-day 1: Nice 0 Schalke 1 (Rahman 75). Att: 21,378. Salzburg 0 Krasnodar 1 (Joaozinho 37). Att: 6,507
Match-day 2: Krasnodar 5 (Smolov 22, Joaozinho 33, 65 pen, Ari 86, 90) Nice 2 (Balotelli 42, Cyprien 71). Att: 10,750. Schalke 3 (Goretzka 15, Caleta-Car 47 og, Howedes 58) Salzburg 1 (Soriano 72). Att: 48,374
Match-day 3: Krasnodar 0 Schalke 1 (Konoplyanka 10). Att: 33,550. Salzburg 0 Nice 1 (Plea 13). Att: 9,473
Match-day 4: Nice 0 Salzburg 2 (Hwang 72, 73). Att: 17,582. Schalke 2 (Caicara 24, Bentaleb 28) Krasnodar 0. Att: 42,210
Match-day 5: Krasnodar 1 (Smolov 85) Salzburg 1 (Dabour 37). Att: 19,150. Schalke 2 (Konoplyanka 14, Aogo 80 pen) Nice 0. Att: 51,504
Match-day 6: Nice 2 (Bosetti 64 pen, Le Marchand 77) Krasnodar 1 (Smolov 51). Att: 12,722. Salzburg 2 (Schlager 22, Radosevic 90) Schalke 0. Att: 23,133

	P	W	D	L	F	A	Pts
Schalke Q	6	5	0	1	9	3	15
Krasnodar Q	6	2	1	3	8	8	7
Salzburg	6	2	1	3	6	6	7
Nice	6	2	0	4	5	11	6

GROUP J

Match-day 1: PAOK Salonika 0 Fiorentina 0. Att: 20,904. Qarabag 2 (Michel 7, Amirguliev 90)
Slovan Liberec 2 (Sykora 1, Baros 68). Att: 6,200
Match-day 2: Fiorentina 5 (Babacar 39, 45, Kalinic 43, Zarate 63, 78) Qarabag 1 (Ndlovu
90). Att: 14,145. Slovan Liberec 1 (Komlichenko 1) PAOK Salonika 2 (Athanasiadis 10 pen,
82). Att: 8,880
Match-day 3: Qarabag 2 (Sosa 56, Amirquliyev 87) PAOK Salonika 0. Att: 26,784. Slovan
Liberec 1 (Sevcik 58) Fiorentina 3 (Kalinic 8, 23, Babacar 70). Att: 9,037
Match-day 4: Fiorentina 3 (Ilicic 30 pen, Kalinic 42, Pepe 73) Slovan Liberec 0. Att: 11,583.
PAOK Salonika 0 Qarabag 1 (Michel 69). Att: 11,476
Match-day 5: Fiorentina 2 (Bernarderschi 33, Babacar 50) PAOK Salonika 3 (Shakhov 5,
Djalma 26, Rodrigues 90). Att: 12,793. Slovan Liberec 3 (Vuch 11, Komlichenko 57 pen, 63)
Qarabag 0. Att: 4,942
Match-day 6: PAOK Salonika 2 (Rodrigues 29, Pelekas 67) Slovan Liberec 0. Att: 11,463.
Qarabag 1 (Reynaldo 73) Fiorentina 2 (Vecino 60, Chiesa 76). Att: 21,750

	P	W	D	L	F	A	Pts
Fiorentina Q	6	4	1	1	15	6	13
PAOK Salonika Q	6	3	1	2	7	6	10
Qarabag	6	2	1	3	7	12	7
Slovan Liberec	6	1	1	4	7	12	4

GROUP K

Match-day 1: Inter Milan 0 Hapoel Beer Sheva 2 (Vitor 54, Buzaglo 69). Att: 16,778.
Southampton 3 (Austin 5 pen, 27, Rodriguez 90) Sparta Prague 0. Att: 25,125
Match-day 2: Hapoel Beer Sheva 0 Southampton 0. Att: 16,138. Sparta Prague 3 (Kadlec 7,
25, Holek 76) Inter Milan 1 (Palacio 71). Att: 14,051
Match-day 3: Hapoel Beer Sheva 0 Sparta Prague 1 (Pulkrab 71). Att: 15,607. Inter Milan 1
(Candreva 67) Southampton 0. Att: 26,719
Match-day 4: Southampton 2 (Van Dijk 64, Nagatomo 69 og) Inter Milan 1 (Icardi 33). Att:
30,389. Sparta Prague 2 (Dockal 23, Lafata 38) Hapoel Beer Sheva 0. Att: 12,891
Match-day 5: Hapoel Beer Sheva 3 (Soares 58, Nwakaeme 71 pen, Sahar 90) Inter Milan 2
(Icardi 13, Brozovic 25). Att: 15,973. Sparta Prague 1 (Nhamoinesu 11) Southampton 0. Att:
17,429
Match-day 6: Inter Milan 2 (Eder 23, 90) Sparta Prague 1 (Maracek 54). Att: 6,449.
Southampton 1 (Van Dijk 90) Hapoel Beer Sheva 1 (Buzaglo 78). Att: 30,416

	P	W	D	L	F	A	Pts
Sparta Prague Q	6	4	0	2	8	6	12
Hapoel Beer Sheva Q	6	2	2	2	6	6	8
Southampton	6	2	2	2	6	4	8
Inter Milan	6	2	0	4	7	11	6

GROUP L

Match-day 1: Osmanlispor 2 (Diabate 64 pen, Umar 74) Steaua Bucharest 0. Att: 11,807.
Villarreal 2 (Pato 28, Dos Santos 45) Zurich 1 (Sadiku 2). Att: 16,384
Match-day 2: Steaua Bucharest 1 (Muniru 20) Villarreal 1 (Santos Borre 9). Att: 13,231.
Zurich 2 (Schonbachler 45, Cavusevic 79) Osmanlispor 1 (Maher 73). Att: 7,473
Match-day 3: Osmanlispor 2 (Rusescu 23, 24) Villarreal 2 (Ndiaye 55, Pato 74). Att: 11,692.
Steaua Bucharest 1 (Golubovic 63) Zurich 0 (Kone 88). Att: 13,154
Match-day 4: Villarreal 1 (Hernandez Cascante 48) Osmanlispor 2 (Webo 8, Rusescu 75). Att:
15,386. Zurich 0 Steaua Bucharest 0. Att: 8,060
Match-day 5: Steaua Bucharest 2 (Momcilovic 68, Tamas 86) Osmanlispor 1 (Ndiaye 30). Att:
6,020. Zurich 1 (Rodriguez 87 pen) Villarreal 1 (Bruno 14). Att: 10,069

Match-day 6: Osmanlispor 2 (Delarge 73, Kilicaslan 89) Zurich 0. Att: 10,250. Villarreal 2 (Sansone 15, Trigueros 88) Steaua Bucharest 1 (Achim 55). Att: 19,471

	P	W	D	L	F	A	Pts
Osmanlispor Q	6	3	1	2	10	7	10
Villarreal Q	6	2	3	1	9	8	9
Steaua Bucharest	6	1	3	2	5	7	6
Zurich	6	1	3	2	5	7	6

ROUND OF 32, FIRST LEG

Alkmaar 1 (Jahanbakhsh 68 pen) Lyon 4 (Tousart 26, Lacazette 45, 57, Ferri 90). Att: 16,098. Anderlecht 2 (Acheampong 5, 31) Zenit St Petersburg 0. Att: 13,415. Athletic Bilbao 3 (Merkis 38 og, Aduriz 61, Williams 72) Apoel Nicosia 2 (Efrem 36, Gianniotas 89). Att: 32,675. Astra Giurgiu 2 (Budescu 43, Seto 90) Genk 2 (Castagne 25, Trossard 83). Att: 3,775 Borussia Monchengladbach 0 Fiorentina 1 (Bernarderschi 44). Att: 46,283. Celta Vigo 0 Shakhtar Donetsk 1 (Bianco 26). Att: 18,318. Gent 1 (Osorio 59) **Tottenham** 0. Att: 19,267. Hapoel Beer Sheva 1 (Barda 44) Besiktas 3 (Soares 42 og, Tosun 60, Hutchinson 90). Att: 15,347 Krasnodar 1 (Claesson 4) Fenerbahce 0. Att: 32,460. Legia Warsaw 0 Ajax 0. Att: 28,742. Ludogorets 1 (Keseru 81) Copenhagen 2 (Andrianantenaina 2 og, Toutouh 53). Att: 14,501. **Manchester Utd** 3 (Ibrahimovic 15, 75, 88 pen) St Etienne 0 (Manchester Utd won). Att: 67,192. Olympiacos 0 Osmanlispor 0. Att: 24,478. PAOK Salonika 0 Schalke 3 (Burgstaller 27, Meyer 82, Huntelaar 90). Att: 25,593. Rostov 4 (Mevlja 15, Poloz 38, Noboa 40, Azmoun 68) Sparta Prague 0. Att: 6,160. Villarreal 0 Roma 4 (Emerson 32, Dzeko 65, 79, 86). Att: 17,960

ROUND OF 32, SECOND LEG

Ajax 1 (Viergever 49) Legia Warsaw 0. Att: 52,285 (Ajax won 1-0 on agg). Apoel Nicosia 2 (Soteriou 46, Gianniotas 54) Athletic Bilbao 0. Att: 15,275 (Apoel Niosia won 4-3 on agg). Besiktas 2 (Aboubakar 17, Tosun 87) Hapoel Beer Sheva 1 (Nwakaeme 64). Att: 27.892 (Besiktas won 5-2 on agg). Copenhagen 0 Ludogorets 0. Att: 17,064 (Copenhagen won 2-1 on agg) Fenerbahce 1 (Souza 41) Krasnodar 1 (Smolov 7). Att 21,788 (Krasnodar won 2-1 on agg). Fiorentina 2 (Kalinic 15, Valero 28) Borussia Monchengladbach 4 (Stindl 44, 47, 55, Christensen 60). Att: 24,712 (Borussia Monchengladbach won 4-3 on agg). Genk 1 (Pozuelo 67) Astra Giurgiu 0. Att: 8,804 (Genk won 3-2 on agg). Lyon 7 (Fekir 4, 27, 78, Cornet 17, Darder 34, Aouar 86, Diakhaby 89) Alkmaar 1 (Garcia 26). Att: 25,743 (Lyon won 11-2 on agg) Osmanlispor 0 Olympiacos 3 (Ansarifard 47, 86, Elyounoussi 70). Att: 17,502 (Olympiacos won 3-0 on agg). Roma 0 Villarreal 1 (Borre 15). Att: 19,495 (Roma won 4-1 on agg). Schalke 1 (Schopf 23) PAOK Salonika 1 (Nastasic 25 og). Att: 50,619 (Schalke won 4-1 on agg). Shakhtar Donetsk 0 Celta Vigo 2 (Aspas 90, Cabral 108). Att: 33,117 (aet, Celta Vigo won 2-1 on agg) Sparta Prague 1 (Karavaev 83) Rostov 1 (Poloz 13). Att: 13,413 (Rostov won 5-1 on agg). St Etienne 0 **Manchester Utd** 1 (Mkhitaryan 16). Att: 41,492 (Manchester Utd won 4-0 on agg. **Tottenham** 2 (Eriksen 10, Wanyama 61) Gent 2 (Kane 20 og, Perbet 82). Att: 80,465 (at Wembley – Gent won 3-2 on agg). Zenit St Petersburg 3 (Giuliano 24, 78, Dzyuba 72) Anderlecht 1 (Thelin 90). Att: 17,992 (agg 3-3, Anderlecht won on away goal)

ROUND OF 16, FIRST LEG

Apoel Nicosia 0 Anderlecht 1 (Stanciu 29). Att: 19,327. Celta Vigo 2 (Wass 50, Веапvue 90) Krasnodar 1 (Claesson 56). Att: 18,414. Copenhagen 2 (Jensen 1, Cornelius 59) Ajax 1 (Dolberg 32). Att: 31,189. Gent 2 (Kalu 27, Coulibaly 61) Genk 5 (Malinovskyi 21, Colley 33, Samatta 41, 72, Uronen 45). Att: 17,112 Lyon 4 (Diakhaby 8, Tolisso 47, Fekir 74, Lacazette 90) Roma 2 (Salah 20, Fazio 33). Att:

50,588. Olympiacos 1 (Cambiasso 36) Besiktas 1 (Aboubakar 53). Att: 25,515. Rostov 1 (Bukharov 53) **Manchester Utd** 1 (Mkhitaryan 35). Att: 14,223. Schalke 1 (Burgstaller 25) Borussia Monchengladbach 1 (Hofmann 15). Att: 52,412

ROUND OF 16, SECOND LEG

Ajax 2 (Traore 23, Dolberg 45 pen) Copenhagen 0. Att: 52,270 (Ajax won 3-2 on agg). Anderlecht 1 (Acheampong 65) Apoel Nicosia 0. Att: 15,662 (Anderlecht won 2-0 on agg). Besiktas 4 (Aboubakar 11, Babel 22, 75, Tosun 84) Olympiacos 1 (Elyounoussi 31). Att: 37,966 (Besiktas won 5-2 on agg). Borussia Monchengladbach 2 (Christensen 27, Dahoud 45) Schalke 2 (Goretzka 54, Bentaleb 68 pen). Att: 46,283 (agg 3-3, Schalke won on away goals) Genk 1 (Castagne 20) Gent 1 (Verstraete 84). Att: 16,028 (Genk won 6-3 on agg). Krasnodar 0 Celta Vigo 2 (Hugh Mallo 52, Aspas 80). Att: 33,318 (Celta Vigo won 4-1 on agg). **Manchester Utd** 1 (Mata 70) Rostov 0. Att: 64,361 (Manchester Utd won 2-1 on agg). Roma 2 (Strootman 18, Tousart 60 og) Lyon 1 (Diakhaby 16). Att: 46,453 (Lyon won 5-4 on agg)

QUARTER-FINALS, FIRST LEG

Ajax 2 (Klaassen 23 pen, 52) Schalke 0. Att: 52,384. Anderlecht 1 (Dendoncker 87) **Manchester Utd** 1 (Mkhitaryan 37). Att: 20,060. Celtic Vigo 3 (Sisto 14, Aspas 17, Guidetti 38) Genk 2 (Boetius 10, Buffel 68). Att: 21,608. Lyon 2 (Tolisso 83, Morel 84) Besiktas 1 (Babel 15). Att: 55,452

QUARTER-FINALS, SECOND LEG

Beiktas 2 (Talisca 27, 58) Lyon 1 (Lacazette 34). Att: 39,623 (aet, agg 3-3, Lyon won 7-6 on pens). Genk 1 (Trossard 67) Celtic Vigo 1 (Sisto 63). Att: 18,833 (Celta Vigo won 4-3 on agg). **Manchester Utd** 2 (Mkhitaryan 10, Rashford 107) Anderlecht 1 (Hanni 32). Att: 71,496 (aet, Manchester Utd won 3-2 on agg). Schalke 3 (Goretzka 53, Burgstaller 56, Caligiuri 101) Ajax 2 (Viergever 111, Younes 120). Att: 53,701 (aet, Ajax won 4-3 on agg)

SEMI-FINALS, FIRST LEG

Ajax 4 (Traore 25, 71, Dolberg 34, Younes 49) Lyon 1 (Valbuena 66). Att: 52,141. Celta Vigo 0 **Manchester Utd** 1 (Rashford 67). Att: 26,202

SEMI-FINALS, SECOND LEG

Lyon 3 (Lacazette 45 pen, 45, Ghezzal 81) Ajax 1 (Dolberg 27). Att: 53,810 (Ajax won 5-4 on agg). **Manchester Utd** 1 (Fellaini 17) Celta Vigo 1 (Roncaglia 05). Att: 75,138 (Manchester Utd won 2-1 on agg)

FINAL

AJAX 0 MANCHESTER UNITED 2
Friends Arena, Stockholm (46,961); Wednesday, May 24 2017

Ajax (4-3-3): Onana, Veltman, Sanchez, De Ligt, Riedewald (De Jong 80), Ziyech, Schone (Van de Beek 70), Klaassen (capt), Traore, Dolberg (Neres 62), Younes. **Subs not used:** Boer, Tete, Westermann, Kluivert. **Booked:** Veltman, Younes, Riedewald. **Coach:** Peter Bosz **Manchester United** (4-3-3): Romero, Valencia (capt), Smalling, Blind, Darmian, Fellaini, Herrera, Pogba, Mata (Rooney 90), Rashford (Martial 84), Mkhitaryan (Lingard 74). **Subs not used:** De Gea, Jones, Carrick, Fosu-Mensah. **Scorers:** Pogba (18), Mkhitaryan (48). **Booked:** Mkhitaryan, Fellaini, Mata. **Manager:** Jose Mourinho **Referee:** D Skomina (Slovenia). **Half-time:** 0-1

Not just a trophy for the club, but a tribute to the city. Manchester United players overcame private grief on a public stage to win the Europa League Final and dedicate it to the victims of the bomb attack at home just 48 hours earlier. They conducted themselves commendably in a difficult, demanding build-up to the match in Stockholm, then displayed the professionalism and pride needed to bring the one piece of silverware missing from the Old Trafford honours cabinet. Big-match experience quelled the youthful energy Ajax brought to the final. United were never in trouble. Paul Pogba opened the scoring after 18 minutes and long before Henrikh Mkhitaryan's second goal three minutes into the second half, they were totally in control. The reward was a place in the Champions League with Chelsea, Tottenham, Manchester City and Liverpool to go alongside the season's League Cup and, at Jose Mourinho's insistence, the Community Shield. It was a vindication of the manager's decision, in the latter stages of the campaign, to target this competition, rather than the Premier League, as United's best chance of qualifying for the elite tournament. It meant they joined a select band of teams, Bayern Munich, Juventus, Chelsea and Ajax, in winning all the major European trophies. More importantly, the prospect of Champions League football strengthened his hand in securing top players in an increasingly competitive summer transfer market.

Leading scorers: 8 Dzeko (Roma), Giuliano (Zenit St Petersburg); 7 Aduriz (Athletic Bilbao); 6 Dolberg (Ajax), Mkhitaryan (Manchester Utd), Lacazette (Lyon); 5 Hoarau (Young Boys), Aspas (Celta Vigo), Ibrahimovic (Manchester Utd), Kalinic (Fiorentina), Teodorczyk (Anderlecht)

FIFA CLUB WORLD CUP – JAPAN 2016

QUALIFYING MATCHES

Jeonbuk Motors (South Korea) 1 (Bo-Kyung Kim 23) Club America (Mexico) 2 (Romero 58, 74). Att: 14,587 (Suita). Mamelodi Sundowns (South Africa) 0 Kashima Antlers (Japan) 2 (Endo 63, Kanazaki 88). Att: 21,702 (Suita)

SEMI-FINALS

Atletico Nacional (Colombia) 0 Kashima Antlers 3 (Doi 33, Endo 83, Suzuki 85). Att: 15,050 (Suita). Club America 0 Real Madrid 2 (Benzema 45, Ronaldo 90). Att: 50,117 (Yokohama)

FINAL

REAL MADRID 4 KASHIMA ANTLERS 2 (aet)
Yokohama (68,742); Sunday, December 18, 2016

Real Madrid (4-3-3): Navas, Daniel Carvajal, Varane, Sergio Ramos (capt), Marcelo, Modric (Kovacic 105), Casemiro, Kroos, Lucas Vazquez (Isco 81), Benzema, Ronaldo (Alvaro Morata 112). **Subs not used**: Kiko Casilla, Ruben Yanez, Pepe, Rodriguez, Fabio Coentrao, Diaz, Marco Asensio, Danilo. **Scorers**: Benzema (9), Ronaldo (60 pen, 97, 104). **Booked**: Sergio Ramos, Casemiro, Daniel Carvajal. **Coach**: Zinedine Zidane
Kasima Antlers (4-4-2): Sogahata, Nishi, Ueda, Shoji, Yamamoto, Endo (Ito 103), Nagaki (Akasaki 114), Ogasawara (capt) (Fabricio 68), Shibasaki, Kanasaki, Doi (Suzuki 88). **Subs not used**: Kushibiki, Kawamata, Nakamura, Seok-Ho Hwang, Bueno, Misao, Sugimoto, Hirato. **Scorer**: Shibasaki (44, 52). **Booked**: Yamamoto, Fabricio. **Coach**: Masatada Ishii
Referee: J Sikazwe (Zambia). **Half-time**: 1-1

EUROPEAN SUPER CUP 2016

REAL MADRID 3 SEVILLA 2 (aet)
Trondheim (17,939); Tuesday, August 9 2016

Real Madrid (4-3-3): Kiko Casilla, Daniel Carvajal, Varane, Sergio Ramos, Marcelo, Isco (Modric 66) Casemiro, Kovacic (Rodriguez 93), Lucas Vazquez, Alvaro Morata (Benzema 62), Marco Asensio. **Subs not used**: Ruben Yanez, Danilo, Marcos Llorente, Nacho. **Scorers**: Marco Asensio (21), Sergio Ramos (90), Daniel Carvajal (119). **Booked**: Daniel Carvajal, Marco Asensio, Rodriguez. **Coach**: Zinedine Zidane
Sevilla (3-4-3): Sergio Rico, Pareja, Daniel Carrico (Rami 51), Kolodziejczak, Mariano, N'Zonzi,

Iborra (Kranevitter 74), Vazquez, Kiyotake, Vietto (Konoplyanka 67), Vitolo. **Subs not used:** David Soria, Sergio Escudero, Pablo Sarabia, Ben Yedder. **Scorers:** Vazquez (41), Konoplyanka (72). **Booked:** Vitolo, Kolodziejczak. **Sent off:** Kolodziejczak (93). **Coach:** Jorge Sampaoli **Referee:** M Mazic (Serbia). **Half-time:** 1-1

UEFA CUP FINALS

1972	Tottenham beat Wolves 3-2 on agg (2-1a, 1-1h)
1973	Liverpool beat Borussia Moenchengladbach 3-2 on agg (3-0h, 0-2a)
1974	Feyenoord beat Tottenham 4-2 on agg (2-2a, 2-0h)
1975	Borussia Moenchengladbach beat Twente Enschede 5-1 on agg (0-0h, 5-1a)
1976	Liverpool beat Brugge 4-3 on agg (3-2h, 1-1a)
1977	Juventus beat Atletico Bilbao on away goals after 2-2 agg (1-0h, 1-2a)
1978	PSV Eindhoven beat Bastia 3-0 on agg (0-0a, 3-0h)
1979	Borussia Moenchengladbach beat Red Star Belgrade 2-1 on agg (1-1a, 1 0h)
1980	Eintracht Frankfurt beat Borussia Moenchengladbach on away goals after 3-3 agg (2-3a, 1-0h)
1981	Ipswich Town beat AZ 67 Alkmaar 5-4 on agg (3-0h, 2-4a)
1982	IFK Gothenburg beat SV Hamburg 4-0 on agg (1-0h, 3-0a)
1983	Anderlecht beat Benfica 2-1 on agg (1-0h, 1-1a)
1984	Tottenham beat Anderlecht 4-3 on penalties after 2-2 agg (1-1a, 1-1h)
1985	Real Madrid beat Videoton 3-1 on agg (3-0a, 0-1h)
1986	Real Madrid beat Cologne 5-3 on agg (5-1h, 0-2a)
1987	IFK Gothenburg beat Dundee Utd 2-1 on agg (1-0h, 1-1a)
1988	Bayer Leverkusen beat Espanol 3-2 on penalties after 3-3 agg (0-3a, 3-0h)
1989	Napoli beat VfB Stuttgart 5-4 on agg (2-1h, 3-3a)
1990	Juventus beat Fiorentina 3-1 on agg (3-1h, 0-0a)
1991	Inter Milan beat AS Roma 2-1 on agg (2-0h, 0-1a)
1992	Ajax beat Torino on away goals after 2-2 agg (2-2a, 0-0h)
1993	Juventus beat Borussia Dortmund 6-1 on agg (3-1a, 3-0h)
1994	Inter Milan beat Salzburg 2-0 on agg (1-0a, 1-0h)
1995	Parma beat Juventus 2-1 on agg (1-0h, 1-1a)
1996	Bayern Munich beat Bordeaux 5-1 on agg (2-0h, 3-1a)
1997	FC Schalke beat Inter Milan 4-1 on penalties after 1-1 agg (1-0h, 0-1a)
1998	Inter Milan beat Lazio 3-0 (one match) – Paris
1999	Parma beat Marseille 3-0 (one match) – Moscow
2000	Galatasaray beat Arsenal 4-1 on penalties after 0-0 (one match) – Copenhagen
2001	Liverpool beat Alaves 5-4 on golden goal (one match) – Dortmund
2002	Feyenoord beat Borussia Dortmund 3-2 (one match) – Rotterdam
2003	FC Porto beat Celtic 3-2 on silver goal (one match) – Seville
2004	Valencia beat Marseille 2-0 (one match) – Gothenburg
2005	CSKA Moscow beat Sporting Lisbon 3-1 (one match) – Lisbon
2006	Sevilla beat Middlesbrough 4-0 (one match) – Eindhoven
2007	Sevilla beat Espanyol 3-1 on penalties after 2-2 (one match) – Hampden Park
2008	Zenit St Petersburg beat Rangers 2-0 (one match) – City of Manchester Stadium
2009†	Shakhtar Donetsk beat Werder Bremen 2-1 (one match) – Istanbul

EUROPA LEAGUE FINALS

2010†	Atletico Madrid beat Fulham 2-1 (one match) Hamburg
2011	Porto beat Braga 1-0 (one match) – Dublin
2012	Atletico Madrid beat Athletic Bilbao 3-0 (one match) – Bucharest
2013	Chelsea beat Benfica 2-1 (one match) – Amsterdam
2014	Sevilla beat Benfica 4-2 on penalties after 0-0 (one match) – Turin

2015	Sevilla beat Dnipro 3-2 (one match) – Warsaw
2016	Sevilla beat Liverpool 3-1 (one match) – Basle
2017	Manchester Utd beat Ajax 2-0 (one match) – Stockholm

(† After extra-time)

FAIRS CUP FINALS

(As UEFA Cup previously known)

1958	Barcelona beat London 8-2 on agg (2-2a, 6-0h)
1960	Barcelona beat Birmingham 4-1 on agg (0-0a, 4-1h)
1961	AS Roma beat Birmingham City 4-2 on agg (2-2a, 2-0h)
1962	Valencia beat Barcelona 7-3 on agg (6-2h, 1-1a)
1963	Valencia beat Dynamo Zagreb 4-1 on agg (2-1a, 2-0h)
1964	Real Zaragoza beat Valencia 2-1 (Barcelona)
1965	Ferencvaros beat Juventus 1-0 (Turin)
1966	Barcelona beat Real Zaragoza 4-3 on agg (0-1h, 4-2a)
1967	Dinamo Zagreb beat Leeds Utd 2-0 on agg (2-0h, 0-0a)
1968	Leeds Utd beat Ferencvaros 1-0 on agg (1-0h, 0-0a)
1969	Newcastle Utd beat Ujpest Dozsa 6-2 on agg (3-0h, 3-2a)
1970	Arsenal beat Anderlecht 4-3 on agg (1-3a, 3-0h)
1971	Leeds Utd beat Juventus on away goals after 3-3 agg (2-2a, 1-1h)

CUP-WINNERS' CUP FINALS

1961	Fiorentina beat Rangers 4-1 on agg (2-0 Glasgow first leg, 2-1 Florence second leg)
1962	Atletico Madrid beat Fiorentina 3-0 (replay Stuttgart, after a 1-1 draw, Glasgow)
1963	Tottenham beat Atletico Madrid 5-1 (Rotterdam)
1964	Sporting Lisbon beat MTK Budapest 1-0 (replay Antwerp, after a 3-3 draw, Brussels)
1965	West Ham Utd beat Munich 1860 2-0 (Wembley)
1966†	Borussia Dortmund beat Liverpool 2-1 (Glasgow)
1967†	Bayern Munich beat Rangers 1-0 (Nuremberg)
1968	AC Milan beat SV Hamburg 2-0 (Rotterdam)
1969	Slovan Bratislava beat Barcelona 3-2 (Basle)
1970	Manchester City beat Gornik Zabrze 2-1 (Vienna)
1971†	Chelsea beat Real Madrid 2-1 (replay Athens, after a 1-1 draw, Athens)
1972	Rangers beat Moscow Dynamo 3-2 (Barcelona)
1973	AC Milan beat Leeds Utd 1-0 (Salonika)
1974	Magdeburg beat AC Milan 2-0 (Rotterdam)
1975	Dynamo Kiev beat Ferencvaros 3-0 (Basle)
1976	Anderlecht beat West Ham Utd 4-2 (Brussels)
1977	SV Hamburg beat Anderlecht 2-0 (Amsterdam)
1978	Anderlecht beat Austria WAC 4-0 (Paris)
1979†	Barcelona beat Fortuna Dusseldorf 4-3 (Basle)
1980†	Valencia beat Arsenal 5-4 on penalties after a 0-0 draw (Brussels)
1981	Dinamo Tbilisi beat Carl Zeiss Jena 2-1 (Dusseldorf)
1982	Barcelona beat Standard Liege 2-1 (Barcelona)
1983†	Aberdeen beat Real Madrid 2-1 (Gothenburg)
1984	Juventus beat Porto 2-1 (Basle)
1985	Everton beat Rapid Vienna 3-1 (Rotterdam)
1986	Dynamo Kiev beat Atletico Madrid 3-0 (Lyon)
1987	Ajax beat Lokomotiv Leipzig 1-0 (Athens)
1988	Mechelen beat Ajax 1-0 (Strasbourg)
1989	Barcelona beat Sampdoria 2-0 (Berne)
1990	Sampdoria beat Anderlecht 2-0 (Gothenburg)

1991	Manchester Utd beat Barcelona 2-1 (Rotterdam)
1992	Werder Bremen beat Monaco 2-0 (Lisbon)
1993	Parma beat Royal Antwerp 3-1 (Wembley)
1994	Arsenal beat Parma 1-0 (Copenhagen)
1995†	Real Zaragoza beat Arsenal 2-1 (Paris)
1996	Paris St Germain beat Rapid Vienna 1-0 (Brussels)
1997	Barcelona beat Paris St Germain 1-0 (Rotterdam)
1998	Chelsea beat VfB Stuttgart 1-0 (Stockholm)
1999	Lazio beat Real Mallorca 2-1 (Villa Park, Birmingham)

(† After extra time)

EUROPEAN SUPER CUP RESULTS

1972*	Ajax beat Rangers 6-3 on agg (3-1, 3-2)
1973	Ajax beat AC Milan 6-1 on agg (0-1, 6-0)
1974	Bayern Munich and Magdeburg did not play
1975	Dynamo Kiev beat Bayern Munich 3-0 on agg (1-0, 2-0)
1976	Anderlecht beat Bayern Munich 5-3 on agg (1-2, 4-1)
1977	Liverpool beat Hamburg 7-1 on agg (1-1, 6-0)
1978	Anderlecht beat Liverpool 4-3 on agg (3-1, 1-2)
1979	Nottm Forest beat Barcelona 2-1 on agg (1-0, 1-1)
1980	Valencia beat Nottm Forest on away goal after 2-2 agg (1-2, 1-0)
1981	Liverpool and Dinamo Tbilisi did not play
1982	Aston Villa beat Barcelona 3-1 on agg (0-1, 3-0 aet)
1983	Aberdeen beat Hamburg 2-0 on agg (0-0, 2-0)
1984	Juventus beat Liverpool 2-0 – one match (Turin)
1985	Juventus and Everton did not play
1986	Stéaua Bucharest beat Dynamo Kiev 1-0 – one match (Monaco)
1987	Porto beat Ajax 2-0 on agg (1-0, 1-0)
1988	Mechelen beat PSV Eindhoven 3-1 on agg (3-0, 0-1)
1989	AC Milan beat Barcelona 2-1 on agg (1-1, 1-0)
1990	AC Milan beat Sampdoria 3-1 on agg (1-1, 2-0)
1991	Manchester Utd beat Red Star Belgrade 1-0 – one match (Old Trafford)
1992	Barcelona beat Werder Bremen 3-2 on agg (1-1, 2-1)
1993	Parma beat AC Milan 2-1 on agg (0-1, 2-0 aet)
1994	AC Milan beat Arsenal 2-0 on agg (0-0, 2-0)
1995	Ajax beat Real Zaragoza 5-1 on agg (1-1, 4-0)
1996	Juventus beat Paris St Germain 9-2 on agg (6-1, 3-1)
1997	Barcelona beat Borussia Dortmund 3-1 on agg (2-0, 1-1)
1998	Chelsea beat Real Madrid 1-0 (Monaco)
1999	Lazio beat Manchester Utd 1-0 (Monaco)
2000	Galatasaray beat Real Madrid 2-1 – aet, golden goal (Monaco)
2001	Liverpool beat Bayern Munich 3-2 (Monaco)
2002	Real Madrid beat Feyenoord 3-1 (Monaco)
2003	AC Milan beat Porto 1-0 (Monaco)
2004	Valencia beat Porto 2-1 (Monaco)
2005	Liverpool beat CSKA Moscow 3-1 – aet (Monaco)
2006	Sevilla beat Barcelona 3-0 (Monaco)
2007	AC Milan beat Sevilla 3-1 (Monaco)
2008	Zenit St Petersburg beat Manchester Utd 2-1 (Monaco)
2009	Barcelona beat Shakhtar Donetsk 1-0 – aet (Monaco)
2010	Atletico Madrid beat Inter Milan 2-0 (Monaco)
2011	Barcelona beat Porto 2-0 (Monaco)
2012	Atletico Madrid beat Chelsea 4-1 (Monaco)

2013	Bayern Munich beat Chelsea 5-4 on pens, aet – 2-2 (Prague)		
2014	Real Madrid beat Sevilla 2-0 (Cardiff)		
2015	Barcelona beat Sevilla 5-4 – aet (Tbilisi)		
2016	Real Madrid beat Sevilla 3-2 – aet (Trondheim)		

*not recognised by UEFA; from 1998 one match

INTER-CONTINENTAL CUP

Year	Winners	Runners-up	Score
1960	Real Madrid (Spa)	Penarol (Uru)	0-0 5-1
1961	Penarol (Uru)	Benfica (Por)	0-1 2-1 5-0
1962	Santos (Bra)	Benfica (Por)	3-2 5-2
1963	Santos (Bra)	AC Milan (Ita)	2-4 4-2 1-0
1964	Inter Milan (Ita)	Independiente (Arg)	0-1 2-0 1-0
1965	Inter Milan (Ita)	Independiente (Arg)	3-0 0-0
1966	Penarol (Uru)	Real Madrid (Spa)	2-0 2-0
1967	Racing (Arg)	Celtic (Sco)	0-1 2-1 1-0
1968	Estudiantes (Arg)	Manchester Utd (Eng)	1-0 1-1
1969	AC Milan (Ita)	Estudiantes (Arg)	3-0 1-2
1970	Feyenoord (Hol)	Estudiantes (Arg)	2-2 1-0
1971	Nacional (Uru)	Panathanaikos (Gre)	* 1-1 2-1
1972	Ajax (Hol)	Independiente (Arg)	1-1 3-0
1973	Independiente (Arg)	Juventus* (Ita)	1-0 #
1974	Atletico Madrid (Spa)*	Independiente (Arg)	0-1 2-0
1975	Not played		
1976	Bayern Munich (WGer)	Cruzeiro (Bra)	2-0 0-0
1977	Boca Juniors (Arg)	Borussia Mönchengladbach* (WGer)	2-2 3-0
1978	Not played		
1979	Olimpia Asuncion (Par)	Malmö* (Swe)	1-0 2-1
1980	Nacional (Arg)	Nott'm Forest (Eng)	1-0
1981	Flamengo (Bra)	Liverpool (Eng)	3-0
1982	Penarol (Uru)	Aston Villa (Eng)	2-0
1983	Porto Alegre (Bra)	SV Hamburg (WGer)	2-1
1984	Independiente (Arg)	Liverpool (Eng)	1-0
1985	Juventus (Ita)	Argentinos Juniors (Arg)	2-2 (aet)
	(Juventus won 4-2 on penalties)		
1986	River Plate (Arg)	Steaua Bucharest (Rom)	1-0
1987	Porto (Por)	Penarol (Uru)	2-1 (aet)
1988	Nacional (Uru)	PSV Eindhoven (Hol)	1-1 (aet)
	(Nacional won 7-6 on penalties)		
1989	AC Milan (Ita)	Nacional (Col)	1-0 (aet)
1990	AC Milan (Ita)	Olimpia Asuncion (Par)	3-0
1991	Red Star (Yug)	Colo Colo (Chi)	3-0
1992	Sao Paulo (Bra)	Barcelona (Spa)	2-1
1993	Sao Paulo (Bra)	AC Milan (Ita)	3-2
1994	Velez Sarsfield (Arg)	AC Milan (Ita)	2-0
1995	Ajax (Hol)	Gremio (Bra)	0-0 (aet)
	(Ajax won 4-3 on penalties)		
1996	Juventus (Ita)	River Plate (Arg)	1-0
1997	Borussia Dortmund (Ger)	Cruzeiro (Arg)	2-0
1998	Real Madrid (Spa)	Vasco da Gama (Bra)	2-1
1999	Manchester Utd (Eng)	Palmeiras (Bra)	1-0
2000	Boca Juniors (Arg)	Real Madrid (Spa)	2-1

2001	Bayern Munich (Ger)	Boca Juniors (Arg)	1-0
2002	Real Madrid (Spa)	Olimpia Ascuncion (Par)	2-0
2003	Boca Juniors (Arg)	AC Milan (Ita)	1-1
	(Boca Juniors won 3-1 on penalties)		
2004	FC Porto (Por)	Caldas (Col)	0-0

(FC Porto won 8-7 on penalties)
Played as a single match in Japan since 1980
* European Cup runners-up # One match only
Summary: 43 contests; South America 22 wins, Europe 23 wins

CLUB WORLD CHAMPIONSHIP

2005	Sao Paulo beat Liverpool	1-0
2006	Internacional (Bra) beat Barcelona	1-0
2007	AC Milan beat Boca Juniors (Arg)	4-2

CLUB WORLD CUP

2008	Manchester Utd beat Liga de Quito	1-0
2009	Barcelona beat Estudiantes	2-1 (aet)
2010	Inter Milan beat TP Mazembe	3-0
2011	Barcelona beat Santos	4-0
2012	Corinthians beat Chelsea	1-0
2013	Bayern Munich beat Raja Casablanca	2-0
2014	Real Madrid beat San Lorenzo	2-0
2015	Barcelona beat River Plate	3-0
2016	Real Madrid beat Kashima Antlers	4-2 (aet)

REMEMBERING THE FIRST LEAGUE GOAL

The first ever goal scored in league football was commemorated last season by a plaque unveiled in the Pikes Lane area of Bolton. For more than a century, it was thought that an own goal by Aston Villa's Gershom Cox against Wolves held that distinction. But research by author and historian Mark Metcalf and librarian Robert Boylng revealed the kick-off in that game had been delayed. It meant Kenny Davenport's goal at 3.47pm for Bolton against Derby on September 8, 1888, was the first. A local business agreed to have the plaque on their building in memory of Davenport, who holds a special place in Bolton Wanderers' history. He was the first from the club to play for England and part of the first group of footballers to become professionals. Results on that day were: Bolton 3 Derby 6, Everton 2 Accrington 1, Preston 5 Burnley 2, Stoke 0 West Bromwich Albion 2, Wolves 1 Aston Villa 1. Blackburn and Notts County played the following week. The English Football League is the world's original league competition.

EUROPEAN TABLES 2016–2017

FRANCE – LIGUE 1

	P	W	D	L	F	A	GD	Pts
Monaco	38	30	5	3	107	31	76	95
Paris SG	38	27	6	5	83	27	56	87
Nice	38	22	12	4	63	36	27	78
Lyon	38	21	4	13	77	48	29	67
Marseille	38	17	11	10	57	41	16	62
Bordeaux	38	15	14	9	53	43	10	59
Nantes	38	14	9	15	40	54	-14	51
St Etienne	38	12	14	12	41	42	-1	50
Rennes	38	12	14	12	36	42	-6	50
Guingamp	38	14	8	16	46	53	-7	50
Lille	38	13	7	18	40	47	-7	46
Angers	38	13	7	18	40	49	-9	46
Toulouse	38	10	14	14	37	41	-4	44
Metz	38	11	10	17	39	72	-33	43
Montpellier	38	10	9	19	48	66	-18	39
Dijon	38	8	13	17	46	58	-12	37
Caen	38	10	7	21	36	65	-29	37
Lorient	38	10	6	22	44	70	-26	36
Nancy	38	9	8	21	29	52	-23	35
Bastia	38	8	10	20	29	54	-25	34

Leading league scorers: 35 Cavani (Paris SG); 28 Lacazette (Lyon); 21 Falcao (Monaco); 20 Gomis (Marseille); 16 Thauvin (Marseille); 15 Balotelli (Nice), Mbappe-Lottin (Monaco), Santini (Caen); 14 De Preville (Lille), Mounie (Montpellier)
Cup Final: Paris SG 1 (Cissokho 90 og) Angers 0

HOLLAND – EREDIVISIE

	P	W	D	L	F	A	GD	Pts
Feyenoord	34	26	4	4	86	25	61	82
Ajax	34	25	6	3	79	23	56	81
PSV Eindhoven	34	22	10	2	68	23	45	76
Utrecht	34	18	8	8	54	38	16	62
Vitesse Arnhem	34	15	6	13	51	40	11	51
Alkmaar	34	12	13	9	56	52	4	49
Twente	34	12	9	13	48	50	-2	45
Groningen	34	10	13	11	55	51	4	43
Heerenveen	34	12	7	15	54	53	1	43
Heracles	34	12	7	15	53	55	-2	43
Den Haag	34	11	5	18	37	59	-22	38
Excelsior	34	9	10	15	43	60	-17	37
Willem	34	9	9	16	29	44	-15	36
Zwolle	34	9	8	17	39	67	-28	35
Sparta	34	9	7	18	42	61	-19	34
NEC*	34	9	7	18	32	59	-27	34
Roda	34	7	12	15	26	51	-25	33
Go Ahead*	34	6	5	23	32	73	-41	23

*relegated

Leading league scorers: 21 Jorgensen (Feyenoord); 20 Van Wolfswinkel (Vitesse Arnhem); 19 Armenteros (Heracles), Ghoochannejhad (Heerenveen); 18 Unal (Twente); 17 Mahi (Groningen); 16 Dolberg (Ajax); 14 Klaasen (Ajax), Toornstra (Feyenoord)
Cup Final: Vitesse Arnhem 2 (Van Wolfswinkel 80, 88) Alkmaar 0

GERMANY – BUNDESLIGA

	P	W	D	L	F	A	GD	Pts
Bayern Munich	34	25	7	2	89	22	67	82
Leipzig	34	20	7	7	66	39	27	67
Borussia Dortmund	34	18	10	6	72	40	32	64
Hoffenheim	34	16	14	4	64	37	27	62
Cologne	34	12	13	9	51	42	9	49
Hertha	34	15	4	15	43	47	-4	49
Freiburg	34	14	6	14	42	60	-18	48
Werder Bremen	34	13	6	15	61	64	-3	45
Borussia M'gladbach	34	12	9	13	45	49	4	45
Schalke	34	11	10	13	45	40	5	43
Eintracht Frankfurt	34	11	9	14	36	43	-7	42
Bayer Leverkusen	34	11	8	15	53	55	-2	41
Augsburg	34	9	11	14	35	51	-16	38
Hamburg	34	10	8	16	33	61	-28	38
Mainz	34	10	7	17	44	55	-11	37
Wolfsburg	34	10	7	17	34	52	-18	37
Ingolstadt	34	8	8	18	36	57	-21	32
Darmstadt	34	7	4	23	28	63	-35	25

Leading league scorers: 31 Aubameyang (Borussia Dortmund); 30 Lewandowski (Bayern Munich); 25 Modeste (Cologne); 21 Werner (Leipzig); 16 Gomez (Wolfsburg); 15 Kramaric (Hoffenheim), Kruse (Werder Bremen); 13 Robben (Bayern Munich); 12 Ibisevic (Hertha)
Cup Final: Borussia Dortmund 2 (Dembele 8, Aubameyang 67 pen) Eintracht Frankfurt 1 (Rebic 29)

ITALY – SERIE A

	P	W	D	L	F	A	GD	Pts
Juventus	38	29	4	5	77	27	50	91
Roma	38	28	3	7	90	38	52	87
Napoli	38	26	8	4	94	39	55	86
Atalanta	38	21	9	8	62	41	21	72
Lazio	38	21	7	10	74	51	23	70
AC Milan	38	18	9	11	57	45	12	63
Inter Milan	38	19	5	14	72	49	23	62
Fiorentina	38	16	12	10	63	57	6	60
Torino	38	13	14	11	71	66	5	53
Sampdoria	38	12	12	14	49	55	-6	48
Cagliari	38	14	5	19	55	76	-21	47
Sassuolo	38	13	7	18	58	63	-5	46
Udinese	38	12	9	17	47	56	-9	45
Chievo	38	12	7	19	43	61	-18	43
Bologna	38	11	8	19	40	58	-18	41
Genoa	38	9	9	20	38	64	-26	36
Crotone	38	9	7	22	34	58	-24	34
Empoli	38	8	8	22	29	61	-32	32
Palermo	38	6	8	24	33	77	-44	26
Pescara	38	3	9	26	37	81	-44	18

Leading league scorers: 29 Dzeko (Roma); 28 Mertens (Napoli); 26 Belotti (Torino); 24 Higuain (Juventus), Icardi (Inter Milan); 23 Immobile (Lazio/Roma); 18 Insigne (Napoli); 16 Borriello (Cagliari/Calcio), Gomez (Atalanta), Keita (Lazio/Roma)
Cup Final: Juventus 2 (Dani Alves 12, Bonucci 24) Lazio 0

PORTUGAL – PRIMEIRA LIGA

	P	W	D	L	F	A	GD	Pts
Benfica	34	25	7	2	72	18	54	82
Porto	34	22	10	2	71	19	52	76
Sporting Lisbon	34	21	7	6	68	36	32	70
Guimaraes	34	18	8	8	50	39	11	62
Sporting Braga	34	15	9	10	51	36	15	54
Maritimo	34	13	11	10	34	32	2	50
Rio Ave	34	14	7	13	41	39	2	49
Feirense	34	14	6	14	31	45	-14	48
Boavista	34	10	13	11	33	36	-3	43
Estoril	34	10	8	16	36	42	-6	38
Chaves	34	8	14	12	35	42	-7	38
Setubal	34	10	8	16	30	39	-9	38
Pacos Ferreira	34	8	12	14	32	45	-13	36
Belenenses	34	9	9	16	27	45	-18	36
Moreirense	34	8	9	17	33	48	-15	33
Tondela	34	8	8	18	29	52	-23	32
Arouca	34	9	5	20	33	57	-24	32
Nacional	34	4	9	21	22	58	-36	21

Leading league scorers: 34 Bas Dost (Sporting Lisbon); 19 Soares (Porto/Guimaraes); 16 Andre Silva (Porto), Mitroglou (Benfica); 13 Jonas (Benfica), Marega (Guimaraes); 11 Rui Fonte (Sporting Braga), Welthon (Pacos Ferreira); 10 Pizzi (Benfica)

Cup Final: Benfica 2 (Jimenez 48, Savio 53) Guimaraes 1 (Zunga 79)

SPAIN – LA LIGA

	P	W	D	L	F	A	GD	Pts
Real Madrid	38	29	6	3	106	41	65	93
Barcelona	38	28	6	4	116	37	79	90
Atletico Madrid	38	23	9	6	70	27	43	78
Sevilla	38	21	9	8	69	49	20	72
Villarreal	38	19	10	9	56	33	23	67
Real Sociedad	38	19	7	12	59	53	6	64
Athletic Bilbao	38	19	6	13	53	43	10	63
Espanyol	38	15	11	12	49	50	-1	56
Alaves	38	14	13	11	41	43	-2	55
Eibar	38	15	9	14	56	51	5	54
Malaga	38	12	10	16	49	55	-6	46
Valencia	38	13	7	18	56	65	-9	46
Celta Vigo	38	13	6	19	53	69	-16	45
Las Palmas	38	10	9	19	53	74	-21	39
Real Betis	38	10	9	19	41	64	-23	39
Deportivo	38	8	12	18	43	61	-18	36
Leganes	38	8	11	19	36	55	-19	35
Sporting Gijon	38	7	10	21	42	72	-30	31
Osasuna	38	4	10	24	40	94	-54	22
Granada	38	4	8	26	30	82	-52	20

Leading league scorers: 37 Messi (Barcelona); 29 Suarez (Barcelona); 25 Ronaldo (Real Madrid); 19 Aspas (Celta Vigo); 16 Aduriz (Athletic Bilbao), Griezmann (Atletico Madrid); 15 Alvaro Morata (Real Madrid); 14 Sandro (Malaga); 13 Gerard (Espanyol), Neymar (Barcelona), Ruben Castro (Real Betis)

Cup Final: Barcelona 3 (Messi 30, Neymar 45, Alcacer 45) Alaves 1 (Hernandez 33)

BRITISH & IRISH INTERNATIONALS 2016–2017

* denotes new cap

SLOVAKIA 0 ENGLAND 1
Group F: Trnava (18,111); Sunday, September 4 2016
Slovakia (4-3-2-1): Kozacik, Pekarik, Skrtel, Durica, Hubocan, Pecovsky (Gyomber 56), Gregus, Hamsik, Svento (Kiss 78), Mak (Kubik 71), Duris. **Booked**: Skrtel, Hubocan. **Sent off**: Skrtel (57)
England (4-2-3-1): Hart, Walker, Stones, Cahill, Rose, Dier, Henderson (Alli 64), Lallana, Rooney, Sterling (Walcott 71), Kane (Sturridge 82). **Scorer**: Lallana (90)
Referee: M Mazic (Serbia). **Half-time**: 0-0
(Sam Allardyce's only game as England manager)

MALTA 1 SCOTLAND 5
Group F: Ta'Qali (15,069); Sunday, September 4 2016
Malta (3-5-1-1): Hogg, Caruana, Agius, Borg, Scicluna (Camilleri 79), Fenech, Sciberras, Gambin, Zerafa, Schembri (Briffa 66), Effiong (Mifsud 89). **Scorer**: Effiong (14). **Booked**: Fenech, Effiong. **Sent off**: Caruana (60), Gambin (90)
Scotland (4-2-3-1): Marshall, Paterson, Hanley, R Martin, Robertson, D Fletcher, Bannan, Burke (Forest 66), Snodgrass, Ritchie (Anya 86), C Martin (S Fletcher 69). **Scorers**: Snodgrass (10, 61 pen, 85), C Martin (53), S Fletcher (78)
Referee: E Aranovskiy (Ukraine). **Half-time**: 1-1

CZECH REPUBLIC 0 NORTHERN IRELAND 0
Group C: Prague (10,731); Sunday, September 4 2016
Czech Republic (4-1-4-1): Vaclik, Kaderabek, Suchy, M Kadlec, Novak, Pavelka, Skalak (Kopic 77), Darida, V Kadlec (Vydra 84), Krejci, Skoda (Necid 68). **Booked**: Pavelka
Northern Ireland (4-1-4-1): McGovern, McLaughlin, McAuley, J Evans, Ferguson (Hodson 66), McNair, Ward (McGinn 74), Davis, Norwood, Dallas, Lafferty (Magennis 59). **Booked**: Norwood, Ward
Referee: I Sidiropoulos (Greece)

WALES 4 MOLDOVA 0
Group D: Cardiff City Stadium (31,731); Monday, September 5 2016
Wales (3-4-2-1): Hennessey, Chester, A Williams (Collins 82), Davies, Gunter, Allen, Ledley (Huws 67), Taylor, King, Bale, Vokes (Robson-Kanu 75). **Scorers**: Vokes (38), Allen (44), Bale (51, 90 pen)
Moldova (4-4-1-1): Cebanu, Jardan, Cascaval, Epureanu, Armas, Ionita, Gatcan, Cojocari, Dedov (Mihailov 85), Cebotaru (Sidorenco 75), Ginsari (Bugaev 75). **Booked**: Dedov
Referee: L Liany (Israel). **Half-time**: 2-0

SERBIA 2 REPUBLIC OF IRELAND 2
Group D: Belgrade (7,896); Monday, September 5 2016
Serbia (5-4-1): Rajkovic, Ivanovic, Nastasic, Vukovic, Rukavina, Milivojevic, Gudelj, Mladenovic (Tosic 77), Tadic, Mitrovic (Pavlovic 59), Kostic (Katai 81). **Scorers**: Kostic (62), Tadic (69 pen). **Booked**: Nastasic, Katai
Republic of Ireland (4-3-3): Randolphs, Coleman, O'Shea, Keogh, Ward (Quinn 70), Hendrick (Murphy 76), Whelan, Brady, Walters, S Long (Clark 90), McClean **Scorers**: Hendrick (3), Murphy (80). **Booked**: Ward, Hendrick, Brady, Whelan
Referee: V Kassai (Hungary). **Half-time**: 0-1

AUSTRIA 2 WALES 2
Group D: Vienna (44,200): Thursday, October 6 2016
Austria (4-2-3-1): Almer (Ozcan 57), Klein, Dragovic, Hinteregger, Wimmer, Baumgartlinger, Alaba, Sabitzer, Junuzovic, Arnautovic (Schaub 87), Janko. **Scorer**: Arnautovic (28, 48). **Booked**: Arnautovic, Janko
Wales (5-2-2-1): Hennessey, Gunter, Chester, A Williams, Davies, Taylor (Huws 90), Allen

(Edwards 55), Ledley, King, Bale, Vokes (Robson-Kanu 77). **Scorers**: Allen (22), Wimmer (45 og). **Booked**: Davies
Referee: C Cakir (Turkey). **Half-time**: 1-2

REPUBLIC OF IRELAND 1 GEORGIA 0
Group D: Aviva Stadium (39,793); Thursday, October 6 2016
Republic of Ireland (4-1-4-1): Randolph, Coleman, Clark, Duffy, Ward, McCarthy, Walters, Hendrick, Brady (Whelan 81), McClean, S Long (O'Shea 90). **Scorer**: Coleman (56). **Booked**: Hendrick
Georgia (4-2-3-1): Loria, Kakabadze, Kashia, Kverkvelia, Novalovski (Kobakhidze 89), Daushvili (Kacharava 90), Gvilla, Okriashvili, Kazaishvili, Ananidze (Skhirtiadze 74), Mchedlidze. **Booked**: Mchedlidze
Referee: T Chapron (France). **Half-time**: 0-0

ENGLAND 2 MALTA 0
Group F: Wembley (81,787); Saturday, October 8 2016
England (4-2-3-1): Hart, Walker, Cahill, Stones, Bertrand (Rose 19), Henderson, Rooney, Walcott (Rashford 68), Alli, *Lingard, Sturridge (Vardy 74). **Scorers**: Sturridge (29), Alli (38)
Malta (4-5-1): Hogg, Borg, Camilleri, Agius, Z Muscat, A Muscat, Kristensen, Sciberras, Schembri (R Muscat 86), Fenech, Effiong (Mifsud 76). **Booked**: Borg
Referee: S Johannesson (Sweden). **Half-time**: 2-0
(Gareth Southgate's first match as interim England manager)

SCOTLAND 1 LITHUANIA 1
Group F: Hampden Park (35,966); Saturday, October 8 2016
Scotland (4-2-3-1): Marshall, Paterson, R Martin, Hanley, Robertson, D Fletcher (McArthur 46), Bannan, Burke (Forrest 57), Snodgrass, Ritchie (Griffiths 71), C Martin. **Scorer**: McArthur (89). **Booked**: Hanley, McArthur
Lithuania (4-2-3-1): Setkus, Vaitkunas, Freidgemas, Girdvainas, Slavickas (Andriuskevicius 63), Kuklys, Zulpa (Chvedukas 66), Cernych, Slivka, Novikovas, Valskis (Grigarivivius 85). **Scorer**: Cernych (59). **Booked**: Vaitkunas, Freidgemas, Kuklys
Referee: T Stieler (Germany). **Half-time**: 0-0

NORTHERN IRELAND 4 SAN MARINO 0
Group C: Windsor Park (18,234); Saturday, October 8 2016
Northern Ireland (4-4-1-1): McGovern, McLaughlin (McNair 77), McAuley, J Evans, Ferguson, McGinn, Davis, Norwood, Dallas (Washington 65), Ward, Magennis (Lafferty 73). **Scorers**: Davis (26 pen), Lafferty (79, 90), Ward (85)
San Marino (4-5-1): A Simoncini, Berardi, F Vitaioli, D Simoncini, Palazzi, Hirsch (Cesarini 56), Coppini (Golinucci 71), Tosi, M Vitaioli, Stefanelli (Zafferani 87), Della Valle. **Booked**: Palazzi, F Vitaioli, Berardi, M Vitaioli. **Sent off**: Palazzi (49)
Referee: I Kovacs (Romania). **Half-time**: 1-0

WALES 1 GEORGIA 1
Group D: Cardiff City Stadium (32,652): Sunday, October 9 2016
Wales (3-4-2-1): Hennessey, Chester, A Williams, Davies, Gunter, Edwards, Ledley (Huws 73), Taylor (Cotterill 70), King (Robson-Kanu 61), Bale, Vokes. **Scorer**: Bale (10)
Georgia (4-2-3-1): Loria, Kakabadze, Kashia, Kverkvelia, Novalovski, Daushvili, Gvilia, Okriashvili (Jigauri 90), Kazaishvili, Ananidze (Kacharava 90), Mchedlidze (Dvalishvili 75). **Scorer**: Okriashvili (57). **Booked**: Daushvili, Gvilia, Okriasvili, Kashia
Referee: P Mazzoleni (Italy). **Half-time**: 1-0

MOLDOVA 1 REPUBLIC OF IRELAND 3
Group D: Chisinau (6,089); Sunday, October 9 2016
Moldova (4-2-3-1): Calancea, Bordian, Posmac, Armas (Colovatenco 35), Bolohan, Gatcan,

Cojocari, Andronic (Sidorenco 83), Zasavitchi (Cebotaru 61), Dedov, Bugaev. **Scorer**: Bugaev (45). **Booked**: Cojocari, Bugaev, Gatcan. Dedov
Republic of Ireland (4-2-3-1): Randolph, Coleman, Clark, Duffy, Ward, McCarthy (Meyler 82), Whelan, Walters, Hoolahan (O'Kane 86), McClean, S Long (O'Dowda 63). **Scorers**: Long (2), McClean (69, 76). **Booked**: Walters, Coleman
Referee: J Kehlet (Denmark). **Half-time**: 1-1

SLOVENIA 0 ENGLAND 0
Group F: Ljubljana (13,274); Tuesday, October 11 2016
Slovenia (4-3-1-2): Oblak, Struna, Samardzic, Cesar (Mevlja 68), Jokic, Krhin (Omladic 84), Verbic, Birsa (Kronaveter 59), Kurtic, Bezjak, Ilicic. **Booked**: Birsa, Kronaveter, Struna
England (4-2-3-1): Hart, Walker, Cahill, Stones, Rose, Henderson, Dier, Walcott (Townsend 62), Alli (Rooney 73), Lingard, Sturridge (Rashford 82). **Booked**: Dier, Sturridge, Cahill, Lingard
Referee: D Aytekin (Germany)

SLOVAKIA 3 SCOTLAND 0
Group F: Trnava (11,098); Tuesday, October 11 2016
Slovakia (4-4-1-1): Kozacic, Sabo, Skrtel, Durica, Holubek, Duris, Kucka, Skriniar, Mak (Svento 81), Hamsik (Kiss 87), Nemec (Bakos 69). **Scorers**: Mak (18, 56), Nemec (68). **Booked**: Sabo
Scotland (4-3-3): Marshall, Paterson, R Martin, Hanley, Tierney, McArthur, D Fletcher (Griffiths 64), Bannan, Snodgrass, S Fletcher (McGinn 76), Ritchie (Anya 64)
Referee: M Strombergsson (Sweden). **Half-time**: 1-0

GERMANY 2 NORTHERN IRELAND 0
Group C: Hannover (42,132); Tuesday, October 11 2016
Germany (4-2-3-1): Neuer, Kimmich, Boateng (Mustafi 69), Hummels, Hector (Volland 81), Khedira, Kroos, Muller, Ozil (Gundogan 46), Draxler, Gotze. **Scorers**: Draxler (13), Khedira (17)
Northern Ireland (4-5-1): McGovern, Hodson, Hughes, McAuley, J Evans, Ferguson, C Evans, Norwood (McNair 72), Davis, Ward (McGinn 61), Magennis (Lafferty 76). **Booked**: Ferguson
Referee: P Tagliavento (Italy). **Half-time**: 2-0

ENGLAND 3 SCOTLAND 0
Group F: Wembley (87,258); Friday, November 11 2016
England (4-2-3-1): Hart, Walker, Cahill, Stones, Rose, Henderson, Dier, Sterling, Rooney, Lallana, Sturridge (Vardy 76). **Scorers**: Sturridge (25), Lallana (51), Cahill (61). **Booked**: Cahill, Rooney
Scotland (4-2-3-1): Gordon, Anya (Paterson 80), Hanley, Berra, Wallace, Brown, D Fletcher, Forrest, Snodgrass (Ritchie 82), Morrison (McArthur 66), Griffiths. **Booked**: Griffiths
Referee: C Cakir (Turkey). **Half-time**: 1-0

NORTHERN IRELAND 4 AZERBAIJAN 0
Group C: Windsor Park (18,404); Friday, November 11 2016
Northern Ireland (4-4-1-1): McGovern, McLaughlin, McAuley, J Evans, Brunt, Magennis, Davis, C Evans (McNair 81), Ferguson (McGinn 73), Norwood, Lafferty (Grigg 62). **Scorers**: Lafferty (27), McAuley (40), McLaughlin (66), Brunt (83). **Booked**: Ferguson, C Evans
Referee: C Turpin (France). **Half-time**: 2-0

WALES 1 SERBIA 1
Group D: Cardiff City Stadium (32,879); Saturday, November 12 2016
Wales (4-1-2-1-2): Hennessey, Gunter, A Williams, Chester, Taylor, Ledley (Edwards 84), Allen, Ramsey, Bale, Robson-Kanu (Lawrence 68), Vokes. **Scorer**: Bale (30). **Booked**: Bale, Allen, Ledley, A Williams

Serbia (3-4-2-1): Stojkovic, Ivanovic, Maksimovic, Nastasic, Rukavina, Milivojevic, Matic, Obradovic, Tadic, Kostic (Katai 69) Mitrovic (Gudelj 88). **Scorer:** Mitrovic (86). **Booked:** Nastasic, Stojkovic, Katai
Referee: A Undiano (Spain). **Half-time:** 1-0

AUSTRIA 0 REPUBLIC OF IRELAND 1
Group D: Vienna (48,500); Saturday, November 12 2016
Austria (4-2-3-1): Ozcan, Klein, Dragovic, Hinterriger, Wimmer, Baumgartlinger, Alaba, Sabitzer (Harnik 73), Schopf (Schaub 57), Arnautovic, Janko. **Booked:** Dragovic, Baumgartlinger
Republic of Ireland (4-1-3-2): Randolph, Coleman, Clark, Duffy, Brady, Whelan (Meyler 24), Arter, Hendrick, Hoolahan (McGoldrick 78), Walters, McClean. **Scorer:** McClean (48). **Booked:** Duffy, Brady
Referee: S Karasev (Russia). **Half-time:** 0-0

REPUBLIC OF IRELAND 0 WALES 0
Group D: Aviva Stadium (49,989); Friday, March 24 2017
Republic of Ireland (4-2-3-1): Randolph, Coleman (Christie 72), Keogh, O'Shea, Ward. Meyler (McGeady 80), Whelan, Walters, Hendrick, McClean, S Long. **Booked:** Meyler, McGeady
Wales (3-4-2-1): Hennessey, Chester, A Williams, Davies, Gunter, Allen, Ledley (Richards 72), Taylor, Bale, Ramsey, Robson-Kanu (Vokes 46). **Booked:** Ramsey, Bale. **Sent off:** Taylor (69)
Referee: N Rizzoli (Italy)

ENGLAND 2 LITHUANIA 0
Group F: Wembley (77,690); Sunday, March 26 2017
England (4-2-3-1): Hart, Walker, Keane, Stones, Bertrand, Dier, Oxlade-Chamberlain, Sterling (Rashford 60), Alli, Lallana, Defoe (Vardy 60). **Scorers:** Defoe (21), Vardy (66). **Booked:** Rashford
Lithuania (4-4-1-1): Setkus, Vaitkunas, Kijanskas, Klimavicius, Slavickas, Novikovas (Grigaravicius 54), Zulpa, Kuklys, Cernych, Slivka (Paulius 87), Valskis (Matulevicius 73). **Booked:** Vaitkunas, Zulpa
Referee: R Buquet (France). **Half-time:** 1-0

SCOTLAND 1 SLOVENIA 0
Group F; Hampden Park (20,435); Sunday, March 26 2017
Scotland (4-2-3-1): Gordon, Tierney, Mulgrew, R Martin, Robertson, Brown, Morrison (C Martin 80), Forrest, *Armstrong, Snodgrass (Anya 73), Griffiths (Naismith 49). **Scorer:** C Martin (88)
Slovenia (4-3-3): Oblak, Struna, Samardzic, Cesar, Jokic, Kampl (Omladic 87), Krhin, Kurtic, Birsa (Beric 68), Ilicic, Bezjak (Verbic 58). **Booked:** Jokic, Cesar, Bezjak, Birsa, Samardzic
Referee: B Kuipers (Holland). **Half-time:** 0-0

NORTHERN IRELAND 2 NORWAY 0
Windsor Park (18,161); Sunday, March 26 2017
Northern Ireland (3-5-2): McGovern, Cathcart, McAuley, J Evans, McLaughlin, Davis, Norwood, Brunt, Dallas (Lund 88), Ward (McGinn 80), Washington (Lafferty 85). **Scorers:** Ward (2), Washington (33). **Booked:** Dallas
Norway (4-1-3-2): Jarstein, Elabdellaoui, Hovland, Valsvik, Skjelvik, Nordtveit, M Elyounoussi, Johansen (Berge 75),'T Elyounoussi (Daehli 54), Soderlund (Diomande 64), King. **Booked:** Nordtveit
Referee: H Gocek (Turkey). **Half-time:** 2-0

SCOTLAND 2 ENGLAND 2
Group F: Hampden Park (48,520); Saturday, June 10 2017
Scotland (3-4-2-1): Gordon, Berra, Mulgrew, Tierney, Anya (C Martin 81), Morrison (McArthur 46), Brown, Robertson, Snodgrass (*Fraser 67), Armstrong, Griffiths. **Scorer:** Griffiths (87, 90). **Booked:** Brown

England (4-2-3-1): Hart, Walker, Smalling, Cahill, Bertrand, Livermore (Defoe 90), Dier, Rashford (Oxlade-Chamberlain 65), Alli (Sterling 84), Lallana, Kane. **Scorers**: Oxlade-Chamberlain (70), Kane (90). **Booked**: Livermore, Dier
Referee: P Tagliavento (Italy). **Half-time**: 0-0

AZERBAIJAN 0 NORTHERN IRELAND 1
Group C: Baku (27,978); Saturday, June 10 2017

Azerbaijan (4-3-3): Agayev, Medvedev, Guseinov, Sadygov, Pashaev, Huseynov, Qarayev, Almeida, Ismayilov (Amirquliev 84), Sheydaev (Abdullayev 90), Nazarov (Alasgarov 77).
Bookings: Medvedev, Huseynov, Qarayev
Northern Ireland (5-3-2): McGovern, McLaughlin, Hughes, McAuley (McGinn 25) (Hodson 86), J Evans, Dallas, Brunt, Norwood, Davis, Boyce (K Lafferty 77), Magennis. **Scorer**: Dallas (90).
Booked: Magennis, Davis
Referee: J Estrada (Spain). **Half-time**: 0-0

SERBIA 1 WALES 1
Group D: Belgrade (42,100); Sunday, June 11 2017

Serbia (3-4-2-1): Stojkovic, Ivanovic, Nastasic, Vukovic, Rukavina, Matic, Milivojevic (Gudelj 63), Kolarov, Kostic (Prijovic 67), Tadic, Mitrovic. **Scorer**: Mitrovic (73). **Booked**: Stojkovic, Milivojevic, Matic
Wales (3-4-2-1): Hennessey, Chester, A Williams, Davies, Gunter, Allen, Ledley, Richards, Ramsey, Edwards (Huws 73), Vokes (Lawrence 86). **Scorer**: Ramsey (35). **Booked**: Allen, Richards
Referee: J Sousa (Portugal). **Half-time**: 0-1

REPUBLIC OF IRELAND 1 AUSTRIA 1
Group D: Aviva Stadium (51,000); Sunday, June 11 2017

Republic of Ireland (4-2-3-1): Randolph, Christie, K Long, Duffy, Ward (Murphy 56), Whelan (McGeady 77), Arter (Hoolahan 71), Brady, Hendrick, McClean, Walters. **Scorer**: Walters (85).
Booked: Brady, Christie
Austria (4-3-3): Lindner, Lainer, Dragovic, Prodl, Hinteregger, Baumgartlinger, Junuzovic (Grillitsch 79), Alaba, Lazaro, Burgstaller (Harnik 75), Kainz (Gregoritsch 90). **Scorer**: Hinteregger (31)
Referee: D Borbalan (Spain). **Half-time**: 0-1

THE THINGS THEY SAY ...

'It will not be long before we see a £150m or £200m signing'   **Arsene Wenger**, Arsenal manager, forecasting that transfer fees will continue to spiral.

'This is part of football. It is something which you have to go through and I am big enough to deal with it. I will just keep working. I feel I still have a lot to offer' – **Wayne Rooney** vowing to win back his England place.

'There's nobody happier or any higher in this ether than me. I could be an astronaut with how I feel' – **Ian Holloway** after being appointed Queens Park Rangers manager for the second time.

'At least we are guaranteed a game' – **Robert Snodgrass**, midfielder, with Hull down to 13 fit senior players for the start of the season.

'I look forward now to sitting back and watching the team as a fan' – **Robbie Keane** after calling time on a record-breaking international career of 146 appearances and 68 goals for the Republic of Ireland.

FRIENDLY INTERNATIONALS

REPUBLIC OF IRELAND 4 OMAN 0
Aviva Stadium (27,000): Wednesday, August 31 2016
Republic of Ireland (4-2-3-1): Westwood (Randolph 46), Christie, Wilson, Clark, Brady (Ward 46), Whelan (Hendrick 46), Quinn (O'Dowda 65), S Long (McClean 46), Arter, Walters, Keane (Hoolahan 57). **Scorers**: Brady (8), Keane (30), Walters (34, 63). **Booked**: Wilson
Oman (4-4-1): Al-Rushaidi, Al Mushaifri (Al-Mukhainiat 46), Al-Mukhaini, Bait Mabrook, Raboh Bait (Al Busaidi 57), Al-Hadhri (Al Shuabi 75), Al-Yahyaei, Al Saadi, Saleh, Johar (Al Farsi 57), Al Muqbali (Absulsalam 87). **Booked**: Al Saadi
Referee: D Masias (Cyprus). **Half-time**: 3-0

ENGLAND 2 SPAIN 2
Wembley (83,716); Tuesday, November 15 2016
England (4-2-3-1): Hart (Heaton 46), Clyne, Cahill (Jagielka 46), Stones, Rose (*Cresswell 79), Henderson, Dier, Lingard, Lallana (Walcott 27), Sterling (Townsend 65), Vardy (Rashford 67). **Scorers**: Lallana (9 pen), Vardy (48). **Booked**: Sterling, Walcott, Rose
Spain (3-4-2-1): Reina, Azpilicueta, Martinez, Nacho, Carvajal, Busquets (Nolito 78), Thiago Alcantara (Herrera 56), Vitolo (Koke 46), Mata (Aspas 46), Silva (Isco 64), Aduriz (Alvaro Morata 64). **Scorers**: Aspas (89), Isco (90). **Booked**: Martinez, Aspas, Carvajal
Referee: O Hategan (Romania). **Half-time**: 1-0

NORTHERN IRELAND 0 CROATIA 3
Windsor Park (16,893); Tuesday, November 15 2016
Northern Ireland (4-1-4-1): Mannus, Hodson, McAuley (McGivern 46), J Evans, Brunt, Norwood, Magennis (Lafferty 56), *Lund (Davis 46), McNair, McGinn (Paton 62), Boyce (Grigg 68)
Croatia (4-4-2): Kalinic (Vargic 82), Jedvaj, Leovac, Vida (Vrsaljko 60), Mitrovic, Badelj (Brozovic 51), Bradaric, Rog (Pivaric 87), Cop, Kramaric, Mandzukic (Coric 72). **Scorers**: Mandzukic (9), Cop (35), Kramaric (67)
Referee: M Clattenburg (England). **Half-time**: 0-2

GERMANY 1 ENGLAND 0
Dortmund (60,109); Wednesday, March 22 2017
Germany (4-2-3-1): Ter Stegen, Kimmich, Rudiger, Hummels, Hector, Kroos, Weigl (Emre Can 66), Sane, Podolski (Rudy 84), Brandt (Schurrle 59), Werner (Muller 77). **Scorer**: Podolski (69)
England (3-4-2-1): Hart, *Keane, Smalling (Stones 84), Cahill, Walker, Livermore (*Ward-Prowse 83), Dier, Bertrand (Shaw 84), Lallana (*Redmond 66), Alli (Lingard 71), Vardy (Rashford 70)
Referee: D Skomina (Slovenia). **Half-time**: 0-0
(Gareth Southgate's first match as permanent England manager)

SCOTLAND 1 CANADA 1
Easter Road, Edinburgh (9,158); Wednesday, March 22 2017
Scotland (4-2-3-1): McGregor, Anya, Berra, Mulgrew, Wallace (Robertson 46), *Cairney (McGinn 75), D Fletcher, Snodgrass, Naismith (Rhodes 61), Burke (Bannan 46), C Martin (Griffiths 61). **Scorer**: Naismith (34)
Canada (4-2-3-1): Thomas (Leutwiler 46), Ledgerwood, Straith, James, Tissot (Corbin-Ong 46), Arfield (Trafford 90), Piette, Aird, Bustos, Hoilett, Jackson (Fisk 76). **Scorer**: Aird (10)
Referee: J Kehlet (Denmark). **Half-time**: 1-1

REPUBLIC OF IRELAND 0 ICELAND 1
Aviva Stadium (37,241); Tuesday, March 28 2017
Republic of Ireland (4-4-1-1): Westwood, Christie *Egan (*Boyle 64), Pearce, Brady, McGeady

(O'Dowda 73), Hendrick (Gleeson 63), *Hourihane (O'Kane 63), Hayes (*Horgan 63), McClean (Long 72), Doyle. **Booked**: Egan
Iceland (4-4-2): Kristinsson, Saevarsson (Jonsson 85), Ingason, R Sigurdsson (Eyjolfsson 53), Magnusson, Gislason, Gunnarsson, Skulason (Smarason 79), A Sigurdsson (Omarsson 65), Bodvarsson, Finnbogason (Karlsson 72). **Scorer**: Magnusson (21). **Booked**: Ingason
Referee: J Kehlet (Denmark). **Half-time**: 0-1

NORTHERN IRELAND 1 NEW ZEALAND 0
Windsor Park (16,815); Friday, June 2 2017
Northern Ireland (3-5-2): McGovern (Carroll 84), *Flanagan, Hughes, J Evans, McLaughlin, Lund (Davis 46), Norwood, Brunt (Ferguson 46), Dallas (Paton 74), Boyce (Lafferty 46), Magennis (*McCartan 83), **Scorer**: Boyce (6)
New Zealand (3-5-1-1): Marinovic, Boxall, Durante, Smith, Colvey (Barbaraouses 63), Lewis (Tuiloma 46), McGlinchey, Thomas (Smeltz 79), Doyle (Wynne 72), Rojas (Patterson 63), Wood. **Booked**: Durante
Referee: L Kopriwa (Luxembourg). **Half-time**: 1-0

MEXICO 3 REPUBLIC OF IRELAND 1
New Jersey (42,017); Friday, June 2 2017
Mexico (4-4-2): Cota, Salcedo (Layun 46), Reyes, Moreno (Alanis 46), Gallardo, Vela (Marquez 68), Herrera (Peralta 46), Hernandez, Dos Santos (Pineda 58), Corona (Aquino 58), Jimenez. **Scorers**: Corona (16), Jimenez (25 pen), Vela (54). **Booked**: Salcedo
Republic of Ireland (3-5-2): Randolph, Keogh, Duffy, Egan (*K Long 64), Christie (*Browne 73), Horgan (Gleeson 73), Hourihane (O'Kane 64), O'Dowda, McClean, McGoldrick, Murphy (Hoolahan 64). **Scorer**: Gleeson (76). **Booked**: McClean
Referee: E Unkel (USA). **Half-time**: 2-0

REPUBLIC OF IRELAND 3 URUGUAY 1
Aviva Stadium (27,193); Sunday, June 4 2017
Republic of Ireland (4-2-3-1): Randolph (Westwood 46), Christie, Duffy (Pearce 61), K Long, Ward, Whelan (Hoolahan 46), Arter, Brady, Hendrick (McClean 74), Hayes (McGeady 61), Walters (Murphy 61). **Scorers**: Walters (27), Christie (51), McClean (77). **Booked**: Hendrick
Uruguay (3-4-2-1): Conde, Gimenez, Coates, Caceres, Pereira (Ricca 62), Vecino, Arevalo (Gonzalez 46), Laxalt (Silva 46), Sanchez (Nandez 46), Urreta, Cavani (Stuani 13). **Scorer**: Gimenez (38)
Referee: C Thompson (Scotland). **Half-time**: 1-1

FRANCE 3 ENGLAND 2
Paris (80,000); Tuesday, June 13 2017
France (4-4-2): Lloris, Sidibe (Jallet 89), Varane, Umtiti, Mendy (Digne 21), Dembele, Kante, Pogba, Lemar, Giroud (Koscielny 52), Mbappe Lottin. **Scorers**: Umtiti (22), Sidibe (43), Dembele (78). **Sent off**: Varane (47)
England (3-4-2-1): Heaton (Butland 46), Jones (Cresswell 81), Stones, Cahill, *Trippier (Lallana 75), Oxlade-Chamberlain, Dier, Bertrand (Walker 46), Sterling, Alli, Kane. **Scorer**: Kane (9, 48 pen). **Booked**: Stones, Alli
Referee: D Massa (Italy). **Half-time**: 2-1

OTHER BRITISH & IRISH INTERNATIONAL RESULTS

ENGLAND

v ALBANIA

		E	A
1989	Tirana (WC)	2	0
1989	Wembley (WC)	5	0
2001	Tirana (WC)	3	1
2001	Newcastle (WC)	2	0

v ALGERIA

		E	A
2010	Cape Town (WC)	0	0

v ANDORRA

		E	A
2006	Old Trafford (EC)	5	0
2007	Barcelona (EC)	3	0
2008	Barcelona (WC)	2	0
2009	Wembley (WC)	6	0

v ARGENTINA

		E	A
1951	Wembley	2	1
1953*	Buenos Aires	0	0
1962	Rancagua (WC)	3	1
1964	Rio de Janeiro	0	1
1966	Wembley (WC)	1	0
1974	Wembley	2	2
1977	Buenos Aires	1	1
1980	Wembley	3	1
1986	Mexico City (WC)	1	2
1991	Wembley	2	2
1998†	St Etienne (WC)	2	2
2000	Wembley	0	0
2002	Sapporo (WC)	1	0
2005	Geneva	3	2

(*Abandoned after 21 mins – rain)
(† England lost 3-4 on pens)

v AUSTRALIA

		E	A
1980	Sydney	2	1
1983	Sydney	0	0
1983	Brisbane	1	0
1983	Melbourne	1	1
1991	Sydney	1	0
2003	West Ham	1	3
2016	Sunderland	2	1

v AUSTRIA

		E	A
1908	Vienna	6	1
1908	Vienna	11	1
1909	Vienna	8	1
1930	Vienna	0	0
1932	Stamford Bridge	4	3
1936	Vienna	1	2
1951	Wembley	2	2
1952	Vienna	3	2
1958	Boras (WC)	2	2
1961	Vienna	1	3
1962	Wembley	3	1
1965	Wembley	2	3
1967	Vienna	1	0
1973	Wembley	7	0

1979	Vienna	3	4
2004	Vienna (WC)	2	2
2005	Old Trafford (WC)	1	0
2007	Vienna	1	0

v AZERBAIJAN

		E	A
2004	Baku (WC)	1	0
2005	Newcastle (WC)	2	0

v BELARUS

		E	B
2008	Minsk (WC)	3	1
2009	Wembley (WC)	3	0

v BELGIUM

		E	B
1921	Brussels	2	0
1923	Highbury	6	1
1923	Antwerp	2	2
1924	West Bromwich	4	0
1926	Antwerp	5	3
1927	Brussels	9	1
1928	Antwerp	3	1
1929	Brussels	5	1
1931	Brussels	4	1
1936	Brussels	2	3
1947	Brussels	5	2
1950	Brussels	4	1
1952	Wembley	5	0
1954	Basle (WC)	4	4
1964	Wembley	2	2
1970	Brussels	3	1
1980	Turin (EC)	1	1
1990	Bologna (WC)	1	0
1998*	Casablanca	0	0
1999	Sunderland	2	1
2012	Wembley	1	0

(*England lost 3-4 on pens)

v BOHEMIA

		E	B
1908	Prague	4	0

v BRAZIL

		E	B
1956	Wembley	4	2
1958	Gothenburg (WC)	0	0
1959	Rio de Janeiro	0	2
1962	Vina del Mar (WC)	1	3
1963	Wembley	1	1
1964	Rio de Janeiro	1	5
1969	Rio de Janeiro	1	2
1970	Guadalajara (WC)	0	1
1976	Los Angeles	0	1
1977	Rio de Janeiro	0	0
1978	Wembley	1	1
1981	Wembley	0	1
1984	Rio de Janeiro	2	0
1987	Wembley	1	1
1990	Wembley	1	0
1992	Wembley	1	1
1993	Washington	1	1
1995	Wembley	1	3
1997	Paris (TF)	0	1

2000	Wembley	1	1
2002	Shizuoka (WC)	1	2
2007	Wembley	1	1
2009	Doha	0	1
2013	Wembley	2	1
2013	Rio de Janeiro	2	2

v BULGARIA

		E	B
1962	Rancagua (WC)	0	0
1968	Wembley	1	1
1974	Sofia	1	0
1979	Sofia (EC)	3	0
1979	Wembley (EC)	2	0
1996	Wembley	1	0
1998	Wembley (EC)	0	0
1999	Sofia (EC)	1	1
2010	Wembley (EC)	4	0
2011	Sofia (EC)	3	0

v CAMEROON

		E	C
1990	Naples (WC)	3	2
1991	Wembley	2	0
1997	Wembley	2	0
2002	Kobe (Japan)	2	2

v CANADA

		E	C
1986	Vancouver	1	0

v CHILE

		E	C
1950	Rio de Janeiro (WC)	2	0
1953	Santiago	2	1
1984	Santiago	0	0
1989	Wembley	0	0
1998	Wembley	0	2
2013	Wembley	0	2

v CHINA

		E	C
1996	Beijing	3	0

v CIS
(formerly Soviet Union)

		E	CIS
1992	Moscow	2	2

v COLOMBIA

		E	C
1970	Bogota	4	0
1988	Wembley	1	1
1995	Wembley	0	0
1998	Lens (WC)	2	0
2005	New York	3	2

v COSTA RICA

		E	CR
2014	Belo Horizonte (WC)	0	0

v CROATIA

		E	C
1995	Wembley	0	0
2003	Ipswich	3	1
2004	Lisbon (EC)	4	2
2006	Zagreb (EC)	0	2
2007	Wembley (EC)	2	3
2008	Zagreb (WC)	4	1
2009	Wembley (WC)	5	1

v CYPRUS

		E	C
1975	Wembley (EC)	5	0
1975	Limassol (EC)	1	0

v CZECH REPUBLIC

		E	C
1998	Wembley	2	0
2008	Wembley	2	2

v CZECHOSLOVAKIA

		E	C
1934	Prague	1	2
1937	White Hart Lane	5	4
1963	Bratislava	4	2
1966	Wembley	0	0
1970	Guadalajara (WC)	1	0
1973	Prague	1	1
1974	Wembley (EC)	3	0
1975*	Bratislava (EC)	1	2
1978	Wembley (EC)	1	0
1982	Bilbao (WC)	2	0
1990	Wembley	4	2
1992	Prague	2	2
(* Aband 0-0, 17 mins prev day – fog)			

v DENMARK

		E	D
1948	Copenhagen	0	0
1955	Copenhagen	5	1
1956	W'hampton (WC)	5	2
1957	Copenhagen (WC)	4	1
1966	Copenhagen	2	0
1978	Copenhagen (EC)	4	3
1979	Wembley (EC)	1	0
1982	Copenhagen (EC)	2	2
1983	Wembley (EC)	0	1
1988	Wembley	1	0
1989	Copenhagen	1	1
1990	Wembley	1	0
1992	Malmo (EC)	0	0
1994	Wembley	1	0
2002	Niigata (WC)	3	0
2003	Old Trafford	2	3
2005	Copenhagen	1	4
2011	Copenhagen	2	1
2014	Wembley	1	0

v EAST GERMANY

		E	EG
1963	Leipzig	2	1
1970	Wembley	3	1
1974	Leipzig	1	1
1984	Wembley	1	0

v ECUADOR

		E	Ec
1970	Quito	2	0
2006	Stuttgart (WC)	1	0
2014	Miami	2	2

v EGYPT

		E	Eg
1986	Cairo	4	0
1990	Cagliari (WC)	1	0
2010	Wembley	3	1

v ESTONIA

		E	Est
2007	Tallinn (EC)	3	0
2007	Wembley (EC)	3	0
2014	Tallinn (EC)	1	0
2015	Wembley (EC)	2	0

v FIFA

		E	F
1938	Highbury	3	0
1953	Wembley	4	4
1963	Wembley	2	1

v FINLAND

		E	F
1937	Helsinki	8	0
1956	Helsinki	5	1
1966	Helsinki	3	0
1976	Helsinki (WC)	4	1
1976	Wembley (WC)	2	1
1982	Helsinki	4	1
1984	Wembley (WC)	5	0
1985	Helsinki (WC)	1	1
1992	Helsinki	2	1
2000	Helsinki (WC)	0	0
2001	Liverpool (WC)	2	1

v FRANCE

		E	F
1923	Paris	4	1
1924	Paris	3	1
1925	Paris	3	2
1927	Paris	6	0
1928	Paris	5	1
1929	Paris	4	1
1931	Paris	2	5
1933	White Hart Lane	4	1
1938	Paris	4	2
1947	Highbury	3	0
1949	Paris	3	1
1951	Highbury	2	2
1955	Paris	0	1
1957	Wembley	4	0
1962	Hillsborough (EC)	1	1
1963	Paris (EC)	2	5
1966	Wembley (WC)	2	0
1969	Wembley	5	0
1982	Bilbao (WC)	3	1
1984	Paris	0	2
1992	Wembley	2	0
1992	Malmo (EC)	0	0
1997	Montpellier (TF)	1	0
1999	Wembley	0	2
2000	Paris	1	1
2004	Lisbon (EC)	1	2
2008	Paris	0	1
2010	Wembley	1	2
2012	Donetsk (EC)	1	1
2015	Wembley	2	0
2017	Paris	2	3

v GEORGIA

		E	G
1996	Tbilisi (WC)	2	0
1997	Wembley (WC)	2	0

v GERMANY/WEST GERMANY

		E	G
1930	Berlin	3	3
1935	White Hart Lane	3	0
1938	Berlin	6	3
1954	Wembley	3	1
1956	Berlin	3	1
1965	Nuremberg	1	0
1966	Wembley	1	0
1966	Wembley (WCF)	4	2
1968	Hanover	0	1
1970	Leon (WC)	2	3
1972	Wembley (EC)	1	3
1972	Berlin (EC)	0	0
1975	Wembley	2	0
1978	Munich	1	2
1982	Madrid (WC)	0	0
1982	Wembley	1	2
1985	Mexico City	3	0
1987	Dusseldorf	1	3
1990*	Turin (WC)	1	1
1991	Wembley	0	1
1993	Detroit	1	2
1996†	Wembley (EC)	1	1
2000	Charleroi (EC)	1	0
2000	Wembley (WC)	0	1
2001	Munich (WC)	5	1
2007	Wembley	1	2
2008	Berlin	2	1
2010	Bloemfontein (WC)	1	4
2012	Donetsk (EC)	1	1
2013	Wembley	0	1
2016	Berlin	3	2
2017	Dortmund	0	1

(*England lost 3-4 on pens)
(† England lost 5-6 on pens)

v GHANA

		E	G
2011	Wembley	1	1

v GREECE

		E	G
1971	Wembley (EC)	3	0
1971	Athens (EC)	2	0
1982	Salonika (EC)	3	0
1983	Wembley (EC)	0	0
1989	Athens	2	1
1994	Wembley	5	0
2001	Athens (WC)	2	0
2001	Old Trafford (WC)	2	2
2006	Old Trafford	4	0

v HOLLAND

		E	H
1935	Amsterdam	1	0
1946	Huddersfield	8	2
1964	Amsterdam	1	1
1969	Amsterdam	1	0
1970	Wembley	0	0
1977	Wembley	0	2
1982	Wembley	2	0
1988	Wembley	2	2
1988	Dusseldorf (EC)	1	3
1990	Cagliari (WC)	0	0
1993	Wembley (WC)	2	2

1993	Rotterdam (WC)	0	2
1996	Wembley (EC)	4	1
2001	White Hart Lane	0	2
2002	Amsterdam	1	1
2005	Villa Park	0	0
2006	Amsterdam	1	1
2009	Amsterdam	2	2
2012	Wembley	2	3
2016	Wembley	1	2

v HONDURAS

		E	H
2014	Miami	0	0

v HUNGARY

		E	H
1908	Budapest	7	0
1909	Budapest	4	2
1909	Budapest	8	2
1934	Budapest	1	2
1936	Highbury	6	2
1953	Wembley	3	6
1954	Budapest	1	7
1960	Budapest	0	2
1962	Rancagua (WC)	1	2
1965	Wembley	1	0
1978	Wembley	1	1
1981	Budapest (WC)	3	1
1981	Wembley (WC)	1	0
1983	Wembley (EC)	2	0
1983	Budapest (EC)	3	0
1988	Budapest	0	0
1990	Wembley	1	0
1992	Budapest	1	0
1996	Wembley	3	0
1999	Budapest	1	1
2006	Old Trafford	3	1
2010	Wembley	2	1

v ICELAND

		E	I
1982	Reykjavik	1	1
2004	City of Manchester	6	1
2016	Nice (EC)	1	2

v ISRAEL

		E	I
1986	Tel Aviv	2	1
1988	Tel Aviv	0	0
2006	Tel Aviv (EC)	0	0
2007	Wembley (EC)	3	0

v ITALY

		E	I
1933	Rome	1	1
1934	Highbury	3	2
1939	Milan	2	2
1948	Turin	4	0
1949	White Hart Lane	2	0
1952	Florence	1	1
1959	Wembley	2	2
1961	Rome	3	2
1973	Turin	0	2
1973	Wembley	0	1
1976	New York	3	2
1976	Rome (WC)	0	2
1977	Wembley (WC)	2	0
1980	Turin (EC)	0	1

1985	Mexico City	1	2
1989	Wembley	0	0
1990	Bari (WC)	1	2
1996	Wembley (WC)	0	1
1997	Nantes (TF)	2	0
1997	Rome (WC)	0	0
2000	Turin	0	1
2002	Leeds	1	2
2012*	Kiev (EC)	0	0
2012	Berne	2	1
2014	Manaus (WC)	1	2
2015	Turin	1	1

(*England lost 2-4 on pens)

v JAMAICA

		E	J
2006	Old Trafford	6	0

v JAPAN

		E	J
1995	Wembley	2	1
2004	City of Manchester	1	1
2010	Graz	2	1

v KAZAKHSTAN

		E	K
2008	Wembley (WC)	5	1
2009	Almaty (WC)	4	0

v KUWAIT

		E	K
1982	Bilbao (WC)	1	0

v LIECHTENSTEIN

		E	L
2003	Vaduz (EC)	2	0
2003	Old Trafford (EC)	2	0

v LITHUANIA

		E	L
2015	Wembley (EC)	4	0
2015	Vilnius (EC)	3	0
2017	Wembley (WC)	2	0

v LUXEMBOURG

		E	L
1927	Luxembourg	5	2
1960	Luxembourg (WC)	9	0
1961	Highbury (WC)	4	1
1977	Wembley (WC)	5	0
1977	Luxembourg (WC)	2	0
1982	Wembley (EC)	9	0
1983	Luxembourg (EC)	4	0
1998	Luxembourg (EC)	3	0
1999	Wembley (EC)	6	0

v MACEDONIA

		E	M
2002	Southampton (EC)	2	2
2003	Skopje (EC)	2	1
2006	Skopje (EC)	1	0
2006	Old Trafford (EC)	0	0

v MALAYSIA

		E	M
1991	Kuala Lumpur	4	2

v MALTA

		E	M
1971	Valletta (EC)	1	0
1971	Wembley (EC)	5	0

| 2000 | Valletta | 2 | 1 |
| 2016 | Wembley (WC) | 2 | 0 |

v MEXICO

		E	M
1959	Mexico City	1	2
1961	Wembley	8	0
1966	Wembley (WC)	2	0
1969	Mexico City	0	0
1985	Mexico City	0	1
1986	Los Angeles	3	0
1997	Wembley	2	0
2001	Derby	4	0
2010	Wembley	3	1

v MOLDOVA

		E	M
1996	Kishinev	3	0
1997	Wembley (WC)	4	0
2012	Chisinu (WC)	5	0
2013	Wembley (WC)	4	0

v MONTENEGRO

		E	M
2010	Wembley (EC)	0	0
2011	Podgorica (EC)	2	2
2013	Podgorica (WC)	1	1
2013	Wembley (WC)	4	1

v MOROCCO

		E	M
1986	Monterrey (WC)	0	0
1998	Casablanca	1	0

v NEW ZEALAND

		E	NZ
1991	Auckland	1	0
1991	Wellington	2	0

v NIGERIA

		E	NZ
1994	Wembley	1	0
2002	Osaka (WC)	0	0

v NORWAY

		E	NZ
1937	Oslo	6	0
1938	Newcastle	4	0
1949	Oslo	4	1
1966	Oslo	6	1
1980	Wembley (WC)	4	0
1981	Oslo (WC)	1	2
1992	Wembley (WC)	1	1
1993	Oslo (WC)	0	2
1994	Wembley	0	0
1995	Oslo	0	0
2012	Oslo	1	0
2014	Wembley	1	0

v PARAGUAY

		E	P
1986	Mexico City (WC)	3	0
2002	Anfield	4	0
2006	Frankfurt (WC)	1	0

v PERU

		E	P
1959	Lima	1	4
1961	Lima	4	0
2014	Wembley	3	0

v POLAND

		E	P
1966	Goodison Park	1	1
1966	Chorzow	1	0
1973	Chorzow (WC)	0	2
1973	Wembley (WC)	1	1
1986	Monterrey (WC)	3	0
1989	Wembley (WC)	3	0
1989	Katowice (WC)	0	0
1990	Wembley (EC)	2	0
1991	Poznan (EC)	1	1
1993	Chorzow (WC)	1	1
1993	Wembley (WC)	3	0
1996	Wembley (WC)	2	1
1997	Katowice (WC)	2	0
1999	Wembley (EC)	3	1
1999	Warsaw (EC)	0	0
2004	Katowice (WC)	2	1
2005	Old Trafford (WC)	2	1
2012	Warsaw (WC)	1	1
2013	Wembley (WC)	2	0

v PORTUGAL

		E	P
1947	Lisbon	10	0
1950	Lisbon	5	3
1951	Goodison Park	5	2
1955	Oporto	1	3
1958	Wembley	2	1
1961	Lisbon (WC)	1	1
1961	Wembley (WC)	2	0
1964	Lisbon	4	3
1964	Sao Paulo	1	1
1966	Wembley (WC)	2	1
1969	Wembley	1	0
1974	Lisbon	0	0
1974	Wembley (EC)	0	0
1975	Lisbon (EC)	1	1
1986	Monterrey (WC)	0	1
1995	Wembley	1	1
1998	Wembley	3	0
2000	Eindhoven (EC)	2	3
2002	Villa Park	1	1
2004	Faro	1	1
2004*	Lisbon (EC)	2	2
2006†	Gelsenkirchen (WC)	0	0
2016	Wembley	1	0

(† England lost 1–3 on pens)
(*England lost 5–6 on pens)

v REPUBLIC OF IRELAND

		E	RoI
1946	Dublin	1	0
1949	Goodison Park	0	2
1957	Wembley (WC)	5	1
1957	Dublin (WC)	1	1
1964	Dublin	3	1
1977	Wembley	1	1
1978	Dublin (EC)	1	1
1980	Wembley (EC)	2	0
1985	Wembley	2	1
1988	Stuttgart (EC)	0	1
1990	Cagliari (WC)	1	1
1990	Dublin (EC)	1	1
1991	Wembley (EC)	1	1

1995*	Dublin	0	1
2013	Wembley	1	1
2015	Dublin	0	0

(*Abandoned 27 mins – crowd riot)

v ROMANIA

		E	R
1939	Bucharest	2	0
1968	Bucharest	0	0
1969	Wembley	1	1
1970	Guadalajara (WC)	1	0
1980	Bucharest (WC)	1	2
1981	Wembley (WC)	0	0
1985	Bucharest (WC)	0	0
1985	Wembley (WC)	1	1
1994	Wembley	1	1
1998	Toulouse (WC)	1	2
2000	Charleroi (EC)	2	3

v RUSSIA

		E	R
2007	Wembley (EC)	3	0
2007	Moscow (EC)	1	2
2016	Marseille (EC)	1	1

v SAN MARINO

		E	SM
1992	Wembley (WC)	6	0
1993	Bologna (WC)	7	1
2012	Wembley (WC)	5	0
2013	Serravalle (WC)	8	0
2014	Wembley (EC)	5	0
2015	Serravalle (EC)	6	0

v SAUDI ARABIA

		E	SA
1988	Riyadh	1	1
1998	Wembley	0	0

v SERBIA-MONTENEGRO

		E	S-M
2003	Leicester	2	1

v SLOVAKIA

		E	S
2002	Bratislava (EC)	2	1
2003	Middlesbrough (EC)	2	1
2009	Wembley	4	0
2016	St Etienne (EC)	0	0
2016	Trnava (WC)	1	0

v SLOVENIA

		E	S
2009	Wembley	2	1
2010	Port Elizabeth (WC)	1	0
2014	Wembley (EC)	3	1
2015	Ljubljana (EC)	3	2
2016	Ljubljana (WC)	0	0

v SOUTH AFRICA

		E	SA
1997	Old Trafford	2	1
2003	Durban	2	1

v SOUTH KOREA

		E	SK
2002	Seoguipo	1	1

v SOVIET UNION (see also CIS)

		E	SU
1958	Moscow	1	1
1958	Gothenburg (WC)	2	2

1958	Gothenburg (WC)	0	1
1958	Wembley	5	0
1967	Wembley	2	2
1968	Rome (EC)	2	0
1973	Moscow	2	1
1984	Wembley	0	2
1986	Tbilisi	1	0
1988	Frankfurt (EC)	1	3
1991	Wembley	3	1

v SPAIN

		E	S
1929	Madrid	3	4
1931	Highbury	7	1
1950	Rio de Janeiro (WC)	0	1
1955	Madrid	1	1
1955	Wembley	4	1
1960	Madrid	0	3
1960	Wembley	4	2
1965	Madrid	2	0
1967	Wembley	2	0
1968	Wembley (EC)	1	0
1968	Madrid (EC)	2	1
1980	Barcelona	2	0
1980	Naples (EC)	2	1
1981	Wembley	1	2
1982	Madrid (WC)	0	0
1987	Madrid	4	2
1992	Santander	0	1
1996*	Wembley (EC)	0	0
2001	Villa Park	3	0
2004	Madrid	0	1
2007	Old Trafford	0	1
2009	Seville	0	2
2011	Wembley	1	0
2015	Alicante	0	2
2016	Wembley	2	2

(*England won 4-2 on pens)

v SWEDEN

		E	S
1923	Stockholm	4	2
1923	Stockholm	3	1
1937	Stockholm	4	0
1948	Highbury	4	2
1949	Stockholm	1	3
1956	Stockholm	0	0
1959	Wembley	2	3
1965	Gothenburg	2	1
1968	Wembley	3	1
1979	Stockholm	0	0
1986	Stockholm	0	1
1988	Wembley (WC)	0	0
1989	Stockholm (WC)	0	0
1992	Stockholm (EC)	1	2
1995	Leeds	3	3
1998	Stockholm (EC)	1	2
1999	Wembley (EC)	0	0
2001	Old Trafford	1	1
2002	Saitama (WC)	1	1
2004	Gothenburg	0	1
2006	Cologne (WC)	2	2
2011	Wembley	1	0
2012	Kiev (EC)	3	2
2012	Stockholm	2	4

v SWITZERLAND

		E	S
1933	Berne	4	0
1938	Zurich	1	2
1947	Zurich	0	1
1949	Highbury	6	0
1952	Zurich	3	0
1954	Berne (WC)	2	0
1962	Wembley	3	1
1963	Basle	8	1
1971	Basle (EC)	3	2
1971	Wembley (EC)	1	1
1975	Basle	2	1
1977	Wembley	0	0
1980	Wembley (WC)	2	1
1981	Basle (WC)	1	2
1988	Lausanne	1	0
1995	Wembley	3	1
1996	Wembley (EC)	1	1
1998	Berne	1	1
2004	Coimbra (EC)	3	0
2008	Wembley	2	1
2010	Basle (EC)	3	1
2011	Wembley (EC)	2	2
2014	Basle (EC)	2	0
2015	Wembley (EC)	2	0

v TRINIDAD & TOBAGO

		E	T
2006	Nuremberg (WC)	2	0
2008	Port of Spain	3	0

v TUNISIA

		E	T
1990	Tunis	1	1
1998	Marseille (WC)	2	0

v TURKEY

		E	T
1984	Istanbul (WC)	8	0
1985	Wembley (WC)	5	0
1987	Izmir (EC)	0	0
1987	Wembley (EC)	8	0
1991	Izmir (EC)	1	0
1991	Wembley (EC)	1	0
1992	Wembley (WC)	4	0
1993	Izmir (WC)	2	0
2003	Sunderland (EC)	2	0
2003	Istanbul (EC)	0	0
2016	Etihad Stadium	2	1

v UKRAINE

		E	U
2000	Wembley	2	0
2004	Newcastle	3	0
2009	Wembley (WC)	2	1
2009	Dnipropetrovski (WC)	0	1
2012	Donetsk (EC)	1	0
2012	Wembley (WC)	1	1
2013	Kiev (WC)	0	0

v URUGUAY

		E	U
1953	Montevideo	1	2
1954	Basle (WC)	2	4
1964	Wembley	2	1
1966	Wembley (WC)	0	0
1969	Montevideo	2	1
1977	Montevideo	0	0
1984	Montevideo	0	2
1990	Wembley	1	2
1995	Wembley	0	0
2006	Anfield	2	1
2014	Sao Paulo (WC)	1	2

v USA

		E	USA
1950	Belo Horizonte (WC)	0	1
1953	New York	6	3
1959	Los Angeles	8	1
1964	New York	10	0
1985	Los Angeles	5	0
1993	Boston	0	2
1994	Wembley	2	0
2005	Chicago	2	1
2008	Wembley	2	0
2010	Rustenburg (WC)	1	1

v YUGOSLAVIA

		E	Y
1939	Belgrade	1	2
1950	Highbury	2	2
1954	Belgrade	0	1
1956	Wembley	3	0
1958	Belgrade	0	5
1960	Wembley	3	3
1965	Belgrade	1	1
1966	Wembley	2	0
1968	Florence (EC)	0	1
1972	Wembley	1	1
1974	Belgrade	2	2
1986	Wembley (EC)	2	0
1987	Belgrade (EC)	4	1
1989	Wembley	2	1
1937	Stockholm	4	0
1948	Highbury	4	2
1949	Stockholm	1	3
1956	Stockholm	0	0
1959	Wembley	2	3
1965	Gothenburg	2	1
1968	Wembley	3	1
1979	Stockholm	0	0
1986	Stockholm	0	1
1988	Wembley (WC)	0	0
1989	Stockholm (WC)	0	0
1992	Stockholm (EC)	1	2
1995	Leeds	3	3
1998	Stockholm (EC)	1	2
1999	Wembley (EC)	0	0
2001	Old Trafford	1	1
2002	Saitama (WC)	1	1
2004	Gothenburg	0	1
2006	Cologne (WC)	2	2

ENGLAND'S RECORD England's first international was a 0-0 draw against Scotland in Glasgow, on the West of Scotland cricket ground, Partick, on November 30, 1872 Their complete record at the start of 2017–18 is:

P	W	D	L	F	A
968	549	236	183	21251	958

ENGLAND'S 'B' TEAM RESULTS

England scores first

1949	Finland (A)	4	0	1980	USA (H)	1	0
1949	Holland (A)	4	0	1980	Spain (H)	1	0
1950	Italy (A)	0	5	1980	Australia (H)	1	0
1950	Holland (H)	1	0	1981	Spain (A)	2	3
1950	Holland (H)	0	3	1984	N Zealand (H)	2	0
1950	Luxembourg (A)	2	1	1987	Malta (A)	2	0
1950	Switzerland (H)	5	0	1989	Switzerland (A)	2	0
1952	Holland (A)	1	0	1989	Iceland (A)	2	0
1952	France (H)	1	7	1989	Norway (A)	1	0
1953	Scotland (A)	2	2	1989	Italy (H)	1	1
1954	Scotland (H)	1	1	1989	Yugoslavia (H)	2	1
1954	Germany (A)	4	0	1990	Rep of Ireland (A)	1	4
1954	Yugoslavia (A)	1	2	1990	Czechoslovakia (H)	2	0
1954	Switzerland (A)	0	2	1990	Algeria (A)	0	0
1955	Germany (H)	1	1	1991	Wales (A)	1	0
1955	Yugoslavia (H)	5	1	1991	Iceland (H)	1	0
1956	Switzerland (H)	4	1	1991	Switzerland (H)	2	1
1956	Scotland (A)	2	2	1991	Spanish XI (A)	1	0
1957	Scotland (H)	4	1	1992	France (H)	3	0
1978	W Germany (A)	2	1	1992	Czechoslovakia (A)	1	0
1978	Czechoslovakia (A)	1	0	1992	CIS (A)	1	1
1978	Singapore (A)	0	0	1994	N Ireland (H)	4	2
1978	Malaysia (A)	1	1	1995	Rep of Ireland (H)	2	0
1978	N Zealand (H)	4	0	1998	Chile (H)	1	2
1978	N Zealand (A)	3	1	1998	Russia (H)	4	1
1978	N Zealand (A)	4	0	2006	Belarus (H)	1	2
1979	Austria (A)	1	0	2007	Albania	3	1
1979	N Zealand (H)	4	1				

GREAT BRITAIN v REST OF EUROPE (FIFA)

		GB	RofE				GB	RofE
1947	Glasgow	6	1	1955	Belfast		1	4

SCOTLAND

v ARGENTINA

		S	A
1977	Buenos Aires	1	1
1979	Glasgow	1	3
1990	Glasgow	1	0
2008	Glasgow	0	1

v AUSTRALIA

		S	A
1985*	Glasgow (WC)	2	0
1985^	Melbourne (WC)	0	0
1996	Glasgow	1	0
2000	Glasgow	0	2
2012	Edinburgh	3	1
(* World Cup play-off)			

v AUSTRIA

		S	A
1931	Vienna	0	5
1933	Glasgow	2	2
1937	Vienna	1	1
1950	Glasgow	0	1
1951	Vienna	0	4
1954	Zurich (WC)	0	1
1955	Vienna	4	1
1956	Glasgow	1	1
1960	Vienna	1	4
1963*	Glasgow	4	1
1968	Glasgow (WC)	2	1
1969	Vienna (WC)	0	2
1978	Vienna (EC)	2	3
1979	Glasgow (EC)	1	1
1994	Vienna	2	1
1996	Vienna (WC)	0	0
1997	Glasgow (WC)	2	0
(* Abandoned after 79 minutes)			
2003	Glasgow	0	2
2005	Graz	2	2
2007	Vienna	1	0

v BELARUS

		S	B
1997	Minsk (WC)	1	0
1997	Aberdeen (WC)	4	1
2005	Minsk (WC)	0	0
2005	Glasgow (WC)	0	1

v BELGIUM

		S	B
1947	Brussels	1	2
1948	Glasgow	2	0
1951	Brussels	5	0
1971	Liege (EC)	0	3
1971	Aberdeen (EC)	1	0
1974	Brugge	1	2
1979	Brussels (EC)	0	2
1979	Glasgow (EC)	1	3
1982	Brussels (EC)	2	3
1983	Glasgow (EC)	1	1
1987	Brussels (EC)	1	4
1987	Glasgow (EC)	2	0
2001	Glasgow (WC)	2	2
2001	Brussels (WC)	0	2
2012	Brussels (WC)	0	2
2013	Glasgow (WC)	0	2

v BOSNIA

		S	B
1999	Sarajevo (EC)	2	1
1999	Glasgow (EC)	1	0

v BRAZIL

		S	B
1966	Glasgow	1	1
1972	Rio de Janeiro	0	1
1973	Glasgow	0	1
1974	Frankfurt (WC)	0	0
1977	Rio de Janeiro	0	2
1982	Seville (WC)	1	4
1987	Glasgow	0	2
1990	Turin (WC)	0	1
1998	St Denis (WC)	1	2
2011	Arsenal	0	2

v BULGARIA

		S	B
1978	Glasgow	2	1
1986	Glasgow (EC)	0	0
1987	Sofia (EC)	1	0
1990	Sofia (EC)	1	1
1991	Glasgow (EC)	1	1
2006	Kobe	5	1

v CANADA

		S	C
1983	Vancouver	2	0
1983	Edmonton	3	0
1983	Toronto	2	0
1992	Toronto	3	1
2002	Edinburgh	3	1
2017	Edinburgh	1	1

v CHILE

		S	C
1977	Santiago	4	2
1989	Glasgow	2	0

v CIS (formerly Soviet Union)

		S	C
1992	Norrkoping (EC)	3	0

v COLOMBIA

		S	C
1988	Glasgow	0	0
1996	Miami	0	1
1998	New York	2	2

v COSTA RICA

		S	C
1990	Genoa (WC)	0	1

v CROATIA

		S	C
2000	Zagreb (WC)	1	1
2001	Glasgow (WC)	0	0
2008	Glasgow	1	1
2013	Zagreb (WC)	1	0
2013	Glasgow (WC)	2	0

v CYPRUS

		S	C
1968	Nicosia (WC)	5	0
1969	Glasgow (WC)	8	0
1989	Limassol (WC)	3	2
1989	Glasgow (WC)	2	1
2011	Larnaca	2	1

v CZECH REPUBLIC

		S	C
1999	Glasgow (EC)	1	2
1999	Prague (EC)	2	3
2008	Prague	1	3
2010	Glasgow	1	0
2010	Prague (EC)	0	1
2011	Glasgow (EC)	2	2
2016	Prague	1	0

v CZECHOSLOVAKIA

		S	C
1937	Prague	3	1
1937	Glasgow	5	0
1961	Bratislava (WC)	0	4
1961	Glasgow (WC)	3	2
1961*	Brussels (WC)	2	4
1972	Porto Alegre	0	0
1973	Glasgow (WC)	2	1
1973	Bratislava (WC)	0	1
1976	Prague (WC)	0	2
1977	Glasgow (WC)	3	1

(*World Cup play-off)

v DENMARK

		S	D
1951	Glasgow	3	1
1952	Copenhagen	2	1
1968	Copenhagen	1	0
1970	Glasgow (EC)	1	0
1971	Copenhagen (EC)	0	1
1972	Copenhagen (WC)	4	1
1972	Glasgow (WC)	2	0
1975	Copenhagen (EC)	1	0
1975	Glasgow (EC)	3	1
1986	Neza (WC)	0	1
1996	Copenhagen	0	2
1998	Glasgow	0	1
2002	Glasgow	0	1
2004	Copenhagen	0	1
2011	Glasgow	2	1
2016	Glasgow	1	0

v EAST GERMANY

		S	EG
1974	Glasgow	3	0
1977	East Berlin	0	1
1982	Glasgow (EC)	2	0

1983	Halle (EC)	1	2
1986	Glasgow	0	0
1990	Glasgow	0	1

v ECUADOR

		S	E
1995	Toyama, Japan	2	1

v EGYPT

		S	E
1990	Aberdeen	1	3

v ESTONIA

		S	E
1993	Tallinn (WC)	3	0
1993	Aberdeen	3	1
1996	Tallinn (WC)	*No result	
1997	Monaco (WC)	0	0
1997	Kilmarnock (WC)	2	0
1998	Edinburgh (EC)	3	2
1999	Tallinn (EC)	0	0
(* Estonia absent)			
2004	Tallinn	1	0
2013	Aberdeen	1	0

v FAROE ISLANDS

		S	F
1994	Glasgow (EC)	5	1
1995	Toftir (EC)	2	0
1998	Aberdeen (EC)	2	1
1999	Toftir (EC)	1	1
2002	Toftir (EC)	2	2
2003	Glasgow (EC)	3	1
2006	Glasgow (EC)	6	0
2007	Toftir (EC)	2	0
2010	Aberdeen	3	0

v FINLAND

		S	F
1954	Helsinki	2	1
1964	Glasgow (WC)	3	1
1965	Helsinki (WC)	2	1
1976	Glasgow	6	0
1992	Glasgow	1	1
1994	Helsinki (EC)	2	0
1995	Glasgow (EC)	1	0
1998	Edinburgh	1	1

v FRANCE

		S	F
1930	Paris	2	0
1932	Paris	3	1
1948	Paris	0	3
1949	Glasgow	2	0
1950	Paris	1	0
1951	Glasgow	1	0
1958	Orebro (WC)	1	2
1984	Marseilles	0	2
1989	Glasgow (WC)	2	0
1990	Paris (WC)	0	3
1997	St Etienne	1	2
2000	Glasgow	0	2
2002	Paris	0	5
2006	Glasgow (EC)	1	0
2007	Paris (EC)	1	0
2016	Metz	0	3

v GEORGIA

		S	G
2007	Glasgow (EC)	2	1
2007	Tbilisi (EC)	0	2
2014	Glasgow (EC)	1	0
2015	Tbilisi (EC)	0	1

v GERMANY/WEST GERMANY

		S	G
1929	Berlin	1	1
1936	Glasgow	2	0
1957	Stuttgart	3	1
1959	Glasgow	3	2
1964	Hanover	2	2
1969	Glasgow (WC)	1	1
1969	Hamburg (WC)	2	3
1973	Glasgow	1	1
1974	Frankfurt	1	2
1986	Queretaro (WC)	1	2
1992	Norrkoping (EC)	0	2
1993	Glasgow	0	1
1999	Bremen	1	0
2003	Glasgow (EC)	1	1
2003	Dortmund (EC)	1	2
2014	Dortmund (EC)	1	2
2015	Glasgow (EC)	2	3

v GIBRALTAR

		S	G
2015	Glasgow (EC)	6	1
2015	Faro (EC)	6	0

v GREECE

		S	G
1994	Athens (EC)	0	1
1995	Glasgow	1	0

v HOLLAND

		S	H
1929	Amsterdam	2	0
1938	Amsterdam	3	1
1959	Amsterdam	2	1
1966	Glasgow	0	3
1968	Amsterdam	0	0
1971	Amsterdam	1	2
1978	Mendoza (WC)	3	2
1982	Glasgow	2	1
1986	Eindhoven	0	0
1992	Gothenburg (EC)	0	1
1994	Glasgow	0	1
1994	Utrecht	1	3
1996	Birmingham (EC)	0	0
2000	Arnhem	0	0
2003*	Glasgow (EC)	1	0
2003*	Amsterdam (EC)	0	6
2009	Amsterdam (WC)	0	3
2009	Glasgow (WC)	0	1
(*Qual Round play-off)			

v HUNGARY

		S	H
1938	Glasgow	3	1
1955	Glasgow	2	4
1955	Budapest	1	3
1958	Glasgow	1	1
1960	Budapest	3	3
1980	Budapest	1	3

v ICELAND

		S	I
1984	Glasgow (WC)	3	0
1985	Reykjavik (WC)	1	0
2002	Reykjavik (EC)	2	0
2003	Glasgow (EC)	2	1
2008	Reykjavik (WC)	2	1
2009	Glasgow (WC)	2	1

v IRAN

		S	I
1978	Cordoba (WC)	1	1

v ISRAEL

		S	I
1981	Tel Aviv (WC)	1	0
1981	Glasgow (WC)	3	1
1986	Tel Aviv	1	0

v ITALY

		S	I
1931	Rome	0	3
1965	Glasgow (WC)	1	0
1965	Naples (WC)	0	3
1988	Perugia	0	2
1992	Glasgow (WC)	0	0
1993	Rome (WC)	1	3
2005	Milan (WC)	0	2
2005	Glasgow (WC)	1	1
2007	Bari (EC)	0	2
2007	Glasgow (EC)	1	2
2016	Ta'Qali	0	1

v JAPAN

		S	J
1995	Hiroshima	0	0
2006	Saitama	0	0
2009	Yokohama	0	2

v LATVIA

		S	L
1996	Riga (WC)	2	0
1997	Glasgow (WC)	2	0
2000	Riga (WC)	1	0
2001	Glasgow (WC)	2	1

v LIECHTENSTEIN

		S	L
2010	Glasgow (EC)	2	1
2011	Vaduz (EC)	1	0

v LITHUANIA

		S	L
1998	Vilnius (EC)	0	0
1999	Glasgow (EC)	3	0
2003	Kaunus (EC)	0	1
2003	Glasgow (EC)	1	0
2006	Kaunas (EC)	2	1
2007	Glasgow (EC)	3	1
2010	Kaunas (EC)	0	0
2011	Glasgow (EC)	1	0
2016	Glasgow (WC)	1	1

v LUXEMBOURG

		S	L
1947	Luxembourg	6	0
1986	Glasgow (EC)	3	0
1987	Esch (EC)	0	0
2012	Josy Barthel	2	1

v MACEDONIA

		S	M
2008	Skopje (WC)	0	1
2009	Glasgow (WC)	2	0
2012	Glasgow (WC)	1	1
2013	Skopje (WC)	2	1

v MALTA

		S	M
1988	Valletta	1	1
1990	Valletta	2	1
1993	Glasgow (WC)	3	0
1993	Valletta (WC)	2	0
1997	Valletta	3	2
2016	Ta'Qali (WC)	5	1

v MOLDOVA

		S	M
2004	Chisinau (WC)	1	1
2005	Glasgow (WC)	2	0

v MOROCCO

		S	M
1998	St Etienne (WC)	0	3

v NEW ZEALAND

		S	NZ
1982	Malaga (WC)	5	2
2003	Edinburgh	1	1

v NIGERIA

		S	N
2002	Aberdeen	1	2
2014	Fulham	2	2

v NORWAY

		S	N
1929	Bergen	7	3
1954	Glasgow	1	0
1954	Oslo	1	1
1963	Bergen	3	4
1963	Glasgow	6	1
1974	Oslo	2	1
1978	Glasgow (EC)	3	2
1979	Oslo (EC)	4	0
1988	Oslo (WC)	2	1
1989	Glasgow (WC)	1	1
1992	Oslo	0	0
1998	Bordeaux (WC)	1	1
2003	Oslo	0	0
2004	Glasgow (WC)	0	1
2005	Oslo (WC)	2	1
2008	Glasgow (WC)	0	0
2009	Oslo (WC)	0	4
2013	Molde	1	0

v PARAGUAY

		S	P
1958	Norrkoping (WC)	2	3

v PERU

		S	P
1972	Glasgow	2	0
1978	Cordoba (WC)	1	3
1979	Glasgow	1	1

v POLAND

		S	P
1958	Warsaw	2	1
1960	Glasgow	2	3
1965	Chorzow (WC)	1	1
1965	Glasgow (WC)	1	2

1980	Poznan	0	1
1990	Glasgow	1	1
2001	Bydgoszcz	1	1
2014	Warsaw	1	0
2014	Warsaw (EC)	2	2
2015	Glasgow (EC)	2	2

v PORTUGAL

		S	P
1950	Lisbon	2	2
1955	Glasgow	3	0
1959	Lisbon	0	1
1966	Glasgow	0	1
1971	Lisbon (EC)	0	2
1971	Glasgow (EC)	2	1
1975	Glasgow	1	0
1978	Lisbon (EC)	0	1
1980	Glasgow (EC)	4	1
1980	Glasgow (WC)	0	0
1981	Lisbon (WC)	1	2
1992	Glasgow (WC)	0	0
1993	Lisbon (WC)	0	5
2002	Braga	0	2

v QATAR

		S	Q
2015	Edinburgh	1	0

v REPUBLIC OF IRELAND

		S	RoI
1961	Glasgow (WC)	4	1
1961	Dublin (WC)	3	0
1963	Dublin	0	1
1969	Dublin	1	1
1986	Dublin (EC)	0	0
1987	Glasgow (EC)	0	1
2000	Dublin	2	1
2003	Glasgow (EC)	0	2
2011	Dublin (CC)	0	1
2014	Glasgow (EC)	1	0
2015	Dublin (EC)	1	1

v ROMANIA

		S	R
1975	Bucharest (EC)	1	1
1975	Glasgow (EC)	1	1
1986	Glasgow	3	0
1990	Glasgow (EC)	2	1
1991	Bucharest (EC)	0	1
2004	Glasgow	1	2

v RUSSIA

		S	R
1994	Glasgow (EC)	1	1
1995	Moscow (EC)	0	0

v SAN MARINO

		S	SM
1991	Serravalle (EC)	2	0
1991	Glasgow (EC)	4	0
1995	Serravalle (EC)	2	0
1995	Glasgow (EC)	5	0
2000	Serravalle (WC)	2	0
2001	Glasgow (WC)	4	0

v SAUDI ARABIA

		S	SA
1988	Riyadh	2	2

v SERBIA

		S	Se
2012	Glasgow (WC)	0	0
2013	Novi Sad (WC)	0	2

v SLOVAKIA

		S	Sl
2016	Trnava (WC)	0	3

v SLOVENIA

		S	SL
2004	Glasgow (WC)	0	0
2005	Celje (WC)	3	0
2012	Koper	1	1
2017	Glasgow (WC)	1	0

v SOUTH AFRICA

		S	SA
2002	Hong Kong	0	2
2007	Aberdeen	1	0

v SOUTH KOREA

		S	SK
2002	Busan	1	4

v SOVIET UNION (see also CIS and RUSSIA)

		S	SU
1967	Glasgow	0	2
1971	Moscow	0	1
1982	Malaga (WC)	2	2
1991	Glasgow	0	1

v SPAIN

		S	Sp
1957	Glasgow (WC)	4	2
1957	Madrid (WC)	1	4
1963	Madrid	6	2
1965	Glasgow	0	0
1975	Glasgow (EC)	1	2
1975	Valencia (EC)	1	1
1982	Valencia	0	3
1985	Glasgow (WC)	3	1
1985	Seville (WC)	0	1
1988	Madrid	0	0
2004*	Valencia	1	1

(*Abandoned after 59 mins – floodlight failure)

| 2010 | Glasgow (EC) | 2 | 3 |
| 2011 | Alicante (EC) | 1 | 3 |

v SWEDEN

		S	Swe
1952	Stockholm	1	3
1953	Glasgow	1	2
1975	Gothenburg	1	1
1977	Glasgow	3	1
1980	Stockholm (WC)	1	0
1981	Glasgow (WC)	2	0
1990	Genoa (WC)	2	1
1995	Solna	0	2
1996	Glasgow (WC)	1	0
1997	Gothenburg (WC)	1	2
2004	Edinburgh	1	4
2010	Stockholm	0	3

v SWITZERLAND

		S	Sw
1931	Geneva	3	2
1948	Berne	1	2
1950	Glasgow	3	1
1957	Basle (WC)	2	1

1957	Glasgow (WC)	3	2
1973	Berne	0	1
1976	Glasgow	1	0
1982	Berne (EC)	0	2
1983	Glasgow (EC)	2	2
1990	Glasgow (EC)	2	1
1991	Berne (EC)	2	2
1992	Berne (WC)	1	3
1993	Aberdeen (WC)	1	1
1996	Birmingham (EC)	1	0
2006	Glasgow	1	3

v TRINIDAD & TOBAGO

		S	T
2004	Hibernian	4	1

v TURKEY

		S	T
1960	Ankara	2	4

v UKRAINE

		S	U
2006	Kiev (EC)	0	2
2007	Glasgow (EC)	3	1

v USA

		S	USA
1952	Glasgow	6	0
1992	Denver	1	0
1996	New Britain, Conn	1	2
1998	Washington	0	0
2005	Glasgow	1	1
2012	Jacksonville	1	5
2013	Glasgow	0	0

v URUGUAY

		S	U
1954	Basle (WC)	0	7
1962	Glasgow	2	3
1983	Glasgow	2	0
1986	Neza (WC)	0	0

v YUGOSLAVIA

		S	Y
1955	Belgrade	2	2
1956	Glasgow	2	0
1958	Vaasteras (WC)	1	1
1972	Belo Horizonte	2	2
1974	Frankfurt (WC)	1	1
1984	Glasgow	6	1
1988	Glasgow (WC)	1	1
1989	Zagreb (WC)	1	3

v ZAIRE

		S	Z
1974	Dortmund (WC)	2	0

WALES

v ALBANIA

		W	A
1994	Cardiff (EC)	2	0
1995	Tirana (EC)	1	1

v ANDORRA

		W	A
2014	La Vella (EC)	2	1
2015	Cardiff (EC)	2	0

v ARGENTINA

		W	A
1992	Gifu (Japan)	0	1
2002	Cardiff	1	1

v ARMENIA

		W	A
2001	Yerevan (WC)	2	2
2001	Cardiff (WC)	0	0

v AUSTRALIA

		W	A
2011	Cardiff	1	2

v AUSTRIA

		W	A
1954	Vienna	0	2
1955	Wrexham	1	2
1975	Vienna (EC)	1	2
1975	Wrexham (EC)	1	0
1992	Vienna	1	1
2005	Cardiff	0	2
2005	Vienna	0	1
2013	Swansea	2	1
2016	Vienna (WC)	2	2

v AZERBAIJAN

		W	A
2002	Baku (EC)	2	0
2003	Cardiff (EC)	4	0
2004	Baku (WC)	1	1
2005	Cardiff (WC)	2	0
2008	Cardiff (WC)	1	0
2009	Baku (WC)	1	0

v BELARUS

		W	B
1998	Cardiff (EC)	3	2
1999	Minsk (EC)	2	1
2000	Minsk (WC)	1	2
2001	Cardiff (WC)	1	0

v BELGIUM

		W	B
1949	Liege	1	3
1949	Cardiff	5	1
1990	Cardiff (EC)	3	1
1991	Brussels (EC)	1	1
1992	Brussels (WC)	0	2
1993	Cardiff (WC)	2	0
1997	Cardiff (WC)	1	2
1997	Brussels (WC)	2	3
2012	Cardiff (WC)	0	2
2013	Brussels (WC)	1	1
2014	Brussels (EC)	0	0
2015	Cardiff (EC)	1	0
2016	Lille (EC)	3	1

v BOSNIA-HERZEGOVINA

		W	B-H
2003	Cardiff	2	2
2012	Llanelli	0	2
2014	Cardiff (EC)	0	0
2015	Zenica (EC)	0	2

v BRAZIL

		W	B
1958	Gothenburg (WC)	0	1
1962	Rio de Janeiro	1	3

1962	Sao Paulo	1	3
1966	Rio de Janeiro	1	3
1966	Belo Horizonte	0	1
1983	Cardiff	1	1
1991	Cardiff	1	0
1997	Brasilia	0	3
2000	Cardiff	0	3
2006	White Hart Lane	0	2

v BULGARIA

		W	B
1983	Wrexham (EC)	1	0
1983	Sofia (EC)	0	1
1994	Cardiff (EC)	0	3
1995	Sofia (EC)	1	3
2006	Swansea	0	0
2007	Bourgas	1	0
2010	Cardiff (EC)	0	1
2011	Sofia (EC)	1	0

v CANADA

		W	C
1986	Toronto	0	2
1986	Vancouver	3	0
2004	Wrexham	1	0

v CHILE

		W	C
1966	Santiago	0	2

v COSTA RICA

		W	C
1990	Cardiff	1	0
2012	Cardiff	0	1

v CROATIA

		W	C
2002	Varazdin	1	1
2010	Osijek	0	2
2012	Osijek (WC)	0	2
2013	Swansea (WC)	1	2

v CYPRUS

		W	C
1992	Limassol (WC)	1	0
1993	Cardiff (WC)	2	0
2005	Limassol	0	1
2006	Cardiff (EC)	3	1
2007	Nicosia (EC)	1	3
2014	Cardiff (EC)	2	1
2015	Nicosia	1	0

v CZECHOSLOVAKIA (see also RCS)

		W	C
1957	Cardiff (WC)	1	0
1957	Prague (WC)	0	2
1971	Swansea (EC)	1	3
1971	Prague (EC)	0	1
1977	Wrexham (WC)	3	0
1977	Prague (WC)	0	1
1980	Cardiff (WC)	1	0
1981	Prague (WC)	0	2
1987	Wrexham (EC)	1	1
1987	Prague (EC)	0	2

v CZECH REPUBLIC

		W	CR
2002	Cardiff	0	0
2006	Teplice (EC)	1	2
2007	Cardiff (EC)	0	0

v DENMARK

		W	D
1964	Copenhagen (WC)	0	1
1965	Wrexham (WC)	4	2
1987	Cardiff (EC)	1	0
1987	Copenhagen (EC)	0	1
1990	Copenhagen	0	1
1998	Copenhagen (EC)	2	1
1999	Anfield (EC)	0	2
2008	Copenhagen	1	0

v EAST GERMANY

		W	EG
1957	Leipzig (WC)	1	2
1957	Cardiff (WC)	4	1
1969	Dresden (WC)	1	2
1969	Cardiff (WC)	1	3

v ESTONIA

		W	E
1994	Tallinn	2	1
2009	Llanelli	1	0

v FAROE ISLANDS

		W	FI
1992	Cardiff (WC)	6	0
1993	Toftir (WC)	3	0

v FINLAND

		W	F
1971	Helsinki (EC)	1	0
1971	Swansea (EC)	3	0
1986	Helsinki (EC)	1	1
1987	Wrexham (EC)	4	0
1988	Swansea (WC)	2	2
1989	Helsinki (WC)	0	1
2000	Cardiff	1	2
2002	Helsinki (EC)	2	0
2003	Cardiff (EC)	1	1
2009	Cardiff (WC)	0	2
2009	Helsinki (WC)	1	2
2013	Cardiff	1	1

v FRANCE

		W	F
1933	Paris	1	1
1939	Paris	1	2
1953	Paris	1	6
1982	Toulouse	1	0

v GEORGIA

		W	G
1994	Tbilisi (EC)	0	5
1995	Cardiff (EC)	0	1
2008	Swansea	1	2
2016	Cardiff (WC)	1	1

v GERMANY/WEST GERMANY

		W	G
1968	Cardiff	1	1
1969	Frankfurt	1	1
1977	Cardiff	0	2
1977	Dortmund	1	1
1979	Wrexham (EC)	0	2
1979	Cologne (EC)	1	5
1989	Cardiff (WC)	0	0
1989	Cologne (WC)	1	2
1991	Cardiff (EC)	1	0
1991	Nuremberg (EC)	1	4

1995	Dusseldorf (EC)	1	1
1995	Cardiff (EC)	1	2
2002	Cardiff	1	0
2007	Cardiff (EC)	0	2
2007	Frankfurt (EC)	0	0
2008	Moenchengladbach (WC)	0	1
2009	Cardiff (WC)	0	2

v GREECE

		W	G
1964	Athens (WC)	0	2
1965	Cardiff (WC)	4	1

v HOLLAND

		W	H
1988	Amsterdam (WC)	0	1
1989	Wrexham (WC)	1	2
1992	Utrecht	0	4
1996	Cardiff (WC)	1	3
1996	Eindhoven (WC)	1	7
2008	Rotterdam	0	2
2014	Amsterdam	0	2
2015	Cardiff	2	3

v HUNGARY

		W	H
1958	Sanviken (WC)	1	1
1958	Stockholm (WC)	2	1
1961	Budapest	2	3
1963	Budapest (EC)	1	3
1963	Cardiff (EC)	1	1
1974	Cardiff (EC)	2	0
1975	Budapest (EC)	2	1
1986	Cardiff	0	3
2004	Budapest	2	1
2005	Cardiff	2	0

v ICELAND

		W	I
1980	Reykjavik (WC)	4	0
1981	Swansea (WC)	2	2
1984	Reykjavik (WC)	0	1
1984	Cardiff (WC)	2	1
1991	Cardiff	1	0
2008	Reykjavik	1	0
2014	Cardiff	3	1

v IRAN

		W	I
1978	Tehran	1	0

v ISRAEL

		W	I
1958	Tel Aviv (WC)	2	0
1958	Cardiff (WC)	2	0
1984	Tel Aviv	0	0
1989	Tel Aviv	3	3
2015	Haifa (EC)	3	0
2015	Cardiff (EC)	0	0

v ITALY

		W	I
1965	Florence	1	4
1968	Cardiff (WC)	0	1
1969	Rome (WC)	1	4
1988	Brescia	1	0
1996	Terni	0	3
1998	Anfield (EC)	0	2
1999	Bologna (EC)	0	4

| 2002 | Cardiff (EC) | 2 | 1 |
| 2003 | Milan (EC) | 0 | 4 |

v JAMAICA

		W	J
1998	Cardiff	0	0

v JAPAN

		W	J
1992	Matsuyama	1	0

v KUWAIT

		W	K
1977	Wrexham	0	0
1977	Kuwait City	0	0

v LATVIA

		W	L
2004	Riga	2	0

v LIECHTENSTEIN

		W	L
2006	Wrexham	4	0
2008	Cardiff (WC)	2	0
2009	Vaduz (WC)	2	0

v LUXEMBOURG

		W	L
1974	Swansea (EC)	5	0
1975	Luxembourg (EC)	3	1
1990	Luxembourg (EC)	1	0
1991	Luxembourg (EC)	1	0
2008	Luxembourg	2	0
2010	Llanelli	5	1

v MACEDONIA

		W	M
2013	Skopje (WC)	1	2
2013	Cardiff (WC)	1	1

v MALTA

		W	M
1978	Wrexham (EC)	7	0
1979	Valletta (EC)	2	0
1988	Valletta	3	2
1998	Valletta	3	0

v MEXICO

		W	M
1958	Stockholm (WC)	1	1
1962	Mexico City	1	2
2012	New York	0	2

v MOLDOVA

		W	M
1994	Kishinev (EC)	2	3
1995	Cardiff (EC)	1	0
2016	Cardiff (WC)	4	0

v MONTENEGRO

		W	M
2009	Podgorica	1	2
2010	Podgorica (EC)	0	1
2011	Cardiff (EC)	2	1

v NEW ZEALAND

		W	NZ
2007	Wrexham	2	2

v NORWAY

		W	N
1982	Swansea (EC)	1	0
1983	Oslo (EC)	0	0

1984	Trondheim	0	1
1985	Wrexham	1	1
1985	Bergen	2	4
1994	Cardiff	1	3
2000	Cardiff (WC)	1	1
2001	Oslo (WC)	2	3
2004	Oslo	0	0
2008	Wrexham	3	0
2011	Cardiff	4	1

v PARAGUAY

		W	P
2006	Cardiff	0	0

v POLAND

		W	P
1973	Cardiff (WC)	2	0
1973	Katowice (WC)	0	3
1991	Radom	0	0
2000	Warsaw (WC)	0	0
2001	Cardiff (WC)	1	2
2004	Cardiff (WC)	2	3
2005	Warsaw (WC)	0	1
2009	Vila-Real (Por)	0	1

v PORTUGAL

		W	P
1949	Lisbon	2	3
1951	Cardiff	2	1
2000	Chaves	0	3
2016	Lyon (EC)	0	2

v QATAR

		W	Q
2000	Doha	1	0

v RCS (formerly Czechoslovakia)

		W	RCS
1993	Ostrava (WC)	1	1
1993	Cardiff (WC)	2	2

v REPUBLIC OF IRELAND

		W	RI
1960	Dublin	3	2
1979	Swansea	2	1
1981	Dublin	3	1
1986	Dublin	1	0
1990	Dublin	0	1
1991	Wrexham	0	3
1992	Dublin	1	0
1993	Dublin	1	2
1997	Cardiff	0	0
2007	Dublin (EC)	0	1
2007	Cardiff (EC)	2	2
2011	Dublin (CC)	0	3
2013	Cardiff	0	0
2017	Dublin (WC)	0	0

v REST OF UNITED KINGDOM

		W	UK
1951	Cardiff	3	2
1969	Cardiff	0	1

v ROMANIA

		W	R
1970	Cardiff (EC)	0	0
1971	Bucharest (EC)	0	2
1983	Wrexham	5	0
1992	Bucharest (WC)	1	5
1993	Cardiff (WC)	1	2

v RUSSIA (See also Soviet Union)

		W	R
2003*	Moscow (EC)	0	0
2003*	Cardiff (EC)	0	1
2008	Moscow (WC)	1	2
2009	Cardiff (WC)	1	3
2016	Toulouse (EC)	3	0

(*Qual Round play-offs)

v SAN MARINO

		W	SM
1996	Serravalle (WC)	5	0
1996	Cardiff (WC)	6	0
2007	Cardiff (EC)	3	0
2007	Serravalle (EC)	2	1

v SAUDI ARABIA

		W	SA
1986	Dahran	2	1

v SERBIA

		W	S
2012	Novi Sad (WC)	1	6
2013	Cardiff (WC)	0	3
2016	Cardiff (WC)	1	1
2017	Belgrade (WC)	1	1

v SERBIA & MONTENEGRO

		W	S
2003	Belgrade (EC)	0	1
2003	Cardiff (EC)	2	3

v SLOVAKIA

		W	S
2006	Cardiff (EC)	1	5
2007	Trnava (EC)	5	2
2016	Bordeaux (EC)	2	1

v SLOVENIA

		W	S
2005	Swansea	0	0

v SOVIET UNION (See also Russia)

		W	SU
1965	Moscow (WC)	1	2
1965	Cardiff (WC)	2	1
1981	Wrexham (WC)	0	0
1981	Tbilisi (WC)	0	3
1987	Swansea	0	0

v SPAIN

		W	S
1961	Cardiff (WC)	1	2
1961	Madrid (WC)	1	1
1982	Valencia	1	1
1984	Seville (WC)	0	3
1985	Wrexham (WC)	3	0

v SWEDEN

		W	S
1958	Stockholm (WC)	0	0
1988	Stockholm	1	4
1989	Wrexham	0	2
1990	Stockholm	2	4
1994	Wrexham	0	2
2010	Swansea	0	1
2016	Stockholm	0	3

v SWITZERLAND

		W	S
1949	Berne	0	4
1951	Wrexham	3	2
1996	Lugano	0	2

1999	Zurich (EC)	0	2
1999	Wrexham (EC)	0	2
2010	Basle (EC)	1	4
2011	Swansea (EC)	2	0

v TRINIDAD & TOBAGO

		W	T
2006	Graz	2	1

v TUNISIA

		W	T
1998	Tunis	0	4

v TURKEY

		W	T
1978	Wrexham (EC)	1	0
1979	Izmir (EC)	0	1
1980	Cardiff (WC)	4	0
1981	Ankara (WC)	1	0
1996	Cardiff (WC)	0	0
1997	Istanbul (WC)	4	6

v UKRAINE

		W	U
2001	Cardiff (WC)	1	1
2001	Kiev (WC)	1	1
2015	Kiev	0	1

v URUGUAY

		W	U
1986	Wrexham	0	0

v USA

		W	USA
2003	San Jose	0	2

v YUGOSLAVIA

		W	Y
1953	Belgrade	2	5
1954	Cardiff	1	3
1976	Zagreb (EC)	0	2
1976	Cardiff (EC)	1	1
1982	Titograd (EC)	4	4
1983	Cardiff (EC)	1	1
1988	Swansea	1	2

NORTHERN IRELAND

v ALBANIA

		NI	A
1965	Belfast (WC)	4	1
1965	Tirana (WC)	1	1
1983	Tirana (EC)	0	0
1983	Belfast (EC)	1	0
1992	Belfast (WC)	3	0
1993	Tirana (WC)	2	1
1996	Belfast (WC)	2	0
1997	Zurich (WC)	0	1
2010	Tirana	0	1

v ALGERIA

		NI	A
1986	Guadalajara (WC)	1	1

v ARGENTINA

		NI	A
1958	Halmstad (WC)	1	3

v ARMENIA

		NI	A
1996	Belfast (WC)	1	1
1997	Yerevan (WC)	0	0
2003	Yerevan (EC)	0	1
2003	Belfast (EC)	0	1

v AUSTRALIA

		NI	A
1980	Sydney	2	1
1980	Melbourne	1	1
1980	Adelaide	2	1

v AUSTRIA

		NI	A
1982	Madrid (WC)	2	2
1982	Vienna (EC)	0	2
1983	Belfast (EC)	3	1
1990	Vienna (EC)	0	0
1991	Belfast (EC)	2	1
1994	Vienna (EC)	2	1
1995	Belfast (EC)	5	3
2004	Belfast (WC)	3	3
2005	Vienna (WC)	0	2

v AZERBAIJAN

		NI	A
2004	Baku (WC)	0	0
2005	Belfast (WC)	2	0
2012	Belfast (WC)	1	1
2013	Baku (WC)	0	2
2016	Belfast (WC)	4	0
2017	Baku (WC)	1	0

v BARBADOS

		NI	B
2004	Bridgetown	1	1

v BELARUS

		NI	B
2016	Belfast	3	0

v BELGIUM

		NI	B
1976	Liege (WC)	0	2
1977	Belfast (WC)	3	0
1997	Belfast	3	0

v BRAZIL

		NI	B
1986	Guadalajara (WC)	0	3

v BULGARIA

		NI	B
1972	Sofia (WC)	0	3
1973	Sheffield (WC)	0	0
1978	Sofia (EC)	2	0
1979	Belfast (EC)	2	0
2001	Sofia (WC)	3	4
2001	Belfast (WC)	0	1
2008	Belfast	0	1

v CANADA

		NI	C
1995	Edmonton	0	2
1999	Belfast	1	1
2005	Belfast	0	1

v CHILE

		NI	C
1989	Belfast	0	1
1995	Edmonton, Canada	0	2
2010	Chillan	0	1
2014	Valparaiso	0	2

v COLOMBIA

		NI	C
1994	Boston, USA	0	2

v CROATIA

		NI	C
2016	Belfast	0	3

v CYPRUS

		NI	C
1971	Nicosia (EC)	3	0
1971	Belfast (EC)	5	0
1973	Nicosia (WC)	0	1
1973	Fulham (WC)	3	0
2002	Belfast	0	0
2014	Nicosia	0	0

v CZECHOSLOVAKIA/CZECH REP

		NI	C
1958	Halmstad (WC)	1	0
1958	Malmo (WC)	2	1
2001	Belfast (WC)	0	1
2001	Teplice (WC)	1	3
2008	Belfast (WC)	0	0
2009	Prague (WC)	0	0
2016	Prague (WC)	0	0

v DENMARK

		NI	D
1978	Belfast (EC)	2	1
1979	Copenhagen (EC)	0	4
1986	Belfast	1	1
1990	Belfast (EC)	1	1
1991	Odense (EC)	1	2
1992	Belfast (WC)	0	1
1993	Copenhagen (WC)	0	1
2000	Belfast (WC)	1	1
2001	Copenhagen (WC)	1	1
2006	Copenhagen (EC)	0	0
2007	Belfast (EC)	2	1

v ESTONIA

		NI	E
2004	Tallinn	1	0
2006	Belfast	1	0
2011	Tallinn (EC)	1	4
2011	Belfast (EC)	1	2

v FAROE ISLANDS

		NI	FI
1991	Belfast (EC)	1	1
1991	Landskrona, Sw (EC)	5	0
2010	Toftir (EC)	1	1
2011	Belfast (EC)	4	0
2014	Belfast (EC)	2	0
2015	Torshavn (EC)	3	1

v FINLAND

		NI	F
1984	Pori (WC)	0	1
1984	Belfast (WC)	2	1
1998	Belfast (EC)	1	0
1999	Helsinki (EC)	1	4
2003	Belfast	0	1
2006	Helsinki	2	1
2012	Belfast	3	3
2015	Belfast (EC)	2	1
2015	Helsinki (EC)	1	1

v FRANCE

		NI	F
1951	Belfast	2	2
1952	Paris	1	3
1958	Norrkoping (WC)	0	4
1982	Paris	0	4
1982	Madrid (WC)	1	4
1986	Paris	0	0
1988	Belfast	0	0
1999	Belfast	0	1

v GEORGIA

		NI	G
2008	Belfast	4	1

v GERMANY/WEST GERMANY

		NI	G
1958	Malmo (WC)	2	2
1960	Belfast (WC)	3	4
1961	Berlin (WC)	1	2
1966	Belfast	0	2
1977	Cologne	0	5
1982	Belfast (EC)	1	0
1983	Hamburg (EC)	1	0
1992	Bremen	1	1
1996	Belfast	1	1
1997	Nuremberg (WC)	1	1
1997	Belfast (WC)	1	3
1999	Belfast (EC)	0	3
1999	Dortmund (EC)	0	1
2005	Belfast	1	4
2016	Paris (EC)	0	1
2016	Hannover (WC)	0	2

v GREECE

		NI	G
1961	Athens (WC)	1	0
1961	Belfast (WC)	2	0
1988	Athens	2	3
2003	Belfast (EC)	0	2
2003	Athens (EC)	0	1
2014	Piraeus (EC)	2	0
2015	Belfast (EC)	3	1

v HOLLAND

		NI	H
1962	Rotterdam	0	4
1965	Belfast (WC)	2	1
1965	Rotterdam (WC)	0	0
1976	Rotterdam (WC)	2	2
1977	Belfast (WC)	0	1
2012	Amsterdam	0	6

v HONDURAS

		NI	H
1982	Zaragoza (WC)	1	1

v HUNGARY

		NI	H
1988	Budapest (WC)	0	1
1989	Belfast (WC)	1	2
2000	Belfast	0	1

2008	Belfast	0	2
2014	Budapest (EC)	2	1
2015	Belfast (EC)	1	1

v ICELAND

		NI	I
1977	Reykjavik (WC)	0	1
1977	Belfast (WC)	2	0
2000	Reykjavik (WC)	0	1
2001	Belfast (WC)	3	0
2006	Belfast (EC)	0	3
2007	Reykjavik (EC)	1	2

v ISRAEL

		NI	I
1968	Jaffa	3	2
1976	Tel Aviv	1	1
1980	Tel Aviv (WC)	0	0
1981	Belfast (WC)	1	0
1984	Belfast	3	0
1987	Tel Aviv	1	1
2009	Belfast	1	1
2013	Belfast (WC)	0	2
2013	Ramat Gan (WC)	1	1

v ITALY

		NI	I
1957	Rome (WC)	0	1
1957	Belfast	2	2
1958	Belfast (WC)	2	1
1961	Bologna	2	3
1997	Palermo	0	2
2003	Campobasso	0	2
2009	Pisa	0	3
2010	Belfast (EC)	0	0
2011	Pescara (EC)	0	3

v LATVIA

		NI	L
1993	Riga (WC)	2	1
1993	Belfast (WC)	2	0
1995	Riga (EC)	1	0
1995	Belfast (EC)	1	2
2006	Belfast (EC)	1	0
2007	Riga (EC)	0	1
2015	Belfast	1	0

v LIECHTENSTEIN

		NI	L
1994	Belfast (EC)	4	1
1995	Eschen (EC)	4	0
2002	Vaduz	0	0
2007	Vaduz (EC)	4	1
2007	Belfast (EC)	3	1

v LITHUANIA

		NI	L
1992	Belfast (WC)	2	2

v LUXEMBOURG

		NI	L
2000	Luxembourg	3	1
2012	Belfast (WC)	1	1
2013	Luxembourg (WC)	2	3

v MALTA

		NI	M
1988	Belfast (WC)	3	0
1989	Valletta (WC)	2	0
2000	Ta'Qali	3	0
2000	Belfast (WC)	1	0
2001	Valletta (WC)	1	0
2005	Valletta	1	1
2013	Ta'Qali	0	0

v MEXICO

		NI	M
1966	Belfast	4	1
1994	Miami	0	3

v MOLDOVA

		NI	M
1998	Belfast (EC)	2	2
1999	Kishinev (EC)	0	0

v MONTENEGRO

		W	M
2010	Podgorica	0	2

v MOROCCO

		NI	M
1986	Belfast	2	1
2010	Belfast	1	1

v NEW ZEALAND

		NI	NZ
2017	Belfast	1	0

v NORWAY

		NI	N
1974	Oslo (EC)	1	2
1975	Belfast (EC)	3	0
1990	Belfast	2	3
1996	Belfast	0	2
2001	Belfast	0	4
2004	Belfast	1	4
2012	Belfast	0	3
2017	Belfast (WC)	2	0

v POLAND

		NI	P
1962	Katowice (EC)	2	0
1962	Belfast (EC)	2	0
1988	Belfast	1	1
1991	Belfast	3	1
2002	Limassol (Cyprus)	1	4
2004	Belfast (WC)	0	3
2005	Warsaw (WC)	0	1
2009	Belfast (WC)	3	2
2009	Chorzow (WC)	1	1
2016	Nice (EC)	0	1

v PORTUGAL

		NI	P
1957	Lisbon (WC)	1	1
1957	Belfast (WC)	3	0
1973	Coventry (WC)	1	1
1973	Lisbon (WC)	1	1
1980	Lisbon (WC)	0	1
1981	Belfast (WC)	1	0
1994	Belfast (EC)	1	2
1995	Oporto (EC)	1	1
1997	Belfast (WC)	0	0
1997	Lisbon (WC)	0	1
2005	Belfast	1	1
2012	Porto (WC)	1	1
2013	Belfast (WC)	2	4

v QATAR

		NI	Q
2015	Crewe	1	1

v REPUBLIC OF IRELAND

		NI	RI
1978	Dublin (EC)	0	0
1979	Belfast (EC)	1	0
1988	Belfast (WC)	0	0
1989	Dublin (WC)	0	3
1993	Dublin (WC)	0	3
1993	Belfast (WC)	1	1
1994	Belfast (EC)	0	4
1995	Dublin (EC)	1	1
1999	Dublin	1	0
2011	Dublin (CC)	0	5

v ROMANIA

		NI	R
1984	Belfast (WC)	3	2
1985	Bucharest (WC)	1	0
1994	Belfast	2	0
2006	Chicago	0	2
2014	Bucharest (EC)	0	2
2015	Belfast (EC)	0	0

v RUSSIA

		NI	R
2012	Moscow (WC)	0	2
2013	Belfast (WC)	1	0

v SAN MARINO

		NI	SM
2008	Belfast (WC)	4	0
2009	Serravalle (WC)	3	0
2016	Belfast (WC)	4	0

v SERBIA & MONTENEGRO

		NI	S
2004	Belfast	1	1

v SERBIA

		NI	S
2009	Belfast	0	1
2011	Belgrade (EC)	1	2
2011	Belfast (EC)	0	1

v SLOVAKIA

		NI	S
1998	Belfast	1	0
2008	Bratislava (WC)	1	2
2009	Belfast (WC)	0	2
2016	Trnava	0	0

v SLOVENIA

		NI	S
2008	Maribor (WC)	0	2
2009	Belfast (WC)	1	0
2010	Maribor (EC)	1	0
2011	Belfast (EC)	0	0
2016	Belfast	1	0

v SOVIET UNION

		NI	SU
1969	Belfast (WC)	0	0
1969	Moscow (WC)	0	2
1971	Moscow (EC)	0	1
1971	Belfast (EC)	1	1

v SPAIN

		NI	S
1958	Madrid	2	6
1963	Bilbao	1	1
1963	Belfast	0	1
1970	Seville (EC)	0	3
1972	Hull (EC)	1	1
1982	Valencia (WC)	1	0
1985	Palma, Majorca	0	0
1986	Guadalajara (WC)	1	2
1988	Seville (WC)	0	4
1989	Belfast (WC)	0	2
1992	Belfast (WC)	0	0
1993	Seville (WC)	1	3
1998	Santander	1	4
2002	Belfast	0	5
2002	Albacete (EC)	0	3
2003	Belfast (EC)	0	0
2006	Belfast (EC)	3	2
2007	Las Palmas (EC)	0	1

v ST KITTS & NEVIS

		NI	SK
2004	Basseterre	2	0

v SWEDEN

		NI	S
1974	Solna (EC)	2	0
1975	Belfast (EC)	1	2
1980	Belfast (WC)	3	0
1981	Stockholm (WC)	0	1
1996	Belfast	1	2
2007	Belfast (EC)	2	1
2007	Stockholm (EC)	1	1

v SWITZERLAND

		NI	S
1964	Belfast (WC)	1	0
1964	Lausanne (WC)	1	2
1998	Belfast	1	0
2004	Zurich	0	0
2010	Basle (EC)	1	4

v THAILAND

		NI	T
1997	Bangkok	0	0

v TRINIDAD & TOBAGO

		NI	T
2004	Port of Spain	3	0

v TURKEY

		NI	T
1968	Belfast (WC)	4	1
1968	Istanbul (WC)	3	0
1983	Belfast (EC)	2	1
1983	Ankara (EC)	0	1
1985	Belfast (WC)	2	0
1985	Izmir (WC)	0	0
1986	Izmir (EC)	0	0
1987	Belfast (EC)	1	0
1998	Istanbul (EC)	0	3
1999	Belfast (EC)	0	3
2010	Connecticut	0	2
2013	Adana	0	1

v UKRAINE

		NI	U
1996	Belfast (WC)	0	1

1997	Kiev (WC)	1	2
2002	Belfast (EC)	0	0
2003	Donetsk (EC)	0	0
2016	Lyon (FC)	2	0

v URUGUAY

		NI	U
1964	Belfast	3	0
1990	Belfast	1	0
2006	New Jersey	0	1
2014	Montevideo	0	1

v YUGOSLAVIA

		NI	Y
1975	Belfast (EC)	1	0
1975	Belgrade (EC)	0	1
1982	Zaragoza (WC)	0	0
1987	Belfast (EC)	1	2
1987	Sarajevo (EC)	0	3
1990	Belfast (EC)	0	2
1991	Belgrade (EC)	1	4
2000	Belfast	1	2

REPUBLIC OF IRELAND

v ALBANIA

		RI	A
1992	Dublin (WC)	2	0
1993	Tirana (WC)	2	1
2003	Tirana (EC)	0	0
2003	Dublin (EC)	2	1

v ALGERIA

		RI	A
1982	Algiers	0	2
2010	Dublin	3	0

v ANDORRA

		RI	A
2001	Barcelona (WC)	3	0
2001	Dublin (WC)	3	1
2010	Dublin (EC)	3	1
2011	La Vella (EC)	2	0

v ARGENTINA

		RI	A
1951	Dublin	0	1
1979*	Dublin	0	0
1980	Dublin	0	1
1998	Dublin	0	2
2010	Dublin	0	1
(*Not regarded as full Int)			

v ARMENIA

		RI	A
2010	Yerevan (EC)	1	0
2011	Dublin (EC)	2	1

v AUSTRALIA

		RI	A
2003	Dublin	2	1
2009	Limerick	0	3

v AUSTRIA

		RI	A
1952	Vienna	0	6
1953	Dublin	4	0
1958	Vienna	1	3
1962	Dublin	2	3
1963	Vienna (EC)	0	0
1963	Dublin (EC)	3	2
1966	Vienna	0	1
1968	Dublin	2	2
1971	Dublin (EC)	1	4
1971	Linz (EC)	0	6
1995	Dublin (EC)	1	3
1995	Vienna (EC)	1	3
2013	Dublin (WC)	2	2
2013	Vienna (WC)	0	1
2016	Vienna (WC)	1	0
2017	Dublin (WC	1	1

v BELARUS

		RI	B
2016	Cork	1	2

v BELGIUM

		RI	B
1928	Liege	4	2
1929	Dublin	4	0
1930	Brussels	3	1
1934	Dublin (WC)	4	4
1949	Dublin	0	2
1950	Brussels	1	5
1965	Dublin	0	2
1966	Liege	3	2
1980	Dublin (WC)	1	1
1981	Brussels (WC)	0	1
1986	Brussels (EC)	2	2
1987	Dublin (EC)	0	0
1997*	Dublin (WC)	1	1
1997*	Brussels (WC)	1	2
2016	Bordeaux (EC)	0	3
(*World Cup play-off)			

v BOLIVIA

		RI	B
1994	Dublin	1	0
1996	East Rutherford, NJ	3	0
2007	Boston	1	1

v BOSNIA HERZEGOVINA

		RI	B-H
2012	Dublin	1	0
2015	Zenica (EC)	1	1
2015	Dublin (EC)	2	0

v BRAZIL

		RI	B
1974	Rio de Janeiro	1	2
1982	Uberlandia	0	7
1987	Dublin	1	0
2004	Dublin	0	0
2008	Dublin	0	1
2010	Arsenal	0	2

v BULGARIA

		RI	B
1977	Sofia (WC)	1	2
1977	Dublin (WC)	0	0
1979	Sofia (EC)	0	1

1979	Dublin (EC)	3	0
1987	Sofia (EC)	1	2
1987	Dublin (EC)	2	0
2004	Dublin	1	1
2009	Dublin (WC)	1	1
2009	Sofia (WC)	1	1

v CAMEROON

		RI	C
2002	Niigata (WC)	1	1

v CANADA

		RI	C
2003	Dublin	3	0

v CHILE

		RI	C
1960	Dublin	2	0
1972	Recife	1	2
1974	Santiago	2	1
1982	Santiago	0	1
1991	Dublin	1	1
2006	Dublin	0	1

v CHINA

		RI	C
1984	Sapporo	1	0
2005	Dublin	1	0

v COLOMBIA

		RI	C
2008	Fulham	1	0

v COSTA RICA

		RI	CR
2014	Chester, USA	1	1

v CROATIA

		RI	C
1996	Dublin	2	2
1998	Dublin (EC)	2	0
1999	Zagreb (EC)	0	1
2001	Dublin	2	2
2004	Dublin	1	0
2011	Dublin	0	0
2012	Poznan (EC)	1	3

v CYPRUS

		RI	C
1980	Nicosia (WC)	3	2
1980	Dublin (WC)	6	0
2001	Nicosia (WC)	4	0
2001	Dublin (WC)	4	0
2004	Dublin (WC)	3	0
2005	Nicosia (WC)	1	0
2006	Nicosia (EC)	2	5
2007	Dublin (EC)	1	1
2008	Dublin (WC)	1	0
2009	Nicosia (WC)	2	1

v CZECHOSLOVAKIA/CZECH REP

		RI	C
1938	Prague	2	2
1959	Dublin (EC)	2	0
1959	Bratislava (EC)	0	4
1961	Dublin	1	3
1961	Prague (WC)	1	7
1967	Dublin (EC)	0	2
1967	Prague (EC)	2	1
1969	Dublin (WC)	1	2

1969	Prague (WC)	0	3
1979	Prague	1	4
1981	Dublin	3	1
1986	Reykjavik	1	0
1994	Dublin	1	3
1996	Prague	0	2
1998	Olomouc	1	2
2000	Dublin	3	2
2004	Dublin	2	1
2006	Dublin (EC)	1	1
2007	Prague (EC)	0	1
2012	Dublin	1	1

v DENMARK

		RI	D
1956	Dublin (WC)	2	1
1957	Copenhagen (WC)	2	0
1968*	Dublin (WC)	1	1
1969	Copenhagen (WC)	0	2
1969	Dublin (WC)	1	1
1978	Copenhagen (EC)	3	3
1979	Dublin (EC)	2	0
1984	Copenhagen (WC)	0	3
1985	Dublin (WC)	1	4
1992	Copenhagen (WC)	0	0
1993	Dublin (WC)	1	1
2002	Dublin	3	0

(*Abandoned after 51 mins – fog)

2007	Aarhus	4	0

v ECUADOR

		RI	E
1972	Natal	3	2
2007	New York	1	1

v EGYPT

		RI	E
1990	Palermo (WC)	0	0

v ESTONIA

		RI	E
2000	Dublin (WC)	2	0
2001	Tallinn (WC)	2	0
2011	Tallinn (EC)	4	0
2011	Dublin (EC)	1	1

v FAROE ISLANDS

		RI	F
2004	Dublin (WC)	2	0
2005	Torshavn (WC)	2	0
2012	Torshavn (WC)	4	1
2013	Dublin (WC)	3	0

v FINLAND

		RI	F
1949	Dublin (WC)	3	0
1949	Helsinki (WC)	1	1
1990	Dublin	1	1
2000	Dublin	3	0
2002	Helsinki	3	0

v FRANCE

		RI	F
1937	Paris	2	0
1952	Dublin	1	1
1953	Dublin (WC)	3	5
1953	Paris (WC)	0	1
1972	Dublin (WC)	2	1

265

1973	Paris (WC)	1	1
1976	Paris (WC)	0	2
1977	Dublin (WC)	1	0
1980	Paris (WC)	0	2
1981	Dublin (WC)	3	2
1989	Dublin	0	0
2004	Paris (WC)	0	0
2005	Dublin (WC)	0	1
2009	Dublin (WC)	0	1
2009	Paris (WC)	1	1
2016	Lyon (EC)	1	2

v GEORGIA

		RI	G
2002	Tbilisi (EC)	2	1
2003	Dublin (EC)	2	0
2008	Mainz (WC)	2	1
2009	Dublin (WC)	2	1
2013	Dublin	4	0
2014	Tbilisi (EC)	2	1
2015	Dublin (EC)	1	0
2016	Dublin (WC)	1	0

v GERMANY/WEST GERMANY

		RI	G
1935	Dortmund	1	3
1936	Dublin	5	2
1939	Bremen	1	1
1951	Dublin	3	2
1952	Cologne	0	3
1955	Hamburg	1	2
1956	Dublin	3	0
1960	Dusseldorf	1	0
1966	Dublin	0	4
1970	Berlin	1	2
1975*	Dublin	1	0
1979	Dublin	1	3
1981	Bremen	0	3
1989	Dublin	1	1
1994	Hanover	2	0
2002	Ibaraki (WC)	1	1
2006	Stuttgart (EC)	0	1
2007	Dublin (EC)	0	0
2012	Dublin (WC)	1	6
2013	Cologne (WC)	0	3
2014	Gelsenkirchen (EC)	1	1
2015	Dublin (EC)	1	0

(*v W Germany 'B')

v GIBRALTAR

		RI	G
2014	Dublin (EC)	7	0
2015	Faro (EC)	4	0

v GREECE

		RI	G
2000	Dublin	0	1
2002	Athens	0	0
2012	Dublin	0	1

v HOLLAND

		RI	H
1932	Amsterdam	2	0
1934	Amsterdam	2	5
1935	Dublin	3	5
1955	Dublin	1	0
1956	Rotterdam	4	1
1980	Dublin (WC)	2	1
1981	Rotterdam (WC)	2	2
1982	Rotterdam (EC)	1	2
1983	Dublin (EC)	2	3
1988	Gelsenkirchen (EC)	0	1
1990	Palermo (WC)	1	1
1994	Tilburg	1	0
1994	Orlando (WC)	0	2
1995*	Liverpool (EC)	0	2
1996	Rotterdam	1	3

(*Qual Round play-off)

2000	Amsterdam (WC)	2	2
2001	Dublin (WC)	1	0
2004	Amsterdam	1	0
2006	Dublin	0	4
2016	Dublin	1	1

v HUNGARY

		RI	H
1934	Dublin	2	4
1936	Budapest	3	3
1936	Dublin	2	3
1939	Cork	2	2
1939	Budapest	2	2
1969	Dublin (WC)	1	2
1969	Budapest (WC)	0	4
1989	Budapest (WC)	0	0
1989	Dublin (WC)	2	0
1992	Gyor	2	1
2012	Budapest	0	0

v ICELAND

		RI	I
1962	Dublin (EC)	4	2
1962	Reykjavik (EC)	1	1
1982	Dublin (EC)	2	0
1983	Reykjavik (EC)	3	0
1986	Reykjavik	2	1
1996	Dublin (WC)	0	0
1997	Reykjavik (WC)	4	2
2017	Dublin	0	1

v IRAN

		RI	I
1972	Recife	2	1
2001*	Dublin (WC)	2	0
2001*	Tehran (WC)	0	1

(*Qual Round play-off)

v ISRAEL

		RI	I
1984	Tel Aviv	0	3
1985	Tel Aviv	0	0
1987	Dublin	5	0
2005	Tel Aviv (WC)	1	1
2005	Dublin (WC)	2	2

v ITALY

		RI	I
1926	Turin	0	3
1927	Dublin	1	2
1970	Florence (EC)	0	3
1971	Dublin (EC)	1	2
1985	Dublin	1	2
1990	Rome (WC)	0	1
1992	Boston, USA	0	2
1994	New York (WC)	1	0

2005	Dublin	1	2
2009	Bari (WC)	1	1
2009	Dublin (WC)	2	2
2011	Liege	2	0
2012	Poznan (EC)	0	2
2014	Fulham	0	0
2016	Lille (EC)	1	0

v JAMAICA

		RI	J
2004	Charlton	1	0

v KAZAKHSTAN

		RI	K
2012	Astana (WC)	2	1
2013	Dublin (WC)	3	1

v LATVIA

		RI	L
1992	Dublin (WC)	4	0
1993	Riga (WC)	2	0
1994	Riga (EC)	3	0
1995	Dublin (EC)	2	1
2013	Dublin	3	0

v LIECHTENSTEIN

		RI	L
1994	Dublin (EC)	4	0
1995	Eschen (EC)	0	0
1996	Eschen (WC)	5	0
1997	Dublin (WC)	5	0

v LITHUANIA

		RI	L
1993	Vilnius (WC)	1	0
1993	Dublin (WC)	2	0
1997	Dublin (WC)	0	0
1997	Zalgiris (WC)	2	1

v LUXEMBOURG

		RI	L
1936	Luxembourg	5	1
1953	Dublin (WC)	4	0
1954	Luxembourg (WC)	1	0
1987	Luxembourg (EC)	0	0
1987	Luxembourg (EC)	2	1

v MACEDONIA

		RI	M
1996	Dublin (WC)	3	0
1997	Skopje (WC)	2	3
1999	Dublin (EC)	1	0
1999	Skopje (EO)	1	1
2011	Dublin (EC)	2	1
2011	Skopje (EC)	2	0

v MALTA

		RI	M
1983	Valletta (EC)	1	0
1983	Dublin (WC)	8	0
1989	Dublin (WC)	2	0
1989	Valletta (WC)	2	0
1990	Valletta	3	0
1998	Dublin (EC)	1	0
1999	Valletta (EC)	3	2

v MEXICO

		RI	M
1984	Dublin	0	0
1994	Orlando (WC)	1	2
1996	New Jersey	2	2

1998	Dublin	0	0
2000	Chicago	2	2
2017	New Jersey	1	3

v MOLDOVA

		RI	M
2016	Chisinau (WC)	3	1

v MONTENEGRO

		RI	M
2008	Podgorica (WC)	0	0
2009	Dublin (WC)	0	0

v MOROCCO

		RI	M
1990	Dublin	1	0

v NIGERIA

		RI	N
2002	Dublin	1	2
2004	Charlton	0	3
2009	Fulham	1	1

v NORWAY

		RI	N
1937	Oslo (WC)	2	3
1937	Dublin (WC)	3	3
1950	Dublin	2	2
1951	Oslo	3	2
1954	Dublin	2	1
1955	Oulo	3	1
1960	Dublin	3	1
1964	Oslo	4	1
1973	Oslo	1	1
1976	Dublin	3	0
1978	Oslo	0	0
1984	Oslo (WC)	0	1
1985	Dublin (WC)	0	0
1988	Oslo	0	0
1994	New York (WC)	0	0
2003	Dublin	1	0
2008	Oslo	1	1
2010	Dublin	1	2

v OMAN

		RI	O
2012	Fulham	4	1
2014	Dublin	2	0
2016	Dublin	4	0

v PARAGUAY

		RI	P
1999	Dublin	2	0
2010	Dublin	2	1

v POLAND

		RI	P
1938	Warsaw	0	6
1938	Dublin	3	2
1958	Katowice	2	2
1958	Dublin	2	2
1964	Cracow	1	3
1964	Dublin	3	2
1968	Dublin	2	2
1968	Katowice	0	1
1970	Dublin	1	2
1970	Poznan	0	2
1973	Wroclaw	0	2
1973	Dublin	1	0
1976	Poznan	2	0

1977	Dublin	0	0
1978	Lodz	0	3
1981	Bydgoszcz	0	3
1984	Dublin	0	0
1986	Warsaw	0	1
1988	Dublin	3	1
1991	Dublin (EC)	0	0
1991	Poznan (EC)	3	3
2004	Bydgoszcz	0	0
2008	Dublin	2	3
2013	Dublin	2	0
2013	Poznan	0	0
2015	Dublin (EC)	1	1
2015	Warsaw (EC)	1	2

v PORTUGAL

		RI	P
1946	Lisbon	1	3
1947	Dublin	0	2
1948	Lisbon	0	2
1949	Dublin	1	0
1972	Recife	1	2
1992	Boston, USA	2	0
1995	Dublin (EC)	1	0
1995	Lisbon (EC)	0	3
1996	Dublin	0	1
2000	Lisbon (WC)	1	1
2001	Dublin (WC)	1	1
2005	Dublin	1	0
2014	East Rutherford, USA	1	5

v ROMANIA

		RI	R
1988	Dublin	2	0
1990*	Genoa	0	0
1997	Bucharest (WC)	0	1
1997	Dublin (WC)	1	1
2004	Dublin	1	0

(*Rep won 5-4 on pens)

v RUSSIA (See also Soviet Union)

		RI	R
1994	Dublin	0	0
1996	Dublin	0	2
2002	Dublin	2	0
2002	Moscow (EC)	2	4
2003	Dublin (EC)	1	1
2010	Dublin (EC)	2	3
2011	Moscow (EC)	0	0

v SAN MARINO

		RI	SM
2006	Dublin (EC)	5	0
2007	Rimini (EC)	2	1

v SAUDI ARABIA

		RI	SA
2002	Yokohama (WC)	3	0

v SERBIA

		RI	S
2008	Dublin	1	1
2012	Belgrade	0	0
2014	Dublin	1	2
2016	Belgrade (WC)	2	2

v SLOVAKIA

		RI	S
2007	Dublin (EC)	1	0
2007	Bratislava (EC)	2	2
2010	Zilina (EC)	1	1
2011	Dublin (EC)	0	0
2016	Dublin	2	2

v SOUTH AFRICA

		RI	SA
2000	New Jersey	2	1
2009	Limerick	1	0

v SOVIET UNION (See also Russia)

		RI	SU
1972	Dublin (WC)	1	2
1973	Moscow (WC)	0	1
1974	Dublin (EC)	3	0
1975	Kiev (EC)	1	2
1984	Dublin (WC)	1	0
1985	Moscow (WC)	0	2
1988	Hanover (EC)	1	1
1990	Dublin	1	0

v SPAIN

		RI	S
1931	Barcelona	1	1
1931	Dublin	0	5
1946	Madrid	1	0
1947	Dublin	3	2
1948	Barcelona	1	2
1949	Dublin	1	4
1952	Madrid	0	6
1955	Dublin	2	2
1964	Seville (EC)	1	5
1964	Dublin (EC)	0	2
1965	Dublin (WC)	1	0
1965	Seville (WC)	1	4
1965	Paris (WC)	0	1
1966	Dublin (EC)	0	0
1966	Valencia (EC)	0	2
1977	Dublin	0	1
1982	Dublin (EC)	3	3
1983	Zaragoza (EC)	0	2
1985	Cork	0	0
1988	Seville (WC)	0	2
1989	Dublin (WC)	1	0
1992	Seville (WC)	0	0
1993	Dublin (WC)	1	3
2002*	Suwon (WC)	1	1

(*Rep lost 3-2 on pens)

2012	Gdansk (EC)	0	4
2013	New York	0	2

v SWEDEN

		RI	S
1949	Stockholm (WC)	1	3
1949	Dublin (WC)	1	3
1959	Dublin	3	2
1960	Malmo	1	4
1970	Dublin (EC)	1	1
1970	Malmo (EC)	0	1
1999	Dublin	2	0
2006	Dublin	3	0
2013	Stockholm (WC)	0	0
2013	Dublin (WC)	1	2
2016	Paris (EC)	1	1

v SWITZERLAND

		RI	S
1935	Basle	0	1
1936	Dublin	1	0
1937	Berne	1	0
1938	Dublin	4	0
1948	Dublin	0	1
1975	Dublin (EC)	2	1
1975	Berne (EC)	0	1
1980	Dublin	2	0
1985	Dublin (WC)	3	0
1985	Berne (WC)	0	0
1992	Dublin	2	1
2002	Dublin (EC)	1	2
2003	Basle (EC)	0	2
2004	Basle (WC)	1	1
2005	Dublin (WC)	0	0
2016	Dublin	1	0

v TRINIDAD & TOBAGO

		RI	T&T
1982	Port of Spain	1	2

v TUNISIA

		RI	T
1988	Dublin	4	0

v TURKEY

		RI	T
1966	Dublin (EC)	2	1
1967	Ankara (EC)	1	2
1974	Izmir (EC)	1	1
1975	Dublin (EC)	4	0
1976	Ankara	3	3

1978	Dublin	4	2
1990	Izmir	0	0
1990	Dublin (EC)	5	0
1991	Istanbul (EC)	3	1
1999	Dublin (EC)	1	1
1999	Bursa (EC)	0	0
2003	Dublin	2	2
2014	Dublin	1	2

v URUGUAY

		RI	U
1974	Montevideo	0	2
1986	Dublin	1	1
2011	Dublin	2	3
2017	Dublin	3	1

v USA

		RI	USA
1979	Dublin	3	2
1991	Boston	1	1
1992	Dublin	4	1
1992	Washington	1	3
1996	Boston	1	2
2000	Foxboro	1	1
2002	Dublin	2	1
2014	Dublin	4	1

v YUGOSLAVIA

		RI	Y
1955	Dublin	1	4
1988	Dublin	2	0
1998	Belgrade (EC)	0	1
1999	Dublin (EC)	2	1

THE THINGS THEY SAY ...

'What a night, what a moment and what a journey. Getting on the pitch for that match was worth every gruelling moment' – **Shaun Barker**, former Derby captain, making his first appearance for nearly four-and-a-half-years after a knee injury in Burton's victory over his old club.

'Never did I think when I left home at 15 to go to Southampton to be a professional footballer that one day I would have a statue' – **Alan Shearer**, the Premier League's record scorer with 260 goals, at the unveiling of the bronze sculpture at St James' Park, Newcastle, another of his former clubs.

'I thought it was dark yellow, the referee though light red' – **Arsene Wenger**, Arsenal manager, on Granit Xhaka's sending off against Swansea.

'The Premier League is the best league in the world to work in, to play in. This is the NBA, this is Hollywood. We are human, so we want to be part of something big' – **Slaven Bilic**, West Ham manager.

'The Champions League is empty when Manchester United are not there. It is their natural habitat' – **Jose Mourinho**, United manager.

BRITISH AND IRISH INTERNATIONAL APPEARANCES SINCE THE WAR (1946–2017)

(As at start of season 2017–18; in year shown 2017 = season 2016–17
*Also a pre-war International player. Totals include appearances as substitute)

ENGLAND

Agbonlahor G (Aston Villa, 2009–10)	3	Beckham D (Manchester Utd, Real Madrid, LA Galaxy, AC Milan 1997–2010)	115
A'Court A (Liverpool, 1958–59)	5	Bell C (Manchester City, 1968–76)	48
Adams T (Arsenal, 1987–2001)	66	Bent D (Charlton, Tottenham Sunderland, Aston Villa, 2006–12)	13
Alli D (Tottenham, 2016–17)	19	Bentley D (Blackburn, 2008–09)	7
Allen A (Stoke, 1960)	3	Bentley R (Chelsea, 1949–55)	12
Allen C (QPR, Tottenham, 1984–88)	5	Berry J (Manchester Utd, 1953–56)	4
Allen R (WBA, 1952–55)	5	Bertrand R (Chelsea, Southampton, 2013–17)	14
Anderson S (Sunderland, 1962)	2	Birtles G (Nottm Forest, 1980–81)	3
Anderson V (Nottm Forest, Arsenal, Manchester Utd, 1979–88)	30	Blissett L (Watford, AC Milan, 1983–84)	14
Anderton D (Tottenham, 1994–2002)	30	Blockley J (Arsenal, 1973)	1
Angus J (Burnley, 1961)	1	Blunstone F (Chelsea, 1955–57)	5
Armfield J (Blackpool, 1959–66)	43	Bonetti P (Chelsea, 1966–70)	7
Armstrong D (Middlesbrough, Southampton, 1980–4)	3	Bothroyd J (Cardiff, 2011)	1
Armstrong K (Chelsea, 1955)	1	Bould S (Arsenal, 1994)	2
Ashton D (West Ham, 2008)	1	Bowles S (QPR, 1974–77)	5
Astall G (Birmingham, 1956)	2	Bowyer L (Leeds, 2003)	1
Astle J (WBA, 1969–70)	5	Boyer P (Norwich, 1976)	1
Aston J (Manchester Utd, 1949–51)	17	Brabrook P (Chelsea, 1958–60)	3
Atyeo J (Bristol City, 1956–57)	6	Bracewell P (Everton, 1985–86)	3
		Bradford G (Bristol Rov, 1956)	1
Bailey G (Manchester Utd, 1985)	2	Bradley W (Manchester Utd, 1959)	3
Bailey M (Charlton, 1964–5)	2	Bridge W (Southampton, Chelsea, Manchester City 2002–10)	36
Baily E (Tottenham, 1950–3)	9	Bridges B (Chelsea, 1965–66)	4
Baines L (Everton, 2010–15)	30	Broadbent P (Wolves, 1958–60)	7
Baker J (Hibernian, Arsenal, 1960–6)	8	Broadis I (Manchester City, Newcastle, 1952–54)	14
Ball A (Blackpool, Everton, Arsenal, 1965–75)	72	Brooking T (West Ham, 1974–82)	47
Ball M (Everton, 2001)	1	Brooks J (Tottenham, 1957)	3
Banks G (Leicester, Stoke, 1963–72)	73	Brown A (WBA, 1971)	1
Banks T (Bolton, 1958–59)	6	Brown K (West Ham, 1960)	1
Bardsley D (QPR, 1993)	2	Brown W (Manchester Utd, 1999–2010)	23
Barham M (Norwich, 1983)	2	Bull S (Wolves, 1989–91)	13
Barkley R (Everton, 2014–16)	22	Butcher T (Ipswich, Rangers, 1980–90)	77
Barlow R (WBA, 1955)	1	Butland J (Birmingham, Stoke, 2013–17)	5
Barmby N (Tottenham, Middlesbrough, Everton, Liverpool, 1995–2002)	23	Butt N (Manchester Utd, Newcastle, 1997–2005)	39
Barnes J (Watford, Liverpool, 1983–96)	79	Byrne G (Liverpool, 1963–66)	2
Barnes P (Manchester City, WBA, Leeds, 1978–82)	22	Byrne J (Crystal Palace, West Ham, 1962–65)	11
Barrass M (Bolton, 1952–53)	3	Byrne R (Manchester Utd, 1954–58)	33
Barrett E (Oldham, Aston Villa, 1991–93)	3		
Barry G (Aston Villa, Manchester City, 2000–12)	53	Cahill G (Bolton, Chelsea, 2011–17)	55
Barton J (Manchester City, 2007)	1	Callaghan I (Liverpool, 1966–78)	4
Barton W (Wimbledon, Newcastle, 1995)	3	Campbell F (Sunderland, 2012)	1
Batty D (Leeds, Blackburn, Newcastle, Leeds, 1991–2000)	42	Campbell S (Tottenham, Arsenal, Portsmouth, 1996–2008)	73
Baynham R (Luton, 1956)	3	Carragher J (Liverpool, 1999–2010)	38
Beardsley P (Newcastle, Liverpool, Newcastle, 1986–96)	59	Carrick M (West Ham, Tottenham, Manchester Utd, 2001–16)	34
Beasant D (Chelsea, 1990)	2	Carroll A (Newcastle, Liverpool 2011– 13)	9
Beattie J (Southampton, 2003–04)	5	Carson S (Liverpool, Aston Villa WBA, Bursaspor 2008–12)	4
Beattie K (Ipswich, 1975–58)	9	*Carter H (Derby, 1947)	7

Gray A (Crystal Palace, 1992) 1
Gray M (Sunderland, 1999) 3
Greaves J (Chelsea, Tottenham, 1959–67) 57
Green R (Norwich, West Ham 2005–12) 12
Greenhoff B (Manchester Utd, Leeds, 1976–80) 18
Gregory J (QPR, 1983–84) 6
Guppy S (Leicester, 2000) 1

Hagan J (Sheffield Utd, 1949) 1
Haines J (WBA, 1949) 1
Hall J (Birmingham, 1956–57) 17
Hancocks J (Wolves, 1949–50) 3
Hardwick G (Middlesbrough, 1947–48) 13
Harford M (Luton, 1988–89) 2
Hargreaves O (Bayern Munich, Manchester Utd, 2002–08) 42
Harris G (Burnley, 1966) 1
Harris P (Portsmouth, 1950–54) 2
Hart J (Manchester City, 2010–17) 71
Harvey C (Everton, 1971) 1
Hassall H (Huddersfield, Bolton, 1951–54) 5
Hateley M (Portsmouth, AC Milan, Monaco, Rangers, 1984–92) 32
Haynes J (Fulham, 1955–62) 56
Heaton T (Burnley, 2016–17) 3
Hector K (Derby, 1974) 2
Hellawell M (Birmingham, 1963) 2
Henderson J (Sunderland, Liverpool, 2011–17) 32
Hendrie L (Aston Villa, 1999) 1
Henry R (Tottenham, 1963) 1
Heskey E (Leicester, Liverpool, Birmingham, Wigan, Aston Villa 1999–2010) 62
Hill F (Bolton, 1963) 2
Hill G (Manchester Utd, 1976–78) 6
Hill R (Luton, 1983–86) 3
Hinchcliffe A (Everton, Sheffield Wed, 1997–99) 7
Hinton A (Wolves, Nottm Forest, 1963–65) 3
Hirst D (Sheffield Wed, 1991–92) 3
Hitchens G (Aston Villa, Inter Milan, 1961–62) 7
Hoddle G (Tottenham, Monaco, 1980–88) 53
Hodge S (Aston Villa, Tottenham, Nottm Forest, 1986–91) 24
Hodgkinson A (Sheffield Utd, 1957–61) 5
Holden D (Bolton, 1959) 5
Holliday E (Middlesbrough, 1960) 3
Hollins J (Chelsea, 1967) 1
Hopkinson E (Bolton, 1958–60) 14
Howe D (WBA, 1958–60) 23
Howe J (Derby, 1948–49) 3
Howey S (Newcastle, 1995–96) 4
Huddlestone T (Tottenham, 2010–13) 4
Hudson A (Stoke, 1975) 2
Hughes E (Liverpool, Wolves, 1970–80) 62
Hughes L (Liverpool, 1950) 3
Hunt R (Liverpool, 1962–69) 34
Hunt S (WBA, 1984) 2
Hunter N (Leeds, 1966–75) 28
Hurst G (West Ham, 1966–72) 49

Ince P (Manchester Utd, Inter Milan, Liverpool, Middlesbrough, 1993–2000) 53
Ings D (Liverpool 2016) 1

Jagielka P (Everton, 2008–17) 40
James D (Liverpool, Aston Villa, West Ham, Manchester City, Portsmouth, 1997–2010) 53
Jarvis M (Wolves, 2011) 1
Jeffers F (Arsenal, 2003) 1
Jenas J (Newcastle, Tottenham, 2003–10) 21
Jenkinson C (Arsenal, 2013) 1
Jezzard B (Fulham, 1954–56) 2
Johnson A (Crystal Palace, Everton, 2005–08) 8
Johnson A (Manchester City, 2010–13) 12
Johnson D (Ipswich, Liverpool, 1975–80) 8
Johnson G (Chelsea, Portsmouth, Liverpool, 2004–14) 54
Johnson S (Derby, 2001) 1
Johnston H (Blackpool, 1947–54) 10
Jones M (Leeds, Sheffield Utd, 1965–70) 3
Jones P (Manchester Utd, 2012–17) 21
Jones R (Liverpool, 1992–95) 8
Jones W H (Liverpool, 1950) 2

Kane H (Tottenham, 2015–17) 19
Kay A (Everton, 1963) 1
Keane M (Burnley, 2017) 2
Keegan K (Liverpool, Hamburg, Southampton, 1973–82) 63
Kelly, M (Liverpool, 2012) 1
Kennedy A (Liverpool, 1984) 2
Kennedy R (Liverpool, 1976–80) 17
Keown M (Everton, Arsenal, 1992–2002) 43
Kevan D (WBA, 1957–61) 14
Kidd B (Manchester Utd, 1970) 2
King L (Tottenham, 2002–10) 21
Kirkland C (Liverpool, 2007) 1
Knight Z (Fulham, 2005) 2
Knowles C (Tottenham, 1968) 4
Konchesky P (Charlton, 2003–06) 2

Labone B (Everton, 1963–70) 26
Lallana A (Southampton, Liverpool, 2014–17) 33
Lambert R (Southampton, Liverpool, 2014–15) 11
Lampard F Snr (West Ham, 1973–80) 2
Lampard F Jnr (West Ham, Chelsea, 2000–14) 106
Langley J (Fulham, 1958) 3
Langton R (Blackburn, Preston, Bolton, 1947–51) 11
Latchford R (Everton, 1978–9) 12
Lawler C (Liverpool, 1971–72) 4
*Lawton T (Chelsea, Notts Co, 1947–49) 15
Lee F (Manchester City, 1969–72) 27
Lee J (Derby, 1951) 1
Lee R (Newcastle, 1995–99) 21
Lee S (Liverpool, 1983–84) 14
Lennon A (Tottenham, 2006–13) 21
Le Saux G (Blackburn, Chelsea, 1994–2001) 36
Lescott J (Everton, Manchester City, 2008–13) 26
Le Tissier M (Southampton, 1994–97) 8
Lindsay A (Liverpool, 1974) 4
Lineker G (Leicester, Everton, Barcelona, Tottenham, 1985–92) 80
Lingard J (Manchester Utd, 2017) 4

Rimmer J (Arsenal, 1976) — 1
Ripley S (Blackburn, 1994–97) — 2
Rix G (Arsenal, 1981–84) — 17
Robb G (Tottenham, 1954) — 1
Roberts G (Tottenham, 1983–84) — 6
Robinson P (Leeds, Tottenham, 2003–08) — 41
Robson B (WBA, Manchester Utd, 1980–92) — 90
Robson R (WBA, 1958–62) — 20
Rocastle D (Arsenal, 1989–92) — 14
Rodriguez J (Southampton, 2014) — 1
Rodwell J (Everton, Manchester City, 2012–13) — 3
Rooney W (Everton, Manchester Utd, 2003–17) — 119
Rose D (Tottenham, 2016–17) — 12
Rowley J (Manchester Utd, 1949–52) — 6
Royle J (Everton, Manchester City, 1971–77) — 6
Ruddock N (Liverpool, 1995) — 1
Ruddy J (Norwich, 2013) — 1

Sadler D (Manchester Utd, 1968–71) — 4
Salako J (Crystal Palace, 1991–92) — 5
Sansom K (Crystal Palace, Arsenal, 1979–88) — 86
Scales J (Liverpool, 1995) — 3
Scholes P (Manchester Utd, 1997–2004) — 66
Scott L (Arsenal, 1947–49) — 17
Seaman D (QPR, Arsenal, 1989–2003) — 75
Sewell J (Sheffield Wed, 1952–54) — 6
Shackleton L (Sunderland, 1949–55) — 5
Sharpe L (Manchester Utd, 1991–94) — 8
Shaw G (Sheffield Utd, 1959–63) — 5
Shaw L (Southampton, Manchester Utd, 2014–17) — 7
Shawcross, R (Stoke, 2013) — 1
Shearer A (Southampton, Blackburn, Newcastle, 1992–2000) — 63
Shellito K (Chelsea, 1963) — 1
Shelvey J (Liverpool, Swansea, 2013–16) — 6
Sheringham E (Tottenham, Manchester Utd, Tottenham, 1993–2002) — 51
Sherwood T (Tottenham, 1999) — 3
Shilton P (Leicester, Stoke, Nottm Forest, Southampton, Derby, 1971–90) — 125
Shimwell E (Blackpool, 1949) — 1
Shorey N (Reading, 2007) — 2
Sillett P (Chelsea, 1955) — 3
Sinclair T (West Ham, Manchester City, 2002–04) — 12
Sinton A (QPR, Sheffield Wed, 1992–94) — 12
Slater W (Wolves, 1955–60) — 12
Smalling C (Manchester Utd, 2012–17) — 31
Smith A (Arsenal, 1989–92) — 13
Smith A (Leeds, Manchester Utd, Newcastle, 2001–08) — 19
Smith L (Arsenal, 1951–53) — 6
Smith R (Tottenham, 1961–64) — 15
Smith T (Birmingham, 1960) — 2
Smith T (Liverpool, 1971) — 1
Southgate G (Aston Villa, Middlesbrough, 1996–2004) — 57
Spink N (Aston Villa, 1983) — 1

Springett R (Sheffield Wed, 1960–66) — 33
Staniforth R (Huddersfield, 1954–55) — 8
Statham D (WBA, 1983) — 3
Stein B (Luton, 1984) — 1
Stepney A (Manchester Utd, 1968) — 1
Sterland M (Sheffield Wed, 1989) — 1
Sterling R (Liverpool, Manchester City, 2013–17) — 32
Steven T (Everton, Rangers, Marseille, 1985–92) — 36
Stevens G (Everton, Rangers, 1985–92) — 46
Stevens G (Tottenham, 1985–86) — 7
Stewart P (Tottenham, 1992) — 3
Stiles N (Manchester Utd, 1965–70) — 28
Stone S (Nottm Forest, 1996) — 9
Stones J (Everton, Manchester City, 2014–17) — 18
Storey P (Arsenal, 1971–73) — 19
Storey–Moore I (Nottm Forest, 1970) — 1
Streten B (Luton, 1950) — 1
Sturridge D (Chelsea, Liverpool, 2012–17) — 25
Summerbee M (Manchester City, 1968–73) — 8
Sunderland, A (Arsenal, 1980) — 1
Sutton C (Blackburn, 1997) — 1
Swan P (Sheffield Wed, 1960–62) — 19
Swift F (Manchester City, 1947–79) — 19

Talbot B (Ipswich, Arsenal, 1977–80) — 6
Tambling R (Chelsea, 1963–66) — 3
Taylor E (Blackpool, 1954) — 1
Taylor J (Fulham, 1951) — 2
Taylor P (Liverpool, 1948) — 3
Taylor P (Crystal Palace, 1976) — 4
Taylor T (Manchester Utd, 1953–58) — 19
Temple D (Everton, 1965) — 1
Terry J (Chelsea, 2003–13) — 78
Thomas D (QPR, 1975–76) — 8
Thomas D (Coventry, 1983) — 2
Thomas G (Crystal Palace, 1991–92) — 9
Thomas M (Arsenal, 1989–90) — 2
Thompson A (Celtic, 2004) — 1
Thompson Peter (Liverpool, 1964–70) — 16
Thompson Phil (Liverpool, 1976–83) — 42
Thompson T (Aston Villa, Preston, 1952–57) — 2
Thomson R (Wolves, 1964–65) — 8
Todd C (Derby, 1972–77) — 27
Towers A (Sunderland, 1978) — 3
Townsend A (Tottenham, Newcastle, Crystal Palace, 2014–17) — 13
Trippier K (Tottenham, 2017) — 1
Tueart D (Manchester City, 1975–77) — 6

Ufton D (Charlton, 1954) — 1
Unsworth D (Everton, 1995) — 1
Upson M (Birmingham, West Ham, 2003–10) — 21

Vardy J (Leicester, 2015–17) — 16
Vassell D (Aston Villa, 2002–04) — 22
Venables T (Chelsea, 1965) — 2
Venison B (Newcastle, 1995) — 2
Viljoen C (Ipswich, 1975) — 2
Viollet D (Manchester Utd, 1960) — 2

Waddle C (Newcastle, Tottenham, Marseille, 1985–92) 62
Waiters A (Blackpool, 1964–65) 5
Walcott T (Arsenal, 2006–17) 47
Walker D (Nottm Forest, Sampdoria, Sheffield Wed, 1989–94) 59
Walker I (Tottenham, Leicester, 1996–2004) 4
Walker K (Tottenham, 2012–17) 27
Wallace D (Southampton, 1986) 1
Walsh P (Luton, 1983–4) 5
Waiters M (Rangers, 1991) 1
Ward P (Brighton, 1980) 1
Ward T (Derby, 1948) 2
Ward–Prowse J (Southampton, 2017) 1
Warnock S (Blackburn, Aston Villa, 2008–11) 2
Watson D (Sunderland, Manchester City, Werder Bremen, Southampton, Stoke, 1974–82) 65
Watson D (Norwich, Everton, 1984–8) 12
Watson W (Sunderland, 1950–1) 4
Webb N (Nottm Forest, Manchester Utd, 1988–92) 26
Welbeck D (Manchester Utd, Arsenal, 2011–16) 34
Weller K (Leicester, 1974) 4
West G (Everton, 1969) 3
Wheeler J (Bolton, 1955) 1
White D (Manchester City, 1993) 1
Whitworth S (Leicester, 1975–76) 7
Whymark T (Ipswich, 1978) 1
Wignall F (Nottm Forest, 1965) 2
Wilcox J (Blackburn, Leeds, 1996–2000) 3
Wilkins R (Chelsea, Manchester Utd, AC Milan, 1976–87) 84
Williams R (Wolves, 1949–56) 24

Williams S (Southampton, 1983–85) 6
Willis A (Tottenham, 1952) 1
Wilshaw D (Wolves, 1954–57) 12
Wilshere J (Arsenal, 2011–16) 34
Wilson R (Huddersfield, Everton, 1960–8) 63
Winterburn N (Arsenal, 1990–93) 2
Wise D (Chelsea, 1991–2001) 21
Withe P (Aston Villa, 1981–85) 11
Wood R (Manchester Utd, 1955–56) 3
Woodcock A (Nottm Forest, Cologne, Arsenal, 1977–86) 42
Woodgate J (Leeds, Newcastle, Middlesbrough, Tottenham, 1999–2008) 8
Woods C (Norwich, Rangers, Sheffield Wed, 1984–93) 43
Worthington F (Leicester, 1974–75) 8
Wright I (Crystal Palace, Arsenal, West Ham, 1991–99) 33
Wright M (Southampton, Derby, Liverpool, 1984–96) 45
Wright R (Ipswich, Arsenal, 2000–02) 2
Wright T (Everton, 1968–70) 11
Wright W (Wolves, 1947–59) 105
Wright–Phillips S (Manchester City, Chelsea, Manchester City, 2005–11) 36

Young A (Aston Villa, Manchester Utd, 2008–14) 30
Young G (Sheffield Wed, 1965) 1
Young L (Charlton, 2005) 7

Zaha W (Manchester Utd, 2013–14) 2
Zamora R (Fulham, 2011–12) 2

SCOTLAND

Adam C (Rangers, Blackpool, Liverpool, Stoke, 2007–15) 26
Aird J (Burnley, 1954) 4
Aitken G (East Fife, 1949–54) 8
Aitken R (Celtic, Newcastle, St Mirren, 1980–92) 57
Albiston A (Manchester Utd, 1982–6) 14
Alexander G (Preston, Burnley, 2002–10) 40
Alexander N (Cardiff, 2006) 2
Allan T (Dundee, 1974) 2
Anderson J (Leicester, 1954) 1
Anderson R (Aberdeen, Sunderland, 2003–08) 11
Anya, I (Watford, Derby, 2014–17) 27
Archibald S (Aberdeen, Tottenham, Barcelona, 1980–86) 27
Armstrong S (Celtic, 2017) 2
Auld B (Celtic, 1959–60) 3

Baird H (Airdrie, 1956) 1
Baird S (Rangers, 1957–58) 7
Bannan B (Aston Villa, Crystal Palace, Sheffield Wed, 2011–17) 25
Bannon E (Dundee Utd, 1980–86) 11
Bardsley P (Sunderland, 2011–14) 13

Barr D (Falkirk, 2009) 1
Bauld W (Hearts, 1950) 3
Baxter J (Rangers, Sunderland, 1961–68) 34
Beattie C (Celtic, WBA, 2006–08) 7
Bell C (Kilmarnock, 2011) 1
Bell W (Leeds, 1966) 2
Bernard P (Oldham, 1995) 2
Berra C (Hearts, Wolves, Ipswich, 2008–17) 36
Bett J (Rangers, Lokeren, Aberdeen, 1982–90) 26
Black E (Metz, 1988) 2
Black I (Southampton, 1948) 1
Black I (Rangers, 2013) 1
Blacklaw A (Burnley, 1963–66) 3
Blackley J (Hibernian, 1974–77) 7
Blair J (Blackpool, 1947) 1
Blyth J (Coventry, 1978) 2
Bone J (Norwich, 1972–73) 2
Booth S (Aberdeen, Borussia Dortmund, Twente Enschede 1993–2002) 22
Bowman D (Dundee Utd, 1992–94) 6
Boyd G (Peterborough, Hull, 2013–14) 2
Boyd K (Rangers, Middlesbrough, 2006–11) 18
Boyd T (Motherwell, Chelsea, Celtic, 1991–2002) 72

Brand R (Rangers, 1961–62) 8
Brazil A (Ipswich, Tottenham, 1980–83) 13
Bremner D (Hibernian, 1976) 1
Bremner W (Leeds, 1965–76) 54
Brennan F (Newcastle, 1947–54) 7
Bridcutt L (Brighton, Sunderland, 2013–16) 2
Broadfoot K (Rangers, 2009–11) 4
Brogan J (Celtic, 1971) 4
Brown A (East Fife, Blackpool, 1950–54) 13
Brown H (Partick, 1947) 3
Brown J (Sheffield Utd, 1975) 1
Brown R (Rangers, 1947–52) 3
Brown S (Hibernian, Celtic, 2007–17) 53
Brown W (Dundee, Tottenham, 1958–66) 28
Brownlie J (Hibernian, 1971–76) 7
Bryson C (Kilmarnock, Derby, 2011–16) 3
Buchan M (Aberdeen, Manchester Utd, 1972–8) 34
Buckley P (Aberdeen, 1954–55) 3
Burchill M (Celtic, 2000) 6
Burke C (Rangers, Birmingham, 2006–14) 7
Burke O (Nottm Forest, Leipzig, 2016–17) 5
Burley C (Chelsea, Celtic, Derby, 1995–2003) 46
Burley G (Ipswich, 1979–82) 11
Burns F (Manchester Utd, 1970) 1
Burns K (Birmingham, Nottm Forest, 1974–81) 20
Burns T (Celtic, 1981–88) 8

Caddis P (Birmingham, 2016) 1
Cairney T (Fulham, 2017) 1
Calderwood C (Tottenham, Aston Villa, 1995–2000) 36
Caldow E (Rangers, 1957–63) 40
Caldwell G (Newcastle, Sunderland, Hibernian, Wigan, 2002–13) 55
Caldwell S (Newcastle, Sunderland, Celtic, Wigan, 2001–11) 12
Callaghan T (Dunfermline, 1970) 2
Cameron C (Hearts, Wolves, 1999–2005) 28
Campbell R (Falkirk, Chelsea, 1947–50) 5
Campbell W (Morton, 1947–48) 5
Canero P (Leicester, 2004) 1
Carr W (Coventry, 1970–73) 6
Chalmers S (Celtic, 1965–67) 5
Clark J (Celtic, 1966–67) 4
Clark R (Aberdeen, 1968–73) 17
Clarke S (Chelsea, 1988–94) 6
Clarkson D (Motherwell, 2008–09) 2
Collins J (Hibernian, Celtic, Monaco, Everton, 1988–2000) 58
Collins R (Celtic, Everton, Leeds, 1951–65) 31
Colquhoun E (Sheffield Utd, 1972–73) 9
Colquhoun J (Hearts, 1988) 2
Combe J (Hibernian, 1948) 3
Commons K (Derby, Celtic, 2009–13) 12
Conn A (Hearts, 1956) 1
Conn A (Tottenham, 1975) 2
Connachan E (Dunfermline, 1962) 2
Connelly G (Celtic, 1974) 2

Connolly J (Everton, 1973) 1
Connor R (Dundee, Aberdeen, 1986–91) 4
Conway C (Dundee Utd, Cardiff, 2010–14) 7
Cooke C (Dundee, Chelsea, 1966–75) 16
Cooper D (Rangers, Motherwell, 1980–90) 22
Cormack P (Hibernian, 1966–72) 9
Cowan J (Morton, 1948–52) 25
Cowie D (Dundee, 1953–58) 20
Cowie D (Watford, 2010–12) 10
Cox C (Hearts, 1948) 1
Cox S (Rangers, 1948–54) 25
Craig JP (Celtic, 1968) 1
Craig J (Celtic, 1977) 1
Craig T (Newcastle, 1976) 1
Crainey S (Celtic, Southampton, Blackpool, 2002–12) 12
Crawford S (Raith, Dunfermline, Plymouth Argyle, 1995–2005) 25
Crerand P (Celtic, Manchester Utd, 1961–66) 16
Cropley A (Hibernian, 1972) 2
Cruickshank J (Hearts, 1964–76) 6
Cullen M (Luton, 1956) 1
Cumming J (Hearts, 1955–60) 9
Cummings W (Chelsea, 2002) 1
Cunningham W (Preston, 1954–55) 8
Curran H (Wolves, 1970–71) 5

Dailly C (Derby, Blackburn, West Ham, 1997–2008) 67
Dalglish K (Celtic, Liverpool, 1972–87) 102
Davidson C (Blackburn, Leicester, Preston, 1999–2010) 19
Davidson M (St Johnstone, 2013) 1`
Davidson J (Partick, 1954–55) 8
Dawson A (Rangers, 1980–83) 5
Deans J (Celtic, 1975)` 2
*Delaney J (Manchester Utd, 1947–48) 4
Devlin P (Birmingham, 2003–04) 10
Dick J (West Ham, 1959) 1
Dickov P (Manchester City, Leicester, Blackburn, 2001–05) 10
Dickson W (Kilmarnock, 1970–71) 5
Dixon P (Huddersfield, 2013) 3
Dobie S (WBA, 2002–03) 6
Docherty T (Preston, Arsenal, 1952–59) 25
Dodds D (Dundee Utd, 1984) 2
Dodds W (Aberdeen, Dundee Utd, Rangers, 1997–2002) 26
Donachie W (Manchester City, 1972–79) 35
Donnelly S (Celtic, 1997–99) 10
Dorrans G (WBA, Norwich, 2010–16) 12
Dougall C (Birmingham, 1947) 1
Dougan R (Hearts, 1950) 1
Douglas R (Celtic, Leicester, 2002–06) 19
Doyle J (Ayr, 1976) 1
Duncan A (Hibernian, 1975–76) 6
Duncan D (East Fife, 1948) 3
Duncanson J (Rangers, 1947) 1
Durie G (Chelsea, Tottenham, Rangers, 1988–98) 43
Durrant I (Rangers, Kilmarnock, 1988–2000) 20

Elliott M (Leicester, 1997–2002) — 18
Evans A (Aston Villa, 1982) — 4
Evans R (Celtic, Chelsea, 1949–60) — 48
Ewing T (Partick, 1958) — 2

Farm G (Blackpool, 1953–59) — 10
Ferguson B (Rangers, Blackburn, Rangers, 1999–2009) — 45
Ferguson D (Dundee Utd, Everton, 1992–97) — 7
Ferguson D (Rangers, 1988) — 2
Ferguson I (Rangers, 1989–97) — 9
Ferguson R (Kilmarnock, 1966–67) — 7
Fernie W (Celtic, 1954–58) — 12
Flavell R (Airdrie, 1947) — 2
Fleck R (Norwich, 1990–91) — 4
Fleming C (East Fife, 1954) — 1
Fletcher D (Manchester Utd, WBA, 2004–17) — 78
Fletcher S (Hibernian, Burnley, Wolves, Sunderland, Sheffield Wed, 2008–17) — 30
Forbes A (Sheffield Utd, Arsenal, 1947–52) — 14
Ford D (Hearts, 1974) — 3
Forrest J (Motherwell, 1958) — 1
Forrest J (Rangers, Aberdeen, 1966–71) — 5
Forrest J (Celtic, 2011–17) — 17
Forsyth A (Partick, Manchester Utd, 1972–76) — 10
Forsyth C (Kilmarnock, 1964) — 4
Forsyth C (Derby, 2014–15) — 4
Forsyth T (Motherwell, Rangers, 1971–78) — 22
Fox D (Burnley, Southampton, 2010–13) — 4
Fraser D (WBA, 1968–69) — 2
Fraser R (Bournemouth, 2017) — 1
Fraser W (Sunderland, 1955) — 2
Freedman D (Crystal Palace, 2002) — 2

Gabriel J (Everton, 1961–64) — 2
Gallacher K (Dundee Utd, Coventry, Blackburn, Newcastle, 1988–2001) — 53
Gallacher P (Dundee Utd, 2003–04) — 8
Gallagher P (Blackburn, 2004) — 1
Galloway M (Celtic, 1992) — 1
Gardiner I (Motherwell, 1958) — 1
Gemmell T (St Mirren, 1955) — 2
Gemmell T (Celtic, 1966–71) — 18
Gemmill A (Derby, Nottm Forest, Birmingham, 1971–81) — 43
Gemmill S (Nottm Forest, Everton, 1995–2003) — 26
Gibson D (Leicester, 1963–65) — 7
Gilks M (Blackpool, 2013–14) — 3
Gillespie G (Liverpool, 1988–91) — 13
Gilzean A (Dundee, Tottenham, 1964–71) — 22
Glass S (Newcastle Utd 1999) — 1
Glavin R (Celtic, 1977) — 1
Glen A (Aberdeen, 1956) — 2
Goodwillie D (Dundee Utd, Blackburn, 2011–12) — 3
Goram A (Oldham, Hibernian, Rangers, 1986–98) — 43
Gordon C (Hearts, Sunderland, Celtic, 2004–17) — 47

Gough R (Dundee Utd, Tottenham, Rangers, 1983–93) — 61
Gould J (Celtic, 2000–01) — 2
Govan J (Hibernian, 1948–49) — 6
Graham A (Leeds, 1978–81) — 10
Graham G (Arsenal, Manchester Utd, 1972–73) — 12
Gray A (Aston Villa, Wolves, Everton, 1976–85) — 20
Gray A (Bradford City, 2003) — 2
Gray E (Leeds, 1969–77) — 12
Gray F (Leeds, Nottm Forest, 1976–83) — 32
Grant J (Hibernian, 1958) — 2
Grant P (Celtic, 1989) — 2
Green A (Blackpool, Newcastle, 1971–72) — 6
Greer G (Brighton, 2014–16) — 11
Greig J (Rangers, 1964–76) — 44
Griffiths L (Wolves, Celtic, 2013–17) — 13
Gunn B (Norwich, 1990–94) — 6

Haddock H (Clyde, 1955–58) — 6
Haffey F (Celtic, 1960–61) — 2
Hamilton A (Dundee, 1962–66) — 24
Hamilton G (Aberdeen, 1947–54) — 5
Hamilton W (Hibernian, 1965) — 1
Hammell S (Motherwell, 2005) — 1
Hanley G (Blackburn, Newcastle, 2011–17) — 27
Hansen A (Liverpool, 1979–87) — 26
Hansen J (Partick, 1972) — 2
Harper J (Aberdeen, Hibernian, 1973–78) — 4
Hartford A (WBA, Manchester City, Everton, 1972–82) — 50
Hartley P (Hearts, Celtic, Bristol City, 2005–10) — 25
Harvey D (Leeds, 1973–77) — 16
Haughney M (Celtic, 1954) — 1
Hay D (Celtic, 1970–74) — 27
Hegarty P (Dundee Utd, 1979–83) — 8
Henderson J (Portsmouth, Arsenal, 1953–59) — 7
Henderson W (Rangers, 1963–71) — 29
Hendry C (Blackburn, Rangers, Coventry, Bolton, 1994–2001) — 51
Herd D (Arsenal, 1959–61) — 5
Herd G (Clyde, 1958–61) — 5
Herriot J (Birmingham, 1969–70) — 8
Hewie J (Charlton, 1956–60) — 19
Holt D (Hearts, 1963–64) — 5
Holt G (Kilmarnock, Norwich, 2001–05) — 10
Holton J (Manchester Utd, 1973–75) — 15
Hope R (WBA, 1968–69) — 2
Hopkin D (Crystal Palace, Leeds, 1997–2000) — 7
Houliston W (Queen of the South, 1949) — 3
Houston S (Manchester Utd, 1976) — 1
Howie H (Hibernian, 1949) — 1
Hughes J (Celtic, 1965–70) — 8
Hughes R (Portsmouth, 2004–06) — 5
Hughes S (Norwich, 2010) — 1
Hughes W (Sunderland, 1975) — 1
Humphries W (Motherwell, 1952) — 1

Hunter A (Kilmarnock, Celtic, 1972–74) 4
Hunter W (Motherwell, 1960–61) 3
Husband J (Partick, 1947) 1
Hutchison D (Everton, Sunderland,
West Ham, 1999–2004) 26
Hutchison T (Coventry, 1974–76) 17
Hutton A (Rangers, Tottenham,
Aston Villa, 2007–16) 50

Imlach S (Nottm Forest, 1958) 4
Irvine B (Aberdeen, 1991–94) 9
Iwelumo C (Wolves, Burnley, 2009–11) 4

Jackson C (Rangers, 1975–77) 8
Jackson D (Hibernian, Celtic, 1995–99) 28
Jardine A (Rangers, 1971–80) 38
Jarvie A (Airdrie, 1971) 3
Jess E (Aberdeen, Coventry,
Aberdeen, 1993–99) 18
Johnston A (Sunderland, Rangers,
Middlesbrough, 1999–2003) 18
Johnston L (Clyde, 1948) 2
Johnston M (Watford, Celtic, Nantes,
Rangers, 1984–92) 38
Johnston W (Rangers, WBA, 1966–78) 21
Johnstone D (Rangers, 1973–80) 14
Johnstone J (Celtic, 1965–75) 23
Johnstone R (Hibernian, Manchester City,
1951–56) 17
Jordan J (Leeds, Manchester Utd, AC Milan,
1973–82) 52

Kelly H (Blackpool, 1952) 1
Kelly J (Barnsley, 1949) 2
Kelly L (Kilmarnock, 2013) 1
Kennedy J (Celtic, 1964–65) 6
Kennedy J (Celtic, 2004) 1
Kennedy S (Rangers, 1975) 5
Kennedy S (Aberdeen, 1978–82) 8
Kenneth G (Dundee Utd, 2011) 2
Kerr A (Partick, 1955) 2
Kerr B (Newcastle, 2003–04) 3
Kingsley S (Swansea, 2016) 1
Kyle K (Sunderland, Kilmarnock,
2002–10) 10

Lambert P (Motherwell, Borussia Dortmund,
Celtic, 1995–2003) 40
Law D (Huddersfield, Manchester City,
Torino, Manchester Utd, 1959–74) 55
Lawrence T (Liverpool, 1963–69) 3
Leggat G (Aberdeen, Fulham, 1956–60) 18
Leighton J (Aberdeen, Manchester Utd,
Hibernian, Aberdeen, 1983–99) 91
Lennox R (Celtic, 1967–70) 10
Leslie L (Airdrie, 1961) 5
Levein C (Hearts, 1990–95) 16
Liddell W (Liverpool, 1947–55) 28
Linwood A (Clyde, 1950) 1
Little R (Rangers, 1953) 1
Logie J (Arsenal, 1953) 1
Long H (Clyde, 1947) 1
Lorimer P (Leeds, 1970–76) 21

Macari L (Celtic, Manchester Utd, 1972–78) 24
Macaulay A (Brentford, Arsenal, 1947–48) 7
MacDonald A (Rangers, 1976) 1
MacDougall E (Norwich, 1975–76) 7
Mackail-Smith C (Peterborough, Brighton
2011–12) 7
MacKay D (Celtic, 1959–62) 14
Mackay D (Hearts, Tottenham, 1957–66) 22
Mackay G (Hearts, 1988) 4
Mackay M (Norwich, 2004–05) 5
Mackay–Steven G (Dundee Utd, 2014) 1
MacKenzie J (Partick, 1954–56) 9
Mackie J (QPR, 2011–13) 9
MacLeod J (Hibernian, 1961) 4
MacLeod M (Celtic, Borussia Dortmund,
Hibernian, 1985–91) 20
Maguire C (Aberdeen, 2011) 2
Maloney S (Celtic, Aston Villa, Celtic,
Wigan, Chicago, Hull, 2006–16) 47
Malpas M (Dundee Utd, 1984–93) 55
Marshall D (Celtic, Cardiff, Hull, 2005–17) 27
Marshall G (Celtic, 1992) 1
Martin B (Motherwell, 1995) 2
Martin C (Derby, 2014–17) 13
Martin F (Aberdeen, 1954–55) 6
Martin N (Hibernian, Sunderland, 1965–66) 3
Martin R (Norwich, 2011–17) 29
Martis J (Motherwell, 1961) 1
Mason J (Third Lanark 1949–51) 7
Masson D (QPR, Derby, 1976–78) 17
Mathers D (Partick, 1954) 1
Matteo D (Leeds, 2001–02) 6
May S (Sheffield Wed, 2015) 1
McAllister B (Wimbledon, 1997) 3
McAllister G (Leicester, Leeds,
Coventry, 1990–99) 57
McAllister J (Livingston, 2004) 1
McArthur J (Wigan, Crystal Palace, 2011–17) 28
McAvennie F (West Ham, Celtic, 1986–88) 5
McBride J (Celtic, 1967) 2
McCall S (Everton, Rangers, 1990–98) 40
McCalliog J (Sheffield Wed, Wolves,
1967–71) 5
McCann N (Hearts, Rangers,
Southampton, 1999–2006) 26
McCann R (Motherwell, 1959–61) 5
McClair B (Celtic, Manchester Utd,
1987–93) 30
McCloy P (Rangers, 1973) 4
McCoist A (Rangers, Kilmarnock,
1986–99) 61
McColl I (Rangers, 1950–58) 14
McCormack R (Motherwell, Cardiff,
Leeds, Fulham, 2008–16) 13
McCreadie E (Chelsea, 1965–9) 23
McCulloch L (Wigan, Rangers, 2005–11) 18
McDonald J (Sunderland, 1956) 2
McEveley, J (Derby, 2008) 3
McFadden J (Motherwell, Everton,
Birmingham, 2002–11) 48
McFarlane W (Hearts, 1947) 1
McGarr E (Aberdeen, 1970) 2

McGarvey F (Liverpool, Celtic, 1979 84) — 7
McGhee M (Aberdeen, 1983–84) — 4
McGinlay J (Bolton, 1995–97) — 13
McGinn J (Hibernian, 2016–17) — 3
McGrain D (Celtic, 1973–82) — 62
McGregor A (Rangers, Besiktas, Hull, 2007–17) — 36
McGrory J (Kilmarnock, 1965–66) — 3
McInally A (Aston Villa, Bayern Munich, 1989–90) — 8
McInally J (Dundee Utd, 1987–93) — 10
McInnes D (WBA, 2003) — 2
McKay B (Rangers, 2016) — 1
McKean R (Rangers, 1976) — 1
McKimmie S (Aberdeen, 1989–96) — 40
McKinlay T (Celtic, 1996–98) — 22
McKinlay W (Dundee Utd, Blackburn, 1994–99) — 29
McKinnon R (Rangers, 1966–71) — 28
McKinnon R (Motherwell, 1994–95) — 3
McLaren A (Preston, 1947–48) — 4
McLaren A (Hearts, Rangers, 1992 96) — 24
McLaren A (Kilmarnock, 2001) — 1
McLean G (Dundee, 1968) — 1
McLean K (Aberdeen, 2016) — 1
McLean T (Kilmarnock, Rangers, 1969–71) — 6
McLeish A (Aberdeen, 1980–93) — 77
McLintock F (Leicester, Arsenal, 1963–71) — 9
McManus S (Celtic, Middlesbrough, 2007–11) — 26
McMillan I (Airdrie, 1952–61) — 6
McNamara J (Celtic, Wolves, 1997–2006) — 33
McNamee D (Livingston, 2004–06) — 4
McNaught W (Raith, 1951–55) — 5
McNaughton K (Aberdeen, Cardiff, 2002–08) — 4
McNeill W (Celtic, 1961–72) — 29
McPhail J (Celtic, 1950 54) — 5
McPherson D (Hearts, Rangers, 1989–93) — 27
McQueen G (Leeds, Manchester Utd, 1974–81) — 30
McStay P (Celtic, 1984–97) — 76
McSwegan G (Hearts, 2000) — 2
Millar J (Rangers, 1963) — 2
Miller C (Dundee Utd, 2001) — 1
Miller K (Rangers, Wolves, Celtic, Derby, Rangers, Bursaspor, Cardiff, Vancouver, 2001–14) — 69
Miller L (Dundee Utd, Aberdeen 2006–10) — 3
Miller W (Celtic, 1946–47) — 6
Miller W (Aberdeen, 1975–90) — 65
Mitchell R (Newcastle, 1951) — 2
Mochan N (Celtic, 1954) — 1
Moir W (Bolton, 1950) — 1
Moncur R (Newcastle, 1968–72) — 16
Morgan W (Burnley, Manchester Utd, 1968–74) — 21
Morris H (East Fife, 1950) — 1
Morrison J (WBA, 2008–17) — 44
Mudie J (Blackpool, 1957–58) — 17

Mulgrew C (Celtic, Blackburn, 2012–17) — 27
Mulhall G (Aberdeen, Sunderland, 1960–64) — 3
Munro F (Wolves, 1971–75) — 9
Munro I (St Mirren, 1979–80) — 7
Murdoch R (Celtic, 1966–70) — 12
Murray I (Hibernian, Rangers, 2003–06) — 6
Murray J (Hearts, 1958) — 5
Murray S (Aberdeen, 1972) — 1
Murty G (Reading, 2004–08) — 4
Naismith S (Kilmarnock, Rangers, Everton, Norwich, 2007–17) — 45
Narey D (Dundee Utd, 1977–89) — 35
Naysmith G (Hearts, Everton, Sheffield Utd, 2000–09) — 46
Neilson R (Hearts, 2007) — 1
Nevin P (Chelsea, Everton, Tranmere, 1987–96) — 28
Nicholas C (Celtic, Arsenal, Aberdeen, 1983–89) — 20
Nicholson B (Dunfermline, 2001–05) — 3
Nicol S (Liverpool, 1985–92) — 27
O'Connor G (Hibernian, Lokomotiv Moscow, Birmingham, 2002–10) — 16
O'Donnell P (Motherwell, 1994) — 1
O'Hare J (Derby, 1970–72) — 13
O'Neil B (Celtic, VfL Wolfsburg, Derby, Preston, 1996–2006) — 7
O'Neil J (Hibernian, 2001) — 1
Ormand W (Hibernian, 1954 60) — 6
Orr T (Morton, 1952) — 2
Parker A (Falkirk, Everton, 1955–56) — 15
Parlane D (Rangers, 1973–77) — 12
Paterson C (Hearts, Cardiff, 2016–17) — 5
Paton A (Motherwell, 1952) — 2
Pearson S (Motherwell, Celtic, Derby, 2004–07) — 10
Pearson T (Newcastle, 1947) — 2
Penman A (Dundee, 1966) — 1
Pettigrew W (Motherwell, 1976–77) — 5
Phillips M (Blackpool, QPR, 2012–16) — 4
Plenderleith J (Manchester City, 1961) — 1
Pressley S (Hearts, 2000–07) — 32
Provan D (Rangers, 1964–66) — 5
Provan D (Celtic, 1980–82) — 10
Quashie N (Portsmouth, Southampton, WBA, 2004–07) — 14
Quinn P (Motherwell, 1961–62) — 4
Rae G (Dundee, Rangers, Cardiff, 2001–09) — 14
Redpath W (Motherwell, 1949–52) — 9
Reilly L (Hibernian, 1949–57) — 38
Rhodes J (Huddersfield, Blackburn, Sheffield Wed, 2012–17) — 14
Ring T (Clyde, 1953–58) — 12
Rioch B (Derby, Everton, 1975–78) — 24
Riordan D (Hibernian, 2006–10) — 3
Ritchie M (Bournemouth, Newcastle, 2015–17) — 14
Ritchie P (Hearts, Bolton, 1999–2000) — 7

Ritchie W (Rangers, 1962) — 1
Robb D (Aberdeen, 1971) — 5
Robertson A (Clyde, 1955) — 5
Robertson A (Dundee Utd, Hull, 2014–17) — 15
Robertson D (Rangers, 1992–94) — 3
Robertson H (Dundee, 1962) — 1
Robertson J (Tottenham, 1964) — 1
Robertson J (Nottm Forest, Derby, 1978–84) — 28
Robertson J (Hearts, 1991–96) — 16
Robertson S (Dundee Utd, 2009–11) — 2
Robinson R (Dundee, 1974–75) — 4
Robson B (Celtic, Middlesbrough, 2008–12) — 17
Ross M (Rangers, 2002–04) — 13
Rough A (Partick, Hibernian, 1976–86) — 53
Rougvie D (Aberdeen, 1984) — 1
Russell J (Derby, 2015–16) — 4
Rutherford E (Rangers, 1948) — 1

Saunders S (Motherwell, 2011) — 1
Schaedler E (Hibernian, 1974) — 1
Scott A (Rangers, Everton, 1957–66) — 16
Scott J (Hibernian, 1966) — 1
Scott J (Dundee, 1971) — 2
Scoular J (Portsmouth, 1951–53) — 9
Severin S (Hearts, Aberdeen, 2002–07) — 15
Sharp G (Everton, 1985–88) — 12
Shaw D (Hibernian, 1947–49) — 8
Shaw J (Rangers, 1947) — 4
Shearer D (Aberdeen, 1994–96) — 7
Shearer R (Rangers, 1961) — 4
Shinnie A (Inverness, 2013) — 1
Simpson N (Aberdeen, 1983–88) — 5
Simpson R (Celtic, 1967–69) — 5
Sinclair J (Leicester, 1966) — 1
Smith D (Aberdeen, Rangers, 1966–68) — 2
Smith G (Hibernian, 1947–57) — 18
Smith H (Hearts, 1988–92) — 3
Smith JE (Celtic, 1959) — 2
Smith J (Aberdeen, Newcastle, 1968–74) — 4
Smith J (Celtic, 2003) — 2
Snodgrass R (Leeds, Norwich, West Ham, 2011–17) — 24
Souness G (Middlesbrough, Liverpool, Sampdoria, Rangers, 1975–86) — 54
Speedie D (Chelsea, Coventry, 1985–89) — 10
Spencer J (Chelsea, QPR, 1995–97) — 14
Stanton P (Hibernian, 1966–74) — 16
Steel W (Morton, Derby, Dundee, 1947–53) — 30
Stein C (Rangers, Coventry, 1969–73) — 21
Stephen J (Bradford Park Avenue, 1947–48) — 2
Stewart D (Leeds, 1978) — 1
Stewart J (Kilmarnock, Middlesbrough, 1977–79) — 2
Stewart M (Manchester Utd, Hearts 2002–09) — 4
Stewart R (West Ham, 1981–7) — 10
St John I (Motherwell, Liverpool, 1959–65) — 21

Stockdale R (Middlesbrough, 2002–03) — 5
Strachan G (Aberdeen, Manchester Utd, Leeds, 1980–92) — 50
Sturrock P (Dundee Utd, 1981–87) — 20
Sullivan N (Wimbledon, Tottenham, 1997–2003) — 28
Teale G (Wigan, Derby, 2006–09) — 13
Telfer P (Coventry, 2000) — 1
Telfer W (St Mirren, 1954) — 1
Thomson K (Rangers, Middlesbrough, 2009–11) — 3
Thompson S (Dundee Utd, Rangers, 2002–05) — 16
Thomson W (St Mirren, 1980–84) — 7
Thornton W (Rangers, 1947–52) — 7
Tierney K (Celtic, 2016–17) — 4
Toner W (Kilmarnock, 1959) — 2
Turnbull E (Hibernian, 1948–58) — 8

Ure I (Dundee, Arsenal, 1962–68) — 11

Waddell W (Rangers, 1947–55) — 17
Walker A (Celtic, 1988–95) — 3
Walker N (Hearts, 1993–96) — 2
Wallace I (Coventry, 1978–79) — 3
Wallace L (Hearts, Rangers, 2010–17) — 10
Wallace R (Preston, 2010) — 1
Wallace W (Hearts, Celtic, 1965–69) — 7
Wardhaugh J (Hearts, 1955–57) — 2
Wark J (Ipswich, Liverpool, 1979–85) — 29
Watson J (Motherwell, Huddersfield, 1948–54) — 2
Watson R (Motherwell, 1971) — 1
Watt T (Charlton, 2016) — 1
Webster A (Hearts, Rangers, Hearts, 2003–13) — 28
Weir A (Motherwell, 1959–60) — 6
Weir D (Hearts, Everton, Rangers, 1997–2011) — 69
Weir P (St Mirren, Aberdeen, 1980–84) — 6
White J (Falkirk, Tottenham, 1959–64) — 22
Whittaker S (Rangers, Norwich, 2010–16) — 31
Whyte D (Celtic, Middlesbrough, Aberdeen, 1988–99) — 12
Wilkie L (Dundee, 2002–03) — 11
Williams S (Nottm Forest, 2002–03) — 5
Wilson A (Portsmouth, 1954) — 1
Wilson D (Liverpool, 2011–12) — 5
Wilson D (Rangers, 1961–65) — 22
Wilson I (Leicester, Everton, 1987–8) — 5
Wilson M (Celtic, 2011) — 1
Wilson P (Celtic, 1975) — 1
Wilson R (Arsenal, 1972) — 2
Wood G (Everton, Arsenal, 1978–82) — 4
Woodburn W (Rangers, 1947–52) — 24
Wright K (Hibernian, 1992) — 1
Wright S (Aberdeen, 1993) — 2
Wright T (Sunderland, 1953) — 3

Yeats R (Liverpool, 1965–66) — 2
Yorston H (Aberdeen, 1955) — 1
Young A (Hearts, Everton, 1960–66) — 8
Young G (Rangers, 1947–57) — 53
Younger T (Hibernian, Liverpool, 1955–58) — 24

WALES

Aizlewood M (Charlton, Leeds, Bradford City, Bristol City, Cardiff, 1986–95) 39

Allchurch I (Swansea City, Newcastle, Cardiff, 1951–66) 68

Allchurch L (Swansea City, Sheffield Utd, 1955–64) 11

Allen B (Coventry, 1951) 2

Allen J (Swansea, Liverpool, Stoke, 2009–17) 37

Allen M (Watford, Norwich, Millwall, Newcastle, 1986–94) 14

Baker C (Cardiff, 1958–62) 7

Baker W (Cardiff, 1948) 1

Bale G (Southampton, Tottenham, Real Madrid, 2006–17) 66

Barnard D (Barnsley, Grimsby, 1998–2004) 24

Barnes W (Arsenal, 1948–55) 22

Bellamy C (Norwich, Coventry, Newcastle, Blackburn, Liverpool, West Ham, Manchester City, Liverpool, Cardiff, 1998–2014) 78

Berry G (Wolves, Stoke, 1979–83) 5

Blackmore C (Manchester Utd, Middlesbrough, 1985–97) 39

Blake D (Cardiff, Crystal Palace, 2011–13) 14

Blake N (Sheffield Utd, Bolton, Blackburn, Wolves, 1994–2004) 29

Bodin P (Swindon, Crystal Palace, Swindon, 1990–95) 23

Bowen D (Arsenal, 1955–59) 19

Bowen J (Swansea City, Birmingham, 1994–97) 2

Bowen M (Tottenham, Norwich, West Ham, 1986–97) 41

Boyle T (Crystal Palace, 1981) 2

Bradley M (Walsall, 2010) 1

Bradshaw T (Walsall, 2016) 1

Brown J (Gillingham, Blackburn, Aberdeen, 2006–12) 3

Browning M (Bristol Rov, Huddersfield, 1996–97) 5

Burgess R (Tottenham, 1947–54) 32

Burton A (Norwich, Newcastle, 1963–72) 9

Cartwright L (Coventry, Wrexham, 1974–79) 7

Charles Jeremy (Swansea City, QPR, Oxford Utd, 1981–87) 19

Charles John (Leeds, Juventus, Cardiff, 1950–65) 38

Charles M (Swansea City, Arsenal, Cardiff, 1955–63) 31

Chester J (Hull, WBA, Aston Villa, 2014–17) 23

Church S (Reading, Nottm Forest, Charlton, MK Dons 2009–16) 38

Clarke R (Manchester City, 1949–56) 22

Coleman C (Crystal Palace, Blackburn, Fulham, 1992–2002) 32

Collins D (Sunderland, Stoke, 2005–11) 12

Collins J (Cardiff, West Ham, Aston Villa, West Ham, 2004–17) 50

Collison J (West Ham, 2008–14) 17

Cornforth J (Swansea City, 1995) 2

Cotterill D (Bristol City, Wigan, Sheffield Utd, Swansea, Doncaster, Birmingham, 2006–17) 24

Coyne D (Tranmere, Grimsby, Leicester, Burnley, Tranmere, 1996–2008) 16

Crofts A (Gillingham, Brighton, Norwich, Brighton, 2006–16) 28

Crossley M (Nottm Forest, Middlesbrough, Fulham, 1997–2005) 8

Crowe V (Aston Villa, 1959–63) 16

Curtis A (Swansea City, Leeds, Southampton, Cardiff, 1976–87) 35

Daniel R (Arsenal, Sunderland, 1951–57) 21

Davies A (Manchester Utd, Newcastle, Swansea City, Bradford City, 1983–90) 13

Davies A (Yeovil 2006) 1

Davies B (Swansea, Tottenham, 2013–17) 30

Davies C (Charlton, 1972) 1

Davies C (Oxford, Verona, Oldham, Barnsley, Bolton, 2006–14) 7

Davies D (Everton, Wrexham, Swansea City 1975–83) 52

Davies ER (Newcastle, 1953–58) 6

Davies G (Fulham, Chelsea, Manchester City, 1980–86) 16

Davies RT (Norwich, Southampton, Portsmouth, 1964–74) 29

Davies RW (Bolton, Newcastle, Man Utd, Man City, Blackpool, 1964–74) 34

Davies S (Manchester Utd, 1996) 1

Davies S (Tottenham, Everton, Fulham, 2001–10) 58

Davis G (Wrexham, 1978) 3

Deacy N (PSV Eindhoven, Beringen, 1977–79) 12

Delaney M (Aston Villa, 2000–07) 36

Derrett S (Cardiff, 1969–71) 4

Dibble A (Luton, Manchester City, 1986–89) 3

Dorman A (St Mirren, Crystal Palace, 2010–11) 3

Dummett P (Newcastle, 2014–16) 2

Duffy R (Portsmouth, 2006–08) 13

Durban A (Derby, 1966–72) 27

Dwyer P (Cardiff, 1978–80) 10

Eardley N (Oldham, Blackpool, 2008–11) 16

Farnshaw R (Cardiff, WBA, Norwich, Derby, Nottm Forest, Cardiff, 2002–13) 59

Easter J (Wycombe, Crystal Palace, Millwall, 2007–14) 12

Eastwood F (Wolves, Coventry, 2008–11) 11

Edwards C (Swansea City, 1996) 1

Edwards D (Luton, Wolves, 2007–17) 39

Edwards, G (Birmingham, Cardiff, 1947–50) 12

Edwards, I (Chester, Wrexham, 1978–80) 4

Edwards, L (Charlton, 1957) 2

Edwards, R (Bristol City, 1997–98) 4

Edwards, R (Aston Villa, Wolves, 2003–07) 15

Emmanuel W (Bristol City, 1973) 2

England M (Blackburn, Tottenham, 1962–75) 44

THE THINGS THEY SAY …

'I can honestly say I'm delighted for Wayne. He deserves his place in the history books. He is a true great for club and country' – **Sir Bobby Charlton** after watching Wayne Rooney overtake his all-time scoring record of 249 goals for Manchester United.

NORTHERN IRELAND

Aherne T (Belfast Celtic, Luton, 1947–50) 4

Anderson T (Manchester Utd, Swindon, Peterborough, 1973–79) 22

Armstrong G (Tottenham, Watford, Real Mallorca, WBA, 1977–86) 63

Baird C (Southampton, Fulham, Burnley, WBA, Derby, 2003–16) 79

Barr H (Linfield, Coventry, 1962–63) 3

Barton A (Preston, 2011) 1

Best G (Manchester Utd, Fulham, 1964–77) 37

Bingham W (Sunderland, Luton, Everton, Port Vale, 1951–64) 56

Black K (Luton, Nottm Forest, 1988–94) 30

Blair R (Oldham, 1975–76) 5

Blanchflower RD (Barnsley, Aston Villa, Tottenham, 1950–63) 56

Blanchflower J (Manchester Utd, 1954–58) 12

Blayney A (Doncaster, Linfield, 2006–11) 5

Bowler G (Hull, 1950) 3

Boyce L (Werder Bremen, Ross Co, 2011–17) 10

Braithwaite R (Linfield, Middlesbrough, 1962–65) 10

Braniff K (Portadown, 2010) 2

Brennan R (Luton, Birmingham, Fulham, 1949–51) 5

Briggs W (Manchester Utd, Swansea, 1962–65) 2

Brotherston N (Blackburn, 1980–85) 27

Bruce A (Hull, 2013–14) 2

Bruce W (Glentoran, 1961–67) 2

Brunt C (Sheffield Wed, WBA, 2005–17) 59

Bryan M (Watford, 2010) 2

Camp L (Nottm Forest, 2011–13) 9

Campbell D (Nottm Forest, Charlton, 1987–88) 10

Campbell J (Fulham, 1951) 2

Campbell R (Crusaders, 1963–65) 2

Campbell R (Bradford City, 1982) 2

Campbell W (Dundee, 1968–70) 6

Capaldi A (Plymouth Argyle, Cardiff, 2004–08) 22

Carey J (Manchester Utd, 1947–49) 7

Carroll R (Wigan, Manchester Utd, West Ham, Olympiacos, Notts Co, Linfield, 1997–2017) 45

Carson J (Ipswich, 2011–13) 4

Carson S (Coleraine, 2009) 1

Casey T (Newcastle, Portsmouth, 1955–59) 12

Casement C (Ipswich, 2009) 1

Caskey W (Derby, Tulsa, Roughnecks, 1979–82) 7

Cassidy T (Newcastle, Burnley, 1971–82) 24

Cathcart C (Blackpool, Watford, 2011–17) 33

Caughey M (Linfield, 1986) 2

Clarke C (Bournemouth, Southampton, QPR, Portsmouth, 1986–93) 38

Cleary J (Glentoran, 1982–85) 5

Clements D (Coventry, Sheffield Wed, Everton, New York Cosmos, 1965–76) 48

Clingan S (Nottm Forest, Norwich, Coventry, Kilmarnock, 2006–15) 39

Clyde, M (Wolves, 2005) 3

Coates C (Crusaders, 2009–11) 6

Cochrane A (Coleraine, Burnley, Middlesbrough, Gillingham, 1976–84) 26

Cochrane D (Leeds, 1947–50) 10

Connell T (Coleraine, 1978) 1

Coote A (Norwich, 1999–2000) 6

Cowan J (Newcastle, 1970) 1

Coyle F (Coleraine, Nottm Forest, 1956–58) 4

Coyle L (Derry City, 1989) 1

Coyle R (Sheffield Wed, 1973–74) 5

Craig D (Newcastle, 1967–75) 25

Craigan S (Partick, Motherwell, 2003–11) 54

Crossan E (Blackburn, 1950–55) 3

Crossan J (Sparta Rotterdam, Sunderland, Manchester City, Middlesbrough, 1960–68) 24

Cunningham W (St Mirren, Leicester, Dunfermline, 1951–62) 30

Cush W (Glenavon, Leeds, Portadown, 1951–62) 26

Dallas S (Crusaders, Brentford, Leeds, 2011–17) 22

D'Arcy S (Chelsea, Brentford, 1952–53) 5

Davis S (Aston Villa, Fulham, Rangers, Southampton, 2005–17) 95

Davison A (Bolton, Bradford City, Grimsby, 1996–97) 3

Dennison R (Wolves, 1988–97) 18

Devine J (Glentoran, 1990) 1

Dickson D (Coleraine, 1970–73) 4

Dickson T (Linfield, 1957) 1

Dickson W (Chelsea, Arsenal, 1951–55) 12

Doherty L (Linfield, 1985–88) 2

*Doherty P (Derby, Huddersfield, Doncaster, 1946–50) 6

Doherty T (Bristol City, 2003–05) 9

Donaghy M (Luton, Manchester Utd, Chelsea, 1980–94) 91

Donnelly L (Fulham, 2014) 1

Donnelly M (Crusaders, 2009) 1

Dougan D (Portsmouth, Blackburn, Aston Villa, Leicester, Wolves, 1958–73) 43

Douglas J (Belfast Celtic, 1947) 1

Dowd H (Glenavon, 1974) 3

Dowie I (Luton, Southampton, Crystal Palace, West Ham, QPR, 1990–2000) 59

Duff M (Cheltenham, Burnley, 2002–12) 24

Dunlop G (Linfield, 1985–90) 4

Eglington T (Everton, 1947–49) 6

Elder A (Burnley, Stoke, 1960–70) 40

Elliott S (Motherwell, Hull, 2001–08) 38

Evans C (Manchester Utd, Hull, Blackburn, 2009–17) 39

Evans J (Manchester Utd, WBA, 2007–17) 61

Farrell P (Everton, 1947–49) 7

Quinn J (Blackburn, Swindon, Leicester, Bradford City, West Ham, Bournemouth, Reading, 1985–96) 46

Quinn SJ (Blackpool, WBA, Willem 11, Sheffield Wed, Peterborough, Northampton, 1996–2007) 50

Rafferty P (Linfield, 1979) 1
Ramsey P (Leicester, 1984–89) 14
Reeves B (MK Dons, 2015) 2
Rice P (Arsenal, 1969–80) 49
Robinson S (Bournemouth, Luton, 1997–2008) 7
Rogan A (Celtic, Sunderland, Millwall, 1988–97) 18
Ross W (Newcastle, 1969) 1
Rowland K (West Ham, QPR, 1994–99) 19
Russell A (Linfield, 1947) 1
Ryan R (WBA, 1950) 1

Sanchez L (Wimbledon, 1987–89) 3
Scott J (Grimsby, 1958) 2
Scott P (Everton, York, Aldershot, 1976–79) 10
Sharkey P (Ipswich, 1976) 1
Shields J (Southampton, 1957) 1
Shiels M (Hibernian, Doncaster, Kilmarnock, Rangers, 2006–13) 14
Simpson W (Rangers, 1951–59) 12
Sloan D (Oxford Utd, 1969–71) 2
Sloan J (Arsenal, 1947) 1
Sloan T (Manchester Utd, 1979) 3
Smith A (Glentoran, Preston, 2003–05) 18
Smith M (Peterborough, 2016) 1
Smyth S (Wolves, Stoke, 1948–52) 9
Smyth W (Distillery, 1949–54) 4
Sonner D (Ipswich, Sheffield Wed, Birmingham, Nottm Forest, Peterborough, 1997–2005) 13
Spence D (Bury, Blackpool, Southend, 1975–82) 29
Sproule I (Hibernian, 2006–08) 11
*Stevenson A (Everton, 1947–48) 3
Steele J (New York Bulls, 2014) 3
Stewart A (Glentoran, Derby, 1967–69) 7
Stewart D (Hull, 1978) 1
Stewart I (QPR, Newcastle, 1982–87) 31
Stewart T (Linfield, 1961) 1

Taggart G (Barnsley, Bolton, Leicester, 1990–2003) 51
Taylor M (Fulham, Birmingham, 1999–2012) 88
Thompson A (Watford, 2011) 2
Thompson P (Linfield, 2006–08) 8
Todd S (Burnley, Sheffield Wed, 1966–71) 11
Toner C (Leyton Orient, 2003) 2
Trainor D (Crusaders, 1967) 1
Tuffey J (Partick, Inverness, 2009–11) 8
Tully C (Celtic, 1949–59) 10
Uprichard W (Swindon, Portsmouth, 1952–59) 18
Vernon J (Belfast Celtic, WBA, 1947–52) 17

Walker J (Doncaster, 1955) 1
Walsh D (WBA, 1947–50) 9
Walsh W (Manchester City, 1948–49) 5
Ward J (Derby, Nottm Forest, 2012–17) 30
Washington C (QPR, 2016–17) 10
Watson P (Distillery, 1971) 1
Webb S (Ross Co, 2006–07) 4
Welsh E (Carlisle, 1966–67) 4
Whiteside N (Manchester Utd, Everton, 1982–90) 38
Whitley Jeff (Manchester City, Sunderland, Cardiff, 1997–2006) 20
Whitley Jim (Manchester City, 1998–2000) 3
Williams M (Chesterfield, Watford, Wimbledon, Stoke, Wimbledon, MK Dons, 1999–2005) 36
Williams M (Chesterfield, Watford Wimbledon, Stoke, Wimbledon MK Dons 1999–2005) 36
Williams P (WBA, 1991) 1
Wilson D (Brighton, Luton, Sheffield Wed, 1987–92) 24
Wilson K (Ipswich, Chelsea, Notts Co, Walsall, 1987–95) 42
Wilson S (Glenavon, Falkirk, Dundee, 1962–68) 12
Winchester C (Oldham, 2011) 1
Wood T (Walsall, 1996) 1
Worthington N (Sheffield Wed, Leeds, Stoke, 1984–97) 66
Wright T (Newcastle, Nottm Forest, Reading, Manchester City, 1989–2000) 31

REPUBLIC OF IRELAND

Aherne T (Belfast Celtic, Luton, 1946–54) 16
Aldridge J (Oxford Utd, Liverpool, Real Sociedad, Tranmere, 1986–97) 69
Ambrose P (Shamrock R, 1955–64) 5
Anderson J (Preston, Newcastle, 1980–89) 16
Andrews K (Blackburn, WBA, 2009–13) 35
Arter H (Bournemouth, 2015–17) 6

Babb P (Coventry, Liverpool, Sunderland, 1994–2003) 35
Bailham E (Shamrock R, 1964) 1
Barber E (Bohemians, Birmingham, 1966) 2
Barrett G (Arsenal, Coventry, 2003–05) 6
Beglin J (Liverpool, 1984–87) 15

Bennett A (Reading, 2007) 2
Best L (Coventry, 2009–10) 7
Braddish S (Dundalk, 1978) 2
Branagan K (Bolton, 1997) 1
Bonner P (Celtic, 1981–96) 80
Boyle A (Preston, 2017) 1
Brady L (Arsenal, Juventus, Sampdoria, Inter–Milan, Ascoli, West Ham, 1975–90) 72
Brady R (QPR, 1964) 6
Brady R (Manchester Utd, Hull, Burnley, 2013–17) 34
Breen G (Birmingham, Coventry, West Ham, Sunderland, 1996–2006) 63
*Breen T (Shamrock R, 1947) 3

Farrelly G (Aston Villa, Everton, Bolton, 1996–2000) 6

Finnan S (Fulham, Liverpool, Espanyol 2000–09) 53

Finucane A (Limerick, 1967–72) 11

Fitzgerald F (Waterford, 1955–6) 2

Fitzgerald P (Leeds, 1961–2) 5

Fitzpatrick K (Limerick, 1970) 1

Fitzsimons A (Middlesbrough, Lincoln, 1950–59) 26

Fleming C (Middlesbrough, 1996–8) 10

Fogarty A (Sunderland, Hartlepool Utd, 1960–64) 11

Folan C (Hull, 2009–10) 7

Foley D (Watford, 2000–01) 6

Foley K (Wolves, 2009–11) 8

Foley T (Northampton, 1964–67) 9

Fullam J (Preston, Shamrock R, 1961–70) 11

Forde D (Millwall, 2011–16) 24

Fullam J (Preston, Shamrock, 1961–70) 11

Gallagher C (Celtic, 1967) 2

Gallagher M (Hibernian, 1954) 1

Galvin A (Tottenham, Sheffield Wed, Swindon, 1983–90) 29

Gamble J (Cork City, 2007) 2

Gannon E (Notts Co, Sheffield Wed, Shelbourne, 1949–55) 14

Gannon M (Shelbourne, 1972) 1

Gavin J (Norwich, Tottenham, Norwich, 1950–57) 7

Gibbons A (St Patrick's Ath, 1952–56) 4

Gibson D (Manchester Utd, Everton, 2008–16) 27

Gilbert R (Shamrock R, 1966) 1

Giles C (Doncaster, 1951) 1

Giles J (Manchester Utd, Leeds, WBA, Shamrock R, 1960–79) 59

Given S (Blackburn, Newcastle, Manchester City, Aston Villa, Stoke, 1996–2016) 134

Givens D (Manchester Utd, Luton, QPR, Birmingham, Neuchatel, 1969–82) 56

Gleeson S (Wolves, Birmingham, 2007–17) 4

Glynn D (Drumcondra, 1952–55) 2

Godwin T (Shamrock R, Leicester, Bournemouth, 1949–58) 13

Goodman J (Wimbledon, 1997) 4

Goodwin J (Stockport, 2003) 1

*Gorman W (Brentford, 1947) 2

Grealish A (Orient Luton, Brighton, WBA, 1976–86) 45

Green P (Derby, Leeds, 2010–14) 22

Gregg E (Bohemians, 1978–80) 8

Grimes A (Manchester Utd, Coventry, Luton, 1978–88) 18

Hale A (Aston Villa, Doncaster, Waterford, 1962–72) 14

Hamilton T (Shamrock R, 1959) 2

Hand E (Portsmouth, 1969–76) 20

Harte I (Leeds, Levante, 1996–2007) 64

Hartnett J (Middlesbrough, 1949–54) 2

Haverty J (Arsenal, Blackburn, Millwall, Celtic, Bristol Rov, Shelbourne, 1956–67) 32

Hayes A (Southampton, 1979) 1

Hayes J (Aberdeen, 2016–17) 4

*Hayes W (Huddersfield, 1947) 2

Hayes W (Limerick, 1949) 1

Healey R (Cardiff, 1977–80) 2

Healy C (Celtic, Sunderland, 2002–04) 13

Heighway S (Liverpool, Minnesota, 1971–82) 34

Henderson B (Drumcondra, 1948) 2

Henderson W (Brighton, Preston, 2006–08) 6

Hendrick J (Derby, Burnley, 2013–17) 33

Hennessy J (Shelbourne, St Patrick's Ath, 1956–69) 5

Herrick J (Cork Hibernian, Shamrock R, 1972–73) 3

Higgins J (Birmingham, 1951) 1

Holland M (Ipswich, Charlton, 2000–06) 49

Holmes J (Coventry, Tottenham, Vancouver W'caps, 1971–81) 30

Hoolahan W (Blackpool, Norwich, 2008–17) 40

Horgan D (Preston, 2017) 2

Houghton R (Oxford Utd, Liverpool, Aston Villa, Crystal Palace, Reading, 1986–97) 73

Hourihane C (Aston Villa, 2017) 2

Howlett G (Brighton, 1984) 1

Hughton C (Tottenham, West Ham, 1980–92) 53

Hunt N (Reading, 2009) 2

Hunt S (Reading, Hull, Wolves, 2007–12) 39

Hurley C (Millwall, Sunderland, Bolton, 1957–69) 40

Ireland S (Manchester City, 2006–08) 6

Irwin D (Manchester Utd, 1991–2000) 56

Judge A (Brentford, 2016) 1

Kavanagh G (Stoke, Cardiff, Wigan, 1998–2007) 16

Keane, R (Wolves, Coventry, Inter Milan, Leeds Tottenham, Liverpool, LA Galaxy, 1998–2017) 146

Keane R (Nottm Forest, Manchester Utd, 1991–2006) 67

Keane T (Swansea, 1949) 4

Kearin M (Shamrock R, 1972) 1

Kearns F (West Ham, 1954) 1

Kearns M (Oxford Utd, Walsall, Wolves, 1970–80) 18

Kelly A (Sheffield Utd, Blackburn, 1993–2002) 34

Kelly D (Walsall, West Ham, Leicester, Newcastle, Wolves, Sunderland, Tranmere, 1988–98) 26

Kelly G (Leeds, 1994–2003) 52

Kelly JA (Drumcondra, Preston, 1957–73) 47

Kelly M (Portsmouth, 1988–91) 4

Kelly N (Nottm Forest, 1954) 1

Kelly P (Wolves, 1961–62) 5

O'Callaghan B (Stoke, 1979–82) 6
O'Callaghan K (Ipswich, Portsmouth, 1981–87) 21
O'Cearuill J (Arsenal, 2007) 2
O'Connell A (Dundalk, Bohemians, 1967–71) 2
O'Connor T (Shamrock R, 1950) 4
O'Connor T (Fulham, Dundalk, Bohemians, 1968–73) 7
O'Dowda C (Oxford, Bristol City, 2016–7) 5
O'Dea D (Celtic, Toronto, Metalurh Donetsk, 2010–14) 20
O'Driscoll J (Swansea, 1949) 3
O'Driscoll S (Fulham, 1982) 3
O'Farrell F (West Ham, Preston, 1952–59) 9
*O'Flanagan Dr K (Arsenal, 1947) 3
O'Flanagan M (Bohemians, 1947) 1
O'Halloran S (Aston Villa, 2007) 2
O'Hanlon K (Rotherham, 1988) 1
O'Kane E (Bournemouth, Leeds, 2016–17) 6
O'Keefe E (Everton, Port Vale, 1981–85) 5
O'Leary D (Arsenal, 1977–93) 68
O'Leary P (Shamrock R, 1980–1) 7
O'Neill F (Shamrock R, 1962–72) 20
O'Neill J (Everton, 1952–59) 17
O'Neill J (Preston, 1961) 1
O'Neill N (Norwich, Middlesbrough, 1996–2000) 13
O'Regan K (Brighton, 1984–85) 4
O'Reilly J (Cork Utd, 1946) 2
O'Shea J (Manchester Utd, Sunderland, 2002–17) 117

Pearce A (Reading, Derby, 2013–17) 9
Peyton G (Fulham, Bournemouth, Everton, 1977–92) 33
Peyton N (Shamrock R, Leeds, 1957–61) 6
Phelan T (Wimbledon, Manchester City, Chelsea, Everton, Fulham, 1992–2000) 42
Pilkington A (Norwich, Cardiff, 2014–16) 9
Potter D (Wolves, 2007–08) 5
Quinn A (Sheffield Wed, Sheffield Utd, 2003–07) 7
Quinn B (Coventry, 2000) 4
Quinn N (Arsenal, Manchester City, Sunderland, 1986–2002) 92
Quinn S (Hull, Reading, 2013–17) 18

Randolph D (Motherwell, West Ham, 2013–17) 22
Reid A (Nottm Forest, Tottenham, Charlton, Sunderland, Nottm Forest, 2004–14) 29
Reid S (Millwall, Blackburn, 2002–09) 23
Richardson D (Shamrock R, Gillingham, 1972–80) 3
Ringstead A (Sheffield Utd, 1951–59) 20
Robinson M (Brighton, Liverpool, QPR, 1981–86) 24
Roche P (Shelbourne, Manchester Utd, 1972–76) 8
Rogers E (Blackburn, Charlton, 1968–73) 19
Rowlands M (QPR, 2004–10) 5

Ryan G (Derby, Brighton, 1978–85) 18
Ryan R (WBA, Derby, 1950–56) 16

Sadlier R (Millwall, 2002) 1
Sammon C (Derby, 2013–14) 9
Savage D (Millwall, 1996) 5
Saward P (Millwall, Aston Villa, Huddersfield, 1954–63) 18
Scannell T (Southend, 1954) 1
Scully P (Arsenal, 1989) 1
Sheedy K (Everton, Newcastle, 1984–93) 46
Sheridan C (Celtic, CSKA Sofia, 2010–11) 3
Sheridan J (Leeds, Sheffield Wed, 1988–96) 34
Slaven B (Middlesbrough, 1990–93) 7
Sloan P (Arsenal, 1946) 2
Smyth M (Shamrock R, 1969) 1
St Ledger S (Preston, Leicester, 2009–14) 37
Stapleton F (Arsenal, Manchester Utd, Ajax Derby, Le Havre, Blackburn, 1977–90) 71
Staunton S (Liverpool, Aston Villa, Liverpool, Crystal Palace, Aston Villa, 1989–2002) 102
*Stevenson A (Everton, 1947–49) 6
Stokes A (Sunderland, Celtic, 2007–15) 9
Strahan F (Shelbourne, 1964–65) 5
Swan M (Drumcondra, 1960) 1
Synnott N (Shamrock R, 1978–79) 3
Taylor T (Waterford, 1959) 1
Thomas P (Waterford, 1974) 2
Thompson J (Nottm Forest, 2004) 1
Townsend A (Norwich, Chelsea, Aston Villa, Middlesbrough, 1989–97) 70
Traynor T (Southampton, 1954–64) 8
Treacy K (Preston, Burnley 2011–12) 6
Treacy R (WBA, Charlton, Swindon, Preston, Shamrock R, 1966–80) 42
Tuohy L (Shamrock R, Newcastle, Shamrock R, 1956–65) 8
Turner A (Celtic, 1963) 2

Vernon J (Belfast Celtic, 1946) 2

Waddock G (QPR, Millwall, 1980–90) 21
Walsh D (WBA, Aston Villa, 1946–54) 20
Walsh J (Limerick, 1982) 1
Walsh M (Blackpool, Everton, QPR, Porto, 1976–85) 21
Walsh M (Everton, Norwich, 1982–83) 4
Walsh W (Manchester City, 1947–50) 9
Walters J (Stoke 2011–17) 49
Ward S (Wolves, Burnley, 2011–17) 43
Waters J (Grimsby, 1977–80) 2
Westwood K (Coventry, Sunderland, Sheffield Wed, 2009–17) 21
Whelan G (Stoke 2009–17) 81
Whelan R (St Patrick's Ath, 1964) 2
Whelan R (Liverpool, Southend, 1981–95) 53
Whelan L (Manchester Utd, 1956–57) 4
Whittaker R (Chelsea, 1959) 1
Wilson M (Stoke, Bournemouth, 2011–17) 25

INTERNATIONAL GOALSCORERS 1946–2017
(start of season 2017–18)

ENGLAND

Rooney	53
Charlton R	49
Lineker	48
Greaves	44
Owen	40
Finney	30
Lofthouse	30
Shearer	30
Lampard Frank jnr	29
Platt	27
Robson B	26
Hurst	24
Mortensen	23
Crouch	22
Channon	21
Gerrard	21
Keegan	21
Defoe	20
Peters	20
Haynes	18
Hunt R	18
Beckham	17
Lawton	16
Taylor T	16
Woodcock	16
Scholes	14
Welbeck	14
Chivers	13
Mariner	13
Smith R	13
Francis T	12
Barnes J	11
Douglas	11
Mannion	11
Sheringham	11
Clarke A	10
Cole J	10
Flowers R	10
Gascoigne	10
Lee F	10
Milburn	10
Wilshaw	10
Beardsley	9
Bell	9
Bentley	9
Hateley	9
Wright I	9
Ball	8
Broadis	8
Byrne J	8
Hoddle	8
Kane	8
Kevan	8
Sturridge	8
Anderton	7
Connelly	7
Coppell	7
Fowler	7
Heskey	7
Paine	7
Walcott	7
Young A	7
Charlton J	6
Macdonald	6
Mullen	6
Oxlade-Chamberlain	6
Rowley	6
Terry	6
Vardy	6
Vassell	6
Waddle	6
Wright-Phillips S	6
Adams	5
Atyeo	5
Baily	5
Brooking	5
Carter	5
Edwards	5
Ferdinand L	5
Hitchens	5
Johnson D	5
Latchford	5
Neal	5
Pearce	5
Pearson Stan	5
Pearson Stuart	5
Pickering F	5
Barmby	4
Barnes P	4
Bent	4
Cahill	4
Dixon K	4
Hassall	4
Revie	4
Robson R	4
Steven	4
Watson Dave (Sunderland)	4
Baker	3
Blissett	3
Butcher	3
Currie	3
Elliott	3
Francis G	3
Grainger	3
Jagielka	3
Kennedy R	3
Lallana	3
Lambert	3
McDermott	3
McManaman	3
Matthews S	3
Merson	3
Morris	3
O'Grady	3
Peacock	3
Ramsey	3
Sewell	3
Townsend	3
Webb	3
Wilkins	3
Wright W	3
Allen R	2
Alli	2
Anderson	2
Barkley	2
Barry	2
Bradley	2
Broadbent	2
Brooks	2
Carroll	2
Cowans	2
Dier	2
Eastham	2
Ferdinand R	2
Froggatt J	2
Froggatt R	2
Haines	2
Hancocks	2
Hunter	2
Ince	2
Johnson A	2
Keown	2
Lee R	2
Lee S	2
Moore	2
Perry	2
Pointer	2
Richardson	2
Royle	2
Smith A (1989-92)	2
Southgate	2
Sterling	2
Stone	2
Taylor P	2
Tueart	2
Upson	2
Wignall	2
Wilshere	2
Worthington	2
A'Court	1
Astall	1
Baines	1
Beattie K	1
Bowles	1
Bradford	1
Bridge	1

SCOTLAND

Duff	8	Farrell	3	Dempsey	1
Dunne R	8	Fogarty	3	Duffy	1
Grealish	8	Haverty	3	Elliott	1
Kilbane	8	Hoolahan	3	Fitzgerald F	1
McGrath P	8	Kennedy Mark	3	Fullam	1
Staunton	8	Kinsella	3	Galvin	1
Brady R	7	McAteer	3	Gibson	1
Breen G	7	O'Shea	3	Gleeson	1
Fitzsimons	7	Ryan R	3	Glynn	1
Ringstead	7	St Ledger S	3	Green	1
Townsend	7	Waddock	3	Grimes	1
Coyne	6	Walsh M	3	Healy	1
Houghton	6	Ward	3	Hendrick	1
McEvoy	6	Whelan R	3	Holmes	1
Martin C	6	Barrett	2	Hughton	1
Moran	6	Clark	2	Hunt S	1
Cummins	5	Conroy	2	Gibson	1
Fagan F	5	Christie	2	Kavanagh	1
Giles	5	Dennehy	2	Keogh R	1
Hulland	5	Eglington	2	Kernaghan	1
Lawrenson	5	Fallon	2	Mancini	1
McGeady	5	Finnan	2	McCann	1
Rogers	5	Fitzgerald P	2	McPhail	1
Sheridan	5	Foley	2	Miller	1
Treacy	5	Gavin	2	Mooney	1
Walsh D	5	Hale	2	Moroney	1
Walters	5	Hand	2	Mulligan	1
Byrne J	4	Hurley	2	Murphy	1
Cox	4	Kelly G	2	O'Brien A	1
Doherty	4	Keogh A	2	O'Dea	1
Ireland	4	Lawrence	2	O'Callaghan K	1
Irwin	4	Leech	2	O'Keefe	1
McGee	4	McCarthy	2	O'Leary	1
Martin M	4	McLoughlin	2	O'Neill F	1
O'Neill K	4	O'Connor (1968-73	2	O'Reilly J	1
Reid A	4	O'Farrell	2	Pilkington	1
Robinson	4	Pearce	2	Ryan G	1
Tuohy	4	Reid S	2	Slaven	1
Andrews	3	Whelan G	2	Sloan	1
Carey J	3	Ambrose	1	Strahan	1
Coad	3	Anderson	1	Waters	1
Conway	3	Carroll	1	Wilson	1
Fahey	3	Coleman	1		

HOME INTERNATIONAL RESULTS

Note: In the results that follow, WC = World Cup, EC = European Championship, CC = Carling Cup
TF = Tournoi de France For Northern Ireland read Ireland before 1921

ENGLAND V SCOTLAND

Played 114; England won 48; Scotland 41; drawn 25 Goals: England 203, Scotland 174

Year	Venue	E	S	Year	Venue	E	S
1872	Glasgow	0	0	1882	Glasgow	1	5
1873	The Oval	4	2	1883	Sheffield	2	3
1874	Glasgow	1	2	1884	Glasgow	0	1
1875	The Oval	2	2	1885	The Oval	1	1
1876	Glasgow	0	3	1886	Glasgow	1	1
1877	The Oval	1	3	1887	Blackburn	2	3
1878	Glasgow	2	7	1888	Glasgow	5	0
1879	The Oval	5	4	1889	The Oval	2	3
1880	Glasgow	4	5	1890	Glasgow	1	1
1881	The Oval	1	6	1891	Blackburn	2	1
				1892	Glasgow	4	1

Year	Venue	E	S		Year	Venue	E	S
1893	Richmond	5	2		1952	Glasgow	2	1
1894	Glasgow	2	2		1953	Wembley	2	2
1895	Goodison Park	3	0		1954	Glasgow (WC)	4	2
1896	Glasgow	1	2		1955	Wembley	7	2
1897	Crystal Palace	1	2		1956	Glasgow	1	1
1898	Glasgow	3	1		1957	Wembley	2	1
1899	Birmingham	2	1		1958	Glasgow	4	0
1900	Glasgow	1	4		1959	Wembley	1	0
1901	Crystal Palace	2	2		1960	Glasgow	1	1
1902	Birmingham	2	2		1961	Wembley	9	3
1903	Sheffield	1	2		1962	Glasgow	0	2
1904	Glasgow	1	0		1963	Wembley	1	2
1905	Crystal Palace	1	0		1964	Glasgow	0	1
1906	Glasgow	1	2		1965	Wembley	2	2
1907	Newcastle	1	1		1966	Glasgow	4	3
1908	Glasgow	1	1		1967	Wembley (EC)	2	3
1909	Crystal Palace	2	0		1968	Glasgow (EC)	1	1
1910	Glasgow	0	2		1969	Wembley	4	1
1911	Goodison Park	1	1		1970	Glasgow	0	0
1912	Glasgow	1	1		1971	Wembley	3	1
1913	Stamford Bridge	1	0		1972	Glasgow	1	0
1914	Glasgow	1	3		1973	Glasgow	5	0
1920	Sheffield	5	4		1973	Wembley	1	0
1921	Glasgow	0	3		1974	Glasgow	0	2
1922	Birmingham	0	1		1975	Wembley	5	1
1923	Glasgow	2	2		1976	Glasgow	1	2
1924	Wembley	1	1		1977	Wembley	1	2
1925	Glasgow	0	2		1978	Glasgow	1	0
1926	Manchester	0	1		1979	Wembley	3	1
1927	Glasgow	2	1		1980	Glasgow	2	0
1928	Wembley	1	5		1981	Wembley	0	1
1929	Glasgow	0	1		1982	Glasgow	1	0
1930	Wembley	5	2		1983	Wembley	2	0
1931	Glasgow	0	2		1984	Glasgow	1	1
1932	Wembley	3	0		1985	Glasgow	0	1
1933	Glasgow	1	2		1986	Wembley	2	1
1934	Wembley	3	0		1987	Glasgow	0	0
1935	Glasgow	0	2		1988	Wembley	1	0
1936	Wembley	1	1		1989	Glasgow	2	0
1937	Glasgow	1	3		1996	Wembley (EC)	2	0
1938	Wembley	0	1		1999	Glasgow (EC)	2	0
1939	Glasgow	2	1		1999	Wembley (EC)	0	1
1947	Wembley	1	1		2013	Wembley	3	2
1948	Glasgow	2	0		2014	Glasgow	3	1
1949	Wembley	1	3		2016	Wembley (WC)	3	0
1950	Glasgow (WC)	1	0		2017	Glasgow (WC)	2	2
1951	Wembley	2	3					

ENGLAND v WALES

Played 102; England won 67; Wales 14; drawn 21; Goals: England 247 Wales 91

Year	Venue	E	W		Year	Venue	E	W
1879	The Oval	2	1		1891	Sunderland	4	1
1880	Wrexham	3	2		1892	Wrexham	2	0
1881	Blackburn	0	1		1893	Stoke	6	0
1882	Wrexham	3	5		1894	Wrexham	5	1
1883	The Oval	5	0		1895	Queens Club, London	1	1
1884	Wrexham	4	0		1896	Cardiff	9	1
1885	Blackburn	1	1		1897	Bramall Lane	4	0
1886	Wrexham	3	1		1898	Wrexham	3	0
1887	The Oval	4	0		1899	Bristol	4	0
1888	Crewe	5	1		1900	Cardiff	1	1
1889	Stoke	4	1		1901	Newcastle	6	0
1890	Wrexham	3	1		1902	Wrexham	0	0
					1903	Portsmouth	2	1

Year	Venue				Year	Venue		
1904	Wrexham	2	2		1954	Wembley	3	2
1905	Anfield	3	1		1955	Cardiff	1	2
1906	Cardiff	1	0		1956	Wembley	3	1
1907	Fulham	1	1		1957	Cardiff	4	0
1908	Wrexham	7	1		1958	Villa Park	2	2
1909	Nottingham	2	0		1959	Cardiff	1	1
1910	Cardiff	1	0		1960	Wembley	5	1
1911	Millwall	3	0		1961	Cardiff	1	1
1912	Wrexham	2	0		1962	Wembley	4	0
1913	Bristol	4	3		1963	Cardiff	4	0
1914	Cardiff	2	0		1964	Wembley	2	1
1920	Highbury	1	2		1965	Cardiff	0	0
1921	Cardiff	0	0		1966	Wembley (EC)	5	1
1922	Anfield	1	0		1967	Cardiff (EC)	3	0
1923	Cardiff	2	2		1969	Wembley	2	1
1924	Blackburn	1	2		1970	Cardiff	1	1
1925	Swansea	2	1		1971	Wembley	0	0
1926	Selhurst Park	1	3		1972	Cardiff	3	0
1927	Wrexham	3	3		1972	Cardiff (WC)	1	0
1927	Burnley	1	2		1973	Wembley (WC)	1	1
1928	Swansea	3	2		1973	Wembley	3	0
1929	Stamford Bridge	6	0		1974	Cardiff	2	0
1930	Wrexham	4	0		1975	Wembley	2	2
1931	Anfield	3	1		1976	Wrexham	2	1
1932	Wrexham	0	0		1976	Cardiff	1	0
1933	Newcastle	1	2		1977	Wembley	0	1
1934	Cardiff	4	0		1978	Cardiff	3	1
1935	Wolverhampton	1	2		1979	Wembley	0	0
1936	Cardiff	1	2		1980	Wrexham	1	4
1937	Middlesbrough	2	1		1981	Wembley	0	0
1938	Cardiff	2	4		1982	Cardiff	1	0
1946	Maine Road	3	0		1983	Wembley	2	1
1947	Cardiff	3	0		1984	Wrexham	0	1
1948	Villa Park	1	0		2004	Old Trafford (WC)	2	0
1949	Cardiff (WC)	4	1		2005	Cardiff (WC)	1	0
1950	Sunderland	4	2		2011	Cardiff (EC)	2	0
1951	Cardiff	1	1		2011	Wembley (EC)	1	0
1952	Wembley	5	2		2016	Lens (EC)	2	1
1953	Cardiff (WC)	4	1					

ENGLAND v N IRELAND

Played 98; England won 75; Ireland 7; drawn 16 Goals: England 323, Ireland 81

Year	Venue	E	I		Year	Venue	E	I
1882	Belfast	13	0		1902	Belfast	1	0
1883	Aigburth, Liverpool	7	0		1903	Wolverhampton	4	0
1884	Belfast	8	1		1904	Belfast	3	1
1885	Whalley Range	4	0		1905	Middlesbrough	1	1
1886	Belfast	6	1		1906	Belfast	5	0
1887	Bramall Lane	7	0		1907	Goodison Park	1	0
1888	Belfast	5	1		1908	Belfast	3	1
1889	Goodison Park	6	1		1909	Bradford PA	4	0
1890	Belfast	9	1		1910	Belfast	1	1
1891	Wolverhampton	6	1		1911	Derby	2	1
1892	Belfast	2	0		1912	Dublin	6	1
1893	Perry Barr	6	1		1913	Belfast	1	2
1894	Belfast	2	2		1914	Middlesbrough	0	3
1895	Derby	9	0		1919	Belfast	1	1
1896	Belfast	2	0		1920	Sunderland	2	0
1897	Nottingham	6	0		1921	Belfast	1	1
1898	Belfast	3	2		1922	West Bromwich	2	0
1899	Sunderland	13	2		1923	Belfast	1	2
1900	Dublin	2	0		1924	Goodison Park	3	1
1901	Southampton	3	0		1925	Belfast	0	0
					1926	Anfield	3	3

1927	Belfast	0	2
1928	Goodison Park	2	1
1929	Belfast	3	0
1930	Bramall Lane	5	1
1931	Belfast	6	2
1932	Blackpool	1	0
1933	Belfast	3	0
1935	Goodison Park	2	1
1935	Belfast	3	1
1936	Stoke	3	1
1937	Belfast	5	1
1938	Old Trafford	7	0
1946	Belfast	7	2
1947	Goodison Park	2	2
1948	Belfast	6	2
1949	Maine Road (WC)	9	2
1950	Belfast	4	1
1951	Villa Park	2	0
1952	Belfast	2	2
1953	Goodison Park (WC)	3	1
1954	Belfast	2	0
1955	Wembley	3	0
1956	Belfast	1	1
1957	Wembley	2	3
1958	Belfast	3	3
1959	Wembley	2	1
1960	Belfast	5	2
1961	Wembley	1	1
1962	Belfast	3	1
1963	Wembley	8	3
1964	Belfast	4	3
1965	Wembley	2	1
1966	Belfast (EC)	2	0
1967	Wembley (EC)	2	0
1969	Belfast	3	1
1970	Wembley	3	1
1971	Belfast	1	0
1972	Wembley	0	1
1973	*Goodison Park	2	1
1974	Wembley	1	0
1975	Belfast	0	0
1976	Wembley	4	0
1977	Belfast	2	1
1978	Wembley	1	0
1979	Wembley (EC)	4	0
1979	Belfast	2	0
1979	Belfast (EC)	5	1
1980	Wembley	1	1
1982	Wembley	4	0
1983	Belfast	0	0
1984	Wembley	1	0
1985	Belfast (WC)	1	0
1985	Wembley (WC)	0	0
1986	Wembley (EC)	3	0
1987	Belfast (EC)	2	0
2005	Old Trafford (WC)	4	0
2005	Belfast (WC)	0	1

(*Switched from Belfast because of political situation)

SCOTLAND v WALES

Played 107; Scotland won 61; Wales 23; drawn 23; Goals: Scotland 243, Wales 124

		S	W
1876	Glasgow	4	0
1877	Wrexham	2	0
1878	Glasgow	9	0
1879	Wrexham	3	0
1880	Glasgow	5	1
1881	Wrexham	5	1
1882	Glasgow	5	0
1883	Wrexham	3	0
1884	Glasgow	4	1
1885	Wrexham	8	1
1886	Glasgow	4	1
1887	Wrexham	2	0
1888	Edinburgh	5	1
1889	Wrexham	0	0
1890	Paisley	5	0
1891	Wrexham	4	3
1892	Edinburgh	6	1
1893	Wrexham	8	0
1894	Kilmarnock	5	2
1895	Wrexham	2	2
1896	Dundee	4	0
1897	Wrexham	2	2
1898	Motherwell	5	2
1899	Wrexham	6	0
1900	Aberdeen	5	2
1901	Wrexham	1	1
1902	Greenock	5	1
1903	Cardiff	1	0
1904	Dundee	1	1
1905	Wrexham	1	3
1906	Edinburgh	0	2
1907	Wrexham	0	1
1908	Dundee	2	1
1909	Wrexham	2	3
1910	Kilmarnock	1	0
1911	Cardiff	2	2
1912	Tynecastle	1	0
1913	Wrexham	0	0
1914	Glasgow	0	0
1920	Cardiff	1	1
1921	Aberdeen	2	1
1922	Wrexham	1	2
1923	Paisley	2	0
1924	Cardiff	0	2
1925	Tynecastle	3	1
1926	Cardiff	3	0
1927	Glasgow	3	0
1928	Wrexham	2	2
1929	Glasgow	4	2
1930	Cardiff	4	2
1931	Glasgow	1	1
1932	Wrexham	3	2
1933	Edinburgh	2	5
1934	Cardiff	2	3
1935	Aberdeen	3	2
1936	Cardiff	1	1
1937	Dundee	1	2
1938	Cardiff	1	2
1939	Edinburgh	3	2
1946	Wrexham	1	3
1947	Glasgow	1	2

Year	Venue			Year	Venue		
1948	Cardiff (WC)	3	1	1972	Glasgow	1	0
1949	Glasgow	2	0	1973	Wrexham	2	0
1950	Cardiff	3	1	1974	Glasgow	2	0
1951	Glasgow	0	1	1975	Cardiff	2	2
1952	Cardiff (WC)	2	1	1976	Glasgow	3	1
1953	Glasgow	3	3	1977	Glasgow (WC)	1	0
1954	Cardiff	1	0	1977	Wrexham	0	0
1955	Glasgow	2	0	1977	Anfield (WC)	2	0
1956	Cardiff	2	2	1978	Glasgow	1	1
1957	Glasgow	1	1	1979	Cardiff	0	3
1958	Cardiff	3	0	1980	Glasgow	1	0
1959	Glasgow	1	1	1981	Swansea	0	2
1960	Cardiff	0	2	1982	Glasgow	1	0
1961	Glasgow	2	0	1983	Cardiff	2	0
1962	Cardiff	3	2	1984	Glasgow	2	1
1963	Glasgow	2	1	1985	Glasgow (WC)	0	1
1964	Cardiff	2	3	1985	Cardiff (WC)	1	1
1965	Glasgow (EC)	4	1	1997	Kilmarnock	0	1
1966	Cardiff (EC)	1	1	2004	Cardiff	0	4
1967	Glasgow	3	2	2009	Cardiff	0	3
1969	Wrexham	0	3	2011	Dublin (CC)	3	1
1970	Glasgow	0	0	2012	Cardiff (WC)	1	2
1971	Cardiff	0	0	2013	Glasgow (WC	1	2

SCOTLAND v NORTHERN IRELAND

Played 96; Scotland won 64; Northern Ireland 15; drawn 17; Goals: Scotland 258, Northern Ireland 80

Year	Venue	S	I	Year	Venue	S	I
1884	Belfast	5	0	1924	Glasgow	2	0
1885	Glasgow	8	2	1925	Belfast	3	0
1886	Belfast	7	2	1926	Glasgow	4	0
1887	Belfast	4	1	1927	Belfast	2	0
1888	Belfast	10	2	1928	Glasgow	0	1
1889	Glasgow	7	0	1929	Belfast	7	3
1890	Belfast	4	1	1930	Glasgow	3	1
1891	Glasgow	2	1	1931	Belfast	0	0
1892	Belfast	3	2	1932	Glasgow	3	1
1893	Glasgow	6	1	1933	Belfast	4	0
1894	Belfast	2	1	1934	Glasgow	1	2
1895	Glasgow	3	1	1935	Belfast	1	2
1896	Belfast	3	3	1936	Edinburgh	2	1
1897	Glasgow	5	1	1937	Belfast	3	1
1898	Belfast	3	0	1938	Aberdeen	1	1
1899	Glasgow	9	1	1939	Belfast	2	0
1900	Belfast	3	0	1946	Glasgow	0	0
1901	Glasgow	11	0	1947	Belfast	0	2
1902	Belfast	5	1	1948	Glasgow	3	2
1902	Belfast	3	0	1949	Belfast	8	2
1903	Glasgow	0	2	1950	Glasgow	6	1
1904	Dublin	1	1	1951	Belfast	3	0
1905	Glasgow	4	0	1952	Glasgow	1	1
1906	Dublin	1	0	1953	Belfast	3	1
1907	Glasgow	3	0	1954	Glasgow	2	2
1908	Dublin	5	0	1955	Belfast	1	2
1909	Glasgow	5	0	1956	Glasgow	1	0
1910	Belfast	0	1	1957	Belfast	1	1
1911	Glasgow	2	0	1958	Glasgow	2	2
1912	Belfast	4	1	1959	Belfast	4	0
1913	Dublin	2	1	1960	Glasgow	5	1
1914	Belfast	1	1	1961	Belfast	6	1
1920	Glasgow	3	0	1962	Glasgow	5	1
1921	Belfast	2	0	1963	Belfast	1	2
1922	Glasgow	2	1	1964	Glasgow	3	2
1923	Belfast	1	0	1965	Belfast	2	3
				1966	Glasgow	2	1

Year	Venue			Year	Venue		
1967	Belfast	0	1	1980	Belfast	0	1
1969	Glasgow	1	1	1981	Glasgow (WC)	1	1
1970	Belfast	1	0	1981	Glasgow	2	0
1971	Glasgow	0	1	1981	Belfast (WC)	0	0
1972	Glasgow	2	0	1982	Belfast	1	1
1973	Glasgow	1	2	1983	Glasgow	0	0
1974	Glasgow	0	1	1984	Belfast	0	2
1975	Glasgow	3	0	1992	Glasgow	1	0
1976	Glasgow	3	0	2008	Glasgow	0	0
1977	Glasgow	3	0	2011	Dublin (CC)	3	0
1978	Glasgow	1	1	2015	Glasgow	1	0
1979	Glasgow	1	0			W	I

WALES v NORTHERN IRELAND

Played 97; Wales won 45; Northern Ireland won 27; drawn 25; Goals: Wales 191 Northern Ireland 132

Year	Venue			Year	Venue		
1882	Wrexham	7	1	1936	Belfast	2	3
1883	Belfast	1	1	1937	Wrexham	4	1
1884	Wrexham	6	0	1938	Belfast	0	1
1885	Belfast	8	2	1939	Wrexham	3	1
1886	Wrexham	5	0	1947	Belfast	1	2
1887	Belfast	1	4	1948	Wrexham	2	0
1888	Wrexham	11	0	1949	Belfast	2	0
1889	Belfast	3	1	1950	Wrexham (WC)	0	0
1890	Shrewsbury	5	2	1951	Belfast	2	1
1891	Belfast	2	7	1952	Swansea	3	0
1892	Bangor	1	1	1953	Belfast	3	2
1893	Belfast	3	4	1954	Wrexham (WC)	1	2
1894	Swansea	4	1	1955	Belfast	3	2
1895	Belfast	2	2	1956	Cardiff	1	1
1896	Wrexham	6	1	1957	Belfast	0	0
1897	Belfast	3	4	1958	Cardiff	1	1
1898	Llandudno	0	1	1959	Belfast	1	4
1899	Belfast	0	1	1960	Wrexham	3	2
1900	Llandudno	2	0	1961	Belfast	5	1
1901	Belfast	1	0	1962	Cardiff	4	0
1902	Cardiff	0	3	1963	Belfast	4	1
1903	Belfast	0	2	1964	Swansea	2	3
1904	Bangor	0	1	1965	Belfast	5	0
1905	Belfast	2	2	1966	Cardiff	1	4
1906	Wrexham	4	4	1967	Belfast (EC)	0	0
1907	Belfast	3	2	1968	Wrexham (EC)	2	0
1908	Aberdare	0	1	1969	Belfast	0	0
1909	Belfast	3	2	1970	Swansea	1	0
1910	Wrexham	4	1	1971	Belfast	0	1
1911	Belfast	2	1	1972	Wrexham	0	0
1912	Cardiff	2	3	1973	*Goodison Park	0	1
1913	Belfast	1	0	1974	Belfast	1	0
1914	Wrexham	1	2	1975	Belfast	0	1
1920	Belfast	2	2	1976	Swansea	1	0
1921	Swansea	2	1	1977	Belfast	1	1
1922	Belfast	1	1	1978	Wrexham	1	0
1923	Wrexham	0	3	1979	Belfast	1	1
1924	Belfast	1	0	1980	Cardiff	0	1
1925	Wrexham	0	0	1982	Wrexham	3	0
1926	Belfast	0	3	1983	Belfast	1	0
1927	Cardiff	2	2	1984	Swansea	1	1
1928	Belfast	2	1	2004	Cardiff (WC)	2	2
1929	Wrexham	2	2	2005	Belfast (WC)	3	2
1930	Belfast	0	7	2007	Belfast	0	0
1931	Wrexham	3	2	2008	Glasgow	0	0
1932	Belfast	0	4	2011	Dublin (CC)	2	0
1933	Wrexham	4	1	2016	Cardiff	1	1
1934	Belfast	1	1	2016	Paris (EC)	1	0
1935	Wrexham	3	1	(*Switched from Belfast because of political situation)			

WORLD CUP 2018 QUALIFYING

For England, the continuation of a near eight-year unbeaten run in qualifying matches. For Scotland, a case of so near, yet so far. Gordon Strachan's team were on the brink of forcing their way into contention for a place in the World Cup in Russia when two identical free-kicks from Celtic's Leigh Griffiths established a 2-1 lead going into extra-time at Hampden Park. That would have left them neck-and-neck with Slovakia and Slovenia for the runners-up spot in Group F and the chance of progressing to the play-offs. Instead, new captain Harry Kane's 92nd equaliser for England left them trailing and probably needing three wins in the final four group matches. England still have work to do to ensure automatic qualification, notably against Slovakia at Wembley on September 4, with two points separating the two sides. They have not lost in 35 qualifiers since a 1-0 defeat by Ukraine in October 2009, but questions remain about the team's performance, not least whether Joe Hart remains the No 1 choice of goalkeeper. An injury-time winner by Stuart Dallas in Azerbaijan left Northern Ireland with a four-point cushion in second place in Group C. Victory in San Marino, when the group resumes on September 1, could extend that lead to seven points, with the Czech Republic facing Germany on the same day. If so, the Irish would have a golden chance of guaranteeing a place in the play-offs three days later when facing the Czechs at Windsor Park. For Wales, five draws in six qualifiers have dampened the euphoria of reaching the European Championship semi-finals. They trail Serbia and the Republic of Ireland by four points and need to resume with a victory over Austria in Cardiff on September 2. If so, their return fixture with the Republic will begin to assume huge significance for Chris Coleman and Martin O'Neill.

Russia is staging the tournament for the first time. Draw for the finals will be held in the Kremlin on December 1. The opening match, involving Russia, is on Thursday, June 14, 2018 in the capital's 81,000-capacity Luzhniki Stadium. It will also stage the final on Sunday, July 15. Other venues, with provisional capacities, are Moscow's Spartak Stadium (42,000), St Petersburg (68,000), Sochi (47,000), Ekaterinburg (45,000), Kazan (45,000), Nizhny Novgorod (45,000), Rostov-on-Don (45,000), Samara (45,000), Saransk (45,000), Volgograd (45,000), Kaliningrad (35,000).

QUALIFYING TO-DATE

EUROPE
(Group winners qualify, plus winners of play-off matches involving eight best runners up. Russia qualify as hosts)

GROUP A

	P	W	D	L	F	A	Pts
Sweden	6	4	1	1	12	4	13
France	6	4	1	1	11	5	13
Holland	6	3	1	2	13	6	10
Bulgaria	6	3	0	3	9	12	9
Belarus	6	1	2	3	4	11	5
Luxembourg	6	0	1	5	6	17	1

Results: Belarus 0 France 0, Bulgaria 4 Luxembourg 3, Sweden 1 Holland 1, France 4 Bulgaria 1, Luxembourg 0 Sweden 1, Holland 4 Belarus 1, Belarus 1 Luxembourg 1, Holland 0 France 1, Sweden 3 Bulgaria 0, France 2 Sweden 1, Bulgaria 1 Belarus 0, Luxembourg 1 Holland 3, Sweden 4 Belarus 0, Bulgaria 2 Holland 0, Luxembourg 1 France 3, Belarus 2 Bulgaria 1, Holland 5 Luxembourg 0, Sweden 2 France 1

To play – Aug 31: Bulgaria v Sweden, France v Holland, Luxembourg v Belarus; Sep 3: Belarus v Sweden, Holland v Bulgaria, France v Luxembourg; Oct 7: Sweden v Luxembourg, Belarus v Holland, Bulgaria v France; Oct 10: France v Belarus, Luxembourg v Bulgaria, Holland v Sweden

GROUP B

	P	W	D	L	F	A	Pts
Switzerland	6	6	0	0	12	3	18
Portugal	6	5	0	1	22	3	15
Hungary	6	2	1	3	8	7	7
Faroe Is	6	1	2	3	2	10	5
Andorra	6	1	1	4	2	13	4
Latvia	6	1	0	5	2	12	3

Results: Switzerland 2 Portugal 0, Andorra 0 Latvia 1, Faroe Is 0 Hungary 0, Latvia 0 Faroe Is 2, Hungary 2 Switzerland 3, Portugal 6 Andorra 0, Andorra 1 Switzerland 2, Faroe Is 0 Portugal 6, Latvia 0 Hungary 2, Switzerland 2 Faroe Is 0, Hungary 4 Andorra 0, Portugal 4 Latvia 1, Andorra 0 Faroe Is 0, Switzerland 1 Latvia 0, Portugal 3 Hungary 0, Andorra 1 Hungary 0, Faroe Is 0 Switzerland 2, Latvia 0 Portugal 3
To play – Aug 31: Hungary v Latvia, Portugal v Faroe Is, Switzerland v Andorra; Sep 3: Faroe Is v Andorra, Hungary v Portugal, Latvia v Switzerland; Oct 7: Faroe Is v Latvia, Andorra v Portugal, Switzerland v Hungary; Oct 10: Hungary v Faroe Is, Latvia v Andorra, Portugal v Switzerland

GROUP C

	P	W	D	L	F	A	Pts
Germany	6	6	0	0	27	1	18
N Ireland	6	4	1	1	11	2	13
Czech Rep	6	2	3	1	9	5	9
Azerbaijan	6	2	1	3	3	9	7
Norway	6	1	1	4	6	10	4
San Marino	6	0	0	6	1	30	0

Results: San Marino 0 Azerbaijan 1, Czech Republic 0 N Ireland 0, Norway 0 Germany 3, Azerbaijan 1 Norway 0, Germany 3 Czech Rep 0, N Ireland 4 San Marino 0, Czech Rep 0 Azerbaijan 0, Germany 2 N Ireland 0, Norway 4 San Marino 1, Czech Rep 2 Norway 1, N Ireland 4 Azerbaijan 0, San Marino 0 Germany 8, Azerbaijan 1 Germany 4, San Marino 0 Czech Rep 6, N Ireland 2 Norway 0, Azerbaijan 0 N Ireland 1, Germany 7 San Marino 0, Norway 1 Czech Rep 1
To play – Sep 1: San Marino v N Ireland, Czech Rep v Germany, Norway v Azerbaijan; Sep 4: N Ireland v Czech Rep, Azerbaijan v San Marino, Germany v Norway; Oct 5: N Ireland v Germany, Azerbaijan v Czech Rep, San Marino v Norway; Oct 8: Norway v Northern Ireland, Czech Rep v San Marino, Germany v Azerbaijan

GROUP D

	P	W	D	L	F	A	Pts
Serbia	6	3	3	0	13	7	12
Rep of Ireland	6	3	3	0	8	4	12
Wales	6	1	5	0	9	5	8
Austria	6	2	2	2	9	8	8
Georgia	6	0	3	3	6	10	3
Moldova	6	0	2	4	4	15	2

Results: Georgia 1 Austria 2, Serbia 2 Rep of Ireland 2, Wales 4 Moldova 0, Austria 2 Wales 2, Moldova 0 Serbia 3, Rep of Ireland 1 Georgia 0, Serbia 3 Austria 2, Wales 1 Georgia 1, Moldova 1 Rep of Ireland 3, Wales 1 Serbia 1, Austria 0 Rep of Ireland 1, Georgia 1 Moldova 1, Georgia 1 Serbia 3, Austria 2 Moldova 0, Rep of Ireland 0 Wales 0, Moldova 2 Georgia 2, Rep of Ireland 1 Austria 1, Serbia 1 Wales 1
To play – Sep 2: Wales v Austria, Georgia v Rep of Ireland, Serbia v Moldova; Sept 5: Moldova v

Wales, Republic of Ireland v Serbia, Austria v Georgia; Oct 6: Georgia v Wales, Rep of Ireland v Moldova, Austria v Serbia Oct 9: Wales v Rep of Ireland, Moldova v Austria, Serbia v Georgia

GROUP E

	P	W	D	L	F	A	Pts
Poland	6	5	1	0	15	7	16
Montenegro	6	3	1	2	14	7	10
Denmark	6	3	1	2	10	6	10
Romania	6	1	3	2	7	7	6
Armenia	6	2	0	4	7	14	6
Kazakhstan	6	0	2	4	4	16	2

Results: Denmark 1 Armenia 0, Kazakhstan 2 Poland 2, Romania 1 Montenegro 1, Armenia 0 Romania 5, Montenegro 5 Kazakhstan 0, Poland 3 Denmark 2, Kazakhstan 0 Romania 0, Denmark 0 Montenegro 1, Poland 2 Armenia 1, Denmark 4 Kazakhstan 1, Romania 0 Poland 3, Armenia 3 Montenegro 2, Armenia 2 Kazakhstan 0, Montenegro 1 Poland 2, Romania 0 Denmark 0, Kazakhstan 1 Denmark 3, Montenegro 4 Armenia 1, Poland 3 Romania 1
To play – Sep 1: Kazakhstan v Montenegro, Denmark v Poland, Romania v Armenia; Sep 4: Armenia v Denmark, Montenegro v Romania, Poland v Kazakhstan; Oct 5: Armenia v Poland, Montenegro v Denmark, Romania v Kazakhstan; Oct 8: Denmark v Romania, Kazakhstan v Armenia, Poland v Montenegro

GROUP F

	P	W	D	L	F	A	Pts
England	6	4	2	0	10	2	14
Slovakia	6	4	0	2	12	4	12
Slovenia	6	3	2	1	6	3	11
Scotland	6	2	2	2	9	10	8
Lithuania	6	1	2	3	6	11	5
Malta	6	0	0	6	2	15	0

Results: Lithuania 2 Slovenia 2, Slovakia 0 England 1, Malta 1 Scotland 5, England 2 Malta 0, Scotland 1 Lithuania 1, Slovenia 1 Slovakia 0, Slovenia 0 England 0, Malta 0 Slovenia 1, England 0 Scotland 0, Slovakia 4 Lithuania 0, Slovakia 0 Scotland 0, Lithuania 2 Malta 0, England 2 Lithuania 0, Malta 1 Slovakia 3, Scotland 1 Slovenia 0, Scotland 2 England 2, Slovenia 2 Malta 0, Lithuania 1 Slovakia 2
To play – Sep 1: Malta v England, Lithuania v Scotland, Slovakia v Slovenia; Sep 4: England v Slovakia, Scotland v Malta, Slovenia v Lithuania; Oct 5: England v Slovenia, Scotland v Slovakia, Malta v Lithuania; Oct 8: Lithuania v England, Slovenia v Scotland, Slovakia v Malta

GROUP G

	P	W	D	L	F	A	Pts
Spain	6	5	1	0	21	3	16
Italy	6	5	1	0	18	4	16
Albania	6	3	0	3	7	8	9
Israel	6	3	0	3	9	12	9
Macedonia	6	1	0	5	8	13	3
Liechtenstein	6	0	0	6	1	24	0

Results: Israel 1 Italy 3, Spain 8 Liechtenstein 0, Albania 2 Macedonia 1, Italy 1 Spain 1, Liechtenstein 0 Albania 2, Macedonia 1 Israel 2, Israel 2 Liechtenstein 1, Albania 0 Spain 2, Macedonia 2 Italy 3, Albania 0 Israel 3, Liechtenstein 0 Italy 4, Spain 4 Macedonia 0, Italy 2 Albania 0, Liechtenstein 0 Macedonia 3, Spain 4 Israel 1, Italy 5 Liechtenstein 0, Israel 0 Albania 3, Macedonia 1 Spain 2

305

To play – Sep 2: Albania v Liechtenstein, Israel v Macedonia, Spain v Italy; Sep 5: Italy v Israel, Liechtenstein v Spain, Macedonia v Albania; Oct 6: Italy v Macedonia, Liechtenstein v Israel, Spain v Albania; Oct 9: Albania v Italy, Israel v Spain, Macedonia v Liechtenstein

GROUP H

	P	W	D	L	F	A	Pts
Belgium	6	5	1	0	24	2	16
Greece	6	3	3	0	10	3	12
Bosnia-Herz	6	3	2	1	13	5	11
Cyprus	6	2	1	3	5	9	7
Estonia	6	1	1	4	5	17	4
Gibraltar	6	0	0	6	3	24	0

Results: Bosnia-Herz 5 Estonia 0, Cyprus 0 Belgium 3, Gibraltar 1 Greece 4, Belgium 4 Bosnia-Herz 0, Estonia 4 Gibraltar 0, Greece 2 Cyprus 0, Bosnia-Herz 2 Cyprus 0, Estonia 0 Greece 2, Gilbraltar 0 Belgium 6, Cyprus 3 Gibraltar 1, Belgium 8 Estonia 1, Greece 1 Bosnia-Herz 1, Cyprus 0 Estonia 0, Bosnia-Herz 5 Gibraltar 0, Belgium 1 Greece 1, Bosnia-Herz 0 Greece 0, Estonia 0 Belgium 2, Gibraltar 1 Cyprus 2
To play- Aug 31: Belgium v Gibraltar, Cyprus v Bosnia-Herz, Greece v Estonia; Sep 3: Estonia v Cyprus, Gibraltar v Bosnia-Herz, Greece v Belgium; Oct 7: Bosnia-Herz v Belgium, Gibraltar v Estonia, Cyprus v Greece; Oct 10: Belgium v Cyprus,, Estonia v Bosnia-Herz, Greece v Gibraltar

GROUP I

	P	W	D	L	F	A	Pts
Croatia	6	4	1	1	11	2	13
Iceland	6	4	1	1	9	6	13
Turkey	6	3	2	1	11	6	11
Ukraine	6	3	2	1	9	5	11
Finland	6	0	1	5	4	10	1
Kosovo	6	0	1	5	3	18	0

Results: Croatia 1 Turkey 1, Finland 1 Kosovo 1, Ukraine 1 Iceland 1, Kosovo 0 Croatia 6, Iceland 3 Finland 2, Turkey 2 Ukraine 2, Finland 0 Croatia 1, Ukraine 3 Kosovo 0, Iceland 2 Turkey 0, Croatia 2 Iceland 0, Turkey 2 Kosovo 0, Ukraine 1 Finland 0, Turkey 2 Finland 0, Croatia 1 Ukraine 0, Kosovo 1 Iceland 2, Finland 1 Ukraine 2, Iceland 1 Croatia 0, Kosovo 1 Turkey 4
To play – Sep 2: Finland v Iceland, Croatia v Kosovo, Ukraine v Turkey; Sep 5: Iceland v Ukraine, Kosovo v Finland, Turkey v Croatia; Oct 6: Croatia v Finland, Kosovo v Ukraine, Turkey v Iceland; Oct 9: Finland v Turkey, Iceland v Kosovo, Ukraine v Croatia

SOUTH AMERICA
(Top four qualify. Fifth team meet winner of Oceania group in play-off)

	P	W	D	L	F	A	Pts
Brazil	14	10	3	1	35	10	33
Colombia	14	7	3	4	18	15	24
Uruguay	14	7	2	5	26	17	23
Chile	14	7	2	5	24	19	23
Argentina	14	6	4	4	15	14	22
Ecuador	14	6	2	6	23	20	20
Peru	14	5	3	6	22	23	18
Paraguay	14	5	3	6	13	21	18
Bolivia	14	3	1	10	12	32	10
Venezuela	14	1	3	10	17	34	6

AFRICA
(Group winners qualify)

GROUP A

	P	W	D	L	F	A	Pts
DR Congo	2	2	0	0	6	1	6
Tunisia	2	2	0	0	3	0	6
Guinea	2	0	0	2	1	4	0
Libya	2	0	0	2	0	5	0

GROUP B

	P	W	D	L	F	A	Pts
Nigeria	2	2	0	0	5	2	6
Cameroon	2	0	2	0	2	2	2
Zambia	2	0	1	1	2	3	1
Algeria	2	0	1	1	2	4	1

GROUP C

	P	W	D	L	F	A	Pts
Ivory Coast	2	1	1	0	3	1	4
Gabon	2	0	2	0	0	0	2
Morocco	2	0	2	0	0	0	2
Mali	2	0	1	1	1	3	1

GROUP D

	P	W	D	L	F	A	Pts
Burkina Faso	2	1	1	0	3	1	4
South Africa	2	1	1	0	3	2	4
Senegal	2	1	0	1	3	2	3
Cape Verde	2	0	0	2	0	4	0

GROUP E

	P	W	D	L	F	A	Pts
Egypt	2	2	0	0	4	1	6
Uganda	2	1	1	0	1	0	4
Ghana	2	0	1	1	0	2	1
Rep Congo	2	0	0	2	1	3	0

ASIA
(Top two from each group qualify. Third-placed teams in play-off - winner meeting fourth-placed CONCACAF side)

GROUP A

	P	W	D	L	F	A	Pts
Iran	7	5	2	0	6	0	17
South Korea	7	4	1	2	9	7	13
Uzbekistan	7	4	0	3	6	4	12
Syria	7	2	2	3	2	3	8
China	7	1	2	4	3	7	5
Qatar	7	1	1	5	3	8	4

GROUP B

	P	W	D	L	F	A	Pts
Japan	7	5	1	1	14	5	16
Saudi Arabia	8	5	1	2	15	8	16
Australia	8	4	4	0	14	8	16
UAE	7	3	0	4	7	10	9
Iraq	7	1	1	5	7	10	4
Thailand	7	0	1	6	3	19	1

NORTH, CENTRAL AMERICA AND CARIBBEAN (CONCACAF)
(Top three qualify, fourth in play-off with Asia play-off winner)

	P	W	D	L	F	A	Pts
Mexico	6	4	2	0	9	2	14
Costa Rica	5	2	2	1	7	3	8
USA	6	2	2	2	11	8	8
Panama	5	1	3	1	2	2	6
Honduras	5	1	1	3	4	12	4
Trinidad & Tobago	5	1	0	4	2	8	3

OCEANIA
(Top team in each group meet, winner in play-off with fifth side in South America group)

GROUP A

	P	W	D	L	F	A	Pts
New Zealand	4	3	1	0	6	0	10
New Caledonia	4	1	2	1	4	5	5
Fiji	4	0	1	3	3	8	1

GROUP B

	P	W	D	L	F	A	Pts
Tahiti	4	2	0	2	7	4	6
Solomon Is	3	2	0	1	4	5	6
Papua New Guinea	3	1	0	2	5	7	3

THE THINGS THEY SAY ...

'It was the most abject, embarrassing 45 minutes of football I have seen from any team at any level' – **Alan Shearer**, Match of the Day pundit, on Swansea's first-half performance against Manchester United when they trailed 3-0.

'Great win, nice story, unfortunately we were on the end of it' – **Jurgen Klopp**, Liverpool manager, after his side surrendered a 3-1 lead to lose 4-3 at Bournemouth.

'This is arguably the most significant and most exciting appointment the club has made in its modern history' – **Carolyn Radford**, Mansfield's chief executive officer, on Steve Evans becoming the club's new manager.

'It shows just how far the ordinary fan has slipped down the pecking order in the modern game. Picking a time of 11.30am is particularly insulting' – **Fulham Supporters Trust** criticising a Sunday morning kick-off for the club's FA Cup tie at Cardiff.

WORLD CUP SUMMARIES 1930–2014

1930 – URUGUAY

WINNERS: Uruguay **RUNNERS-UP:** Argentina **THIRD:** USA **FOURTH:** Yugoslavia
Other countries taking part: Belgium, Bolivia, Brazil, Chile, France, Mexico, Paraguay, Peru, Romania. **Total entries:** 13
Venue: All matches played in Montevideo
Top scorer: Stabile (Argentina) 8 goals
Final (30/7/30): **Uruguay 4** (Dorado 12, Cea 55, Iriarte 64, Castro 89) **Argentina 2** (Peucelle 29, Stabile 35). **Att:** 90,000
Uruguay: Botasso; Nasazzi (capt), Mascheroni, Andrade, Fernandez, Gestido, Dorado, Scarone, Castro, Cea, Iriarte
Argentina: Botasso; Della Torre, Paternoster, J Evaristo, Monti, Suarez, Peucelle, Varallo, Stabile, Ferreira (capt), M Evaristo
Referee: Langenus (Belgium). **Half-time:** 1-2

1934 – ITALY

WINNERS: Italy **RUNNERS-UP:** Czechoslovakia **THIRD:** Germany **FOURTH:** Austria
Other countries in finals: Argentina, Belgium, Brazil, Egypt, France, Holland, Hungary, Romania, Spain, Sweden, Switzerland, USA. **Total entries:** 29 (16 qualifiers)
Venues: Bologna, Florence, Genoa, Milan, Naples, Rome, Trieste, Turin
Top scorers: Conen (Germany), Nejedly (Czechoslovakia), Schiavio (Italy), each 4 goals. **Final** (Rome, 10/6/34): **Italy 2** (Orsi 82, Schiavio 97) **Czechoslovakia 1** (Puc 70) after extra-time.
Att: 50,000
Italy: Combi (capt); Monzeglio, Allemandi, Ferraris, Monti, Bertolini, Guaita, Meazza, Schiavio, Ferrari, Orsi
Czechoslovakia: Planicka (capt); Zenisek, Ctyroky, Kostalek, Cambal, Krcil, Junek, Svoboda, Sobotka, Nejedly, Puc
Referee: Eklind (Sweden). **Half-time:** 0-0 (90 mins: 1-1)

1938 – FRANCE

WINNERS: Italy **RUNNERS-UP:** Hungary **THIRD:** Brazil **FOURTH:** Sweden
Other countries in finals: Belgium, Cuba, Czechoslovakia, Dutch East Indies, France, Germany, Holland, Norway, Poland, Romania, Switzerland. **Total entries:** 25 (15 qualifiers)
Venues: Antibes, Bordeaux, Le Havre, Lille, Marseille, Paris, Reims, Strasbourg, Toulouse
Top scorer: Leonidas (Brazil) 8 goals
Final (Paris, 19/6/38): **Italy 4** (Colaussi 6, 36, Piola 15, 81) **Hungary 2** (Titkos 7, Sarosi 65). **Att:** 45,000
Italy: Olivieri; Foni, Rava, Serantoni, Andreolo, Locatelli, Biavati, Meazza (capt), Piola, Ferrari, Colaussi
Hungary: Szabo; Polgar, Biro, Szalay, Szucs, Lazar, Sas, Vincze, Sarosi (capt), Szengeller, Titkos
Referee: Capdeville (France). **Half-time:** 3-1

1950 – BRAZIL

WINNERS: Uruguay **RUNNERS-UP:** Brazil **THIRD:** Sweden **FOURTH:** Spain
Other countries in finals: Bolivia, Chile, England, Italy, Mexico, Paraguay, Switzerland, USA, Yugoslavia. **Total entries:** 29 (13 qualifiers)
Venues: Belo Horizonte, Curitiba, Porto Alegre, Recife, Rio de Janeiro, Sao Paulo
Top scorer: Ademir (Brazil) 9 goals
Deciding Match (Rio de Janeiro, 16/7/50): **Uruguay 2** (Schiaffino 64, Ghiggia 79) **Brazil 1** (Friaca 47). **Att:** 199,850
(For the only time, the World Cup was decided on a final pool system, in which the winners of the four qualifying groups met in a six-match series So, unlike previous and subsequent

tournaments, there was no official final as such, but Uruguay v Brazil was the deciding match in the final pool)

Uruguay: Maspoli; Gonzales, Tejera, Gambetta, Varela (capt), Andrade, Ghiggia, Perez, Miguez, Schiaffino, Moran

Brazil: Barbosa; Augusto (capt), Juvenal, Bauer, Danilo, Bigode, Friaca, Zizinho, Ademir, Jair, Chico

Referee: Reader (England). **Half-time:** 0-0

1954 – SWITZERLAND

WINNERS: West Germany RUNNERS-UP: Hungary THIRD: Austria FOURTH: Uruguay
Other countries in finals: Belgium, Brazil, Czechoslovakia, England, France, Italy, Korea, Mexico, Scotland, Switzerland, Turkey, Yugoslavia. **Total entries:** 35 (16 qualifiers)
Venues: Basle, Berne, Geneva, Lausanne, Lugano, Zurich
Top scorer: Kocsis (Hungary) 11 goals
Final (Berne, 4/7/54): **West Germany 3** (Morlock 12, Rahn 17, 84) **Hungary 2** (Puskas 4, Czibor 9). **Att:** 60,000
West Germany: Turek; Posipal, Kohlmeyer, Eckel, Liebrich, Mai, Rahn, Morlock, O Walter, F Walter (capt), Schaefer
Hungary: Grosics; Buzansky, Lantos, Bozsik, Lorant, Zakarias, Czibor, Kocsis, Hidegkuti, Puskas (capt), J Toth
Referee: Ling (England). **Half-time:** 2-2

1958 – SWEDEN

WINNERS: Brazil RUNNERS-UP: Sweden THIRD: France FOURTH: West Germany
Other countries in finals: Argentina, Austria, Czechoslovakia, England, Hungary, Mexico, Northern Ireland, Paraguay, Scotland, Soviet Union, Wales, Yugoslavia. **Total entries:** 47 (16 qualifiers)
Venues: Boras, Eskilstuna, Gothenburg, Halmstad, Helsingborgs, Malmo, Norrkoping, Orebro, Sandviken, Stockholm, Vasteras
Top scorer: Fontaine (France) 13 goals
Final (Stockholm, 29/6/58): **Brazil 5** (Vava 10, 32, Pele 55, 88, Zagalo 76) **Sweden 2** (Liedholm 4, Simonsson 83). **Att:** 49,737
Brazil: Gilmar; D Santos, N Santos, Zito, Bellini (capt), Orlando, Garrincha, Didi, Vava, Pele, Zagalo
Sweden: Svensson; Bergmark, Axbom, Boerjesson, Gustavsson, Parling, Hamrin, Gren, Simonsson, Liedholm (capt), Skoglund
Referee: Guigue (France). **Half-time:** 2-1

1962 – CHILE

WINNERS: Brazil RUNNERS-UP: Czechoslovakia THIRD: Chile FOURTH: Yugoslavia
Other countries in finals: Argentina, Bulgaria, Colombia, England, Hungary, Italy, Mexico, Soviet Union, Spain, Switzerland, Uruguay, West Germany. **Total entries:** 53 (16 qualifiers)
Venues: Arica, Rancagua, Santiago, Vina del Mar
Top scorer: Jerkovic (Yugoslavia) 5 goals
Final (Santiago, 17/6/62): **Brazil 3** (Amarildo 17, Zito 69, Vava 77) **Czechoslovakia 1** (Masopust 16). **Att:** 68,679
Brazil: Gilmar; D Santos, Mauro (capt), Zozimo, N Santos, Zito, Didi, Garrincha, Vava, Amarildo, Zagalo
Czechoslovakia: Schroiff; Tichy, Novak, Pluskal, Popluhar, Masopust (capt), Pospichal, Scherer, Kvasnak, Kadraba, Jelinek
Referee: Latychev (Soviet Union). **Half-time:** 1-1

1966 – ENGLAND

WINNERS: England RUNNERS-UP: West Germany THIRD: Portugal FOURTH: USSR
Other countries in finals: Argentina, Brazil, Bulgaria, Chile, France, Hungary, Italy, Mexico, North Korea, Spain, Switzerland, Uruguay. **Total entries:** 53 (16 qualifiers)

Venues: Birmingham (Villa Park), Liverpool (Goodison Park), London (Wembley and White City), Manchester (Old Trafford), Middlesbrough (Ayresome Park), Sheffield (Hillsborough), Sunderland (Roker Park)
Top scorer: Eusebio (Portugal) 9 goals
Final (Wembley, 30/7/66): **England 4** (Hurst 19, 100, 120, Peters 78) **West Germany 2** (Haller 13, Weber 89) after extra-time. **Att:** 93,802
England: Banks; Cohen, Wilson, Stiles, J Charlton, Moore (capt), Ball, Hurst, Hunt, R Charlton, Peters
West Germany: Tilkowski; Hottges, Schnellinger, Beckenbauer, Schulz, Weber, Haller, Held, Seeler (capt), Overath, Emmerich
Referee: Dienst (Switzerland). **Half-time:** 1-1 (90 mins: 2-2)

1970 – MEXICO

WINNERS: Brazil **RUNNERS-UP:** Italy **THIRD:** West Germany **FOURTH:** Uruguay
Other countries in finals: Belgium, Bulgaria, Czechoslovakia, El Salvador, England, Israel, Mexico, Morocco, Peru, Romania, Soviet Union, Sweden. **Total entries:** 68 (16 qualifiers)
Venues: Guadalajara, Leon, Mexico City, Puebla, Toluca
Top scorer: Muller (West Germany) 10 goals
Final (Mexico City, 21/6/70): **Brazil 4** (Pele 18, Gerson 66, Jairzinho 71, Carlos Alberto 87) **Italy 1** (Boninsegna 38). **Att:** 107,412
Brazil: Felix, Carlos Alberto (capt), Brito, Piazza, Everaldo, Clodoaldo, Gerson, Jairzinho, Tostao, Pele, Rivelino
Italy: Albertosi; Burgnich, Facchetti (capt), Cera, Rosato, Bertini (Juliano 72), Domenghini, De Sisti, Mazzola, Boninsegna (Rivera 84), Riva
Referee: Glockner (East Germany). **Half-time:** 1-1

1974 – WEST GERMANY

WINNERS: West Germany **RUNNERS-UP:** Holland **THIRD:** Poland **FOURTH:** Brazil
Other countries in finals: Argentina, Australia, Bulgaria, Chile, East Germany, Haiti, Italy, Scotland, Sweden, Uruguay, Yugoslavia, Zaire. **Total entries:** 98 (16 qualifiers)
Venues: Berlin, Dortmund, Dusseldorf, Frankfurt, Gelsenkirchen, Hamburg, Hanover, Munich, Stuttgart
Top scorer: Lato (Poland) 7 goals
Final (Munich, 7/7/74): **West Germany 2** (Breitner 25 pen, Muller 43) **Holland 1** (Neeskens 2 pen). **Att:** 77,833
West Germany: Maier; Vogts, Schwarzenbeck, Beckenbauer (capt), Breitner, Bonhof, Hoeness, Overath, Grabowski, Muller, Holzenbein
Holland: Jongbloed; Suurbier, Rijsbergen (De Jong 69), Haan, Krol, Jansen, Van Hanegem, Neeskens, Rep, Cruyff (capt), Rensenbrink (R Van der Kerkhof 46)
Referee: Taylor (England). **Half-time:** 2-1

1978 – ARGENTINA

WINNERS: Argentina **RUNNERS-UP:** Holland **THIRD:** Brazil **FOURTH:** Italy
Other countries in finals: Austria, France, Hungary, Iran, Mexico, Peru, Poland, Scotland, Spain, Sweden, Tunisia, West Germany. **Total entries:** 102 (16 qualifiers)
Venues: Buenos Aires, Cordoba, Mar del Plata, Mendoza, Rosario
Top scorer: Kempes (Argentina) 6 goals
Final (Buenos Aires, 25/6/78): **Argentina 3** (Kempes 38, 104, Bertoni 115) **Holland 1** (Nanninga 82) after extra-time. **Att:** 77,000
Argentina: Fillol; Passarella (capt), Olguin, Galvan, Tarantini, Ardiles (Larrosa 66), Gallego, Ortiz (Houseman 74), Bertoni, Luque, Kempes
Holland: Jongbloed; Krol (capt), Poortvliet, Brandts, Jansen (Suurbier 73), Haan, Neeskens, W Van der Kerkhof, Rep (Nanninga 58), R Van der Kerkhof, Rensenbrink
Referee: Gonella (Italy). **Half-time:** 1-0 (90 mins: 1-1)

1982 – SPAIN

WINNERS: Italy RUNNERS-UP: West Germany THIRD: Poland FOURTH: France
Other countries in finals: Algeria, Argentina, Austria, Belgium, Brazil, Cameroon, Chile, Czechoslovakia, El Salvador, England, Honduras, Hungary, Kuwait, New Zealand, Northern Ireland, Peru, Scotland, Soviet Union, Spain, Yugoslavia. **Total entries:** 109 (24 qualifiers)
Venues: Alicante, Barcelona, Bilbao, Coruna, Elche, Gijon, Madrid, Malaga, Oviedo, Seville, Valencia, Valladolid, Vigo, Zaragoza
Top scorer: Rossi (Italy) 6 goals
Final (Madrid, 11/7/82): **Italy** 3 (Rossi 57, Tardelli 69, Altobelli 81) **West Germany** 1 (Breitner 84). **Att:** 90,089
Italy: Zoff (capt); Bergomi, Scirea, Collovati, Cabrini, Oriali, Gentile, Tardelli, Conti, Rossi, Graziani (Altobelli 18 – Causio 88)
West Germany: Schumacher; Kaltz, Stielike, K-H Forster, B Forster, Dremmler (Hrubesch 63), Breitner, Briegel, Rummenigge (capt) (Muller 70), Fischer, Littbarski
Referee: Coelho (Brazil). **Half-time:** 0-0

1986 – MEXICO

WINNERS: Argentina RUNNERS-UP: West Germany THIRD: France FOURTH: Belgium
Other countries in finals: Algeria, Brazil, Bulgaria, Canada, Denmark, England, Hungary, Iraq, Italy, Mexico, Morocco, Northern Ireland, Paraguay, Poland, Portugal, Scotland, South Korea, Soviet Union, Spain, Uruguay. **Total entries:** 118 (24 qualifiers)
Venues: Guadalajara, Irapuato, Leon, Mexico City, Monterrey, Nezahualcoyotl, Puebla, Queretaro, Toluca
Top scorer: Lineker (England) 6 goals
Final (Mexico City, 29/6/86): **Argentina** 3 (Brown 23, Valdano 56, Burruchaga 85) **West Germany** 2 (Rummenigge 74, Voller 82). **Att:** 115,026
Argentina: Pumpido; Cuciuffo, Brown, Ruggeri, Olarticoechea, Batista, Giusti, Maradona (capt), Burruchaga (Trobbiani 89), Enrique, Valdano
West Germany: Schumacher; Berthold, K-H Forster, Jakobs, Brehme, Briegel, Eder, Matthaus, Magath (Hoeness 62), Allofs (Voller 45), Rummenigge (capt)
Referee: Filho (Brazil). **Half-time:** 1-0

1990 – ITALY

WINNERS: West Germany RUNNERS-UP: Argentina THIRD: Italy FOURTH: England
Other countries in finals: Austria, Belgium, Brazil, Cameroon, Colombia, Costa Rica, Czechoslovakia, Egypt, Holland, Republic of Ireland, Romania, Scotland, Spain, South Korea, Soviet Union, Sweden, United Arab Emirates, USA, Uruguay, Yugoslavia. **Total entries:** 103 (24 qualifiers)
Venues: Bari, Bologna, Cagliari, Florence, Genoa, Milan, Naples, Palermo, Rome, Turin, Udine, Verona
Top scorer: Schillaci (Italy) 6 goals
Final (Rome, 8/7/90): **Argentina** 0 **West Germany** 1 (Brehme 85 pen). **Att:** 73,603
Argentina: Goycochea; Ruggeri (Monzon 45), Simon, Serrizuela, Lorenzo, Basualdo, Troglio, Burruchaga (Calderon 53), Sensini, Maradona (capt), Dezotti **Sent-off**: Monzon (65), Dezotti (86) – first players ever to be sent off in World Cup Final
West Germany: Illgner; Berthold (Reuter 75), Buchwald, Augenthaler, Kohler, Brehme, Matthaus (capt), Littbarski, Hassler, Klinsmann, Voller
Referee: Codesal (Mexico). **Half-time:** 0-0

1994 – USA

WINNERS: Brazil RUNNERS-UP: Italy THIRD: Sweden FOURTH: Bulgaria
Other countries in finals: Argentina, Belgium, Bolivia, Cameroon, Colombia, Germany, Greece, Holland, Mexico, Morocco, Nigeria, Norway, Republic of Ireland, Romania, Russia, Saudi Arabia, South Korea, Spain, Switzerland, USA. **Total entries:** 144 (24 qualifiers)

Venues: Boston, Chicago, Dallas, Detroit, Los Angeles, New York City, Orlando, San Francisco, Washington
Top scorers: Salenko (Russia), Stoichkov (Bulgaria), each 6 goals
Final (Los Angeles, 17/7/94): **Brazil** 0 **Italy** 0 after extra-time; Brazil won 3-2 on pens
Att: 94,194
Brazil: Taffarel; Jorginho (Cafu 21), Aldair, Marcio Santos, Branco, Mazinho, Mauro Silva, Dunga (capt), Zinho (Viola 105), Romario, Bebeto
Italy: Pagliuca; Mussi (Apolloni 35), Baresi (capt), Maldini, Benarrivo, Berti, Albertini, D Baggio (Evani 95), Donadoni, R Baggio, Massaro
Referee: Puhl (Hungary)
Shoot-out: Baresi missed, Marco Santos saved, Albertini 1-0, Romario 1-1, Evani 2-1, Branco 2-2, Massaro saved, Dunga 2-3, R Baggio missed

1998 – FRANCE

WINNERS: France RUNNERS-UP: Brazil **THIRD:** Croatia **FOURTH:** Holland
Other countries in finals: Argentina, Austria, Belgium, Bulgaria, Cameroon, Chile, Colombia, Denmark, England, Germany, Iran, Italy, Jamaica, Japan, Mexico, Morocco, Nigeria, Norway, Paraguay, Romania, Saudi Arabia, Scotland, South Africa, South Korea, Spain, Tunisia, USA, Yugoslavia. **Total entries:** 172 (32 qualifiers)
Venues. Bordeaux, Lens, Lyon, Marseille, Montpellier, Nantes, Paris (St Denis, Parc des Princes), Saint-Etienne, Toulouse
Top scorer: Davor Suker (Croatia) 6 goals
Final (Paris St Denis, 12/7/98): **Brazil** 0 **France** 3 (Zidane 27, 45, Petit 90). **Att:** 75,000
Brazil: Taffarel; Cafu, Junior Baiano, Aldair, Roberto Carlos; Dunga (capt), Leonardo (Denilson 46), Cesar Sampaio (Edmundo 74), Rivaldo; Bebeto, Ronaldo
France: Barthez; Thuram, Leboeuf, Desailly, Lizarazu; Karembeu (Boghossian 56), Deschamps (capt), Petit, Zidane, Djorkaeff (Viera 75); Guivarc'h (Dugarry 66) **Sent-off:** Desailly (68)
Referee: Belqola (Morocco). **Half-time:** 0-2

2002 – JAPAN/SOUTH KOREA

WINNERS: Brazil **RUNNERS-UP:** Germany **THIRD:** Turkey **FOURTH:** South Korea
Other countries in finals: Argentina, Belgium, Cameroon, China, Costa Rica, Croatia, Denmark, Ecuador, England, France, Italy, Japan, Mexico, Nigeria, Paraguay, Poland, Portugal, Republic of Ireland, Russia, Saudi Arabia, Senegal, Slovenia, South Africa, Spain, Sweden, Tunisia, USA, Uruguay. **Total entries:** 195 (32 qualifiers)
Venues: Japan – Ibaraki, Kobe, Miyagi, Niigata, Oita, Osaka, Saitama, Sapporo, Shizuoka, Yokohama. **South Korea** – Daegu, Daejeon, Gwangju, Incheon, Jeonju, Busan, Seogwipo, Seoul, Suwon Ulsan
Top scorer: Ronaldo (Brazil) 8 goals
Final (Yokohama, 30/6/02): **Germany** 0 **Brazil** 2 (Ronaldo 67, 79). **Att:** 69,029
Germany: Kahn (capt), Linke, Ramelow, Metzelder, Frings, Jeremies (Asamoah 77), Hamann, Schneider, Bode (Zeige 84), Klose (Bierhoff 74), Neuville
Brazil: Marcos, Lucio, Edmilson, Roque Junior, Cafu (capt) Kleberson, Gilberto Silva, Roberto Carlos, Ronaldinho (Juninho 85), Rivaldo, Ronaldo (Denilson 90)
Referee: Collina (Italy). **Half-time:** 0-0

2006 – GERMANY

WINNERS: Italy **RUNNERS-UP:** France **THIRD:** Germany **FOURTH:** Portugal
Other countries in finals: Angola, Argentina, Australia, Brazil, Costa Rica, Croatia, Czech Republic, Ecuador, England, Ghana, Holland, Iran, Ivory Coast, Japan, Mexico, Paraguay, Poland, Saudi Arabia, Serbia & Montenegro, South Korea, Spain, Sweden, Switzerland, Trinidad & Tobago, Togo, Tunisia, Ukraine, USA. **Total entries:** 198 (32 qualifiers)
Venues: Berlin, Cologne, Dortmund, Frankfurt, Gelsenkirchen, Hamburg, Hanover, Kaiserslautern, Leipzig, Munich, Nuremberg, Stuttgart

Top scorer: Klose (Germany) 5 goals
Final (Berlin, 9/7/06): **Italy** 1 (Materazzi 19) **France** 1 (Zidane 7 pen) after extra-time: Italy won 5-3 on pens. **Att:** 69,000
Italy: Buffon; Zambrotta, Cannavaro (capt), Materazzi, Grosso, Perrotta (De Rossi 61), Pirlo, Gattuso, Camoranesi (Del Piero 86), Totti (Iaquinta 61), Toni
France: Barthez; Sagnol, Thuram, Gallas, Abidal, Makelele, Vieira (Diarra 56), Ribery (Trezeguet 100), Malouda, Zidane (capt), Henry (Wiltord 107) **Sent-off:** Zidane (110)
Referee: Elizondo (Argentina). **Half-time:** 1-1 90 mins: 1-1
Shoot-out: Pirlo 1-0, Wiltord 1-1, Materazzi 2-1, Trezeguet missed, De Rossi 3-1, Abidal 3-2, Del Piero 4-2, Sagnol 4-3, Grosso 5-3

2010 – SOUTH AFRICA
WINNERS: Spain RUNNERS-UP: Holland THIRD: Germany FOURTH: Uruguay
Other countries in finals: Algeria, Argentina, Australia, Brazil, Cameroon, Chile, Denmark, England, France, Ghana, Greece, Honduras, Italy, Ivory Coast, Japan, Mexico, New Zealand, Nigeria, North Korea, Paraguay, Portugal, Serbia, Slovakia, Slovenia, South Africa, South Korea, Switzerland, USA. **Total entries:** 204 (32 qualifiers)
Venues: Bloemfontein, Cape Town, Durban, Johannesburg (Ellis Park), Johannesburg (Soccer City), Nelspruit, Polokwane, Port Elizabeth, Pretoria, Rustenburg
Top scorers: Forlan (Uruguay), Muller (Germany), Sneijder (Holland), Villa (Spain) 5 goals
Final (Johannesburg, Soccer City, 11/7/10): **Holland** 0 **Spain** 1 (Iniesta 116) after extra-time; **Att:** 84,490
Holland: Stekelenburg; Van der Wiel, Heitinga, Mathijsen, Van Bronckhorst (capt) (Braafheid 105), Van Bommel, De Jong (Van der Vaart 99), Robben, Sneijder, Kuyt (Elia 71), Van Persie. **Sent off:** Heitinga (109)
Spain: Casillas (capt); Sergio Ramos, Puyol, Piquet, Capdevila, Busquets, Xabi Alonso (Fabregas 87), Iniesta, Xavi, Pedro (Jesus Navas 60), Villa (Torres 106)
Referee: Webb (England). **Half-time:** 0-0

2014 – BRAZIL
WINNERS: Germany RUNNERS-UP: Argentina THIRD: Holland FOURTH: Brazil
Other countries in finals: Algeria, Argentina, Australia, Belgium, Bosnia-Herzegovina, Brazil, Cameroon, Chile, Colombia, Costa Rica, Croatia, Ecuador, England, France, Germany, Ghana, Greece, Holland, Honduras, Iran, Italy, Ivory Coast, Japan, Mexico, Nigeria, Portugal, Russia, South Korea, Spain, Switzerland, Uruguay, USA. **Total entries:** 204 (32 qualifiers)
Venues: Belo Horizonte, Brasilia, Cuiaba, Curitiba, Fortaleza, Manaus, Natal, Porto Alegre, Recife, Rio de Janeiro, Salvador, Sao Paulo
Top scorer: Rodriguez (Colombia) 6 goals
Final (Rio de Janeiro, 13/7/14): **Germany** 1 (Gotze 113) **Argentina** 0 after extra-time; **Att:** 74,738
Germany: Neuer; Lahm (capt), Boateng, Hummels, Howedes, Kramer (Schurrle 32), Schweinsteiger, Muller, Kroos, Ozil (Mertesacker 120), Klose (Gotze 88)
Argentina: Romero; Zabaleta, Demichelis, Garay, Rojo, Biglia, Mascherano, Perez (Gago 86), Messi (capt), Lavezzi (Aguero 46), Higuain (Palacio 78)
Referee: Rizzoli (Italy). **Half-time:** 0-0

BAD WEEK FOR DUFFY

Shane Duffy scored three own goals and was sent off in the space of five days at the start of last season's Championship. Blackburn's Republic of Ireland central defender conceded one to Wigan in their 3-0 victory and both to Cardiff, who won 2-1. Duffy was then shown a second yellow card for kicking the ball at a Cardiff player.

BRITISH AND IRISH UNDER-21 INTERNATIONALS 2016–17

EUROPEAN CHAMPIONSHIP 2017 QUALIFYING

SCOTLAND 0 MACEDONIA 1
Group 3: Tynecastle (4,557); September 2, 2016
Scotland. Kelly (Rangers), Smith (Hearts) (Nicholson, Hearts 75), Kingsley (Swansea), Souttar (Hearts), McGhee (Hearts), Slater (Colchester) (McBurnie, Swansea 58), Fraser (Bournemouth) (King, Hearts 87), Gauld (Sporting Club), Cummings (Hibernian), Christie (Celtic), Henderson (Celtic). **Booked**: Christie, Cummings
Scorer – Macedonia: Markoski (18). **Half-time**: 0-1

WALES 0 DENMARK 4
Group 5: Racecourse Ground, Wrexham (668); September 2, 2016
Wales: O'Brien (Manchester City), Lockyer (Bristol Rov), Smith (Shrewsbury), Jones (Everton), O'Sullivan (Cardiff), Sheehan (Swansea) (Poole, Manchester Utd 61), Wilson (Liverpool), Harrison (Bristol Rov) (James, Swansea 51), Evans (Wrexham), Burns (Bristol City) (Charles, Barnsley 71), Hedges (Swansea). **Booked**: Evans
Scorers – Denmark: Ingvartsen (21), Siston (40, 49), Dolberg (83). **Half-time**: 0-2

NORTHERN IRELAND 0 ICELAND 1
Group 3: Mourneview Park, Lurgan (572); September 2, 2016
Northern Ireland: Mitchell (Burnley), Donnelly (Hartlepool), Marshall (Glenavon), Dummigan (Oldham), Nolan (Southport), Johnson (Stevenage) (Gendles-White, Swindon 62), Gorman (Stevenage), Thompson (Rangers), Cooper (Glenavon) (Charles, Fleetwood, 65), Lavery (Everton) (Rooney, Plymouth 78), Whyte (Crusaders). **Booked**: Cooper, Nolan, Donnelly
Scorer – Iceland: Egisson (87). **Half-time**: 0-0

REPUBLIC OF IRELAND 2 SLOVENIA 0
Group 2: Sports Centre, Waterford (510); September 2, 2016
Republic of Ireland: Rogers (Aberdeen), Hoban (Watford), O'Connor (Cork), O'Connell (Celtic), Rea (Luton), Byrne (Manchester City), Browne (Preston) (Dimaio, Chesterfield 90), Charsley (Everton), Cullen (West Ham), Duffus (Everton) (Maguire, Cork 89), Shodipo (QPR). **Booked**: Duffus, Browne
Scorers – Republic of Ireland: Charsley (87), Maguire (90 pen). **Half-time**: 0-0

ENGLAND 6 NORWAY 1
Group 9: Community Stadium, Colchester (8,454); September 6, 2016
England: Gunn (Manchester City), Iorfa (Wolves), Chambers (Arsenal), Hause (Wolves), Targett (Southampton), Ward-Prowse (Southampton), Chalobah (Chelsea), Redmond (Southampton) (Gray, Leicester 81), Loftus-Cheek (Chelsea) (Watmore, Sunderland 80), Baker (Chelsea), Rashford (Manchester Utd) (Akpom, Arsenal 84).
Scorers – England: Rashford (29, 66, 72 pen), Chalobah (38), Loftus-Cheek (64), Baker (86).
Norway: Zahid (68). **Half-time**: 2-0

UKRAINE 4 SCOTLAND 0
Group 3: Kiev (2,150); September 6, 2016
Scotland: Kelly (Rangers), Souttar (Hearts), McGhee (Hearts) (Storie, Aberdeen 78), Gauld (Sporting Club) (O'Hara, Dundee 83), McBurnie (Swansea), Hyam (Reading), Chalmers (Motherwell), Henderson (Celtic), King (Hearts), Nicholson (Hearts) (Cummings, Hibernian 65), Cadden (Motherwell). **Booked**: Gauld, McBurnie, Chalmers. **Sent off**: Souttar (90)
Scorers – Ukraine: Bliznichenko (26), Besedin (69, 77), Boriachuk (90 pen). **Half-time**: 1-0

WALES 1 LUXEMBOURG 1
Group 5: Book People Stadium, Bangor (768); September 6, 2016

Wales: O'Brien (Manchester City), Lockyer (Bristol Rov), Poole (Manchester Utd), Rodon (Swansea), Jones (Everton), Sheehan (Swansea), James (Swansea) (Charles, Barnsley 76), Wilson (Liverpool), Evans (Wrexham), Burns (Bristol City) (Harrison, Bristol Rov 83), Hedges (Swansea) (O'Sullivan, Cardiff 46). **Booked**: Burns
Scorers – Wales: Charles (90). **Luxembourg**: Kerger (15). **Half-time**: 0-1

MACEDONIA 2 NORTHERN IRELAND 0
Group 3: Skopje (5,082); September 6, 2016

Northern Ireland: Mitchell (Burnley), Conlan (Morecambe), Sendles-White (Swindon), Dummigan (Oldham), Doherty (Leyton Orient), Gorman (Stevenage) (Paul, QPR 87), Thompson (Rangers), Sykes (Glenavon), Lavery (Everton) (Whyte, Crusaders 75), Charles (Fleetwood), Smyth (Linfield) (Cooper, Glenavon 46). **Booked**: Lavery, Thompson
Scorers – Macedonia: Doherty (37 og), Markoski (85). **Half-time**: 1-0

SERBIA 3 REPUBLIC OF IRELAND 2
Group 2: Novi Sad (1,943); September 6, 2016

Republic of Ireland: Rogers (Aberdeen), Lenihan (Blackburn), Rea (Luton), Hoban (Watford), O'Connor (Cork), Charsley (Everton), Cullen (West Ham), Byrne (Manchester City) (Dimaio, Chesterfield 76), O'Dowda (Bristol City), Duffus (Everton) (Maguire, Cork 72), Shodipo (QPR) (Mulraney, Inverness 66). **Booked**: Lenihan, Rogers, Hoban
Scorers – Serbia: Djurdevic (12, 72 pen), Lazic (65). **Republic of Ireland**: O'Dowda (69), Maguire (81). **Half-time**: 1-0

ICELAND 2 SCOTLAND 0
Group 3: Reykjavik (332); October 5, 2016

Scotland: Fulton (Liverpool), McGhee (Hearts), Cameron (Newcastle), Henderson (Celtic), Iacovitti (Nottm Forest), Jules (Reading), Nesbitt (Celtic) (Sammut, Chelsea 69), Hardie (Rangers), McBurnie (Swansea) (Wighton, Dundee 78), Jones (Crewe), Docherty (Hamilton) (Burt, Rangers 63). **Booked**: Iacovitti, McGhee, Burt
Scorers – Iceland: Thrandarson (47), Omarsson (66). **Half-time**: 0-0

KAZAKHSTAN 0 ENGLAND 1
Group 9: Aktobe (12,720); October 6, 2016

England: Woodman (Newcastle), Holgate (Everton), Chambers (Arsenal), Holding (Arsenal), Galloway (Everton), Ward-Prowse (Southampton), Chalobah (Chelsea), Baker (Chelsea), Redmond (Southampton), Loftus-Cheek (Chelsea) (Watmore, Sunderland 75), Gray (Leicester) (Abraham, Chelsea 85). **Booked**: Holding
Scorer – England: Gray (6). **Half-time**: 0-1

UKRAINE 1 NORTHERN IRELAND 1
Group 3: Kiev (1,150); October 6, 2016

Northern Ireland: Mitchell (Burnley), Conlan (Morecambe), Donnelly (Hartlepool), Dummigan (Oldham), Nolan (Southport), Quigley (Dundee), B Kennedy (Stevenage), Thompson (Rangers) (McKnight, Stalybridge 90), Sykes (Glenavon), Duffy (Celtic) (Charles, Fleetwood 90), Smyth (Linfield) (M Kennedy, Charlton 78). **Booked**: Thompson
Scorers – Ukraine: Besedin (15). **Northern Ireland**: Smyth (12). **Half-time**: 1-1

REPUBLIC OF IRELAND 1 SERBIA 3
Group 2: Sports Centre, Waterford (650); October 7, 2016

Republic of Ireland: Bossin (Anderlecht), O'Connell (Celtic), O'Connor (Cork), Lenihan (Blackburn), Hoban (Watford), Browne (Preston), Charsley (Everton), Cullen (West Ham), Duffus (Everton) (Maguire, Cork 71), Byrne (Manchester City) (Mulraney, Inverness 71), Shodipo (QPR) (Kavanagh, Fulham 79). **Booked**: Browne, Hoban, O'Connell
Scorers – Republic of Ireland: Duffus (49). **Serbia**: Mihajlovic (64), Gacinovic (67), Lukic (88). **Half-time**: 0-0

ENGLAND 5 BOSNIA-HERZEGOVINA 0
Group 9: Banks's Stadium, Walsall (5,263); October 11, 2016

England: Walton (Brighton), Iorfa (Wolves), Stephens (Southampton), Chalobah (Chelsea), Chambers, Arsenal 46), Galloway (Everton), Hayden (Newcastle), Onomah (Tottenham), Swift (Reading), Grealish (Aston Villa) (Redmond, Southampton 74), Watmore (Sunderland), Loraham (Chelsea). **Booked**: Hayden, Swift

Scorers – England: Swift (14), Abraham (18, 68), Onomah (49), Watmore (62). **Half-time**: 2-0

MACEDONIA 2 SCOTLAND 0
Group 3: Skopje (12,000); October 11, 2016

Scotland: Fulton (Liverpool), Sheppard (Reading) (McCrorie, Rangers 58), Cameron (Newcastle), Iacovitti (Nottm Forest), Jules (Reading), Henderson (Celtic), Burt (Rangers), Jones (Crewe) (Sammut, Chelsea 88), Wighton (Dundee), McBurnie (Swansea), Hardy (Rangers) (MacDonald, Derby 81). **Booked**: Henderson, Jones

Scorers – Macedonia: Markoski (18), Bardi (22). **Half-time**: 2-0

ARMENIA 1 WALES 3
Group 5: Yerevan (645); October 11, 2016

Wales: Crowe (Ipswich), Jones (Everton), John (Cardiff), Poole (Manchester Utd) (Roberts, Swansea 86), Rodon (Swansea), Smith (Shrewsbury), Wilson (Liverpool), Sheehan (Swansea), Harrison (Bristol Rov) (Charles, Barnsley 73), O'Sullivan (Cardiff), Williams (Fulham) (James, Swansea 65). **Booked**: Wilson, John

Scorers – Armenia: Simonyan (69). **Wales**: Harrison (19), Shakhnazaryan (67 og), O'Sullivan (90). **Half-time**: 0-1

NORTHERN IRELAND 0 FRANCE 3
Group 3 Windsor Park (412); October 11, 2016

Northern Ireland: Mitchell (Burnley), Conlan (Morecambe), Donnelly (Hartlepool), Dummigan (Oldham), Nolan (Southport), Quigley (Dundee) (Duffy, Celtic 46), McLaughlin (Oldham), B Kennedy (Stevenage), (M Kennedy, Charlton 86), Sykes (Glenavon) (Gorman, Stevenage 65), Smyth (Linfield), McDermott (Derry). **Booked**: Smyth, Gorman

Scorers – France: Augustin (16, 42), Dembele (89). **Half-time**: 0-2

QUALIFYING TABLES
Group winners qualify for finals; four best runners-up to two play off matches to determine two more finalists; Poland qualify as hosts)

GROUP 1

	P	W	D	L	F	A	Pts
Czech Rep Q	10	7	2	1	29	10	23
Belgium	10	6	0	4	14	11	18
Montenegro	10	4	4	2	13	11	16
Malta	10	3	2	5	9	20	11
Latvia	10	2	3	5	10	13	9
Moldova	10	2	1	7	8	18	7

GROUP 2

	P	W	D	L	F	A	Pts
Italy Q	10	7	3	0	17	3	24
Serbia Q	10	7	2	1	27	8	23
Slovenia	10	5	0	5	18	11	15
Rep of Ireland	10	4	0	6	14	17	12
Lithuania	10	3	1	6	5	17	10
Andorra	10	1	0	9	1	26	3

GROUP 3

Macedonia Q	10	6	3	1	13	7	21
France	10	6	2	2	17	8	20
Iceland	10	5	3	2	13	9	18
Ukraine	10	4	2	4	14	12	14
Scotland	10	2	2	6	8	17	8
Northern Ireland	10	0	2	8	6	18	2

GROUP 4

Portugal Q	10	8	2	0	34	5	26
Israel	10	6	3	1	21	4	21
Greece	10	4	1	5	13	14	13
Albania	10	3	3	4	11	20	12
Hungary	10	3	3	4	19	16	12
Liechtenstein	10	0	0	10	1	40	0

GROUP 5

Denmark Q	10	9	1	0	24	3	28
Bulgaria	10	5	2	3	11	7	17
Romania	10	5	1	4	15	14	16
Wales	10	4	4	2	14	12	16
Luxembourg	10	1	3	6	5	18	6
Armenia	10	0	1	9	6	21	1

GROUP 6

Sweden Q	10	7	3	0	24	7	24
Spain Q	10	7	2	1	31	9	23
Croatia	10	6	2	2	24	11	20
Georgia	10	4	1	5	17	17	13
Estonia	10	1	1	8	3	26	4
San Marino	10	0	1	9	1	30	1

GROUP 7

Germany Q	10	10	0	0	35	8	30
Austria	10	7	1	2	22	12	22
Finland	10	4	2	4	13	10	14
Azerbaijan	10	2	3	5	8	19	9
Russia	10	2	3	5	15	19	9
Faroe Is	10	0	1	9	3	28	1

GROUP 8

Slovakia Q	8	6	1	1	21	6	19
Holland	8	4	2	2	15	10	14
Turkey	8	3	2	3	7	8	11
Belarus	8	2	2	4	7	11	8
Cyprus	8	1	1	6	4	19	4

GROUP 9

England Q	8	6	2	0	20	3	20
Norway	8	5	1	2	12	10	16
Switzerland	8	3	3	2	11	8	12
Kazakhstan	8	1	1	6	3	14	4
Bosnia-Herz	8	0	3	5	2	13	3

Play-offs (on agg): Austria 1 Spain 1 (Spain won on away goal); Serbia 2 Norway 1

EUROPEAN CHAMPIONSHIP 2019 – QUALIFYING

ESTONIA 1 NORTHERN IRELAND 2
Group 2: Tallinn (312); June 8, 2017

Northern Ireland: Mitchell (Burnley), Dummigan (Oldham), McDermott (Derry), Donnelly (Hartlepool), Johnson (Stevenage), Gorman (Stevenage) (Cooper, Glenavon 64), Thompson (Rangers), Smyth (Linfield) (McGonigle, Coleraine 75), Lewis (Norwich), Dunwoody (Stoke) (Gordon, Motherwell 79), Parkhouse (Sheffield Utd). **Booked**: Dunwoody, Smyth, Dummigan
Scorers – Estonia: Sappinen (50). **Northern Ireland**: Parkhouse (74), Donnelly (90 pen). **Half-time**: 0-0

FRIENDLY INTERNATIONALS

SLOVAKIA 4 SCOTLAND 0
Myjava (1,200); November 9, 2016

Scotland: Fulton (Liverpool), Smith (Hearts) (Sheppard, Reading 71), Cameron (Newcastle), (MacDonald, Derby) 71), Souttar (Hearts), Iacovitti (Nottm Forest), Jules (Reading) (Sammut, Chelsea 67), Henderson (Celtic), (Quitongo, Morton, 46), Cadden (Motherwell) (Nesbitt, Celtic, 67), Jones (Crewe), Brophy (Hamilton), (Hardie, Rangers 46), Docherty (Hamilton) (Forrest, Ayr 67)
Scorers   Slovakia: Rusnak (9), Iacovitti (59og), Ninaj (77), Balaj (82). **Half-time**: 1-0

ENGLAND 3 ITALY 2
St Mary's Stadium, Southampton (11,550); November 10, 2016

England: Gunn (Manchester City), Hayden (Newcastle), Chambers (Arsenal), Stephens (Southampton), Galloway (Everton), Chalobah (Chelsea), Ward-Prowse (Southampton), Redmond (Southampton), Swift (Reading) (Hughes, Derby 30), Baker (Chelsea), (Abraham, Chelsea 77), Gray (Leicester) (Watmore, Sunderland 71)
Scorers – England: Gray (6), Baker (60), Stephens (90). **Italy**: Conti (14), Di Francesco (29).
Half-time: 1-2

FRANCE 3 ENGLAND 2
Bondoufle (5,000); November 14, 2016

England: Mitchell (Derby), Iorfa (Wolves), Holding (Arsenal) (Redmond, Southampton 82), Mawson (Swansea), Hause (Wolves), Winks (Tottenham) (Ward-Prowse, Southampton 65), Chalobah (Chelsea) (Hayden, Newcastle 82), Baker (Chelsea), Watmore (Sunderland), Abraham (Chelsea), Grealish (Aston Villa) (Hughes, Derby 89)
Scorers – France: Dembele (18, 64), Cyprian (83). **England**: Watmore (9), Baker (81) **Half-time**: 1 1

GERMANY 1 ENGLAND 0
Wiesbaden (9,547); March 24, 2017

England: Pickford (Sunderland), Holgate (Everton), Mawson (Swansea), Stephens (Southampton), Chilwell (Leicester), Chalobah (Chelsea), Baker (Chelsea), Gray (Leicester) (Loftus-Cheek, Chelsea 58), Murphy (Norwich), Winks (Tottenham) (Swift, Reading 72), Abraham (Chelsea). **Booked**: Baker
Scorer – Germany: Amiri (23). **Half-time**: 1 0

DENMARK 0 ENGLAND 4
Randers (5,367); March 27, 2017

England: Gunn (Manchester City), Gomez (Liverpool), Holding (Arsenal), Hause (Wolves), McQueen (Southampton), Hughes (Derby), Swift (Reading), March (Brighton) (Gray, Leicester 61), Loftus-Cheek (Chelsea), Murphy (Norwich) (Grealish, Aston Villa 38), Woodrow (Fulham) (Abraham, Chelsea 74).
Scorers – England: Loftus-Cheek (10, 69), March (15), Woodrow (61). **Half-time**: 0-2

SCOTLAND 0 ESTONIA 0
Paisley Stadium (1,100): March 28, 2017

Scotland: Fulton (Liverpool) (Ruddy, Wolves 46), Smith (Hearts), Taylor (Kilmarnock), McGhee (Celtic) (Iacovitti, Nottm Forest 59), McCart (Celtic), Henderson (Celtic), McMullan (Celtic) (Thomas, Motherwell 59), Jones (Crewe) (Thomson (Celtic 74), McBurnie (Swansea) (Hardie, Rangers 59), Mallan (St Mirren), Morgan (St Mirren) (Wighton, Dundee 81)

CONFEDERATIONS CUP – RUSSIA 2017

GROUP A
Match-day 1
Portugal 2 (Ricardo Quaresma 34, Soares 86) **Mexico** 2 (Hernandez 42, Moreno 90). Att 34,372 (Kazan). **Russia** 2 (Boxall 31 og, Smolov 69) **New Zealand** 0 Att: 50,251 (St Petersburg)

Match-day 2
Mexico 2 (Jimenez 54, Peralta 72) **New Zealand** 1 (Wood). Att: 25,133 (Sochi). **Russia** 0 **Portugal** 1 (Ronaldo 8). Att: 42,759 (Moscow)

Match-day 3
Mexico 2 (Araujo 30, Lozano 52) **Russia** 1 (Samedov 25). Att: 41,585 (Kazan). **New Zealand** 0 **Portugal** 4 (Ronaldo 33, Bernardo Silva 37, Andre Silva 80, Nani 90). Att: 56,290 (St Petersburg)

	P	W	D	L	F	A	Pts
Portugal Q	3	2	1	0	7	2	7
Mexico Q	3	2	1	0	6	4	7
Russia	3	1	0	2	3	3	3
New Zealand	3	0	0	3	1	8	0

GROUP B
Match-day 1
Australia 2 (Rogic 41, Juric 56) **Germany** 3 (Stindl 5, Draxler 44, Goretzka 48). Att: 28,605 (Sochi). **Cameroon** 0 **Chile** 2 (Vidal 81, Vargas 90). Att: 33,492 (Moscow)

Match-day 2
Cameroon 1 (Anguissa 45) **Australia** 1 (Milligan 60). Att: 35,021 (St Petersburg). **Germany** 1 (Stindl 41) **Chile** 1 (Sanchez 6). Att: 38,222 (Kazan)

Match-day 3
Chile 1 (Rodriguez 67) **Australia** 1 (Troisi 42). Att: 33,639 (Moscow). **Germany** 3 (Demirbay 48, Werner 66, 81) **Cameroon** 1 (Aboubakar 78). Att: 30,230 (Sochi)

	P	W	D	L	F	A	Pts
Germany Q	3	2	1	0	7	4	7
Chile Q	3	1	2	0	4	2	5
Australia	3	0	2	1	4	5	2
Cameroon	3	0	1	2	2	6	1

SEMI-FINALS
Germany 4 (Goretzka 6, 8, Werner 59, Younes 90) **Mexico** 1 (Fabian 89). Att: 37,923 (Sochi). **Portugal** 0 **Chile** 0 – aet, Chile won 3-0 on pens. Att: 40,855 (Kazan)

THIRD/FOURTH PLACE
Portugal 2 (Pepe 90, Adrien Silva 104) **Mexico** 1 (Neto 54 og) – aet. Att: 42,659 (Moscow)

FINAL
CHILE 0 GERMANY 1
St Petersburg (57,268); Sunday, July 2 2017

Chile (4-3-3): Bravo (capt), Isla, Medel, Jara, Beausejour, Aranguiz (Sagal 81), Diaz (Valencia 53), Hernandez, Vargas (Puch 81), Vidal, Sanchez. **Booked:** Vidal, Jara, Vargas, Bravo. **Coach:** Juan Antonio Pizzi
Germany (3-4-2-1): ter Stegen, Ginter, Mustafi, Rudiger, Kimmich, Goretzka (Sule 90), Rudy, Hector, Stindl, Draxler (capt), Werner (Emre Can 79). **Scorer:** Stindl (20). **Booked:** Kimmich, Emre Can, Rudy. **Coach:** Joachim Low
Referee: M Mazic (Serbia). **Half-time:** 0-1

OLYMPIC TOURNAMENT – BRAZIL 2016

MEN
GROUP A

	P	W	D	L	F	A	Pts
Brazil Q	3	1	2	0	4	0	5
Denmark Q	3	1	1	1	1	4	4
Iraq	3	0	3	0	1	1	3
South Africa	3	0	2	1	1	2	2

GROUP B

Nigeria Q	3	2	0	1	6	6	6
Colombia Q	3	1	2	0	6	4	5
Japan	3	1	1	1	7	7	4
Sweden	3	0	1	2	2	4	1

GROUP C

South Korea Q	3	2	1	0	12	3	7
Germany Q	3	1	2	0	15	5	5
Mexico	3	1	1	1	7	4	4
Fiji	3	0	0	3	1	23	0

GROUP D

Portugal Q	3	2	1	0	5	2	7
Honduras Q	3	1	1	1	5	5	4
Argentina	3	1	1	1	3	4	4
Algeria	3	0	1	2	4	6	1

Quarter-finals: Portugal 0 Germany 4; Nigeria 2 Denmark 0; South Korea 0 Honduras 1; Brazil 2 Colombia 0. **Semi-finals:** Brazil 6 Honduras 0; Nigeria 0 Germany 2. **Third/fourth place:** Honduras 2 Nigeria 3

Final: Brazil 1 (Neymar 27) Germany 1 (Meyer 59) – aet, Brazil won 5-4 on pens. Maracana Stadium, Rio de Janeiro (63,707), August 20, 2016

WOMEN
GROUP A

Brazil Q	3	2	1	0	8	1	7
China Q	3	1	1	1	2	3	4
Sweden Q	3	1	1	1	2	5	4
South Africa	3	0	1	2	0	3	1

GROUP B

Canada Q	3	3	0	0	7	2	9
Germany Q	3	1	1	1	9	5	4
Australia Q	3	1	1	1	8	5	4
Zimbabwe	3	0	0	3	3	15	0

GROUP C

USA Q	3	2	1	0	5	2	7
France Q	3	2	0	1	7	1	6
New Zealand	3	1	0	2	1	5	3
Colombia	3	0	1	2	2	7	1

Quarter-finals: USA 1 Sweden 1 (aet, Sweden won 4-3 on pens); China 0 Germany 1; Canada 1 France 0; Brazil 0 Australia 0 (aet, Brazil won 7-6 on pens). **Semi-finals:** Brazil 0 Sweden 0 (aet, Sweden won 4-3 on pens); Canada 0 Germany 2. **Third/fourth place:** Brazil 1 Canada 2

Final: Sweden 1 (Blackstenius 66) Germany 2 (Marozsan 48, Sembrant 61 og). Maracana Stadium, Rio de Janeiro (52,432), August 19, 2016

TRANSFER TRAIL

Player	From	To	Date	£
Paul Pogba	Juventus	Manchester Utd	8/16	89,300,000
Gareth Bale	Tottenham	Real Madrid	8/13	85,300,000
Cristiano Ronaldo	Manchester Utd	Real Madrid	7/09	80,000,000
Romelu Lukaku	Everton	Manchester Utd	7/17	75,000,000
Luis Suarez	Liverpool	Barcelona	7/14	65,000,000
Angel di Maria	Real Madrid	Manchester Utd	8/14	59,700,000
Kevin De Bruyne	Wolfsburg	Manchester City	8/15	54,500,000
Oscar	Chelsea	Shanghai Shenhua	1/17	52,000,000
Fernando Torres	Liverpool	Chelsea	1/11	50,000,000
David Luiz	Chelsea	Paris SG	6/14	50,000,000
Raheem Sterling	Liverpool	Manchester City	7/15	49,000,000
John Stones	Everton	Manchester City	8/16	47,500,000
Alexandre Lacazette	Lyon	Arsenal	7/17	46,500,000
Kyle Walker	Tottenham	Manchester City	7/17	45,000,000
Angel di Maria	Manchester Utd	Paris SG	8/15	44,300,000
Bernardo Silva	Monaco	Manchester City	6/17	43,000,000
Mesut Ozil	Real Madrid	Arsenal	9/13	42,400,000
Tiemoue Bakayoko	Monaco	Chelsea	7/17	39,700,000
Sergio Aguero	Atletico Madrid	Manchester City	7/11	38,500,000
Juan Mata	Chelsea	Manchester Utd	1/14	37,100,000
Leroy Sane	Schalke	Manchester City	7/16	37,000,000
Anthony Martial	Monaco	Manchester Utd	9/15	36,000,000
Andy Carroll	Newcastle	Liverpool	1/11	35,000,000
Cesc Fabregas	Arsenal	Barcelona	8/11	35,000,000
Alexis Sanchez	Barcelona	Arsenal	7/14	35,000,000
Granit Xhaka	Borussia M'gladbach	Arsenal	6/16	35,000,000
Shkodran Mustafi	Valencia	Arsenal	8/16	35,000,000
Ederson	Benfica	Manchester City	6/17	34,900,000
Mohamed Salah	Roma	Liverpool	7/17	34,300,000
Sadio Mane	Southampton	Liverpool	6/16	34,000,000
Michy Batshuayi	Marseille	Chelsea	7/16	33,000,000
Robinho	Real Madrid	Manchester City	9/08	32,500,000
Christian Benteke	Aston Villa	Liverpool	7/15	32,500,000
Eden Hazard	Lille	Chelsea	6/12	32,000,000
Diego Costa	Atletico Madrid	Chelsea	7/14	32,000,000
N'Golo Kante	Leicester	Chelsea	7/16	32,000,000
David Luiz	Paris SG	Chelsea	8/16	32,000,000
Eliaquim Mangala	Porto	Manchester City	8/14	31,900,000
Dimitar Berbatov	Tottenham	Manchester Utd	9/08	30,750,000
Victor Lindelof	Benfica	Manchester Utd	6/17	30,700,000
Andriy Shevchenko	AC Milan	Chelsea	5/06	30,800,000
Xabi Alonso	Liverpool	Real Madrid	8/09	30,000,000
Fernandinho	Shakhtar Donetsk	Manchester City	6/13	30,000,000
Willian	Anzhi Makhachkala	Chelsea	8/13	30,000,000
Erik Lamela	Roma	Tottenham	8/13	30,000,000
Luke Shaw	Southampton	Manchester Utd	6/14	30,000,000
Eric Bailly	Villarreal	Manchester Utd	6/16	30,000,000
Moussa Sissoko	Newcastle	Tottenham,	8/16	30,000,000
Jordan Pickford	Sunderland	Everton	6/17	30,000,000
Islam Slimani	Sporting Lisbon	Leicester	8/16	29,700,000
Rio Ferdinand	Leeds	Manchester Utd	7/02	29,100,000
Antonio Rudiger	Roma	Chelsea	7/17	29,000,000
Ander Herrara	Athletic Bilbao	Manchester Utd	6/14	28,800,000

Nicolas Otamendi	Valencia	Manchester City	8/15	28,500,000
Juan Sebastian Veron	Lazio	Manchester Utd	7/01	28,100,000
Romelu Lukaku	Chelsea	Everton	7/14	28,000,000
Yaya Toure	Barcelona	Manchester City	7/10	28,000,000
Wilfried Bony	Swansea	Manchester City	1/15	28,000,000
Roberto Firmino	Hoffenheim	Liverpool	6/15	28,000,000
Marouane Fellaini	Everton	Manchester Utd	9/13	27,500,000
Wayne Rooney	Everton	Manchester Utd	8/04	27,000,000
Edin Dzeko	Wolfsburg	Manchester City	1/11	27,000,000
Luka Modric	Tottenham	Real Madrid	8/12	27,000,000
Cesc Fabregas	Barcelona	Chelsea	6/14	27,000,000
Gabriel Jesus	Palmeiras	Manchester City	7/16	27,000,000
Christian Benteke	Liverpool	Crystal Palace	8/16	27,000,000
Roberto Soldado	Valencia	Tottenham	8/13	26,000,000
Henrikh Mkhitaryan	Borussia Dortmund	Manchester Utd	7/16	26,000,000
Marc Overmars	Arsenal	Barcelona	7/00	25,000,000
Carlos Tevez	Manchester Utd	Manchester City	7/09	25,000,000
Emmanuel Adebayor	Arsenal	Manchester City	7/09	25,000,000
Samir Nasri	Arsenal	Manchester City	8/11	25,000,000
Oscar	Internacional	Chelsea	7/12	25,000,000
Adam Lallana	Southampton	Liverpool	7/14	25,000,000
Memphis Depay	PSV Eindhoven	Manchester Utd	6/15	25,000,000
Morgan Schneiderlin	Southampton	Manchester Utd	7/15	25,000,000
Ramires	Chelsea	Jiangsu Suning	2/16	25,000,000
Georginio Wijnaldum	Newcastle	Liverpool	7/16	25,000,000
Yannick Bolasie	Crystal Palace	Everton	8/16	25,000,000
Michael Keane	Burnley	Everton	7/17	25,000,000
Arjen Robben	Chelsea	Real Madrid	8/07	24,500,000
Michael Essien	Lyon	Chelsea	8/05	24,400,000
David Silva	Valencia	Manchester City	7/10	24,000,000
James Milner	Aston Villa	Manchester City	8/10	24,000,000
Mario Balotelli	Inter Milan	Manchester City	8/10	24,000,000
Robin van Persie	Arsenal	Manchester Utd	8/12	24,000,000
Alvaro Negredo	Manchester City	Valencia	7/15	23,800,000
Davy Klaassen	Ajax	Everton	6/17	23,600,000
Juan Mata	Valencia	Chelsea	8/11	23,500,000
David Beckham	Manchester Utd	Real Madrid	7/03	23,300,000
Juan Cuadrado	Fiorentina	Chelsea	2/15	23,300,000
Didier Drogba	Marseille	Chelsea	7/04	23,200,000
Andre Schurrle	Chelsea	Wolfsburg	2/15	23,000,000
Marcos Alonso	Fiorentina	Chelsea	8/16	23,000,000
Luis Suarez	Ajax	Liverpool	1/11	22,700,000
Nicolas Anelka	Arsenal	Real Madrid	8/99	22,300,000
Fernando Torres	Atletico Madrid	Liverpool	7/07	22,000,000
Joleon Lescott	Everton	Manchester City	8/09	22,000,000
Stevan Jovetic	Fiorentina	Manchester City	7/13	22,000,000
Son Heung-min	Bayer Leverkusen	Tottenham	8/15	21,900,000
Baba Rahman	Augsburg	Chelsea	8/15	21,700,000
David Luiz	Benfica	Chelsea	1/11	21,300,000
Shaun Wright-Phillips	Manchester City	Chelsea	7/05	21,000,000
Nemanja Matic	Benfica	Chelsea	01/14	21,000,000
Pedro	Barcelona	Chelsea	8/15	21,000,000
Ilkay Gundogan	Borussia Dortmund	Manchester City	6/16	21,000,000
Andre Ayew	Swansea	West Ham	8/16	20,500,000
Lassana Diarra	Portsmouth	Real Madrid	12/08	20,000,000
Alberto Aquilani	Roma	Liverpool	8/09	20,000,000

Player	From	To	Date	£
Stewart Downing	Aston Villa	Liverpool	7/11	20,000,000
Lazar Markovic	Benfica	Liverpool	7/14	20,000,000
Dejan Lovren	Southampton	Liverpool	7/14	20,000,000
Odion Ighalo	Watford	Changchun Yatai	1/17	20,000,000
Nathan Ake	Chelsea	Bournemouth	6/17	20,000,000
Ricardo Carvalho	Porto	Chelsea	7/04	19,850,000
Mario Balotelli	Manchester City	AC Milan	1/13	19,500,000
Ruud van Nistelrooy	PSV Eindhoven	Manchester Utd	4/01	19,000,000
Robbie Keane	Tottenham	Liverpool	7/08	19,000,000
Michael Carrick	Tottenham	Manchester Utd	8/06	18,600,000
Javier Mascherano	Media Sports	Liverpool	2/08	18,600,000
Giannelli Imbula	Porto	Stoke	2/11	18,300,000
Rio Ferdinand	West Ham	Leeds	11/00	18,000,000
Anderson	Porto	Manchester Utd	7/07	18,000,000
Jo	CSKA Moscow	Manchester City	6/08	18,000,000
Yuri Zhirkov	CSKA Moscow	Chelsea	7/09	18,000,000
Ramires	Benfica	Chelsea	8/10	18,000,000
Darren Bent	Sunderland	Aston Villa	1/11	18,000,000
Romelu Lukaku	Anderlecht	Chelsea	8/11	18,000,000
Andre Schurrle	Bayer Leverkusen	Chelsea	6/13	18,000,000
Mamadou Sakho	Paris SG	Liverpool	9/13	18,000,000
David De Gea	Atletico Madrid	Manchester Utd	6/11	17,800,000
Roque Santa Cruz	Blackburn	Manchester City	6/09	17,500,000
Jose Reyes	Sevilla	Arsenal	1/04	17,400,000
Javier Mascherano	Liverpool	Barcelona	8/10	17,250,000
Damien Duff	Blackburn	Chelsea	7/03	17,000,000
Owen Hargreaves	Bayern Munich	Manchester Utd	6/07	17,000,000
Glen Johnson	Portsmouth	Liverpool	6/09	17,000,000
Paulinho	Corinthians	Tottenham	7/13	17,000,000
Harry Maguire	Hull	Leicester	6/17	17,000,000
Andrey Arshavin	Zenit St Petersburg	Arsenal	2/09	16,900,000
Hernan Crespo	Inter Milan	Chelsea	8/03	16,800,000
Claude Makelele	Real Madrid	Chelsea	9/03	16,600,000
Luka Modric	Dinamo Zagreb	Tottenham	6/08	16,600,000
Darren Bent	Charlton	Tottenham	6/07	16,500,000
Phil Jones	Blackburn	Manchester Utd	6/11	16,500,000
Santi Cazorla	Malaga	Arsenal	8/12	16,500,000
Jose Bosingwa	Porto	Chelsea	6/08	16,200,000
Michael Owen	Real Madrid	Newcastle	8/05	16,000,000
Thierry Henry	Arsenal	Barcelona	6/07	16,000,000
Aleksandar Kolarov	Lazio	Manchester City	7/10	16,000,000
Robinho	Manchester City	AC Milan	8/10	16,000,000
Jordan Henderson	Sunderland	Liverpool	6/11	16,000,000
Ashley Young	Aston Villa	Manchester Utd	6/11	16,000,000
Calum Chambers	Southampton	Arsenal	7/14	16,000,000
Mario Balotelli	AC Milan	Liverpool	8/14	16,000,000
Danny Welbeck	Manchester Utd	Arsenal	8/14	16,000,000
Sofiane Boufal	Lille	Southampton	8/16	16,000,000
Adrian Mutu	Parma	Chelsea	8/03	15,800,000
Samir Nasri	Marseille	Arsenal	7/08	15,800,000
Javi Garcia	Benfica	Manchester City	8/12	15,800,000
Jermain Defoe	Portsmouth	Tottenham	1/09	15,750,000

BRITISH RECORD TRANSFERS FROM FIRST £1,000 DEAL

Player	From	To	Date	£
Alf Common	Sunderland	Middlesbrough	2/1905	1,000

Syd Puddefoot	West Ham	Falkirk	2/22	5,000
Warney Cresswell	South Shields	Sunderland	3/22	5,500
Bob Kelly	Burnley	Sunderland	12/25	6,500
David Jack	Bolton	Arsenal	10/28	10,890
Bryn Jones	Wolves	Arsenal	8/38	14,500
Billy Steel	Morton	Derby	9/47	15,000
Tommy Lawton	Chelsea	Notts Co	11/47	20,000
Len Shackleton	Newcastle	Sunderland	2/48	20,500
Johnny Morris	Manchester Utd	Derby	2/49	24,000
Eddie Quigley	Sheffield Wed	Preston	12/49	26,500
Trevor Ford	Aston Villa	Sunderland	10/50	30,000
Jackie Sewell	Notts Co	Sheffield Wed	3/51	34,500
Eddie Firmani	Charlton	Sampdoria	7/55	35,000
John Charles	Leeds	Juventus	4/57	65,000
Denis Law	Manchester City	Torino	6/61	100,000
Denis Law	Torino	Manchester Utd	7/62	115,000
Allan Clarke	Fulham	Leicester	6/68	150,000
Allan Clarke	Leicester	Leeds	6/69	165,000
Martin Peters	West Ham	Tottenham	3/70	200,000
Alan Ball	Everton	Arsenal	12/71	220,000
David Nish	Leicester	Derby	8/72	250,000
Bob Latchford	Birmingham	Everton	2/74	350,000
Graeme Souness	Middlesbrough	Liverpool	1/78	352,000
Kevin Keegan	Liverpool	Hamburg	6/77	500,000
David Mills	Middlesbrough	WBA	1/79	516,000
Trevor Francis	Birmingham	Nottm Forest	2/79	1,180,000
Steve Daley	Wolves	Manchester City	9/79	1,450,000
Andy Gray	Aston Villa	Wolves	9/79	1,469,000
Bryan Robson	WBA	Manchester Utd	10/81	1,500,000
Ray Wilkins	Manchester Utd	AC Milan	5/84	1,500,000
Mark Hughes	Manchester Utd	Barcelona	5/86	2,300,000
Ian Rush	Liverpool	Juventus	6/87	3,200,000
Chris Waddle	Tottenham	Marseille	7/89	4,250,000
David Platt	Aston Villa	Bari	7/91	5,500,000
Paul Gascoigne	Tottenham	Lazio	6/92	5,500,000
Andy Cole	Newcastle	Manchester Utd	1/95	7,000,000
Dennis Bergkamp	Inter Milan	Arsenal	6/95	7,500,000
Stan Collymore	Nottm Forest	Liverpool	6/95	8,500,000
Alan Shearer	Blackburn	Newcastle	7/96	15,000,000
Nicolas Anelka	Arsenal	Real Madrid	8/99	22,500,000
Juan Sebastian Veron	Lazio	Manchester Utd	7/01	28,100,000
Rio Ferdinand	Leeds	Manchester Utd	7/02	29,100,000
Andriy Shevchenko	AC Milan	Chelsea	5/06	30,800,000
Robinho	Real Madrid	Manchester City	9/08	32,500,000
Cristiano Ronaldo	Manchester Utd	Real Madrid	7/09	80,000,000
Gareth Bale	Tottenham	Real Madrid	9/13	85,300,000

• World's first £1m transfer: GuiseppeSavoldi, Bologna to Napoli, July 1975

TOP FOREIGN SIGNINGS

Player	From	To	Date	£
Gonzalo Higuain	Napoli	Juventus	7/16	75,300,000
Zlatan Ibrahimovic	Inter Milan	Barcelona	7/09	60,300,000
James Rodriguez	Monaco	Real Madrid	7/14	60,000,000
Kaka	AC Milan	Real Madrid	6/08	56,000,000
Edinson Cavani	Napoli	Paris SG	7/13	53,000,000
Radamel Falcao	Atletico Madrid	Monaco	6/13	51,000,000
Neymar	Santos	Barcelona	6/13	48,600,000

Zinedine Zidane	Juventus	Real Madrid	7/01	47,200,000
Hulk	Zenit St Petersburg	Shanghai SIPG	7/16	46,100,000
James Rodriguez	Porto	Monaco	5/13	38,500,000
Alex Teixeira	Shekhtar Donetsk	Jiangsu Suning	2/16	38,400,000
Joao Mario	Sporting Lisbon	Inter Milan	8/16	38,400,000
Luis Figo	Barcelona	Real Madrid	7/00	37,200,000
Javier Pastore	Palermo	Paris SG	8/11	36,600,000
Corentin Tolisso	Lyon	Bayern Munich	6/17	36,500,000
Karim Benzema	Lyon	Real Madrid	7/09	35,800,000
Julian Draxler	Wolfsburg	Paris SG	1/17	35,500,000
Hernan Crespo	Parma	Lazio	7/00	35,000,000
Radamel Falcao	Porto	Atletico Madrid	8/11	34,700,000
Gonzalo Higuain	Real Madrid	Napoli	7/13	34,500,000
David Villa	Valencia	Barcelona	5/10	34,000,000
Thiago Silva	AC Milan	Paris SG	7/12	34,000,000
Lucas Moura	Sao Paulo	Paris SG	1/13	34,000,000
Asier Illarramendi	Real Sociedad	Real Madrid	7/13	34,000,000
Ronaldo	Inter Milan	Real Madrid	8/02	33,000,000
Gianluigi Buffon	Parma	Juventus	7/01	32,600,000
Axel Witsel	Benfica	Zenit St Petersburg	8/12	32,500,000
Hulk	Porto	Zenit St Petersburg	8/12	32,000,000
Javi Martinez	Athletic Bilbao	Bayern Munich	8/12	31,600,000
Mario Gotze	Borussia Dortmund	Bayern Munich	6/13	31,500,000
Christian Vieri	Lazio	Inter Milan	6/99	31,000,000
Jackson Martinez	Atletico Madrid	Guangzhou Evergrande	2/16	31,000,000
Alessandro Nesta	Lazio	AC Milan	8/02	30,200,000

WORLD'S MOST EXPENSIVE TEENAGER
£36m: Anthony Martial, 19, Monaco to Manchester Utd, Aug 2015

WORLD RECORD FOR 16-YEAR-OLD
£12m: Theo Walcott, Southampton to Arsenal, Jan 2006

RECORD TRIBUNAL FEE
£6.5m: Danny Ings, Burnley to Liverpool, Jun 2016

RECORD FEE BETWEEN SCOTTISH CLUBS
£4.4m: Scott Brown, Hibernian to Celtic, May 2007

RECORD NON-LEAGUE FEE
£1m: Jamie Vardy, Fleetwood to Leicester, May 2012

RECORD FEE BETWEEN NON-LEAGUE CLUBS
£275,000: Richard Brodie, York to Crawley, Aug 2010

MILESTONES

1848: First code of rules compiled at Cambridge University.

1857: Sheffield FC, world's oldest football club, formed.

1862: Notts Co (oldest League club) formed.

1863: Football Association founded – their first rules of game agreed.

1871: FA Cup introduced.

1872: First official International: Scotland 0 England 0. Corner-kick introduced.

1873: Scottish FA formed; Scottish Cup introduced.

1874: Shinguards introduced.

1875: Crossbar introduced (replacing tape).

1876: FA of Wales formed.

1877: Welsh Cup introduced.

1878: Referee's whistle first used.

1880: Irish FA founded; Irish Cup introduced.

1883: Two-handed throw-in introduced.

1885: Record first-class score (Arbroath 36 Bon Accord 0 – Scottish Cup). Professionalism legalised.

1886: International Board formed.

1887: Record FA Cup score (Preston 26 Hyde 0).

1888: Football League founded by William McGregor. First matches on Sept 8.

1889: Preston win Cup and League (first club to complete Double).

1890: Scottish League and Irish League formed.

1891: Goal-nets introduced. Penalty-kick introduced.

1892: Inter-League games began. Football League Second Division formed.

1893: FA Amateur Cup launched.

1894: Southern League formed.

1895: FA Cup stolen from Birmingham shop window – never recovered.

1897: First Players' Union formed. Aston Villa win Cup and League.

1899: Promotion and relegation introduced.

1901: Maximum wage rule in force (£4 a week). Tottenham first professional club to take FA Cup south. First six-figure attendance (110,802) at FA Cup Final.

1902: Ibrox Park disaster (25 killed). Welsh League formed.

1904: FIFA founded (7 member countries).

1905: First £1,000 transfer (Alf Common, Sunderland to Middlesbrough).

1907: Players' Union revived.

1908: Transfer fee limit (£350) fixed in January and withdrawn in April.

1911: New FA Cup trophy – in use to 1991. Transfer deadline introduced.

1914: King George V first reigning monarch to attend FA Cup Final.

1916: Entertainment Tax introduced.

1919: League extended to 44 clubs.

1920: Third Division (South) formed.

1921: Third Division (North) formed.

1922: Scottish League (Div II) introduced.

1923: Beginning of football pools. First Wembley Cup Final.

1924: First International at Wembley (England 1 Scotland 1). Rule change allows goals to be scored direct from corner-kicks.

1925: New offside law.

1926: Huddersfield complete first League Championship hat-trick.

1927: First League match broadcast (radio): Arsenal v Sheffield United. First radio broadcast of Cup Final (winners Cardiff City). Charles Clegg, president of FA, becomes first knight of football.

1928: First £10,000 transfer – David Jack (Bolton to Arsenal). WR ('Dixie') Dean (Everton) creates League record – 60 goals in season. Britain withdraws from FIFA

1930: Uruguay first winners of World Cup.

1931: WBA win Cup and promotion.

1933: Players numbered for first time in Cup Final (1-22).

1934: Sir Frederick Wall retires as FA secretary; successor Stanley Rous. Death of Herbert Chapman (Arsenal manager).

1935: Arsenal equal Huddersfield's Championship hat-trick record. Official two-referee trials.

1936: Joe Payne's 10-goal League record (Luton 12 Bristol Rov 0).

1937: British record attendance: 149,547 at Scotland v England match.

1938: First live TV transmission of FA Cup Final. Football League 50th Jubilee. New pitch marking – arc on edge of penalty-area. Laws of Game re-drafted by Stanley Rous. Arsenal pay record £14,500 fee for Bryn Jones (Wolves).

1939: Compulsory numbering of players in Football League. First six-figure attendance for League match (Rangers v Celtic 118,567). All normal competitions suspended for duration of Second World War.

1945: Scottish League Cup introduced.

1946: British associations rejoin FIFA. Bolton disaster (33 killed) during FA Cup tie with Stoke. Walter Winterbottom appointed England's first director of coaching.

1947: Great Britain beat Rest of Europe 6-1 at Hampden Park, Glasgow. First £20,000 transfer – Tommy Lawton, Chelsea to Notts Co

1949: Stanley Rous, secretary FA, knighted. England's first home defeat outside British Champ. (0-2 v Eire).

1950: Football League extended from 88 to 92 clubs. World record crowd (203,500) at World Cup Final, Brazil v Uruguay, in Rio. Scotland's first home defeat by foreign team (0-1 v Austria).

1951: White ball comes into official use.

1952: Newcastle first club to win FA Cup at Wembley in successive seasons.

1953: England's first Wembley defeat by foreign opponents (3-6 v Hungary).

1954: Hungary beat England 7-1 in Budapest.

1955: First FA Cup match under floodlights (prelim round replay): Kidderminster v Brierley Hill Alliance.

1956: First FA Cup ties under floodlights in competition proper. First League match by floodlight (Portsmouth v Newcastle). Real Madrid win the first European Cup.

1957: Last full Football League programme on Christmas Day. Entertainment Tax withdrawn.

1958: Manchester United air crash at Munich. League re-structured into four divisions.

1960: Record transfer fee: £55,000 for Denis Law (Huddersfield to Manchester City). Wolves win Cup, miss Double and Championship hat-trick by one goal. For fifth time in ten years FA Cup Final team reduced to ten men by injury. FA recognise Sunday football. Football League Cup launched.

1961: Tottenham complete the first Championship–FA Cup double this century. Maximum wage (£20 a week) abolished in High Court challenge by George Eastham. First British £100-a-week wage paid (by Fulham to Johnny Haynes). First £100,000 British transfer – Denis Law, Manchester City to Torino. Sir Stanley Rous elected president of FIFA.

1962: Manchester United raise record British transfer fee to £115,000 for Denis Law.

1963: FA Centenary. Season extended to end of May due to severe winter. First pools panel. English "retain and transfer" system ruled illegal in High Court test case.

1964: Rangers' second great hat-trick – Scottish Cup, League Cup and League. Football League and Scottish League guaranteed £500,000 a year in new fixtures copyright agreement with Pools. First televised 'Match of the Day' (BBC2): Liverpool 3 Arsenal 2.

1965: Bribes scandal – ten players jailed (and banned for life by FA) for match-fixing 1960–63. Stanley Matthews knighted in farewell season. Arthur Rowley (Shrewsbury) retires with record of 434 League goals. Substitutes allowed for injured players in Football League matches (one per team).

1966: England win World Cup (Wembley).

1967: Alf Ramsey, England manager, knighted; OBE for captain Bobby Moore. Celtic become first British team to win European Cup. First substitutes allowed in FA Cup Final (Tottenham v Chelsea) but not used. Football League permit loan transfers (two per club).

1968: First FA Cup Final televised live in colour (BBC2 – WBA v Everton). Manchester United first English club to win European Cup.

1970: FIFA/UEFA approve penalty shoot-out in deadlocked ties.

1971: Arsenal win League Championship and FA Cup.

1973: Football League introduce 3-up, 3-down promotion/relegation between Divisions 1, 2 and 3 and 4-up, 4-down between Divisions 3 and 4.

1974: First FA Cup ties played on Sunday. League football played on Sunday for first time. Last FA Amateur Cup Final. Joao Havelange (Brazil) succeeds Sir Stanley Rous as FIFA president.

1975: Scottish Premier Division introduced.

1976: Football League introduce goal difference (replacing goal average) and red/yellow cards.

1977: Liverpool achieve the double of League Championship and European Cup. Don Revie defects to United Arab Emirates when England manager – successor Ron Greenwood.

1978: Freedom of contract for players accepted by Football League. PFA lifts ban on foreign players in English football. Football League introduce Transfer Tribunal. Viv Anderson (Nottm Forest) first black player to win a full England cap. Willie Johnston (Scotland) sent home from World Cup Finals in Argentina after failing dope test.

1979: First all-British £500,000 transfer – David Mills, Middlesbrough to WBA. First British million pound transfer (Trevor Francis – Birmingham to Nottm Forest). Andy Gray moves from Aston Villa to Wolves for a record £1,469,000 fee.

1981: Tottenham win 100th FA Cup Final. Liverpool first British side to win European Cup three times. Three points for a win introduced by Football League. QPR install Football League's first artificial pitch. Death of Bill Shankly, manager–legend of Liverpool 1959–74. Record British transfer – Bryan Robson (WBA to Manchester United), £1,500,000.

1982: Aston Villa become sixth consecutive English winners of European Cup. Tottenham retain FA Cup – first club to do so since Tottenham 1961 and 1962. Football League Cup becomes the (sponsored) Milk Cup.

1983: Liverpool complete League Championship–Milk Cup double for second year running. Manager Bob Paisley retires. Aberdeen first club to do Cup-Winners' Cup and domestic Cup double. Football League clubs vote to keep own match receipts. Football League sponsored by Canon, Japanese camera and business equipment manufacturers – 3-year agreement starting 1983–4. Football League agree two-year contract for live TV coverage of ten matches per season (5 Friday night, BBC, 5 Sunday afternoon, ITV).

1984: One FA Cup tie in rounds 3, 4, 5 and 6 shown live on TV (Friday or Sunday). Aberdeen take Scottish Cup for third successive season, win Scottish Championship, too. Tottenham win UEFA Cup on penalty shoot-out. Liverpool win European Cup on penalty shoot-out to complete unique treble with Milk Cup and League title (as well as Championship hat-trick). N Ireland win the final British Championship. France win European Championship – their first honour. FA National Soccer School opens at Lilleshall. Britain's biggest score this century: Stirling Alb 20 Selkirk 0 (Scottish Cup).

1985: Bradford City fire disaster – 56 killed. First £1m receipts from match in Britain (FA Cup Final). Kevin Moran (Manchester United) first player to be sent off in FA Cup Final. Celtic win 100th Scottish FA Cup Final. European Cup Final horror (Liverpool v Juventus, riot in Brussels) 39 die. UEFA ban all English clubs indefinitely from European competitions. No TV coverage at start of League season – first time since 1963 (resumption delayed until January 1986). Sept: first ground-sharing in League history – Charlton Athletic move from The Valley to Selhurst Park (Crystal Palace).

1986: Liverpool complete League and Cup double in player-manager Kenny Dalglish's first season in charge. Swindon (4th Div Champions) set League points record (102). League approve reduction of First Division to 20 clubs by 1988. Everton chairman Philip Carter elected president of Football League. Death of Sir Stanley Rous (91). 100th edition of News of the World Football Annual. League Cup sponsored for next three years by Littlewoods (£2m). Football League voting majority (for rule changes) reduced from three-quarters to two-thirds. Wales move HQ from Wrexham to Cardiff after 110 years. Two substitutes in FA Cup and League (Littlewoods) Cup. Two-season League/TV deal (£6.2m):- BBC and ITV each show seven live League matches per season, League Cup semi-finals and Final. Football League sponsored by Today newspaper. Luton first club to ban all visiting supporters; as sequel are themselves banned from League Cup. Oldham and Preston install artificial pitches, making four in Football League (following QPR and Luton).

1987: League introduce play-off matches to decide final promotion/relegation places in all divisions. Re-election abolished – bottom club in Div 4 replaced by winners of GM Vauxhall Conference. Two substitutes approved for Football League 1987–8. Red and yellow disciplinary cards (scrapped 1981) re-introduced by League and FA Football League sponsored by Barclays. First Div reduced to 21 clubs.

1988: Football League Centenary. First Division reduced to 20 clubs.

1989: Soccer gets £74m TV deal: £44m over 4 years, ITV; £30m over 5 years, BBC/BSB. But it costs Philip Carter the League Presidency. Ted Croker retires as FA chief executive; successor Graham Kelly, from Football League. Hillsborough disaster: 95 die at FA Cup semi-final (Liverpool v Nottm Forest). Arsenal win closest-ever Championship with last kick. Peter Shilton sets England record with 109 caps.

1990: Nottm Forest win last Littlewoods Cup Final. Both FA Cup semi-finals played on Sunday and televised live. Play-off finals move to Wembley; Swindon win place in Div 1, then relegated back to Div 2 (breach of financial regulations) – Sunderland promoted instead. England reach World Cup semi-final in Italy and win FIFA Fair Play Award. Peter Shilton retires as England goalkeeper with 125 caps (world record). Graham Taylor (Aston Villa) succeeds Bobby Robson as England manager. International Board amend offside law (player 'level' no longer offside). FIFA make "professional foul" a sending-off offence. English clubs back in Europe (Manchester United and Aston Villa) after 5-year exile.

1991: First FA Cup semi-final at Wembley (Tottenham 3 Arsenal 1). Bert Millichip (FA chairman) and Philip Carter (Everton chairman) knighted. End of artificial pitches in Div 1 (Luton, Oldham). Scottish League reverts to 12-12-14 format (as in 1987–8). Penalty shoot-out introduced to decide FA Cup ties level after one replay.

1992: FA launch Premier League (22 clubs). Football League reduced to three divisions (71 clubs). Record TV-sport deal: BSkyB/BBC to pay £304m for 5-year coverage of Premier League. ITV do £40m, 4-year deal with Football League. Channel 4 show Italian football live (Sundays). FIFA approve new back-pass rule (goalkeeper must not handle ball kicked to him by team-mate). New League of Wales formed. Record all-British transfer, £3.3m: Alan Shearer (Southampton to Blackburn). Charlton return to The Valley after 7-year absence.

1993: Barclays end 6-year sponsorship of Football League. For first time both FA Cup semi-finals at Wembley (Sat, Sun). Arsenal first club to complete League Cup/FA Cup double. Rangers pull off Scotland's domestic treble for fifth time. FA in record British sports sponsorship deal (£12m over 4 years) with brewers Bass for FA Carling Premiership, from Aug. Brian Clough retires after 18 years as Nottm Forest manager; as does Jim McLean (21 years manager of Dundee Utd). Football League agree 3-year, £3m sponsorship with Endsleigh Insurance. Premier League introduce squad numbers with players' names on shirts. Record British transfer: Duncan Ferguson, Dundee Utd to Rangers (£4m). Record English-club signing: Roy Keane, Nottm Forest to Manchester United (£3.75m). Graham Taylor resigns as England manager after World Cup exit (Nov). Death of Bobby Moore (51), England World Cup winning captain 1966.

1994: Death of Sir Matt Busby. Terry Venables appointed England coach. Manchester United complete the Double. Last artificial pitch in English football goes – Preston revert to grass, summer 1994. Bobby Charlton knighted. Scottish League format changes to four divisions of ten clubs. Record British transfer: Chris Sutton, Norwich to Blackburn

(£5m). FA announce first sponsorship of FA Cup – Littlewoods Pools (4-year, £14m deal, plus £6m for Charity Shield). Death of Billy Wright.

1995: New record British transfer: Andy Cole, Newcastle to Manchester United (£7m). First England match abandoned through crowd trouble (v Republic of Ireland, Dublin). Blackburn Champions for first time since 1914. Premiership reduced to 20 clubs. British transfer record broken again: Stan Collymore, Nottm Forest to Liverpool (£8.5m). Starting season 1995–6, teams allowed to use 3 substitutes per match, not necessarily including a goalkeeper. European Court of Justice upholds Bosman ruling, barring transfer fees for players out of contract and removing limit on number of foreign players clubs can field.

1996: Death of Bob Paisley (77), ex-Liverpool, most successful manager in English Football. FA appoint Chelsea manager Glenn Hoddle to succeed Terry Venables as England coach after Euro 96. Manchester United first English club to achieve Double twice (and in 3 seasons). Football League completes £125m, 5-year TV deal with BSkyB starting 1996–7. England stage European Championship, reach semi-finals, lose on pens to tournament winners Germany. Keith Wiseman succeeds Sir Bert Millichip as FA Chairman. Linesmen become known as 'referees' assistants'. Alan Shearer football's first £15m player (Blackburn to Newcastle). Nigeria first African country to win Olympic soccer. Nationwide Building Society sponsor Football League in initial 3-year deal worth £5.25m Peter Shilton first player to make 1000 League appearances.

1997: Howard Wilkinson appointed English football's first technical director. England's first home defeat in World Cup (0-1 v Italy). Ruud Gullit (Chelsea) first foreign coach to win FA Cup. Rangers equal Celtic's record of 9 successive League titles. Manchester United win Premier League for fourth time in 5 seasons. New record World Cup score: Iran 17, Maldives 0 (qualifying round). Season 1997–8 starts Premiership's record £36m, 4-year sponsorship extension with brewers Bass (Carling).

1998: In French manager Arsene Wenger's second season at Highbury, Arsenal become second English club to complete the Double twice. Chelsea also win two trophies under new player-manager Gianluca Vialli (Coca-Cola Cup, Cup Winners' Cup). In breakaway from Scottish League, top ten clubs form new Premiership under SFA, starting season 1998–9. Football League celebrates its 100th season, 1998–9. New FA Cup sponsors – French insurance giants AXA (25m, 4-year deal). League Cup becomes Worthington Cup in £23m, 5-year contract with brewers Bass. Nationwide Building Society's sponsorship of Football League extended to season 2000–1.

1999: FA buy Wembley Stadium (£103m) for £320m, plan rebuilding (Aug 2000–March 2003) as new national stadium (Lottery Sports fund contributes £110m) Scotland's new Premier League takes 3-week mid-season break in January. Sky screen Oxford Utd v Sunderland (Div 1) as first pay-per-view match on TV. FA sack England coach Glenn Hoddle; Fulham's Kevin Keegan replaces him at £1m a year until 2003. Sir Alf Ramsey, England's World Cup-winning manager, dies aged 79. With effect 1999, FA Cup Final to be decided on day (via penalties, if necessary). Hampden Park re-opens for Scottish Cup Final after £63m refit. Alex Ferguson knighted after Manchester United complete Premiership, FA Cup, European Cup treble. Starting season 1999–2000, UEFA increase Champions League from 24 to 32 clubs. End of Cup-Winners' Cup (merged into 121-club UEFA Cup). FA allow holders Manchester United to withdraw from FA Cup to participate in FIFA's inaugural World Club Championship in Brazil in January. Chelsea first British club to field an all-foreign line-up – at Southampton (Prem). FA vote in favour of streamlined 14-man board of directors to replace its 92-member council.

2000: Scot Adam Crozier takes over as FA chief executive. Wales move to Cardiff's £125m Millennium Stadium (v Finland). Brent Council approve plans for new £475m Wembley Stadium (completion target spring 2003); demolition of old stadium to begin after England v Germany (World Cup qual.). Fulham Ladies become Britain's first female professional team. FA Premiership and Nationwide League to introduce (season 2000–01) rule whereby referees advance free-kick by 10 yards and caution player who shows dissent, delays kick or fails to retreat 10 yards. Scottish football increased to 42 League clubs in 2000–01 (12 in Premier League and 3 divisions of ten; Peterhead and Elgin elected from Highland League). France win European Championship – first time a major international tournament has been jointly hosted (Holland/ Belgium). England's £10m bid to stage 2006 World Cup fails; vote goes to Germany. England manager Kevin Keegan resigns after 1-0 World Cup defeat by Germany in Wembley's last International. Lazio's Swedish coach Sven-Goran Eriksson agrees to become England head coach.

2001: Scottish Premier League experiment with split into two 5-game mini leagues (6 clubs in each) after 33 matches completed. New transfer system agreed by FIFA/UEFA is ratified. Barclaycard begin £48m, 3-year sponsorship of the Premiership, and Nationwide's contract with the Football League is extended by a further 3 years (£12m). ITV, after winning auction against BBC's Match of the Day, begin £183m, 3-season contract for highlights of Premiership matches; BSkyB's live coverage (66 matches per season) for next 3 years will cost £1.1bn. BBC and BSkyB pay £400m (3-year contract) for live coverage of FA Cup and England home matches. ITV and Ondigital pay £315m to screen Nationwide League and Worthington Cup matches. In new charter for referees, top men can earn up to £60,000 a season in Premiership. Real Madrid break world transfer record, buying Zinedine Zidane from Juventus for £47.2m. FA introduce prize money, round by round, in FA Cup.

2002: Scotland appoint their first foreign manager, Germany's former national coach Bertie Vogts replacing Craig Brown. Collapse of ITV Digital deal, with Football League owed £178m, threatens lower-division clubs. Arsenal complete Premiership/FA Cup Double for second time in 5 seasons, third time in all. Newcastle manager Bobby Robson knighted in Queen's Jubilee Honours. New record British transfer and world record for defender, £29.1m Rio Ferdinand (Leeds to Manchester United). Transfer window introduced to British football. FA Charity Shield renamed FA Community Shield. After 2-year delay, demolition of Wembley Stadium begins. October: Adam Crozier, FA chief executive, resigns.

2003: FA Cup draw (from 4th Round) reverts to Monday lunchtime. Scottish Premier League decide to end mid-winter shut-down. Mark Palios appointed FA chief executive. For first time, two Football League clubs demoted (replaced by two from Conference). Ban lifted on loan transfers between Premiership clubs. July: David Beckham becomes record British export (Manchester United to Real Madrid, £23.3m). Biggest takeover in British football history – Russian oil magnate Roman Abramovich buys control of Chelsea for £150m Wimbledon leave rented home at Selhurst Park, become England's first franchised club in 68-mile move to Milton Keynes.

2004: Arsenal first club to win Premiership with unbeaten record and only the third in English football history to stay undefeated through League season. Trevor Brooking knighted in Queen's Birthday Honours. Wimbledon change name to Milton Keynes Dons. Greece beat hosts Portugal to win European Championship as biggest outsiders (80-1 at start) ever to succeed in major international tournament. New contracts – Premiership in £57m deal with Barclays, seasons 2004–07. Coca-Cola replace Nationwide as Football League sponsors (£15m over 3 years), rebranding Div 1 as Football League Championship, with 2nd and 3rd Divisions, becoming Leagues 1 and 2. All-time League record of 49 unbeaten Premiership matches set by Arsenal. Under new League rule, Wrexham forfeit 10 points for going into administration.

2005: Brian Barwick, controller of ITV Sport, becomes FA chief executive. Foreign managers take all major trophies for English clubs: Chelsea, in Centenary year, win Premiership (record 95 points) and League Cup in Jose Mourinho's first season; Arsene Wenger's Arsenal win FA Cup in Final's first penalty shoot-out; under new manager Rafael Benitez, Liverpool lift European Cup on penalties after trailing 0-3 in Champions League Final. Wigan, a League club only since 1978, promoted to Premiership. In new record British-club take-over, American tycoon Malcolm Glazer buys Manchester United for £790m Tributes are paid world-wide to George Best, who dies aged 59.

2006: Steve Staunton succeeds Brian Kerr as Republic of Ireland manager. Chelsea post record losses of £140m. Sven-Goran Eriksson agrees a settlement to step down as England coach. Steve McClaren replaces him. The Premier League announce a new 3-year TV deal worth £1.7 billion under which Sky lose their monopoly of coverage. Chelsea smash the British transfer record, paying £30.8m for Andriy Shevchenko. Clydesdale Bank replace Bank of Scotland as sponsor of the SPL.

2007: Michel Platini becomes the new president of UEFA. Walter Smith resigns as Scotland manager to return to Rangers and is replaced by Alex McLeish. The new £800m Wembley Stadium is finally completed. The BBC and Sky lose TV rights for England's home matches and FA Cup ties to ITV and Setanta. World Cup-winner Alan Ball dies aged 61. Lawrie Sanchez resigns as Northern Ireland manager to take over at Fulham. Nigel Worthington succeeds him. Lord Stevens names five clubs in his final report into alleged transfer irregularities. Steve McClaren is sacked after England fail to qualify for the European Championship Finals and is replaced by Fabio Capello. The Republic of Ireland's Steve Staunton also goes. Scotland's Alex McLeish resigns to become Birmingham manager.

2008: The Republic of Ireland follow England's lead in appointing an Italian coach – Giovanni Trapattoni. George Burley leaves Southampton to become Scotland manager. Manchester United beat Chelsea in the first all-English Champions League Final. Manchester City smash the British transfer record when signing Robinho from Real Madrid for £32.5m.

2009: Sky secure the rights to five of the six Premier League packages from 2010–13 with a bid of £1.6bn. Reading's David Beckham breaks Bobby Moore's record number of caps for an England outfield player with his 109th appearance. A British league record for not conceding a goal ends on 1,311 minutes for Manchester United's Edwin van der Sar. AC Milan's Kaka moves to Real Madrid for a world record fee of £56m. Nine days later, Manchester United agree to sell Cristiano Ronaldo to Real for £80m. Sir Bobby Robson dies aged 76 after a long battle with cancer. Shay Given and Kevin Kilbane win their 100th caps for the Republic of Ireland. The Premier League vote for clubs to have eight home-grown players in their squads. George Burley is sacked as Scotland manager and replaced by Craig Levein.

2010: npower succeed Coca-Cola as sponsors of the Football League. Portsmouth become the first Premier League club to go into administration. Chelsea achieve the club's first League and FA Cup double. Lord Triesman resigns as chairman of the FA and of England's 2018 World Cup bid. John Toshack resigns as Wales manager and is replaced by former captain Gary Speed. England are humiliated in the vote for the 2018 World Cup which goes to Russia, with the 2022 tournament awarded to Qatar.

2011: Seven club managers are sacked in a week. The transfer record between British clubs is broken twice in a day, with Liverpool buying Newcastle's Andy Carroll for £35m and selling Fernando Torres to Chelsea for £50m. Vauxhall replace Nationwide as sponsors of England and the other home nations. John Terry is restored as England captain. Football League clubs vote to reduce the number of substitutes from seven to five. Nigel Worthington steps down as Northern Ireland manager and is succeeded by Michael O'Neill. Sir Alex Ferguson completes 25 years as Manchester United manager. Manchester City post record annual losses of nearly £195m. Huddersfield set a Football League record of 43 successive unbeaten league games. Football mourns Gary Speed after the Wales manager is found dead at his home.

2012: Chris Coleman is appointed the new Wales manager. Fabio Capello resigns as manager after John Terry is stripped of the England captaincy for the second time. Roy Hodgson takes over. Rangers are forced into liquidation by crippling debts and a newly-formed club are demoted from the Scottish Premier League to Division Three. Manchester City become champions for the first time since 1968 after the tightest finish to a Premier League season. Chelsea win a penalty shoot-out against Bayern Munich in the Champions League Final. Capital One replace Carling as League Cup sponsors. Steven Gerrard (England) and Damien Duff (Republic of Ireland) win their 100th caps. The FA's new £120m National Football Centre at Burton upon Trent is opened. Scotland manager Craig Levein is sacked.

2013: Gordon Strachan is appointed Scotland manager. FIFA and the Premier League announce the introduction of goal-line technology. Energy company npower end their sponsorship of the Football League and are succeeded by Sky Bet. Sir Alex Ferguson announces he is retiring after 26 years as Manchester United manager. Wigan become the first club to lift the FA Cup and be relegated in the same season. Chelsea win the Europa League. Ashley Cole and Frank Lampard win their 100th England caps. Robbie Keane becomes the most capped player in the British Isles on his 126th appearance for the Republic of Ireland. Scottish Football League clubs agree to merge with the Scottish Premier League. Greg Dyke succeeds David Bernstein as FA chairman. Real Madrid sign Tottenham's Gareth Bale for a world record £85.3m. Giovanni Trapatonni is replaced as Republic of Ireland manager by Martin O'Neill.

2014: Sir Tom Finney, one of the finest British players of all-time, dies aged 91. England experience their worst-ever World Cup, finishing bottom the group with a single point. Germany deliver one of the most remarkable scorelines in World Cup history – 7-1 against Brazil in the semi-finals. Manchester United announce a world-record kit sponsorship with adidas worth £750m. United break the incoming British transfer record by paying £59.7m for Real Madrid's Angel di Maria, part of a record £835m spending by Premier League clubs in the summer transfer window. England's Wayne Rooney and the Republic of Ireland's John O'Shea win their 100th caps.

2015: The Premier League sell live TV rights for 2016-19 to Sky and BT for a record £5.13bn. Bournemouth, a club on the brink of folding in 2008, win promotion to the Premier League. FIFA president Sepp Blatter resigns as a bribery and corruption scandal engulfs the world governing body. Blatter and suspended UEFA president Michel Platini are banned for eight years, reduced on appeal to six years.

2016: An inquest jury rules that the 96 Liverpool fans who died in the Hillsborough disaster of 1989 were unlawfully killed. Leicester, 5,000-1 outsiders become Premier League champions in one of the game's biggest-ever surprises. Aaron Hughes wins his 100th cap for Northern Ireland. FA Cup quarter-final replays are scrapped. England manager Roy Hodgson resigns. He is replaced by Sam Allardyce, who is forced out after one match for 'inappropriate conduct' and succeeded by Gareth Southgate. Manchester United sign Paul Pogba for a world record £89.3m.

2017 Celtic retain the Scottish Premiership title without losing a game. Manchester United win the Europa League. Arsenal win a record 13th FA Cup and manager Arsenal Wenger lifts the trophy for a record seventh time.

THE THINGS THEY SAY ...

'The mascot was out of order' – **Sam Allardyce** on cheeky Watford mascot Harry the Hornet who threw himself in front of Wilfried Zaha after the CrystalPalace forward was booked for diving.

'Watford FC has reminded Harry the Hornet of his responsibilities, which include continuing to have fun and entertain supporters' – **Watford** statement.

'He was like a brother to me. We shared an unbreakable bond since we first met. We went on an incredible journey and it will stay with me forever' – **Sir Elton John** on the success he shared with the late Graham Taylor at Watford.

'I will love Gareth Southgate forever' – **Paul Doswell**, manager of National League Sutton, after the England manager gave his side a home tie against Arsenal when making the draw for the FA Cup fifth round.

FINAL WHISTLE – OBITUARIES 2016–17

JULY 2016

JACKIE MCINALLY, 79, played a key role in Kilmarnock's only Scottish League title success, achieved on a dramatic final day of the 1964–65 season when they overtook Hearts on goal average by winning 2-0 at Tynecastle. The inside-forward featured in 32 of the 34 games and scored 11 goals. He was also part of the team beaten by Rangers in the 1960 Scottish Cup final and defeated by Rangers and Hearts in League Cup finals. McInally made 309 appearances for the club, netting 132 times, then helped Motherwell become Division Two champions in 1969 and finished his career with Hamilton. His son, Alan, also played for Kilmarnock, along with Celtic, Aston Villa and Bayern Munich, and won eight Scottish caps.

JOHN HOPE, 67, won promotion to the old First Division with Sheffield United in 1971 when they finished runners-up to Leicester. The goalkeeper kept seven successive clean sheets, a record for the club until Mark Howard achieved eight in 2014. Hope made his Football League debut, aged 16, for Darlington and both his sons, Chris and Richard, played for the club. He also had spells with Newcastle and Hartlepool.

DAVID STRIDE, 58, spent his career with teams in London and the United States. The full-back started out at Chelsea in 1976 and established himself with 33 appearances in the 1978–79 relegation season. He moved Memphis for a £90,000 transfer fee and went on to win the Major Indoor League title with Dallas in 1987. On his return, Stride had spells with Millwall and Leyton Orient and was briefly manager of non-league Bashley.

GEORGE ALLEN, 84, was a member of the Birmingham side beaten 4-1 on aggregate by Barcelona in the 1960 final of the Fairs Cup, forerunner of the UEFA Cup and Europa Cup. He made 165 appearances in a decade at the club, a total which would have been much greater but for the club's full-back pairing of Ken Green and Jeff Hall. Allen eventually established himself in the team before a fractured skull set him back and he later moved on to play for Torquay.

DAVE SYRETT, 60, played for Mansfield in their only season in the game's second tier – 1977-78. Highlight was his hat-trick in a 3-3 draw with Tottenham. The England youth international also had spells with Swindon, Walsall, Peterborough and Northampton.

RAY SPENCER, 82, scored the first goal for Darlington in a 3-2 victory over West Ham in a League Cup tie watched by a crowd of 17,000 at Feethams in 1960. A record crowd for the club of more than 21,000 saw the third round match against Bolton, who won it 2-1. Allen, a right-half, was an England schoolboy international who started his career at Aston Villa and later played for Torquay.

DICK DONNELLY, 74, was a goalkeeper with East Fife, Brechin and Arbroath in the 1960s, but became better known as a journalist and radio broadcaster across Tayside. Dundee United described him as 'a hugely important figure in covering matches.'

AUGUST 2016

DALIAN ATKINSON, 48, died in tragic circumstances 24 years to the day after scoring Aston Villa's first goal in the Premier League. It was a late equaliser against Ipswich at the start of a season which ended with his side finishing runners-up to Manchester United. The striker made more headlines when he won the league's inaugural goal of the season competition on *Match of the Day*, running half the length of the pitch before chipping Wimbledon goalkeeper Hans Segers. He was also a key figure in Villa's 1994 League Cup success, with goals in each of the two-leg semi-final against Tranmere and another to put them on the way to a 3-1 victory over United at Wembley. Atkinson was previously with Ipswich, Sheffield Wednesday and Real Sociedad. He left Villa Park for Fenerbahce in Turkey, had spells on loan with Metz and Manchester City and also played in Saudi Arabia and South Korea. He made one appearance for England B and would almost certainly have gained full international honours but for the presence of Alan Shearer. Teddy Sheringham, Les Ferdinand and Robbie Fowler. He died on August 15, 2016 after being shot with a taser by police at his father's home in Telford.

JOAO HAVELANGE, 100, succeeded Britain's Sir Stanley Rouse as president of FIFA in 1974, having marshalled support from national federations unhappy about the perceived European domination of the world governing body, He held the position for nearly a quarter of a century, during which the World Cup expanded from 16 to 32 teams, a women's tournament was established and the Confederations Cup introduced. The Brazilian lawyer's tenure was also mired in controversy over bribery allegations. He made way for Sepp Blatter in 1998 and resigned as honorary president in 2013.

REG MATTHEWSON, 77, scored on his league debut for Sheffield United and spent ten years at his home-town club before joining Fulham under Bobby Robson for a £30,000 fee in 1968. The centre-half's best season was in 1970–71 when he played every match but one in the Third Division promotion-winning side under Robson's successor, Bill Dodgin junior. Matthewson then captained Chester to promotion from Division Four in 1975, when they also reached the League Cup semi-finals, losing 5-4 on aggregate to the eventual winners Aston Villa.

RONNIE COPE, 81, was an England schoolboy international who captained Manchester United to victory over Wolves in the first FA Youth Cup Final in 1953. The centre-half made his senior debut under Matt Busby three years later, but spent most of his time in the reserves until the 1958 Munich Air Disaster which claimed the lives of eight of United's team. He helped the club rebuild, playing in that season's FA Cup Final, which Bolton won 2-0, and both legs of the European Cup semi-final against AC Milan, United losing that one 5-2 on aggregate. Cope made 108 appearances before joining Luton in 1961 and later managing Northwich Victoria.

LIAM TUOHY, 83, won eight Republic of Ireland caps while playing for Shamrock Rovers and Newcastle. He was then manager of the national team from 1971–73. The left-winger had two spells with Rovers, winning four league titles and eight FAI Cups. He also managed the club, along with spells in charge of Dundalk, Shelbourne and Dublin University.

KEITH BLUNT, 77, was inducted into the FA's coaching hall of fame in 2014. He was at the forefront of English coaching during the 1970s and 80s, including pioneering work for the FA's national school at Lilleshall. Alongside it, he had spells as assistant manager of Gillingham and Plymouth, youth team coach at Tottenham and manager of Sutton United and Swedish club Malmo. Blunt also held various coaching roles in China.

ROY SUMMERSBY, 81, scored 25 goals for Crystal Palace in their Fourth Division promotion-winning season of 1960–61. The inside-forward partnered Johnny Byrne, who netted 30 in the team's total of 110. Summersby signed from Millwall and went on to join his former Palace manager George Smith at Portsmouth.

NEIL WILKINSON, 61, helped his home-town team Blackburn win the Third Division title in the 1974–75 season when they finished a point ahead of Plymouth. The right-back left Ewood Park in 1977 to play for Cape Town in South Africa, then had spells with Port Vale and Crewe.

RUSSELL COUGHLIN, 56, was a much-travelled midfielder who played for nine clubs and made a total of 673 appearances. He started his career with Manchester City in 1977 and went on to serve Blackburn, Carlisle, Plymouth, Blackpool, Shrewsbury (loan), home-town team Swansea, Exeter and Torquay.

JOE DAVIS, 75, achieved remarkable consistency with Hibernian after Jock Stein signed him from Third Lanark. In four seasons from 1965–69 he made 273 successive appearances and also scored 43 penalties. Had it not been for Celtic's Tommy Gemmell and Chelsea's Eddie McCreadie, the talk might have won international recognition. Davis, part of the Hibernian side beaten 6-2 by Celtic in the 1969 Scottish League Cup Final, later played for Carlisle.

ALAN SMITH, 77, made 303 Football League and Cup appearances for Torquay, his only club, between 1958–69. Most of them were at centre-half, although he played in both full-back positions on occasions. Smith was never booked in his career.

MEL SLACK, 72, played a leading role in the Cambridge United side that replaced Bradford Park Avenue in the Football League in 1970. The wing-half was on Burnley's books as a youngster, had spells with Sunderland and Southend and also played for Cambridge City.

RAB STEWART, 54, scored the goal which put Dunfermline within reach of a Scottish Cup upset against Rangers in 1984. They led at Ibrox until the last ten minutes when Rangers recovered to win the third-round tie 2-1. Stewart, a forward, later played for Motherwell, Falkirk and Queen of the South.

SEPTEMBER 2016

MEL CHARLES, 81, won 31 caps for Wales and was a key figure in the side that reached the quarter-finals of the 1958 World Cup in Sweden. He was complimented on his performance in the 1-0 defeat by Brazil by match-winner Pele, who said he was one of the tournament's outstanding defenders. Yet the Swansea and Arsenal player always admitted that his elder brother and international team-mate John Charles was the real star of the family. The title of his autobiography, 'In the Shadow of a Giant', acknowledged that. Mel, who like his brother was equally at home in central defence or at centre-forward, scored six international goals, four of them in a 4-0 Home International win over Northern Ireland. He joined Arsenal for a £46,750 fee in 1959 and later served Cardiff and Port Vale in a club career spanning 401 matches (122 goals). His son Jeremy won 19 caps and also played for Swansea.

JACKIE SEWELL, 89, was a prolific marksman, an FA Cup winner and a 'double' international. In 557 matches for Notts County, Sheffield Wednesday, Aston Villa and Hull, the inside forward scored 244 goals. He helped County win the Third Division South title in 1950 and Wednesday return to the top division as champions in his first season following a record British record transfer of £34,500. Sewell then lifted the FA Cup with Aston Villa, who defeated Manchester United 2-1 in the 1957 final. He won six caps with England, one of his three goals coming in the 6-3 Wembley defeat by Hungary in 1953 – their first at home by a non British or Irish team. He came out of retirement to become player coach of the Zambian club Lusaka and made ten appearances for the country's fledgling national team.

GRAHAM HAWKINS, 70, fulfilled the young football fan's dream – playing for and managing his local club. He joined Wolves as an apprentice from grammar school, turned professional in 1963 and helped them gain promotion to the top flight as runners-up to Coventry in 1967. Hawkins then led Preston to the Third Division championship in 1971, playing all 46 games, and four years later helped Blackburn to the same title. The central defender finished his career with Port Vale, having made 502 appearances in all. A spell as assistant manager at Shrewsbury was followed by the top job back at Molineux. Wolves returned to the top division in 1983, finishing second to Queens Park Rangers, but he was sacked as they went straight back down. Hawkins later coached in the Middle East and became head of player development at the Football League.

ALAN COUSIN, 78, was an ever-present as Dundee became Scottish champions for the first, and only time, in 1962. They totalled 54 points to finish ahead of Rangers (51) and Celtic (46), with Cousin's partnership up front alongside Alan Gilzean a key factor. The pair were equally influential in their team's run the following season to the semi-finals of the European Cup, beating Cologne, Sporting Lisbon and Anderlecht before losing to AC Milan. They also led Dundee to the 1964 Scottish Cup Final, which Rangers won 3-1. Cousin, a part-timer throughout, combining his career with university studies and teaching, made 384 appearances and scored 141 goals in 11 years at Dens Park. The Scotland under-23 international followed manager Bob Shankly to Hibernian in 1965 and also played for Falkirk.

SHAY DUNNE, 86, made 326 appearances for Luton after signing from League of Ireland club Shelbourne in 1950. The right-back was a mainstay in promotion to the top division in 1955 when they finished runners-up to Birmingham on goal average. His biggest disappointment was missing out through injury on the run to the 1959 FA Cup Final. Dunne, capped 15 times by the Republic of Ireland, later had a spell as player-manager of Dunstable.

BERT LLEWELLYN, 77, marked his Everton debut as a 17-year-old with a goal against Blackpool in 1956. The centre-forward made 11 appearances for the club, netting once more, before prolific spells with Crewe (58 goals in 106 games) and Port Vale (50 in 103 matches). A move to Northampton, cut short by a leg injury 11 minutes into his debut, was followed by spells at Walsall and Wigan.

MAX MURRAY, 80, helped Rangers become Scottish champions in the 1956–57 and 1958–59 seasons. He also scored their first goal in Europe, against Nice in a European Cup first round tie which his side won 2-1. In eight years at the club, the Scottish under-23 international centre-forward netted 130 goals in 183 matches and was the club's leading marksman for three successive campaigns. Murray, who started his career with Queen's Park, made an unsuccessful £15,000 move to West Bromwich Albion in 1962. He went on to play for Third Lanark, Clyde and the Irish side Distillery.

DAVE DURIE, 85, made 301 appearances and scored 88 goals in 12 seasons with his home-town club Blackpool. Among the highlights was a 22-goal tally as his side finished fourth in the old First Division in the 1956–57 season. Durie's main position was inside-forward, but his versatility meant he was able to play in a variety of roles. He was never booked or sent off in a career which also took in a spell with Chester.

MATT GRAY, 80, signed for Manchester City from the now defunct Third Lanark for a Scottish record £30,001 in 1963. The extra pound was added to surpass the fee for team-mate Dave Hilley's move to Newcastle. Gray, who scored in Third Lanark's 2-1 defeat by Hearts in the 1959–60 Scottish League Cup Final, spent four years at Maine Road. The inside forward then played for South African clubs in Port Elizabeth and Johannesburg.

DAVE PACEY, 79, stood on the terraces at Kenilworth Road as a boy, played for Luton's schoolboys' team and made his league debut for his home-town club in a 3-0 defeat by Manchester United at Old Trafford on Christmas Day, 1957. The wing-half went on to make 280 appearances, including the 1959 FA Cup Final when Pacey scored his side's goal in a 2-1 defeat by Nottingham Forest. He also played non-league football for Hitchin and Kettering.

DENIS ATKINS, 77, joined Huddersfield from school as an amateur in 1953, signed professional forms two years later and made 214 appearances for the club. He joined Bradford City in a four-player swop in 1968 which also took Tony Leighton to Valley Parade, with Paul Aimson and Alex Smith going in the opposite direction. The right-back helped them win promotion from the Fourth Division the following year.

GORDON GUTHRIE, 86, served Derby in various roles for six decades. After his playing career was cut short by injury, he became physio, trainer and kit manager. He was awarded an MBE for services to football and has a stand named after him at Pride Park.

SYLVIA GORE, 71, was a pioneer of women's football and scorer of England's first official goal, in a 3-2 win over Scotland in 1972. In 2000, she was awarded an MBE for her services to the game. In 2014, she was inducted into the National Football Museum's Hall of Fame. Gore played for Manchester Corinthians and Fodens, originally a works team from Sandbach, once scoring 134 goals in a season. After retiring, she was manager of Wales.

OCTOBER 2016

DAVID HERD, 82, won two League titles and the FA Cup during a prolific career in which he averaged more than a goal every two games for Arsenal and Manchester United. The centre-forward forged a formidable partnership with fellow-Scot Denis Law as United became champions in 1965, finishing ahead of Leeds on goal average, and two years later when four points clear of Nottingham Forest. Herd's father, Alec, had previously won the title with Manchester City. United defeated Leicester 3-1 at Wembley in 1963, with two-goal Herd again emulating his father by lifting the trophy. He also had the distinction of scoring in his first appearances for the club in the FA Cup, League Cup and all three European competitions. But he missed their biggest triumph, against Benfica in the 1968 European Cup Final, having sustained a broken leg. Herd, who started his career at Stockport before joining Arsenal, left United for Stoke and finished his playing career at the Irish club Waterford, having accumulated 269 goals in 511 appearances. He was also on the mark three times in five games for Scotland. Later, he had a brief spell as manager of Lincoln.

GARY SPRAKE, 71, won domestic and European honours with Leeds during their time as one of the dominant forces in English football under Don Revie. The goalkeeper was an ever-present in the First Division title-winning season of 1968–69 when his team finished six points ahead of Liverpool. In the previous campaign, Leeds beat Arsenal 1-0 to win the League Cup at Wembley and Ferencvaros 1-0 on aggregate in the final of the Fairs Cup – forerunner of the UEFA Cup and Europa League. They lifted that trophy again in 1971, defeating Juventus on away goals after a 3-3 aggregate score over the two legs. Sprake made 508 appearances in 11 years at the club before losing his place to David Harvey and joining Birmingham for £100,000 – then a world record fee for his position. He won 37 Wales caps after becoming their youngest-ever goalkeeper when making his debut against Scotland in 1963 aged 18. His relationship with Revie and several members of the squad soured in the years after leaving Elland Road because of an involvement in a newspaper investigation into allegations of match-fixing against the manager.

CARLOS ALBERTO, 72, led Brazil to the 1970 World Cup in Mexico with a team regarded as the finest in the tournament's history. The captain also completed a 4-1 victory over Italy in the final with one of its most spectacular goals, accelerating on to Pele's lay-off to finish off a flowing move throughout with a tremendous cross-shot. The right-back, who had been controversially overlooked for the 1966 tournament in England, played 53 times for his country and was named in the world team of the 20th Century. At club level, he won domestic titles with Santos – for whom he made 445 appearances – and Fluminense, before finishing his playing days with New York Cosmos. Carlos Alberto went on to coach 15 clubs, among them Brazil champions Flamengo, ending his football career in charge of the Azerbaijan national side in 2005. He was one of Brazil's ambassadors for the 2014 World Cup in Brazil.

GERRY GOW, 64, was a combative, tough-tackling midfielder who made his debut for Bristol City as a 17-year-old in 1970 and went on to play 445 games, scoring 54 goals, in 12 years at the club. They included the 1975–76 promotion season when City reached the old First Division as runners-up to Sunderland. Gow left Ashton Gate for Manchester City and was part of their team for the 100th FA Cup Final in 1981 against Tottenham, who won it 3-2 in a replay. He also played for Rotherham and Burnley and managed Yeovil in their non-league days

SAMMY SMYTH, 91, was the last survivor of Wolves' 1949 FA Cup-winning side. In that final, the inside forward ran from the halfway line to seal a 3-1 win over Leicester. He joined the club from Irish football and scored 43 goals in 115 appearances. Smyth went on to play for Stoke and Liverpool and won nine caps with Northern Ireland.

RAY MABBUTT, 80, signed for Bristol Rovers in 1955, made nearly 400 appearances and served the club through the majority of their successful years in the old Second Division. The wing-half had a spell with Newport towards the end of his career, then continued well into his 40s in non-league football. Son Gary played for Rovers and Tottenham, winning 16 England caps. Gary's brother Kevin was with Bristol City and Crystal Palace.

GEORGE PEEBLES, 80, played a key role in Dunfermline's 1961 Scottish Cup Final success. The right-winger supplied the cross for Davie Thomson to head their first goal in a 2-0 replay win over Celtic after the teams' first meeting ended goalless. Peebles, who featured in every round, made 413 appearances in 11 years at the club, scoring 85 goals, before playing for and managing Stirling Albion.

MERVYN JONES, 85, scored one of Crewe's goals when they held Tottenham 2-2 in an FA Cup fourth round tie in 1960. In the replay, his side were beaten 13-2 at White Hart Lane. The left-winger previously played for Liverpool, then Scunthorpe where he was a Third Division North title winner in the 1957–58 season. He later served Chester and Lincoln, making a total of 392 Football League appearances.

EDDIE O'HARA, 80, won the 1957 Scottish Cup with Falkirk, who defeated Kilmarnock 2-1 in a replay after the teams had drawn 1-1. The left-winger, a Scottish under-23 international, then joined Everton and later Rotherham, Morton and Barnsley. After emigrating to South Africa, he played for Bloemfontein.

BRIAN HILL, 75, became Coventry's youngest-ever debutant and goalscorer in the final match of the 1957–58 Division Three South season against Gillingham. He was aged 16 years and 273 days. Hill's career really took off under Jimmy Hill, who switched him to a more defensive role as a successful man-marker. He made 244 appearances in 13 years at the club, had a spell on loan with Bristol City, then played for Torquay.

ROY JENNINGS, 84, was an England youth international who made 297 appearances for Brighton between 1952–64. During that time, he was converted from full-back to centre half, helped them win promotion to the old Second Division and scored 13 penalties. After moving to Crawley, then a non-league club, he netted 38 goals in 220 games, all penalties, and never missed from a spot-kick. He later managed the club.

JIMMY McINTOSH, 79, served Falkirk throughout his senior career and was a squad member in their Scottish Cup-winning season of 1956–57. He also gained Scottish under-23 honours. In 1958, the wing-half was denied the chance of a World Cup place in Sweden by a serious knee injury.

PETER DENTON, 70, signed for Jimmy Hill's Coventry from home-town club Gorleston and made his debut in 1965. He was in competition for the right-wing spot with Welsh international Ronnie Rees, moved on to Luton, then played non-league football.

NOVEMBER 2016

PAUL FUTCHER, 60, became the most expensive defender in English football and Manchester City's record buy in 1978. The £350,000 move from Luton was not a success. His new side failed to live up to expectations, Futcher himself came under criticism and after a single season he joined Oldham for £150,000. The centre-half, who started his career with Chester, went on to play for Derby, Barnsley, Halifax and Grimsby, making nearly 700 league appearances An England under-21 international, he was twice called up to the senior squad, but withdrew each time with injuries. He later played and managed at non-league level, taking Southport to the 1998 FA Trophy Final against Cheltenham (0-1). Twin brother Ron, a centre-forward, served ten league clubs, while son Ben was a central defender like his father and also had spells with Oldham and Grimsby.

LEN ALLCHURCH, 83, played alongside some of the finest Welsh talent that emerged from the Swansea Town side – as they were then called – of the 1950s. They included his legendary brother Ivor Allchurch, Mel Charles, Cliff Jones and Terry Medwin. The right-winger spent a decade there before joining Sheffield United and scored five goals in the final seven games to help them gain promotion to the old First Division in 1961. He won the Fourth Division title with Stockport in 1967, before returning to his home-town club, now known as Swansea City, who went up from Division Four in 1970. Len made 604 league appearances, won 11 Wales caps and was a non-playing member of the 1958 World Cup squad in Sweden.

BOBBY CAMPBELL, 60, shared Bradford City's triumph and tragedy at the end of the 1984–85 season. He was in the team presented with the Third Division title trophy before the final fixture against Lincoln at Valley Parade. Shortly before half-time, fire engulfed the wooden main stand, causing the death of 56 people. The Football League decided the abandoned game should not be replayed, with the 0-0 scoreline standing. Campbell was in his second spell at the club, having won promotion from Division Four during his first in 1982. He made more than 300 appearances and remains their all-time record scorer with 143 goals. The centre-forward began his career with Aston Villa, followed by spells at Huddersfield, Sheffield United, Halifax, Derby and Wigan, along with teams in Canada and Australia. He won two Northern Ireland caps and was among the non-playing members of Billy Bingham's squad at the 1982 World Cup in Spain

DAVIE PROVAN, 75, was part of Rangers' treble-winning team of the 1963–64 season. The Scottish champions finished six points clear of second-place Kilmarnock, beat Dundee 3-1 in the Scottish Cup Final and defeated Morton 5-0 to lift the League Cup. Provan won two more Scottish Cups and one other League Cup during 12 years and 268 appearances at the club. He was also in the side beaten by Bayern Munich in the 1967 European Cup-Winners' Cup Final. Provan later played for Crystal Palace, Plymouth and St Mirren and won five Scotland caps. He was then assistant manager to John Greig at Ibrox and Alex Ferguson at St Mirren, and also managed Albion Rovers.

MICK GRANGER, 86, was part of York's squad that reached the semi-finals of the FA Cup in 1955 before losing in a replay to Newcastle, who went on to beat Manchester City at Wembley. He played in the first two rounds for the Third Division North side, deputising for the injured Tommy Forgan. Granger later had spells with Hull and Halifax and during his time in the Forces was named Hong Kong Footballer of the Year.

RAY BRADY, 79, was part of a notable football family, headed by younger brother Liam, one of Ireland's finest players. He, himself, won six caps for the Republic and a Fourth Division title medal with Millwall in the 1961–62 season when he missed only one match. The centre-half also played for Queens Park Rangers before finishing his career with St Patrick's in the League of Ireland. Brother Pat had spells with the two London clubs, while Frank was with Shamrock Rovers.

IAN COWAN, 71, was a much-travelled right-winger who started his career at Falkirk and returned for a second spell with the club after playing for Partick and St Johnstone. He later served Dunfermline, Southend and Albion Rovers, along with clubs in Belgium and Hong Kong.

DANIEL PRODAN, 44, joined Rangers from Atletico Madrid for £2.2m in 1998. A knee injury prevented him playing a single competitive match in two-and-a-half years at the club and it was revealed he had not undergone a medical examination. The central defender won 54 caps for Romania, playing in the 1994 World Cup and Euro 96. After retiring, he took up a sporting director role with the Romanian FA. He died of a heart attack.

DECEMBER 2016

PETER DRABROOK, 79, won league and cup honours with Chelsea and West Ham and played in the World Cup for England. As an 18-year-old, Brabrook helped bring the title to Stamford Bridge in 1955 when his team finished four points ahead of Wolves and Portsmouth. He made 271 appearances and scored 57 goals for the club before a £35,000 move to Upton Park in 1964, the right-winger provided the cross for Ronnie Boyce to head a last-minute winner in the FA Cup Final against Preston (3-2). After £215 appearances and 43 goals, Brabrook finished his career at Leyton Orient, having won three international caps. One came at the 1968 finals in Sweden – a group play-off match against the Soviet Union which England lost 1-0. Later, he coached some of West Ham's most notable academy graduates, including Joe Cole, Michael Carrick and Frank Lampard junior.

DAVE MACLAREN, 82, started his career with Dundee, moved to Leicester in 1957 and immediately helped them win the Second Division title, seven points ahead of Nottingham Forest. After losing his place to England's Gordon Banks, the goalkeeper played for Plymouth, then joined his former manager Andy Beattie at Wolves. MacLaren finished his career at Southampton and later coached in Malaysia and Australia.

IAN CARTWRIGHT, 52, came through the youth ranks at Wolves and was a regular in the side that won promotion to the old First Division as runners-up to Queens Park Rangers in 1983. He remained at Molineux as they suffered three successive relegations, but was forced to retire with an ankle injury in 1986. The midfield player contracted kidney cancer in 2005 and the club staged a special match against West Bromwich Albion a year later to raised money.

ALBERT BENNETT, 72, joined Newcastle from Rotherham for £27,000 in 1965 and had two claims to fame during his time at St James' Park. The England-under 23 international was the club's first player to be named as a substitute, against Nottingham Forest later that year.

And it was the rugby-style tackle on him by Emlyn Hughes that earned the Liverpool captain the nickname of 'crazy horse.' Bennett, a centre-forward, moved to Norwich for £25,000 in 1969 and had his career ended by injury two years later.

BRIAN BULLESS, 83, signed for Hull straight from school, turned professional with his home-town team in 1951 and made 357 appearances before a leg injury forced him to retire in 1963. High spot came in the 1958–59 season when the wing-half, one of the most versatile players to have served the club, helped them win promotion to the old Second Division.

MATT CARRAGHER, 40, captained Port Vale to victory in the 2001 LDV Vans Trophy, his side beating Brentford 2-1 in the final at the Millennium Stadium. The defender joined the club from Wigan, where he was part of the Division Three title-winning side of 1996–97. Carragher, who also played for Macclesfield and made 423 career appearances, died of cancer.

TOMMY MCCULLOCH, 82, joined Clyde in 1957 and was a Scottish Cup winner in his first season, his team defeating Hibernian 1-0 in the final. The goalkeeper made 505 appearances in 15 years at the club before finishing his career at Hamilton.

NORMAN OAKLEY, 77, signed for Hartlepool from Doncaster in 1958 and spent six years there. The goalkeeper then joined Swindon for £6,000, a fee which helped keep his old club afloat. He also played for Grimsby and Boston.

NORMAN RIMMINGTON, 93, served his home-town club Barnsley in various roles spread over seven decades. He joined them at the end of the Second World War, also kept goal for Hartlepool, then returned to Oakwell after his playing career was ended by a broken leg. In turn, he was head coach, physio, assistant manager, groundsman and kitman. Shortly after his death, he was awarded the British Empire Medal posthumously in the New Year Honours for his services to football.

BARRIE HILLIER, 80, made his debut for Southampton in 1957 in a 5-0 win over Queens Park Rangers. The full-back made nine first-team appearances, mainly as a stand-in for long-serving Tommy Traynor, spending most of his time in the reserves. Hillier, whose father Joe kept goal for Middlesbrough, Cardiff and Newport, later played for Southern League Poole.

EDDIE BAILHAM, 75, was a prolific marksman in the League of Ireland who won one international cap with the Republic – a 3-1 defeat by England at Dalymount Park in 1964. He helped Shamrock Rovers to a league and cup double that year, scoring twice in the final against Cork Celtic. He later had spells in English non-league football with Cambridge City, Worcester and Wimbledon.

JANUARY 2017

GRAHAM TAYLOR, 72, was, by his own admission, never going to be more than a journeyman player. But he went on to become a coach and manager of the highest quality, held the England job for three years and was respected throughout the game for his ability and integrity. The son of a sports journalist, he made 339 league appearances at full-back for Grimsby and Lincoln before retiring with a hip injury. He had prepared for the future by attaining the full FA coaching badge at 21 and led Lincoln to the Division Four title in 1976. The following year, Taylor joined Elton John's Watford, embarking on what the singer called 'an incredible journey' during which they won three promotions in five seasons to reach the top flight. Watford finished runners-up to Liverpool, qualified for Europe for the first time and reached an FA Cup Final. Taylor then led Aston Villa to second place behind Liverpool and in 1990 succeeded Bobby Robson as manager of the national team. It proved a step too far. England failed to qualify for the 1994 World Cup, he mistakenly allowed a fly-on-the-wall television crew unprecedented access to him at work for a documentary and was eventually forced out by abuse from supporters and media criticism. Returning to club football, he took charge of Wolves and led Watford into the Premier League before retiring at the end of the 2000–01 season. He joined Villa's board of directors, but came back for a second spell on the touchline before finishing after more than 1,000 games as a manager. Taylor, who went on to become a radio summariser, was awarded an OBE in 2002. He was also a stalwart worker for charities.

BRIAN WHITEHOUSE, 81, scored both goals for West Bromwich Albion in an FA Cup semi-final against Aston Villa in 1957. The tie was drawn, with Villa winning the replay 1-0. The centre-forward left for Norwich because of strong competition for places at the club and also played for Wrexham, Crystal Palace, Charlton and Leyton Orient. He retired in 1968, joined Arsenal's coaching staff under Don Howe and led their youngsters to the FA Youth Cup. Whitehouse returned to The Hawthorns when his former Albion team-mate became manager, later taking over as caretaker after Howe's departure and giving a debut to a young Bryan Robson. After serving under subsequent managers Johnny Giles, Ronnie Allen and Ron Atkinson, he joined Atkinson's coaching team at Manchester United and later became chief scout for Coventry.

PAUL WENT, 67, became Leyton Orient's youngest-ever first-team player when making his debut, aged 15 years, 327 days, against Preston in 1965. The central defender's transfer to Charlton two years later helped keep the club afloat and there were further moves to Fulham, where he scored on his debut against Burnley, Portsmouth, for a then record club fee of £154,000, and Cardiff. Went finished his playing career back at Orient, having made more than 500 appearances. He became reserve coach and scout, then had a 21 day spell as manager in the 1980–81 season.

GRAHAM ATKINSON, 73, was a record-breaking figure in the rise of Oxford United. He joined the club, then Headington United, in 1959, making his debut against Chelmsford in the Southern League and becoming their youngest player – and scorer – at 16 years, 108 days. The inside-forward scored their first Football League goal, against Barrow, in 1962 and went on to accumulate a club-record 107 in 394 appearances. During that time, he played alongside elder brother Ron, who followed a record 561 appearances for the club with a top-flight managerial career. Graham left Oxford in 1974 to join Kettering.

BILLY SIMPSON, 87, joined Rangers from Linfield for a club-record fee of £11,500 in 1950 and scored a hat-trick on his debut against East Fife. He went on to win three titles in eight years at Ibrox, netting 174 goals in 262 appearances. The centre-forward also secured a Scottish Cup winners' medal with the only one of the 1953 replays against Aberdeen in 1953. Another winner gave Northern Ireland a famous 3-2 victory over England at Wembley in 1957, one of five goals in his 12 international appearances. He won a place in their squad for the following year's World Cup in Sweden, but did not feature because of injury. Simpson, who grew up in the shadow of Windsor Park and gained league and cup honours with Linfield, played for Stirling, Partick and Oxford after leaving Rangers.

LINDY DELAPENHA, 89, became the first Jamaican to play professional football in England. He joined Portsmouth in 1948 after leaving the army and helped them win back-to-back titles in the old First Division. The outside-right went on to made 270 appearances and score 93 goals for Middlesbrough after a £7,000 transfer, had a spell with Mansfield, then played for non-league Hereford and Burton.

DAVE SHIPPERLEY, 64, was Charlton's record scorer for an out-and-out central defender with 16 goals in two spells at the club in the 1970s. In between, he played for Gillingham and Plymouth. Shipperley left for a second time for Reading, who paid a then club-record fee of £50,000 in 1979. His son, Neil, served nine clubs, including Chelsea, Southampton and Crystal Palace.

JOHNNY LITTLE, 86, joined Rangers from Queen's Park in 1951 and in a decade at the club won two League titles and two Scottish Cups. The Canadian-born left-back made 327 appearances before finishing his career with Morton. He won one Scotland cap, against Sweden in 1953.

HARRY TAYLOR, 81, made his debut for Newcastle against Sheffield United in 1955. He played 29 first-team games, spending most of the time as back-up to Jackie Milburn and Len White. The right-winger had a spell on loan with Fulham and was also with non-league Chelmsford and Cambridge United.

FEBRUARY 2017

ALEX YOUNG, 80, was a deep-lying centre-forward whose style and artistry made him one of the most popular players in Everton's history. He joined the club for £40,000 in 1960 after a Scottish championship win with Hearts and in eight years at Goodison Park scored 87 goals in 273 appearances. Young, nicknamed 'The Golden Vision,' scored 22 goals and created many more for his captain Roy Vernon, who netted 24, as Everton became champions in 1963, finishing six points clear of Tottenham. Three years later, he was a key member of the successful FA Cup side that defeated Sheffield Wednesday 3-2 in the final – the first to retrieve a two-goal deficit to win at Wembley. Young, who gained eight Scotland caps, left to become player-manager of the Irish club Glentoran in 1968, then had a brief spell with Stockport.

PAUL McCARTHY, 45, had a leading role in Wycombe's run to the semi-finals of the FA Cup in 2001. The central defender scored against Millwall and Grimsby and was on the mark again in their sixth round win over Leicester. That took his side to Villa Park, where they were beaten 2-1 by Liverpool goals from Emile Heskey and Robbie Fowler. McCarthy spent seven years at the club after moving from Brighton. He later played for Oxford and won the FA Trophy with Ebbsfleet in 2008

ROGER HYND, 75, played as a makeshift centre-forward for Rangers in the 1967 European Cup-Winners' Cup Final against Bayern Munich (0-1). He was largely a squad player at Ibrox, left to join Crystal Palace, then became one of Birmingham's finest centre-halves in five years with the club. Highlight was the 1971–72 season when Hynd was an ever-present as Birmingham won promotion from the old Second Division and reached the semi-finals of the FA Cup, losing 3-0 to Leeds. The nephew of Liverpool legend Bill Shankly later played for Walsall, briefly managed Motherwell and was a coach at St Johnstone.

BOBBY MURDOCH, 81, signed for Liverpool, initially as an amateur, in 1955, turned professional two years later and spent four years at the club before leaving, two months before the arrival of Bill Shankly as manager. The forward went on to play for Bolton, Barrow, Stockport, Carlisle, Southport and Wigan.

BOBBY LUMLEY, 84, scored twice on his debut for Hartlepool in 1955 and was part of the squad that finished runners-up to Derby in the Third Division North two years later. The inside-right, who signed from Charlton, went on to play for Chesterfield and Gateshead before returning to Victoria Park. He later had a spell as the club's reserve team manager.

ROY PROVERBS, 84, started his career with Coventry, had a spell with Bournemouth, then spent four years with Gillingham. The half-back later played non-league football.

BOBBY GRANT, 76, was a winger who spent two seasons with St Johnstone in the 1960s and also played for Carlisle and Leyton Orient. His son, Roddy, won promotion to the Scottish Premier Division with St Johnstone in the 1989–90 season.

MARCH 2017

RONNIE MORAN, 83, was one of the most influential figures in Liverpool's distinguished history. He served the club for 49 years as player, coach, physio and caretaker-manager, was part of the famed Anfield boot room and had a hand in 44 trophies. They included 13 league titles, four European Cup triumphs, two UEFA Cups, five FA Cup successes and five League Cups. Moran signed as a part-timer in 1949, turned professional three years later and made his debut in a 3-2 defeat at Derby. The left-back went on to make 379 appearances, 47 as captain, notably as Liverpool regained top division status in 1962 and became First Division champions two years later, four points ahead of Manchester United and five clear of Everton. Moran, invited to join the backroom staff by Bill Shankly in 1966, worked under nine managers. He twice filled in as caretaker, following the resignation of Kenny Dalglish, then when Graeme Souness had heart surgery. With Souness recovering, he led the team out at Wembley for the 1992 FA Cup Final against Sunderland, which Liverpool won 2-0. He retired in 1998. Three weeks before his death, a book was published telling his story – its title 'Mr Liverpool.'

TOMMY GEMMELL, 73, played a key part in Celtic's historic European Cup triumph of 1967. The right-footed left-back scored the equaliser against Inter Milan and helped set up the decider for Steve Chalmers – a 2-1 success for the team known as 'The Lisbon Lions' after becoming the first from Britain to win the tournament. He also scored in the 1970 final which Celtic lost by the same scoreline to Feyenoord. Gemmell collected six titles, along with three Scottish Cups and four League Cups, during ten years at the club. After 418 appearances and 63 goals, he joined Nottingham Forest in 1971, had a spell in the United States with Miami Toros, then led Dundee to a 1-0 League Cup Final victory over Celtic in 1973. After that came three years managing Dundee and two spells in charge of Albion Rovers. His career also embraced 18 Scotland caps, with a debut against England in 1966 and the following year's 3-2 victory over the world champions at Wembley.

RAYMOND KOPA, 85, was one of the most skilful and graceful players of his era, winning the European Cup three times in succession with Real Madrid. They had signed him from Reims after defeating the French side in the tournament's first final in 1956. Kopa, who also shared two Spanish title successes, played 45 times for France, notably as a deep-lying centre-forward in the 1958 World Cup when his side reached the semi-finals. He returned to Reims the following year and remained until retiring in 1967.

JOHN PHILLIPS, 65, was a ball boy when England beat Portugal in the semi-finals of the 1966 World Cup – and he returned to Wembley seven years later for his international debut for Wales. It was the first of four caps for the Chelsea goalkeeper, who came to Stamford Bridge after spells with home-town club Shrewsbury and Aston Villa. He was understudy to Peter Bonetti, but still played 149 games before moving on to Crewe, then Brighton, Charlton and Crystal Palace.

JIM MCANEARNEY, 81, joined Sheffield Wednesday in 1951 with elder brother Tom and spent eight years at the club. The inside-forward went on to play for Plymouth, Watford and Bradford City. After coaching Bradford and managing Rotherham, he returned to Hillsborough in 1974 to take charge of the reserve team and was caretaker-manager following the departure of Steve Burtenshaw.

BILLY HAILS, 82, helped Peterborough win five successive Midland League titles prior to their election to the Football League in 1960. And he was an ever-present in the side that became champions of the Fourth Division at the first attempt, scoring 24 goals. The right-winger, who was signed from Lincoln, made 318 appearances for the club. Hails was then part of Northampton's Third Division title win in 1963. He also played for Luton before returning to Peterborough as physio and briefly managed the club following the departure of John Barnwell in 1978. After that, he was part of part of Watford's backroom staff under Graham Taylor.

PAUL BOWLES, 59, was a centre-half who started as a youth player at Manchester United. He spent five years at Crewe, then had spells with Port Vale and Stockport before finishing his career with Barrow.

KEN CURRIE, 91, broke into the Hearts team during War-time football and helped them reach the semi-finals of the Scottish League Cup when the game returned to normal in 1946. The inside-forward later played for Third Lanark, Raith, Dunfermline and Stranraer.

DAVE TAYLOR, 76, scored a post-War club record 284 goals in 436 matches, for non-league Yeovil between 1960–69. The inside-forward previously played for Gillingham and Portsmouth.

APRIL 2017

UGO EHIOGU, 44, suffered a cardiac arrest at Tottenham's training centre and died in hospital. Tributes were led by England manager Gareth Southgate, his defensive partner in Aston Villa's League Cup Final win over Leeds in 1996 and Middlesbrough's victory over Bolton in the same competition in 2004. They also shared Villa's FA Cup Final defeat by Chelsea in 2000. Ehiogu won four England caps, making his debut against China and scoring against Spain – Sven-Goran Eriksson's first game as manager. Had England not been blessed with several top-class centre-halves, he would almost certainly have gained more. His club career also embraced West Bromwich Albion, Leeds on loan, Rangers and Sheffield United. In his first Old Firm derby for Rangers against Celtic, he scored with an overhead kick – a goal voted by Ibrox supporters the best of the season. Ehiogu came out of retirement in 2012 to play for Wembley FC in the FA Cup. He joined Tottenham's coaching staff on a full-time basis in 2014 and was put in charge of the under-23 team.

STAN ANSLOW, 86, was converted from full-back to centre-forward by Millwall and scored five goals in their FA Cup run of season 1956–57. They defeated Newcastle, Wembley winners three times in the previous six seasons, 2-1 in front of a crowd of more than 45,000 on the way to the fifth round before losing to Birmingham. Anslow spent seven years at The Den – his only club.

FRED FURNISS, 94, made 433 appearances for Sheffield United. The full-back played a key role in United winning the War-time League North title of 1945–46 and the Football League Division Two title in the 1952–53 season. He was also with Chesterfield and Worksop and played local football well into his 50s.

STUART MARKLAND, 69, was a centre-half who also played in every other defensive position during his time with Dundee United from 1968–71. He joined the club from Berwick, had two spells with Montrose and was also with Cowdenbeath and Sydney Olympic in Australia.

MAY 2017

PETER NOBLE, 72, was a member of Swindon's League Cup-winning team in 1969 when they defeated Arsenal 3-1 in the final. He played every match on the road to Wembley, scoring the extra-time winner in the semi-final replay against Burnley. Noble, who joined the club from Newcastle, also helped them win the Anglo-Italian Cup in 1970 and gain promotion to the Second Division for the first time. The forward went on to play for Burnley and Blackpool.

NOEL KINSEY, 91, helped Birmingham become Second Division champions, then reach their highest-ever place of sixth in the old top division in 1956. He also scored in that year's FA Cup Final, won 3-1 by Manchester City in a match notable for City goalkeeper Bert Trautmann playing on with a broken bone in his neck. The inside-right, who joined the club from Norwich, won seven caps with Wales and played in their qualifying campaign for the 1954 World Cup. He finished his career at Port Vale.

TOMMY ROSS, 71, went into the record books when scoring a hat-trick in 90 seconds for Highland League club Ross County in November 1964. It was listed as the world's fastest and still stands. The 18-year-old inside-forward achieved the feat against Nairn County in a season which brought him 44 goals. Ross had been with the Dingwall club – now in the Scottish Premiership - since he was 15. He went on to play for Peterborough, York, Wigan and Scaborough and later scouted for Tottenham.

CORBETT CRESSWELL, 84, won the FA Amateur Cup three years in succession with Bishop Auckland between 1955-57. The centre-half also gained ten amateur international caps. Cresswell died three days before home-town club South Shields won the FA Vase at Wembley. In 1922, his father Warney Cresswell joined Sunderland from South Shields for a world record fee of £5,500.

TONY CONWELL, 85, was a full-back who played for Sheffield Wednesday, Huddersfield Derby. and finally Doncaster, where he sustained a broken leg in an FA Cup tie and retired in 1964.

ERIC STEVENSON, 74, signed for Hearts as a schoolboy, but a contract irregularity took him to Hibernian, where he made 390 appearances and scored 79 goals in ten years at the club. Two of them game in a 4-0 win over their Edinburgh rivals in 1965. The winger, comfortable on either flank. later played for Ayr.

CAMMY DUNCAN, 51, started his goalkeeping career at Sunderland. He played for Motherwell and Partick, was signed by Ayr's future Scotland manager George Burley and finished with Albion Rovers.

ROY GATER, 76, was a tough-tackling centre-half who captained Bournemouth during his six years at the club. He joined them from Port Vale and went on to play for Crewe before finishing his career in non-league football.

JUNE 2017

CHEICK TIOTE, 30, suffered a heart attack four months after leaving Newcastle to join the Chinese club Beijing Enterprises. Tiote, who collapsed during a training session, spent nearly seven years on Tyneside following a £3.5m move from FC Twente, where he had just won the Dutch title under Steve McClaren. The defensive midfielder made 156 appearances for the club, the last one in an FA Cup third round replay against Birmingham on January 18. He will be best remembered for a spectacular volley which completed Newcastle's Premier League comeback from 4-0 down to 4-4 in 2011. Tiote won 52 international caps with the Ivory Coast, playing in two World Cups and four Africa Cup on Nations.

RALPH WETTON, 89, signed professional forms with Tottenham in 1950 as the club's famous 'push and run' team under Arthur Rowe were putting together back-to-back titles – first in Division Two, then becoming Division One champions for the first time. The wing-half made his debut against Aston Villa and his final appearance against Arsenal in 1954. In between, he provided cover for Bill Nicholson and Ron Burgess. Wetton also played for Plymouth and Aldershot.

JOHN HIGGINS, 87, was in the Hibernian team that became the first in Britain to play in the European Cup when facing German club Rot-Weiss Essen in 1955. They went on to reach the semi-finals before losing to the French side Reims. Higgins spent five years at the club before moving to St Mirren, where he missed out on a Scottish Cup winners' medal against Aberdeen in 1959 with a viral infection. The right-back later played for Swindon.

ERNIE EDDS, 91, started out as an amateur with home town club Portsmouth before the War. The centre-forward signed professional forms with Millwall, then joined Plymouth in 1946 for the first of two spells with the club. He also played for Blackburn, Torquay and Swindon.

ALBERT FRANKS, 80, joined Newcastle from Sunderland Amateurs and made his debut against Luton in 1957. He left the club for Rangers in 1960 and also played for Morton, Lincoln and Queen of the South.

JULY 2017

JOHN MACKENZIE, 91, won nine Scotland caps and was the only native Gaelic speaker to have played for the national team. Two of them came in the 1954 World Cup in Switzerland – defeats by Austria and Uruguay. Another was an international friendly against Hungary, whose legendary captain Ferenc Puskas said afterwards that he gave 'the most magnificent display of wing play I have ever seen.' Mackenzie made 396 appearances for Partick, scoring 53 goals. He was on the losing side in three League Cup Finals, against East Fife, Celtic and Hearts, winning his only trophy – the Irish Cup – with Derry. He also had spells with Bournemouth and Fulham.

JOHN MCCORMICK, 80, helped Crystal Palace win promotion to the old First Division as runners-up to Derby in 1969. He formed a strong partnership alongside Mel Blyth at the heart of the defence and won the club's first Player of the Year award in 1972. McCormick joined Palace from Aberdeen and made 225 appearances in seven years at Selhurst Park.

KEN WIMSHURST, 79, was part of Southampton's squad that won promotion to the First Division as runners-up to Manchester City in the 1965-66 season. The wing-half spent five years at the club, then a similar period with Bristol City. He was previously with Newcastle, Gateshead and Wolves.

RAY SMITH, 88, was spotted by Luton's north-east scout playing amateur football and signed professional forms with the club in 1950. He had to wait 18 months for his league debut. Then, a knee injury restricted him to reserve team football. The wing-half had a run of senior games after Luton were promoted to the First Division, before joining Southend.

RECORDS SECTION

Compiled by Albert Sewell

INDEX

GOALSCORING

(†Football League pre-1992–93)

Highest: Arbroath 36 Bon Accord (Aberdeen) 0 in Scottish Cup 1, Sep 12, 1885. On same day, also in Scottish Cup 1, Dundee Harp beat Aberdeen Rov 35-0.

Internationals: France 0 England 15 in Paris, 1906 (Amateur); Ireland 0 England 13 in Belfast Feb 18, 1882 (record in UK); England 9 Scotland 3 at Wembley, Apr 15, 1961; Biggest England win at Wembley: 9-0 v Luxembourg (Euro Champ), Dec 15, 1982.

Other record wins: Scotland: 11-0 v Ireland (Glasgow, Feb 23, 1901); **Northern Ireland:** 7-0 v Wales (Belfast, Feb 1, 1930); **Wales:** 11-0 v Ireland (Wrexham, Mar 3, 1888); **Rep of Ireland:** 8-0 v Malta (Euro Champ, Dublin, Nov 16, 1983).

Record international defeats: England: 1-7 v Hungary (Budapest, May 23, 1954); **Scotland:** 3-9 v England (Wembley, Apr 15, 1961); **Ireland:** 0-13 v England (Belfast, Feb 18, 1882); **Wales:** 0-9 v Scotland (Glasgow, Mar 23, 1878); **Rep of Ireland:** 0-7 v Brazil (Uberlandia, May 27, 1982).

World Cup: Qualifying round – Australia 31 American Samoa 0, world record international score (Apr 11, 2001); Australia 22 Tonga 0 (Apr 9, 2001); Iran 19 Guam 0 (Nov 25, 2000); Maldives 0 Iran 17 (Jun 2, 1997). **Finals – highest scores:** Hungary 10 El Salvador 1 (Spain, Jun 15, 1982); Hungary 9 S Korea 0 (Switzerland, Jun 17, 1954); Yugoslavia 9 Zaire 0 (W Germany, Jun 18, 1974).

European Championship: Qualifying round – highest scorers: San Marino 0 Germany 13 (Serravalle, Sep 6, 2006). **Finals – highest score:** Holland 6 Yugoslavia 1 (quarter-final, Rotterdam, Jun 25, 2000).

Biggest England U-21 win: 9-0 v San Marino (Shrewsbury, Nov 19, 2013).

FA Cup: Preston 26 Hyde 0 1st round, Oct 15, 1887.

League Cup: West Ham 10 Bury 0 (2nd round, 2nd leg, Oct 25, 1983); Liverpool 10 Fulham 0 (2nd round, 1st leg, Sep 23, 1986). **Record aggregates:** Liverpool 13 Fulham 2 (10-0h, 3-2a), Sep 23, Oct 7, 1986; West Ham 12 Bury 0 (2-1a, 10-0h), Oct 4, 25, 1983; Liverpool 11 Exeter 0 (5-0h, 6-0a), Oct 7, 28, 1981.

League Cup – most goals in one match: 12 Reading 5 Arsenal 7 aet (4th round, Oct 30, 2012). Dagenham & Redbridge 6 Brentford 6 aet (Brentford won 4-2 on pens; 1st round, Aug 12, 2014)

Premier League (beginning 1992–93): Manchester Utd 9 Ipswich 0, Mar 4, 1995. **Record away win:** Nottm Forest 1 Manchester Utd 8 Feb 6, 1999.

Highest aggregate scores in Premier League – 11: Portsmouth 7 Reading 4, Sep 29, 2007; **10:** Tottenham 6 Reading 4, Dec 29, 2007; Tottenham 9 Wigan 1, Nov 22, 2009; Manchester Utd 8 Arsenal 2, Aug 28, 2011; Arsenal 7 Newcastle 3, Dec 29, 2012; WBA 5 Manchester Utd 5, May 19, 2013.

†Football League (First Division): Aston Villa 12 Accrington 2, Mar 12, 1892; Tottenham 10 Everton 4, Oct 11, 1958 (highest Div 1 aggregate that century); WBA 12 Darwen 0, Apr 4, 1892; Nottm Forest 12 Leicester Fosse 0, Apr 21, 1909. **Record away win:** Newcastle 1 Sunderland 9, Dec 5, 1908; Cardiff 1 Wolves 9, Sep 3, 1955; Wolves 0 WBA 8, Dec 27, 1893.

New First Division (beginning 1992–93): Bolton 7 Swindon 0, Mar 8, 1997, Sunderland 7 Oxford Utd 0, Sep 19, 1998. **Record away win:** Stoke 0 Birmingham 7, Jan 10, 1998; Oxford Utd 0 Birmingham 7, Dec 12, 1998. **Record aggregate:** Grimsby 6 Burnley 5, Oct 29, 2002; Burnley 4 Watford 4, Apr 5, 2003.

Championship (beginning 2004–05): Birmingham 0 Bournemouth 8, Oct 25, 2014. **Record away win:** Birmingham 0 Bournemouth 8, Oct 25, 2014. **Record aggregate:** Leeds 4 Preston 6, Sep 29, 2010; Leeds 3 Nottm Forest 7, Mar 20, 2012.

†**Second Division:** Newcastle 13 Newport Co 0, Oct 5, 1946; Small Heath 12 Walsall Town Swifts 0, Dec 17, 1892; Darwen 12 Walsall 0, Dec 26, 1896; Woolwich Arsenal 12 Loughborough 0, Mar 12, 1900; Small Heath 12 Doncaster 0, Apr 11, 1903. **Record away win:** *Burslem Port Vale 0 Sheffield Utd 10, Dec 10, 1892. **Record aggregate:** Manchester City 11 Lincoln 3, Mar 23, 1895.

New Second Division (beginning 1992–93): Hartlepool 1 Plymouth Argyle 8, May 7, 1994; Hartlepool 8 Grimsby 1, Sep 12, 2003.

New League 1 (beginning 2004–05): MK Dons 7 Oldham 0, Dec 20, 2014. **Record aggregate:** Hartlepool 4 Wrexham 6, Mar 5, 2005; Wolves 6 Rotherham 4, Apr 18, 2014; Bristol City 8 Walsall 2, May 3, 2015.

†**Third Division:** Gillingham 10 Chesterfield 0, Sep 5, 1987; Tranmere 9 Accrington 0, Apr 18, 1959; Brentford 9 Wrexham 0, Oct 15, 1963. **Record away win:** Halifax 0 Fulham 8, Sep 16, 1969. **Record aggregate:** Doncaster 7 Reading 5, Sep 25, 1982.

New Third Division (beginning 1992–93): Barnet 1 Peterborough 9, Sep 5, 1998. **Record aggregate:** Hull 7 Swansea 4, Aug 30, 1997.

New League 2 (beginning 2004–05): Peterborough 7 Brentford 0, Nov 24, 2007 Shrewsbury 7 Gillingham 0, Sep 13, 2008; Crewe 7 Barnet 0, Aug 21, 2010; Crewe 8 Cheltenham 1, Apr 2, 2011; Cambridge 7 Morecambe 0, Apr 19, 2016. **Record away win:** Boston 0 Grimsby 6, Feb 3, 2007; Macclesfield 0 Darlington 6, Aug 30, 2008; Lincoln 0 Rotherham 6, Mar 25, 2011. **Record aggregate:** Burton 5 Cheltenham 6, Mar 13, 2010; Accrington 7 Gillingham 4, Oct 2, 2010.

†**Third Division (North):** Stockport 13 Halifax 0 (still joint biggest win in Football League – see Div 2) Jan 6, 1934; Tranmere 13 Oldham 4, Dec 26, 1935. (17 is highest Football League aggregate score). **Record away win:** Accrington 0 Barnsley 9, Feb 3, 1934.

†**Third Division (South):** Luton 12 Bristol Rov 0, Apr 13, 1936; Bristol City 9 Gillingham 4, Jan 15, 1927; Gillingham 9 Exeter 4, Jan 7, 1951. **Record away win:** Northampton 0 Walsall 8, Apr 8, 1947.

†**Fourth Division:** Oldham 11 Southport 0, Dec 26, 1962. **Record away win:** Crewe 1 Rotherham 8, Sep 8, 1973. **Record aggregate:** Hartlepool 10 Barrow 1, Apr 4, 1959; Crystal Palace 9 Accrington 2, Aug 20, 1960; Wrexham 10 Hartlepool 1, Mar 3, 1962; Oldham 11 Southport 0, Dec 26, 1962; Torquay 8 Newport 3, Oct 19, 1963; Shrewsbury 7 Doncaster 4, Feb 1, 1975; Barnet 4 Crewe 7, Aug 17, 1991.

Scottish Premier – Highest aggregate: 12: Motherwell 6 Hibernian 6, May 5, 2010; 11: Celtic 8 Hamilton 3, Jan 3, 1987; Motherwell 5 Aberdeen 6, Oct 20, 1999. **Other highest team scores:** Aberdeen 8 Motherwell 0 (Mar 26, 1979); Hamilton 0 Celtic 8 (Nov 5, 1988); Celtic 9 Aberdeen 0 (Nov 6, 2010).

Scottish League Div 1: Celtic 11 Dundee 0, Oct 26, 1895. **Record away win:** Hibs 11 *Airdrie 1, Oct 24, 1959.

Scottish League Div 2: Airdrieonians 15 Dundee Wanderers 1, Dec 1, 1894 (biggest win in history of League football in Britain).

Record modern Scottish League aggregate: 12 – Brechin 5 Cowdenbeath 7, Div 2, Jan 18, 2003.

Record British score since 1900: Stirling 20 Selkirk 0 (Scottish Cup 1, Dec 8, 1984). Winger Davie Thompson (7 goals) was one of 9 Stirling players to score.

LEAGUE GOALS – BEST IN SEASON (Before restructure in 1992)

Div		Goals	Games
1	WR (Dixie) Dean, Everton, 1927–28	60	39
2	George Camsell, Middlesbrough, 1926–27	59	37

3(S)	Joe Payne, Luton, 1936–37	....	55	39
3(N)	Ted Harston, Mansfield, 1936–37	....	55	41
3	Derek Reeves, Southampton, 1959–60	....	39	46
4	Terry Bly, Peterborough, 1960–61	....	52	46

(Since restructure in 1992)

Div			Goals	Games
1	Guy Whittingham, Portsmouth, 1992–93	....	42	46
2	Jimmy Quinn, Reading, 1993–94	....	35	46
3	Andy Morrell, Wrexham, 2002–03	....	34	45

Premier League – BEST IN SEASON
Andy Cole **34 goals** (Newcastle – 40 games, 1993–94); Alan Shearer **34 goals** (Blackburn – 42 games, 1994–95).

FOOTBALL LEAGUE – BEST MATCH HAULS

(Before restructure in 1992)

Div		Goals
1	Ted Drake (Arsenal), away to Aston Villa, Dec 14, 1935	7
	James Ross (Preston) v Stoke, Oct 6, 1888	7
2	*Neville (Tim) Coleman (Stoke) v Lincoln, Feb 23, 1957	7
	Tommy Briggs (Blackburn) v Bristol Rov, Feb 5, 1955	7
3(S)	Joe Payne (Luton) v Bristol Rov, Apr 13, 1936	10
3(N)	Robert ('Bunny') Bell (Tranmere) v Oldham, Dec 26, 1935 he also missed a penalty	9
3	Barrie Thomas (Scunthorpe) v Luton, Apr 24, 1965	5
	Keith East (Swindon) v Mansfield, Nov 20, 1965	5
	Steve Earle (Fulham) v Halifax, Sep 16, 1969	5
	Alf Wood (Shrewsbury) v Blackburn, Oct 2, 1971	5
	Tony Caldwell (Bolton) v Walsall, Sep 10, 1983	5
	Andy Jones (Port Vale) v Newport Co., May 4, 1987	5
4	Bert Lister (Oldham) v Southport, Dec 26, 1962	6
	*Scored from the wing	

(Since restructure in 1992)

Div Goals
1   **4** in match – John Durnin (Oxford Utd v Luton, 1992–93); Guy Whittingham (Portsmouth v Bristol Rov 1992–93); Craig Russell (Sunderland v Millwall, 1995–96); David Connolly (Wolves at Bristol City 1998–99); Darren Byfield (Rotherham at Millwall, 2002–03); David Connolly (Wimbledon at Bradford City, 2002–03); Marlon Harewood (Nottm Forest v Stoke, 2002–03); Michael Chopra (Watford at Burnley, 2002–03); Robert Earnshaw (Cardiff v Gillingham, 2003–04).

2   **5** in match – Paul Barnes (Burnley v Stockport, 1996–97); Robert Taylor (all 5, Gillingham at Burnley, 1998–99); Lee Jones (all 5, Wrexham v Cambridge Utd, 2001–02).

3   **5** in match – Tony Naylor (Crewe v Colchester, 1992–93); Steve Butler (Cambridge Utd v Exeter, 1993–4); Guiliano Grazioli (Peterborough at Barnet, 1998–99).

Champ **4** in match – Garath McCleary (Nottm Forest at Leeds 2011–12); Nikola Zigic (Birmingham at Leeds 2011–12; Craig Davies (Barnsley at Birmingham 2012–13; Ross McCormack (Leeds at Charlton 2013–14), Jesse Lingard (Birmingham v Sheffield Wed 2013–14); Odion Ighalo (Watford v Blackpool, 2014-15).

Lge 1 **4** in match – Jordan Rhodes (all 4, Huddersfield at Sheffield Wed, 2011–12); Ellis Harrison (Bristol Rov v Northampton, 2016–17); James Vaughan (Bury v Peterborough, 2016–17).
5 in match – Juan Ugarte (Wrexham at Hartlepool, 2004–05); Jordan Rhodes (Huddersfield at Wycombe, 2011–12).

Last player to score 6 in English League match: Geoff Hurst (West Ham 8 Sunderland 0, Div 1 Oct 19,1968.

PREMIER LEAGUE – BEST MATCH HAULS

5 goals in match: Andy Cole (Manchester Utd v Ipswich, Mar 4, 1995); Alan Shearer (Newcastle v Sheffield Wed, Sep 19, 1999); Jermain Defoe (Tottenham v Wigan, Nov 22, 2009); Dimitar Berbatov (Manchester Utd v Blackburn, Nov 27, 2010), Sergio Aguero (Manchester City v Newcastle, Oct 3, 2015).

SCOTTISH LEAGUE

Div		Goals
Prem	Gary Hooper (Celtic) v Hearts, May 13, 2012	5
	Kris Boyd (Rangers) v Dundee Utd, Dec 30, 2009	5
	Kris Boyd (Kilmarnock) v Dundee Utd, Sep 25, 2004	5
	Kenny Miller (Rangers) v St Mirren, Nov 4, 2000	5
	Marco Negri (Rangers) v Dundee Utd, Aug. 23, 1997	5
	Paul Sturrock (Dundee Utd) v Morton, Nov 17, 1984	5
1	Jimmy McGrory (Celtic) v Dunfermline, Jan 14, 1928	8
1	Owen McNally (Arthurlie) v Armadale, Oct 1, 1927	8
2	Jim Dyet (King's Park) v Forfar, Jan 2, 1930 on his debut for the club	8
2	John Calder (Morton) v Raith, Apr 18, 1936	8
2	Norman Haywood (Raith) v Brechin, Aug. 20, 1937	8

SCOTTISH LEAGUE – BEST IN SEASON

Prem	Brian McClair (Celtic, 1986–87) **35**	
	Henrik Larsson (Celtic, 2000–01)	35
1	William McFadyen (Motherwell, 1931–32)	53
2	*Jimmy Smith (Ayr, 1927–28 – 38 appearances)	66
	(*British record)	

CUP FOOTBALL

Scottish Cup: John Petrie (Arbroath) v Bon Accord, at Arbroath, 1st round,
Sep 12, 1885 — 13
FA Cup: Ted MacDougall (Bournemouth) v Margate, 1st round, Nov 20,1971 — 9
FA Cup Final: Billy Townley (Blackburn) v Sheffield Wed, at Kennington
Oval, 1890; Jimmy Logan (Notts Co) v Bolton, at Everton, 1894;
Stan Mortensen (Blackpool) v Bolton, at Wembley, 1953 — 3
League Cup: Frank Bunn (Oldham) v Scarborough (3rd round), Oct 25, 1989 — 6
Scottish League Cup: Willie Penman (Raith) v Stirling, Sep 18, 1949 — 6
Scottish Cup: Most goals in match since war: 10 by **Gerry Baker** (St Mirren) in 15-0 win (1st round) v Glasgow Univ, Jan 30, 1960; 9 by his brother **Joe Baker** (Hibernian) in 15-1 win (2nd round) v Peebles, Feb 11, 1961.

AGGREGATE LEAGUE SCORING RECORDS

	Goals
*Arthur Rowley (1947–65, WBA, Fulham, Leicester, Shrewsbury)	434
†Jimmy McGrory (1922–38, Celtic, Clydebank)	410
Hughie Gallacher (1921–39, Airdrieonians, Newcastle, Chelsea, Derby, Notts Co, Grimsby, Gateshead)	387
William ('Dixie') Dean (1923–37, Tranmere, Everton, Notts Co)	379
Hugh Ferguson (1916–30, Motherwell, Cardiff, Dundee)	362
● Jimmy Greaves (1957–71, Chelsea, Tottenham, West Ham)	357
Steve Bloomer (1892–1914, Derby, Middlesbrough, Derby)	352
George Camsell (1923–39, Durham City, Middlesbrough)	348

Dave Halliday (1920–35, St Mirren, Dundee, Sunderland, Arsenal,
   Manchester City, Clapton Orient) **338**
John Aldridge (1979–98, Newport, Oxford Utd, Liverpool, Tranmere) **329**
Harry Bedford (1919–34), Nottm Forest, Blackpool, Derby, Newcastle,
   Sunderland, Bradford PA, Chesterfield **326**
John Atyeo (1951–66, Bristol City) **315**
Joe Smith (1908–29, Bolton, Stockport) **315**
Victor Watson (1920–36, West Ham, Southampton) **312**
Harry Johnson (1919–36, Sheffield Utd, Mansfield) **309**
Bob McPhail (1923–1939, Airdrie, Rangers) **306**
(*Rowley scored 4 for WBA, 27 for Fulham, 251 for Leicester, 152 for Shrewsbury.

● **Greaves'** 357 is record top-division total (he also scored 9 League goals for AC Milan).
Aldridge also scored 33 League goals for Real Sociedad. †McGrory scored 397 for Celtic, 13
for Clydebank).

Most League goals for one club: 349 – **Dixie Dean** (Everton 1925–37); **326** – **George Camsell**
(Middlesbrough 1925–39); **315** – **John Atyeo** (Bristol City 1951–66); **306** – **Vic Watson**
(West Ham 1920–35); **291** – **Steve Bloomer** (Derby 1892–1906, 1910–14); **259** – **Arthur
Chandler** (Leicester 1923–35); **255** – **Nat Lofthouse** (Bolton 1946–61); **251** – **Arthur Rowley**
(Leicester 1950–58).

More than 500 goals: Jimmy McGrory (Celtic, Clydebank and Scotland) scored a total of **550**
goals in his first-class career (1922–38).

More than 1,000 goals: Brazil's **Pele** is reputedly the game's all-time highest scorer with **1,283**
goals in 1,365 matches (1956–77), but many of them were scored in friendlies for his club,
Santos. He scored his 1,000th goal, a penalty, against Vasco da Gama in the Maracana
Stadium, Rio, on Nov 19, 1969. ● Pele (born Oct 23, 1940) played regularly for Santos from
the age of 16. During his career, he was sent off only once. He played 95 'A' internationals
for Brazil and in their World Cup-winning teams in 1958 and 1970. † Pele (Edson Arantes do
Nascimento) was subsequently Brazil's Minister for Sport. He never played at Wembley, apart
from being filmed there scoring a goal for a commercial. Aged 57, Pele received an 'honorary
knighthood' (Knight Commander of the British Empire) from the Queen at Buckingham
Palace on Dec 3, 1997.

Romario (retired Apr, 2008, aged 42) scored more than 1,000 goals for Vasco da Gama,
Barcelona, PSV Eindhoven, Valencia and Brazil (56 in 73 internationals).

MOST LEAGUE GOALS IN SEASON: DEAN'S 60

WR ('Dixie') Dean, Everton centre-forward, created a League scoring record in 1927–28 with 60
in 39 First Division matches. He also scored three in FA Cup ties, and 19 in representative
games, totalling 82 for the season.

George Camsell, of Middlesbrough, previously held the record with 59 goals in 37 Second
Division matches in 1926–27, his total for the season being 75.

SHEARER'S RECORD 'FIRST'

Alan Shearer (Blackburn) is the only player to score more than 30 top-division goals in 3
successive seasons since the War: 31 in 1993–94, 34 in 1994–95, 31 in 1995–96.

Thierry Henry (Arsenal) is the first player to score more than 20 Premiership goals in five
consecutive seasons (2002–06). **David Halliday** (Sunderland) topped 30 First Division goals
in 4 consecutive seasons with totals of 38, 36, 36 and 49 from 1925–26 to 1928–29.

MOST GOALS IN A MATCH

Sep 12, 1885: John Petrie set the all-time British individual record for a first-class match when,
in Arbroath's 36-0 win against Bon Accord (Scottish Cup 1), he scored **13**.

Apr 13, 1936: Joe Payne set the still-existing individual record on his debut as a centre-forward,
for Luton v Bristol Rov (Div 3 South). In a 12-0 win he scored **10**.

ROWLEY'S ALL-TIME RECORD

Arthur Rowley is English football's top club scorer with a total of 464 goals for WBA, Fulham, Leicester and Shrewsbury (1947–65). There were 434 in the League, 26 FA Cup, 4 League Cup.

Jimmy Greaves is second with a total of 420 goals for Chelsea, AC Milan, Tottenham and West Ham, made up of 366 League, 35 FA Cup, 10 League Cup and 9 in Europe. He also scored nine goals for AC Milan.

John Aldridge retired as a player at the end of season 1997–98 with a career total of 329 League goals for Newport, Oxford Utd, Liverpool and Tranmere (1979–98). In all competitions for those clubs he scored 410 in 737 appearances. He also scored 45 in 63 games for Real Sociedad.

MOST GOALS IN INTERNATIONAL MATCHES

13 by **Archie Thompson** for Australia v American Samoa in World Cup (Oceania Group qualifier) at Coff's Harbour, New South Wales, Apr 11, 2001. Result: 31-0.

7 by **Stanley Harris** for England v France in Amateur International in Paris, Nov 1, 1906. Result: 15-0.

6 by **Nat Lofthouse** for Football League v Irish League, at Wolverhampton, Sep 24, 1952. Result: 7-1.

Joe Bambrick for Northern Ireland against Wales (7 0) in Belfast, Feb 1, 1930 – a record for a Home Nations International.

WC Jordan in Amateur International for England v France, at Park Royal, Mar 23, 1908. Result: 12-0.

Vivian Woodward for England v Holland in Amateur International, at Chelsea, Dec 11,1909. Result: 9-1.

5 by **Howard Vaughton** for England v Ireland (Belfast) Feb 18, 1882. Result: 13-0.

Steve Bloomer for England v Wales (Cardiff) Mar 16, 1896. Result: 9-1.

Hughie Gallacher for Scotland against Ireland (Belfast), Feb 23, 1929. Result: 7-3.

Willie Hall for England v Northern Ireland, at Old Trafford, Nov 16, 1938. Five in succession (first three in 3'5 mins – fastest international hat-trick). Result: 7-0.

Malcolm Macdonald for England v Cyprus (Wembley) Apr 16, 1975. Result: 5-0.

Hughie Gallacher for Scottish League against Irish League (Belfast) Nov 11, 1925. Result: 7-3.

Barney Battles for Scottish League against Irish League (Firhill Park, Glasgow) Oct 31, 1928. Result: 8-2.

Bobby Flavell for Scottish League against Irish League (Belfast) Apr 30, 1947. Result: 7-4.

Joe Bradford for Football League v Irish League (Everton) Sep 25, 1929. Result: 7-2

Albert Stubbins for Football League v Irish League (Blackpool) Oct 18, 1950. Result: 6-3.

Brian Clough for Football League v Irish League (Belfast) Sep 23, 1959. Result: 5-0.

LAST ENGLAND PLAYER TO SCORE ...

3 goals: Jermain Defoe v Bulgaria (4-0), Euro Champ qual, Wembley, Sep 3, 2010.

4 goals: Ian Wright v San Marino (7-1), World Cup qual, Bologna, Nov 17, 1993.

5 goals: Malcolm Macdonald v Cyprus (5-0), Euro Champ qual, Wembley, Apr 16, 1975.

INTERNATIONAL TOP SHOTS

		Goals	Games
England	Wayne Rooney (2003–2017)	53	119
N Ireland	David Healy (2000–13)	36	95
Scotland	Denis Law (1958–74)	30	55
	Kenny Dalglish (1971–86)	30	102
Wales	Ian Rush (1980–96)	28	73
Rep of Ire	Robbie Keane (1998–2017)	68	146

ENGLAND'S TOP MARKSMEN
(As at start of season 2017–18)

	Goals	Games
Wayne Rooney (2003–17)	53	119
Bobby Charlton (1958–70)	49	106
Gary Lineker (1984–92)	48	80
Jimmy Greaves (1959–67)	44	57
Michael Owen (1998–2008)	40	89
Tom Finney (1946–58)	30	76
Nat Lofthouse (1950–58)	30	33
Alan Shearer (1992–2000)	30	63
Vivian Woodward (1903–11)	29	23
Frank Lampard (2003–14)	29	106
Steve Bloomer (1895–1907)	28	23
David Platt (1989–96)	27	62
Bryan Robson (1979–91)	26	90
Geoff Hurst (1966–72)	24	49
Stan Mortensen (1947–53)	23	25
Tommy Lawton (1938–48)	22	23
Peter Crouch (2005–11)	22	42
Mike Channon (1972–77)	21	46
Kevin Keegan (1972–82)	21	63

ROONEY'S ENGLAND RECORD

Wayne Rooney reached 50 international goals with a penalty against Switzerland at Wembley on September 8, 2015 to become England's record scorer, surpassing Bobby Charlton's mark. Charlton's record was set in 106 games, Rooney's tally in 107.

CONSECUTIVE GOALS FOR ENGLAND

Steve Bloomer scored in **10** consecutive appearances (19 goals) between Mar 1895 and Mar 1899.
Jimmy Greaves scored 11 goals in five consecutive matches from the start of season 1960–61.
Paul Mariner scored in five consecutive appearances (7 goals) between Nov 1981 and Jun 1982.
Wayne Rooney scored in five consecutive appearances (6 goals) between Oct 2012 and Mar 2013.

ENGLAND'S TOP FINAL SERIES MARKSMAN

Gary Lineker with 6 goals at 1986 World Cup in Mexico.

ENGLAND TOP SCORERS IN COMPETITIVE INTERNATIONALS

Michael Owen 26 goals in 53 matches; **Gary Lineker** 22 in 39; **Alan Shearer** 20 in 31.

MOST ENGLAND GOALS IN SEASON

13 – **Jimmy Greaves** (1960–61 in 9 matches); **12** – **Dixie Dean** (1926–27 in 6 matches); **10** – **Gary Lineker** (1990–91 in 10 matches); **10** – **Wayne Rooney** – (2008–09 in 9 matches).

MOST ENGLAND HAT-TRICKS

Jimmy Greaves 6; **Gary Lineker** 5, **Bobby Charlton** 4, **Vivian Woodward** 4, **Stan Mortensen** 3.

MOST GOALS FOR ENGLAND U-21s

13 – Alan Shearer (11 apps) Francis Jeffers (13 apps).

GOLDEN GOAL DECIDERS

The Football League, in an experiment to avoid penalty shoot-outs, introduced a new golden goal system in the 1994–95 **Auto Windscreens Shield** to decide matches in the knock-out stages of the competition in which scores were level after 90 minutes. The first goal scored in overtime ended play.

Iain Dunn (Huddersfield) became the first player in British football to settle a match by this sudden-death method. His 107th-minute goal beat Lincoln 3-2 on Nov 30, 1994, and to mark his 'moment in history' he was presented with a golden football trophy.

The AWS Final of 1995 was decided when Paul Tait headed the only goal for Birmingham against Carlisle 13 minutes into overtime – the first time a match at Wembley had been decided by the 'golden goal' formula.

First major international tournament match to be decided by sudden death was the Final of the **1996 European Championship** at Wembley in which Germany beat Czech Rep 2-1 by **Oliver Bierhoff's** goal in the 95th minute.

In the **1998 World Cup Finals** (2nd round), host country France beat Paraguay 1-0 with **Laurent Blanc's** goal (114).

France won the **2000 European Championship** with golden goals in the semi-final, 2-1 v Portugal (Zinedine Zidane pen, 117), and in the Final, 2-1 v Italy (David Trezeguet, 103).

Galatasaray (Turkey) won the **European Super Cup** 2-1 against Real Madrid (Monaco, Aug 25, 2000) with a 103rd minute golden goal, a penalty.

Liverpool won the **UEFA Cup** 5-4 against Alaves with a 117th-min golden goal, an own goal, in the Final in Dortmund (May 19, 2001).

In the **2002 World Cup Finals**, 3 matches were decided by Golden Goals: in the 2nd round Senegal beat Sweden 2-1 (Henri Camara, 104) and South Korea beat Italy 2-1 (Ahn Jung-hwan, 117); in the quarter-final, Turkey beat Senegal 1-0 (Ilhan Mansiz, 94).

France won the 2003 **FIFA Confederations Cup Final** against Cameroon (Paris, Jun 29) with a 97th-minute golden goal by Thierry Henry.

Doncaster won promotion to Football League with a 110th-minute golden goal winner (3-2) in the Conference Play-off Final against Dagenham at Stoke (May 10, 2003).

Germany won the **Women's World Cup Final** 2-1 v Sweden (Los Angeles, Oct 12, 2003) with a 98th-minute golden goal.

GOLD TURNS TO SILVER

Starting with the 2003 Finals of the UEFA Cup and Champions League/European Cup, UEFA introduced a new rule by which a silver goal could decide the winners if the scores were level after 90 minutes.

Team leading after 15 minutes' extra time win match. If sides level, a second period of 15 minutes to be played. If still no winner, result to be decided by penalty shoot-out.

UEFA said the change was made because the golden goal put too much pressure on referees and prompted teams to play negative football.

Although both 2003 European Finals went to extra-time, neither was decided by a silver goal. The new rule applied in the 2004 European Championship Finals, and Greece won their semi-final against the Czech Republic in the 105th minute.

The **International Board** decided (Feb 28 2004) that the golden/silver goal rule was 'unfair' and that from July 1 competitive international matches level after extra-time would, when necessary, be settled on penalties.

PREMIER LEAGUE TOP SHOTS (1992–2017)

Alan Shearer	260	Les Ferdinand	149
Wayne Rooney	198	Teddy Sheringham	146
Andy Cole	187	Robin van Persie	144
Frank Lampard	177	Jimmy Floyd Hasselbaink	127
Thierry Henry	175	Robbie Keane	126
Robbie Fowler	163	Nicolas Anelka	125
Jermain Defoe	158	Dwight Yorke	123
Michael Owen	150	Sergio Aguero	122

Steven Gerrard	120	Paul Scholes	107
Ian Wright	113	Darren Bent	106
Dion Dublin	111	Didier Drogba	104
Emile Heskey	110	Peter Crouch	103
Ryan Giggs	109	Matt Le Tissier	100

LEAGUE GOAL RECORDS

The highest goal-scoring aggregates in the Football League, Premier and Scottish League are as follows:

For

	Goals	Games	Club	Season
Prem	103	38	Chelsea	2009–10
Div 1	128	42	Aston Villa	1930–31
New Div 1	108	46	Manchester City	2001–02
New Champ	99	46	Reading	2005–06
Div 2	122	42	Middlesbrough	1926–27
New Div 2	89	46	Millwall	2000–01
New Lge 1	106	46	Peterborough	2010–11
Div 3(S)	127	42	Millwall	1927–28
Div 3(N)	128	42	Bradford City	1928–29
Div 3	111	46	QPR	1961–62
New Div 3	96	46	Luton	2001–02
New Lge 2	96	46	Notts Co	2009–10
Div 4	134	46	Peterborough	1960–61
Scot Prem	105	38	Celtic	2003–04
Scot L 1	132	34	Hearts	1957–58
Scot L 2	142	34	Raith Rov	1937–38
Scot L 3 (Modern)	130	36	Gretna	2004–05

Against

	Goals	Games	Club	Season
Prem	100	42	Swindon	1993–94
Div 1	125	42	Blackpool	1930–31
New Div 1	102	46	Stockport	2001–02
New Champ	86	46	Crewe	2004–05
Div 2	141	34	Darwen	1898–99
New Div 2	102	46	Chester	1992–93
New Lge 1	98	46	Stockport	2004–05
Div 3(S)	135	42	Merthyr T	1929–30
Div 3(N)	136	42	Nelson	1927–28
Div 3	123	46	Accrington Stanley	1959–60
New Div 3	113	46	Doncaster	1997–98
New Lge 2	96	46	Stockport	2010–11
Div 4	109	46	Hartlepool Utd	1959–60
Scot Prem	100	36	Morton	1984–85
Scot Prem	100	44	Morton	1987–88
Scot L 1	137	38	Leith A	1931–32
Scot L 2	146	38	Edinburgh City	1931–32
Scot L 3 (Modern)	118	36	East Stirling	2003–04

BEST DEFENSIVE RECORDS

Denotes under old offside law

Div	Goals Agst	Games	Club	Season
Prem	15	38	Chelsea	2004–05
1	16	42	Liverpool	1978–79

1	*15	22	Preston	1888–89
New Div 1	28	46	Sunderland	1998–99
New Champ	30	46	Preston	2005–06
2	18	28	Liverpool	1893–94
2	*22	34	Sheffield Wed	1899–1900
2	24	42	Birmingham	1947–48
2	24	42	Crystal Palace	1978–79
New Div 2	25	46	Wigan	2002–03
New Lge 1	32	46	Nottm Forest	2007–08
3(S)	*21	42	Southampton	1921–22
3(S)	30	42	Cardiff	1946–47
3(N)	*21	38	Stockport	1921–22
3(N)	21	46	Port Vale	1953–54
3	30	46	Middlesbrough	1986–87
New Div 3	20	46	Gillingham	1995–96
New Lge 2	31	46	Notts Co	2009–10
4	25	46	Lincoln	1980–81

SCOTTISH LEAGUE

Div	Goals Agst	Games	Club	Season
Prem	17	38	Celtic	2014–15
1	*12	22	Dundee	1902–03
1	^14	38	Celtic	1913–14
2	20	38	Morton	1966–67
2	*29	38	Clydebank	1922–23
2	29	36	East Fife	1995–96
New Div 3	21	36	Brechin	1995–96

TOP SCORERS (LEAGUE ONLY)

		Goals	Div
2016–17	Billy Sharp (Sheffield Utd)	30	Lge 1
2015–16	Matt Taylor (Bristol Rov)	27	Lge 2
2014–15	Daryl Murphy (Ipswich)	27	Champ
2013–14	Luis Suarez (Liverpool)	31	Prem
2012–13	Tom Pope (Port Vale)	31	Lge 2
2011–12	Jordan Rhodes (Huddersfield)	36	Lge 1
2010–11	Clayton Donaldson (Crewe)	28	Lge 2
2009–10	Rickie Lambert (Southampton)	31	Lge 1
2008–09	Simon Cox (Swindon)		
	Rickie Lambert (Bristol Rov)	29	Lge 1
2007–08	Cristiano Ronaldo (Manchester Utd)	31	Prem
2006–07	Billy Sharp (Scunthorpe)	30	Lge 1
2005–06	Thierry Henry (Arsenal)	27	Prem
2004–05	Stuart Elliott (Hull)	27	1
	Phil Jevons (Yeovil)	27	2
	Dean Windass (Bradford City)	27	1
2003–04	Thierry Henry (Arsenal)	30	Prem
2002–03	Andy Morrell (Wrexham)	34	3
2001–02	Shaun Goater (Manchester City)	28	1
	Bobby Zamora (Brighton)	28	2
2000–01	Bobby Zamora (Brighton)	28	3
1999–00	Kevin Phillips (Sunderland)	30	Prem
1998–99	Lee Hughes (WBA)	31	1
1997–98	Pierre van Hooijdonk (Nottm Forest)	29	1
	Kevin Phillips (Sunderland)	29	1

1996–97	Graeme Jones (Wigan)	31	3
1995–96	Alan Shearer (Blackburn)	31	Prem
1994–95	Alan Shearer (Blackburn)	34	Prem
1993–94	Jimmy Quinn (Reading)	35	2
1992–93	Guy Whittingham (Portsmouth)	42	1
1991–92	Ian Wright (Crystal Palace 5, Arsenal 24)	29	1
1990–91	Teddy Sheringham (Millwall)	33	2
1989–90	Mick Quinn (Newcastle)	32	2
1988–89	Steve Bull (Wolves)	37	3
1987–88	Steve Bull (Wolves)	34	4
1986–87	Clive Allen (Tottenham)	33	1
1985–86	Gary Lineker (Everton)	30	1
1984–85	Tommy Tynan (Plymouth Argyle)	31	3
	John Clayton (Tranmere)	31	4
1983–84	Trevor Senior (Reading)	36	4
1982–83	Luther Blissett (Watford)	27	1
1981–82	Keith Edwards (Hull 1, Sheffield Utd 35)	36	4
1980–81	Tony Kellow (Exeter)	25	3
1979–80	Clive Allen (Queens Park Rangers)	28	2
1978–79	Ross Jenkins (Watford)	29	3
1977–78	Steve Phillips (Brentford)	32	4
	Alan Curtis (Swansea City)	32	4
1976–77	Peter Ward (Brighton)	32	3
1975–76	Dixie McNeil (Hereford)	35	3
1974–75	Dixie McNeil (Hereford)	31	3
1973–74	Brian Yeo (Gillingham)	31	4
1972–73	Bryan (Pop) Robson (West Ham)	28	1
1971–72	Ted MacDougall (Bournemouth)	35	3
1970–71	Ted MacDougall (Bournemouth)	42	4
1969–70	Albert Kinsey (Wrexham)	27	4
1968–69	Jimmy Greaves (Tottenham)	27	1
1967–68	George Best (Manchester Utd)	28	1
	Ron Davies (Southampton)	28	1
1966–67	Ron Davies (Southampton)	37	1
1965–66	Kevin Hector (Bradford PA)	44	4
1964–65	Alick Jeffrey (Doncaster)	36	4
1963–64	Hugh McIlmoyle (Carlisle)	39	4
1962–63	Jimmy Greaves (Tottenham)	37	1
1961–62	Roger Hunt (Liverpool)	41	2
1960–61	Terry Bly (Peterborough)	52	4

100 LEAGUE GOALS IN SEASON

Manchester City, First Div Champions in 2001–02, scored 108 goals.

Bolton, First Div Champions in 1996–97, reached 100 goals, the first side to complete a century in League football since 103 by **Northampton** (Div 4 Champions) in 1986–87.

Last League Champions to reach 100 League goals: Chelsea (103 in 2009–10). Last century of goals in the top division: 111 by runners-up **Tottenham** in 1962–63.

Clubs to score a century of Premier League goals in season: **Chelsea** 103 in 2009–10, Manchester City (102) and Liverpool (101) in 2013–14.

Wolves topped 100 goals in four successive First Division seasons (1957–58, 1958–59, 1959–60, 1960–61).

In **1930–31,** the top three all scored a century of League goals: 1 Arsenal (127), 2 Aston Villa (128), 3 Sheffield Wed (102).

Latest team to score a century of League goals: Peterborough with 106 in 2010–11 (Lge 1).

100 GOALS AGAINST

Swindon, relegated with 100 goals against in 1993–94, were the first top-division club to concede a century of League goals since Ipswich (121) went down in 1964. Most goals conceded in the top division: 125 by Blackpool in 1930–31, but they avoided relegation.

MOST LEAGUE GOALS ON ONE DAY

A record of 209 goals in the four divisions of the Football League (43 matches) was set on **Jan 2, 1932**: 56 in Div 1, 53 in Div 2, 57 in Div 3 South and 43 in Div 3 North.

There were two 10-goal aggregates: Bradford City 9, Barnsley 1 in Div 2 and Coventry City 5, Fulham 5 in Div 3 South.

That total of 209 League goals on one day was equalled on **Feb 1, 1936** (44 matches): 46 in Div 1, 46 in Div 2, 49 in Div 3 South and 69 in Div 3 North. Two matches in the Northern Section produced 23 of the goals: Chester 12, York 0 and Crewe 5, Chesterfield 6.

MOST GOALS IN TOP DIV ON ONE DAY

This record has stood since **Dec 26, 1963**, when 66 goals were scored in the ten First Division matches played.

MOST PREMIER LEAGUE GOALS ON ONE DAY

47, in nine matches on **May 8, 1993** (last day of season). For the first time, all 20 clubs scored in the Premier League programme over the weekend of Nov 27-28, 2010.

FEWEST PREMIER LEAGUE GOALS IN ONE WEEK-END

10, in 10 matches on **Nov 24/25, 2001**.

FEWEST FIRST DIV GOALS ON ONE DAY

For full/near full programme: **Ten goals**, all by home clubs, in ten matches on Apr 28, 1923 (day of Wembley's first FA Cup Final).

SCORER OF LEAGUE'S FIRST GOAL

Kenny Davenport (2 mins) for Bolton v Derby, Sep 8, 1888.

VARDY'S RECORD

Jamie Vardy set a Premier League record by scoring in 11 consecutive matches for Leicester (Aug-Nov 2015). The all-time top division record of scoring in 12 successive games was set by **Jimmy Dunne** for Sheffield Utd in the old First Division in season 1931-32. **Stan Mortensen** scored in 15 successive matches for Blackpool (First Division) in season 1950-51, but that sequence included two injury breaks.

SCORERS FOR 7 PREMIER LEAGUE CLUBS

Craig Bellamy (Coventry, Newcastle, Blackburn, Liverpool, West Ham, Manchester City, Cardiff).

SCORERS FOR 6 PREMIER LEAGUE CLUBS

Les Ferdinand (QPR, Newcastle, Tottenham, West Ham, Leicester, Bolton); **Andy Cole** (Newcastle, Manchester Utd, Blackburn, Fulham, Manchester City, Portsmouth); **Marcus Bent** (Crystal Palace, Ipswich, Leicester, Everton, Charlton, Wigan); **Nick Barmby** (Tottenham, Middlesbrough, Everton, Liverpool, Leeds, Hull); **Peter Crouch** (Tottenham, Aston Villa, Southampton, Liverpool, Portsmouth, Stoke); **Robbie Keane** (Coventry, Leeds, Tottenham, Liverpool, West Ham, Aston Villa); **Nicolas Anelka** (Arsenal, Liverpool, Manchester City, Bolton, Chelsea, WBA); **Darren Bent** (Ipswich, Charlton, Tottenham, Sunderland, Aston Villa, Fulham).

SCORERS FOR 5 PREMIER LEAGUE CLUBS

Stan Collymore (Nottm Forest, Liverpool, Aston Villa, Leicester, Bradford); **Mark Hughes** (Manchester

Utd, Chelsea, Southampton, Everton, Blackburn); **Benito Carbone** (Sheffield Wed, Aston Villa, Bradford, Derby, Middlesbrough); **Ashley Ward** (Norwich, Derby, Barnsley, Blackburn Bradford); **Teddy Sheringham** (Nottm Forest, Tottenham, Manchester Utd, Portsmouth, West Ham); **Chris Sutton** (Norwich, Blackburn, Chelsea, Birmingham, Aston Villa).

SCORERS IN MOST CONSECUTIVE LEAGUE MATCHES

Arsenal broke the record by scoring in 55 successive Premiership fixtures: the last match in season 2000–01, then all 38 games in winning the title in 2001–02, and the first 16 in season 2002–03. The sequence ended with a 2-0 defeat away to Manchester Utd on December 7, 2002.

Chesterfield previously held the record, having scored in 46 consecutive matches in Div 3 (North), starting on Christmas Day, 1929 and ending on December 27, 1930.

SIX-OUT-OF-SIX HEADERS

When **Oxford Utd** beat Shrewsbury 6-0 (Div 2) on Apr 23, 1996, all six goals were headers.

ALL–ROUND MARKSMEN

Alan Cork scored in four divisions of the Football League and in the Premier League in his 18-season career with Wimbledon, Sheffield Utd and Fulham (1977–95).

Brett Ormerod scored in all four divisions (2, 1, Champ and Prem Lge) for Blackpool in two spells (1997–2002, 2008–11). **Grant Holt** (Sheffield Wed, Rochdale, Nottm Forest, Shrewsbury, Norwich) has scored in four Football League divisions and in the Premier League.

MOST CUP GOALS

FA Cup – most goals in one season: 20 by **Jimmy Ross** (Preston, runners-up 1887–88); 15 by **Alex (Sandy) Brown** (Tottenham, winners 1900–01).

Most FA Cup goals in individual careers: 49 by **Harry Cursham** (Notts Co 1877–89); 20th century: 44 by **Ian Rush** (39 for Liverpool, 4 for Chester, 1 for Newcastle 1979–98). **Denis Law** was the previous highest FA Cup scorer in the 20th century with 41 goals for Huddersfield Town, Manchester City and Manchester Utd (1957–74).

Most FA Cup Final goals by individual: 5 by **Ian Rush** for Liverpool (2 in 1986, 2 in 1989, 1 in 1992).

HOTTEST CUP HOT-SHOT

Geoff Hurst scored 21 cup goals in season 1965–66: 11 League Cup, 4 FA Cup and 2 Cup-Winners' Cup for West Ham, and 4 in the World Cup for England.

SCORERS IN EVERY ROUND

Twelve players have scored in every round of the FA Cup in one season, from opening to Final inclusive: **Archie Hunter** (Aston Villa, winners 1887); **Sandy Brown** (Tottenham, winners 1901); **Harry Hampton** (Aston Villa, winners 1905); **Harold Blackmore** (Bolton, winners 1929); **Ellis Rimmer** (Sheffield Wed, winners 1935); **Frank O'Donnell** (Preston, beaten 1937); **Stan Mortensen** (Blackpool, beaten 1948); **Jackie Milburn** (Newcastle, winners 1951); **Nat Lofthouse** (Bolton, beaten 1953); **Charlie Wayman** (Preston, beaten 1954); **Jeff Astle** (WBA, winners 1968); **Peter Osgood** (Chelsea, winners 1970).

Blackmore and the next seven completed their 'set' in the Final at Wembley; Osgood did so in the Final replay at Old Trafford.

Only player to score in every **Football League Cup** round possible in one season: **Tony Brown** for WBA, winners 1965–66, with 9 goals in 10 games (after bye in Round 1).

TEN IN A ROW

Dixie McNeill scored for Wrexham in ten successive FA Cup rounds (18 goals): 11 in Rounds 1-6, 1977–78; 3 in Rounds 3-4, 1978–79; 4 in Rounds 3-4, 1979–80.

Stan Mortensen (Blackpool) scored 25 goals in 16 FA Cup rounds out of 17 (1946–51).

TOP MATCH HAULS IN FA CUP

Ted MacDougall scored nine goals, a record for the competition proper, in the FA Cup first round on Nov 20, 1971, when Bournemouth beat Margate 11-0. On Nov 23, 1970 he had scored six in an 8-1 first round replay against Oxford City.

Other six-goal FA Cup scorers include **George Hilsdon** (Chelsea v Worksop, 9-1, 1907–08), **Ronnie Rooke** (Fulham v Bury, 6-0, 1938–39), **Harold Atkinson** (Tranmere v Ashington, 8-1, 1952–53), **George Best** (Manchester Utd v Northampton 1969–70, 8-2 away), **Duane Darby** (Hull v Whitby, 8-4, 1996–97).

Denis Law scored all six for Manchester City at Luton (6-2) in an FA Cup 4th round tie on Jan 28, 1961, but none of them counted – the match was abandoned (69 mins) because of a waterlogged pitch. He also scored City's goal when the match was played again, but they lost 3 1.

Tony Philliskirk scored **five** when Peterborough beat Kingstonian 9-1 in an FA Cup 1st round replay on Nov 25, 1992, but had them wiped from the records.

With the score at 3-0, the Kingstonian goalkeeper was concussed by a coin thrown from the crowd and unable to play on. The FA ordered the match to be replayed at Peterborough behind closed doors, and Kingstonian lost 1-0.

• Two players have scored **ten goals** in FA Cup preliminary round matches: **Chris Marron** for South Shields against Radcliffe in Sep 1947; **Paul Jackson** when Sheffield-based club Stocksbridge Park Steels beat Oldham Town 17-1 on Aug 31, 2002. He scored 5 in each half and all ten with his feet – goal times 6, 10, 22, 30, 34, 68, 73, 75, 79, 84 mins.

QUICKEST GOALS AND RAPID SCORING

A goal in **4 sec** was claimed by **Jim Fryatt**, for Bradford PA v Tranmere (Div 4, Apr 25, 1965), and by **Gerry Allen** for Whitstable v Danson (Kent League, Mar 3,1989). **Damian Mori** scored in **4 sec** for Adelaide v Sydney (Australian National League, December 6, 1995).

Goals after **6 sec** – **Albert Mundy** for Aldershot v Hartlepool, Oct 25, 1958; **Barrie Jones** for Notts Co v Torquay, Mar 31, 1962; **Keith Smith** for Crystal Palace v Derby, Dec 12, 1964.

9.6 sec by **John Hewitt** for Aberdeen at Motherwell, 3rd round, Jan 23, 1982 (fastest goal in Scottish Cup history).

Colin Cowperthwaite reputedly scored in **3.5 sec** for Barrow v Kettering (Alliance Premier League) on Dec 8, 1979, but the timing was unofficial.

Phil Starbuck for Huddersfield **3 sec** after entering the field as 54th min substitute at home to Wigan (Div 2) on Easter Monday, Apr 12, 1993. Corner was delayed, awaiting his arrival and he scored with a header.

Malcolm Macdonald after **5 sec** (officially timed) in Newcastle's 7-3 win in a pre-season friendly at St Johnstone on Jul 29, 1972.

World's fastest goal: 2.8 sec, direct from kick-off, Argentinian **Ricardo Olivera** for Rio Negro v Soriano (Uruguayan League), December 26, 1998.

Fastest international goal: 7 sec, Christian Benteke for Belgium v Gibraltar (World Cup qual, Faro), Oct 10, 2016.

Fastest England goals: 17 sec, Tommy Lawton v Portugal in Lisbon, May 25, 1947. **27 sec, Bryan Robson** v France in World Cup at Bilbao, Spain on Jun 16, 1982; **37 sec, Gareth Southgate** v South Africa in Durban, May 22, 2003; **30 sec, Jack Cock** v Ireland, Belfast, Oct 25, 1919; **30 sec, Bill Nicholson** v Portugal at Goodison Park, May 19, 1951. **38 sec, Bryan Robson** v Yugoslavia at Wembley, Dec 13, 1989; **42 sec, Gary Lineker** v Malaysia in Kuala Lumpur, Jun 12, 1991.

Fastest international goal by substitute: 5 sec, John Jensen for Denmark v Belgium (Euro Champ), Oct 12, 1994.

Fastest goal by England substitute: 10 sec, Teddy Sheringham v Greece (World Cup qualifier) at Old Trafford, Oct 6, 2001.

Fastest FA Cup goal: 4 sec, Gareth Morris (Ashton Utd) v Skelmersdale, 1st qual round, Sep 15, 2001.

Fastest FA Cup goal (comp proper): 9.7 sec, Jimmy Kebe for Reading v WBA, 5th Round, Feb 13, 2010.

Fastest FA Cup Final goal: 25 sec, **Louis Saha** for Everton v Chelsea at Wembley, May 30, 2009.

Fastest goal by substitute in FA Cup Final: 96 sec, **Teddy Sheringham** for Manchester Utd v Newcastle at Wembley, May 22, 1999.

Fastest League Cup Final goal: 45 sec, **John Arne Riise** for Liverpool v Chelsea, 2005.

Fastest goal on full League debut: 7.7 sec, **Freddy Eastwood** for Southend v Swansea (Lge 2), Oct 16, 2004. He went on to score hat-trick in 4-2 win.

Fastest goal in cup final: 4.07 sec, 14-year-old **Owen Price** for Ernest Bevin College, Tooting, beaten 3-1 by Barking Abbey in Heinz Ketchup Cup Final at Arsenal on May 18, 2000. Owen, on Tottenham's books, scored from inside his own half when the ball was played back to him from kick-off.

Fastest Premier League goals: 10 sec, **Ledley King** for Tottenham away to Bradford, Dec 9, 2000; **10.4 sec, Alan Shearer** for Newcastle v Manchester City, Jan 18, 2003; **11 sec, Mark Viduka** for Leeds v Charlton, Mar 17, 2001; **12.5 sec. James Beattie** for Southampton at Chelsea, Aug 28, 2004; **13 sec, Chris Sutton** for Blackburn at Everton, Apr 1, 1995; **13 sec, Dwight Yorke** for Aston Villa at Coventry, Sep 30, 1995; **13 sec Asmir Begovic** (goalkeeper) for Stoke v Southampton, Nov 2, 2013; **13 sec Jay Rodriguez** for Southampton at Chelsea, Dec 1, 2013.

Fastest top-division goal: 7 sec, **Bobby Langton** for Preston v Manchester City (Div 1), Aug 25, 1948.

Fastest goal in Champions League: 10 sec, **Roy Makaay** for Bayern Munich v Real Madrid (1st ko rd), Mar 7, 2007.

Fastest Premier League goal by substitute: 9 sec, **Shaun Goater,** Manchester City's equaliser away to Manchester Utd (1-1), Feb 9, 2003. In Dec, 2011, Wigan's **Ben Watson** was brought off the bench to take a penalty against Stoke and scored.

Fastest goal on Premier League debut: 36 sec, **Thievy Bifouma** on as sub for WBA away to Crystal Palace, Feb 8, 2014.

Fastest Scottish Premiership goal: 10 sec, **Kris Boyd** for Kilmarnock v Ross Co, Jan 28, 2017.

Fastest-ever hat-trick: 90 sec, credited to 18-year-old **Tommy Ross** playing in a Highland match for Ross County against Nairn County on Nov 28, 1964.

Fastest goal by goalkeeper in professional football: 13 sec, **Asmir Begovic** for Stoke v Southampton (Prem Lge), Nov 2, 2013.

Fastest goal in Olympic Games: 14 sec, **Neymar** for Brazil in semi-finals v Honduras, Aug 17, 2016, Rio de Janeiro.

Fastest goal in women's football: 7 sec, **Angie Harriott** for Launton v Thame (Southern League, Prem Div), season 1998–99.

Fastest hat-trick in League history: 2 min 20 sec, Bournemouth's 84th-minute substitute **James Hayter** in 6-0 home win v Wrexham (Div 2) on Feb 24, 2004 (goal times 86, 87, 88 mins).

Fastest First Division hat-tricks since war: Graham Leggat, 3 goals in 3 minutes (first half) when Fulham beat Ipswich 10-1 on Boxing Day, 1963; **Nigel Clough**, 3 goals in **4 minutes** (81, 82, 85 pen) when Nottm Forest beat QPR 4-0 on Dec 13, 1987.

Fastest Premier League hat-trick: 2 min 56 sec (13, 14, 16) by **Sadio Mane** in Southampton 6, Aston Villa 1 on May 16, 2015.

Fastest international hat-trick: 2 min 35 sec, Abdul Hamid Bassiouny for Egypt in 8-2 win over Namibia in Abdallah, Libya, (African World Cup qual), Jul 13, 2001.

Fastest international hat-trick in British matches: 3.5 min, Willie Hall for England v N Ireland at Old Trafford, Manchester, Nov 16, 1938. (Hall scored 5 in 7-0 win); **3min 30 sec, Arif Erdem** for Turkey v N Ireland, European Championship qualifier, at Windsor Park, Belfast, on Sep 4, 1999.

Fastest FA Cup hat-tricks: In 3 min, Billy Best for Southend v Brentford (2nd round, Dec 7, 1968); **2 min 20 sec, Andy Locke** for Nantwich v Droylsden (1st Qual round, Sep 9, 1995).

Fastest Scottish hat-trick: 2 min 30 sec, **Ian St John** for Motherwell away to Hibernian (Scottish League Cup), Aug 15, 1959.

Fastest hat-trick of headers: Dixie Dean's 5 goals in Everton's 7-2 win at home to Chelsea (Div 1) on Nov 14, 1931 included 3 headers between **5th** and **15th**-min.

Scored first kick: Billy Foulkes (Newcastle) for Wales v England at Cardiff, Oct 20, 1951, in his first international match.

Preston scored six goals in **7 min** in record 26-0 FA Cup 1st round win v Hyde, Oct 15, 1887.

Notts Co scored six second-half goals in **12 min** (Tommy Lawton 3, Jackie Sewell 3) when beating Exeter 9-0 (Div 3 South) at Meadow Lane on Oct 16, 1948.

Arsenal scored six in **18 min** (71-89 mins) in 7-1 home win (Div 1) v Sheffield Wed, Feb 15, 1992.

Tranmere scored six in first **19 min** when beating Oldham 13-4 (Div 3 North), December 26, 1935.

Sunderland scored eight in **28 min** at Newcastle (9-1 Div 1), December 5, 1908. Newcastle went on to win the title.

Southend scored all seven goals in **29 min** in 7-0 win at home to Torquay (Leyland Daf Cup, Southern quarter-final), Feb 26, 1991. Score was 0-0 until 55th minute.

Plymouth scored five in first **18 min** in 7-0 home win v Chesterfield (Div 2), Jan 3, 2004.

Five in 20 min: Frank Keetley in Lincoln's 9-1 win over Halifax in Div 3 (North), Jan 16, 1932; **Brian Dear** for West Ham v WBA (6-1, Div 1) Apr 16, 1965. **Kevin Hector** for Bradford PA v Barnsley (7-2, Div 4), Nov 20, 1965.

Four in 5 min: John McIntyre for Blackburn v Everton (Div 1), Sep 16, 1922; **WG (Billy) Richardson** for WBA v West Ham (Div 1), Nov 7, 1931.

Three in 2·5 min: Jimmy Scarth for Gillingham v Leyton Orient (Div 3S), Nov 1, 1952.

Three in three minutes: Billy Lane for Watford v Clapton Orient (Div 3S), December 20, 1933; **Johnny Hartburn** for Leyton Orient v Shrewsbury (Div 3S), Jan 22, 1955; **Gary Roberts** for Brentford v Newport, (Freight Rover Trophy, South Final), May 17, 1985; **Gary Shaw** for Shrewsbury v Bradford City (Div 3), December 22, 1990.

Two in 9 sec: Jamie Bates with last kick of first half, **Jermaine McSporran** 9 sec into second half when Wycombe beat Peterborough 2-0 at home (Div 2) on Sep 23, 2000.

Premier League – fastest scoring: Four goals in 4 min 44 sec, Tottenham home to Southampton on Sunday, Feb 7, 1993.

Premiership – fast scoring away: When **Aston Villa** won 5-0 at Leicester (Jan 31, 2004), all goals scored in **18 second-half min** (50-68).

Four in 13 min by Premier League sub: Ole Gunnar Solskjaer for Manchester Utd away to Nottm Forest, Feb 6, 1999.

Five in 9 mins by substitute: Robert Lewandowski for Bayern Munich v Wolfsburg (5-1, Bundesliga), Sep 22, 2015.

FASTEST GOALS IN WORLD CUP FINAL SERIES

10.8 sec, Hakan Sukur for Turkey against South Korea in 3rd/4th-place match at Taegu, Jun 29, 2002; **15 sec, Vaclav Masek** for Czechoslovakia v Mexico (in Vina, Chile, 1962); **27 sec, Bryan Robson** for England v France in Bilbao, Spain, 1982).

TOP MATCH SCORES SINCE WAR

By English clubs: 13-0 by Newcastle v Newport (Div 2, Oct 1946); 13-2 by Tottenham v Crewe (FA Cup 4th. Rd replay, Feb 1960); 13-0 by Chelsea v Jeunesse Hautcharage, Lux. (Cup-Winners' Cup 1st round, 2nd leg, Sep 1971).

By Scottish club: 20-0 by Stirling v Selkirk (E. of Scotland League) in Scottish Cup 1st round (Dec 1984). That is the highest score in British first-class football since Preston beat Hyde 26-0 in FA Cup, Oct 1887.

MOST GOALS IN CALENDAR YEAR

88 by Lionel Messi in 2012 (76 Barcelona, 12 Argentina).

ROONEY'S DOUBLE TOP

Wayne Rooney ended season 2016–17 as top scorer for England (53) and Manchester Utd (253).

PREMIER LEAGUE LONGEST-RANGE GOALS BY OUTFIELD PLAYERS

66 yards: Charlie Adam (Stoke at Chelsea, Apr 4, 2015)
64 yards: Xabi Alonso (Liverpool v Newcastle, Sep 20, 2006)
62 yards: Maynor Figueroa (Wigan at Stoke, Dec 12, 2009)

59 yards: **David Beckham** (Manchester Utd at Wimbledon, Aug 17, 1996)
55 yards: **Wayne Rooney** (Manchester Utd at West Ham, Mar 22, 2014)

GOALS BY GOALKEEPERS

(Long clearances unless stated)

Pat Jennings for Tottenham v Manchester Utd (goalkeeper Alex Stepney), Aug 12, 1967 (FA Charity Shield).
Peter Shilton for Leicester v Southampton (Campbell Forsyth), Oct 14, 1967 (Div 1).
Ray Cashley for Bristol City v Hull (Jeff Wealands), Sep 18, 1973 (Div 2).
Steve Sherwood for Watford v Coventry (Raddy Avramovic), Jan 14, 1984 (Div 1).
Steve Ogrizovic for Coventry v Sheffield Wed (Martin Hodge), Oct 25, 1986 (Div 1).
Andy Goram for Hibernian v Morton (David Wylie), May 7, 1988 (Scot Prem Div).
Andy McLean, on Irish League debut, for Cliftonville v Linfield (George Dunlop), Aug 20, 1988.
Alan Paterson for Glentoran v Linfield (George Dunlop), Nov 30, 1988 (Irish League Cup Final - only instance of goalkeeper scoring winner in a senior cup final in UK).
Ray Charles for East Fife v Stranraer (Bernard Duffy), Feb 28, 1990 (Scot Div 2).
Iain Hesford for Maidstone v Hereford (Tony Elliott), Nov 2, 1991 (Div 4).
Chris Mackenzie for Hereford v Barnet (Mark Taylor), Aug 12, 1995 (Div 3).
Peter Schmeichel for Manchester Utd v Rotor Volgograd, Sep 26, 1995 (header, UEFA Cup 1).
Mark Bosnich (Aston Villa) for Australia v Solomon Islands, Jun 11, 1997 (penalty in World Cup qual – 13-0).
Peter Keen for Carlisle away to Blackpool (goalkeeper John Kennedy), Oct 24, 2000 (Div 3).
Steve Mildenhall for Notts Co v Mansfield (Kevin Pilkington), Aug 21, 2001 (free-kick inside own half, League Cup 1).
Peter Schmeichel for Aston Villa v Everton (Paul Gerrard), Oct 20, 2001 (volley, first goalkeeper to score in Premiership).
Mart Poom for Sunderland v Derby (Andy Oakes), Sep 20, 2003 (header, Div 1).
Brad Friedel for Blackburn v Charlton (Dean Kiely), Feb 21, 2004 (shot, Prem).
Paul Robinson for Leeds v Swindon (Rhys Evans), Sep 24, 2003 (header, League Cup 2).
Andy Lonergan for Preston v Leicester (Kevin Pressman), Oct 2, 2004 (Champ).
Matt Glennon for St Johnstone away to Ross Co (Joe Malin), Mar 11, 2006 (shot, Scot Div 1).
Gavin Ward for Tranmere v Leyton Orient (Glenn Morris), Sep 2, 2006 (free-kick Lge 1).
Mark Crossley for Sheffield Wed v Southampton (Kelvin Davis), Dec 23, 2006 (header, Champ).
Paul Robinson for Tottenham v Watford (Ben Foster), Mar 17, 2007 (Prem).
Adam Federici for Reading v Cardiff (Peter Enckelman), Dec 28, 2008 (shot, Champ).
Chris Weale for Yeovil v Hereford (Peter Gulacsi), Apr 21, 2009 (header, Lge 1).
Scott Flinders for Hartlepool v Bournemouth (Shwan Jalal), Apr 30, 2011 (header, Lge 1).
Iain Turner for Preston v Notts Co (Stuart Nelson), Aug 27 2011 (shot, Lge 1).
Andy Leishman for Auchinleck v Threave (Vinnie Parker), Oct 22, 2011 (Scot Cup 2).
Tim Howard for Everton v Bolton (Adam Bogdan), Jan 4, 2012 (Prem).
Asmir Begovic for Stoke v Southampton (Artur Boruc), Nov 2, 2013 (Prem).
Mark Oxley for Hibernian v Livingston (Darren Jamieson), Aug 9, 2014 (Scot Champ).
Jesse Joronen for Stevenage v Wycombe (Matt Ingram), Oct 17, 2015 (Lge 2).
Barry Roche for Morecambe v Portsmouth (Ryan Fulton), Feb 2, 2016 (header, Lge 2).

MORE GOALKEEPING HEADLINES

Arthur Wilkie, sustained a hand injury in Reading's Div 3 match against Halifax on Aug 31, 1962, then played as a forward and scored twice in a 4-2 win.
Alex Stepney was Manchester Utd's joint top scorer for two months in season 1973–74 with two penalties.
Dundee Utd goalkeeper Hamish McAlpine scored three penalties in a ten-month period between 1976–77, two against Hibernian, home and away, and one against Rangers at Ibrox.
Alan Fettis scored twice for Hull in 1994–95 Div 2 season, as a substitute in 3-1 home win over Oxford Utd (Dec 17) and, when selected outfield, with last-minute winner (2-1) against Blackpool on May 6.

Roger Freestone scored for Swansea with a penalty at Oxford Utd (Div 2, Apr 30, 1995) and twice from the spot the following season against Shrewsbury (Aug 12) and Chesterfield (Aug 26).

Jimmy Glass, on loan from Swindon, kept Carlisle in the Football League on May 8, 1999. With ten seconds of stoppage-time left, he went upfield for a corner and scored the winner against Plymouth that sent Scarborough down to the Conference instead.

Paul Smith, Nottm Forest goalkeeper, was allowed to run through Leicester's defence unchallenged and score direct from the kick-off of a Carling Cup second round second match on Sep 18, 2007. It replicated the 1-0 score by which Forest had led at half-time when the original match was abandoned after Leicester defender Clive Clarke suffered a heart attack. Leicester won the tie 3-2?

Tony Roberts (Dagenham), is the only known goalkeeper to score from open play in the FA Cup, his last-minute goal at Basingstoke in the fourth qualifying round on Oct 27, 2001 earning a 2-2 draw. Dagenham won the replay 3-0 and went on to reach the third round proper.

The only known instance in first-class football in Britain of a goalkeeper scoring direct from a goal-kick was in a First Division match at Roker Park on Apr 14, 1900. The kick by Manchester City's **Charlie Williams** was caught in a strong wind and Sunderland keeper J. E Doig fumbled the ball over his line.

Jose Luis Chilavert, Paraguay's international goalkeeper, scored a hat-trick of penalties when his club Velez Sarsfield beat Ferro Carril Oeste 6-1 in the Argentine League on Nov 28, 1999. In all, he scored 8 goals in 72 internationals. He also scored with a free-kick from just inside his own half for Velez Sarsfield against River Plate on Sep 20, 2000.

Most goals by a goalkeeper in a League season: 5 (all penalties) by **Arthur Birch** for Chesterfield (Div 3 North), 1923-24.

When Brazilian goalkeeper **Rogerio Ceni** (37) converted a free-kick for Sao Paulo's winner (2-1) v Corinthians in a championship match on Mar 27, 2011, it was his 100th goal (56 free-kicks, 44 pens) in a 20-season career.

OWN GOALS

Most goals by player in one season: 5 by **Robert Stuart** (Middlesbrough) in 1934-35.

Three in match by one team: Sheffield Wed's **Vince Kenny**, **Norman Curtis** and **Eddie Gannon** in 5-4 defeat at home to WBA (Div 1) on Dec 26, 1952; Rochdale's **George Underwood**, **Kenny Boyle** and **Danny Murphy** in 7-2 defeat at Carlisle (Div 3 North), Dec 25, 1954; Sunderland's **Stephen Wright** and **Michael Proctor** (2) at home to Charlton (1-3, Prem), Feb 1, 2003; Brighton's **Liam Bridcutt** (2) and **Lewis Dunk** in 6-1 FA Cup 5th rd defeat at Liverpool, Feb 19, 2012.; Sunderland's **Santiago Vergini**, **Liam Bridcutt** and **Patrick van Aanholt** in 8-0 defeat at Southampton (Prem), Oct 18, 2014,

Two in match by one player: Chris Nicholl (Aston Villa) scored all 4 goals in 2-2 draw away to Leicester (Div 1), Mar 20, 1976; Jamie Carragher (Liverpool) in first half at home to Manchester Utd (2-3) in Premiership, Sep 11, 1999; Jim Goodwin (Stockport) in 1-4 defeat away to Plymouth (Div 2), Sep 23, 2002; Michael Proctor (Sunderland) in 1-3 defeat at home to Charlton (Premiership), Feb 1, 2003. Michael Duberry (Oxford) scored two own goals against Hereford on Jan 21, 2012, then rescued a point for his side with a 90th minute equaliser. Jonathan Walters (Stoke) headed the first 2 Chelsea goals in their 4-0 Premier League win at the Britannia Stadium, Jan 12, 2013. He also missed a penalty. Newport's **Tom Naylor** conceded two own goals and gave away a penalty in a 3-2 defeat by Morecambe on Sept 14, 2013.

Fastest own goals: 8 sec by **Pat Kruse** of Torquay, for Cambridge Utd (Div 4), Jan 3, 1977; in First Division, **16 sec** by **Steve Bould** (Arsenal) away to Sheffield Wed, Feb 17, 1990.

Late own-goal man: Frank Sinclair (Leicester) put through his own goal in the 90th minute of Premiership matches away to Arsenal (L1-2) and at home to Chelsea (2-2) in Aug 1999.

Half an own goal each: Chelsea's second goal in a 3-1 home win against Leicester on December 18, 1954 was uniquely recorded as 'shared own goal'. Leicester defenders **Stan Milburn** and **Jack Froggatt**, both lunging at the ball in an attempt to clear, connected simultaneously and sent it rocketing into the net.

Match of 149 own goals: When Adama, Champions of Malagasy (formerly Madagascar) won a League match 149-0 on Oct 31, 2002, all 149 were own goals scored by opponents Stade Olympique De L'Emryne. They repeatedly put the ball in their own net in protest at a refereeing decision.

MOST SCORERS IN MATCH

Liverpool set a Football League record with **eight** scorers when beating Crystal Palace 9-0 (Div 1) on Sep 12, 1989. Marksmen were: Steve Nicol (7 and 88 mins), Steve McMahon (16), Ian Rush (45), Gary Gillespie (56), Peter Beardsley (61), John Aldridge (67 pen), John Barnes (79), Glenn Hysen (82).

Fifteen years earlier, **Liverpool** had gone one better with **nine** different scorers when they achieved their record win, 11-0 at home to Stromsgodset (Norway) in the Cup-Winners' Cup 1st round, 1st leg on Sep 17, 1974.

Eight players scored for **Swansea** when they beat Sliema, Malta, 12-0 in the Cup-Winners' Cup 1st round, 1st leg on Sep 15, 1982.

Nine Stirling players scored in the 20-0 win against Selkirk in the Scottish Cup 1st Round on December 8, 1984.

Premier League record: **Seven Chelsea** scorers in 8-0 home win over Aston Villa, Dec 23, 2012. An eighth player missed a penalty.

LONG SCORING RUNS

Tom Phillipson scored in 13 consecutive matches for Wolves (Div 2) in season 1926-27, which is still an English League record. In the same season, **George Camsell** scored in 12 consecutive matches for Middlesbrough (Div 2). **Bill Prendergast** scored in 13 successive League and Cup appearances for Chester (Div 3 North) in season 1938-39.

Dixie Dean scored in 12 consecutive games (23 goals) for Everton in Div 2 in 1930-31.

Danish striker **Finn Dossing** scored in 15 consecutive matches (Scottish record) for Dundee Utd (Div 1) in 1964-65.

50-GOAL PLAYERS

With **52** goals for **Wolves** in 1987-78 (34 League, 12 Sherpa Van Trophy, 3 Littlewoods Cup, 3 FA Cup), **Steve Bull** became the first player to score 50 in a season for a League club since **Terry Bly** for Div 4 newcomers Peterborough in 1960-61. Bly's 54 comprised 52 League goals and 2 in the FA Cup, and included 7 hat-tricks, still a post-war League record. Bull was again the country's top scorer with 50 goals in season 1988-89: 37 League, 2 Littlewoods Cup and 11 Sherpa Van Trophy. Between Bly and Bull, the highest individual scoring total for a season was 49 by two players: **Ted MacDougall** (Bournemouth 1970-71, 42 League, 7 FA Cup) and **Clive Allen** (Tottenham 1986-87, 33 League, 12 Littlewoods Cup, 4 FA Cup).

HOT SHOTS

Jimmy Greaves was top Div 1 scorer (League goals) six times in 11 seasons: 32 for Chelsea (1958-59), 41 for Chelsea (1960-61) and, for Tottenham, 37 in 1962-63, 35 in 1963-64, 29 in 1964-65 (joint top) and 27 in 1968-69.

Brian Clough (Middlesbrough) was leading scorer in Div 2 in three successive seasons: 40 goals in 1957-58, 42 in 1958-59 and 39 in 1959-60.

John Hickton (Middlesbrough) was top Div 2 scorer three times in four seasons: 24 goals in 1967-68, 24 in 1969-70 and 25 in 1970-71.

MOST HAT-TRICKS

Nine by George Camsell (Middlesbrough) in Div 2, 1926-27, is the record for one season. Most League hat-tricks in career: 37 by **Dixie Dean** for Tranmere and Everton (1924-38).

Most top division hat-tricks in a season since last War: six by **Jimmy Greaves** for Chelsea (1960-61). **Alan Shearer** scored five hat-tricks for Blackburn in the Premier League, season 1995-96.

Frank Osborne (Tottenham) scored three consecutive hat-tricks in Div 1 in Oct-Nov 1925, against Liverpool, Leicester (away) and West Ham.

Tom Jennings (Leeds) scored hat-tricks in three successive Div 1 matches (Sep–Oct, 1926): 3 goals v Arsenal, 4 at Liverpool, 4 v Blackburn. Leeds were relegated that season.

Jack Balmer (Liverpool) scored his three hat-tricks in a 17-year career in successive Div 1 matches (Nov 1946): 3 v Portsmouth, 4 at Derby, 3 v Arsenal. No other Liverpool player scored during that 10-goal sequence by Balmer.

Gilbert Alsop scored hat-tricks in three successive matches for Walsall in Div 3 South in Apr 1939: 3 at Swindon, 3 v Bristol City and 4 v Swindon.

Alf Lythgoe scored hat-tricks in three successive games for Stockport (Div 3 North) in Mar 1934: 3 v Darlington, 3 at Southport and 4 v Wrexham.

TRIPLE HAT-TRICKS

There have been at least three instances of 3 hat-tricks being scored for one team in a Football League match:

Apr 21, 1909: Enoch West, Billy Hooper and Alfred Spouncer for Nottm Forest (12-0 v Leicester Fosse, Div 1).

Mar 3, 1962: Ron Barnes, Wyn Davies and Roy Ambler in Wrexham's 10-1 win against Hartlepool (Div 4).

Nov 7, 1987: Tony Adcock, Paul Stewart and David White for Manchester City in 10-1 win at home to Huddersfield (Div 2).

For the first time in the Premiership, **three** hat-tricks were completed on one day (Sep 23, 1995): **Tony Yeboah** for Leeds at Wimbledon; **Alan Shearer** for Blackburn v Coventry; **Robbie Fowler** with 4 goals for Liverpool v Bolton.

In the FA Cup, **Jack Carr, George Elliott** and **Walter Tinsley** each scored 3 in Middlesbrough's 9-3 first round win against Goole in Jan, 1915. **Les Allen** scored 5, **Bobby Smith** 4 and **Cliff Jones** 3 when Tottenham beat Crewe 13-2 in a fourth-round replay in Feb 1960.

HAT-TRICKS v THREE 'KEEPERS

When West Ham beat Newcastle 8-1 (Div 1) on Apr 21, 1986 **Alvin Martin** scored 3 goals against different goalkeepers: Martin Thomas injured a shoulder and was replaced, in turn, by outfield players Chris Hedworth and Peter Beardsley.

Jock Dodds of Lincoln had done the same against West Ham on Dec 18, 1948, scoring past Ernie Gregory, Tommy Moroney and George Dick in 4-3 win.

David Herd (Manchester Utd) scored against Sunderland's Jim Montgomery, Charlie Hurley and Johnny Parke in 5-0 First Division home win on Nov 26, 1966.

Brian Clark, of Bournemouth, scored against Rotherham's Jim McDonagh, Conal Gilbert and Michael Leng twice in 7-2 win (Div 3) on Oct 10, 1972.

On Oct 16, 1999 (Div 3) **Chris Pike** (Hereford) scored a hat-trick in 5-0 win over Colchester, who became the first team in league history to have two keepers sent off in the same game.

On Dec 18, 2004 (Lge 1), in 6-1 defeat at Hull, Tranmere used **John Achterberg** and **Russell Howarth**, both retired injured, and defender **Theo Whitmore**.

On Mar 9, 2008, Manchester Utd had three keepers in their 0-1 FA Cup quarter-final defeat by Portsmouth. **Tomasz Kuszczak** came on at half-time for **Edwin van der Sar** but was sent off when conceding a penalty. **Rio Ferdinand** went in goal and was beaten by Sulley Muntari's spot-kick.

Derby used three keepers in a 4-1 defeat at Reading (Mar 10, 2010, Champ). **Saul Deeney**, who took over when **Stephen Bywater** was injured, was sent off for a foul and **Robbie Savage** replaced him.

EIGHT-DAY HAT-TRICK TREBLE

Joe Bradford, of Birmingham, scored three hat-tricks in eight days in Sep 1929-30 v Newcastle (won 5-1) on the 21st, 5 for the Football League v Irish League (7-2) on the 25th, and 3 in his club's 5-7 defeat away to Blackburn on the 28th.

PREMIERSHIP DOUBLE HAT-TRICK

Robert Pires and **Jermaine Pennant** each scored 3 goals in Arsenal's 6-1 win at home to Southampton (May 7, 2003).

TON UP – BOTH ENDS

Manchester City are the only club to score and concede a century of League goals in the same season. When finishing fifth in the 1957–58 season, they scored 104 and gave away 100.

TOURNAMENT TOP SHOTS

Most individual goals in a World Cup Final series: 13 by **Just Fontaine** for France, in Sweden 1958. Most in European Championship Finals: 9 by **Michel Platini** for France, in France 1984.

MOST GOALS ON CLUB DEBUT

Jim Dyet scored eight in King's Park's 12-2 win against Forfar (Scottish Div 2, Jan 2, 1930). **Len Shackleton** scored six times in Newcastle's 13-0 win v Newport (Div 2, Oct 5, 1946) in the week he joined them from Bradford Park Avenue.

MOST GOALS ON LEAGUE DEBUT

Five by **George Hilsdon**, for Chelsea (9-2) v Glossop, Div 2, Sep 1, 1906. **Alan Shearer,** with three goals for Southampton (4-2) v Arsenal, Apr 9, 1988, became, at 17, the youngest player to score a First Division hat-trick on his full debut.

FOUR-GOAL SUBSTITUTE

James Collins (Swindon), sub from 60th minute, scored 4 in 5-0 home win v Portsmouth (Lge 1) on Jan 1, 2013.

CLEAN-SHEET RECORDS

On the way to promotion from Div 3 in season 1995–96, Gillingham's ever-present goalkeeper **Jim Stannard** set a clean-sheet record. In 46 matches. He achieved 29 shut-outs (17 at home, 12 away), beating the 28 by **Ray Clemence** for Liverpool (42 matches in Div 1, 1978–79) and the previous best in a 46-match programme of 28 by Port Vale (Div 3 North, 1953–54). In conceding only 20 League goals in 1995–96, Gillingham created a defensive record for the lower divisions.

Chris Woods, Rangers' England goalkeeper, set a British record in season 1986–87 by going 1,196 minutes without conceding a goal. The sequence began in the UEFA Cup match against Borussia Moenchengladbach on Nov 26, 1986 and ended when Rangers were sensationally beaten 1-0 at home by Hamilton in the Scottish Cup 3rd round on Jan 31, 1987 with a 70th-minute goal by **Adrian Sprott**. The previous British record of 1,156 minutes without a goal conceded was held by Aberdeen goalkeeper **Bobby Clark** (season 1970–71).

Manchester Utd set a new Premier League clean-sheet record of 1,333 minutes (including 14 successive match shut-outs) in season 2008–09 (Nov 15–Feb 21). **Edwin van der Sar's** personal British record of 1,311 minutes without conceding ended when United won 2-1 at Newcastle on Mar 4, 2009.

Most clean sheets in season in top English division: **28** by Liverpool (42 matches) in 1978–79; **25** by Chelsea (38 matches) in 2004–05.

There have been three instances of clubs keeping 11 consecutive clean sheets in the Football League: **Millwall** (Div 3 South, 1925–26), **York** (Div 3, 1973–74) and **Reading** (Div 4, 1978–79). In his sequence, Reading goalkeeper **Steve Death** set the existing League shut-out record of 1,103 minutes.

Sasa Ilic remained unbeaten for over 14 hours with 9 successive shut-outs (7 in Div 1, 2 in play-offs) to equal a Charlton club record in Apr/May 1998. He had 12 clean sheets in 17 first team games after winning promotion from the reserves with 6 successive clean sheets.

Sebastiano Rossi kept a clean sheet in 8 successive away matches for AC Milan (Nov 1993–Apr 1994). A world record of 1,275 minutes without conceding a goal was set in 1990–01 by **Abel Resino,**

the Atletico Madrid goalkeeper. He was finally beaten by Sporting Gijon's Enrique in Atletico's 3-1 win on Mar 19, 1991.

In international football, the record is held by **Dino Zoff** with a shut-out for Italy (Sep 1972 to Jun 1974) lasting 1,142 minutes.

LOW SCORING

Fewest goals by any club in season in Football League: 18 by **Loughborough** (Div 2, 34 matches, 1899–1900); in 38 matches 20 by **Derby** (Prem Lge, 2007–08); in 42 matches, 24 by **Watford** (Div 2, 1971–72) and by **Stoke** (Div 1, 1984–85)); in 46-match programme, 27 by **Stockport** (Div 3, 1969–70).

Arsenal were the lowest Premier League scorers in its opening season (1992–93) with 40 goals in 42 matches, but won both domestic cup competitions. In subsequent seasons the lowest Premier League scorers were **Ipswich** (35) in 1993–94, **Crystal Palace** (34) in 1994–95, **Manchester City** (33) in 1995–96 and **Leeds** (28) in 1996–97 until **Sunderland** set the Premiership's new fewest-goals record with only 21 in 2002–03. Then, in 2007–08, **Derby** scored just 20.

LONG TIME NO SCORE

The world international non-scoring record was set by **Northern Ireland** when they played 13 matches and 1,298 minutes without a goal. The sequence began against Poland on Feb 13, 2002 and ended 2 years and 5 days later when David Healy scored against Norway (1-4) in Belfast on Feb 18, 2004.

Longest non-scoring sequences in Football League: 11 matches by **Coventry** in 1919–20 (Div 2); 11 matches in 1992–93 (Div 2) by **Hartlepool**, who after beating Crystal Palace 1-0 in the FA Cup 3rd round on Jan 2, went 13 games and 2 months without scoring (11 League, 1 FA Cup, 1 Autoglass Trophy). The sequence ended after 1,227 blank minutes with a 1-1 draw at Blackpool (League) on Mar 6.

In the Premier League (Oct–Jan season 1994–95) **Crystal Palace** failed to score in nine consecutive matches.

The British non-scoring club record is held by **Stirling:** 14 consecutive matches (13 League, 1 Scottish Cup) and 1,292 minutes play, from Jan 31 1981 until Aug 8, 1981 (when they lost 4-1 to Falkirk in the League Cup).

In season 1971–72, **Mansfield** did not score in any of their first nine home games in Div 3. They were relegated on goal difference of minus two.

FA CUP CLEAN SHEETS

Most consecutive FA Cup matches without conceding a goal, 11 by **Bradford City**. The sequence spanned 8 rounds, from 3rd in 1910–11 to 4th. Round replay in 1911–12, and included winning the Cup in 1911.

GOALS THAT WERE WRONGLY GIVEN

Tottenham's last minute winner at home to Huddersfield (Div 1) on Apr 2, 1952: Eddie Baily's corner-kick struck referee WR Barnes in the back, and the ball rebounded to Baily, who crossed for Len Duquemin to head into the net. Baily had infringed the Laws by playing the ball twice, but the result (1-0) stood. Those two points helped Spurs to finish Championship runners-up; Huddersfield were relegated.

The second goal (66 mins) in **Chelsea's** 2-1 home win v Ipswich (Div 1) on Sep 26, 1970: Alan Hudson's shot hit the stanchion on the outside of goal and the ball rebounded on to the pitch. But instead of the goal-kick, referee Roy Capey gave a goal, on a linesman's confirmation. TV pictures proved otherwise. The Football League quoted from the Laws of the Game: 'The referee's decision on all matters is final.'

When **Watford** John Eustace and **Reading's** Noel Hunt challenged for a 13th minute corner at Vicarage Road on Sep 20, 2008, the ball was clearly diverted wide. But referee Stuart Attwell signalled for a goal on the instruction his assistant and it went down officially as a Eustace own goal. The Championship match ended 2-2.

Sunderland's 1-0 Premier League win over **Liverpool** on Oct 17, 2009 was decided by one of the most bizarre goals in football history when Darren Bent's shot struck a red beach ball thrown from the crowd and wrong-footed goalkeeper Jose Reina. Referee Mike Jones wrongly allowed it to stand. The Laws of the Game state: 'An outside agent interfering with play should result in play being stopped and restarted with a drop ball.'

Blackburn's 59th minute equaliser (2-2) in 3-3 draw away to Wigan (Prem) on Nov 19, 2011 was illegal. Morten Gamst Pedersen played the ball to himself from a corner and crossed for Junior Hoilett to net.

The Republic of Ireland were deprived of the chance of a World Cup place in the second leg of their play-off with France on Nov 18, 2009. They were leading 1-0 in Paris when Thierry Henry blatantly handled before setting up William Gallas to equalise in extra-time time and give his side a 2-1 aggregate victory. The FA of Ireland's call for a replay was rejected by FIFA.

• The most notorious goal in World Cup history was fisted in by Diego Maradona in **Argentina's** 2-1 quarter-final win over England in Mexico City on Jun 22, 1986.

ATTENDANCES

GREATEST WORLD CROWDS

World Cup, Maracana Stadium, Rio de Janeiro, Jul 16, 1950. Final match (Brazil v Uruguay) attendance 199,850; receipts £125,000.

Total attendance in three matches (including play-off) between Santos (Brazil) and AC Milan for the Inter-Continental Cup (World Club Championship) 1963, exceeded 375,000.

BRITISH RECORD CROWDS

Most to pay: 149,547, Scotland v England, at Hampden Park, Glasgow, Apr 17, 1937. This was the first all-ticket match in Scotland (receipts £24,000).

At Scottish FA Cup Final: 146,433, Celtic v Aberdeen, at Hampden Park, Apr 24, 1937. Estimated another 20,000 shut out.

For British club match (apart from a Cup Final): 143,470, Rangers v Hibernian, at Hampden Park, Mar 27, 1948 (Scottish Cup semi-final).

FA Cup Final: 126,047, Bolton v West Ham, Apr 28, 1923. Estimated 150,000 in ground at opening of Wembley Stadium.

New Wembley: 89,874, FA Cup Final, Cardiff v Portsmouth, May 17, 2008.

World Cup Qualifying ties: 120,000, Cameroon v Morocco, Yaounde, Nov 29, 1981; 107,580, Scotland v Poland, Hampden Park, Oct 13, 1965.

European Cup: 135,826, Celtic v Leeds (semi-final, 2nd leg) at Hampden Park, Apr 15, 1970.

European Cup Final: 127,621, Real Madrid v Eintracht Frankfurt, at Hampden Park, May 18, 1960.

European Cup-Winners' Cup Final: 100,000, West Ham v TSV Munich, at Wembley, May 19, 1965.

Scottish League: 118,567, Rangers v Celtic, Jan 2, 1939.

Scottish League Cup Final: 107,609, Celtic v Rangers, at Hampden Park, Oct 23, 1965.

Football League old format: First Div: 83,260, Manchester Utd v Arsenal, Jan 17, 1948 (at Maine Road); **Div 2** 70,302 Tottenham v Southampton, Feb 25, 1950; **Div 3S:** 51,621, Cardiff v Bristol City, Apr 7, 1947; **Div 3N:** 49,655, Hull v Rotherham, Dec 25, 1948; **Div 3:** 49,309, Sheffield Wed v Sheffield Utd, Dec 26, 1979; **Div 4:** 37,774, Crystal Palace v Millwall, Mar 31, 1961.

Premier League: 76,098, Manchester Utd v Blackburn, Mar 31, 2007.

Football League – New Div 1: 41,214, Sunderland v Stoke, Apr 25, 1998; **New Div2:** 32,471, Manchester City v York, May 8, 1999; **New Div 3:** 22,319, Hull v Hartlepool Utd, Dec 26, 2002. **New Champs:** 52,181, Newcastle v Ipswich, Apr 24, 2010; **New Lge 1:** 38,256, Leeds v Gillingham, May 3, 2008; **New Lge 2:** 18,746, Portsmouth v Northampton, May 7, 2016.

In English Provinces: 84,569, Manchester City v Stoke (FA Cup 6), Mar 3, 1934.

Record for Under-21 International: 55,700, England v Italy, first match at New Wembley, Mar 24, 2007.

Record for friendly match: 104,679, Rangers v Eintracht Frankfurt, at Hampden Park, Glasgow, Oct 17, 1961.

FA Youth Cup: 38,187, Arsenal v Manchester Utd, at Emirates Stadium, Mar 14, 2007.

Record Football League aggregate (season): 41,271,414 (1948–49) – 88 clubs.

Record Football League aggregate (single day): 1,269,934, December 27, 1949, previous day, 1,226,098.

Record average home League attendance for season: 75,691 by Manchester Utd in 2007–08.

Long-ago League attendance aggregates: 10,929,000 in 1906–07 (40 clubs); 28,132,933 in 1937–38 (88 clubs).

Last 1m crowd aggregate, League (single day): 1,007,200, December 27, 1971.

Record Amateur match attendance: 100,000 for FA Amateur Cup Final, Pegasus v Harwich & Parkeston at Wembley, Apr 11, 1953.

Record Cup-tie aggregate: 265,199, at two matches between Rangers and Morton, in Scottish Cup Final, 1947–48.

Abandoned match attendance records: In England – 63,480 at Newcastle v Swansea City FA Cup 3rd round, Jan 10, 1953, abandoned 8 mins (0-0), fog.

In Scotland: 94,596 at Scotland v Austria (4-1), Hampden Park, May 8, 1963. Referee Jim Finney ended play (79 minutes) after Austria had two players sent off and one carried off.

Colchester's record crowd (19,072) was for the FA Cup 1st round tie v Reading on Nov 27, 1948, abandoned 35 minutes (0-0), fog.

SMALLEST CROWDS

Smallest League attendances: 450 Rochdale v Cambridge Utd (Div 3, Feb 5, 1974); 469, Thames v Luton (Div 3 South, December 6, 1930).

Only 13 people paid to watch Stockport v Leicester (Div 2, May 7, 1921) at Old Trafford, but up to 2,000 stayed behind after Manchester Utd v Derby earlier in the day. Stockport's ground was closed.

Lowest Premier League crowd: 3,039 for Wimbledon v Everton, Jan 26, 1993 (smallest top-division attendance since War).

Lowest Saturday post-war top-division crowd: 3,231 for Wimbledon v Luton, Sep 7, 1991 (Div 1).

Lowest Football League crowds, new format – Div 1: 849 for Wimbledon v Rotherham, (Div 1) Oct 29, 2002 (smallest attendance in top two divisions since War); 1,054 Wimbledon v Wigan (Div 1), Sep 13, 2003 in club's last home match when sharing Selhurst Park; **Div 2:** 1,077, Hartlepool Utd v Cardiff, Mar 22, 1994; **Div 3:** 739, Doncaster v Barnet, Mar 3, 1998.

Lowest top-division crowd at a major ground since the war: 4,554 for Arsenal v Leeds (May 5, 1966) – fixture clashed with live TV coverage of Cup-Winners' Cup Final (Liverpool v Borussia Dortmund).

Smallest League Cup attendances: 612, Halifax v Tranmere (1st round, 2nd leg) Sep 6, 2000; 661, Wimbledon v Rotherham (3rd round), Nov 5, 2002.

Smallest League Cup attendance at top-division ground: 1,987 for Wimbledon v Bolton (2nd Round, 2nd Leg) Oct 6, 1992.

Smallest Wembley crowds for England matches: 15,628 v Chile (Rous Cup, May 23, 1989 – affected by Tube strike); 20,038 v Colombia (Friendly, Sep 6, 1995); 21,432 v Czech. (Friendly, Apr 25, 1990); 21,142 v Japan (Umbro Cup, Jun 3, 1995); 23,600 v Wales (British Championship, Feb 23, 1983); 23,659 v Greece (Friendly, May 17, 1994); 23,951 v East Germany (Friendly, Sep 12, 1984); 24,000 v N Ireland (British Championship, Apr 4, 1984); 25,756 v Colombia (Rous Cup, May 24, 1988); 25,837 v Denmark (Friendly, Sep 14, 1988).

Smallest international modern crowds: 221 for Poland v N Ireland (4-1, friendly) at Limassol, Cyprus, on Feb 13, 2002. Played at neutral venue at Poland's World Cup training base. 265 (all from N Ireland) at their Euro Champ qual against Serbia in Belgrade on Mar 25, 2011. Serbia ordered by UEFA to play behind closed doors because of previous crowd trouble.

Smallest international modern crowds at home: N Ireland: 2,500 v Chile (Belfast, May 26, 1989 – clashed with ITV live screening of Liverpool v Arsenal Championship decider); Scotland: 7,843 v N Ireland (Hampden Park, May 6, 1969); Wales: 2,315 v N Ireland (Wrexham, May 27, 1982).

Smallest attendance for post-war England match: 2,378 v San Marino (World Cup) at Bologna (Nov 17, 1993). Tie clashed with Italy v Portugal (World Cup) shown live on Italian TV.

Lowest England attendance at New Wembley: 40,181 v Norway (friendly), Sep 3, 2014
Smallest paid attendance for British first-class match: 29 for Clydebank v East Stirling, CIS Scottish League Cup 1st round, Jul 31, 1999. Played at Morton's Cappielow Park ground, shared by Clydebank. Match clashed with the Tall Ships Race which attracted 200,000 to the area.

FA CUP CROWD RECORD (OUTSIDE FINAL)

The first FA Cup-tie shown on closed-circuit TV (5th round, Saturday, Mar 11, 1967, kick-off 7pm) drew a total of 105,000 spectators to Goodison Park and Anfield. At Goodison, 64,851 watched the match 'for real', while 40,149 saw the TV version on eight giant screens at Anfield. Everton beat Liverpool 1-0.

LOWEST SEMI-FINAL CROWD

The smallest FA Cup semi-final attendance since the War was 17,987 for the Manchester Utd–Crystal Palace replay at Villa Park on Apr 12, 1995. Palace supporters largely boycotted tie after a fan died in car-park clash outside pub in Walsall before first match.
Previous lowest: 25,963 for Wimbledon v Luton, at Tottenham on Apr 9, 1988.
Lowest quarter-final crowd since the war: 8,735 for Chesterfield v Wrexham on Mar 9, 1997.
Smallest FA Cup 3rd round attendances for matches between League clubs: 1,833 for Chester v Bournemouth (at Macclesfield) Jan 5, 1991; 1,966 for Aldershot v Oxford Utd, Jan 10, 1987.

PRE-WEMBLEY CUP FINAL CROWDS

AT CRYSTAL PALACE

1895	42,560	1902	48,036	1908	74,967
1896	48,036	Replay	33,050	1909	67,651
1897	65,891	1903	64,000	1910	76,980
1898	62,017	1904	61,734	1911	69,098
1899	73,833	1905	101,117	1912	54,434
1900	68,945	1906	75,609	1913	120,028
1901	110,802	1907	84,584	1914	72,778

AT OLD TRAFFORD

1915	50,000

AT STAMFORD BRIDGE

1920	50,018	1921	72,805	1922	53,000

England women's record crowd: 45,619 v Germany, 0-3 (Wembley, Nov 23, 2014) – Karen Carney's 100th cap.

INTERNATIONAL RECORDS

MOST APPEARANCES

Peter Shilton, England goalkeeper, then aged 40, retired from international football after the 1990 World Cup Finals with the European record number of caps – 125. Previous record (119) was set by **Pat Jennings,** Northern Ireland's goalkeeper from 1964–86, who retired on his 41st birthday during the 1986 World Cup in Mexico. Shilton's England career spanned 20 seasons from his debut against East Germany at Wembley on Nov 25, 1970.

Nine players have completed a century of appearances in full international matches for England. **Billy Wright** of Wolves, was the first, retiring in 1959 with a total of 105 caps. **Bobby Charlton,** of Manchester Utd, beat Wright's record in the World Cup match against West Germany in Leon, Mexico, in Jun 1970 and **Bobby Moore,** of West Ham, overtook Charlton's 106 caps against Italy in Turin, in Jun 1973. Moore played 108 times for England, a record that stood until **Shilton** reached 109 against Denmark in Copenhagen (Jun 7, 1989). In season 2008–09, **David Beckham** (LA Galaxy/AC Milan) overtook Moore as England's most-capped outfield player. In the vastly different selection processes of their eras, Moore played 108 full games for his country, whereas Beckham's total of 115 to the end of season 2009–10, included 58 part matches, 14 as substitute and 44 times substituted. **Steven Gerrard** won his 100th cap against Sweden in Stockholm on Nov 14, 2012 and **Ashley Cole** reached 100 appearances against Brazil at Wembley on Feb 6, 2013. **Frank Lampard** played his 100th game against Ukraine in Kiev (World Cup qual) on Sep 10, 2013. **Wayne Rooney**'s 100th appearance was against Slovenia at Wembley (Euro Champ qual) on Nov 15, 2014.

Robbie Keane won his 126th Republic of Ireland cap, overtaking Shay Given's record, In a World Cup qualifier against the Faroe Islands on Jun 7, 2013. Keane scored all his team's three goals in a 3-0 win.

Kenny Dalglish became Scotland's first 100-cap international v Romania (Hampden Park, Mar 26, 1986).

World's most-capped player: Ahmed Hassan, 184 for Egypt (1995–2012).

Most-capped European player: Vitalijs Astafjevs, 167 for Latvia (1992–2010).

Most capped European goalkeeper: Thomas Ravelli, 143 Internationals for Sweden (1981–97).

Gillian Coultard, (Doncaster Belles). England Women's captain, received a special presentation from Geoff Hurst to mark 100 caps when England beat Holland 1-0 at Upton Park on Oct 30, 1997. She made her international debut at 18 in May 1981, and retired at the end of season 1999–2000 with a record 119 caps (30 goals).

BRITAIN'S MOST-CAPPED PLAYERS

(As at start of season 2017–18)

England		Alex McLeish	77	David Healy	95
Peter Shilton	125	Paul McStay	76	Steven Davis	95
Wayne Rooney	119	Tommy Boyd	72	Mal Donaghy	91
David Beckham	115	**Wales**		Sammy McIlroy	88
Steven Gerrard	114	Neville Southall	92	Maik Taylor	88
Bobby Moore	108	Gary Speed	85		
Ashley Cole	107	Craig Bellamy	78	**Republic of Ireland**	
Bobby Charlton	106	Dean Saunders	75	Robbie Keane	146
Frank Lampard	106	Peter Nicholas	73	Shay Given	134
Billy Wright	105	Ian Rush	73	John O'Shea	117
Scotland				Kevin Kilbane	110
Kenny Dalglish	102	**Northern Ireland**		Steve Staunton	102
Jim Leighton	91	Pat Jennings	119	Damien Duff	100
Darren Fletcher	78	Aaron Hughes	106		

ENGLAND'S MOST-CAPPED PLAYER (either gender)

Fara Williams (Liverpool midfielder) with 155 appearances for the England's women's team to end of season 2015–16.

MOST ENGLAND CAPS IN ROW

Most consecutive international appearances: 70 by **Billy Wright,** for England from Oct 1951 to May 1959. He played 105 of England's first 108 post-war matches.

England captains most times: Billy Wright and **Bobby Moore,** 90 each.

England captains – 4 in match (v Serbia & Montenegro at Leicester Jun 3, 2003): **Michael Owen** was captain for the first half and after the interval the armband passed to **Emile Heskey** (for 15 minutes), **Phil Neville** (26 minutes) and substitute **Jamie Carragher** (9 minutes, including time added).

MOST SUCCESSIVE ENGLAND WINS

10 (Jun 1908–Jun 1909. Modern: 8 (Oct 2005–Jun 2006).

ENGLAND'S LONGEST UNBEATEN RUN

19 matches (16 wins, 3 draws), Nov 1965–Nov 1966.

ENGLAND'S TALLEST

At **6ft 7in, Peter Crouch** became England's tallest-ever international when he made his debut against Colombia in New Jersey, USA on May 31, 2005.

MOST PLAYERS FROM ONE CLUB IN ENGLAND SIDES

Arsenal supplied seven men (a record) to the England team v Italy at Highbury on Nov 14, 1934. They were: Frank Moss, George Male, Eddie Hapgood, Wilf Copping, Ray Bowden, Ted Drake and Cliff Bastin. In addition, Arsenal's Tom Whittaker was England's trainer.

Since then until 2001, the most players from one club in an England team was six from **Liverpool** against Switzerland at Wembley in Sep 1977. The side also included a Liverpool old boy, Kevin Keegan (Hamburg).

Seven **Arsenal** men took part in the England – France (0-2) match at Wembley on Feb 10, 1999. Goalkeeper David Seaman and defenders Lee Dixon, Tony Adams and Martin Keown lined up for England. Nicolas Anelka (2 goals) and Emmanuel Petit started the match for France and Patrick Vieira replaced Anelka.

Manchester Utd equalled Arsenal's 1934 record by providing England with seven players in the World Cup qualifier away to Albania on Mar 28, 2001. Five started the match – David Beckham (captain), Gary Neville, Paul Scholes, Nicky Butt and Andy Cole – and two went on as substitutes: Wes Brown and Teddy Sheringham.

INTERNATIONAL SUBS RECORDS

Malta substituted all 11 players in their 1-2 home defeat against England on Jun 3, 2000. Six substitutes by England took the total replacements in the match to 17, then an international record.

Most substitutions in match by **England:** 11 in second half by Sven-Goran Eriksson against Holland at Tottenham on Aug 15, 2001; 11 against Italy at Leeds on Mar 27, 2002; Italy sent on 8 players from the bench – the total of 19 substitutions was then a record for an England match; 11 against Australia at Upton Park on Feb 12, 2003 (entire England team changed at half-time); 11 against Iceland at City of Manchester Stadium on Jun 5, 2004.

Forty three players, a record for an England match, were used in the international against Serbia & Montenegro at Leicester on Jun 3, 2003. England sent on 10 substitutes in the second half and their opponents changed all 11 players.

The **Republic of Ireland** sent on 12 second-half substitutes, using 23 players in all, when they beat Russia 2-0 in a friendly international in Dublin on Feb 13, 2002.

First England substitute: Wolves winger **Jimmy Mullen** replaced injured Jackie Milburn (15 mins) away to Belgium on May 18, 1950. He scored in a 4-1 win.

ENGLAND'S WORLD CUP-WINNERS

At Wembley, Jul 30, 1966, 4-2 v West Germany (2-2 after 90 mins), scorers Hurst 3, Peters. Team: Banks; Cohen, Wilson, Stiles, Jack Charlton, Moore (capt), Ball, Hurst, Bobby Charlton, Hunt, Peters. Manager **Alf Ramsey** fielded that same eleven in six successive matches (an England record): the World Cup quarter-final, semi-final and Final, and the first three games of the following season. England wore red shirts in the Final and The Queen presented the Cup to Bobby Moore. The players each received a £1,000 bonus, plus £60 World Cup Final appearance money, all less tax, and Ramsey a £6,000 bonus from the FA. The match was shown live on TV (in black and white).

England's non-playing reserves – there were no substitutes – also received the £1,000 bonus, but no medals. That remained the case until FIFA finally decided that non-playing members and staff of World Cup-winning squads should be given replica medals. England's 'forgotten heroes' received theirs at a reception in Downing Street on June 10, 2009 and were later guests of honour at the World Cup qualifier against Andorra at Wembley. The 11 reserves were: Springett, Bonetti, Armfield, Byrne, Flowers, Hunter, Paine, Connelly, Callaghan, Greaves, Eastham.

BRAZIL'S RECORD RUN

Brazil hold the record for the longest unbeaten sequence in international football: 45 matches from 1993–97. The previous record of 31 was held by Hungary between Jun 1950 and Jul 1954.

ENGLAND MATCHES ABANDONED

May 17, 1953 v **Argentina** (Friendly, Buenos Aires) after 23 mins (0-0) – rain.

Oct 29, 1975 v **Czechoslovakia** (Euro Champ qual, Bratislava) after 17 mins (0-0) – fog. Played next day.

Feb 15, 1995 v **Rep of Ireland** (Friendly, Dublin) after 27 mins (1-0) crowd disturbance.

ENGLAND POSTPONEMENTS

Nov 21, 1979 v **Bulgaria** (Euro Champ qual, Wembley, postponed for 24 hours – fog; Aug 10, 2011 v **Holland** (friendly), Wembley, postponed after rioting in London.

Oct 16, 2012 v **Poland** (World Cup qual, Warsaw) postponed to next day – pitch waterlogged.

The friendly against **Honduras** (Miami, Jun 7, 2014) was suspended midway through the first half for 44 minutes – thunderstorm.

ENGLAND UNDER COVER

England played indoors for the first time when they beat Argentina 1-0 in the World Cup at the Sapporo Dome, Japan, on Jun 7, 2002.

ALL-SEATED INTERNATIONALS

The first **all-seated crowd** (30,000) for a full international in Britain saw **Wales** and **West Germany** draw 0-0 at Cardiff Arms Park on May 31, 1989. The terraces were closed.

England's first all-seated international at Wembley was against Yugoslavia (2-1) on December 13, 1989 (attendance 34,796). The terracing behind the goals was closed for conversion to seating

The first **full-house all-seated** international at Wembley was for England v Brazil (1-0) on Mar 28, 1990, when a capacity 80,000 crowd paid record British receipts of £1,200,000.

MOST NEW CAPS IN ENGLAND TEAM

6, by Sir Alf Ramsey (v Portugal, Apr 3, 1974) and **by Sven-Goran Eriksson** (v Australia, Feb 12, 2003; 5 at half-time when 11 changes made).

PLAYED FOR MORE THAN ONE COUNTRY

Multi-nationals in senior international football include. **Johnny Carey** (1938–53) – caps Rep of Ireland 29, N Ireland 7; **Ferenc Puskas** (1945-62) – caps Hungary 84, Spain 4; **Alfredo di Stefano** (1950–56) – caps Argentina 7, Spain 31; **Ladislav Kubala** (1940–58) – caps, Hungary 3, Czechoslovakia 11, Spain 19, only player to win full international honours with 3 countries. Kubala also played in a fourth international team, scoring twice for FIFA v England at Wembley in 1953. Eleven players, including **Carey**, appeared for both N Ireland and the Republic of Ireland in seasons directly after the last war.

Cecil Moore, capped by N Ireland in 1949 when with Glentoran, played for USA v England in 1953.

Hawley Edwards played for England v Scotland in 1874 and for Wales v Scotland in 1876.

Jack Reynolds (Distillery and WBA) played for both Ireland (5 times) and England (8) in the 1890s.

Bobby Evans (Sheffield Utd) had played 10 times for Wales when capped for England, in 1910–11. He was born in Chester of Welsh parents.

In recent years, several players have represented USSR and one or other of the breakaway republics. The same applies to Yugoslavia and its component states. **Josip Weber** played for Croatia in 1992 and made a 5-goal debut for Belgium in 1994.

THREE-GENERATION INTERNATIONAL FAMILY

When Bournemouth striker **Warren Feeney** was capped away to Liechtenstein on Mar 27, 2002, he became the third generation of his family to play for Northern Ireland. He followed in the footsteps of his grandfather James (capped twice in 1950) and father Warren snr. (1 in 1976).

FATHERS & SONS CAPPED BY ENGLAND

George Eastham senior (pre-war) and **George Eastham junior**; **Brian Clough** and **Nigel Clough**; **Frank Lampard snr** and **Frank Lampard jnr**; **Mark Chamberlain** and **Alex Oxlade-Chamberlain**.

FATHER & SON SAME-DAY CAPS

Iceland made father-and-son international history when they beat Estonia 3-0 in Tallin on Apr 24, 1996. **Arnor Gudjohnsen** (35) started the match and was replaced (62 mins) by his 17-year-old son **Eidur**.

LONGEST UNBEATEN START TO ENGLAND CAREER

Steven Gerrard, 21 matches (W16, D5) 2000–03.

SUCCESSIVE ENGLAND HAT-TRICKS

The last player to score a hat-trick in consecutive England matches was **Dixie Dean** on the summer tour in May 1927, against Belgium (9-1) and Luxembourg (5-2).

SCORED ON ENGLAND DEBUT

Marcus Rashford, against Australia on May 27, 2016, joined a list which includes **Stanley Matthews**, **Tom Finney**, **Jimmy Greaves**, **Bobby Charlton**, **Alan Shearer** and **Rickie Lambert**.

MOST GOALS BY PLAYER v ENGLAND

4 by **Zlatan Ibrahimovic** (Sweden 4 England 2, Stockholm, Nov 14, 2012).

POST-WAR HAT-TRICKS v ENGLAND

Nov 25, 1953, **Nandor Hidegkuti** (England 3, Hungary 6, Wembley); May 11, 1958, **Aleksandar Petakovic** (Yugoslavia 5, England 0, Belgrade); May 17, 1959, **Juan Seminario** (Peru 4, England 1, Lima); Jun 15, 1988, **Marco van Basten** (Holland 3, England 1, European Championship, Dusseldorf). Six other players scored hat-tricks against England (1878–1930).

NO-SAVE GOALKEEPERS

Chris Woods did not have one save to make when England beat San Marino 6-0 (World Cup) at Wembley on Feb 17, 1993. He touched the ball only six times.

Gordon Banks had a similar no-save experience when England beat Malta 5-0 (European Championship) at Wembley on May 12, 1971. Malta did not force a goal-kick or corner, and the four times Banks touched the ball were all from back passes.

Robert Green was also idle in the 6-0 World Cup qualifying win over Andorra at Wembley on Jun 10, 2009.

Joe Hart was untroubled in England's 5-0 win over San Marino in a World Cup qualifier at Wembley on Oct 12, 2012.

WORLD/EURO MEMBERS

FIFA has 209 member countries, **UEFA** 53

NEW FIFA PRESIDENT

The 18-year reign of FIFA president **Sepp Blatter** ended in December 2015 amid widespread allegations of corruption. He was replaced in February 2016 by Gianni Infantino, a 45-year-old Swiss-Italian lawyer, who was previously general secretary of UEFA. Under new rules, he will serve four years.

FIFA WORLD YOUTH CUP (UNDER-20)

Finals: 1977 (Tunis) Soviet Union 2 Mexico 2 (Soviet won 9-8 on pens.); **1979** (Tokyo) Argentina 3 Soviet Union 1; **1981** (Sydney) W Germany 4 Qatar 0; **1983** (Mexico City) Brazil 1

Argentina 0; **1985** (Moscow) Brazil 1 Spain 0; **1987** (Santiago) Yugoslavia 1 W Germany 1 (Yugoslavia won 5-4 on pens.); **1989** (Riyadh) Portugal 2 Nigeria 0; **1991** (Lisbon) Portugal 0 Brazil 0 (Portugal won 4-2 on pens.); **1993** (Sydney) Brazil 2 Ghana 1; **1995** (Qatar) Argentina 2 Brazil 0; **1997** (Kuala Lumpur) Argentina 2 Uruguay 1; **1999** (Lagos) Spain 4 Japan 0; **2001** (Buenos Aires) Argentina 3 Ghana 0; **2003** (Dubai) Brazil 1 Spain 0; **2005** (Utrecht) Argentina 2 Nigeria 1; **2007** (Toronto) Argentina 2 Czech Republic 1; **2009** (Cairo) Ghana 0 Brazil 0 (aet, Ghana won 4-3 on pens); **2011** (Bogota) Brazil 3 Portugal 2 (aet); **2013** (Istanbul) France 0 Uruguay 0 (aet, France won 4-1 on pens), **2015** (Auckland) Serbia 2 Brazil 1 (aet); **2017** (Suwon) England 1 Venezuela 0.

FAMOUS CLUB FEATS

Chelsea were Premiership winners in 2004–05, their centenary season with the highest points total (95) ever recorded by England Champions. They set these other records: Most Premiership wins in season (29); most clean sheets (25) and fewest goals conceded (15) in top-division history. They also won the League Cup in 2005.

Arsenal created an all-time English League record sequence of 49 unbeaten Premiership matches (W36, D13), spanning 3 seasons, from May 7, 2003 until losing 2-0 away to Manchester Utd on Oct 24, 2004. It included all 38 games in season 2003–04.

The Double: There have been 11 instances of a club winning the Football League/Premier League title and the FA Cup in the same season. **Manchester Utd** and **Arsenal** have each done so three times: **Preston** 1888–89; **Aston Villa** 1896–97; **Tottenham** 1960–61; **Arsenal** 1970–71, 1997–98, 2001–02; **Liverpool** 1985–86; **Manchester Utd** 1993–94, 1995–96, 1998–99; **Chelsea** 2009–10.

The Treble: Liverpool were the first English club to win three major competitions in one season when in 1983–84, Joe Fagan's first season as manager, they were League Champions, League Cup winners and European Cup winners.

Sir Alex Ferguson's **Manchester Utd** achieved an even more prestigious treble in 1998–99, completing the domestic double of Premiership and FA Cup and then winning the European Cup. In season 2008–09, they completed another major triple success – Premier League, Carling Cup and World Club Cup.

Liverpool completed a unique treble by an English club with three cup successes under Gerard Houllier in season 2000–01: the League Cup, FA Cup and UEFA Cup.

Liverpool the first English club to win five major trophies in one calendar year (Feb– Aug 2001): League Cup, FA Cup, UEFA Cup, Charity Shield, UEFA Super Cup.

As Champions in season 2001–02, **Arsenal** set a Premiership record by winning the last 13 matches. They were the first top-division club since Preston in the League's inaugural season (1888–89) to maintain an unbeaten away record.

(See Scottish section for treble feats by Rangers and Celtic).

Record Home Runs: Liverpool went 85 competitive first-team games unbeaten at home between losing 2-3 to Birmingham on Jan 21, 1978 and 1-2 to Leicester on Jan 31, 1981. They comprised 63 in the League, 9 League Cup, 7 in European competition and 6 FA Cup.

Chelsea hold the record unbeaten home League sequence of 86 matches (W62, D24) between losing 1-2 to Arsenal, Feb 21, 2004, and 0-1 to Liverpool, Oct 26, 2008.

Third to First: Charlton, in 1936, became the first club to advance from the Third to First Division in successive seasons. **Queens Park Rangers** were the second club to achieve the feat in 1968, and **Oxford Utd** did it in 1984 and 1985 as Champions of each division. Subsequently, **Derby** (1987), **Middlesbrough** (1988), **Sheffield Utd** (1990) and **Notts Co** (1991) climbed from Third Division to First in consecutive seasons.

Watford won successive promotions from the modern Second Division to the Premier League in 1997–98, 1998–99. **Manchester City** equalled the feat in 1998–99, 1999–2000. **Norwich** climbed from League 1 to the Premier League in seasons 2009–10, 2010–11. **Southampton** did the same in 2010–11 and 2011–12.

Fourth to First: Northampton , in 1965 became the first club to rise from the Fourth to the

First Division. **Swansea** climbed from the Fourth Division to the First (three promotions i four seasons), 1977–78 to 1980–81. **Wimbledon** repeated the feat, 1982–83 to 1985–8 **Watford** did it in five seasons, 1977–8 to 1981–82. **Carlisle** climbed from Fourth Divisio to First, 1964–74.

Non-League to First: When **Wimbledon** finished third in the Second Division in 1986, the completed the phenomenal rise from non-League football (Southern League) to the Firs Division in nine years. Two years later they won the FA Cup.

Tottenham, in 1960–61, not only carried off the First Division Championship and the FA Cu for the first time that century but set up other records by opening with 11 successive wins registering most First Division wins (31), most away wins in the League's history (16), an equalling Arsenal's First Division records of 66 points and 33 away points. They already hel the Second Division record of 70 points (1919–20).

Arsenal, in 1993, became the first club to win both English domestic cup competitions (FA Cup and League Cup) in the same season. **Liverpool** repeated the feat in 2001. **Chelsea** did it in 2007.

Chelsea achieved the FA Cup/Champions League double in May 2012.

Preston, in season 1888–89, won the first League Championship without losing a match and the FA Cup without having a goal scored against them. Only other English clubs to remain unbeaten through a League season were **Liverpool** (Div 2 Champions in 1893–94) and **Arsenal** (Premiership Champions 2003–04).

Bury, in 1903, also won the FA Cup without conceding a goal.

Everton won Div 2, Div 1 and the FA Cup in successive seasons, 1930–31, 1931–32, 1932–33.

Wolves won the League Championship in 1958 and 1959 and the FA Cup in 1960.

Liverpool won the title in 1964, the FA Cup in 1965 and the title again in 1966. In 1978 they became the first British club to win the European Cup in successive seasons. Nottm Fores repeated the feat in 1979 and 1980.

Liverpool won the League Championship six times in eight seasons (1976–83) under **Bob Paisley's** management.

Sir Alex Ferguson's **Manchester Utd** won the Premier League in 13 of its 21 seasons (1992–2013). They were runners-up five times and third three times.

Most Premier League wins in season: 30 by **Chelsea** 2016–17.

Biggest points-winning margin by League Champions: 18 by **Manchester Utd** (1999–2000).

Leicester, champions of England for first time, won Premier League, season 2015-16, by 10 points.

Most consecutive Premier League wins in season: 13 by **Arsenal** in 2001–02, **Chelsea** 2016–17.

FA CUP/PROMOTION DOUBLE

WBA are the only club to achieve this feat in the same season (1930–31).

COVENTRY UNIQUE

Coventry are the only club to have played in the Premier League, all four previous divisions of the Football League, in both sections (North and South) of the old Third Division and in the modern Championship.

FAMOUS UPS & DOWNS

Sunderland: Relegated in 1958 after maintaining First Division status since their election to the Football League in 1890. They dropped into Division 3 for the first time in 1987.

Aston Villa: Relegated with Preston to the Third Division in 1970.

Arsenal up: When the League was extended in 1919, Woolwich Arsenal (sixth in Division Two in 1914–15, last season before the war) were elected to Division One. Arsenal have been in the top division ever since.

Tottenham down: At that same meeting in 1919 Chelsea (due for relegation) retained their place in Division One but the bottom club (Tottenham) had to go down to Division Two.

Preston and **Burnley down:** Preston, the first League Champions in season 1888–89, dropped into the Fourth Division in 1985. So did Burnley, also among the League's original members in 1888. In 1986, Preston had to apply for re-election.

Wolves' fall: Wolves, another of the Football League's original members, completed the fall from First Division to Fourth in successive seasons (1984–85–86).

Lincoln out: Lincoln became the first club to suffer automatic demotion from the Football League when they finished bottom of Div 4, on goal difference, in season 1986–87. They were replaced by Scarborough, champions of the GM Vauxhall Conference. Lincoln regained their place a year later.

Swindon up and down: In the 1990 play-offs, Swindon won promotion to the First Division for the first time, but remained in the Second Division because of financial irregularities.

MOST CHAMPIONSHIP WINS

Manchester Utd have been champions of England a record 20 times (7 Football League, 13 Premier League).

LONGEST CURRENT MEMBERS OF TOP DIVISION

Arsenal (since 1919), **Everton** (1954), **Liverpool** (1962), **Manchester Utd** (1975).

CHAMPIONS: FEWEST PLAYERS

Liverpool used only **14** players (five ever-present) when they won the League Championship in season 1965–66. **Aston Villa** also called on no more than 14 players to win the title in 1980–81, with seven ever-present.

UNBEATEN CHAMPIONS

Only two clubs have become Champions of England with an unbeaten record: **Preston** as the Football League's first winners in 1888–89 (22 matches) and **Arsenal**, Premiership winners in 2003–04 (38 matches).

LEAGUE HAT-TRICKS

Huddersfield created a record in 1924–25–26 by winning the League Championship three years in succession.

Arsenal equalled this hat-trick in 1933–34–35, **Liverpool** in 1982–83–84 and **Manchester Utd** in 1999–2000–01. Sir Alex Ferguson's side became the first to complete two hat-tricks (2007–08–09).

'SUPER DOUBLE' WINNERS

Since the War, there have been three instances of players appearing in and then managing FA Cup and Championship-winning teams:

Joe Mercer: Player in Arsenal Championship teams 1948, 1953 and in their 1950 FA Cup side; manager of Manchester City when they won Championship 1968, FA Cup 1969.

Kenny Dalglish: Player in Liverpool Championship-winning teams 1979, 1980, 1982, 1983, 1984, player-manager 1986, 1988, 1990; player-manager when Liverpool won FA Cup (to complete Double) 1986; manager of Blackburn, Champions 1995.

George Graham: Played in Arsenal's Double-winning team in 1971, and as manager took them to Championship success in 1989 and 1991 and the FA Cup – League Cup double in 1993.

ORIGINAL TWELVE

The original 12 members of the Football League (formed in 1888) were: **Accrington, Aston Villa, Blackburn, Bolton, Burnley, Derby, Everton, Notts Co, Preston, Stoke, WBA and Wolves.**

Results on the opening day (Sep 8, 1888): Bolton 3, Derby 6; Everton 2, Accrington 1; Preston 5, Burnley 2; Stoke 0, WBA 2; Wolves 1, Aston Villa 1. Preston had the biggest first-day crowd: 6,000. Blackburn and Notts Co did not play that day. They kicked off a week later (Sep 15) – Blackburn 5, Accrington 5; Everton 2, Notts Co 1.

Accrington FC resigned from the league in 1893 and later folded. A new club, Accrington Stanley, were members of the league from 1921 until 1962 when financial problems forced their demise. The current Accrington Stanley were formed in 1968 and gained league status in 2007.

FASTEST CLIMBS

Three promotions in four seasons by two clubs – **Swansea City**: 1978 third in Div 4; 1979 third in Div 3; 1981 third in Div 2; **Wimbledon**: 1983 Champions of Div 4; 1984 second in Div 3; 1986 third in Div 2.

MERSEYSIDE RECORD

Liverpool is the only city to have staged top-division football – through Everton and/or Liverpool – **in every season** since League football began in 1888.

EARLIEST PROMOTIONS TO TOP DIVISION POST-WAR

Mar 23, 1974, **Middlesbrough;** Mar 25, 2006, **Reading.**

EARLIEST RELEGATIONS POST-WAR

From top division: **QPR** went down from the old First Division on Mar 29, 1969; **Derby** went down from the Premier League on Mar 29, 2008, with 6 matches still to play. From modern First Division: **Stockport** on Mar 16, 2002, with 7 matches still to play; **Wimbledon** on Apr 6, 2004, with 7 matches to play.

LEAGUE RECORDS

CHAMPIONS OF ENGLAND 1888–2017

Football League and Premier league

Manchester Utd 20, Liverpool 18, Arsenal 13, Everton 9, Aston Villa 7, Chelsea 6, Sunderland 6, Manchester City 4, Newcastle 4, Sheffield Wed 4, Blackburn 3, Huddersfield 3, Leeds 3, Wolves 3, Burnley 2, Derby 2, Portsmouth 2, Preston 2, Tottenham 2, Ipswich 1, Leicester 1, Nottm Forest 1, Sheffield Utd 1, WBA 1

DOUBLE CHAMPIONS

Nine men have played in and managed League Championship-winning teams:

Ted Drake Player – Arsenal 1934, 1935, 1938. Manager – Chelsea 1955.
Bill Nicholson Player – Tottenham 1951. Manager – Tottenham 1961.
Alf Ramsey Player – Tottenham 1951. Manager – Ipswich 1962.
Joe Mercer Player – Everton 1939, Arsenal 1948, 1953. Manager – Manchester City 1968.
Dave Mackay Player – Tottenham 1961. Manager – Derby 1975.
Bob Paisley Player – Liverpool 1947. Manager – Liverpool 1976, 1977, 1979, 1980, 1982, 1983.
Howard Kendall Player – Everton 1970. Manager – Everton 1985, 1987.
Kenny Dalglish Player – Liverpool 1979, 1980, 1982, 1983, 1984. Player-manager – Liverpool 1986, 1988, 1990. Manager – Blackburn 1995.
George Graham Player – Arsenal 1971. Manager – Arsenal 1989, 1991.

CANTONA'S FOUR-TIMER

Eric Cantona played in four successive Championship-winning teams: Marseille 1990–01, Leeds 1991–92, Manchester Utd 1992–93 and 1993–94.

ARRIVALS AND DEPARTURES

The following are the Football League arrivals and departures since 1923:

Year	In	Out
1923	Doncaster	Stalybridge Celtic
	New Brighton	
1927	Torquay	Aberdare Athletic
1928	Carlisle	Durham
1929	York	Ashington
1930	Thames	Merthyr Tydfil

1931	Mansfield	Newport Co
	Chester	Nelson
1932	Aldershot	Thames
	Newport Co	Wigan Borough
1938	Ipswich	Gillingham
1950	Colchester, Gillingham	
	Scunthorpe, Shrewsbury	
1951	Workington	New Brighton
1960	Peterborough	Gateshead
1962	Oxford Utd	Accrington (resigned)
1970	Cambridge Utd	Bradford PA
1972	Hereford	Barrow
1977	Wimbledon	Workington
1978	Wigan	Southport
1987	Scarborough	Lincoln
1988	Lincoln	Newport Co
1989	Maidstone	Darlington
1990	Darlington	Colchester
1991	Barnet	
1992	Colchester	Aldershot, Maidstone (resigned)
1993	Wycombe	Halifax
1997	Macclesfield	Hereford
1998	Halifax	Doncaster
1999	Cheltenham	Scarborough
2000	Kidderminster	Chester
2001	Rushden	Barnet
2002	Boston	Halifax
2003	Yeovil, Doncaster	Exeter, Shrewsbury
2004	Chester, Shrewsbury	Carlisle, York
2005	Barnet, Carlisle	Kidderminster, Cambridge Utd
2006	Accrington, Hereford	Oxford Utd, Rushden & Diamonds
2007	Dagenham, Morecambe	Torquay, Boston
2008	Aldershot, Exeter	Wrexham, Mansfield
2009	Burton, Torquay	Chester, Luton
2010	Stevenage, Oxford Utd	Grimsby, Darlington
2011	Crawley, AFC Wimbledon	Lincoln, Stockport
2012	Fleetwood, York	Hereford, Macclesfield
2013	Mansfield, Newport	Barnet, Aldershot
2014	Luton, Cambridge Utd	Bristol Rov, Torquay
2015	Barnet, Bristol Rov	Cheltenham, Tranmere
2016	Cheltenham, Grimsby	Dagenham & Redbridge, York
2017	Lincoln, Forest Green	Hartlepool, Leyton Orient

Leeds City were expelled from Div 2 in Oct, 1919; Port Vale took over their fixtures.

EXTENSIONS TO FOOTBALL LEAGUE

Clubs	Season	Clubs	Season
12 to 14	1891–92	44 to 66†	1920–21
14 to 28*	1892–93	66 to 86†	1921–22
28 to 31	1893–94	86 to 88	1923–24
31 to 32	1894–95	88 to 92	1950–51
32 to 36	1898–99	92 to 93	1991–92
36 to 40	1905–06	(Reverted to 92 when Aldershot closed, Mar 1992)

*Second Division formed. † Third Division (South) formed from Southern League clubs.
†Third Division (North) formed.

Football League reduced to 70 clubs and three divisions on the formation of the FA Premier League in 1992; increased to 72 season 1994–95, when Premier League reduced to 20 clubs.

RECORD RUNS

Arsenal hold the record unbeaten sequence in the English League – 49 Premiership matches (36 wins, 13 draws) from May 7, 2003 until Oct 24, 2004 when beaten 2-0 away to Manchester Utd. The record previously belonged to **Nottm Forest** – 42 First Division matches (21 wins, 21 draws) from Nov 19, 1977 until beaten 2-0 at Liverpool on December 9, 1978.

Huddersfield set a new Football League record of 43 League 1 matches unbeaten from Jan 1, 2011 until Nov 28, 2011 when losing 2-0 at Charlton.

Best debuts: Ipswich won the First Division at their first attempt in 1961–62.

Peterborough in their first season in the Football League (1960–01) not only won the Fourth Division but set the all-time scoring record for the League of 134 goals. **Hereford** were promoted from the Fourth Division in their first League season, 1972–73.

Wycombe were promoted from the Third Division (via the play-offs) in their first League season, 1993–94. **Stevenage** were promoted from League 2 (via the play-offs) in their first League season, 2010–11. **Crawley** gained automatic promotion in their first season in 2011–12.

Record winning sequence in a season: 14 consecutive League victories (all in Second Division): **Manchester Utd** 1904–05, **Bristol City** 1905–06 and **Preston** 1950–51.

Best winning start to League season: 13 successive victories in Div 3 by **Reading,** season 1985–86.

Best starts in 'old' First Division: 11 consecutive victories by **Tottenham** in 1960–61; 10 by **Manchester Utd in** 1985–86. In 'new' First Division, 11 consecutive wins by **Newcastle** in 1992–93 and by **Fulham** in 2000–01.

Longest unbeaten sequence (all competitions): 40 by **Nottm Forest,** Mar–December 1978. It comprised 21 wins, 19 draws (in 29 League matches, 6 League Cup, 4 European Cup, 1 Charity Shield).

Longest unbeaten starts to League season: 38 matches (26 wins, 12 draws) in **Arsenal's** undefeated Premiership season, 2003–04; 29 matches – **Leeds,** Div 1 1973–74 (19 wins, 10 draws); **Liverpool,** Div 1 1987–88 (22 wins, 7 draws).

Most consecutive League matches unbeaten in a season: 38 **Arsenal** Premiership season 2003–04 (see above); 33 **Reading** (25 wins, 8 draws) 2005–06.

Longest winning sequence in Div 1: 13 matches by **Tottenham** – last two of season 1959–60, first 11 of 1960–61.

Longest winning one-season sequences in League Championship: 13 matches by **Preston,** 1891–92; **Sunderland,** also 1891–92; **Arsenal** 2001–02.

Longest unbeaten home League sequence in top division: 86 matches (62 wins, 24 draws) by **Chelsea** (Mar 2004–Oct 2008).

League's longest winning sequence with clean sheets: 9 matches by **Stockport** (Lge 2, 2006–07 season).

Premier League – best starts to season: Arsenal, 38 games, 2003–04; **Manchester City,** 14 games, 2011–12.

Best winning start to Premiership season: 9 consecutive victories by **Chelsea** in 2005–06.

Premier League – most consecutive wins (two seasons): 14 by **Arsenal,** Feb–Aug, 2002. Single season: 13 by **Arsenal** (Feb–May, 2002).

Premier League – most consecutive home wins: 20 by **Manchester City** (last 5 season 2010–11, first 15 season 2011–12).

Most consecutive away League wins in top flight: 11 by **Chelsea** (3 at end 2007–08 season, 8 in 2008–09).

Premier League – longest unbeaten away run: 27 matches (W17, D10) by **Arsenal** (Apr 5, 2003– Sep 25, 2004).

Record home-win sequences: Bradford Park Avenue won 25 successive home games in Div 3 North – the last 18 in 1926–27 and the first 7 the following season. Longest run of home wins in the top division is 21 by **Liverpool** – the last 9 of 1971–72 and the first 12 of 1972–73.

British record for successive League wins: 25 by **Celtic** (Scottish Premier League), 2003–04.

WORST SEQUENCES

Derby experienced the longest run without a win in League history in season 2007–08 – 32 games from Sep 22 to the end of the campaign (25 lost, 7 drawn). They finished bottom by a 24-pt margin. The sequence increased to 36 matches (28 lost, 8 drawn) at the start of the following season.

Cambridge Utd had the previous worst of 31 in 1983–84 (21 lost, 10 drawn). They were bottom of Div 2.

Worst losing start to a League season : 12 consecutive defeats by **Manchester Utd** (Div 1), 1930–31.

Worst Premier League start: QPR 16 matches without win (7 draws, 9 defeats), 2012–13.

Premier League – most consecutive defeats: 20 **Sunderland** last 15 matches, 2002–03, first five matches 2005–06.

Longest non-winning start to League season: 25 matches (4 draws, 21 defeats) by **Newport**, Div 4. Worst no-win league starts since then: 16 matches by **Burnley** (9 draws, 7 defeats in Div 2, 1979–80); 16 by **Hull** (10 draws, 6 defeats in Div 2, 1989–90); 16 by **Sheffield Utd** (4 draws, 12 defeats in Div 1, 1990–91).

Most League defeats in season: 34 by **Doncaster** (Div 3) 1997–98.

Fewest League wins in season: 1 by **Loughborough** (Div 2, season 1899–1900). They lost 27, drew 6, goals 18-100 and dropped out of the League. (See also Scottish section.) 1 by **Derby** (Prem Lge, 2007–08). They lost 29, drew 8, goals 20-89.

Most consecutive League defeats in season: 18 by **Darwen** (Div 1, 1898–99); 17 by **Rochdale** (Div 3 North, 1931–32).

Fewest home League wins in season: 1 by **Loughborough** (Div 2, 1899–1900), **Notts Co** (Div 1, 1904–05), **Woolwich Arsenal** (Div 1, 1912–13), **Blackpool** (Div 1, 1966–67), **Rochdale** (Div 3, 1973–74), **Sunderland** (Prem Lge, 2005–06); **Derby** (Prem Lge, 2007–08).

Most home League defeats in season: 18 by **Cambridge Utd** (Div 3, 1984–85).

Away League defeats record: 24 in row by **Crewe** (Div 2) – all 15 in 1894–95 followed by 9 in 1895–96; by **Nelson** (Div 3 North) – 3 in Apr 1930 followed by all 21 in season 1930–31. They then dropped out of the League.

Biggest defeat in Champions' season· During **Newcastle's** title-winning season in 1908–09, they were beaten 9-1 at home by Sunderland on December 5.

WORST START BY EVENTUAL CHAMPIONS

Sunderland took only 2 points from their first 7 matches in season 1912–13 (2 draws, 5 defeats). They won 25 of the remaining 31 games to clinch their fifth League title.

DISMAL DERBY

Derby were relegated in season 2007–08 as the worst ever team in the Premier League: fewest wins (1), fewest points (11), fewest goals (20), first club to go down in March (29th).

UNBEATEN LEAGUE SEASON

Only three clubs have completed an English League season unbeaten: **Preston** (22 matches in 1888–89, the League's first season), **Liverpool** (28 matches in Div 2, 1893–94) and **Arsenal** (38 matches in Premiership, 2003–04).

100 PER CENT HOME RECORDS

Six clubs have won every home League match in a season: **Sunderland** (13 matches)' in 1891–92 and four teams in the old Second Division: **Liverpool** (14) in 1893–94, **Bury** (15) in 1894–95, **Sheffield Wed** (17) in 1899–1900 and **Small Heath,** subsequently **Birmingham** (17) in 1902–03. The last club to do it, **Brentford,** won all 21 home games in Div 3 South in 1929–30. **Rotherham** just failed to equal that record in 1946–47. They won their first 20 home matches in Div 3 North, then drew the last 3-3 v Rochdale.

BEST HOME LEAGUE RECORDS IN TOP FLIGHT

Sunderland, 1891–92 (P13, W13); **Newcastle,** 1906–07 (P19, W18, D1); **Chelsea,** 2005–06 (P19, W18, D1); **Manchester Utd,** 2010–11 (P19, W18, D1); **Manchester City,** 2011–12 (P19, W18, D1).

MOST CONSECUTIVE CLEAN SHEETS

Premier League – 14: **Manchester Utd** (2008–09); **Football League** – 11: **Millwall** (Div 3 South 1925–26); **York** (Div 3 1973–74); **Reading** (Div 4, 1978–79).

WORST HOME RUNS

Most consecutive home League defeats: 14 **Rochdale** (Div 3 North) seasons 1931–32 and 1932–33; 10 **Birmingham** (Div 1) 1985–86; 9 **Darwen** (Div 2) 1897–98; 9 **Watford** (Div 2) 1971–72.

Between Nov 1958 and Oct 1959 **Portsmouth** drew 2 and lost 14 out of 16 consecutive home games.

West Ham did not win in the Premiership at Upton Park in season 2002–03 until the 13th home match on Jan 29.

MOST AWAY WINS IN SEASON

Doncaster won 18 of their 21 away League fixtures when winning Div 3 North in 1946–47.

AWAY WINS RECORD

Most consecutive away League wins: 11 **Chelsea** (Prem Lge) – 8 at start of 2008–09 after ending previous season with 3.

100 PER CENT HOME WINS ON ONE DAY

Div 1 – All 11 home teams won on Feb 13, 1926 and on Dec 10, 1955. **Div 2** – All 12 home teams won on Nov 26, 1988. **Div 3**, all 12 home teams won in the week-end programme of Oct 18–19, 1968.

NO HOME WINS IN DIV ON ONE DAY

Div 1 – 8 away wins, 3 draws in 11 matches on Sep 6, 1986. **Div 2** – 7 away wins, 4 draws in 11 matches on Dec 26, 1987. **Premier League** – 6 away wins, 5 draws in 11 matches on Dec 26, 1994.

The week-end **Premiership** programme on Dec 7–8–9, 1996 produced no home win in the ten games (4 aways, 6 draws). There was again no home victory (3 away wins, 7 draws) in the week-end **Premiership** fixtures on Sep 23–24, 2000.

MOST DRAWS IN A SEASON (FOOTBALL LEAGUE)

23 by **Norwich** (Div 1, 1978–79), **Exeter** (Div 4, 1986–87). **Cardiff** and **Hartlepool** (both Div 3, 1997–98). **Norwich** played 42 matches, the others 46.

MOST DRAWS IN PREMIER LEAGUE SEASON

18 (in 42 matches) by **Manchester City** (1993–94), **Sheffield Utd** (1993–94), **Southampton** (1994–95).

MOST DRAWS IN ONE DIV ON ONE DAY

On Sep 18, 1948 **nine** out of 11 First Division matches were drawn.

MOST DRAWS IN PREMIER DIV PROGRAMME

Over the week-ends of December 2–3–4, 1995, and Sep 23–24, 2000, **seven** out of the ten matches finished level.

FEWEST DRAWS IN SEASON

In 46 matches: 3 by **Reading** (Div 3 South, 1951–52); **Bradford Park Avenue** (Div 3 North, 1956–57); **Tranmere** (Div 4, 1984–85); **Southend** (Div 3, 2002–03); in 42 matches: 2 by **Reading** (Div 3 South, 1935–36); **Stockport** (Div 3 North, 1946–47); in 38 matches: 2 by **Sunderland** (Div 1, 1908–09).

HIGHEST-SCORING DRAWS IN LEAGUE

Leicester 6, **Arsenal** 6 (Div 1 Apr 21, 1930); **Charlton** 6, **Middlesbrough** 6 (Div 2. Oct 22, 1960)

Latest **6-6** draw in first-class football was between **Tranmere** and **Newcastle** in the Zenith Data Systems Cup 1st round on Oct 1, 1991. The score went from 3-3 at 90 minutes to 6-6 after extra time, and Tranmere won 3-2 on penalties. In Scotland: **Queen of the South** 6, **Falkirk** 6 (Div 1, Sep 20, 1947).

Most recent **5-5** draws in top division: **Southampton v Coventry** (Div 1, May 4, 1982); **QPR v Newcastle** (Div 1, Sep 22, 1984); **WBA v Manchester Utd** (Prem Lge, May 19, 2013).

DRAWS RECORDS

Most consecutive drawn matches in Football League: 8 by **Torquay** (Div 3, 1969-70), **Middlesbrough** (Div 2, 1970-71), **Peterborough** (Div 4, 1971-72), **Birmingham** (Div 3 (1990-91), **Southampton** (Champ, 2005-06), **Chesterfield** (Lge 1, 2005-06), **Swansea** (Champ, 2008-09).

Longest sequence of draws by the same score: six 1-1 results by **QPR** in season 1957-58. **Tranmere** became the first club to play **five consecutive 0-0 League draws**, in season 1997-98.

IDENTICAL RECORDS

There is only **one instance** of two clubs in one division finishing a season with identical records. In 1907-08, **Blackburn** and **Woolwich Arsenal** were bracketed equal 14th in the First Division with these figures: P38, W12, D12, L14, Goals 51-63, Pts. 36.

The total of **1195 goals** scored in the Premier League in season 1993-94 was repeated in 1994-95.

DEAD LEVEL

Millwall's record in Division Two in season 1973-74 was P42, W14, D14, L14, F51, A51, Pts 42

CHAMPIONS OF ALL DIVISIONS

Wolves, Burnley and **Preston** are the only clubs to have won titles in the old Divisions 1, 2, 3 and 4. Wolves also won the Third Division North and the new Championship.

POINTS DEDUCTIONS

2000-01: Chesterfield 9 for breach of transfer regulations and falsifying gate receipts.
2002-03: Boston 4 for contractual irregularities.
2004-05: Wrexham, Cambridge Utd 10 for administration.
2005-06: Rotherham 10 for administration
2006-07: Leeds, Boston 10 for administration; **Bury** 1 for unregistered player.
2007-08: Leeds 15 over insolvency rules; **Bournemouth, Luton, Rotherham** 10 for administration
2008-09: Luton 20 for failing Insolvency rules, 10 over payments to agents; **Bournemouth, Rotherham** 17 for breaking administration rules; **Southampton, Stockport** 10 for Administration – **Southampton** with effect from season 2009-10 **Crystal Palace** 1 for ineligible player.
2009-10: Portsmouth 9, **Crystal Palace** 10 for administration; **Hartlepool** 3 for ineligible player.
2010-11: Plymouth 10 for administration; **Hereford** 3, **Torquay** 1, each for ineligible player
2011-12: Portsmouth and **Port Vale** both 10 for administration – Portsmouth from following season.
2013-14: Coventry 10 for administration; **AFC Wimbledon** 3 for ineligible player.
2014-15: Rotherham 3 for ineligible player.
2015-16: Bury 3 for ineligible player.

Among previous points penalties imposed:
Nov 1990: Arsenal 2, **Manchester Utd** 1 following mass players' brawl at Old Trafford.
Dec 1996: Brighton 2 for pitch invasions by fans.
Jan 1997: Middlesbrough 3 for refusing to play Premiership match at Blackburn because of injuries and illness.

Jun 1994: Tottenham 12 (reduced to 6) and banned from following season's FA Cup for making illegal payments to players. On appeal, points deduction annulled and club re-instated in Cup.

NIGHTMARE STARTS

Most goals conceded by a goalkeeper on League debut: 13 by **Steve Milton** when Halifax lost 13-0 at Stockport (Div 3 North) on Jan 6, 1934.

Post-war: 11 by Crewe's new goalkeeper **Dennis Murray** (Div 3 North) on Sep 29, 1951, when Lincoln won 11-1.

RELEGATION ODD SPOTS

None of the Barclays Premiership relegation places in season 2004–05 were decided until the last day (Sunday, May 15). **WBA** (bottom at kick-off) survived with a 2-0 home win against Portsmouth, and the three relegated clubs were **Southampton** (1-2 v Manchester Utd), **Norwich** (0-6 at Fulham) and **Crystal Palace** (2-2 at Charlton).

In season 1937–38, **Manchester City** were the highest-scoring team in the First Division with 80 goals (3 more than Champions Arsenal), but they finished in 21st place and were relegated – a year after winning the title. They scored more goals than they conceded (77).

That season produced the **closest relegation battle** in top-division history, with only 4 points spanning the bottom 11 clubs in Div 1. **WBA** went down with **Manchester City**.

Twelve years earlier, in 1925–26, City went down to Division 2 despite totalling 89 goals – still the most scored in any division by a relegated team. Manchester City also scored 31 FA Cup goals that season, but lost the Final 1-0 to Bolton Wanderers.

Cardiff were relegated from Div 1 in season 1928–29, despite conceding fewest goals in the division (59). They also scored fewest (43).

On their way to relegation from the First Division in season 1984–85, **Stoke** twice lost ten matches in a row.

RELEGATION TREBLES

Two Football League clubs have been relegated three seasons in succession. **Bristol City** fell from First Division to Fourth in 1980–81–82 and **Wolves** did the same in 1984–85–86.

OLDEST CLUBS

Oldest Association Football Club is **Sheffield FC** (formed in 1857). The oldest Football League clubs are **Notts Co,** 1862; **Nottm Forest,** 1865; and **Sheffield Wed,** 1866.

FOUR DIVISIONS

In **May, 1957**, the Football League decided to re-group the two sections of the Third Division into Third and Fourth Divisions in **season 1958–59**.

The Football League was reduced to three divisions on the formation of the Premier League in **1992**.

In season 2004–05, under new sponsors Coca-Cola, the titles of First, Second and Third Divisions were changed to League Championship, League One and League Two.

THREE UP – THREE DOWN

The Football League annual general meeting of Jun 1973 agreed to adopt the promotion and relegation system of three up and three down.

The **new system** came into effect in **season 1973–74** and applied only to the first three divisions; four clubs were still relegated from the Third and four promoted from the Fourth.

It was the first change in the promotion and relegation system for the top two divisions in 81 years.

MOST LEAGUE APPEARANCES

Players with more than 700 English League apps (as at end of season 2016–17)

1005   Peter Shilton 1966–97 (286 Leicester, 110 Stoke, 202 Nottm Forest, 188 Southampton, 175 Derby, 34 Plymouth Argyle, 1 Bolton, 9 Leyton Orient).

931	Tony Ford 1975–2002 (423 Grimsby, 9 Sunderland, 112 Stoke, 114 WBA, 5 Bradford City, 76 Scunthorpe, 103 Mansfield, 89 Rochdale).
840	Graham Alexander 1991–2012 (159 Scunthorpe, 152 Luton, 372 Preston, 157 Burnley)
824	Terry Paine 1956–77 (713 Southampton, 111 Hereford).
795	Tommy Hutchison 1968–91 (165 Blackpool, 314 Coventry City, 46 Manchester City, 92 Burnley, 178 Swansea). In addition, 68 Scottish League apps for Alloa 1965–68, giving career League app total of 863.
790	Neil Redfearn 1982–2004 (35 Bolton, 100 Lincoln, 46 Doncaster, 57 Crystal Palace, 24 Watford, 62 Oldham, 292 Barnsley, 30 Charlton, 17 Bradford City, 22 Wigan, 42 Halifax, 54 Boston, 9 Rochdale).
782	Robbie James 1973–94 (484 Swansea, 48 Stoke, 87 QPR, 23 Leicester, 89 Bradford City, 51 Cardiff).
777	Alan Oakes 1959–84 (565 Manchester City, 211 Chester, 1 Port Vale).
773	Dave Beasant 1980–2003 (340 Wimbledon, 20 Newcastle, 6 Grimsby, 4 Wolves, 133 Chelsea, 88 Southampton, 139 Nottm F, 27 Portsmouth, 16 Brighton).
770	John Trollope 1960–80 (all for Swindon, record total for one club).
769	David James 1990–2012 (89 Watford, 214 Liverpool, 67 Aston Villa, 91 West Ham, 93 Manchester City, 134 Portsmouth, 81 Bristol City).
764	Jimmy Dickinson 1946–65 (all for Portsmouth).
761	Roy Sproson 1950–72 (all for Port Vale).
760	Mick Tait 1974–97 (64 Oxford Utd, 106 Carlisle, 33 Hull, 240 Portsmouth, 99 Reading, 79 Darlington, 139 Hartlepool Utd).
758	Billy Bonds 1964–88 (95 Charlton, 663 West Ham).
758	Ray Clemence 1966–88 (48 Scunthorpe, 470 Liverpool, 240 Tottenham).
757	Pat Jennings 1963–86 (48 Watford, 472 Tottenham, 237 Arsenal).
757	Frank Worthington 1966–88 (171 Huddersfield Town, 210 Leicester, 84 Bolton, 75 Birmingham, 32 Leeds, 19 Sunderland, 34 Southampton, 31 Brighton, 60 Tranmere, 23 Preston, 19 Stockport).
755	Wayne Allison 1986–2008 (84 Halifax, 7 Watford, 195 Bristol City, 103 Swindon, 76 Huddersfield, 102 Tranmere, 73 Sheffield Utd, 115 Chesterfield).
749	Ernie Moss 1968–88 (469 Chesterfield, 35 Peterborough, 57 Mansfield, 74 Port Vale, 11 Lincoln, 44 Doncaster, 26 Stockport, 23 Scarborough, 10 Rochdale).
746	Les Chapman 1966–88 (263 Oldham, 133 Huddersfield Town, 70 Stockport, 139 Bradford City, 88 Rochdale, 53 Preston).
744	Asa Hartford 1967–90 (214 WBA, 260 Manchester City, 3 Nottm Forest, 81 Everton, 28 Norwich, 81 Bolton, 45 Stockport, 7 Oldham, 25 Shrewsbury).
743	Alan Ball 1963–84 (146 Blackpool, 208 Everton, 177 Arsenal, 195 Southampton, 17 Bristol Rov).
743	John Hollins 1963–84 (465 Chelsea, 151 QPR, 127 Arsenal).
743	Phil Parkes 1968–91 (52 Walsall, 344 QPR, 344 West Ham, 3 Ipswich).
737	Steve Bruce 1979–99 (205 Gillingham, 141 Norwich, 309 Manchester Utd 72 Birmingham, 10 Sheffield Utd).
734	Teddy Sheringham 1983–2007 (220 Millwall, 5 Aldershot, 42 Nottm Forest, 104 Manchester Utd, 236 Tottenham, 32 Portsmouth, 76 West Ham, 19 Colchester)
732	Mick Mills 1966–88 (591 Ipswich, 103 Southampton, 38 Stoke).
731	Ian Callaghan 1959–81 (640 Liverpool, 76 Swansea, 15 Crewe).
731	David Seaman 1982–2003 (91 Peterborough, 75 Birmingham, 141 QPR, 405 Arsenal, 19 Manchester City).
725	Steve Perryman 1969–90 (655 Tottenham, 17 Oxford Utd, 53 Brentford).
722	Martin Peters 1961–81 (302 West Ham, 189 Tottenham, 207 Norwich, 24 Sheffield Utd).
718	Mike Channon 1966–86 (511 Southampton, 72 Manchester City, 4 Newcastle, 9 Bristol Rov, 88 Norwich, 34 Portsmouth).
716	Ron Harris 1961–83 (655 Chelsea, 61 Brentford).

716   Mike Summerbee 1959–79 (218 Swindon, 357 Manchester City, 51 Burnley, 3 Blackpool, 87 Stockport).

714   Glenn Cockerill 1976–98 (186 Lincoln, 26 Swindon, 62 Sheffield Utd, 387 Southampton, 90 Leyton Orient, 40 Fulham, 23 Brentford).

705   Keith Curle 1981–2003 (32 Bristol Rov, 16 Torquay, 121 Bristol City, 40 Reading, 93 Wimbledon, 171 Manchester City, 150 Wolves, 57 Sheffield Utd, 11 Barnsley, 14 Mansfield.

705   Phil Neal 1968–89 (186 Northampton, 455 Liverpool, 64 Bolton).

705   John Wile 1968–86 (205 Peterborough, 500 WBA).

701   Neville Southall 1980–2000 (39 Bury, 578 Everton, 9 Port Vale, 9 Southend, 12 Stoke, 53 Torquay, 1 Bradford City).

● **Stanley Matthews** made 701 League apps 1932–65 (322 Stoke, 379 Blackpool), incl. 3 for Stoke at start of 1939–40 before season abandoned (war).

● Goalkeeper **John Burridge** made a total of 771 League appearances in a 28-season career in English and Scottish football (1968–96). He played 691 games for 15 English clubs (Workington, Blackpool, Aston Villa, Southend, Crystal Palace, QPR, Wolves, Derby, Sheffield Utd, Southampton, Newcastle, Scarborough, Lincoln, Manchester City and Darlington) and 80 for 5 Scottish clubs (Hibernian, Aberdeen, Dumbarton, Falkirk and Queen of the South).

LONGEST LEAGUE APPEARANCE SEQUENCE

Harold Bell, centre-half of Tranmere, was ever-present for the first nine post-war seasons (1946–55), achieving a League record of 401 consecutive matches. Counting FA Cup and other games, his run of successive appearances totalled 459.

The longest League sequence since Bell's was 394 appearances by goalkeeper **Dave Beasant** for Wimbledon, Newcastle and Chelsea. His nine-year run began on Aug 29, 1981 and was ended by a broken finger sustained in Chelsea's League Cup-tie against Portsmouth on Oct 31, 1990. Beasant's 394 consecutive League games comprised 304 for Wimbledon (1981–88), 20 for Newcastle (1988–89) and 70 for Chelsea (1989–90).

Phil Neal made 366 consecutive First Division appearances for Liverpool between December 1974 and Sep 1983, a remarkable sequence for an outfield player in top-division football.

MOST CONSECUTIVE PREMIER LEAGUE APPEARANCES

310 by goalkeeper **Brad Friedel** (152 Blackburn, 114 Aston Villa, 44 Tottenham, May 2004–Oct 2012). He played in 8 **ever-present seasons** (2004–12, Blackburn 4, Villa 3, Tottenham 1).

EVER-PRESENT DEFENCE

The **entire defence** of **Huddersfield** played in all 42 Second Division matches in season 1952–53, namely, Bill Wheeler (goal), Ron Staniforth and Laurie Kelly (full-backs), Bill McGarry, Don McEvoy and Len Quested (half-backs). In addition, Vic Metcalfe played in all 42 League matches at outside-left.

FIRST SUBSTITUTE USED IN LEAGUE

Keith Peacock (Charlton), away to Bolton (Div 2) on Aug 21, 1965.

FROM PROMOTION TO CHAMPIONS

Clubs who have become Champions of England a year after winning promotion: **Liverpool** 1905, 1906; **Everton** 1931, 1932; **Tottenham** 1950, 1951; **Ipswich** 1961, 1962; **Nottm Forest** 1977, 1978. The first four were placed top in both seasons: Forest finished third and first.

PREMIERSHIP'S FIRST MULTI-NATIONAL LINE-UP

Chelsea made history on December 26, 1999 when starting their Premiership match at Southampton without a single British player in the side.

Fulham's Unique XI: In the Worthington Cup 3rd round at home to Bury on Nov 6, 2002, Fulham fielded 11 players of 11 different nationalities. Ten were full Internationals, with Lee Clark an England U–21 cap.

On Feb 14, 2005 **Arsenal** became the first English club to select an all-foreign match squad when Arsene Wenger named 16 non-British players at home to Crystal Palace (Premiership).

Fifteen nations were represented at Fratton Park on Dec 30, 2009 (Portsmouth 1 Arsenal 4) when, for the first time in Premier League history, not one Englishman started the match. The line-up comprised seven Frenchmen, two Algerians and one from each of 13 other countries.

Players from 22 nationalities (subs included) were involved in the Blackburn–WBA match at Ewood Park on Jan 23, 2011.

PREMIER LEAGUE'S FIRST ALL-ENGLAND LINE-UP

On Feb 27, 1999 **Aston Villa** (at home to Coventry) fielded the first all-English line up seen in the Premier League (starting 11 plus 3 subs).

ENTIRE HOME-GROWN TEAM

Crewe Alexandra's starting 11 in the 2-0 home win against Walsall (Lge 1) on Apr 27, 2013 all graduated from the club's academy.

THREE-NATION CHAMPIONS

David Beckham won a title in four countries: with Manchester Utd six times (1996–97–99–2000–01–03), Real Madrid (2007), LA Galaxy (2011) and Paris St Germain (2013).

Trevor Steven earned eight Championship medals in three countries: two with Everton (1985, 1987); five with Rangers (1990, 1991, 1993, 1994, 1995) and one with Marseille in 1992.

LEEDS NO WIN AWAY

Leeds, in 1992–93, provided the first instance of a club failing to win an away League match as reigning Champions.

PIONEERS IN 1888 AND 1992

Three clubs among the twelve who formed the Football League in 1888 were also founder members of the Premier League: **Aston Villa, Blackburn** and **Everton.**

CHAMPIONS (MODERN) WITH TWO CLUBS – PLAYERS

Francis Lee (Manchester City 1968, Derby 1975); **Ray Kennedy** (Arsenal 1971, Liverpool 1979, 1980, 1982); **Archie Gemmill** (Derby 1972, 1975, Nottm Forest 1978); **John McGovern** (Derby 1972, Nottm Forest 1978) **Larry Lloyd** (Liverpool 1973, Nottm Forest 1978); **Peter Withe** (Nottm Forest 1970, Aston Villa 1981); **John Lukic** (Arsenal 1989, Leeds 1992); **Kevin Richardson** (Everton 1985, Arsenal 1989); **Eric Cantona** (Leeds 1992, Manchester Utd 1993, 1994, 1996, 1997); **David Batty** (Leeds 1992, Blackburn 1995); **Bobby Mimms** (Everton 1987, Blackburn 1995), **Henning Berg** (Blackburn 1995, Manchester Utd 1999, 2000); **Nicolas Anelka** (Arsenal 1998, Chelsea 2010); **Ashley Cole** (Arsenal 2002, 2004, Chelsea 2010); **Gael Clichy** (Arsenal 2004, Manchester City 2012); **Kolo Toure** (Arsenal 2004, Manchester City 2012); **Carlos Tevez** (Manchester Utd 2008, 2009, Manchester City 2012).

TITLE TURNABOUTS

In Jan 1996, **Newcastle** led the Premier League by 13 points. They finished runners-up to Manchester Utd.

At Christmas 1997, **Arsenal** were 13 points behind leaders Manchester Utd and still 11 points behind at the beginning of Mar 1998. But a run of 10 wins took the title to Highbury.

On Mar 2, 2003, **Arsenal,** with 9 games left, went 8 points clear of Manchester Utd, who had a match in hand. United won the Championship by 5 points.

In Mar 2002, **Wolves** were in second (automatic promotion) place in Nationwide Div 1, 11 points ahead of WBA, who had 2 games in hand. They were overtaken by Albion on the run-in, finished third, then failed the play-offs. A year later they won promotion to the Premiership via the play-offs.

CLUB CLOSURES

Four clubs have left the Football League in mid-season: **Leeds City** (expelled Oct 1919); **Wigan Borough** (Oct 1931, debts of £20,000); **Accrington Stanley** (Mar 1962, debts £62,000); **Aldershot** (Mar 1992, debts £1.2m). **Maidstone**, with debts of £650,000, closed Aug 1992, on the eve of the season.

FOUR-DIVISION MEN

In season 1986–87, goalkeeper **Eric Nixon**, became the first player to appear in **all four divisions** of the Football League **in one season**. He served two clubs in Div 1: Manchester City (5 League games) and Southampton (4); in Div 2 Bradford City (3); in Div 3 Carlisle (16); and in Div 4 Wolves (16). Total appearances: 44.

Harvey McCreadie, a teenage forward, played in four divisions over two seasons inside a calendar year – from Accrington (Div 3) to Luton (Div 1) in Jan 1960, to Div 2 with Luton later that season and to Wrexham (Div 4) in Nov.

Tony Cottee played in all four divisions in season 2000–01, for Leicester (Premiership), Norwich (Div 1), Barnet (Div 3, player-manager) and Millwall (Div 2).

FATHERS AND SONS

When player-manager **Ian** (39) and **Gary** (18) **Bowyer** appeared together in the **Hereford** side at Scunthorpe (Div 4, Apr 21, 1990), they provided the first instance of father and son playing in the same team in a Football League match for 39 years. Ian played as substitute, and Gary scored Hereford's injury-time equaliser in a 3-3 draw.

Alec (39) and **David** (17) **Herd** were among previous father-and-son duos in league football – for Stockport, 2-0 winners at Hartlepool (Div 3 North) on May 5, 1951.

When Preston won 2-1 at Bury in Div 3 on Jan 13, 1990, the opposing goalkeepers were brothers: **Alan Kelly** (21) for Preston and **Gary** (23) for Bury. Their father, **Alan** (who kept goal for Preston in the 1964 FA Cup Final and won 47 Rep of Ireland caps) flew from America to watch the sons he taught to keep goal line up on opposite sides.

Other examples: **Bill Dodgin Snr** (manager, Bristol Rov) faced son **Bill Jnr** (manager of Fulham) four times between 1969 and 1971. On Apr 16, 2013 (Lge 1), Oldham, under **Lee Johnson,** won 1-0 at home to Yeovil, managed by his father **Gary.**

George Eastham Snr (manager) and son **George Eastham Jnr** were inside-forward partners for Ards in the Irish League in season 1954–55.

FATHER AND SON REFEREE PLAY-OFF FINALS

Father and son refereed two of the 2009 Play-off Finals. **Clive Oliver**, 46, took charge of Shrewsbury v Gillingham (Lge 2) and **Michael Oliver**, 26, refereed Millwall v Scunthorpe (Lge 1) the following day.

FATHER AND SON BOTH CHAMPIONS

John Aston snr won a Championship medal with Manchester Utd in 1952 and **John Aston jnr** did so with the club in 1967. **Ian Wright** won the Premier League title with Arsenal in 1998 and **Shaun Wright-Phillips** won with Chelsea in 2006.

FATHER AND SON RIVAL MANAGERS

When **Bill Dodgin snr** took Bristol Rov to Fulham for an FA Cup 1st Round tie in Nov 1971, the opposing manager was his son, **Bill jnr.** Rovers won 2-1. Oldham's new manager, **Lee Johnson**, faced his father **Gary's** Yeovil in a Lge 1 match in April, 2013. Oldham won 1-0.

FATHER AND SON ON OPPOSITE SIDES

It happened for the first time in FA Cup history (1st Qual Round on Sep 14, 1996) when 21-year-old **Nick Scaife** (Bishop Auckland) faced his father **Bobby** (41), who played for Pickering. Both were in midfield. Home side Bishops won 3-1.

THREE BROTHERS IN SAME SIDE

Southampton provided the first instance for 65 years of three brothers appearing together in a Div 1 side when **Danny Wallace** (24) and his 19-year-old twin brothers **Rodney** and **Ray** played against Sheffield Wed on Oct 22, 1988. In all, they made 25 appearances together for Southampton until Sep 1989.

A previous instance in Div 1 was provided by the Middlesbrough trio, **William, John** and **George Carr** with 24 League appearances together from Jan 1920 to Oct 1923.

The **Tonner** brothers, **Sam, James** and **Jack,** played together in 13 Second Division matches for Clapton Orient in season 1919–20.

Brothers **David, Donald** and **Robert Jack** played together in Plymouth's League side in 1920.

TWIN TEAM-MATES (see also Wallace twins above)

Twin brothers **David** and **Peter Jackson** played together for three League clubs (Wrexham, Bradford City and Tranmere) from 1954–62. The **Morgan** twins, **Ian** and **Roger**, played regularly in the QPR forward line from 1964–68. WBA's **Adam** and **James Chambers**, 18, were the first twins to represent England (v Cameroon in World Youth Championship, Apr 1999). They first played together in Albion's senior team, aged 19, in the League Cup 2nd. Round against Derby in Sep 2000. Brazilian identical twins **Rafael** and **Fabio Da Silva** (18) made first team debuts at full-back for Manchester Utd in season 2008–09. Swedish twins **Martin** and **Marcus Olsson** played together for Blackburn in season 2011–12. **Josh** and **Jacob Murphy**, 19, played for Norwich in season 2013–2014.

SIR TOM DOES THE HONOURS

Sir Tom Finney, England and Preston legend, opened the Football League's new headquarters on their return to Preston on Feb 23, 1999. Preston had been the League's original base for 70 years before the move to Lytham St Annes in 1959.

SHORTENED MATCHES

The 0-0 score in the **Bradford City v Lincoln** Third Division fixture on May 11, 1985, abandoned through fire after 40 minutes, was subsequently confirmed as a result. It is the shortest officially- completed League match on record, and was the fourth of only five instances in Football League history of the score of an unfinished match being allowed to stand.

The other occasions: **Middlesbrough 4, Oldham 1** (Div 1, Apr 3, 1915), abandoned after 55 minutes when Oldham defender Billy Cook refused to leave the field after being sent off; **Barrow 7, Gillingham 0** (Div 4, Oct 9, 1961), abandoned after 75 minutes because of bad light, the match having started late because of Gillingham's delayed arrival.

A crucial **Manchester** derby (Div 1) was abandoned after 85 minutes, and the result stood, on Apr 27, 1974, when a pitch invasion at Old Trafford followed the only goal, scored for City by Denis Law, which relegated United, Law's former club.

The only instance of a first-class match in England being abandoned **'through shortage of players'** occurred in the First Division at Bramall Lane on Mar 16, 2002. Referee Eddie Wolstenholme halted play after 82 minutes because **Sheffield Utd** were reduced to 6 players against **WBA.** They had had 3 men sent off (goalkeeper and 2 substitutes), and with all 3 substitutes used and 2 players injured, were left with fewer than the required minimum of 7 on the field. Promotion contenders WBA were leading 3-0, and referee Ordered the result to stand.

The last 60 seconds of **Birmingham v Stoke** (Div 3, 1-1, on Feb 29, 1992) were played behind locked doors. The ground had been cleared after a pitch invasion.

A First Division fixture, **Sheffield Wed v Aston Villa** (Nov 26, 1898), was abandoned through bad light after 79 mins with Wednesday leading 3-1. The Football League ruled that the match should be completed, and the remaining 10.5 minutes were played four months later (Mar 13, 1899), when Wednesday added another goal to make the result 4-1.

FA CUP RECORDS
(See also Goalscoring section)

CHIEF WINNERS

13 Arsenal, **12** Manchester Utd, **8** Tottenham; **7** Aston Villa, Chelsea, Liverpool; **6** Blackburn, Newcastle.

Three times in succession: The Wanderers (1876–77–78) and Blackburn (1884–85–86).

Trophy handed back: The FA Cup became the Wanderers' absolute property in 1878, but they handed it back to the Association on condition that it was not to be won outright by any club.

In successive years by professional clubs: Blackburn (1890 and 1891); Newcastle (1951 and 1952); Tottenham (1961 and 1962); Tottenham (1981 and 1982); Arsenal (2002 and 2003); Chelsea (2009–10).

Record Final-tie score: Bury 6, Derby 0 (1903).

Most FA Cup Final wins at Wembley: Arsenal 10, Manchester Utd 10, Chelsea 6, Tottenham 6, Liverpool 5, Newcastle 5.

SECOND DIVISION WINNERS

Notts Co (1894), **Wolves** (1908), **Barnsley** (1912), **WBA** (1931), **Sunderland** (1973), **Southampton** (1976), **West Ham** (1980). When **Tottenham** won the Cup in 1901 they were a Southern League club.

'OUTSIDE' SEMI-FINALISTS

Sheffield Utd, in 2014, became the ninth team from outside the top two divisions to reach the semi-finals, following **Millwall** (1937), **Port Vale** (1954), **York** (1955), **Norwich** (1959), **Crystal Palace** (1976), **Plymouth** (1984), **Chesterfield** (1997) and **Wycombe** (2001). None reached the Final.

FOURTH DIVISION QUARTER-FINALISTS

Oxford Utd (1964), **Colchester** (1971), **Bradford City** (1976), **Cambridge Utd** (1990).

FOURTH ROUND – NO REPLAYS

No replays were necessary in the 16 fourth round ties in January 2008 (7 home wins, 9 away). This had not happened for 51 years, since 8 home and 8 away wins in season 1956–57.

FIVE TROPHIES

The trophy which Arsenal won in 2014 was the fifth in FA Cup history. These were its predecessors:

1872–95: First Cup stolen from shop in Birmingham while held by Aston Villa. Never seen again.

1910: Second trophy presented to Lord Kinnaird on completing 21 years as FA president.

1911–91: Third trophy used until replaced ('battered and fragile') after 80 years' service.

1992–2013 Fourth FA Cup lasted 21 years – now retained at FA headquarters at Wembley Stadium.

Traditionally, the Cup stays with the holders until returned to the FA in March.

FINALISTS RELEGATED

Six clubs have reached the FA Cup Final and been relegated. The first five all lost at Wembley – **Manchester City** 1926, **Leicester** 1969, **Brighton** 1983, **Middlesbrough** 1997 and **Portsmouth** 2010. Wigan, Cup winners for the first time in 2013, were relegated from the Premier League three days later.

FA CUP – TOP SHOCKS

(2017 = season 2016–17; rounds shown in brackets; R = replay)

1922 (1)	Everton	0	Crystal Palace	6
1933 (3)	Walsall	2	Arsenal	0
1939 (F)	Portsmouth	4	Wolves	1

1948 (3)	Arsenal	0	Bradford PA	1
1948 (3)	Colchester	1	Huddersfield	0
1949 (4)	Yeovil	2	Sunderland	1
1954 (4)	Arsenal	1	Norwich	2
1955 (5)	York	2	Tottenham	1
1957 (4)	Wolves	0	Bournemouth	1
1957 (5)	Bournemouth	3	Tottenham	1
1958 (4)	Newcastle	1	Scunthorpe	3
1959 (3)	Norwich	3	Manchester Utd	0
1959 (3)	Worcester	2	Liverpool	1
1961 (3)	Chelsea	1	Crewe	2
1964 (3)	Newcastle	1	Bedford	2
1965 (4)	Peterborough	2	Arsenal	1
1971 (5)	Colchester	3	Leeds	2
1972 (3)	Hereford	2	Newcastle	1R
1973 (F)	Sunderland	1	Leeds	0
1975 (3)	Burnley	0	Wimbledon	1
1976 (F)	Southampton	1	Manchester Utd	0
1978 (F)	Ipswich	1	Arsenal	0
1980 (3)	Chelsea	0	Wigan	1
1980 (3)	Halifax	1	Manchester City	0
1980 (F)	West Ham	1	Arsenal	0
1981 (4)	Exeter	4	Newcastle	0R
1984 (3)	Bournemouth	2	Manchester Utd	0
1985 (4)	York	1	Arsenal	0
1986 (3)	Birmingham	1	Altrincham	2
1988 (F)	Wimbledon	1	Liverpool	0
1989 (3)	Sutton	2	Coventry	1
1991 (3)	WBA	2	Woking	4
1992 (3)	Wrexham	2	Arsenal	1
1994 (3)	Liverpool	0	Bristol City	1R
1994 (3)	Birmingham	1	Kidderminster	2
1997 (5)	Chesterfield	1	Nottm Forest	0
2001 (4)	Everton	0	Tranmere	3
2003 (3)	Shrewsbury	2	Everton	1
2005 (3)	Oldham	1	Manchester City	0
2008 (6)	Barnsley	1	Chelsea	0
2009 (2)	Histon	1	Leeds	0
2010 (4)	Liverpool	1	Reading	2R
2011 (3)	Stevenage	3	Newcastle	1
2012 (3)	Macclesfield	2	Cardiff	1
2013 (4)	Norwich	0	Luton	1
2013 (4)	Oldham	3	Liverpool	2
2013 (F)	Wigan	1	Manchester City	0
2014 (3)	Rochdale	2	Leeds	0
2015 (3)	Chelsea	2	Bradford City	4
2015 (5)	Bradford City	2	Sunderland	0
2016 (3)	Oxford	3	Swansea	2
2017 (5)	Burnley	0	Lincoln	1

YEOVIL TOP GIANT-KILLERS

Yeovil's victories over Colchester and Blackpool in season 2000–01 gave them a total of 20 FA Cup wins against League opponents. They set another non-League record by reaching the third round 13 times.

This was Yeovil's triumphant (non-League) Cup record against League clubs: 1924–25 Bournemouth 3-2; 1934–35 Crystal Palace 3-0, Exeter 4-1; 1938–39 Brighton 2-1; 1948–49 Bury 3-1, Sunderland 2-1; 1958–59 Southend 1-0; 1960–61 Walsall 1-0; 1963–64 Southend 1-0, Crystal Palace 3-1; 1970–71 Bournemouth 1-0; 1972–73 Brentford 2-1; 1987–88 Cambridge Utd 1-0; 1991–92 Walsall 1-0; 1992–93 Torquay 5-2, Hereford 2-1; 1993–94 Fulham 1-0; 1998–99 Northampton 2-0; 2000–01 Colchester 5-1, Blackpool 1-0.

NON-LEAGUE BEST

Since League football began in 1888, three non-League clubs have reached the FA Cup Final. **Sheffield Wed** (Football Alliance) were runners-up in 1890, as were **Southampton** (Southern League) in 1900 and 1902. **Tottenham** won the Cup as a Southern League team in 1901.

Lincoln won 1-0 at Burnley on Feb 18, 2017, to become the first non-league club to reach the last eight in 103 years. Two non-league sides – **Lincoln** and **Sutton** – had reached the last 16 for the first time.

Otherwise, the furthest progress by non-League clubs has been to the 5th round on 7 occasions: **Colchester** 1948, **Yeovil** 1949, **Blyth** 1978, **Telford** 1985, **Kidderminster** 1994, **Crawley** 2011, **Luton** 2013.

Greatest number of non-League sides to reach the **3rd round** is **8** in 2009: **Barrow, Blyth, Eastwood, Forest Green, Histon, Kettering, Kidderminster** and **Torquay.**

Most to reach **Round 4: 3** in 1957 (**Rhyl, New Brighton, Peterborough**) and 1975 (**Leatherhead, Stafford** and **Wimbledon**).

Five non-League clubs reaching **round 3** in 2001 was a Conference record. They were **Chester, Yeovil, Dagenham, Morecambe** and **Kingstonian**.

In season 2002–03, **Team Bath** became the first University-based side to reach the FA Cup 1st Round since **Oxford University** (Finalists in 1880).

NON-LEAGUE 'LAST TIMES'

Last time no non-League club reached round 3: 1951. Last time only one did so: 1969 (**Kettering**).

TOP-DIVISION SCALPS

Victories in FA Cup by non-League clubs over top-division teams since 1900 include: 1900–01 (Final, replay): **Tottenham** 3 Sheffield Utd 1 (Tottenham then in Southern League); 1919–20 **Cardiff** 2, Oldham 0; Sheffield Wed 0, **Darlington** 2; 1923–24 **Corinthians** 1, Blackburn 0; 1947–48 **Colchester** 1, Huddersfield 0; 1948–9 **Yeovil** 2, Sunderland 1; 1971–72 **Hereford** 2, Newcastle 1; 1974–75 Burnley 0, **Wimbledon** 1; 1985–86 Birmingham 1, **Altrincham** 2; 1988–89 **Sutton** 2, Coventry 1; 2012–13 Norwich 0, **Luton** 1.

MOST WINNING MEDALS

Ashley Cole has won the trophy seven times, with (Arsenal 2002–03–05) and Chelsea (2007–09–10–12). **The Hon Arthur Kinnaird** (The Wanderers and Old Etonians), **Charles Wollaston** (The Wanderers) and **Jimmy Forrest** (Blackburn) each earned five winners' medals. Kinnaird, later president of the FA, played in nine of the first 12 FA Cup Finals, and was on the winning side three times for The Wanderers, in 1873 (captain), 1877, 1878 (captain), and twice as captain of Old Etonians (1879, 1882).

MANAGERS' MEDALS BACKDATED

In 2010, the FA agreed to award Cup Final medals to all living managers who took their teams to the Final before 1996 (when medals were first given to Wembley team bosses). Lawrie McMenemy had campaigned for the award since Southampton's victory in 1976.

MOST WINNERS' MEDALS AT WEMBLEY

4 – Mark Hughes (3 for Manchester Utd, 1 for Chelsea), **Petr Cech, Frank Lampard, John Terry, Didier Drogba, Ashley Cole** (all Chelsea).

3 – Dick Pym (3 clean sheets in Finals), **Bob Haworth, Jimmy Seddon, Harry Nuttall, Billy Butler** (all Bolton); **David Jack** (2 Bolton, 1 Arsenal); **Bob Cowell, Jack Milburn, Bobby Mitchell** (all

Newcastle); **Dave Mackay** (Tottenham); **Frank Stapleton** (1 Arsenal, 2 Manchester Utd); **Bryan Robson** (3 times winning captain); **Arthur Albiston, Gary Pallister** (all Manchester Utd); **Bruce Grobbelaar, Steve Nicol, Ian Rush** (all Liverpool); **Roy Keane, Peter Schmeichel, Ryan Giggs** (all Manchester Utd); **Dennis Wise** (1 Wimbledon, 2 Chelsea).

Arsenal's **David Seaman** and **Ray Parlour** have each earned 4 winners' medals (2 at Wembley, 2 at Cardiff) as have Manchester Utd's **Roy Keane** and **Ryan Giggs** (3 at Wembley, 1 at Cardiff).

MOST WEMBLEY FINALS

Nine players appeared in five FA Cup Finals at Wembley, replays excluded:

- **Joe Hulme** (Arsenal: 1927 lost, 1930 won, 1932 lost, 1936 won; Huddersfield: 1938 lost).
- **Johnny Giles** (Manchester Utd: 1963 won; Leeds: 1965 lost, 1970 drew at Wembley, lost replay at Old Trafford, 1972 won, 1973 lost).
- **Pat Rice** (all for Arsenal: 1971 won, 1972 lost, 1978 lost, 1979 won, 1980 lost).
- **Frank Stapleton** (Arsenal: 1978 lost, 1979 won, 1980 lost; Manchester Utd: 1983 won, 1985 won).
- **Ray Clemence** (Liverpool: 1971 lost, 1974 won, 1977 lost; Tottenham: 1982 won, 1987 lost).
- **Mark Hughes** (Manchester Utd: 1985 won, 1990 won, 1994 won, 1995 lost; Chelsea: 1997 won).
- **John Barnes** (Watford: 1984 lost; Liverpool: 1988 lost, 1989 won, 1996 lost; Newcastle: 1998 sub, lost): – first player to lose Wembley FA Cup Finals with three different clubs.
- **Roy Keane** (Nottm Forest: 1991 lost; Manchester Utd: 1994 won, 1995 lost, 1996 won, 1999 won).
- **Ryan Giggs** (Manchester Utd: 1994 won, 1995 lost, 1996 won, 1999 won, 2007 lost).
- Clemence, Hughes and Stapleton also played in a replay, making six actual FA Cup Final appearances for each of them.
- **Glenn Hoddle** also made six appearances at Wembley: 5 for Tottenham (incl. 2 replays), in 1981 won, 1982 won and 1987 lost, and 1 for Chelsea as sub in 1994 lost.
- **Paul Bracewell** played in four FA Cup Finals without being on the winning side – for Everton 1985, 1986, 1989, Sunderland 1992.

MOST WEMBLEY/CARDIFF FINAL APPEARANCES

8 by **Ashley Cole** (Arsenal: 2001 lost; 2002 won; 2003 won; 2005 won; Chelsea: 2007 won; 2009 won; 2010 won, 2012 won).

7 by **Roy Keane** (Nottm Forest: 1991 lost; Manchester Utd: 1994 won, 1995 lost, 1996 won; 1999 won; 2004 won; 2005 lost).

7 by **Ryan Giggs** (Manchester Utd): 1994 won; 1995 lost; 1996 won; 1999 won; 2004 won; 2005 lost; 2007 lost.

6 by **Paul Scholes** (Manchester Utd): 1995 lost; 1996 won; 1999 won; 2004 won; 2005 lost; 2007 lost.

5 by **David Seaman** and **Ray Parlour** (Arsenal): 1993 won; 1998 won; 2001 lost; 2002 won; 2003 won; **Dennis Wise** (Wimbledon 1988 won; Chelsea 1994 lost; 1997 won; 2000 won; Millwall 2004 lost); Patrick Vieira (Arsenal): 1998 won; 2001 lost; 2002 won; 2005 won; (Manchester City) 2011 won.

BIGGEST FA CUP SCORE AT WEMBLEY

5-0 by Stoke v Bolton (semi-final, Apr 17, 2011).

WINNING GOALKEEPER-CAPTAINS

1988 **Dave Beasant** (Wimbledon); 2003 **David Seaman** (Arsenal).

MOST WINNING MANAGERS

7 Arsene Wenger (Arsenal) 1998, 2002, 2003, 2005, 2014, 2015, 2017; **6 George Ramsay** (Aston Villa) 1887, 1895, 1897, 1905, 1913, 1920; **5 Sir Alex Ferguson** (Manchester Utd) 1990, 1994, 1996, 1999, 2004.

PLAYER-MANAGERS IN FINAL

Kenny Dalglish (Liverpool, 1986); **Glenn Hoddle** (Chelsea, 1994); **Dennis Wise** (Millwall, 2004).

DEBUTS IN FINAL

Alan Davies (Manchester Utd v Brighton, 1983); **Chris Baird** (Southampton v Arsenal, 2003); **Curtis Weston** (Millwall sub v Manchester Utd, 2004).

SEMI-FINALS AT WEMBLEY

1991 Tottenham 3 Arsenal 1; **1993** Sheffield Wed 2 Sheffield Utd 1, Arsenal 1 Tottenham 0; **1994** Chelsea 2 Luton 0, Manchester Utd 1 Oldham 1; **2000** Aston Villa beat Bolton 4-1 on pens (after 0-0), Chelsea 2 Newcastle 1; **2008** Portsmouth 1 WBA 0, Cardiff 1 Barnsley 0; **2009** Chelsea 2 Arsenal 1, Everton beat Manchester Utd 4-2 on pens (after 0-0); **2010** Chelsea 3 Aston Villa 0, Portsmouth 2 Tottenham 0; **2011** Manchester City 1 Manchester Utd 0, Stoke 5 Bolton 0; **2012** Liverpool 2 Everton 1, Chelsea 5 Tottenham 1; **2013** Wigan 2 Millwall 0, Manchester City 2 Chelsea 1; **2014** Arsenal beat Wigan 4-2 on pens (after 1-1), Hull 5 Sheffield Utd 3; **2015** Arsenal 2 Reading 1, Aston Villa 2 Liverpool 1; **2016** Manchester Utd 2 Everton 1, Crystal Palace 2 Watford 1; **2017** Arsenal 2 Manchester City 1, Chelsea 4 Tottenham 2

CHELSEA'S FA CUP MILESTONES

Their victory over Liverpool in the 2012 Final set the following records:
Captain **John Terry** first player to lift the trophy four times for one club; **Didier Drogba** first to score in four Finals; **Ashley Cole** first to earn seven winner's medals (Arsenal 3, Chelsea 4); **Roberto Di Matteo** first to score for and manage the same winning club (player for Chelsea 1997, 2000, interim manager 2012).
Chelsea's four triumphs in six seasons (2007–12) the best winning sequence since Wanderers won five of the first seven competitions (1872–78) and Blackburn won five out of eight (1884–91).

FIRST ENTRANTS (1871–72)

Barnes, Civil Service, Crystal Palace, Clapham Rov, Donnington School (Spalding), Hampstead Heathens, Harrow Chequers, Hitchin, Maidenhead, Marlow, Queen's Park (Glasgow), Reigate Priory, Royal Engineers, Upton Park and Wanderers. Total 15.

LAST ALL-ENGLISH WINNERS

Manchester City, in 1969, were the last club to win the final with a team of all English players.

FA CUP FIRSTS

Out of country: Cardiff, by defeating Arsenal 1-0 in the 1927 Final at Wembley, became the first and only club to take the FA Cup out of England.
All-English Winning XI: First club to win the FA Cup with all-English XI: Blackburn Olympic in 1883. Others since: WBA in 1888 and 1931, Bolton (1958), Manchester City (1969), West Ham (1964 and 1975).
Non-English Winning XI: Liverpool in 1986 (Mark Lawrenson, born Preston, was a Rep of Ireland player).
Won both Cups: Old Carthusians won the FA Cup in 1881 and the FA Amateur Cup in 1894 and 1897. Wimbledon won Amateur Cup in 1963, FA Cup in 1988.

MOST GAMES NEEDED TO WIN

Barnsley played a record 12 matches (20 hours' football) to win the FA Cup in season 1911–12. All six replays (one in round 1, three in round 4 and one in each of semi-final and Final) were brought about by goalless draws.
Arsenal played 11 FA Cup games when winning the trophy in 1979. Five of them were in the 3rd round against Sheffield Wed.

LONGEST TIES

6 matches: (11 hours): Alvechurch v Oxford City (4th qual round, 1971–72). Alvechurch won 1–0.

5 matches: (9 hours, 22 mins – record for competition proper): Stoke v Bury (3rd round, 1954–55). Stoke won 3–2.

5 matches: Chelsea v Burnley (4th round, 1955–56). Chelsea won 2–0.

5 matches: Hull v Darlington (2nd round, 1960–61). Hull won 3–0.

5 matches: Arsenal v Sheffield Wed (3rd round, 1978–79). Arsenal won 2–0.

Other marathons (qualifying comp, all 5 matches, 9 hours): Barrow v Gillingham (last qual round, 1924–25) – winners Barrow; Leyton v Ilford (3rd qual round, 1924–25) – winners Leyton; Falmouth v Bideford (3rd qual round, 1973–74) winners Bideford.

End of Cup Final replays: The FA decided that, with effect from 1999, there would be no Cup Final replays. In the event of a draw after extra-time, the match would be decided on penalties. This happened for the first time in 2005, when Arsenal beat Manchester Utd 5–4 on penalties after a 0–0 draw. A year later, Liverpool beat West Ham 3–1 on penalties after a 3–3 draw.

FA Cup marathons ended in season 1991–92, when the penalty shoot-out was introduced to decide ties still level after one replay and extra-time.

In 1932–33 **Brighton** (Div 3 South) played 11 FA Cup games, including replays, and scored 43 goals, without getting past round 5. They forgot to claim exemption and had to play from 1st qual round.

LONGEST ROUND

The longest round in FA Cup history was the **3rd round** in **1962–63**. It took 66 days to complete, lasting from Jan 5 to Mar 11, and included 261 postponements because of bad weather.

LONGEST UNBEATEN RUN

23 matches by Blackburn In winning the Cup in three consecutive years (1884–05–06), they won 21 ties (one in a replay), and their first Cup defeat in four seasons was in a first round replay of the next competition.

RE-STAGED TIES

Sixth round, Mar 9, 1974: Newcastle 4, Nottm Forest 3. Match declared void by FA and ordered to be replayed following a pitch invasion after Newcastle had a player sent off. Forest claimed the hold-up caused the game to change its pattern. The tie went to two further matches at Goodison Park (0–0, then 1–0 to Newcastle).

Third round, Jan 5, 1985: Burton 1, Leicester 6 (at Derby). Burton goalkeeper Paul Evans was hit on the head by a missile thrown from the crowd and continued in a daze. The FA ordered the tie to be played again, behind closed doors at Coventry (Leicester won 1–0).

First round replay, Nov 25, 1992: Peterborough 9 (Tony Philliskirk 5), Kingstonian 1. Match expunged from records because, at 3–0 after 57 mins, Kingstonian were reduced to ten men when goalkeeper Adrian Blake was concussed by a 50 pence coin thrown from the crowd. The tie was re-staged on the same ground behind closed doors (Peterborough won 1–0).

Fifth round: Within an hour of holders Arsenal beating Sheffield Utd 2–1 at Highbury on Feb 13, 1999, the FA took the unprecedented step of declaring the match void because an unwritten rule of sportsmanship had been broken. With United's Lee Morris lying injured, their goalkeeper Alan Kelly kicked the ball into touch. Play resumed with Arsenal's Ray Parlour throwing it in the direction of Kelly, but Nwankwo Kanu took possession and centred for Marc Overmars to score the 'winning' goal. After four minutes of protests by manager Steve Bruce and his players, referee Peter Jones confirmed the goal. Both managers absolved Kanu of cheating but Arsenal's Arsène Wenger offered to replay the match. With the FA immediately approving, it was re-staged at Highbury ten days later (ticket prices halved) and Arsenal again won 2–1.

PRIZE FUND

The makeover of the FA Cup competition took off in 2001–02 with the introduction of round-by-round prize-money.

FA CUP FOLLIES

1999–2000 The FA broke with tradition by deciding the 3rd round be moved from its regular Jan date and staged before Christmas. Criticism was strong, gates poor and the 3rd round in 2000–01 reverted to the New Year. By allowing the holders Manchester Utd to withdraw from the 1999–2000 competition in order to play in FIFA's inaugural World Club Championship in Brazil in Jan, the FA were left with an odd number of clubs in the 3rd round. Their solution was a 'lucky losers' draw among clubs knocked out in round 2. Darlington, beaten at Gillingham, won it to re-enter the competition, then lost 2-1 away to Aston Villa.

HAT-TRICKS IN FINAL

There have been three in the history of the competition: **Billy Townley** (Blackburn, 1890), **Jimmy Logan** (Notts Co, 1894) and **Stan Mortensen** (Blackpool, 1953).

MOST APPEARANCES

88 by **Ian Callaghan** (79 for Liverpool, 7 for Swansea City, 2 for Crewe); **87** by **John Barnes** (31 for Watford, 51 for Liverpool, 5 for Newcastle); **86** by **Stanley Matthews** (37 for Stoke, 49 for Blackpool); **84** by **Bobby Charlton** (80 for Manchester Utd, 4 for Preston); **84** by **Pat Jennings** (3 for Watford, 43 for Tottenham, 38 for Arsenal); **84** by **Peter Shilton** for seven clubs (30 for Leicester, 5 for Stoke, 18 for Nottm Forest, 17 for Southampton, 10 for Derby, 1 for Plymouth Argyle, 1 for Leyton Orient); **82** by **David Seaman** (5 for Peterborough, 5 for Birmingham, 17 for QPR, 54 for Arsenal, 1 for Manchester City).

THREE-CLUB FINALISTS

Five players have appeared in the FA Cup Final for three clubs: **Harold Halse** for Manchester Utd (1909), Aston Villa (1913) and Chelsea (1915); **Ernie Taylor** for Newcastle (1951), Blackpool (1953) and Manchester Utd (1958); **John Barnes** for Watford (1984), Liverpool (1988, 1989, 1996) and Newcastle (1998); **Dennis Wise** for Wimbledon (1988), Chelsea (1994, 1997, 2000), Millwall (2004); **David James** for Liverpool (1996), Aston Villa (2000) and Portsmouth (2008, 2010).

CUP MAN WITH TWO CLUBS IN SAME SEASON

Stan Crowther, who played for Aston Villa against Manchester Utd in the 1957 FA Cup Final, appeared for both Villa and United in the 1957–58 competition. United signed him directly after the Munich air crash and, in the circumstances, he was given dispensation to play for them in the Cup, including the Final.

CAPTAIN'S CUP DOUBLE

Martin Buchan is the only player to have captained Scottish and English FA Cup-winning teams – Aberdeen in 1970 and Manchester Utd in 1977.

MEDALS BEFORE AND AFTER

Two players appeared in FA Cup Final teams before and after the Second World War: **Raich Carter** was twice a winner (Sunderland 1937, Derby 1946) and **Willie Fagan** twice on the losing side (Preston 1937, Liverpool 1950).

DELANEY'S COLLECTION

Scotland winger **Jimmy Delaney** uniquely earned Scottish, English, Northern Ireland and Republic of Ireland Cup medals. He was a winner with Celtic (1937), Manchester Utd (1948) and Derry City (1954) and a runner-up with Cork City (1956).

STARS WHO MISSED OUT

Internationals who never won an FA Cup winner's medal include: Tommy Lawton, Tom Finney, Johnny Haynes, Gordon Banks, George Best, Terry Butcher, Peter Shilton, Martin Peters, Nobby Stiles, Alan Ball, Malcolm Macdonald, Alan Shearer, Matthew Le Tissier, Stuart Pearce, Des Walker, Phil Neal, Ledley King.

CUP WINNERS AT NO COST

Not one member of **Bolton**'s 1958 FA Cup-winning team cost the club a transfer fee. Each joined the club for a £10 signing-on fee.

11-NATIONS LINE-UP

Liverpool fielded a team of 11 different nationalities in the FA Cup 3rd round at Yeovil on Jan 4, 2004.

HIGH-SCORING SEMI-FINALS

The **record team score** in FA Cup semi-finals is **6**: 1891–92 WBA 6, Nottm Forest 2; 1907–08 Newcastle 6, Fulham 0; 1933–34 Manchester City 6, Aston Villa 1.

Most goals in semi-finals (aggregate): 17 in 1892 (4 matches) and 1899 (5 matches). In modern times: 15 in 1958 (3 matches, including Manchester Utd 5, Fulham 3 – highest-scoring semi-final since last war); 16 in 1989–90 (Crystal Palace 4, Liverpool 3; Manchester Utd v Oldham 3-3, 2-1. All **16 goals** in those three matches were scored by **different players**.

Stoke's win against Bolton at Wembley in 2011 was the first 5-0 semi-final result since Wolves beat Grimsby at Old Trafford in 1939. In 2014, Hull defeated Sheffield Utd 5-3.

Last hat-trick in an FA Cup semi-final was scored by **Alex Dawson** for Manchester Utd in 5-3 replay win against Fulham at Highbury in 1958.

SEMI-FINAL VENUES

Villa Park has staged more such matches (55 including replays) than any other ground. Next is Hillsborough (33).

ONE IN A HUNDRED

The 2008 semi-finals included only one top-division club, Portsmouth, for the first time in 100 years – since Newcastle in 1908.

FOUR SPECIAL AWAYS

For the only time in FA Cup history, **all four quarter-finals** in season 1986–87 were won by the away team.

DRAWS RECORD

In season 1985–86, **seven** of the eight 5th round ties went to replays – a record for that stage of the competition.

SHOCK FOR TOP CLUBS

The fourth round on Jan 24, 2015 produced an astonishing set of home defeats for leading clubs. The top three in the Premier League, Chelsea, Manchester City and Southampton were all knocked out and sixth-place Tottenham also lost at home. Odds against this happening were put at 3825-1.

LUCK OF THE DRAW

In the FA Cup on Jan 11, 1947, eight of **London**'s ten Football League clubs involved in the 3rd round were drawn at home (including Chelsea v Arsenal). Only Crystal Palace played outside the capital (at Newcastle).

In the 3rd round in Jan 1992, Charlton were the only London club drawn at home (against Barnet), but the venue of the Farnborough v West Ham tie was reversed on police instruction. So Upton Park staged Cup ties on successive days, with West Ham at home on the Saturday and Charlton (who shared the ground) on Sunday.

Arsenal were drawn away in every round on the way to reaching the Finals of 1971 and 1972. **Manchester Utd** won the Cup in 1990 without playing once at home.

The 1999 finalists, **Manchester Utd** and **Newcastle,** were both drawn at home every time in Rounds 3–6.

On their way to the semi-finals of both domestic Cup competitions in season 2002–03, **Sheffield Utd** were drawn at home ten times out of ten and won all ten matches – six in the League's Worthington Cup and four in the FA Cup.

On their way to winning the Cup in 2014, **Arsenal** did not play once outside London. Home draws in rounds 3, 4, 5 and 6 were followed by the semi-final at Wembley.

ALL TOP-DIVISION VICTIMS

The only instance of an FA Cup-winning club meeting top-division opponents in every round was provided by Manchester Utd in 1947–48. They beat Aston Villa, Liverpool, Charlton, Preston, then Derby in the semi-final and Blackpool in the Final.

In contrast, these clubs have reached the Final without playing top-division opponents on the way: West Ham (1923), Bolton (1926), Blackpool (1948), Bolton (1953), Millwall (2004).

WON CUP WITHOUT CONCEDING GOAL

1873 **The Wanderers** (1 match; as holders, exempt until Final); 1889 **Preston** (5 matches); 1903 **Bury** (5 matches). In 1966 **Everton** reached Final without conceding a goal (7 matches), then beat Sheffield Wed 3-2 at Wembley.

HOME ADVANTAGE

For the first time in FA Cup history, all eight ties in the 1992–93 5th round were won (no replays) by the **clubs drawn at home.** Only other instance of eight home wins at the last 16 stage was in 1889–90, in what was then the 2nd round.

NORTH-EAST WIPE-OUT

For the first time in 54 years, since the 4th round in Jan, 1957, the North-East's 'big three' were knocked out on the same date, Jan 8, 2011 (3rd round). All lost to lower-division opponents – Newcastle 3-1 at Stevenage, **Sunderland** 2-1 at home to Notts County and **Middlesbrough** 2-1 at Burton.

FEWEST TOP-DIVISION CLUBS IN LAST 16 (5th ROUND)

5 in 1958; **6** in 1927, 1970, 1982; **7** in 1994, 2003; **8** in 2002, 2004.

SIXTH-ROUND ELITE

For the first time in FA Cup 6th round history, dating from 1926 when the format of the competition changed, all **eight quarter-finalists** in 1995–96 were from the top division.

SEMI-FINAL – DOUBLE DERBIES

There have been three instances of both FA Cup semi-finals in the same year being local derbies: **1950** Liverpool beat Everton 2-0 (Maine Road), Arsenal beat Chelsea 1-0 after 2-2 draw (both at Tottenham); **1993** Arsenal beat Tottenham 1-0 (Wembley), Sheffield Wed beat Sheffield Utd 2-1 (Wembley); **2012** Liverpool beat Everton 2-1 (Wembley), Chelsea beat Tottenham 5-1 (Wembley).

TOP CLUB DISTINCTION

Since the Football League began in 1888, there has never been an FA Cup Final in which **neither club** represented the top division.

CLUBS THROWN OUT

Bury expelled (Dec 2006) for fielding an ineligible player in 3-1 2nd rd replay win at Chester. **Droylsden** expelled for fielding a suspended player in 2-1 2nd rd replay win at home to Chesterfield (Dec 2008).

SPURS OUT – AND IN

Tottenham were banned, pre-season, from the 1994–95 competition because of financial irregularities, but were re-admitted on appeal and reached the semi-finals.

FATHER & SON FA CUP WINNERS

Peter Boyle (Sheffield Utd 1899, 1902) and **Tommy Boyle** (Sheffield Utd 1925); **Harry Johnson Snr** (Sheffield Utd 1899, 1902) and **Harry Johnson Jnr** (Sheffield Utd 1925); **Jimmy Dunn Snr** (Everton 1933) and **Jimmy Dunn Jnr** (Wolves 1949); **Alec Herd** (Manchester City 1934) and **David Herd** (Manchester Utd 1963); **Frank Lampard Snr** (West Ham 1975, 1980) and **Frank Lampard Jnr** (Chelsea 2007, 2009, 2010, 2012).

BROTHERS IN FA CUP FINAL TEAMS (modern times)

1950 **Denis and Leslie Compton** (Arsenal); 1952 **George and Ted Robledo** (Newcastle); 1967 **Ron and Allan Harris** (Chelsea); 1977 **Jimmy and Brian Greenhoff** (Manchester Utd); 1996 and 1999 **Gary and Phil Neville** (Manchester Utd).

FA CUP SPONSORS

Littlewoods Pools became the first sponsors of the FA Cup in season 1994–95 in a £14m, 4-year deal. French insurance giants **AXA** took over (season 1998–99) in a sponsorship worth £25m over 4 years. German energy company **E.ON** agreed a 4-year deal worth £32m from season 2006–07 and extended it for a year to 2011. American beer company **Budweiser** began a three-year sponsorship worth £24m in season 2011–12. The **Emirates** airline became the first title sponsor (2015-18) in a reported £30m deal with the FA.

FIRST GOALKEEPER-SUBSTITUTE IN FINAL

Paul Jones (Southampton), who replaced injured Antti Niemi against Arsenal in 2003.

LEAGUE CUP RECORDS
(See also Goalscoring section)

Most winning managers: 4 Brian Clough (Nottm Forest), Sir Alex Ferguson (Manchester Utd), Jose Mourinho (3 Chelsea, 1 Manchester Utd).

Highest scores: West Ham 10-0 v Bury (2nd round, 2nd leg 1983–84; agg 12-1); Liverpool 10-0 v Fulham (2nd round, 1st leg 1986–87; agg 13-2).

Most League Cup goals (career): 49 Geoff Hurst (43 West Ham, 6 Stoke, 1960–75); 49 Ian Rush (48 Liverpool, 1 Newcastle, 1981–98).

Highest scorer (season): 12 Clive Allen (Tottenham 1986–87 in 9 apps).

Most goals in match: 6 Frank Bunn (Oldham v Scarborough, 3rd round, 1989–90).

Most winners' medals: 5 Ian Rush (Liverpool).

Most appearances in Final: 6 Kenny Dalglish (Liverpool 1978–87), Ian Rush (Liverpool 1981–95). Emile Heskey (Leicester 1997, 1999, 2000), Liverpool (2001, 2003), Aston Villa (2010)

Biggest Final win: Swansea City 5 Bradford City 0 (2013).

League Cup sponsors: Milk Cup 1981–86, Littlewoods Cup 1987–90, Rumbelows Cup 1991–92, Coca-Cola Cup 1993–98, Worthington Cup 1999–2003, Carling Cup 2003–12; Capital One Cup from season 2012–16.

Up for the cup, then down: In 2011, Birmingham became only the second club to win a major trophy (the Carling Cup) and be relegated from the top division. It previously happened to Norwich in 1985 when they went down from the old First Division after winning the Milk Cup.

Liverpool's League Cup records: Winners a record 8 times. **Ian Rush** only player to win 5 times. Rush also first to play in 8 winning teams in Cup Finals **at Wembley**, all with Liverpool (FA Cup 1986–89–92; League Cup 1981–82–83–84–95).

Britain's first under-cover Cup Final: Worthington Cup Final between Blackburn and Tottenham at Cardiff's Millennium Stadium on Sunday, Feb 24, 2002. With rain forecast, the retractable roof was closed on the morning of the match.

Record penalty shoot-out: Liverpool beat Middlesbrough 14-13 (3rd round, Sep 23, 2014) after 2-2. Derby beat Carlisle 14-13 (2nd round, Aug 23, 2016) after 1-1.

DISCIPLINE

SENDINGS-OFF

Season 2003–04 set an **all-time record** of 504 players sent off in English domestic football competitions. There were 58 in the Premiership, 390 Nationwide League, 28 FA Cup (excluding non-League dismissals), 22 League Cup, 2 in Nationwide play-offs, 4 in LDV Vans Trophy.

Most sendings-off in Premier League programme (10 matches): 9 (8 Sat, 1 Sun, Oct 31–Nov 1, 2009).

The 58 Premiership red cards was 13 fewer than the record English **top-division** total of 71 in 2002–03. **Bolton** were the only club in the English divisions without a player sent off in any first-team competition that season.

Worst day for dismissals in English football was Boxing Day, 2007, with **20 red cards** (5 Premier League and 15 Coca-Cola League). Three players, Chelsea's Ashley Cole and Ricardo Carvalho and Aston Villa's Zat Knight were sent off in a 4-4 draw at Stamford Bridge. Luton had three men dismissed in their game at Bristol Rov, but still managed a 1-1 draw.

Previous worst day was Dec 13, 2003, with **19 red cards** (2 Premiership and the 17 Nationwide League).

In the entire first season of post-war League football (1946–47) only 12 players were sent off, followed by 14 in 1949–50, and the total League dismissals for the first nine seasons after the War was 104.

The worst pre-War total was 28 in each of seasons 1921–22 and 1922–23.

ENGLAND SENDINGS-OFF

In a total of 15 England dismissals, David Beckham and Wayne Rooney have been red-carded twice. Beckham and Steven Gerrard are the only England captains to be sent off and Robert Green the only goalkeeper.

Jun 5, 1968	**Alan Mullery**	v Yugoslavia (Florence, Euro Champ)
Jun 6, 1973	**Alan Ball**	v Poland (Chorzow, World Cup qual)
Jun 12, 1977	**Trevor Cherry**	v Argentina (Buenos Aires, friendly)
Jun 6, 1986	**Ray Wilkins**	v Morocco (Monterrey, World Cup Finals)
Jun 30, 1998	**David Beckham**	v Argentina (St Etienne, World Cup Finals)
Sep 5, 1998	**Paul Ince**	v Sweden (Stockholm, Euro Champ qual)
Jun 5, 1999	**Paul Scholes**	v Sweden (Wembley, Euro Champ qual)
Sep 8, 1999	**David Batty**	v Poland (Warsaw, Euro Champ qual)
Oct 16, 2002	**Alan Smith**	v Macedonia (Southampton, Euro Champ qual)
Oct 8, 2005	**David Beckham**	v Austria (Old Trafford, World Cup qual)
Jul 1, 2006	**Wayne Rooney**	v Portugal (Gelsenkirchen, World Cup Finals)
Oct 10, 2009	**Robert Green**	v Ukraine (Dnipropetrovsk, World Cup qual)
Oct 7, 2011	**Wayne Rooney**	v Montenegro (Podgorica, Euro Champ qual)
Sep 11, 2012	**Steven Gerrard**	v Ukraine (Wembley, World Cup qual)
Jun 4, 2014	**Raheem Sterling**	v Ecuador (Miami, friendly)

Other countries: Most recent sendings-off of players representing other Home Countries:
N Ireland – Chris Baird (European Champ qual v Hungary, Belfast, Sep 7, 2015).
Scotland – Charlie Mulgrew (European Champ qual v Germany, Dortmund, Sep 7, 2014).
Wales – Neil Taylor (World Cup qual v Republic of Ireland, Dublin, Mar 24, 2017).
Rep of Ireland – Shane Duffy (European Champ v France, Lyon, June 26, 2016).
England dismissals at other levels:
U-23: Stan Anderson (v Bulgaria, Sofia, May 19, 1957); **Alan Ball** (v Austria, Vienna, Jun 2, 1965); **Kevin Keegan** (v E Germany, Magdeburg, Jun 1, 1972); **Steve Perryman** (v Portugal, Lisbon, Nov 19, 1974).

U-21: Sammy Lee (v Hungary, Keszthely, Jun 5, 1981); **Mark Hateley** (v Scotland, Hampden Park, Apr 19, 1982); **Paul Elliott** (v Denmark, Maine Road, Manchester, Mar 26, 1986); **Tony Cottee** (v W Germany, Ludenscheid, Sep 8, 1987); **Julian Dicks** (v Mexico, Toulon, France, Jun 12, 1988); **Jason Dodd** (v Mexico, Toulon, May 29, 1991; 3 Mexico players also sent off in that match); **Matthew Jackson** (v France, Toulon, May 28, 1992); **Robbie Fowler** (v Austria, Kafkenberg, Oct 11, 1994); **Alan Thompson** (v Portugal, Oporto, Sep 2, 1995); **Terry Cooke** (v Portugal, Toulon, May 30, 1996); **Ben Thatcher** (v Italy, Rieti, Oct 10, 1997); **John Curtis** (v Greece, Heraklion, Nov 13, 1997); **Jody Morris** (v Luxembourg, Grevenmacher, Oct 13, 1998); **Stephen Wright** (v Germany, Derby, Oct 6, 2000); **Alan Smith** (v Finland, Valkeakoski, Oct 10, 2000); **Luke Young** and **John Terry** (v Greece, Athens, Jun 5, 2001); **Shola Ameobi** (v Portugal, Rio Maior, Mar 28, 2003); **Jermaine Pennant** (v Croatia, Upton Park, Aug 19, 2003); **Glen Johnson** (v Turkey, Istanbul, Oct 10, 2003); **Nigel Reo-Coker** (v Azerbaijan, Baku, Oct 12, 2004); **Glen Johnson** (v Spain, Henares, Nov 16, 2004); **Steven Taylor** (v Germany, Leverkusen, Oct 10, 2006); **Tom Huddlestone** (v Serbia & Montenegro, Nijmegen, Jun 17, 2007); **Tom Huddlestone** (v Wales, Villa Park, Oct 14, 2008); **Michael Mancienne** (v Finland, Halmstad, Jun 15, 2009); **Fraizer Campbell** (v Sweden, Gothenburg, Jun 26, 2009); **Ben Mee** (v Italy, Empoli, Feb 8, 2011); **Danny Rose** (v Serbia, Krusevac, Oct 16, 2012); **Andre Wisdom** (v Finland, Tampere, Sep 9, 2013); **Jack Stephens** (v Bosnia Herz, Sarajevo, Nov 12, 2015); **Jordon Ibe** (vSwitzerland, Thun, Mar 26, 2016).
England 'B' (1): **Neil Webb** (v Algeria, Algiers, Dec 11, 1990).

MOST DISMISSALS IN INTERNATIONAL MATCHES

19 (10 Chile, 9 Uruguay), Jun 25, 1975; **6** (2 Mexico, 4 Argentina), 1956; **6** (5 Ecuador, 1 Uruguay), Jan 4, 1977 (4 Ecuadorians sent off in 78th min, match abandoned, 1-1); **5** (Holland 3, Brazil 2), Jun 6, 1999 in Goianio, Brazil.

INTERNATIONAL STOPPED THROUGH DEPLETED SIDE

Portugal v Angola (5-1), friendly international in Lisbon on Nov 14, 2001, abandoned (68 mins) because Angola were down to 6 players (4 sent off, 1 carried off, no substitutes left).

MOST 'CARDS' IN WORLD CUP FINALS MATCH

20 in Portugal v Holland quarter-final, Nuremberg, Jun 25, 2006 (9 yellow, 2 red, Portugal; 7 yellow, 2 red, Holland).

FIVE OFF IN ONE MATCH

For the first time since League football began in 1888, five players were sent off in one match (two Chesterfield, three Plymouth) in Div 2 at Saltergate on **Feb 22, 1997**. Four were dismissed (two from each side) in a goalmouth brawl in the last minute. Five were sent off on Dec 2, 1997 (4 Bristol Rov, 1 Wigan) in Div 2 match at Wigan, four in the 45th minute. The third instance occurred at Exeter on **Nov 23, 2002** in Div 3 (three Exeter, two Cambridge United) all in the last minute. On **Mar 27, 2012** (Lge 2) three Bradford players and two from Crawley were shown red cards in the dressing rooms after a brawl at the final whistle at Valley Parade.

Matches with **four** Football League club players being sent off in one match:
Jan 8, 1955: Crewe v Bradford City (Div 3 North), two players from each side.
Dec 13, 1986: Sheffield Utd (1 player) v Portsmouth (3) in Div 2.
Aug 18, 1987: Port Vale v Northampton (Littlewoods Cup 1st Round, 1st Leg), two players from each side.
Dec 12, 1987: Brentford v Mansfield (Div 3), two players from each side.
Sep 6, 1992: First instance in British first-class football of four players from one side being sent off in one match. Hereford's seven survivors, away to Northampton (Div 3), held out for a 1-1 draw.
Mar 1, 1977: Norwich v Huddersfield (Div 1), two from each side.
Oct 4, 1977: Shrewsbury (1 player), Rotherham (3) in Div 3.
Aug 22, 1998: Gillingham v Bristol Rov (Div 2), two from each side, all after injury-time brawl.

Mar 16, 2001: Bristol City v Millwall (Div 2), two from each side.
Aug 17, 2002: Lincoln (1 player), Carlisle (3) in Div 3.
Aug 26, 2002: Wycombe v QPR (Div 2), two from each side.
Nov 1, 2005: Burnley (1 player) v Millwall (3) in Championship.
Nov 24, 2007: Swindon v Bristol Rov (Lge 1), two from each side.
Mar 4, 2007: Hull v Burnley (Champ) two from each side.

Four Stranraer players were sent off away to Airdrie (Scottish Div 1) on Dec 3, 1994, and that Scottish record was equalled when four Hearts men were ordered off away to Rangers (Prem Div) on Sep 14, 1996. Albion had four players sent off (3 in last 8 mins) away to Queen's Park (Scottish Div 3) on Aug 23, 1997.

In the **Island Games** in Guernsey (Jul 2003), five players (all from Rhodes) were sent off against Guernsey for violent conduct and the match was abandoned by referee Wendy Toms.

Most dismissals one team, one match: Five players of America Tres Rios in first ten minutes after disputed goal by opponents Itaperuna in Brazilian cup match in Rio de Janeiro on Nov 23, 1991. Tie then abandoned and awarded to Itaperuna.

Eight dismissals in one match: Four on each side in South American Super Cup quarter-final (Gremio, Brazil v Penarol, Uruguay) in Oct 1993.

Five dismissals in one season – Dave Caldwell (2 with Chesterfield, 3 with Torquay) in 1987–88.

First instance of four dismissals in Scottish match: three Rangers players (all English – Terry Hurlock, Mark Walters, Mark Hateley) and Celtic's Peter Grant in Scottish Cup quarter-final at Parkhead on Mar 17, 1991 (Celtic won 2-0).

Four players (3 Hamilton, 1 Airdrie) were sent off in Scottish Div 1 match on Oct 30, 1993.
Four players (3 Ayr, 1 Stranraer) were sent off in Scottish Div 1 match on Aug 27, 1994.

In Scottish Cup first round replays on Dec 16, 1996, there were two instances of three players of one side sent off: Albion Rov (away to Forfar) and Huntly (away to Clyde).

FASTEST SENDINGS-OFF

World record – 10 sec: Giuseppe Lorenzo (Bologna) for striking opponent in Italian League match v Parma, Dec 9, 1990. Goalkeeper **Preston Edwards** (Ebbsfleet) for bringing down opponent and conceding penalty in Blue Square Premier League South match v Farnborough, Feb 5, 2011.

World record (non-professional) – 3 sec: David Pratt (Chippenham) at Bashley (British Gas Southern Premier League, Dec 27, 2008).

Domestic – 13 sec: Kevin Pressman Sheffield Wed goalkeeper at Wolves, Div 1, Sunday, Aug 14, 2000); **15 sec: Simon Rea** (Peterborough at Cardiff, Div 2, Nov 2, 2002). **19 sec: Mark Smith** (Crewe goalkeeper at Darlington, Div 3, Mar 12, 1994). **Premier League – 72 sec: Tim Flowers** (Blackburn goalkeeper v Leeds Utd, Feb 1, 1995).

In World Cup – 55 sec: Jose Batista (Uruguay v Scotland at Neza, Mexico, Jun 13, 1986).

In European competition – 90 sec: Sergei Dirkach (Dynamo Moscow v Ghent UEFA Cup 3rd round, 2nd leg, Dec 11, 1991).

Fastest FA Cup dismissal – 52 sec: Ian Culverhouse (Swindon defender, deliberate hand-ball on goal-line, away to Everton, 3rd Round, Sunday Jan 5, 1997).

Fastest League Cup dismissal – 33 sec: Jason Crowe (Arsenal substitute v Birmingham, 3rd Round, Oct 14, 1997). Also fastest sending off on debut.

Fastest Sending-off of substitute – 0 sec: Walter Boyd (Swansea City) for striking opponent before ball in play after he went on (83 mins) at home to Darlington, Div 3, Nov 23, 1999. **15 secs: Keith Gillespie** (Sheffield Utd) for striking an opponent at Reading (Premiership), Jan 20, 2007. **90 sec: Andreas Johansson** (Wigan), without kicking a ball, for shirt-pulling (penalty) away to Arsenal (Premiership), May 7, 2006.

MOST SENDINGS-OFF IN CAREER

21	**Willie Johnston** , 1964–82 (Rangers 7, WBA 6, Vancouver Whitecaps 4, Hearts 3, Scotland 1)
21	**Roy McDonough**, 1980–95 (13 in Football League – Birmingham, Walsall, Chelsea, Colchester, Southend, Exeter, Cambridge Utd plus 8 non-league)
13	**Steve Walsh** (Wigan, Leicester, Norwich, Coventry)
13	**Martin Keown** (Arsenal, Aston Villa, Everton)

13	**Alan Smith** (Leeds, Manchester Utd, Newcastle, England U-21, England)
12	**Dennis Wise** (Wimbledon, Chelsea, Leicester, Millwall)
12	**Vinnie Jones** (Wimbledon, Leeds, Sheffield Utd, Chelsea, QPR)
12	**Mark Dennis** (Birmingham, Southampton, QPR)
12	**Roy Keane** (Manchester Utd, Rep of Ireland)
10	**Patrick Vieira** (Arsenal)
10	**Paul Scholes** (Manchester Utd, England)

Most Premier League sendings-off: Patrick Vieira 9, Duncan Ferguson 8, Richard Dunne 8, Vinnie Jones 7, Roy Keane 7, Alan Smith 7. Lee Cattermole 7.

● **Carlton Palmer** holds the unique record of having been sent off with each of his five Premiership clubs: Sheffield Wed, Leeds, Southampton, Nottm Forest and Coventry.

FA CUP FINAL SENDINGS-OFF

Kevin Moran (Manchester Utd) v Everton, Wembley, 1985; **Jose Antonio Reyes** (Arsenal) v Manchester Utd, Cardiff, 2005; **Pablo Zabaleta** (Manchester City) v Wigan, Wembley 2013; **Chris Smalling** (Manchester Utd) v Crystal Palace , Wembley, 2016; **Victor Moses** (Chelsea) v Arsenal, Wembley, 2017

WEMBLEY SENDINGS-OFF

Aug 1948	**Branko Stankovic** (Yugoslavia) v Sweden, Olympic Games
Jul 1966	**Antonio Rattin** (Argentina captain) v England, World cup quarter-final
Aug 1974	**Billy Bremner** (Leeds) and **Kevin Keegan** (Liverpool), Charity Shield
Mar 1977	**Gilbert Dresch** (Luxembourg) v England, World Cup
May 1985	**Kevin Moran** (Manchester Utd) v Everton, FA Cup Final
Apr 1993	**Lee Dixon** (Arsenal) v Tottenham, FA Cup semi-final
May 1993	**Peter Swan** (Port Vale) v WBA, Div 2 Play-off Final
Mar 1994	**Andrei Kanchelskis** (Manchester Utd) v Aston Villa, League Cup Final
May 1994	**Mike Wallace, Chris Beaumont** (Stockport) v Burnley, Div 2 Play-off Final
Jun 1995	**Tetsuji Hashiratani** (Japan) v England, Umbro Cup
May 1997	**Brian Statham** (Brentford) v Crewe, Div 2 Play-off Final
Apr 1998	**Capucho** (Portugal) v England, friendly
Nov 1998	**Ray Parlour** (Arsenal) and **Tony Vareilles** (Lens), Champions League
Mar 1999	**Justin Edinburgh** (Tottenham) v Leicester, League Cup Final
Jun 1999	**Paul Scholes** (England) v Sweden, European Championship qual
Feb 2000	**Clint Hill** (Tranmere) v Leicester, League Cup Final
Apr 2000	**Mark Delaney** (Aston Villa) v Bolton, FA Cup semi-final
May 2000	**Kevin Sharp** (Wigan) v Gillingham, Div 2 Play-off Final
Aug 2000	**Roy Keane** (Manchester Utd captain) v Chelsea, Charity Shield
May 2007	**Marc Tierney** (Shrewsbury) v Bristol Rov, Lge 2 Play-off Final
May 2007	**Matt Gill** (Exeter) v Morecambe, Conf Play-off Final
May 2009	**Jamie Ward** (Sheffield Utd) and **Lee Hendrie** (Sheffield Utd) v Burnley, Champ Play-off Final (Hendrie after final whistle)
May 2009	**Phil Bolland** (Cambridge Utd) v Torquay, Blue Square Prem Lge Play-off Final
May 2010	**Robin Hulbert** (Barrow) and **David Bridges** (Stevenage), FA Trophy Final
Apr 2011	**Paul Scholes** (Manchester Utd) v Manchester City, FA Cup semi-final
Apr 2011	**Toumani Diagouraga** (Brentford) v Carlisle, Johnstone's Paint Trophy Final
Sep 2012	**Steven Gerrard** (England) v Ukraine, World Cup qual
Feb 2013	**Matt Duke** (Bradford) v Swansea, League Cup Final
May 2013	**Pablo Zabaleta** (Manchester City) v Wigan, FA Cup Final
Mar 2014	**Joe Newell** (Peterborough) v Chesterfield, Johnstone's Paint Trophy Final
May 2014	**Gary O'Neil** (QPR) v Derby, Champ Play-off Final
May 2016	**Chris Smalling** (Manchester Utd) v Crystal Palace, FA Cup Final
May 2017	**Victor Moses** (Chelsea) v Arsenal, FA Cup Final

WEMBLEY'S SUSPENDED CAPTAINS

Suspension prevented four **club captains** playing at Wembley in modern finals, in successive years. Three were in FA Cup Finals – **Glenn Roeder** (QPR, 1982), **Steve Foster** (Brighton, 1983), **Wilf Rostron** (Watford, 1984). Sunderland's **Shaun Elliott** was banned from the 1985 Milk Cup Final. Roeder was banned from QPR's 1982 Cup Final replay against Tottenham, and Foster was ruled out of the first match in Brighton's 1983 Final against Manchester Utd.

RED CARD FOR KICKING BALL-BOY

Chelsea's **Eden Hazard** was sent off (80 mins) in the League Cup semi-final, second leg at Swansea on Jan 23, 2013 for kicking a 17-year-old ball-boy who refused to hand over the ball that had gone out of play. The FA suspended Hazard for three matches.

BOOKINGS RECORDS

Most players of one Football League club booked in one match is **TEN** – members of the Mansfield team away to Crystal Palace in FA Cup third round, Jan 1963. Most yellow cards for one team in Premier League match – **9** for Tottenham away to Chelsea, May 2, 2016.

Fastest bookings – 3 seconds after kick-off, **Vinnie Jones** (Chelsea, home to Sheffield Utd, FA Cup fifth round, Feb 15, 1992); 5 seconds after kick-off: **Vinnie Jones** (Sheffield Utd, away to Manchester City, Div 1, Jan 19, 1991). He was sent-off (54 mins) for second bookable offence.

FIGHTING TEAM-MATES

Charlton's **Mike Flanagan** and **Derek Hales** were sent off for fighting each other five minutes from end of FA Cup 3rd round tie at home to Southern League Maidstone on Jan 9, 1979.

Bradford City's **Andy Myers** and **Stuart McCall** had a fight during the 1-6 Premiership defeat at Leeds on Sunday, May 13, 2001.

On Sep 28, 1994 the Scottish FA suspended Hearts players **Graeme Hogg** and **Craig Levein** for ten matches for fighting each other in a pre-season 'friendly' v Raith.

Blackburn's England players **Graeme Le Saux** and **David Batty** clashed away to Spartak Moscow (Champions League) on Nov 22, 1995. Neither was sent off.

Newcastle United's England Internationals **Lee Bowyer** and **Kieron Dyer** were sent off for fighting each other at home to Aston Villa (Premiership on Apr 2, 2005).

Arsenal's **Emmanuel Adebayor** and **Nicklas Bendtner** clashed during the 5-1 Carling Cup semi-final 2nd leg defeat at Tottenham on Jan 22, 2008. Neither was sent off; each fined by their club.

Stoke's **Richardo Fuller** was sent off for slapping his captain, Andy Griffin, at West Ham in the Premier League on Dec 28, 2008.

Preston's **Jermaine Beckford** and **Eoin Doyle** clashed in the Championship game against Sheffield Wednesday on Dec 3, 2016, and were both sent off.

St Johnstone's **Richard Foster** and **Danny Swanson** were dismissed for brawling in the Scottish Premiership match with Hamilton on Apr 1, 2017.

FOOTBALL'S FIRST BETTING SCANDAL

A Football League investigation into the First Division match which ended Manchester Utd 2, Liverpool 0 at Old Trafford on Good Friday, Apr 2, 1915 proved that the result had been 'squared' by certain players betting on the outcome. Four members of each team were suspended for life, but some of the bans were lifted when League football resumed in 1919 in recognition of the players' war service.

PLAYERS JAILED

Ten professional footballers found guilty of conspiracy to fraud by 'fixing' matches for betting purposes were given prison sentences at Nottingham Assizes on Jan 26, 1965.

Jimmy Gauld (Mansfield), described as the central figure, was given four years. Among the others sentenced, **Tony Kay** (Sheffield Wed, Everton & England), **Peter Swan** (Sheffield Wed & England) and **David 'Bronco' Layne** (Sheffield Wed) were suspended from football for life by the FA.

DRUGS BANS

Abel Xavier (Middlesbrough) was the first Premiership player found to have taken a performance-enchancing drug. He was banned by UEFA for 18 months in Nov 2005 after testing positive for an anabolic steroid. The ban was reduced to a year in Jul 2006 by the Court of Arbitration for Sport. **Paddy Kenny** (Sheffield Utd goalkeeper) was suspended by an FA commission for 9 months from July, 2009 for failing a drugs test the previous May. Kolo Toure (Manchester City) received a 6-month ban in May 2011 for a doping offence. It was backdated to Mar 2.

LONG SUSPENSIONS

The longest suspension (8 months) in modern times for a player in British football was imposed on two Manchester Utd players. First was **Eric Cantona** following his attack on a spectator as he left the pitch after being sent off at Crystal Palace (Prem League) on Jan 25, 1995. The club immediately suspended him to the end of the season and fined him 2 weeks' wages (est £20,000). Then, on a disrepute charge, the FA fined him £10,000 (Feb 1995) and extended the ban to Sep 30 (which FIFA confirmed as world-wide). A subsequent 2-weeks' jail sentence on Cantona for assault was altered, on appeal, to 120 hours' community service, which took the form of coaching schoolboys in the Manchester area.

On **Dec 19, 2003** an FA Commission, held at Bolton, suspended **Rio Ferdinand** from football for 8 months (plus £50,000 fine) for failing to take a random drug test at the club's training ground on Sep 23. The ban operated from Jan 12, 2004.

Aug 1974: Kevin Keegan (Liverpool) and Billy Bremner (Leeds) both suspended for 10 matches and fined £500 after being sent off in FA Charity Shield at Wembley.

Jan 1988: Mark Dennis (QPR) given 8-match ban after 11th sending-off of his career.

Oct 1988: Paul Davis (Arsenal) banned for 9 matches for breaking the jaw of Southampton's Glenn Cockerill.

Oct 1998: Paolo Di Canio (Sheff Wed) banned for 11 matches and fined £10,000 for pushing referee Paul Alcock after being sent off at home to Arsenal (Prem), Sep 26.

Mar 2005: David Prutton (Southampton) banned for 10 matches (plus 1 for red card) and fined £6,000 by FA for shoving referee Alan Wiley when sent off at home to Arsenal (Prem), Feb 26.

Aug 2006: Ben Thatcher (Manchester City) banned for 8 matches for elbowing Pedro Mendes (Portsmouth).

Sep 2008: Joey Barton (Newcastle) banned for 12 matches (6 suspended) and fined £25,000 by FA for training ground assault on former Manchester City team-mate Ousmane Dabo.

May 2012: Joey Barton (QPR) suspended for 12 matches and fined £75,000 for violent conduct when sent off against Manchester City on final day of Premier League season.

Mar 2014: Joss Labadie (Torquay) banned for 10 matches and fined £2,000 for biting Chesterfield's Ollie Banks (Lge 2) on Feb 15, 2014.

Seven-month ban: Frank Barson, 37-year-old Watford centre-half, sent off at home to Fulham (Div 3 South) on Sep 29, 1928, was suspended by the FA for the remainder of the season.

Twelve-month ban: Oldham full-back Billy Cook was given a 12-month suspension for refusing to leave the field when sent off at Middlesbrough (Div 1), on Apr 3, 1915. The referee abandoned the match with 35 minutes still to play, and the score (4-1 to Middlesbrough) was ordered to stand.

Long Scottish bans: Sep 1954: Willie Woodburn, Rangers and Scotland centre-half, suspended for rest of career after fifth sending-off in 6 years.

Billy McLafferty, Stenhousemuir striker, was banned (Apr 14) for 8 and a half months, to Jan 1, 1993, and fined £250 for failing to appear at a disciplinary hearing after being sent off against Arbroath on Feb 1.

Twelve-match ban: On May 12, 1994 Scottish FA suspended Rangers forward Duncan Ferguson for 12 matches for violent conduct v Raith on Apr 16. On Oct 11, 1995, Ferguson (then with Everton) sent to jail for 3 months for the assault (served 44 days); Feb 1, 1996 Scottish judge quashed 7 matches that remained of SFA ban on Ferguson.

On Sep 29, 2001 the SFA imposed a **17-match suspension** on Forfar's former Scottish international **Dave Bowman** for persistent foul and abusive language when sent off against

Stranraer on Sep 22. As his misconduct continued, he was shown **5 red cards** by the referee

On Apr 3, 2009, captain **Barry Ferguson** and goalkeeper **Allan McGregor** were banned for life from playing for Scotland for gestures towards photographers while on the bench for a World Cup qualifier against Iceland.

On Dec 20, 2011 Liverpool and Uruguay striker **Luis Suarez** was given an 8-match ban and fined £40,000 by the FA for making 'racially offensive comments' to Patrice Evra of Manchester Utd (Prem Lge, Oct 15).

On Apr 25, 2013 **Luis Suarez** was given a 10-match suspension by the FA for 'violent conduct' – biting Chelsea defender Branislav Ivanovic, Prem Lge, Apr 21. The Liverpool player was also fined £200,000 by Liverpool. His ban covered the last 4 games of that season and the first 6 of 2013–14. On Jun 26, 2014, Suarez, while still a Liverpool player, received the most severe punishment in World Cup history – a four-month ban from 'all football activities' and £66,000 fine from FIFA for biting Giorgio Chiellini during Uruguay's group game against Italy.

On Nov 4, 2016 Rochdale's **Calvin Andrew** was banned by the FA for 12 matches – reduced to 9 on appeal – for elbowing Peter Clarke (Oldham) in the face.

On Apr 16, 2017 **Joey Barton** was banned by the FA for 18 months and fined £30,000 for breaching betting rules. The Burnley player admitted placing 1,260 bets on matches.

TOP FINES

Clubs: £49,000,000 (World record) Manchester City: May 2014 for breaking UEFA Financial Fair Play rules **(£32,600,000** suspended subject to City meeting certain conditions over two seasons). **£7.6m** Bournemouth: May 2016, for breaking Financial Fair Play rules; **£5,500,000** West Ham: Apr 2007, for breaches of regulations involving 'dishonesty and deceit' over Argentine signings Carlos Tevez and Javier Mascherano; **£1,500,000** (increased from original £600,000) Tottenham: Dec 1994, financial irregularities; **£875,000** QPR: May 2011 for breaching rules when signing Argentine Alejandro Faurlin; **£375,000** (reduced to £290,000 on appeal) Chelsea: May 2016, players brawl v Tottenham; **£300,000** (reduced to £75,000 on appeal) Chelsea: Jun 2005, illegal approach to Arsenal's Ashley Cole; **£300,000** (plus 2-year ban on signing academy players, part suspended) Manchester City: May 2017, approaching young players; **£225,000** (reduced to £175,000 on appeal) Tottenham: May 2016, players brawl v Chelsea; **£200,000** Aston Villa: May 2015 for fans' pitch invasion after FA Cup quarter-final v WBA; **£175,000** Arsenal: Oct 2003, players' brawl v Manchester Utd; **£150,000** Leeds: Mar 2000, players' brawl v Tottenham; **£150,000** Tottenham: Mar 2000, players brawl v Leeds; **£145,000** Hull: Feb 2015, breaching Financial Fair Play rules; **£115,000** West Ham: Aug 2009, crowd misconduct at Carling Cup; v Millwall; **£105,000** Chelsea: Jan 1991, irregular payments; **£100,000** Boston Utd: Jul 2002, contract irregularities; **£100,000** Arsenal and Chelsea: Mar 2007 for mass brawl after Carling Cup Final; **£100,000** (including suspended fine) Blackburn: Aug 2007, poor disciplinary record; **£100,000** Sunderland: May 2014, breaching agents' regulations; **£100,000** Reading: Aug 2015, pitch invasion, FA Cup tie v Bradford (reduced to £40,000 on appeal); **£100,000** Chelsea: Dec 2016, players brawl v Manchester City; **£100,000** (plus 2-year ban on signing academy players, part suspended) Liverpool: Apr 2017, approaching young player; **£90,000** Brighton: Feb 2015, breaching rules on agents; **£71,000** West Ham: Feb 2015 for playing Diafra Sakho in FA Cup 4th round tie against Bristol City after declaring him unfit for Senegal's Africa Cup of Nations squad; **£65,000** Chelsea: Jan 2016, players brawl v WBA; **£62,000** Macclesfield: Dec 2005, funding of a stand at club's ground.

Players: £220,000 (plus 4-match ban) John Terry (Chelsea): Sep 2012, racially abusing Anton Ferdinand (QPR); **£150,000** Roy Keane (Manchester Utd): Oct 2002, disrepute offence over autobiography; **£100,000** (reduced to £75,000 on appeal) Ashley Cole (Arsenal): Jun 2005, illegal approach by Chelsea; **£100,000** (plus 5-match ban) Jonjo Shelvey (Newcastle): Dec 2016, racially abusing Romain Saiss (Wolves); **£90,000** Ashley Cole (Chelsea): Oct 2012, offensive Tweet against FA; **£80,000 (plus 5-match ban)** Nicolas Anelka (WBA): Feb 2014, celebrating goal at West Ham with racially-offensive 'quenelle' gesture; **£75,000 (plus 12-match ban)** Joey Barton (QPR): May 2012, violent conduct v Manchester City; **£60,000 (plus 3-match ban)** John Obi Mikel (Chelsea): Dec 2012, abusing referee Mark Clattenburg after Prem Lge v Manchester Utd); **£60,000** Dexter Blackstock (Nottm Forest): May 2014, breaching betting rules; **£50,000** Cameron Jerome (Stoke): Aug 2013, breaching FA betting rules; **£50,000** Benoit Assou-Ekotto (Tottenham): Sep 2014, publicly backing Nicolas Anelka's controversial 'quenelle' gesture; **£45,000** Patrick Vieira (Arsenal): Oct 1999, tunnel incidents v West Ham; **£45,000** Rio Ferdinand (Manchester Utd): Aug 2012, improper comments about Ashley Cole on Twitter; **£40,000** Lauren (Arsenal): Oct 2003, players' fracas v Manchester Utd; **£40,000 (plus 8-match ban)** Luis Suarez (Liverpool): Dec 2011, racially abusing Patrice Evra (Manchester Utd); **£40,000 (plus 3-match ban)** Dani Osvaldo (Southampton): Jan 2014, violent conduct, touchline Newcastle; **£40,000** Bacary Sagna (Manchester City): Jan 2017, questioning integrity of referee Lee Mason.

*In eight seasons with Arsenal (1996–2004) **Patrick Vieira** was fined a total of £122,000 by the FA for disciplinary offences.

Managers: £200,000 (reduced to £75,000 on appeal) Jose Mourinho (Chelsea): Jun 2005, illegal approach to Arsenal's Ashley Cole; **£60,000 (plus 7-match ban)** Alan Pardew (Newcastle): head-butting Hull player David Meyler (also fined £100,000 by club); **£58,000** Jose Mourinho (Manchester Utd): Nov 2016, misconduct involving referees Mark Clattenburg and Anthony Taylor; **£50,000** Jose Mourinho (Chelsea): Oct 2015, accusing referees of bias; **£40,000 (plus 1 match stadium ban)** Jose Mourinho (Chelsea): Nov 2015, abusive behaviour towards referee Jon Moss v West Ham, **£33,000 (plus 3-match Euro ban)** Arsene Wenger (Arsenal): Mar 2012, criticising referee after Champions League defeat by AC Milan; **£30,000** Sir Alex Ferguson (Manchester Utd): Mar 2011 criticising referee Martin Atkinson v Chelsea; **£30,000 (plus 6-match ban ((plus 6-match ban reduced to 4 on appeal);** Rui Faria (Chelsea assistant): May 2014, confronting match officials v Sunderland.

• Jonathan Barnett, Ashley Cole's agent was fined **£100,000** in Sep 2006 for his role in the 'tapping up' affair involving the player and Chelsea.

• Gillingham and club chairman Paul Scally each fined £75,000 in Jul 2015 for 'racial victimisation' towards player Mark McCammon. Club fine reduced to £50,000 on appeal.

• Leyton Orient owner Francesco Becchetti fined £40,000 and given six-match stadium ban in Jan 2016 for violent conduct towards assistant manager Andy Hessenthaler.

***£68,000** FA: May 2003, pitch invasions and racist chanting by fans during England v Turkey, Sunderland.

£50,000 FA: Dec 2014, for Wigan owner-chairman Dave Whelan, plus six-week ban from all football activity, for remarks about Jewish and Chinese people in newspaper interview.

***£250,000** FA: Dec 2016, for Leeds owner Massimo Cellino, plus 18-month ban, for breaking agent regulations (reduced to £100,000 and one year on appeal). Club fined £250,000 (reduced to £200,000 on appeal). Agent Derek Day fined £75,000 and banned for 18 months (11 months suspended).

MANAGERS

INTERNATIONAL RECORDS

(As at start of season 2017–18)

	P	W	D	L	F	A
Gareth Southgate (England – appointed Sep 2016)	8	3	3	2	13	8
Gordon Strachan (Scotland – appointed Jan 2013)	36	17	8	11	53	39
Chris Coleman (Wales – appointed Jan 2012)	43	16	12	15	48	52
Michael O'Neill (Northern Ireland – appointed Oct 2011)	47	16	14	17	49	52
Martin O'Neill (Republic of Ireland – appointed Nov 2013)	40	16	14	10	59	39

ENGLAND MANAGERS

		P	W	D	L
1946–62	**Walter Winterbottom**	139	78	33	28
1963–74	**Sir Alf Ramsey**	113	69	27	17
1974	**Joe Mercer**, caretaker	7	3	3	1
1974–77	**Don Revie**	29	14	8	7

1977–82	**Ron Greenwood**	55	33	12	10
1982–90	**Bobby Robson**	95	47	30	18
1990–93	**Graham Taylor**	38	18	13	7
1994–96	**Terry Venables**	23	11	11	1
1996–99	**Glenn Hoddle**	28	17	6	5
1999	**Howard Wilkinson**, caretaker	1	0	0	1
1999–2000	**Kevin Keegan**	18	7	7	4
2000	**Howard Wilkinson**, caretaker	1	0	1	0
2000	**Peter Taylor**, caretaker	1	0	0	1
2001–06	**Sven–Goran Eriksson**	67	40	17	10
2006–07	**Steve McClaren**	18	9	4	5
2007–12	**Fabio Capello**	42	28	8	6
2012	**Stuart Pearce**, caretaker	1	0	0	1
2012–16	**Roy Hodgson**	56	33	15	8
2016	**Sam Allardyce**	1	1	0	0

INTERNATIONAL MANAGER CHANGES

England: Walter Winterbottom 1946–62 (initially coach); **Alf Ramsey** (Feb 1963–May 1974); **Joe Mercer** (caretaker May 1974); **Don Revie** (Jul 1974–Jul 1977); **Ron Greenwood** (Aug 1977–Jul 1982); **Bobby Robson** (Jul 1982–Jul 1990); **Graham Taylor** (Jul 1990–Nov 1993); **Terry Venables**, coach (Jan 1994–Jun 1996); **Glenn Hoddle**, coach (Jun 1996–Feb 1999); **Howard Wilkinson** (caretaker Feb 1999); **Kevin Keegan** coach (Feb 1999–Oct 2000); **Howard Wilkinson** (caretaker Oct 2000); **Peter Taylor** (caretaker Nov 2000); **Sven–Goran Eriksson** (Jan 2001–Aug 2006); **Steve McClaren** (Aug 2006–Nov 2007); **Fabio Capello** (Dec 2007–Feb 2012); **Roy Hodgson** (May 2012– Jun 2016); **Sam Allardyce** (Jul-Sep 2016); **Gareth Southgate** (Sep-Nov 2016 interim, then permanent appointment).

Scotland (modern): Bobby Brown (Feb 1967–Jul 1971); **Tommy Docherty** (Sep 1971–Dec 1972); **Willie Ormond** (Jan 1973–May 1977); **Ally MacLeod** (May 1977–Sep 1978); **Jock Stein** (Oct 1978–Sep 1985); **Alex Ferguson** (caretaker Oct 1985–Jun 1986); **Andy Roxburgh**, coach (Jul 1986–Sep 1993); **Craig Brown** (Sep 1993–Oct 2001); **Berti Vogts** (Feb 2002–Oct 2004); **Walter Smith** (Dec 2004–Jan 2007); **Alex McLeish** (Jan 2007–Nov 2007); **George Burley** (Jan 2008–Nov 2009); **Craig Levein** (Dec 2009–Nov 2012); **Billy Stark** (caretaker Nov–Dec 2012); **Gordon Strachan** (since Jan 2013).

Northern Ireland (modern): Peter Doherty (1951–62); **Bertie Peacock** (1962–67); **Billy Bingham** (1967–Aug 1971); **Terry Neill** (Aug 1971–Mar 1975); **Dave Clements** (player-manager Mar 1975–1976); **Danny Blanchflower** (Jun 1976–Nov 1979); **Billy Bingham** (Feb 1980–Nov 1993); **Bryan Hamilton** (Feb 1994–Feb 1998); **Lawrie McMenemy** (Feb 1998–Nov 1999); **Sammy McIlroy** (Jan 2000–Oct 2003); **Lawrie Sanchez** (Jan 2004–May 2007); **Nigel Worthington** (May 2007–Oct 2011); **Michael O'Neill** (since Oct 2011).

Wales (modern): Mike Smith (Jul 1974–Dec 1979); **Mike England** (Mar 1980–Feb 1988); **David Williams** (caretaker Mar 1988); **Terry Yorath** (Apr 1988–Nov 1993); **John Toshack** (Mar 1994, one match); **Mike Smith** (Mar 1994–Jun 1995); **Bobby Gould** (Aug 1995–Jun 1999); **Mark Hughes** (Aug 1999 – Oct 2004); **John Toshack** (Nov 2004–Sep 2010); Brian Flynn (caretaker Sep–Dec 2010); **Gary Speed** (Dec 2010–Nov 2011); **Chris Coleman** (since Jan 2012).

Republic of Ireland (modern): Liam Tuohy (Sep 1971–Nov 1972); **Johnny Giles** (Oct 1973–Apr 1980, initially player–manager); **Eoin Hand** (Jun 1980–Nov 1985); **Jack Charlton** (Feb 1986–Dec 1995); **Mick McCarthy** (Feb 1996–Oct 2002); **Brian Kerr** (Jan 2003–Oct 2005); **Steve Staunton** (Jan 2006–Oct 2007); **Giovanni Trapattoni** (May 2008–Sep 2013); **Martin O'Neill** (since Nov 2013).

WORLD CUP-WINNING MANAGERS

1930 Uruguay (Alberto Suppici); 1934 and 1938 Italy (Vittorio Pozzo); 1950 Uruguay (Juan Lopez Fontana); 1954 West Germany (Sepp Herberger); 1958 Brazil (Vicente Feola); 1962 Brazil (Aymore Moreira); 1966 England (Sir Alf Ramsey); 1970 Brazil (Mario Zagallo); 1974 West Germany (Helmut Schon); 1978 Argentina (Cesar Luis Menotti); 1982 Italy

(Enzo Bearzot), 1986 Argentina (Carlos Bilardo); 1990 West Germany (Franz Beckenbauer); 1994 Brazil (Carlos Alberto Parreira); 1998 France (Aimee Etienne Jacquet); 2002 Brazil (Luiz Felipe Scolari); 2006 Italy (Marcello Lippi); 2010 Spain (Vicente Del Bosque); 2014 Germany (Joachim Low).
Each of the 20 winning teams had a manager/coach of that country's nationality.

YOUNGEST LEAGUE MANAGERS

Ivor Broadis, 23, appointed player-manager of Carlisle, Aug 1946; **Chris Brass**, 27, appointed player-manager of York, Jun 2003; **Terry Neill**, 28, appointed player manager of Hull, Jun 1970; **Graham Taylor**, 28, appointed manager of Lincoln, Dec 1972.

LONGEST-SERVING LEAGUE MANAGERS – ONE CLUB

Fred Everiss, secretary–manager of WBA for 46 years (1902–48); **George Ramsay**, secretary–manager of Aston Villa for 42 years (1884–1926); **John Addenbrooke**, Wolves, for 37 years (1885–1922). Since last war: **Sir Alex Ferguson** at Manchester Utd for 27 seasons (1986–2013); **Sir Matt Busby**, in charge of Manchester Utd for 25 seasons (1945–69, 1970–71); **Dario Gradi** at Crewe for 26 years (1983–2007, 2009–11); **Jimmy Seed** at Charlton for 23 years (1933–56); **Brian Clough** at Nottm Forest for 18 years (1975–93); **Arsene Wenger** at Arsenal for 21 years (1996-to-date).

LAST ENGLISH MANAGER TO WIN CHAMPIONSHIP

Howard Wilkinson (Leeds), season 1991–92.

1,000-TIME MANAGERS

Only six have managed in more than **1,000 English League** games: Alec Stock, Brian Clough, Jim Smith, Graham Taylor, Dario Gradi and Sir Alex Ferguson.
Sir Matt Busby, Dave Bassett, Lennie Lawrence, Alan Buckley, Denis Smith, Joe Royle, Ron Atkinson, Brian Horton, Neil Warnock, Harry Redknapp, Graham Turner, Steve Coppell, Roy Hodgson, Arsene Wenger, Len Ashurst, Lawrie McMenemy, Sir Bobby Robson, Danny Wilson and Tony Pulis have each managed more than **1,000 matches in all first class competitions**.

SHORT-TERM MANAGERS

Departed

3 days	Bill Lambton (Scunthorpe)	Apr 1959
6 days	Tommy McLean (Raith Rov)	Sep 1996
7 days	Tim Ward (Exeter)	Mar 1953
7 days	Kevin Cullis (Swansea City)	Feb 1996
8 days	Billy McKinlay (Watford)	Oct 2014
10 days	Dave Cowling (Doncaster)	Oct 1997
10 days	Peter Cormack (Cowdenbeath)	Dec 2000
13 days	Johnny Cochrane (Reading)	Apr 1939
13 days	Micky Adams (Swansea City)	Oct 1997
16 days	Jimmy McIlroy (Bolton)	Nov 1970
19 days	Martin Allen (Barnet)	Apr 2011
20 days	Paul Went (Leyton Orient)	Oct 1981
27 days	Malcolm Crosby (Oxford Utd)	Jan 1998
27 days	Oscar Garcia (Watford)	Sep 2014
28 days	Tommy Docherty (QPR)	Dec 1968
28 days	Paul Hart (QPR)	Jan 2010
32 days	Steve Coppell (Manchester City)	Nov 1996
32 days	Darko Milanic (Leeds)	Oct 2014
34 days	Niall Quinn (Sunderland)	Aug 2006
36 days	Steve Claridge (Millwall)	Jul 2005
39 days	Paul Gascoigne (Kettering)	Dec 2005
39 days	Kenny Jackett (Rotherham)	Nov 2016

40 days	Alex McLeish (Nottm Forest)	Feb 2013
41 days	Steve Wicks (Lincoln)	Oct 1995
41 days	Les Reed (Charlton)	Dec 2006
43 days	Mauro Milanese (Leyton Orient)	Dec 2014
44 days	Brian Clough (Leeds)	Sep 1974
44 days	Jock Stein (Leeds)	Oct 1978
45 days	Paul Murray (Hartlepool)	Dec 2014
48 days	John Toshack (Wales)	Mar 1994
48 days	David Platt (Sampdoria coach)	Feb 1999
49 days	Brian Little (Wolves)	Oct 1986
49 days	Terry Fenwick (Northampton)	Feb 2003
52 days	Alberto Cavasin (Leyton Orient)	Nov 2016
54 days	Craig Levein (Raith Rov)	Oct 1996
57 days	Henning Berg (Blackburn)	Dec 2012
59 days	Kevin Nugent (Barnet)	Apr 2017
61 days	Bill McGarry (Wolves)	Nov 1985

- In May 1984, Crystal Palace named **Dave Bassett** as manager, but he changed his mind four days later, without signing the contract, and returned to Wimbledon.
- In May 2007, **Leroy Rosenior** was reportedly appointed manager of Torquay after relegation and sacked ten minutes later when the club came under new ownership.
- **Brian Laws** lost his job at Scunthorpe on Mar 25, 2004 and was reinstated three weeks later.
- In an angry outburst after a play-off defeat in May 1992, Barnet chairman Stan Flashman sacked manager **Barry Fry** and re-instated him a day later.

EARLY-SEASON MANAGER SACKINGS

2012: Andy Thorn (Coventry) 8 days; John Sheridan (Chesterfield) 10 days; **2011:** Jim Jefferies (Hearts) 9 days; **2010** Kevin Blackwell (Sheffield Utd) 8 days; **2009** Bryan Gunn (Norwich) 6 days; **2007:** Neil McDonald (Carlisle) 2 days; Martin Allen (Leicester) 18 days; **2004** Paul Sturrock (Southampton) 9 days; **2004:** Sir Bobby Robson (Newcastle) 16 days; **2003** Glenn Roeder (West Ham) 15 days; **2000:** Alan Buckley (Grimsby) 10 days; **1997:** Kerry Dixon (Doncaster) 12 days; **1996:** Sammy Chung (Doncaster) on morning of season's opening League match; **1996:** Alan Ball (Manchester City) 12 days; **1994:** Kenny Hibbitt (Walsall) and Kenny Swain (Wigan) 20 days; **1993:** Peter Reid (Manchester City) 12 days; **1991:** Don Mackay (Blackburn) 14 days; **1989:** Mick Jones (Peterborough) 12 days; **1980:** Bill McGarry (Newcastle) 13 days; **1979:** Dennis Butler (Port Vale) 12 days; **1977:** George Petchey (Leyton O) 13 days; **1977:** Willie Bell (Birmingham) 16 days; **1971:** Len Richley (Darlington) 12 days

BRUCE'S FOUR-TIMER

Steve Bruce is the only manager to win four promotions to the Premier League – with Birmingham in 2002 and 2007 and with Hull in 2013 and 2016.

RECORD START FOR MANAGER

Russ Wilcox, appointed by Scunthorpe in Nov 2013, remained unbeaten in his first 28 league matches (14 won, 14 drawn) and took the club to promotion from League Two. It was the most successful start to a managerial career In English football, beating the record of 23 unbeaten games by Preston's William Sudell in 1889.

RECORD TOP DIVISION START

Arsenal were unbeaten in 17 league matches from the start of season 1947-48 under new manager **Tom Whittaker**.

SACKED, REINSTATED, FINISHED

Brian McDermott was sacked as Leeds manager on Jan 31, 2014. The following day, he was reinstated. At the end of the season, with the club under new ownership, he left by 'mutual consent.'

CARETAKER SUPREME

As Chelsea's season collapsed, Andre Villas-Boas was sacked in March 2012 after eight months as manager, 2012. Roberto Di Matteo was appointed caretaker and by the season's end his team had won the FA Cup and the Champions League.

MANAGER DOUBLES

Four managers have won the League Championship with different clubs: **Tom Watson**, secretary-manager with Sunderland (1892–93–95) and **Liverpool** (1901); **Herbert Chapman** with Huddersfield (1923–24, 1924–25) and Arsenal (1930–31, 1932–33); **Brian Clough** with Derby (1971–72) and Nottm Forest (1977–78); **Kenny Dalglish** with Liverpool (1985–86, 1987–88, 1989–90) and Blackburn (1994–95).

Managers to win the FA Cup with different clubs: **Billy Walker** (Sheffield Wed 1935, Nottm Forest 1959); **Herbert Chapman** (Huddersfield 1922, Arsenal 1930).

Kenny Dalglish (Liverpool) and **George Graham** (Arsenal) completed the Championship/FA Cup double as both player and manager with a single club. **Joe Mercer** won the title as a player with Everton, the title twice and FA Cup as a player with Arsenal and both competitions as manager of Manchester City.

CHAIRMAN-MANAGER

On Dec 20, 1988, after two years on the board, Dundee Utd manager **Jim McLean** was elected chairman, too. McLean, Scotland's longest-serving manager (appointed on Nov 24, 1971), resigned at end of season 1992–93 (remained chairman).

Ron Noades was chairman-manager of Brentford from Jul 1998–Mar 2001. **John Reames** did both jobs at Lincoln from Nov 1998–Apr 2000)

Niall Quinn did both jobs for five weeks in 2006 before appointing Roy Keane as manager of Sunderland.

TOP DIVISION PLAYER-MANAGERS

Les Allen (QPR 1968–69); **Johnny Giles** (WBA 1976–77); **Howard Kendall** (Everton 1981–82); **Kenny Dalglish** (Liverpool, 1985–90; **Trevor Francis** (QPR, 1988–89); **Terry Butcher** (Coventry, 1990–91), **Peter Reid** (Manchester City, 1990–93), **Trevor Francis** (Sheffield Wed, 1991–94), **Glenn Hoddle**, (Chelsea, 1993–95); **Bryan Robson** (Middlesbrough, 1994–97); **Ray Wilkins** (QPR, 1994–96), **Ruud Gullit** (Chelsea, 1996 98), **Gianluca Vialli** (Chelsea, 1998–2000).

FIRST FOREIGN MANAGER IN ENGLISH LEAGUE

Uruguayan **Danny Bergara** (Rochdale 1988–89).

COACHING KINGS OF EUROPE

Five coaches have won the European Cup/Champions League with two different clubs: **Ernst Happel** with Feyenoord (1970) and Hamburg (1983); **Ottmar Hitzfeld** with Borussia Dortmund (1997) and Bayern Munich (2001); **Jose Mourinho** with Porto (2004) and Inter Milan (2010), **Jupp Heynckes** with Real Madrid (1998) and Bayern Munich (2013); **Carlo Ancelotti** with AC Milan (2003, 2007) and Real Madrid (2014).

FOREIGN TRIUMPH

Former Dutch star **Ruud Gullit** became the first foreign manager to win a major English competition when Chelsea took the FA Cup in 1997.

Arsene Wenger and **Gerard Houllier** became the first foreign managers to receive recognition when they were awarded honorary OBEs in the Queen's Birthday Honours in Jun 2003 'for their contribution to English football and Franco–British relations'.

MANAGERS OF POST-WAR CHAMPIONS (*Double winners)

1947 George Kay (Liverpool); **1948** Tom Whittaker (Arsenal); **1949** Bob Jackson (Portsmouth). **1950** Bob Jackson (Portsmouth); **1951** Arthur Rowe (Tottenham); **1952** Matt Busby (Manchester

Utd); **1953** Tom Whittaker (Arsenal); **1954** Stan Cullis (Wolves); **1955** Ted Drake (Chelsea); **1956** Matt Busby (Manchester Utd); **1957** Matt Busby (Manchester Utd); **1958** Stan Cullis (Wolves); **1959** Stan Cullis (Wolves).

1960 Harry Potts (Burnley); **1961** *Bill Nicholson (Tottenham); **1962** Alf Ramsey (Ipswich); **1963** Harry Catterick (Everton); **1964** Bill Shankly (Liverpool); **1965** Matt Busby (Manchester Utd); **1966** Bill Shankly (Liverpool); **1967** Matt Busby (Manchester Utd); **1968** Joe Mercer (Manchester City); **1969** Don Revie (Leeds).

1970 Harry Catterick (Everton); **1971** *Bertie Mee (Arsenal); **1972** Brian Clough (Derby); **1973** Bill Shankly (Liverpool); **1974** Don Revie (Leeds); **1975** Dave Mackay (Derby); **1976** Bob Paisley (Liverpool); **1977** Bob Paisley (Liverpool); **1978** Brian Clough (Nottm Forest); **1979** Bob Paisley (Liverpool).

1980 Bob Paisley (Liverpool); **1981** Ron Saunders (Aston Villa); **1982** Bob Paisley (Liverpool); **1983** Bob Paisley (Liverpool); **1984** Joe Fagan (Liverpool); **1985** Howard Kendall (Everton); **1986** *Kenny Dalglish (Liverpool – player/manager); **1987** Howard Kendall (Everton); **1988** Kenny Dalglish (Liverpool – player/manager); **1989** George Graham (Arsenal).

1990 Kenny Dalglish (Liverpool); **1991** George Graham (Arsenal); **1992** Howard Wilkinson (Leeds); **1993** Alex Ferguson (Manchester Utd); **1994** *Alex Ferguson (Manchester Utd); **1995** Kenny Dalglish (Blackburn); **1996** *Alex Ferguson (Manchester Utd); **1997** Alex Ferguson (Manchester Utd); **1998** *Arsene Wenger (Arsenal); **1999** *Alex Ferguson (Manchester Utd).

2000 Sir Alex Ferguson (Manchester Utd); **2001** Sir Alex Ferguson (Manchester Utd); **2002** *Arsene Wenger (Arsenal); **2003** Sir Alex Ferguson (Manchester Utd); **2004** Arsene Wenger (Arsenal); **2005** Jose Mourinho (Chelsea); **2006** Jose Mourinho (Chelsea); **2007** Sir Alex Ferguson (Manchester Utd); **2008** Sir Alex Ferguson (Manchester Utd); **2009** Sir Alex Ferguson (Manchester Utd); **2010** *Carlo Ancelotti (Chelsea); **2011** Sir Alex Ferguson (Manchester Utd); **2012** Roberto Mancini (Manchester City); **2013** Sir Alex Ferguson (Manchester Utd); **2014** Manuel Pellegrini (Manchester City); **2015** Jose Mourinho (Chelsea); **2016** Claudio Ranieri (Leicester); **2017** Antonio Conte (Chelsea)

WORLD NO 1 MANAGER

When **Sir Alex Ferguson**, 71, retired in May 2013, he ended the most successful managerial career in the game's history. He took Manchester United to a total of 38 prizes – 13 Premier League titles, 5 FA Cup triumphs, 4 League Cups, 10 Charity/Community Shields (1 shared), 2 Champions League wins, 1 Cup-Winners' Cup, 1 FIFA Club World Cup, 1 Inter-Continental Cup and 1 UEFA Super Cup. Having played centre-forward for Rangers, the Glaswegian managed 3 Scottish clubs, East Stirling, St Mirren and then Aberdeen, where he broke the Celtic/Rangers duopoly with 9 successes: 3 League Championships, 4 Scottish Cups, 1 League Cup and 1 UEFA Cup. Appointed at Old Trafford in November 1986, when replacing Ron Atkinson, he did not win a prize there until his fourth season (FA Cup 1990), but thereafter the club's trophy cabinet glittered with silverware. His total of 1,500 matches in charge ended with a 5-5 draw away to West Bromwich Albion. The longest-serving manager in the club's history, he constructed 4 triumphant teams. Sir Alex was knighted in 1999 and in 2012 he received the FIFA award for services to football. On retirement from management, he became a director and club ambassador. United maintained the dynasty of long-serving Scottish managers (Sir Matt Busby for 24 seasons) by appointing David Moyes, who had been in charge at Everton for 11 years.

MANAGERS' EURO TREBLES

Two managers have won the European Cup/Champions League three times. **Bob Paisley** did it with Liverpool (1977,78, 81).

Carlo Ancelotti's successes were with AC Milan in 2003 and 2007 and with Real Madrid in 2014.

WINNER MOURINHO

In winning the Premier League and League Cup in 2015, Jose Mourinho embellished his reputation as Chelsea's most successful manager. Those achievements took his total of honours in two spells at the club to 8: 3 Premier League, 3 League Cup, 1 FA Cup, 1 Community Shield. Joining from Portuguese champions Porto, Mourinho was initially with Chelsea from June 2004 to September 2007. He then successfully coached Inter Milan and Real Madrid before returning to Stamford Bridge in June 2013. His Premier League triumph in 2015 was his eighth title in 11 years in four countries (England 3, Portugal 2, Italy 2, Spain 1). In his first season with Manchester Utd (2016–17), he won three trophies – League Cup, Europa League and Community Shield.

WENGER'S CUP AGAIN

Arsenal's win against Aston Villa in the 2015 Final was a record 12th success for them in the FA Cup and a sixth triumph in the competition for manager Arsene Wenger, equalling the record of George Ramsay for Villa (1887–1920). With his sixth victory in seven Finals, Wenger made history as the first manager to win the Cup in successive seasons twice (previously in 2002 and 2003). He won it for a record seventh time – in eight finals – in 2017.

RECORD MANAGER FEE

Chelsea paid Porto a record £13.25m compensation when they appointed **Andre Villas-Boas** as manager in June 2011. He lasted less than nine months at Stamford Bridge.

FATHER AND SON MANAGERS WITH SAME CLUB

Fulham: Bill Dodgin Snr 1949–53; Bill Dodgin Jnr 1968–72. **Brentford:** Bill Dodgin Snr 1953–57; Bill Dodgin Jnr 1976–80. **Bournemouth:** John Bond 1970–73; Kevin Bond 2006–08. **Derby:** Brian Clough 1967–73; Nigel Clough 2009–2013. **Bristol City:** Gary Johnson 2005–10; Lee Johnson 2016–present.

SIR BOBBY'S HAT-TRICK

Sir Bobby Robson, born and brought up in County Durham, achieved a unique hat-trick when he received the Freedom of Durham in Dec 2008. He had already been awarded the Freedom of Ipswich and Newcastle. He died in July 2009 and had an express loco named after him on the East Coast to London line.

MANAGERS WITH MOST FA CUP SUCCESSES

7 Arsene Wenger (Arsenal); **George Ramsay** (Aston Villa); **5 Sir Alex Ferguson** (Manchester Utd); **3 Charles Foweraker** (Bolton); **John Nicholson** (Sheffield Utd); **Bill Nicholson** (Tottenham).

RELEGATION 'DOUBLES'

Managers associated with two clubs relegated in same season: **John Bond** in 1985–86 (Swansea City and Birmingham); **Ron Saunders** in 1985–86 (WBA – and their reserve team – and Birmingham); **Bob Stokoe** in 1986-87 (Carlisle and Sunderland); **Billy McNeill** in 1986–87 (Manchester City and Aston Villa); **Dave Bassett** in 1987–88 (Watford and Sheffield Utd); **Mick Mills** in 1989–90 (Stoke and Colchester); **Gary Johnson** in 2014–15 (Yeovil and Cheltenham)

THREE FA CUP DEFEATS IN ONE SEASON

Manager **Michael Appleton** suffered three FA Cup defeats in season 2012-13, with Portsmouth (v Notts Co, 1st rd); Blackpool (v Fulham, 3rd rd); Blackburn (v Millwall, 6th rd).

WEMBLEY STADIUM

NEW WEMBLEY

A new era for English football began in March 2007 with the completion of the new national stadium. The 90,000-seater arena was hailed as one of the world's finest – but came at a price. Costs soared, the project fell well behind schedule and disputes involving the FA, builders Multiplex and the Government were rife. The old stadium, opened in 1923, cost £750,000. The new one, originally priced at £326m in 2000, ended up at around £800m. The first international after completion was an Under-21 match between England and Italy. The FA Cup Final returned to its spiritual home after being staged at the Millennium Stadium in Cardiff for six seasons. Then, England's senior team were back for a friendly against Brazil.

DROGBA'S WEMBLEY RECORD

Didier Drogba's FA Cup goal for Chelsea against Liverpool in May 2012 meant that he had scored in all his 8 competitive appearances for the club at Wembley. (7 wins, 1 defeat). They came in: 2007 FA Cup Final (1-0 v Manchester Utd); 2008 League Cup Final (1-2 v Tottenham); 2009 FA Cup semi-final (2-1 v Arsenal); 2009 FA Cup Final (2-1 v Everton); 2010 FA Cup semi-final (3-0 v Aston Villa); 2010 FA Cup Final (1-0 v Portsmouth); 2012 FA Cup semi-final (5-1 v Tottenham); 2012 FA Cup Final (2-1 v Liverpool).

INVASION DAY

Memorable scenes were witnessed at the first **FA Cup Final at Wembley**, Apr 28, 1923, between **Bolton** and **West Ham**. An accurate return of the attendance could not be made owing to thousands breaking in, but there were probably more than 200,000 spectators present. The match was delayed for 40 minutes by the crowd invading the pitch. Official attendance was 126,047. Gate receipts totalled £27,776. The two clubs and the FA each received £6,365 and the FA refunded £2,797 to ticket-holders who were unable to get to their seats. Cup Final admission has since been by ticket only.

REDUCED CAPACITY

Capacity of the all-seated Wembley Stadium was 78,000. The last 100,000 attendance was for the 1985 FA Cup Final between Manchester Utd and Everton. Crowd record for New Wembley: 89,874 for 2008 FA Cup Final (Portsmouth v Cardiff).

WEMBLEY'S FIRST UNDER LIGHTS

Nov 30, 1955 (England 4, Spain 1), when the floodlights were switched on after 73 minutes (afternoon match played in damp, foggy conditions).
First Wembley international played throughout under lights: England 8, N Ireland 3 on evening of Nov 20, 1963 (att: 55,000).

MOST WEMBLEY APPEARANCES

59 by **Tony Adams** (35 England, 24 Arsenal); 57 by **Peter Shilton** (52 England, 3 Nottm Forest, 1 Leicester, 1 Football League X1).

WEMBLEY HAT-TRICKS

Three players have scored hat-tricks in major finals at Wembley: **Stan Mortensen** for Blackpool v Bolton (FA Cup Final, 1953), **Geoff Hurst** for England v West Germany (World Cup Final, 1966) and **David Speedie** for Chelsea v Manchester City (Full Members Cup, 1985).

ENGLAND'S WEMBLEY DEFEATS

England have lost 25 matches to foreign opponents at Wembley:

Nov 1953	3-6 v Hungary	**Jun 1995**	1-3 v Brazil
Oct 1959	2-3 v Sweden	**Feb 1997**	0-1 v Italy
Oct 1965	2-3 v Austria	**Feb 1998**	0-2 v Chile
Apr 1972	1-3 v W Germany	**Feb 1999**	0-2 v France
Nov 1973	0-1 v Italy	**Oct 2000**	0-1 v Germany
Feb 1977	0-2 v Holland	**Aug 2007**	1-2 v Germany
Mar 1981	1-2 v Spain	**Nov 2007**	2-3 v Croatia
May 1981	0-1 v Brazil	**Nov 2010**	1-2 v France
Oct 1982	1-2 v W Germany	**Feb 2012**	2-3 v Holland
Sep 1983	0-1 v Denmark	**Nov 2013**	0-2 v Chile
Jun 1984	0-2 v Russia	**Nov 2013**	0-1 v Germany
May 1990	1-2 v Uruguay	**Mar 2016**	1-2 v Holland
Sep 1991	0-1 v Germany		

A further defeat came in **Euro 96**. After drawing the semi-final with Germany 1-1, England went out 6-5 on penalties.

FASTEST GOALS AT WEMBLEY

In first-class matches: **25 sec** by **Louis Saha** for Everton in 2009 FA Cup Final against Chelsea; **38 sec** by **Bryan Robson** for England's against Yugoslavia in 1989; **42 sec** by **Roberto Di Matteo** for Chelsea in 1997 FA Cup Final v Middlesbrough; **44 sec** by **Bryan Robson** for England v Northern Ireland in 1982.

Fastest goal in **any** match at Wembley: **20 sec** by **Maurice Cox** for Cambridge University against Oxford in 1979.

FOUR WEMBLEY HEADERS

When **Wimbledon** beat Sutton 4-2 in the FA Amateur Cup Final at Wembley on May 4, 1963, Irish centre-forward **Eddie Reynolds** headed all four goals.

WEMBLEY ONE-SEASON DOUBLES

In 1989, **Nottm Forest** became the first club to win two Wembley Finals in the same season (Littlewoods Cup and Simod Cup).

In 1993, **Arsenal** made history there as the first club to win the League (Coca-Cola) Cup and the FA Cup in the same season. They beat Sheffield Wed 2-1 in both finals.

In 2012, **York** won twice at Wembley in nine days at the end of the season, beating Newport 2-0 in the FA Trophy Final and Luton 2-1 in the Conference Play-off Final to return to the Football League.

SUDDEN-DEATH DECIDERS

First Wembley Final decided on sudden death (first goal scored in overtime): Apr 23, 1995 – **Birmingham** beat Carlisle (1-0, Paul Tait 103 mins) to win Auto Windscreens Shield.

First instance of a golden goal deciding a major international tournament was at Wembley on Jun 30, 1996, when **Germany** beat the Czech Republic 2-1 in the European Championship Final with Oliver Bierhoff's goal in the 95th minute.

WEMBLEY'S MOST ONE-SIDED FINAL (in major domestic cups)

Swansea 5 Bradford City 0 (League Cup, Feb 24, 2013).

FOOTBALL TRAGEDIES

DAYS OF TRAGEDY – CLUBS

Season 1988–89 brought the worst disaster in the history of British sport, with the death of 96 Liverpool supporters (200 injured) at the **FA Cup semi-final** against Nottm Forest at **Hillsborough, Sheffield**, on Saturday, Apr 15. The tragedy built up in the minutes preceding kick-off, when thousands surged into the ground at the Leppings Lane end. Many were crushed in the tunnel between entrance and terracing, but most of the victims were trapped inside the perimeter fencing behind the goal. The match was abandoned without score after six minutes' play. The dead included seven women and girls, two teenage sisters and two teenage brothers. The youngest victim was a boy of ten, the oldest 67-year-old Gerard Baron, whose brother Kevin played for Liverpool in the 1950 Cup Final. (*Total became 96 in Mar 1993, when Tony Bland died after being in a coma for nearly four years). A two-year Inquest at Warrington ended on April 26, 2016 with the verdict that the 96 were 'unlawfully killed.' It cleared Liverpool fans of any blame and ruled that South Yorkshire Police and South Yorkshire Ambulance Service 'caused or contributed' to the loss of life.

The two worst disasters in one season in British soccer history occurred at the end of 1984–85. On May 11, the last Saturday of the League season, 56 people (two of them visiting supporters) were burned to death – and more than 200 taken to hospital – when fire destroyed the main stand at the **Bradford City–Lincoln** match at Valley Parade.

The wooden, 77-year-old stand was full for City's last fixture before which, amid scenes of celebration, the club had been presented with the Third Division Championship trophy. The fire broke out just before half-time and, within five minutes, the entire stand was engulfed.

Heysel Tragedy

Eighteen days later, on May 29, at the European Cup Final between **Liverpool** and **Juventus** at the Heysel Stadium, Brussels, 39 spectators (31 of them Italian) were crushed or trampled to death and 437 injured. The disaster occurred an hour before the scheduled kick-off when Liverpool supporters charged a Juventus section of the crowd at one end of the stadium, and a retaining wall collapsed. The sequel was a 5-year ban by UEFA on English clubs generally in European competition, with a 6-year ban on Liverpool.

On May 26 1985 ten people were trampled to death and 29 seriously injured in a crowd panic on the way into the **Olympic Stadium, Mexico City** for the Mexican Cup Final between local clubs National University and America.

More than 100 people died and 300 were injured in a football disaster at **Nepal's national stadium** in Katmandu in Mar 1988. There was a stampede when a violent hailstorm broke over the capital. Spectators rushed for cover, but the stadium exits were locked, and hundreds were trampled in the crush.

In South Africa, on Jan 13 1991 40 black fans were trampled to death (50 injured) as they tried to escape from fighting that broke out at a match in the gold-mining town of Orkney, 80 miles from Johannesburg. The friendly, between top teams **Kaiser Chiefs** and **Orlando Pirates**, attracted a packed crowd of 20,000. Violence erupted after the referee allowed Kaiser Chiefs a disputed second-half goal to lead 1-0.

Disaster struck at the French Cup semi-final (May 5, 1992), with the death of 15 spectators and 1,300 injured when a temporary metal stand collapsed in the Corsican town of Bastia. The tie between Second Division **Bastia** and French Champions **Marseille** was cancelled. Monaco, who won the other semi-final, were allowed to compete in the next season's Cup-Winners' Cup.

A total of 318 died and 500 were seriously injured when the crowd rioted over a disallowed goal at the National Stadium in Lima, Peru, on May 24, 1964. **Peru** and **Argentina** were competing to play in the Olympic Games in Tokyo.

That remained **sport's heaviest death** toll until Oct 20, 1982, when (it was revealed only in Jul 1989) 340 Soviet fans were killed in Moscow's Lenin Stadium at the UEFA Cup second round first leg match between **Moscow Spartak** and **Haarlem** (Holland). They were crushed on an open stairway when a last-minute Spartak goal sent departing spectators surging back into the ground.

Among other crowd disasters abroad: Jun, 1968 – 74 died in Argentina. Panic broke out at the end of a goalless match between River Plate and Boca Juniors at Nunez, Buenos Aires, when Boca supporters threw lighted newspaper torches on to fans in the tiers below.

Feb 1974 – 49 killed in **Egypt** in crush of fans clamouring to see Zamalek play Dukla Prague.

Sep 1971 – 44 died in **Turkey**, when fighting among spectators over a disallowed goal (Kayseri v Siwas) led to a platform collapsing.

The then worst disaster in the history of British football, in terms of loss of life, occurred at Glasgow Rangers' ground at **Ibrox Park**, Jan 2 1971. Sixty-six people were trampled to death (100 injured) as they tumbled down Stairway 13 just before the end of the **Rangers v Celtic** New Year's match. That disaster led to the 1975 Safety of Sports Grounds legislation.

The Ibrox tragedy eclipsed even the Bolton disaster in which 33 were killed and about 500 injured when a wall and crowd barriers collapsed near a corner-flag at the **Bolton v Stoke** FA Cup sixth round tie on Mar 9 1946. The match was completed after half an hour's stoppage.

In a previous crowd disaster at **Ibrox** on Apr 5, 1902, part of the terracing collapsed during the Scotland v England international and 25 people were killed. The match, held up for 20 minutes, ended 1-1, but was never counted as an official international.

Eight leading players and three officials of **Manchester Utd** and eight newspaper representatives were among the 23 who perished in the air crash at **Munich** on Feb 6, 1958, during take-off following a European Cup-tie in Belgrade. The players were Roger Byrne, Geoffrey Bent, Eddie Colman, Duncan Edwards, Mark Jones, David Pegg, Tommy Taylor and Liam Whelan, and the officials were Walter Crickmer (secretary), Tom Curry (trainer) and Herbert Whalley (coach). The newspaper representatives were Alf Clarke, Don Davies, George Follows, Tom Jackson, Archie Ledbrooke, Henry Rose, Eric Thompson and Frank Swift (former England goalkeeper of Manchester City).

On May 14, 1949, the entire team of Italian Champions **Torino**, 8 of them Internationals, were killed when the aircraft taking them home from a match against Benfica in Lisbon crashed at Superga, near Turin. The total death toll of 28 included all the club's reserve players, the manager, trainer and coach.

On Feb 8, 1981, 24 spectators died and more than 100 were injured at a match in **Greece**. They were trampled as thousands of the 40,000 crowd tried to rush out of the stadium at Piraeus after Olympiacos beat AEK Athens 6-0.

On Nov 17, 1982, 24 people (12 of them children) were killed and 250 injured when fans stampeded at the end of a match at the Pascual Guerrero stadium in **Cali, Colombia**. Drunken spectators hurled fire crackers and broken bottles from the higher stands on to people below and started a rush to the exits.

On Dec 9, 1987, the 18-strong team squad of **Alianza Lima**, one of Peru's top clubs, were wiped out, together with 8 officials and several youth players, when a military aircraft taking them home from Puccalpa crashed into the sea off Ventillana, ten miles from Lima. The only survivor among 43 on board was a member of the crew.

On Apr 28, 1993, 18 members of **Zambia's international squad** and 5 ZFA officials died when the aircraft carrying them to a World Cup qualifying tie against Senegal crashed into the Atlantic soon after take-off from Libreville, Gabon.

On Oct 16 1996, 81 fans were crushed to death and 147 seriously injured in the '**Guatemala Disaster**' at the World Cup qualifier against Costa Rica in Mateo Flores stadium. The tragedy happened an hour before kick-off, allegedly caused by ticket forgery and overcrowding – 60,000 were reported in the 45,000-capacity ground – and safety problems related to perimeter fencing.

On Jul 9, 1996, 8 people died, 39 injured in riot after derby match between **Libya's two top clubs** in Tripoli. Al-Ahli had beaten Al-Ittihad 1-0 by a controversial goal.

On Apr 6, 1997, 5 spectators were crushed to death at **Nigeria's national stadium** in Lagos after the 2-1 World Cup qualifying victory over Guinea. Only two of five gates were reported open as the 40,000 crowd tried to leave the ground.

It was reported from the **Congo** (Oct 29, 1998) that a bolt of lightning struck a village match, killing all 11 members of the home team Benatshadi, but leaving the opposing players from Basangana unscathed. It was believed the surviving team wore better-insulated boots.

On Jan 10, 1999, eight fans died and 13 were injured in a stampede at **Egypt's Alexandria Stadium**. Some 25,000 spectators had pushed into the ground. Despite the tragedy, the cup-tie between Al-Ittihad and Al-Koroum was completed.

Three people suffocated and several were seriously injured when thousands of fans forced their way into **Liberia's national stadium** in Monrovia at a goalless World Cup qualifying match against Chad on Apr 23, 2000. The stadium (capacity 35,000) was reported 'heavily overcrowded'.

On Jul 9, 2000, 12 spectators died from crush injuries when police fired tear gas into the 50,000 crowd after South Africa scored their second goal in a World Cup group qualifier against Zimbabwe in **Harare**. A stampede broke out as fans scrambled to leave the national stadium. Players of both teams lay face down on the pitch as fumes swept over them. FIFA launched an investigation and decided that the result would stand, with South Africa leading 2-0 at the time of the 84th-minute abandonment.

On Apr 11, 2001, at one of the biggest matches of the South African season, 43 died and 155 were injured in a crush at **Ellis Park, Johannesburg**. After tearing down a fence, thousands of fans surged into a stadium already packed to its 60,000 capacity for the Premiership derby between top Soweto teams Kaizer Chiefs and Orlando Pirates. The match was abandoned at 1-1 after 33 minutes. In Jan 1991, 40 died in a crowd crush at a friendly between the same clubs at Orkney, 80 miles from Johannesburg.

On Apr 29, 2001, seven people were trampled to death and 51 injured when a riot broke out at a match between two of Congo's biggest clubs, Lupopo and Mazembe at **Lubumbashi**, southern Congo.

On May 6, 2001, two spectators were killed in Iran and hundreds were injured when a glass fibre roof collapsed at the over-crowded Mottaqi Stadium at Sari for the match between Pirouzi and Shemshak Noshahr.

On May 9, 2001, in Africa's worst football disaster, 123 died and 93 were injured in a stampede at the national stadium in **Accra, Ghana**. Home team Hearts of Oak were leading 2-1 against Asanti Kotoko five minutes from time, when Asanti fans started hurling bottles on to the pitch. Police fired tear gas into the stands, and the crowd panicked in a rush for the exits, which were locked. It took the death toll at three big matches in Africa in Apr/May to 173.

On Aug 12, 2001, two players were killed by lightning and ten severely burned at a **Guatemala** Third Division match between Deportivo Culquimulilla and Pueblo Nuevo Vinas.

On Nov 1, 2002, two players died from injuries after lightning struck Deportivo Cali's training ground in **Colombia**.

On Mar 12 2004, five people were killed and more than 100 injured when spectators stampeded shortly before the Syrian Championship fixture between Al-Jihad and Al-Fatwa in **Qameshli**, Northern Syria. The match was cancelled.

On Oct 10, 2004, three spectators died in a crush at the African Zone World Cup qualifier between **Guinea** and **Morocco** (1-1) at Conakry, Guinea.

On Mar 25, 2005, five were killed as 100,000 left the Azadi Stadium, **Tehran**, after Iran's World Cup qualifying win (2-1) against Japan.

On Jun 2, 2007, 12 spectators were killed and 46 injured in a crush at the Chillabombwe Stadium, **Zambia**, after an African Nations Cup qualifier against Congo.

On Mar 29, 2009, 19 people died and 139 were injured after a wall collapsed at the Ivory Coast stadium in **Abidjan** before a World Cup qualifier against Malawi. The match went ahead, Ivory Coast winning 5-0 with two goals from Chelsea's Didier Drogba. The tragedy meant that, in 13 years, crowd disasters at club and internationals at ten different grounds across Africa had claimed the lives of 283 people.

On Jan 8, 2010, terrorists at **Cabinda**, Angola machine-gunned the Togo team buses travelling to the Africa Cup of Nations. They killed a driver, an assistant coach and a media officer and injured several players. The team were ordered by their Government to withdraw from the tournament.

On Oct 23, 2010, seven fans were trampled to death when thousands tried to force their way into the Nyayo National Stadium in **Nairobi** at a Kenya Premier League match between the Gor Mahia and AFC Leopards clubs.

On Feb 1, 2012, 74 died and nearly 250 were injured in a crowd riot at the end of the Al-Masry v Al-Ahly match in **Port Said** – the worst disaster in Egyptian sport.

On Nov 28, 2016, 19 players and staff of the Brazilian club Chapecoense were among 71 people killed in a plane crash in Colombia. An electrical fault was blamed.

DAYS OF TRAGEDY – PERSONAL

Sam Wynne, Bury right-back, collapsed five minutes before half-time in the First Division match away to Sheffield Utd on Apr 30, 1927, and died in the dressing-room.

John Thomson, Celtic and Scotland goalkeeper, sustained a fractured skull when diving at an opponent's feet in the Rangers v Celtic League match on Sep 5, 1931, and died the same evening.

Sim Raleigh (Gillingham), injured in a clash of heads at home to Brighton (Div 3 South) on Dec 1, 1934, continued to play but collapsed in second half and died in hospital the same night.

James Thorpe, Sunderland goalkeeper, was injured during the First Division match at home to Chelsea on Feb 1, 1936 and died in a diabetic coma three days later.

Derek Dooley, Sheffield Wed centre-forward and top scorer in 1951–52 in the Football League with 46 goals in 30 matches, broke a leg in the League match at Preston on Feb 14, 1953, and, after complications set in, had to lose the limb by amputation.

John White, Tottenham's Scottish international forward, was killed by lightning on a golf course at Enfield, North London in Jul, 1964.

Tony Allden, Highgate centre-half, was struck by lightning during an Amateur Cup quarter-final with Enfield on Feb 25, 1967. He died the following day. Four other players were also struck but recovered.

Roy Harper died while refereeing the York v Halifax (Div 4) match on May 5, 1969.

Jim Finn collapsed and died from a heart attack while refereeing Exeter v Stockport (Div 4) on Sep 16, 1972.

Scotland manager Jock Stein, 62, collapsed and died at the end of the Wales-Scotland World Cup qualifying match (1-1) at Ninian Park, Cardiff on Sep 10, 1985.

David Longhurst, York forward, died after being carried off two minutes before half-time in the Fourth Division fixture at home to Lincoln on Sep 8, 1990. The match was abandoned (0-0). The inquest revealed that Longhurst suffered from a rare heart condition.

Mike North collapsed while refereeing Southend v Mansfield (Div 3) on Apr 16, 2001 and died shortly afterwards. The match was abandoned and re-staged on May 8, with the receipts donated to his family.

Marc-Vivien Foe, on his 63rd appearance in Cameroon's midfield, collapsed unchallenged in the centre circle after 72 minutes of the FIFA Confederations Cup semi-final against Colombia in Lyon, France, on Jun 26, 2003, and despite the efforts of the stadium medical staff he could not be revived. He had been on loan to Manchester City from Olympique Lyonnais in season 2002–03, and poignantly scored the club's last goal at Maine Road.

Paul Sykes, Folkestone Invicta (Ryman League) striker, died on the pitch during the Kent Senior Cup semi-final against Margate on Apr 12, 2005. He collapsed after an innocuous off-the-ball incident.

Craig Gowans, Falkirk apprentice, was killed at the club's training ground on Jul 8, 2005 when he came into contact with power lines.

Peter Wilson, Mansfield goalkeeping coach, died of a heart attack after collapsing during the warm-up of the League Two game away to Shrewsbury on Nov 19, 2005.

Matt Gadsby, Hinckley defender, collapsed and died while playing in a Conference North match at Harrogate on Sep 9, 2006.

Phil O'Donnell, 35-year-old Motherwell captain and Scotland midfield player, collapsed when about to be substituted near the end of the SPL home game against Dundee Utd on Dec 29, 2007 and died shortly afterwards in hospital.

GREAT SERVICE

'For services to Association Football', **Stanley Matthews** (Stoke, Blackpool and England), already a CBE, became the first professional footballer to receive a knighthood. This was bestowed in 1965, his last season. Before he retired and five days after his 50th birthday, he played for Stoke to set a record as the oldest First Division footballer (v Fulham, Feb 6, 1965).

Over a brilliant span of 33 years, he played in 886 first-class matches, including 54 full Internationals (plus 31 in war time), 701 League games (including 3 at start of season 1939-40, which was abandoned on the outbreak of war) and 86 FA Cup-ties, and scored 95 goals. He was never booked in his career.

Sir Stanley died on Feb 23, 2000, three weeks after his 85th birthday. His ashes were buried under the centre circle of Stoke's Britannia Stadium. After spending a number of years in Toronto, he made his home back in the Potteries in 1989, having previously returned to his home town, Hanley in Oct, 1987 to unveil a life-size bronze statue of himself. The inscription reads: 'Sir Stanley Matthews, CBE. Born Hanley, 1 Feb 1915.

His name is symbolic of the beauty of the game, his fame timeless and international, his sportsmanship and modesty universally acclaimed. A magical player, of the people, for the people.' On his home-coming in 1989, Sir Stanley was made President of Stoke, the club he joined as a boy of 15 and served as a player for 20 years between 1931 and 1965, on either side of his spell with Blackpool.

In Jul 1992 FIFA honoured him with their 'Gold merit award' for outstanding services to the game.

Former England goalkeeper **Peter Shilton** has made more first-class appearances (1,387) than any other footballer in British history. He played his 1,000th League game in Leyton Orient's 2-0 home win against Brighton on Dec 22, 1996 and made 9 appearances for Orient in his final season. He retired from international football after the 1990 World Cup in Italy with 125 caps, then a world record. Shilton kept a record 60 clean sheets for England.

Shilton's career spanned 32 seasons, 20 of them on the International stage. He made his League debut for Leicester in May 1966, two months before England won the World Cup.

His 1,387 first-class appearances comprise a record 1,005 in the Football League, 125 Internationals, 102 League Cup, 86 FA Cup, 13 for England U-23s, 4 for the Football League and 52 other matches (European Cup, UEFA Cup, World Club Championship, Charity Shield, European Super Cup, Full Members' Cup, Play-offs, Screen Sports Super Cup, Anglo-Italian Cup, Texaco Cup, Simod Cup, Zenith Data Systems Cup and Autoglass Trophy).

Shilton appeared 57 times at Wembley, 52 for England, 2 League Cup Finals, 1 FA Cup Final, 1 Charity Shield match, and 1 for the Football League. He passed a century of League appearances with each of his first five clubs: Leicester (286), Stoke (110), Nottm Forest (202), Southampton (188) and Derby (175) and subsequently played for Plymouth, Bolton and Leyton Orient.

He was awarded the MBE and OBE for services to football. At the Football League Awards ceremony in March 2013, he received the League's Contribution award.

Six other British footballers have made more than 1,000 first-class appearances:

Ray Clemence, formerly for Tottenham, Liverpool and England, retired through injury in season 1987–88 after a goalkeeping career of 1,119 matches starting in 1965–66.

Clemence played 50 times for his first club, Scunthorpe; 665 for Liverpool; 337 for Tottenham; his 67 representative games included 61 England caps.

A third great British goalkeeper, **Pat Jennings**, ended his career (1963–86) with a total of 1,098 first-class matches for Watford, Tottenham, Arsenal and N Ireland. They were made up of 757 in the Football League, 119 full Internationals, 84 FA Cup appearances, 72 League/ Milk Cup, 55 European club matches, 2 Charity Shield, 3 Other Internationals, 1 Under-23 cap, 2 Texaco Cup, 2 Anglo-Italian Cup and 1 Super Cup. Jennings played his 119th and final international on his 41st birthday, Jun 12, 1986, against Brazil in Guadalajara in the Mexico World Cup.

Yet another outstanding 'keeper, **David Seaman**, passed the 1,000 appearances milestone for clubs and country in season 2002–03, reaching 1,004 when aged 39, he captained Arsenal to FA Cup triumph against Southampton.

With Arsenal, Seaman won 3 Championship medals, the FA Cup 4 times, the Double twice, the League Cup and Cup-Winners' Cup once each. After 13 seasons at Highbury, he joined Manchester City (Jun 2003) on a free transfer. He played 26 matches for City before a shoulder injury forced his retirement in Jan 2004, aged 40.

Seaman's 22-season career composed 1,046 first-class matches: 955 club apps (Peterborough 106, Birmingham 84, QPR 175, Arsenal 564, Manchester City 26); 75 senior caps for England, 6 'B' caps and 10 at U-21 level.

Defender **Graeme Armstrong**, 42-year-old commercial manager for an Edinburgh whisky company and part-time assistant-manager and captain of Scottish Third Division club Stenhousemuir, made the 1000th first team appearance of his career in the Scottish Cup 3rd Round against Rangers at Ibrox on Jan 23, 1999. He was presented with the Man of the Match award before kick-off.

Against East Stirling on Boxing Day, he had played his 864th League game, breaking the British record for an outfield player set by another Scot, Tommy Hutchison, with Alloa, Blackpool, Coventry, Manchester City, Burnley and Swansea City.

Armstrong's 24-year career, spent in the lower divisions of the Scottish League, began as a 1-match trialist with Meadowbank Thistle in 1975 and continued via Stirling Albion, Berwick Rangers, Meadowbank and, from 1992, Stenhousemuir.

Tony Ford became the first English outfield player to reach 1000 senior appearances in Rochdale's 1-0 win at Carlisle (Auto Windscreens Shield) on Mar 7, 2000. Grimsby-born, he began his 26-season midfield career with Grimsby and played for 7 other League clubs: Sunderland (loan), Stoke, WBA, Bradford City (loan), Scunthorpe, Mansfield and Rochdale. He retired, aged 42, in 2001 with a career record of 1072 appearances (121 goals) and his total of 931 League games is exceeded only by Peter Shilton's 1005.

On Apr 16, 2011, **Graham Alexander** reached 1,000 appearances when he came on as a sub for Burnley at home to Swansea. Alexander, 40, ended a 22-year career with the equaliser for

Preston against Charlton (2-2, Lge 1) on Apr 28, 2012 – his 1,023rd appearance. He also played for Luton and Scunthorpe and was capped 40 times by Scotland.

GIGGS RECORD COLLECTION

Ryan Giggs (Manchester Utd) has collected the most individual honours in English football with a total of 34 prizes. They comprise: 13 Premier League titles, 4 FA Cups, 3 League Cups, 2 European Cups, 1 UEFA Super Cup, 1 Inter-Continental Cup, 1 World Club Cup, 9 Charity Shields/Community Shields. One-club man Giggs played 24 seasons for United, making a record 963 appearances. He won 64 Wales caps and on retiring as a player, aged 40, in May 2014, became the club's assistant manager. He ended a 29-year association with the club in June 2016.

KNIGHTS OF SOCCER

Players, managers and administrators who have been honoured for their services to football: **Charles Clegg** (1927), **Stanley Rous** (1949), **Stanley Matthews** (1965), **Alf Ramsey** (1967), **Matt Busby** (1968), **Walter Winterbottom** (1978) **Bert Millichip** (1991), **Bobby Charlton** (1994), **Tom Finney** (1998), **Geoff Hurst** (1998), **Alex Ferguson** (1999), **Bobby Robson** (2002), **Trevor Brooking** (2004), **Dave Richards** (2006), **Doug Ellis** (2011).

● On Nov 6, 2014, **Karren Brady**, vice-chairman of West Ham, was elevated to the Lords as Karren, Baroness Brady, OBE, of Knightsbridge, life peer

PENALTIES

The **penalty-kick** was introduced to the game, following a proposal to the Irish FA in 1890 by William McCrum, son of the High Sheriff for Co Omagh, and approved by the International Football Board on Jun 2, 1891.

First penalty scored in a first-class match in England was by John Heath, for Wolves v Accrington Stanley (5-0 in Div 1, Sep 14, 1891).

The greatest influence of the penalty has come since the 1970s, with the introduction of the shoot-out to settle deadlocked ties in various competitions.

Manchester Utd were the first club to win a competitive match in British football via a shoot-out (4-3 away to Hull, Watney Cup semi-final, Aug 5, 1970); in that penalty contest, George Best was the first player to score, Denis Law the first to miss.

The shoot-out was adopted by FIFA and UEFA the same year (1970).

In season 1991-92, penalty shoot-outs were introduced to decide FA Cup ties still level after one replay and extra time.

Wembley saw its first penalty contest in the 1974 Charity Shield. Since then many major matches across the world have been settled in this way, including:

1976	**European Championship Final (Belgrade):** Czechoslovakia beat West Germany 5-3 (after 2-2)
1980	**Cup-Winners' Cup Final (Brussels):** Valencia beat Arsenal 5-4 (after 0-0)
1984	**European Cup Final (Rome):** Liverpool beat Roma 4-2 (after 1-1)
1984	**UEFA Cup Final:** Tottenham (home) beat Anderlecht 4-3 (2-2 agg)
1986	**European Cup Final (Seville):** Steaua Bucharest beat Barcelona 2-0 (after 0-0).
1987	**Freight Rover Trophy Final (Wembley):** Mansfield beat Bristol City 5-4 (after 1-1)
1987	**Scottish League Cup Final (Hampden Park):** Rangers beat Aberdeen 5-3 (after 3-3)
1988	**European Cup Final (Stuttgart):** PSV Eindhoven beat Benfica 6-5 (after 0-0)
1988	**UEFA Cup Final:** Bayer Leverkusen (home) beat Espanyol 3-2 after 3-3 (0-3a, 3-0h)
1990	**Scottish Cup Final (Hampden Park):** Aberdeen beat Celtic 9-8 (after 0-0)
1991	**European Cup Final (Bari):** Red Star Belgrade beat Marseille 5-3 (after 0-0)
1991	**Div 4 Play-off Final (Wembley):** Torquay beat Blackpool 5-4 (after 2-2)
1992	**Div 4 Play-off Final (Wembley):** Blackpool beat Scunthorpe 4-3 (after 1-1)
1993	**Div 3 Play-off Final(Wembley):** York beat Crewe 5-3 (after 1-1)
1994	**Autoglass Trophy Final (Wembley):** Swansea City beat Huddersfield 3-1 (after 1-1)

1994	**World Cup Final (Los Angeles):** Brazil beat Italy 3-2 (after 0-0)
1994	**Scottish League Cup Final (Ibrox Park):** Raith beat Celtic 6-5 (after 2-2)
1995	**Copa America Final (Montevideo):** Uruguay beat Brazil 5-3 (after 1-1)
1996	**European Cup Final (Rome):** Juventus beat Ajax 4-2 (after 1-1)
1996	**European U-21 Champ Final (Barcelona):** Italy beat Spain 4-2 (after 1-1)
1997	**Auto Windscreens Shield Final (Wembley):** Carlisle beat Colchester 4-3 (after 0-0)
1997	**UEFA Cup Final:** FC Schalke beat Inter Milan 4-1 (after 1-1 agg)
1998	**Div 1 Play-off Final (Wembley):** Charlton beat Sunderland 7-6 (after 4-4)
1999	**Div 2 Play-off Final (Wembley):** Manchester City beat Gillingham 3-1 (after 2-2)
1999	**Women's World Cup Final (Pasedena):** USA beat China 5-4 (after 0-0)
2000	**African Nations Cup Final (Lagos):** Cameroon beat Nigeria 4-3 (after 0-0)
2000	**UEFA Cup Final (Copenhagen):** Galatasaray beat Arsenal 4-1 (after 0-0)
2000	**Olympic Final (Sydney):** Cameroon beat Spain 5-3 (after 2-2)
2001	**League Cup Final (Millennium Stadium):** Liverpool beat Birmingham 5-4 (after 1-1)
2001	**Champions League Final (Milan):** Bayern Munich beat Valencia 5-4 (after 1-1)
2002	**Euro U-21 Champ Final (Basle):** Czech Republic beat France 3-1 (after 0-0)
2002	**Div 1 Play-off Final (Millennium Stadium):** Birmingham beat Norwich 4-2 (after 1-1)
2003	**Champions League Final (Old Trafford):** AC Milan beat Juventus 3-2 (after 0-0)
2004	**Div 3 Play-off Final (Millennium Stadium):** Huddersfield beat Mansfield 4-1 (after 0-0)
2004	**Copa America Final (Lima):** Brazil beat Argentina 4-2 (after 2-2)
2005	**FA Cup Final (Millennium Stadium):** Arsenal beat Manchester Utd 5-4 (after 0-0)
2005	**Champions League Final (Istanbul):** Liverpool beat AC Milan 3-2 (after 3-3)
2006	**African Cup of Nations Final (Cairo):** Egypt beat Ivory Coast 4-2 (after 0-0)
2006	**FA Cup Final (Millennium Stadium):** Liverpool beat West Ham 3-1 (after 3-3)
2006	**Scottish Cup Final (Hampden Park):** Hearts beat Gretna 4-2 (after 1-1)
2006	**Lge 1 Play-off Final (Millennium Stadium):** Barnsley beat Swansea City 4-3 (after 2-2)
2006	**World Cup Final (Berlin):** Italy beat France 5-3 (after 1-1)
2007	**UEFA Cup Final (Hampden Park):** Sevilla beat Espanyol 3-1 (after 2-2)
2008	**Champions League Final (Moscow):** Manchester Utd beat Chelsea 6-5 (after 1-1)
2008	**Scottish League Cup Final (Hampden Park):** Rangers beat Dundee Utd 3-2 (after 2-2)
2009	**League Cup Final (Wembley):** Manchester Utd beat Tottenham 4-1 (after 0-0)
2011	**Women's World Cup Final (Frankfurt):** Japan beat USA 3-1 (after 2-2)
2012	**League Cup Final (Wembley):** Liverpool beat Cardiff 3-2 (after 2-2)
2012	**Champions League Final (Munich):** Chelsea beat Bayern Munich 4-3 (after 1-1)
2012	**Lge 1 Play-off Final (Wembley):** Huddersfield beat Sheffield Utd 8-7 (after 0-0)
2012	**Africa Cup of Nations Final (Gabon):** Zambia beat Ivory Coast 8-7 (after 0-0)
2013	**FA Trophy Final (Wembley):** Wrexham beat Grimsby 4-1 (after 1-1)
2013	**European Super Cup (Prague):** Bayern Munich beat Chelsea 5-4 (after 2-2)
2014	**Scottish League Cup Final (Celtic Park):** Aberdeen beat Inverness 4-2 (after 0-0)
2014	**Lge 1 Play-off Final (Wembley):** Rotherheam beat Leyton Orient 4-3 (after 2-2)
2014	**Europa Lge Final (Turin):** Sevilla beat Benfica 4-2 (after 0-0)
2015	**Africa Cup of Nations Final (Equ Guinea):** Ivory Coast beat Ghana 9-8 (after 0-0)
2015	**Conference Play-off Final (Wembley):** Bristol Rov beat Grimsby 5-3 (after 1-1)
2015	**Lge 2 Play-off Final (Wembley):** Southend beat Wycombe 7-6 (after 1-1)
2015	**FA Trophy Final (Wembley):** North Ferriby beat Wrexham 5-4 (after3-3)
2015	**Euro U-21 Champ Final (Prague):** Sweden beat Portugal 4-3 (after 0-0)
2015	**Copa America Final (Santiago):** Chile beat Argentina 4-1 (after 0-0)
2016	**League Cup Final (Wembley):** Manchester City beat Liverpool 3-1 (after 1-1)
2016	**Champions League Final (Milan):** Real Madrid beat Atletico Madrid 5-3 (after 1-1)
2016	**Olympic Men's Final (Rio de Janeiro):** Brazil beat Germany 5-4 (after 1-1)
2017	**Champ Play-off Final (Wembley):** Huddersfield beat Reading 4-3 (after 0-0)

In South America in 1992, in a 26-shot competition, **Newell's Old Boys** beat America 11-10 in the Copa Libertadores.

Longest-recorded penalty contest in first-class matches was in Argentina in 1988 – from 44 shots, **Argentinos Juniors** beat Racing Club 20-19. Genclerbirligi beat Galatasaray 17-16 in a Turkish Cup-tie in 1996. Only one penalty was missed.

Highest-scoring shoot-outs in international football: **North Korea** beat Hong Kong 11-10 (after 3-3 draw) in an Asian Cup match in 1975; and **Ivory Coast** beat Ghana 11-10 (after 0-0 draw) in African Nations Cup Final, 1992.

Most penalties needed to settle an adult game in Britain: **44** in Norfolk Primary Cup 4th round replay, Dec 2000. Aston Village side **Freethorpe** beat Foulsham 20-19 (5 kicks missed). All 22 players took 2 penalties each, watched by a crowd of 20. The sides had drawn 2-2, 4-4 in a tie of 51 goals.

Penalty that took 24 days: That was how long elapsed between the award and the taking of a penalty in an Argentine Second Division match between **Atalanta** and Defensores in 2003. A riot ended the original match with 5 minutes left. The game resumed behind closed doors with the penalty that caused the abandonment. Lucas Ferreiro scored it to give Atalanta a 1-0 win.

INTERNATIONAL PENALTIES, MISSED

Four penalties out of five were missed when **Colombia** beat Argentina 3-0 in a Copa America group tie in Paraguay in Jul 1999. Martin Palmermo missed three for Argentina and Colombia's Hamilton Ricard had one spot-kick saved.

In the European Championship semi-final against Italy in Amsterdam on Jun 29, 2000, **Holland** missed five penalties – two in normal time, three in the penalty contest which Italy won 3-1 (after 0-0). Dutch captain Frank de Boer missed twice from the spot.

ENGLAND'S SHOOT-OUT RECORD

England have been beaten in seven of nine penalty shoot outs in major tournaments:

1990	(World Cup semi-final, Turin) 3-4 v West Germany after 1-1.
1996	(Euro Champ quarter-final, Wembley) 4-2 v Spain after 0-0.
1996	(Euro Champ semi-final, Wembley) 5-6 v Germany after 1-1.
1998	(World Cup 2nd round., St Etienne) 3-4 v Argentina after 2-2.
2004	(Euro Champ quarter-final, Lisbon) 5-6 v Portugal after 2-2.
2006	(World Cup quarter-final, Gelsenkirchen) 1-3 v Portugal after 0-0.
2007	(Euro U-21 Champ semi-final, Heerenveen) 12-13 v Holland after 1-1.
2009	(Euro U-21 Champ semi-final, Gothenburg) 5-4 v Sweden after 3-3.
2012	(Euro Champ quarter-final, Kiev) 2-4 v Italy after 0-0.
2017	(Euro-21 Champ semi-final, Tychy) 3-4 v Germany after 2-2.

FA CUP SHOOT-OUTS

First penalty contest in the FA Cup took place in 1972. In the days of the play-off for third place, the match was delayed until the eve of the following season when losing semi-finalists Birmingham and Stoke met at Ol Andrew's on Aug 5. The score was 0-0 and Birmingham won 4-3 on penalties.

Highest-scoring: Preliminary round replay (Aug 30, 2005): Tunbridge Wells beat Littlehampton 16-15 after 40 spot-kicks (9 missed).

Competition proper: Scunthorpe beat Worcester 14-13 in 2nd round replay (Dec 17, 2014) after 1-1 (32 kicks).

Shoot-out abandoned: The FA Cup 1st round replay between Oxford City and Wycombe at Wycombe on Nov 9, 1999 was abandoned (1-1) after extra-time. As the penalty shoot-out was about to begin, a fire broke out under a stand. Wycombe won the second replay 1-0 at Oxford Utd's ground.

First FA Cup Final to be decided by shoot-out was in 2005 (May 21), when Arsenal beat Manchester Utd 5-4 on penalties at Cardiff's Millennium Stadium (0-0 after extra time). A year later (May 13) Liverpool beat West Ham 3-1 (3-3 after extra-time).

MARATHON SHOOT-OUT BETWEEN LEAGUE CLUBS

Highest recorded score in shoot-out between league clubs: Dagenham & Redbridge 14-13 against Leyton Orient (after 1-1) in Johnstone's Paint Trophy southern section on Sep 7, 2011

SHOOT-OUT RECORD WINNERS AND LOSERS

When **Bradford** beat Arsenal 3-2 on penalties in a League Cup fifth round tie, it was the club's ninth successive shoot-out victory in FA Cup, League Cup and Johnstone's Paint Trophy ties between Oct 2009 and Dec 2012.

Tottenham's 4-1 spot-kick failure against Basel in the last 16 of the Europa League was their seventh successive defeat in shoot-outs from Mar 1996 to Apr 2013 (FA Cup, League Cup, UEFA Cup, Europa League)

MISSED CUP FINAL PENALTIES

John Aldridge (Liverpool) became the first player to miss a penalty in an FA Cup Final at Wembley when Dave Beasant saved his shot in 1988 to help Wimbledon to a shock 1-0 win. Seven penalties before had been scored in the Final at Wembley.

Previously, **Charlie Wallace**, of Aston Villa, had failed from the spot in the 1913 Final against Sunderland at Crystal Palace, which his team won 1-0

Gary Lineker (Tottenham) had his penalty saved by Nottm Forest's Mark Crossley in the 1991 FA Cup Final.

For the first time, two spot-kicks were missed in an FA Cup Final. In 2010, Petr Cech saved from Portsmouth's **Kevin-Prince Boateng** while Chelsea's **Frank Lampard** put his kick wide.

Another miss at Wembley was by Arsenal's **Nigel Winterburn**, Luton's Andy Dibble saving his spot-kick in the 1988 Littlewoods Cup Final, when a goal would have put Arsenal 3-1 ahead. Instead, they lost 3-2.

Winterburn was the third player to fail with a League Cup Final penalty at Wembley, following **Ray Graydon** (Aston Villa) against Norwich in 1975 and **Clive Walker** (Sunderland), who shot wide in the 1985 Milk Cup Final, also against Norwich who won 1-0. Graydon had his penalty saved by Kevin Keelan, but scored from the rebound and won the cup for Aston Villa (1-0).

Derby's Martin Taylor saved a penalty from **Eligio Nicolini** in the Anglo-Italian Cup Final at Wembley on Mar 27, 1993, but Cremonese won 3-1.

LEAGUE PENALTIES RECORD

Most penalties in Football League match: Five – 4 to Crystal Palace (3 missed), 1 to Brighton (scored) in Div 2 match at Selhurst Park on Mar 27 (Easter Monday), 1989. Crystal Palace won 2-1. Three of the penalties were awarded in a 5-minute spell. The match also produced 5 bookings and a sending-off. Other teams missing 3 penalties in a match: Burnley v Grimsby (Div 2), Feb 13, 1909; Manchester City v Newcastle (Div 1), Jan 17, 1912.

HOTTEST MODERN SPOT-SHOTS

Matthew Le Tissier ended his career in season 2001–02 with the distinction of having netted 48 out of 49 first-team penalties for Southampton. He scored the last 27 after his only miss when Nottm Forest keeper Mark Crossley saved in a Premier League match at The Dell on Mar 24, 1993.

Graham Alexander scored 78 out of 84 penalties in a 22-year career (Scunthorpe, Luton, Preston twice and Burnley) which ended in 2012.

SPOT-KICK HAT-TRICKS

Right-back **Joe Willetts** scored three penalties when Hartlepool beat Darlington 6-1 (Div 3N) on Good Friday 1951.

Danish international **Jan Molby's** only hat-trick in English football, for Liverpool in a 3-1 win at home to Coventry (Littlewoods Cup, 4th round replay, Nov 26, 1986) comprised three goals from the penalty spot.

It was the first such hat-trick in a major match for two years – since **Andy Blair** scored three penalties for Sheffield Wed against Luton (Milk Cup 4th round, Nov 20 1984).

Portsmouth's **Kevin Dillon** scored a penalty hat-trick in the Full Members' Cup (2nd round) at home to Millwall (3-2) on Nov 4, 1986.

Alan Slough scored a hat-trick of penalties in an away game, but was on the losing side, when Peterborough were beaten 4-3 at Chester (Div 3, Apr 29, 1978).

Penalty hat-tricks in **international football**: Dimitris Saravakos (in 9 mins) for Greece v Egypt in 1990. He scored 5 goals in match. Henrik Larsson, among his 4 goals in Sweden's 6-0 home win v Moldova in World Cup qualifying match, Jun 6, 2001.

MOST PENALTY GOALS (LEAGUE) IN SEASON

13 out of 13 by **Francis Lee** for Manchester City (Div 1) in 1971–72. His goal total for the season was 33. In season 1988–89, **Graham Roberts** scored 12 League penalties for Second Division Champions Chelsea. In season 2004–05, **Andrew Johnson** scored 11 Premiership penalties for Crystal Palace, who were relegated.

PENALTY-SAVE SEQUENCES

Ipswich goalkeeper **Paul Cooper** saved eight of the ten penalties he faced in 1979–80. **Roy Brown** (Notts Co) saved six in a row in season 1972–73.

Andy Lomas, goalkeeper for Chesham (Diadora League) claimed a record eighth **consecutive** penalty saves – three at the end of season 1991–92 and five in 1992–93.

Mark Bosnich (Aston Villa) saved five in two consecutive matches in 1993–94: three in Coca-Cola Cup semi-final penalty shoot-out v Tranmere (Feb 26), then two in Premiership at Tottenham (Mar 2).

MISSED PENALTIES SEQUENCE

Against Wolves in Div 2 on Sep 28, 1991, **Southend** missed their seventh successive penalty (five of them the previous season).

SCOTTISH RECORDS

(See also under 'Goals' & 'Discipline')

CELTIC SUPREME

In winning the Treble for the fourth time in 2016–17, **Celtic** rewrote the Scottish records. In the first season under **Brendan Rodgers**, previously Liverpool manager, they did not lose a domestic match and were the first to stay unbeaten in the league since Rangers in 1899. They set new records for points (106), goals (106), wins (34) and for a 30-point winning margin. Celtic have won the title 48 times, the SFA Cup on 37 occasions and the League Cup 16 times. Their 25 consecutive wins in season 2003–04 is a British record. The club's record in 1966–67 was the most successful by a British side in one season. They won the Treble and became the first to win the European Cup. Under Jock Stein, there were nine consecutive championships (1966–74).

RANGERS' MANY RECORDS

Rangers' record-breaking feats include:

League Champions: 54 times (once joint holders) – world record.

Winning every match in Scottish League (18 games, 1898–99 season).

Major hat-tricks: Rangers have completed the domestic treble (League Championship, League Cup and Scottish FA Cup) a record seven times (1948–49, 1963–64, 1975–76, 1977–78, 1992–93, 1998–99, 2002–03).

League & Cup double: 17 times.

Nine successive Championships (1989–97). Four men played in all nine sides: Richard Gough, Ally McCoist, Ian Ferguson and Ian Durrant.

115 major trophies: Championships 54, Scottish Cup 33, League Cup 27, Cup-Winners' Cup 1.

UNBEATEN SCOTTISH CHAMPIONS

Celtic and **Rangers** have each won the Scottish Championship with an unbeaten record: Celtic in 1897–98 (P18, W15, D3), Rangers in 1898–99 (P18, W18).

FORSTER'S SHUT-OUT RECORD

Celtic goalkeeper **Fraser Forster** set a record in Scottish top-flight football by not conceding a goal for 1,256 consecutive minutes in season 2013–14.

TRIO OF TOP CLUBS MISSING

Three of Scotland's leading clubs were missing from the 2014-15 Premiership season. With **Hearts** finishing bottom and **Rangers** still working their way back through the divisions after being demoted, they were joined in the second tier by **Hibernian**, who lost the play-off final on penalties to Hamilton.

SCOTTISH CUP HAT-TRICKS

Aberdeen's feat of winning the Scottish FA Cup in 1982–83–84 made them only the third club to achieve that particular hat-trick. **Queen's Park** did it twice (1874–75–76 and 1880–81–82), and **Rangers** have won the Scottish Cup three years in succession on three occasions: 1934–35–36, 1948–49–50 and 1962–63–64.

SCOTTISH CUP FINAL DISMISSALS

Five players have been sent off in the Scottish FA Cup Final: **Jock Buchanan** (Rangers v Kilmarnock, 1929); **Roy Aitken** (Celtic v Aberdeen, 1984); **Walter Kidd** (Hearts captain v Aberdeen, 1986); **Paul Hartley** (Hearts v Gretna, 2006); **Pa Kujabi** (Hibernian v Hearts, 2012).

HIGHEST-SCORING SHOOT-OUT

In Scottish football's highest-scoring penalty shoot-out, **Stirling Albion** beat junior club Hurlford 13-12 after 28 spot-kicks in a third round replay. The tie, on Nov 8, 2014, had ended 2-2 after extra-time.

RECORD SEQUENCES

Celtic hold Britain's League record of 62 matches undefeated, from Nov 13, 1915 to Apr 21, 1917, when Kilmarnock won 2-0 at Parkhead. They won 49, drew 13 (111 points) and scored 126 goals to 26.

Greenock Morton in 1963–64 accumulated 67 points out of 72 and scored 135 goals.

Queen's Park did not have a goal scored against them during the first seven seasons of their existence (1867–74, before the Scottish League was formed).

EARLIEST PROMOTIONS IN SCOTLAND

Dundee promoted from Div 2, Feb 1, 1947; **Greenock Morton** promoted from Div 2, Mar 2, 1964; **Gretna** promoted from Div 3, Mar 5, 2005; **Hearts** promoted from Championship, Mar 21, 2015.

WORST HOME SEQUENCE

After gaining promotion to Div 1 in 1992, **Cowdenbeath** went a record 38 consecutive home League matches without a win. They ended the sequence (drew 8, lost 30) when beating Arbroath 1-0 on Apr 2, 1994, watched by a crowd of 225.

ALLY'S RECORDS

Ally McCoist became the first player to complete 200 goals in the Premier Division when he scored Rangers' winner (2-1) at Falkirk on Dec 12, 1992. His first was against Celtic in Sep 1983, and he reached 100 against Dundee on Boxing Day 1987.

When McCoist scored twice at home to Hibernian (4-3) on Dec 7, 1996, he became Scotland's record post-war League marksman, beating Gordon Wallace's 264.

Originally with St Johnstone (1978–81), he spent two seasons with Sunderland (1981–83), then joined Rangers for £200,000 in Jun 1983.

In 15 seasons at Ibrox, he scored 355 goals for Rangers (250 League), and helped them win 10 Championships (9 in succession), 3 Scottish Cups and earned a record 9 League Cup winner's medals. He won the European Golden Boot in consecutive seasons (1991–92, 1992–93).

His 9 Premier League goals in three seasons for Kilmarnock gave him a career total of 281 Scottish League goals when he retired at the end of 2000–01. McCoist succeeded Walter Smith as manager of Rangers in May 2011.

SCOTLAND'S MOST SUCCESSFUL MANAGER

Bill Struth, 30 trophies for Rangers, 1920–54 (18 Championships, 10 Scottish Cups, 2 League Cups.

SMITH'S IBROX HONOURS

Walter Smith, who retired in May, 2011, won a total of 21 trophies in two spells as Rangers manager (10 League titles, 5 Scottish Cups, 6 League Cups).

RANGERS PUNISHED

In April 2012, **Rangers** (in administration) were fined £160,000 by the Scottish FA and given a 12-month transfer ban on charges relating to their finances. The ban was later overturned in court. The club had debts estimated at around £135m and on June 12, 2012 were forced into liquidation. A new company emerged, but Rangers were voted out of the Scottish Premier League and demoted to Division Three for the start of the 2012-13 season. They returned to the top division in 2016 via three promotions in four seasons.

FIVE IN A MATCH

Paul Sturrock set an individual scoring record for the Scottish Premier Division with 5 goals in Dundee Utd's 7-0 win at home to Morton on Nov 17, 1984. **Marco Negri** equalled the feat with all 5 when Rangers beat Dundee Utd 5-1 at Ibrox (Premier Division) on Aug 23, 1997, and **Kenny Miller** scored 5 in Rangers' 7-1 win at home to St Mirren on Nov 4, 2000. **Kris Boyd** scored all Kilmarnock's goals in a 5-2 SPL win at home to Dundee Utd on Sep 25, 2004. **Boyd** scored another 5 when Rangers beat Dundee Utd 7-1 on Dec 30, 2009. That took his total of SPL goals to a record 160. **Gary Hooper** netted all Celtic's goals in 5-0 SPL win against Hearts on May 13, 2012

NEGRI'S TEN-TIMER

Marco Negri scored in Rangers' first ten League matches (23 goals) in season 1997–98, a Premier Division record. The previous best was 8 by **Ally MacLeod** for Hibernian in 1978.

DOUBLE SCOTTISH FINAL

Rangers v Celtic drew **129,643** and **120,073** people to the Scottish Cup Final and replay at Hampden Park, Glasgow, in 1963. Receipts for the two matches totalled £50,500.

MOST SCOTTISH CHAMPIONSHIP MEDALS

13 by **Sandy Archibald** (Rangers, 1918–34). Post-war record: 10 by **Bobby Lennox** (Celtic, 1966–79).

Alan Morton won **nine** Scottish Championship medals with Rangers in 1921 23–24–25–27–28–29–30–31. **Ally McCoist** played in the Rangers side that won nine successive League titles (1989–97).

Between 1927 and 1939 **Bob McPhail** helped Rangers win nine Championships, finish second twice and third once. He scored 236 League goals but was never top scorer in a single season.

TOP SCOTTISH LEAGUE SCORERS IN SEASON

Raith Rovers (Div 2) 142 goals in 1937–38; **Morton** (Div 2) 135 goals in 1963–64; **Hearts** (Div 1) 132 goals in 1957–58; **Falkirk** (Div 2) 132 goals in 1935–36; **Gretna** (Div 3) 130 goals in 2004–05.

SCOTTISH CUP – NO DECISION

The **Scottish FA** withheld their Cup and medals in 1908–09 after Rangers and Celtic played two drawn games in the Final. Spectators rioted.

FEWEST LEAGUE WINS IN SEASON

In modern times: 1 win by **Ayr** (34 matches, Div 1, 1966–67); **Forfar** (38 matches, Div 2, 1973–74); **Clydebank** (36 matches, Div 1, 1999–2000).

Vale of Leven provided the only instance of a British team failing to win a single match in a league season (Div 1, 18 games, 1891–92).

HAMPDEN'S £63M REDEVELOPMENT

On completion of redevelopment costing £63m **Hampden Park**, home of Scottish football and the oldest first-class stadium in the world, was re-opened full scale for the Rangers-Celtic Cup Final on May 29, 1999.

Work on the 'new Hampden' (capacity 52,000) began in 1992. The North and East stands were restructured (£12m); a new South stand and improved West stand cost £51m. The Millennium Commission contributed £23m and the Lottery Sports Fund provided a grant of £3.75m.

FIRST FOR INVERNESS

Inverness Caledonian Thistle won the Scottish Cup for the Highlands for the first time when beating Falkirk 2-1 in the Final on May 30, 2015.

FASTEST GOALS IN SPL

10.4 sec by **Kris Boyd** for Kilmarnock in 3-2 win over Ross Co, Jan 28, 2017; 12.1 sec by **Kris Commons** for Celtic in 4-3 win over Aberdeen, Mar 16, 2013; 12.4 sec by **Anthony Stokes** for Hibernian in 4-1 home defeat by Rangers, Dec 27, 2009.

YOUNGEST SCORER IN SPL

Fraser Fyvie, aged 16 years and 306 days, for Aberdeen v Hearts (3-0) on Jan 27, 2010.

12 GOALS SHARED

There was a record aggregate score for the SPL on May 5, 2010, when **Motherwell** came from 6-2 down to draw 6-6 with **Hibernian**.

25-POINT DEDUCTION

Dundee were deducted 25 points by the Scottish Football League in November 2010 for going into administration for the second time. It left the club on minus 11 points, but they still managed to finish in mid-table in Division One.

GREAT SCOTS

In Feb 1988, the Scottish FA launched a national **Hall of Fame**, initially comprising the first 11 Scots to make 50 international appearances, to be joined by all future players to reach that number of caps. Each member receives a gold medal, invitation for life at all Scotland's home matches, and has his portrait hung at Scottish FA headquarters in Glasgow.

MORE CLUBS IN 2000

The **Scottish Premier League** increased from 10 to 12 clubs in season 2000–01. The **Scottish Football League** admitted two new clubs – Peterhead and Elgin City from the Highland League – to provide three divisions of 10 in 2000–01.

FIRST FOR EDINBURGH CITY

In May 2016, **Edinburgh City** became the first club to be promoted to Scottish League Two through the pyramid system with a 2-1 aggregate play-off aggregate win over East Stirling, whose 61 years in senior football came to an end.

NOTABLE SCOTTISH 'FIRSTS'

- The father of League football was a Scot, **William McGregor**, a draper in Birmingham. The 12-club Football League kicked off in Sep 1888, and McGregor was its first president.
- **Hibernian** were the first British club to play in the European Cup, by invitation. They reached the semi-final when it began in 1955–56.
- **Celtic** were Britain's first winners of the European Cup, in 1967.
- Scotland's First Division became the **Premier Division** in season 1975–76.
- Football's **first international** was staged at the West of Scotland cricket ground, Partick, on Nov 30, 1872: Scotland 0, England 0.
- Scotland introduced its **League Cup** in 1945–46, the first season after the war. It was another 15 years before the Football League Cup was launched.
- Scotland pioneered the use in British football of **two subs** per team in League and Cup matches.
- The world's **record football score** belongs to Scotland: Arbroath 36, Bon Accord 0 (Scottish Cup 1st rd) on Sep 12, 1885.
- The Scottish FA introduced the penalty **shoot-out** to their Cup Final in 1990.
- On Jan 22, 1994 all six matches in the **Scottish Premier Division** ended as draws.
- Scotland's new Premier League introduced a **3-week shut down** in Jan 1999 – first instance of British football adopting the winter break system that operates in a number of European countries. The SPL ended its New Year closure after 2003.
- **Rangers** made history at home to St Johnstone (Premier League, 0-0, Mar 4, 2000) when fielding a team entirely without Scottish players.
- **John Fleck**, aged 16 years, 274 days, became the youngest player in a Scottish FA Cup Final when he came on as a substitute for Rangers in their 3-2 win over Queen of the South at Hampden Park on May 24, 2008

SCOTTISH CUP SHOCK RESULTS

1885–86	(1)	Arbroath 36 Bon Accord 0
1921–22	(F)	Morton 1 Rangers 0
1937–38	(F)	East Fife 4 Kilmarnock 2 (replay, after 1-1)
1960–61	(F)	Dunfermline 2 Celtic 0 (replay, after 0-0)
1966–67	(1)	Berwick 1 Rangers 0
1979–80	(3)	Hamilton 2 Keith 3
1984–85	(1)	Stirling 20 Selkirk 0
1984–85	(3)	Inverness 3 Kilmarnock 0
1986–87	(3)	Rangers 0 Hamilton 1
1994–95	(4)	Stenhousemuir 2 Aberdeen 0
1998–99	(3)	Aberdeen 0 Livingston 1
1999–2000	(3)	Celtic 1 Inverness 3
2003–04	(5)	Inverness 1 Celtic 0
2005–06	(3)	Clyde 2 Celtic 1
2008–09	(6)	St Mirren 1 Celtic 0
2009–10	(SF)	Ross Co 2 Celtic 0
2013–14	(4)	Albion 1 Motherwell 0

Scottish League (Coca-Cola) Cup Final

| 1994–95 | Raith 2, Celtic 2 (Raith won 6-5 on pens) |

Europa League first qualifying round

| 2017-18 | Progres Niederkorn (Luxembourg) 2 Rangers 1 (on agg) |

WINTER BREAK

Scotland's top league employed a winter break, or winter shutdown, in 1998–99, 1999–2000, 2000–01, 2002–03 and 2012–13 (shorter break). It returned in season 2016–17.

MISCELLANEOUS

NATIONAL ASSOCIATIONS FORMED

FA	**1863**
FA of Wales	**1876**
Scottish FA	**1873**
Irish FA	**1904**
Federation of International Football Associations (FIFA)	**1904**

NATIONAL & INTERNATIONAL COMPETITIONS LAUNCHED

FA Cup	**1871**
Welsh Cup	**1877**
Scottish Cup	**1873**
Irish Cup	**1880**
Football League	**1888**
Premier League	**1992**
Scottish League	**1890**
Scottish Premier League	**1998**
Scottish League Cup	**1945**
Football League Cup	**1960**
Home International Championship	**1883–84**
World Cup	**1930**
European Championship	**1958**
European Cup	**1955**
Fairs/UEFA Cup	**1955**
Cup-Winners' Cup	**1960**
European Champions League	**1992**
Olympic Games Tournament, at Shepherd's Bush	**1908**

INNOVATIONS

Size of Ball: Fixed in **1872**.

Shinguards: Introduced and registered by Sam Weller Widdowson (Nottm Forest & England) in **1874**.

Referee's whistle: First used on Nottm Forest's ground in **1878**.

Professionalism: Legalised in England in the summer of **1885** as a result of agitation by Lancashire clubs.

Goal-nets: Invented and patented in **1890** by Mr JA Brodie of Liverpool. They were first used in the North v South match in Jan, **1891**.

Referees and linesmen: Replaced umpires and referees in Jan, **1891**.

Penalty-kick: Introduced at Irish FA's request in the season **1891–92**. The penalty law ordering the goalkeeper to remain on the goal-line came into force in Sep, **1905**, and the order to stand on his goal-line until the ball is kicked arrived in **1929–30**.

White ball: First came into official use in **1951**.

Floodlighting: First FA Cup-tie (replay), Kidderminster Harriers v Brierley Hill Alliance, **1955**. First Football League match: Portsmouth v Newcastle (Div 1), **1956**.

Heated pitch to beat frost tried by Everton at Goodison Park in **1958**.

First soccer closed-circuit TV: At Coventry ground in Oct **1965** (10,000 fans saw their team win at Cardiff, 120 miles away).

Substitutes (one per team) were first allowed in Football League matches at the start of season **1965–66**. Three substitutes (one a goalkeeper) allowed, two of which could be used, in Premier League matches, **1992–93**. The Football League introduced three substitutes for **1993–94**.

Three points for a win: Introduced by the Football League in **1981–82**, by FIFA in World Cup games in **1994**, and by the Scottish League in the same year.

Offside law amended, player 'level' no longer offside, and 'professional foul' made sending-off offence, **1990**.

Penalty shoot-outs introduced to decide FA Cup ties level after one replay and extra time, **1991–92**.

New back-pass rule: goalkeeper must not handle ball kicked to him by team-mate, **1992**.

Linesmen became 'referees' assistants', **1998**.

Goalkeepers not to hold ball longer than 6 seconds, **2000**.

Free-kicks advanced by ten yards against opponents failing to retreat, **2000**. This experimental rule in England was scrapped in 2005).

YOUNGEST AND OLDEST

Youngest Caps

Harry Wilson (Wales v Belgium, Oct 15, 2013)	**16 years 207 days**
Norman Whiteside (N Ireland v Yugoslavia, Jun 17, 1982)	**17 years 41 days**
Theo Walcott (England v Hungary, May 30, 2006)	**17 years 75 days**
Johnny Lambie (Scotland v Ireland, Mar 20, 1886)	**17 years 92 days**
Jimmy Holmes (Rep of Ireland v Austria, May 30, 1971)	**17 years 200 days**

Youngest England scorer: Wayne Rooney (17 years, 317 days) v Macedonia, Skopje, Sep 6, 2003

Youngest scorer on England debut: Marcus Rashford (18 years, 208 days) v Australia, Sunderland, May 27, 2016.

Youngest England hat-trick scorer: Theo Walcott (19 years, 178 days) v Croatia, Zagreb, Sep 10, 2008.

Youngest England captains: Bobby Moore (v Czech., Bratislava, May 29, 1963), 22 years, 47 days; Michael Owen (v Paraguay, Anfield, Apr 17, 2002), 22 years, 117 days.

Youngest England goalkeeper: Jack Butland (19 years, 158 days) v Italy, Bern, Aug 15, 2012

Youngest England players to reach 50 caps: Michael Owen (23 years, 6 months) v Slovakia at Middlesbrough, Jun 11, 2003, Bobby Moore (25 years, 7 months) v Wales at Wembley, Nov 16, 1966.

Youngest player in World Cup Final: Pele (Brazil) aged 17 years, 237 days v Sweden in Stockholm, Jun 12, 1958.

Youngest player to appear in World Cup Finals: Norman Whiteside (N Ireland v Yugoslavia in Spain Jun 17, 1982, age 17 years and 42 days.

Youngest First Division player: Derek Forster (Sunderland goalkeeper v Leicester, Aug 22, 1964) aged 15 years, 185 days.

Youngest First Division scorer: At 16 years and 57 days, schoolboy Jason Dozzell (substitute after 30 minutes for Ipswich at home to Coventry on Feb 4, 1984). Ipswich won 3-1 and Dozzell scored their third goal.

Youngest Premier League player: Matthew Briggs (Fulham sub at Middlesbrough, May 13, 2007) aged 16 years and 65 days.

Youngest Premier League scorer: James Vaughan (Everton, home to Crystal Palace, Apr 10, 2005), 16 years, 271 days.

Youngest Premier League captain: Lee Cattermole (Middlesbrough away to Fulham, May 7, 2006) aged 18 years, 47 days.

Youngest player sent off in Premier League: Wayne Rooney (Everton, away to Birmingham, Dec 26, 2002) aged 17 years, 59 days.

Youngest First Division hat-trick scorer: Alan Shearer, aged 17 years, 240 days, in Southampton's 4-2 home win v Arsenal (Apr 9, 1988) on his full debut. Previously, Jimmy Greaves (17 years, 309 days) with 4 goals for Chelsea at home to Portsmouth (7-4), Christmas Day, 1957.

Youngest to complete 100 Football League goals: Jimmy Greaves (20 years, 261 days) when he did so for Chelsea v Manchester City, Nov 19, 1960.

Youngest players in Football League: Reuben Noble-Lazarus (Barnsley 84th minute sub at Ipswich, Sep 30, 2008, Champ) aged 15 years, 45 days; Mason Bennett (Derby at Middlesbrough, Champ, Oct 22, 2011) aged 15 years, 99 days; Albert Geldard (Bradford PA v Millwall, Div 2, Sep 16, 1929) aged 15 years, 158 days; Ken Roberts (Wrexham v Bradford Park Avenue, Div 3 North, Sep 1, 1951) also 15 years, 158 days.

Youngest Football League scorer: Ronnie Dix (for Bristol Rov v Norwich, Div 3 South, Mar 3, 1928) aged 15 years, 180 days.

Youngest player in Scottish League: Goalkeeper Ronnie Simpson (Queens Park) aged 15 in 1946.

Youngest player in FA Cup: Andy Awford, Worcester City's England Schoolboy defender, aged 15 years, 88 days when he substituted in second half away to Boreham Wood (3rd qual round) on Oct 10, 1987.

Youngest player in FA Cup proper: Luke Freeman, Gillingham substitute striker (15 years, 233 days) away to Barnet in 1st round, Nov 10, 2007.

Youngest FA Cup scorer: Sean Cato (16 years, 25 days), second half sub in Barrow Town's 7-2 win away to Rothwell Town (prelim rd), Sep 3, 2011.

Youngest Wembley Cup Final captain: Barry Venison (Sunderland v Norwich, Milk Cup Final, Mar 24, 1985 – replacing suspended captain Shaun Elliott) – aged 20 years, 220 days.

Youngest FA Cup-winning captain: Bobby Moore (West Ham, 1964, v Preston), aged 23 years, 20 days.

Youngest FA Cup Final captain: David Nish aged 21 years and 212 days old when he captained Leicester against Manchester City at Wembley on Apr 26, 1969.

Youngest FA Cup Final player: Curtis Weston (Millwall sub last 3 mins v Manchester Utd, 2004) aged 17 years, 119 days.

Youngest FA Cup Final scorer: Norman Whiteside (Manchester Utd v Brighton, 1983 replay, Wembley), aged 18 years, 19 days.

Youngest FA Cup Final managers: Stan Cullis, Wolves (32) v Leicester, 1949; Steve Coppell, Crystal Palace (34) v Manchester Utd, 1990; Ruud Gullit, Chelsea (34) v Middlesbrough, 1997.

Youngest player in Football League Cup: Chris Coward (Stockport) sub v Sheffield Wed, 2nd Round, Aug 23, 2005, aged 16 years and 31 days.

Youngest Wembley scorer: Norman Whiteside (Manchester Utd v Liverpool, Milk Cup Final, Mar 26, 1983) aged 17 years, 324 days.

Youngest Wembley Cup Final goalkeeper: Chris Woods (18 years, 125 days) for Nottm Forest v Liverpool, League Cup Final on Mar 18, 1978.

Youngest Wembley FA Cup Final goalkeeper: Peter Shilton (19 years, 219 days) for Leicester v Manchester City, Apr 26, 1969.

Youngest senior international at Wembley: Salomon Olembe (sub for Cameroon v England, Nov 15, 1997), aged 16 years, 342 days.

Youngest winning manager at Wembley: Stan Cullis, aged 32 years, 187 days, as manager of Wolves, FA Cup winners on April 30 1949.

Youngest scorer in full international: Mohamed Kallon (Sierra Leone v Congo, African Nations Cup, Apr 22, 1995), reported as aged 15 years, 192 days.

Youngest English scorer in Champions League: Alex Oxlade-Chamberlain (Arsenal v Olympiacos, Sep 28, 2011) aged 18 years 1 month, 13 days

Youngest player sent off in World Cup Final series: Rigobert Song (Cameroon v Brazil, in USA, Jun 1994) aged 17 years, 358 days.

Youngest FA Cup Final referee: Kevin Howley, of Middlesbrough, aged 35 when in charge of Wolves v Blackburn, 1960.

Youngest player in England U-23 team: Duncan Edwards (v Italy, Bologna, Jan 20, 1954), aged 17 years, 112 days.

Youngest player in England U-21 team: Theo Walcott (v Moldova, Ipswich, Aug 15, 2006), aged 17 years, 152 days.

Youngest player in Scotland U-21 team: Christian Dailly (v Romania, Hampden Park, Sep 11, 1990), aged 16 years, 330 days.

Youngest player in senior football: Cameron Campbell Buchanan, Scottish-born outside right, aged 14 years, 57 days when he played for Wolves v WBA in War-time League match, Sep 26, 1942.

Youngest player in peace-time senior match: Eamon Collins (Blackpool v Kilmarnock, Anglo-Scottish Cup quarter-final 1st leg, Sep 9, 1980) aged 14 years, 323 days.

World's youngest player in top division match: Centre-forward Fernando Rafael Garcia, aged 13, played for 23 minutes for Peruvian club Juan Aurich in 3-1 win against Estudiantes on May 19, 2001.

Oldest player to appear in Football League: New Brighton manager Neil McBain (51 years, 120 days) as emergency goalkeeper away to Hartlepool (Div 3 North, Mar 15, 1947).

Other oldest post-war League players: Sir Stanley Matthews (Stoke, 1965, 50 years, 5 days); Peter Shilton (Leyton Orient 1997, 47 years, 126 days); Kevin Poole (Burton, 2010, 46 years, 291 days); Dave Beasant (Brighton 2003, 44 years, 46 days); Alf Wood (Coventry, 1958, 43 years, 199 days); Tommy Hutchison (Swansea City, 1991, 43 years, 172 days).

Oldest Football League debutant: Andy Cunningham, for Newcastle at Leicester (Div 1) on Feb 2, 1929, aged 38 years, 2 days.

Oldest post-war debut in English League: Defender David Donaldson (35 years, 7 months, 23 days) for Wimbledon on entry to Football League (Div 4) away to Halifax, Aug 20, 1977.

Oldest player to appear in First Division: Sir Stanley Matthews (Stoke v Fulham, Feb 6, 1965), aged 50 years, 5 days – on that his last League appearance, the only 50-year-old ever to play in the top division.

Oldest players in Premier League: Goalkeepers John Burridge (Manchester City v QPR, May 14, 1995), 43 years, 5 months, 11 days; Alec Chamberlain (Watford v Newcastle, May 13, 2007) 42 years, 11 months, 23 days; Steve Ogrizovic (Coventry v Sheffield Wed, May 6, 2000), 42 years, 7 months, 24 days; Brad Friedel (Tottenham v Newcastle, Nov 10, 2013) 42 years, 4 months, 22 days; Neville Southall (Bradford City v Leeds, Mar 12, 2000), 41 years, 5 months, 26 days. Outfield: Teddy Sheringham (West Ham v Manchester City, Dec 30, 2006), 40 years, 8 months, 28 days; Ryan Giggs (Manchester Utd v Hull, May 6, 2014), 40 years, 5 months, 7 days; Gordon Strachan (Coventry City v Derby, May 3, 1997), 40 years, 2 months, 24 days.

Oldest player for British professional club: John Ryan (owner-chairman of Conference club Doncaster, played as substitute for last minute in 4-2 win at Hereford on Apr 26, 2003), aged 52 years, 11 months, 3 weeks.

Oldest FA Cup Final player: Walter (Billy) Hampson (Newcastle v Aston Villa on Apr 26, 1924), aged 41 years, 257 days.

Oldest captain and goalkeeper in FA Cup Final: David James (Portsmouth v Chelsea, May 15, 2010) aged 39 years, 287 days.

Oldest FA Cup Final scorers: Bert Turner (Charlton v Derby, Apr 27, 1946) aged 36 years, 312 days. Scored for both sides. Teddy Sheringham (West Ham v Liverpool, May 13, 2006) aged 40 years, 41 days. Scored in penalty shoot-out.

Oldest FA Cup-winning team: Arsenal 1950 (average age 31 years, 2 months). Eight of the players were over 30, with the three oldest centre-half Leslie Compton 37, and skipper Joe Mercer and goalkeeper George Swindin, both 35.

Oldest World Cup-winning captain: Dino Zoff, Italy's goalkeeper v W Germany in 1982 Final, aged 40 years, 92 days.

Oldest player capped by England: Stanley Matthews (v Denmark, Copenhagen, May 15, 1957), aged 42 years, 103 days.

Oldest England scorer: Stanley Matthews (v N Ireland, Belfast, Oct 6, 1956), aged 41 years, 248 days.

Oldest British international player: Billy Meredith (Wales v England at Highbury, Mar 15, 1920), aged 45 years, 229 days.

Oldest 'new caps': Goalkeeper Alexander Morten, aged 41 years, 113 days when earning his only England Cap against Scotland on Mar 8, 1873; Arsenal centre-half Leslie Compton, at 38 years, 64 days when he made his England debut in 4-2 win against Wales at Sunderland on Nov 15, 1950. **For Scotland:** Goalkeeper Ronnie Simpson (Celtic) at 36 years, 186 days v England at Wembley, Apr 15, 1967.

Oldest scorer in Wembley Final: Chris Swailes, 45, for Morpeth in 4-1 win over Hereford (FA Vase), May 22, 2016.

Longest Football League career: This spanned 32 years and 10 months, by Stanley Matthews (Stoke, Blackpool, Stoke) from Mar 19, 1932 until Feb 6, 1965.

Shortest FA Cup-winning captain: 5ft 4in – Bobby Kerr (Sunderland v Leeds, 1973).

SHIRT NUMBERING

Numbering players in Football League matches was made compulsory in 1939. Players wore numbered shirts (1-22) in the FA Cup Final as an experiment in 1933 (Everton 1-11 v Manchester City 12-22).

Squad numbers for players were introduced by the Premier League at the start of season 1993–94. They were optional in the Football League until made compulsory in 1999–2000.

Names on shirts: For first time, players wore names as well as numbers on shirts in League Cup and FA Cup Finals, 1993.

SUBSTITUTES

In **1965**, the Football League, by 39 votes to 10, agreed that **one substitute** be allowed for an injured player at any time during a League match. First substitute used in Football League: Keith Peacock (Charlton), away to Bolton in Div 2, Aug 21, 1965.

Two substitutes per team were approved for the League (Littlewoods) Cup and FA Cup in season 1986–87 and two were permitted in the Football League for the first time in 1987–88.

Three substitutes (one a goalkeeper), two of which could be used, introduced by the Premier League for 1992–93. The Football League followed suit for 1993–94.

Three substitutes (one a goalkeeper) were allowed at the World Cup Finals for the first time at US '94.

Three substitutes (any position) introduced by Premier League and Football League in 1995–96.

Five named substitutes (three of which could be used) introduced in Premier League in 1996–97, in FA Cup in 1997–98, League Cup in 1998–99 and Football League in 1999–2000.

Seven named substitutes for Premier League, FA Cup and League Cup in 2008–09. Still only three to be used. Football League adopted this rule for 2009–10, reverted to five in 2011–12 and went back to seven for the 2012–13 season.

First substitute to score in FA Cup Final: Eddie Kelly (Arsenal v Liverpool, 1971). The **first recorded use** of a substitute was in 1889 (Wales v Scotland at Wrexham on Apr 15) when Sam Gillam arrived late – although he was a Wrexham player – and Allen Pugh (Rhostellyn) was allowed to keep goal until he turned up. The match ended 0-0.

When **Dickie Roose**, the Welsh goalkeeper, was injured against England at Wrexham, Mar 16, 1908, **Dai Davies** (Bolton) was allowed to take his place as substitute. Thus Wales used 12 players. England won 7-1.

END OF WAGE LIMIT

Freedom from the maximum wage system – in force since the formation of the Football League in 1888 – was secured by the Professional Footballers' Association in 1961. About this time Italian clubs renewed overtures for the transfer of British stars and Fulham's **Johnny Haynes** became the first British player to earn £100 a week.

THE BOSMAN RULING

On Dec 15, 1995 the **European Court of Justice** ruled that clubs had no right to transfer fees for out-of-contract players, and the outcome of the 'Bosman case' irrevocably changed football's player-club relationship. It began in 1990, when the contract of 26-year-old **Jean-Marc Bosman**, a midfield player with FC Liege, Belgium, expired. French club Dunkirk wanted him but were unwilling to pay the £500,000 transfer fee, so Bosman was compelled to remain with Liege. He responded with a lawsuit against his club and UEFA on the grounds of 'restriction of trade', and after five years at various court levels the European Court of Justice ruled not only in favour of Bosman but of all professional footballers.

The end of restrictive labour practices revolutionised the system. It led to a proliferation of transfers, rocketed the salaries of elite players who, backed by an increasing army of agents, found themselves in a vastly improved bargaining position as they moved from team to team, league to league, nation to nation. Removing the limit on the number of foreigners clubs could field brought an increasing ratio of such signings, not least in England and Scotland.

Bosman's one-man stand opened the way for footballers to become millionaires, but ended his own career. All he received for his legal conflict was 16 million Belgian francs (£312,000) in compensation, a testimonial of poor reward and martyrdom as the man who did most to change the face of football.

By 2011, he was living on Belgian state benefits, saying: 'I have made the world of football rich and shifted the power from clubs to players. Now I find myself with nothing.'

INTERNATIONAL SHOCK RESULTS

1950	USA 1 England 0 (World Cup).
1953	England 3 Hungary 6 (friendly).
1954	Hungary 7 England 1 (friendly)
1966	North Korea 1 Italy 0 (World Cup).
1982	Spain 0, Northern Ireland 1; Algeria 2, West Germany 1 (World Cup).
1990	Cameroon 1 Argentina 0; Scotland 0 Costa Rica 1; Sweden 1 Costa Rica 2 (World Cup).
1990	Faroe Islands 1 Austria 0 (European Champ qual).
1992	Denmark 2 Germany 0 (European Champ Final).
1993	USA 2 England 0 (US Cup tournament).
1993	Argentina 0 Colombia 5 (World Cup qual).
1993	France 2 Israel 3 (World Cup qual)
1994	Bulgaria 2 Germany 1 (World Cup).
1994	Moldova 3 Wales 2; Georgia 5 Wales 0 (European Champ qual).
1995	Belarus 1 Holland 0 (European Champ qual).
1996	Nigeria 4 Brazil 3 (Olympics).
1998	USA 1 Brazil 0 (Concacaf Gold Cup).
1998	Croatia 3 Germany 0 (World Cup).
2000	Scotland 0 Australia 2 (friendly).
2001	Australia 1 France 0; Australia 1, Brazil 0 (Confederations Cup).
2001	Honduras 2 Brazil 0 (Copa America).
2001	Germany 1 England 5 (World Cup qual).
2002	France 0 Senegal 1; South Korea 2 Italy 1 (World Cup).
2003:	England 1 Australia 3 (friendly)
2004:	Portugal 0 Greece 1 (European Champ Final).
2005:	Northern Ireland 1 England 0 (World Cup qual).
2014:	Holland 5 Spain 1 (World Cup).
2014:	Brazil 1 Germany 7 (World Cup).
2016	England 1 Iceland 2 (European Champ)

GREAT RECOVERIES – DOMESTIC FOOTBALL

On Dec 21, 1957, **Charlton** were losing 5-1 against Huddersfield (Div 2) at The Valley with only 28 minutes left, and from the 15th minute, had been reduced to ten men by injury, but they won 7-6, with left-winger Johnny Summers scoring five goals. **Huddersfield** (managed by Bill Shankly) remain the only team to score six times in a League match and lose. On Boxing Day, 1927 in Div 3 South, **Northampton** won 6-5 at home to Luton after being 1-5 down at half-time.

Season 2010-11 produced a Premier League record for **Newcastle**, who came from 4-0 down at home to Arsenal to draw 4-4. Previous instance of a team retrieving a four-goal deficit in the top division to draw was in 1984 when Newcastle trailed at QPR in a game which ended 5-5.

In the 2012-13 League Cup, **Arsenal** were 0-4 down in a fourth round tie at Reading, levelled at 4-4 and went on to win 7-5 in extra-time.

MATCHES OFF

Worst day for postponements: Feb 9, 1963, when 57 League fixtures in England and Scotland were frozen off. Only 7 Football League matches took place, and the entire Scottish programme was wiped out.

Other weather-hit days:
Jan 12, 1963 and Feb 2, 1963 – on both those Saturdays, only 4 out of 44 Football League matches were played.

Jan 1, 1979 – 43 out of 46 Football League fixtures postponed.

Jan 17, 1987 – 37 of 45 scheduled Football League fixtures postponed; only 2 Scottish matches survived.

Feb 8–9, 1991 – only 4 of the week-end's 44 Barclays League matches survived the freeze-up (4 of the postponements were on Friday night). In addition, 11 Scottish League matches were off.

Jan 27, 1996 – 44 Cup and League matches in England and Scotland were frozen off.

On the weekend of Jan 9, 10, 11, 2010, 46 League and Cup matches in England and Scotland were victims of the weather. On the weekend of Dec 18-21, 2010, 49 matches were frozen off in England and Scotland.

Fewest matches left on one day by postponements was during the Second World War – Feb 3, 1940 when, because of snow, ice and fog only one out of 56 regional league fixtures took place. It resulted Plymouth Argyle 10, Bristol City 3.

The Scottish Cup second round tie between Inverness Thistle and Falkirk in season 1978–79 was **postponed 29 times** because of snow and ice. First put off on Jan 6, it was eventually played on Feb 22. Falkirk won 4-0.

Pools Panel's busiest days: Jan 17, 1987 and Feb 9, 1991 – on both dates they gave their verdict on 48 postponed coupon matches.

FEWEST 'GAMES OFF'

Season 1947–48 was the best since the war for English League fixtures being played to schedule. Only six were postponed.

LONGEST SEASON

The latest that League football has been played in a season was **Jun 7, 1947** (six weeks after the FA Cup Final). The season was extended because of mass postponements caused by bad weather in mid-winter.

The latest the FA Cup competition has been completed was in season 2014–15 when Arsenal beat Aston Villa 4-0 in the Final on May 30, kick-off 5.30pm

Worst winter hold-up was in season 1962–63. The Big Freeze began on Boxing Day and lasted until Mar, with nearly 500 first-class matches postponed. The FA Cup 3rd round was the longest on record – it began with only three out of 32 ties playable on Jan 5 and ended 66 days and 261 postponements later on Mar 11. The Lincoln–Coventry tie was put off 15 times. The Pools Panel was launched that winter, on Jan 26, 1963.

HOTTEST DAYS

The Nationwide League kicked off season 2003–04 on Aug 9 with pitch temperatures of 102 degrees recorded at Luton v Rushden and Bradford v Norwich. On the following day, there was a pitch temperature of 100 degrees for the Community Shield match between Manchester Utd and Arsenal at Cardiff's Millennium Stadium. Wembley's pitch-side thermometer registered 107 degrees for the 2009 Chelsea–Everton FA Cup Final.

FOOTBALL LEAGUE NAME CHANGE

From the start of the 2016-17 season, the Football League was renamed the English Football League, as part of a corporate and competition rebranding.

FOOTBALL ASSOCIATION SECRETARIES/CHIEF EXECUTIVES

1863–66 Ebenezer Morley; 1866–68 Robert Willis; 1868–70 RG Graham; 1870–95 **Charles Alcock** (paid from 1887); 1895–1934 **Sir Frederick Wall**; 1934–62 **Sir Stanley Rous**; 1962–73 **Denis Follows**; 1973–89 **Ted Croker** (latterly chief executive); 1989–99 **Graham Kelly** (chief executive); 2000–02 **Adam Crozier** (chief executive); 2003–04 **Mark Palios** (chief executive); 2005–08: **Brian Barwick** (chief executive); 2009–10 **Ian Watmore** (chief executive); 2010-15 **Alex Horne** (chief executive); 2015 **Martin Glenn** (chief executive).

FOOTBALL'S SPONSORS

Football League: Canon 1983–86; Today Newspaper 1986–87; Barclays 1987–93; Endsleigh Insurance 1993–96; Nationwide Building Society 1996–2004; Coca-Cola 2004–10; npower

2010–14; Sky Bet from 2014.

League Cup: Milk Cup 1982–86; Littlewoods 1987–90; Rumbelows 1991–92; Coca-Cola 1993–98; Worthington 1998–2003; Carling 2003–12; Capital One 2012–16; Carabao from 2017.

Premier League: Carling 1993–2001; Barclaycard 2001–04; Barclays 2004–16.

FA Cup: Littlewoods 1994–98; AXA 1998–2002; E.ON 2006–11; Budweiser 2011–15; Emirates (title sponsor) from 2015.

NEW HOMES FOR CLUBS

Newly-constructed League grounds in England since the war: 1946 Hull (Boothferry Park); 1950 Port Vale (Vale Park); 1955 Southend (Roots Hall); 1988 Scunthorpe (Glanford Park); 1990 Walsall (Bescot Stadium); 1990 Wycombe (Adams Park); 1992 Chester (Deva Stadium); 1993 Millwall (New Den); 1994 Huddersfield (McAlpine Stadium); 1994 Northampton (Sixfields Stadium); 1995 Middlesbrough (Riverside Stadium); 1997 Bolton (Reebok Stadium); 1997 Derby (Pride Park); 1997 Stoke (Britannia Stadium); 1997 Sunderland (Stadium of Light); 1998 Reading (Madejski Stadium); 1999 Wigan (JJB Stadium); 2001 Southampton (St Mary's Stadium); 2001 Oxford Utd (Kassam Stadium); 2002 Leicester (Walkers Stadium); 2002 Hull (Kingston Communications Stadium); 2003 Manchester City (City of Manchester Stadium); 2003 Darlington (New Stadium); 2005 Coventry (Ricoh Arena); Swansea (Stadium of Swansea, Morfa); 2006 Arsenal (Emirates Stadium), 2007 Milton Keynes Dons (Stadium: MK); Shrewsbury (New Meadow); 2008 Colchester (Community Stadium); 2009 Cardiff City Stadium; 2010 Chesterfield (b2net Stadium), Morecambe (Globe Arena); 2011 Brighton (American Express Stadium), 2012 Rotherham (New York Stadium).

Bolton now Macron Stadium; Chesterfield now Proact Stadium; Derby now iPro Stadium; Huddersfield now John Smith's Stadium; Leicester now King Power Stadium; Manchester City now Etihad Stadium; Shrewsbury now Greenhous Meadow Stadium; Stoke now bet365 Stadium; Swansea now Liberty Stadium; Walsall now Banks's Stadium; Wigan now DW Stadium; 2016 West Ham (Olympic Stadium).

NATIONAL FOOTBALL CENTRE

The FA's new £120m centre at St George's Park, Burton upon Trent, was opened on Oct 9, 20012 by the Duke of Cambridge, president of the FA. The site covers 330 acres, has 12 full-size pitches (5 with undersoil heating and floodlighting). There are 5 gyms, a 90-seat lecture theatre, a hydrotherapy unit with swimming pool for the treatment of injuries and two hotels. It is the base for England teams, men and women, at all levels.

GROUND-SHARING

Manchester Utd played their home matches at **Manchester City's** Maine Road ground for 8 years after Old Trafford was bomb-damaged in Aug 1941. **Crystal Palace** and **Charlton** shared Selhurst Park (1985–91); **Bristol Rov** and **Bath City** (Twerton Park, Bath, 1986–96); **Partick Thistle** and **Clyde** (Firhill Park, Glasgow, 1986–91; in seasons 1990–01, 1991–92 **Chester** shared **Macclesfield's** ground (Moss Rose).

Crystal Palace and **Wimbledon** shared Selhurst Park, from season 1991–92, when **Charlton** (tenants) moved to rent Upton Park from **West Ham**, until 2003 when Wimbledon relocated to Milton Keynes. **Clyde** moved to Douglas Park, **Hamilton Academical's** home, in 1991–92. **Stirling Albion** shared **Stenhousemuir's** ground, Ochilview Park, in 1992–93. In 1993–94, **Clyde** shared **Partick's** home until moving to Cumbernauld. In 1994–95, **Celtic** shared Hampden Park with **Queen's Park** (while Celtic Park was redeveloped); **Hamilton** shared **Partick's** ground. **Airdrie** shared **Clyde's** Broadwood Stadium. **Bristol Rov** left **Bath City's** ground at the start of season 1996–97, sharing Bristol Rugby Club's Memorial Ground. **Clydebank** shared **Dumbarton's** Boghead Park from 1996–97 until renting Greenock Morton's Cappielow Park in season 1999–2000. **Brighton** shared **Gillingham's** ground in seasons 1997–98, 1998–99. **Fulham** shared **QPR's** home at Loftus Road in seasons 2002–03, 2003–04, returning to Craven Cottage in Aug 2004. **Coventry** played home fixtures at Northampton in season 2013–14, returning to their own ground, the Ricoh Arena, in Sept 2014.

Inverness Caledonian Thistle moved to share Aberdeen's Pittodrie Stadium in 2004–05 after being promoted to the SPL; Gretna's home matches on arrival in the SPL in 2007–08 were held at Motherwell and Livingston. Stenhousemuir (owners) share Ochilview with East Stirling (tenants).

ARTIFICIAL TURF

QPR were the first British club to install an artificial pitch, in 1981. They were followed by Luton in 1985, and Oldham and Preston in 1986. QPR reverted to grass in 1988, as did Luton and promoted Oldham in season 1991–92 (when artificial pitches were banned in Div 1). Preston were the last Football League club playing 'on plastic' in 1993–94, and their Deepdale ground was restored to grass for the start of 1994–95.

Stirling were the first Scottish club to play on plastic, in season 1987–88.

DOUBLE RUNNERS-UP

There have been nine instances of clubs finishing runner-up in both the League Championship and FA Cup in the same season: 1928 Huddersfield; 1932 Arsenal; 1939 Wolves; 1962 Burnley; 1965 and 1970 Leeds; 1986 Everton; 1995 Manchester Utd; 2001 Arsenal.

CORNER-KICK RECORDS

Not a single corner-kick was recorded when Newcastle drew 0-0 at home to Portsmouth (Div 1) on Dec 5, 1931.

The record for most corners in a match for one side is believed to be Sheffield Utd's 28 to West Ham's 1 in Div 2 at Bramall Lane on Oct 14, 1989. For all their pressure, Sheffield Utd lost 2-0.

Nottm Forest led Southampton 22-2 on corners (Premier League, Nov 28, 1992) but lost the match 1-2.

Tommy Higginson (Brentford, 1960s) once passed back to his own goalkeeper from a corner kick.

When Wigan won 4-0 at home to Cardiff (Div 2) on Feb 16, 2002, all four goals were headed in from corners taken by N Ireland international Peter Kennedy.

Steve Staunton (Rep of Ireland) is believed to be the only player to score direct from a corner in two Internationals.

In the 2012 Champions League Final, Bayern Munich forced 20 corners without scoring, while Chelsea scored from their only one.

SACKED AT HALF-TIME

Leyton Orient sacked Terry Howard on his 397th appearance for the club – at half-time in a Second Division home defeat against Blackpool (Feb 7, 1995) for 'an unacceptable performance'. He was fined two weeks' wages, given a free transfer and moved to Wycombe.

Bobby Gould resigned as Peterborough's head coach at half-time in their 1-0 defeat in the LDV Vans Trophy 1st round at Bristol City on Sep 29, 2004.

Harald Schumacher, former Germany goalkeeper, was sacked as Fortuna Koln coach when they were two down at half-time against Waldhof Mannheim (Dec 15, 1999). They lost 5-1.

MOST GAMES BY 'KEEPER FOR ONE CLUB

Alan Knight made 683 League appearances for Portsmouth, over 23 seasons (1978–2000), a record for a goalkeeper at one club. The previous holder was Peter Bonetti with 600 League games for Chelsea (20 seasons, 1960–79).

PLAYED TWO GAMES ON SAME DAY

Jack Kelsey played full-length matches for both club and country on Wednesday Nov 26, 1958. In the afternoon he kept goal for Wales in a 2-2 draw against England at Villa Park, and he then drove to Highbury to help Arsenal win 3-1 in a prestigious floodlit friendly against Juventus.

On the same day, winger Danny Clapton played for England (against Wales and Kelsey) and then in part of Arsenal's match against Juventus.

On Nov 11, 1987, Mark Hughes played for Wales against Czechoslovakia (European Championship) in Prague, then flew to Munich and went on as substitute that night in a winning Bayern Munich team, to whom he was on loan from Barcelona.

On Feb 16, 1993 goalkeeper **Scott Howie** played in Scotland's 3-0 U-21 win v Malta at Tannadice Park, Dundee (ko 1.30pm) and the same evening played in Clyde's 2-1 home win v Queen of South (Div 2).

Ryman League **Hornchurch**, faced by end-of-season fixture congestion, played **two matches** on the same night (May 1, 2001). They lost 2-1 at home to Ware and drew 2-2 at Clapton.

RECORD LOSS

Manchester City made a record loss of £194.9m in the 2010–11 financial year.

FIRST 'MATCH OF THE DAY'

BBC TV (recorded highlights): Liverpool 3, Arsenal 2 on Aug 22, 1964. **First complete match to be televised:** Arsenal 3, Everton 2 on Aug 29, 1936. **First League match televised in colour:** Liverpool 2, West Ham 0 on Nov 15, 1969.

'MATCH OF THE DAY' – BIGGEST SCORES

Football League: Tottenham 9, Bristol Rov 0 (Div 2, 1977–78). **Premier League:** Nottm Forest 1, Manchester Utd 8 (1998–99); Portsmouth 7 Reading 4 (2007–08).

FIRST COMMENTARY ON RADIO

Arsenal 1 Sheffield Utd 1 (Div 1) broadcast on BBC, Jan 22, 1927.

OLYMPIC FOOTBALL WINNERS

1908 Great Britain (in London); **1912** Great Britain (Stockholm); **1920** Belgium (Antwerp); **1924** Uruguay (Paris); **1928** Uruguay (Amsterdam); **1932** No soccer in Los Angeles Olympics; **1936** Italy (Berlin); **1948** Sweden (London); **1952** Hungary (Helsinki); **1956** USSR (Melbourne); **1960** Yugoslavia (Rome); **1964** Hungary (Tokyo); **1968** Hungary (Mexico City); **1972** Poland (Munich); **1976** E Germany (Montreal); **1980** Czechoslovakia (Moscow); **1984** France (Los Angeles); **1988** USSR (Seoul); **1992** Spain (Barcelona); **1996** Nigeria (Atlanta); **2000** Cameroon (Sydney); **2004** Argentina (Athens); **2008** Argentina (Beijing); **2012** Mexico (Wembley); **2016** Brazil (Rio de Janeiro).

Highest scorer in Final tournament: Ferenc Bene (Hungary) 12 goals, 1964.

Record crowd for Olympic Soccer Final: 108,800 (France v Brazil, Los Angeles 1984).

MOST AMATEUR CUP WINS

Bishop Auckland set the FA Amateur Cup record with 10 wins, and in 1957 became the only club to carry off the trophy in three successive seasons. The competition was discontinued after the Final on Apr 20, 1974. (Bishop's Stortford 4, Ilford 1, at Wembley).

FOOTBALL FOUNDATION

This was formed (May 2000) to replace the **Football Trust**, which had been in existence since 1975 as an initiative of the Pools companies to provide financial support at all levels, from schools football to safety and ground improvement work throughout the game.

SEVEN-FIGURE TESTIMONIALS

The first was **Sir Alex Ferguson**'s at Old Trafford on Oct 11, 1999, when a full-house of 54,842 saw a Rest of the World team beat Manchester Utd 4-2. United's manager pledged that a large percentage of the estimated £1m receipts would go to charity.

Estimated receipts of £1m and over came from testimonials for **Denis Irwin** (Manchester Utd) against Manchester City at Old Trafford on Aug 16, 2000 (45,158); **Tom Boyd** (Celtic) against Manchester Utd at Celtic Park on May 15, 2001 (57,000) and **Ryan Giggs** (Manchester Utd) against Celtic on Aug 1, 2001 (66,967).

Tony Adams' second testimonial (1-1 v Celtic on May 13, 2002) two nights after Arsenal completed the Double, was watched by 38,021 spectators at Highbury. Of £1m receipts, he donated £500,000 to Sporting Chance, the charity that helps sportsmen/women with drink, drug, gambling problems.

Sunderland and a Republic of Ireland XI drew 0-0 in front of 35,702 at the Stadium of Light on May 14, 2002. The beneficiary, **Niall Quinn**, donated his testimonial proceeds, estimated at £1m, to children's hospitals in Sunderland and Dublin, and to homeless children in Africa and Asia.

A record testimonial crowd of 69,591 for **Roy Keane** at Old Trafford on May 9, 2006 netted more than £2m for charities in Dublin, Cork and Manchester. Manchester Utd beat Celtic 1-0, with Keane playing for both teams.

Alan Shearer's testimonial on May 11, 2006, watched by a crowd of 52,275 at St James' Park, raised more than £1m. The club's record scorer, in his farewell match, came off the bench in stoppage time to score the penalty that gave Newcastle a 3-2 win over Celtic. Total proceeds from his testimonial events, £1.64m, were donated to 14 charities in the north-east.

Ole Gunnar Solskjaer, who retired after 12 years as a Manchester Utd player, had a crowd of 68,868, for his testimonial on Aug 2, 2008 (United 1 Espanyol 0). He donated the estimated receipts of £2m to charity, including the opening of a dozen schools In Africa.

Liverpool's **Jamie Carragher** had his testimonial against Everton (4-1) on Sep 4, 2010. It was watched by a crowd of 35,631 and raised an estimated £1m for his foundation, which supports community projects on Merseyside.

Gary Neville donated receipts of around £1m from his testimonial against Juventus (2-1) in front of 42,000 on May 24, 2011, to charities and building a Supporters' Centre near Old Trafford.

Paul Scholes had a crowd of 75,000 for his testimonial, Manchester United against New York Cosmos, on Aug 5, 2011. Receipts were £1.5m.

Steven Gerrard, Liverpool captain, donated £500,000 from his testimonial to the local Alder Hey Children's Hospital after a match against Olympiacos was watched by a crowd of 44,362 on Aug 3, 2013. Gerrard chose the Greek champions because he scored a special goal against them in the season Liverpool won the 2005 Champions League.

Wayne Rooney's match against Everton on Aug 3, 2016, raised £1.2m, which the Manchester United captain donated to local children's charities.

WHAT IT USED TO COST

Minimum admission to League football was one shilling in 1939 After the war, it was increased to 1s 3d in 1946; 1s 6d in 1951; 1s 9d in 1952; 2s in 1955; 2s 6d; in 1960; 4s in 1965; 5s in 1968; 6s in 1970; and 8s (40p) in 1972 After that, the fixed minimum charge was dropped.

Wembley's first Cup Final programme in 1923 cost three pence ($1\frac{1}{4}$p in today's money). The programme for the 'farewell' FA Cup Final in May, 2000 was priced £10.

FA Cup Final ticket prices in 2011 reached record levels – £115, £85, £65 and £45.

WHAT THEY USED TO EARN

In the 1930s, First Division players were on £8 a week (£6 in close season) plus bonuses of £2 win, £1 draw. The maximum wage went up to £12 when football resumed post-war in 1946 and had reached £20 by the time the limit was abolished in 1961.

EUROPEAN TROPHY WINNERS

European Cup/Champions League: 12 Real Madrid; 7 AC Milan; 5 Liverpool, Barcelona, Bayern Munich; 4 Ajax; 3 Inter Milan, Manchester Utd; 2 Benfica, Juventus, Nottm Forest, Porto; 1 Aston Villa, Borussia Dortmund, Celtic, Chelsea, Feyenoord, Hamburg, Marseille, PSV Eindhoven, Red Star Belgrade, Steaua Bucharest

Cup-Winners' Cup: 4 Barcelona; 2 Anderlecht, Chelsea, Dynamo Kiev, AC Milan; 1 Aberdeen, Ajax, Arsenal, Atletico Madrid, Bayern Munich, Borussia Dortmund, Dynamo Tbilisi, Everton, Fiorentina, Hamburg, Juventus, Lazio, Magdeburg, Manchester City, Manchester Utd, Mechelen, Paris St Germain, Parma, Rangers, Real Zaragoza, Sampdoria, Slovan Bratislava, Sporting Lisbon, Tottenham, Valencia, Werder Bremen, West Ham.

UEFA Cup: 3 Barcelona, Inter Milan, Juventus, Liverpool, Valencia; 2 Borussia Moenchengladbach, Feyenoord, Gothenburg, Leeds, Parma, Real Madrid, Sevilla, Tottenham; 1 Anderlecht,

Ajax, Arsenal, Bayer Leverkusen, Bayern Munich, CSKA Moscow, Dynamo Zagreb, Eintracht Frankfurt, Ferencvaros, Galatasaray, Ipswich, Napoli, Newcastle, Porto, PSV Eindhoven, Real Zaragoza, Roma, Schalke, Shakhtar Donetsk, Zenit St Petersburg.
Europa League: 3 Sevilla; **2** Atletico Madrid, **1** Chelsea, Manchester Utd, Porto.
● The Champions League was introduced into the European Cup in 1992–93 to counter the threat of a European Super League. The UEFA Cup became the Europa League, with a new format, in season 2009–10.

BRITAIN'S 35 TROPHIES IN EUROPE

Euro Cup/Champs Lge (13)	Cup-Winners' Cup (10)	Fairs/UEFA Cup/Europa Lge (12)
1967 Celtic	1963 Tottenham	1968 Leeds
1968 Manchester Utd	1965 West Ham	1969 Newcastle
1977 Liverpool	1970 Manchester City	1970 Arsenal
1978 Liverpool	1971 Chelsea	1971 Leeds
1979 Nottm Forest	1972 Rangers	1972 Tottenham
1980 Nottm Forest	1983 Aberdeen	1973 Liverpool
1981 Liverpool	1985 Everton	1976 Liverpool
1982 Aston Villa	1991 Manchester Utd	1981 Ipswich
1984 Liverpool	1994 Arsenal	1984 Tottenham
1999 Manchester Utd	1998 Chelsea	2001 Liverpool
2005 Liverpool		2013 Chelsea
2008 Manchester Utd		2017 Manchester Utd
2012 Chelsea		

ENGLAND'S EUROPEAN RECORD

Manchester Utd, Chelsea, Arsenal and Liverpool all reached the Champions League quarter-finals in season 2007–08 – the first time one country had provided four of the last eight. For the first time, England supplied both finalists in 2008 (Manchester Utd and Chelsea) and have provided three semi-finalists in 2007–08–09).

END OF CUP-WINNERS' CUP

The **European Cup-Winners' Cup**, inaugurated in 1960–61, terminated with the 1999 Final. The competition merged into a revamped **UEFA Cup**.
From its inception in 1955, the **European Cup** comprised only championship winning clubs until 1998–99, when selected runners-up were introduced. Further expansion came in 1999–2000 with the inclusion of clubs finishing third in certain leagues and fourth in 2002.

EUROPEAN CLUB COMPETITIONS – SCORING RECORDS

European Cup – record aggregate: 18-0 by Benfica v Dudelange (Lux) (8-0a, 10-0h), prelim rd, 1965–66.
Record single-match score: 11-0 by Dinamo Bucharest v Crusaders (rd 1, 2nd leg, 1973-74 (agg 12-0).
Champions League – record single-match score: Liverpool 8-0 v Besiktas, Group A qual (Nov 6, 2007).
Highest match aggregate: 19 = Bayern Munich 12 Sporting Lisbon 1 (5-0 away, 7-1 at home, 1st ko rd, 2008–09)
Cup-Winners' Cup – *record aggregate: 21-0 by Chelsea v Jeunesse Hautcharage (Lux) (8-0a, 13-0h), 1st rd, 1971–72.
Record single-match score: 16-1 by Sporting Lisbon v Apoel Nicosia, 2nd round, 1st leg, 1963–64 (aggregate was 18-1).
UEFA Cup (prev Fairs Cup) – *Record aggregate: 21-0 by Feyenoord v US Rumelange (Lux) (9-0h, 12-0a), 1st round, 1972–73.
Record single-match score: 14-0 by Ajax Amsterdam v Red Boys (Lux) 1st rd, 2nd leg, 1984–85 (aggregate also 14-0).
Record British score in Europe: 13-0 by **Chelsea** at home to Jeunesse Hautcharage (Lux) in Cup-

Winners' Cup 1st round, 2nd leg, 1971–72. Chelsea's overall 21-0 win in that tie is highest aggregate by British club in Europe.

Individual scoring record for European tie (over two legs): 10 goals (6 home, 4 away) by **Kiril Milanov** for Levski Spartak in 19-3 agg win Cup-Winners' Cup 1st round v Lahden Reipas, 1976–77. Next highest: **8 goals** by Jose Altafini for AC Milan v US Luxembourg (European Cup, prelim round, 1962–63, agg 14-0) and by **Peter Osgood** for Chelsea v Jeunesse Hautcharage (Cup-Winners' Cup, first round 1971–72, agg 21-0). Altafini and Osgood each scored 5 goals at home, 3 away.

Individual single-match scoring record in European competition: **6** by **Mascarenhas** for Sporting Lisbon in 16-1 Cup-Winner's Cup 2nd round, 1st leg win v Apoel, 1963–64; and by **Lothar Emmerich** for Borussia Dortmund in 8-0 CWC 1st round, 2nd leg win v Floriana 1965–66; and by **Kiril Milanov** for Levski Spartak in 12-2 CWC 1st round, 1st leg win v Lahden Reipas, 1976–77.

Most goals in single European campaign: 15 by **Jurgen Klinsmann** for Bayern Munich (UEFA Cup 1995–96).

Most goals by British player in European competition: 30 by **Peter Lorimer** (Leeds, in 9 campaigns).

Most individual goals in Champions League match: 5 by **Lionel Messi** (Barcelona) in 7-1 win at home to Bayer Leverkusen in round of 16 second leg, 2011–12.

Most European Cup goals by individual player: 49 by **Alfredo di Stefano** in 58 apps for Real Madrid (1955–64).

(*Joint record European aggregate)

First European treble: Clarence Seedorf became the first player to win the European Cup with three clubs: Ajax in 1995, Real Madrid in 1998 and AC Milan in 2003.

EUROPEAN FOOTBALL – BIG RECOVERIES

In the most astonishing Final in the history of the European Cup/Champions League, **Liverpool** became the first club to win it from a 3-0 deficit when they beat AC Milan 3-2 on penalties after a 3-3 draw in Istanbul on May 25, 2005. Liverpool's fifth triumph in the competition meant that they would keep the trophy.

The following season, **Middlesbrough** twice recovered from three-goal aggregate deficits in the **UEFA Cup**, beating Basel 4-3 in the quarter finals and Steaua Bucharest by the same scoreline in the semi-finals. In 2010, **Fulham** beat Juventus 5-4 after trailing 1-4 on aggregate in the second leg of their Europa League, Round of 16 match at Craven Cottage.

Two Scottish clubs have won a European tie from a 3-goal, first leg deficit: **Kilmarnock** 0-3, 5-1 v Eintracht Frankfurt (Fairs Cup 1st round, 1964–65); **Hibernian** 1-4, 5-0 v Napoli (Fairs Cup 2nd Round, 1967–68).

English clubs have three times gone out of the **UEFA Cup** after leading 3-0 from the first leg: 1975–76 (2nd Rd) **Ipswich** lost 3-4 on agg to Bruges; 1976–77 (quarter-final) **QPR** lost on penalties to AEK Athens after 3-3 agg; 1977–78 (3rd round) **Ipswich** lost on penalties to Barcelona after 3-3 agg.

On Oct 16, 2012, Sweden recovered from 0-4 down to draw 4-4 with Germany (World Cup qual) in Berlin.

● In the **1966 World Cup quarter-final** (Jul 23) at Goodison Park, North Korea led Portugal 3-0, but Eusebio scored 4 times to give **Portugal** a 5-3 win.

RONALDO'S EURO CENTURY

Cristiano Ronaldo became the first player to reach a century of goals in European club competitions when scoring twice for Real Madrid away to Bayern Munich on Apr 12, 2017. He reached the hundred in 143 matches (84 for Real, 16 for Manchester Utd) in the Champions League (97), UEFA Super Cup (2) and Champions League qualifying round (1).

RECORD COMEBACK

The greatest turnaround in Champions League history took place in a round of 16 match on Mar 8, 2017. **Barcelona**, 0-4 down to Paris St Germain, won the return leg 6-1, scoring three goals in the last seven minutes.

HEAVIEST ENGLISH-CLUB DEFEATS IN EUROPE

(Single-leg scores)

Champions League: Porto 5 Leicester 0 (group, Dec 6, 2016)

European Cup: Artmedia Bratislava 5, **Celtic** 0 (2nd qual round), Jul 2005 (agg 5-4); Ajax 5, **Liverpool** 1 (2nd round), Dec 1966 (agg 7-3); Real Madrid 5, Derby 1 (2nd round), Nov 1975 (agg 6-5).

Cup-Winners' Cup: Sporting Lisbon 5, **Manchester Utd** 0 (quarter-final), Mar 1964 (agg 6-4).

Fairs/UEFA Cup: Bayern Munich 6, **Coventry** 1 (2nd round), Oct 1970 (agg 7-3). **Combined London** team lost 6-0 (agg 8-2) in first Fairs Cup Final in 1958. Barcelona 5, **Chelsea** 0 in Fairs Cup semi-final play-off, 1966, in Barcelona (after 2-2 agg)

SHOCK ENGLISH CLUB DEFEATS

1968–69 (Eur Cup, 1st round): **Manchester City** beaten by Fenerbahce, 1-2 agg.

1971–72 (CWC, 2nd round): **Chelsea** beaten by Atvidaberg on away goals.

1993–94 (Eur Cup, 2nd round): **Manchester Utd** beaten by Galatasaray on away goals.

1994–95 (UEFA Cup, 1st round): **Blackburn** beaten by Trelleborgs, 2-3 agg.

2000–01 (UEFA Cup, 1st round): **Chelsea** beaten by St Gallen, Switz 1-2 agg.

PFA FAIR PLAY AWARD (Bobby Moore Trophy from 1993)

1988	Liverpool	2003	Crewe
1989	Liverpool	2004	Crewe
1990	Liverpool	2005	Crewe
1991	Nottm Forest	2006	Crewe
1992	Portsmouth	2007	Crewe
1993	Norwich	2008	Crewe
1994	Crewe	2009	Stockport
1995	Crewe	2010	Rochdale
1996	Crewe	2011	Rochdale
1997	Crewe	2012	Chesterfield
1998	Cambridge Utd	2013	Crewe
1999	Grimsby	2014	Exeter
2000	Crewe	2015	Exeter
2001	Hull	2016	Walsall
2002	Crewe		

RECORD MEDAL SALES

At Sotherby's in London on Nov 11, 2014, the FA Cup winner's medal which **Sir Stanley Matthews** earned with Blackpool in 1953 was sold for £220,000 – the most expensive medal in British sporting history. At the same auction, **Ray Wilson's** 1966 World Cup winner's medal fetched £136,000, while **Jimmy Greaves**, who was left out of the winning England team, received £44,000 for the medal the FA belatedly awarded him in 2009

West Ham bought (Jun 2000) the late **Bobby Moore's** collection of medals and trophies for £1.8m at Christie's auction. It was put up for sale by his first wife Tina and included his World Cup-winner's medal.

A No. 6 duplicate red shirt made for England captain **Bobby Moore** for the 1966 World Cup Final fetched £44,000 at an auction at Wolves' ground in Sep, 1999. Moore kept the shirt he wore in that Final and gave the replica to England physio Harold Shepherdson.

Sir Geoff Hurst's 1966 World Cup-winning shirt fetched a record £91,750 at Christie's in Sep, 2000. His World Cup Final cap fetched £37,600 and his Man of the Match trophy £18,800. Proceeds totalling £274,410 from the 129 lots went to Hurst's three daughters and charities of his choice, including the Bobby Moore Imperial Cancer Research Fund.

In Aug, 2001, Sir Geoff sold his World Cup-winner's medal to his former club West Ham Utd (for their museum) at a reported £150,000.

'The **Billy Wright** Collection' – caps, medals and other memorabilia from his illustrious career – fetched over £100,000 at Christie's in Nov, 1996.

At the sale in Oct 1993, trophies, caps and medals earned by **Ray Kennedy**, former England, Arsenal and Liverpool player, fetched a then record total of £88,407. Kennedy, suffering from Parkinson's Disease, received £73,000 after commission. The PFA paid £31,080 for a total of 60 lots – including a record £16,000 for his 1977 European Cup winner's medal – to be exhibited at their Manchester museum. An anonymous English collector paid £17,000 for the medal and plaque commemorating Kennedy's part in the Arsenal Double in 1971.

Previous record for one player's medals, shirts etc collection: £30,000 (**Bill Foulkes**, Manchester Utd in 1992). The sale of **Dixie Dean**'s medals etc in 1991 realised £28,000.

In Mar, 2001, **Gordon Banks**' 1966 World Cup-winner's medal fetched a new record £124,750. TV's Nick Hancock, a Stoke fan, paid £23,500 for **Sir Stanley Matthews's** 1953 FA Cup-winner's medal. He also bought one of Matthews's England caps for £3,525 and paid £2,350 for a Stoke Div 2 Championship medal (1963).

Dave Mackay's 1961 League Championship and FA Cup winner's medals sold for £18,000 at Sotherby's. Tottenham bought them for their museum.

A selection of England World Cup-winning manager **Sir Alf Ramsey**'s memorabilia – England caps, championship medals with Ipswich etc. – fetched more than £80,000 at Christie's. They were offered for sale by his family, and his former clubs Tottenham and Ipswich were among the buyers.

Ray Wilson's 1966 England World Cup-winning shirt fetched £80,750. Also in Mar, 2002, the No. 10 shirt worn by **Pele** in Brazil's World Cup triumph in 1970 was sold for a record £157,750 at Christies. It went to an anonymous telephone bidder.

In Oct, 2003, **George Best**'s European Footballer of the Year (1968) trophy was sold to an anonymous British bidder for £167,250 at Bonham's. It was the then most expensive item of sporting memorabilia ever auctioned in Britain.

England captain **Bobby Moore**'s 1970 World Cup shirt, which he swapped with Pele after Brazil's 1-0 win in Mexico, was sold for £60,000 at Christie's in Mar, 2004.

Sep, 2004: England shirt worn by tearful **Paul Gascoigne** in 1990 World Cup semi-final v Germany sold at Christie's for £28,680. At same auction, shirt worn by Brazil's **Pele** in 1958 World Cup Final in Sweden sold for £70,505.

May, 2005: The **second FA Cup** (which was presented to winning teams from 1896 to 1909) was bought for £420,000 at Christie's by Birmingham chairman David Gold, a world record for an item of football memorabilia. It was presented to the National Football Museum, Preston. At the same auction, the World Cup-winner's medal earned by England's **Alan Ball** in 1966 was sold for £164,800.

Oct, 2005: At auction at Bonham's, the medals and other memorabilia of Hungary and Real Madrid legend **Ferenc Puskas** were sold for £85,000 to help pay for hospital treatment.

Nov, 2006: A ball used in the 2006 World Cup Final and signed by the winning **Italy** team was sold for £1.2m (a world record for football memorabilia) at a charity auction in Qatar. It was bought by the Qatar Sports Academy.

Feb, 2010: A pair of boots worn by **Sir Stanley Matthews** in the 1953 FA Cup Final was sold at Bonham's for £38,400.

Oct, 2010: Trophies and memorabilia belonging to **George Best** were sold at Bonham's for £193,440. His 1968 European Cup winner's medal fetched £156,000.

Oct–Nov 2010: **Nobby Stiles** sold his 1966 World Cup winner's medal at an Edinburgh auction for a record £188,200. His old club, Manchester Utd, also paid £48,300 for his 1968 European Cup medal to go to the club's museum at Old Trafford. In London, the shirt worn by Stiles in the 1966 World Cup Final went for £75,000. A total of 45 items netted £424,438. **George Cohen** and **Martin Peters** had previously sold their medals from 1966.

Oct 2011: **Terry Paine** (who did not play in the Final) sold his 1966 World Cup medal for £27,500 at auction.

Mar 2013: **Norman Hunter** (Leeds and England) sold his honours' collection on line for nearly £100,000

Nov 2013: A collection of **Nat Lofthouse's** career memorabilia was sold at auction for £100,000. Bolton Council paid £75,000 for items including his 1958 FA Cup winner's medal to go on show at the local museum.

LONGEST UNBEATEN CUP RUN

Liverpool established the longest unbeaten Cup sequence by a Football League club: 25 successive rounds in the League/Milk Cup between semi-final defeat by Nottm Forest (1-2 agg) in 1980 and defeat at Tottenham (0-1) in the third round on Oct 31, 1984. During this period Liverpool won the tournament in four successive seasons, a feat no other Football League club has achieved in any competition.

BIG HALF-TIME SCORES

Tottenham 10, Crewe 1 (FA Cup 4th round replay, Feb 3, 1960; result 13-2); Tranmere 8, Oldham 1 (Div 3N., Dec 26, 1935; result 13-4); **Chester City 8, York 0** (Div 3N., Feb 1, 1936; result 12-0; believed to be record half-time scores in League football).

Nine goals were scored in the first half – **Burnley 4, Watford 5** in Div 1 on Apr 5, 2003. Result: 4-7.

Stirling Albion led Selkirk 15-0 at half-time (result 20-0) in the Scottish Cup 1st round, Dec 8, 1984.

World record half-time score: **16-0** when **Australia** beat **American Samoa** 31-0 (another world record) in the World Cup Oceania qualifying group at Coff's Harbour, New South Wales, on Apr 11 2001.

* On Mar 4 1933 **Coventry** beat QPR (Div 3 South) 7-0, having led by that score at half-time. This repeated the half-time situation in Bristol City's 7 0 win over Grimsby on Dec 26, 1914.

TOP SECOND-HALF TEAM

Most goals scored by a team in one half of a League match is **11. Stockport** led Halifax 2-0 at half-time in Div 3 North on Jan 6 1934 and won 13-0.

FIVE NOT ENOUGH

Last team to score **5** in League match and lose: **Burton**, beaten 6-5 by Cheltenham (Lge 2, Mar 13, 2010).

LONG SERVICE WITH ONE CLUB

Bill Nicholson, OBE, was associated with Tottenham for 67 years – as a wing-half (1938–55), then the club's most successful manager (1958–74) with 8 major prizes, subsequently chief advisor and scout. He became club president, and an honorary freeman of the borough, had an executive suite named after him at the club, and the stretch of roadway from Tottenham High Road to the main gates has the nameplate Bill Nicholson Way. He died, aged 85, in Oct 2004.

Ted Bates, the Grand Old Man of Southampton with 66 years of unbroken service to the club, was awarded the Freedom of the City in Apr, 2001. He joined Saints as an inside-forward from Norwich in 1937, made 260 peace-time appearances for the club, became reserve-team trainer in 1953 and manager at The Dell for 18 years (1955–73), taking Southampton into the top division in 1966. He was subsequently chief executive, director and club president. He died in Oct 2003, aged 85.

Bob Paisley was associated with Liverpool for 57 years from 1939, when he joined them from Bishop Auckland, until he died in Feb 1996. He served as player, trainer, coach, assistant-manager, manager, director and vice-president. He was Liverpool's most successful manager, winning 13 major trophies for the club (1974–83).

Dario Gradi, MBE, stepped down after completing 24 seasons and more than 1,000 matches as manager of Crewe (appointed Jun 1983). Never a League player, he previously managed Wimbledon and Crystal Palace. At Crewe, his policy of finding and grooming young talent has earned the club more than £20m in transfer fees. He stayed with Crewe as technical director, and twice took charge of team affairs again following the departure of the managers who succeeded him, Steve Holland and Gudjon Thordarson.

Ronnie Moran, who joined Liverpool as a player 1952, retired from the Anfield coaching staff in season 1998–99.

Ernie Gregory served West Ham for 52 years as goalkeeper and coach. He joined them as boy of 14 from school in 1935, retired in May 1987.

Ryan Giggs played 24 seasons for Manchester Utd (1990-2014), then became assistant manager under Louis van Gaal.

Ted Sagar, Everton goalkeeper, 23 years at Goodison Park (1929-52, but only 16 League seasons because of war).

Alan Knight, goalkeeper, played 23 seasons (1977-2000) for his only club, Portsmouth.

Sam Bartram was recognised as one of the finest goalkeepers never to play for England, apart from unofficial wartime games. He was with Charlton from 1934-56

Jack Charlton, England World Cup winner, served Leeds from 1952-73.

Roy Sproson, defender, played 21 League seasons for his only club, Port Vale (1950-71).

John Terry had a 22-year association with Chelsea from 1994-2017.

TIGHT AT HOME

Fewest home goals conceded in League season (modern times): 4 by **Liverpool** (Div 1, 1978-9); 4 by **Manchester Utd** (Premier League, 1994-95) – both in 21 matches.

VARSITY MATCH

First played in 1873, this is the game's second oldest contest (after the FA Cup). Played 133, Oxford 52 wins, Cambridge 49, Draws 32. Goals: Oxford 211, Cambridge 207. Latest result: Oxford 3 Cambridge 2 (Mar 19, 2017) at Barnet.

TRANSFER WINDOW

This was introduced to Britain in Sep 2002 via FIFA regulations to bring uniformity across Europe (the rule previously applied in a number of other countries).

The transfer of contracted players is restricted to two periods: Jun 1-Aug 31 and Jan 1-31).

On appeal, Football League clubs continued to sign/sell players (excluding deals with Premiership clubs).

PROGRAMME PIONEERS

Chelsea pioneered football's magazine-style programme by introducing a 16-page issue for the First Division match against Portsmouth on Christnmas Day 1948. It cost sixpence (2.5p). A penny programme from the 1909 FA Cup Final fetched £23,500 at a London auction in May, 2012.

FOOTBALL POOLS

Littlewoods launched them in 1923 with capital of £100. Coupons (4,000 of them) were first issued outside Manchester United's ground, the original 35 investors staking a total of £4 7s 6d (pay-out £2 12s). Vernons joined Littlewoods as leading promoters. The Treble Chance, leading to bonanza dividends, was introduced in 1946 and the Pools Panel began in January 1963 to counter mass fixture postponements caused by the Big Freeze winter.

But business was hard hit by the launch of the National Lottery in 1994. Dividends slumped, the work-force was cut severely and in June 2000 the Liverpool-based Moores family sold Littlewoods Pools in a £161m deal. After 85 years, the name Littlewoods disappeared from Pools betting in August 2008. The New Football Pools was formed. Vernons and Zetters continued to operate in their own name under the ownership of Sportech. The record prize remains the £2,924,622 paid to a syndicate in Worsley, Manchester, in November 1994.

WORLD'S OLDEST FOOTBALL ANNUAL

Now in its 131st edition, this publication begawn as the 16-page Athletic News Football Supplement & Club Directory in 1887. From the long-established Athletic News, it became the Sunday Chronicle Annual in 1946, the Empire News in 1956, the News of the World & Empire News in 1961 and the News of the World Annual from 1965 until becoming the Nationwide Annual in 2008.

PREMIER LEAGUE CLUB DETAILS AND SQUADS 2017–18

(at time of going to press)

ARSENAL

Ground: Emirates Stadium, Highbury, London, N5 1BU
Telephone: 0207 619 5000. **Club nickname:** Gunners
Capacity: 60,432. **Colours:** Red and white. **Main sponsor:** Emirates
Record transfer fee: £46.5m to Lyon for Alexandre Lacazette, Jul 201
Record fee received: £35m from Barcelona for Cesc Fabregas, Aug 2011
Record attendance: Highbury: 73,295 v Sunderland (Div 1) Mar 9, 1935. Emirates Stadium: 60,161 v Manchester Utd (Prem Lge) Nov 3, 2007. Wembley: 73,707 v Lens (Champ Lge) Nov 25, 1998
League Championship: Winners 1930–31, 1932–33, 1933–34, 1934–35, 1937–38, 1947–48, 1952–53, 1970–71, 1988–89, 1990–91, 1997–98, 2001–02, 2003–04
FA Cup: Winners 1930, 1936, 1950, 1971, 1979, 1993, 1998, 2002, 2003, 2005, 2014, 2015, 2017
League Cup: Winners 1987, 1993
European competitions: Winners Fairs Cup 1969–70; Cup-Winners' Cup 1993–94
Finishing positions in Premier League: 1992–93 10th, 1993–94 4th, 1994–95 12th, 1995–96 5th, 1996–97 3rd, 1997–98 1st, 1998–99 2nd, 1999–2000 2nd, 2000–01 2nd, 2001–02 1st, 2002–03 2nd, 2003–04 1st, 2004–05 2nd, 2005–06 4th, 2006–07 4th, 2007–08 3rd, 2008–09 4th, 2009–10 3rd, 2010–11 4th, 2011–12 3rd, 2012–13 4th, 2013–14 4th, 2014–15 3rd, 2015–16 2nd, 2016–17 5th
Biggest win: 12-0 v Loughborough (Div 2) Mar 12, 1900
Biggest defeat: 0-8 v Loughborough (Div 2) Dec 12, 1896
Highest League scorer in a season: Ted Drake 42 (1934–35)
Most League goals in aggregate: Thierry Henry 176 (1999–2007) (2012)
Longest unbeaten League sequence: 49 matches (2003–04)
Longest sequence without a League win: 23 matches (1912–13)
Most capped player: Thierry Henry (France) 81

Name	Height ft in	Previous club	Birthplace	Birthdate
Goalkeepers				
Cech, Petr	6.5	Chelsea	Plzen, Cz	20.05.82
Martinez, Damian	6.4	Independiente	Mar del Plata, Arg	02.09.92
Ospina, David	6.0	Nice	Medellin, Col	31.08.88
Defenders				
Bellerin, Hector	5.10	Barcelona	Barcelona, Sp	19.03.95
Chambers, Calum	6.0	Southampton	Petersfield	20.01.95
Debuchy, Mathieu	5.10	Newcastle	Fretin, Fr	28.07.85
Gabriel Paulista	6.2	Villarreal	Sao Paulo, Br	26.11.90
Gibbs, Kieran	5.10	–	Lambeth	26.09.89
Holding, Rob	6.0	Bolton	Tameside	12.09.95
Jenkinson, Carl	6.1	Charlton	Harlow	08.02.92
Kolasinac, Sead	6.0	Schalke	Karlsruhe, Ger	20.06.93
Koscielny, Laurent	6.1	Lorient	Tulle, Fr	10.09.85
Mertesacker, Per	6.6	Werder Bremen	Hannover, Ger	29.09.84
Monreal, Nacho	5.10	Malaga	Pamplona, Sp	26.02.86
Mustafi, Shkodran	6.1	Valencia	Bad Hersfeld, Ger	17.04.92
Midfielders				
Cazorla, Santi	5.6	Malaga	Llanera, Sp	13.12.84
Coquelin, Francis	5.10	–	Laval, Fr	13.05.91

Elneny, Mohamed	5.11	Basle	El-Mahalla, Egy	11.07.92
Oxlade-Chamberlain, Alex	5.11	Southampton	Portsmouth	15.08.93
Ozil, Mesut	5.11	Real Madrid	Gelsenkirchen, Ger	15.10.88
Ramsey, Aaron	5.11	Cardiff	Caerphilly	26.12.90
Wilshere, Jack	5.8	–	Stevenage	01.01.92
Xhaka, Granit	6.1	Borussia M'gladbach	Basle, Swi	27.09.92
Forwards				
Akpom, Chuba	6.0	Southend	Canning Town	09.10.95
Campbell, Joel	5.10	Saprissa	San Jose, CRica	26.06.92
Giroud, Olivier	6.4	Montpellier	Chambery, Fr	30.09.86
Iwobi, Alex	5.11	–	Lagos, Nig	03.05.96
Lucas Perez	6.0	Deportivo La Coruna	La Coruna, Sp	10.09.88
Sanchez, Alexis	5.7	Barcelona	Tocopilla, Chil	19.12.88
Walcott, Theo	5.8	Southampton	Newbury	16.03.89
Welbeck, Danny	5.10	Manchester Utd	Manchester	26.11.90

BOURNEMOUTH

Ground: Vitality Stadium, Dean Court, Bournemouth BH7 7AF
Telephone: 0344 576 1910. **Club nickname**: Cherries
Capacity: 11,464. **Colours**: Red and black. **Main sponsor**: M88
Record transfer fee: £20m to Chelsea for Nathan Ake, Jun 2017
Record fee received: £3m from Norwich for Lewis Grabban, Jun 2014
Record attendance: 28,799 v Manchester Utd (FA Cup 6) Mar 2, 1957
FA Cup: Sixth round 1957
League Cup: Fifth round 2014
Finishing position in Premier League: 2015–16 16th, 2016–17 9th
Biggest win: 8-0 v Birmingham (Champ) Oct 15, 2014. Also: 11-0 v Margate (FA Cup 1) Nov20, 1971
Biggest defeat: 0-9 v Lincoln (Div 3) Dec 18, 1982
Highest League scorer in a season: Ted MacDougall 42 (1970–71)
Most League goals in aggregate: Ron Eyre 202 (1924–33)
Longest unbeaten League sequence: 18 (1982)
Longest sequence without a League win: 14 (1974)
Most capped player: Gerry Peyton (Republic of Ireland) 7

Goalkeepers				
Allsop, Ryan	6.3	Leyton Orient	Birmingham	17.06.92
Begovic, Asmir	6.5	Chelsea	Trebinje, Bos	20.06.87
Boruc, Artur	6.4	Southampton	Siedice, Pol	20.02.80
Federici, Adam	6.2	Reading	Nowra, Aus	31.01.85
Defenders				
Ake, Nathan	5.11	Chelsea	The Hague, Hol	18.02.95
Cargill, Baily	6.2	–	Winchester	05.07.95
Cook, Steve	6.1	Brighton	Hastings	19.04.91
Daniels, Charlie	5.10	Leyton Orient	Harlow	07.09.86
Francis, Simon	6.0	Charlton	Nottingham	16.02.85
Mings, Tyrone	6.3	Ipswich	Bath	13.03.93
Smith, Adam	5.11	Tottenham	Leystonstone	29.04.91
Smith, Brad	5.10	Liverpool	Penrith, Aus	09.04.94
Wiggins, Rhoys	5.9	Sheffield Wed	Hillingdon	04.11.87
Wilson, Marc	6.2	Stoke	Belfast	17.08.87
Midfielders				
Arter, Harry	5.9	Woking	Eltham	28.12.89
Cook, Lewis	5.9	Leeds	Leeds	28.03.97

Fraser, Ryan	5.4	Aberdeen	Aberdeen	24.02.94
Gosling, Dan	5.10	Newcastle	Brixham	02.02.90
Hyndman, Emerson	5.8	Fulham	Dallas, US	09.04.96
Ibe, Jordon	5.7	Liverpool	Bermondsey	08.12.95
Mahoney, Connor	5.9	Blackburn	Blackburn	12.02.97
Pugh, Marc	5.11	Hereford	Bacup	02.04.87
Stanislas, Junior	6.0	Burnley	Eltham	26.11.89
Surman, Andrew	5.11	Norwich	Johannesburg, SA	20.08.86
Forwards				
Afobe, Benik	6.0	Wolves	Waltham Forest	12.02.93
Defoe, Jermain	5.8	Sunderland	Beckton	07.10.82
Grabban, Lewis	6.0	Norwich	Croydon	12.01.88
Gradel, Max	5.10	St Etienne	Abidjan, Iv C	30.11.87
King, Josh	5.11	Blackburn	Oslo, Nor	15.01.92
Mousset, Lys	6.0	Le Havre	Montivilliers, Fr	08.12.96
Wilson, Callum	5.11	Coventry	Coventry	27.02.92

BRIGHTON AND HOVE ALBION

Ground: Amex Stadium, Village Way, Brighton BN1 9BL
Telephone: 01273 878288. **Club nickname:** Seagulls
Capacity: 30,750. **Colours:** Blue and white. **Main sponsor:** American Express
Record transfer fee: £2.5m to Peterborough for Craig Mackail-Smith, Jul 2011
Record fee received: £1.5m from Tottenham for Bobby Zamora, Jul 2003; from Celtic for Adam Virgo, Jul 2005; from Norwich for Elliott Bennett, Jun 2011
Record attendance: Goldstone Ground: 36,747 v Fulham (Div 2) Dec 27, 1958; Withdean Stadium: 8,729 v Manchester City (League Cup 2) Sep 24, 2008; Amex Stadium: 30,338 v Bristol City (Champ) Apr 29, 2017
League Championship: 13th 1981–92
FA Cup: Runners-up 1983
League Cup: Fifth round 1979
Biggest win: 10-1 v Wisbech (FA Cup 1) Nov 13, 1965
Biggest defeat: 0-9 v Middlesbrough (Div 2) Aug 23, 1958
Highest League scorer in a season: Peter Ward 32 (1976–77)
Most League goals in aggregate: Tommy Cook 114 (1922–29)
Longest unbeaten League sequence: 22 matches (2015)
Longest sequence without a League win: 15 matches (1972–73)
Most capped player: Gerry Ryan (Republic of Ireland) 17, Steve Penney (Northern Ireland) 17

Goalkeepers				
Maenpaa, Niki	6.3	Venlo	Espoo, Fin	23.01.85
Ryan, Mathew	6.1	Valencia	Plumpton, Aus	08.04.92
Defenders				
Bong, Gaetan	6.2	Wigan	Sakbayeme, Cam	25.04.88
Bruno	5.11	Valencia	El Masnou, Sp	01.10.80
Duffy, Shane	6.4	Blackburn	Derry	01.01.92
Dunk, Lewis	6.4	–	Brighton	1.11.91
Goldson, Conor	6.3	Shrewsbury	Wolverhampton	18.12.92
Hall, Ben	6.1	Motherwell	Enniskillen	16.01.97
Hunemeier, Uwe	6.2	Paderborn	Rietberg, Ger	09.01.86
Hunt, Robert	–	–	Dagenham	07.07.95
Rosenior, Liam	5.10	Hull	Wandsworth	09.07.84
Suttner, Markus	5.10	Ingolstadt	Hollabrunn, Aut	16.04.87
Midfielders				
Gross, Pascal	6.0	Ingolstadt	Mannheim, Ger	15.06.91

Hornby-Forbes, Tyler	5.11	Fleetwood	Preston	08.03.96
Ince, Rohan	6.3	Chelsea	Whitechapel	08.11.92
Kayal, Beram	5.10	Celtic	Jadeidi, Isr	02.05.88
Knockaert, Anthony	5.8	Standard Liege	Roubaix, Fr	20.11.91
LuaLua, Kazenga	5.11	Newcastle	Kinshasa, DR Cong	10.12.90
March, Solly	5.11	–	Eastbourne	20.07.94
Murphy, Jamie	5.10	Sheffield Utd	Glasgow	28.08.89
Norwood, Oliver	5.11	Reading	Burnley	12.04.91
Sidwell, Steve	5.10	Stoke	Wandsworth	14.12.82
Skalak, Jiri	5.9	Mlada Boleslav	Pardubice, Cz	12.03.92
Stephens, Dale	5.7	Charlton	Bolton	12.06.89
Towell, Richie	5.8	Dundalk	Dublin, Ire	17.07.91
Forwards				
Baldock, Sam	5.8	Bristol City	Bedford	15.03.89
Hemed, Tomer	6.0	Almeria Kiryat	Tivon, Isr	02.05.87
Murray, Glenn	6.1	Bournemouth	Maryport	25.09.83

BURNLEY

Ground: Turf Moor, Harry Potts Way, Burnley BB10 4BX
Telephone: 0871 221 1882. **Club nickname:** Clarets
Capacity: 22,546. **Colours:** Claret and blue. **Main sponsor:** Dafabet
Record transfer fee: £13m to Norwich for Robbie Brady, Jan 2017
Record fee received: £25m from Everton for Michael Keane, Jul 2017
Record attendance: 54,775 v Huddersfield (FA Cup 3) Feb 23, 1924
League Championship: Winners 1920–21, 1959–60
FA Cup: Winners 1914
League Cup: Semi-finals 1961, 1969, 1983, 2009
European competitions: European Cup quarter-finals 1960–61
Finishing position in Premier League: 2014–15 19th, 2016–17 16th
Biggest win: 9-0 v Darwen (Div 1) Jan 9, 1892, v Crystal Palace (FA Cup 2) Feb 10, 1909, v New Brighton (FA Cup 4) Jan 26, 1957, v Penrith (FA Cup 1) Nov 17, 1984
Biggest defeat: 0-10 v Aston Villa (Div 1) Aug 29, 1925, v Sheffield Utd (Div 1) Jan 19, 1929
Highest League scorer in a season: George Beel 35 (1927–28)
Highest League scorer in aggregate: George Beel 178 (1923–32)
Longest unbeaten League sequence: 30 matches (1920–21)
Longest sequence without a League win: 24 matches (1979)
Most capped player: Jimmy McIlroy (Northern Ireland) 51

Goalkeepers				
Heaton, Tom	6.1	Bristol City	Chester	15.04.86
Pope, Nick	6.3	Charlton	Cambridge	19.04.92
Defenders				
Darikwa, Tendayi	6.2	Chesterfield	Nottingham	13.12.91
Long, Kevin	6.2	Cork	Cork, Ire	18.08.90
Lowton, Matthew	5.11	Aston Villa	Chesterfield	09.06.89
Mee, Ben	5.11	Manchester City	Sale	23.09.89
Taylor, Charlie	5.9	Leeds	York	18.09.93
Ward, Stephen	5.11	Wolves	Dublin, Ire	20.08.85
Midfielders				
Arfield, Scott	5.10	Huddersfield	Livingston	01.11.88
Brady, Robbie	5.10	Norwich	Dublin, Ire	14.01.92
Cork, Jack	6.1	Swansea	Carshalton	25.06.89
Defour, Steven	5.9	Anderlecht	Mechelen, Bel	15.04.88
Gudmundsson, Johann Berg	6.1	Charlton	Reykjavik, Ice	27.10.90

Hendrick, Jeff	6.1	Derby	Dublin, Ire	31.01.92
Marney, Dean	5.11	Hull	Barking	31.01.84
O'Neill, Aiden	5.10	Brisbane	Brisbane, Aus	04.07.98
Tarkowski, James	6.1	Brentford	Manchester	19.11.92
Ulvestad, Fredrik	6.0	Aalesund	Aalesund, Nor	17.06.92
Westwood, Ashley	5.7	Aston Villa	Nantwich	01.04.90
Forwards				
Agyei, Dan	6.0	AFC Wimbledon	Kingston upon Thames	01.06.97
Barnes, Ashley	6.0	Brighton	Bath	31.10.89
Gray, Andre	5.10	Brentford	Wolverhampton	26.06.91
Long, Chris	5.7	Everton	Huyton	25.02.95
Vokes, Sam	5.11	Wolves	Lymington	21.10.89
Walters, Jon	6.0	Stoke	Birkenhead	20.09.83

CHELSEA

Ground: Stamford Bridge Stadium, London SW6 1HS
Telephone: 0871 984 1905. **Club nickname:** Blues
Capacity: 41,326. **Colours:** Blue. **Main sponsor:** Yokohama
Record transfer fee: £50m to Liverpool for Fernando Torres, Jan 2011
Record fee received: £52m from Shanghai Shenhua for Oscar, Jan 2017
Record attendance: 82,905 v Arsenal (Div 1) Oct 12, 1935
League Championship: Winners 1954–55, 2004–05, 2005–06, 2009–10, 2014–15, 2016–17
FA Cup: Winners 1970, 1997, 2000, 2007, 2009, 2010, 2012
League Cup: Winners 1965, 1998, 2005, 2007, 2015
European competitions: Winners Champions League 2011–12; Cup-Winners' Cup 1970–71, 1997–98; Europa League 2012–13; European Super Cup 1998
Finishing positions in Premier League: 1992–93 11th, 1993–94 14th, 1994–95 11th, 1995–96 11th, 1996–97 6th, 1997–98 4th, 1998–99 3rd, 1999–2000 5th, 2000–01 6th, 2001–02 6th, 2002–03 4th, 2003–04 2nd, 2004–05 1st, 2005–06 1st, 2006–07 2nd, 2007–08 2nd, 2008–09 3rd, 2009–10 1st, 2010–11 2nd, 2011–12 6th, 2012–13 3rd, 2013–14 3rd, 2014–15 1st, 2015–16 10th, 2016–17 1st
Biggest win: 8-0 v Aston Villa (Prem Lge) Dec 23, 2012. Also: 13-0 v Jeunesse Hautcharage, (Cup-Winners' Cup 1) Sep 29, 1971
Biggest defeat: 1-8 v Wolves (Div 1) Sep 26, 1953; 0-7 v Leeds (Div 1) Oct 7, 1967, v Nottm Forest (Div 1) Apr 20, 1991
Highest League scorer in a season: Jimmy Greaves 41 (1960–61)
Most League goals in aggregate: Bobby Tambling 164 (1958–70)
Longest unbeaten League sequence: 40 matches (2004–05)
Longest sequence without a League win: 21 matches (1987–88)
Most capped player: Frank Lampard (England) 104

Goalkeepers				
Caballero, Willy	6.1	Manchester City	Santa Elena, Arg	28.09.81
Courtois, Thibaut	6.6	Genk	Bree, Bel	11.05.92
Eduardo	6.2	Dinamo Zagreb	Mirandela, Port	19.09.82
Defenders				
Aina, Ola	5.9	–	Southwark	08.10.96
Alonso, Marcos	6.2	Fiorentina	Madrid, Sp	28.12.90
Azpilicueta, Cesar	5.10	Marseille	Pamplona, Sp	28.08.89
Cahill, Gary	6.2	Bolton	Sheffield	19.12.85
Christensen, Andreas	6.2	Brondby	Lillerod, Den	10.04.96
Hector, Michael	6.4	Reading	East Ham	19.07.92
Luiz, David	6.3	Paris SG	Diadema, Br	22.04.87
Rudiger, Antonio	6.3	Roma	Berlin, Ger	03.03.93
Zouma, Kurt	6.3	St Etienne	Lyon, Fr	27.10.94

Midfielders

Bakayoko, Tiemoue	6.1	Monaco	Paris, Fr	17.08.94
Fabregas, Cesc	5.11	Barcelona	Arenys de Mar,Sp	04.05.87
Hazard, Eden	5.8	Lille	La Louviere, Bel	07.01.91
Kante, N'Golo	5.7	Leicester	Paris, Fr	29.03.91
Musconda, Charly	5.8	Anderlecht	Brussels, Bel	15.10.96
Matic, Nemanja	6.4	Benfica	Sabac, Serb	01.08.88
Moses, Victor	5.10	Wigan	Lagos, Nig	12.12.90
Pedro	5.6	Barcelona	Santa Cruz, Ten	28.07.87
Willian	5.9	Anzhi Makhachkala	Ribeirao Pires, Br	09.08.88

Forwards

Batshuayi, Michy	6.0	Marseille	Brussels, Bel	02.10.93
Diego Costa	6.2	Atletico Madrid	Lagarto, Br	07.10.88
Remy, Loic	6.1	QPR	Rilleux, Fr	02.01.87

CRYSTAL PALACE

Ground: Selhurst Park, Whitehorse Lane, London SE25, 6PU
Telephone: 0208 768 6000. **Club nickname:** Eagles
Capacity: 26,309. **Colours:** Red and blue. **Main sponsor:** ManBetX
Record transfer fee: £27m to Liverpool for Christian Benteke, Aug 2016
Record fee received: £25m from Everton for Yannick Bolasie, Aug 2016
Record attendance: 51,482 v Burnley (Div 2), May 11, 1979
League Championship: 3rd 1990–91
FA Cup: Runners-up 1990, 2016
League Cup: Semi-finals 1993, 1995, 2001, 2012
Finishing positions in Premier League: 1992–93 20th, 1994–95 19th, 1997–98 20th, 2004–05 18th, 2013–14 11th, 2014–15 10th, 2015–16 15th, 2016–17 14th
Biggest win: 9-0 v Barrow (Div 4) Oct 10, 1959
Biggest defeat: 0-9 v Liverpool (Div 1) Sep 12, 1989. Also: 0-9 v Burnley (FA Cup 2 rep) Feb 10, 1909
Highest League scorer in a season: Peter Simpson 46 (1930–31)
Most League goals in aggregate: Peter Simpson 153 (1930–36)
Longest unbeaten League sequence: 18 matches (1969)
Longest sequence with a League win: 20 matches (1962)
Most capped player: Mile Jedinak (Australia) 37

Goalkeepers

Hennessey, Wayne	6.5	Wolves	Bangor, Wal	24.01.87
Speroni, Julian	6.1	Dundee	Buenos Aires, Arg	18.05.79

Defenders

Dann, Scott	6.2	Blackburn	Liverpool	14.02.87
Delaney, Damien	6.2	Ipswich	Cork, Ire	29.07.81
Kelly, Martin	6.3	Liverpool	Whiston	27.04.90
Schlupp, Jeffrey	5.8	Leicester	Hamburg, Ger	23.12.92
Souare, Pape	5.10	Lille	Mbao, Sen	06.06.90
Tomkins, James	6.3	West Ham	Basildon	29.03.89
Van Aanholt, Patrick	5.9	Sunderland	Hertogenbosch, Hol	29.08.90
Ward, Joel	6.2	Portsmouth	Portsmouth	29.10.89

Midfielders

Boateng, Hiram	5.7	–	Wandsworth	08.01.96
Cabaye, Yohan	5.9	Paris SG	Tourcoing, Fr	14.01.86
Kaikai, Sullay	6.0	–	Southwark	26.08.95
Lee Chung–Yong	5.11	Bolton	Seoul, S Kor	02.07.88
Loftus-Cheek, Ruben	6.3	Chelsea (loan)	Lewisham	23.01.96
McArthur, James	5.7	Wigan	Glasgow	07.10.87

Milivojevic, Luka	6.0	Olympiacos	Kragujevac, Serb	07.04.91
Mutch, Jordon	5.9	QPR	Birmingham	02.12.91
Puncheon, Jason	5.8	Southampton	Croydon	26.06.86
Sako, Bakary	5.11	Wolves	Ivry-sur-Seine, Fr	26.04.88
Townsend, Andros	6.0	Newcastle	Leytonstone	16.07.91
Williams, Jonathan	5.7	–	Pembury	09.10.93
Zaha, Wilfried	5.10	Manchester Utd	Abidjan, Iv C	10.11.92
Forwards				
Benteke, Christian	6.3	Liverpool	Kinshasa, DR Cong	03.12.90
Keshi Anderson	5.10	Barton	Luton	06.04.95
Ladapo, Freddie	6.0	Margate	Romford	01.02.93
Wickham, Connor	6.3	Sunderland	Colchester	31.03.93

EVERTON

Ground: Goodison Park, Liverpool L4 4EL
Telephone: 0151 556 1878. **Club nickname:** Toffees
Capacity: 40,569. **Colours:** Blue and white. **Main sponsor:** SportPesa
Record transfer fee: £30m to Sunderland for Jordan Pickford, Jun 2017
Record fee received: £75m from Manchester Utd for Romelu Lukaku, Jul 2017
Record attendance: 78,299 v Liverpool (Div 1) Sep 18, 1948
League Championship: Winners 1890–91, 1914–15, 1927–28, 1931–31, 1938–39,
1962–63, 1969–70, 1984–85, 1986–87
FA Cup: Winners 1906, 1933, 1966, 1984, 1995
League Cup: Runners-up 1977, 1984
European competitions: Winners Cup Winners' Cup 1984–85
Finishing positions in Premier League: 1992–93 13th, 1993–94 17th, 1994–95 15th,
1995–96 6th 1996–97 15th 1997–98 17th 1998–99 14th, 1999–2000 13th, 2000–01
16th, 2001–02 15th, 2002–03 7th, 2003–04 17th, 2004–05 4th, 2005–06 11th, 2006–07
6th, 2007–08 5th, 2008–09 5th, 2009–10 8th, 20010–11 7th, 2011–12 7th, 2012–13 6th,
2013–14 5th, 2014–15 11th, 2015–16 11th, 2016–17 8th
Biggest win: 9-1 v Manchester City (Div 1) Sep 3, 1906, v Plymouth (Div 2) Dec 27, 1930.
Also: 11-2 v Derby (FA Cup 1) Jan 18, 1890
Biggest defeat: 0-7 v Portsmouth (Div 1) Sep 10, 1949, v Arsenal (Prem Lge) May 11, 2005
Highest League scorer in a season: Ralph 'Dixie' Dean 60 (1927–28)
Most League goals in aggregate: Ralph 'Dixie' Dean 349 (1925–37)
Longest unbeaten League sequence: 20 matches (1978)
Longest sequence without a League win: 14 matches (1937)
Most capped player: Neville Southall (Wales) 92

Goalkeepers

Pickford, Jordan	6.1	Sunderland	Washington, Co Dur	07.03.94
Robles, Joel	6.5	Atletico Madrid	Getafe, Sp	17.06.90
Stekelenburg, Maarten	6.6	Fulham	Haarlem, Hol	22.09.82
Defenders				
Baines, Leighton	5.7	Wigan	Liverpool	11.12.84
Browning, Tyias	5.11	–	Liverpool	27.05.94
Coleman, Seamus	5.10	Sligo	Donegal, Ire	11.10.88
Funes Mori, Ramiro	6.1	River Plate	Mendoza, Arg	01.07.91
Holgate, Mason	5.11	Barnsley	Doncaster	22.10.96
Kenny, Jonjoe	5.10	–	Liverpool	15.03.97
Jagielka, Phil	5.11	Sheffield Utd	Manchester	17.08.82
Keane, Michael	6.3	Burnley	Stockport	11.01.93
Pennington, Matthew	6.1	–	Warrington	06.10.94
Williams, Ashley	6.0	Swansea	Wolverhampton	23.08.84

Midfielders

Barkley, Ross	6.2	–	Liverpool	05.12.93
Barry, Gareth	6.0	Manchester City	Hastings	23.02.81
Besic, Muhamed	5.10	Ferencvaros	Berlin, Ger	10.09.92
Bolasie, Yannick	6.2	Crystal Palace	Kinshasa, DR Cong	24.05.89
Davies, Tom	5.11	–	Liverpool	30.06.98
Gueye, Idrissa	5.9	Aston Villa	Dakar, Sen	26.09.89
Klaassen, Davy	5.11	Ajax	Hilversum, Hol	21.02.93
Lennon, Aaron	5.5	Tottenham	Leeds	16.04.87
McCarthy, James	5.11	Wigan	Glasgow	12.11.90
Mirallas, Kevin	6.0	Olympiacos	Liege, Bel	05.10.87
Schneiderlin, Morgan	5.11	Manchester Utd	Zellwiller, Fr	08.11.89
Williams, Joe	6.1	–	Liverpool	08.12.96

Forwards

Calvert-Lewin, Dominic	6.2	Sheffield Utd	Sheffield	16.03.97
Lookman, Ademola	5.9	Charlton	Wandsworth	20.10.97
Niasse, Oumar	6.1	Lokomotiv Moscow	Oukam, Sen	18.04.90
Rooney, Wayne	5.10	Manchester Utd	Liverpool	24.10.85
Sandro	5.10	Malaga	Las Palmas, Sp	09.07.95

HUDDERSFIELD TOWN

Ground: John Smith's Stadium, Huddersfield HD1 6PX
Telephone: 0870 444 4677. **Club nickname**: Terriers.
Capacity: 24,500. **Colours**: Blue and White. **Main sponsor**: Ope Sports
Record transfer fee: £11.4m to Montpellier for Steve Mounie, Jul 2017
Record fee received: £8m from Blackburn for Jordan Rhodes, Aug 2012
Record attendance: Leeds Road: 67,037 v Arsenal (FA Cup 6) Feb 27, 1932; John Smith's Stadium: 24,129 v Manchester City (FA Cup 5) Feb 18, 2017
League Championship: Winners 1923–24, 1924–25, 1925–26
FA Cup: Winners 1922
League Cup: Semi-finalists 1968
Biggest win: 10-1 v Blackpool (Div 1) Dec 13, 1930
Biggest defeat: 1-10 v Manchester City (Div 2) Nov 7, 1987
Highest League scorer in a season: Jordan Rhodes 36 (2011–12)
Most League goals in aggregate: George Brown (1921–29) 142, Jimmy Glazzard (1946–56) 142
Longest unbeaten League sequence: 43 matches (2011)
Longest sequence without a League win: 22 matches (1971–72)
Most capped player: Jimmy Nicholson (Northern Ireland) 31

Goalkeepers

Coleman, Joel	6.4	Oldham	Bolton	06.09.95
Lossl, Jonas	6.5	Mainz	Kolding, Den	01.02.89
Schofield, Ryan	6.3	–	Huddersfield	11.12.99

Defenders

Cranie, Martin	6.0	Barnsley	Yeovil	23.09.86
Hefele, Michael	6.3	Dynamo Dresden	Pfaffenhofen, Ger	01.09.90
Hudson, Mark	6.3	Cardiff	Guildford	30.03.82
Jorgensen, Mathias	6.3	FC Copenhagen	Copenhagen, Den	23.04.90
Lowe, Chris	5.8	Kaiserslautern	Plauen, Ger	16.04.89
Malone, Scott	6.2	Fulham	Rowley Regis	25.03.91
Schindler, Christopher	6.2	1860 Munich	Munich, Ger	29.04.90
Smith, Tommy	6.1	Manchester City	Warrington	14.04.92
Stankovic, Jon Gorenc	6.3	Borussia Dortmund	Ljubljana, Sloven	14.01.96
Holmes-Dennis, Tareiq	5.9	Charlton	Farnborough	31.10.95

Midfielders

Billing, Philip	6.4	–	Esbjerg, Den	11.06.96
Hogg, Jonathan	5.7	Watford	Middlesbrough	06.12.88
Ince, Tom	5.10	Derby	Stockport	30.01.92
Lolley, Joe	5.10	Kidderminster	Redditch	25.08.92
Mooy, Aaron	5.11	Manchester City	Sydney, Aus	15.09.90
Palmer, Kasey	5.10	Chelsea (loan)	London	09.11.96
Payne, Jack	5.6	Southend	Tower Hamlets	25.10.94
Scannell, Sean	5.9	Crystal Palace	Croydon	21.03.89
Whitehead, Dean	5.11	Middlesbrough	Abingdon	12.01.82
Williams, Danny	6.0	Reading	Karlsruhe, Ger	08.03.89

Forwards

Bunn, Harry	5.9	Manchester City	Oldham	21.11.92
Depoitre, Laurent	6.3	Porto	Tournai, Bel	07.12.88
Kachunga, Elias	5.10	Ingolstadt	Haan, Ger	22.04.92
Mounie, Steve	6.3	Montpellier	Parakin, Benin	29.09.94
Quaner, Collin	6.3	Union Berlin	Dusseldorf, Ger	18.06.91
Van La Parra, Rajiv	5.11	Wolves	Rotterdam, Hol	04.06.91
Wells, Nahki	6.7	Bradford	Hamilton, Berm	01.06.90

LEICESTER CITY

Ground: King Power Stadium, Filbert Way, Leicester, LE2 7FL
Telephone: 0844 815 5000. **Club nickname:** Foxes
Capacity: 32,500. **Colours:** Blue and white. **Main sponsor:** King Power
Record transfer fee: £29.7m to Sporting Lisbon for Islam Slimani, Aug 2016
Record fee received: £32m from Chelsea for N'Golo Kante, Jul, 2016
Record attendance: Filbert Street: 47,298 v. Tottenham (FA Cup 5) Fb 18, 1928; King Power Stadium: 32,148 v Newcastle (Prem Lge) Dec 26, 2003. Also: 32,188 v Real Madrid (friendly) Jul 30, 2011
League Championship: Winners 2015–16
FA Cup: Runners-up 1949, 1961, 1963, 1969
League Cup: Winners 1964, 1997, 2000
European competitions: Champions League quarter-finals 2016-17
Finishing positions in Premier League: 1994–95 21st, 1996–97 9th, 1997-98 10th, 1998–99 10th, 1999-2000 8th, 2000–01 13th, 2001–02 20th, 2003–04 18th, 2014–15 14th, 2015–16 1st, 2016–17 12th
Biggest win: 10-0 v Portsmouth (Div 1) Oct 20, 1928. Also: 13-0 v Notts Olympic (FA Cup) Oct 13, 1894
Biggest defeat (while Leicester Fosse): 0-12 v Nottm Forest (Div 1) Apr 21, 1909
Highest League scorer in a season: Arthur Rowley 44 (1956–57)
Most League goals in aggregate: Arthur Chandler 259 (1923–35)
Longest unbeaten League sequence: 23 matches (2008–09)
Longest sequence without a League win: 19 matches (1975)
Most capped player: John O'Neill (Northern Ireland), Andy King (Wales) 39

Goalkeepers

Hamer, Ben	6.4	Charlton	Taunton	20.11.87
Schmeichel, Kasper	6.0	Leeds	Copenhagen, Den	05.11.86

Defenders

Benalouane, Yohan	6.2	Atalatna	Bagnols-sur-Ceze, Fr	28.03.87
Chilwell, Ben	5.10	–	Milton Keynes	21.12.96
Fuchs, Christian	6.1	Schalke	Neunkirchen, Aut	07.04.86
Huth, Robert	6.3	Stoke	Berlin, Ger	18.08.84
Maguire, Harry	6.2	Hull	Sheffield	05.03.93

Morgan, Wes	6.1	Nottm Forest	Nottingham	21.01.84
Simpson, Danny	6.0	QPR	Salford	04.01.87
Midfielders				
Albrighton, Mark	6.1	Aston Villa	Tamworth	18.11.89
Amartey, Daniel	6.0	Copenhagen	Accra, Gh	01.12.94
Drinkwater, Danny	5.10	Manchester Utd	Manchester	05.03.90
Gray, Demarai	5.10	Birmingham	Birmingham	28.06.96
Iborra, Vicente	6.3	Sevilla	Moncada, Sp	16.01.88
James, Matty	5.10	Manchester Utd	Bacup	22.07.91
Kapustka, Bartosz	5.11	Cracovia	Tarnow, Pol	23.12.96
King, Andy	6.0	–	Maidenhead	29.10.88
Mahrez, Riyad	5.11	Le Havre	Sarcelles, Fr	21.02.91
Mendy, Nampalys	5.6	Nice	La Seyne, Fr	23.06.92
Ndidi, Wilfred	6.0	Genk	Lagos, Nig	16.12.96
Forwards				
Lawrence, Tom	5.10	Manchester Utd	Wrexham	13.01.94
Musa, Ahmed	5.7	CSKA Moscow	Jos, Nig	14.10.92
Okazaki, Shinji	5.9	Mainz	Takarazuka, Jap	16.04.86
Slimani, Islam	6.2	Sporting Lisbon	Algiers, Alg	18.06.88
Ulloa, Leonardo	6.2	Brighton	General Roca, Arg	26.07.86
Vardy, Jamie	5.10	Fleetwood	Sheffield	11.01.87

LIVERPOOL

Ground: Anfield, Liverpool L4 OTH
Telephone: 0151 263 2361. **Club nickname**: Reds or Pool
Capacity: 54,074. **Colours**: Red. **Main sponsor**: Standard Chartered
Record transfer fee: £35m to Newcastle for Andy Carroll, Jan 2011
Record fee received: £65m from Barcelona for Luis Suarez, Jul 2014
Record attendance: 61,905 v Wolves, (FA Cup 4), Feb 2, 1952
League Championship: Winners 1900–01, 1905–06, 1921–22, 1922–23, 1946–47, 1963–64, 1965–66, 1972–73, 1975–76, 1976–77, 1978–79, 1979–80, 1981–82, 1982–83,1983–84, 1985–86, 1987–88, 1989–90
FA Cup: Winners 1965, 1974, 1986, 1989, 1992, 2001, 2006
League Cup: Winners 1981, 1982, 1983, 1984, 1995, 2001, 2003, 2012
European competitions: Winners European Cup/Champions League 1976–77, 1977–78,1980–81, 1983–84, 2004–05; UEFA Cup 1972–73, 1975–76, 2000–01; European Super Cup 1977, 2001, 2005
Finishing positions in Premier League: 1992–93 6th, 1993–94 8th, 1994–95 4th, 1995–96 3rd, 1996–97 4th, 1997–98 3rd, 1998–99 7th, 1999–2000 4th, 2000–01 3rd, 2001–02 2nd, 2002–03 5th, 2003–04 4th, 2004–05 5th, 2005–06 3rd, 2006–07 3rd, 2007–08 4th, 2008–09 2nd, 2009–10 7th, 2010–11 6th, 2011–12 8th, 2012–13 7th, 2013–14 2nd, 2014–15 6th, 2015–16 8th, 2016–17 4th
Biggest win: 10-1 v Rotherham (Div 2) Feb 18, 1896. Also: 11-0 v Stromsgodset (Cup-Winners' Cup) Sep 17, 1974
Biggest defeat: 1-9 v Birmingham (Div 2) Dec 11, 1954
Highest League scorer in a season: Roger Hunt 41 (1961–62)
Most League goals in aggregate: Roger Hunt 245 (1959–69)
Longest unbeaten League sequence: 31 matches (1987–88))
Longest sequence without a League win: 14 matches (1953–54))
Most capped player: Steven Gerrard (England) 114

Goalkeepers				
Bogdan, Adam	6.4	Stoke	Budapest, Hun	27.09.87
Karius, Loris	6.3	Mainz	Biberach, Ger	22.06.93

Mignolet, Simon	6.4	Sunderland	Sint-Truiden, Bel	06.08.88
Ward, Danny	6.4	Wrexham	Wrexham	22.06.93
Defenders				
Clyne, Nathaniel	5.9	Southampton	Stockwell	05.04.91
Flanagan, Jon	5.11	–	Liverpool	01.01.93
Gomez, Joe	6.1	Charlton	Catford	23.05.97
Klavan, Ragnar	6.2	Augsburg	Viljandi, Est	30.10.85
Lovren, Dejan	6.2	Southampton	Zenica, Bos	05.07.89
Matip, Joel	6.5	Schalke	Bochum, Ger	08.08.91
Moreno, Alberto	5.7	Sevilla	Seville, Sp	05.07.92
Sakho, Mamadou	6.2	Paris SG	Paris, Fr	13.02.90
Midfielders				
Brannagan, Cameron	5.11	–	Manchester	09.05.96
Coutinho, Philippe	5.8	Inter Milan	Rio de Janeiro, Br	12.06.92
Ejaria, Ovie	5.11	Arsenal	Southwark	18.11.97
Emre Can	6.1	Bayer Leverkusen	Frankfurt, Ger	12.01.94
Grujic, Marko	6.3	Red Star Belgrade	Belgrade, Serb	13.04.96
Henderson, Jordan	5.10	Sunderland	Sunderland	17.06.90
Lallana, Adam	5.10	Southampton	Bournemouth	10.05.88
Markovic, Lazar	5.9	Benfica	Cacak, Serb	02.03.94
Milner, James	5.11	Manchester City	Leeds	04.01.86
Ojo, Sheyi	5.10	–	Hemel Hempstead	19.06.97
Salah, Mohamed	5.9	Roma	Basyoun, Egy	15.06.92
Stewart, Kevin	5.7	Tottenham	Enfield	07.09.93
Wijnaldum, Georginio	5.9	Newcastle	Rotterdam, Hol	11.11.90
Forwards				
Firmino, Roberto	6.0	Hoffenheim	Maceio, Br	02.10.91
Ings, Danny	5.10	Burnley	Winchester	16.03.92
Mane, Sadio	5.9	Southampton	Sedhiou, Sen	10.04.92
Origi, Divock	6.1	Lille	Ostend, Bel	18.04.95
Solanke, Dominic	6.1	Chelsea	Reading	14.09.97
Sturridge, Daniel	6.2	Chelsea	Birmingham	01.09.89
Woodburn, Ben	5.11	–	Nottingham	15.10.99

MANCHESTER CITY

Ground: Etihad Stadium, Etihad Campus, Manchester M11 3FF
Telephone 0161 444 1894. **Club nickname:** City
Capacity: 55,097. **Colours:** Sky blue and white. **Main sponsor:** Etihad
Record transfer fee: £54.5m to Wolfsburg for Kevin De Bruyne, Aug 2015
Record fee received: £23.8m from Valencia for Alvaro Negredo, Jul 2015
Record attendance: Maine Road: 84,569 v Stoke (FA Cup 6) Mar 3, 1934 (British record for any game outside London or Glasgow). Etihad Stadium: 54,693 v Leicester (Prem Lge) February 6, 2016
League Championship: Winners 1936–37, 1967–68, 2011–12, 2013–14
FA Cup: Winners 1904, 1934, 1956, 1969, 2011
League Cup: Winners 1970, 1976, 2014, 2016
European competitions: Winners Cup-Winners' Cup 1969–70
Finishing positions in Premier League: 1992–93 9th, 1993–94 16th, 1994–95 17th, 1995–96 18th, 2000–01: 18th, 2002–03 9th, 2003–04 16th, 2004–05 8th, 2005–06 15th, 2006–07 14th, 2007–08 9th, 2008–09 10th, 2009–10 5th, 2010–11 3rd, 2011–12 1st, 2012–13 2nd, 2013–14 1st, 2014–15 2nd, 2015–16 4th, 2016–17 3rd
Biggest win: 10-1 Huddersfield (Div 2) Nov 7, 1987. Also: 10-1 v Swindon (FA Cup 4) Jan 29, 1930
Biggest defeat: 1-9 v Everton (Div 1) Sep 3, 1906
Highest League scorer in a season: Tommy Johnson 38 (1928–29)

Most League goals in aggregate: Tommy Johnson, 158 (1919–30)
Longest unbeaten League sequence: 22 matches (1946–47)
Longest sequence without a League win: 17 matches (1979–80)
Most capped player: Joe Hart (England) 63

Goalkeepers

Bravo, Claudio	6.1	Barcelona	Viluco, Chil	13.04.83
Ederson	6.2	Benfica	Osasco, Br	17.08.93

Defenders

Adarabioyo, Tosin	6.5	–	Manchester	24.09.97
Denayer, Jason	6.1	–	Jette, Bel	28.06.95
Kompany, Vincent	6.4	Hamburg	Uccle, Bel	10.04.86
Kolarov, Aleksandar	6.2	Lazio	Belgrade, Serb	10.11.85
Maffeo, Pablo	5.8	Girona	Sant Joan, Sp	12.07.97
Mangala, Eliaquim	6.2	Porto	Colombes, Fr	13.02.91
Otamendi, Nicolas	6.0	Valencia	Buenos Aires, Arg	12.02.88
Stones, John	6.2	Everton	Barnsley	28.05.94
Walker, Kyle	6.0	Tottenham	Sheffield	28.05.90

Midfielders

De Bruyne, Kevin	5.11	Wolfsburg	Drongen, Bel	28.06.91
Delph, Fabian	5.9	Aston Villa	Bradford	21.11.89
Fernandinho	5.10	Shakhtar Donetsk	Londrina, Br	04.05.85
Fernando	6.0	Porto Alto	Paraiso, Br	25.07.87
Garcia, Aleix	5.8	Villarreal	Ulldecona, Sp	28.06.97
Gundogan, Ilkay	5.11	Borussia Dortmund	Gelsenkirchen, Ger	24.10.90
Moreno, Marlos	5.7	Nacional	Medellin, Col	20.09.96
Nasri, Samir	5.10	Arsenal	Marseille, Fr	26.06.87
Roberts, Patrick	5.7	Fulham	Kingston upon Thames	05.02.97
Sane, Leroy	6.0	Schalke	Essen, Ger	11.01.96
Silva, Bernardo	5.8	Monaco	Lisbon, Port	10.08.94
Silva, David	5.7	Valencia	Arguineguin, Sp	08.01.86
Sterling, Raheem	5.7	Liverpool	Kingston, Jam	08.12.94
Toure, Yaya	6.3	Barcelona	Bouake, Iv C	13.05.83
Zinchenko, Oleksandr	5.9	FC Ufa	Radomyshi, Ukr	15.12.96

Forwards

Aguero, Sergio	5.8	Atletico Madrid	Quilmes, Arg	02.06.88
Bony, Wilfried	6.0	Swansea	Bingerville, Iv C	10.12.88
Gabriel Jesus	5.9	Palmeiras	Sao Paulo, Br	03.04.97
Iheanacho, Kelechi	6.2	–	Owerri, Nig	03.10.96
Nolito	5.9	Celta Vigo	Sanlucar, Sp	15.10.86

MANCHESTER UNITED

Ground: Old Trafford Stadium, Sir Matt Busby Way, Manchester, M16 0RA
Telephone: 0161 868 8000. **Club nickname:** Red Devils
Capacity: 75,365. **Colours:** Red and white. **Main sponsor:** Chevrolet
Record transfer fee: £89.3m to Juventus for Paul Pogba, Aug 2016
Record fee received: £80m from Real Madrid for Cristiano Ronaldo, Jun 2009
Record attendance: 75,811 v Blackburn (Prem Lge), Mar 31, 2007. Also: 76,962 Wolves v Grimsby (FA Cup semi-final) Mar 25, 1939. Crowd of 83,260 saw Manchester Utd v Arsenal (Div 1) Jan 17, 1948 at Maine Road – Old Trafford out of action through bomb damage
League Championship: Winners 1907–08, 1910–11, 1951–52, 1955–56, 1956–7, 1964–65, 1966–67, 1992–93, 1993–94, 1995–96, 1996–97, 1998–99, 1999–2000, 2000–01, 2002–03, 2006–07, 2007–08, 2008–09, 2010–11, 2012–13
FA Cup: Winners 1909, 1948, 1963, 1977, 1983, 1985, 1990, 1994, 1996, 1999, 2004, 2016

League Cup: Winners 1992, 2006, 2009, 2010, 2017
European competitions: Winners European Cup/Champions League 1967–68, 1998–99, 2007–08; Cup-Winners' Cup 1990–91; European Super Cup 1991; Europa League 2016–17
World Club Cup: Winners 2008
Finishing positions in Premier League: 1992–93 1st, 1993–94 1st, 1994–95 2nd, 1995–96 1st, 1996–97 1st, 1997–98 2nd, 1998–99 1st, 1999–2000 1st, 2000–01 1st, 2001–02 3rd, 2002–03 1st, 2003–04 3rd, 2004–05 3rd, 2005–06 2nd, 2006–07 1st, 2007–08 1st, 2008–09 1st, 2009–10 2nd, 2010–11 1st, 2011–12 2nd, 2012–13 1st, 2013–14 7th, 2014–15 4th, 2015–16 5th, 2016–17 6th
Biggest win: As Newton Heath: 10 1 v Wolves (Div 1) Oct 15, 1892. As Manchester Utd: 9-0 v Ipswich (Prem Lge), Mar 4, 1995. Also: 10-0 v Anderlecht (European Cup prelim rd) Sep 26, 1956
Biggest defeat: 0-7 v Blackburn (Div 1) Apr 10, 1926, v Aston Villa (Div 1) Dec 27, 1930, v Wolves (Div 2) 26 Dec, 1931
Highest League scorer in a season: Dennis Viollet 32 (1959–60)
Most League goals in aggregate: Bobby Charlton 199 (1956–73)
Longest unbeaten League sequence: 29 matches (1998–99)
Longest sequence without a League win: 16 matches (1930)
Most capped player: Sir Bobby Charlton (England) 106

Goalkeepers

De Gea, David	6.4	Atletico Madrid	Madrid, Sp	07.11.90
Romero, Sergio	6.4	Sampdoria	Bernardo, Arg	22.02.87

Defenders

Bailly, Eric	6.1	Villarreal	Bingerville, Iv C	12.04.94
Darmian, Matteo	6.0	Torino	Legnano, It	02.12.89
Fosu-Mensah, Tim	6.1	–	Amsterdam, Hol	02.01.98
Jones, Phil	5.11	Blackburn	Blackburn	21.02.92
Lindelof, Victor	6.2	Benfica	Vasteras, Swe	17.07.94
Rojo, Marcos	6.2	Sporting Lisbon	La Plata, Arg	20.03.90
Shaw, Luke	6.1	Southamptonn	Kingston upon Thames	12.07.95
Smalling, Chris	6.1	Fulham	Greenwich	22.11.89

Midfielders

Blind, Daley	5.11	Ajax	Amsterdam, Hol	09.03.90
Carrick, Michael	6.0	Tottenham	Wallsend	28.07.81
Fellaini, Marouane	6.4	Everton	Etterbeek, Bel	22.11.87
Herrera, Ander	6.0	Athletic Bilbao	Bilbao, Sp	14.08.89
Januzaj, Adnan	5.11	Anderlecht	Brussels, Bel	05.02.95
Mata, Juan	5.7	Chelsea	Burgos, Sp	28.04.88
Mkhitaryan, Henrikh	5.10	Borussia Dortmund	Yerevan, Arm	21.01.89
Pereira, Andreas	5.10	PSV Eindhoven	Duffel, Bel	01.01.96
Pogba, Paul	6.3	Juventus	Lagny-sur-Marne, Fr	15.03.93
Valencia, Antonio	5.10	Wigan	Lago Agrio, Ec	04.08.85
Varela, Guillermo	5.8	Penarol	Montevideo, Uru	24.03.93
Young, Ashley	5.10	Aston Villa	Stevenage	09.07.85

Forwards

Lingard, Jesse	6.2	–	Warrington	15.12.92
Lukaku, Romelu	6.3	Everton	Antwerp, Bel	13.05.93
Martial, Anthony	5.11	Monaco	Massy, Fr	05.12.95
Rashford, Marcus	6.0	–	Wythenshawe	31.10.97

NEWCASTLE UNITED

Ground: St James' Park, Newcastle-upon-Tyne, NE1 4ST
Telephone: 0844 372 1892. **Club nickname**: Magpies
Capacity: 52,401.**Colours**: Black and white. **Main sponsor**: FUN88
Record attendance: 68,386 v Chelsea (Div 1) Sep 3, 1930

Record transfer fee: £16m to Real Madrid for Michael Owen, Aug 2005
Record fee received: £35m from Liverpool for Andy Carroll, Jan 2011
League Championship: Winners 1904–05, 1906–07, 1908–09, 1926–27
FA Cup: Winners: 1910, 1924, 1932, 1951, 1952,1955
League Cup: Runners-up 1976
European competitions: Winners Fairs Cup 1968–69; Anglo-Italian Cup 1972–73
Finishing positions in Premier League: 1993–94 3rd, 1994–95 6th, 1995–96 2nd, 1996–97 2nd, 1997–98 13th, 1998–99 13th, 1999–2000 11th, 2000–01 11th, 2001–02 4th, 2002–03 3rd, 2003–04 5th, 2004–05 14th, 2005–06 7th, 2006–07 13th, 2007–08 12th, 2008–09 18th, 2010–11 12th, 2011–12 5th, 2012–13 16th, 2013–14 10th, 2014–15 15th, 2015–16 18th
Biggest win: 13-0 v Newport (Div 2) Oct 5, 1946
Biggest defeat: 0-9 v Burton (Div 2) Apr 15, 1895
Highest League scorer in a season: Hughie Gallacher 36 (1926–27)
Most League goals in aggregate: Jackie Milburn 177 (1946–57)
Longest unbeaten League sequence: 14 matches (1950)
Longest sequence without a League win: 21 matches (1978)
Most capped player: Shay Given (Republic of Irelnd) 83

Goalkeepers

Darlow, Karl	6.1	Nottm Forest	Northampton	08.10.90
Elliot, Rob	6.3	Charlton	Chatham	30.04.86
Woodman, Freddie	6.2	Crystal Palace	Croydon	04.03.97

Defenders

Clark, Ciaran	6.2	Aston Villa	Harrow	26.09.89
Dummett, Paul	6.0	–	Newcastle	26.09.91
Findlay, Stuart	6.3	Celtic	Rutherglen	14.09.95
Gamez, Jesus	6.0	Atletico Madrid	Fuengirola, Sp	10.04.85
Hanley, Grant	6.2	Blackburn	Dumfries	20.11.91
Haidara, Massado	5.10	Nancy	Trappes, Fr	02.12.92
Lascelles, Jamaal	6.2	Nottm Forest	Derby	11.11.93
Lazaar, Achraf	6.1	Palermo	Casablanca, Mor	22.01.92
Lejeune, Florian	6.3	Eibar	Paris, Fr	20.05.91
Mbemba, Chancel	6.0	Anderlecht	Kinshasa, DR Cong	08.08.94
Yedlin, DeAndre	5.9	Tottenham	Seattle, US	09.07.93

Midfielders

Aarons, Rolando	5.9	Bristol City	Kingston, Jam	16.11.95
Atsu, Christian	5.8	Chelsea	Ada Foah, Gh	10.01.92
Colback, Jack	5.10	Sunderland	Killingworth	24.10.89
De Jong, Siem	6.1	Ajax	Aigle, Swi	28.01.89
Diame, Mohamed	6.1	Hull	Creteil, Fr	14.06.87
Hayden, Isaac	6.1	Arsenal	Chelmsford	22.03.95
Ritchie, Matt	5.8	Bournemouth	Gosport	10.09.89
Shelvey, Jonjo	6.0	Swansea	Romford	27.02.92

Forwards

Armstrong, Adam	5.8	–	Newcastle	10.02.97
Ayoze Perez	5.11	Tenerife	Santa Cruz, Ten	23.07.93
Gayle, Dwight	5.10	Crystal Palace	Walthamstow	20.10.90
Gouffran, Yoan	5.10	Bordeaux	Villeneuve Georges, Fr	25.05.86
Mitrovic, Aleksandar	6.3	Anderlecht	Smederevo, Serb	16.09.94
Murphy, Daryl	6.2	Ipswich	Waterford, Ire	15.03.83
Riviere, Emmanuel	6.0	Monaco	La Lamentin, Mart	03.03.90

SOUTHAMPTON

Ground: St Mary's Stadium, Britannia Road, Southampton, SO14 5FP
Telephone: 0845 688 9448. **Club nickname**: Saints
Capacity: 32,689. **Colours**: Red and white. **Main sponsor**: Virgin Media
Record transfer fee: £16m to Lille for Sofiane Boufal, Aug 2016
Record fee received: £34m from Liverpool for Sadio Mane, Jun 2016
Record attendance: The Dell: 31,044 v Manchester Utd (Div 1) Oct 8, 1969. St Mary's: 32,363 v Coventry (Champ) Apr 28, 2012
League Championship: Runners-up 1983–84
FA Cup: Winners 1976
League Cup: Runners-up 1979, 2017
European competitions: Fairs Cup rd 3 1969–70; Cup-Winners' Cup rd 3 1976–77
Finishing positions in Premier League: 1992 93 18th, 1993–94 18th, 1994–5 10th, 1995–96 17th, 1996–97 16th, 1997–98 12th, 1998–99 17th, 1999–200 15th, 2000–01 10th, 2001–02 11th, 2002–03 8th, 2003–04 12th, 2004–05 20th, 2012–13 14th, 2013–14 8th, 2014–15 7th, 2015–16 6th, 2016–17 8th
Biggest win: 8-0 v Northampton (Div 3S) Dec 24, 1921, v Sunderland (Prem Lge) Oct 18, 2014
Biggest defeat: 0-8 v Tottenham (Div 2) Mar 28, 1936, v Everton (Div 1) Nov 20, 1971
Highest League scorer in a season: Derek Reeves 39 (1959–60)
Most League goals in aggregate: Mick Channon 185 (1966–82)
Longest unbeaten League sequence: 19 matches (1921)
Longest unbeaten League sequence: 20 matches (1969)
Most capped player: Peter Shilton (England) 49

Goalkeepers

Forster, Fraser	6.7	Celtic	Hexham	17.03.88
McCarthy, Alex	6.4	Crystal Palace	Guildford	03.12.89

Defenders

Bednarek, Jan	6.2	Lech Poznan	Slupca, Pol	12.04.96
Bertrand, Ryan	5.10	Chelsea	Southwark	05.08.89
Gardos, Florin	6.4	Steaua Bucharest	Satu Mare, Rom	29.10.88
Pied, Jeremy	5.8	Nice	Grenoble, Fr	23.02.89
Soares, Cedric	5.8	Sporting Lisbon	Singen, Ger	31.08.91
Stephens, Jack	6.1	Plymouth	Torpoint	27.01.94
Targett, Matt	6.0		Eastleigh	18.09.95
Van Dijk, Virgil	6.4	Celtic	Breda, Hol	08.07.91
Yoshida, Maya	6.2	Venlo	Nagasaki, Jap	24.08.88

Midfielders

Boufal, Sofiann	5.9	Lille	Paris, Fr	17.09.93
Clasie, Jordy	5.7	Feyenoord	Haarlem, Hol	27.06.91
Davis, Steven	5.8	Rangers	Ballymena	01.01.85
Hesketh, Jake	5.6	–	Stockport	27.03.96
Hojbjerg, Pierre-Emile	6.1	Bayern Munich	Copenhagen, Den	05.08.95
McQueen, Sam	5.11	–	Southampton	06.02.95
Redmond, Nathan	5.8	Norwich	Birmingham	06.03.94
Romeu, Oriol	6.0	Chelsea	Ulldecona, Sp	24.09.91
Sims, Joshua	5.9	–	Yeovil	28.03.97
Tadic, Dusan	5.11	Twente Backa	Topola, Serb	20.11.88
Ward-Prowse, James	5.8	–	Portsmouth	01.11.94

Forwards

Austin, Charlie	6.2	QPR	Hungerford	05.07.89
Gabbiadini, Manolo	6.1	Napoli	Calcinate, It	26.11.91
Gallagher, Sam	6.4	–	Crediton	15.09.95
Long, Shane	5.10	Hull	Gortnahoe, Ire	22.01.87
Seager, Ryan	5.9	–	Yeovil	05.02.96

STOKE CITY

Ground: bet365 Stadium, Stanley Matthews Way, Stoke-on-Trent ST4 7EG
Telephone: 01782 367598. **Club nickname:** Potters
Capacity: 30,183. **Colours:** Red and white. **Main sponsor:** bet365
Record transfer fee: £18.3m to Porto for Giannelli Imbula, Feb 2016
Record fee received: £8m from Chelsea for Asmir Begovic, Jul 2015
Record attendance: Victoria Ground: 51,380 v Arsenal (Div 1) Mar 29, 1937. bet365 Stadium: 28,218 v Everton (FA Cup 3) Jan 5, 2002
League Championship: 4th 1935–36, 1946–47
FA Cup: Runners-up 2011
League Cup: Winners 1972
European competitions: Europa League rd of 32 2011–12
Finishing positions in Premier League: 2008–09 12th, 2009–10 11th, 2010–11 13th, 2011–12 14th, 2012–13 13th, 2013–14 9th, 2014–15 9th, 2015–16 9th, 2016–17 13th
Biggest win: 10-3 v WBA (Div 1) Feb 4, 1937
Biggest defeat: 0-10 v Preston (Div 1) Sep 14, 1889
Highest League scorer in a season: Freddie Steele 33 (1936–37)
Most League goals in aggregate: Freddie Steele 142 (1934–49)
Longest unbeaten League sequence: 25 matches (1992–93)
Longest sequence without a League win: 17 matches (1989)
Most capped player: Glenn Whelan (Republic of Ireland) 81

Goalkeepers

Butland, Jack	6.4	Birmingham	Bristol	10.03.93
Grant, Lee	6.2	Derby	Hemel Hempstead	27.01.83
Haugaard, Jakob	6.6	Midtjylland	Sundby, Den	01.05.92

Defenders

Bardsley, Phil	5.11	Sunderland	Salford	28.06.85
Cameron, Geoff	6.3	Houston	Attleboro, US	11.07.85
Johnson, Glen	6.0	Liverpool	Greenwich	23.08.84
Muniesa, Marc	5.11	Barcelona	Lloret de Mar, Sp	27.03.92
Pieters, Erik	6.1	PSV Eindhoven	Tiel, Hol	07.08.88
Shawcross, Ryan	6.3	Manchester Utd	Chester	04.10.87
Tymon, Josh	5.10	Hull	Hull	22.05.99
Wollscheid, Philipp	6.4	Bayer Leverkusen	Wadern, Ger	06.03.89

Midfielders

Adam, Charlie	6.1	Liverpool	Dundee	10.12.85
Afellay, Ibrahim	5.11	Barcelona	Utrecht, Hol	02.04.86
Allen, Joe	5.7	Liverpool	Carmarthen	14.03.90
El Ouriachi, Moha	5.10	Barcelona	Nador, Mor	13.01.96
Fletcher, Darren	6.0	WBA	Edinburgh	01.02.84
Imbula, Giannelli	6.1	Porto	Vilvoorde, Bel	12.09.92
Ireland, Stephen	5.8	Aston Villa	Cork, Ire	22.08.86
Shaqiri, Xherdan	5.7	Inter Milan	Gjilan, Kos	10.10.91
Sobhi, Ramadan	6.0	Al Ahly	Cairo, Egy	23.01.97
Whelan, Glenn	5.10	Sheffield Wed	Dublin, Ire	3.01.84

Forwards

Arnautovic, Marko	6.4	Werder Bremen	Vienna, Aut	19.04.89
Berahino, Saido	5.10	WBA	Bujumbura, Bur	04.08.93
Biram Diouf, Mame	6.1	Hannover	Dakar, Sen	16.12.87
Crouch, Peter	6.7	Tottenham	Macclesfield	30.01.81
Joselu	6.3	Hannover	Stuttgart, Ger	27.03.90
Krkic, Bojan	5.7	Barcelona	Linyola, Sp	28.08.90
Ngoy, Julien	6.2	Bruges	Antwerp, Bel	02.11.97

SWANSEA CITY

Ground: Liberty Stadium, Morfa, Swansea SA1 2FA
Telephone: 01792 616600. **Club nickname**: Swans
Capacity: 20,972. **Colours**: White. **Main sponsor**: Letou
Record transfer fee: £15.5m to Atletico Madrid for Borja Baston, Aug 2016
Record fee received: £28m from Manchester City for Wilfried Bony, Aug 2012
Record attendance: Vetch Field: 32,796 v Arsenal (FA Cup 4) Feb 17, 1968. Liberty Stadium: 20,972 v Liverpool (Prem Lge) May 1, 2016
League Championship: 6th 1981–82
FA Cup: Semi-finals 1926, 1964
League Cup: Winners 2013
Finishing positions in Premier League: 2011–12 11th, 2012–13 9th, 2013–14 12th, 2014–15 8th, 2015–16 12th, 2016 17 15th
European competitions: Cup-Winners' Cup rd 2 1982–83; Europa Lge rd of 32 2013–14
Biggest win: 8-0 v Hartlepool (Div 4) Apr 1, 1978. Also: 12-0 v Sliema (Cup-Winners' Cup rd 1, 1st leg), Sep 15, 1982
Biggest defeat: 0-8 v Liverpool (FA Cup 3) Jan 9, 1990, 0-8 v Monaco (Cup-Winners' Cup rd 1, 2nd leg) Oct 1, 1991
Highest League scorer in a season: Cyril Pearce 35 (1931–32)
Most League goals in aggregate: Ivor Allchurch 166 (1949–58, 1965–68)
Longest unbeaten League sequence: 19 matches (1970–71)
Longest sequence without a League win: 15 matches (1989)
Most capped player: Ashley Williams (Wales) 64

Goalkeepers

Birighitti, Mark	6.2	Newcastle Jets	Perth, Aus	17.04.91
Fabianski, Lukasz	6.3	Arsenal	Kostrzyn, Pol	18.04.85
Mulder, Erwin	6.4	Heerenveen	Pannerden, Hol	03.03.09
Nordfeldt, Kristoffer	6.3	Heerenveen	Stockholm, Swe	23.06.89

Defenders

Bartley, Kyle	6.1	Arsenal	Stockport	22.05.91
Fernandez, Federico	6.3	Napoli	Tres Algarrobos, Arg	21.02.89
Kingsley, Stephen	5.10	Falkirk	Stirling	23.07.94
Mawson, Alfie	6.2	Barnsley	Hillingdon	19.01.94
Naughton, Kyle	5.10	Tottenham	Sheffield	11.11.88
Olsson, Martin	5.10	Norwich	Gavle, Swe	17.05.88
Reid Tyler	6.11	Manchester Utd	Luton	02.09.97
Rangel, Angel	5.11	Terrassa	Tortosa, Sp	28.10.82
van der Hoorn, Mike	6.3	Ajax	Almere, Hol	15.10.92

Midfielders

Britton, Leon	5.5	Sheffield Utd	Merton	16.09.82
Carroll, Tom	5.10	Tottenham	Watford	28.05.92
Dyer, Nathan	5.10	Southampton	Trowbridge	29.11.87
Fer, Leroy	6.2	QPR	Zoetermeer, Hol	05.01.90
Fulton, Jay	5.10	Falkirk	Bolton	04.04.94
Grimes, Matt	5.10	Exeter	Exeter	15.07.95
Ki Sung-Yueng	6.2	Celtic	Gwangju, S Kor	24.01.89
Mesa, Roque	5.7	Las Palmas	Las Palmas, Gran Can	07.06.89
Montero, Jefferson	5.7	Morelia	Babahoyo, Ec	01.09.89
Narsingh, Luciano	5.10	PSV Eindhoven	Amsterdam, Hol	13.09.90
Routledge, Wayne	5.7	Newcastle	Sidcup	07.01.85
Sigurdsson, Gylfi	6.1	Tottenham	Hafnarfjordur, Ice	08.09.89

Forwards

Abraham, Tammy	6.4	Chelsea (loan)	Camberwell	02.10.97

Ayew, Jordan	6.0	Aston Villa	Marseille, Fr	11.09.91
Barrow, Modou	5.10	Ostersunds	Banjul, Gam	13.10.92
Llorente, Fernando	6.5	Sevilla	Pamplona, Sp	26.02.85
McBurnie, Oliver	6.2	Bradford	Leeds	04.06.96

TOTTENHAM HOTSPUR

Ground: Wembley Stadium (temporary)
Telephone: 0344 499 5000. **Club nickname:** Spurs
Capacity: 90,000. **Colours:** White. **Main sponsor:** AIA
Record transfer fee: £30m to Roma for Erik Lamela, Aug 2013
Record fee received: £85.3m from Real Madrid for Gareth Bale, Aug 2013
Record attendance: White Hart Lane: 75,038 v Sunderland (FA Cup 6) Mar 5, 1938. Wembley: 85,512 v Bayer Leverkusen (Champs Lge) Nov 2, 2016
League Championship: Winners 1950–51, 1960–61
FA Cup: Winners 1901, 1921, 1961, 1962, 1967, 1981, 1982, 1991
League Cup: Winners 1971, 1973, 1999, 2008
European competitions: Winners Cup-Winners' Cup 1962–63; UEFA Cup 1971–72, 1983–84
Finishing positions in Premier League: 1992–93 8th, 1993–94 15th, 1994–95 7th, 1995–96 8th, 1996–97 10th, 1997–98 14th, 1998–99 11th, 1999–2000 10th, 2000–01 12th, 2001–02 9th, 2002–03 10th, 2003–04 14th, 2004–05 9th, 2005–06 5th, 2006–07 5th, 2007–08 11th, 2008–09 8th, 2009–10 4th, 2010–11 5th, 2011–12 4th, 2012–13 5th, 2013–14 6th, 2014–15 5th, 2015–16 3rd, 2016–17 2nd
Biggest win: 9-0 v Bristol Rov (Div 2) Oct 22, 1977. Also: 13-2 v Crewe (FA Cup 4 replay) Feb 3, 1960
Biggest defeat: 0-7 v Liverpool (Div 1) Sep 2, 1979. Also: 0-8 v Cologne (Inter Toto Cup) Jul 22, 1995
Highest League scorer in a season: Jimmy Greaves 37 (1962–63)
Most League goals in aggregate: Jimmy Greaves 220 (1961–70)
Longest unbeaten League sequence: 22 matches (1949)
Longest sequence without a League win: 16 matches (1934–35)
Most capped player: Pat Jennings (Northern Ireland) 74

Goalkeepers				
Lloris, Hugo	6.2	Lyon	Nice, Fr	26.12.86
Vorm, Michel	6.0	Swansea	Nieuwegein, Hol	20.10.83
Defenders				
Alderweireld, Toby	6.2	Atletico Madrid	Antwerp, Bel	02.03.89
Davies, Ben	5.6	Swansea	Neath	24.04.93
Dier, Eric	6.2	Sporting Lisbon	Cheltenham	15.01.94
Fazio, Federico	6.5	Sevilla	Buenos Aires, Arg	17.03.87
Rose, Danny	5.8	Leeds	Doncaster	02.07.90
Trippier, Kieran	5.10	Burnley	Bury	19.09.90
Vertonghen, Jan	6.2	Ajax	Sint-Niklaas, Bel	24.04.87
Wimmer, Kevin	6.2	Cologne	Wels, Aut	15.11.92
Midfielders				
Alli, Dele	6.1	MK Dons	Milton Keynes	11.04.96
Dembele, Mousa	6.1	Fulham	Wilrijk, Bel	16.07.87
Eriksen, Christian	5.10	Ajax	Middelfart, Den	14.02.92
Lamela, Erik	6.0	Roma	Buenos Aires, Arg	04.03.92
Nkoudou, Georges-Kevin	5.8	Marseille	Versailles, Fr	13.02.95
Onomah, Josh	5.11	–	Enfield	27.04.97
Sissoko, Moussa	6.2	Newcastle	Le Blanc-Mesnil, Fr	16.08.89
Wanyama, Victor	6.2	Southampton	Nairobi, Ken	25.06.91
Winks, Harry	5.10	–	Hemel Hempstead	02.02.96
Forwards				
Janssen, Vincent	5.11	Alkmaar	Heesch, Hol	15.06.94

| Kane, Harry | 6.2 | – | | Walthamstow | 28.07.93 |
| Son Heung-Min | 6.1 | Bayer Leverkusen | | Chuncheon, S Kor | 08.07.92 |

WATFORD

Ground: Vicarage Road Stadium, Vicarage Road, Watford WD18 0ER
Telephone: 01923 496000. **Club nickname:** Hornets
Capacity: 21,977. **Colours:** Yellow and black. **Main sponsor:** FxPro
Record transfer fee: £13m to Juventus for Roberto Pereyra, Aug 2016
Record fee received: £20m from Changchun Yatai for Odion Ighalo, Jan 2017
Record attendance: 34,099 v Manchester Utd (FA Cup 4 rep) Feb 3, 1969
League Championship: Runners-up 1982–83
FA Cup: Runners-up 1984
League Cup: Semi-finals 1979, 2005
European competitions: UEFA Cup rd 3 1983–84
Finishing positions in Premier League: 1999–2000 20th, 2006–07 20th, 2015–16 13th, 2016–17 17th
Biggest win: 8-0 v Sunderland (Div 1) Sep 25, 1982. Also: 10-1 v Lowestoft (FA Cup 1) Nov 27, 1926
Biggest defeat: 0-10 v Wolves (FA Cup 1 replay) Jan 24, 1912
Highest League scorer in a season: Cliff Holton 42 (1959–60)
Most League goals in aggregate: Luther Blissett 148 (1976–83, 1984–88, 1991–92)
Longest unbeaten League sequence: 22 matches (1996–97)
Longest sequence without a League win: 19 matches (1971–72)
Most capped players: John Barnes (England) 31, Kenny Jackett (Wales) 31

Goalkeepers

Arlauskis, Giedrius	6.4	Steaua Bucharest		Telsiai, Lith	01.12.87
Bachmann, Daniel	6.3	Stoke		Vienna, Aut	09.07.94
Gomes, Heurelho	6.2	PSV Eindhoven		Joao Pinheiro, Br	15.12.81
Pantilimon, Costel	6.0	Sunderland		Bacau, Rom	01.02.87

Defenders

Britos, Miguel	6.2	Napoli		Maldonado, Uru	17.07.85
Cathcart, Craig	6.2	Blackpool		Belfast	06.02.89
Dja Djedje, Brice	5.7	Marseille		Aboude, Iv C	23.12.90
Femenia, Kiko	5.9	Alaves		Sanet Neprals, Sp	02.02.91
Hoban, Tommie	6.2			Waltham Forest	24.01.94
Holebas, José	6.1	Roma		Aschaffenburg, Ger	27.06.84
Janmaat, Daryl	6.1	Newcastle		Leidschendam, Hol	22.07.89
Kabasele, Christian	6.1	Genk		Lubumbashi, DR Cong	24.02.91
Kaboul, Younes	6.3	Sunderland		St Julien, Fr	04.01.86
Mariappa, Adrian	5.11	Crystal Palace		Harrow	03.10.86
Paredes, Juan Carlos	5.9	Granada		Esmeraldas, Ec	08.07.87
Prodl, Sebastian	6.4	Werder Bremen		Graz, Aut	21.06.87

Midfielders

Amrabat, Nordin	5.11	Malaga		Naarden, Hol	31.03.87
Behrami, Valon	6.1	Hamburg		Mitrovica, Kos	19.04.85
Berghuis, Steven	6.0	Alkmaar		Apeldoorn, Hol	19.12.91
Capoue, Etienne	6.2	Tottenham		Niort, Fr	11.07.88
Chalobah, Nathaniel	6.1	Chelsea		Freetown, Sl eone	12.12.94
Cleverley, Tom	5.10	Everton		Basingstoke	12.08.89
Doucoure, Abdoulaye	6.0	Rennes		Meulan, Fr	01.01.93
Hughes, Will	6.1	Derby		Weybridge	07.04.95
Pereyra, Roberto	6.0	Juventus		San Miguel, Arg	07.01.91
Watson, Ben	5.10	Wigan		Camberwell	09.07.85
Zarate, Mauro	5.10	Fiorentina		Haedo, Arg	18.03.87

Forwards

Deeney, Troy	6.0	Walsall	Birmingham	29.06.88
Okaka, Stefano	6.1	Anderlecht	Castiglione, It	09.08.89
Oulare, Obbi	6.5	Club Bruges	Waregem, Bel	08.01.96
Penaranda, Adalberto	6.0	Udinese	El Vigia, Ven	31.05.97
Sinclair, Jerome	6.0	Liverpool	Birmingham	20.09.96
Success, Isaac	6.0	Granada	Benin City, Nig	07.01.96

WEST BROMWICH ALBION

Ground: The Hawthorns, Halfords Lane, West Bromwich B71 4LF
Telephone: 0871 271 1100. **Club nickname:** Baggies
Capacity: 26,500. **Colours:** Blue and white. **Main sponsor:** UK-K8
Record transfer fee: £13m to Tottenham for Nacer Chadli, Aug 2016
Record fee received: £11.8m from Stoke for Saido Berahino, Jan 2017
Record attendance: 64,815 v Arsenal (FA Cup 6) Mar 6, 1937
League Championship: Winners 1919–20
FA Cup: Winners 1888, 1892, 1931, 1954, 1968
League Cup: Winners 1966
European competitions: Cup-Winners' Cup quarter-finals 1968–69; UEFA Cup quarter-finals 1978–79
Finishing positions in Premier League: 2002–03 19th, 2004–5 17th, 2005–6 19th; 2008–09 20th, 2010–11 11th, 2011–12 10th, 2012–13 8th, 2013–14 17th, 2014–15 13th, 2015–16 14th, 2016–17 10th
Biggest win: 12-0 v Darwen (Div 1) Apr 4, 1892
Biggest defeat: 3-10 v Stoke (Div 1) Feb 4, 1937
Highest League scorer in a season: William Richardson 39 (1935–36)
Most League goals in aggregate: Tony Brown 218 (1963–79)
Longest unbeaten League sequence: 17 matches (1957)
Longest sequence without a League win: 14 matches (1995)
Most capped player: Chris Brunt (Northern Ireland) 49

Goalkeepers

Foster, Ben	6.2	Birmingham	Leamington	03.04.83
Myhill, Boaz	6.3	Hull	Modesto, US	09.11.82
Palmer, Alex	6.0	–	Kidderminster	10.08.96
Defenders				
Dawson, Craig	6.2	Rochdale	Rochdale	06.05.90
Evans, Jonny	6.2	Manchester Utd	Belfast	02.01.88
McAuley, Gareth	6.3	Ipswich	Larne	05.12.79
Nyom, Allan	6.2	Watford	Neuilly-sur-Seine, Fr	10.05.88
Wilson, Kane	6.0	–	Birmingham	11.03.00
Midfielders				
Brunt, Chris	6.1	Sheffield Wed	Belfast	14.12.84
Chadli, Nacer	6.2	Tottenham	Liege, Bel	02.08.89
Field, Sam	5.11	–	Stourbridge	08.05.98
Harper, Rekeem	6.0	–	Birmingham	08.03.00
Leko, Jonathan	6.0	–	Kinshasa, DR Cong	24.04.99
Livermore, Jake	6.0	Hull	Enfield	14.11.89
McClean, James	5.11	Wigan	Derry	22.04.89
Morrison, James	5.10	Middlesbrough	Darlington	25.05.86
Phillips, Matt	6.0	QPR	Aylesbury	13.03.91
Yacob, Claudio	5.11	Racing Club	Carcarana, Arg	18.07.87
Forwards				
McManaman, Callum	5.11	Wigan	Knowsley	25.04.91
Roberts, Tyler	5.11	–	Gloucester	12.01.99

Robson-Kanu, Hal	6.0	Reading	Acton	21.05.89
Rodriguez, Jay	6.1	Southampton	Burnley	29.07.89
Rondon, Salomon	6.2	Zenit St Petersburg	Caracas, Ven	16.09.89

WEST HAM UNITED

Ground: Queen Elizabeth Olympic Park, London E20 2ST
Telephone: 0208 548 2748. **Club nickname:** Hammers
Capacity: 60,000. **Colours:** Claret and blue. **Main sponsor:** Betway
Record transfer fee: £20.5m to Swansea for Andre Ayew, Aug 2016
Record fee received: £25m from Marseille for Dimitri Payet, Jan 2017
Record attendance: Upton Park: 43,322 v Tottenham (Div 1) Oct 17, 1970. Olympic Stadium: 56,996 v Manchester Utd (Prem Lge) Jan 2, 2017
League Championship: 3rd 1985–86
FA Cup: Winners 1964, 1975, 1980
League Cup: Runners-up 1966, 1981
European competitions: Winners Cup-Winners' Cup 1964–65
Finishing positions in Premier League: 1993–94 13th, 1994–95 14th, 1995–96 10th, 1996–97 14th, 1997–98 8th, 1998–99 5th, 1999–2000 9th, 2000–01 15th, 2001–02 7th, 2002–03 18th, 2005–06 9th, 2006–07 15th, 2007–08 10th, 2008–09: 9th, 2009 10 17th, 2010–11 20th, 2012–13 10th, 2013–14 13th, 2014–15 12th, 2015–16 7th, 2016–17 11th
Biggest win: 8-0 v Rotherham (Div 2) Mar 8, 1958, v Sunderland (Div 1) Oct 19, 1968. Also: 10-0 v Bury (League Cup 2) Oct 25, 1983
Biggest defeat: 0-7 v Barnsley (Div 2) Sep 1, 1919, v Everton (Div 1) Oct 22, 1927, v Sheffield Wed (Div 1) Nov 28, 1959
Highest League scorer in a season: Vic Watson 42 (1929–30)
Most League goals in aggregate: Vic Watson 298 (1920–35)
Longest unbeaten League sequence: 27 matches (1980–81)
Longest sequence without a League win: 17 matches (1976)
Most capped player: Bobby Moore (England) 108

Goalkeepers
| Adrian | 6.3 | Real Betis | Seville, Sp | 03.01.87 |
| Randolph, Darren | 6.1 | Birmingham | Bray, Ire | 12.06.87 |

Defenders
Byram, Sam	5.11	Leeds	Thurrock	16.09.93
Burke, Reece	6.2		Newham	02.09.96
Collins, James	6.2	Aston Villa	Newport	23.08.83
Cresswell, Aaron	5.7	Ipswich	Liverpool	15.12.89
Fonte, Jose	6.2	Southampton	Penafiel, Por	22.12.83
Henry, Doneil	6.2	Apollon Limassol	Brampton, Can	20.04.93
Masuaku, Arthur	5.11	Olympiacos	Lille, Fr	07.11.93
Ogbonna, Angelo	6.3	Juventus	Cassino, It	23.05.88
Reid, Winston	6.3	Midtjylland	Auckland, NZ	03.07.88
Zabaleta, Pablo	5.10	Manchester City	Buenos Aires, Arg	16.01.85

Midfielders
Antonio, Michail	5.11	Nottm Forest	Wandsworth	28.03.90
Feghouli, Sofiane	5.10	Valencia	Levallois Perret, Fr	26.12.89
Fernandes, Edimilson	6.3	FC Sion	Sion, Switz	15.04.96
Kouyate, Cheikhou	6.4	Anderlecht	Dakar, Sen	21.12.89
Lanzini, Manuel	5.6	Al Jazira	Ituzaingo, Arg	15.02.93
Noble, Mark	5.11	–	West Ham	08.05.87
Nordtveit, Havard	6.2	Borussia M'gladbach	Vats, Nor	21.06.90
Obiang, Pedro	6.1	Sampdoria	Alcala, Sp	27.03.92
Snodgrass, Robert	6.0	Hull	Glasgow	07.09.87

Forwards

Ayew, Andre	5.10	Swansea	Seclin, Fr	17.12.89
Carroll, Andy	6.3	Liverpool	Gateshead	06.01.89
Fletcher, Ashley	6.1	Manchester Utd	Keighley	02.10.95
Sakho, Diafra	6.1	Metz	Guediawaye, Sen	24.12.89

ENGLISH FOOTBALL LEAGUE PLAYING STAFFS 2017–18

(At time of going to press)

CHAMPIONSHIP

ASTON VILLA

Ground: Villa Park, Trinity Road, Birmingham, B6 6HE
Telephone: 0800 612 0970. **Club nickname**: Villans
Colours: Claret and blue. **Capacity**: 42,785
Record attendance: 76,588 v Derby (FA Cup 6) Mar 2, 1946

Goalkeepers

Bunn, Mark	6.0	Norwich	Southgate	16.11.84
Johnstone, Sam	6.3	Manchester Utd (loan)	Preston	25.03.93
Steer, Jed	6.3	Norwich	Norwich	23.09.92
Defenders				
Amavi, Jordan	5.9	Nice	Toulon, Fr	09.03.94
Baker, Nathan	6.3	–	Worcester	23.04.91
Bree, James	5.10	Barnsley	Wakefield	11.10.97
Chester, James	5.11	WBA	Warrington	23.01.89
Cissokho, Aly	5.11	Valencia	Blois, Fr	15.09.87
De Laet, Ritchie	6.1	Leicester	Antwerp, Bel	28.11.88
Elphick, Tommy	5.11	Bournemouth	Brighton	07.09.87
Hutton, Alan	6.1	Tottenham	Glasgow	30.11.84
Richards, Micah	5.11	Manchester City	Birmingham	24.06.88
Taylor, Neil	5.9	Swansea	St Asaph	07.02.89
Terry, John	6.1	Chelsea	Barking	07.12.80
Midfielders				
Adomah, Albert	6.1	Middlesbrough	Lambeth	13.12.87
Bacuna, Leandro	6.2	Groningen	Groningen, Hol	21.08.91
Bjarnason, Birkir	6.0	Basle	Akureyri, Ice	27.05.88
Gardner, Gary	6.2	–	Solihull	29.06.92
Grealish, Jack	5.9	–	Solihull	10.09.95
Green, Andre	5.11	–	Solihull	26.07.98
Hourihane, Conor	6.0	Barnsley	Cork, Ire	02.02.91
Jedinak, Mile	6.3	Crystal Palace	Sydney, Aus	03.08.84
Lansbury, Henri	6.0	Nottm Forest	Enfield	12.10.90
Lyden, Jordan	6.0	–	Perth, Aus	30.01.96
Sanchez, Carlos	6.0	Elche	Quibdo, Col	06.02.86
Tshibola, Aaron	6.3	Reading	Newham	02.01.95
Veretout, Jordan	5.10	Nantes	Ancenis, Fr	01.03.93
Forwards				
Agbonlahor, Gabriel	5.11	–	Birmingham	13.10.86
Hogan, Scott	5.11	Brentford	Salford	13.04.92

| Kodjia, Jonathan | 6.2 | Bristol City | St Denis, Fr | 22.10.89 |
| McCormack, Ross | 5.10 | Fulham | Glasgow | 18.08.86 |

BARNSLEY

Ground: Oakwell Stadium, Barnsley S71 1ET
Telephone: 01226 211211. **Club nickname:** Tykes
Colours: Red and white. **Capacity:** 23,009
Record attendance: 40,255 v Stoke (FA Cup 5) Feb 15, 1936

Goalkeepers

Davies, Adam	6.1	Sheffield Wed	Rinteln, Ger	17.07.92
Townsend, Nick	5.11	Birmingham	Solihull	01.11.94
Defenders				
Fryers, Zeki	6.0	Crystal Palace	Manchester	09.09.92
Jackson, Adam	6.3	Middlesbrough	Darlington	18.05.94
Kpekawa, Cole	6.3	QPR	Blackpool	20.05.96
Lindsay, Liam	6.3	Partick	Paisley	12.10.95
MacDonald, Angus	6.2	Torquay	Winchester	15.10.92
Pinnock, Ethan	6.2	Forest Green	Lambeth	29.05.93
McCarthy, Jason	6.1	Southampton	Southampton	07.11.95
Yiadom, Andy	5.11	Barnet	Holloway	09.12.91
Midfielders				
D'Almeida, Sessi	5.10	Paris SG	Bordeaux, Fr	22.11.95
Hammill, Adam	5.10	Huddersfield	Liverpool	25.01.88
Hedges, Ryan	6.1	Swansea	Northampton	08.07.95
Isgrove, Lloyd	5.10	Southampton	Yeovil	12.01.93
Mallan, Stevie	5.11	St Mirren	Glasgow	25.03.96
McGeehan, Cameron	5.11	Luton	Kingston upon Thames	06.04.95
Moncur, George	5.9	Colchester	Swindon	18.08.93
Mowatt, Alex	5.10	Leeds	Doncaster	13.02.95
Forwards				
Bradshaw, Tom	5.10	Walsall	Shrewsbury	27.07.92
Jackson, Kayden	5.11	Wrexham	Bradford	22.02.94
Payne, Stefan	5.10	Dover	Lambeth	10.08.91
Iuton, Shaun	6.1	Halifax	Sheffield	03.12.91

BIRMINGHAM CITY

Ground: St Andrew's, Birmingham B9 4NH
Telephone: 0844 557 1875. **Club nickname:** Blues
Colours: Blue and white. **Capacity:** 30,016
Record attendance: 66,844 v Everton (FA Cup 5) Feb 11, 1939

Goalkeepers

Kuszczak, Tomasz	6.3	Wolves	Krosno, Pol	20.03.82
Legzdins, Adam	6.0	Leyton Orient	Penkridge	28.11.86
Stockdale, David	6.3	Brighton	Leeds	28.09.85
Trueman, Connal	6.1	–	Birmingham	26.03.96
Defenders				
Grounds, Jonathan	6.1	Oldham	Thornaby	02.02.88
Keita, Cheick	5.7	Virtus Entella	Paris, Fr	16.11.96
Morrison, Michael	6.1	Charlton	Bury St Edmunds	03.03.88
Nsue, Emilio	6.0	Middlesbrough	Palma, Sp	30.09.89
O'Keefe, Corey	6.0	–	Birmingham	05.06.98
Roberts, Marc	6.0	Barnsley	Wakefield	26.07.90

Robinson, Paul	5.9	Bolton	Watford	14.12.78
Shotton, Ryan	6.3	Derby	Stoke	30.09.88
Midfielders				
Cotterill, David	5.9	Doncaster	Cardiff	04.12.87
Davis, David	5.8	Wolves	Smethwick	20.02.91
Fabbrini, Diego	6.0	Watford	Pisa, It	31.07.90
Frei, Kerim	5.7	Besiktas	Feldkirch, Aut	19.11.93
Gardner, Craig	5.10	WBA	Solihull	25.11.86
Gleeson, Stephen	6.2	MK Dons	Dublin, Ire	03.08.88
Kieftenbeld, Maikel	5.10	Groningen	Dalfsen, Hol	26.06.90
Maghoma, Jacques	5.11	Sheffield Wed	Lubumbashi, DR Cong	23.10.87
N'Doye, Cheikh	6.3	Angers	Rufisque, Sen	29.03.86
Solomon-Otabor, Viv	5.9	–	London	02.01.96
Storer, Jack	6.1	Stevenage	Birmingham	02.01.98
Tesche, Robert	5.11	Nottm Forest	Wismar, Ger	27.05.87
Forwards				
Adams, Che	5.10	Sheffield Utd	Leicester	13.07.96
Brock-Madsen, Nicolai	6.4	Randers	Randers, Den	09.01.93
Donaldson, Clayton	6.1	Brentford	Bradford	07.02.84
Jutkiewicz, Lukas	6.1	Burnley	Southampton	20.03.89

BOLTON WANDERERS

Ground: Macron Stadium, Burnden Way, Lostock, Bolton BL6 6JW
Telephone: 0844 871 2932. **Club nickname**: Trotters
Colours: White and navy. **Capacity**: 28,723
Record attendance: Burnden Park: 69,912 v Manchester City (FA Cup 5) Feb 18, 1933.
Macron Stadium: 28,353 v Leicester (Prem Lge) Dec 28, 2003

Goalkeepers				
Alnwick, Ben	6.2	Peterborough	Prudhoe	01.01.87
Amos, Ben	6.3	Manchester Utd	Macclesfield	10.04.90
Howard, Mark	6.1	Sheffield Utd	Southwark	21.09.86
Defenders				
Beevers, Mark	6.4	Millwall	Barnsley	21.11.89
Darby, Stephen	6.0	Bradford	Liverpool	06.10.88
Dervite, Dorian	6.3	Charlton	Lille, Fr	25.07.88
Little, Mark	6.1	Bristol City	Worcester	20.08.88
Osede, Derik	6.0	Real Madrid	Madrid, Sp	21.02.93
Wheater, David	6.5	Middlesbrough	Redcar	14.02.87
Midfielders				
Ameobi, Sammy	6.4	Newcastle	Newcastle	01.05.92
Buckley, Will	6.0	Sunderland	Oldham	12.08.88
Davies, Mark	5.11	Wolves	Wolverhampton	18.02.88
Karacan, Jem	5.10	Galatasaray	Catford	21.02.89
Morais, Filipe	5.9	Bradford	Benavente, Por	21.11.85
Pratley, Darren	6.0	Swansea	Barking	22.04.85
Samizadeh, Alex	5.9	Curzon Ashton	Tehran, Ira	10.11.98
Taylor, Chris	6.0	Blackburn	Oldham	20.12.86
Vela, Josh	5.11	–	Salford	14.12.93
Forwards				
Le Fondre, Adam	5.9	Cardiff	Stockport	02.12.86
Madine, Gary	6.3	Sheffield Wed	Gateshead	24.08.90

BRENTFORD

Ground: Griffin Park, Braemar Road, Brentford TW8 0NT
Telephone: 0845 345 6442. **Club nickname**: Bees
Colours: Red, white and black. **Capacity**: 12,763
Record attendance: 38,678 v Leicester (FA Cup 6) Feb 26, 1949

Goalkeepers

Bentley, Daniel	6.2	Southend	Basildon	13.07.93
Daniels, Luke	6.4	Scunthorpe	Bolton	05.01.88
Defenders				
Barbet, Yoann	6.2	Chamois	Libourne, Fr	10.05.93
Bjelland, Andreas	6.2	Twente	Vedbaek, Den	11.07.88
Clarke, Josh	5.8	–	Walthamstow	05.07.94
Colin, Maxime	5.11	Anderlecht	Arras, Fr	15.11.91
Dalsgaard, Henrik	6.3	Zulte Waregem	Roum, Den	27.07.89
Dean, Harlee	5.10	Southampton	Basingstoke	26.07.91
Egan, John	6.2	Gillingham	Cork, Ire	20.10.92
Field, Tom	5.10	–	Kingston upon Thames	14.03.97
Henry, Rico	5.8	Walsall	Birmingham	08.07.97
Jota	5.11	Celta Vigo	Pobra do Caraminal, Sp	16.06.91
Yennaris, Nico	5.9	Arsenal	Leytonstone	24.05.93
Midfielders				
Canos, Sergi	5.9	Norwich	Nules, Sp	02.02.97
Judge, Alan	6.0	Blackburn	Dublin, Ire	11.11.88
Kerschbaumer, Konstantin	5.11	Admira Wacker	Tulln Donau, Aut	01.07.92
MacLeod, Lewis	5.9	Rangers	Wishaw	16.06.94
Maupay, Neal	5.7	St Etienne	Versailles, Fr	14.08.96
McEachran, Josh	5.10	Chelsea	Oxford	01.03.93
Mokotjo, Kamo	5.7	Twente	Odendaalsrus, SA	11.03.91
Sawyers, Romaine	5.9	Walsall	Birmingham	02.11.91
Woods, Ryan	5.8	Shrewsbury	Norton Canes	13.12.93
Forwards				
Jozefzoom, Florian	5.8	PSV Eindhoven	Saint Laurent, Fr Guin	09.02.91
Shaibu, Justin	6.0	Kope	Denmark	20.10.97
Vibe, Lasse	6.0	Gothenburg	Aarhus, Den	22.02.87

BRISTOL CITY

Ground: Ashton Gate, Bristol BS3 2EJ
Telephone: 0871 222 6666. **Club nickname**: Robins
Colours: Red and white. **Capacity**: 27,000
Record attendance: 43,335 v Preston (FA Cup 5) Feb 16, 1935

Goalkeepers

Fielding, Frank	6.0	Derby	Blackburn	04.04.88
Lucic, Ivan	6.4	Bayern Munich	Vienna, Aut	23.03.95
O'Leary, Max	6.1	–	Bath	10.10.96
Defenders				
Flint, Aden	6.2	Swindon	Pinxton	11.07.89
Kelly, Lloyd	5.10	–	Bristol	01.10.98
Magnusson, Hordur	6.3	Juventus	Reykjavik, Ice	11.02.93
Moore, Taylor	6.1	Lens	Walthamstow	12.05.97
Pisano, Eros	6.1	Hellas Verona	Busto Arsizio, It	31.03.87
Vyner, Zak	5.11	–	Bath	14.05.95
Wright, Bailey	5.10	Preston	Melbourne, Aus	28.07.92

Midfielders

Brownhill, Josh	5.10	Preston	Warrington	19.12.95
Bryan, Joe	5.7	–	Bristol	17.09.93
Golbourne, Scott	5.9	Wolves	Bristol	29.02.88
Hegeler, Jens	6.4	Hertha Berlin	Cologne, Ger	22.01.88
O'Dowda, Callum	5.11	Oxford	Oxford	23.04.95
O'Neil, Gary	5.8	Norwich	Beckenham	18.05.83
Pack, Marlon	6.2	Cheltenham	Portsmouth	25.03.91
Reid, Bobby	5.7	–	Bristol	02.02.93
Smith, Korey	6.0	Oldham	Hatfield	31.01.91

Forwards

De Girolamo, Diego	5.10	Sheffield Utd	Chesterfield	05.10.95
Diedhiou, Famara	6.2	Angers	Saint-Louis, Sen	15.12.92
Djuric, Milan	6.6	Cesena	Tuzia, Bos	22.05.90
Engvall, Gustav	6.1	Gothenburg	Kalmar, Swe	29.04.96
Garita, Paul-Arnold	6.2	Chateauroux	Douala, Cam	18.06.95
McCoulsky, Shawn	6.0	Dulwich Hamlet	Lewisham	06.01.97
Paterson, Jamie	5.9	Nottm Forest	Coventry	20.12.91
Taylor, Matty	5.9	Bristol Rov	Oxford	30.03.90
Wilbrahan, Aaron	6.3	Crystal Palace	Knutsford	21.10.79

BURTON ALBION

Ground: Pirelli Stadium, Princess Way, Burton upon Trent DE13 AR
Telephone: 01283 565938. **Club nickname**: Brewers
Colours: Yellow and black. **Capacity**: 6,912
Record attendance: 6,192 v Oxford Utd (Blue Square Prem Lge) Apr 17, 2009

Goalkeepers

Bywater, Stephen	6.3	Kerala	Oldham	07.06.81
Campbell, Harry	6.1	Bolton	Blackburn	16.11.95

Defenders

Barker, Shaun	6.3	Derby	Trowell	19.09.82
Buxton, Jake	5.11	Wigan	Sutton-in-Ashfield	04.03.85
Delaney, Ryan	6.0	Wexford	Wexford, Ire	06.09.96
McFadzean, Kyle	6.1	MK Dons	Sheffield	28.02.87
McCrory, Damien	6.2	Dagenham	Croom, Ire	23.02.90
Mousinho, John	6.1	Preston	Isleworth	30.04.86
Naylor, Tom	6.0	Derby	Sutton-in-Ashfield	28.06.91
Turner, Ben	6.4	Cardiff	Birmingham	21.08.88
Warnock, Stephen	5.10	Wigan	Ormskirk	12.12.81

Midfielders

Dyer, Lloyd	5.8	Burnley	Birmingham	13.09.82
Fox, Ben	5.11	–	Burton	01.02.98
Harness, Marcus	6.0	–	Coventry	01.08.94
Irvine, Jackson	6.2	Ross Co	Melbourne, Aus	07.03.93
Lund, Matt	6.0	Rochdale	Manchester	21.11.90
Murphy, Luke	6.2	Leeds (loan)	Alsager	21.10.89
Palmer, Matt	5.10	–	Derby	01.08.93

Forwards

Akins, Lucas	6.0	Stevenage	Huddersfield	25.02.89
Boyce, Liam	6.1	Ross Co	Belfast	08.04.91
Sbarra, Joe	5.10	–	Lichfield	21.12.98
Sordell, Marvin	5.10	Coventry	Harrow	17.02.91
Varney, Luke	5.11	Ipswich	Leicester	28.09.82

CARDIFF CITY

Ground: Cardiff City Stadium, Leckwith Road, Cardiff CF11 8AZ
Telephone: 0845 365 1115. **Club nickname:** Bluebirds
Colours: Blue. **Capacity:** 33,300
Record attendance: Ninian Park: 62,634 Wales v England, Oct 17, 1959; Club: 57,893 v Arsenal (Div 1) Apr 22, 1953, Cardiff City Stadium: 33,280 (Wales v Belgium) Jun 12, 2015. Club: 28,680 v Derby (Champ) Apr 2, 2016

Goalkeepers

Camp, Lee	6.1	Rotherham	Derby	22.08.84
Etheridge, Neil	6.3	Walsall	Enfield	07.02.90
Murphy, Brian	6.1	Portsmouth	Waterford, Ire	07.05.83
Wilson, Ben	6.1	Accrington	Stanley	09.08.92

Defenders

Bamba, Sol	6.3	Leeds	Ivry-sur-Seine, Fr	13.01.85
Bennett, Joe	5.10	Aston Villa	Rochdale	28.03.90
Connolly, Matthew	6.2	QPR	Barnet	24.09.87
Halford, Greg	6.4	Rotherham	Chelmsford	08.12.84
John, Declan	5.10		Merthyr Tydfil	30.06.95
Manga, Bruno	6.1	Lorient	Libreville, Gab	16.07.88
Morrison, Sean	6.1	Reading	Plymouth	08.01.91
Paterson, Callum	6.0	Hearts	London	13.10.94
Peltier, Lee	5.11	Huddersfield	Liverpool	11.12.86
Richards, Jazz	6.1	Fulham	Swansea	12.04.91

Midfielders

Damour, Loic	5.11	Bourg Peronnas	Chantilly, Fr	08.01.91
Gunnarsson, Aron	5.11	Coventry	Akureyri, Ice	22.04.89
Harris, Kadeem	5.9	Wycombe	Westminster	08.06.93
Hoilett, Junior	5.8	QPR	Brampton, Can	05.06.90
Kennedy, Matthew	5.9	Everton	Dundonald	01.11.94
Mendez-Laing, Nathaniel	5.10	Rochdale	Birmingham	15.04.92
Noone, Craig	6.3	Brighton	Fazakerly	17.11.87
O'Keefe, Stuart	5.8	Crystal Palace	Norwich	04.03.91
Pilkington, Anthony	6.0	Norwich	Blackburn	06.06.88
Ralls, Joe	6.0	–	Aldershot	13.10.93

Forwards

Gounongbe, Frederic	6.3	Westerlo	Brussels, Bel	01.05.88
Healey, Rhys	5.11	Connah's Quay	Manchester	06.12.94
Saadi, Idriss	5.10	Clermont	Valence, Fr	08.02.92
Tomlin, Lee	5.11	Bristol City	Leicester	12.01.89
Ward, Danny	5.11	Rotherham	Bradford	09.12.90
Zohore, Kenneth	6.3	Kortrijk	Copenhagen, Den	31.01.94

DERBY COUNTY

Ground: Pride Park, Derby DE24 8XL
Telephone: 0871 472 1884. **Club nickname:** Rams
Colours: White and black. **Capacity:** 33,597
Record attendance: Baseball Ground: 41,826 v Tottenham (Div 1) Sep 20, 1969; Pride Park: 33,597 (England v Mexico) May 25, 2011; Club: 33,475 v Rangers (Ted McMinn testimonial) May 1, 2006

Goalkeepers

Carson, Scott	6.3	Wigan	Whitehaven	03.09.85
Mitchell, Jonathan	6.2	Newcastle	Hartlepool	24.11.94
Roos, Kelle	6.5	Nuneaton	Rijkevoort, Hol	31.05.92

Defenders

Baird, Chris	5.11	WBA	Rasharkin	25.02.82
Davies, Curtis	6.2	Hull	Waltham Forest	15.03.85
Forsyth, Craig	6.0	Watford	Carnoustie	24.02.89
Keogh, Richard	6.2	Coventry	Harlow	11.08.86
Lowe, Max	5.9	–	Birmingham	11.05.97
Olsson, Marcus	6.0	Blackburn	Gavle, Swe	17.05.88
Pearce, Alex	6.2	Reading	Wallingford	09.11.88
Shackell, Jason	6.4	Burnley	Stevenage	27.09.83
Wisdom, Andre	6.1	Liverpool	Leeds	09.05.93

Midfielders

Anya, Ikechi	5.7	Watford	Glasgow	03.01.88
Butterfield, Jacob	5.11	Huddersfield	Bradford	10.06.90
Bryson, Craig	5.8	Kilmarnock	Rutherglen	06.11.86
Hanson, Jamie	6.3	–	Burton upon Trent	10.11.95
Huddlestone, Tom	6.1	Hull	Nottingham	28.12.86
Johnson, Bradley	5.10	Norwich	Hackney	28.04.87
Thorne, George	6.2	WBA	Chatham	04.01.93

Forwards

Bennett, Mason	5.10	–	Shirebrook	15.07.96
Bent, Darren	5.11	Aston Villa	Wandsworth	06.02.84
Blackman, Nick	6.1	Reading	Whitefield	11.11.89
Martin, Chris	5.10	Norwich	Beccles	04.11.88
Nugent, David	5.11	Middlesbrough	Liverpool	02.05.85
Russell, Johnny	5.10	Dundee Utd	Glasgow	08.04.90
Vydra, Matej	5.11	Watford	Chotebor, Cz	01.05.92
Weimann, Andreas	6.2	Aston Villa	Vienna, Aut	05.08.91

FULHAM

Ground: Craven Cottage, Stevenage Road, London SW6 6HH
Telephone: 0870 442 1222. **Club nickname**: Cottagers
Colours: White and black. **Capacity**: 25,678
Record attendance: 49,335 v Millwall (Div 2) Oct 8, 1938

Goalkeepers

| Bettinelli, Marcus | 6.4 | Simpeleen | Camberwell | 24.05.92 |
| Button, David | 6.3 | Brentford | Stevenage | 27.02.89 |

Defenders

Fredericks, Ryan	5.8	Bristol City	Potters Bar	10.10.92
Madl, Michael	6.0	Sturm Graz	Judenburg, Aut	21.03.88
Marcelo	6.4	CD Lugo	Barcelona, Sp	08.10.93
Odoi, Denis	5.10	Lokeren	Leuven, Bel	27.05.88
Ream, Tim	6.1	Bolton	St Louis, US	05.10.87
Sessegnon, Ryan	5.10	–	Roehampton	18.05.2000
Sigurdsson, Ragnar	6.2	Krasnodar	Reykjavik, Ice	19.06.86

Midfielders

Ayite, Floyd	5.9	Bastia	Bordeaux, Fr	15.12.88
Cairney, Tom	6.0	Blackburn	Nottingham	20.01.91
Christensen, Lasse	5.1	Midtjylland	Esbjerg, Den	15.08.94
Cisse, Ibrahima	6.0	Standard Liege	Liege, Bel	28.02.94
Johansen, Stefan	6.0	Celtic	Vardo, Nor	08.01.91
Kavanagh, Sean	5.9	Belvedere	Dublin, Ire	20.01.94
Kebano, Neeskens	5.11	Genk	Montereau, Fr	10.03.92
McDonald, Kevin	6.2	Wolves	Carnoustie	04.11.88

Forwards

Aluko, Sone	5.8	Hull	Hounslow	19.12.89
Piazon, Lucas	6.0	Chelsea (loan)	Sao Paulo, Br	20.01.94
Williams, George	5.8	MK Dons	Milton Keynes	07.09.95
Woodrow, Cauley	6.1	Luton	Hemel Hempstead	02.12.94

HULL CITY

Ground: KCom Stadium, Anlaby Road, Hull, HU3 6HU
Telephone: 01482 504 600. **Club nickname:** Tigers
Capacity: 25,404. **Colours:** Amber and black
Record attendance: Boothferry Park: 55,019 v Manchester Utd (FA Cup 6) Feb 26, 1949. KC Stadium: 25,030 v Liverpool (Prem Lge) May 9, 2010. Also: 25,280 (England U21 v Holland) Feb 17, 2004

Goalkeepers

Jakupovic, Eldin	6.3	Aris	Sarajevo, Bos	02.10.84
Marshall, David	6.3	Cardiff	Glasgow	05.03.85
McGregor, Allan	6.0	Besiktas	Edinburgh	31.01.82

Defenders

Aina, Ola	5.9	Chelsea (loan)	Southwark	08.10.96
Dawson, Michael	6.2	Tottenham	Northallerton	18.11.83
Lenihan, Brian	5.10	Cork	Cork	08.06.94
Odubajo, Moses	5.10	Brentford	Greenwich	28.07.93
Robertson, Andrew	5.10	Dundee Utd	Glasgow	11.03.94

Midfielders

Batty, Daniel	5.11	–	Pontefract	10.12.97
Clucas, Sam	5.10	Chesterfield	Lincoln	25.09.90
Elmohamady, Ahmed	5.11	Sunderland	Basyoun, Egy	09.09.87
Evandro	5.10	Porto	Blumenau, Br	23.08.86
Grosicki, Kamil	5.11	Rennes	Szczecin, Pol	08.06.88
Henriksen, Markus	6.2	Alkmaar	Trondheim, Nor	25.07.92
Maloney, Shaun	5.7	Chicago Fire	Miri, Malay	24.01.83
Mason, Ryan	5.9	Tottenham	Enfield	13.06.91
Meyler, David	6.2	Sunderland	Cork, Ire	29.05.89
Olley, Greg	5.10	–	Durham	02.02.96
Weir, Jamee	5.11	Manchester Utd	Preston	04.08.95

Forwards

Bowen, Jarrod	5.9	Hereford	Leominster	20.12.96
Diomande, Adama	5.11	Stabaek	Oslo, Nor	14.02.90
Hernandez, Abel	6.1	Palermo	Pando, Uru	08.08.90
Keane, Will	6.2	Manchester Utd	Stockport	11.01.93
Luer, Greg	5.11	Burgess Hill	Brighton	06.12.94

IPSWICH TOWN

Ground: Portman Road, Ipswich IP1 2DA
Telephone: 01473 400500. **Club nickname:** Blues/Town
Colours: Blue and white. **Capacity:** 30,300
Record attendance: 38,010 v Leeds (FA Cup 6) Mar 8, 1975

Goalkeepers

Bialkowski, Bartosz	6.0	Notts Co	Braniewo, Pol	06.07.87
Gerken, Dean	6.2	Bristol City	Southend	04.08.85

Defenders

Chambers, Luke	5.11	Nottm Forest	Kettering	29.08.85

Iorfa, Dominic	6.2	Wolves (loan)	Southend	08.07.95
Kenlock, Myles	6.1	–	Croydon	29.11.96
Knudsen, Jonas	6.1	Esbjerg	Esbjerg, Den	16.09.92
Smith, Tommy	6.1	–	Macclesfield	31.03.90
Spence, Jordan	6.2	MK Dons	Woodford	24.05.90
Webster, Adam	6.3	Portsmouth	Chichester	04.01.95
Midfielders				
Adeyemi, Tom	6.1	Cardiff	Norwich	24.10.91
Bru, Kevin	6.0	Levski Sofia	Paris, Fr	12.12.88
Bishop, Teddy	5.11	–	Cambridge	15.07.96
Celina, Bersant	5.11	Manchester City (loan)	Prizren, Kos	09.09.96
Dozzell, Andre	5.10	–	Ipswich	02.05.99
Huws, Emyr	5.10	Cardiff	Llanelli	30.09.93
Hyam, Luke	5.10	–	Ipswich	24.10.91
Rowe, Danny	6.0	Macclesfield	Wythenshawe	09.03.92
Skuse, Cole	5.9	Bristol City	Bristol	29.03.86
Ward, Grant	5.10	Tottenham	Lewisham	05.12.94
Forwards				
Gaarner, Joe	5.10	Rangers	Blackburn	12.04.88
McGoldrick, David	6.1	Nottm Forest	Nottingham	29.11.87
Sears, Freddie	5.10	Colchester	Hornchurch	27.11.89

LEEDS UNITED

Ground: Elland Road, Leeds LS11 OES
Telephone: 0871 334 1919. **Club nickname**: Whites
Colours: White. **Capacity**: 37,900
Record attendance: 57,892 v Sunderland (FA Cup 5 rep) Mar 15, 1967

Goalkeepers				
Green, Robert	6.3	QPR	Chertsey	18.01.80
Peacock-Farrell, Bailey	6.2	–	Darlington	29.10.96
Silvestri, Marco	6.3	Chievo	Castelnovo, It	02.03.91
Wiedwald, Felix	6.3	Werder Bremen	Thedinghausen, Ger	15.03.90
Defenders				
Ayling, Luke	6.1	Bristol City	Lambeth	25.08.91
Berardi, Gaetano	5.11	Sampdoria	Sorengo, Swi	21.08.88
Cooper, Liam	6.0	Chesterfield	Hull	30.08.91
Denton, Tyler	5.8	–	Dewsbury	06.09.95
Jansson, Pontus	6.5	Torino	Arlov, Swe	13.02.91
Midfielders				
Alioski, Ezgjan	5.8	Lugano	Prilep, Maced	12.02.92
Anita, Vurnon	5.6	Newcastle	Willemstad, Cur	04.04.89
Bridcutt, Liam	5.9	Sunderland	Reading	08.05.89
Dallas, Stuart	6.0	Brentford	Cookstown	19.04.91
Hernandez, Pablo	5.8	Al-Arabi	Castellon, Sp	11.04.85
Klich, Mateusz	6.0	FC Twente	Tarnow, Pol	13.06.90
O'Kane, Eunan	5.8	Bournemouth	Derry	10.07.90
Phillips, Kalvin	5.10	–	Leeds	02.12.95
Sacko, Hadi	6.0	Sporting Lisbon	Corbeil, Fr	24.03.94
Saiz, Samuel	5.9	Huesca	Madrid, Sp	22.01.91
Vieira, Ronaldo	5.11	–	Bissau, Guin	20.07.98
Forwards				
Antonsson, Marcus	6.1	Kalmar	Sweden	08.05.91
Doukara, Souleymane	6.1	Catania	Meudon, Fr	29.09.91

Ekuban, Caleb	6.2	Chievo	Villafranca, It	23.03.94
Roofe, Kemar	5.10	Oxford	Walsall	06.01.93
Wood, Chris	6.3	Leicester	Auckland, NZ	07.12.91

MIDDLESBROUGH

Ground: Riverside Stadium, Middlesbrough, TS3 6RS
Telephone: 0844 499 6789. **Club nickname:** Boro
Capacity: 35,100. **Colours:** Red
Record attendance: Ayresome Park. 53,596 v Newcastle (Div 1) Dec 27, 1949; Riverside Stadium: 35,000 (England v Slovakia) Jun 11, 2003. Club: 34,836 v Norwich (Prem Lge) Dec 28, 2004

Goalkeepers
Konstantopoulos, Dimi	6.5	AEK Athens	Thessaloniki, Gre	29.11.79
Mejias, Tomas	6.5	Real Madrid	Madrid, Sp	30.01.89
Ripley, Connor	6.3	–	Middlesbrough	13.02.93

Defenders
Ayala, Daniel	6.3	Norwich	El Saucejo, Sp	07.11.90
Baptiste, Alex	5.11	Bolton	Sutton-in-Ashfield	31.01.86
Barragan, Antonio	6.1	Valencia	Pontedeume, Sp	12.06.87
Christie, Cyrus	6.2	Derby	Coventry	30.09.92
Fabio	5.6	Cardiff	Petropolis, Br	09.07.90
Friend, George	6.0	Doncaster	Barnstaple	19.10.87
Fry, Dael	6.0	–	Middlesbrough	30.08.97
Gibson, Ben	6.1	–	Nunthorpe	06.01.93
Roberts, Connor	5.9	Swansea (loan)	Neath	23.09.95

Midfielders
Clayton, Adam	5.9	Huddersfield	Manchester	14.01.89
De Pena, Carlos	5.10	Nacional	Montevideo, Uru	11.03.92
De Roon, Marten	6.1	Atalanta	Zwijndrecht, Hol	29.03.91
De Sart, Julien	6.2	Standard Liege	Waremme, Bel	23.12.94
Downing, Stewart	6.0	West Ham	Middlesbrough	02.07.84
Forshaw, Adam	6.1	Wigan	Liverpool	08.10.91
Guedioura, Adlene	6.0	Watford	La Roche, Fr	12.11.85
Howson, Jonny	5.11	Norwich	Leeds	21.05.88
Leadbitter, Grant	5.9	Ipswich	Chester le Street	07.01.86
Ramirez, Gaston	6.0	Southampton	Fray Bentos, Uru	02.12.90
Traore, Adama	5.10	Aston Villa	L'Hospitalet, Sp	25.01.96

Forwards
Bamford, Patrick	6.1	Chelsea	Grantham	05.09.93
Braithwaite, Martin	5.11	Toulouse	Esbjerg, Den	05.06.91
Gestede, Rudy	6.4	Aston Villa	Nancy, Fr	10.10.88
Miller, George	5.10	Bury	Bolton	11.08.98
Stuani, Cristhian	6.1	Espanyol	Tala, Uru	12.10.86

MILLWALL

Ground: The Den, Zampa Road, London SE16 3LN
Telephone: 0207 232 1222. **Club nickname:** Lions
Colours: Blue. **Capacity:** 20,146
Record attendance: The Den: 48,672 v Derby (FA Cup 5) Feb 20, 1937. New Den: 20,093 v Arsenal (FA Cup 3) Jan 10, 1994

Goalkeepers
| Archer, Jordan | 6.3 | Tottenham | Walthamstow | 12.04.93 |
| King, Tom | 6.1 | Crystal Palace | Plymouth | 09.03.95 |

Defenders

Craig, Tony	6.0	Brentford	Greenwich	20.04.85
Cummings, Shaun	6.0	Reading	Hammersmith	28.02.89
Hutchinson, Shaun	6.2	Fulham	Newcastle	23.11.90
McLaughlin, Conor	6.0	Fleetwood	Belfast	26.07.91
Meredith, James	6.1	Bradord	Albury, Aus	04.04.88
Romeo, Mahlon	5.10	Gillingham	Westminster	19.09.95
Webster, Byron	6.4	Yeovil	Leeds	31.03.87

Midfielders

Butcher, Calum	6.0	Burton	Rochford	26.02.91
Ferguson, Shane	5.11	Newcastle	Derry	12.07.91
Oyedinma, Fred	6.1	–	Plumstead	24.11.96
Saville, George	5.9	Wolves	Camberley	01.06.93
Thompson, Ben	5.10	–	Sidcup	03.10.95
Wallace, Jed	5.10	Wolves	Reading	26.03.94
Williams, Shaun	6.0	MK Dons	Dublin, Ire	19.09.86
Worrall, David	6.0	Southend	Manchester	12.06.90

Forwards

Elliott, Tom	6.4	AFC Wimbledon	Leeds	09.11.90
Gregory, Lee	6.2	Halifax	Sheffield	26.08.88
Morison, Steve	6.2	Leeds	Enfield	29.08.83
O'Brien, Aiden	5.8	–	Islington	04.10.93

NORWICH CITY

Ground: Carrow Road, Norwich NR1 1JE
Telephone: 01603 760760. **Club nickname:** Canaries
Colours: Yellow and green. **Capacity:** 27,220
Record attendance: 43,984 v Leicester City (FA Cup 6), Mar 30, 1963

Goalkeepers

Jones, Paul	6.3	Portsmouth	Maidstone	28.06.86
McGovern, Michael	6.3	Hamilton	Enniskillen	12.07.84

Defenders

Franke, Marcel	6.4	Greuther Furth	Dresden, Ger	05.04.93
Husband, James	5.11	Middlesbrough	Leeds	03.01.94
Klose, Timm	6.4	Wolfsburg	Frankfurt, Ger	09.05.88
Martin, Russell	6.0	Peterborough	Brighton	04.01.86
Pinto, Ivo	6.1	Dinamo Zagreb	Lourosa, Por	07.01.90
Toffolo, Harry	6.0	–	Welwyn Garden City	19.08.95
Zimmermann, Christoph	6.4	Borussia Dortmund	Dusseldorf, Ger	12.01.93

Midfielders

Godfrey, Ben	6.2	York	York	15.01.98
Hoolahan, Wes	5.7	Blackpool	Dublin, Ire	10.08.83
Jarvis, Matt	5.8	West Ham	Middlesbrough	22.05.86
Maddison, James	5.10	Coventry	Coventry	23.11.96
Murphy, Jacob	5.10	–	Wembley	24.02.95
Murphy, Josh	5.9	–	Wembley	24.02.95
Pritchard, Alex	5.8	Tottenham	Orsett	03.05.93
Reed, Harrison	5.7	Southampton (loan)	Worthing	27.01.95
Tettey, Alexander	5.11	Rennes	Accra, Gh	04.04.86
Thompson, Louis	5.11	Swindon	Bristol	19.12.94
Vrancic, Mario	6.1	Darmstadt	Slavonski Brod, Croa	23.05.89
Wildschut, Yanic	6.2	Wigan	Amsterdam, Hol	01.11.91

Forwards

Jerome, Cameron	6.1	Stoke	Huddersfield	14.08.86
Naismith, Steven	5.10	Everton	Irvine	14.09.86
Oliveira, Nelson	6.1	Benfica	Barcelos, Por	08.08.91
Watkins, Marley	6.1	Barnsley	Lewisham	17.10.90

NOTTINGHAM FOREST

Ground: City Ground, Pavilion Road, Nottingham NG2 5FJ
Telephone: 0115 982 4444. **Club nickname**: Forest
Colours: Red and white. **Capacity**: 30,576
Record attendance: 49,946 v Manchester Utd (Div 1) Oct 28, 1967

Goalkeepers

Evtimov, Dimitar	6.3	Etropole	Shumen, Bul	07.09.93
Henderson, Stephen	6.3	Charlton	Dublin, Ire	02.05.88
Smith, Jordan	6.1	–	Nottingham	08.12.94
Stojkovic, Vladimir	6.5	Maccabi Haifa	Loznica, Serb	28.07.83

Defenders

Fox, Danny	6.0	Southampton	Winsford	29.05.86
Hobbs, Jack	6.3	Hull	Portsmouth	18.08.88
Lam, Thomas	6.2	Zwolle	Amsterdam, Hol	18.12.93
Lichaj, Eric	5.10	Aston Villa	Downers Grove, US	17.11.88
Mancienne, Michael	6.0	Hamburg	Feltham	08.01.88
Mills, Matt	6.3	Bolton	Swindon	14.07.86
Perquis, Damien	6.1	Toronto	Troyes, Fr	10.04.84
Traore, Armand	6.1	QPR	Paris, Fr	08.10.89
Worrall, Joe	6.4	–	Hucknall	10.01.97

Midfielders

Arlyibi, Gboly	6.0	Chesterfield	Arlington, US	18.01.95
Carayol, Mustapha	6.10	Middlesbrough	Banjul, Gam	04.09.88
Cash, Matty	6.1	–	Slough	07.08.97
Cohen, Chris	5.11	Yeovil	Norwich	05.03.87
Grant, Jorge	5.9	–	Banbury	19.12.94
Lica	6.0	Porto	Lamelan, Por	08.09.88
Osborn, Ben	6.10	–	Derby	05.08.94
McKay, Barrie	5.9	Rangers	Paisley	30.12.94
Vaughan, David	5.7	Sunderland	Rhuddlan	18.02.83
Ward, Jamie	5.5	Derby	Birmingham	12.05.86

Forwards

Assombalonga, Britt	5.10	Peterborough	Kinshasa, DR Cong	06.12.92
Brereton, Ben	6.0	–	Blythe Bridge	18.04.99
Clough, Zach	5.8	Bolton	Manchester	08.03.95
Cummings, Jason	5.10	Hibernian	Edinburgh	01.08.95
Vellios, Apostolos	6.4	Iraklis	Thessaloniki, Gre	08.01.92
Walker, Tyler	5.10	–	Nottingham	07.10.96

PRESTON NORTH END

Ground: Deepdale, Sir Tom Finney Way, Preston PR1 6RU
Telephone: 0844 856 1964. **Club nickname**: Lilywhites
Colours: White and navy. **Capacity**: 23,404
Record attendance: 42,684 v Arsenal (Div 1) Apr 23, 1938

Goalkeepers

Hudson, Matthew	6.4	–	Southport	29.07.98
Maxwell, Chris	6.2	Fleetwood	St Asaph	30.07.90

Rudd, Declan	6.3	Norwich	Diss	16.01.91

Defenders

Boyle, Andy	5.11	Dundalk	Dublin, Ire	07.03.91
Clarke, Tom	5.11	Huddersfield	Halifax	21.12.87
Cunningham, Greg	6.0	Bristol City	Carnmore, Ire	31.01.91
Davies, Ben	5.11	–	Barrow	11.08.95
Huntington, Paul	6.2	Yeovil	Carlisle	17.09.87
O'Connor, Kevin	6.2	Cork	Enniscorthy, Ire	07.05.95
Spurr, Tommy	6.1	Blackburn	Leeds	30.09.87
Vermijl, Marnick	5.11	Sheffield Wed	Peer, Bel	13.01.92
Woods, Calum	5.11	Huddersfield	Liverpool	05.02.87

Midfielders

Browne, Alan	5.8	Cork	Cork, Ire	15.04.95
Grimshaw, Liam	5.10	Manchester Utd	Burnley	02.02.95
Harrop, Josh	5.9	Manchester Utd	Stockport	15.12.95
Horgan, Daryl	5.7	Dundalk	Galway, Ire	10.08.92
Johnson, Daniel	5.8	Aston Villa	Kingston, Jam	08.10.92
Pearson, Ben	5.5	Manchester Utd	Oldham	04.01.95
Pringle, Ben	5.8	Fulham	Newcastle	25.07.89
Welsh, John	6.0	Tranmere	Liverpool	10.01.84

Forwards

Barkhuizen, Tom	5.11	Preston	Blackpool	04.07.93
Doyle, Eoin	6.0	Cardiff	Dublin, Ire	12.03.88
Gallagher, Paul	6.0	Leicester	Glasgow	09.08.84
Hugill, Jordan	6.0	Port Vale	Middlesbrough	04.06.92
Maguire, Sean	5.9	Cork	Luton	01.05.94
May, Stevie	5.10	Sheffield Wed	Perth, Scot	03.11.92
Robinson, Callum	5.10	Aston Villa	Northampton	02.02.95

QUEENS PARK RANGERS

Ground: Loftus Road Stadium, South Africa Road, London W12 7PA
Telephone: 0208 743 0262. **Club nickname:** Hoops
Colours: Blue and white. **Capcity:** 18,360
Record attendance: 35,353 v Leeds (Div 1) 27 Apr, 1974

Goalkeepers

Ingram, Matt	6.3	Wycombe	High Wycombe	18.12.93
Smithies, Alex	6.3	Huddersfield	Huddersfield	05.03.90

Defenders

Bidwell, Jake	6.0	Brentford	Southport	21.03.93
Caulker, Steven	6.3	Cardiff	Feltham	29.12.91
Furlong, Darnell	5.11	–	Luton	31.10.95
Hall, Grant	6.4	Tottenham	Brighton	29.10.91
Lynch, Joel	6.1	Huddersfield	Eastbourne	03.10.87
Onuoha, Nedum	6.2	Manchester City	Warri, Nig	12.11.86
Perch, James	6.0	Wigan	Mansfield	28.09.85
Robinson, Jack	5.7	Liverpool	Warrington	01.09.93

Midfielders

Borysiuk, Ariel	5.10	Legia Warsaw	Biala Podlaska, Pol	28.07.91
Cousins, Jordan	5.10	Charlton	Greenwich	06.03.94
Freeman, Luke	5.10	Bristol City	Dartford	22.03.92
Goss, Sean	5.10	Manchester Utd	Wegberg, Ger	01.10.95
Luongo, Massimo	5.10	Swindon	Sydney, Aus	25.09.92
Petrasso, Michael	5.6	–	Toronto, Can	09.07.95

| Scowen, Josh | 5.10 | Barnsley | Enfield | 28.03.93 |
| Wszolek, Pawel | 6.1 | Hellas Verona | Tczew, Pol | 30.04.92 |

Forwards

El Khayati, Abdenasser	6.1	Burton	Rotterdam, Hol	07.02.89
Emmanuel-Thomas, Jay	6.3	Bristol City	Forest Gate	27.12.90
Grego-Cox, Reece	5.7	–	Hammersmith	02.11.96
Mackie, Jamie	5.8	Nottm Forest	Dorking	22.09.85
Ngbakoto, Yeni	5.8	Metz	Croix, Fr	23.01.92
Smith, Matt	6.6	Fulham	Birmingham	07.06.89
Sylla, Idrissa	6.2	Anderlecht	Conakry, Guin	03.12.90
Washington, Conor	5.10	Peterborough	Chatham	18.05.92

READING

Ground: Madejski Stadium, Junction 11 M4, Reading RG2 0FL
Telephone: 0118 968 1100. **Club nickname:** Royals
Colours: Blue and white. **Capacity:** 24,200
Record attendance: Elm Park: 33,042 v Brentford (FA Cup 5) Feb 19, 1927; Madejski
Stadium: 24,184 v Everton (Prem Lge) Nov 17, 2012

Goalkeepers

| Al Habsi, Ali | 6.4 | Wigan | Al-Mudhaibi, Om | 30.12.81 |
| Jaakkola, Anssi | 6.5 | Ajax Cape Town | Kemi, Fin | 13.03.87 |

Defenders

Blackett, Tyler	6.1	Manchester Utd	Manchester	02.04.94
Cooper, Jake	6.4	–	Bracknell	03.02.95
Gunter, Chris	5.11	Nottm Forest	Newport	21.07.89
Ilori, Tiago	6.3	Liverpool	Hampstead	26.02.93
McShane, Paul	6.0	Hull	Kilpedder, Ire	06.01.86
Moore, Liam	6.1	Leicester	Leicester	31.01.93
Obita, Jordan	5.11	–	Oxford	08.12.93
Watson, Tennai	6.0	–	Hillingdon	04.03.97

Midfielders

Barrett, Josh	5.8	–	Oxford	21.06.90
Beerens, Roy	5.9	Hertha Berlin	Bladel, Hol	22.12.87
Clement, Pelle	5.10	Ajax	Amsterdam, Hol	19.05.96
Evans, George	6.1	Manchester City	Cheadle	13.12.94
Harriott, Callum	5.6	Charlton	Norbury	04.03.94
Hurtado, Paolo	5.10	Pacos de Ferreira	Callao, Per	27.07.90
Kelly, Liam	5.6	–	Basingstoke	22.11.95
McCleary, Garath	5.11	Nottm Forest	Bromley	15.05.87
Popa, Adrian	5.7	Steaua Bucharest	Bucharest, Rom	24.07.88
Quinn, Stephen	5.6	Hull	Dublin, Ire	04.04.86
Swift, John	6.0	Chelsea	Portsmouth	23.06.95
Van den Berg, Joey	6.1	Heerenveen	Nijeveen, Hol	13.02.86
Wieser, Sando	6.1	FC Thun	Vaduz, Liech	03.02.93

Forwards

Bodvarsson, Jon Dadi	6.3	Wolves	Selfoss, Ice	25.05.92
Kermorgant, Yann	6.1	Bournemouth	Vannes, Fr	08.11.81
Mendes, Joseph	6.1	Le Havre	Evreux, Fr	30.03.91
Samuel, Dominic	6.0	–	Southwark	01.04.94

SHEFFIELD UNITED

Ground: Bramall Lane, Sheffield S2 4SU
Telephone: 0871 995 1899. **Club nickname:** Blades

Colours: Red and white. **Capacity:** 32,702
Record attendance: 68,287 v Leeds (FA Cup 5) Feb 15, 1936

Goalkeepers

Eastwood, Jake	6.1	–	Sheffield	03.10.96
Moore, Simon	6.3	Cardiff	Sandown, IOW	19.05.90

Defenders

Baldock, George	5.9	MK Dons	Buckingham	09.03.93
Basham, Chris	5.11	Blackpool	Hebburn	18.02.88
Brayford, John	5.8	Cardiff	Stoke	29.12.87
Freeman, Kieron	6.1	Derby	Bestwood	21.03.92
Lafferty, Daniel	6.1	Burnley	Derry	01.04.89
O'Connell, Jack	6.3	Brentford	Liverpool	29.03.94
Stearman, Richard	6.2	Fulham	Wolverhampton	19.08.87
Stevens, Enda	6.0	Portsmouth	Dublin, Ire	09.07.90
Wilson, James	6.2	Oldham	Chepstow	26.02.89
Wright, Jake	5.11	Oxford	Keighley	11.03.86

Midfielders

Carruthers, Samir	5.8	MK Dons	Islington	04.04.93
Coutts, Paul	6.1	Derby	Aberdeen	22.07.88
Done, Matt	5.10	Rochdale	Oswestry	22.07.88
Duffy, Mark	5.9	Birmingham	Liverpool	07.10.85
Fleck, John	5.7	Coventry	Glasgow	24.08.91
Thomas, Nathan	5.10	Hartlepool	Ingleby Barwick	27.09.94

Forwards

Clarke, Leon	6.2	Bury	Birmingham	10.02.85
Evans, Ched	6.0	Chesterfield	St Asaph	28.12.88
Hanson, James	6.4	Bradford	Bradford	09.11.87
Lavery, Caolan	5.11	Sheffield Wed	Alberta, Can	22.10.92
Sharp, Billy	5.9	Leeds	Sheffield	05.02.86

SHEFFIELD WEDNESDAY

Ground: Hillsborough, Sheffield, S6 1SW
Telephone: 0871 995 1867. **Club nickname:** Owls
Colours: Blue and white. **Capacity:** 39,812
Record attendance: 72,841 v Manchester City (FA Cup 5) Feb 17, 1934

Goalkeepers

Dawson, Cameron	6.0	Sheffield Utd	Sheffield	07.07.95
Kean, Jake	6.4	Norwich	Derby	04.02.91
Westwood, Keiren	6.1	Sunderland	Manchester	23.10.84
Wildsmith, Joe	6.1	–	Sheffield	28.12.95

Defenders

Fox, Morgan	6.1	Charlton	Chelmsford	21.09.93
Hunt, Jack	5.9	Crystal Palace	Rothwell	06.12.90
Hutchinson, Sam	6.0	Chelsea	Windsor	03.08.89
Lees, Tom	6.1	Leeds	Warwick	18.11.90
Loovens, Glenn	6.2	Zaragoza	Doetinchem, Hol	22.10.83
Palmer, Liam	6.2	–	Worksop	19.09.91
Pudil, Daniel	6.1	Watford	Prague, Cz	27.09.85

Midfielders

Abdi, Almen	5.11	Watford	Prizren, Kos	21.10.86
Bannan, Barry	5.11	Crystal Palace	Airdrie	01.12.89
Boyd, George	5.10	Burnley	Chatham	02.10.85
Filipe Melo	6.2	Moreirenses	Santa Maria, Por	03.11.89

Jones, David	6.0	Burnley	Southport	04.11.84
Lee, Kieran	6.1	Oldham	Tameside	22.06.88
Reach, Adam	6.1	Middlesbrough	Gateshead	03.02.93
Wallace, Ross	5.6	Burnley	Dundee	23.05.85
Forwards				
Fletcher, Steven	6.1	Sunderland	Shrewsbury	26.03.87
Forestieri, Fernando	5.8	Watford	Rosario, Arg	15.01.90
Hooper, Gary	5.10	Norwich	Loughton	26.01.88
Lucas Joao	6.4	Nacional	Luanda, Ang	04.09.93
Matias, Marco	5.10	Nacional	Barreiro, Por	10.05.89
Nuhiu, Atdhe	6.6	Rapid Vienna	Prishtina, Kos	29.07.89
Rhodes, Jordan	6.1	Middlesbrough	Oldham	05.02.90
Winnall, Sam	5.9	Barnsley	Wolverhampton	19.01.91

SUNDERLAND

Ground: Stadium of Light, Sunderland SR5 1SU
Telephone: 0871 911 1200. **Club nickname**: Black Cats
Capacity: 48,707. **Colours**: Red and white
Record attendance: Roker Park: 75,118 v Derby (FA Cup 6 rep) Mar 8, 1933. Stadium of Light: 48,353 v Liverpool (Prem Lge) Apr 13, 2002

Goalkeepers				
Mannone, Vito	6.3	Arsenal	Desio, It	02.03.88
Mika	6.1	Boavista	Yverdon, Switz	08.03.91
Defenders				
Djilobodji, Papy	6.4	Chelsea	Kaolack, Sen	11.12.88
Galloway, Brendan	6.2	Everton (loan)	Harare, Zimb	17.03.96
Jones, Billy	5.11	WBA	Shrewsbury	24.03.87
Kone, Lamine	6.3	Lorient	Paris, Fr	01.02.88
Love, Donald	5.10	Manchester Utd	Rochdale	02.12.94
Matthews, Adam	5.10	Celtic	Swansea	13.01.92
O'Shea, John	6.3	Manchester Utd	Waterford, Ire	30.04.81
Oviedo, Bryan	5.8	Everton	San Jose, C Rica	18.02.90
Midfielders				
Cattermole, Lee	5.10	Wigan	Stockton	21.03.88
Gibson, Darron	6.0	Everton	Derry	25.10.87
Gooch, Lynden	5.8	–	Santa Cruz, US	24.12.95
Honeyman, George	5.8	–	Prudhoe	02.09.94
Khazri, Wahbi	6.0	Bordeaux	Ajaccio, Fr	08.02.91
Lens, Jeremain	5.10	Dynamo Kiev	Amsterdam, Hol	24.11.87
McGeady, Aiden	5.11	Everton	Paisley	04.04.86
McNair, Paddy	6.0	Manchester Utd	Ballyclare	27.04.95
Ndong, Didier	5.10	Lorient	Lambarene, Gab	17.06.94
Rodwell, Jack	6.1	Manchester City	Birkdale	17.09.89
Forwards				
Asoro, Joel	5.9	–	Stockholm, Swe	27.04.99
Vaughan, James	5.11	Bury	Birmingham	14.07.88
Watmore, Duncan	5.9	Altrincham	Cheadle Hulme	08.03.94

WOLVERHAMPTON WANDERERS

Ground: Molineux Stadium, Waterloo Road, Wolverhampton WV1 4QR
Telephone: 0871 222 2220. **Club nickname**: Wolves
Colours: Gold and black. **Capacity**: 31,700
Record attendance: 61,315 v Liverpool (FA Cup 5) Feb 11, 1939

Goalkeepers

Lonergan, Andy	6.3	Fulham	Preston	19.10.83
Norris, Will	6.5	Cambridge	Watford	12.08.93
Ruddy, Jack	6.5	Bury	Glasgow	27.12.97
Ruddy, John	6.4	Norwich	St Ives, Camb	24.10.86

Defenders

Batth, Danny	6.3	–	Brierley Hill	21.09.90
Bennett, Ryan	6.2	Wolves	Orsett	06.03.90
Boly, Willy	6.2	Porto (loan)	Melun, Fr	03.02.91
Doherty, Matt	5.11	–	Dublin, Ire	16.01.92
Douglas, Barry	5.9	Konyaspor	Glasgow	04.09.89
Hause, Kortney	6.3	Wycombe	Goodmayes	16.07.95
Miranda, Roderick	6.3	Rio Ave	Odivelas, Port	30.03.91
Ofosu-Ayeh, Phil	6.0	Eintracht Braunschweig	Moers, Ger	15.09.91

Midfielders

Cavaleiro, Ivan	5.9	Monaco	Vila Franca de Xira, Por	18.10.93
Coady, Conor	6.1	Huddersfield	St Helens	25.02.93
Edwards, David	5.11	Luton	Pontesbury	03.02.85
Evans, Lee	6.1	Newport	Newport	24.07.94
Graham, Jordan	6.0	Aston Villa	Coventry	05.03.95
Helder Costa	5.10	Benfica	Luandra, Ang	12.01.94
Marshall, Ben	6.0	Blackburn	Salford	29.09.91
Neves, Ruben	5.11	Porto	Santa Maria, Port	13.03.97
Price, Jack	5.7	–	Shrewsbury	19.12.92
Prince Oniangue	6.3	Reims	Paris, Fr	04.11.88
Ronan, Connor	5.8	–	Rochdale	06.03.98
Saiss, Romain	6.3	Angers	Bourg-de-Peage, Fr	26.03.90
Zyro, Michal	6.2	Legia Warsaw	Warsaw, Pol	20.09.92

Forwards

Enobakhare, Bright	6.0	–	Nigeria	08.02.98
Dicko, Nouha	5.8	Wigan	Paris, Fr	14.05.92
Mason, Joe	5.10	Cardiff	Plymouth	13.05.91

LEAGUE ONE

AFC WIMBLEDON

Ground: Cherry Red Stadium, Kingston Road, Kingston upon Thames KT1 3PB
Telephone: 0208 547 3528. **Club nickname:** Dons
Colours: Blue. **Capacity:** 4,850
Record attendance: 4,749 v Exeter (Lge 2) Apr 23, 2013

Goalkeepers

Long, George	6.4	Sheffield Utd (loan)	Sheffield	05.11.93
McDonnell, Joe	5.11	Basingstoke	Basingstoke	19.05.94
Tzanev, Nik	6.4	Brentford	Wellington, NZ	23.12.96

Defenders

Charles, Darius	6.1	Burton	Ealing	10.12.87
Fuller, Barry	5.10	Barnet	Ashford, Kent	25.09.84
Kennedy, Callum	6.1	Leyton Orient	Chertsey	09.11.89
Meades, Jon	6.1	Oxford	Cardiff	02.03.92
Nightingale, Will	6.1	–	Wandsworth	02.08.95
Oshilaja, Adedeji	6.0	Cardiff	Bermondsey	26.02.93

Owens, Seth	5.10	Brentford	Hackney	06.11.98
Robinson, Paul	6.1	Portsmouth	Barnet	07.01.82
Sibbick, Toby	6.0	–	Isleworth	23.05.99

Midfielders

Abdou, Jimmy	5.10	Millwall (loan)	Martigues, Fr	13.07.84
Barcham, Andy	5.10	Portsmouth	Basildon	16.12.86
Egan, Alfie	5.10	–	Lambeth	03.09.97
Francomb, George	6.0	Norwich	Hackney	08.09.91
Kaja, Egli	5.10	Kingstonian	Albania	26.07.97
Parrett, Dean	5.9	Stevenage	Hampstead	16.11.91
Soares, Tom	6.0	Bury	Reading	10.07.86
Whelpdale, Chris	6.0	Stevenage	Harold Wood	27.01.87

Forwards

Appiah, Kwesi	5.11	Crystal Palace	Thamesmead	12.08.90
McDonald, Cody	6.0	Gillingham	Witham	30.05.86
Taylor, Lyle	6.2	Scunthorpe	Greenwich	29.03.90

BLACKBURN ROVERS

Ground: Ewood Park, Blackburn BB2 4JF
Telephone: 0871 702 1875. **Club nickname:** Rovers
Colours: Blue and white. **Capacity:** 31,367
Record attendance: 62,522 v Bolton (FA Cup 6) Mar 2, 1929

Goalkeepers

| Raya, David | 6.0 | Cornella | Barcelona, Sp | 15.09.95 |
| Steele, Jason | 6.2 | Middlesbrough | Newton Aycliffe | 18.08.90 |

Defenders

Lenihan, Darragh	5.10	Belvedere	Dunboyne, Ire	16.03.94
Mulgrew, Charlie	6.3	Celtic	Glasgow	06.03.86
Nyambe, Ryan	6.0	–	Katima Mulilo, Nam	04.12.97
Ward, Elliott	6.1	Bournemouth	Harrow	19.01.85
Williams, Derrick	6.2	Bristol City	Waterford, Ire	17.01.93

Midfielders

Bennett, Elliott	5.9	Norwich	Telford	18.12.88
Conway, Craig	5.8	Cardiff	Irvine	02.05.85
Duck, Bradley	5.8	Gillingham	Greenwich	31.12.97
Evans, Corry	5.11	Hull	Belfast	30.07.90
Feeney, Liam	6.0	Bolton	Hammersmith	28.04.86
Gladwin, Ben	6.3	QPR	Reading	08.06.92
Smallwood, Richie	5.11	Rotherham	Redcar	29.12.90
Whittingham, Peter	5.10	Cardiff	Nuneaton	08.09.84

Forwards

| Graham, Danny | 6.1 | Sunderland | Gateshead | 12.08.85 |
| Stokes, Anthony | 6.1 | Celtic | Dublin, Ire | 25.07.88 |

BLACKPOOL

Ground: Bloomfield Road, Blackpool FY1 6JJ
Telephone: 0871 622 1953. **Club nickname:** Seasiders
Colours: Tangerine and white. **Capacity:** 17,338
Record attendance: 38,098 v Wolves (Div 1) Sep 17, 1955

Goalkeepers

| Boney, Myles | 5.11 | – | Blackpool | 01.02.98 |
| Williams, Ben | 6.1 | Bury | Manchester | 27.08.82 |

Defenders

Aimson, Will	5.10	Hull	Christchurch	01.01.94
Anderton, Nick	6.2	Barrow	Preston	22.04.96
Hartley, Peter	6.2	Bristol Rov	Hartlepool	03.04.88
Mellor, Kelvin	6.2	Plymouth	Crewe	25.01.91
Robertson, Clark	6.2	Aberdeen	Aberdeen	05.09.93
Taylor, Andy	5.11	Walsall	Blackburn	14.03.86
Tilt, Curtis	6.4	Wrexham	Walsall	04.08.91

Midfielders

Daniel, Colin	5.11	Port Vale	Nottingham	15.02.88
Des Pres, Sebastien	–	Salt Lake	Encinitas, US	11.11.98
McAlister, Jim	5.11	Dundee	Rothesay	02.11.85
Osayi-Samuel, Bright	5.9	–	Nigeria	01.02.97
Potts, Brad	6.2	Carlisle	Hexham	07.03.94
Ryan, Jimmy	5.10	Fleetwood	Maghull	06.09.88
Turton, Ollie	5.11	Crewe	Manchester	06.12.92

Forwards

Clayton, Max	5.9	Bolton	Crewe	09.08.94
Cullen, Mark	5.9	Luton	Stakeford	21.04.92
Delfouneso, Nathan	6.1	Swindon	Birmingham	02.02.91
Gnanduillet, Armand	6.3	Leyton Orient	Angers, Fr	13.02.92
Matt, Jamille	6.2	Fleetwood	Walsall	02.12.90
Philliskirk, Danny	5.10	Oldham	Oldham	10.04.91
Vassell, Kyle	6.0	Peterborough	Milton Keynes	07.02.93

BRADFORD CITY

Ground: Northern Commercials Stadium, Valley Parade, Bradford BD8 7DY
Telephone: 01274 773355. **Club nickname:** Bantams
Colours: Yellow and claret. **Capacity:** 25,136
Record attendance: 39,146 v Burnley (FA Cup 4) Mar 11, 1911

Goalkeepers

Doyle, Colin	6.5	Blackpool	Cork, Ire	12.08.85
Sattelmaier, Rouven	6.2	Stuttgart Kickers	Ludwigsburg, Ger	07.08.87

Defenders

Boateng, Kwame	5.10	–	Leeds	21.11.98
Chicksen, Adam	5.8	Charlton	Milton Keynes	27.09.91
Hanson, Jacob	6.0	Huddersfield	Kirkburton	30.11.97
Kilgallon, Matt	6.1	Blackburn	York	08.01.84
Knight-Percival, Nat	6.0	Shrewsbury	Cambridge	31.03.87
McMahon, Tony	5.10	Blackpool	Bishop Auckland	24.03.86
Vincelot, Romain	5.10	Coventry	Poitiers, Fr	29.10.85

Midfielders

Devine, Danny	5.11	–	Bradford	04.09.97
Dieng, Timothee	6.2	Oldham	Grenoble, Fr	09.04.92
Gillieard, Alex	6.0	Newcastle (loan)	Shotley Bridge	11.02.96
Law, Nicky	5.10	Rangers	Plymouth	29.03.88
Pybus, Dan	5.11	Sunderland	South Shields	12.12.97
Reeves, Jake	5.7	AFC Wimbledon	Greenwich	30.05.93
Wright, Sam	5.9	–	Bradford	28.09.97

Forwards

Jones, Alex	6.1	Birmingham	Sutton Coldfield	28.09.94
McCartan, Shay	5.10	Accrington	Newry	18.05.94
Poleon, Dominic	6.2	AFC Wimbledon	Newham	07.09.93

Taylor, Paul	5.11	Peterborough	Liverpool	04.10.87
Webb-Foster, Reece	5.11	–	Keighley	07.03.98
Wyke, Charlie	5.11	Carlisle	Middlesbrough	06.12.92

BRISTOL ROVERS

Ground: Memorial Stadium, Filton Avenue, Horfield, Bristol BS7 0BF
Telephone: 0117 909 6648. **Club nickname:** Pirates
Colours: Blue and white. **Capacity:** 12,011
Record attendance: Eastville: 38,472 v Preston (FA Cup 4) Jan 30, 1960. Memorial Stadium:
12,011 v WBA (FA Cup 6) Mar 9, 2008

Goalkeepers

| Slocombe, Sam | 6.0 | Blackpool | Scunthorpe | 05.06.88 |
| Smith, Adam | 5.11 | Northampton | Sunderland | 23.01.92 |

Defenders

Bola, Marc	6.1	Arsenal (loan)	Greenwich	09.12.97
Broom, Ryan	5.10	–	Newport	04.09.96
Brown, Lee	6.0	QPR	Farnborough	10.08.90
Burn, Jonathan	6.1	Middlesbrough	Darlington	01.08.95
Clarke, James	6.0	Woking	Aylesbury	17.11.89
Kilgour, Alfie	5.10	–	Bath	18.05.98
Leadbitter, Daniel	6.0	Hereford	Newcastle	24.06.01
Lockyer, Tom	6.1	–	Cardiff	03.12.94
Partington, Joe	6.2	Eastleigh	Portsmouth	01.04.90

Midfielders

Clarke, Ollie	5.11	–	Bristol	29.06.92
Lines, Chris	6.2	Port Vale	Bristol	30.11.85
Moore, Byron	6.0	Port Vale	Stoke	24.08.88
Sercombe, Liam	5.10	Oxford	Exeter	25.04.90
Sinclair, Stuart	5.8	Salisbury	Houghton Conquest	09.11.87

Forwards

Bodin, Billy	5.11	Northampton	Swindon	24.03.92
Gaffney, Rory	6.0	Cambridge Utd	Tuam, Ire	23.10.89
Harrison, Ellis	5.11		Newport	29.01.94

BURY

Ground: Gigg Lane, Bury BL9 9HR
Telephone: 08445 790009. **Club nickname:** Shakers
Colours: White and blue. **Capacity:** 11,640
Record attendance: 35,000 v Bolton (FA Cup 3) Jan 9, 1960

Goalkeepers

| Murphy, Joe | 6.2 | Huddersfield | Dublin, Ire | 21.08.81 |

Defenders

Aldred, Tom	6.2	Blackpool	Bolton	11.09.90
Cameron, Nathan	6.2	Coventry	Birmingham	21.11.91
Edwards, Phil	5.9	Burton	Bootle	08.11.85
Jones, Craig	5.8	New Saints	Chester	20.03.87
Leigh, Greg	5.11	Bradford	Manchester	30.09.94
O'Connell, Eoghan	6.2	Celtic	Cork, Ire	13.08.95
Skarz, Joe	6.0	Oxford	Huddersfield	13.07.89
Thompson, Adam	6.2	Southend	Harlow	28.09.92

Midfielders

| Dawson, Stephen | 5.6 | Scunthorpe | Dublin, Ire | 04.12.85 |

Humphrey, Chris	5.11	Hibernian	Saint Catherine, Jam	19.09.87
Ismail, Zeli	5.9	Wolves	Kukes, Alb	12.12.93
Mayor, Danny	6.0	Sheffield Wed	Leyland	18.10.90
O'Shea, Jay	6.0	Chesterfield	Dublin, Ire	10.08.88
Reilly, Callum	6.1	Burton	Warrington	03.10.93
Tutte, Andrew	5.9	Rochdale	Liverpool	21.09.90
Forwards				
Ajose, Nicky	5.10	Charlton (loan)	Bury	07.10.91
Beckford, Jermaine	6.2	Preston	Ealing	09.12.83
Heardman, Tom	6.4	Newcastle (loan)	Gosforth	12.09.95
Lowe, Ryan	5.11	Crewe	Liverpool	18.09.78

CHARLTON ATHLETIC
Ground: The Valley, Floyd Road, London SE7 8BL
Telephone: 0208 333 4000. **Club nickname:** Addicks
Colours: Red and white. **Capacity:** 27,111
Record attendance: 75,031 v Aston Villa (FA Cup 5) Feb 12, 1938

Goalkeepers				
Phillips, Dillon	6.2	–	Hornchurch	11.06.95
Defenders				
Bauer, Patrick	6.4	Maritimo	Backnang, Ger	28.10.92
Lennon, Harry	6.3	–	Romford	16.12.94
Page, Lewis	5.10	West Ham	Enfield	20.05.96
Pearce, Jason	5.11	Wigan	Hillingdon	06.12.87
Sarr, Naby	6.5	Sporting Lisbon	Marseille, Fr	13.08.93
Solly, Chris	5.8	–	Rochester	20.01.90
Teixeira, Jorge	6.2	Standard Liege	Lisbon, Por	27.08.86
Midfielders				
Aribo, Joe	6.0	Staines	Camberwell	21.07.96
Ceballos, Cristian	5.8	Tottenham	Barcelona, Sp	03.12.92
Crofts, Andrew	5.9	Brighton	Chatham	29.05.84
Forster-Caskey, Jake	5.10	Brighton	Southend	05.04.94
Fosu, Tarique	5.8	Reading	Wandsworth	05.11.95
Jackson, Johnnie	6.1	Notts Co	Camden	15.08.82
Kashi, Ahmed	5.10	Metz	Aubervilliers, Fr	18.11.88
Marshall, Mark	5.7	Bradford	Manchester, Jam	05.05.87
Forwards				
Ahearne-Grant, Karlan	6.0	–	Greenwich	19.12.97
Clarke, Billy	5.7	Bradford	Cork, Ire	13.12.87
Holmes, Ricky	6.2	Northampton	Uxbridge	19.06.87
Magennis, Josh	6.2	Kilmarnock	Bangor, NI	15.08.90
Novak, Lee	6.0	Birmingham	Newcastle	28.09,88
Watt, Tony	6.0	Standard Liege	Coatbridge	29.12.93

DONCASTER ROVERS
Ground: Keepmoat Stadium, Stadium Way, Doncaster DN4 5JW
Telephone: 01302 764664. **Club nickname:** Rovers
Colours: Red and white. **Capacity:** 15,231
Record attendance: Belle Vue: 37,149 v Hull (Div 3 N) Oct 2, 1948. Keepmoat Stadium: 15,001 v Leeds (Lge 1) Apr 1, 2008

Goalkeepers				
Etheridge, Ross	6.2	Accrington	–	04.09.94

| Lawlor, Ian | 6.4 | Manchester City | Dublin, Ire | 27.10.94 |
| Marosi, Marko | 6.3 | Wigan | Slovakia | 23.10.93 |

Defenders

Alcock, Craig	5.8	Sheffield Utd	Truro	08.12.87
Andrew, Danny	5.11	Grimsby	Holbeach	23.12.90
Baudry, Mathieu	6.2	Leyton Orient	Le Havre, Fr	24.02.88
Butler, Andy	6.0	Sheffield Utd	Doncaster	04.11.83
Fielding, Reece	6.2	–	Doncaster	23.10.98
Garratt, Tyler	6.0	Bolton	Lincoln	20.10.96
Mason, Niall	5.11	Aston Villa	Bromley	10.01.97
McCullough, Luke	6.1	Manchester Utd	Portadown	15.02.94
Wright, Joe	6.4	Huddersfield	Monk Fryston	26.02.95

Midfielders

Blair, Matty	5.10	Mansfield	Warwick	30.11.87
Coppinger, James	5.7	Exeter	Middlesbrough	10.01.81
Middleton, Harry	5.11	–	Doncaster	12.04.95
Rowe, Tommy	5.11	Wolves	Manchester	01.05.89
Whiteman, Ben	6.0	Sheffield Utd (loan)	Rochdale	17.06.96

Forwards

Beestin, Alfie	5.10	Tadcaster	Leeds	01.10.97
Kiwomya, Alex	5.11	Chelsea	Sheffield	20.05.96
Mandeville, Liam	5.11	–	Lincoln	17.02.97
Marquis, John	6.1	Millwall	Lewisham	16.05.92
May, Alfie	5.10	Hythe	–	02.07.93
Williams, Andy	5.10	Swindon	Hereford	14.08.86

FLEETWOOD TOWN

Ground: Highbury Stadium, Park Avenue, Fleetwod FY7 6TX
Telephone: 01253 775080. **Club nickname:** Fishermen
Colours: Red and white. **Capacity:** 5,311
Record attendance: 5,194 v York (Lge 2 play-off semi-final, 2nd leg) May 16, 2014

Goalkeepers

Cairns, Alex	6.0	Rotherham	Doncaster	04.01.93
Neal, Chris	6.2	Port Vale	St Albans	23.10.85

Defenders

Bell, Amari'i	5.11	Birmingham	Burton	05.05.94
Bolger, Cian	6.4	Southend	Cullbridge, Ire	12.03.92
Charles, Dion	5.10	Blackpool	Preston	07.10.95
Coyle, Lewie	5.8	Leeds (loan)	Hull	15.10.95
Eastham, Ashley	6.3	Rochdale	Preston	22.03.91
Ekpolo, Godswill	5.11	Barcelona	Benin City, Nig	14.05.95
Maguire, Joe	5.10	Liverpool	Manchester	18.01.96
Pond, Nathan	6.2	Lancaster	Preston	05.01.85
Rodgers, Harvey	5.11	Hull	York	20.10.96

Midfielders

Dempsey, Kyle	5.10	Huddersfield	Whitehaven	17.09.95
Duckworth, Michael	5.11	Hartlepool	Rinteln, Ger	28.04.92
Grant, Bobby	5.11	Blackpool	Litherland	01.07.90
Nirennold, Victor	6.0	Nova Univ	Rennes, Fr	05.04.91
Glendon, George	5.10	Manchester City	Manchester	03.05.95
Schwabl, Markus	6.0	Aalen	Tegernsee, Ger	26.08.90
Sowerby, Jack	5.9	–	Preston	23.03.95
Wright, Akil	6.0	Ilkeston	Derby	13.05.96

Forwards

Burns, Wes	5.8	Bristol City	Cardiff	23.11.94
Cole, Devante	6.1	Bradford	Alderley Edge	10.05.95
Hiwula, Jordy	5.10	Huddersfield (loan)	Manchester	21.09.94
Hunter, Ashley	5.10	Ilkeston	Derby	29.09.95
McAleny, Conor	5.10	Everton	Liverpool	12.08.92

GILLINGHAM

Ground: Mems Priestfield Stadium, Redfern Avenue, Gillingham ME7 4DD
Telephone: 01634 300000. **Club nickname**: Gills
Colours: Blue and white. **Capacity**: 11,582
Record attendance: 23,002 v QPR. (FA Cup 3) Jan 10, 1948

Goalkeepers

Hadler, Tom	6.2	–	–	30.0796
Holy, Tomas	6.9	Sparta Prague	Rychnov, Cz	10.12.91
Nelson, Stuart	6.1	Notts Co	Stroud	17.09.81

Defenders

Ehmer, Max	6.2	QPR	Frankfurt, Ger	03.02.92
Garmston, Bradley	5.11	WBA	Chorley	18.01.94
Lacey, Alex	6.0	Yeovil	Milton Keynes	31.05.93
Morris, Aaron	6.0	Wimbledon	Rumney	30.12.89
Ogilvie, Connor	6.0	Tottenham (loan)	Waltham Abbey	14.02.96
O'Neill, Luke	6.0	Southend	Slough	20.08.91
Zakuani, Gabriel	6.1	Northampton	Kinshasa, DR Cong	31.05.86

Midfielders

Byrne, Mark	5.9	Newport	Dublin, Ire	09.11.88
Hessenthaler, Jake	5.10	–	Gravesend	20.04.90
List, Elliott	5.10	Crystal Palace	Camberwell	12.05.97
Martin, Lee	5.10	Millwall	Taunton	09.02.87
Oldaker, Darren	5.9	QPR	London	01.04.99
Wagstaff, Scott	5.9	Bristol City	Maidstone	31.03.90
Wright, Josh	6.0	Leyton Orient	Bethnal Green	06.11.89

Forwards

Eaves, Tom	6.4	Yeovil	Liverpool	14.01.92
Parker, Josh	5.11	Wealdstone	Slough	01.12.90
Wilkinson, Conor	6.3	Bolton	Croydon	23.01.95

MILTON KEYNES DONS

Ground: stadiummk, Stadium Way West, Milton Keynes MK1 1ST
Telephone: 01908 622922. **Club nickname**: Dons
Colours: White. **Capacity**: 30,500
Record attendance: 28,127 v Chelsea (FA Cup 4) Jan 31, 2016

Goalkeepers

Nicholls, Lee	6.3	Wigan	Huyton	05.10.92
Sietsma, Wieger	6.3	Heerenveen	Groningen, Hol	11.07.95

Defenders

Brittain, Callum	5.10	–	Bedford	12.03.98
Downing, Paul	6.1	Walsall	Taunton	26.10.91
Ebanks-Landell, Ethan	6.2	Wolves (loan)	Smethwick	12.12.92
Jackson, Oran	6.0	–	Milton Keynes	16.10.98
Lewington, Dean	5.11	Wimbledon	Kingston upon Thames	18.05.84
Tilney, Ben	5.9	–	Luton	28.02.97
Walsh, Joe	5.11	Crawley	Cardiff	13.05.92

| Williams, George | 5.9 | Barnsley | Hillingdon | 14.04.93 |
| Wootton, Scott | 6.2 | Leeds | Birkenhead | 12.09.91 |

Midfielders

Aneke, Chuks	6.3	Zulte Waregem	Newham	03.07.93
Cisse, Ousseynou	6.4	Tours	Suresnes, Fr	07.04.91
McGrandles, Conor	6.0	Norwich	Falkirk	24.09.95
Pawlett, Peter	5.10	Aberdeen	Hull	03.02.91
Rasulo, Giorgio	5.10	–	Banbury	23.01.97
Reeves, Ben	5.10	Southampton	Verwood	19.11.91
Upson, Ed	5.10	Millwall	Bury St Edmunds	21.11.89

Forwards

Agard, Kieran	5.10	Bristol City	Newham	10.10.89
Muirhead, Robbie	6.3	Hearts	Irvine	08.03.96
Thomas-Asante, Brandon	5.11	–	Milton Keynes	29.12.98

NORTHAMPTON TOWN

Ground: Sixfields Stadium, Upton Way, Northampton NN5 5QA
Telephone: 01604 683700. **Club nickname:** Cobblers
Colours: Claret and white. **Capacity:** 7,750
Record attendance: County Ground: 24,523 v Fulham (Div 1) Apr 23, 1966. Sixfields
Stadium: 7,798 v Manchester Utd (Lge Cup 3) Sep 21, 2016

Goalkeepers

| Cornell, David | 6.0 | Oldham | Swansea | 28.03.91 |
| Goff, James | 6.0 | – | Huntingdon | 18.03.99 |

Defenders

Barnett, Leon	6.1	Bury	Luton	30.11.85
Buchanan, David	5.9	Preston	Rochdale	06.05.86
Hanley, Raheem	5.8	Swansea	Blackburn	24.03.94
Moloney, Brendan	6.1	Yeovil	Beaufort, Ire	18.01.89
Phillips, Aaron	5.8	Coventry	Warwick	20.11.93
Poole, Regan	5.11	Manchester Utd	Cardiff	18.06.98
Smith, George	6.0	Gateshead	Barnsley	14.08.96
Taylor, Ash	6.0	Aberdeen	Bromborough	02.09.90

Midfielders

Foley, Sam	6.0	Port Vale	Upton-on-Severn	17.10.86
Kasim, Yaser	5.11	Swindon	Baghdad, Irq	16.05.91
McWilliams, Shaun	5.11		Northampton	14.08.98
O'Toole, John-Joe	6.2	Bristol Rov	Harrow	30.09.88
Powell, Daniel	6.2	MK Dons	Luton	12.03.91
Taylor, Matt	5.10	Burnley	Oxford	27.11.81

Forwards

Bowditch, Dean	5.11	MK Dons	Bishop's Stortford	15.06.86
Hoskins, Sam	5.8	Yeovil	Dorchester	04.02.93
Iaciofano, Joe	5.10	–	Northampton	10.09.98
Lobjoit, Leon	5.10	Buckingham	–	04.01.95
Revell, Alex	6.3	MK Dons	Cambridge	07.07.83
Richards, Marc	5.11	Chesterfield	Wolverhampton	08.07.82
Waters, Billy	5.9	Cheltenham	Epsom	15.10.94

OLDHAM ATHLETIC

Ground: SportsDirect Park, Oldham OL1 2PA
Telephone: 0161 624 4972. **Club nickname:** Latics
Colours: Blue and white. **Capacity:** 13,500

Record attendance: 47,761 v Sheffield Wed (FA Cup 4) Jan 25, 1930

Goalkeepers

Kettings, Chris	6.4	Crystal Palace	Glasgow	25.10.92

Defenders

Clarke, Peter	6.0	Bury	Southport	03.01.82
Dummigan, Cameron	5.11	Burnley	Lurgan	02.06.96
Edmundson, George	6.1	–	Wythenshawe	15.08.97
Gerrard, Anthony	6.2	Shrewsbury	Liverpool	06.02.86
Hunt, Rob	5.8	Brighton	Dagenham	07.07.95
McLaughlin, Ryan	5.9	Liverpool	Belfast	30.09.94
Stott, Jamie	6.1	–	Failsworth	22.12.97
Wilson, Brian	5.10	Colchester	Manchester	09.05.83

Midfielders

Banks, Ollie	6.3	Chesterfield	Rotherham	21.09.92
Fane, Ousmane	6.4	Kidderminster	Paris, Fr	13.12.93
Flynn, Ryan	5.7	Sheffield Utd	Edinburgh	04.09.88
Gardner, Dan	6.1	Chesterfield	Gorton	05.04.90
Green, Paul	5.9	Rotherham	Pontefract	10.04.83
Obadeyi, Temitope	5.10	Dundee Utd	Birmingham	29.10.89

Forwards

Amadi-Holloway, Aaron	6.2	Fleetwood	Cardiff	01.02.93
Davies, Craig	6.2	Scunthorpe	Burton	09.01.86

OXFORD UNITED

Ground: Kassam Stadium, Grenoble Road, Oxford OX4 4XP
Telephone: 01865 337500. **Club nickname:** U's
Colours: Yellow. **Capacity:** 12,500
Record attendance: Manor Ground: 22,750 v Preston (FA Cup 6) Feb 29, 1964. Kassam Stadium: 12,243 v Leyton Orient (Lge 2) May 6, 2006

Goalkeepers

Eastwood, Simon	6.2	Blackburn	Luton	26.06.89
Shearer, Scott	6.3	Mansfield	Glasgow	15.02.81

Defenders

Carroll, Canice	6.0	–	Oxford	26.01.99
Kelleher, Fiacre	6.5	Celtic	Cork, Ire	10.03.96
Long, Sam	5.10	–	Oxford	16.01.95
Lundstram, John	5.11	Everton	Liverpool	18.02.94
Martin, Aaron	6.1	Coventry	Newport IOW	29.09.89
Nelson, Curtis	6.0	Plymouth	Newcastle-under-Lyme	21.05.93
Raglan, Charlie	6.0	Chesterfield	Wythenshawe	28.04.93
Ribeiro, Christian	6.0	Exeter	Neath	14.12.89
Tiendalli, Dwight	5.11	Swansea	Paramaribo, Sur	21.10.85

Midfielders

Ashby, Josh	5.11	–	Oxford	03.05.96
Henry, James	6.1	Wolves	Reading	10.06.89
Johnson, Marvin	5.10	Motherwell	Birmingham	01.12.90
Ledson, Ryan	5.10	Everton	Liverpool	19.08.87
Rothwell, Joe	6.1	Manchester Utd	Manchester	11.01.95
Ruffels, Josh	5.10	Coventry	Oxford	23.10.93

Forwards

Hall, Rob	6.2	Bolton	Aylesbury	20.10.93
Hemmings Kane	6.1	Dundee	Burton	08.04.92

Maguire, Chris	5.8	Rotherham	Bellshill	16.01.89
Obika, Jonathan	6.0	Swindon	Enfield	12.09.90
Roberts, James	5.11	Wycombe	Stoke Mandeville	21.06.96
Thomas, Wes	5.11	Birmingham	Barking	23.01.87

PETERBOROUGH UNITED

Ground: Abax Stadium, London Road, Peterborough PE2 8AL
Telephone: 01733 563947. **Club nickname**: Posh
Colours: Blue and white. **Capacity**: 14,319
Record attendance: 30,096 v Swansea (FA Cup 5) Feb 20, 1965

Goalkeepers

Bond, Jonathan	6.3	Reading (loan)	Hemel Hempstead	19.05.93
Tibbetts, Josh	6.0	Birmingham	Stourbridge	02.11.94
Defenders				
Baldwin, Jack	6.1	Hartlepool	Barking	30.06.93
Hughes, Andrew	5.11	Newport	Cardiff	05.06.92
Tafazolli, Ryan	6.5	Mansfield	Sutton	28.09.91
Midfielders				
Anderson, Harry	5.7	Crawley	Slough	09.01.97
Anderson, Jermaine	5.11	–	Camden	16.05.96
Bostwick, Michael	6.1	Stevenage	Greenwich	17.05.88
Chettle, Callum	5.10	Nuneaton	Nottingham	28.08.96
Da Silva-Lopes, Leon	5.7	–	Lisbon, Por	30.11.98
Doughty, Michael	6.1	QPR	Westminster	20.11.92
Edwards, Gwion	5.9	Crawley	Lampeter	01.03.93
Forrester Chris	5.11	St Patrick's	Dublin, Ire	17.12.92
Grant, Anthony	5.10	Port Vale	Lambeth	04.06.87
Maddison, Marcus	5.11	Gateshead	Durham	26.09.93
Forwards				
Coulthirst, Shaquile	5.11	Tottenham	Hackney	02.11.94
Lloyd, Danny	–	Stockport	Liverpool	03.12.91
Marriott, Jack	5.9	Luton	Beverley	09.09.84
Miller, Ricky	6.2	Dover	Hatfield	19.03.89
Morias, Junior	5.8	St Albans	Kingston, Jam	04.07.95
Nabi, Adil	5.9	WBA	Birmingham	20.02.94
Nichols, Tom	5.10	Exeter	Taunton	28.08.93
Nicholson, Jordan	5.10	Histon	Godmanchester	29.09.93
Stevens, Matty	5.11	Barnet	Surrey	12.02.98

PLYMOUTH ARGYLE

Ground: Home Park, Plymouth PL2 3DQ
Telephone: 01752 562561. **Club nickname**: Pilgrims
Colours: Green and white. **Capacity**: 16,388
Record attendance: 43,596 v Aston Villa (Div 2) Oct 10, 1936

Goalkeepers

McCormick, Luke	6.0	Oxford	Coventry	15.08.83
Te Loeke, Robbert	6.4	Achilles 29	Arnhem, Hol	01.12.88
Defenders				
Bradley, Sonny	6.4	Crawley	Hull	13.09.91
Edwards, Ryan	5.11	Morecambe	Liverpool	07.10.93
Miller, Gary	6.0	Partick	Glasgow	15.04.87
Songo'o, Yann	6.2	Blackburn	Yaounde, Cam	19.11.91

Sawyer, Gary	6.0	Leyton Orient	Bideford	05.07.85
Taylor-Sinclair, Aaron	6.1	Doncaster	Aberdeen	08.04.91
Threlkeld, Oscar	6.0	Bolton	Bolton	15.12.94

Midfielders

Ainsworth, Lionel	5.9	Motherwell	Nottingham	01.10.87
Carey, Graham	6.0	Ross Co	Dublin, Ire	02.05.89
Fox, David	5.10	Crewe	Leek	13.12.83
Lameiras, Ruben	5.9	Coventry	Lisbon, Por	22.12.94
Ness, Jamie	6.1	Scunthorpe	Irvine	02.03.91
Sarcevic, Antoni	6.0	Shrewsbury	Manchester	13.03.92
Sokolik, Jakub	6.2	Southend	Ostrava, Cz	28.08.93
Wylde, Gregg	5.10	Millwall	Kirkintilloch	23.03.91

Forwards

Blissett, Nathan	6.4	Torquay	West Bromwich	29.06.90
Grant, Joel	6.0	Exeter	Acton	26.08.87
Jervis, Jake	6.3	Ross Co	Birmingham	17.09.91
Taylor, Ryan	6.2	Oxford	Rotherham	04.05.88

PORTSMOUTH

Ground: Fratton Park, Frogmore Road, Portsmouth, PO4 8RA
Telephone: 0239 273 1204. **Club nickname**: Pompey
Colours: Blue and white. **Capacity**: 20,700
Record attendance: 51,385 v Derby (FA Cup 6) Feb 26, 1949

Goalkeepers

| Bass, Alex | 6.2 | – | Southampton | 01.04.98 |
| McGee, Luke | 6.2 | Tottenham | Edgware | 02.09.95 |

Defenders

Burgess, Christian	6.5	Peterborough	Barking	07.10.91
Clarke, Matt	5.11	Ipswich	Ipswich	22.09.96
Davies, Tom	5.11	Accrington	Warrington	18.04.92
Haunstrup, Brandon	5.8	–	Waterlooville	26.10.96
Holmes-Dennis, Tareiq	5.9	Huddersfield (loan)	Farnborough	31.10.95
Talbot, Drew	5.10	Chesterfield	Barnsley	19.07.86
Thompson, Nathan	5.10	Swindon	Chester	22.04.91
Whatmough, Jack	6.0	–	Gosport	19.08.96

Midfielders

Baker, Carl	6.2	MK Dons	Whiston	26.12.82
Bennett, Kyle	5.5	Doncaster	Telford	09.09.90
Evans, Gareth	6.0	Fleetwood	Macclesfield	26.04.88
Close, Ben	5.9	–	Portsmouth	08.08.96
Lalkovic, Milan	5.10	Walsall	Kosice, Slovak	09.12.92
Lowe, Jamal	6.0	Hampton	Harrow	21.07.94
May, Adam	6.0	–	Southampton	06.12.97
Naismith, Kai	6.1	Accrington	Glasgow	18.02.92
Oxlade-Chamberlain, Christian	6.2	–	Port Solent	24.06.98
Roberts, Gary	5.10	Chesterfield	Chester	18.03.84
Rose, Danny	5.8	Northampton	Bristol	21.02.88

Forwards

Chaplin, Conor	5.10	–	Worthing	16.02.97
Kabamba, Nicke	6.3	Hampton	Brent	01.02.93
Main, Curtis	5.10	Doncaster	South Shields	20.06.92
Pitman, Brett	6.0	Ipswich	St Helier, Jer	03.01.88
Smith, Michael	6.4	Swindon	Wallsend	17.10.91

ROCHDALE

Ground: Crown Oil Arena, Wilbutts Lane, Rochdale OL11 5DS
Telephone: 01706 644648. **Club nickname:** Dale
Colours: Blue and black. **Capacity:** 10,249
Record attendance: 24,231 v Notts Co (FA Cup 2) Dec 10, 1949

Goalkeepers

Collis, Steve	6.3	Macclesfield	Harrow	18.03.81
Lillis, Josh	6.0	Scunthorpe	Derby	24.06.87
Moore, Brendan	6.2	Torquay	Elmira, USA	16.04.92

Defenders

Brown, Reece	6.2	Bury	Manchester	01.11.91
Canavan, Niall	6.3	Scunthorpe	Leeds	11.04.91
Kitching, Mark	6.2	Middlesbrough	Guisborough	04.09.95
McGahey, Harrison	6.1	Sheffield Utd	Preston	26.09.95
McNulty, Jim	6.0	Bury	Liverpool	13.02.85
Rafferty, Joe	6.0	Liverpool	Liverpool	06.10.93

Midfielders

Allen, Jamie	5.11	–	Rochdale	29.01.95
Barry-Murphy, Brian	6.0	Bury	Cork, Ire	27.07.78
Camps, Callum	5.11	–	Stockport	14.03.96
Cannon, Andy	5.9	–	Tameside	14.03.96
Inman, Brad	5.9	Peterborough (loan)	Adelaide, Aus	10.12.91
Keane, Keith	5.9	Cambridge	Luton	20.11.86
Noble-Lazarus, Reuben	6.2	Barnsley	Huddersfield	16.08.93
Rathbone, Oliver	5.11	Manchester Utd	Blackburn	10.10.96
Thompson, Joe	6.0	Carlisle	Rochdale	05.03.89
Williams, Jordan	5.11	Barrow	Warrington	13.12.92

Forwards

Andrew, Calvin	6.2	York	Luton	19.12.86
Bunney, Joe	5.10		Northwich	26.09.93
Davies, Steven	6.1	Bradford	Liverpool	29.12.87
Henderson, Ian	5.10	Colchester	Thetford	24.01.85

ROTHERHAM UNITED

Ground: New York Stadium, New York Way, Rotherham S60 1AH
Telephone: 08444 140733. **Club nickname:** Millers
Colours: Red and white. **Capacity:** 12,021
Record attendance: Millmoor: 25,170 v Sheffield Wed (Div 2) Jan 26, 1952 and v Sheffield Wed (Div 2) Dec 13, 1952; **Don Valley Stadium:** 7,082 v Aldershot (Lge 2 play-off semi-final, 2nd leg) May 19, 2010; **New York Stadium:** 11,758 v Sheffield Utd (Lge 1) Sep 7, 2013

Goalkeepers

O'Donnell, Richard	6.2	Bristol City	Sheffield	12.09.88
Price, Lewis	6.3	Sheffield Wed	Bournemouth	19.07.84

Defenders

Ajayi, Semi	6.4	Cardiff	Crayford	09.11.93
Ball, Dominic	6.1	Tottenham	Welwyn Garden City	02.08.95
Belaid, Aymen	6.2	Levski Sofia	Paris, Fr	02.01.89
Emmanuel, Josh	5.11	Ipswich	London	18.08.97
Fisher, Darnell	5.9	Celtic	Reading	04.04.94
Ihiekwe, Michael	6.1	Tranmere	Liverpool	20.11.92
Mattock, Joe	6.0	Sheffield Wed	Leicester	15.05.90
Purrington, Ben	5.9	Plymouth	Exeter	05.05.96

Warren, Mason	5.8	–	Doncaster	28.03.97
Wood, Richard	6.3	Charlton	Ossett	05.07.85
Midfielders				
Bailey-King, Darnelle	5.9	Fulham	Lambeth	17.10.97
Forde, Anthony	5.9	Walsall	Ballingarry, Ire	16.11.93
Frecklington, Lee	5.8	Peterborough	Lincoln	08.09.85
Newell, Joe	5.11	Peterborough	Tamworth	15.03.93
Potter, Darren	5.10	MK Dons	Liverpool	21.12.84
Taylor, Jon	5.11	Peterborough	Liverpool	20.07.92
Vaulks, Will	5.11	Falkirk	Wirral	13.09.93
Williams, Ryan	5.8	Barnsley	Perth, Aus	28.10.93
Forwards				
Ball, David	6.0	Fleetwood	Whitefield	14.12.89
Procter, Jamie	6.2	Bolton	Preston	25.03.92
Clarke-Harris, Jonson	6.0	Oldham	Leicester	20.07.94
Moore, Kieffer	6.5	Ipswich (loan)	Torquay	08.08.92
Yates, Jerry	5.9	–	Doncaster	10.11.96

SCUNTHORPE UNITED

Ground: Glanford Park, Doncaster Road, Scunthorpe DN15 8TD
Telephone: 0871 221 1899. **Club nickname**: Iron
Colours: Claret and blue. **Capacity**: 9,183
Record attendance: Old Show Ground: 23,935 v Portsmouth (FA Cup 4) Jan 30, 1954.
Glanford Park: 8,921 v Newcastle (Champ) Oct 20, 2009

Goalkeepers				
Gilks, Matt	6.1	Wigan	Rochdale	04.06.82
Watson, Rory	6.3	Hull	York	05.02.96
Defenders				
Burgess, Cameron	6.4	Fulham	Aberdeen	21.10.95
Clarke, Jordan	6.0	Coventry	Coventry	19.11.91
Goode, Charlie	6.5	Hendon	Watford	03.08.95
McArdle, Rory	6.1	Bradford	Sheffield	01.05.87
Townsend, Conor	5.6	Hull	Hessle	04.03.93
Wallace, Murray	6.2	Huddersfield	Glasgow	10.01.93
Midfielders				
Adelakun, Hakeeb	6.0	–	Hackney	11.06.96
Bishop, Neal	6.0	Blackpool	Stockton	07.08.81
Holmes, Duane	5.6	Huddersfield	Columbus, US	06.11.94
Mantom, Sam	5.9	Walsall	Stourbridge	20.02.92
Morris, Josh	5.10	Bradford	Preston	30.09.91
Sutton, Levi	5.11	–	Scunthorpe	24.03.96
Forwards				
Burdett, Noel	5.10	–	Scunthorpe	13.11.97
Dyche, Jack	5.9	–	Leeds	11.10.97
Hopper, Tom	6.1	Leicester	Boston	14.12.93
Madden, Paddy	6.0	Yeovil	Dublin, Ire	04.03.90
Margetts, Jonny	5.9	Lincoln	Doncaster	28.09.93
Van Veen, Kevin	6.0	FC Oss	Eindhovern, Hol	01.06.91
Williams, Luke	6.1	Middlesbrough	Middlesbrough	11.06.93
Wootton, Kyle	6.2	–	Epworth	11.10.96

SHREWSBURY TOWN

Ground: Greenhous Meadow Stadium, Oteley Road, Shrewsbury SY2 6ST

Telephone: 01743 289177. **Club nickname:** Shrews
Colours: Blue and yellow. **Capacity:** 9,875
Record attendance: Gay Meadow: 18,917 v Walsall (Div 3) Apr 26, 1961. Greenhous Meadow: 10,210 v Chelsea (Lge Cup 4) Oct 28, 2014

Goalkeepers

Henderson, Dean	6.3	Manchester Utd (loan)	Whitehaven	12.03.97
Leutwiler, Jayson	6.4	Middlesbrough	Neuchatel, Switz	25.04.89
MacGillivray, Craig	6.2	Walsall	Harrogate	12.01.93

Defenders

Brown, Junior	5.9	Mansfield	Crewe	07.05.89
Jules, Zak	6.3	Reading	Islington	07.02.97
McGivern, Ryan	6.2	Port Vale	Newry	08.01.90
Nsiala, Aristote	6.4	Hartlepool	Kinshasa, DR Cong	25.03.92
Riley, Joe	6.0	Bury	Salford	13.10.91
Sadler, Mat	5.11	Rotherham	Birmingham	26.02.85
Smith, Dominic	6.0	–	Shrewsbury	09.02.96

Midfielders

Adams, Ebou	5.11	Norwich (loan)	Greenwich	15.01.96
Dodds, Louis	5.10	Port Vale	Sheffield	08.10.86
Morris, Bryn	6.0	Middlesbrough	Hartlepool	25.04.96
Nolan, Jon	5.10	Chesterfield	Huyton	22.04.92
O'Brien, Jim	6.0	Coventry	Vale of Leven	28.09.87
Ogogo, Abu	5.10	Dagenham	Epsom	03.11.89
Rodman, Alex	6.2	Notts Co	Sutton Coldfield	15.12.87
Whalley, Shaun	5.9	Luton	Whiston	07.08.87

Forwards

Gnahoua, Arthur	6.2	Kidderminster	London	18.09.92
John-Lewis, Lenell	5.10	Newport	Hammersmith	17.05.89
Leitch-Smith AJ	5.11	Port Vale	Crewe	06.03.90
Morris, Carlton	6.2	Norwich (loan)	Cambridge	16.12.95

SOUTHEND UNITED

Ground: Roots Hall, Victoria Avenue, Southend SS2 6NQ
Telephone: 01702 304050. **Club nickname:** Shrimpers
Colours: Blue and white. **Capacity:** 12,392
Record attendance: 31,090 v Liverpool (FA Cup 3) Jan 10, 1979

Goalkeepers

Oxley, Mark	6.2	Hibernian	Sheffield	28.09.90
Smith, Ted	6.1	–	Bentleet	18.01.96

Defenders

Barrett, Adam	5.10	Gillingham	Dagenham	29.11.79
Coker, Ben	5.11	Colchester	Cambridge	01.07.90
Demetriou, Jason	5.11	Walsall	Newham	18.11.87
Ferdinand, Anton	6.0	Reading	Peckham	18.02.85
Hendrie, Stephen	5.11	West Ham	Glasgow	08.01.95
Kyprianou, Harry	6.0	Watford	Enfield	16.03.97
Leonard, Ryan	6.1	Plymouth	Plymouth	24.05.92
White, John	6.0	Colchester	Colchester	25.07.86

Midfielders

Kightly, Michael	5.11	Burnley	Basildon	24.01.86
Leonard, Ryan	6.1	Plymouth	Plympton	24.05.92
McGlashan, Jermaine	5.7	Gillingham	Croydon	14.04.88
McLaughlin, Stephen	5.10	Nottm Forest	Donegal, Ire	14.06.90

Timlin, Michael	5.8	Swindon	Lambeth	19.03.85
Wordsworth, Anthony	6.1	Ipswich	Camden	03.01.89
Forwards				
Cox, Simon	5.11	Reading	Reading	28.04.87
Fortune, Marc-Antoine	6.0	Coventry	Cayenne, Fr Guin	02.07.81
Ranger, Nile	6.2	Blackpool	Wood Green	11.04.91
Robinson, Theo	5.10	Lincoln	Birmingham	22.01.89

WALSALL

Ground: Banks's Stadium, Bescot Crescent, Walsall WS1 4SA
Telephone: 01922 622791. **Club nickname**: Saddlers
Colours: Red and white. **Capacity**: 11,300
Record attendance: Fellows Park: 25,453 v Newcastle (Div 2) Aug 29, 1961. Banks's
Stadium: 11,049 v Rotherham (Div 1) May 10, 2004

Goalkeepers				
Evans, Owen	6.1	Hereford	Newport	28.11.96
Gillespie, Mark	6.0	Carlisle	Newcastle	27.03.92
Roberts, Liam	6.0	–	Walsall	24.11.94
Defenders				
Cockerill-Mollett, Callum	5.10	–	Leicester	15.01.99
Devlin, Nicky	6.0	Ayr	Bishopbriggs	17.10.93
Edwards, Joe	5.9	Colchester	Gloucester	31.10.90
Guthrie, Jon	5.10	Crewe	Devizes	29.07.92
Leahy, Luke	5.10	Falkirk	Coventry	19.11.92
O'Connor, James	5.10	Derby	Birmingham	20.11.84
Preston, Matt	6.0	–	Birmingham	16.03.95
Roberts, Kory	6.1	–	Birmingham	17.12.97
Vann, Dan	6.0	–	Solihull	09.06.99
Midfielders				
Chambers, Adam	5.10	Leyton Orient	Sandwell	20.11.80
Cuvelier, Florent	6.0	Sheffield Utd	Brussels, Bel	12.09.92
Flanagan, Reece	5.11	–	Birmingham	19.10.94
Kinsella, Liam	5.9	–	Colchester	23.02.96
Morris, Kieron	5.10	–	Hereford	03.06.94
Oztumer, Erhun	5.3	Peterborough	Greenwich	29.05.91
Sangha, Jordon	6.0	–	West Bromwich	04.01.98
Forwards				
Bakayoko, Amadou	6.3	–	Sierra Leone	01.01.96
Jackson, Simeon	5.8	Blackburn	Kingston, Jam	28.03.87

WIGAN ATHLETIC

Ground: DW Stadium, Robin Park, Wigan WN5 0UZ
Telephone: 01942 774000. **Club nickname**: Latics
Colours: Blue and white. **Capacity**: 25,023
Record attendance: Springfield Park: 27,526 v Hereford (FA Cup 2) Dec 12, 1953;
DW Stadium: 25,133 v Manchester Utd (Prem Lge) May 11, 2008

Goalkeepers				
Walton, Christian	6.5	Brighton (loan)	Truro	09.11.95
Defenders				
Burn, Dan	6.7	Fulham	Blyth	09.05.92
Burke, Luke	5.7	–	Liverpool	22.02.98
Daniels, Donervon	6.1	WBA	Montserrat	24.11.93

Dunkley, Chey	6.2	Oxford	Wolverhampton	13.02.92
James, Reece	5.6	Manchester Utd	Bacup	07.11.93
Kellett, Andy	5.8	Bolton	Bolton	10.11.93
Morgan, Craig	6.0	Rotherham	Flint	16.06.85
Terell, Thomas	6.0	Charlton	Redbridge	13.10.97
Midfielders				
Byrne, Jack	5.9	Manchester City	Dublin, Ire	24.04.96
Byrne, Nathan	5.11	Wolves	St Albans	05.06.92
Colclough, Ryan	6.0	Crewe	Burslem	27.12.94
Flores, Jordan	5.11	–	Wigan	04.10.95
Gilbey, Alex	6.0	Colchester	Dagenham	09.12.94
Jacobs, Michael	5.9	Wolves	Rothwell	04.11.91
Laurent, Josh	6.2	Hartlepool	Leystonstone	06.05.95
MacDonald, Shaun	6.1	Bournemouth	Swansea	17.06.88
Morsy, Sam	5.9	Chesterfield	Wolverhampton	10.09.91
Perkins, David	5.6	Blackpool	Heysham	21.06.82
Powell, Nick	6.0	Manchester Utd	Crewe	23.03.94
Power, Max	5.11	Tranmere	Birkenhead	27.07.93
Whitehead, Danny	5.10	Macclesfield	Trafford	23.10.93
Forwards				
Barrigan, James	5.11	–	Liverpool	25.01.98
Bogle, Omar	6.3	Grimsby	Birmingham	26.07.92
Grigg, Will	5.11	Brentford	Solihull	03.07.91
Mandron, Mikael	6.3	Eastleigh	Boulogne, Fr	11.10.94
Massey, Gavin	5.10	Leyton Orient	Watford	14.10.92
McKay, Billy	5.9	Inverness	Corby	22.10.88
Odelusi, Sanmi	6.0	Bolton	Dagenham	11.06.93
Woolery, Kaiyne	5.10	Bolton	Hackney	11.01.95

LEAGUE TWO

ACCRINGTON STANLEY

Ground: Wham Stadium, Livingstone Road, Accrington BB5 5BX
Telephone: 0871 434 1968. **Club nickname:** Stanley
Colours: Red and white. **Capacity:** 5,057
Record attendance: 4,368 v Colchester (FA Cup 3) Jan 3, 2004

Goalkeepers				
Chapman, Aaron	6.8	Chesterfield	Rotherham	29.05.90
Defenders				
Beckles, Omar	6.3	Aldershot	Kettering	19.10.91
Conneely, Seamus	6.1	Sligo	Lambeth	09.07.88
Donacien, Janoi	6.0	Aston Villa	Castries, St Luc	03.11.93
Hughes, Mark	6.3	Stevenage	Kirkby	09.12.86
Ogle, Reagan	5.9	–	–	29.03.99
Pearson, Matty	6.3	Halifax	Keighley	03.08.93
Richards-Everton, Ben	6.4	Dunfermline	Birmingham	17.10.91
Sykes, Ross	6.5	–	Burnley	26.03.99
Midfielders				
Boco, Romuald	5.10	Portsmouth	Bernay, Fr	08.07.85
Brown, Scott	5.9	Grimsby	Runcorn	08.05.85
Clark, Jordan	6.0	Shrewsbury	Hoyland	22.09.93
McConville, Sean	5.11	Chester	Burscough	06.03.89
Nolan, Liam	5.10	Southport	Liverpool	20.09.94

Sousa, Erico	5.7	Tranmere	Vale da Amoreira, Por	12.03.95
Forwards				
Edwards, Jonny	5.11	Hull (loan)	Luton	24.11.96
Kee, Billy	5.9	Scunthorpe	Leicester	01.12.90

BARNET

Ground: The Hive, Camrose Avenue, London HA8 6AG
Telephone: 0208 381 3800. **Club nickname**: Bees
Colours: Gold and black. **Capacity**: 6,205
Record attendance:Underhill:11,026 v Wycombe (FA Amateur Cup 4) Feb 23, 1952. The Hive: 5,233 v Gateshead (Conf) Apr 25, 2015

Goalkeepers				
McKenzie-Lyle, Kai	6.5	–	Haringey	30.11.97
Ross, Craig	6.2	Macclesfield	–	29.01.90
Stephens, Jamie	6.1	Newport	Wotton-under-Edge	24.08.93
Defenders				
Brindley, Richard	5.11	Colchester	Norwich	05.05.93
Clough, Charlie	6.2	Forest Green	Taunton	04.09.90
Johnson, Elliot	5.10	Norwich	Edgware	17.08.94
Nelson, Michael	6.2	Cambridge Utd	Bishop Auckland	23.03.80
Payne, Joe	6.1	–	Enfield	02.04.99
Santos, Ricardo	6.5	Peterborough	Almada, Por	18.06.95
Taylor, Harry	6.2	–	Hammersmith	05.05.97
Tutonda, David	5.11	Cardiff	Kinshasa, DR Con	11.10.95
Midfielders				
Bover, Ruben	5.10	New York Cosmos	Mallorca, Sp	24.06.92
Campbell-Ryce, Jamal	5.7	Sheffield Utd	Lambeth	06.04.83
Kyei, Nana	5.11	–	Hackney	10.01.98
Sweeney, Dan	6.3	Maidstone	Kingston upon Thames	25.04.94
Taylor, Jack	6.1	Chelsea	Hammersmith	23.06.98
Vilhete, Mauro	5.9	–	Rio de Mauro, Por	10.05.93
Watson, Ryan	6.1	Leicester	Crewe	07.07.93
Weston, Curtis	5.11	Gillingham	Greenwich	24.01.87
Forwards				
Akinde, John	6.2	Alfreton	Gravesend	08.07.89
Akinola, Simeon	5.10	Braintree	–	06.08.92
Akpa Akpro, Jean-Louis	6.0	Shrewsbury	Toulouse, Fr	04.01.85
Nicholls, Alex	5.10	Exeter	Stourbridge	09.12.87

CAMBRIDGE UNITED

Ground: Cambs Glass Stadium, Newmarket Road, Cambridge CB5 8LN
Telephone: 01223 566500. **Club nickname**: U's
Colours: Yellow and black. **Capacity**: 9,617
Record attendance: 14,000 v Chelsea (friendly) May 1, 1970

Goalkeepers				
Mitov, Dimitar	6.2	Charlton	–	22.01.97
Defenders				
Carroll, Jake	6.0	Hartlepool	Dublin, Ire	11.08.91
Coulson, Josh	6.3	–	Cambridge	28.01.89
Legge, Leon	6.1	Gillingham	Hastings	28.04.85
O'Neil, Liam	5.11	Chesterfield	Cambridge	31.07.93
Roberts, Mark	6.1	Stevenage	Northwich	16.10.83

| Taylor, Greg | 6.1 | Luton | Bedford | 15.01.90 |

Midfielders

Berry, Luke	5.9	Barnsley	Cambridge	12.07.92
Deegan, Gary	5.9	Shrewsbury	Dublin, Ire	28.09.87
Elito, Medy	6.0	Newport	Kinshasa, DR Cong	20.03.90
Halliday, Brad	5.11	Middlesbrough	Redcar	10.07.95
Lewis, Paul	6.1	Macclesfield	–	17.12.94
Mingoia, Piero	5.7	Accrington	Enfield	20.10.91
Osadebe, Emmanuel	6.2	Gillingham	Dundalk, Ire	01.10.96

Forwards

Amoo, David	5.10	Partick	Southwark	13.04.91
Azeez, Ade	6.0	Partick	Orpington	08.01.94
Dunk, Harrison	6.0	Bromley	London	25.10.90
Ibehre, Jabo	6.2	Carlisle	Islington	28.01.83
Ikpeazu, Uche	6.3	Watford	Harrow	28.02.95
Maris, George	5.11	Barnsley	Sheffield	06.03.96
McGurk, Adam	5.10	Portsmouth	St Helier	24.01.89

CARLISLE UNITED

Ground: Brunton Park, Warwick Road, Carlisle CA1 1LL
Telephone: 01228 526237. **Club nickname**: Cumbrians
Colours: Blue and white. **Capacity**: 17,949
Record attendance: 27,500 v Birmingham City (FA Cup 3) Jan 5, 1957, v Middlesbrough (FA Cup 5) Jan 7, 1970

Goalkeepers

| Bacon, Morgan | 6.2 | – | Bury | 01.06.98 |
| Bonham, Jack | 6.3 | Brentford (loan) | Stevenage | 14.09.93 |

Defenders

Brisley, Shaun	6.2	Peterborough	Macclesfield	06.05.90
Ellis, Mark	6.2	Shrewsbury	Plymouth	30.09.88
Grainger, Danny	5.10	Dunfermline	Penrith	28.07.86
Miller, Tom	5.11	Lincoln	Ely	29.06.90
Parkes, Tom	6.3	Leyton Orient	Sutton-in-Ashfield	15.01.92

Midfielders

Adams, Nicky	5.10	Northampton	Bolton	16.10.86
Devitt, Jamie	5.10	Morecambe	Dublin, Ire	06.07.90
Lluriu, Kelvin	6.1	Bury	Kano, Nig	30.05.88
Jones, Mike	6.0	Oldham	Birkenhead	15.08.87
Joyce, Luke	5.11	Accrington	Bolton	09.07.87
Kennedy, Jason	6.1	Bradford	Roseworth	11.09.86
Lambe, Reggie	5.8	Mansfield	Hamilton, Berm	04.02.91
Liddle, Gary	6.1	Chesterfield	Middlesbrough	15.06.86
Nabi, Samir	5.11	Delhi	Birmingham	16.12.96
O'Sullivan, John	5.11	Blackburn	Dublin, Ire	18.09.93

Forwards

Hope, Hallam	5.11	Bury	Manchester	17.03.94
Miller, Shaun	5.8	Morecambe	Alsager	25.09.87
Salkeld, Cameron	6.0	–	Newcastle	01.12.98

CHELTENHAM TOWN

Ground: LCI Stadium, Whaddon Road, Cheltenham GL52 5NA
Telephone: 01242 573558
Colours: Red and black. **Capacity**: 7,066

Record attendance: 8,326 v Reading (FA Cup 1) Nov 17, 1956

Goalkeepers

Flatt, Jon	6.1	Wolves (loan)	Wolverhampton	12.09.94

Defenders

Bower, Matt	6.5	–	–	11.12.98
Boyle, Will	6.2	Huddersfield	Garforth	01.09.95
Cranston, Jordan	5.11	Gateshead	Wednesfield	11.11.93
Downes, Aaron	6.1	Torquay	Mudgee, Aus	15.05.85
Forster, Jordon	6.2	Hibernian	Edinburgh	23.09.93
Grimes, Jamie	6.1	Dover	Nottingham	22.12.90
O'Shaughnessy, Daniel	6.2	Brentford	Riihimaki, Fin	14.09.94

Midfielders

Atangana, Nigel	6.2	Leyton Orient	Corbeil-Essonnes, Fr	09.09.89
Dawson, Kevin	5.11	Yeovil	Dublin, Ire	30.06.90
Pell, Harry	6.4	Eastleigh	Tilbury	21.10.91
Storer, Kyle	5.11	Wrexham	Nuneaton	30.04.87
Thomas, Josh	5.8	–	–	17.04.99
Winchester, Carl	6.0	Oldham	Belfast	12.04.93

Forwards

Eisa, Mohamed	6.1	Greenwich	Khartoum, Sud	15.06.90
Holman, Dan	5.11	Colchester	Northampton	05.06.90
Sellars, Jerell	5.9	Aston Villa	Lincoln	28.04.95
Wright, Danny	6.2	Kidderminster	Southampton	10.09.84

CHESTERFIELD

Ground: Proact Stadium, Whittington Moor, Chesterfield S41 8NZ
Telephone: 01246 209765. **Club nickname**: Spireites
Colours: Blue and white. **Capacity**: 10,400
Record attendance: Saltergate: 30,561 v Tottenham (FA Cup 5) Feb 12, 1938. Proact Stadium: 10,089 v Rotherham (Lge 2) Mar 18, 2011

Goalkeepers

Anyon, Joe	6.2	Scunthorpe	Lytham St Annes	29.12.86
Lee, Tommy	6.2	Macclesfield	Keighley	03.01.86

Defenders

Barry, Brad	6.0	Swindon	Hastings	13.02.95
Binnom-Williams, Jerome	5.11	Peterborough	Croydon	07.03.95
Evatt, Ian	6.3	Blackpool	Coventry	19.11.81
Hird Sam	6.0	Doncaster	Doncaster	07.09.87
McGinn, Paul	5.8	Dundee	Glasgow	22.10.90
Maguire, Laurence	5.10	–	Sheffield	08.02.97
Ofoegbu, Ify	5.11	–	Nigeria	05.01.00
Wiseman, Scott	6.0	Scunthorpe	Hull	13.12.85

Midfielders

Dimaio, Connor	5.10	Sheffield Utd	Chesterfield	28.01.96
Donohue, Dion	5.10	Sutton Coldfield	Anglesey	26.08.93
McCourt, Jak	5.10	Northampton	Liverpool	06.07.95
Reed, Louis	5.8	Sheffield Utd (loan)	Barnsley	25.07.97
Sinnott, Jordan	5.11	Halifax	Bradford	14.02.94

Forwards

Brewster, Delial	5.11	Everton	Southport	07.11.97
Dennis, Kristian	5.11	Stockport	Manchester	12.03.90
German, Ricky	5.11	–	Brent	13.01.99
Mitchell, Reece	5.9	Chelsea	Westminster	19.09.95

O'Grady, Chris	6.1	Brighton	Nottingham	25.01.86
Simons, Rai	6.0	Ilkeston	Hamilton, Berm	11.01.96
Ugwu, Gozie	6.1	Woking	Oxford	22.04.93

COLCHESTER UNITED

Ground: Weston Homes Community Stadium, United Way, Colchester CO4 5HE
Telephone: 01206 755100. **Club nickname**: U's
Colours: Blue and white. **Capacity**: 10,105
Record attendance: Layer Road:19,072 v Reading (FA Cup 1) Nov 27, 1948.
Community Stadium: 10,064 v Norwich (Lge 1) Jan 16, 2010

Goalkeepers

Barnes, Dillon	6.4	Bedford	Enfield	08.04.96
Gilmartin, Rene	6.5	Watford	Dublin, Ire	31.05.87
Walker, Sam	6.6	Chelsea	Gravesend	02.10.91

Defenders

Eastman, Tom	6.3	Ipswich	Colchester	21.10.91
James, Cameron	6.0	–	Chelmsford	11.02.98
Kent, Frankie	6.2	–	Romford	21.11.95
Kinsella, Lewis	5.9	Aston Villa	Watford	02.09.94
Prosser, Luke	6.3	Southend	Enfield	28.05.88
Vincent Young, Kane	5.11	Tottenham	Camden	15.03.06
Wynter, Alex	6.1	Crystal Palace	Croydon	16.09.93

Midfielders

Lapslie, Tom	5.6	–	Waltham Forest	05.10.95
Loft, Doug	6.0	Gillingham	Maidstone	25.12.86
Murray, Sean	5.9	Swindon	Abbots Langley	11.10.93
O'Sullivan, Tommy	5.10	Cardiff	Mountain Ash	18.01.96
Sembie-Ferris, Dion	5.8	St Neots	Peterborough	23.05.96
Slater, Craig	5.10	Kilmarnock	Glasgow	20.04.94
Szmodics, Sammie	5.7	–	Colchester	24.09.95
Wright, Drey	5.9	–	Greenwich	30.04.95

Forwards

Dickenson, Drennan	6.0	Gillingham	Ferndown	26.03.97
Guthrie, Kurtis	6.3	Forest Green	Jersey	21.04.93
Johnstone, Denny	6.2	Birmingham	Dumfries	09.01.95

COVENTRY CITY

Ground: Ricoh Arena, Phoenix Way, Coventry CV6 6GE.
Telephone: 02476 992326. **Club nickname**: Sky Blues
Colours: Sky blue. **Capacity**: 32,500
Record attendance: Highfield Road: 51,455 v Wolves (Div 2) Apr 29, 1967. Ricoh Arena:
31,407 v Chelsea (FA Cup 6), Mar 7, 2009

Goalkeepers

Burge, Lee	5.11	–	Hereford	09.01.93
Charles-Cook, Reice	6.1	Bury	Lewisham	08.04.94
Liam O'Brien	6.4	Portsmouth	Ruislip	30.11.91

Defenders

Grimmer, Jackk	6.1	Fulham	Aberdeen	25.01.94
Harries, Cian	6.1	–	Birmingham	01.04.97
Haynes, Ryan	5.7	–	Northampton	27.09.95
Hyam, Dominic	6.2	Reading	Dundee	20.12.95
Kelly-Evans, Dion	5.10	–	Coventry	21.09.96

McDonald, Rod	6.3	Northampton	Crewe	11.04.92
Stokes, Chris	6.1	Forest Green	Trowbridge	08.03.91
Willis, Jordan	5.11	–	Coventry	24.08.94
Midfielders				
Doyle, Michael	5.10	Portsmouth	Dublin, Ire	08.07.81
Jones, Jodi	5.10	Dagenham	Bow	22.10.97
Kelly, Liam	5.10	Leyton Orient	Milton Keynes	10.02.90
Reid, Kyel	5.10	Preston	Deptford	26.11.87
Stevenson, Ben	6.0	–	Leicester	23.03.97
Vincenti, Peter	6.2	Rochdale	St Peter, Jer	07.07.86
Forwards				
Beavon, Stuart	5.7	Burton	Reading	05.05.84
Biamou, Maxime	6.1	Sutton	Creteil, Fr	13.11.90
McNulty, Marc	5.10	Sheffield Utd	Edinburgh	14.09.92
Thomas, Kwame	5.10	Derby	Nottingham	28.09.95
Thomas, George	5.8	–	Leicester	24.03.97

CRAWLEY TOWN

Ground: Checkatrade Stadium, Winfield Way, Crawley RH11 9RX
Telephone: 01293 410000. **Club nickname:** Reds
Colours: Red. **Capacity:** 6,134
Record attendance: 5,880 v Reading (FA Cup 3) Jan 5, 2013

Goalkeepers				
Mersin, Yusuf	6.4	Kasimpasa	Greenwich	23.09.94
Morris, Glenn	6.0	Gillingham	Woolwich	20.12.83
Defenders				
Blackman, Andre	5.11	Blackpool	Lambeth	10.11.90
Connolly, Mark	6.1	Kilmarnock	Monaghan, Ire	16.12.91
Evina, Cedric	5.9	Doncaster	Cameroon	16.11.91
Garnett, Addison	6.2	Hendon	London	13.09.96
Lelan, Josh	6.1	Northampton	Church Broughton	21.12.94
McNerney, Joe	6.4	Woking	–	24.01.90
Randall, Mark	6.0	Newport	Milton Keynes	28.09.89
Yorwerth, Josh	6.0	Ipswich	Bridgend	28.02.95
Midfielders				
Arthur, Chris	5.10	Woking	Enfield	25.01.90
Bulman, Dannie	5.8	AFC Wimbledon	Ashford, Surrey	24.01.79
Clifford, Billy	5.7	Boreham Wood	Slough	18.10.92
Cox, Dean	5.4	Leyton Orient	Haywards Heath	12.08.87
Djalo, Aliu	5.7	PS Kemi	Bissau, Guin	05.02.92
Payne, Josh	6.0	Eastleigh	Basingstoke	25.11.90
Roberts, Jordan	6.1	Inverness	Watford	05.01.94
Sanoh, Moussa	5.9	Waalwijk	Nijmegen, Hol	20.07.95
Smith, Jimmy	6.1	Stevenage	Newham	07.01.87
Tajbakhsh, Aryan	6.1	Cray	Hendon	20.10.90
Young, Lewis	5.9	Bury	Stevenage	27.09.89
Forwards				
Boldewijn, Enzio	6.1	Almere City	Almere, Hol	17.11.92
Camara, Panutche	6.1	Dulwich Hamlet	Guin-Bassau	28.02.97
Harrold, Matt	6.1	Bristol Rov	Leyton	25.07.84
Verheydt, Thomas	6.3	Maastricht	The Hague, Hol	24.01.92

CREWE ALEXANDRA

Ground: Alexandra Stadium, Gresty Road, Crewe CW2 6EB
Telephone: 01270 213014. **Club nickname:** Railwaymen
Colours: Red and white. **Capacity:** 10,066
Record attendance: 20,000 v Tottenham (FA Cup 4) Jan 30, 1960

Goalkeepers

Garratt, Ben	6.1		Shrewsbury	25.04.93
Richards, David	6.0	Bristol City	Abergavenny	31.12.93

Defenders

Bakayogo, Zoumana	5.9	Leicester	Paris, Fr	11.08.86
Ng, Perry	5.11	–	Liverpool	27.04.96
Nolan, Eddie	6.0	Blackpool	Waterford, Ire	05.08.88
Ray, George	6.0	–	Warrington	03.10.93
Raynes, Michael	6.3	Carlisle	Wythenshawe	15.10.87

Midfielders

Ainley, Callum	5.8	–	Middlewich	02.11.97
Cooper, George	5.9	–	Warrington	02.11.96
Finney, Oliver	5.7	–	Stoke	15.12.97
Jones, James	5.9	–	Winsford	01.02.96
Kirk, Charlie	5.7	–	Winsford	24.12.97
Lowery, Tom	–	–	Holmes Chapel	31.12.97
Pickering, Harry	–	–	Chester	29.12.98
Walker, Brad	6.1	Hartlepool	Billingham	25.04.96
Wintle, Ryan	5.6	Alsager	Newcastle-under-Lyme	13.06.97

Forwards

Bowery, Jordan	6.1	Leyton Orient	Nottingham	02.07.91
Dagnall, Chris	5.8	Hibernian	Liverpool	15.04.86
Dale, Owen	5.9	–	Warrington	01.11.98
Porter, Chris	6.1	Colchester	Wigan	12.12.83
Udoh, Daniel	6.1	Ilkeston	Lagos, Nig	30.08.96

EXETER CITY

Ground: St James Park, Stadium Way, Exeter EX4 6PX
Telephone: 01392 411243. **Club nickname:** Grecians
Colours: Red and white. **Capacity:** 8,830
Record attendance: 20,984 v Sunderland (FA Cup 6 replay) Mar 4, 1931

Goalkeepers

Hamon, James	6.1	Guernsey	Guernsey	01.07.95
Pym, Christy	5.11	–	Exeter	24.04.95

Defenders

Archibald-Henville, Troy	6.2	Carlisle	Newham	04.11.88
Brown, Troy	6.1	Cheltenham	Croydon	17.09.90
Croll, Luke	6.1	Crystal Palace	Lambeth	10.01.95
Moore-Taylor, Jordan	5.10	–	Exeter	21.01.94
Moxey, Dean	5.11	Bolton	Exeter	14.01.86
Storey, Jordan	6.2	–	Yeovil	02.09.97
Sweeney, Pierce	5.11	Reading	Dublin, Ire	11.09.94
Woodman, Craig	5.9	Brentford	Tiverton	22.12.82

Midfielders

Byrne, Alex	5.9	–	–	05.02.97
Harley, Ryan	5.9	Swindon	Bristol	22.01.85
Holmes, Lee	5.9	Preston	Mansfield	02.04.87
James, Lloyd	5.11	Leyton Orient	Bristol	16.02.88

| Taylor, Jake | 5.10 | Reading | Ascot | 01.12.91 |
| Tillson, Jordan | 6.0 | Bristol Rov | Bath | 05.03.93 |

Forwards

Jay, Matt	5.10	–	Torbay	27.02.96
McAlinden, Liam	6.1	Wolves	Cannock	26.09.93
Reid, Reuben	6.0	Plymouth	Bristol	26.07.88
Simpson, Robbie	6.1	Cambridge	Poole	15.03.85
Watkins, Ollie	5.10	–	Torbay	30.12.95
Wheeler, David	5.11	Staines	Brighton	04.10.90

FOREST GREEN ROVERS

Ground: New Lawn, Another Way, Nailsworth GL6 0FG
Telephone: 01453 835291. **Club nickname**: Green Devils
Capacity: 5,140. **Record attendance**: 4,836 v Derby (FA Cup 3, Jan 3, 2009)

Goalkeepers

| Lefebvre, Simon | 6.7 | Bordeaux | Tarbes, Fr | 06.05.97 |
| Russell, Sam | 6.0 | Gateshead | Middlesbrough | 04.10.82 |

Defenders

Bennett, Dale	5.11	Watford	Enfield	06.01.90
Collins, Lee	5.11	Mansfield	Telford	28.09.88
Evans, Callum	5.10	Barnsley	Bristol	11.10.95
Laird, Scott	5.9	Scunthorpe	Taunton	15.05.88
Monthe, Manny	6.1	Bath	Cameroon	26.01.95
Moran, Jon	6.1	Nantwich	Warrington	20.06.97
Racine, Aaran	6.2	Torquay	Worthing	30.10.91
Wishart, Dan	5.11	Sutton		28.05.92

Midfielders

Brown, Reece	5.9	Birmingham	Dudley	03.03.96
Cooper, Charlie	5.9	Birmingham	Stockton	01.05.97
James, Luke	6.0	Peterborough	Amble	04.11.94
Noble, Liam	5.8	Notts Co	Cramlington	08.05.91
Robert, Fabien	5.9	Swindon	Hennebont, Fr	06.01.89
Sinclair, Rob	5.10	Salisbury	Bedford	29.08.89
Traore, Drissa	5.8	Swindon	Bouake, Iv C	25.03.92

Forwards

Bugiel, Omar	6.2	Worthing	Germany	25.09.84
Doidge, Christian	6.1	Dagenham	Newport	25.08.92
Mehew, Olly	5.10	Bristol Rov	Bristol	03.11.97
Mullings, Shamir	6.1	Sutton	Hillingdon	30.10.93
Murphy, Rhys	6.1	Oldham	Shoreham	06.11.90

GRIMSBY TOWN

Ground: Blundell Park, Cleethorpes DN35 7PY
Telephone: 01472 605050
Colours: Black and white. **Capacity**: 9,052
Record attendance: 31,651 v Wolves (FA Cup 5) 20 February, 1937

Goalkeepers

| Killip, Ben | 6.0 | Norwich | Isleworth | 24.11.95 |
| McKeown, James | 6.1 | Peterborough | Birmingham | 24.07.89 |

Defenders

| Boyce, Andrew | 6.2 | Scunthorpe | Doncaster | 05.11.89 |
| Clarke, Nathan | 5.11 | Coventry | Halifax | 30.07.83 |

Collins, Danny	6.0	Rotherham	Chester	06.08.80
Davies, Ben	5.7	Portsmouth	Birmingham	27.05.81
Mills, Zak	6.0	Boston	Peterborough	28.05.92
Midfielders				
Berrett, James	5.10	York	Halifax	13.01.89
Bolarinwa, Tom	5.11	Sutton	Greenwich	21.01.90
Clements, Chris	5.9	Mansfield	Birmingham	06.02.90
Clifton, Harry	5.11	–	Grimsby	12.06.98
Kelly, Sam	5.10	Port Vale	Huntingdon	21.10.93
McAllister, Sean	5.8	Scunthorpe	Bolton	15.08.87
Osborne, Jamey	6.0	Solihull	Solihull	07.06.92
Rose, Mitch	5.9	Newport	Doncaster	04.07.94
Summerfield, Luke	6.0	York	Ivybridge	06.12.87
Wright, Max	5.8	–	Grimsby	06.04.98
Forwards				
Asante, Akwasi	6.0	Solihull	Amsterdam, Hol	06.09.92
Jones, Sam	6.2	Gateshead	Barnsley	18.09.91
Vernon, Scott	6.1	Shrewsbury	Manchester	13.12.83
Yussuf, Adi	6.1	Mansfield	Zanzibar, Tanz	20.02.92

LINCOLN CITY

Ground: Sincil Bank Stadium, Lincoln LN5 8LD
Telephone: 01522 880011. **Club nickname**: Imps
Colours: Red and white. **Capacity**: 10,130
Record attendance: 23,196 v Derby (League Cup 4) Nov 15, 1967

Goalkeepers				
Farman, Paul	6.5	Gateshead	North Shields	02.11.89
Vickers, Josh	6.0	Swansea	Basildon	01.12.95
Defenders				
Beevers, Lee	6.2	Mansfield	Doncaster	04.12.83
Habergham, Sam	6.0	Braintree	Doncaster	20.02.92
Howe, Callum	6.0	Scunthorpe	Doncaster	09.04.94
Long, Sean	5.10	Reading	Dublin	02.06.95
Raggett, Sean	6.5	Dover	Gillingham	17.04.93
Waterfall, Luke	6.2	Wrexham	Sheffield	30.07.90
Wood, Bradley	5.10	Alfreton	Leicester	02.09.91
Midfielders				
Arnold, Nathan	5.7	Grimsby	Mansfield	26.07.87
Ginnelly, Josh	5.8	Burnley (loan)	Coventry	24.03.97
Knott, Billy	5.8	Gillingham	Canvey Island	28.11.92
Maguire-Drew, Jordan	6.0	Brighton (loan)	Crawley	15.09.97
Whitehouse, Elliott	5.11	Nuneaton	Worksop	27.10.93
Woodyard, Alex	5.9	Braintree	Gravesend	03.05.93
Forwards				
Green, Matt	6.0	Mansfield	Bath	02.01.87
Marriott, Adam	5.9	Stevenage	Brandon	14.04.91
Palmer, Ollie	6.5	Leyton Orient	Epsom	21.01.92
Rhead, Matt	6.4	Mansfield	Stoke	31.05.84

LUTON TOWN

Ground: Kenilworth Road, Maple Road, Luton LU4 8AW
Telephone: 01582 411622. **Club nickname**: Hatters
Colours: Orange and black. **Capacity**: 10,226

Goalkeepers

Shea, James	5.11	AFC Wimbledon	Islington	16.06.91
Stech, Marek	6.5	Sparta Prague	Prague, Cz	28.01.90

Defenders

Cuthbert, Scott	6.2	Leyton Orient	Alexandria, Sco	15.06.87
Famewo, Akin	5.11	–	Lewisham	09.11.98
Justin, James	6.3	–	Luton	11.07.97
Mullins, Johnny	5.11	Oxford	Hampstead	06.11.85
Musonda, Frankie	6.0	–	Bedford	12.12.97
Potts, Dan	5.8	West Ham	Romford	13.04.94
Rea, Glen	6.1	Brighton	Brighton	03.09.94
Senior, Jack	5.8	Huddersfield	Halifax	13.01.97
Sheehan, Alan	5.11	Bradford	Athlone, Ire	14.09.86
Stacey, Jack	5.11	Reading	Ascott	06.04.96

Midfielders

Bakinson, Tyreeq	6.1	–	Camden	08.01.98
Cook, Jordan	5.9	Walsall	Sunderland	20.03.90
D'Ath, Lawson	5.9	Northampton	Witney	24.12.92
Gambin, Luke	5.7	Barnet	Sutton	16.03.93
Lee, Olly	6.0	Birmingham	Hornchurch	11.07.91
McCormack, Alan	5.8	Brentford	Dublin, Ire	10.01.84
Ruddock, Pelly	5.9	West Ham	Hendon	17.07.93
Shinnie, Andrew	5.11	Birmingham (loan)	Aberdeen	17.07.89

Forwards

Collins, James	6.2	Crawley	Coventry	01.12.90
Hylton, Danny	6.0	Oxford	Camden	25.02.89
Lee, Elliot	5.11	Barnsley	Durham	16.12.94
Vassell, Isaac	5.8	Truro	Newquay	09.09.93

MANSFIELD TOWN

Ground: One Call Stadium, Quarry Lane, Mansfield NG18 5DA
Telephone: 01623 482482. **Club nickname**: Stags
Colours: Amber and blue. **Capacity**: 10,000
Record attendance: 24,467 v Nottm Forest (FA Cup 3) Jan 10, 1953

Goalkeepers

Logan, Conrad	6.2	Rochdale	Ramelton, Ire	18.04.86
Olejnik, Bobby	6.0	Exeter	Vienna, Aut	26.11.86

Defenders

Bennett, Rhys	6.3	Rochdale	Manchester	01.09.91
Benning, Malvind	5.10	Walsall	Sandwell	02.11.93
Diamond, Zander	6.2	Northampton	Alexandria, Sco	03.12.85
Hunt, Johnny	5.10	Chester	Liverpool	23.08.90
Mirfin, David	6.1	Scunthorpe	Sheffield	18.04.85
Pearce, Krystian	6.2	Torquay	Birmingham	05.01.90
Shires, Corbin	6.3	Hallam	Sheffield	31.12.97
Taft, George	6.3	Burton	Leicester	29.07.93
White, Hayden	6.1	Peterborough	Greenwich	15.04.95

Midfielders

Anderson, Paul	5.9	Northampton	Leicester	23.07.88
Atkinson, Will	5.10	Southend	Beverley	14.10.88
Byrom, Joel	6.0	Northampton	Oswaldtwistle	14.09.86
Chapman, Adam	5.10	Newport	Doncaster	29.11.89

Digby, Paul	6.3	Ipswich	Sheffield	02.02.95
Hakeem, Zayn	5.10	Nottm Forest	–	15.02.99
MacDonald, Alex	5.7	Oxford	Warrington	14.04.90
Mellis, Jacob	5.11	Bury	Nottingham	08.01.91
Potter, Alfie	5.7	Northampton	Islington	09.01.89
Thomas, Jack	5.9	–	Sutton-in-Ashfield	03.06.96
Forwards				
Angol, Lee	6.2	Peterborough	Sutton	04.08.94
Hakeem, Zayn	6.2	Nottm Forest	Leicester	15.02.99
Hamilton CJ	5.7	Sheffield Utd	Harrow	23.03.95
Rose, Danny	5.10	Bury	Barnsley	10.12.93
Spencer, Jimmy	6.1	Plymouth	Leeds	13.12.91
Sterling-James, Omari	5.10	Solihull	Birmingham	15.09.93

MORECAMBE

Ground: Globe Arena, Christie Way, Westgate, Morecambe LA4 4TB
Telephone: 01524 411797. **Club nickname**: Shrimps
Colours: Red and white **Capacity**: 6,476
Record attendance: Christie Park: 9,234 v Weymouth (FA Cup 3) Jan 6, 1962. Globe Arena: 5,003 v Burnley (League Cup 2) Aug 24, 2010

Goalkeepers				
Nizic, Dan	6.5	Burnley	Sydney, Aus	15.03.95
Roche, Barry	6.4	Chesterfield	Dublin, Ire	06.04.82
Defenders				
Conlan, Luke	5.11	Burnley	Portaferry	31.10.94
Lund, Mitchell	6.1	Doncaster (loan)	Leeds	27.08.96
McGowan, Aaron	5.9	–	Kirkby	24.07.96
Rose, Michael	5.11	Rochdale	Salford	28.07.82
Winnard, Dean	5.9	Accrington	Wigan	20.08.89
Midfielders				
Brough, Patrick	6.3	Carlisle	Carlisle	20.02.96
Ellison, Kevin	6.0	Rotherham	Liverpool	23.02.79
Fleming, Andy	5.11	Wrexham	Liverpool	05.10.87
Kenyon, Alex	6.0	Stockport	Euxton	17.07.92
Wildig, Aaron	5.9	Shrewsbury	Hereford	15.04.92
Forwards				
Campbell, Adam	5.9	Notts Co	North Shields	01.01.95
Mullin, Paul	5.10	Huddersfield	Liverpool	06.11.94
Oliver, Vadaine	6.1	York	Sheffield	21.10.91
Thompson, Garry	5.11	Wycombe	Kendal	24.11.80
Turner, Rhys	5.11	Oldham	Preston	22.07.95

NEWPORT COUNTY

Ground: Rodney Parade, Newport NP19 0UU
Telephone: 01633 670690. **Club nickname**: Exiles
Colours: Amber and black. **Capacity**: 7,850
Record attendance: Somerton Park: 24,268 v Cardiff (Div 3S) Oct 16, 1937. Rodney Parade: 6,615 v Grimsby (Conf play-off semi-finals 2nd leg) Apr 28, 2013

Goalkeepers				
Bittner, James	6.1	Plymouth	Devizes	02.02.82
Day, Joe	6.0	Peterborough	Brighton	13.08.90

Defenders

Barnum-Bobb, Jazzi	5.11	Cardiff	Enfield	15.09.95
Bennett, Scott	5.10	Notts Co	Newquay	30.11.90
Butler, Dan	5.9	Torquay	Cowes	26.08.94
Demetriou, Mickey	6.2	Shrewsbury	Dorrington	12.03.90
O'Brien, Mark	5.11	Luton	Dublin, Ire	20.11.92
Pipe, David	5.9	Eastleigh	Caerphilly	05.11.83
Turley, Jamie	6.1	Eastleigh	Reading	07.04.90

Midfielders

Dolan, Matt	5.9	Yeovil	Hartlepool	11.02.93
Labadie, Joss	6.3	Dagenham	Croydon	30.08.90
Rigg, Sean	5.9	Wimbledon	Bristol	01.10.88
Tozer, Ben	6.1	Yeovil	Plymouth	01.03.90
Willmott, Robbie	5.9	Chelmsford	Harlow	16.05.90

Forwards

Jackson, Marlon	6.1	Oxford City	Bristol	06.12.90
Nouble, Frank	6.3	Southend	Lewisham	24.09.91
Reynolds, Lamar	5.10	Brentwood	Jamaica	16.08.95
Williams, Aaron	5.10	Peterborough	Sandwell	21.10.93

NOTTS COUNTY

Ground: Meadow Lane, Nottingham NG2 3HJ
Telephone: 0115 952 9000. **Club nickname:** Magpies
Colours: White and black. **Capacity:** 20,300
Record attendance: 47,310 v York (FA Cup 6) Mar 12, 1955

Goalkeepers

Collin, Adam	6.1	Rotherham	Carlisle	09.12.84
Searson, Joe	6.2	–	Nottingham	08.09.98

Defenders

Dickinson, Carl	6.1	Port Vale	Swadlincote	31.03.8
Duffy, Richard	5.11	Port Vale	Swansea	30.08.85
Edwards, Mike	6.0	Carlisle	Hessle	25.04.80
Hewitt, Elliott	5.11	Ipswich	Bodelwyddan	30.05.94
Hollis, Haydn	6.4	–	Selston	14.10.92
Jones, Dan	6.2	Chesterfield	Wordsley	23.12.86
Richards, Jordan	5.9	–	Nottingham	06.07.97
Tootle, Matt	5.9	Shrewsbury	Knowsley	11.10.90

Midfielders

Hawkridge, Terry	5.6	Lincoln	Nottingham	23.02.90
Milsom, Rob	5.10	Rotherham	Redhill	02.01.87
O'Connor, Michael	6.1	Port Vale	Belfast	06.10.87
Smith, Alan	5.10	MK Dons	Rothwell	28.10.80
Thompson, Curtis	5.7	–	Nottingham	02.09.93

Forwards

Alessandra, Lewis	5.10	Hartlepool	Heywood	08.02.89
Ameobi, Shola	6.3	Fleetwood	Zaria, Nig	12.10.81
Forte, Jonathan	6.0	Oldham	Sheffield	25.07.86
Stead, Jon	6.3	Huddersfield	Huddersfield	07.04.83

PORT VALE

Ground: Vale Park, Hamil Road, Burslem, Stoke-on-Trent ST6 1AW
Telephone: 01782 655800. **Club nickname:** Valiants
Colours: Black and white. **Capacity:** 18,947

Record attendance: 49,768 v Aston Villa (FA Cup 5) Feb 20, 1960

Goalkeepers

Boot, Ryan	6.1	Stoke	Rocester	09.11.94
Hornby, Sam	6.2	Burton	Sutton Coldfield	14.02.95
Lainton, Rob	6.2	Bury	Ashton-under-Lyme	12.10.89

Defenders

Davis, Joe	6.3	Fleetwood	Burnley	10.11.93
Gibbons, James	5.9	–	Stoke	16.03.98
Kay, Antony	5.11	Bury	Barnsley	21.10.82
Kelly, Graham	5.10	Sheffield Utd	Dublin, Ire	16.10.97
Smith, Nathan	6.0	–	Madeley	03.04.96

Midfielders

Brown, Michael	5.10	Leeds	Hartlepool	25.01.77
De Freitas, Anthony	5.11	Monaco	Lyon, Fr	10.05.94
Montano, Cristian	5.11	Bristol Rov	Cali, Col	11.12.91
Pugh, Danny	6.0	Blackpool	Cheadle Hulme	19.10.82
Reeves, Billy	6.0	–	Wrexham	18.12.96

Forwards

Barnett, Tyrone	6.3	AFC Wimbledon	Stevenage	28.10.85
Forrester, Anton	6.0	Blackburn	Liverpool	11.02.94
Pope, Tom	6.3	Bury	Stoke	27.08.85
Pyke, Rekeil	5.10	Huddersfield (loan)	Leeds	01.09.97
Turner, Dan	5.11	–	Stone	23.06.98

STEVENAGE

Ground: Lamex Stadium, Broadhall Way, Stevenage SG2 8RH
Telephone: 01438 223223. **Club nickname:** Doro
Colours: White and red. **Capacity:** 6,920
Record attendance: 8,040 v Newcastle (FA Cup 4) January 25, 1998

Goalkeepers

Day, Chris	6.2	Millwall	Walthamstow	28.07.75
Fryer, Joe	6.1	Middlesbrough (loan)	Chester le Street	14.11.95

Defenders

Franks, Fraser	6.0	Luton	Hammersmith	22.11.90
Henry, Ronnie	5.11	Luton	Hemel Hempstead	02.01.84
Johnson, Ryan	6.2	–	Birmingham	09.10.96
King, Jack	6.0	Scunthorpe	Oxford	20.08.85
Martin, Joe	6.0	Millwall	Dagenham	29.11.88
Wilkinson, Luke	6.2	Luton	Wells	02.12.91

Midfielders

Beautyman, Harry	5.10	Nothamptonm	Newham	01.04.92
Conlon, Tom	5.9	Peterborough	Stoke	03.02.96
Ferry, James	5.11	Brenford	–	20.04.97
Gorman, Dale	5.11	–	Letterkenny, Ire	28.06.96
McAnuff, Jobi	5.11	Leyton Orient	Edmonton	09.11.81
Schumacher, Steven	6.0	Fleetwood	Liverpool	30.04.84
Turgott, Blair	6.0	Bromley	Bromley	22.05.94

Forwards

Godden, Matt	6.1	Ebbsfleet	Canterbury	29.07.91
Kennedy, Ben	5.10	–	Belfast	12.01.97
Liburd, Rowan	6.3	Reading	Croydon	28.08.92
Pett, Tom	5.8	Wealdstone	Potters Bar	03.12.91
Samuel, Alex	6.0	Swansea	Neath	20.09.95

SWINDON TOWN

Ground: County Ground, County Road, Swindon SN1 2ED
Telephone: 0871 423 6433. **Club nickname**: Robins
Colours: Red and white. **Capacity**: 15,728
Record attendance: 32,000 v Arsenal (FA Cup 3) Jan 15, 1972

Goalkeepers

Henry, Will	5.11	–	Bristol	06.07.98
Vigouroux, Lawrence	6.4	Liverpool	Camden	19.11.93

Defenders

Conroy, Dion	6.0	Chelsea	Redhill	11.12.95
Hussey, Chris	6.0	Sheffield Utd (loan)	Hammersmith	02.01.89
Lancashire, Olly	6.1	Shrewsbury	Basingstoke	13.12.88
Purkiss, Ben	6.2	Port Vale	Sheffield	01.04.84
Robertson, Chris	6.3	AFC Wimbledon	Dundee	11.10.86
Starkey, Jesse	5.10	Brighton	Brighton	01.09.95
Thompson, Nathan	5.10	–	Chester	22.04.91

Midfielders

Brophy, James	5.11	Edgware	London	25.07.94
Dunne, James	5.11	Cambridge	Farnborough	18.09.89
Goddard, John	5.10	Woking	Sandhurst	02.06.93
Iandolo, Ellis	5.10	–	Chatham	22.08.97
Linganzi, Amine	6.1	Portsmouth	Algiers, Alg	16.11.89
Thomas, Conor	6.1	Coventry	Coventry	29.10.93
Smith, Tom	5.10	–	Swindon	25.01.98

Forwards

McDermott, Donal	5.10	Rochdale	Dublin, Ire	19.10.89
Mullin, Paul	5.10	Morecambe	Liverpool	06.11.94
Norris, Luke	6.1	Gillingham	Stevenage	03.06.93
Smith Harry	6.5	Millwall (loan)	–	18.05.95

WYCOMBE WANDERERS

Ground: Adams Park, Hillbottom Road, High Wycombe HP12 4HJ
Telephone: 01494 472100. **Club nickname**: Chairboys
Colours: Light and dark blue. **Capacity**: 10,300
Record attendance: 10,000 v Chelsea (friendly) July 13, 2005

Goalkeepers

Brown, Scott	6.1	Aberdeen	Wolverhampton	26.04.85

Defenders

De Havilland, Will	6.0	Sheffield Wed	Huntingdon	08.11.94
El–Abd, Adam	6.0	Shrewsbury	Brighton	11.09.84
Harriman, Michael	5.6	QPR	Chichester	23.10.92
Jacobson, Joe	5.11	Shrewsbury	Cardiff	17.11.86
Jombati, Sido	6.1	Cheltenham	Lisbon, Por	20.08.87
Muller, Max	6.3	Salzburg	Speyer, Ger	16.05.94
Pierre, Aaron	6.1	Brentford	Southall	17.02.93
Stewart, Anthony	6.0	Crewe	Lambeth	18.09.92

Midfielders

Bean, Marcus	5.11	Colchester	Hammersmith	02.11.84
Bloomfield, Matt	5.8	Ipswich	Felixstowe	08.02.84
Cowan-Hall, Paris	5.8	Millwall	Hillingdon	05.10.90
Gape, Dominic	5.11	Southampton	Burton Bradstock	09.09.94
O'Nien, Luke	5.9	Watford	Hemel Hempstead	21.11.94

| Rowe, Danny | 6.2 | Rotherham | Middlesbrough | 24.10.95 |
| Saunders, Sam | 5.8 | Brentford | Erith | 29.08.83 |

Forwards

Akinfenwa, Adebayo	6.0	Wimbledon	Islington	10.05.82
Hayes, Paul	6.0	Scunthorpe	Dagenham	20.09.83
Kashket, Scott	5.9	Leyton Orient	Chigwell	25.02.96
Southwell, Dayle	5.11	Boston	Grimsby	20.10.93

YEOVIL TOWN

Ground: Huish Park, Lufton Way, Yeovil BA22 8YF
Telephone: 01935 423662. **Club nickname:** Glovers
Colours: Green and white. **Capacity:** 9,665
Record attendance: 9,527 v Leeds (Lge 1) Apr 25, 2008

Goalkeepers

| Krysiak, Artur | 6.4 | Exeter | Lodz, Pol | 11.08.89 |
| Maddison, Jonny | 6.1 | Leicester | Chester-le-Street | 04.09.94 |

Defenders

Davies, Keston	6.2	Swansea (loan)	Swansea	02.10.96
Dickson, Ryan	5.10	Crawley	Saltash	14.12.86
James, Tom	5.11	Cardiff	Cardiff	15.04.96
Mugabi, Bevis	6.2	Southampton	Harrow	01.05.95
Shephard, Liam	5.10	Swansea (loan)	Pentre	22.11.94
Smith, Nathan	6.0	Chesterfield	Enfield	11.01.87
Zubar, Stephane	6.1	Weymouth	Pointe-a-Pitre, Guad	09.10.86

Midfielders

Bailey, James	6.0	Carlisle	Bollington	18.09.88
Browne, Rhys	5.9	Grimsby	Romford	16.11.95
Gray, Jake	5.11	Luton	Aylesbury	25.12.95
Khan, Otis	5.9	Barnsley	Ashton-under-Lyne	05.09.95
Smith, Connor	5.11	Plymouth	Mullingar, Ire	18.02.93

Forwards

Olomola, Olufela	5.8	Southampton (loan)	London	05.09.97
Sowunmi, Omar	6.6	Ipswich	Colchester	07.11.95
Zoko, Francois	6.0	Blackpool	Daloa, Iv C	13.09.83

THE THINGS THEY SAY ...

'Society's gone soft. Two games in three days playing football, for the money they get? Ask their grandads who worked 12 hours down the pit. They never got tired' – **Tony Pulis**, West Bromwich Albion manager, has no sympathy for critics of the Christmas and New Year programme.

'This is a crazy sport. There is nothing else like it' – **Luis Enrique**, Barcelona coach, after his side made Champions League history by retrieving a 4-0 deficit from the first leg against Paris Saint-Germain and winning the return match 6-5 to reach the quarter-finals.

'People can't focus if they are not getting paid' – **Omer Riza**, Leyton Orient's fifth manager of a torrid season which ended with relegation to the National League.

SCOTTISH PREMIERSHIP SQUADS 2017–18

(at time of going to press)

ABERDEEN

Ground: Pittodrie Stadium, Pittodrie Street, Aberdeen AB24 5QH. **Capacity**: 22,199.
Telephone: 01224 650400. **Manager**: Derek McInnes. **Colours**: Red and white. **Nickname**: Dons
Goalkeepers: Joe Lewis, Danny Rogers
Defenders: Kari Arnason, Andrew Considine, Daniel Harvie, Shaleum Logan, Scott McKenna, Anthony O'Connor, Mark Reynolds, Graeme Shinnie
Midfielders: Ryan Christie (loan), Gary Mackay-Steven, Kenny McLean, Frank Ross, Craig Storie, Greg Tansey
Forwards: Adam Rooney, Nicky Maynard, Connor McLennan, Greg Stewart (loan), Miles Storey, Jayden Stockley, Scott Wright

CELTIC

Ground: Celtic Park, Glasgow G40 3RE. **Capacity**: 60,832. **Telephone**: 0871 226 1888
Manager: Brendan Rodgers. **Colours**: Green and white. **Nickname**: Bhoys
Goalkeepers: Dorus de Vries, Craig Gordon
Defenders: Kristoffer Ajer, Dedryck Boyata, Cristian Gamboa, Emilio Izaguirre, Mikael Lustig, Jozo Simunovic, Erik Sviatchenko, Kieran Tierney
Midfielders: Stuart Armstrong, Kundai Benyu, Nir Bitton, Scott Brown, James Forrest, Jonny Hayes, Liam Henderson, Eboue Kouassi, Callum McGregor, Olivier Ntcham, Tom Rogic, Scott Sinclair
Forwards: Nadir Ciftci, Moussa Dembele, Leigh Griffiths

DUNDEE

Ground: Dens Park, Sandeman Street, Dundee DD3 7JY. **Capacity**: 11,850. **Telephone**: 01382 889966. **Manager**: Neil McCann. **Colours**: Blue and white. **Nickname**: Dark Blues
Goalkeepers: Scott Bain
Defenders: Julen Etxabeguren, Kostadin Gadzhalov, Jack Hendry, Kevin Holt, Cammy Kerr, Darren O'Dea, James McPake
Midfielders: Scott Allan (loan), Jesse Curran, Roarie Deacon, Tom Hateley, Glen Kamara, Nicky Low, Paul McGowan, Mark O'Hara, Lewis Spence, James Vincent, Randy Wolters, Danny Williams
Forwards: Faissal El Bakhtaoui, Marcus Haber, Sofien Moussa, Craig Wighton

HAMILTON ACADEMICAL

Ground: New Douglas Park, Hamilton ML3 OFT. **Capacity**: 6,000. **Telephone**: 01698 368652.
Manager: Martin Canning. **Colours**: Red and white. **Nickname**: Accies
Goalkeepers: Darren Jamieson, Alex Marshall, Gary Woods
Defenders: Michael Devlin, Alex Gogic, Jordan McGregor, Scott McMann, Georgios Sarris, Shaun Want
Midfielders: Steven Boyd, Ali Crawford, Greg Docherty, Massimo Donati, Grant Gillespie, Ronan Hughes, Doug Imrie, Darren Lyon, Louis Longridge, Darian MacKinnon, Danny Redmond, David Templeton
Forwards: Rakish Bingham, Eamonn Brophy, Ross Cunningham, Ryan Tierney

HEART OF MIDLOTHIAN

Ground: Tynecastle Stadium, McLeod Street Edinburgh EH11 2NL. **Capacity**: 18,008.
Telephone: 0871 663 1874. **Manager**: Ian Cathro. **Colours**: Maroon and white. **Nickname**: Jam Tarts

Goalkeepers: Jack Hamilton, Viktor Noring
Defenders: Christophe Berra, Aaron Hughes, Jordan McGhee, Krystian Nowak, Liam Smith, Michael Smith, Ashley Smith-Brown, John Souttar
Midfielders: Angus Beith, Prince Buaben, Don Cowie, Arnaud Djoum, Rafal Grzelak, Malaury Martin, Jamie Walker
Forwards: Roy Currie, Esmael Goncalves, Bjorn Johnsen, Kyle Lafferty, Conor Sammon, Cole Stockton, Dario Zanatta

HIBERNIAN

Ground: Easter Road Stadium, Albion Place, Edinburgh EH7 5QG. **Capacity:** 20,451.
Telephone: 0131 661 2159. **Manager:** Neil Lennon. **Colours:** Green and white. **Nickname:** Hibees
Goalkeepers: Ross Laidlaw, Ofir Marciano
Defenders: Efe Ambrose, Callum Crane, Liam Fontaine, David Gray, Paul Hanlon, Darren McGregor, Lewis Stevenson, Steven Whittaker
Midfielders: Marvin Bartley, Scott Martin, Dylan McGeouch, John McGinn, Fraser Murray, Danny Swanson
Forwards. Lewis Allan, Martin Boyle, Brian Graham, Simon Murray, Oli Shaw

KILMARNOCK

Ground: Rugby Park, Kilmarnock KA 1 2DP. **Capacity:** 18,128. **Telephone:** 01563 545300
Manager: Lee McCulloch. **Colours:** Blue and white. **Nickname:** Killie
Goalkeepers: Jamie MacDonald, Devlin MacKay
Defenders: Miles Addison, Scott Boyd, Kirk Broadfoot, Daniel Higgins, Stephen O'Donnell, Karleigh Osborne, Steven Smith, Greg Taylor, Calum Waters
Midfielders: Gary Dicker, Adam Frizzell, Dean Hawkshaw, Jordan Jones, Martin Smith, Alan Power, Dom Thomas, Iain Wilson
Forwards: Kris Doyd, Greg Kiltie, Rory McKenzie

MOTHERWELL

Ground: Fir Park, Firpark Street, Motherwell ML1 2QN. **Capacity:** 13,742. **Telephone:** 01698 333333. **Manager:** Stephen Robinson. **Colours:** Claret and amber. **Nickname:** Well
Goalkeepers: Trevor Carson, Russell Griffiths
Defenders: Charles Dunne, Steven Hammell, Ben Heneghan, Cedric Kipre, Stephen McManus, Jack McMillan, Andy Rose, Richard Tait, Luke Watt
Midfielders: Gael Bigirimana, Chris Cadden, Allan Campbell, Craig Clay, Elliott Frear, Shea Gordon, Jake Hastie, Carl McHugh, Keith Lasley, Ross MacLean
Forwards: Ryan Bowman, Jacob Blyth, Alex Fisher, Louis Moult, Craig Tanner

PARTICK THISTLE

Ground: Firhill Stadium, Firhill Road, Glasgow G20 7BA. **Capacity:** 13,079. **Telephone:** 0141 579 1971. **Manager:** Alan Archibald. **Colours:** Yellow, red and black. **Nickname:** Jags
Goalkeepers: Tomas Cerny, Ryan Scully, Jamie Sneddon
Defenders: Callum Booth, Mustapha Dumbuya, Danny Devine, Niall Keown, James Penrice
Midfielders: Stuart Bannigan, Adam Barton, Ryan Edwards, Christie Elliott, Chris Erskine, Gary Fraser, Steven Lawless, Abdul Osman, Blair Spittal
Forwards: Kris Doolan, Kevin Nisbet

RANGERS

Ground: Ibrox Park, Edmison Drive, Glasgow G51 2XD. **Capacity:** 50,411.
Telephone: 0871 702 1972. **Manager:** Pedro Caixinha. **Colours:** Blue. **Nickname:** Gers
Goalkeepers: Jak Alnwick, Wes Foderingham, Liam Kelly

Defenders: Bruno Alves, David Bates, Myles Beerman, Fabio Cardoso, Lee Hodson, Rob Kiernan, Ross McCrorie, James Tavernier, Lee Wallace, Aidan Wilson, Danny Wilson
Midfielders: Jamie Barjonas, Liam Burt, Daniel Candeias, Matt Crooks, Dalcio (loan), Graham Dorrans, Harry Forrester, Jason Holt, Ryan Jack, Perry Kitchen, Niko Kranjcar, Carlos Pena, Jordan Rossiter, Jordan Thompson, Tom Walsh, Josh Windass
Forwards: Joe Dodoo, Ryan Hardie, Eduardo Herrera, Kenny Miller, Alfredo Morelos, Michael O'Halloran, Martin Waghorn

ROSS COUNTY

Ground: Global Energy Stadium, Victoria Park, Jubilee Road, Dingwall IV15 9QZ. **Capacity:** 6,541. **Telephone:** 01349 860860. **Manager:** Jim McIntyre. **Colours:** Blue. **Nickname:** Staggies
Goalkeepers: Scott Fox, Aaron McCarey
Defenders: Andrew Davies, Marcus Fraser, Sean Kelly, Jamie Lindsay (loan), Jay McEveley, Thomas Mikkelsen, Jason Naismith, Christopher Routis, Reghan Tumilty, Kenny van der Weg
Midfielders: Tim Chow, Tony Dingwall
Forwards: Craig Curran, Ryan Dow, Michael Gardyne, Greg Morrison, Alex Schalk

ST JOHNSTONE

Ground: McDiarmid Park, Crieff Road, Perth PH1 2SJ. **Capacity:** 10,673. **Telephone:** 01738 459090. **Manager:** Tommy Wright. **Colours:** Blue and white. **Nickname:** Saints
Goalkeepers: Zander Clark, Mark Hurst, Alan Mannus
Defenders: Steven Anderson, Aaron Comrie, Brian Easton, Richard Foster, Ally Gilchrist, Liam Gordon, Jason Kerr, Joe Shaughnessy, Scott Tanser, Keith Watson
Midfielders: Blair Alston, Liam Craig, Murray Davidson, Kyle McCean, Chris Millar, Paul Paton, Stefan Scougall, Craig Thomson, David Wotherspoon
Forwards: Graham Cummins, Greg Hurst, Chris Kane, Steven MacLean

ENGLISH FIXTURES 2017–2018
Premier League and Football League

Friday, 4 August
Championship
Sunderland v Derby
Nottm Forest v Millwall

Saturday, 5 August
Championship
Aston Villa v Hull
Bristol City v Barnsley
Burton v Cardiff
Fulham v Norwich
Ipswich v Birmingham
Preston v Sheffield Wed
QPR v Reading
Sheffield Utd v Brentford
Wolves v Middlesbrough

League One
Bradford v Blackpool
Bury v Walsall
Charlton v Bristol Rov
Doncaster v Gillingham
Fleetwood v Rotherham
MK Dons v Wigan
Oldham v Oxford
Peterborough v Plymouth
Portsmouth v Rochdale
Scunthorpe v AFC Wimbledon
Shrewsbury v Northampton
Southend v Blackburn

League Two
Accrington v Colchester
Carlisle v Swindon
Chesterfield v Grimsby
Coventry v Notts Co
Crawley v Port Vale
Crewe v Mansfield
Exeter v Cambridge
Forest Green v Barnet
Luton v Yeovil
Morecambe v Cheltenham
Stevenage v Newport
Wycombe v Lincoln

Sunday, 6 August
Championship
Bolton v Leeds

Friday, 11 August
Premier League
Arsenal v Leicester

Saturday, 12 August
Premier League
Brighton v Man City
Chelsea v Burnley
Crystal Palace v Huddersfield
Everton v Stoke
Southampton v Swansea
Watford v Liverpool
WBA v Bournemouth

Championship
Barnsley v Ipswich
Birmingham v Bristol City
Brentford v Nottm Forest
Cardiff v Aston Villa
Derby v Wolves
Hull v Burton
Leeds v Preston
Middlesbrough v Sheffield Utd
Millwall v Bolton
Reading v Fulham
Sheffield Wed v QPR

League One
AFC Wimbledon v Shrewsbury
Blackburn v Doncaster
Blackpool v MK Dons
Bristol Rov v Peterborough
Gillingham v Bradford
Northampton v Fleetwood
Oxford v Portsmouth
Plymouth v Charlton
Rochdale v Scunthorpe
Rotherham v Southend
Walsall v Oldham

League Two
Barnet v Luton
Cambridge v Carlisle
Cheltenham v Crawley
Colchester v Stevenage
Grimsby v Coventry
Lincoln v Morecambe
Mansfield v Forest Green
Newport v Crewe
Notts Co v Chesterfield
Port Vale v Wycombe
Swindon v Exeter
Yeovil v Accrington

Sunday, 13 August
Premier League

Saturday, 12 August
Manchester Utd v West Ham
Newcastle v Tottenham

Championship
Norwich v Sunderland

League One
Wigan v Bury

Tuesday, 15 August
Championship
Barnsley v Nottm Forest
Birmingham v Bolton
Brentford v Bristol City
Cardiff v Sheffield Utd
Derby v Preston
Hull v Wolves
Leeds v Fulham
Middlesbrough v Burton
Millwall v Ipswich
Reading v Aston Villa

Wednesday, 16 August
Championship
Norwich v QPR
Sheffield Wed v Sunderland

Friday, 18 August
Championship
Burton v Birmingham

Saturday, 19 August
Premier League
Bournemouth v Watford
Burnley v WBA
Leicester v Brighton
Liverpool v Crystal Palace
Stoke v Arsenal
Swansea v Man Utd
West Ham v Southampton

Championship
Aston Villa v Norwich
Bolton v Derby
Bristol City v Millwall
Fulham v Sheffield Wed
Ipswich v Brentford
Nottm Forest v Middlesbrough
Preston v Reading
QPR v Hull
Sheffield Utd v Barnsley
Sunderland v Leeds
Wolves v Cardiff

League One
Bradford v Blackburn
Bury v Bristol Rov
Charlton v Northampton
Doncaster v Blackpool
Fleetwood v AFC Wimbledon
MK Dons v Gillingham
Oldham v Wigan
Peterborough v Rotherham
Portsmouth v Walsall
Scunthorpe v Oxford
Shrewsbury v Rochdale
Southend v Plymouth

League Two
Accrington v Mansfield
Carlisle v Cheltenham
Chesterfield v Port Vale
Coventry v Newport
Crawley v Cambridge
Crewe v Barnet
Exeter v Lincoln
Forest Green v Yeovil
Luton v Colchester
Morecambe v Swindon
Stevenage v Grimsby
Wycombe v Notts Co

Sunday, 20 August
Premier League
Huddersfield v Newcastle
Tottenham v Chelsea

Monday, 21 August
Premier League
Man City v Everton

Friday, 25 August
Championship
Bristol City v Aston Villa

League Two
Notts Co v Accrington

Saturday, 26 August
Premier League
Bournemouth v Man City
Chelsea v Everton
Crystal Palace v Swansea
Huddersfield v Southampton
Man Utd v Leicester
Newcastle v West Ham
Watford v Brighton

Championship
Barnsley v Sunderland
Birmingham v Reading
Brentford v Wolves
Burton v Sheffield Wed
Cardiff v QPR
Hull v Bolton
Ipswich v Fulham
Middlesbrough v Preston
Millwall v Norwich
Nottm Forest v Leeds
Sheffield Utd v Derby

League One
AFC Wimbledon v Doncaster
Blackburn v MK Dons
Blackpool v Oldham
Bristol Rov v Fleetwood
Gillingham v Southend
Northampton v Peterborough
Oxford v Shrewsbury
Plymouth v Scunthorpe
Rochdale v Bury
Rotherham v Charlton
Walsall v Bradford
Wigan v Portsmouth

League Two
Barnet v Stevenage
Cambridge v Morecambe
Cheltenham v Exeter
Colchester v Forest Green
Grimsby v Wycombe
Lincoln v Carlisle
Mansfield v Luton
Newport v Chesterfield
Port Vale v Crewe
Swindon v Crawley
Yeovil v Coventry

Sunday, 27 August
Premier League
Liverpool v Arsenal
Tottenham v Burnley
WBA v Stoke

Saturday, 2 September
League One
Blackpool v AFC Wimbledon
Bradford v Bristol Rov
Bury v Scunthorpe
Doncaster v Peterborough
Gillingham v Shrewsbury
MK Dons v Oxford
Oldham v Charlton
Southend v Rochdale

Walsall v Plymouth
Wigan v Northampton

League Two
Cambridge v Colchester
Carlisle v Mansfield
Cheltenham v Stevenage
Chesterfield v Coventry
Crawley v Yeovil
Exeter v Newport
Grimsby v Crewe
Lincoln v Luton
Morecambe v Accrington
Port Vale v Notts Co
Swindon v Barnet
Wycombe v Forest Green

Sunday, 3 September
League One
Blackburn v Fleetwood
Portsmouth v Rotherham

Friday, 8 September
Championship
Derby v Hull

Saturday, 9 September
Premier League
Arsenal v Bournemouth
Brighton v WBA
Everton v Tottenham
Leicester v Chelsea
Man City v Liverpool
Southampton v Watford
Stoke v Man Utd

Championship
Aston Villa v Brentford
Bolton v Middlesbrough
Fulham v Cardiff
Leeds v Burton
Norwich v Birmingham
Preston v Barnsley
QPR v Ipswich
Reading v Bristol City
Sheffield Wed v Nottm Forest
Sunderland v Sheffield Utd
Wolves v Millwall

League One
AFC Wimbledon v Portsmouth
Bristol Rov v Walsall
Charlton v Southend
Fleetwood v Oldham
Northampton v Doncaster

xford v Gillingham
eterborough v Bradford
lymouth v MK Dons
ochdale v Blackburn
otherham v Bury
cunthorpe v Blackpool
hrewsbury v Wigan

eague Two
ccrington v Carlisle
arnet v Cambridge
olchester v Crawley
oventry v Port Vale
rewe v Chesterfield
orest Green v Exeter
uton v Swindon
1ansfield v Grimsby
1ewport v Wycombe
lotts Co v Morecambe
tevenage v Lincoln
eovil v Cheltenham

iunday, 10 September
remier League
Burnley v Crystal Palace
iwansea v Newcastle

1onday, 11 September
Premier League
Vest Ham v Huddersfield

1uesday, 12 September
Championship
Aston Villa v Middlesbrough
Bolton v Sheffield Utd
Derby v Ipswich
ulham v Hull
eeds v Birmingham
Norwich v Burton
Preston v Cardiff
QPR v Millwall
Reading v Barnsley
Sheffield Wed v Brentford
Sunderland v Nottm Forest
Wolves v Bristol City

League One
AFC Wimbledon v Gillingham
Bristol Rov v Oldham
Charlton v Wigan
Fleetwood v Bury
Northampton v Portsmouth
Oxford v Bradford
Peterborough v MK Dons
Plymouth v Blackpool
Rochdale v Doncaster

Rotherham v Walsall
Scunthorpe v Blackburn
Shrewsbury v Southend

League Two
Accrington v Grimsby
Colchester v Chesterfield
Coventry v Carlisle
Crewe v Cambridge
Forest Green v Lincoln
Luton v Port Vale
Mansfield v Wycombe
Newport v Cheltenham
Notts Co v Swindon
Stevenage v Crawley
Yeovil v Morecambe
Barnet v Exeter

Friday, 15 September
Premier League
Bournemouth v Brighton

Saturday, 16 September
Premier League
Crystal Palace v Southampton
Huddersfield v Leicester
Liverpool v Burnley
Newcastle v Stoke
Tottenham v Swansea
Watford v Man City
WBA v West Ham

Championship
Barnsley v Aston Villa
Birmingham v Preston
Brentford v Reading
Bristol City v Derby
Burton v Fulham
Cardiff v Sheffield Wed
Hull v Sunderland
Ipswich v Bolton
Middlesbrough v QPR
Millwall v Leeds
Nottm Forest v Wolves
Sheffield Utd v Norwich

League One
Blackburn v AFC Wimbledon
Blackpool v Oxford
Bradford v Rotherham
Bury v Plymouth
Gillingham v Charlton
MK Dons v Rochdale
Oldham v Shrewsbury
Portsmouth v Fleetwood
Southend v Northampton
Walsall v Peterborough
Wigan v Bristol Rov

League Two
Cambridge v Coventry
Carlisle v Barnet
Cheltenham v Colchester
Chesterfield v Accrington
Crawley v Notts Co
Exeter v Crewe
Grimsby v Yeovil
Lincoln v Mansfield
Morecambe v Newport
Port Vale v Forest Green
Swindon v Stevenage
Wycombe v Luton

Sunday, 17 September
Premier League
Chelsea v Arsenal
Man Utd v Everton

League One
Doncaster v Scunthorpe

Friday, 22 September
League One
AFC Wimbledon v MK Dons

Saturday, 23 September
Premier League
Arsenal v WBA
Burnley v Huddersfield
Everton v Bournemouth
Leicester v Liverpool
Man City v Crystal Palace
Southampton v Man Utd
Stoke v Chelsea
Swansea v Watford
West Ham v Tottenham

Championship
Aston Villa v Nottm Forest
Bolton v Brentford
Derby v Birmingham
Fulham v Middlesbrough
Leeds v Ipswich
Norwich v Bristol City
Preston v Millwall
QPR v Burton
Reading v Hull
Sheffield Wed v Sheffield Utd
Sunderland v Cardiff
Wolves v Barnsley

League One
Bristol Rov v Blackpool
Charlton v Bury

Fleetwood v Southend
Northampton v Bradford
Oxford v Walsall
Peterborough v Wigan
Plymouth v Doncaster
Rochdale v Gillingham
Rotherham v Oldham
Scunthorpe v Portsmouth
Shrewsbury v Blackburn

League Two
Accrington v Cheltenham
Barnet v Crawley
Colchester v Wycombe
Coventry v Exeter
Crewe v Carlisle
Forest Green v Swindon
Luton v Chesterfield
Mansfield v Cambridge
Newport v Grimsby
Notts Co v Lincoln
Stevenage v Morecambe
Yeovil v Port Vale

Sunday, 24 September
Premier League
Brighton v Newcastle

Tuesday, 26 September
Championship
Barnsley v QPR
Birmingham v Sheffield Wed
Brentford v Derby
Bristol City v Bolton
Burton v Aston Villa
Cardiff v Leeds
Hull v Preston
Ipswich v Sunderland
Middlesbrough v Norwich
Millwall v Reading
Nottm Forest v Fulham
Sheffield Utd v Wolves

League One
Blackburn v Rotherham
Blackpool v Rochdale
Bradford v Fleetwood
Bury v Oxford
Doncaster v Shrewsbury
Gillingham v Scunthorpe
MK Dons v Northampton
Oldham v Peterborough
Portsmouth v Bristol Rov
Southend v AFC Wimbledon
Walsall v Charlton
Wigan v Plymouth

League Two
Cambridge v Forest Green
Carlisle v Stevenage
Cheltenham v Mansfield
Chesterfield v Yeovil
Crawley v Newport
Exeter v Notts Co
Grimsby v Colchester
Lincoln v Barnet
Morecambe v Luton
Port Vale v Accrington
Swindon v Coventry
Wycombe v Crewe

Saturday, 30 September
Premier League
Bournemouth v Leicester
Chelsea v Man City
Huddersfield v Tottenham
Man Utd v Crystal Palace
Stoke v Southampton
WBA v Watford
West Ham v Swansea

Championship
Aston Villa v Bolton
Burton v Wolves
Cardiff v Derby
Hull v Birmingham
Ipswich v Bristol City
Middlesbrough v Brentford
Millwall v Barnsley
Nottm Forest v Sheffield Utd
Preston v Sunderland
QPR v Fulham
Reading v Norwich
Sheffield Wed v Leeds

League One
AFC Wimbledon v Rochdale
Blackburn v Gillingham
Bradford v Doncaster
Bristol Rov v Plymouth
Bury v MK Dons
Fleetwood v Charlton
Peterborough v Oxford
Portsmouth v Oldham
Rotherham v Northampton
Shrewsbury v Scunthorpe
Southend v Blackpool
Wigan v Walsall

League Two
Chesterfield v Cheltenham
Coventry v Crewe
Crawley v Carlisle

Exeter v Morecambe
Forest Green v Accrington
Grimsby v Lincoln
Luton v Newport
Mansfield v Notts Co
Stevenage v Port Vale
Swindon v Cambridge
Wycombe v Barnet
Yeovil v Colchester

Sunday, 1 October
Premier League
Arsenal v Brighton
Everton v Burnley
Newcastle v Liverpool

Saturday, 7 October
League One
Blackpool v Blackburn
Charlton v Peterborough
Doncaster v Southend
Gillingham v Portsmouth
MK Dons v Bradford
Northampton v Bristol Rov
Oldham v Bury
Oxford v AFC Wimbledon
Plymouth v Fleetwood
Rochdale v Rotherham
Scunthorpe v Wigan
Walsall v Shrewsbury

League Two
Accrington v Luton
Barnet v Coventry
Cambridge v Wycombe
Carlisle v Exeter
Cheltenham v Swindon
Colchester v Mansfield
Crewe v Stevenage
Lincoln v Chesterfield
Morecambe v Crawley
Newport v Yeovil
Notts Co v Forest Green
Port Vale v Grimsby

Saturday, 14 October
Premier League
Brighton v Everton
Burnley v West Ham
Crystal Palace v Chelsea
Leicester v WBA
Liverpool v Man Utd
Man City v Stoke
Southampton v Newcastle
Swansea v Huddersfield
Tottenham v Bournemouth
Watford v Arsenal

Championship

Barnsley v Middlesbrough
Birmingham v Cardiff
Bolton v Sheffield Wed
Brentford v Millwall
Bristol City v Burton
Derby v Nottm Forest
Fulham v Preston
Leeds v Reading
Norwich v Hull
Sheffield Utd v Ipswich
Sunderland v QPR
Wolves v Aston Villa

League One

Bristol Rov v Oxford
Bury v Bradford
Charlton v Doncaster
Fleetwood v Rochdale
Northampton v AFC Wimbledon
Oldham v Blackburn
Peterborough v Gillingham
Plymouth v Shrewsbury
Portsmouth v MK Dons
Rotherham v Scunthorpe
Walsall v Blackpool
Wigan v Southend

League Two

Accrington v Coventry
Chesterfield v Morecambe
Colchester v Carlisle
Forest Green v Newport
Grimsby v Crawley
Lincoln v Cambridge
Luton v Stevenage
Mansfield v Swindon
Notts Co v Barnet
Port Vale v Cheltenham
Wycombe v Exeter
Yeovil v Crewe

Tuesday, 17 October
League One

AFC Wimbledon v Rotherham
Blackburn v Plymouth
Blackpool v Bury
Bradford v Oldham
Doncaster v Portsmouth
Gillingham v Wigan
MK Dons v Walsall
Oxford v Charlton
Rochdale v Northampton
Scunthorpe v Fleetwood
Shrewsbury v Bristol Rov
Southend v Peterborough

League Two

Cambridge v Yeovil
Carlisle v Wycombe
Cheltenham v Grimsby
Coventry v Forest Green
Crawley v Chesterfield
Crewe v Notts Co
Exeter v Luton
Morecambe v Port Vale
Newport v Colchester
Stevenage v Accrington
Swindon v Lincoln
Barnet v Mansfield

Saturday, 21 October
Premier League

Chelsea v Watford
Everton v Arsenal
Huddersfield v Man Utd
Man City v Burnley
Newcastle v Crystal Palace
Southampton v WBA
Stoke v Bournemouth
Swansea v Leicester
Tottenham v Liverpool
West Ham v Brighton

Championship

Aston Villa v Fulham
Barnsley v Hull
Bolton v QPR
Brentford v Sunderland
Bristol City v Leeds
Derby v Sheffield Wed
Middlesbrough v Cardiff
Millwall v Birmingham
Nottm Forest v Burton
Sheffield Utd v Reading
Wolves v Preston

League One

AFC Wimbledon v Plymouth
Blackburn v Portsmouth
Blackpool v Wigan
Bradford v Charlton
Doncaster v Walsall
Gillingham v Northampton
MK Dons v Oldham
Oxford v Rotherham
Rochdale v Bristol Rov
Scunthorpe v Peterborough
Shrewsbury v Fleetwood
Southend v Bury

League Two

Barnet v Yeovil

Cambridge v Chesterfield
Carlisle v Notts Co
Cheltenham v Lincoln
Coventry v Colchester
Crawley v Luton
Crewe v Accrington
Exeter v Port Vale
Morecambe v Grimsby
Newport v Mansfield
Stevenage v Forest Green
Swindon v Wycombe

Sunday, 22 October
Championship

Ipswich v Norwich

Saturday, 28 October
Premier League

Arsenal v Swansea
Bournemouth v Chelsea
Brighton v Southampton
Burnley v Newcastle
Crystal Palace v West Ham
Leicester v Everton
Liverpool v Huddersfield
Man Utd v Tottenham
Watford v Stoke
WBA v Man City

Championship

Burton v Ipswich
Cardiff v Millwall
Fulham v Bolton
Hull v Nottm Forest
Leeds v Sheffield Utd
Norwich v Derby
Preston v Brentford
QPR v Wolves
Reading v Middlesbrough
Sheffield Wed v Barnsley
Sunderland v Bristol City

League One

Bristol Rov v MK Dons
Bury v Doncaster
Charlton v AFC Wimbledon
Fleetwood v Oxford
Northampton v Blackpool
Oldham v Scunthorpe
Peterborough v Shrewsbury
Plymouth v Rochdale
Portsmouth v Bradford
Rotherham v Gillingham
Walsall v Southend
Wigan v Blackburn

League Two
Accrington v Barnet
Chesterfield v Carlisle
Colchester v Crewe
Forest Green v Morecambe
Grimsby v Cambridge
Lincoln v Crawley
Luton v Coventry
Mansfield v Exeter
Notts Co v Newport
Port Vale v Swindon
Wycombe v Cheltenham
Yeovil v Stevenage

Sunday, 29 October
Championship
Birmingham v Aston Villa

Tuesday, 31 October
Championship
Burton v Barnsley
Cardiff v Ipswich
Fulham v Bristol City
Hull v Middlesbrough
Leeds v Derby
Norwich v Wolves
QPR v Sheffield Utd
Reading v Nottm Forest
Sheffield Wed v Millwall
Sunderland v Bolton

Wednesday, 1 November
Championship
Birmingham v Brentford
Preston v Aston Villa

Saturday, 4 November
Premier League
Chelsea v Man Utd
Everton v Watford
Huddersfield v WBA
Man City v Arsenal
Newcastle v Bournemouth
Southampton v Burnley
Stoke v Leicester
Swansea v Brighton
Tottenham v Crystal Palace
West Ham v Liverpool

Championship
Aston Villa v Sheffield Wed
Barnsley v Birmingham
Bolton v Norwich
Brentford v Leeds
Bristol City v Cardiff

Derby v Reading
Ipswich v Preston
Middlesbrough v Sunderland
Millwall v Burton
Nottm Forest v QPR
Sheffield Utd v Hull
Wolves v Fulham

Saturday, 11 November
League One
AFC Wimbledon v Peterborough
Blackburn v Walsall
Blackpool v Portsmouth
Bradford v Plymouth
Doncaster v Rotherham
Gillingham v Bury
MK Dons v Fleetwood
Oxford v Northampton
Rochdale v Wigan
Scunthorpe v Bristol Rov
Shrewsbury v Charlton
Southend v Oldham

League Two
Barnet v Colchester
Cambridge v Accrington
Carlisle v Yeovil
Cheltenham v Luton
Coventry v Mansfield
Crawley v Forest Green
Crewe v Lincoln
Exeter v Grimsby
Morecambe v Wycombe
Newport v Port Vale
Stevenage v Notts Co
Swindon v Chesterfield

Friday, 17 November
Championship
Burton v Sheffield Utd

Saturday, 18 November
Premier League
Arsenal v Tottenham
Bournemouth v Huddersfield
Brighton v Stoke
Burnley v Swansea
Crystal Palace v Everton
Leicester v Man City
Liverpool v Southampton
Man Utd v Newcastle
Watford v West Ham
WBA v Chelsea

Championship
Birmingham v Nottm Forest

Cardiff v Brentford
Fulham v Derby
Hull v Ipswich
Leeds v Middlesbrough
Norwich v Barnsley
Preston v Bolton
QPR v Aston Villa
Reading v Wolves
Sheffield Wed v Bristol City
Sunderland v Millwall

League One
Bristol Rov v AFC Wimbledon
Bury v Blackburn
Charlton v MK Dons
Fleetwood v Doncaster
Northampton v Scunthorpe
Oldham v Rochdale
Peterborough v Blackpool
Plymouth v Oxford
Portsmouth v Southend
Rotherham v Shrewsbury
Walsall v Gillingham
Wigan v Bradford

League Two
Accrington v Newport
Chesterfield v Exeter
Colchester v Morecambe
Forest Green v Crewe
Grimsby v Carlisle
Lincoln v Coventry
Luton v Cambridge
Mansfield v Stevenage
Notts Co v Cheltenham
Port Vale v Barnet
Wycombe v Crawley
Yeovil v Swindon

Tuesday, 21 November
Championship
Aston Villa v Sunderland
Barnsley v Cardiff
Bolton v Reading
Brentford v Burton
Bristol City v Preston
Derby v QPR
Ipswich v Sheffield Wed
Middlesbrough v Birmingham
Millwall v Hull
Nottm Forest v Norwich
Sheffield Utd v Fulham
Wolves v Leeds

League One
Blackpool v Gillingham

Bradford v Scunthorpe
Bristol Rov v Rotherham
Bury v Shrewsbury
Charlton v Rochdale
MK Dons v Southend
Oldham v AFC Wimbledon
Oxford v Blackburn
Peterborough v Portsmouth
Plymouth v Northampton
Walsall v Fleetwood
Wigan v Doncaster

League Two
Accrington v Wycombe
Cheltenham v Cambridge
Chesterfield v Forest Green
Colchester v Lincoln
Crawley v Exeter
Grimsby v Swindon
Luton v Carlisle
Morecambe v Crewe
Newport v Barnet
Port Vale v Mansfield
Stevenage v Coventry
Yeovil v Notts Co

Saturday, 25 November
Premier League
Crystal Palace v Stoke
Huddersfield v Man City
Liverpool v Chelsea
Man Utd v Brighton
Newcastle v Watford
Southampton v Everton
Swansea v Bournemouth
Tottenham v WBA
West Ham v Leicester

Championship
Aston Villa v Ipswich
Barnsley v Leeds
Burton v Sunderland
Fulham v Millwall
Hull v Bristol City
Middlesbrough v Derby
Norwich v Preston
Nottm Forest v Cardiff
QPR v Brentford
Reading v Sheffield Wed
Sheffield Utd v Birmingham
Wolves v Bolton

League One
AFC Wimbledon v Walsall
Blackburn v Bristol Rov
Doncaster v MK Dons

Fleetwood v Blackpool
Gillingham v Oldham
Northampton v Bury
Portsmouth v Plymouth
Rochdale v Peterborough
Rotherham v Wigan
Scunthorpe v Charlton
Shrewsbury v Bradford
Southend v Oxford

League Two
Barnet v Grimsby
Cambridge v Stevenage
Carlisle v Morecambe
Coventry v Crawley
Crewe v Luton
Exeter v Accrington
Forest Green v Cheltenham
Lincoln v Port Vale
Mansfield v Chesterfield
Swindon v Newport
Wycombe v Yeovil

Sunday, 26 November
Premier League
Burnley v Arsenal

League Two
Notts Co v Colchester

Tuesday, 28 November
Premier League
Brighton v Crystal Palace
Leicester v Tottenham
Watford v Man Utd
WBA v Newcastle

Wednesday, 29 November
Premier League
Arsenal v Huddersfield
Bournemouth v Burnley
Chelsea v Swansea
Everton v West Ham
Man City v Southampton
Stoke v Liverpool

Friday, 1 December
Championship
Cardiff v Norwich

Saturday, 2 December
Premier League
Arsenal v Man Utd
Bournemouth v Southampton
Brighton v Liverpool

Chelsea v Newcastle
Everton v Huddersfield
Leicester v Burnley
Man City v West Ham
Stoke v Swansea
Watford v Tottenham
WBA v Crystal Palace

Championship
Birmingham v Wolves
Bolton v Barnsley
Brentford v Fulham
Bristol City v Middlesbrough
Derby v Burton
Ipswich v Nottm Forest
Leeds v Aston Villa
Millwall v Sheffield Utd
Preston v QPR
Sheffield Wed v Hull
Sunderland v Reading

Saturday, 9 December
Premier League
Burnley v Watford
Crystal Palace v Bournemouth
Huddersfield v Brighton
Liverpool v Everton
Man Utd v Man City
Newcastle v Leicester
Swansea v WBA
Tottenham v Stoke
West Ham v Chelsea

Championship
Aston Villa v Millwall
Barnsley v Derby
Burton v Preston
Fulham v Birmingham
Hull v Brentford
Middlesbrough v Ipswich
Norwich v Sheffield Wed
Nottm Forest v Bolton
QPR v Leeds
Reading v Cardiff
Sheffield Utd v Bristol City
Wolves v Sunderland

League One
Blackpool v Rotherham
Bradford v Rochdale
Bristol Rov v Southend
Bury v AFC Wimbledon
Charlton v Portsmouth
MK Dons v Shrewsbury
Oldham v Northampton
Oxford v Doncaster

Peterborough v Blackburn
Plymouth v Gillingham
Walsall v Scunthorpe
Wigan v Fleetwood

League Two
Accrington v Swindon
Cheltenham v Crewe
Chesterfield v Barnet
Colchester v Exeter
Crawley v Mansfield
Grimsby v Forest Green
Luton v Notts Co
Morecambe v Coventry
Newport v Carlisle
Port Vale v Cambridge
Stevenage v Wycombe
Yeovil v Lincoln

Sunday, 10 December
Premier League
Southampton v Arsenal

Tuesday, 12 December
Premier League
Burnley v Stoke
Crystal Palace v Watford
Huddersfield v Chelsea
Man Utd v Bournemouth
Swansea v Man City

Wednesday, 13 December
Premier League
Liverpool v WBA
Newcastle v Everton
Southampton v Leicester
Tottenham v Brighton
West Ham v Arsenal

Saturday, 16 December
Premier League
Arsenal v Newcastle
Bournemouth v Liverpool
Brighton v Burnley
Chelsea v Southampton
Everton v Swansea
Leicester v Crystal Palace
Man City v Tottenham
Stoke v West Ham
Watford v Huddersfield
WBA v Man Utd

Championship
Birmingham v QPR
Bolton v Burton

Brentford v Barnsley
Bristol City v Nottm Forest
Cardiff v Hull
Derby v Aston Villa
Ipswich v Reading
Leeds v Norwich
Millwall v Middlesbrough
Preston v Sheffield Utd
Sheffield Wed v Wolves
Sunderland v Fulham

League One
AFC Wimbledon v Wigan
Blackburn v Charlton
Doncaster v Oldham
Fleetwood v Peterborough
Gillingham v Bristol Rov
Northampton v Walsall
Portsmouth v Bury
Rochdale v Oxford
Rotherham v Plymouth
Scunthorpe v MK Dons
Shrewsbury v Blackpool
Southend v Bradford

League Two
Barnet v Morecambe
Cambridge v Newport
Carlisle v Port Vale
Coventry v Cheltenham
Crewe v Crawley
Exeter v Stevenage
Forest Green v Luton
Lincoln v Accrington
Mansfield v Yeovil
Notts Co v Grimsby
Swindon v Colchester
Wycombe v Chesterfield

Friday, 22 December
Championship
Norwich v Brentford

League Two
Coventry v Wycombe

Saturday, 23 December
Premier League
Arsenal v Liverpool
Brighton v Watford
Burnley v Tottenham
Everton v Chelsea
Leicester v Man Utd
Man City v Bournemouth
Southampton v Huddersfield
Stoke v WBA

Swansea v Crystal Palace
West Ham v Newcastle

Championship
Aston Villa v Sheffield Utd
Bolton v Cardiff
Derby v Millwall
Fulham v Barnsley
Leeds v Hull
Preston v Nottm Forest
QPR v Bristol City
Reading v Burton
Sheffield Wed v Middlesbrough
Sunderland v Birmingham
Wolves v Ipswich

League One
AFC Wimbledon v Bradford
Bristol Rov v Doncaster
Charlton v Blackpool
Fleetwood v Gillingham
Northampton v Blackburn
Oxford v Wigan
Peterborough v Bury
Plymouth v Oldham
Rochdale v Walsall
Rotherham v MK Dons
Scunthorpe v Southend
Shrewsbury v Portsmouth

League Two
Accrington v Crawley
Barnet v Cheltenham
Colchester v Port Vale
Crewe v Swindon
Forest Green v Carlisle
Luton v Grimsby
Mansfield v Morecambe
Newport v Lincoln
Notts Co v Cambridge
Stevenage v Chesterfield
Yeovil v Exeter

Tuesday, 26 December
Premier League
Bournemouth v West Ham
Chelsea v Brighton
Crystal Palace v Arsenal
Huddersfield v Stoke
Liverpool v Swansea
Man Utd v Burnley
Newcastle v Man City
Tottenham v Southampton
Watford v Leicester
WBA v Everton

Championship
Barnsley v Preston
Birmingham v Norwich
Brentford v Aston Villa
Bristol City v Reading
Burton v Leeds
Cardiff v Fulham
Hull v Derby
Ipswich v QPR
Middlesbrough v Bolton
Millwall v Wolves
Nottm Forest v Sheffield Wed
Sheffield Utd v Sunderland

League One
Blackburn v Rochdale
Blackpool v Scunthorpe
Bradford v Peterborough
Bury v Rotherham
Doncaster v Northampton
Gillingham v Oxford
MK Dons v Plymouth
Oldham v Fleetwood
Portsmouth v AFC Wimbledon
Southend v Charlton
Walsall v Bristol Rov
Wigan v Shrewsbury

League Two
Cambridge v Barnet
Carlisle v Accrington
Cheltenham v Yeovil
Chesterfield v Crewe
Crawley v Colchester
Exeter v Forest Green
Grimsby v Mansfield
Lincoln v Stevenage
Morecambe v Notts Co
Port Vale v Coventry
Swindon v Luton
Wycombe v Newport

Friday, 29 December
Championship
Millwall v QPR

League One
Doncaster v Rochdale
Wigan v Charlton

League Two
Morecambe v Yeovil

Saturday, 30 December
Premier League
Bournemouth v Everton

Chelsea v Stoke
Crystal Palace v Man City
Huddersfield v Burnley
Liverpool v Leicester
Man Utd v Southampton
Newcastle v Brighton
Tottenham v West Ham
Watford v Swansea
WBA v Arsenal

Championship
Barnsley v Reading
Birmingham v Leeds
Brentford v Sheffield Wed
Bristol City v Wolves
Burton v Norwich
Cardiff v Preston
Hull v Fulham
Ipswich v Derby
Middlesbrough v Aston Villa
Nottm Forest v Sunderland
Sheffield Utd v Bolton

League One
Blackburn v Scunthorpe
Blackpool v Plymouth
Bradford v Oxford
Bury v Fleetwood
Gillingham v AFC Wimbledon
MK Dons v Peterborough
Oldham v Bristol Rov
Portsmouth v Northampton
Southend v Shrewsbury
Walsall v Rotherham

League Two
Cambridge v Crewe
Carlisle v Coventry
Cheltenham v Newport
Chesterfield v Colchester
Crawley v Stevenage
Exeter v Barnet
Grimsby v Accrington
Lincoln v Forest Green
Port Vale v Luton
Swindon v Notts Co
Wycombe v Mansfield

Monday, 1 January
Premier League
Arsenal v Chelsea
Brighton v Bournemouth
Burnley v Liverpool
Everton v Man Utd
Leicester v Huddersfield
Man City v Watford

Southampton v Crystal Palace
Stoke v Newcastle
Swansea v Tottenham
West Ham v WBA

Championship
Aston Villa v Bristol City
Bolton v Hull
Derby v Sheffield Utd
Leeds v Nottm Forest
Norwich v Millwall
Preston v Middlesbrough
QPR v Cardiff
Sheffield Wed v Burton
Sunderland v Barnsley
Wolves v Brentford

League One
AFC Wimbledon v Southend
Bristol Rov v Portsmouth
Charlton v Gillingham
Fleetwood v Bradford
Northampton v Wigan
Oxford v MK Dons
Peterborough v Doncaster
Plymouth v Walsall
Rochdale v Blackpool
Rotherham v Blackburn
Scunthorpe v Bury
Shrewsbury v Oldham

League Two
Accrington v Morecambe
Barnet v Swindon
Colchester v Cambridge
Coventry v Chesterfield
Crewe v Grimsby
Forest Green v Wycombe
Luton v Lincoln
Mansfield v Carlisle
Newport v Exeter
Notts Co v Port Vale
Stevenage v Cheltenham
Yeovil v Crawley

Tuesday, 2 January
Championship
Fulham v Ipswich
Reading v Birmingham

Saturday, 6 January
League One
AFC Wimbledon v Blackburn
Bristol Rov v Wigan
Charlton v Oldham
Fleetwood v Portsmouth

Northampton v Southend
Oxford v Blackpool
Peterborough v Walsall
Plymouth v Bury
Rochdale v MK Dons
Rotherham v Bradford
Scunthorpe v Doncaster
Shrewsbury v Gillingham

League Two
Accrington v Chesterfield
Barnet v Carlisle
Colchester v Cheltenham
Coventry v Cambridge
Crewe v Exeter
Forest Green v Port Vale
Luton v Wycombe
Mansfield v Lincoln
Newport v Morecambe
Notts Co v Crawley
Stevenage v Swindon
Yeovil v Grimsby

Saturday, 13 January
Premier League
Bournemouth v Arsenal
Chelsea v Leicester
Crystal Palace v Burnley
Huddersfield v West Ham
Liverpool v Man City
Man Utd v Stoke
Newcastle v Swansea
Tottenham v Everton
Watford v Southampton
WBA v Brighton

Championship
Barnsley v Wolves
Birmingham v Derby
Brentford v Bolton
Bristol City v Norwich
Burton v QPR
Cardiff v Sunderland
Hull v Reading
Ipswich v Leeds
Middlesbrough v Fulham
Millwall v Preston
Nottm Forest v Aston Villa
Sheffield Utd v Sheffield Wed

League One
Blackburn v Shrewsbury
Blackpool v Bristol Rov
Bradford v Northampton
Bury v Charlton
Doncaster v Plymouth

Gillingham v Rochdale
MK Dons v AFC Wimbledon
Oldham v Rotherham
Portsmouth v Scunthorpe
Southend v Fleetwood
Walsall v Oxford
Wigan v Peterborough

League Two
Cambridge v Mansfield
Carlisle v Crewe
Cheltenham v Accrington
Chesterfield v Luton
Crawley v Barnet
Exeter v Coventry
Grimsby v Newport
Lincoln v Notts Co
Morecambe v Stevenage
Port Vale v Yeovil
Swindon v Forest Green
Wycombe v Colchester

Saturday, 20 January
Premier League
Arsenal v Crystal Palace
Brighton v Chelsea
Burnley v Man Utd
Everton v WBA
Leicester v Watford
Man City v Newcastle
Southampton v Tottenham
Stoke v Huddersfield
Swansea v Liverpool
West Ham v Bournemouth

Championship
Aston Villa v Barnsley
Bolton v Ipswich
Derby v Bristol City
Fulham v Burton
Leeds v Millwall
Norwich v Sheffield Utd
Preston v Birmingham
QPR v Middlesbrough
Reading v Brentford
Sheffield Wed v Cardiff
Sunderland v Hull
Wolves v Nottm Forest

League One
AFC Wimbledon v Blackpool
Bristol Rov v Bradford
Charlton v Walsall
Fleetwood v Blackburn
Northampton v MK Dons
Oxford v Bury

Peterborough v Oldham
Plymouth v Wigan
Rochdale v Southend
Rotherham v Portsmouth
Scunthorpe v Gillingham
Shrewsbury v Doncaster

League Two
Accrington v Port Vale
Barnet v Lincoln
Colchester v Grimsby
Coventry v Swindon
Crewe v Wycombe
Forest Green v Cambridge
Luton v Morecambe
Mansfield v Cheltenham
Newport v Crawley
Notts Co v Exeter
Stevenage v Carlisle
Yeovil v Chesterfield

Saturday, 27 January
Championship
Barnsley v Fulham
Birmingham v Sunderland
Brentford v Norwich
Bristol City v QPR
Burton v Reading
Cardiff v Bolton
Hull v Leeds
Ipswich v Wolves
Middlesbrough v Sheffield Wed
Millwall v Derby
Nottm Forest v Preston
Sheffield Utd v Aston Villa

League One
Blackburn v Northampton
Blackpool v Charlton
Bradford v AFC Wimbledon
Bury v Peterborough
Doncaster v Bristol Rov
Gillingham v Fleetwood
MK Dons v Rotherham
Oldham v Plymouth
Portsmouth v Shrewsbury
Southend v Scunthorpe
Walsall v Rochdale
Wigan v Oxford

League Two
Cambridge v Notts Co
Carlisle v Forest Green
Cheltenham v Barnet
Chesterfield v Stevenage
Crawley v Accrington

Exeter v Yeovil
Grimsby v Luton
Lincoln v Newport
Morecambe v Mansfield
Port Vale v Colchester
Swindon v Crewe
Wycombe v Coventry

Tuesday, 30 January
Premier League
Huddersfield v Liverpool
Swansea v Arsenal
West Ham v Crystal Palace

Wednesday, 31 January
Premier League
Chelsea v Bournemouth
Everton v Leicester
Newcastle v Burnley
Southampton v Brighton
Man City v WBA
Stoke v Watford
Tottenham v Man Utd

Saturday, 3 February
Premier League
Arsenal v Everton
Bournemouth v Stoke
Brighton v West Ham
Burnley v Man City
Crystal Palace v Newcastle
Leicester v Swansea
Liverpool v Tottenham
Man Utd v Huddersfield
Watford v Chelsea
WBA v Southampton

Championship
Aston Villa v Burton
Bolton v Bristol City
Derby v Brentford
Fulham v Nottm Forest
Leeds v Cardiff
Norwich v Middlesbrough
Preston v Hull
QPR v Barnsley
Reading v Millwall
Sheffield Wed v Birmingham
Sunderland v Ipswich
Wolves v Sheffield Utd

League One
Bristol Rov v Shrewsbury
Bury v Blackpool
Charlton v Oxford
Fleetwood v Scunthorpe

Northampton v Rochdale
Oldham v Bradford
Peterborough v Southend
Plymouth v Blackburn
Portsmouth v Doncaster
Rotherham v AFC Wimbledon
Walsall v MK Dons
Wigan v Gillingham

League Two
Accrington v Stevenage
Chesterfield v Crawley
Colchester v Newport
Forest Green v Coventry
Grimsby v Cheltenham
Lincoln v Swindon
Luton v Exeter
Mansfield v Barnet
Notts Co v Crewe
Port Vale v Morecambe
Wycombe v Carlisle
Yeovil v Cambridge

Friday, 9 February
League Two
Cambridge v Lincoln

Saturday, 10 February
Premier League
Chelsea v WBA
Everton v Crystal Palace
Huddersfield v Bournemouth
Man City v Leicester
Newcastle v Man Utd
Southampton v Liverpool
Stoke v Brighton
Swansea v Burnley
Tottenham v Arsenal
West Ham v Watford

Championship
Barnsley v Sheffield Wed
Bolton v Fulham
Brentford v Preston
Bristol City v Sunderland
Derby v Norwich
Ipswich v Burton
Middlesbrough v Reading
Millwall v Cardiff
Nottm Forest v Hull
Sheffield Utd v Leeds
Wolves v QPR

League One
AFC Wimbledon v Northampton
Blackburn v Oldham

Blackpool v Walsall
Bradford v Bury
Doncaster v Charlton
Gillingham v Peterborough
MK Dons v Portsmouth
Oxford v Bristol Rov
Rochdale v Fleetwood
Scunthorpe v Rotherham
Shrewsbury v Plymouth
Southend v Wigan

League Two
Barnet v Notts Co
Carlisle v Colchester
Cheltenham v Port Vale
Coventry v Accrington
Crawley v Grimsby
Crewe v Yeovil
Exeter v Wycombe
Morecambe v Chesterfield
Newport v Forest Green
Stevenage v Luton
Swindon v Mansfield

Sunday, 11 February
Championship
Aston Villa v Birmingham

Tuesday, 13 February
League One
Bristol Rov v Rochdale
Bury v Southend
Charlton v Bradford
Fleetwood v Shrewsbury
Northampton v Gillingham
Oldham v MK Dons
Peterborough v Scunthorpe
Plymouth v AFC Wimbledon
Portsmouth v Blackburn
Rotherham v Oxford
Walsall v Doncaster
Wigan v Blackpool

League Two
Accrington v Crewe
Chesterfield v Cambridge
Colchester v Coventry
Forest Green v Stevenage
Grimsby v Morecambe
Lincoln v Cheltenham
Luton v Crawley
Mansfield v Newport
Notts Co v Carlisle
Port Vale v Exeter
Wycombe v Swindon
Yeovil v Barnet

Saturday, 17 February

Championship
Birmingham v Millwall
Burton v Nottm Forest
Cardiff v Middlesbrough
Fulham v Aston Villa
Hull v Barnsley
Leeds v Bristol City
Preston v Wolves
QPR v Bolton
Reading v Sheffield Utd
Sheffield Wed v Derby
Sunderland v Brentford

League One
AFC Wimbledon v Bristol Rov
Blackburn v Bury
Bradford v Wigan
Doncaster v Fleetwood
Gillingham v Walsall
MK Dons v Charlton
Oxford v Plymouth
Rochdale v Oldham
Scunthorpe v Northampton
Shrewsbury v Rotherham
Southend v Portsmouth

League Two
Barnet v Accrington
Cambridge v Grimsby
Carlisle v Chesterfield
Cheltenham v Wycombe
Coventry v Luton
Crawley v Lincoln
Crewe v Colchester
Exeter v Mansfield
Morecambe v Forest Green
Newport v Notts Co
Stevenage v Yeovil
Swindon v Port Vale

Sunday, 18 February

Championship
Norwich v Ipswich

League One
Blackpool v Peterborough

Tuesday, 20 February

Championship
Aston Villa v Preston
Barnsley v Burton
Bolton v Sunderland
Brentford v Birmingham
Bristol City v Fulham

Derby v Leeds
Ipswich v Cardiff
Middlesbrough v Hull
Millwall v Sheffield Wed
Nottm Forest v Reading
Sheffield Utd v QPR

Wednesday. 21 February

Championship
Wolves v Norwich

Saturday, 24 February

Premier League
Arsenal v Man City
Bournemouth v Newcastle
Brighton v Swansea
Burnley v Southampton
Crystal Palace v Tottenham
Leicester v Stoke
Liverpool v West Ham
Man Utd v Chelsea
Watford v Everton
WBA v Huddersfield

Championship
Birmingham v Barnsley
Burton v Millwall
Cardiff v Bristol City
Fulham v Wolves
Hull v Sheffield Utd
Leeds v Brentford
Norwich v Bolton
Preston v Ipswich
QPR v Nottm Forest
Reading v Derby
Sheffield Wed v Aston Villa
Sunderland v Middlesbrough

League One
Bristol Rov v Scunthorpe
Bury v Gillingham
Charlton v Shrewsbury
Fleetwood v MK Dons
Northampton v Oxford
Oldham v Southend
Peterborough v AFC Wimbledon
Plymouth v Bradford
Portsmouth v Blackpool
Rotherham v Doncaster
Walsall v Blackburn
Wigan v Rochdale

League Two
Accrington v Cambridge
Chesterfield v Swindon
Colchester v Barnet

Forest Green v Crawley
Grimsby v Exeter
Lincoln v Crewe
Luton v Cheltenham
Mansfield v Coventry
Notts Co v Stevenage
Port Vale v Newport
Wycombe v Morecambe
Yeovil v Carlisle

Saturday, 3 March

Premier League
Brighton v Arsenal
Burnley v Everton
Crystal Palace v Man Utd
Leicester v Bournemouth
Liverpool v Newcastle
Man City v Chelsea
Southampton v Stoke
Swansea v West Ham
Tottenham v Huddersfield
Watford v WBA

Championship
Aston Villa v QPR
Barnsley v Norwich
Bolton v Preston
Brentford v Cardiff
Bristol City v Sheffield Wed
Derby v Fulham
Ipswich v Hull
Middlesbrough v Leeds
Millwall v Sunderland
Nottm Forest v Birmingham
Sheffield Utd v Burton
Wolves v Reading

League One
AFC Wimbledon v Charlton
Blackpool v Northampton
Bradford v Portsmouth
Doncaster v Bury
Gillingham v Rotherham
MK Dons v Bristol Rov
Oxford v Fleetwood
Rochdale v Plymouth
Scunthorpe v Oldham
Shrewsbury v Peterborough
Southend v Walsall

League Two
Barnet v Port Vale
Cambridge v Luton
Carlisle v Grimsby
Cheltenham v Notts Co
Coventry v Lincoln

Crawley v Wycombe
Crewe v Forest Green
Exeter v Chesterfield
Morecambe v Colchester
Newport v Accrington
Stevenage v Mansfield
Swindon v Yeovil

Sunday, 4 March
League One
Blackburn v Wigan

Tuesday, 6 March
Championship
Birmingham v Middlesbrough
Burton v Brentford
Cardiff v Barnsley
Fulham v Sheffield Utd
Hull v Millwall
Leeds v Wolves
Norwich v Nottm Forest
Preston v Bristol City
QPR v Derby
Reading v Bolton
Sheffield Wed v Ipswich
Sunderland v Aston Villa

Saturday, 10 March
Premier League
Arsenal v Watford
Bournemouth v Tottenham
Chelsea v Crystal Palace
Everton v Brighton
Huddersfield v Swansea
Man Utd v Liverpool
Newcastle v Southampton
Stoke v Man City
WBA v Leicester
West Ham v Burnley

Championship
Aston Villa v Wolves
Burton v Bristol City
Cardiff v Birmingham
Hull v Norwich
Ipswich v Sheffield Utd
Middlesbrough v Barnsley
Millwall v Brentford
Nottm Forest v Derby
Preston v Fulham
QPR v Sunderland
Reading v Leeds
Sheffield Wed v Bolton

League One
AFC Wimbledon v Oxford
Blackburn v Blackpool
Bradford v MK Dons
Bristol Rov v Northampton
Bury v Oldham
Fleetwood v Plymouth
Peterborough v Charlton
Portsmouth v Gillingham
Rotherham v Rochdale
Shrewsbury v Walsall
Southend v Doncaster
Wigan v Scunthorpe

League Two
Chesterfield v Lincoln
Coventry v Barnet
Crawley v Morecambe
Exeter v Carlisle
Forest Green v Notts Co
Grimsby v Port Vale
Luton v Accrington
Mansfield v Colchester
Stevenage v Crewe
Swindon v Cheltenham
Wycombe v Cambridge
Yeovil v Newport

Friday, 16 March
League Two
Newport v Luton

Saturday, 17 March
Premier League
Bournemouth v WBA
Burnley v Chelsea
Huddersfield v Crystal Palace
Leicester v Arsenal
Liverpool v Watford
Man City v Brighton
Stoke v Everton
Swansea v Southampton
Tottenham v Newcastle
West Ham v Man Utd

Championship
Barnsley v Millwall
Birmingham v Hull
Bolton v Aston Villa
Brentford v Middlesbrough
Bristol City v Ipswich
Derby v Cardiff
Fulham v QPR
Leeds v Sheffield Wed
Norwich v Reading
Sheffield Utd v Nottm Forest

Sunderland v Preston
Wolves v Burton

League One
Blackpool v Southend
Charlton v Fleetwood
Doncaster v Bradford
Gillingham v Blackburn
MK Dons v Bury
Northampton v Rotherham
Oldham v Portsmouth
Oxford v Peterborough
Plymouth v Bristol Rov
Rochdale v AFC Wimbledon
Scunthorpe v Shrewsbury
Walsall v Wigan

League Two
Accrington v Forest Green
Barnet v Wycombe
Cambridge v Swindon
Carlisle v Crawley
Cheltenham v Chesterfield
Colchester v Yeovil
Crewe v Coventry
Lincoln v Grimsby
Morecambe v Exeter
Notts Co v Mansfield
Port Vale v Stevenage

Saturday, 24 March
League One
Bradford v Gillingham
Bury v Wigan
Charlton v Plymouth
Doncaster v Blackburn
Fleetwood v Northampton
MK Dons v Blackpool
Oldham v Walsall
Peterborough v Bristol Rov
Portsmouth v Oxford
Scunthorpe v Rochdale
Shrewsbury v AFC Wimbledon
Southend v Rotherham

League Two
Accrington v Yeovil
Carlisle v Cambridge
Chesterfield v Notts Co
Coventry v Grimsby
Crawley v Cheltenham
Crewe v Newport
Exeter v Swindon
Forest Green v Mansfield
Luton v Barnet
Morecambe v Lincoln

Stevenage v Colchester
Wycombe v Port Vale

Thursday, 29 March
League One
Gillingham v MK Dons

Friday, 30 March
Championship
Barnsley v Bristol City
Brentford v Sheffield Utd
Cardiff v Burton
Derby v Sunderland
Hull v Aston Villa
Middlesbrough v Wolves
Millwall v Nottm Forest
Norwich v Fulham
Reading v QPR
Sheffield Wed v Preston

League One
AFC Wimbledon v Fleetwood
Blackburn v Bradford
Blackpool v Doncaster
Bristol Rov v Bury
Northampton v Charlton
Oxford v Scunthorpe
Plymouth v Southend
Rochdale v Shrewsbury
Rotherham v Peterborough

League Two
Barnet v Crewe
Cambridge v Crawley
Cheltenham v Carlisle
Colchester v Luton
Grimsby v Stevenage
Lincoln v Exeter
Mansfield v Accrington
Newport v Coventry
Notts Co v Wycombe
Port Vale v Chesterfield
Swindon v Morecambe
Yeovil v Forest Green

Saturday, 31 March
Premier League
Arsenal v Stoke
Brighton v Leicester
Chelsea v Tottenham
Crystal Palace v Liverpool
Everton v Man City
Man Utd v Swansea
Newcastle v Huddersfield
Southampton v West Ham

Watford v Bournemouth
WBA v Burnley

Championship
Birmingham v Ipswich
Leeds v Bolton

League One
Walsall v Portsmouth
Wigan v Oldham

Monday, 2 April
Championship
Aston Villa v Reading
Bolton v Birmingham
Bristol City v Brentford
Burton v Middlesbrough
Ipswich v Millwall
Nottm Forest v Barnsley
Preston v Derby
QPR v Norwich
Sheffield Utd v Cardiff
Sunderland v Sheffield Wed
Wolves v Hull

League One
Bradford v Walsall
Charlton v Rotherham
Doncaster v AFC Wimbledon
Fleetwood v Bristol Rov
MK Dons v Blackburn
Oldham v Blackpool
Peterborough v Northampton
Portsmouth v Wigan
Scunthorpe v Plymouth
Shrewsbury v Oxford
Southend v Gillingham

League Two
Accrington v Notts Co
Carlisle v Lincoln
Chesterfield v Newport
Coventry v Yeovil
Crawley v Swindon
Crewe v Port Vale
Exeter v Cheltenham
Forest Green v Colchester
Luton v Mansfield
Morecambe v Cambridge
Stevenage v Barnet
Wycombe v Grimsby

Tuesday, 3 April
Championship
Fulham v Leeds

League One
Bury v Rochdale

Saturday, 7 April
Premier League
Arsenal v Southampton
Bournemouth v Crystal Palace
Brighton v Huddersfield
Chelsea v West Ham
Everton v Liverpool
Leicester v Newcastle
Man City v Man Utd
Stoke v Tottenham
Watford v Burnley
WBA v Swansea

Championship
Barnsley v Sheffield Utd
Birmingham v Burton
Brentford v Ipswich
Cardiff v Wolves
Derby v Bolton
Hull v QPR
Leeds v Sunderland
Middlesbrough v Nottm Forest
Millwall v Bristol City
Norwich v Aston Villa
Reading v Preston
Sheffield Wed v Fulham

League One
AFC Wimbledon v Scunthorpe
Blackburn v Southend
Blackpool v Bradford
Bristol Rov v Charlton
Gillingham v Doncaster
Northampton v Shrewsbury
Oxford v Oldham
Plymouth v Peterborough
Rochdale v Portsmouth
Rotherham v Fleetwood
Walsall v Bury
Wigan v MK Dons

League Two
Barnet v Forest Green
Cambridge v Exeter
Cheltenham v Morecambe
Colchester v Accrington
Grimsby v Chesterfield
Lincoln v Wycombe
Mansfield v Crewe
Newport v Stevenage
Notts Co v Coventry
Port Vale v Crawley
Swindon v Carlisle
Yeovil v Luton

Tuesday, 10 April

Championship

Aston Villa v Cardiff
Bolton v Millwall
Bristol City v Birmingham
Burton v Hull
Fulham v Reading
Ipswich v Barnsley
Nottm Forest v Brentford
Preston v Leeds
QPR v Sheffield Wed
Sheffield Utd v Middlesbrough
Sunderland v Norwich
Wolves v Derby

Saturday, 14 April

Premier League

Burnley v Leicester
Crystal Palace v Brighton
Huddersfield v Watford
Liverpool v Bournemouth
Man Utd v WBA
Newcastle v Arsenal
Southampton v Chelsea
Swansea v Everton
Tottenham v Man City
West Ham v Stoke

Championship

Aston Villa v Leeds
Barnsley v Bolton
Burton v Derby
Fulham v Brentford
Hull v Sheffield Wed
Middlesbrough v Bristol City
Norwich v Cardiff
Nottm Forest v Ipswich
QPR v Preston
Reading v Sunderland
Sheffield Utd v Millwall

League One

Blackpool v Fleetwood
Bradford v Shrewsbury
Bristol Rov v Blackburn
Bury v Northampton
Charlton v Scunthorpe
MK Dons v Doncaster
Oldham v Gillingham
Oxford v Southend
Peterborough v Rochdale
Plymouth v Portsmouth
Walsall v AFC Wimbledon
Wigan v Rotherham

League Two

Accrington v Exeter
Cheltenham v Forest Green
Chesterfield v Mansfield
Colchester v Notts Co
Crawley v Coventry
Grimsby v Barnet
Luton v Crewe
Morecambe v Carlisle
Newport v Swindon
Port Vale v Lincoln
Stevenage v Cambridge
Yeovil v Wycombe

Sunday, 15 April

Championship

Wolves v Birmingham

Saturday, 21 April

Premier League

Arsenal v West Ham
Bournemouth v Man Utd
Brighton v Tottenham
Chelsea v Huddersfield
Everton v Newcastle
Leicester v Southampton
Man City v Swansea
Stoke v Burnley
Watford v Crystal Palace
WBA v Liverpool

Championship

Birmingham v Sheffield Utd
Bolton v Wolves
Brentford v QPR
Bristol City v Hull
Cardiff v Nottm Forest
Derby v Middlesbrough
Ipswich v Aston Villa
Leeds v Barnsley
Millwall v Fulham
Preston v Norwich
Sheffield Wed v Reading
Sunderland v Burton

League One

AFC Wimbledon v Oldham
Blackburn v Peterborough
Doncaster v Oxford
Fleetwood v Wigan
Gillingham v Blackpool
Northampton v Plymouth
Portsmouth v Charlton
Rochdale v Bradford
Rotherham v Bristol Rov
Scunthorpe v Walsall

Shrewsbury v Bury
Southend v MK Dons

League Two

Barnet v Newport
Cambridge v Cheltenham
Carlisle v Luton
Coventry v Stevenage
Crewe v Morecambe
Exeter v Crawley
Forest Green v Chesterfield
Lincoln v Colchester
Mansfield v Port Vale
Notts Co v Yeovil
Swindon v Grimsby
Wycombe v Accrington

Saturday, 28 April

Premier League

Burnley v Brighton
Crystal Palace v Leicester
Huddersfield v Everton
Liverpool v Stoke
Man Utd v Arsenal
Newcastle v WBA
Southampton v Bournemouth
Swansea v Chelsea
Tottenham v Watford
West Ham v Man City

Championship

Aston Villa v Derby
Barnsley v Brentford
Burton v Bolton
Fulham v Sunderland
Hull v Cardiff
Middlesbrough v Millwall
Norwich v Leeds
Nottm Forest v Bristol City
QPR v Birmingham
Reading v Ipswich
Sheffield Utd v Preston
Wolves v Sheffield Wed

League One

Blackpool v Shrewsbury
Bradford v Southend
Bristol Rov v Gillingham
Bury v Portsmouth
Charlton v Blackburn
MK Dons v Scunthorpe
Oldham v Doncaster
Oxford v Rochdale
Peterborough v Fleetwood
Plymouth v Rotherham
Walsall v Northampton
Wigan v AFC Wimbledon

League Two
Accrington v Lincoln
Cheltenham v Coventry
Chesterfield v Wycombe
Colchester v Swindon
Crawley v Crewe
Grimsby v Notts Co
Luton v Forest Green
Morecambe v Barnet
Newport v Cambridge
Port Vale v Carlisle
Stevenage v Exeter
Yeovil v Mansfield

Saturday, 5 May
Premier League
Arsenal v Burnley
Bournemouth v Swansea
Brighton v Man Utd
Chelsea v Liverpool
Everton v Southampton
Leicester v West Ham
Man City v Huddersfield
Stoke v Crystal Palace
Watford v Newcastle
WBA v Tottenham

League One
AFC Wimbledon v Bury
Blackburn v Oxford
Doncaster v Wigan
Fleetwood v Walsall
Gillingham v Rochdale
Northampton v Oldham
Portsmouth v Peterborough
Rochdale v Charlton
Rotherham v Blackpool
Scunthorpe v Bradford
Shrewsbury v MK Dons
Southend v Bristol Rov

League Two
Barnet v Chesterfield
Cambridge v Port Vale
Carlisle v Newport
Coventry v Morecambe
Crewe v Cheltenham
Exeter v Colchester
Forest Green v Grimsby
Lincoln v Yeovil
Mansfield v Crawley
Notts Co v Luton
Swindon v Accrington
Wycombe v Stevenage

Sunday, 6 May
Championship
Birmingham v Fulham
Bolton v Nottm Forest
Brentford v Hull
Bristol City v Sheffield Utd
Cardiff v Reading
Derby v Barnsley
Ipswich v Middlesbrough
Leeds v QPR
Millwall v Aston Villa
Preston v Burton
Sheffield Wed v Norwich
Sunderland v Wolves

Sunday, 13 May
Premier League
Burnley v Bournemouth
Crystal Palace v WBA
Huddersfield v Arsenal
Liverpool v Brighton
Man Utd v Watford
Newcastle v Chelsea
Southampton v Man City
Swansea v Stoke
Tottenham v Leicester
West Ham v Everton

SCOTTISH FIXTURES 2017–2018
Premiership, Championship, League One and League Two

Saturday, 5 August
Premiership
Aberdee v Hamilton
Celtic v Hearts
Dundee v Ross Co
Hibernian v Partick
Kilmarnock v St Johnstone

Championship
Dumbarton v Morton
Inverness v Dundee Utd
Livingston v Dunfermline
Queen of South v Brechin
St Mirren v Falkirk

League One
Albion v Ayr
Alloa v Raith
Arbroath v Queen's Park
Forfar v Airdrieonians
Stranraer v East Fife

League Two
Annan v Peterhead

Berwick v Clyde
Edinburgh v Montrose
Elgin v Cowdenbeath
Stenhousemuir v Stirling

Sunday, 6 August
Premiership
Motherwell v Rangers

Friday, 11 Aug
Premiership
Partick v Celtic

Saturday, 12 August
Premiership
Hamilton v Dundee
Kilmarnock v Hearts
Rangers v Hibernian
Ross Co v Aberdeen
St Johnstone v Motherwell

Championship
Brechin v Livingston
Dundee Utd v Queen of South

Dunfermline v Inverness
Falkirk v Dumbarton
Morton v St Mirren

League One
Airdrieonians v Arbroath
Ayr v Forfar
East Fife v Alloa
Queen's Park v Albion
Raith v Stranraer

League Two
Clyde v Annan
Cowdenbeath v Edinburgh
Montrose v Stenhousemuir
Peterhead v Elgin
Stirling v Berwick

Saturday, 19 August
Premiership
Aberdeen v Dundee
Hibernian v Hamilton
Kilmarnock v Celtic
Motherwell v Ross Co

Rangers v Hearts
St Johnstone v Partick

Championship
Dundee Utd v Brechin
Dunfermline v Falkirk
Inverness v Morton
Livingston v St Mirren
Queen of South v Dumbarton

League One
Albion v Airdrieonians
Alloa v Queen's Park
Arbroath v East Fife
Raith v Forfar
Stranraer v Ayr

League Two
Berwick v Annan
Elgin v Clyde
Montrose v Cowdenbeath
Stenhousemuir v Peterhead
Stirling v Edinburgh

Saturday, 26 August
Premiership
Celtic v St Johnstone
Kilmarnock v Hamilton
Motherwell v Hearts
Partick v Aberdeen

Championship
Brechin v Inverness
Dumbarton v Dunfermline
Falkirk v Queen of South
Morton v Livingston
St Mirren v Dundee Utd

League One
Airdrieonians v Alloa
Ayr v Arbroath
East Fife v Raith
Forfar v Albion
Queen's Park v Stranraer

League Two
Annan v Montrose
Clyde v Stenhousemuir
Cowdenbeath v Berwick
Edinburgh v Elgin
Peterhead v Stirling

Sunday, 27 August
Premiership
Dundee v Hibernian
Ross Co v Rangers

Saturday, 9 September
Premiership
Hamilton v Celtic
Hearts v Aberdeen
Motherwell v Kilmarnock
Rangers v Dundee
Ross Co v Partick
St Johnstone v Hibernian

Championship
Brechin v Falkirk
Dundee Utd v Dumbarton
Livingston v Queen of South
Morton v Dunfermline
St Mirren v Inverness

League One
Alloa v Forfar
Arbroath v Albion
East Fife v Queen's Park
Raith v Ayr
Stranraer v Airdrieonians

League Two
Edinburgh v Berwick
Elgin v Annan
Peterhead v Montrose
Stenhousemuir v Cowdenbeath
Stirling v Clyde

Saturday, 16 September
Premiership
Aberdeen v Kilmarnock
Celtic v Ross Co
Dundee v St Johnstone
Hamilton v Hearts
Hibernian v Motherwell
Partick v Rangers

Championship
Dumbarton v Brechin
Dunfermline v St Mirren
Falkirk v Dundee Utd
Inverness v Livingston
Queen of South v Morton

League One
Airdrieonians v East Fife
Albion v Stranraer
Ayr v Alloa
Forfar v Arbroath
Queen's Park v Raith

League Two
Annan v Stenhousemuir
Berwick v Elgin

Clyde v Edinburgh
Cowdenbeath v Peterhead
Montrose v Stirling

Saturday, 23 September
Premiership
Hearts v Partick
Kilmarnock v Dundee
Motherwell v Aberdeen
Rangers v Celtic
Ross Co v Hibernian
St Johnstone v Hamilton

Championship
Brechin v Dunfermline
Dumbarton v Inverness
Dundee Utd v Morton
Falkirk v Livingston
St Mirren v Queen of South

League One
Alloa v Albion
East Fife v Forfar
Queen's Park v Ayr
Raith v Airdrieonians
Stranraer v Arbroath

League Two
Clyde v Cowdenbeath
Edinburgh v Peterhead
Elgin v Montrose
Stenhousemuir v Berwick
Stirling v Annan

Saturday, 30 September
Premiership
Aberdeen v St Johnstone
Celtic v Hibernian
Dundee v Hearts
Hamilton v Rangers
Kilmarnock v Ross Co
Motherwell v Partick

Championship
Dunfermline v Dundee Utd
Inverness v Queen of South
Livingston v Dumbarton
Morton v Falkirk
St Mirren v Brechin

League One
Airdrieonians v Queen's Park
Albion v Raith
Arbroath v Alloa
Ayr v East Fife
Forfar v Stranraer

League Two
Annan v Cowdenbeath
Montrose v Clyde
Peterhead v Berwick
Stenhousemuir v Edinburgh
Stirling v Elgin

Saturday, 14 October
Premiership
Celtic v Dundee
Hamilton v Motherwell
Hibernian v Aberdeen
Partick v Kilmarnock
Ross Co v Hearts
St Johnstone v Rangers

Championship
Brechin v Morton
Dumbarton v St Mirren
Falkirk v Inverness
Livingston v Dundee Utd
Queen of South v Dunfermline

League One
Ayr v Airdrieonians
East Fife v Albion
Queen's Park v Forfar
Raith v Arbroath
Stranraer v Alloa

Saturday, 21 October
Premiership
Hearts v St Johnstone
Kilmarnock v Hibernian
Motherwell v Celtic
Partick v Dundee
Rangers v Aberdeen
Ross Co v Hamilton

Championship
Brechin v Queen of South
Dundee Utd v Inverness
Dunfermline v Livingston
Falkirk v St Mirren
Morton v Dumbarton

League One
Albion v Queen's Park
Alloa v East Fife
Arbroath v Airdrieonians
Forfar v Ayr
Stranraer v Raith

League Two
Berwick v Montrose

Clyde v Peterhead
Cowdenbeath v Stirling
Edinburgh v Annan
Elgin v Stenhousemuir

Wednesday, 25 October
Premiership
Aberdeen v Celtic
Dundee v Motherwell
Hamilton v Partick
Hibernian v Hearts
Rangers v Kilmarnock
St Johnstone v Ross Co

Saturday, 28 October
Premiership
Aberdeen v Ross Co
Celtic v Kilmarnock
Dundee v Hamilton
Hearts v Rangers
Motherwell v Hibernian
Partick v St Johnstone

Championship
Dumbarton v Dundee Utd
Inverness v Dunfermline
Livingston v Brechin
Queen of South v Falkirk
St Mirren v Morton

League One
Airdrieonians v Albion
Ayr v Stranraer
East Fife v Arbroath
Forfar v Raith
Queen's Park v Alloa

League Two
Berwick v Cowdenbeath
Clyde v Elgin
Montrose v Edinburgh
Peterhead v Annan
Stirling v Stenhousemuir

Saturday, 4 November
Premiership
Hamilton v Aberdeen
Hearts v Kilmarnock
Hibernian v Dundee
Rangers v Partick
Ross Co v Motherwell
St Johnstone v Celtic

Championship
Brechin v Dumbarton

Dundee Utd v St Mirren
Falkirk v Dunfermline
Livingston v Inverness
Morton v Queen of South

League One
Albion v Forfar
Alloa v Airdrieonians
Arbroath v Ayr
Raith v East Fife
Stranraer v Queen's Park

League Two
Annan v Berwick
Cowdenbeath v Montrose
Edinburgh v Stirling
Elgin v Peterhead
Stenhousemuir v Clyde

Saturday, 11 November
Championship
Dumbarton v Queen of South
Dundee Utd v Falkirk
Dunfermline v Morton
Inverness v Brechin
St Mirren v Livingston

League One
Airdrieonians v Stranraer
Albion v Alloa
Ayr v Raith
Forfar v East Fife
Queen's Park v Arbroath

League Two
Berwick v Edinburgh
Clyde v Stirling
Cowdenbeath v Elgin
Montrose v Annan
Peterhead v Stenhousemuir

Saturday, 18 November
Premiership
Aberdeen v Motherwell
Dundee v Kilmarnock
Hibernian v St Johnstone
Partick v Hearts
Rangers v Hamilton
Ross Co v Celtic

Saturday, 25 November
Premiership
Celtic v Partick
Dundee v Rangers
Hamilton v Hibernian

Hearts v Ross Co
Kilmarnock v Aberdeen
Motherwell v St Johnstone

Championship
Brechin v Dundee Utd
Dunfermline v Dumbarton
Falkirk v Morton
Inverness v St Mirren
Queen of South v Livingston

League One
Alloa v Ayr
Arbroath v Forfar
East Fife v Airdrieonians
Raith v Queen's Park
Stranraer v Albion

League Two
Annan v Clyde
Edinburgh v Cowdenbeath
Elgin v Berwick
Stenhousemuir v Montrose
Stirling v Peterhead

Saturday, 2 December
Premiership
Aberdeen v Rangers
Celtic v Motherwell
Hearts v Hamilton
Partick v Hibernian
Ross Co v Dundee
St Johnstone v Kilmarnock

Championship
Dundee Utd v Dunfermline
Livingston v Falkirk
Morton v Brechin
Queen of South v Inverness
St Mirren v Dumbarton

League One
Airdrieonians v Forfar
Arbroath v Stranraer
Ayr v Albion
Queen's Park v East Fife
Raith v Alloa

League Two
Annan v Elgin
Berwick v Stirling
Clyde v Montrose
Cowdenbeath v Stenhousemuir
Peterhead v Edinburgh

Saturday, 9 December
Premiership
Dundee v Aberdeen
Hamilton v St Johnstone
Hearts v Motherwell
Hibernian v Celtic
Kilmarnock v Partick
Rangers v Ross Co

Championship
Brechin v St Mirren
Dumbarton v Livingston
Dunfermline v Queen of South
Inverness v Falkirk
Morton v Dundee Utd

League One
Airdrieonians v Raith
Albion v Arbroath
Ayr v Queen's Park
East Fife v Stranraer
Forfar v Alloa

League Two
Elgin v Edinburgh
Montrose v Berwick
Peterhead v Clyde
Stenhousemuir v Annan
Stirling v Cowdenbeath

Wednesday, 13 December
Premiership
Celtic v Hamilton
Hearts v Dundee
Hibernian v Rangers
Partick v Motherwell
Ross Co v Kilmarnock
St Johnstone v Aberdeen

Saturday, 16 December
Premiership
Aberdeen v Hibernian
Dundee v Partick
Hamilton v Ross Co
Hearts v Celtic
Kilmarnock v Motherwell
Rangers v St Johnstone

Championship
Falkirk v Brechin
Inverness v Dumbarton
Livingston v Morton
Queen of South v Dundee Utd
St Mirren v Dunfermline

League One
Alloa v Arbroath
East Fife v Ayr
Queen's Park v Airdrieonians
Raith v Albion
Stranraer v Forfar

League Two
Annan v Stirling
Berwick v Peterhead
Cowdenbeath v Clyde
Edinburgh v Stenhousemuir
Montrose v Elgin

Saturday, 23 December
Premiership
Celtic v Aberdeen
Hibernian v Ross Co
Kilmarnock v Rangers
Motherwell v Dundee
Partick v Hamilton
St Johnstone v Hearts

Championship
Dumbarton v Falkirk
Dundee Utd v Livingston
Dunfermline v Brechin
Morton v Inverness
Queen of South v St Mirren

League One
Airdrieonians v Ayr
Albion v East Fife
Alloa v Stranraer
Arbroath v Raith
Forfar v Queen's Park

League Two
Annan v Edinburgh
Clyde v Berwick
Peterhead v Cowdenbeath
Stenhousemuir v Elgin
Stirling v Montrose

Wednesday, 27 December
Premiership
Aberdeen v Partick
Dundee v Celtic
Hamilton v Kilmarnock
Hearts v Hibernian
Rangers v Motherwell
Ross Co v St Johnstone

Saturday, 30 December
Premiership
Aberdeen v Hearts
Celtic v Rangers
Hibernian v Kilmarnock
Motherwell v Hamilton
Partick v Ross Co
St Johnstone v Dundee

Championship
Brechin v Inverness
Dumbarton v Morton
Falkirk v Queen of South
Livingston v Dunfermline
St Mirren v Dundee Utd

League One
Airdrieonians v Alloa
Arbroath v East Fife
Ayr v Forfar
Queen's Park v Albion
Raith v Stranraer

League Two
Berwick v Stenhousemuir
Cowdenbeath v Annan
Edinburgh v Clyde
Elgin v Stirling
Montrose v Peterhead

Tuesday 2 January
Championship
Dundee Utd v Brechin
Dunfermline v Falkirk
Inverness v Livingston
Morton v St Mirren
Queen of South v Dumbarton

League One
Albion v Airdrieonians
Alloa v Queen's Park
East Fife v Raith
Forfar v Arbroath
Stranraer v Ayr

League Two
Clyde v Annan
Edinburgh v Berwick
Montrose v Cowdenbeath
Peterhead v Elgin
Stenhousemuir v Stirling

Saturday, 6 January
Championship
Brechin v Morton

Dumbarton v Dunfermline
Falkirk v Dundee Utd
Livingston v Queen of South
St Mirren v Inverness

League One
Airdrieonians v East Fife
Alloa v Albion
Ayr v Arbroath
Queen's Park v Stranraer
Raith v Forfar

League Two
Annan v Montrose
Cowdenbeath v Edinburgh
Elgin v Clyde
Stenhousemuir v Peterhead
Stirling v Berwick

Saturday, 13 January
Championship
Brechin v Livingston
Dumbarton v St Mirren
Dunfermline v Dundee Utd
Inverness v Queen of South
Morton v Falkirk

League One
Arbroath v Queen's Park
East Fife v Alloa
Forfar v Albion
Raith v Ayr
Stranraer v Airdrieonians

League Two
Berwick v Annan
Clyde v Stenhousemuir
Edinburgh v Montrose
Elgin v Cowdenbeath
Peterhead v Stirling

Saturday, 20 January
League Two
Annan v Peterhead
Berwick v Elgin
Montrose v Clyde
Stenhousemuir v Cowdenbeath
Stirling v Edinburgh

Wednesday, 24 January
Premiership
Dundee v Hibernian
Hamilton v Hearts
Kilmarnock v St Johnstone
Motherwell v Ross Co

Partick v Celtic
Rangers v Aberdeen

Saturday, 27 January
Premiership
Aberdeen v Kilmarnock
Celtic v Hibernian
Hamilton v Dundee
Hearts v Motherwell
Ross Co v Rangers
St Johnstone v Partick

Championship
Dundee Utd v Morton
Dunfermline v St Mirren
Falkirk v Inverness
Livingston v Dumbarton
Queen of South v Brechin

League Two
Clyde v Peterhead
Cowdenbeath v Berwick
Edinburgh v Annan
Elgin v Stenhousemuir
Montrose v Stirling

Wednesday, 31 January
Premiership
Celtic v Hearts
Hibernian v Motherwell
Kilmarnock v Dundee
Partick v Rangers
Ross Co v Aberdeen
St Johnstone v Hamilton

Saturday, 3 February
Premiership
Aberdeen v Hamilton
Dundee v Ross Co
Hearts v St Johnstone
Kilmarnock v Celtic
Motherwell v Partick
Rangers v Hibernian

Championship
Dumbarton v Brechin
Falkirk v Livingston
Inverness v Dundee Utd
Morton v Dunfermline
St Mirren v Queen of South

League Two
Annan v Cowdenbeath
Clyde v Edinburgh
Peterhead v Montrose

tenhousemuir v Berwick
tirling v Elgin

Saturday, 10 February
League Two
Berwick v Clyde
Cowdenbeath v Stirling
Edinburgh v Peterhead
Elgin v Annan
Montrose v Stenhousemuir

Saturday, 17 February
Premiership
Celtic v St Johnstone
Hamilton v Rangers
Hibernian v Aberdeen
Motherwell v Kilmarnock
Partick v Dundee
Ross Co v Hearts

Championship
Brechin v Falkirk
Dundee Utd v Dumbarton
Dunfermline v Inverness
Livingston v St Mirren
Queen of South v Morton

League Two
Clyde v Cowdenbeath
Elgin v Montrose
Peterhead v Berwick
Stenhousemuir v Edinburgh
Stirling v Annan

Saturday, 24 February
Premiership
Aberdeen v Celtic
Dundee v Motherwell
Hamilton v Partick
Kilmarnock v Hibernian
Rangers v Hearts
St Johnstone v Ross Co

Championship
Falkirk v Dumbarton
Inverness v Morton
Livingston v Dundee Utd
Queen of South v Dunfermline
St Mirren v Brechin

League One
Ayr v Airdrieonians
East Fife v Albion
Queen's Park v Forfar
Raith v Arbroath
Stranraer v Alloa

League Two
Annan v Stenhousemuir
Berwick v Montrose
Cowdenbeath v Peterhead
Edinburgh v Elgin
Stirling v Clyde

Tuesday, 27 February
Championship
Brechin v Dunfermline
Dumbarton v Inverness
Dundee Utd v Queen of South
Morton v Livingston
St Mirren v Falkirk

Wednesday, 28 February
Premiership
Celtic v Dundee
Hearts v Kilmarnock
Hibernian v Hamilton
Motherwell v Aberdeen
Ross Co v Partick
St Johnstone v Rangers

Saturday, 3 March
Championship
Dundee Utd v St Mirren
Dunfermline v Livingston
Inverness v Brechin
Morton v Dumbarton
Queen of South v Falkirk

League One
Airdrieonians v Stranraer
Albion v Queen's Park
Alloa v East Fife
Arbroath v Ayr
Forfar v Raith

League Two
Berwick v Stirling
Clyde v Elgin
Edinburgh v Cowdenbeath
Montrose v Annan
Peterhead v Stenhousemuir

Saturday, 10 March
Premiership
Dundee v St Johnstone
Hamilton v Motherwell
Hibernian v Hearts
Kilmarnock v Ross Co
Partick v Aberdeen
Rangers v Celtic

Championship
Brechin v Dundee Utd
Dumbarton v Queen of South
Falkirk v Morton
Livingston v Inverness
St Mirren v Dunfermline

League One
Arbroath v Forfar
Ayr v Raith
East Fife v Airdrieonians
Queen's Park v Alloa
Stranraer v Albion

League Two
Annan v Edinburgh
Cowdenbeath v Montrose
Elgin v Berwick
Stenhousemuir v Clyde
Stirling v Peterhead

Saturday, 17 March
Premiership
Aberdeen v Dundee
Hearts v Partick
Motherwell v Celtic
Rangers v Kilmarnock
Ross Co v Hamilton
St Johnstone v Hibernian

Championship
Brechin v Dumbarton
Dundee Utd v Inverness
Dunfermline v Morton
Livingston v Falkirk
Queen of South v St Mirren

League One
Albion v Arbroath
Alloa v Airdrieonians
Forfar v Ayr
Raith v East Fife
Stranraer v Queen's Park

League Two
Annan v Clyde
Berwick v Stenhousemuir
Cowdenbeath v Elgin
Edinburgh v Stirling
Montrose v Peterhead

Saturday, 24 March
Championship
Dundee Utd v Dunfermline
Inverness v Falkirk
Morton v Brechin

Queen of South v Livingston
St Mirren v Dumbarton

League One
Airdrieonians v Raith
Albion v Alloa
Arbroath v Stranraer
Ayr v Queen's Park
Forfar v East Fife

League Two
Berwick v Edinburgh
Clyde v Montrose
Peterhead v Annan
Stenhousemuir v Elgin
Stirling v Cowdenbeath

Saturday, 31 March
Premiership
Aberdeen v St Johnstone
Celtic v Ross Co
Dundee v Hearts
Hibernian v Partick
Kilmarnock v Hamilton
Motherwell v Rangers

Championship
Dumbarton v Livingston
Dunfermline v Queen of South
Falkirk v Brechin
Inverness v St Mirren
Morton v Dundee Utd

League One
Alloa v Arbroath
East Fife v Ayr
Queen's Park v Airdrieonians
Raith v Albion
Stranraer v Forfar

League Two
Annan v Berwick
Cowdenbeath v Stenhousemuir
Elgin v Stirling
Montrose v Edinburgh
Peterhead v Clyde

Saturday, 7 April
Premiership
Hamilton v Celtic
Hearts v Aberdeen
Partick v Kilmarnock
Rangers v Dundee
Ross Co v Hibernian
St Johnstone v Motherwell

Championship
Brechin v St Mirren
Dumbarton v Dundee Utd
Falkirk v Dunfermline
Livingston v Morton
Queen of South v Inverness

League One
Airdrieonians v Ayr
Albion v Forfar
Alloa v Stranraer
Arbroath v Raith
Queen's Park v East Fife

League Two
Annan v Elgin
Berwick v Peterhead
Cowdenbeath v Clyde
Edinburgh v Stenhousemuir
Stirling v Montrose

Saturday, 14 April
Championship
Dundee Utd v Falkirk
Dunfermline v Brechin
Inverness v Dumbarton
Morton v Queen of South
St Mirren v Livingston

League One
Airdrieonians v Albion
Ayr v Stranraer
East Fife v Arbroath
Forfar v Alloa
Raith v Queen's Park

League Two
Clyde v Stirling
Elgin v Edinburgh

Montrose v Berwick
Peterhead v Cowdenbeath
Stenhousemuir v Annan

Saturday, 21 April
Championship
Dumbarton v Falkirk
Inverness v Dunfermline
Livingston v Brechin
Queen of South v Dundee Utd
St Mirren v Morton

League One
Albion v East Fife
Alloa v Ayr
Arbroath v Airdrieonians
Forfar v Queen's Park
Stranraer v Raith

League Two
Annan v Stirling
Berwick v Cowdenbeath
Edinburgh v Clyde
Elgin v Peterhead
Stenhousemuir v Montrose

Saturday, 28 April
Championship
Brechin v Queen of South
Dundee Utd v Livingston
Dunfermline v Dumbarton
Falkirk v St Mirren
Morton v Inverness

League One
Airdrieonians v Forfar
Ayr v Albion
East Fife v Stranraer
Queen's Park v Arbroath
Raith v Alloa

League Two
Clyde v Berwick
Cowdenbeath v Annan
Montrose v Elgin
Peterhead v Edinburgh
Stirling v Stenhousemuir

NATIONAL LEAGUE FIXTURES 2017–2018

Saturday, August 5
AFC Fylde v Boreham Wood
Bromley v Eastleigh
Dagenham v Barrow
FC Halifax v Aldershot
Guiseley v Ebbsfleet
Hartlepool v Dover
Maidstone v Maidenhead
Solihull v Chester
Sutton v Leyton Orient
Torquay v Tranmere
Woking v Gateshead
Wrexham v Macclesfield

Tuesday, 8 August
Aldershot v Torquay
Barrow v FC Halifax
Boreham Wood v Dagenham
Chester v AFC Fylde
Dover v Bromley
Eastleigh v Sutton
Ebbsfleet v Maidstone
Gateshead v Guiseley
Leyton Orient v Solihull
Macclesfield v Hartlepool
Maidenhead v Wrexham
Tranmere v Woking

Saturday, 12 August
Aldershot v Guiseley
Barrow v Woking
Boreham Wood v Solihull
Chester v FC Halifax
Dover v Wrexham
Eastleigh v Dagenham
Ebbsfleet v AFC Fylde
Gateshead v Torquay
Leyton Orient v Maidstone
Macclesfield v Bromley
Maidenhead v Hartlepool
Tranmere v Sutton

Tuesday, 15 August
AFC Fylde v Maidenhead
Bromley v Leyton Orient
Dagenham v Ebbsfleet
FC Halifax v Dover
Guiseley v Tranmere
Hartlepool v Chester
Maidstone v Aldershot
Solihull v Barrow
Sutton v Macclesfield

Torquay v Boreham Wood
Woking v Eastleigh
Wrexham v Gateshead

Saturday, 19 August
AFC Fylde v Dagenham
Boreham Wood v Aldershot
Bromley v Hartlepool
Chester v Sutton
Dover v Barrow
Eastleigh v Tranmere
Gateshead v Macclesfield
Guiseley v Torquay
Maidenhead v Ebbsfleet
Maidstone v Wrexham
Solihull v FC Halifax
Woking v Leyton Orient

Saturday, 26 August
Aldershot v Chester
Barrow v Maidenhead
Dagenham v Bromley
Ebbsfleet v Gateshead
FC Halifax v Guiseley
Hartlepool v AFC Fylde
Leyton Orient v Eastleigh
Macclesfield v Dover
Sutton v Maidstone
Torquay v Solihull
Tranmere v Boreham Wood
Wrexham v Woking

Monday, 28 August
AFC Fylde v Barrow
Boreham Wood v Wrexham
Bromley v Sutton
Chester v Macclesfield
Dover v Ebbsfleet
Eastleigh v Aldershot
Gateshead v FC Halifax
Guiseley v Hartlepool
Maidenhead v Leyton Orient
Maidstone v Dagenham
Solihull v Tranmere
Woking v Torquay

Saturday, 2 September
Aldershot v Solihull
Barrow v Boreham Wood
Dagenham v Gateshead
Ebbsfleet v Eastleigh
FC Halifax v AFC Fylde

Hartlepool v Maidstone
Leyton Orient v Guiseley
Macclesfield v Woking
Sutton v Maidenhead
Torquay v Chester
Tranmere v Dover
Wrexham v Bromley

Saturday, 9 September
AFC Fylde v Bromley
Aldershot v Dover
Boreham Wood v Leyton Orient
Chester v Ebbsfleet
FC Halifax v Maidenhead
Guiseley v Eastleigh
Hartlepool v Dagenham
Maidstone v Woking
Solihull v Macclesfield
Sutton v Gateshead
Torquay v Wrexham
Tranmere v Barrow

Tuesday, 12 September
Barrow v Guiseley
Bromley v Torquay
Dagenham v Sutton
Dover v Boreham Wood
Eastleigh v Maidstone
Ebbsfleet v Aldershot
Gateshead v Chester
Leyton Orient v FC Halifax
Macclesfield v AFC Fylde
Maidenhead v Tranmere
Woking v Solihull
Wrexham v Hartlepool

Saturday, 16 September
Barrow v Torquay
Bromley v Solihull
Dagenham v FC Halifax
Dover v Chester
Eastleigh v AFC Fylde
Ebbsfleet v Tranmere
Gateshead v Aldershot
Leyton Orient v Hartlepool
Macclesfield v Maidstone
Maidenhead v Boreham Wood
Woking v Sutton
Wrexham v Guiseley

Saturday, 23 September
AFC Fylde v Woking

541

Aldershot v Leyton Orient
Boreham Wood v Ebbsfleet
Chester v Maidenhead
FC Halifax v Bromley
Guiseley v Dover
Hartlepool v Eastleigh
Maidstone v Gateshead
Solihull v Dagenham
Sutton v Barrow
Torquay v Macclesfield
Tranmere v Wrexham

Saturday, 30 September
Barrow v Maidstone
Bromley v Tranmere
Dagenham v Torquay
Dover v Solihull
Eastleigh v Chester
Ebbsfleet v FC Halifax
Gateshead v Boreham Wood
Leyton Orient v AFC Fylde
Macclesfield v Aldershot
Maidenhead v Guiseley
Woking v Hartlepool
Wrexham v Sutton

Tuesday, 3 October
AFC Fylde v Gateshead
Aldershot v Dagenham
Boreham Wood v Eastleigh
Chester v Woking
FC Halifax v Wrexham
Guiseley v Macclesfield
Hartlepool v Barrow
Maidstone v Bromley
Solihull v Ebbsfleet
Sutton v Dover
Torquay v Maidenhead
Tranmere v Leyton Orient

Saturday, 7 October
Barrow v Leyton Orient
Boreham Wood v FC Halifax
Gateshead v Bromley
Macclesfield v Ebbsfleet
Maidenhead v Aldershot
Maidstone v Guiseley
Solihull v Hartlepool
Sutton v AFC Fylde
Torquay v Dover
Tranmere v Chester
Woking v Dagenham
Wrexham v Eastleigh

Saturday, 21 October
AFC Fylde v Maidstone
Aldershot v Tranmere
Bromley v Woking
Chester v Boreham Wood
Dagenham v Wrexham
Dover v Maidenhead
Eastleigh v Gateshead
Ebbsfleet v Barrow
FC Halifax v Torquay
Guiseley v Solihull
Hartlepool v Sutton
Leyton Orient v Macclesfield

Tuesday, 24 October
AFC Fylde v Wrexham
Aldershot v Sutton
Bromley v Maidenhead
Chester v Barrow
Dagenham v Macclesfield
Dover v Woking
Eastleigh v Solihull
Ebbsfleet v Torquay
FC Halifax v Maidstone
Guiseley v Boreham Wood
Hartlepool v Tranmere
Leyton Orient v Gateshead

Saturday, 28 October
Barrow v Aldershot
Boreham Wood v Bromley
Gateshead v Dover
Macclesfield v Eastleigh
Maidenhead v Dagenham
Maidstone v Chester
Solihull v AFC Fylde
Sutton v Ebbsfleet
Torquay v Hartlepool
Tranmere v FC Halifax
Woking v Guiseley
Wrexham v Leyton Orient

Saturday, 11 November
Aldershot v AFC Fylde
Barrow v Macclesfield
Boreham Wood v Hartlepool
Chester v Wrexham
Dover v Eastleigh
Ebbsfleet v Leyton Orient
FC Halifax v Woking
Guiseley v Bromley
Maidenhead v Gateshead
Solihull v Sutton
Torquay v Maidstone
Tranmere v Dagenham

Saturday, 18 November
AFC Fylde v Torquay
Bromley v Chester
Dagenham v Guiseley
Eastleigh v Barrow
Gateshead v Tranmere
Hartlepool v Aldershot
Leyton Orient v Dover
Macclesfield v Boreham Wood
Maidstone v Solihull
Sutton v FC Halifax
Woking v Maidenhead
Wrexham v Ebbsfleet

Tuesday, 21 November
AFC Fylde v Guiseley
Bromley v Aldershot
Dagenham v Dover
Eastleigh v Maidenhead
Gateshead v Barrow
Hartlepool v FC Halifax
Leyton Orient v Chester
Macclesfield v Tranmere
Maidstone v Boreham Wood
Sutton v Torquay
Woking v Ebbsfleet
Wrexham v Solihull

Saturday, 25 November
Aldershot v Wrexham
Barrow v Bromley
Boreham Wood v Woking
Chester v Dagenham
Dover v AFC Fylde
Ebbsfleet v Hartlepool
FC Halifax v Eastleigh
Guiseley v Sutton
Maidenhead v Macclesfield
Solihull v Gateshead
Torquay v Leyton Orient
Tranmere v Maidstone

Saturday, 2 December
AFC Fylde v Chester
Bromley v Dover
Dagenham v Boreham Wood
FC Halifax v Barrow
Guiseley v Gateshead
Hartlepool v Macclesfield
Maidstone v Ebbsfleet
Solihull v Leyton Orient
Sutton v Eastleigh
Torquay v Aldershot
Woking v Tranmere
Wrexham v Maidenhead

Saturday, 9 December

Aldershot v FC Halifax
Barrow v Dagenham
Boreham Wood v AFC Fylde
Chester v Solihull
Dover v Hartlepool
Eastleigh v Bromley
Ebbsfleet v Guiseley
Gateshead v Woking
Leyton Orient v Sutton
Macclesfield v Wrexham
Maidenhead v Maidstone
Tranmere v Torquay

Saturday, 23 December

AFC Fylde v Ebbsfleet
Bromley v Macclesfield
Dagenham v Eastleigh
FC Halifax v Chester
Guiseley v Aldershot
Hartlepool v Maidenhead
Maidstone v Leyton Orient
Solihull v Boreham Wood
Sutton v Tranmere
Torquay v Gateshead
Woking v Barrow
Wrexham v Dover

Tuesday, 26 December

Aldershot v Woking
Barrow v Wrexham
Boreham Wood v Sutton
Chester v Guiseley
Dover v Maidstone
Eastleigh v Torquay
Ebbsfleet v Bromley
Gateshead v Hartlepool
Leyton Orient v Dagenham
Macclesfield v FC Halifax
Maidenhead v Solihull
Tranmere v AFC Fylde

Saturday, 30 December

Aldershot v Maidstone
Barrow v Solihull
Boreham Wood v Torquay
Chester v Hartlepool
Dover v FC Halifax
Eastleigh v Woking
Ebbsfleet v Dagenham
Gateshead v Wrexham
Leyton Orient v Bromley
Macclesfield v Sutton
Maidenhead v AFC Fylde
Tranmere v Guiseley

Monday, 1 January

AFC Fylde v Tranmere
Bromley v Ebbsfleet
Dagenham v Leyton Orient
FC Halifax v Macclesfield
Guiseley v Chester
Hartlepool v Gateshead
Maidstone v Dover
Solihull v Maidenhead
Sutton v Boreham Wood
Torquay v Eastleigh
Woking v Aldershot
Wrexham v Barrow

Saturday, 6 January

Barrow v Tranmere
Bromley v AFC Fylde
Dagenham v Hartlepool
Dover v Aldershot
Eastleigh v Guiseley
Ebbsfleet v Chester
Gateshead v Sutton
Leyton Orient v Boreham Wood
Macclesfield v Solihull
Maidenhead v FC Halifax
Woking v Maidstone
Wrexham v Torquay

Saturday, 20 January

AFC Fylde v Macclesfield
Aldershot v Ebbsfleet
Boreham Wood v Dover
Chester v Gateshead
FC Halifax v Leyton Orient
Guiseley v Barrow
Hartlepool v Wrexham
Maidstone v Eastleigh
Solihull v Woking
Torquay v Bromley
Tranmere v Maidenhead

Saturday, 27 January

Barrow v Sutton
Bromley v FC Halifax
Dagenham v Solihull
Dover v Guiseley
Eastleigh v Hartlepool
Ebbsfleet v Boreham Wood
Gateshead v Maidstone
Leyton Orient v Aldershot
Macclesfield v Torquay
Maidenhead v Chester
Woking v AFC Fylde
Wrexham v Tranmere

Saturday, 3 February

AFC Fylde v Eastleigh
Aldershot v Gateshead
Boreham Wood v Maidenhead
Chester v Dover
FC Halifax v Dagenham
Guiseley v Wrexham
Hartlepool v Leyton Orient
Maidstone v Macclesfield
Solihull v Bromley
Sutton v Woking
Torquay v Barrow
Tranmere v Ebbsfleet

Saturday, 10 February

Barrow v Hartlepool
Bromley v Maidstone
Dagenham v Aldershot
Dover v Sutton
Eastleigh v Boreham Wood
Ebbsfleet v Solihull
Gateshead v AFC Fylde
Leyton Orient v Tranmere
Macclesfield v Guiseley
Maidenhead v Torquay
Woking v Chester
Wrexham v FC Halifax

Saturday, 17 February

AFC Fylde v Leyton Orient
Aldershot v Macclesfield
Boreham Wood v Gateshead
Chester v Eastleigh
FC Halifax v Ebbsfleet
Guiseley v Maidenhead
Hartlepool v Woking
Maidstone v Barrow
Solihull v Dover
Sutton v Wrexham
Torquay v Dagenham
Tranmere v Bromley

Tuesday, 20 February

Aldershot v Bromley
Barrow v Gateshead
Boreham Wood v Maidstone
Chester v Leyton Orient
Dover v Dagenham
Ebbsfleet v Woking
FC Halifax v Hartlepool
Guiseley v AFC Fylde
Maidenhead v Eastleigh
Solihull v Wrexham
Torquay v Sutton
Tranmere v Macclesfield

Saturday, 24 February
AFC Fylde v Dover
Bromley v Barrow
Dagenham v Chester
Eastleigh v FC Halifax
Gateshead v Solihull
Hartlepool v Ebbsfleet
Leyton Orient v Torquay
Macclesfield v Maidenhead
Maidstone v Tranmere
Sutton v Guiseley
Woking v Boreham Wood
Wrexham v Aldershot

Saturday, 3 March
Aldershot v Hartlepool
Barrow v Eastleigh
Boreham Wood v Macclesfield
Chester v Bromley
Dover v Leyton Orient
Ebbsfleet v Wrexham
FC Halifax v Sutton
Guiseley v Dagenham
Maidenhead v Woking
Solihull v Maidstone
Torquay v AFC Fylde
Tranmere v Gateshead

Saturday, 10 March
AFC Fylde v Aldershot
Bromley v Guiseley
Dagenham v Tranmere
Eastleigh v Dover
Gateshead v Maidenhead
Hartlepool v Boreham Wood
Leyton Orient v Ebbsfleet
Macclesfield v Barrow
Maidstone v Torquay
Sutton v Solihull
Woking v FC Halifax
Wrexham v Chester

Saturday, 17 March
AFC Fylde v Hartlepool
Boreham Wood v Tranmere
Bromley v Dagenham
Chester v Aldershot
Dover v Macclesfield
Eastleigh v Leyton Orient
Gateshead v Ebbsfleet
Guiseley v FC Halifax
Maidenhead v Barrow
Maidstone v Sutton
Solihull v Torquay
Woking v Wrexham

Saturday, 24 March
Aldershot v Boreham Wood
Barrow v Dover
Dagenham v AFC Fylde
Ebbsfleet v Maidenhead
FC Halifax v Solihull
Hartlepool v Bromley
Leyton Orient v Woking
Macclesfield v Gateshead
Sutton v Chester
Torquay v Guiseley
Tranmere v Eastleigh
Wrexham v Maidstone

Friday 30 March
AFC Fylde v FC Halifax
Boreham Wood v Barrow
Bromley v Wrexham
Chester v Torquay
Dover v Tranmere
Eastleigh v Ebbsfleet
Gateshead v Dagenham
Guiseley v Leyton Orient
Maidenhead v Sutton
Maidstone v Hartlepool
Solihull v Aldershot
Woking v Macclesfield

Monday, 2 April
Aldershot v Eastleigh
Barrow v AFC Fylde
Dagenham v Maidstone
Ebbsfleet v Dover
FC Halifax v Gateshead
Hartlepool v Guiseley
Leyton Orient v Maidenhead
Macclesfield v Chester
Sutton v Bromley
Torquay v Woking
Tranmere v Solihull
Wrexham v Boreham Wood

Saturday, 7 April
AFC Fylde v Sutton
Aldershot v Maidenhead
Bromley v Gateshead
Chester v Tranmere
Dagenham v Woking
Dover v Torquay
Eastleigh v Wrexham
Ebbsfleet v Macclesfield
FC Halifax v Boreham Wood
Guiseley v Maidstone
Hartlepool v Solihull
Leyton Orient v Barrow

Saturday, 14 April
Barrow v Ebbsfleet
Boreham Wood v Chester
Gateshead v Eastleigh
Macclesfield v Leyton Orient
Maidenhead v Dover
Maidstone v AFC Fylde
Solihull v Guiseley
Sutton v Hartlepool
Torquay v FC Halifax
Tranmere v Aldershot
Woking v Bromley
Wrexham v Dagenham

Saturday, 21 April
AFC Fylde v Solihull
Aldershot v Barrow
Bromley v Boreham Wood
Chester v Maidstone
Dagenham v Maidenhead
Dover v Gateshead
Eastleigh v Macclesfield
Ebbsfleet v Sutton
FC Halifax v Tranmere
Guiseley v Woking
Hartlepool v Torquay
Leyton Orient v Wrexham

Saturday, 28 April
Barrow v Chester
Boreham Wood v Guiseley
Gateshead v Leyton Orient
Macclesfield v Dagenham
Maidenhead v Bromley
Maidstone v FC Halifax
Solihull v Eastleigh
Sutton v Aldershot
Torquay v Ebbsfleet
Tranmere v Hartlepool
Woking v Dover
Wrexham v AFC Fylde

This book is to be returned the last da

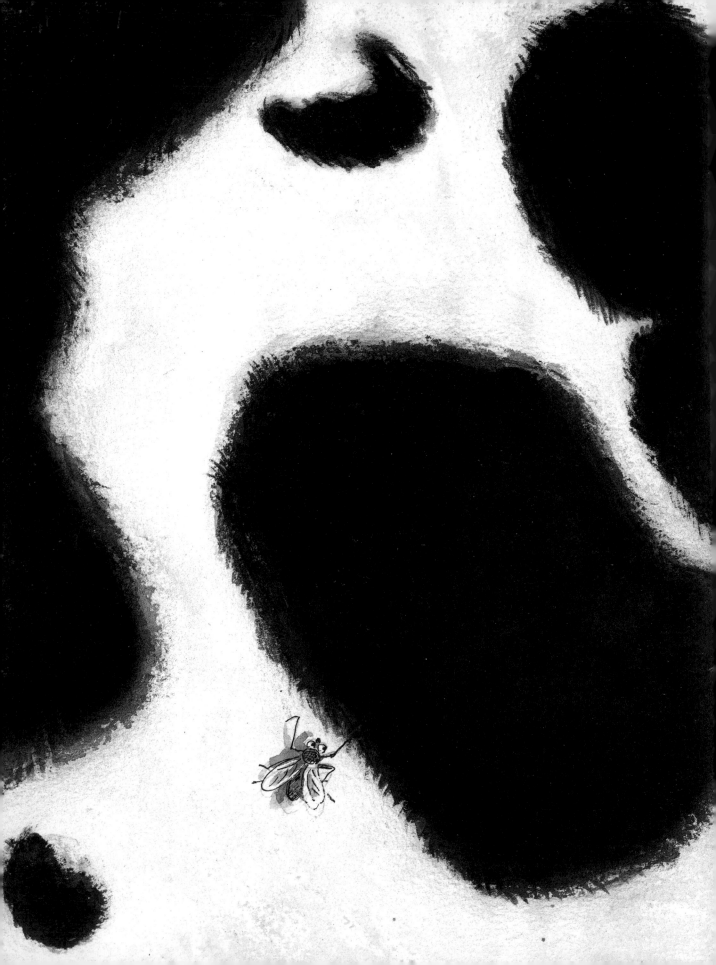